THE OXFORD HAN

POPUL

Cristóbal Rovira Kaltwasser is a Professor of Political Science at Diego Portales University in Santiago de Chile and an Associate Researcher at the Centre for Social Conflict and Cohesion Studies (COES). His publications include *Populism: A Very Short Introduction* (with Cas Mudde, OUP, 2017), and has published articles in journals such as *Comparative European Politics, Comparative Political Studies, Democratization, Government & Opposition, Party Politics* and *Political Studies.*

Paul Taggart is Professor of Politics and Jean Monnet Chair, Director of the Sussex European Institute at the University of Sussex, former editor of *Government and Opposition*, former editor of the journal *Politics*, co-convenor (with Prof. Aleks Szczerbiak) of the European Referendums, Elections and Parties Network (EPERN). His publications include *Populism* (Open University Press, 2000), *The New Populism and The New Politics* (Palgrave, 1996) and *Opposing Europe? The Comparative Party Politics of Euroscepticism, Vols I* and *II* (co-edited with Aleks Szczerbiak, OUP, 2008).

Paulina Ochoa Espejo is an Associate Professor of Political Science at Haverford College. Her publications include *The Time of Popular Sovereignty: Process and the Democratic State* (Penn State University Press, 2011) and has published articles in journals such as the *American Journal of Political Science*, the *Journal of Political Philosophy* and the *Journal of Politics.*

Pierre Ostiguy is Professor of Political Science and International Relations at the Universidad Católica de Córdoba (Argentina). He has published several book chapters on populism, articles in journals including *The Brown Journal of World Affairs* (with Kenneth Roberts), *POSTData* (Argentina), *Politique et Sociétés* (Québec), and the *Revue Internationale de Politique Comparée* (Europe) as well as longer texts as *Kellogg Institute Working Papers.*

THE OXFORD HANDBOOK OF

POPULISM

Edited by

CRISTÓBAL ROVIRA KALTWASSER

PAUL TAGGART

PAULINA OCHOA ESPEJO

and

PIERRE OSTIGUY

OXFORD

UNIVERSITY PRESS

Great Clarendon Street, Oxford, OX2 6DP,
United Kingdom

Oxford University Press is a department of the University of Oxford.
It furthers the University's objective of excellence in research, scholarship,
and education by publishing worldwide. Oxford is a registered trade mark of
Oxford University Press in the UK and in certain other countries

Published in the United States of America by Oxford University Press
198 Madison Avenue, New York, NY 10016, United States of America

British Library Cataloguing in Publication Data
Data available

Library of Congress Cataloging in Publication Data
Data available

ISBN 978–0–19–880356–0 (Hbk.)
ISBN 978–0–19–884628–4 (Pbk.)

Preface

This book project started in 2011 as a cross-regional project of Cristóbal Rovira Kaltwasser and Paul Taggart, then working together at the University of Sussex, and Pierre Ostiguy, at the Catholic University of Chile. In 2014, Paulina Ochoa Espejo joined the project, playing an indispensable role through her coordination and editing of the Handbook's vital political theory section. We would not have been able to finish this book without the generous support of various institutions. To begin with, thanks to the support of the British Academy's International Partnership and Mobility Scheme Award for the project "Populism in Europe and Latin America: A Cross-Regional Perspective" (award number 166098, 2012–2015), between Sussex in the UK and the Católica in Chile, Cristóbal, Paul, and Pierre were able to organize various workshops at both institutions and have several meetings to coordinate the production of this project. In addition, Cristóbal Rovira Kaltwasser would like to acknowledge support from the Chilean National Fund for Scientific and Technological Development (FONDECYT project 1140101), the Chilean Millennium Science Initiative (project NS130008), and the Center for Social Conflict and Cohesion Studies (COES, CONICYT/FONDAP/15130009). He also acknowledges support from Diego Portales University and the Alexander von Humboldt Foundation, which allowed him to undertake a stay during July and August, 2016, at the German Institute of Global and Area Studies (GIGA) in Hamburg to work on this project. Moreover, Pierre Ostiguy would like to thank the Millennium Nucleus for the Study of Stateness and Democracy in Latin America (RS130002), supported by the Millennium Science Initiative of the Ministry of Economy, Development and Tourism of Chile, and Antoine Maillet for their assistance for the conference organized at the Catholic University of Chile in July 2014. Furthermore, Cristóbal, Paul, Paulina, and Pierre want to thank all contributors to this edited volume for their willingness to receive feedback from us and change some aspects of their original contributions. Last but not least, we would like to express our sincere gratitude for the support of the team at Oxford University Press, most notably Dominic Byatt, Sarah Parker, and Olivia Wells.

Cristóbal Rovira Kaltwasser, Paul Taggart,
Paulina Ochoa Espejo, and Pierre Ostiguy
December, 2016

Contents

PART I CONCEPTS

PART II REGIONS

PART III ISSUES

PART IV NORMATIVE DEBATES

LIST OF FIGURES

LIST OF TABLES

LIST OF CONTRIBUTORS

Sahar Abi-Hassan, PhD Candidate, Department of Political Science, Boston University, US

Paris Aslanidis, Lecturer, Political Science Department and Hellenic Studies Program, Yale University, US

Christopher Bickerton, Reader in Modern European Politics, Department of Politics and International Studies, University of Cambridge, UK

Benjamin De Cleen, Assistant Professor, Department of Communication Studies, Vrije Universiteit Brussel, Belgium

Carlos de la Torre, Professor, Department of Sociology, University of Kentucky, US

Roger Eatwell, Emeritus Professor of Comparative Politics, Department of Politics, Languages and International Studies, University of Bath, UK

Jason Frank, Professor and Chair, Department of Government, Cornell University, US

Kirk A. Hawkins, Associate Professor, Department of Political Science, Brigham Young University, US

Olli Hellmann, Senior Lecturer in Political Science and International Relations, University of Waikato, New Zealand

James D. Ingram, Associate Professor, Department of Political Science, McMaster University, Canada

Carlo Invernizzi Accetti, Assistant Professor, Political Science Department, City College, City University of New York, US

Christophe Jaffrelot, Senior Research Fellow at CERI-Sciences Po/CNRS, France, and Professor at the King's India Institute, UK

Duncan Kelly, Professor of Political Thought and Intellectual History, Department of Politics and International Studies, University of Cambridge, UK

Joseph Lowndes, Associate Professor, Department of Political Science, University of Oregon, US

Luca Manucci, Researcher, NCCR Democracy and Institute of Political Science, University of Zurich, Switzerland

Luke March, Professor of Post-Soviet and Comparative Politics, Politics and International Relations, University of Edinburgh, Scotland, UK

Benjamin Moffitt, Senior Lecturer in Politics, National School of Arts, Australian Catholic University, Australia

Cas Mudde, Stanley Wade Shelton UGAF Professor, School of Public and International Affairs, University of Georgia, US, and Professor II at the Center for Research on Extremism (C-REX) of the University of Oslo, Norway

Jan-Werner Müller, Professor, Department of Politics, Princeton University, US

Paulina Ochoa Espejo, Associate Professor, Department of Political Science, Haverford College, US

Kevin Olson, Professor, Department of Political Science, University of California, Irvine, US

Pierre Ostiguy, Professor, Faculty of Political Science and International Relations, Catholic University of Córdoba, Argentina

Francisco Panizza, Professor of Latin American and Comparative Politics, Department of Government, The London School of Economics and Political Science, UK

Teun Pauwels, Scientific Collaborator, Université Libre de Bruxelles, Belgium

Madeleine Read, PhD student, Department of English, University of California, Irvine, USA

Danielle E. Resnick, Senior Research Fellow, Development Strategy and Governance Division, International Food Policy Research Institute (IFPRI), US

Kenneth M. Roberts, Richard J. Schwartz Professor of Government, Cornell University, US

Cristóbal Rovira Kaltwasser, Professor, School of Political Science, Diego Portales University and Associate Researcher at the Centre for Social Conflict and Cohesion Studies (COES), Chile

Stefan Rummens, Professor, Institute of Philosophy, KU Leuven, Belgium

Ben Stanley, Associate Professor, SWPS University of Social Sciences and Humanities, Poland

Yannis Stavrakakis, Professor, School of Political Sciences, Aristotle University of Thessaloniki, Greece

Paul Taggart, Professor of Politics, University of Sussex, UK

Louise Tillin, Reader in Politics, India Institute, King's College London, UK

Nadia Urbinati, Kyriakos Tsakopoulos Professor of Political Theory, Department of Political Science, Columbia University, US

Bertjan Verbeek, Chair and Professor of International Relations, Department of Political Science, Institute for Management Research, Radboud University Nijmegen, The Netherlands

Kurt Weyland, Mike Hogg Professor in Liberal Arts, Department of Government, University of Texas at Austin, US

Andrej Zaslove, Assistant Professor, Department of Political Science, Radboud University, Institute for Management Research, Nijmegen, The Netherlands

José Pedro Zúquete, Research Fellow, the Social Sciences Institute, University of Lisbon, Portugal

CHAPTER 1

POPULISM

An Overview of the Concept and the State of the Art

CRISTÓBAL ROVIRA KALTWASSER, PAUL TAGGART,
PAULINA OCHOA ESPEJO, AND PIERRE OSTIGUY

AT last everyone understands that populism matters. Recent political events have brought the word "populism" to the center of discussions across the globe. And although the term has been making headlines for the last two decades, today a wave of policymakers, pundits, and scholars are gripped by this phenomenon, which both undermines and inspires democracy and therefore usually sparks partisan debates that go beyond academic circles. Yet, many of those who turn to populism for the first time start from scratch, and thus overlook the growing body of scholarly work on this topic. This impulse may make some sense, because the burgeoning literature on populism seems unwieldy. The growth of populism as a phenomenon has led to a proliferation of scholarship: country experts, specialists in comparative politics, and scholars working on normative political theory have been advancing new insights on populism. However, the literature is not as disparate as it is often made out to be. There is a coherent wealth of research that should be used and built upon. As a consequence, the main aim of the *Oxford Handbook of Populism* is to present the state of the art on this topic, and to lay out for the scholarly community not only the knowledge accumulated but also ongoing discussions and research gaps.

From a survey of the literature on populism it is apparent that there is a body of research that shares certain characteristics. First, the literature is fragmentary. The empirical work on populism is almost invariably confined to specific countries or world regions. This is partly inevitable given the costs and difficulty of cross-national and cross-regional comparisons. But what is more concerning is that national and regional studies tend to overlook populism literature focused on other places, and often treat the specificities of national and regional manifestations of populism as generalizable. This means that populism literature is not as cumulative as it should be, and it is prone to exception fallacy. Second, the literature has reached a level of maturity in that it now, across the board, has had to focus on populism in government as well as populism as an insurgent force. Its maturity can also be seen in the gradual movement away from ad hoc theorizing on the basis of single case studies as well as in the construction of theories that aim to have validity for certain world regions and/or specific manifestations of populism, such as populist radical right parties in Western Europe. Third, populism literature has entered the mainstream of the academic debate. This reflects the reality of the political world where populism has become in some senses and some forms a frequent phenomenon. Looking at countries as diverse as Australia, Ecuador, France, Poland, Thailand, and the United States, the rise (and fall) of populist actors seems to be something that has come to stay. As a consequence, the scholarship is gaining maturity and, as we show below, with the partial exception of the US, has become a topic for all fields of political science. The final characteristic of populism scholarship is that it is bound up with practical politics. The term is used to advance or undermine political causes in the media but also sometimes within academia. In other words, the very notion of populism sparks broad discussions and therefore those who study populism are, to a certain extent, forced to engage with the political world and cannot remain removed in ivory towers.

In this introductory chapter to the *Oxford Handbook of Populism*, we are interested in offering an overview of how research on populism has evolved over time and we structure this contribution in four sections. We start by presenting a concise history of populism. After this, we analyze the development of the scholarship since the 1990s, putting special emphasis on the production of academic articles on populism in political science journals. Then we explain the organization of the Handbook and the criteria we have used for selecting the topics covered. Finally, we conclude with some reflections on the future research agenda on populism and hope that scholars will find some of these ideas attractive for their own research.

A CONCISE HISTORY OF POPULISM

The first use of the term "populism" comes from nineteenth-century political movements on both sides of the Atlantic, and we use these instances as the origin of the phenomenon. However, the origins of the term can be traced further back in time through the modern history of democratic legitimacy. If we look at states from either a sociological or a normative perspective, we can conclude that all political associations are in some way created by their members, and the government is ultimately responsive to them. Thus the people are included in any theory of legitimate government in some capacity. Yet, in the history of modern democracy "the people" emerge not only as the source of political authority, but also as a unified entity able to act and to retrieve power from government officials: *the sovereign people*. This popular ground legitimizes democratic politics, but it also paves the way for populism.

The modern theory of popular sovereignty distinguishes between the powers of the government, on the one hand, and the people as the ground of authority in the state,

on the other (Ochoa Espejo, 2011). This theory emerged from the medieval appropriation of Roman Law, which distinguished between the authority of the people and that
of its magistrates (Lee, 2016). Popular sovereignty was later developed in early modern theories of representation (Tuck, 2016). But what was originally a way to separate
the grounds of authority from the exercise of government, in order to keep the latter in
check, became a full-blown source of tension under the assumption that the sovereign
people could shake off the rule of monarchs and retrieve their power (Sabaddini, 2016).
The evolution of the idea of popular sovereignty would eventually allow the creation
of constitutions written in the name of the people, imagined as the ultimate source of
authority in the state (Nelson, 2016). This idea of the people as the ground of authority
would become a beacon for the political imagination of popular movements in every
democratizing government, from the eighteenth century up to this day. The idea that
"the people" can authoritatively recover power from the government to reconstitute
institutions, or wrestle power from corrupt or self-serving elites, would be the ground
from which the earliest movements that could be properly called "populist" emerged in
the nineteenth century.

The term "populism" is now often used pejoratively. But it certainly did not have a
negative connotation at the beginning.[1] It was, in English, a concept that was used about
and by the members of the US People's Party. Its use was first reported in US newspapers
in 1891 and 1892 (Houwen, 2013: 39). The People's Party displayed some of the leitmotifs
of populism. It was a Southern and Western movement based on hostility to the establishment of the railroads and banks, as well as to politicians in Washington. It was also
a third-party force attempting to prise apart US politics by castigating the Democratic
and Republican parties as too close to each other and too tied to special interests. What
they stood for has been variously interpreted by historians. Initially the Populist project
was dismissed as reactionary and regressive (Hofstadter, 1955) but later scholarship has
emphasized its progressive and co-operative basis (Goodwyn, 1976) and even its technical aspirations to move government from the realm of politics into being almost a technocratic process (Postel, 2007). Across the scholarship on the US People's Party, then, we
have examples of how populism is used in very different ways. For Hofstadter the term
was pejorative, equating the Populists with reactionary and regressive politics. For later
historians, like Goodwyn and Postel, there was both a reinterpretation of what the party
stood for as progressive and communitarian and there also, in effect, a reclaiming and
recasting of the term populism.

The term populism has also been used to describe the Russian movement of "going
to the people" under the *narodniki* (Venturi, 1960; Walicki, 1969).[2] This was a movement of idealistic, revolutionary students from the cities who in the tumultuous years
of the 1860s and early 1870s attempted to stir the peasantry in the countryside into over-
throwing the Tsarist regime through living with and learning from them. The movement
was unsuccessful, with the peasantry being suspicious and often turning the students
over to the authorities. In their celebration of the untainted nature of the peasantry and
with the unbridled sense that the establishment needed overturning, these Russian students shared some themes with the populists in the US. Although they had different

versions of agrarian workers—with the *narodniki* drawing on a Slavophile heritage and glorifying natural Russian rural institutions such as *obschina* (Venturi, 1960) and the US Populists focusing on a more robustly hard-working American version of the rural workers (Goodwyn, 1976)—these were parallel versions of populism, albeit shot through with different emphases as a consequence of the different contexts in which they arose.

Although not frequently considered in the history of populism, a third form of foundational populism is the case of Boulangism in France. The notion of populism has been applied to Boulangism by commentators who place it in historical context (Hermet, 2001; 2013; Passmore, 2012; Birnbaum, 2012), by comparative scholars on populism in Europe (Betz, forthcoming; Eatwell, this volume), and by scholars seeking to trace the lineage of contemporary French populism (Winock, 1997; Wolfreys, 2012). Between 1896 and 1898 General Georges Boulanger was a key figure in the politics of the French Third Republic. He rose as an insurgent hero and his rise followed his appointment as Minister for War in 1886. He championed the workers and a resurgent nationalism and also campaigned against the parliamentary regime, looking to overturn it in favor of a radical plebiscitary republicanism (Passmore, 2012). He fled the country before elections in 1889 when he was charged with conspiracy and treason and ended up in Brussels, where he committed suicide in 1891. His campaign and rise to prominence owed much to his opposition to the existing parliamentary regime and his accusations against its corruption and disconnection from the people, and he appealed to a disparate collation of the peasants, workers, monarchists, and radical socialists (Betz, forthcoming; Passmore, 2012). His attack was on an elite still seen as largely monarchist and he advocated for a "heterodox democratic project" with a strong state and plebiscitary and integrative democracy (Betz, forthcoming).

What united the US, Russian, and French populists of the nineteenth century was their shared celebration, to differing extents, of the "true" common rural people—but this reflects the historical context and the importance given to the forms of agriculture and the rural–urban division that suffused the period. Deeper than this and as such something to be seen in later expressions of populism, these three historical examples share some of the common features of populism. There was a direct appeal to "the people" as inherently virtuous and dutiful or disadvantaged. There was also a powerful sense of opposition to an establishment that remained entrenched and a belief that democratic politics needed to be conducted differently and closer to the people. A strong sense of nationalistic or native pride permeated all three cases.[3]

While the three foundational cases of populism discussed above—the US People's Party, the *narodniki*, and Boulangism—took place at the end of the nineteenth century, the emergence of populism in Latin America can be dated to the beginning of the twentieth century, in particular with the rise of Hipólito Yrigoyen in Argentina (1916 and 1922) and Arturo Alessandri in Chile (1920–1925) (Conniff, 2012; Hawkins and Rovira Kaltwasser, 2017). Although Yrigoyen and Alessandri have been analyzed as populist precursors in the region, scholars of Latin American populism have tended to distinguish different waves of populism and they usually describe the 1940s and 1950s as the phase of "classic populism" (Conniff, 2012; de la Torre, this volume; Freidenberg, 2007; Rovira Kaltwasser, 2014a).

What are the particularities of this wave of "classic populism"? There is wide consensus that with the onset of the Great Depression of the 1930s, Latin America underwent a period of significant economic decline that sparked a legitimacy crisis and demands for political incorporation (Collier and Collier, 1991; Roberts, 2008). The combination of economic hardship, rapid migration from rural to urban areas, and increasing demands for the expansion of political and social citizenship facilitated the emergence of populist leaders, who by developing a radical discourse were able to construct heterogeneous class alliances and mobilize excluded sectors of society (Drake, 1978; di Tella, 1965). Paradigmatic examples of populist leaders of this kind are Juan Domingo Perón in Argentina, Getúlio Vargas in Brazil, Victor Raúl Haya de la Torre in Peru, José María Velasco Ibarra in Ecuador, and Jorge Eliécer Gaitán in Colombia (de la Torre and Arnson, 2013: 14). When it comes to the usage of the concept of populism to describe this type of leadership, probably the most influential analysis is the one advanced by Gino Germani, an Italian intellectual who escaped fascism and migrated to Argentina, where he experienced at first hand the rise of Juan Domingo Perón in the 1940s. In dialogue with the work of Lipset (1960), Germani argued that the abrupt modernization process experienced by many Latin American countries during the first half of the twentieth century paved the way for the emergence of populism, which he defined as a multi-class movement that "usually includes contrasting components such as claim for equality of political rights and universal participation for the common people, but fused with some sort of authoritarianism often under charismatic leadership" (Germani, 1978: 88).

Although some scholars have employed the notion of populism to describe fascism in Europe (e.g. Gentile, 2006; Griffin, 1991; see also Eatwell, in this volume), it is perhaps the emergence of Poujadism in the 1950s in France that both marks the first modern form of European populism and, in a very practical sense, provided the basis for the more recent manifestation of populism in that country. Emerging out of an anti-tax protest, Pierre Poujade went on to form a movement (the Union de Défense des Commerçants et Artisans, UDCA) that championed the interests of small business people and of shop keepers and built on anti-establishment sentiment (Priester, 2007: 142–58). The UDCA was successful in getting deputies elected to the National Assembly in 1956 but was a spent force by the time of the subsequent elections in 1958 (Shields, 2004). One of these deputies was Jean-Marie Le Pen, who was the founder of the National Front in the 1970s, which provided the basis for a more enduring form of populism in France and a party that became a standard-bearer for right-wing populism in contemporary Europe (Rydgren, 2005).

As we noted above, populism has also been employed to describe the agrarian movements in Eastern Europe after World War I (Canovan, 1981) but it was from the late 1950s to the early 1970s that we can observe the first real development of a modern body of scholarship on populism. This can be seen in three different spheres. First, various scholars began to employ the notion of populism to pinpoint "societal problems" (Allcock, 1971). For instance, Shils (1956) maintained that populism should be considered an ideology of popular resentment against elites whereby the people are portrayed as better than their rulers, while Dahl (1956) coined the notion of "populistic democracy" to describe a form of government that aims to maximize political equality and popular sovereignty at any cost. In turn, Kornhauser (1959) and Germani (1978) used the concept of populism to highlight how the rise of mass society involves the destruction of social bonds and the emergence of new multitudes available to be mobilized by movements at odds with elites. Another important example is the work of Lipset (1960) on political extremism that drew heavily on the US experience of populism by linking the emergence of McCarthyism back to the reactionary interpretation of the People's Party and in this way reinvigorated the negative connotation of populism.

Secondly, since the 1960s populism has come to be used in a number of different national and regional contexts. This is reflected not only in the work of Germani (1978) already discussed above and the influential book on dependency theory written by Cardoso and Faletto (1969), but also in other contributions with an emphasis beyond Latin America. For example, in his analysis of the electoral rise of Andreas Papandreou's Panhellenic Socialist Movement (PASOK) in Greece in the late 1970s, Mouzelis (1978) claims that the latter represented a unique political force in the European context due to its populism. Mouzelis's main argument is that although PASOK presented itself as a socialist party akin to its West European counterparts, it resemblances were much stronger with Latin American populist parties that are characterized by the presence of a strong leader, whose popularity is related to his ability to mobilize excluded sectors by developing a Manichean rhetoric that distinguishes between the "bad" establishment and the "good" people. At the same time, it was also in the 1970s that Ernesto Laclau published his book *Politics and Ideology in Marxist Theory: Capitalism, Fascism and Populism* (1977), in which he criticized Marxist economic determinism and built the basis of a new theoretical approach for the study of populism. In his subsequent work with Chantal Mouffe, Laclau would build on the Italian Marxist Antonio Gramsci's work to propose, from a post-structuralist standpoint, a theory of radical democracy as the construction of political hegemonies (Laclau and Mouffe, 1985).

Thirdly, in 1968 there was, for the first time, a real attempt to compare usage and to try to reflect on the concept of populism itself. The conference at the London School of Economics that yielded the Ionescu and Gellner (1969) edited volume, brought together scholars from different strands. While it did not attempt, in the book form, to bring together the different scholarship on populism into a unified definition, it fostered a dialogue between scholars working on different world regions and with diverse theoretical backgrounds. This was, therefore, the first academic instance in which scholars tried to advance a truly cross-regional study of populism. It is worth noting that those who participated in this conference and the book that came out of it were not only political scientists, but also anthropologists, economists, historians, philosophers, and sociologists. This shows that the academic interest in populism has been driven by different disciplines within the social sciences and it is only since the 1980s that the political science community began to take ownership of this topic.

In fact, it was in 1982 that William Riker published the book *Liberalism Against Populism*, in which he applied social choice theory to illustrate the impossibility of realizing classical democratic views of collective action. Moreover, at the beginning of the 1980s the British political theorist Margaret Canovan (1981) wrote an influential and empirically wide-ranging book on populism per se. She did in her book what Ionescu and Gellner (1969) didn't, in attempting to draw a comprehensive overview of all instances of populism in order to discern commonalities; in the end, she produced a seven-fold typology of different variants: farmers' populism, peasants' populism, intellectuals' populism, populist dictatorship, populist democracy, reactionary populism, and politicians' populism. However, having drawn out the varieties, Canovan balked at identifying common traits, saying that all the variants of populism were "not reducible to a single core" (Canovan, 1981: 298).

Since the 1990s there has been a huge growth in scholarship on populism and political scientists have been at the forefront of the academic production. Taggart (2000) was an attempt to build on Canovan's general comparative approach but with an argument that drew out central features of populism, seeing it as a response to representative politics, lacking core values, and so having a chameleonic character that reflected the environment in which it arose—and always implicitly and explicitly drawing on notions of a "heartland" as an ideal of something that had been lost. But much subsequent work that was continued in this trend was focused on regions and countries and arose in response to real world developments of populism.

Two regions have particularly been affected by the growth of populism since the early 1990s: South America and Europe. After the transition from military rule to democratic regimes that took place during the 1980s, scholars interested in South American politics distinguished the formation of a new wave of populism in a set of countries of the region. Presidents such as Collor de Mello in Brazil (1990–1992), Fujimori in Peru (1990–2000), and Menem in Argentina (1989–1999) were characterized as populist actors, who in contrast to the emblematic cases of "classic populism" did not implement left-of-center social reforms, but rather favored the introduction of neoliberal policies (Roberts, 1995; Weyland, 1996, 2001). The emergence of this new wave of populism sparked an original debate on not only the concept of populism, but also the ambivalent relationship between populism and democracy (e.g. Carrión, 2006; de la Torre, 2000; Gibson, 1997; Levitsky, 2003; O'Donnell, 1994; Panizza, 2000; Peruzzotti, 2001; Weyland, 1993). This academic discussion about the impact of populism on democracy has been reinforced by the configuration of a new wave of populism since the 2000s, one which is marked by the rise of radical populist projects from the left (Castañeda and Morales, 2008; de la Torre, 2007; Levitsky and Roberts, 2011). The latter have been driven by charismatic leaders such as Rafael Correa in Ecuador, Evo Morales in Bolivia, and Hugo Chávez in Venezuela, who have fostered major institutional reforms that seek to diminish the power of established elites and incorporate excluded sectors. Given that part of the electoral and political success of these populist projects relied on a commodity boom that has come to an end in the last few years, there is open discussion about the future of this wave of radical left populism and its legacies (Weyland, 2013).

In the case of Europe, since the beginning of the 1990s research on populism has been focused on the electoral breakthrough and persistence of populist radical right parties. The early scholarship focused on a small number of parties as insurgent forces challenging the mainstream. The French National Front blazed a trail for such parties, becoming an institutionalized political party and, more importantly, a perennial feature of French politics. But soon there were many countries with some sort of radical right populist party, and now almost all European countries have seen the rise of this party family (Art, 2011; Norris, 2005; Mudde, 2007; 2013). The causes for these parties were seen by some as a consequence of the "silent revolution" that brought to the fore post-material values across Europe (Ignazi, 1992). These have triggered the emergence of identity politics not only through Green parties that defend multiculturalism, but also through populist radical right parties that favor a nativist interpretation of who should belong to the nation. For others the focus was more on the collapse of the European postwar settlement (Taggart, 1995). For both approaches, this newly emerging form of populism on the right was matched by equivalent insurgent non-populist forces on the left of politics paralleling challenging some of the same fault lines of the postwar settlement. In fact, some scholars argue that European countries are experiencing the emergence of a new political cleavage that is centered on cultural issues and is transforming the political landscape across the region (Bornschier, 2010; Kriesi et al., 2008). To a certain extent this holds true not only in Western Europe but also in Central and Eastern Europe (see Stanley, this volume). Nevertheless, in this region political parties are much less institutionalized than in Western Europe, and in consequence, populist forces often emerge here as a way to demonstrate dissatisfaction with the political elite, particularly because of corruption (Kriesi, 2014).

More recent scholarship on populism in Europe then began to deal with populism in new forms. The first change was the ascendency of populist parties into parties in government. This was most dramatically started in Austria in 2000 with the entry of the Austrian Freedom Party into a coalition with the Christian Democrats. This provoked a strong reaction from other governments (Fallend and Heinisch, 2016), but more importantly it marked the breakthrough of the insurgents into the mainstream (Albertazzi and McDonnell, 2015; Akkerman, de Lange, and Roodujin, 2016). The second new form was the identification of a left-wing variant of populism in Europe. This could be seen in parties with an older lineage such as the German party called the Left (*die Linke*) and the Dutch Socialist Party (March, 2012). However, with the onset of the Great Recession a new expression of leftist populism has come to the fore: first through the emergence of anti-austerity social movements that employ a populist frame (Aslanidis, 2016) and later through the formation of leftist populist political parties demanding an end to the austerity policies that have been forced by the European Union (Stavrakakis and Katsambekis, 2014). SYRIZA in Greece and PODEMOS in Spain are the paradigmatic examples of this type of "inclusionary populism" that previous to the Great Recession had been much more common in Latin America than in Europe (Mudde and Rovira Kaltwasser, 2012). At the same time, scholars have been analyzing the impact of the

Great Recession on the political system and have identified different patterns of populist mobilization across Europe (e.g. Kriesi and Pappas, 2015).

In many ways the United States has been the home of populism. It was the site of one of the foundational moments in populism in the People's Party in the late nineteenth century and gave us the very term populism. It has also seen a whole range of populist figures throughout history even after the demise of the People's Party, with politicians like Huey Long, George Wallace, Pat Buchanan, Ross Perot, and Sarah Palin and Donald Trump through the twentieth and twenty-first centuries (Lowndes, this volume). Michael Kazin (1995) goes as far as to trace populism throughout US political history as an endemic feature. But for a country with a political system that both privileges populist discourse and gives rise to so many disparate populist actors, there is a dearth of systematic scholarship of populism as a contemporary phenomenon. The work on populism in the US in reality falls mainly into three categories: (1) historical works on populism, particularly oriented towards the nineteenth century (e.g. Goodwyn, 1976; 1978; Postel, 2007); (2) political critiques of the radical right, often focusing on the extremes (e.g. Lipset, 1960; Berlet and Lyons, 2000); and (3) accounts of populism as a left project of emancipation (e.g. Grattan, 2016). What is remarkable, given the incidences of populism in the US, is that there is a real lack of systematic political science scholarship and that the use of the term populism, where it is invoked, is rather casual and not linked to the study of populism elsewhere. Not by chance, one of the best studies of the populist nature of the so-called Tea Party has been written by a historian (Formisano, 2012). By contrast, the book on the Tea Party written by Skocpol and Williamson (2012) almost does not employ the concept of populism.

Before we draw some lessons from this brief overview of the history of populism, we think that it is important to present a picture of the evolution of the scholarly production on populism. The graph in Figure 1.1 shows the number of books published in English since 1890 in which the word "populism" or "populist" appears in the title.[4] To a certain extent, this graph supports our argument that scholarship on populism started

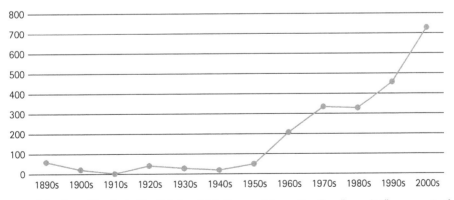

FIG. 1.1 Number of books in English in which the word "populism" or "populist" appears in the title (absolute number per decade).

to expand from the 1950s, when several scholars began to use the notion of populism to pinpoint "societal problems" and analyze different types of political forces in Latin America, Europe, and the United States. This trend toward increasing interest in the study of populism, experienced another fillip in the 1990s due to the rise of populist radical right forces in Europe and different forms of populism in the Americas. Today academic interest in populism is becoming much more global, to the point that scholars have begun to study populist forces in places such as Africa (Resnick, 2014), Asia (Mizuno and Phongpaichit, 2009), and the Middle East (Hadiz, 2016).

What does this brief overview of the history of populism tell us about the current state of the scholarship? In our opinion three key features stand out. First, we can say that there is a huge proliferation in the scholarship. There is extensive coverage of populism where it has emerged as a political force and there is certainly a broader application of the concept across the world. It is a welcome development to see that scholars are employing the term to study not only Europe and the Americas, but also many other regions. Secondly, as much of the interest in populism has been in its challenge to democratic politics and is linked to a perceived distrust of existing politics in certain segments of mass publics, so the focus on populism has become—for better or worse—very much the preserve of political scientists. Finally, despite the growth of literature and its concentration within one discipline, the study of populism still bears the hallmarks of its disparate and atomized origins. This means that the study of populism has not been recognized even by its own scholars and there has been a marked reluctance to systematically and comprehensively make use of work on populism from other regions or other historical periods. Too often the contemporary use of the term makes no reference to or acknowledgement of the existing body of work. We hope that the present volume helps to minimize this problem, as we include here chapters on populism in various regions, focused on a wide range of topics and with different analytical perspectives.

THE POLITICAL SCIENCE SCHOLARSHIP ON POPULISM SINCE 1990

While it is true that research on populism did not start just yesterday, it is important to acknowledge that the expansion of academic studies on this topic began to get greater traction starting in the 1990s. As the graph in Figure 1.1 shows, between 1990 and 2010 approximately twelve hundred books on populism were published in English and there are no signs that this trend toward increasing academic interest in populism will drop off in the near future. Nevertheless, there have been no attempts to examine how the political science community, mostly, has been studying populism. Can we identify if certain conceptual approaches are more dominant than others? Which are the methodologies that scholars prefer when it comes to studying populism? Do certain world regions receive more attention by those who are interested in populism? To answer these types of questions, we discuss in this section a database that considers most of the articles on populism published in political science journals since 1990. This exercise does not aim to offer a perfect picture of how political scientists are analyzing the populist phenomenon. Our goal is much more modest: this is just a first attempt to examine the academic scholarship on populism in the discipline that now most focuses on it.

To accomplish this goal, we constructed a database that includes all the articles published on populism in fourteen selected journals from 1990 to 2015.[5] With the aim of acknowledging the different approaches that exist in the discipline, we selected journals that consider the whole discipline (e.g. *American Journal of Political Science*), focus on comparative politics (e.g. *Comparative Political Studies*), and cover specific world regions (e.g. *Latin American Politics and Society* and *West European Politics*).[6] Moreover, we opted for a very restrictive criterion for selecting the papers: we included in the database only those articles in which the word "populism" or "populist" appears in the title and/or in the abstract. Based on this criterion, the total number of articles considered in the database is 158.

The graph in Figure 1.2 shows the number of articles published across the fourteen selected journals. As can be seen, the journals where we find the largest number of contributions on the topic in question are *West European Politics* (twenty-five articles), followed by *Party Politics* (twenty-two articles) and *Government and Opposition* (twenty articles). Another aspect that is worth mentioning is that some of the most prestigious journals in political science, such as the *American Journal of Political Science* and *American Political Science Review*, have almost no publications on this topic. This is probably related to the fact that mainstream political science in the United States, in part because of the importance of the study of US politics in its own right and an emphasis on certain forms of methodological sophistication, has until very recently devoted little attention to populism. The 2016 presidential election might represent a turning point, since US scholars have argued that two candidates—Bernie Sanders and Donald Trump—can be classified as populist leaders (Hawkins, 2016; Lowndes, 2016).

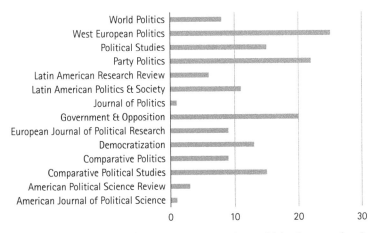

FIG. 1.2 Number of articles on populism, 1990–2015, per journal (absolute numbers).

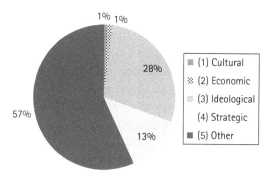

FIG. 1.3 Conceptual approach employed in articles on populism published in fourteen selected political science journals, 1990–2015 (percentage).

Research on populism has always been characterized by an open and ongoing debate about how to define the phenomenon. We examined if these recent articles in political science employed a cultural, economic, ideological, or strategic definition of populism. As can be seen in the graph in Figure 1.3, most contributions cannot be coded within these four categories. The reason for this is that many authors simply do not present a definition of populism or they develop a conceptualization that is very unclear. An important lesson that can be drawn from this is that part of the problem in the populism scholarship in political science (and probably also in other disciplines of the social sciences) is not so much the absence of sharp conceptualizations, but rather the tendency of scholars to avoid specifying their own understandings of populism. Moreover, while this debate is far from reaching an end, the graph also reveals that two types of conceptualizations—ideological and strategic approaches—have a relative degree of dominance within the field.

A more positive note on the evolution of the political science scholarship on populism can be seen in the graph in Figure 1.4, which shows the methodological approaches employed by scholars when it comes to studying the phenomenon in question. Qualitative and quantitative approaches are used almost with the same frequency (35 percent and 34 percent respectively), reflecting methodological pluralism in the analysis of populism. In addition, an important fraction of the published articles is focused on conceptual and/or theoretical debates (22 percent). This is something very peculiar to the study of populism as many scholars delve into abstract questions related to the definition of the phenomenon and its interaction with other phenomena or concepts such as democracy, extremism, hegemony, and popular sovereignty, amongst others.

Finally, we think that it is also relevant to examine which world regions are taken into account by the political science scholarship on populism. As can be seen in the graph in Figure 1.5, Western Europe and Latin America are the two regions that receive the most attention by far. Curiously, there is not much research on populism in North America, something that—as mentioned earlier—is probably related to the dearth of comparative studies of American politics within US political science and the focus on methodological

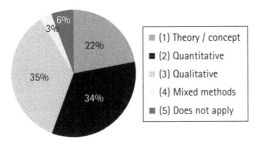

FIG. 1.4 Methodological approach employed in articles on populism published in fourteen selected political science journals, 1990–2015 (percentage).

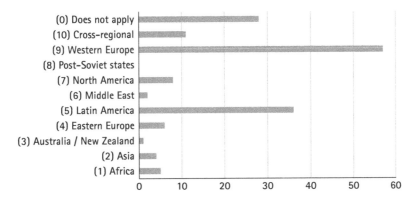

FIG. 1.5 Regions analysed in articles on populism published in fourteen political science journals (absolute numbers).

sophistication in US political science. Work on US populism has been produced mainly by scholars from other disciplines, particularly by historians (e.g. Formisano, 2012; Kazin, 1995; Postel, 2007) and legal scholars (e.g. Krammer, 2004, Michelman, 2001). Another interesting finding is the existence of a small amount of publications that have a cross-regional focus. This is a welcome development, since it allows the generation of cumulative knowledge beyond one specific country or world region.

ORGANIZATION OF THE HANDBOOK

We assembled this volume with the idea of trying to cover all the different aspects of populism that have been studied. For this purpose, we asked both junior and established scholars who are working on populism to write contributions on specific topics. We provided them not only clear guidelines but also feedback on the drafts of their contributions. The volume is organized in four parts. We open up with a short first part that presents the three definitions of populism that in our opinion are the most important in the scholarly debate in political science.[7] These three definitions can be thought of as different conceptual approaches, namely the ideational approach (Cas Mudde), the political-strategic approach (Kurt Weyland), and the socio-cultural approach (Pierre Ostiguy). Each of these approaches proposes a particular understanding of populism and indicates different ways for undertaking empirical analysis. Those who are not familiar with the question of how to define populism would do well to read these contributions in order to get a better sense of the current state of the discussion in political science.

It is worth noting that there is one type of conceptual approach that we have deliberately excluded: definitions centered on the economy. In fact, despite their different understandings of populism, Mudde, Weyland, and Ostiguy share the idea that populism should *not* be defined on the basis of a specific type of economic policies. Nevertheless, some scholars are still influenced by the work of Dornbusch and Edwards, two economists, who at the beginning of the 1990s argued that populism is an economic approach "that emphasizes growth and income distribution and deemphasizes the risks of inflation and deficit finance" (Dornbusch and Edwards, 1991: 9). For instance, Daron Acemoglu and his colleagues have published an article in which they claim that populism should be thought of as "the implementation of policies receiving support from a significant fraction of the population, but ultimately hurting the economic interests of this majority" (Acemoglu, Egorov, and Sonin, 2013: 2). There are two main problems with this type of economic definition. First, it points to the alleged consequences of populism but does not provide clear criteria for conceptualizing populism as such. Secondly, this type of definition limits populism to leftist or inclusionary forms, and in consequence, cannot grasp rightist or exclusionary expressions of populism that are predominant in various places of the world today.

The second part of the Handbook covers populism in different world regions. We have been able to commission contributions on Africa (Danielle E. Resnick), Australia and New Zealand (Benjamin Moffitt), Central and Eastern Europe (Ben Stanley), Latin America (Carlos de la Torre), post-Soviet states (Luke March), East Asia (Olli Hellman), and Western Europe (Paul Taggart). Because of their relevance for the study of populism, we also commissioned pieces on populism in two countries: India (Christophe Jaffrelot and Louise Tillin) and the United Stated (Joseph Lowndes). Unfortunately, we have not been able to include chapters on populism in China and in the Middle East. This omission is related to the fact that there is little current research on populism about those places. Moreover, the few studies that exist on populism in China and the Middle East are inclined to employ economic definitions of populism, which—as we indicated above—are problematic when it comes to conceptualizing the phenomenon and undertaking empirical research. All the chapters of this section work with one (or a combination) of the three conceptual approaches presented in the first section of the Handbook. Regarding the timeframe of the analysis, we asked all the authors to focus their contributions from the 1990s until 2016. The only exceptions are the chapters on Latin America and the US, written by Carlos de la Torre and Joseph Lowndes, respectively. Given that in the Americas there is a long trajectory of different kinds of populist forces, we asked the authors of the pieces on Latin America and the US to provide analyses that start before the 1990s.

For the third part of the Handbook, which is called "Issues," we invited several scholars who are working on different aspects of the populist phenomenon. Selecting the list of topics was not easy as there are many issues that one could find interesting, but not all of them have received enough attention by scholars. In addition, for this part we deliberately wanted to have contributions that do not focus on one specific country or region, but rather advance bold arguments that "travel" to different places. Achieving this criterion was anything but simple, because most scholars are experts on one country or region and therefore are reluctant to develop broad arguments. Take, for instance, the issue of immigration. In the last few years we have seen an explosion of academic publications on the xenophobic tendencies of the populist radical right, but this is *one* particular party family that has been gaining influence in Europe, and in consequence, there is no reason to think that populism is per se against immigration. Just as in Part II, we asked all authors to work with one (or a combination) of the three conceptual approaches presented in the first part of the Handbook.

Kirk A. Hawkins, Madeleine Read, and Teun Pauwels open Part III with a chapter on the causes of populism, which not only offers an overview of the different arguments advanced in the scholarly debate but also proposes a new theory for understanding the emergence of populism. After this, Kenneth M. Roberts examines the difficult relationship between populism and political parties, and then Paris Aslanidis specifies the characteristics of populist social movements. The next chapter is written by Chris Bickerton and Carlo Invernizzi Accetti, who analyze the unexpected parallels between populism and technocracy. In turn, Benjamin De Cleen makes clear that populism and nationalism are two different phenomena that are often confused, while Roger Eatwell disentangles the similitudes and differences between populism and fascism. Subsequently, Bertjan Verbeek and Andrej Zaslove have a contribution that addresses an important dimension that so far has received little attention: the link between populism and foreign policy. Then Francisco Panizza examines the extent to which populism is prone to trigger a peculiar type of identification, as part of its logic. After this, Sahar Abi-Hassan considers the ambivalent relationship between populism and gender. The next chapter is written by José Pedro Zúquete, who explores the extent to which populism bears some resemblance with religion, and then Luca Manucci writes about the links between populism and the media. Finally, this part closes with Cristóbal Rovira Kaltwasser's chapter, which is focused on the question of how to respond to the rise of populism.

In the last part, called "Normative debates," we turn to the analysis of populism from the perspective of normative and critical political theory. Our emphasis here is on what populism ought to be in relation to democracy. The authors in this part concentrate on the connections between populism and the principles and practices of democratic institutions, and they make explicit normative evaluations of populist practices. From a historical perspective, Duncan Kelly argues that populism is part of the history of popular sovereignty, and moreover, that such a history connects European and American democratic politics from the period of the 1848 revolutions through the present. Yannis Stavrakakis draws from Ernesto Laclau and Chantal Mouffe's Gramscian theory to discuss how populism articulates social practices into political identities which seek to build political hegemonies. From a very different theoretical perspective, Stefan Rummens argues that populism is a threat to liberal democracy. In his view, populism is in every case a symptom of a political problem, but not itself a solution. Nadia Urbinati, in turn, argues that populism as a ruling power produces governments that stretch the democratic rules toward an extreme majoritarianism, thus undermining democracy. In a similar vein, Jan-Werner Müller argues that contrary to widely held views, populism is not opposed to constitutionalism; rather, we can talk about a populist constitutionalism. Unlike others, however, populists use constitutions to inhibit pluralism. Paulina Ochoa Espejo further explores the relationship between populism and the people, and argues that the way we conceive of populism depends in great measure on how we conceive "the people" or the *demos* in a democracy. Jason Frank changes the question of *who* the people are, to *how* the people act in order to better appreciate populism's egalitarian praxis. Similarly, James Ingram disrupts the usual associations of populism as an enemy of cosmopolitanism, and explores the possibility of a productive cosmopolitan populism. Finally, Kevin Olson explores the heritage of social democracy since the nineteenth century, which in his view provides the means for a potential reconciliation between populism and democracy, establishing the material conditions for a radically populist politics.

Research Agenda

We would like to finish this introductory chapter to the *Oxford Handbook of Populism* by saying something about the current and future research agenda on populism. If it is true that the political science scholarship on populism is maturing and, in consequence, there is an important body of literature on which to build, it is relevant to know where we stand today, and which are the blind spots that scholars could try to address in the near future. Our first point is that populism has been slowly moving from the margins into the mainstream of the discipline. To a certain extent, this can be explained by the growing relevance of populist forces across the world and, in some cases, the entry of these forces into the political mainstream. As a result, contemporary analyses of populism are becoming much more global than before (e.g. de la Torre, 2014; Moffitt, 2016; Mudde and Rovira Kaltwasser, 2017; Taggart, 2000). Scholars interested in populism are studying not only cases in Europe and the Americas, but also African countries (Resnick, 2014) as well as new forms of Islamic populism (Hadiz, 2016). A further point is that those who research populism engage either implicitly or explicitly in normative discussions. This is related to the fact that populism is partially determined by how individuals and political systems envision the ideals of democracy, including the creation of collectives and the attainment of popular sovereignty. Thus, discussions regarding the definition of populism are influenced by normative standards and ideals that are often expressed in political theory and philosophy.

Furthermore, the increasing amount of research on populism translates into empirical innovation. This is particularly true for those who adhere to the so-called ideational approach, since they have developed new methods to measure both the demand for populism as well as the supply of populism. For instance, Kirk Hawkins (2009) has employed the holistic grading technique to analyze empirically the level of populism in the discourse of presidents, whereas Bart Bonikowski and Noam Gidron (2016) have used automated text analysis to study populist claims-making in US electoral discourse. At the same time, Agnes Akkerman and her colleagues have developed a set of items to measure populist attitudes at the mass level in the Netherlands (Akkermann, Mudde, and Zaslove, 2014), while Eric Oliver and Wendy Rahn have employed a similar set of items to show that Trump supporters hold populist sentiments (Oliver and Rahn 2016). This type of applied empirical research is a welcome development, since it helps to generate cumulative knowledge on how to classify specific leaders and parties as populist or not as well as to better understand why certain segments of the population support populist forces.

Before concluding, let's turn our attention to the future research agenda on populism. The first point that we want to stress is that scholars interested in populism should not overlook the existing body of literature. Cumulative knowledge is necessary for the progress of the field, and the contributions of this Handbook offer a good overview of the current state of the art. At the same time, although there is no consensus on how to define populism, scholars should make an effort to present a clear conceptualization of the phenomenon. This implies clarifying not only what is populism but also what is not. In other words, we are of the opinion that future research needs to put more attention on the family of concepts related to, or opposed to, populism, since this is an important exercise for avoiding conceptual overstretching. We need to make sure that we do not collapse the semantic field, equating populism with other phenomena or categories that are often, but not always, associated with it, such as xenophobia in Europe or clientelism in Latin America or anti-establishment politics in all parts of the world. Part of this can be done through empirical research and measurement, but we also need to think more thoroughly about the differences and similarities between populism and other phenomena that regularly occur together with it but are not necessarily part of it. Populism rarely travels alone. It is necessary to identify what it travels with.

Populism also needs to be considered comparatively. It is no longer adequate to leave the term to those needing a word of abuse in political editorializing in newspapers or to those that construct ad hoc, context-specific definitions. Just as with any other concept we need to see the boundaries and be clear about them but we also need to look at the reach of the term. This means being prepared to reach across different regional and historical contexts and treat the term comparatively. Fortunately, there are some interesting examples of research on populism with a cross-regional focus, such as Weyland's (1999) study on populism in Eastern Europe and Latin America as well as the work of Mudde and Rovira Kaltwasser (2012) on the impact of populism on democracy in Europe and the Americas. Other interesting examples are the comparison between exclusionary vs inclusionary subtypes of populism in Western Europe and Latin America (Mudde and Rovira Kaltwasser, 2013), the analysis of left-wing populism in Argentina and right-wing populism in Turkey (Aytaç and Öniş, 2014), as well as the comparative study on responses to populists in government in Eastern Europe, Latin America, and Western Europe (Rovira Kaltwasser and Taggart, 2016).

In addition, the inherent tension between populism and democracy forces a dialogue between political science and normative political theory. We don't see this as a problem, but rather as a strength of the academic debate that can and should illuminate future research. The debate of the relation between populism and democracy has up to now been conceived in terms of opposition, in order to determine whether populism is good or bad for liberal democratic practices. Yet, this debate has begun to become stale: if something has so far become clear from these debates it is that, as a matter of fact, populism goes hand in hand with democracy (Arditi, 2004; Canovan, 1999; Rovira Kaltwasser, 2014b). This may be true normatively as well. If democracy cannot be detached from populism, can we think of ways to make populism an ally to democratizing forces? This new approach may require that we shift our efforts to understand, evaluate, and critique the *how* of populism, both in government and in opposition, such that populist practices can retain the tendency to expand participation and inclusion, without undermining pluralism and the rights of minorities or the loss of all decorum.

The aspiration for this Handbook is both that it provides a sign-post to the considerable body of work that has been done in the past on populism in the hope that this can be built upon, but also that it may provoke reaction and response in future research. Populism, for some, is a challenge to the functioning of contemporary democratic politics. For others it is an indicator of problems with politics. While, for others, it is a radical and empowering force. Whatever way it is seen, a systematic understanding of populism based on the knowledge of the new body of populism studies that we identify in this Handbook is a necessary part of understanding not only populism but the politics that it generates.

Notes

1. One of the features of the term populism is that it is widely used but loosely applied and so presents some difficulty. The casual use of the term, often as one of opprobrium, is frequent. There is some sense of differentiating between the "vernacular" use of the term where it is employed by politicians and media commentators as a short-hand pejorative word and a more analytical academic usage (which may or may not share the pejorative connotation of the vernacular use). We are focusing here on the second but we are aware of the first.

2. There is a debate about whether populism is the best translation of *narodniki* (Pipes, 1964).

3. Interestingly, the link with agrarianism can also be found in the emergence of populism during the first decades of the twentieth century in Eastern Europe (Ionescu, 1969). Before the communist period, Eastern European societies were mostly rural and only marginally democratic. Therefore, it is not a coincidence that agrarian populism became an important ideology through which different leaders, movements, and parties tried to denounce

the often deplorable situation of the rural population (Canovan, 1981: 98–135; Mudde, 2012: 218–19).

4 The data presented here comes from the catalog WorldCat (https://www.worldcat.org/). We have searched for all books in English from 1890 until 2009 in which the word "populism" or "populist" is used in the title. For practical reasons we decided to present the data in absolute numbers for decades. It is worth mentioning that we made the same search with Google Books Ngram Viewer, which works with percentages instead of absolute numbers, and the results show the same trend of increasing publications on populism.

5 We are very grateful to Cristóbal Sandoval for his work on the construction of this database.

6 The fourteen selected journals are the following (listed in alphabetical order): *American Journal of Political Science, American Political Science Review, Comparative Politics, Comparative Political Studies, Democratization, European Journal of Political Research, Government and Opposition, Journal of Politics, Latin American Research Review, Latin American Politics and Society, Party Politics, Political Studies, West European Politics*, and *World Politics*.

7 Those who are familiar with the work of Ernesto Laclau (2005) might wonder why we didn't include a chapter with the conceptualization of populism advanced in his work. The reason for this is twofold. On the one hand, the so-called ideational approach developed by Mudde in this volume stays in close relationship with the work of Laclau, although it is also true that Mudde and many others who are sympathetic to the ideational approach distance themselves from Laclau's normative impetus and are inclined to undertake empirical knowledge in a more positivist fashion. On the other hand, given that many of the articles that we include across the Handbook propose new insights on the populist phenomenon by relying on the work of Laclau, his impact on the scholarship is well represented.

REFERENCES

Acemoglu, Daron, Georgy Egerov, and Konstantin Sonin. 2013. "A political theory of populism," *The Quarterly Journal of Economics*, 128(2): 771–805.

Akkerman, Agnes, Cas Mudde, and Andrej Zaslove. 2014. "How populist are the people? Measuring populist attitudes in voters," *Comparative Political Studies*, 47(9): 1324–53.

Akkerman, Tjitske, Sarah de Lange, and Matthijs Rooduijn (eds). 2016. *Radical Right-Wing Populist Parties in Western Europe: Into the Mainstream?* London: Routledge.

Albertazzi, Daniele and Duncan McDonnell. 2015. *Populists in Power*. London: Routledge.

Allcock, John. 1971. "Populism: a brief biography," *Sociology*, 5(3): 371–87.

Arditi, Benjamin. 2004. "Populism as a spectre of democracy: a response to Canovan," *Political Studies*, 52(1): 135–43.

Art, David. 2011. *Inside the Radical Right: The Development of Anti-Immigrant Parties in Western Europe*. New York: Cambridge University Press.

Aslanidis, Paris. 2016. "Populist social movements of the Great Recession," *Mobilization: An International Quarterly*, 21(3): 301–21.

Aytaç, Erdem S. and Ziya Öniş. 2014. "Varieties of populism in a changing global context: the divergent paths of Erdoğan and Kirchnerismo," *Comparative Politics*, 47(1): 41–59.

Bale, Tim, Stijn Van Kessel, and Paul Taggart. 2011. "Thrown around with abandon? Popular understandings of populism as conveyed by the print media: a UK case study," *Acta Politica*, 46(2): 111–31.

Berlet, Chip and Matthew N. Lyons. 2000. *Right-wing Populism in America: Too Close for Comfort*. New York: Guilford Press.

Betz, Hans-Georg (forthcoming). "Populist mobilisation across time and space," in Kirk A. Hawkins, Ryan Carlin, Levente Littvay, and Cristóbal Rovira Kaltwasser (eds): *New Directions in Populism Research: Theory, Methods and Cases*. London: Routledge.

Birnbaum, P. 2012. *Genèse du populisme: le peuple et les gros*. Pluriel.

Bonikowski, Bart and Gidron Noam. 2016. "The populist style in American politics: presidential campaign discourse, 1952–1996," *Social Forces* 94(4): 1593–1621.

Bornschier, Simon. 2010. *Cleavage Politics and the Populist Right: The New Cultural Conflict in Western Europe*. Philadelphia: Temple University Press.

Canovan, Margaret. 1981. *Populism*. New York: Harcourt Brace.

Canovan, Margaret. 1999. "Trust the People! Populism and the two faces of democracy," *Political Studies* 47(1): 2–16.

Cardoso, Fernando Henrique and Enzo Faletto. 1969. *Dependencia y desarrollo en América Latina*. Mexico: Editorial Siglo XXI.

Carrión, Julio (ed.). 2006. *The Fujimori Legacy: The Rise of Electoral Authoritarianism in Peru*. University Park: Pennsylvania State University Press.

Castañeda, Jorge and Marco Morales (eds). 2008. *Leftovers: Tales of the Latin American Left*. London: Routledge.

Collier, David and Ruth B. Collier. 1991. *Shaping the Political Arena: Critical Junctures, the Labor Movement, and Regime Dynamics in Latin America*. Princeton: Princeton University Press.

Conniff, Michael L. 2012. "Introduction," in Michael L. Conniff (ed.), *Populism in Latin America*, 2nd edn. Tuscaloosa: University of Alabama Press.

Dahl, Robert. 1956. *A Preface to Democratic Theory*. Chicago: Chicago University Press.

de la Torre, Carlos. 2000. *Populist Seduction in Latin America: The Ecuadorian Experience*. Athens: Ohio State University Press.

de la Torre, Carlos. 2007. "The resurgence of radical populism in Latin America," *Constellations*, 14(3): 384–97.

de la Torre, Carlos (ed.). 2014. *The Promise and Perils of Populism: Global Perspectives*. Lexington: University of Kentucky Press.

de la Torre, Carlos and Cynthia J. Arnson. 2013. "Introduction: the evolution of Latin American populism and the debates over its meaning," in Carlos De la Torre and Cynthia J. Arnson (eds), *Latin American Populism in the Twenty-First Century*. Baltimore: The Johns Hopkins University Press.

di Tella, Torcuato. 1965. "Populism and reform in Latin America," in C. Veliz (ed.), *Obstacles to Change in Latin America*. Oxford: Oxford University Press.

Dornbusch, Rudiger and Sebastian Edwards (eds). 1991. *The Macroeconomics of Populism*. Chicago: University of Chicago Press.

Drake, Paul. 1978. *Socialism and Populism in Chile, 1932–1952*. Urbana: University of Illinois Press.

Fallend, Franz and Reinhard Heinisch. 2016. "Collaboration as successful strategy against right-wing populism? The case of the centre-right coalition in Austria, 2000–2007," *Democratization*, 23(2): 324–44.

Freidenberg, Flavia. 2007. *La tentación populista: una vía al poder en América Latina*. Salamanca: Editorial Síntesis.

Formisano, Ron. 2012. *The Tea Party*. Baltimore: Johns Hopkins University Press.

Gentile, Gino. 2006. *Politics as Religion*. Princeton: Princeton University Press.

Germani, Gino. 1978. *Authoritarianism, Fascism and National Populism*. New Brunswick: Transaction.

Gibson, Edward. 1997. "The Populist road to market reform: policy and electoral coalitions in Mexico and Argentina," *World Politics*, 49(3): 339–70.

Goodwyn, Lawrence. 1976. *Democratic Promise: The Populist Moment in America*. New York: Oxford University Press.

Goodwyn, Lawrence. 1978. *The Populist Moment: A Short History of the Agrarian Revolt in America*. Oxford University Press.

Grattan, Laura. 2016. *Populism's Power: Radical Grassroots Democracy in America*. Oxford: Oxford University Press.

Griffin, Roger. 1991. *The Nature of Fascism*. London: Routledge.

Hadiz, Vedi. 2016. *Islamic Populism in Indonesia and the Middle East*. Cambridge: Cambridge University Press.

Hawkins, Kirk. 2009. "Is Chávez populist? Measuring populist discourse in comparative perspective," *Comparative Political Studies*, 42(8): 1040–67.

Hawkins, Kirk. 2016. "Populism and the 2016 U.S. presidential election in comparative perspective," in Matt Golder and Sona Golder (eds), "Symposium: Populism in Comparative Perspective," *CP: Newsletter of the Comparative Politics Organized Section of the American Political Science Association*, 26(2): 91–7.

Hawkins, Kirk and Cristóbal Rovira Kaltwasser. 2017. "The ideational approach to populism," *Latin American Research Review* (forthcoming).

Hermet, Guy. 2001. *Les populismes dans le monde: une histoire sociologique (XIXe–XXe siècle)*. Paris: Fayard.

Hermet, Guy. 2013. "Foundational populism," in S. Gherghina, S. Mişcoiu, and S. Soare (eds), *Contemporary Populism: A Controversial Concept and Its Diverse Forms*. Newcastle upon Tyne: Cambridge Scholars Publishing.

Hofstadter, Richard. 1955. *The Age of Reform: From Bryan to FDR*. New York: Vintage.

Houwen, Tim. 2013. *Reclaiming Power for the People: Populism in Democracy*. Nijmegen: Radboud University.

Ignazi, Piero. 1992. "The silent counter-revolution: Hypotheses on the emergence of extreme right-wing parties in Europe," *European Journal of Political Research*, 22(1): 3–34.

Ionescu, Ghita. 1969. "Eastern Europe," in Ghita Ionescu and Ernst Gellner (eds), *Populism: Its Meanings and National Characteristics*. London: Weidenfeld and Nicolson.

Ionescu, Ghita and Ernst Gellner (eds). 1969. *Populism: Its Meanings and National Characteristics*. London: Weidenfeld and Nicolson.

Kazin, Michael. 1995. *The Populist Persuasion*, rev. edn. Ithaca: Cornell University Press.

Kornhauser, William. 1959. *The Politics of Mass Society*. Glencoe: The Free Press.

Krammer, Larry. 2004. *The People Themselves: Popular Constitutionalism and Judicial Review*. Oxford: Oxford University Press.

Kriesi, Hanspeter. 2014. "The populist challenge," *West European Politics*, 37(2): 361–78.

Kriesi, Hanspeter and Takis Pappas (eds). 2015. *European Populism in the Shadow of the Great Recession*. Colchester: ECPR Press.

Kriesi, Hanspeter, Edgar Grande, Romain Lachat, Martin Dolezal, Simon Bornschier, and Timotheos Frey. 2008. *West European Politics in the Age of Globalization*. Cambridge: Cambridge University Press.

Laclau, Ernesto. 1977. *Politics and Ideology in Marxist Theory: Capitalism, Fascism and Populism*. London: New Left Books.

Laclau, Ernesto. 2005. *On Populist Reason*. London: Verso.

Laclau, Ernesto and Chantal Mouffe. 1985. *Hegemony and Socialist Strategy: Towards a Radical Democratic Politics*. London: Verso.

Lee, Daniel. 2016. *Popular Sovereignty in Early Modern Constitutional Thought*. Oxford: Oxford University Press.

Levistky, Steven. 2003. *Transforming Labor-Based Parties in Latin America: Argentine Peronism in Comparative Perspective*. Cambridge: Cambridge University Press.

Levitsky, Steven and Kenneth Roberts (eds). 2011. *The Resurgence of the Latin American Left*. Baltimore: Johns Hopkins University Press.

Lipset, Seymour Martin. 1960. *Political Man: The Social Bases of Politics*. Garden City: Doubleday.

Lowndes, Joseph. 2016. "Populism in the 2016 U.S. presidential election," in Matt Golder and Sona Golder (eds), "Symposium: Populism in Comparative Perspective," *CP: Newsletter of the Comparative Politics Organized Section of the American Political Science Association*, 26(2): 97–101.

March, Luke. 2012. *Radical Left Parties in Europe*. London: Routledge.

Michelman, Frank I. 1998. "Constitutional authorship," in L. Alexander (ed.), *Constitutionalism: Philosophical Foundations*. Cambridge: Cambridge University Press, 64–98.

Mizuno, Kosuke and Pasuk Phongpaichit (eds). 2009. *Populism in Asia*. Singapore: Singapore University Press.

Moffitt, Benjamin. 2016. *The Global Rise of Populism: Performance, Political Style, and Representation*. Stanford: Stanford University Press.

Mouzelis, Nikos. 1978. "The Greek elections and the rise of PASOK," *New Left Review*, 108(1): 59–76.

Mudde, Cas. 2007. *Populist Radical Right Parties in Europe*. Cambridge: Cambridge University Press.

Mudde, Cas. 2012. "In the name of the peasantry, the proletariat, and the people: populisms in Eastern Europe," in Yves Meny and Yves Surel (eds), *Democracies and the Populist Challenge*. Basingstoke: Palgrave Macmillan, 33–53.

Mudde, Cas. 2013. "Three decades of populist radical right parties in Western Europe: So what?," *European Journal of Political Research*, 52(1): 1–19.

Mudde, Cas and Cristóbal Rovira Kaltwasser (eds). 2012. *Populism in Europe and the Americas: Threat or Corrective for Democracy?* Cambridge: Cambridge University Press.

Mudde, Cas and Cristóbal Rovira Kaltwasser. 2013. "Exclusionary vs. inclusionary populism: comparing contemporary Europe and Latin America," *Government and Opposition*, 48(2): 147–74.

Mudde, Cas and Cristóbal Rovira Kaltwasser. 2017. *Populism: A Very Short Introduction*. New York: Oxford University Press.

Nelson, Eric. 2016. "Prerogative, Popular Sovereignty and the American Founding," in R. Bourke and Q. Skinner (eds), *Popular Sovereignty in Historical Perspective*. Cambridge: Cambridge University Press.

Norris, P. 2005. *Radical Right: Voters and Parties in the Electoral Market*. New York: Cambridge University Press.

Ochoa Espejo, Paulina. 2011. *The Time of Popular Sovereignty: Process and the Democratic State*. University Park: Pennsylvania State University Press.

O'Donnell, Guillermo. 1994. "Delegative democracy," *Journal of Democracy*, 5(1): 55–69.

Oliver, Eric J. and Wendy M. Rahn. 2016. "Rise of the Trumpenvolk: populism in the 2016 election," *The ANNALS of the American Academy of Political and Social Science* 667(1): 189–206.

Panizza, Francisco. 2000. "Beyond 'delegative democracy': 'old politics' and 'new economics' in Latin America," *Journal of Latin American Studies*, 32(3): 737–63.

Passmore, Kevin. 2012. *The Right in France from the Third Republic to Vichy*. Oxford: Oxford University Press.

Peruzzotti, Enrique. 2001. "The nature of new Argentine democracy: delegative democracy revisited," *Journal of Latin American Studies*, 33(1): 133–55.

Pipes, Richard. 1964. "Narodnichestvo: a semantic inquiry," *Slavic Review*, 23(3): 441–58.

Postel, Charles. 2007. *The Populist Vision*. New York: Oxford University Press.

Priester, Karin. 2007. *Populismus: historische und aktuelle Erscheinungsformen*. Frankfurt/New York: Campus.

Resnick, Danielle E. 2014. *Urban Poverty and Party Populism in African Democracies*. New York: Cambridge University Press.

Roberts, Kenneth. 1995. "Neoliberalism and the transformation of populism in Latin America: the Peruvian case," *World Politics*, 48(1): 82–116.

Roberts, Kenneth. 2008. "The mobilization of opposition to economic liberalization," *Annual Review of Political Science*, 11: 327–49.

Rovira Kaltwasser, Cristóbal. 2014a. "Latin American populism: some conceptual and normative lessons," *Constellations*, 22(4): 494–504.

Rovira Kaltwasser, Cristóbal. 2014b. "The responses of populism to Dahl's democratic dilemmas," *Political Studies*, 62(3): 470–87.

Rovira Kaltwasser, Cristóbal and Paul Taggart. 2016. "Dealing with populists in government: a framework for analysis," *Democratization*, 23(2): 201–20.

Riker, William. 1982. *Liberalism against Populism: A Confrontation between the Theory of Democracy and the Theory of Social Choice*. San Francisco: Waveland.

Rydgren, Jens. 2005. "Is extreme right-wing populism contagious? Explaining the emergence of a new party family," *European Journal of Political Research*, 44(3): 413–37.

Sabbadini, Lorenzo. 2016. "Popular sovereignty in historical perspective," in R. Bourke and Q. Skinner (eds), *Popular Sovereignty in Historical Perspective*. Cambridge: Cambridge University Press, 142–63.

Shields, J. 2004. "An enigma still: Poujadism fifty years on," *French Politics, Culture and Society*, 22(1): 36–56.

Shils, Edward. 1956. *The Torment of Secrecy*. New York: The Free Press.

Skocpol, Theda. and Vanessa Williamson. 2012. *The Tea Party and the Remaking of Republican Conservatism*. New York: Oxford University Press.

Stavrakakis, Yannis and Giorgos Katsambekis. 2014. "Left-wing populism in the European periphery: the case of SYRIZA," *Journal of Political Ideologies*, 19(2): 119–42.

Taggart, Paul. 1995. "New populist parties in Western Europe," *West European Politics*, 18(1): 34–51.

Taggart, Paul. 2000. *Populism*. Buckingham: Open University Press.

Tuck, Richard. 2016. *The Sleeping Sovereign: The Invention of Modern Democracy*. Cambridge: Cambridge University Press.

Venturi, Franco. 1960. *Roots of Revolution: A History of the Populist and Socialist Movements in Nineteenth Century Russia*. London: Weidenfeld and Nicolson.

Walicki, Andrzej. 1969. *The Controversy over Capitalism: Studies in the Social Philosophy of the Russian Populists*. Oxford: Clarendon Press.

Weyland, Kurt. 1993. "The rise and fall of president Collor and its impact on Brazilian democracy," *Journal of Interamerican Studies and World Affairs*, 35(1): 1–37.

Weyland, Kurt. 1996. "Neopopulism and neoliberalism in Latin America: unexpected affinities," *Studies in Comparative International Development*, 31(3): 3–31.

Weyland, Kurt. 1999. "Neoliberal populism in Latin America and Eastern Europe," *Comparative Politics*, 31(4): 379–401.

Weyland, Kurt. 2001. "Clarifying a contested concept: populism in the study of Latin American politics," *Comparative Politics*, 34(1): 1–22.

Weyland, Kurt. 2013. "The threat from the populist left," *Journal of Democracy*, 24(3): 18–32.

Winock, Michel. 1997. "Populismes français," in *Vingtième Siècle, revue d'histoire*, n°56, octobre–décembre, *Les populismes*, 77–91.

Wolfreys, Jim. 2013. "The European extreme right in comparative perspective," in Andrea Mammone, Emmanuel Godin, and Brian Jenkins (eds), *Varieties of Right-Wing Extremism in Europe*. New York and London: Routledge, 19–37.

PART I

CONCEPTS

CHAPTER 2

....

POPULISM

An Ideational Approach

....

CAS MUDDE

INTRODUCTION

MOST concepts in the social sciences are contested, but few are what W. B. Gallie has called essentially contested concepts, i.e. "concepts the proper use of which inevitably involves endless disputes about their proper uses on the part of their users" (1955–6: 169).[1] Populism is undoubtedly an essentially contested concept, given that scholars even contest the essence and usefulness of the concept. While a disturbingly high number of scholars use the concept without ever defining it, others have defined populism as a type of political discourse, ideology, leadership, movement, phenomenon, strategy, style, syndrome, et cetera (e.g. Ionescu and Gellner, 1969). The debate over the true meaning of populism is not just a consequence of the multidisciplinary nature of the research, which includes studies in art history, criminology, economics, education, history, political science, and sociology. Even within one single discipline, like political science, scholars disagree fundamentally about the essence and usefulness of the concept of populism.

But though it has been defined in many different ways, the ideational approach has almost always been at least part of the study of populism. As Ernesto Laclau already observed at the end of the 1970s:

> We can single out four basic approaches to an interpretation of populism. Three of them consider it *simultaneously* as a movement and as an ideology. A fourth reduces it to a purely ideological phenomenon. (1977: 144)

The importance of ideas (and even ideology) can be seen in most studies of the first populist movements, i.e. the Russian *narodniki* (e.g. Karaömerlioglu, 1996; Pipes, 1960) and the US Populists (e.g. Ferkiss, 1957; Kazin, 1995), and in the early studies of generic populism (e.g. Canovan, 1981; Ionescu and Gellner, 1969). And while today organizational definitions remain popular, in studies of Latin American populism in particular (Weyland, 2001), even these studies often include explicitly ideational elements as well (e.g. Roberts, 1995).

In recent years (purely) ideational approaches to populism have gained popularity, particularly within comparative politics. Most notably, a majority of scholars of European populism employ explicitly or implicitly ideational definitions (e.g. Abts and Rummens, 2007; Rooduijn, 2013; Stanley, 2008). But ideational definitions have been successfully employed in studies of non-European populism too. They are even making serious inroads in the well-established study of Latin American populism (e.g. Hawkins, 2009; Rovira Kaltwasser, 2014). Though it is still far too early to speak of an emerging consensus, it is undoubtedly fair to say that the ideational approach to populism is the most broadly used in the field today.

In the next section I will outline the ideational approach to populism, present my own ideological definition, and discuss its key concepts (ideology, the people, the elite, and the general will). This is followed by a section that highlights the main strengths of the approach—i.e. *distinguishability, categorizability, travelability*, and *versatility*—and a section that compares it to other approaches. The chapter is finished with a short conclusion.

AN IDEATIONAL APPROACH TO POPULISM

The argument that ideational definitions of populism date back to the first studies of populism, and have recently become most popular in the field, requires some explanation and qualification. In addition to the many studies that explicitly define populism as an ideology, numerous studies do not include clear definitions, but nevertheless employ implicitly ideational understandings of populism. For example, in one of the first books on the topic, *Errors of Populism*, Hermon Craven, while never explicitly defining the concept, aims to correct "the teachings of Populism as set forth by representative party leaders" (1896: 4). Other early authors include (an undefined) populism in lists of one or more established ideologies, such as anarchism and socialism (e.g. McCormick, 1898; Platt, 1896).

Until the 1960s much of the academic literature that used the term populism was single country studies, most notably of the United States. Authors would use the term exclusively as a descriptor of a specific movement, particularly the US Populist movement and US People's Party, leaving the concept of populism largely undefined and mostly useless outside of that particular geographical and historical context. The consequences of this disparate study of populism were painfully clear in the seminal edited volume *Populism: Its Meanings and National Characteristics* (Ionescu and Gellner, 1969), which featured a bewildering range of definitions of populism. Among them, however, was also probably the first attempt at a generic definition of populism as an ideology (McRae, 1969). Since then, many scholars have defined populism as a set of ideas, but few have provided comprehensive discussions on the topic (though see Mudde and Rovira Kaltwasser, 2013a; Rensmann, 2006; Stanley, 2008).

In addition to those who define populism explicitly as an ideology, there are many scholars who use an ideational approach, even if they shy away from using the term ideology. Many scholars, for example, follow the late Argentine philosopher Ernesto Laclau (1977; 2005) in defining populism essentially as a type of political "discourse" (e.g. Howarth, 2005; Stavrakakis, 2004). Others define populism as a "language" (e.g. Kazin, 2005), "mode of identification" (e.g. Panizza, 2005b), "political frame" (e.g. Lee, 2006), or "political style" (e.g. Jagers and Walgrave, 2007; Moffitt and Tormey, 2014). Whatever the specific term scholars within the ideational approach use, all consider populism to be, first and foremost, about ideas in general, and ideas about "the people" and "the elite" in particular.

The Definition

In his famous chapter "A syndrome, not a doctrine: some elementary theses on populism," Peter Wiles wrote: "Its ideology is loose, and attempts to define it exactly arouse derision and hostility" (1969: 167). While this might still be true to some extent, Margaret Canovan's seminal book *Populism* (1981) has significantly decreased the derision and hostility. Ironically, while Canovan argues that there is no one thing called populism, she also identified the key ideological features that are central to most (ideational) definitions in the field.

My own definition of populism includes most of these features. It defines populism as "an ideology that considers society to be ultimately separated into two homogeneous and antagonistic groups, 'the pure people' versus 'the corrupt elite', and which argues that politics should be an expression of the volonté générale (general will) of the people" (Mudde 2004: 543). This definition includes four "core concepts," which are both central to and constitutive of the populist ideology (Ball, 1999: 391) and require more detailed discussions: ideology, the people, the elite, and general will. Before I discuss these four core concepts, however, an investigation of the essence of the populist division, *morality*, is in order.

Several ideologies are based upon a fundamental opposition between the people and the elite. However, whereas in socialism this opposition is based on the concept of class (Marx and Engels, 1998 [1848]) and in nationalism on the concept of nation (e.g. Hobsbawn, 1990), in populism the opposition is based on the concept of morality. Even within their own nation populists see a fundamental opposition between "the people" and "the elite." And while they may have different socio-economic interests, this is not because of class, a concept that populism deems at best secondary, but because of morality.

The essence of the people is their purity, in the sense that they are "authentic," while the elite are corrupt, because they are not authentic. Purity and authenticity are not defined in (essentially) ethnic or racial terms, but in moral terms. It is about "doing the right thing," which means doing what is right for all the people. This is possible, because populism considers "the people" to be a homogeneous category. By determining the main opposition to be between the *pure* people and the *corrupt* elite, populism presupposes that the elite comes from the same group as the people, but have willingly chosen to betray them, by putting the special interests and inauthentic morals of the elite over those of the people. Because the distinction is based on morality and not class or nation, millionaires like Silvio Berlusconi (Italy) or ethnic minorities like Alberto Fujimori (Peru) can be considered more authentic representatives of the people than leaders with a more common socio-economic status or a majority ethnic background (see Mudde and Rovira Kaltwasser, 2017).

Ideology

The most important, as well as the most controversial, concept in the ideational approach is ideology. Just like populism, "(i)deology is a word that evokes strong emotional responses" (Freeden, 2003: 1). Much of the debate about the usefulness of the concept of ideology is, ironically perhaps, ideological. The term ideology is used here in an inclusive way, i.e. as "a body of normative and normative-related ideas about the nature of man and society as well as the organization and purposes of society" (Sainsbury, 1980: 8). Ideologies, as Michael Freeden (2003: 2) has convincingly argued, "map the political and social worlds for us."

More specifically, populism is a "thin" or "thin-centered" ideology (e.g. Abts and Rummens, 2007; Mudde, 2004; Stanley, 2008). Thin or thin-centered ideologies do not possess the same level of intellectual refinement and consistency as "thick" or "full" ideologies, such as socialism or liberalism.[2] Instead, they exhibit "a restricted core attached to a narrower range of political concepts" (Freeden, 1998: 750). Consequently, thin ideologies have a more limited ambition and scope than thick ideologies; they do not formulate "a broad menu of solutions to major socio-political issues" (Freeden, 2003: 96). For example, while populism speaks to the main division in society (between "the pure people" and "the corrupt elite"), and offers general advice for the best way to conduct politics (i.e. in line with "the general will of the people"), it offers few specific views on political institutional or socio-economic issues.[3]

Reflecting the larger academic community to a large extent, various populism scholars within the ideational approach have serious practical and (meta-)theoretical problems with the term ideology. Although often using almost identical definitions in terms of substance, they explicitly reject the term ideology. Instead, some provide no alternative term (e.g. Hakhverdian and Koop, 2007; Linden, 2008), while others prefer to define populism as essentially claims-making (Bonikowski and Gidron, 2016), a communication style (e.g. Jagers and Walgrave, 2007), discourse (e.g. Lowndes, 2008; Panizza, 2005a), (discursive) frame (e.g. Aslanidis, 2016; Caiani and Della Porta, 2011), political appeal (e.g. Deegan-Krause and Haughton, 2009), political argument (e.g. Bimes and

Mulroy, 2004), political style (e.g. Moffitt, 2016; Moffitt and Tormey, 2014), or rhetoric (e.g. de la Torre, 2010; Kazin, 1995). Many of these authors have a general theoretical aversion to the use of the concept of ideology, arguing that it is too inflexible and mono-lithic (e.g. Caiani and Della Porta, 2011) or, in line with rational choice theory, that polit-ical actors always, in the end, act strategically.

Other populism scholars have no theoretical problems with the concept of ideology, but reject the term specifically for the case of populism. They argue that while populists use a populist *discourse*, they do not really believe in it—often in sharp contrast to their nationalism and xenophobia, which are considered to be genuine ideological features (e.g. Mammone, 2009). Uwe Backes and Eckhard Jesse (1998: 24) literally describe pop-ulism as "a concept to gain power" (*Machteroberungskonzept*). This argument is some-what similar to the front-stage versus back-stage discussion in the literature on extreme right parties (Van Donselaar, 1991: 16–17), which also assumes that these particular poli-ticians are insincere. But whereas right-wing extremists are alleged to say less than they really believe in, populists are supposed to say more. In essence, populists are accused of saying whatever the people want to hear in an opportunistic attempt to gain popularity.

Clearly, it is unscientific to simply presume that *certain* politicians lie—or, to put it more neutrally, act purely strategically—and others do not. The authenticity of their populism should be an empirical question rather than a theoretical assumption. After all, it can be established empirically. For example, if the ideology of so-called populist actors includes key elitist or pluralist features too, it can be concluded that populism is at best a relatively weak ideological feature. Similarly, if a populist comes to power and either drops her or his populist ideology or implements clearly anti-populist measures, one can convincingly argue that her or his populism was merely a strategic tool to gain power. However, given that few populists ever gain the necessary power to fully imple-ment the policies they want, the distinction between ideology and discourse/strategy is fairly irrelevant in most empirical studies of "real existing populism" (see also Havlík and Pinková, 2012: 20).[4]

In the end, whether or not populism is defined as a full ideology rather than a looser set of ideas, centered around the fundamental opposition between "the pure people" and "the corrupt elite," is in most cases of secondary importance to the research ques-tion and often impossible to determine empirically. In essence, the various definitions within the ideational approach share a clear core, which both holds them together and sets them apart from other approaches to populism.

The People

The key core concept of populism is, obviously, "the people." Even the other core con-cepts, "the elite" and the "general will," take their meaning from it—as being its opposite and its expression, respectively.

Much attention and criticism in the literature has been directed at the concept of the people. Many authors have argued that the people do not really exist and are a mere construction of the populists. This is certainly true, but this has also been convincingly argued of core concepts of other ideologies, like class (e.g. Sartori, 1990) and nation (e.g. Brubaker, 1996). Obviously, history has taught us that the fact that core concepts of main ideologies are based on "imagined communities" (Anderson, 1983) has not made them less relevant in actual politics and societies.

What sets the people apart from class or nation, according to some critics, is that it has no real content at all. This critique is largely a response to Laclau's influential work on populism, which refers to the concept of the people (and therefore also the elite) as "empty signifiers" (Laclau, 1977). But while the signifier is certainly very flexible, in my ideological approach it is not completely empty: first of all, as populism is essentially based on a *moral* divide, the people are "pure"; and while purity is a fairly vague term, and the specific understanding is undoubtedly culturally determined, it does provide some content to the signifier.

Moreover, as Paul Taggart has implicitly suggested with his concept of "the heart-land," despite also referring to "the 'empty heart' of populism" (2000: 4), the concept of the people refers to "an idealized conception of the community" (2004: 274). This means that, at least if populists want to become politically relevant, they will have to define the people in terms of some of the key features of the self-identification of the targeted community. For instance, no American populist will describe the people as atheist and no West European populist will define the people as Muslim. In other words, the populist's perception of the people is usually related to the self-perception (or self-idealization) of the targeted people.

Some authors have distinguished different meanings of the people (e.g. Canovan, 2005; Hermet, 1989). They point out that individual populists have referred to the people in terms of the working class, the common people, and the nation. The reason for this differentiation is external to populism, however. In the real world most populists combine populism with (features of) one or more other ideologies. So, while populism merely defines the people as pure, the accompanying "host" ideology can add an additional dimension—such as class in the case of "social populism" (e.g. March, 2011) and nation in "national populism" (e.g. Taguieff, 1995).

The Elite

Although the elite is the anti-thesis of the people, it has received much less theoretical attention in the populism literature. Many scholars seem to imply that the elite is simply defined *ex negativo*. While this is true in theory, it does not always hold in practice. Theoretically, populism distinguishes the people and the elite on the basis of just one dimension, i.e. morality. This pits the *pure* people against the *corrupt* elite—or, in Manichean terms, the *good* people versus the *evil* elite (e.g. Hawkins, 2009). In practice, populists combine populism with other ideologies and apply different meanings to the people. Populists using class or commonness in their definition of the people will normally also use these criteria for the elite. For example, American conservative populists pit the common people against the "latte-drinking, sushi-eating, Volvo-driving, *New York Times*-reading, Hollywood-loving" liberal elite (in Nicholson and Segura 2012: 369).

But this is not always the case with populists who combine populism and nationalism. In fact, most nativist populists distinguish different groups on the basis of their nativism and their populism. Ethnic minorities and immigrants, for example, are primarily excluded from the people (i.e. the nation) on the basis of *ethnic* rather than moral criteria—a consequence of nativism rather than populism. At the same time, the (cultural, economic, political) elite are primarily excluded on the basis of *moral* rather than ethnic criteria—based on populism rather than nativism. Even when nativist populists primarily attack the elite for putting the interests of ethnic minorities over those of the "native" majority, the rejection of the elite is first and foremost moral, not ethnic (e.g. Mudde, 2007: chapter 3). An exception to this relatively general rule can be found in Latin American "ethnopopulism," which more fully merges nativism and populism (e.g. Madrid, 2008). For example, Bolivian president Evo Morales has regularly pitted the indigenous pure people against the mestizo corrupt elite (e.g. Mudde and Rovira Kaltwasser, 2017; Ramirez, 2009).

General Will

Essential to populist politics is the concept of a general will, closely linked to the homogenous interpretation of the people. Based on a kind of vulgar Rousseauian argument, populists argue that politics should follow the general will of the people. After all, as the people are pure and homogeneous, and all internal divisions are rejected as artificial or irrelevant, they have the same interests and preferences. The belief in a general will of the people is linked to two important concepts in the populist ideology: common sense and special interests.

Populists often claim to base their policies on common sense, i.e. the result of the honest and logical priorities of the (common) people (e.g. Betz, 1998; Ridge, 1973). Anyone who opposes common sense is, by definition, devious and part of the corrupt elite. By arguing to propose "common sense solutions" to complex problems, populists often implicitly also argue that the elite creates problems and is out of touch with the people. Moreover, they can present themselves as the voice of the people (*vox populi*), expressing *its* general will, and as non- or reluctantly political (Taggart, 2000). After all, common sense solutions are neither ideological nor partisan, they follow "logically" from the general will.

Whereas the populist's common sense solutions follow the general will of (all) the people, the elite's proposed solutions are representations of "special interests" (Mudde, 2004; Weyland, 1999). Given that populism considers the people as homogeneous, any *group* of people is seen as either artificially created or irrelevant for politics. Hence, every call for policies that benefit specific groups, even if it is to remove existing inequalities (Sawer, 2004), is denounced as "special interest politics." More broadly, the elite is painted as the voice of special interests, in opposition to the populists, who are the genuine voice of the people.

STRENGTHS OF THE APPROACH

The main strengths of the ideational approach in general, and of the specific definition of populism presented here in particular, are: (1) it sets clear boundaries, i.e. there is a "non-populism" (*distinguishability*); (2) it allows for the construction of logical taxonomies (*categorizability*); (3) it enables cross-national and cross-regional "travel" (*travelability*); and (4) it can be applied at different levels of analysis (*versatility*). I will illustrate the various strengths by drawing upon both theoretical arguments and empirical studies.

Distinguishability

One of the main reasons that some scholars have rejected the concept of populism is that it is believed to be too vague. The argument is that the distinction between populists and non-populists is made politically, and that most definitions are too general or vague to apply in a scientific manner. This critique has also been raised against the definition mentioned above, among others by journal reviewers, but it is unfounded. Following Giovanni Sartori (1970: 1039), who argues that the key to any concept is "the logic of either-or," this definition of populism is able to distinguish populists from non-populists. In fact, there are two clear opposites of populism: elitism and pluralism.

Unlike democracy, which is often seen as "the mirror of populism" (Panniza, 2005a, elitism is the true mirror-image of populism. Most notably, it shares with populism the Manichean division between the two antagonistic and homogeneous groups, the people and the elite. Consequently, both elitism and populism reject essential aspects of liberal democracy, particularly the politics of compromise. After all, compromise can only lead to the corruption of the pure. But in contrast to populism, elitism considers the elite to be pure and virtuous, and the people to be impure and corrupt. Hence, much elitism is anti-democratic, while democratic elitists only want a minimal role for the people in the political system (e.g. Schumpeter, 1976). Though elitism has lost most of its popularity among the masses, and even among the political elites, in the twentieth century, it had informed most major political ideologies and philosophers until then (from Plato to José Ortega y Gasset).

Even more fundamentally, pluralism is a direct opposite of populism. Where populism sees the people as essentially homogeneous, pluralism believes them to be internally divided in different groups. And, whereas pluralism appreciates societal divisions and sees politics as "the art of compromise," populism (and elitism) discards societal divisions, denounces social groups as "special interests," and rejects compromise as defeat. By considering the main struggle of politics in moral terms, any compromise with the elite will corrupt the people, making them less or even impure. Unlike elitism, which finds few relevant proponents in contemporary democracies, pluralism is a key feature of liberal democracy and is an essential ideological feature of most political ideologies (including Christian democracy, social democracy, liberalism).

Distinguishability also plays a role at a more concrete level. Many studies define populism in light of a specific actor or movement and apply the concept only to that particular case. While the concept may accurately capture that specific actor/movement, or group of actors/movements, it might also apply to many actors/movements that are not studied and that are not considered populist. In this case the definitions are not so broad that they have no negative cases, but they do include cases that are considered to be both populist and non-populist. A famous historical example is Isaiah Berlin's discussion of the work of Johann Gottfried Herder, in which Berlin defines populism as "the belief in the value of belonging to a group or culture" (in McRae, 1969: 156). A more recent example is the definition of populism as "the election of a personalistic outsider who mobilizes voters with an anti-establishment appeal" (Levitsky and Loxton, 2013: 107). Finally, this is also an important weakness of the many definitions of populism as a highly emotional and simplistic discourse that is directed at the "gut feelings" of the people (e.g. Bergsdorf, 2000), given that sloganesque politics constitute the core of political campaigning, left, right, and center (Mudde, 2004).

In contrast, the ideational approach of populism has proven to be measurable and able to distinguish populism and non-populism in various empirical studies. This applies to both qualitative and quantitative studies. For example, using a qualitative approach I distinguished between populist and non-populist radical right parties (Mudde, 2007) and Jan Jagers (2006) was able to show empirically that, while several Flemish parties shared *some* populist features, only the VB shared all features, and could therefore be rightly classified as a populist party. In addition, quantitative studies of party ideology have found clear distinctions between populist and non-populist actors (e.g. Hawkins, 2009) as well as more and less populist parties (e.g. Pauwels, 2011; Rooduijn and Pauwels, 2011).

In short, the ideational approach to populism (presented here) meets one of the most important rules of conceptualization, i.e. being able to distinguish between populism and non-populism (e.g. Sartori, 1970). This sets it apart from some other popular definitions of populism, most notably the (recent) discursive approach of Ernesto Laclau (2005) and Chantal Mouffe (2005) as well as the "campaign approach," in which populism is defined as the use of "common" language and symbols or as overpromising/saying whatever the people want to hear (which would better be termed demagogy).

In addition to meeting the "either-or" criteria of conceptualization, the ideational approach can also be used in empirical studies that want to establish distinctions of a "more-less" nature. Through both qualitative and quantitative analysis we can measure the extent of populism of a political actor or campaign (see what follows). However, in line with the Sartorian understanding of conceptualization, we should *first* establish whether or not an actor is populist *before* we establish, within the subset of populist actors, who is more or less populist. This is not to say that non-populist actors never use populist discourse, but rather that it makes little sense to label political actors who have a clear pluralist ideology but occasionally use a few populist frames in their campaigns a "weak populist."

Categorizability

In her seminal book *Populism* Canovan (1981: 289) presented "a typology with seven compartments, including three types of agrarian populism—'farmers,' 'peasant,' and 'intellectuals'—and four of political populism: populist dictatorship, populist democracy, reactionary populism, and politicians' populism." Paradoxically, she concluded that while different types of populism could be distinguished, populism per se could not.

> And one important reason why the temptation to force all populist phenomena into one category should be resisted, is that the various populisms we have distinguished are not just different varieties of the same kind of thing: they are in many cases different sorts of things, and not directly comparable at all. (1981: 298)

The argument that a concept cannot be defined, but that different types of that concept can nevertheless be distinguished, makes little sense in mainstream social science, which is based on classical concepts (see Sartori, 1970). However, recent scholarship has criticized the rigidity of classical concepts and has suggested the use of more flexible concepts, such as family resemblance and radial or diminished subtypes (e.g. Collier and Mahon, 1993; Goertz, 2005). Some authors have also made this argument with regard to the concept of populism (e.g. Howarth, 2005; Smilov and Krastev, 2008).[5]

Within the paradigm of classical concepts,[6] a taxonomy of populism requires at least two things: (1) a clear definition of populism; and (2) each type of populism should include all features of the concept of populism plus (at least) one other feature (Sartori, 1970). Such a taxonomy entails that populism is the primary, not the secondary, concept. In other words, populism is the classifier, not the qualifier. In the latter case, populism is used as an adjective (i.e. populist), which serves to qualify another (prime) concept.[7] The use of populism as an adjective is very popular in the field, and some authors argue that it is the best or even the only correct use of the concept (e.g. Cammack, 2000; Deegan-Krause, 2009; Leaman, 2004; Sikk, 2009).

Most studies of populism do not address populism in general, but a specific type of populism. Examples include, among many more, authoritarian populism (Hall, 1985), civic populism (Boyte, 2003), presidential populism (Bimes and Mulroy, 2004), reactionary populism (Ziai, 2004), Republican populism (Shogan, 2007), and xenophobic populism (e.g. DeAngelis, 2003). The popularity of the use of "populism with adjectives" reflects undoubtedly the fact that populism is a relatively narrow ideology, which rarely exists by itself. Populist actors almost always combine populism with other ideological features (e.g. Mudde and Rovira Kaltwasser, 2013b; Taggart, 2000). As discussed in the preceding, this is not uncommon for thin-centered ideologies.

In the case of populism, a combination with other collectivist ideologies, thin or thick, is most logical. Today, most relevant populist actors combine the ideology with nationalism (e.g. populist radical right parties in Europe, see Mudde, 2007) or socialism (left-wing populism in Latin America, see Remmer, 2012). In fact, populism is so often combined with nationalism that some authors argue that nationalism is a defining feature of populism (e.g. Collier and Collier, 1991), or vice versa (e.g. Mansfield and Snyder, 2002). But populism can also be combined with individualist ideologies, such as (neo)liberalism, as we have recently seen in Europe (Betz, 1994; Pauwels, 2010) and Latin America (Roberts, 1995; Weyland, 1999).

While these cases of "populism with adjectives" provide more precise identifications of the particular object of study, they often do little to relate them to the broader phenomenon and study of populism. The best way to achieve this is to construct a proper typology, i.e. one that distinguishes different types on the basis of one or more dimensions, connecting them in a clear and consistent manner. Ideally, typologies are mutually exclusive and collectively exhaustive; in other words, they are able to accommodate each case, and each case only fits one type (e.g. Collier et al., 2008; Elman, 2005; Sartori, 1970).

The ideational approach is particularly suited to construct typologies of populism; in particular those that can be used in line with Sartori's famous ladder of abstraction (Sartori, 1970). The one most often used in the literature, which is of a purely *ideological* nature, distinguishes between left-wing populism and right-wing populism. Unfortunately, this typology is seldom theoretically developed, and most studies focus only on right-wing populism, merely implying the existence of a left-wing populism (for an exception, see Hartleb, 2004). At a theoretical level, the best distinction between left and right is probably put forward by Norbert Bobbio (1996), who discriminates on the basis of the relative propensity toward egalitarianism. Concretely, left-wing populism mostly combines populism with some form of socialism (e.g. March, 2011; Remmer, 2012), while right-wing populism mainly constitutes combinations of populism and neoliberalism and/or nationalism (e.g. Betz, 1994).

Another explicitly ideological typology distinguishes exclusionary and inclusionary populism. This typology is based on the main *effects* of the particular ideologies of populist actors, which are often combinations of populism and other ideological features. Following the pioneering work of Dani Filc (2010), we can distinguish between three dimensions of exclusion/inclusion: material, political, and symbolic (Mudde and Rovira Kaltwasser, 2013b). The material dimension refers to the distribution of state resources, both monetary and non-monetary, to specific groups in society. In political terms, exclusion and inclusion refer essentially to the two key dimensions of democracy identified by Robert Dahl (1971; 1989): political participation and public contestation (see, in more detail, Rovira Kaltwasser, 2014). The symbolic dimension essentially alludes to the ingroup-outgroup differentiation of populism, i.e. setting the boundaries of "the people" and, *ex negativo*, "the elite."

Interestingly, the most popular distinction in the literature on Latin American populism, which is (still) dominated by organizational definitions (e.g. Roberts, 1995; Weyland, 2001), is also essentially ideological—even if it is often portrayed in terms of *economic policy* rather than political ideology. Whereas (classical) populism supported a specific redistributive economic program (import-substituting indus-trialization or ISI), so-called neopopulism combines populism with neoliberal eco-nomic policies (e.g. Philip, 2000; Weyland, 1999), and contemporary left populism with more or less socialist economic policies (e.g. Arnson and de la Torre, 2013).

Travelability

The essence of the "travelling problem" (Sartori, 1970: 1033) is that many definitions are geographically or temporally specific. This is also a major problem in the study of populism, which is highly segregated in terms of disciplines and regions of study. Some studies define populism so specifically that the concept applies only to one case. This is particularly prevalent in historical studies of American populism, both its historical and contemporary variants. Some Latin American studies are similarly idiosyncratic. For example, Héctor Díaz-Polanco and Stephen Gorman (1982: 42) define populism as "the ideology and program of the modern neoindigenistas."

Most definitions of populism are not idiosyncratic, but neither provide "*empirical universals*" (Sartori, 1970: 1035). Some authors define populism in such a way that it is closely linked to a specific period. An extreme example is offered by Edward Gibson (1997: 340), who defines populism as "denoting parties that incorporated labor during the historical and developmental period mentioned above." Slightly less specific, but still very restrictive, is Lenin's definition of populism as the anti-capitalist protest of "small immediate producers" (Walicki, 1969: 65). Other definitions have strongly national or regional characteristics. Finally, several definitions have a combination of regional and temporal specifics. In all cases, the travelability of the concept is restricted to specific geographical areas or historic periods.

The ideational approach has been successfully applied in studies of populism all across the globe. First and foremost, it is increasingly dominating studies of European populism, particularly in empirical political science. The proposed definition has been used in various studies of both left- and right-wing populism in Europe (e.g. March, 2011; Mudde, 2007). In addition, very similar ideational and ideological definitions inform most other studies of European populism (e.g. Albertazzi and McDonnell, 2008; Jagers and Walgrave, 2007; Stanley, 2008) and a growing group of studies of Latin American populism, in particular following the influential work of Kirk Hawkins (2009; 2010).

Most importantly, from the perspective of travelability, the ideational approach has been used effectively in the few truly comparative cross-regional studies in the field (e.g. Mudde and Rovira Kaltwasser, 2013b). The best example of this is the edited volume *Populism in Europe and the Americas: Threat or Corrective for Democracy?* (Mudde and Rovira Kaltwasser, 2012), which includes eight case studies by a total of ten political sci-entists (excluding the editors) using this exact definition, from Eastern Europe, North America, South America, and Western Europe.

Versatility

Versatility is the last major strength of the ideational approach. Most approaches of populism can only be applied to a limited group of political actors, i.e. political elites. They reduce populism to a purely supply-side factor of politics. In other words, populism is something that is adopted by leaders, parties, or states. It does not exist at the mass level, i.e. as an attitude of the individual.

The ideational approach has been applied in a broad variety of empirical studies of populism at the elite and the mass level. As is the case for most other approaches of populism, the bulk of the work is qualitative and aimed at the elite level, i.e. political leaders, movements, and parties (e.g. Albertazzi and McDonnell, 2008; March, 2011; Mudde, 2007; Mudde and Rovira Kaltwasser, 2012). But the ideational approach has also been used in quantitative studies of political elites (e.g. Cranmer, 2011; Jagers and Walgrave, 2007; Vasilopoulou et al., 2014). The most influential such study is Kirk Hawkin's (2009; 2010) analysis of presidential speeches in Latin America, which has recently been expanded to include East and West European cases. The ideological definition presented here was also successfully applied in various quantitative content analyses of party literature in the West European context (e.g. Pauwels, 2011; Rooduijn and Pauwels, 2011).

Importantly, the ideational approach of populism is (so far) unique in its applicability to quantitative studies at the mass level. The first empirical study of populist attitudes at the mass level was published more than forty-five years ago (Axelrod, 1967). It used an ideational approach of populism, although the operationalization was very specific in both geographical and temporal terms. In the last couple of years several new studies have applied ideational definitions very similar to the one presented here to gauge the spread of populist attitudes at the individual level (e.g. Akkerman et al., 2015; Hawkins et al., 2012; Stanley, 2011).

The important advantage of this versatility is that it enables the integration of very different types of populism studies. For example, we can now study whether people with populist attitudes disproportionately support populist parties (e.g. Akkerman et al., 2015), whether countries with more successful populist parties also have more populist citizens, or whether populist attitudes relate strongly to nationalist and socialist attitudes. In other words, the ideational approach allows us to study both the supply-side and the demand-side of populist politics.

COMPARING THE APPROACHES

In this last section I will shortly compare the ideational approach to three other influential approaches: Ernesto Laclau's (original) discursive approach, Kurt Weyland's organizational approach, and Pierre Ostiguy's performative (or cultural) approach. My ambition is not to be comprehensive or exhaustive in the comparison, but rather to highlight the most fundamental differences between the ideological approach and the main alternatives, to enable scholars of populism to make a more informed choice for their specific study.

Ernesto Laclau is often considered the doyen of populism studies and his influential, but highly complex, discursive approach, laid out in *Politics and Ideology in Marxist Theory: Capitalism, Fascism, Populism* (1977), continues to inform many studies of populism today (e.g. Azzarello, 2011; Palonen, 2009; Stavrakakis, 2004; Žižek, 2006). Essentially, Laclau sees populism as a discursive strategy of political elites to provide meaning to the term "the people" (and "the elite") to maximize popular support. As he considers the concept of the people as an "empty signifier," it can be filled with any specific content. The fundamental distinction with the ideational approach presented here is that Laclau's approach is essentially a highly abstract, normative, universal theory in which "the people" has no specific content. In contrast, most of those who adhere to the ideational approach define populism in a specific manner, in which the key opposition is moral, and it is empirically oriented, positivist, and aimed at developing mid-range theoretical levels.[8]

The organizational approach defines populism, fundamentally, as a particular type of popular mobilization, in which leaders relate directly to their followers (e.g. Roberts, 1995; Weyland, 2001). The unmediated relationship between leader and followers can be a result of the lack of a relevant formal organization (e.g. Alberto Fujimori in Peru; see Roberts, 1995) or a choice to circumvent the formal organization (e.g. Tony Blair in the UK; see Mair, 2002). The ideational approach does not deny the importance of leadership or organizational structure, but acknowledges that populism has come in many guises, from leaderless movements like the contemporary Tea Party to well-developed political parties with populist leaders such as the French National Front (Mudde and Rovira Kaltwasser, 2014; 2017). While charismatic leadership is, virtually by definition, an important part of the explanation of popular support for populist actors, it is neither a necessary condition for electoral breakthrough nor a sufficient condition for electoral persistence (Mudde, 2007). Theoretically, the ideological approach suggests that populists are skeptical of both strong leaders and strong organizations, as both can corrupt the power of the people. Empirically, however, populist actors often include charismatic leaders and relatively weak formal organizations. In short, populism has an elective affinity with charismatic leadership and weak formal organizations, but these are not defining features of populism.

Finally, Pierre Ostiguy's (2009) cultural (or "performative") approach defines politics, in part, on the basis of a high-low axis, which essentially refers to the ways in which political actors relate to people. The high-low axis consists of two closely related subdimensions: the socio-cultural dimension "encompasses manners, demeanors, ways of speaking and dressing, vocabulary, and tastes displayed in public" and the political-cultural dimension refers to "forms of political leadership and modes of decision-making" (2009: 5–9). Populism is defined as low on both sub-dimensions, which means that populists behave and speak in a popular manner and emphasize strong personalistic leadership. There is no doubt that populist actors defined by the ideational approach most often fit the low pole of politics on both sub-dimensions. However, this is not always the case (e.g. U.S. People's Party and Pim Fortuyn on the political-cultural dimension).

CONCLUSION

The ideational approach has gained significant popularity in the study of populism in recent years. As the number of populism studies has exploded, the proportion of scholars using relatively similar definitions of populism has increased rather than decreased. Although the organizational approach to populism retains part of its popularity, most notably in studies of Latin American politics, the ideational approach is increasingly used in studies of populism across the globe. Moreover, the ideational approach has proven to be much more versatile than the other approaches, allowing for the use of both qualitative and quantitative methods as well as research into the demand-side and the supply-side of populist politics.

My specific definition of populism is just one of many very similar definitions within the broader ideational approach, which considers populism essentially as a set of ideas— whether or not they constitute an ideology or "only" a discourse or style is of secondary importance for many research questions. At this stage scholarship of populism would profit from focusing more on the many similarities between various ideational definitions than on (over)emphasizing the few differences. This can foster the development of cumulative knowledge across historical periods and geographical areas, which will further the knowledge of populism in general, and of specific populist actors in particular.

If most of us can agree that populism is essentially a set of ideas, connected to an essential struggle between "the good people" and "the corrupt elite," we should also find common ground on the idea that the cultural paradigm can probably inform the debate on populism much more than the rational choice and institutional approaches that dominate mainstream political science and, although to a lesser degree, sociology. After all, it is the national and political cultures in which populist actors mobilize that provide a better understanding of the conditions under which people come to see political reality through the lenses of populism and that can help us better explain which *type* of populism is successful under which conditions.

NOTES

1 An earlier version of this chapter was presented at the workshop "The Concept of Populism," Brighton (UK), June 21, 2013. I want to thank the participants of the workshop, and particularly the editors of the Handbook, for their helpful comments and critiques.

2 In more recent work Freeden (2003) distinguishes between "macro-ideologies" and "micro-ideologies," which roughly equate to his earlier distinction between "thin" and "thick" ideologies.

3 In the ideological approach, in sharp contrast to the economic approach (e.g. Acemoglu et al., 2013; Dornbusch and Edwards, 1991; Sachs, 1989), there is no specific economic model of populism. Consequently, as can be seen in Latin America, populism can be combined with both neoliberal and redistributive economic policies (e.g. Roberts, 1995; Weyland, 1999). Similarly, populism can be combined with another thin ideology, like nationalism, and a thick ideology, like socialism.

4 Empirical studies on the relevance of populism to populists in power have come to opposing conclusions. While some studies show that populism remains a dominant feature in power (e.g. Albertazzi and McDonnell, 2015; Levitsky and Loxton, 2013; Ruzza and Fella, 2009), others argue that it plays little role once populists are in power (e.g. Rooduijn et al., 2014).

5 Although they don't explicitly use the terminology, Jagers and Walgrave's (2007) four-fold typology of populism is based on a radial concept of populism.

6 The argumentation for my choice for classical concepts falls well beyond the scope of this paper (but see Mudde, 2007: chapter 1).

7 Oddly enough, Canovan's taxonomy combines the two: five of the seven are truly types of populism, but two are populist types of other concepts (i.e. populist *dictatorship* and populist *democracy*).

8 I want to thank Cristóbal Rovira Kaltwasser and Pierre Ostiguy for helping me better understand Laclau's discursive approach and the main differences with my ideological approach.

References

Abts, Koen and Stefan Rummens. 2007. "Populism and democracy," *Political Studies*, 55(2): 405–24.

Acemoglu, Daron, Gyorgy Egorov, and Konstantin Sonin. 2013. "A political theory of populism," *Quarterly Journal of Economics*, 128(2): 771–805.

Akkerman, Agnes, Cas Mudde, and Andrej Zaslove. 2015. "How populist are the people? Measuring populist attitudes in voters," *Comparative Political Studies*, 47(9): 1324–53.

Albertazzi, Daniele and Duncan McDonnell (eds). 2008. *Twenty-First Century Populism: The Spectre of Western European Democracy*. Basingstoke: Palgrave Macmillan.

Albertazzi, Daniele and Duncan McDonnell. 2015. *Populists in Power*. London: Routledge.

Anderson, Benedict. 1983. *Imagined Communities: Reflections on the Origin and Spread of Nationalism*. London: Verso.

Arson, Cynthia and Carlos de la Torre (eds). 2013. *Populism of the Twenty First Century*. Baltimore and Washington: Johns Hopkins University Press and Woodrow Wilson Center Press.

Aslanidis, Paris. 2016. "Is populism an ideology? A reflection and a new perspective," *Political Studies*, 64(1): 88–104.

Axelrod, Robert. 1967. "The structure of public opinion on policy issues," *Public Opinion Quarterly*, 31(1): 51–60.

Azzarello, Stefanie. 2011. *"Populist Masculinities:" Power and Sexuality in the Italian Populist Imaginary*. Utrecht: Unpublished MA thesis.

Backes, Uwe and Eckhard Jesse. 1998. "Neue Formen des politischen Extremismus?," in Uwe Backes and Eckhard Jesse (eds), *Jahrbuch Extremismus and Demokratie*, 10. Baden-Baden: Nomos, 15–32.

Ball, Terence. 1999. "From 'core' to 'sore' concepts: ideological innovation and conceptual change," *Journal of Political Ideologies*, 4(3): 391–6.

Bergsdorf, Harald. 2000. "Rhetorik des Populismus am Beispiel rechtsextremer und rechts-populistischer Parteien wie der 'Republikaner', der FPÖ und des 'Front National'," *Zeitschrift für Parlamentsfragen*, 31(3): 620–6.

Betz, Hans-Georg. 1994. *Radical Right-Wing Populism in Western Europe*. Basingstoke: Macmillan.

Betz, Hans-Georg. 1998. "Introduction," in Hans-Georg Betz and Stefan Immerfall (eds), *The New Politics of the Right*. Basingstoke: Palgrave Macmillan.

Bimes, Terri and Quinn Mulroy. 2004. "The rise and decline of presidential populism," *Studies in American Political Development*, 18(2): 136–59.

Bobbio, Norbert. 1996. *Left and Right: The Significance of a Political Distinction*. Chicago: University of Chicago Press.

Bonikowski, Bart and Noam Gidron. 2016. "The populist style in American politics: presidential campaign discourse, 1952–1996," *Social Forces*, 94(4): 1593–1621.

Boyte, Harry C. 2003. "Civic populism," *Perspectives on Politics*, 1(4): 737–42.

Brubaker, Rogers. 1996. *Nationalism Refrained: Nationhood and the National Question in the New Europe*. Cambridge: Cambridge University Press.

Caiani, Manuela and Donatella della Porta. 2011. "The elitist populism and the extreme right: a frame analysis of extreme right-wing discourses in Italy and Germany," *Acta Politica*, 46(2): 180–202.

Collier, David and James E. Mahon, Jr. 1993. "Conceptual 'stretching' revisited: adapting categories in comparative politics," *American Political Science Review*, 87(4): 845–55.

Collier, David, Jody LaPorte, and Jason Seawright. 2008. "Typologies: forming concepts and creating categorical variables," in Janet M. Box-Steffenmeier, Henry Brady, and David Collier (eds), *Oxford Handbook of Political Methodology*. Oxford: Oxford University Press, 152–73.

Collier, Ruth Berins and David Collier. 1991. *Shaping the Political Arena: Critical Junctures, the Labor Movement, and Regime Dynamics in Latin America*. Princeton: Princeton University Press.

Cammack, Paul. 2000. "The resurgence of populism in Latin America," *Bulletin of Latin American Research*, 19(2): 149–61.

Canovan, Margaret. 1981. *Populism*. London: Junction.

Canovan, Margaret. 2004. "Populism for political theorists," *Journal of Political Ideologies*, 9(3): 241–52.

Canovan, Margaret. 2005. *The People*. Cambridge: Polity.

Cranmer, Mirjam. 2011. "Populist communication and publicity: an empirical study of contextual differences in Switzerland," *Swiss Political Science Review*, 17(3): 286–307.

Craven, Hermon W. 1896. *Errors of Populism*. Seattle: Lowman and Hanford S. and P.

Dahl, Robert. 1971. *Polyarchy: Participation and Opposition*. New Haven: Yale University Press.

Dahl, Robert. 1989. *Democracy and Its Critics*. New Haven: Yale University Press.

DeAngelis, Richard A. 2003. "A rising tide for Jean-Marie, Jörg, and Pauline? Xenophobic populism in comparative perspective," *Australian Journal of Politics and History*, 49(1): 75–92.

Deegan-Krause, Kevin and Tim Haughton. 2009. "Toward a more useful conceptualization of populism: types and degrees of populist appeals in the case of Slovakia," *Politics and Policy*, 37(4): 821–41.

de la Torre, Carlos. 2010. *The Populist Seduction in Latin America*, 2nd edn. Athens: Ohio University Press.

Díaz-Polanco, Héctor and Stephen M. Gorman. 1982. "Indigenismo, populism, and Marxism," *Latin American Perspectives*, 9(2): 42–61.

Dornbusch, Rudiger and Sebastian Edwards (eds). 1991. *The Macroeconomics of Populism in Latin America*. Chicago: University of Chicago Press.

Elman, Colin. 2005. "Explanatory typologies in qualitative studies of international politics," *International Organization*, 59: 293–326.

Ferkiss, Victor C. 1957. "Populist influences on American fascism," *The Western Political Quarterly*, 10(2): 350–73.

Filc, Dani. 2010. *The Political Right in Israel: Different Faces of Jewish Populism*. London: Routledge.

Freeden, Michael. 1998. "Is nationalism a distinct ideology?," *Political Studies*, 46(4): 748–65.

Freeden, Michael. 2003. *Ideology*. Oxford: Oxford University Press.

Gallie, W. B. 1955-6. "Essentially contested concepts," *Proceeding of the Aristotelian Society*, 56: 167–98.

Garzia, Diego. 2011. "The personalization of politics in Western democracies: Causes and consequences on leader–follower relationships," *The Leadership Quarterly*, 22(4): 697–709.

Gibson, Edward L. 1997. "The populist road to market reform: policy and electoral coalition in Mexico and Argentina," *World Politics*, 49(3): 339–70.

Goertz, Gary. 2005. *Social Science Concepts: A User's Guide*. Princeton: Princeton University Press.

Hakhverdian, Armèn and Christel Koop. 2007. "Consensus democracy and populist parties in Western Europe," *Acta Politica*, 42(4): 401–20.

Hall, Stuart J. 1985. Authoritarian populism: A reply to Jessop et al.," *New Left Review*, 151: 115–24.

Hartleb, Florian. 2004. *Rechts- und Linkspopulismus: eine Fallstudie anhand von Schill-Partei und PDS*. Opladen: Vs Verlag für Sozialwissenschaften.

Havlík, Vlastimil and Aneta Pinková. 2012. "Seeking a theoretical framework: how to define and identify populist parties," in Vlastimil Havlík and Aneta Pinková (eds), *Populist Political Parties in East-Central Europe*. Brno: MUNI Press, 17–37.

Hawkins, Kirk A. 2009. "Is Chávez populist? Measuring populist discourse in comparative perspective," *Comparative Political Studies*, 42(8): 1040–67.

Hawkins, Kirk A. 2010. *Venezuela's Chavismo and Populism in Comparative Perspective*. Cambridge: Cambridge University Press.

Hawkins, Kirk, Scott Riding, and Cas Mudde. 2012. "Measuring populist attitudes," *Committee on Concepts and Methods Working Papers Series Political Concepts*, 55.

Hermet, Guy. 1989. *Le peuple contre la démocratie*. Paris: Fayard.

Hobsbawm, Eric J. 1990. *Nations and Nationalism since 1780*. Cambridge: Cambridge University Press.

Howarth, David. 2005. "Populism or popular democracy? The UDF, workerism and the struggle for radical democracy in South Africa," in Francisco Panizza (ed.), *Populism and the Mirror of Democracy*. London: Verso, 202–23.

Ionescu, Ghiţa and Ernest Gellner (eds). 1969. *Populism: Its Meanings and National Characteristics*. London: Weidenfeld and Nicolson.

Jager, Jan. 2006. De stem van het volk! Populisme als concept getest bij Vlaamse politieke partijen. Antwerp: Unpublished PhD thesis.

Jagers, Jan and Stefaan Walgrave. 2007. "Populism as political communication style: an empirical study of political parties' discourse in Belgium," *European Journal of Political Research*, 46(3): 319–45.

Karaömerlioglu, M. Asim. 1996. "On Russian populism," *UCLA Historical Journal*, 16(0): 131–48.

Karvonen, Lauri. 2010. *The Personalisation of Politics: A Study of Parliamentary Democracies.* Colchester: ECPR Press.

Kazin, Michael. 1995. *The Populist Persuasion: An American History.* New York: Basic Books.

Laclau, Ernesto. 1977. *Politics and Ideology in Marxist Theory: Capitalism, Fascism, Populism.* London: NLB.

Laclau, Ernesto. 2005. *On Populist Reason.* London: Verso.

Leaman, David. 2004. "Changing faces of populism in Latin America: masks, makeovers, and enduring features," *Latin American Research Review*, 39(3): 312–26.

Lee, Michael J. 2006. "The populist chameleon: the People's Party, Huey Long, George Wallace, and the populist argumentative frame," *Quarterly Journal of Speech*, 92(4): 355–78.

Levitsky, Steven and James Loxton. 2013. "Populism and competitive authoritarianism in the Andes," *Democratization*, 20(1): 107–36.

Linden, Ronald H. 2008. "The new populism in Central and Southeastern Europe," *Problems of Post-Communism*, 55(3): 3–6.

Lowndes, Joe. 2008. "From founding violence to political hegemony; the conservative populism of George Wallace," in Francisco Panizza (ed.), *Populism and the Mirror of Democracy.* London: Verso, 144–71.

Madrid, Raúl L. 2008. "The rise of ethnopopulism in Latin America," *World Politics*, 60(3): 475–508.

Mammone, Andrea. 2009. "*The eternal return*? Faux populism and contemporarization of neo-fascism across Britain, France and Italy," *Journal of Contemporary European Studies*, 17(2): 171–92.

Mansfield, Edward D. and Jack Snyder. 2002. "Incomplete democratization and the outbreak of military disputes," *International Studies Quarterly*, 46: 529–49.

March, Luke. 2011. *Radical Left Parties in Europe.* London: Routledge.

Marx, Karl and Friedrich Engels 1998 [1848]. *The Communist Manifesto.* New York: Penguin.

McAllister, Ian. 2008. "The personalization of politics," in Russell J. Dalton and Hans-Dieter Klingemann (eds), *Oxford Handbook of Political Behavior.* Oxford: Oxford University Press.

McCormick, S. D. 1898. "An economic view of popular loan," *The North American Review*, 167(501): 249–51.

McRae, Donald. 1969. "Populism as an ideology," in Ghiţa Ionescu and Ernest Gellner (eds), *Populism: Its Meanings and National Characteristics.* London: Weidenfeld and Nicolson, 153–65.

Moffitt, Benjamin. 2016. *The Global Rise of Populism: Performance, Political Style and Representation.* Redwood City: Stanford University Press.

Moffitt, Benjamin and Simon Tormey. 2014. "Rethinking populism: politics, mediatisation and political style," *Political Studies*, 62(2): 381–97.

Mouffe, Chantal. 2005. "The 'end of politics' and the challenge of right-wing populism," in Francisco Panizza (ed.), *Populism and the Mirror of Democracy.* London: Verso, 50–71.

Mudde, Cas. 2004. "The populist zeitgeist," *Government and Opposition*, 39(3): 541–63.

Mudde, Cas. 2007. *Populist Radical Right Parties in Europe.* Cambridge: Cambridge University Press.

Mudde, Cas and Cristóbal Rovira Kalywasser. 2012. *Populism in Europe and the Americas: Threat or Corrective for Democracy?* Cambridge: Cambridge University Press.

Mudde, Cas and Cristóbal Rovira Kaltwasser. 2013a. "Populism," in Michael Freeden, Marc Stears and Lyman Tower Sargent (eds), *Oxford Handbook on Political Ideologies.* Oxford: Oxford University Press, 493–512.

Mudde, Cas and Cristóbal Rovira Kaltwasser. 2013b. "Exclusionary vs. inclusionary populism: comparing contemporary Europe and Latin America," *Government and Opposition*, 48(2): 147–74.

Mudde, Cas and Cristóbal Rovira Kaltwasser. 2014. "Populism and political leadership," in R. A. W. Rhodes and Paul 't Hart (eds), *Oxford Handbook on Political Leadership*. Oxford: Oxford University Press, 376–88.

Mudde, Cas and Cristóbal Rovira Kaltwasser. 2017. *Populism: A Very Short Introduction*. Oxford: Oxford University Press.

Nicholson, Stephen P. and Gary M. Segura. 2012. "Who's the party of the people? Economic populism and U.S. public's beliefs about political parties," *Public Behavior*, 34(2): 369–89.

Ostiguy, Pierre. 2009. "The high-low political divide: rethinking populism and anti-populism," *Committee on Concepts and Methods Working Papers Series Political Concepts*, 35.

Palonen, Emilia. 2009. "Political polarization and populism in contemporary Hungary," *Parliamentary Affairs*, 62(2): 318–34.

Panizza, Francisco (ed.). 2005a. *Populism and the Mirror of Democracy*. London: Verso.

Panizza, Francisco. 2005b. "Introduction: populism and the mirror democracy," in Francisco Panizza (ed.), *Populism and the Mirror of Democracy*. London: Verso, 1–31.

Pauwels, Teun. 2010. "Explaining the success of neo-liberal populist parties: the case of Lijst Dedecker in Belgium," *Political Studies*, 58(5): 1009–29.

Pauwels, Teun. 2011. "Measuring populism: a quantitative text analysis of party literature in Belgium," *Journal of Elections, Public Opinion and Parties*, 21(1): 97–117.

Philip, George. 2000. "Populist possibilities and political constraints in Mexico," *Bulletin of Latin American Research*, 19(2): 207–21.

Pipes, Richard. 1960. "Russian Marxism and its populist background: the late nineteenth century," *Russian Review*, 19(4): 316–37.

Platt, T. C. 1896. "The effect of Republican victory," *The North American Review*, 163(480): 513–16.

Ramirez, Lindsay. 2009. Comparative Populism in the Andean State: A Case Study of Ecuador and Bolivia. Eugene, OR: Unpublished MA thesis.

Remmer, Karin. 2012. "The rise of leftist-populist governance in Latin America: the roots of electoral change," *Comparative Political Studies*, 45(8): 947–72.

Rensmann, Lars. 2006. Populismus und Ideologie," in Frank Decker (ed.), *Populismus in Europe*. Berlin: Bundeszentrale für politische Bildung, 59–80.

Ridge, Martin. 1973. "The Populist as a social critic," *Minnesota History*, 43(8): 297–302.

Roberts, Kenneth M. 1995. "Neoliberalism and the transformation of populism in Latin America: the Peruvian case," *World Politics*, 48(1): 82–116.

Rooduijn, Matthijs. 2013. A Populist Zeitgeist? The Impact of Populism on Parties, Media and the Public in Western Europe. Amsterdam: Unpublished PhD thesis.

Rooduijn, Matthijs and Teun Pauwels. 2011. "Measuring populism: comparing two methods of content analysis," *West European Politics*, 34(6): 1272–83.

Rooduijn, Matthijs, Sarah de Lange and Wouter van der Brug. 2014. "A populist Zeitgest? Programmatic contagion by populist parties in Western Europe," *Party Politics*, 20(4), 563–75.

Rovira Katlwasser, Cristóbal. 2014. "The responses of populism to Dahl's democratic dilemma," *Political Studies*, 62(3): 470–87.

Ruzza, Carlo and Stefano Fella. 2009. *Re-Inventing the Italian Right: Territorial Politics, Populism and "Post-Fascism."* London: Routledge.

Sachs, Jeffrey D. 1989. "Social conflict and populist policies in Latin America," *NBER Working Paper*, 2897.

Sainsbury, Diane. 1980. *Swedish Social Democratic Ideology and Electoral Politics 1944–1948. A Study of the Functions of Party Ideology*. Stockholm: Almqvist and Wicksell.

Sartori, Giovanni. 1970. "Concept misformation in comparative politics," *American Political Science Review*, 64(4): 1033–53.

Sartori, Giovanni. 1990. "The sociology of parties: a critical review," in Peter Mair. (ed.), *The West European Party System*. Oxford: Oxford University Press, 150–82.

Sawer, Marian. 2004. "Populism and public choice in Australia and Canada: turning equality-seekers into 'special interests'," in Marian Sawer and Barry Hindess (eds), *Us and Them: Anti-Elitism in Australia*. Perth: API Network, 33–55.

Schumpeter, Joseph. 1976. *Capitalism, Socialism, and Democracy*. London: Allen and Unwin.

Shogan, Colleen J. 2007. "Anti-intellectualism in the modern presidency: a republican populism," *Perspectives on Politics*, 5(2): 295–303.

Sikk, Allan. 2009. "Parties and populism," *CEPSI Working Paper*, 2009-02.

Smilov, Daniel and Ivan Krastev. 2008. "The rise of populism in Eastern Europe: policy paper," in Grigorij Mesežnikov, Oľga Gyárfášová and Daniel Smilov (eds), *Populist Politics and Liberal Democracy in Central and Eastern Europe*. Bratislava: Institute for Public Affairs, 7–13.

Stanley, Ben. 2008. "The thin ideology of populism," *Journal of Political Ideologies*, 13(1): 95–110.

Stanley, Ben. 2011. "Populism, nationalism, or national populism? An analysis of Slovak voting behaviour at the 2010 parliamentary election," *Communist and Post-Communist Studies*, 44(4): 257–70.

Stavrakakis, Yannis. 2004. "Antinomies of formalism: Laclau's theory of populism and the lessons from religious populism in Greece," *Journal of Political Ideologies*, 9(3): 253–67.

Taggart, Paul. 2000. *Populism*. Buckingstone: Open University Press.

Taggart, Paul. 2004. "Populism and representative politics in contemporary Europe," *Journal of Political Ideologies*, 9(3): 269–88.

Taguieff, Pierre-André. 1995. "Political science confronts populism: from a conceptual mirrage to a real problem," *Telos*, 103: 9–43.

Van Donselaar. 1991. *Fout na de oorlog: Fascistische en racistische organisaties in Nederland 1950–1990*. Amsterdam: Bert Bakker.

Vasilopoulou, Sofia, Daphne Halikiopoulou, and Theofanis Exadaktylos. 2014. "Greece in crisis: austerity, populism and the politics of blame," *Journal of Common Market Studies*, 52(2), 388–402.

Walicki, Andrzej. 1969. "Russia," in Ghiţa Ionescu and Ernest Gellner (eds), *Populism: Its Meanings and National Characteristics*. London: Weidenfeld, 62–96.

Weyland, Kurt. 1999. "Neoliberal populism in Latin America and Eastern Europe," *Comparative Politics*, 31(4): 379–401.

Weyland, Kurt. 2001. "Clarifying a contested concept: populism in the study of Latin American politics," *Comparative Politics*, 34(1): 1–22.

Wiles, Peter. 1969. "A syndrome, not a doctrine: some elementary theses on populism," in Ghiţa Ionescu and Ernest Gellner (eds), *Populism: Its Meanings and National Characteristics*. London: Weidenfeld and Nicolson, 166–79.

Ziai, Aram. 2004. "The ambivalence of post-development: between reactionary populism and radical democracy," *Third World Quarterly*, 25(6): 1045–60.

Žižek, Slavoj. 2006. "Against the populist temptation," *Critical Inquiry*, 32(3): 551–74.

CHAPTER 3

POPULISM

A Political-Strategic Approach

KURT WEYLAND

A *Handbook of Populism* is a daring project. By nature, a professional handbook wants to condense and transmit "the state of the art" in an area of scholarship: What has been established by prior studies, and what can serve as the conceptual and theoretical foundation for future research and thinking? The very term "*state* of the art" implies some degree of consolidation. But inherently populism is a shifty concept that a number of scholars have compared to a chameleon (see especially Taggart, 2000: chapter 1): It constantly changes "colors" and threatens to escape analytical grasp. As soon as scholars are confident that they have encircled it with their definitional snares, it resurfaces in a different form in another corner of the impenetrable jungle of politics. No wonder that the proliferation of "populisms with adjectives" or hyphens has continued over the last decade. After Kenneth Roberts (1995) and I drew scholarly attention by coining the term "neoliberal (neo)populism" that postulated "unexpected affinities" (Weyland, 1996) between seeming opposites, proposals of surprising, provocative combinations have multiplied, with notions such as "ethno-populism" (Madrid, 2008) or "techno-populism" (de la Torre, 2013).

As the study of populism has seen "a hundred flowers bloom," some old bulbs have sent up new sprouts as well and brought fading colors back into the picture. In particular, discursive and ideology-centered concepts of populism have made a significant comeback in recent years, due to methodological innovations and changes in "the real world." Traditionally, discursive and ideological notions suffered from the difficulty of assessment and measurement: Given the vagueness of politicians' rhetoric, how can one define and delimit populist discourse? But Kirk Hawkins's interesting reliance on techniques of "holistic grading" and his wide-ranging project of scoring the level of populism in many leaders' speeches have given scholars the confidence that measurement issues can be overcome. Hawkins's accomplishment has thus re-legitimated the discursive approach.

Moreover, the recent wave of left-wing populists in Latin America enunciates a more appealing, progressive discourse than the neoliberal populists of the 1990s with their appeals to conservative virtues such as order and discipline and their anti-intellectual tendencies. In fact, this group of Bolivarian leaders attributes much greater importance to discourse than their right-wing counterparts. Whereas Alberto Fujimori's motto was, "First one acts; then one talks," Hugo Chávez kept talking, talking, talking, and then he sometimes acted. As the endless hours of "Aló Presidente" show, discourse played a central role for Chávez's populism.

This crucial role of discourse has shaped the image of left-wing populists. By contrast to Carlos Menem, Fernando Collor, and Alberto Fujimori, who were despised by sophisticated public opinion, Chávez, Evo Morales, and, in the beginning, Rafael Correa elicited considerable support from segments of the global intelligentsia. Whereas Menem had to make do with blond supermodels and bold racecar drivers, Chávez received backing from MIT professor Noam Chomsky and actor Sean Penn; endorsements from cosmopolitan intellectuality, rather than crass superficiality, boosted the Bolivarian leader. None of these celebrities actually lived in the countries whose presidents they praised; they were thus spared the explosion of crime, stubborn inflation, and frequent scarcities in Venezuela. Instead, their admiration was drawn primarily by the progressive discourse, left-wing ideology, and noble pronouncements of these populist leaders.

The progressive glow and central role of Bolivarian discourse has also helped inspire scholars to take populism's discursive and ideological dimension more seriously and emphasize this dimension as a definitional feature. Indeed, the most outstanding proponent of a discursive approach in Latin America, Ernesto Laclau, has applied his theory to the current crop of left-wing populists (e.g. Laclau, 2012; see also Svampa, 2013) and thus sought to suggest the continued usefulness of his approach (presented systematically in Laclau, 2005). These discursive and theoretical tendencies have also found resonance in Southern Europe, especially with the emergence of PODEMOS in Spain and, less directly, SYRIZA in Greece (Hawkins and Silva, 2016: 11, 15).

In sum, methodological advances in academia and high-profile developments in the real world of politics have given discursive and ideology-centered concepts of populism a new boost in the scholarly community. This has led to the resurrection of an old approach that was being marginalized by the growing adoption of the political-strategic definitions emerging from the analysis of neoliberal populism ("codified" most systematically in Weyland, 2001). Whereas neologisms such as "ethno-populism" (Madrid, 2008), "rentier populism" (Mazzuca, 2013), and "techno-populism" (de la Torre, 2013) capture only localized varieties (the Central Andes, Latin America's "radical" left, and Ecuador, respectively), the discursive and ideology-centered approach constitutes a fundamental alternative to political-strategic definitions in general (see also Rooduijn, 2014).

This chapter therefore starts by assessing the revival of discursive and ideology-centered notions and evaluating their conceptual clarity and validity. Because this analysis uncovers important problems in the ideational approach, an emphasis on political strategy seems preferable. The central section therefore explains and further develops the conceptualization developed in Weyland (2001: 14), which defines populism "as a political strategy through which a personalistic leader seeks or exercises government power based on direct, unmediated, uninstitutionalized support from large numbers of mostly unorganized followers."

This conceptualization focuses not on what populists say, but on what they actually do, especially how they pursue and sustain political power. Populism sees power emanate from "the people." But because this wide-ranging aggregate is much too heterogeneous and amorphous to act on its own, it falls to an outstanding leader to provide direction and mobilize the followers for the goals that the leader identifies as "the will of the people." With a preeminent leader serving as the unifying bond, the relationship to the followers has a quasi-direct, seemingly personal character. The leader reaches the followers directly, for instance through mass rallies and TV, and largely foregoes clientelistic or organizational intermediation.

To compensate for the fickleness of these uninstitutionalized connections, the leader seeks to give these bonds extraordinary intensity, especially by attacking dangerous enemies and mobilizing the followers for heroic missions; many people in turn crave the sense of belonging to the community forged by strong commitment to an outstanding, bold leader. Where the leader commands charisma and large numbers of people therefore feel an internal compulsion ("calling") to follow, a deep personal identification can develop (Zúquete, 2007), as evident in the uncontrolled mass grief after Hugo Chávez's death. While charisma is not a definitional characteristic of populism, it can solidify the quasi-direct relationship of personalistic leader and supporters that constitutes the core of populism.

After explaining this political-strategic concept in depth, I introduce a clarification that emerges from the assessment of European cases. Despite the force of personal leadership, Mussolini's fascism and Hitler's National Socialism do not count as populism; ideological fervor prevailed, whereas populism is fully personalistic and therefore, following the leader's whims, more pragmatic and opportunistic. For the same reason, the hard-core, dogmatic variants of the contemporary European right do not qualify either; only where personalistic leaders put vote maximization ahead of ideological purity can we speak of populism (Mammone, 2009). Personalistic leadership thus comes in two versions, namely a rigidly ideological, "ideocratic"[1] variant that is non-populist, and a flexible, opportunistic variant that qualifies as populist. With this clarification, the strategy-based definition helps delimit the extension of "populism."

The borderline between ideocratic and opportunistic personalism is not easy to draw, however. Moreover, political leaders who rely mainly on populism can use elements of other strategies in a subordinate, secondary fashion. Therefore, the penultimate section flexibilizes the political-strategic definition by drawing on Charles Ragin's (2000) introduction of fuzzy-set concepts to the social sciences, which allows for a gradated scoring of cases of populism. In these ways, the present chapter tries to advance the never-ending discussion on populism. In the spirit of a handbook, it undertakes a renewed effort finally to capture this "shifty eel" (Weyland, 2010: xii).

THE DECLINE OF NOTIONS
OF ECONOMIC POPULISM

Before contrasting discursive and ideology-centered notions with political-strategic concepts of populism, it makes sense to highlight the fading of a third approach that burst onto the academic scene in the late 1980s and early 1990s, namely the notion of economic populism. Impressed by the dramatic boom and bust cycles in José Sarney's Brazil and Alan García's Peru, well-known economists Jeffrey Sachs (1989) and Rüdiger Dornbusch and Sebastian Edwards (1991) identified populism with voluntaristic over-spending and similar politically driven spasms of economic irresponsibility. In this view, a wide variety of political leaders sought to boost their mass support by distribut-ing a plethora of economic benefits. But this short-term maximization of popularity fla-grantly disregarded economic equilibria. This myopia soon caused a spiraling economic crisis that quickly evaporated the presidents' support and resulted in an economic and political collapse, which brought great suffering and worsening poverty for the masses.

Inspired by these dramatic events in the real world, the notion of economic populism drew a good deal of scholarly attention. But from the beginning, the great diversity of politicians who were tagged with this label raised questions about its conceptual validity and analytical usefulness, especially for political science. Classical populist Juan Perón, neopopulist Alan García, Marxist socialist Salvador Allende, and conservative José Sarney—the cases examined by Sachs (1989; see also Dornbusch and Edwards, 1991)—were very different political animals; can a concept be useful that encompasses them all?

Moreover, developments in the real world quickly seemed to disprove the association of populism with economic irresponsibility postulated by Sachs (1989) and Dornbusch and Edwards (1991). Precisely when these authors published their claims, a new wave of political populists embarked on orthodox adjustment and thorough market reform. Carlos Menem, Fernando Collor, and Alberto Fujimori systematically applied populist strategies and tactics to boost their political leadership, but at the same time enacted comprehensive programs of neoliberal reform in close consultation with the global sheriffs of economic orthodoxy, the International Monetary Fund and the World Bank. These "unexpected affinities" of populism and economic liberalism (Weyland, 1996) showed that populism cannot be defined via the disregard of neoliberal principles such as budget discipline and monetary equilibrium.

Even the reappearance of left-wing, radical populism in contemporary Latin America has not restored the usefulness of economic notions of populism. Among the new leaders, Evo Morales has maintained budget discipline and avoided "economic irre-sponsibility" (Edwards, 2010: 171; Madrid, Hunter, and Weyland, 2010: 153–60), while Rafael Correa has refrained from challenging crucial constraints imposed by his neo-liberal predecessors and cemented via dollarization. And although Hugo Chávez clearly engaged in wild overspending, racked up a huge debt, suffocated the domestic economy, and made Venezuela hyper-dependent on imports, the continuing influx of

exorbitant petroleum rents allowed him to postpone the long-predicted day of reckoning (Edwards, 2010: 192–3). Thus, the crash predicted by economists' theories of the
populist cycle was long averted. The resulting lack of a "paradigmatic" case of dramatic
failure has confined economic notions to the margins of the contemporary debate on
populism (Edwards, 2010: part 3).

THE RESURGENCE OF DISCURSIVE
AND IDEOLOGY-CENTERED NOTIONS

The main novelty in the scholarly discussion on populism is the revival of definitions
based on discourse and ideology. These ideational notions seek to grasp populism's
meaning by highlighting the fundamental schemata that structure the populist worldview. These basic patterns of thinking (ideology) shape the ways in which populist politicians appeal to their followers and criticize their adversaries, in their speeches and
discourse (see e.g. Panizza, 2005).

Certainly, however, populist movements are notorious for not espousing a clear, systematic, and comprehensive worldview; they avoid embracing a specific, well-defined
ideology. Advocates of ideational notions therefore call populism a "thin-centered ideology" (Mudde, 2007: 15–26): It comprises only some basic, very generic schemata, not
a fully elaborated edifice of maxims and tenets (see also Rooduijn, 2014; Stanley, 2008;
Taggart, 2000: 1–5).

Ideational conceptualizations highlight the black-and-white contrast informing the
populist worldview, which extols the pure, authentic people in their confrontation with
powerful, dangerous adversaries, especially selfish, corrupt elites. In this heroic struggle, populism promotes the general will of "the people" against rapacious special interests. Who the enemies of the people are varies widely with circumstances. Due to its
generic worldview, populism can combine with a great diversity of specific ideologies.

The "thin" nature of populist ideology makes it difficult to ascertain and delimit this
concept. This problem traditionally plagued ideology-centered and discursive notions
and for years dissuaded political scientists from adopting them.

But a methodological innovation has given the ideational approach a new boost.
Kirk Hawkins has adapted techniques of holistic grading from pedagogy and has
applied them for scoring populist discourse on a numerical scale. These measurements
of elements of the populist worldview in politicians' speeches yield quantitative indicators (Hawkins, 2010: chapter 3). This data in turn allows for statistical analyses of
the causes and consequences of populism (Hawkins, 2010: chapter 5). This methodological advance, which has also helped to open the path for survey research on populist mass attitudes (Akkerman, Mudde, and Zaslove, 2014; Spruyt, Keppens, and Van
Droogenbroek, 2016), seems to overcome the congenital weakness of discursive and
ideology-centered notions: their imprecision. As a result, the ideational approach has
made a comeback among populism scholars.

Nevertheless, discursive and ideology-centered definitions suffer from significant problems. First, even Hawkins's measurement procedure does not succeed in validly delimiting populism's extension. Instead, it produces important "false positives": crucial cases are improperly classified as populist. Second, the recent ideational concepts misunderstand populism's intension and distort its meaning. While populism in its discourse claims to empower "the people," in reality it immediately delegates this popular sovereignty to a personalistic leader—and thus effectively disempowers the citizenry! Ideational notions highlight the progressive, direct-democratic rhetoric and façade but overlook the essence of populism, which revolves around top-down leadership.

Problems of Extension: Excessive Breadth

Despite its careful methodology, Hawkins's measurements yield some striking false positives. George W. Bush earns one of the highest populism scores in Hawkins's disparate sample (Hawkins, 2010: 81–2). But the US president did not rise on the back of a populist mass movement; after all, he infamously lost the popular vote. Nor did Bush act like a populist in office; for instance, he never sought constitutional change to undermine checks and balances and augment presidential power. Thus, how valid and useful is the holistic "grading" of leaders' speeches?

Also, how would Italian fascism and Germany's National Socialism score in Hawkins's procedure (see Hawkins, 2010: 37)? These movements certainly espoused Manichean discourse and pitted "the pure people" against mortal enemies. But subsuming them under populism misconstrues the nature of fascism and National Socialism. The massive use of violence and the imposition of totalitarianism differed fundamentally from the fluid, tenuous approach of populism. Populist leaders do not try to re-mold the people via eugenics, impose ideological homogeneity, and force their followers into all-encompassing mass organizations. Whereas fascism and National Socialism quickly established full-scale despotism, populism hovers in the hybrid zone between democracy and "competitive" authoritarianism: it constitutes a very different political animal (Priester, 2012: chapter 7, especially 177–9; Van Kessel, 2014: 108). Discursive notions of populism miss these crucial differences because they highlight Manichean rhetoric, on which the interwar tyrants could not be outdone.

In sum, despite Hawkins's nifty measurement procedure, discursive and ideology-centered notions continue to have crucial problems in delimiting populism's extension (cf. Van Kessel, 2014).[2] Due to the political attractiveness of "us vs them" rhetoric, these definitions end up with too broad a scope. Thus, the difficulty arises from the focus on discourse itself.

Problems of Intension: Missing Populism's Twisted Meaning

The recent ideational definitions also misunderstand populism's meaning. Populism often displays a significant disjuncture between form and substance, style and strategy, rhetoric and reality. Ideational notions overlook these gulfs by relying on populism's self-depiction as a movement of "the people" confronting corrupt elites. This discourse suggests that the popular sovereign can and should have political agency: "the people" finally take the country's fate into their own hands and shake off domination by selfish elites. Populism thus claims to empower the popular sovereign.

But these self-depictions miss a crucial fact: Because "the people"—a *very* broad aggregate—are amorphous, heterogeneous, and largely unorganized, they cannot exercise effective agency; collective action dilemmas preclude that. Instead, it is the very essence of populism that the rhetorically empowered people necessarily follow a leader who claims to act on their behalf. The typical populist move is to identify "the people" with this leader—and then vest in the leader the power emanating from the people (de la Torre, 2015: 9, 13, 18–19). This populist twist inverts the direction of political influence. Whereas by omitting the crucial role of leadership (see recently Moffitt, 2016: 8, 20, 42–3, 51–5, 68, 101, 147), discourse implicitly depicts populism as a bottom-up mass movement, it really rests on a top-down strategy through which a leader marshals plebiscitarian support for the goals that she determines on her own.[3] By missing this fundamental inversion and not even including personalistic leadership in the definition, discursive and ideology-centered notions fail to capture the central meaning of populism. They focus on the surface and miss the very axis around which populism revolves.

The neglect of personalistic, plebiscitarian leadership is doubly surprising. First, recent ideational approaches are often derived from the analysis of right-wing movements in Europe (Mudde, 2007), where personalistic leadership predominates and empowerment of "the people" is conspicuous by its absence (Pelinka, 2013; case studies in Albertazzi and McDonnell, 2008 and Wodak, KhosraviNik, and Mral, 2013). Second, Hawkins's discursive approach scores speeches delivered by top leaders, not the official pronouncements of the broader movement.[4] Thus, data collection actually focuses on leading politicians—but the conceptual discussion (Hawkins, 2010: 29–69) fails to highlight the decisive role of these politicians!

By neglecting the automatic transfer of "the people's" sovereignty to a personalistic leader, discursive and ideology-centered definitions hinder the understanding of core features of populism. Whereas organized, truly empowered mass movements such as European Social Democracy form lasting collective actors that can systematically pursue a long-term reform strategy, populist leadership sustained by amorphous mass support is inherently unsteady, fickle, and unpredictable. Populism is notorious for its twists and turns, driven by the opportunistic efforts of personalistic leaders to concentrate power and stay in office. The driving force behind populism is political, not ideological. Prototypical populist movements are practically impossible to define in ideological terms. Argentine Peronism for decades spanned the full arch from fascist right to radical left. And who could define the Bolivarianism of Hugo Chávez, who took advice from reactionary Norberto Ceresole as well as Marxist Heinz Dieterich? It does not seem useful to define populism via ideology, however thin-centered it may be.[5]

Instead, it makes sense to conceptualize populism via the decisive role of personalistic, plebiscitarian leadership. That top-down agency forms the axis around which populism revolves becomes obvious where a surging mass movement loses steam and evaporates once its main leader dies, as happened after the death of Carlos Palenque in Bolivia and the assassinations of Jorge Eliécer Gaitán in Colombia and of Pim Fortuyn in the Netherlands (Lucardie, 2008: 151, 162–4; Pelinka, 2013: 10). What is typical of populism is the way in which personalistic leaders relate to their followers, seek to boost their influence, and exercise their power. Accordingly, populism is best defined as a distinctive political strategy.

Populism as a Political Strategy

To do justice to the actual role of "the people" and their personalistic leader and to capture the distinctive connection between the leader and the mass followers that is constitutive of populism, this notion is best conceptualized as a political strategy. Such a strategy comprises "the methods and instruments of winning and exercising power" (Weyland, 2001: 12). It constitutes a coherent set of approaches and mechanisms for structuring relations of political participation, support building, and governmental authority. In other words, a political strategy determines the principal ways and means by which a political actor captures the government and makes and enforces authoritative decisions. Specifically, how does this political ruler sustain the government and ensure the support and obedience of citizens? And what type of political actor—for instance, a personal leader or an organized party—is in command? Thus, there are two central components of a political strategy: namely the type of political actor that seeks and exercises power; and the principal power capability which that political actor mobilizes as support basis.

Table 3.1 Populism in contrast to other strategies of rule, classified by type of ruler, principal power capability, and ruler's relation to support base.

TYPE OF RULER	PRINCIPAL POWER CAPABILITY			RULER'S RELATIONSHIP TO SUPPORT BASE
	Numbers	Special Weight		
		Economic Clout	Military Coercion	
Individual Person	Populism	Patrimonialism	*Caudillismo*	"Direct" and Unorganized
Informal Grouping	Clientelism	Oligarchy	Government by Military Faction	Firm Informal Ties
Formal Organization	Party Government	Corporatism	Government by Military Institution	Stable Organizational Links

Note: The right and left columns refer to the same dimension, but from different angles. Reproduced with slight modifications from Weyland (2001: 13)—with written permission from *Comparative Politics*.

Type of Ruler

One cornerstone of a political strategy concerns the type of political actor that strives for winning and exercising government power. Historically, the main options have been individuals (that is, personal leaders), informal groupings, or formal organizations, especially institutionalized political parties or military establishments (Weyland, 2001: 13). Accordingly, modern democracies are characterized by electoral competition and governmental alternation among reasonably well-organized and programmatic political parties. Latin America's bureaucratic authoritarianism of the 1960s and 1970s was run by the armed forces as an institution (not the traditional "man on horseback"). And the competitive oligarchies that were common in the region during the nineteenth century revolved around informal groupings, especially regional elite factions.

Viewed from this comparative perspective, populism is a political strategy that revolves around an individual politician. Specifically, populism rests on personalistic leadership, seeks to boost its autonomy and power, and contests, pushes aside, or dominates other types of actors, such as elite factions and organized political parties. In particular, populist leaders combat the established "political class" and try to rise above it. Thus, the clear predominance of a powerful leader is a cornerstone of populism (from a Europeanist perspective, see Decker, 2006: 17–18; Pelinka, 2013: 10).

Even a politician who initially emerges as part of an informal clique, a group of party officials, or a cohort of military officers can achieve populist leadership if that leader establishes personal preeminence and independence from erstwhile supporters. In this vein, Juan Perón from 1943 to 1946 quickly rose to political prominence, overcame the constraints that his military comrades sought to impose on him, and gained clear personal predominance. In these ways, he turned into one of Latin America's quintessential populists. Similarly, Colombia's Álvaro Uribe cut his teeth as a leader of the centenarian Liberal Party, won election to governor of Antioquia, and helped to usher major bills, such as pension privatization, through Congress. But in the midst of economic crisis and escalating guerrilla war, he jumped ship at the turn of the millennium, embraced a populist strategy, and as an independent candidate won the presidential election of 2002. In office, he typically promoted constitutional reform to extend presidential powers and won an unprecedented reelection victory in 2006. These examples corroborate that versatile leadership and skillful opportunism are constitutive of populism.

Principal Power Capability

The other dimension of a political strategy concerns the principal power capability that political actors use for winning influence and sustaining their authority. The fundamental options are numbers or special weight (Weyland, 1995: 128–9); special weight comprises primarily economic clout or military coercion (Weyland, 2001: 13). On this dimension, populism clearly prefers numbers. Insisting on the norm of political equality, it criticizes the privileges derived from special weight and attacks elitism. To make numbers count in politics, populism constantly mobilizes "the people," that is, the large majority of the populace. Based on the principle of "one person, one vote," populism seeks to overwhelm its adversaries in the electoral arena and sweep its leader into office with massive victories at the polls.

Populism relies on numbers in other arenas as well. Traditionally, mass rallies were a decisive way for populist leaders to affirm and demonstrate their support from "the people" and push aside their adversaries, symbolically or through forceful street contention. Crowd mobilization in fact allowed populists to emerge unscathed, even strengthened from serious crises, as Hugo Chávez managed to do in the coup attempt of April 2002. Similarly, October 17, 1945, when huge demonstrations forced Juan Perón's liberation from jail, gave a big boost to the Peronist movement, which has celebrated it ever since as its "Day of Loyalty."

Mass rallies have diminished in political importance with the rise of opinion polls, which enable personalistic leaders to prove their wide-ranging support in more representative and scientific ways. Populists constantly commission surveys and brandish their popularity ratings as political weapons. Strong approval bolsters their claim to embody "the will of the people" and helps them delegitimize their adversaries and opponents as "enemies of the people." In the battle over public opinion, poll numbers thus play a crucial role. The increasing reliance on surveys has allowed populism to assume a particularly clear, pure form. Whereas mass mobilization for rallies required some degree of organization, efforts to boost popularity ratings do not depend on organization and revolve even more exclusively around the top leader, who can therefore preserve and enhance her personal autonomy. Contemporary populism thus comes closer to approximating the ideal-type of personalistic leadership sustained by amorphous mass support than historical figures such as Juan Perón, who ended up laying the foundation for a lasting, albeit uninstitutionalized political party.

The alternative type of power capability is special weight: the political preferences of some sectors count disproportionately, based on the resources that back them up. The most common example is the economic clout of private business, which commands a powerful political voice. And of course, political actors will listen if the military rattles its sabers. When sectors demonstrate the particular intensity of their preferences, especially in a costly way—for instance through a hunger strike—they can also acquire special weight and count more than regular citizens. All of these forms of special weight cause deviations from the principle of political equality. While excepting the usage of military firepower, liberal, pluralist democracy has nevertheless opened up avenues and mechanisms for advancing "weighty" preferences, for instance through neocorporatist consultations with business, interest group lobbying in parliament, and nonviolent protests in the streets.

Populism, in contrast, is averse to special weight and singles out widespread mass support as the legitimate base of rule. While for pragmatic reasons personalistic leaders have to talk to business, especially after winning the presidency, they try to affirm and demonstrate their independence from elite groupings, bypass organized civil society, and put the armed forces in their place. Populism criticizes special weight as an elitist mechanism that provides privileges for the few and disadvantages the people. To prove and boost their distance from "the establishment," populist politicians keep mobilizing their mass support, their main base of sustenance. For this purpose, they hold frequent elections and plebiscites, constantly advertise their popularity ratings, and rally their backers for street demonstrations, especially when they confront a political challenge.

Core Elements of Populist Strategy

To win, maintain, and strengthen such backing from large numbers of citizens, ideally the people as a whole, personalistic leaders rely on unmediated, quasi-direct appeals. How else to connect to a broad, heterogeneous aggregate, "the people," which is composed of multiple diverse sectors while lacking an overarching, encompassing organization? For mobilizing such an amorphous, diverse mass, specific programmatic promises have limited effectiveness; diffuse personal appeals that depict the leader as the embodiment of "the people" and its will seem to work better. Leaders therefore promote a direct identification with their followers, which bypasses all forms of intermediation, such as clientelism and party organization. As Venezuela's Bolivarian populism proclaimed, "Chávez is the people, and the people is Chávez."

In this quasi-direct way, contemporary populist leaders reach the mass public especially through TV and increasingly through social communications media. These forms of linking up to the variegated citizenry create the impression of direct contact, face to face. In turn, the leader draws on opinion polls and focus groups to ascertain the "will of the people." All of these mechanisms can give a personalistic leader a daily presence in the lives of millions of followers, which gains special intensity if the leader commands charisma;[6] in that case, the populist bond can reach quasi-religious fervor (Zúquete, 2007) and trigger outbreaks of collective hysteria, as happened after the death of Hugo Chávez. The leader deliberately foments the intensity of the populist bond because the absence of a direct personal exchange relationship (as in clientelism) and the lack of organizational discipline and programmatic commitment (via an institutionalized party) expose populist support inherently to unreliability and fickleness.

Because the absence of an institutionalized connection leaves the leader without a firm, dependable support network, s/he constantly has to mobilize the followers and reinforce their commitment and loyalty. For this purpose, populist leaders seek to direct the people toward a heroic mission such as re-founding the country and combating dangerous adversaries. The best way to engineer mass support is to confront threats to popular well-being and take on "the enemies of the people"; nothing motivates people more than a serious challenge, and the clarion call of a courageous leader to tackle it directly. Anti-elite rhetoric is therefore an important political instrument of populist leaders, who are constantly on the look-out for enemies; the absence of challenges deflates their leadership and risks eroding their following. Therefore, the best thing that could happen to Hugo Chávez was having to face George W. Bush, the "perfect" embodiment of

US imperialism, if not the devil incarnate, as the Venezuelan master populist declared in a famous UN speech. Thus, contrary to discursive and ideology-centered notions, Manichean rhetoric does not form the core of populism as a potentially bottom-up movement, but serves as a top-down instrument for personalistic leaders.

Explaining the Strategic Definition of Populism

These elements add up to the notion presented in the introduction: "Populism is best defined as a political strategy through which a personalistic leader seeks or exercises government power based on direct, unmediated, uninstitutionalized support from large numbers of mostly unorganized followers" (Weyland, 2001: 14). This concept highlights the crucial role of personalistic leadership that is politically sustained through the mobilization of numbers, that is, wide-ranging mass support. Given the personalistic nature of rule and the heterogeneity of the populace, their connection lacks institutionalization and rests on the impression of direct contact. As these components come together, populism forms a coherent political strategy that has often served for winning and maintaining political power.

The central axis of the concept concerns the quasi-direct, unmediated relationship between the outstanding leader and the mass followers: populism mobilizes "the people," but this vast aggregate is so diverse and heterogeneous that rather than representing the multitude of specific interests in a pluralistic fashion, populism claims to advance the general "will of the people," as embodied in the leader. Thus, populism does not conceive of representation as a process, but as ensured via identity, namely the identification of the leader with the people, and vice versa. As the leader personifies the will of the people, the relationship between leader and followers is seen as a personal connection. This deep association gives populism the intensity that provides many followers with a sense of belonging, which liberal, pluralist democracy with its reliance on "cold" procedural mechanisms lacks.

Charisma is not a definitional component of populism,[7] but a widespread belief in a leader's amazing, extra-ordinary, and "supernatural" capacities is a prime way in which the connection between leader and followers can acquire the special intensity that gives rise to and sustains populism. If people are convinced of a leader's salvational and redemptive qualities (Zúquete, 2007), they will offer profound commitment. The resulting bond is direct and bypasses any organizational intermediation; to the extent that there are underlings in the populist movement, they have only borrowed authority as the anointed "disciples" of the leader. Charisma is thus a great example of the "glue" that can hold together a leader's direct relationship to a mass of followers and that can give this connection a deeply personal character.

The strategic definition of populism via the combination of personalistic leadership and the reliance on numbers as the principal power capability also suggests what the principal alternatives to populism are. Where a personalistic leader draws mainly on special weight, patrimonialism (economic clout) or *caudillismo* (military coercion) emerges. On the other hand, a system of rule that rests on large numbers but is headed by an informal grouping is held together by clientelism; whereas the predominance of formal organization gives rise to party government. The polar opposites to populism in this two-dimensional conceptualization are government by the military as an institution (that is, a formal organization relying on the "special weight" of armed coercion) and corporatism (formal organizations relying on economic clout). Table 3.1 (reproduced from Weyland, 2001: 13) systematically clarifies the conceptual field comprising the different strategies of political rule.

Analytical Benefits of the Strategic Definition

The strategic notion is useful for elucidating the central features and tendencies that scholars have long associated with populism and that characterize its contemporary manifestations as well. A prime example is the stark volatility in political fate that populist leaders can experience: after a meteoric rise, their rule can quickly collapse, as happened to Brazil's Fernando Collor (1990–1992) and Ecuador's Abdalá Bucaram (1996–1997); Peru's Alan García experienced a similar roller coaster in his presidential popularity but miraculously managed to serve out his first term (1985–1990). As regards European cases, Austrian leader Jörg Haider, a right-winger who qualifies as populist, faced this kind of dramatic inflection after his party entered the government in 2000 (Heinisch, 2003; Pallaver and Gärtner, 2006: 104–5, 108–10, 115–18; Probst, 2003: 122–4; Fallend 2012). Thus, whereas political organization takes a long time to build but is also slow to erode, the force of personality can rapidly sway masses of followers with its intense direct appeals, but it can deflate with equally stunning speed.

The central role of personalistic leadership, which allows the leader great latitude for opportunistic calculations and maneuverings, also gives populism the striking unpredictability, shiftiness, and disorganization in the exercise of government power and in public policy-making that observers have noted. Populist presidents are not committed to a systematic ideology or clear program, but govern as they see fit, depending on their own tactical considerations, sudden ideas, and even whims; the more they succeed in their goal of concentrating power and enhancing their own autonomy, the fewer constraints they face and the more easily they can engage in "decisionism" (Novaro, 2011). Accordingly, populist leaders like undertaking new initiatives, often with great fanfare; but thorough program elaboration and careful, systematic implementation are often missing. This asymmetry, arising from the limited and shifting attention of the personal leader, accounts for the disjuncture of grand proclamations and generous promises vs meager realizations that is so typical of populism.

Hugo Chávez, for instance, was notorious for starting a panoply of ambitious projects, in both the domestic and international arena. But the follow-through was usually deficient; accordingly, in 2008 this populist leader had to declare an "emergency" in the health program that he had started with grandiose proclamations a mere five years before; and the monumental oil pipeline that was supposed to connect Venezuela with Argentina remained unbuilt. Typical of populist leaders, Chávez placed personal loyalty ahead of technical competence in selecting his aides; no wonder that Bolivarian populism has been disastrous in its policy performance. While less averse to technocracy than his left-leaning counterpart, Fujimori was similarly unpredictable in his policy orientation and also weak in program implementation. After surprisingly switching to neoliberalism at the beginning of his term (in response to catastrophic hyperinflation and a virtual economic collapse), the Peruvian leader turned around again in the late 1990s and promoted economic expansion to facilitate his second reelection. Typically, the opportunistic goal of self-perpetuation won out over programmatic commitments. Political expediency also drove specific measures, such as the sudden, totally unprepared announcement of a health insurance scheme for public school students in 1997; health experts, who do not see adolescents as a priority group, were left scratching their heads, but the president hoped for political payoffs in proudly announcing the new coverage for millions of people at low cost.

In sum, a strategy-based definition of populism seems to have considerable face validity. It sheds light on distinctive features of populism that observers of all stripes have frequently noticed. This notion focuses on effective political action and the foundations of political rule. In their behavior, political leaders are compelled to make real choices; therefore, they have to show "their true colors" more clearly than in speeches and other forms of discourse, which often display considerable vagueness, rhetorical license, and opportunistic dissimulation. For this reason, deeds constitute a firmer base for classification than mere words. A strategic definition therefore promises to yield fewer "false positives" than discursive and ideology-based notions.

"Precising" the Strategic Definition to Specify the Extension of European Populism

Conceiving of populism as a political strategy has an important conceptual and analytical benefit. It delimits populism's extension in a way that avoids the heterogeneity and disparateness associated with the term in recent cross-regional analyses. Authors who rely on discursive and ideology-centered notions have included both Latin America's mass-based, majoritarian populism and the right-wing extremism that has cropped up at the ideological margin of many European polities (Mudde and Rovira Kaltwasser, 2012; 2013).[8] They have then claimed that this broad extension allows for wide-ranging comparisons that shed new light on populism. But these recent analyses have highlighted the important differences among regional variants (Mudde and Rovira

Kaltwasser, 2013; see also Mastropaolo, 2008: 32–3); strikingly, they have not come up with the similarities that such a "different systems" design is—for methodological reasons—supposed to yield (Przeworski and Teune, 1970: 34–9).

These problematic results of an interesting research design suggest that much of Europe's right-wing radicalism may be a different "political animal" and not fall under populism. The definition of populism as a strategy resting on a quasi-direct, unmediated relationship between a personalistic leader and a largely unorganized mass of followers is crucial for understanding this difference: it implies that the established organizational landscape restricts the political space for populism in Europe; correspondingly, it suggests a narrow delimitation of the extension of European populism. In line with the political-strategic approach, the longstanding prevalence of fairly well-organized, program-oriented parties in much of Europe leaves limited room for populist movements. Because social-democratic and Christian-democratic parties decades ago incorporated major sectors of the "popular masses" and have continued to encapsulate a good part of the electorate, populist movements in Western, Northern, and Central Europe are often confined to the margins of the political system: usually, they cluster toward the poles of the ideological spectrum, especially the right (because Communist parties also used to command tight organizations). Thus, with its emphasis on political-organizational factors, the strategic definition "logically" elucidates the constraints facing populism in European politics. Discursive and ideology-centered notions are less useful in this respect and may point in the wrong ideological direction: should not leftist parties critical of established society appeal to "the people" and inveigh against corrupt elites? But outside Greece and Spain, left-leaning populism has been a rarity in contemporary Europe.

Moreover, regarding the right-wing fringe, the strategic definition suggests a stricter delimitation of populism. A number of radical parties, such as Belgium's *Vlaams Belang* (De Lange and Akkerman, 2012: 32–3) and Le Pen's *Front National* (Rooduijn, 2014: 586, 589), are much more firmly institutionalized than loose populist movements; therefore, they fall outside the extension of the strategy-based notion. Also, while fascistoid radicals may appeal to "the people" in their discourse (as they actually seem to do to a limited extent!),[9] usually they captivate only narrow, minoritarian segments of the citizenry. Discursive and ideology-centered notions classify leaders like Jean-Marie Le Pen, Gianfranco Fini, or Andrzej Lepper as populists, whereas these ideological extremists do not qualify under a strategy-based definition, given the clear disjuncture between rhetoric and reality.[10]

This distinction between populism and rightist extremism does not hinge on differential political success as such, but on the underlying reason for right-wingers' lack of mass support. As a thoroughly personalistic strategy, populism tailors its appeals in opportunistic ways to maximize the leader's chances of capturing the government. By contrast, radical right-wingers cling to their resentment-driven ideology even at the cost of remaining confined to the ideological margins. They seek an "ideocracy," that is, rule guided by a dogmatic ideology toward a millenarian goal (Kailitz, 2013: 42–9). Those extremist views predictably draw widespread rejection and hostility, enclose these leaders in an ideological ghetto, and restrict their political success. Even on the infrequent occasions when extreme-right leaders win promising vote shares, their dogmatism hinders their accession to power. Aversion to reactionary radicalism often induces all mainstream forces to close ranks and defeat them in the decisive contest, as happened to Jean-Marie Le Pen in the second round of France's presidential election in 2002.

This distinction between populism and right-wing radicalism (which is in line with the exclusion of interwar fascism above) suggests a "precising" of the strategy-based definition. As proposed by Collier and Levitsky (1997: 442–5), precising highlights a characteristic that had been implicitly associated with a concept and includes it in the explicit definition. Accordingly, this chapter clarifies that populism rests on pure, opportunistic personalism—as distinct from ideocratic personalism, where the leader embodies a dogmatic ideology and acts as its monopolistic interpreter. Bent on ideological purity, ideocratic personalism shuns the flexibility that is crucial for winning over "the people." It does not mobilize numbers as such, but seeks to draw fervent disciples, preferring depth of commitment over breadth of support. Pursuing millenarian goals, ideocratic leaders adopt a long-term perspective, patiently seek to win converts, and do not mind staying in opposition.

Pure personalism, by contrast, is opportunistic and tries to maximize the leader's chances of coming to power. Fully personalistic leaders therefore use ideas, slogans, and campaign promises instrumentally and flexibly shift with changing circumstances. Lacking firm ideological commitments, they seek to mobilize as much mass support as possible. It is this pure, opportunistic personalism that gives rise to populism.

With this clarification, the strategy-based definition of populism excludes extreme-right movements and includes only right-wing leaders who flexibly pursue votes. For example, it leaves out hard-core oppositionist Jean-Marie Le Pen with his fascistoid connections (Mammone, 2009), but subsumes his daughter Marine, as well as Jörg Haider, both of whom pulled their parties out of the neofascist ghetto and redirected them toward the opportunistic quest for votes (for Le Pen, see Shields, 2013: 191–3). For this purpose, they employed the quasi-direct, personalistic appeals that are constitutive of populism.

This conceptual distinction makes analytical sense. Due to its ideocratic strategy, right-wing extremism differs in its political trajectory from populism. These marginal hardcore groupings tend to have greater steadiness and can survive and even thrive for many years in opposition.[11] Ideological extremism and resentment provide strong glue that can keep these movements together over the long run, despite their limited electoral success and minimal chances of winning power. Jean-Marie Le Pen, for instance, haunted French politics for decades, and Gianfranco Fini was a longstanding fixture in Italy.

By contrast, populist movements survive only if they quickly win the top office, as did Hugo Chávez in Venezuela in 1998, Rafael Correa in Ecuador in 2006, and Alberto Fujimori in Peru in 1990. Given the quasi-personal nature of the leader's connection to the heterogeneous mass base, the resulting vagueness of appeals, and the lack of organization of the followers, populist movements tend to evaporate if they do not achieve electoral success, as happened to "Fra-Fra" Errázuriz in Chile after 1989 (Drake, 2012: 81), Irene Sáez in Venezuela in 1997–1998, and Ross Perot in the US after 1992; populism's persistence in opposition, exemplified by Peru's American Popular Revolutionary Alliance (APRA), is rare. Populist movements also tend to disappear if they quickly lose governmental power, as happened in Brazil to Jânio Quadros in 1961 and to Fernando Collor de Mello in 1992, and in Ecuador to Abdalá Bucaram in 1997 and to Lucio Gutiérrez in 2005.

The precised strategy-based definition thus yields a stricter and more useful delimitation of populism than discursive and ideology-centered notions. By concentrating on discourse, those notions overrate the "popular" appeals of right-wing extremists and do not stress the crucial fact that ideological radicalism severely limits their political impact. The overestimation of a marginal phenomenon has stimulated more scholarly interest in Europe's right-wing extremism than it arguably deserves.[12] Right-wingers only win significant vote shares if they soften their ideological commitments and turn into flexible, opportunistic vote-getters—and therefore pose much less of a threat.

Excluding reactionary radicalism from the concept of populism has the analytical advantage of putting cross-regional comparisons among populist movements and governments on a more valid methodological foundation. As mentioned above, such "different systems" designs are supposed to yield similarities in causal factors—not differences, which recent efforts highlight (Mudde and Rovira Kaltwasser, 2013). Commonalities would indeed move to the forefront if students of European populism focused not on sectarian radicals, but on catch-all movements with personalistic leaders who seek to win quasi-direct, unmediated mass support from a broad cross-section of "the people." As Silvio Berlusconi's *Forza Italia* (Edwards, 2005; Pissowotzki, 2003; Ruzza and Balbo, 2013), Andreas Papandreou's Panhellenic Socialist Movement (PASOK: Clogg, 1992: chapters 6–7; Featherstone, 1983), Alexis Tsipras's SYRIZA (Stavrakakis and Katsambekis, 2014), and Victor Orbán's FIDESZ (Pappas, 2014) show,[13] such movements have a good chance of capturing the government, as may Pablo Iglesias's PODEMOS soon have in Spain as well (Kioupkiolis, 2016). Then these majority-seeking leaders exercise power like their Latin American counterparts—in a rather opportunistic, unpredictable, and unaccountable if not arbitrary way. Typically, therefore, their policy performance tends to fall far short of their grand promises (for Haider, see Heinisch, 2003). And due to the tenuous, uninstitutionalized links to their mass base, these leaders' popularity can fluctuate significantly—again, just as in Latin America.

In sum, the similarities between a properly delimited notion of European populism and its Latin American equivalent (recently examined in de la Torre and Arnson, 2013) are noteworthy. A "precised" strategic definition of populism, which excludes "ideocratic" right extremism, helps to rectify the methodological problem in the new flurry of cross-regional analyses and promises significant analytical benefits for the quest to broaden the empirical investigation and theoretical study of populism (for an interesting effort, see Werz, 2003).

Capturing the Fuzziness of Populism?

While the political-strategic definition clarifies the core of populism and usefully delimits its extension, the boundaries of this concept remain difficult to pin down; the distinction of ideocratic vs pure, opportunistic personalism is not clear-cut either. Even more than other political phenomena, populism has fuzzy edges because in their quest for power, leaders flexibly adjust to contextual opportunities and constraints and change color with the circumstances. Whereas biology examines species that are genetically distinct, political phenomena lack clear borderlines. A cat is a cat and a dog a dog—but in politics, contextual complexity and human ingenuity soften or even erase boundaries; there can be partial and mixed types that fixed conceptual categories do not fully capture. Given leaders' opportunism, populism in particular may be a "cat-dog" (cf. Van Kessel, 2014). After all, political leaders can combine features of different identities and strategies. For instance, was Mexico's Pancho Villa a bandit, revolutionary, or populist? Was Hugo Chávez a socialist or populist—that is, partly ideocratic or purely opportunistic? And is Bolivia's Evo Morales a social movement leader or a populist?

The classical conceptualization applied in my 2001 article was inspired by Sartori's European rigor and tried to establish clear boundaries. In this binary approach to categorization, cases are either strictly inside or fully outside a concept's extension. This insistence on conceptual clarity promises analytical benefits. But it may be too blunt for the nuances and grey zones that characterize the political world in its tremendous complexity and fluidity. Especially for a phenomenon that resembles a chameleon as much as populism does, a better procedure may be to rely on the fuzzy-set approach propagated by Charles Ragin (2000). Fuzzy sets introduce conceptual gradations and qualitative thresholds that can capture the shades and mixtures of "real world" politics (Schneider and Wagemann, 2012: 24–40).

Fuzzy sets can thus depict political leaders who rely primarily on one strategy, but also draw on another strategy as a complement. In their opportunistic quest for power and disregard for ideological purity, populist politicians seem especially likely to apply such combinations of strategies. For instance, Carlos Menem in Argentina sought and exercised power first and foremost as the personalistic leader of a heterogeneous mass of citizens. But Menem also marshaled his Peronist Party (Partido Justicialista—PJ) and its affiliated trade unions; he used union support to win the PJ's presidential candidacy for the 1989 contest and relied on the party to help sustain his government for the subsequent decade. The Peronist Party did not constitute a firm, institutionalized base for political rule, however. The PJ is notoriously flexible in its procedures, programmatically ill-defined, deeply factionalized, and therefore always "in need of" personalistic leadership. Lacking institutionalization, the PJ did not constrain Menem's personalistic leadership for many years; instead, the president quickly took control of the party and bent it to his will. Therefore, Menem's strategy was predominantly populist; political organization played a subordinate role.

The Peronist Party did give Menem's rivals a base to guarantee their own political survival, however; by contrast to fully populist movements, such as the shifting electoral vehicles created and discarded by Alberto Fujimori and Hugo Chávez, Menem never managed to suppress or expel all adversaries. Therefore, when his personalistic backing eroded in the late 1990s, Eduardo Duhalde could use his roots in the PJ's traditionalist sectors to block Menem's quest for another re-election and wrested away the candidacy for the 1999 contest. Thus, Menem's reliance on the Peronist Party eventually blocked the further perpetuation of his personalistic leadership.

Menem therefore qualifies as predominantly yet not fully populist. According to a fuzzy-set approach, this case is more inside than outside the category of populism. Charles Ragin's procedures would award Menem a fuzzy-set score of 0.66 on "populism." Peru's Alan García deserves the same score for his first term (1985–1990), during which he subjugated the American Popular Revolutionary Alliance (APRA) to his personalistic leadership and garnered popularity ratings up to 90 percent, albeit temporarily. Álvaro Uribe ranks similarly because his two-term presidency rested on unorganized mass support for his personalistic leadership, but he had a background in and continuing connections to Colombia's traditional parties.

Bolivia's Evo Morales also constitutes a mixed case because he applies various political strategies, but this combination lies more outside than inside populism. Morales deserves a fuzzy-set score of 0.33 because his rule rests largely on the backing of powerful, contentious social movements, which have retained considerable autonomy and mobilizational capacity. This mass base has continued to limit Morales's personal leadership and blocked important governmental initiatives. While the president has personalistic tendencies and populist aspirations, especially self-perpetuation in office, these goals have not achieved a definitive breakthrough; instead, Bolivia's politicized and highly mobilized social movements have insisted on a good deal of accountability and responsiveness, as demonstrated by their furious and effective reaction to the government's "Gasolinazo" of December 2010 (Crabtree, 2013: 282–91). Overall, therefore, Morales and his Movimiento al Socialismo do not qualify as populist (similarly Roberts, 2013: 57–60).

By contrast to these hybrid, partial cases, leaders like Fujimori, Chávez, Fernando Collor in Brazil, and Ecuador's Rafael Correa, who enjoyed tremendous personal autonomy, founded their own flimsy electoral vehicles, and were never constrained by them, count as full-scale populists with a fuzzy-set score of 1.0. At the other extreme, leaders of well-organized parties, such as Luiz Inácio Lula da Silva in Brazil, Michelle Bachelet in Chile, and Tabaré Vázquez in Uruguay, rank at 0 on the populism scale. While these politicians have commanded considerable personal popularity, their organizational and institutional insertion has reliably constrained personal ambitions, for instance precluding constitutional reforms to facilitate their reelection. Contemporary Latin American politics thus spans the whole range of political strategies. A fuzzy-set approach can locate different leaders and their political movements with a useful degree of clarity and precision.

The differentiated scoring of populism via Ragin's measurement approach can also help with the European cases. For example, Silvio Berlusconi with his opportunistic personalism, weak electoral vehicle, and heavy reliance on TV qualifies as a complete populist with a score of 1.0; so would Dutch leader Pim Fortuyn (Lucardie, 2008; Oudenampsen, 2013). Andreas Papandreou, by contrast, faced some constraints from his party PASOK, as does Pablo Iglesias from Spain's PODEMOS (Kioupkiolis, 2016); just like Argentina's Menem, these leaders therefore merit a 0.66. Jörg Haider also qualifies as a populist leader because he decisively reoriented his party, softened its reactionary ideology, pursued vote maximization, and used flashy appeals and telegenic appearances for this purpose (Heinisch, 2003; Wodak, 2013). Due to this transition from ideocratic dogmatism to opportunistic personalism, Haider deserves a score of 0.66 on the populism scale. Hard-core reactionary Jean-Marie Le Pen, by contrast, who for decades put ideological radicalism ahead of popularity and mass appeal, ranks as 0, like most of Europe's right-wing extremists (Mammone, 2009). His daughter Marine, however, has adopted a more flexible posture in order to win votes (Shields, 2013: 191–3), as she ostentatiously highlighted in 2015 via the "costly signal" of expelling her own father from the movement; with her determined advance toward opportunistic personalism, she now qualifies for a populism score of 0.66, as Haider did.

In sum, by capturing the mixed strategies that a number of leaders apply, a fuzzy-set approach is more realistic for measuring the complexity of the "real world," especially the cat-dog of populism. Therefore, it seems preferable to the strict binary classification advocated in Weyland (2001).

CONCLUSION

This chapter has explained and refined a political-strategic conceptualization of populism. Populism is notoriously hard to grasp and has long been one of the most "contested" concepts in the social sciences. Yet upon further reflection, the very shiftiness of this chameleonic notion provides a crucial hint about its nature: populism revolves around the opportunism of personalistic plebiscitarian leaders. The political-strategic approach highlights this wily leadership, which aptly makes use of available opportunities and often turns adversity into advantage. To secure this maneuverability, populist leaders avoid committing to a discourse, worldview, or ideology, however thin-centered it may be; in particular, they do not tie their political fate to ideocratic visions. Instead, the substantive orientation of populist movements and governments remains ill-defined and subject to arbitrary switches, derived from the calculations, choices, and even whims of the personalistic leader.

This political-strategic conceptualization leads the study of populism in a more promising direction than the recent revival of discursive and ideology-centered concepts. Even with Hawkins's innovative measurement procedure, the extension of these notions is problematic. Ideational notions also misconceive the intension of populism by highlighting the claim of popular sovereignty while missing the essential populist twist in which "the people" automatically delegate their sovereignty to a personalistic leader. Moreover, ideational definitions attribute too much importance to extreme rightists' rhetorical appeals to "the people." By contrast, the strategic approach emphasizes that ideological radicalism confines leaders to the political margins and inherently limits their ability to win support from a broad cross-section of the people. Therefore, ideocratic leadership differs from the opportunistic personalism that is typical of populism and falls outside this notion, as "precised" above.

A political-strategic definition that emphasizes patterns of political behavior and actual relations between leaders and citizens avoids the other two problems as well. To reiterate, deeds constitute a firmer and clearer basis of conceptualization than words. The prevalence of top-down leadership, which contrasts with the bottom-up rhetoric, is typical of populism. Correspondingly, there is a plebiscitarian connection between leader and followers that lacks intermediary organization. These features allow for a fairly clear delimitation of populism. With the help of Ragin's fuzzy-set approach, the political-strategic definition can also do justice to the remaining nuances and subtleties of populism, which reflect its constitutive opportunism.

Refined and precised in these ways, the political-strategic definition has important analytical advantages. Above all, it captures the inherent volatility of populism and the rapid shifts in the political fate of populist movements and leaders (Weyland, 2001: 16–17). Moreover, it yields a more precise delimitation of European populism by drawing a distinction from right-wing extremism; reactionary radicalism holds less widespread appeal and is therefore less dangerous than many observers fear. As an added benefit, this clarification puts cross-regional comparisons on a more valid methodological foundation; specifically, it yields underlying similarities across a variety of contextual differences. The political-strategic definition therefore looks like the most productive approach to the study of populism.

Notes

1 I borrow this concept from Kailitz (2013: 41–9). Whereas Kailitz (2013: 47–9) sets ideocracy apart from personalism, I highlight the overlap, given Stalin's unchallenged role as chief interpreter of Communist ideocracy (1929–1953) and the dependence of National Socialist ideology on Hitler.
2 In trying to identify the common "nucleus of populism," Rooduijn (2014) overlooks the other side of concept formation à la Sartori, boundary demarcation. Thus, is his "lowest common denominator" distinctive of populism or more broadly shared, e.g. by fascism?
3 While proposing a cumulative concept that combines features of discourse and political strategy, Barr (2009: 38–9) emphasizes the top-down nature of populism.
4 As Mudde (2007: 36–8) highlights, it is not easy to determine who speaks for a populist movement as a whole, given internal heterogeneity and weak organization.
5 Similarly, Priester (2012: 48) invokes the shifty, chameleonic nature of populism to reject Laclau's definition of populism via Manichean discourse.
6 As Priester (2012: chapter 4) emphasizes, however, charisma is neither a defining characteristic nor a necessary trait of populist leadership.

7   Deep crises, in particular, allow even uncharismatic "managers" to acquire populist leadership by boldly confronting the problems. Peru in the early 1990s is a prime example: Hyperinflation and guerrilla war allowed tight-lipped university professor Alberto Fujimori to establish his personalistic plebiscitarian predominance.

8   Strictly speaking, Europe's right-wing movements do not fit discursive and ideology-centered notions of populism well, as Hawkins and Silva's (2016: 16, 29, 31) recent measurements suggest. Also, the main enemy of "the pure people" is not the established elite, but ethnic "underlings"; hostility is directed mainly downward, not upward.

9   Interestingly, even Hawkins's measurement of discourse yields a strikingly low populism score for many of these right-wing movements (Hawkins and Silva 2016: 16, 29, 31).

10 See Mammone (2009) and Van Kessel (2014: 107–8); and for Britain, Richardson (2013).

11 Heinisch (2003) highlights the political benefits of opposition even for the *Freiheitliche Partei Österreichs*, which Haider pulled away from dogmatic ideology toward vote maximization.

12 According to Bornschier's (2010) interesting argument, however, the rise of right-wing extremism reflects a "new cultural conflict in Western Europe" that is of broader political significance.

13 Mair (2002: 92–7) also subsumes Tony Blair's "New Labour" under populism.

References

Akkerman, Agnes, Cas Mudde, and Andrej Zaslove. 2014. "How populist are the people?," *Comparative Political Studies*, 47(9): 1324–53.

Albertazzi, Daniele and Duncan McDonnell (eds). 2008. *Twenty-First Century Populism*. Houndmills: Palgrave Macmillan.

Barr, Robert. 2009. "Populists, outsiders and anti-establishment politics," *Party Politics*, 15(1): 29–48.

Bornschier, Simon. 2010. *Cleavage Politics and the Populist Right*. Philadelphia: Temple University Press.

Clogg, Richard. 1992. *A Concise History of Greece*, 2nd edn. Cambridge: Cambridge University Press.

Collier, David and Steven Levitsky. 1997. "Democracy with adjectives," *World Politics*, 49(3): 430–51.

Crabtree, John. 2013. "From the MNR to the MAS," in Carlos de la Torre and Cynthia Arnson (eds), *Latin American Populism in the Twenty-First Century*. Washington, DC: Woodrow Wilson Center Press, 269–93.

Decker, Frank. 2006. "Die populistische Herausforderung," in Frank Decker (ed.), *Populismus: Gefahr für die Demokratie oder nützliches Korrektiv?* Wiesbaden: Verlag für Sozialwissenschaften, 9–32.

de la Torre, Carlos. 2013. "El tecnopopulismo de Rafael Correa," *Latin American Research Review*, 48(1): 24–43.

de la Torre, Carlos. 2015. "Introduction," in de la Torre (ed.), *The Promise and Perils of Populism*. Lexington: University Press of Kentucky, 1–28.

de la Torre, Carlos and Cynthia Arnson (eds). 2013. *Latin American Populism in the Twenty-First Century*. Washington, DC: Woodrow Wilson Center Press.

de Lange, Sarah and Tjitske Akkerman. 2012. "Populist parties in Belgium," in Cas Mudde and Cristóbal Rovira Kaltwasser (eds), *Populism in Europe and the Americas*. Cambridge: Cambridge University Press, 27–45.

Dornbusch, Rüdiger and Sebastian Edwards (eds). 1991. *The Macroeconomics of Populism in Latin America*. Chicago: University of Chicago Press.

Drake, Paul. 2012. "Chile's populism reconsidered," in Michael Conniff (ed.), *Populism in Latin America*, 2nd edn. Tuscaloosa: University of Alabama Press, 71–85.

Edwards, Phil. 2005. "The Berlusconi anomaly," *South European Society and Politics*, 10(2): 225–43.

Edwards, Sebastian. 2010. *Left Behind: Latin America and the False Promise of Populism*. Chicago: University of Chicago Press.

Fallend, Franz. 2012. "Populism in government," in Cas Mudde and Cristóbal Rovira Kaltwasser (eds), *Populism in Europe and the Americas*. Cambridge: Cambridge University Press, 113–35.

Featherstone, Kevin. 1983. "The Greek socialists in power," *West European Politics*, 6(3): 237–50.

Hawkins, Kirk. 2010. *Venezuela's Chavismo and Populism in Comparative Perspective*. Cambridge: Cambridge University Press.

Hawkins, Kirk and Bruno Castanho Silva. 2016. "A head-to-head comparison of human-based and automated text analysis for measuring populism in 27 countries," manuscript, Department of Political Science, Brigham Young University, Provo, UT, April 20.

Heinisch, Reinhard. 2003. "Success in opposition—failure in government," *West European Politics*, 26(3): 91–130.

Kailitz, Steffen. 2013. "Classifying political regimes revisited," *Democratization*, 20(1): 39–60.

Kioupkiolis, Alexandros. 2016. "Podemos: the ambiguous promises of left-wing populism in contemporary Spain," *Journal of Political Ideologies*, 21(2): 99–120.

Laclau, Ernesto. 2005. *On Populist Reason*. London: Verso.

Laclau, Ernesto. 2012. "Institucionalismo y populismo," *Tiempo Argentino*, August 29. http://tiempo.infonews.com/2012/08/29/editorial-84541-institutionalismo--y-populismo.php, accessed December 5, 2012.

Lucardie, Paul. 2008. "The Netherlands: populism versus pillarization," in Daniele Albertazzi and Duncan McDonnell (eds), *Twenty-First Century Populism*. Houndmills: Palgrave Macmillan, 151–65.

Madrid, Raúl. 2008. "The rise of ethnopopulism in Latin America," *World Politics*, 60(3): 475–508.

Madrid, Raúl, Wendy Hunter, and Kurt Weyland. 2010. "The policies and performance of the contestatory and moderate left," in Kurt Weyland, Raúl Madrid, and Wendy Hunter (eds), *Leftist Governments in Latin America*. Cambridge: Cambridge University Press, 140–80.

Mair, Peter. 2002. "Populist democracy as party democracy," in Yves Mény and Yves Surel (eds), *Democracies and the Populist Challenge*. Houndmills: Palgrave Macmillan, 81–98.

Mammone, Andrea. 2009. "The eternal return? Faux populism and contemporization of neo-fascism across Britain, France and Italy," *Journal of Contemporary European Studies*, 17(2): 171–92.

Mastropaolo, Alfio. 2008. "Politics against democracy," in Daniele Albertazzi and Duncan McDonnell (eds), *Twenty-First Century Populism*. Houndmills: Palgrave Macmillan, 30–48.

Mazzuca, Sebastián. 2013. "The rise of rentier populism," *Journal of Democracy*, 24(2): 108–22.

Moffitt, Benjamin. 2016. *The Global Rise of Populism*. Stanford: Stanford University Press.

Mudde, Cas. 2007. *Populist Radical Right Parties in Europe.* Cambridge: Cambridge University Press.

Mudde, Cas and Cristóbal Rovira Kaltwasser (eds). 2012. *Populism in Europe and the Americas: Threat or Corrective for Democracy?* Cambridge: Cambridge University Press.

Mudde, Cas and Cristóbal Rovira Kaltwasser. 2013. "Exclusionary vs. inclusionary populism: comparing contemporary Europe and Latin America," *Government and Opposition*, 48(2): 147–74.

Novaro, Marcos. 2011. "Populismo y decisionismo en América Latina," *Diálogo Político*, 28(4): 183–210.

Oudenampsen, Merijn. 2013. "Explaining the swing to the right," in Ruth Wodak, Majid KhosraviNik, and Brigitte Mral (eds), *Right-Wing Populism in Europe*. London: Bloomsbury, 191–207.

Pallaver, Günther and Reinhold Gärtner. 2006. "Populistische Parteien an der Regierung," in Frank Decker (ed.), *Populismus: Gefahr für die Demokratie oder nützliches Korrektiv?* Wiesbaden: Verlag für Sozialwissenschaften, 99–120.

Panizza, Francisco (ed.). 2005. *Populism and the Mirror of Democracy.* London: Verso.

Pappas, Takis. 2014. "Populist democracies: post-authoritarian Greece and post-Communist Hungary," *Government and Opposition*, 49(1): 1–23.

Pelinka, Anton. 2013. "Right-wing populism: concept and typology," in Ruth Wodak, Majid KhosraviNik, and Brigitte Mral (eds), *Right-Wing Populism in Europe*. London: Bloomsbury, 3–22.

Pissowotzki, Jörn. 2003. "Der Populist Silvio Berlusconi," in Nikolaus Werz (ed.), *Populismus: Populisten in Übersee und Europa*. Opladen: Leske + Budrich, 127–43.

Priester, Karin. 2012. *Rechter und linker Populismus.* Frankfurt: Campus.

Probst, Lothar. 2003. "Jörg Haider und die FPÖ," in Nikolaus Werz (ed.), *Populismus: Populisten in Übersee und Europa*. Opladen: Leske + Budrich, 113–25.

Przeworski, Adam and Henry Teune. 1970. *The Logic of Comparative Social Inquiry.* New York: John Wiley.

Ragin, Charles. 2000. *Fuzzy-Set Social Science.* Chicago: University of Chicago Press.

Richardson, John. 2013. "Ploughing the same furrow? Continuity and change on Britain's extreme-right fringe," in Ruth Wodak, Majid KhosraviNik, and Brigitte Mral (eds), *Right-Wing Populism in Europe*. London: Bloomsbury, 105–19.

Roberts, Kenneth. 1995. "Neoliberalism and the transformation of populism in Latin America," *World Politics*, 48(1): 82–116.

Roberts, Kenneth. 2013. "Parties and populism in Latin America," in Carlos de la Torre and Cynthia Arnson (eds), *Latin American Populism in the Twenty-First Century*. Washington, DC: Woodrow Wilson Center Press, 37–60.

Rooduijn, Matthijs. 2014. "The nucleus of populism," *Government and Opposition*, 49(4): 573–99.

Ruzza, Carlo and Laura Balbo. 2013. "Italian populism and the trajectories of two leaders," in Ruth Wodak, Majid KhosraviNik, and Brigitte Mral (eds), *Right-Wing Populism in Europe*. London: Bloomsbury, 163–75.

Sachs, Jeffrey. 1989. "Social conflict and populist policies in Latin America," Cambridge, MA: National Bureau of Economic Research, Working Paper 2897.

Schneider, Carsten and Claudius Wagemann. 2012. *Set-Theoretic Methods for the Social Sciences.* Cambridge: Cambridge University Press.

Shields, James. 2013. "Marine Le Pen and the "new" FN," *Parliamentary Affairs*, 66(1): 179–96.

Spruyt, Bram, Gil Keppens, and Filip Van Droogenbroeck. 2016. "*Who* supports populism and *what* attracts people to it?," *Political Research Quarterly*, 69(2): 335–46.

Stanley, Ben. 2008. "The thin ideology of Populism," *Journal of Political Ideologies*, 13(1): 95–110.

Stavrakakis, Yannis and Giorgos Katsambekis. 2014. "Left-wing populism in the European periphery," *Journal of Political Ideologies*, 19(2): 119–42.

Svampa, Maristella. 2013. "El dilema del populismo plebeyo," *Clarín—Revista Ñ*, March 20. http://www.clarin.com/rn/ideas/Hugo-Chavez-dilema-populismo-plebeyo_0_883711650.html, accessed March 20, 2013.

Taggart, Paul. 2000. *Populism*. Buckingham: Open University Press.

Van Kessel, Stijn. 2014. "The populist cat-dog," *Journal of Political Ideologies*, 19(1): 99–118.

Werz, Nikolaus (ed.). 2003. *Populismus*. Opladen: Leske + Budrich.

Weyland, Kurt. 1995. "Latin America's four political models," *Journal of Democracy*, 6(4): 125–39.

Weyland, Kurt. 1996. "Neo-populism and neo-liberalism in Latin America," *Studies in Comparative International Development*, 32(3): 3–31.

Weyland, Kurt. 2001. "Clarifying a contested concept: 'populism' in the study of Latin American politics," *Comparative Politics*, 34(1): 1–22.

Weyland, Kurt. 2010. "Foreword," in Karen Kampwirth (ed.), *Gender and Populism in Latin America*. University Park: Pennsylvania State University Press, vii–xii.

Wodak, Ruth. 2013. "'Anything goes!'—the Haiderization of Europe," in Ruth Wodak, Majid KhosraviNik, and Brigitte Mral (eds), *Right-Wing Populism in Europe*. London: Bloomsbury, 23–37.

Wodak, Ruth, Majid KhosraviNik, and Brigitte Mral (eds). 2013. *Right-Wing Populism in Europe*. London: Bloomsbury.

Zúquete, José Pedro. 2007. *Missionary Politics in Contemporary Europe*. Syracuse: Syracuse University Press.

....

CHAPTER 4

POPULISM

A Socio-Cultural Approach

....

PIERRE OSTIGUY

THIS chapter lays out a conception of populism that is fundamentally relational, emphasizing a socio-cultural dimension that has been much neglected in political studies, together with a sociological component at the level of populism's reception, absent in the conceptualizations of (for example) Mudde and Weyland. More centrally yet, it introduces a key dimension of differentiation in political appeals that we call the "high" and the "low." In several instances, the resulting high-low dimension in politics is as structuring and as defining as the conceptually orthogonal, much-used dimension of left and right. The high-low dimension is core for understanding what populism is, and it also enables one to locate it (ordinally) in a political space. Populism is characterized by a particular form of political relationship between political leaders and a social basis, one established and articulated through "low" appeals which resonate and receive positive reception within particular sectors of society for social-cultural historical reasons. We define populism, in very few words, as the "flaunting of the 'low.'"

This approach does not downplay the importance of affects in populism. But neither does it reduce the phenomenon to manipulation or "demagogy."[1] It recognizes the centrality of leadership features, but does not treat populism as an exclusively "top-down" phenomenon. Instead, it regards it as a *two-way phenomenon*, centrally defined by the claims articulated and the connection established between the leader and supporters, a relation that displays both a socio-cultural and a politico-cultural component. Because populism is relational, in terms both of the relationship between people and leader and—as or more importantly—of this dyad's hostile relation to a "nefarious" Other, it ends up being about identity creation and identities more than about "world views" or "ideology"—especially if ideology is to have any decontestation effect (Freeden, 2003).

"Populism" carries highly charged normative connotations (including in most "scientific" definitions). Moreover and yet, in some settings it is often associated, in a taken-for-granted way, with either the *right* (or radical right) *or* a popular emancipatory project—often clearly *left* of the center. For almost all European scholars, populism is "obviously" an undesirable phenomenon (for democracy, pluralism, Enlightenment, republican values, tolerance, or even rationality). In contrast, for many left-of-center scholars in the Americas, both North and especially South, populism has often been understood as a radically democratizing, equalizing, incorporating, anti-elitist and rooted, plebeian movement.

This chapter aims to provide a normatively neutral definition of populism and an explanation of its supporters' logic that is as "anthropologically commonsensical" as possible. Conceptually, this definition is based on the notion of the "low," in politics. In "flaunting 'the low,'" there is also a second element: the notion of public *flaunting*. This element recuperates, in a more subjective, identity-centered, and socially connotated way, the notion of "antagonism," so central in many definitions of populism, including that of Laclau (2005).

This approach is thus relational, particularly between popular socio-cultural identities, or traits and ways of doing which can then be articulated as identities, and an "asserting" (or "flaunting") leadership. There is an emphasis on "closeness" (whether in a spectacle or ordinary praxis way); second, and equally important because of the marked contrast with standard "high" ways of doing politics, populist appeals are transgressive, improper, and antagonistic in the sense that they are intended to "shock" or provoke. This approach thus shares many affinities with the family of authors who have understood populism as a style. Populism can be studied empirically by looking at (amongst other things) the performance and praxis of politicians. We are willing to call this approach *performative* provided that, in contrast to a certain post-modernist take on performativity, the political link populist performance creates is popularly understood as being not with the repertoire per se, but with a certain expressive self. And as with any *identification*, the relation created is both vertical and horizontal.

Independently of the populists' own claims but usually as a product of them, populism involves the creation of a very peculiar kind of *rapport*. This kind of rapport is at the core of our understanding of the culturally "low" in politics. With their performative emphasis on *closeness*, populists concretely perform—in an antagonistic way—a *representation* ("acting") of the representation ("portrayal") of the people "*as is*." This specific rapport can of course arise as a byproduct of discourse (Mudde) and of strategy (Weyland). There are thus some affinities between this approach and the other two approaches to populism presented in this volume. Indeed, populism as an ideology can only be studied through discourse, which is, itself, a very central element of political style—a defining element our approach obviously embraces. But viewing populism as a Manichean worldview may cast the net too wide, as discussed later. Similarly, this approach is much compatible with Weyland's, in that he leaves off precisely where we begin: we name and identify the precise nature of this so-called "direct, unmediated support" and of what makes this support possible. But Weyland (2001) may cast too narrow a net to capture various *major* instances of—very organized—populism (Collier and Collier, 1991).

As to the high-low axis or dimension in politics, it is theoretically *orthogonal* to—that is, *neutral* in relation to—the left-right axis, unlike other allegedly likewise orthogonal divides, such as the libertarian-authoritarian divide of Kitschelt (e.g., 1994) or perhaps the post-materialist/materialist divide of Inglehart (e.g., 1990). High and low are analogous to left and right in being "poles," "axis," and "scale." In theory as well as in practice (depending on the polity), the left-right and high-low axes can therefore form a *two-dimensional* political space of appeals. One can therefore picture four quadrants. Defense of the high is certainly the key feature of the much under-studied phenomenon of anti-populism, while the flaunting of the low is the core feature of populism.

Let us start with concrete examples of these quadrants, as cognitive theory has made it clear that it is often easier to think with prototypes, exemplars, or even examples, provided we know they are "only" that, in concept analyses. Examples of the "low-left" would be Hugo Chávez or Huey Long. On the "low-right," one finds Carlos Menem, Sarah Palin, or Silvio Berlusconi. On the "high-left," one finds French Socialist Lionel Jospin, Argentine Socialist Hermes Binner, or George McGovern in the US. And on the "high-right," one finds such figures as Mario Vargas Llosa in Peru, Nelson Rockefeller in the US, Valéry Giscard d'Estaing in France, or David Cameron in the UK. Also, some politicians are just squarely "low," as with the Latin American extreme of Abdala Bucaram in Ecuador; or simply "high," as with Javier Perez de Cuellar in Peru or Mario Monti in Italy. The categories of "high" and "low" in politics, at the core of the conception of populism introduced here, are fully detailed in the third section of this chapter (see also Ostiguy, 1999; 2005; 2009).

The next section introduces this (antagonistic) socio-cultural "performative" approach and its logic through what we call in a Weberian way an "affectual narrative" (Weber, 1978: 25). Despite the very local nature and texture of all populisms, cross-continentally they are characterized by a surprisingly similar affectual narrative. The subsequent section, the core of the chapter, then introduces the rich and applicable notions of the "high" and the "low," in politics. Then, after a brief recapitulation of the two subdimensions empirically and theoretically making up the left-right axis, the chapter lays out the two-dimensional political space that is a product of the perpendicular, high-low and left-right axes. Coherently, we then justify the understanding of populism as an ordinal category, rather than a nominal one.

Populism's Affectual Narrative

Let us begin at the most *abstract* (and perhaps not most helpful) level, by conceptualizing populism, *independently of the continent*, as an antagonistic appropriation for political, mobilizational purposes of an "*unpresentable Other*," itself historically created in the process of a specific "proper" civilizational project. The precise nature of that "proper," civilizational project can vary widely, from liberalism, to multi-culturalism, adapting to the ways and manners of the First World or the West, orthodox "textbook" economics, European integration, racial integration, colonial France's "*mission civilisatrice*," or any other. Its specific nature is not the main point here—and populism will indeed not be the same in France, the US South, Venezuela, Southeastern Europe, or the Philippines. This project's so-called "Other" can be recognized as such if it provokes shame or embarrassment for "decent," "politically correct," "proper," or "well-educated" people. The political entrepreneurs *flaunting this Other*, in turn, claim to be speaking in the name of a "repressed truth" (especially in Europe) or (more often in Latin America) of "previously excluded social sectors" or (in the US) the "silent majority." These political entrepreneurs cast the "Other" as allegedly both *damaged* and "swept under the rug" by official discourse and policies. What these politicians represent is allegedly fetched from "under the rug" and brought to the political fore in a loud, perhaps ugly (or at best, oddly "exotic") but "proud" way—and to many, in a rather annoying way as well. While many would prefer to be without them, the populists insist quite "inappropriately" and loudly on making themselves present in the public sphere.[2] In *that* sense, populism is "performative." Third, this "ugly duckling" (that publicly rears its head this way) claims to be linked to the most profound, "truest," authentic, and most deserving part of the homeland. "Betrayed" by a current or previous well-educated and proper elite—often painted as hypocritical or false—the populist politicians and parties claim, loudly, politically incorrectly, and often vulgarly, to be that (truly) authentic people's "fighting hero." The "Other" mentioned above is thereby in reality *not* an "Other," but rather, the "truest" (too often forgotten) Self of the nation, of "the people." Proper discourse is the reverse of what it claims to be: the Representatives are in fact not representative, and the Other is no Other but the truest Self (of the nation).

Because of the above, populism as such is almost always *transgressive*: of the "proper" way of doing politics, of proper public behavior, or of what can or "should" be publicly said. This transgression ("in bad taste"), as with the utterly incorrect Berlusconi, the speeches of Jean-Marie Le Pen, the biting insults of Hugo Chávez, or the mischievous escapades of Carlos Menem, can be appreciatively received, in certain parts of society. These transgressions, when by a male politician, always figure as "manly," with quite "home grown" elements. Populism claims to speak on behalf of a "truth" or a "reality" that is not accepted in the more official, larger circles of the world. If there is not thus some kind of "scandal," whether in terms of policy practices, public behavior, positions championed, or mode of addressing adversaries, then one is not really looking at a case of populism. When it has the wind in its sails, populism is the celebratory desecration of the "high."

Finally, the populist *script*, across continents, is as follows. There is a majority of people (individuals) of "the people" (the *pueblo*), the most "typically from here," whose authentic voice is not heard, and whose true interests are not safeguarded. They face a *three-way* coalition, comprised of a nefarious, resented minority (the object of greatest hatred and not *necessarily* the elite) at odds with "the people"; hostile (and very powerful) global/international forces; and a government in line with that minority. This situation is a source of moral indignation. These highly generic categories are filled in the most diverse ways. That nefarious minority can be the oligarchy, the Jews, a socially dominant ethnic minority, the financial sector, the immigrants, the liberal elite, white colonizers, or black minorities, depending on the casting of the social antagonist. The empirical set of powerful, allied global/international forces is more limited, but nonetheless diverse: American imperialism, an international Jewish conspiracy, global capitalism, global finance, Soviet infiltration, global migration, European colonialism, and now perhaps even "Europe" (or its "Eurocrats"). The "problem" is that the government, instead of "responding to the 'true' people," has been captured by those nefarious forces. Even in the case of right-wing populism, where the "nefarious minority" that is not integrated with "the people" is clearly socially *subaltern* and (though corrosive) not that socially powerful, the "problem" is that the government has become "hung up" about defending and promoting them for "misguided," politically correct, "proper" reasons.

Provocatively "saying the truth" (loud and clear in public), agitation, and mobilizing are the populist remedies. Marx the social "scientist" believed in the *structurally* unavoidable triumph of the working class, in the course of history; Inglehart is certain of the long-term ascent along Maslow's (1954) hierarchy of needs; Kitschelt (1994) showed that a readaptation on the part of social democratic parties to a new electorate would guarantee their victory. No such "social-scientifically based" certainties or optimism exist with populism. Therefore, agitation, indignation, provocations become ontologically decisive in populism, since willful political action is absolutely "all there is."[3]

THE HIGH AND THE LOW IN POLITICS

The high-low axis has to do with ways of *being* and *acting* in politics. The "high-low" axis, in that sense, is "cultural" and very concrete—perhaps more concrete in fact than left and right. High and low have to do with ways of *relating* to people; as such, they go beyond "discourses" as words. They certainly include issues of accent, levels of language, body language, gestures, and ways of dressing. And as a way of relating to people, they *also* encompass the *way of making decisions*, in politics. These different traits may be in fact more difficult to *credibly* change than left-right positioning. High and low are in many ways about private expressions in the public sphere, or if one prefers, the publicization of the private man. This is why, particularly in the case of low ways and manners expressed in an impudent or imprudent way in a public sphere hegemonized by the high, the low is often about transgression. As importantly, in relation to existing social-cultural identities, high and low political appeals and positions allow the voter to recognize a politician as credibly "one of ours." High and low are thus not superficially or faddishly about style, but connect deeply with a society's history, existing group differences, identities, and resentments. They even involve different criteria for judging what is likeable and morally acceptable in a candidate.

Theoretically and conceptually, the high-low axis consists of two closely related sub-dimensions or components: the *social-cultural* and the *political-cultural*. The latter is "cultural" in the same sense that one can speak of certain political sub-cultures. The former is cultural in a more sociological way, in the sense that Bourdieu (1979), for example, writes about cultural capital when it comes to "distinction." Both are, I argue, theoretically as well as empirically correlated. Their angle to one another, borrowing from the language of statistics, is sharper than that between the two established main dimensions of the left-right axis, i.e., one having to do with "values" and the other one with "socio-economic" issues. The high-low axis thus *appears* more unequivocally uni-dimensional (in a Downsian way) than the left-right one.

A last preliminary clarification regarding terminology: since our approach is basi-cally relational, we prefer to talk (at the most general level) about *appeals*, in politics, as its main currency. Appeals in politics of course apply to both the left-right dimension and the high and low one, not to speak of other dimensions. An appeal in politics is sim-ply a way in which a politician or a political party attempts, usually voluntarily, to *woo* supporters. Programmatic appeals or platforms, usually considered ideologies, are *also* appeals in that very same generic sense. There are, in fact, many reasons why people can feel attracted to (or repelled from) different parties or politicians.[4] Since we focus on representation, appeals are crucial.

If populism is the (antagonistic, mobilizing) flaunting of the "low," we had now better define what is the "low," in politics (Figure 4.1).

The Socio-Cultural Component

The first component of the high-low axis is the *social-cultural* appeal in politics. This component encompasses manners, demeanors, ways of speaking and dressing, vocab-ulary, and tastes displayed in public. On the high, people publicly present themselves as well behaved, proper, composed, and perhaps even bookish. Moreover, politicians on the high are often "well-mannered,"[5] perhaps even polished, in public self-presentation, and tend to use either a rationalist (at times replete with jargon) or ethically oriented dis-course. Negatively, they can appear as stiff, rigid, serious, colorless, somewhat distant, and boring. On the low, people frequently use a language that includes slang or folksy expressions and metaphors, are more demonstrative in their bodily or facial expressions as well as in their demeanor, and display more raw, culturally popular tastes.[6] Politicians on the low are capable of being more uninhibited in public and are also more apt to use coarse or popular language. They appear—to the observer on the high—as more "color-ful" and, in the more extreme cases, somewhat grotesque.[7]

It cannot be stated enough that the "low" in politics is *not* synonymous with poor people or lower social strata. In the US, Ross Perot was immensely richer than Al Gore, but Gore was clearly more "high." Similarly, few politicians have been more "blue blood" and from a richer family background than George W. Bush, but he was clearly to the low (and right) of John Kerry in 2004. The same applied in Italy between Monti (and even more so, Veltroni), on the high, and Berlusconi, on the millionaire low. Even at the level of electorates, levels of wealth and high-low positioning can in no way be made synonymous.

This first, social-cultural, component is in fact a politicization of the social mark-ers emphasized in the sociology of Pierre Bourdieu in his classic work of social theory

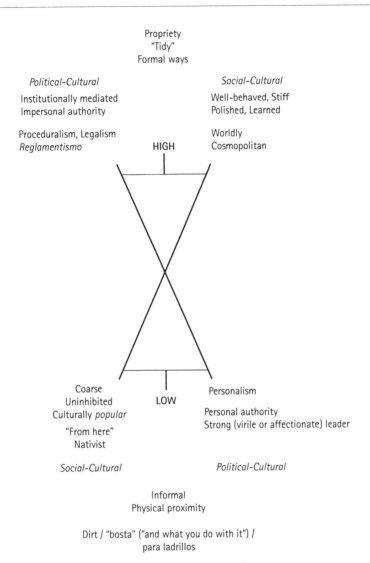

FIG. 4.1 Constitutive dimensions of high-low appeals in politics.

on taste and aesthetics (1979). From a different theoretical perspective, it is a politicization of the—empirically quite similar—differences in concrete manners at the core
of Norbert Elias's seminal work (1982). Bourdieu emphasizes cultural capital as a
"legitimate" form of distinction or credential and marker of respectability. Elias's historical sociology was more concerned about a gradual, irregular, and long-term process of "civilization" in manners. In both sociologists' works, however, one pole of the
spectrum—whether long-term historical or status related—is a kind of propriety (and
even distinction or refinement) that is legitimate by prevailing international standards,
especially in the more developed countries. From that standpoint, the popular classes'
and certain "third-world" practices often appear more "coarse" or less "slick."[8]

Although socio-cultural differences or gaps are present in all societies, and are even at times very sharp and meaningful, these differences are usually not *constitutive* of given political identities and often remain largely outside the political arena. For instance, while heavy drinking and loud singing at the pub is part of a stereotyped British working-class identity, it is not specifically associated with the Labour Party or its leaders. In some cases, socio-cultural differences *do* become politicized. That is, manners, publicized tastes, language, and modes of public behavior do become associated with, and even defining of, political identities. In such cases, *social* identities with their many cultural attributes interact with *political* identities. These interactions occur through politicians' different ways of appealing (or "relating") to supporters, and supporters' different criteria for finding them more likeable or trustworthy.[9] These appeals are not only differences in style, although they certainly are that. They are public manifestations of recognizably social aspects of the self in society (as well as of its desires) that contribute to creating a social sense of trust based on an assumption of sameness, or coded understanding. Politicians, as well as parties (that share certain practices), can be ranked ordinally on the high-low axis, within a society.

Within the social-cultural dimension, one must *also* clearly include not only the proper/refined versus coarser/folksier, but the more "native" or "from here" versus cosmopolitanism, as shown in Figure 4.1 and, especially, 4.2. Certainly, on the more "raw," culturally-popular pole, the *specific* expressions, practices, and repertoires characterizing the socio-cultural component can only be taken from a very particular, culturally bounded and locally developed, repertoire (even though the general themes may be quite common). On the other hand,

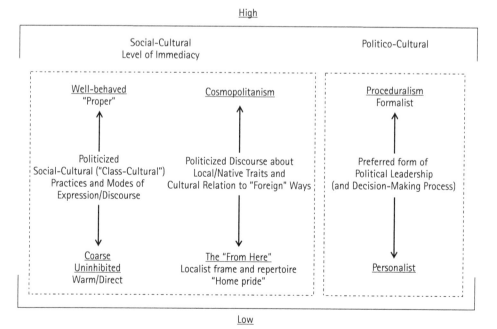

FIG. 4.2 Characteristics and components of the high and the low in politics.

and especially in a world-context of certain "refined" elites who are largely formed and trained in Western institutions of high standing or others emulating them, the appearance, deportment, and mode of discourse of various political elites often share commonalities. There is furthermore something in cosmopolitanism which, by definition, must allow its bearer to "travel" and have an "acceptable" behavior or discourse world-wide. We thus bring in a second element of the social-cultural dimension, included in Figure 4.1 and shown in detail in Figure 4.2: the axis or scale between cosmopolitanism and nationalism or more precisely the "from here".[10] This element figures prominently in populist movements, cross-continentally. Identification with "the heartland," as stated forcefully by Taggart (2000) and in contrast to more impersonal international cultural ways, is indeed a key element of populism.

In fact, as Canovan (1999: 3–5) has highlighted, "the people" as a collective has many meanings: it can refer to the popular sectors, the plebs, the politically subaltern, or it can be the *specific* national community, best embodied by the heartland. The *llaneros* in Venezuela, the hardworking farmers and ranchers of the US heartland, that is, the "typical" and culturally-recognizable working people of the nation's "heartland", are *always* at the core of the "true people" of the populists. Both aspects belong to the socio-cultural dimension.

What all poles of our low dimension (Figure 4.2) share in common is greater emphasis on immediacy (in both discourse and practices), in a more concrete, earthy, and culturally localist ("from here") way, while the reverse is true of abstracting mediation. The high tends to justify its concerns in more abstract terms and to convey them through more "universalizing," less culturally localized language. In a certain way, localist or cosmopolitan cultural emphases and traits are in fact connoted praxes and ways of expressing oneself that *demonstrate* or reveal one's localist *belonging* (in the case of culturally popular nationalism) or one's aptitude as a respectable statesman in the world of today (in the case of cosmopolitanism). One should be clear: "culturally popular nationalism" (like its reverse "cosmopolitanism") is about traits[11] and cultural practices; it does not necessarily and inherently entail *specific policies*, such as anti-immigration policies, nationalization of foreign-owned industries, or anti-imperialist measures. Similarly, a cruder or even vulgar mode of public expression and deportment does not policy-wise imply an intention to "carry on the class struggle" or to redistribute income: to be seen comfortably eating hotdogs (or *choripán*) with "the boys," confidently mounting a horse wearing a poncho, or being a President playing the saxophone and eating fast food are *not* signs of being on the left, but an ability to relate in certain settings.

The Political-Cultural Component

The second component of the high-low axis of appeals in politics is *political-cultural*. This component is about forms of political leadership and preferred (or advocated) modes of decision-making in the polity. On the high, political appeals consist of claims[12] to favor formal, impersonal, legalistic, institutionally mediated models of authority. On the low, political appeals emphasize very personalistic, strong (often male) leadership.[13] Personalistic (and at the Weberian extreme, charismatic) versus procedural authority

(close to Weber´s legal-rationalism) is a good synthesis of this polarity. The high generally claims to represent procedural "normalcy" (at least as a goal to be achieved) in the
conduct of public life, along with formal and generalizable procedures in public administration. The personalist pole generally claims to be much closer to "the people" and
to represent them better than those advocating a more impersonal, procedural, proper
model of authority.

Political science has devoted much attention to this component. It is also, not coincidentally, a central element of the definition of populism proposed by Weyland (1996;
2001). The relevance of this component or element is not surprising since there is a well-
known strong tension, not to say a philosophical opposition, between what populism
and liberal democracy stand for, particularly in terms of Dahl's two features of participation and opposition. While there is a strong "participatory" or rather mobilizational
component in the practices of populism, its respect for rules, division of powers, and the
autonomy of state bodies leaves much to be desired. These classic institutional limitations are explicitly perceived by populist leaders as undesirably limiting popular sovereignty and the people's will.

There is indeed a well-known theoretical contradiction between liberalism and populism. The former, moreover, generally tends to be on the high; while populism, in our
definition, is on the low. The liberal institutional architecture often figures as (and often
is) an *obstacle* to popular will and to the redemptive expectations associated with the
transformative populist projects. But hostility or indifference to a liberal institutional
architecture is not unique to populism; it also exists in (redemptive) revolutionary
socialism. What is unique to populism in that regard is "an appeal … proclaiming the
vox populi … [through] vivid [leaders] who can make politics personal and immediate,
instead of being remote and bureaucratic" (Canovan, 1999: 14). In its strongest form, as
Hugo Chávez stated succinctly in his last electoral campaign: "I am not myself anymore,
I am *not* an individual: I am a people!"

Turning from political theory to the discourse of the actors, a central element on the
populist low is, as often stated in Latin America, the valuation of (strong, personalistic) leaders "with balls." "Ballsyness," however exactly defined, is a central attribute of
the low in this political-cultural dimension.[14] And while the language of populism is at
times definitely steeped in a certain form of popular masculinity, "ballsyness" is clearly
not restricted to men, including in Latin America.[15] That "ballsyness" corresponds to
that of daring "people's fighting heroes." On the populist side, we hear in Latin America
that "Doubt is the boast of intellectuals," "Better than to talk is to do", and bragging that
"He steals but gets things done!" In brief, on the political-cultural dimension, the low
entails a preference for decisive action often at the expense of some "formalities"; while
the high values the "niceties" that accompany the rule of law. Despite the high's claim to
greater propriety, however, it is *not* clear which pole most respects *voting scores*, as the
legitimate mode of determining political power.[16]

The key here is that populist personalized leadership, as a form of rapport, of representation, and of problem solving, is a *way to shorten the distance between the legitimate
authority and the people*. The polar conceptual opposite of personalized populist linkage

is Weberian bureaucracy: impersonal, "fair" in the sense of universal and "the same for everyone," procedural, and overall cold and distant. While one does not expect a bureaucrat to "understand you," one expects "fairness," absence of discrimination and other liberal-rational virtues.

Consequently, the most extreme form of populist representation and linkage is *fusion*, that is, a "fusion" between the leader and the masses. The understudied, positive flip side of the populist fusional discourse, when in power, is that it is often explicitly a discourse of love.[17] The extreme of "fusion"—not particularly liberal or deliberative—bears the question of the relationship of populism to fascism, as at times feared in Western and Eastern Europe. Fascism certainly claimed the same, with the "Führer principle" (and its mass rallies). There are, however, important and highly significant differences. First, populism displays its legitimacy through the repeated counting of votes, empirically "proving" that the populist leader is "what the people want." Fascism (a regime type) ends elections once it wins them; populism appears to *multiply them* and often supplement them with referendums.[18] Second, fascism tended to govern in a disciplined manner, from the state down. Populism is much more ambivalent: though it often uses the state apparatus with little *délicatesse*, it also fosters a myriad of not overly coordinated movements, organizations, circles, with a grassroots component. The "political-cultural" component of the low thus fully incorporates the *lack of formal institutionalization* central to many political scientists' definitions of populism (e.g. Weyland, 2001). But at the very same time, what have just been described are very much political styles, an approach convincingly used to define populism (e.g. de la Torre, 1992; 2000; Knight, 1998) and anti-populism.

The Underlying Commonality and Summary

What do these three components of the high-low axis have in common? As unusual as it may sound, concretely, it is the *level of sublimation* and of suppression judged ideal in the exercise of leadership and authority. The high is definitely more *abstract* and *restrained*, claiming to be more proper, whether in *manners* or in *procedures*. It is also colder, including (comparatively) in the positive reaction it triggers among supporters. The low, in contrast, is more concrete and into immediacy. Perceptions of *immediacy* have important implications with respect to establishing relations with (the) people. Personalism can also be seen as warmer and easier to relate to. The low generally does not worry much about appearing improper in the eyes of the international community, at times even enjoying it.

From an institutionalist standpoint, that is to say that political authority on the low is institutionally less *mediated*,[19] as mediation involves a more sublimated type of practice, whereas behavior on the low (both political-culturally and socio-culturally) is certainly more "crass" and direct. A powerfully accurate typological metaphor, overall, is that of Lévi-Strauss's (1983) famous structural anthropological contrast between "the raw" and "the cooked."

If the level of sublimation and/or suppression matters, it follows that one needs to pay attention to concrete bodies. On the public stage, they will appeal, repel, or leave indifferent. The low is more warm, hot—in the sense of hot-tempered, of openly manifested drives—or physical in its displays.

Undoubtedly, most intellectuals have preferred—and have been located on—the high. On the other hand, poorer and less educated people have often enjoyed and preferred the *less sublimated* cultural expressions and discourse of politicians on the low, as well as the *personalization* of power and social services that have often gone with it. These characteristics are important not only as cultural markers of social differences, but as ways of being that play a role in the economy of affection and dislikes. It comes up in utterances like: "I don't want to associate with *that kind* of people," or "I don't want people *like that* in government," or simpler: "Yes, I can relate to [X]."

A last point, related to social psychology, must be made here regarding identification and desires, in politics. A notable trait of politics on the "low" is its more performative, frequent "soap-opera" aspect. Laclau goes too far in casting the leader as an *empty* signifier, condensing our desire for plenitude. The concrete Carlos Menem publicly fulfilled, crassly but with gusto, many (traditional popular-sector masculine) manly myths. Evita, the radio soap-opera actress, made it *real*, through meeting Perón. Something similar was perhaps at play with Donald Trump's rise to power. That is, importantly, the leader is both *like me* (a "me" with no cultural titles) *and* an ego *ideal*—but one that is accessible and understandable. In populism, those fantasies are coarser and display an antagonistic dimension—a flaunting. Populism is thus a kind of personal (on the part of the leader) and collective (on the part of the movement) narcissistic *affirmation*, with "the middle finger" defiantly raised to the well brought up, the proper, the accepted truths and ways associated with diverse world elites. It is a flaunting of "our" low, in politics.

In summary and overall, populism is defined as the antagonistic, mobilizational flaunting in politics of the culturally popular[20] and native, and of personalism as a mode of decision-making. The culturally popular and the native act as emblematic of what has been "disregarded"[21] in the polity, while personalism is both a mode of identification and of fixing the former. Stated in the most synthetic way, populism is the antagonistic, mobilizational flaunting of the "low."

THE "UNIVERSAL" LEFT-RIGHT AXIS IN POLITICS

The left-right axis is the political axis that orders most party systems and party competitions in democracies around the world (e.g. Huber and Inglehart, 1995; Inglehart and Klingemann, 1976; Huber, 1989; Budge, Robertson, and Hearl, 1987; Laver and Budge, 1992; Gabel and Huber, 2000; and for Latin America, Zechmeister, 2010 or Wiesehomeier, 2010). Left and right are well accepted, much discussed theoretically

(Laponce, 1981; Fuchs and Klingemann, 1989; Bobbio, 1996; Mair, 2009) and also the object of innumerable empirical studies on the structure of values and public opinion. Conceptually, it appears there are also *two* constitutive dimensions of the left-right axis or scale (see Figure 4.3), a finding empirically supported by both survey analysis about that scale and political history. These two constitutive dimensions are, however, at an angle in relation to one another, as illustrated in Figure 4.3. This angle can even be measured statistically through factor analysis or principal component analysis. These two dimensions interact quite distinctively with the high-low dimension.

The first and most well-known dimension is the *socio-economic policy* dimension between, on one pole, appeals for more equal economic distribution and, on the other, appeals that favor established property rights and entitlements. The left pole of this dimension favors a greater role for *politics* in producing *more equal* economic distribution, whether through state intervention, self-management, regulations, or other devices. Over decades and centuries, the specific policies advocated did change, as did some arenas of conflict, but not the conceptualization or idea.

The second dimension of left and right is about the necessary strength of (hierarchical) authority that is indispensable to make life in common functional. It is a more political dimension about *attitudes toward order and authority* or, more precisely, toward the amount of necessary exertion of hierarchical authority that is required for social life. As important politically and theoretically as the first one, it is about attitudes toward hierarchical power relations and public and social order. The right believes that without such exertion, society (and morality) "will go to hell," decay, and face many unwanted problems. The liberal left thinks one should "chill out" and allow for "interesting life-style experiments"; while the radical left is militantly anti-God, anti-patriarchy, and anti-bosses.

With regard to its political sociology, the left-right "materialist" *ideological* cleavage should not be equated with the class or social status *structural* cleavage, as the two have empirically become increasingly *independent* (Knutsen, 1988). And while the latter has

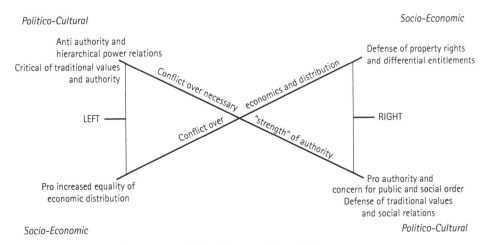

FIG. 4.3 Constitutive dimensions of left-right appeals in politics.

become less significant, the former continues to be highly relevant (ibid.). Inversely, there has been more "sociological anchoring" along the second, politico-cultural dimension than is often assumed, as the right pole is generally stronger amongst rural, family-business owning people (US), small shop-keepers (Europe), and segments of the armed forces in Latin America, while the left pole is always strong amongst students (especially in the social sciences and humanities) and artists.

These two (sub)dimensions of left and right are not theoretically reducible to one another. It is even possible to combine the poles *across* the obtuse angles of Figure 4.3: the influential *New York Times* combined value liberal and pro-free-market economics in the 1990s; similarly, it is often argued that the "neglected" non-unionized white working-class American majority is receptive to both poles shown at the *bottom* of Figure 4.3.[22] That is, it would in fact appear that a class-educational difference is more noticeable *across* a divide *"vertically"* visualized, spatially, in Figure 4.3, rather than horizontally in the customary way across the usual left-right, liberal-conservative axis.

We certainly fully share the conclusions separately reached by Laponce (1981), Bobbio, and Inglehart that "the core meaning of the Left-Right dimension ... is whether one supports or opposes social change in an *egalitarian* direction" (Inglehart, 1990: 293) and that it is about "the attitude of real people in society to the ideal of equality" (Bobbio, 1996: 60). However, we believe that this definition is also quite *left-anchored*. A less skewed perspective about the right is to conceptualize it as political projects and actors aiming to protect a collectively "necessary" societal (i.e. socio-economic *or* other) structure of power that provides order against threats that erode or destroy it. A structuring order is always clothed as a moral order (in what is often *doxa*), and the right usually takes the public defense of this given moral order quite to heart. "Left" are political projects and actors aiming to transform the *structure* of social power, socio-economic or otherwise, in a more egalitarian direction.

A Two-Dimensional Political Space and a "Wheel" of Axes

The orthogonal left-right and high-low axes, *together*, form a two-dimensional political space of appeals, in which we can locate actors, parties, and politicians. This basic political space is illustrated in Figure 4.4. Location along each of those two orthogonal axes making up that space furthermore has significant consequences in the societal or, rather, sociologically differentiated reception of political appeals. It should also be noted that having *two* orthogonal dimensions allows for a much greater variety of possible political or social-political alliances, as well as for quite dissimilar political strategies for appealing to somewhat similar social sectors in the electorate, than a unidimensional space. For example, it is quite possible as a right-wing politician to appeal to broad popular-sectors elements by being on the low and flaunting it, while the task of left-wing politicians seeking to maintain support among those same popular sectors may become more difficult if they are on the

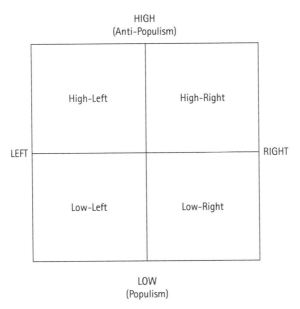

FIG. 4.4 A two-dimensional political space of positions and appeals.

high-left, as is often the case. *Each* of the two constitutive axes, indeed, results in a certain sense from a different way of politically *translating* differential endowments: while a part of the left-right dimension translates social differences in material interests, the high-low axis also translates inequalities in their more cultural-propriety dimension. This space also identifies, and names in the process, the political opposite of populism in politics: the high (and its valuation).

A clear analytical advantage of the political space delineated in Figure 4.4 is that the left-right axis (scale, dimension) and the high-low axis are fully *neutral*, or orthogonal, theoretically, in relation to one another. That is, *any* combination is not only possible, as is commonly the case in spaces configured by non-orthogonal axes, but equally possible. Making this formal neutrality explicit is vital: political scientists of Latin America have regarded populism as *implicitly* left-of-center, since it is said to redistribute income in favor of the popular sectors, oppose orthodox economic policies, and to ally historically with labor unions; while analysts in Northern Europe have understood populism as "obviously" on the right, and even at times as synonymous with "radical right."

There is a delicate conceptual issue in several regions—Europe, Oceania, and arguably the US—as to whether populist parties are "radical right" parties, and also vice versa. To the extent that parties strongly (or even, "radically") promote the "authority pole" (public and social order), on the right of the left-right politico-cultural subdimension (Figure 4.3), it would appear they are not, per se, populist parties but, indeed, "radical right" parties. But in terms of the high-low dimension, such parties are often, and not coincidentally, characterized in the *politico-cultural* subdimension as well (see Figure 4.1) by a strong, personalistic, "one-man"[23] leadership—in contrast to much more bureaucratic or parliamentary European parties. And then, several of these leaders *also* "happen" to be much more *socio-culturally* "low" in their demeanors and praxis: Jean-Marie Le Pen, Umberto Bossi, Vladimir Zhirinovski, Nigel Farage (but not so much Pim Fortuyn). There is in practice a *family resemblance* (or relative proximity) between those three poles.

This empirical pattern is theorized in Figure 4.5, through the superposition of Figure 4.1 and of Figure 4.3—theoretically justified in Ostiguy (2017). This superposition gives rise to a "wheel" of axes of political polarization, made up of the poles of a series of logically *ordered* alternate axes. In this conceptually more sophisticated framework, politicians and parties are located *along the circumference* of the circle (created by such poles). And they empirically cover a given (and continuous) *portion* of such circumference. Regionally, the common populisms of comparatively developed countries combine, as illustrated in Figure 4.5, the politico-cultural right, the politico-cultural low, and the socio-cultural low.[24] In contrast, both the classical and contemporary populisms of Latin America combine the same two components of the low (by definition) with socio-economic redistributionism (the pole at the bottom left of Figure 4.3), in what is only (politically and conceptually) a relatively small clockwise rotation (of one node or rather of one "dot") leftward, along the wheel.

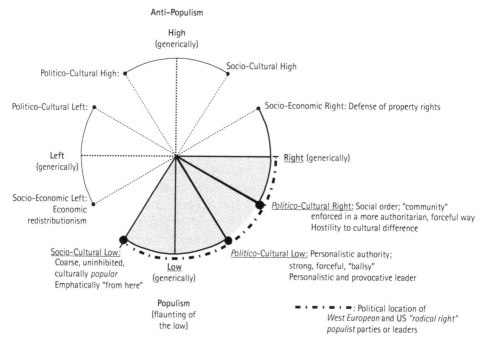

FIG. 4.5 The "wheel" of axes of political polarization: populism and "the right" (Europe and US). Note that since the horizontal axis is about left and right generically (and thus potentially created by any of the two sub-dimensions of left and right), a movement of one node clockwise has the effect of eliminating two shaded areas (on the left) and of adding two shaded areas, clock-wise, on the left.

Populism as an Ordinal Category?

Most publications defining populism have hitherto simply taken for granted that populism is a nominal category. That is, a "referent" (a politician, a party, a regime) is either populist or it is not. The conceptual Sartorian challenge then becomes to create the "net" in category building that catches the precise quantity of fish (the "correct" extension): all populist objects within the net—assuming we *already* know beforehand what a "populist" object is; and all non-populist ones outside the net. But both reality and category construction are more complex than this.

Even if we could *all* agree on a common definition of populism, something unlikely for most contested concepts (Gallie, 1956), it still remains unclear why a nominal category would be the most useful kind. An advantage of understanding populism as a function of the use of the "low" in politics is that it allows clear, *ordinal* categories. To put it differently, it permits us to locate our objects spatially, on a scale. The same certainly routinely happens with left and right.

Understanding populism as an ordinal category is by no mean an option exclusive to this approach. The discursive approach to populism presented in the work of Mudde, laid out for Belgium by Jagers and Walgrave (2007), for Venezuela by Hawkins (2010), or for Latin America in general by Hawkins and Rovira Kaltwasser (2013), is as compatible with an ordinal as with a nominal category, if not even more with the former. Any quantitative textual coding, of the sort pioneered by Hawkins (2010) or of the standard content analysis, is bound to provide an ordinal, and even interval, measure of "populist-ness." The situation is less clear with the approach promoted by Weyland (2001: table 1), as his category is originally derived from a typology, crossed with the categorical notion of "power capability based on numbers" (2001: 13). Nonetheless, his typology about "Type of Ruler" seems ordinal (individual person; informal grouping; formal organization). And in his "ruler's relationship to support base," one can always ask *how* un-institutionalized and *how* unorganized—which would then lead to a more standard ordinal scale. However, difference in degrees in Weyland (2001) becomes—the way Sartori (1970) wants it—a qualitative, and therefore categorical, difference.

Ordinality is particularly useful in politics and political analyses. Whether for high and low or for left and right, it is often indispensable or extremely useful to be able to refer to a "left-of-center" *or* an "extreme left"; or to write about the "extreme right" or the role of the "center." There exist "outflanking on the low," high-low polarizations, or party convergences in the choices of a candidate. The panorama becomes exceedingly rich if the two, orthogonal, ordinalities are combined, when pertinent analytically. Only a portion of politics, to be sure, and only in certain countries and at certain times, is productively analyzed through such a bi-dimensional space. But is Umberto Bossi more right or more low? Is the French Socialist Party more high or more left? Answers to those questions have sociological entailments, as seen when observing the social composition of the vote.

COMPARING THE APPROACHES

Competing dogmatisms notwithstanding, there is a family resemblance among the many conceptualizations of populism circulating. While distinct, the three specific approaches presented in this volume share significant similarities. Nonetheless, Weyland's and Mudde's stand the furthest apart on the importance of personalism and leadership, and on the "sincerity" of the manifested world views. The personalism so central in Weyland's approach is, to us, the very definition of the low pole of the politico-cultural dimension. The leader's *appeals*, which act as "weapon" in the populist *strategy* of Weyland, are for both of our approaches a constitutive feature of populism.

Weyland, however, is quite uneasy epistemologically with style, although he does notice the "similarities in political style and strategy" between different types of populists (2001: 9), even far apart on the left-right axis. Because he is not familiar with, and has little interest in, the empirical study of political style(s), he errs in discarding it, without much justification. Weyland's definition is, fundamentally, "by the negative" (a series of "lack of" and "un-"); but little headway is made regarding what makes even *positively possible* the—somewhat amazing—"direct, unmediated", uninstitutionalized support from "unorganized" followers—besides his own mention of political style and charisma. The focus on political style and performance is in fact a necessary and *essential* corollary to Weyland's approach, thickening it (Coppedge, 1999) and *causally explaining* it. The process of political mobilization that bypasses institutionalized forms of mediation is *embedded* within the very political style of populism. It is ironic that after summarily dismissing political style as "too broad" and "hindering the clear delimitation of cases," Weyland (2001) specifies and causally explains how "populists constantly demonstrate their closeness to common people and stimulate popular identification with their leadership, ... [and] *act in ways* that embody and live out the dreams of the common man ... creat[ing] a particularly intense connection to their followers" (12–14). We really could not have said it better! Without a focus on the actual *content* of the populist appeals, defining populism as a power capability based on numbers and little organization for an individual ruler would simply appear to be a complex way of just referring to demagoguery.

Organizations, Institutionalization, and Numbers

Weyland's definition was inspired by the Latin American populisms of the 1990s. But if there is *one* feature that defined the "classic" (1930–1950s) populisms of that region (the paradigms of populism), it was the remarkably *high* level of *organization* of the populist mode of popular incorporation (as defined in Collier and Collier, 1991). Populist incorporation also meant the creation of, by far, the largest mass political parties—both organizations and institutions—of the entire continent. So either Weyland or Collier and Collier are wrong, definitionally.[25] The definition of populism should *not* center on an organizational criteria. In populism, there usually *is* organization; but formal institutionalization, often not (Levitsky, 1998). One can certainly have personalized

rule based on an individual leader (Weyland, 2001: 13) *and* numbers with highly effective mass *organization*. This is what fascism was, after all.

There is no reason finally why the power capability based on numbers must be fickle
and, thus, why populism necessarily "either fails or, if successful, transcends itself" into
a formally institutionalized form of rule (2001: 14). Hugo Chávez was in power *fourteen* consecutive years as a highly personalistic president with large numbers, and would
have remained so for more years still had he not died.

Like Mudde, we find in discourse a central source of data: from field research and participant observation to audio-visual material and newspaper accounts. We furthermore
examine behavior, body language, expressions, even dress codes, to understand *appeals*.
The question of "sincerity," at times a problem in Mudde's approach, is irrelevant for
us: what is essential is that a *connection* is established. Because the ideology of populism is indeed quite "thin," and the minimal definition perhaps even thinner, Mudde´s
much repeated sentence definition is prone to have too broad of an extension. Its acute
minimalism and thinness inevitably leads to the inclusion of "misleading positives."
His Manichean definition in particular comes ambiguously close to including militant
Marxism and (discursively) the revolutionary rhetoric in Latin America, which considers "society to be ultimately separated into two homogeneous and antagonistic groups,"
the working people versus the parasitic owners, and "which argues that [decision mak-
ing] should be the expression of the volonté générale of the [working] people."

Purity and Corruptness

The emphasized notion of "purity" (Mudde's "pure people") may work well for European
populisms, but does not travel well to other regions. By "pure," we either mean that
the people are "pure" in an ethnic or at least physiologically recognizable way (black
Frenchmen would not be part of the "pure" French people) *or* that the "regular people"
are morally virtuous, have a "pure heart," in contrast to the corrupt elite. If it is the first,
there is certainly no ethnicity or "type" of the "pure" people of Venezuela, for example; "motley" Venezuelans are zambos, mulatos, mestizos, whites, blacks, etc. If it is the
second, as we think, the subordinate strata, the plebs, while certainly "deserving," "suffering," and "being treated unfairly," are most certainly *not* viewed as morally pure and
virtuous (at least in Latin America), whether by themselves or by populists! The world of
the plebs, the *chusma*, the "rabble" in Latin America is the world of petty thieves, of street
smarts, *lazzaroni, patoteros, arrabeleros*. The followers of Abdala Bucaram in Ecuador
may have been many things, but "pure and virtuous" they were not (as the leader himself
also emphasized)! And "angry" populist supporters in the US are not particularly "pure"
either. The word "pure" does not appear in *any* of Chávez's innumerable speeches, nor
in those of Huey Long. Even the fact that the leaders of our "political elite" may be quite
corrupt is not necessarily a problem, provided that, as stated in Brazil's famous populist
slogan, "he [may] steals, but gets things done." Because of the features of personalism,
closeness, *and* disregard for formal rules, the willingness to "get dirty" for the people is
a central discursive feature of many populisms—certainly in the Americas, both North
and South. And dirt is on the "low"!

Mudde's definition would be closer to reality were he to state that populism involves a discursive antagonism between an "*authentic*" people and a *nefarious elite*. This modification, however, shifts the focus away from the morality of the pure people to *representation*—far more crucial in the understanding of populism (see also Taggart, 2004). The key issue here is about connection with, and representation of, the "authentic," "deserving," and "neglected" people of "this place". The moral indignation—and such there is—is that "the people" have been hurt, damaged, ignored, "unrepresented"—not that their "purity" is not sovereign.

Oddly, *just as* Weyland refuses to incorporate theoretically the style that permeates his understanding of populism, Mudde does the same with personalistic leadership. But in his main article on populism (2004), he states that "the current heartland of the populists … wants *leadership* [Mudde's emphasis]. They want politicians who *know* (rather than listen to) the people, and who make their wishes come true" (558). What is needed, Mudde writes, is "a *remarkable* leader … Just look at the flamboyant individuals that lead most of these movements" (559–60). We could not say it better.

Conclusion

The chapter has presented a dynamic cultural-relational approach to populism in politics. This approach takes the notion of appeals seriously, not limiting them exclusively to "ideas" or programs. Through the two-dimensional space, central in this approach, our view of populism can be used in combination with an ideological approach anchored in the notions of left and right, cross-regionally. Like left and right, it views populism as an ordinal category. This approach also highlights strategy, including from a spatial standpoint, without disregarding the political and socio-cultural subjectivities of populists' followers, as Weyland's "strategic" approach arguably does. And it deals with (social, cultural, historical) identities, central in populism, something with which Mudde's approach has theoretical difficulties grappling.

In its rhetoric and praxis, populism carries an emotional charge, which covers the spectrum from the negative *ressentiment* of the *laissés pour compte* to the positive extreme of the fusional love with the leader—an emotional charge akin to the redemptive impulse rightly highlighted by Canovan (1999). At the same time, populism is in many ways a spectacle, a show, a performance; it is a world away from dull bureaucracies and self-enclosed administrations. This approach is thus also a performative one, in which physical and more coded gestures of transgression and closeness figure centrally in generating and perpetuating populism's distinctive bonds and antagonisms.

Populism is always anti-elitist, though it can be quite top-down in its organization and the nature of the elite antagonized can vary widely. If populism is the expression of a plebeian-native "grammar," then not only will it be at ease with the "low" but, in an antagonistic way, it will flaunt it—though it may not be "proper" or "politically correct." In claiming to represent, and at times to embody, a—neglected—true "us-ness," it flaunts a politically or socially "unpresentable Other," a historical byproduct of an allegedly "civilizing process," and champions it as the authentic "Self" of the nation. It should thus come as no surprise that populists are *enfants terribles*, relishing both their transgressions and the much sought-after connections with the "people from here" that they seek to articulate, perform, and display.

NOTES

1   Normatively, it is difficult to avoid a conception of populism in light of which its followers cannot but be apprehended as "lacking sophistication", whether because they easily fall for simplistic Manichean categories (as in Mudde), are easily led astray by ambitious and not overly scrupulous leaders (as in Weyland), or have not incorporated the "civilized" benefits of pluralism, respect for difference, and openness to the world.

2   To put it in crude terms, populism is always a way of "raising the middle finger." This is true from Beppe Grillo's "*vaffanculo*" to Chávez's "*ALCA, ¡al carajo!*" In other words, populism is intentionally and by definition "in your face."

3   This is therefore probably why Laclau equates populism with *politics*.

4   We much prefer to speak of appeals, here, rather than linkages à la Kitschelt (2000), for several reasons. An appeal is an effort to "seduce," to woo, and it may work, *or not*; it does *not* imply a "closed" relation; and it is dependent on the (social) subjectivity and reaction of the receiver. The notion, furthermore, connote does not mutually exclusive motivational categories.

5   "Well-mannered" or "well-bred" is used as translation of "*bien educado*" in Spanish or "*bien élevé*" in French.

6   Heavy local accents and expressive body language are all, in a certain way, difficult-to-ignore intrusions of physicality, of the concrete particular body and locality, in social interaction.

7   Examples of cases on the extreme low include Vladimir Zhirinovsky in Russia and Abdalá Bucaram in Ecuador. In Argentina, there was Carlos Menem and many in his entourage or, even lower, Herminio Iglesias. In the US, on the very low one finds the ex-wrestler Jesse Ventura. In Canada, Camil Samson or Réal Caouette (also a car dealer) of the Social Credit Party were clearly on the low.

8   It does not matter here that Bourdieu views the function of class habitus negatively, while Elias much approved of the "civilizing process": of interest is the axis or spectrum ordering such practices.

9   As Knight wrote, in the 1924 Mexican election, Vasconcelos, a cultured intellectual of the Mexican revolution, faced off against the uncultured Onofre Jimenez. Onofre "guaranteed his election with a populist one-liner: 'The [Doctor] is too big a candidate for Oaxaca; the [Doctor] drinks champagne; I drink mezcal. I ought to be governor!'" (1998: 235, citing Parmenter).

10 Oddly enough, while this component is much visible in Europe, it has been almost entirely neglected by scholars of Latin American politics, more interested in distributional and class issues, despite its overwhelming empirical presence in the discourse of populist leaders: focusing on the *patria*, despising "*vende patrias*," "*cipayos*" in Argentina, "petty-yankees" in Venezuela, etc. Moreover, this *patria* is generally the *patria profunda*, not the *ilustrada*.

11 By "localist," I do *not* mean local in the sense of local community, the town hall meeting, or other types of small-scale localities. Localism refers to an emphasis on particularistic traits, manners, and expressions displayed in public and understood (felt) as an important cultural element of one's own self-definition. In a sense, they are cultural referents.

12 These are *claims* repeatedly made in the political arena, rather than observations of actual behavior along those lines. They are ways of presenting oneself to the public.

13 There is also a strongly affectionate, "caring", female gendered version of that personalistic form of leadership, which can certainly be quite combative, from Evita Perón to Sarah Palin's "grizzly moms." There is no contraction between "love" and "strength/force." The characterization of strongly personalistic leadership is *not* to be equated with "authoritarian," even if politicians on the high often attempt to make that equation for politically motivated purposes.

14 While the more refined term of "audacity" captures a large component of "balls", one appears to also have to add the notion of "fiery indignation," the capacity for anger, for "charging at", in line with ordinary language.

15 Evita Perón, for example, had "much more balls" than most populist male leaders. At the same time, highly personalistic female leaderships have alternatively achieved, empirically, a semi-direct relationship with the people through the very intense public display of affection, love, and nurturing—traditionally also quite gendered. If the high tends to be "gender neutral," the low generally accentuates gendered traits.

16 On the low, electoral success is a clear demonstration and empirical proof of closeness to "the people," of support by the *pueblo*, "the people," "their" "the people." On the high, clean elections with clear rules and without irregularities are an integral part of what they advocate and claim to stand for.

17 Populist leaders and followers have at times claimed to achieve a fusion through love, one toward the other. In Latin America, this fusion is displayed in ads, videos, rallies, from Gaitan to Chávez, Velasco Ibarra to Cristina in 2011, bodies amongst bodies and throughout speeches. Evita repeatedly claimed to be "the bridge of love", between the people and Perón.

18 For example, in Venezuela during the fourteen years of Chávez's rule, there were *ten* major national elections or referendums, where the presidency could have lost.

19 On this specific point, my analysis is identical to that of Weyland (2001) on populism and neopopulism.

20 By "popular" we do not so much mean here "widespread in the population," but *popular* or *populaire*, of "the popular sectors," of "regular folks."

21 The accurate term is, in French, *laissé pour compte*, translating roughly as overlooked, neglected, not taken into account, ignored, left by the wayside.

22 Magazines and books in the US have addressed the phenomenon squarely, publishing electoral sociology articles with titles such as "Joe sixpack's revenge" (Caldwell, 2000) or "Crossing the meatloaf line" (Brooks, 2001).

23 Undisputed, iron-fisted "one-woman" leadership is also possible, as seen in the cases of Marine Le Pen or of Cristina Kirchner in Argentina.

24 This quite coherent pattern along the "wheel" is different from the "less coherent" (and arguably thus, also less frequent) one where a politician combines (more *orthogonally*) a neoliberal, free-trade position on the left-right socio-economic axis (*without* embracing a "radical right" position, politico-culturally) with a praxis visibly on the low, as in the cases of Berlusconi or Menem.

25 While Roberts (2006) quite judiciously explained the *different* levels of organizational density (extreme organization; lack of organization) characterizing the different cases and periods of populism, he still leaves us without a common denominator on that front. Level of organization cannot *thus* be part of the definition.

REFERENCES

Bobbio, Norberto. 1996. *Left and Right: The Significance of a Political Dimension*. Cambridge: Polity Press.

Bourdieu, Pierre. 1979. *La Distinction*. Paris: Les Editions de Minuit.

Brooks, David. 2001. "One nation, slightly divisible," *The Atlantic*, December.

Budge, Ian, David Robertson, and Derek Hearl. 1987. *Ideology, Strategy and Party Change: Spatial Analyses of Post-War Election Programmes in 19 Democracies*. Cambridge: Cambridge University Press.

Caldwell, Christopher. 2000. "Joe sixpack's revenge," *The Atlantic*, June.

Canovan, Margaret. 1999. "Trust the people! Populism and the two faces of democracy," *Political Studies*, 47: 2–16.

Collier, Ruth Berins and David Collier. 1991. *Shaping the Political Arena: Critical Junctures, the Labor Movement, and Regime Dynamics in Latin America*. Princeton: Princeton University Press.

Coppedge, Michael. 1999. "Thickening thin concepts and theories," *Comparative Politics*, 31(4): 465–76.

de la Torre, Carlos. 1992. "The ambiguous meanings of Latin American populisms," *Social Research*, 59(2): 385–414.

de la Torre, Carlos. 2000. *Populist Seduction in Latin America: The Ecuadorian Experience*. Athens: Ohio University Center for International Studies.

Elias, Norbert. [1939] 1982. *The Civilizing Process*. Vol. 1: *The History of Manners* and Vol. 2: *State Formation and Civilization*. Oxford: Basil Blackwell.

Freeden, Michael. 2003. *Ideology: A Very Short Introduction*. Oxford: Oxford University Press.

Fuchs, Dieter and Hans-Dieter Klingemann. 1989. "The left-right schema," in Kent Jennings and Jan van Deth (eds), *Continuities in Political Action*. Berlin: De Gruyter Studies on North America 5.

Gabel, Matthew and John Huber. 2000. "Putting parties in their place: inferring party left-right ideological positions from party manifestos data," *American Journal of Political Science*, 44(1): 94–103.

Gallie, W. B. 1956. "Essentially contested concepts," Meeting of the Aristotelian Society, London.

Hawkins, Kirk. 2010. *Venezuela's Chavismo and Populism in Comparative Perspective*. Cambridge: Cambridge University Press.

Hawkins, Kirk and Cristóbal Rovira Kaltwasser. 2013. "Populism as an ideational concept," paper presented at the Latin American Studies Association (LASA) conference, Washington DC, May 29–June 1.

Huber, John. 1989. "Values and partisanship in left-right orientations: measuring ideology," *European Journal of Political Research*, 17: 599–621.

Huber, John and Ronald Inglehart. 1995. "Expert interpretations of party space and party locations in 42 societies," *Party Politics*, 1(1): 73–111.

Inglehart, Ronald. 1990. *Cultural Shift in Advanced Industrial Society.* Princeton: Princeton University Press.

Inglehart, Ronald and Hans Klingemann. 1976. "Party identification, ideological preference and the left-right dimension among Western mass publics," in I. Budge, I. Crewe, and D. Farlie (eds), *Party Identification and Beyond.* ECPR Classics. London: John Wiley.

Jagers, Jan and Stefaan Walgrave. 2007. "Populism as political communication style: an empirical study of political parties' discourse in Belgium," in *European Journal of Political Research,* 46: 319–45.

Kitschelt, Herbert. 1994. *The Transformation of European Social Democracy.* Cambridge: Cambridge University Press.

Kitschelt, Herbert. 2000. "Linkages between citizens and politicians in democratic polities," *Comparative Political Studies,* 33(6–7): 845–79.

Knight, Alan. 1998. "Populism and neo-populism in Latin America, especially Mexico," *Journal of Latin American Studies,* 30: 223–48.

Knutsen, Oddbjorn. 1988. "The impact of structural and ideological party cleavages in West European democracies: a comparative empirical analysis," *British Journal of Political Science,* 18: 323–52.

Laclau, Ernesto. 2005. *On Populist Reason.* London: Verso.

Laponce, Jean A. 1981. *Left and Right: The Topography of Political Perceptions.* Toronto: University of Toronto Press.

Laver, Michael and Ian Budge (eds). 1992. *Party Policy and Government Coalitions.* Basingstoke: Palgrave.

Lévi-Strauss, Claude. 1983. *The Raw and the Cooked (Mythologiques,* Book 1). Chicago: University of Chicago Press.

Levitsky, Steve. 1998. "Institutionalization and Peronism: the concept, the case, and the case of unpacking the concept," *Party Politics* 4(4): 445–70.

Mair, Peter. 2009. "Left-right orientations," in R. Dalton and H-D. Klingemann (eds), *The Oxford Handbook of Political Behavior.* Oxford: Oxford University Press, 206–22.

Maslow, Abraham. 1954. *Motivation and Personality.* New York: Harper and Row.

Mudde, Cas. 2004. "The populist zeitgeist," *Government and Opposition,* 39(4): 542–63.

Ostiguy, Pierre. 1999. Peronism and anti-Peronism: class-cultural cleavages and political identity in Argentina. PhD dissertation, Department of Political Science, University of California, Berkeley.

Ostiguy, Pierre. 2005. "Gauches péroniste et non péroniste dans le système de partis Argentin," in *Revue Internationale de Politique Comparée* (Paris/Bruxelles) 12(3): 299–330.

Ostiguy, Pierre. 2009. "The high and the low in politics: a two-dimensional political space for comparative analysis and electoral studies," *Kellogg Institute Working Paper* #360. Kellogg Institute for International Studies, Notre Dame. Also published in the Committee on Concepts and Methods Working Paper Series of the International Association of Political Science (IPSA).

Ostiguy, Pierre. 2017. "Party systems and political appeals: populism and anti-populism in Argentina," book manuscript under advanced contract.

Roberts, Kenneth. 2006. "Populism, political conflict, and grass-roots organization in Latin American," *Comparative Politics,* 38(2): 127–48.

Sartori, Giovanni. 1970. "Concept misformation in comparative politics," *American Political Science Review,* 64(4): 1033–53.

Taggart, Paul. 2000. *Populism.* Buckingham: Open University Press.

Taggart, Paul. 2004. "Populism and representative politics in contemporary Europe," *Journal of Political Ideologies*, 9(3): 269–88.

Weber, Max. [1956] 1978. *Economy and Society*. Berkeley: University of California Press.

Weyland, Kurt. 1996. "Neopopulism and neoliberalism in Latin America: unexpected affinities," *Studies in Comparative International Development* 31 (Fall): 3–31.

Weyland, Kurt. 2001. "Clarifying a contested concept: populism in the study of Latin American politics," *Comparative Politics*, 34(1): 1–22.

Wiesehomeier, Nina. 2010. "The meaning of left-right in Latin America: a comparative view," *Kellogg Institute Working Paper #370*. Kellogg Institute for International Studies, Notre Dame.

Zechmeister, Elizabeth. 2010. "Left-right semantics as a facilitator of programmatic structuration," in H. Kitschelt et al. (eds), *Latin American Party Systems*. Cambridge: Cambridge University Press.

PART II

REGIONS

CHAPTER 5

....

POPULISM IN AFRICA

....

DANIELLE E. RESNICK

INTRODUCTION

THE populist modifier has been used to describe many disparate African politicians, ranging across democratic and authoritarian regimes, encompassing both incumbent and opposition leaders, and referring to very different behaviors. Pre-electoral hand-outs, theatrical campaign antics, xenophobic discourse, homophobic rhetoric, promises of valence goods, and declarations of economic nationalization have all been considered as signs of populism. Consequently, there is substantial confusion about what phenom-enon is actually being catalogued and how well it corresponds with its manifestations in other areas of the world.

Many of the cross-regional comparisons of populism have focused on Latin America and Europe (see Mudde and Rovira Kaltwasser, 2012; Mudde and Rovira Kaltwasser, 2013). The African context, however, poses an especially hard case for conceptualizing the core essence of populism given the longstanding absence of well-institutionalized polit-ical parties and the attendant prominence of personalistic rule. This has been facilitated by the dominance of presidential systems with strong executive powers (see van de Walle, 2003), and the tendency of African leaders, many of whom are sexagenarians or older, to view themselves as paternal benefactors (see Schatzberg, 2001). In other words, based on certain conceptualizations, an expectation of populism could be overdetermined.

Three main conceptualizations are discussed in this volume. Weyland (2001; this volume) focuses on populism as ultimately a political strategy based on personalis-tic leaders forging plebscitarian ties with a diverse and unorganized constituency for opportunistic purposes. The political strategy relies on individual politicians who seek to augment their power and autonomy and who depend on mobilizing a large majority of the population. Ostiguy's (this volume) perspective complements this view by stress-ing that populism essentially revolves around socio-cultural performances, includ-ing what he terms "the flaunting of the low." Such performances may rely on the use of popular, coarse, accessible, and sometimes vulgar language and dramatic, colorful, and even politically incorrect acts that grab the public's attention. Mudde (2004; this volume) instead suggests an ideological approach in which populism revolves around a discourse that differentiates the corrupt elite, the pure people, and the general will.

This chapter argues that a cumulative conceptual approach, which combines these three conceptualizations, provides more analytical leverage in discerning African cases of populism than any approach on its own. Cumulative concepts essentially assert that a combination of characteristics need to be jointly present in order for an example to qualify as an instance of a category. Attributes commonly associated with a concept are aggregated and the more attributes that exist, the closer an example fits the conceptual ideal (see Gerring, 2012).

In the remainder of this chapter, I show the utility of applying all three lenses simultaneously by comparing episodes of populism in Africa over time. Particular attention is given to the features of Africa's democratic trajectory since independence with an emphasis on critical junctures in the 1980s through the 2000s. I then discuss key supply-side (party system) and demand-side factors (demographic and economic shifts) underlying the emergence of populist strategies by opposition parties since 2000. Thirdly, I conclude that a cumulative conceptual approach, which views populism as dependent on personalistic leadership dependent on direct ties to the poor bolstered by socio-cultural performances and an inclusive ideology of the people versus the elite, is most useful for delimiting cases of contemporary populist strategies in African democracies.

PEOPLE'S REVOLUTIONS AND POPULIST REGIMES OF THE 1980S

As shown through scholarship on other regions of the world (Demmers et al., 2001; Roberts, 2007; Weyland, 2012), examining manifestations of populism over time aids in delineating its conceptual core in the African context. A first generation of African populism emerged as a consequence of coups in the 1980s that were justified by military leaders as the only means of ousting corrupt incumbents who had exacerbated macroeconomic mismanagement and undermined citizens' welfare (see Chazan et al., 1999; Nugent, 2004).[1]

The first key example of this pattern was in 1981 in Ghana when Flight Lieutenant Jerry Rawlings ousted the civilian government of Hilla Linmann in a popular coup. Ideologically, he espoused the need for a "social revolution," entreating Ghanaians to eliminate exploitation and claiming that his goal was to provide "a chance for the people ... to be part of the decision-making process" (cited in Rothchild and Gyimah-Boadi, 1989: 222). He often toured the country in his military fatigues and would deliver impromptu speeches that aimed to emphasize that he was not only a man of the people but also simultaneously viewed as *above* the people, epitomized by his nickname of "Junior Jesus" (see Chazan et al., 1999). With an eclectic coalition of urban workers, the unemployed, peasants, union members, and the youth, Rawlings established the Provincial National Defense Council (PNDC). The PNDC in turn established lower level institutions to facilitate the voice of the people and provide "popular justice," including People's Defense Committees and Workers Defense Committees. The professional and managerial classes, churches, professional associations, and traditional authorities were all labeled as the neocolonial establishment and faced severe penalties for perceived corruption. Price and rent controls were implemented to protect the most vulnerable, even as such tactics alienated middle- and upper-class Ghanaians.

In Ghana's neighbor to the North, known as Upper Volta at the time, Captain Thomas Sankara adopted a similar approach. A charismatic army officer from the countryside, Sankara overthrew the government of Jean-Baptiste Ouédraogo in 1983, which he justified as a "revolution" intended "to take power out of the hands of our national bourgeoisie and their imperialist allies and put it in the hands of the people" (cited in Martin, 1987: 78). In his view, the "people" referred to the economically and politically marginalized who had been exploited by the country's elite. He was strongly opposed by traditional leaders, particularly since he aimed to abolish private landownership, as well as by the middle class, civil servants, and the country's trade unionists. To implement his people's revolution, he established neighborhood *Comités de Défense de la Révolution* (CDR) that were tied to a national political organ, comprised of key elements of the military, known as the *Conseil National de la Révolution* (CNR). Price controls were enforced, rural taxes were slashed, and housing rents were entirely eliminated (Rothchild and Gyimah-Boadi, 1989).

To dramatically demonstrate his distaste for profligacy, he gave away the state's fleet of Mercedes cars in a national lottery and encouraged civil servants to accept salary reductions in order to re-orient investment to the rural masses (Martin, 1987). He ceremoniously eschewed any signs of privilege, such as having his portrait removed from all public offices, dispensing with limousines to attend meetings in favor of modest cars, regularly playing soccer with his staff in public fields, and declaring his income and assets (Harsch, 2014). An eclectic form of cultural engineering bolstered his "revolution," epitomized by his decision to change the name of the country from Upper Volta to Burkina Faso, meaning "land of the upright (non-corrupt) man."

Yoweri Museveni in Uganda represents a third example of a first generation populist. After successfully mounting a guerrilla campaign against the corrupt regime of Milton Obote in 1986, he took over as president and leader of a movement he founded called the National Resistance Movement (NRM). He promised a clean break with the past and appealed to the common man by emphasizing his own peasant background and through "a frequent use of metaphors and images that are near to people's lives, or proverbs and short phrases taken from vernacular languages" (Carbone, 2005: 5–6). In addition to these performances, Museveni also set up a series of five-tiered "resistance councils," ostensibly to encourage popular participation at the local level, but implicitly to further entrench the NRM's reach at the grassroots level (see Tripp, 2010).

The common characteristics of these populists were fivefold. First, they attempted to establish direct ties with their populations through new, local level, avowedly participatory structures. Secondly, these leaders grounded their populism in an anti-establishment discourse and, by portraying their usurpation of power as people's revolutions, they implied that they were acting in the interests of the "general will" and against the "enemy of the people." The latter encompassed not only the disappointing independence-era political elite but also former colonial powers that had exploited African economies and undermined their prospects for genuine economic liberation. As Chazan et al. (1999: 166) observe of these cases, "Populist thought is fiercely nationalist and anti-imperialist, and its basis is deeply entrenched in frustration, anguish, negation, and protest."

Thirdly, they tended to pursue relatively similar economic strategies focused on heavy state intervention, import substitution industrialization (ISI), and rural collectivization schemes and they were committed to equity and distribution through social welfare spending, subsidized commodities, and attempted land reforms in rural areas (see Young, 1982). Fourthly, they all aimed for a broader societal transformation predicated on modernization and equality by promoting women's rights and attacking traditional patriarchy, especially chiefly privilege in rural areas (Boone, 2003; Skinner, 1988; Tripp, 2010).

Lastly, their populism was not easily compatible with genuine democracy. Both Rawlings and Museveni banned other political parties while Sankara's increasingly iron grip on the CNR alienated other members of the military corps, particularly his deputy, Blaise Compaoré. His populist experiment was cut short when he was assassinated in 1987, allegedly on Compaoré's orders.

Ultimately, this first generation of populism became increasingly unsustainable, often due to economic reasons. For example, Ghana's severe fiscal crisis in 1982 prompted Rawlings to gradually recalibrate his governing style and negotiate an Economic Recovery Plan with the International Monetary Fund (IMF). By 1983, the more radical members of the PNDC were purged and technocrats were appointed into key positions within state corporations. Rawlings reversed his stance, denouncing "populist 'nonsense' and excess" (Rothchild and Gyimah-Boadi, 1989: 241). In 1992, he finally allowed multiparty competition and was freely elected as president, serving until 2000. Similarly, Museveni's ultimate embrace of neoliberal economic reforms in Uganda quickly earned him a reputation as a "donor darling." These developments meant that leaders had less autonomy to pursue interventionist economic policies per se, which in turn had critical political implications not only in these countries but also throughout the African region.

EXCLUSIONARY POPULISM DOMINATED
BY IDEOLOGICAL DISCOURSE

Indeed, macroeconomic crises forced most African governments to embark on structural adjustment programs in the 1980s and 1990s, and the resultant austerity and privatization programs often resulted in reduced consumer subsidies and growing unemployment. These developments often provoked widespread discontent with incumbent governments and, coupled with donor political conditionalities for greater political liberalization, multiparty democracy spread widely across the region during this period as a result (see Bratton and van de Walle, 1997). In some countries, the end of one party rule resulted in a dramatic restructuring of the political party system. In fact, parties that had ruled for a decade or more found that they were facing an uncertain future and needed to either mobilize new supporters or redouble efforts to retain their core constituency base.

These dynamics created fertile ground for a range of electoral tactics in the 1990s and early 2000s that had populist elements but deviated significantly from the factors that characterized the populist regimes of the 1980s. Incumbent parties that felt especially threatened by the prospect of competition pursued what Mudde and Rovira Kaltwasser (2013) characterize as exclusionary populism in order to discredit potential adversaries with support among particular constituencies. A key mechanism for doing this was through strongly ideological terms aimed at strategically redefining citizenship. True citizens were those who were the incumbent parties' historical constituent base while foreigners were those who demonstrated greater support for emerging opposition parties.

For example, labor scarcity in Côte d'Ivoire had long resulted in allowing migrants from predominantly Muslim neighboring countries to farm cocoa plantations in the predominantly Christian, southern part of the country. As the country's first multiparty elections neared in 1995, and as growing discontent with land shortages and rising unemployment emerged, the incumbent Democratic Party of Ivory Coast (PDCI) tried to reverse this policy through the promotion of the principle of *Ivoirité*. Under *Ivoirité*, any resident who lacked two Ivoirian parents, or who was not perceived as indigenous by the local community in which s/he lived, was disenfranchised. The policy was implicitly aimed at disqualifying a strong opposition contender, Alassane Ouattara, whose father was from Burkina Faso, and to discredit his predominantly Muslim supporters, who constituted more than a third of the population. A subsequent land law effectively excluded those deemed non-Ivoirian as ineligible to own land, resulting in the expropriation of farms from approximately 100,000 residents (see Boone, 2009).

Similarly, as Zimbabwe's 2002 elections loomed, citizenship was manipulated by Robert Mugabe and the Zimbabwe African Nation Union-Patriotic Front (ZANU-PF). Two years earlier, Mugabe had lost a referendum that had aimed to expand his powers. In the interim, a competitor emerged with the creation of the Movement for Democratic Change (MDC), which was supported by labor unions and urbanites. While Mugabe launched his Fast Track reform program to gain votes from rural constituents and landless war veterans, the MDC advocated for respect of private property and against land appropriations. In turn, Mugabe argued that the MDC wanted to return land to the whites and portrayed the opposition party as a puppet for the former British colonial regime. In the 2002 elections, many whites and commercial farmworkers were effectively disenfranchised under the Citizenship Amendment Act, which revoked citizenship to those who had foreign ancestry and still possessed another foreign citizenship. Approximately 20 percent of the population was affected, including many Zimbabweans with parents or grandparents from Malawi, Mozambique, or Zambia (see Boone, 2014). The ZANU-PF regime also claimed that only Zimbabweans with a "rural home" were true citizens and used such rhetoric to justify bulldozing urban homes and vending sites in 2005, affecting more than two million people (see Ndlovu-Gatsheni, 2009).

These cases closely conform to Mudde's conceptualization of populism as ideology. In other words, these cases were representative of attempts by leaders to strategically re-characterize a particular demographic group (i.e. Christian Ivoirians and black, rural Zimbabweans) as their countries' genuine citizens and thereby the "pure people." Other groups (i.e. Muslim Ivoirians and white or urban Zimbabweans), who were typically economically advantaged in terms of employment or business opportunities, were by implication portrayed as the "corrupt elite" who benefitted from exploiting the pure people. However, such leaders lacked many of the other characteristics identified in the first generation of populism, including a moral purpose to represent "the people" and direct ties bolstered by socio-cultural performances that reinforce an awareness of the plight of the masses.

Democracy, Demography, and Inequality: Drivers of Contemporary Populism

More recent shifts in Africa's party system, economic circumstances, and demographic trends have provided fertile terrain for the emergence of populism as an electoral strategy used especially by opposition parties. The cases here specifically apply the cumulative conceptual approach to four instances of opposition leaders from the 2000–2015 period who relied on a populist strategy at some stage in their quest for executive power: Raila Odinga of Kenya's Orange Democratic Movement (ODM), Abdoulaye Wade of Senegal's *Parti Démocratique Sénégalais* (PDS), Julius Malema of South Africa's Economic Freedom Front (EFF), and the late Michael Sata of Zambia's Patriotic Front (PF).

Democratization and Critical Junctures in the Party System

Disenchantment with the outcomes of democratization, and especially the inability of opposition parties to oust underperforming incumbent parties, has provided part of the political backdrop for the manifestations of populism in these countries. The experience of disillusionment with representative institutions and mechanisms of accountability, along with particular socioeconomic grievances that are perceived to be ignored by the political class, offers an opportunity for populism to take root (see Laclau, 2005; Roberts, 2015). Empirically, contemporary manifestations of populism appear to be most prominent in Africa's electoral democracies and completely absent in its more authoritarian settings.

In addition to the institutional drivers that facilitate a populist strategy, the nature of the party system has been instructive for explaining when and why these strategies tend to emerge. Roberts (2015: 145–6) argues that there may be three scenarios when the party system plays a role: early stages of democratization when voters are searching for partisan affinities, when party systems are highly fluid and leave voters unattached, and when parties have been so entrenched that they appear to be a "self-reproducing governing caste that is insulated from popular needs and concerns." The latter two scenarios appear to be more important in explaining the supply side drivers of when and where populist strategies have emerged in Africa.

More specifically, in countries such as Kenya and Zambia, many voters initially supported the parties that spearheaded democratization efforts. In Kenya, Mwai Kibaki's National Rainbow Coalition (NARC) ousted the long ruling Kenya African National Union (KANU) in 2002 with great fanfare and 62 percent of the votes. In Zambia, the ability of Frederick Chiluba and the Movement for Multiparty Democracy (MMD) to wrest power from Kenneth Kaunda and the United National Independence Party (UNIP) in 1991 was even more dramatic, with almost 76 percent of Zambians supporting Chiluba. In both countries, however, critical events resulted in fissiparous party dynamics. Chiluba's decision to change the constitution and ultimately failed bid to run for a third term in office in 2001 prompted widespread MMD defections and a proliferation of new parties, including the PF under the leadership of Sata. Opposition within NARC to Kibaki's referendum to strengthen presidential powers in 2005 resulted in a collapse of the coalition, including the defection of one of his ministers, Odinga, who subsequently formed the ODM.

In Senegal and South Africa, however, disillusionment with entrenched parties provided an opportunity for populist strategies. Discontent with the *Parti Socialiste* (PS), which had ruled Senegal since the 1960s, exploded in the 1990s in the wake of deeply flawed presidential elections and growing perceptions of government corruption. The most prominent manifestation of this malaise, especially among unemployed youth and students, was the emergence of the *Set Setal* movement. *Set Setal* represented dual goals, aiming to both mobilize urban youth to clean up rubbish-strewn streets while also figuratively representing a symbol of protest against a non-responsive ruling class (see Diaw and Diouf, 1998). Riots, strikes, and demonstrations targeted against symbols of power in the affluent areas of the capital, Dakar, became increasingly common (Diouf, 1996). Abdoulaye Wade, a lawyer and long-time opposition leader of the PDS, took advantage of this context after returning from self-imposed exile in 1999 to contest the 2000 presidential elections.

In South Africa, the ANC's reputation as a liberation party from white minority rule under apartheid and a representative of the working class became tainted under Thabo

Mbeki's tenure from 1999 to 2008. His pursuit of neoliberal economic policies benefitted a coterie of black business tycoons but showed little impact on the living conditions of a majority of the country's poor. Such policies began to alienate the more avowedly socialist party supporters and its two alliance partners, the Confederation of South African Trade Unions (COSATU) and the Communist Party. Popular dissatisfaction was also palpable, particularly among 18–24-year-olds (known as "Born Frees"), evidenced by gradual reductions in the ANC's vote share in each subsequent election after 1994. Dissatisfaction with Mbeki's leadership resulted in his ouster as ANC party president in 2007. Jacob Zuma proved to be a more palatable ANC president for the party's more leftist members. Yet, corruption scandals during his first term and a massacre of striking workers by police at the Marikana platinum mines in 2012 tainted the ANC's pro-poor and pro-labor credentials. Julius Malema, the former leader of the ANC's Youth League and erstwhile one of Zuma's biggest supporters, seized this opportunity to launch his own party, the EFF.

Urbanization, Inequality, and Youth

Beyond the political context, Africa's changing economic and demographic landscape provide the grievances, or "demand-side" dynamics, upon which savvy politicians can capitalize. After a period of sustained decline, the region has witnessed a resurgence in economic growth, and a handful of countries have now graduated to middle-income status. In fact, since 2000, approximately 300 million more people are believed to have become middle class (AfDB, 2011). The region is also considered one of the fastest urbanizing in the world, and much of this new middle class is concentrated in urban areas. At the same time, however, some analysts have pointed to the growing "urbanization of poverty" (e.g. Ravallion et al., 2007), and African cities are major sites of inequality as gleaming shopping malls abut informal markets and pockets of slums tussle for space with new middle class housing estates.

These challenges are augmented by Africa's persistent high unemployment, especially among young people. For instance, between 1998 and 2006, youth unemployment in urban areas rose from 60 to an astounding 72 percent (World Bank, 2009). In many of the region's countries, this constituency is more likely to be susceptible to ambitious promises by politicians to improve their lives in a very short time span (see Resnick and Casale, 2014). Therefore, unlike in the 1980s, when populist regimes were particularly concerned about exclusion of the peasant class, more contemporary populist strategies have been centered on urban areas.

Consequently, a common feature of contemporary populist strategies is a concentration on mobilizing urbanites and particularly the urban poor. Consisting of heterogeneous, unorganized masses, this constituency is often disillusioned with slum housing, lack of employment, poor service delivery, and frequent harassment by the ruling class. In Zambia, for example, Sata's rise as an increasingly popular opposition leader coincided with episodes of harassment by the MMD of street vendors under the "Keep

Lusaka Clean" campaign and demolitions of shanty compounds. Likewise in Kenya, Odinga's campaign in the 2007 elections was preceded by a range of threatened evictions in the slum of Kibera in Nairobi under Kibaki's government, the bulldozing of hundreds of homes in the capital, and heavy-handed police violence in the slums during the pursuit of gangs.

As evidence of the importance of the urban poor, many of these African politicians strategically focused their campaigns in geographic terms. Sata, for instance, launched and closed his campaigns in either informal markets or shanty compounds while his competitors often chose plush hotels or conference centers. In 2000, Wade focused his peripatetic campaign rallies, known as *les marches bleues* (blue marches), in the main thoroughfares of Dakar where informal workers are concentrated. Odinga finished his 2007 campaigns with closing rallies in the slums of Nairobi, particularly in Langata constituency where he had long been the Member of Parliament. Malema launched his 2014 campaign at the Marikana platinum mine, which had been the site of the deaths of approximately thirty-five miners at the hands of the police in the wake of a labor protest. He also chose to predominantly campaign through the townships, which he would tour with great fanfare after his speeches. Not surprisingly, urban areas tended to be where these leaders and their parties garnered the most votes in the elections that followed their populist campaign strategies.

COMPONENTS OF CONTEMPORARY POPULIST STRATEGIES

The components of contemporary populist strategies witnessed in Africa consist of four key elements: (1) unmediated ties with the urban poor that are facilitated by charisma and socio-cultural performances; (2) anti-elitism that often delineates between the "people" and the establishment; (3) an economically eclectic but relatively programmatic message that consistently centers on promoting employment and services important for the urban poor; and (4) the combination of predominant appeals to the urban poor with ones linked to ethnicity, language, and religion that aim to mobilize a select but sizable group of rural voters. While the former two characteristics nicely complement those found in other regions of the world, the latter two are slightly more distinct to the African context.

Unmediated Ties

The lack of non-mediated rapport between a leader and his/her followers, who singularly claims to represent "the people," closely reflects Weyland's (2001; this volume) differentiation of a populist from a non-populist (see also Barr, 2009; Mouzelis, 1985).

Populist strategies in Africa have attempted to facilitate the impression of unmediated ties through a potent mixture of charismatic leadership along with the socio-cultural practices that Ostiguy (this volume) stresses. At a basic level, this is illustrated by the use of well-known nicknames that aim to endear these politicians to their constituencies. These range from the paternalist *Gorgui* ("old man") for Wade, the biting and acerbic "King Cobra" for Sata, the ambiguous *Agwambo* ("the mysterious one") for Odinga, and the childhood moniker of *Juju* for Malema.

More specifically, each of these leaders has engaged in socio-cultural practices that help differentiate them from other competitors and show their affinity to the "common man," resonating with Ostiguy's notion of "flaunting of the low." Theatrical antics and the strategic use of clothing offer one means of doing this. One example includes Sata's majestic arrival to the High Court in 2008 to register for the elections being tugged in a speedboat because a boat was the PF's campaign symbol. Likewise, instead of the suits favored by the PS, Wade wore the traditional Senegalese *boubou* in his 2000 campaign while his security guards favored blue jeans rather than the typical professional garb of civil servants. The aim was to celebrate and honor Senegal's informal sector workers who typically don denim (see Foucher, 2007). Malema has often been the most fanatic in the use of costume, making the trademark of the EFF a red beret, and aiming to show an affinity with the working class. When he and twenty-four other EFF MPs who were elected in the May, 2014, elections arrived for their first day of Parliament, they dressed up as miners and domestic workers, stating that they refused "to conform to the conventional Western style dress code of suit and tie."[2]

Other particular performance tactics include the use of music and dancing. Given the interest in mobilizing urban youth in particular, campaigns by some of these politicians have involved broadcasting *kwaito* music in South Africa and *Ivoirian* reggae and rap in Wade's blue marches. Sata's 2011 campaign was reinvigorated with a popular rap song called *Donchi Kubeba* ("Don't Tell"), which implied that voters should accept gifts and money from the MMD but not tell the then-incumbent party that they were going to instead vote for the PF.

Even more powerful when communicating with the broader populace was the type of language often employed. The ability to speak in the vernacular, rather than give speeches that were translated from either French or English, was an important distinction for both Wade's and Sata's campaigns vis-à-vis those of their competitors. Sata's quick wit made him extremely popular. When a competitor, Hakainde Hichilema, claimed that he was the "best man" to be president, Sata retorted by asking "then who is the groom?" (cited in Sishuwa, 2011: 65). Wade was also famous for his oratory skills, which sometimes involved drawing on well-known fables to make parallels between literary villains and the incompetence of the PS (see Breuillac, 2000). Malema's one-liners enlivened South Africa's parliamentary proceedings with comments such as "[President Zuma] is a man of tradition, a tradition of empty promises."[3]

Yet, language by some of these politicians and their supporters could also demonstrate violent undertones that truly emphasize their "flaunting of the low." Odinga once emerged from his campaign cavalcade to exclaim that "This [PNU] government needs a hammer … it needs to be hammered out" (cited in Bosire, 2007). Malema gained widespread notoriety by singing *Dubul iBhuni* ("Shoot the Boer") at campaign rallies, which is an old liberation song referring to killing white Afrikaner farmers. He also incorporated elements of sexist discourse, such as when he called the former white leader of the opposition Democratic Alliance, Helen Zille, a "racist little girl."

People Power and Anti-Elite Rhetoric

An anti-elite rhetoric also has been prominent in African instances of populist strategies but also quite ironic given that none of these leaders can truly be considered outsiders to the prevailing political and economic establishment. Wade, for instance, had enjoyed periods of *co-habitation* in the PS government as the Minister of State without Portfolio. Sata was a longtime stalwart in the MMD, serving in various ministerial positions. Odinga has traversed many parties in Kenya, ranging from the Forum for the Restoration of Democracy to the National Democratic Party and the Liberal Democratic Party. As noted earlier, he served in Kibaki's cabinet as part of the NARC coalition. Malema was the leader of the ANC's Youth League until he was effectively suspended by its National Disciplinary Committee in 2012 for sowing divisions within the party by, among other things, calling for regime change in neighboring Botswana. Consequently, in order to suggest that they could offer real change and distance themselves from the ruling establishment, they have had to proclaim a strong affinity to the people and distance themselves from the "elite," following closely Mudde's (2004; this volume) ideological interpretation of populism.

Wade did this mostly by showing how his leadership styles and priorities were more aligned with the people's desires and how the political elite in particular were unable to relate to the poor. Proclaimed *Président de la rue* ("President of the street") because of his popularity with everyday people in the early 2000s (Onishi, 2002), Wade's paternal image helped distinguish him from the PS regime, which had been led by the intellectual poet-president, Leopold Senghor, and the stolid technocrat, Abdou Diouf. With the rallying cry of *Sopi* ("change"), he promised a sharp rupture with the ruling establishment and offered an alternative "which the population could believe in" (Diaw and Diouf, 1998: 134). Responding to questions about his novel campaign approach of blue marches in the 2000 elections, he noted "I have wanted to do what no other candidate can do. *I reach out to the people*" (cited in Foucher, 2007: 113, emphasis added).

For Odinga and Sata, the elite were not just divorced from the concerns of the people but actually to blame for inequality and exploitation. Odinga's campaign manifesto presented stark dichotomies, evoking Manichean discourse and stating, "I give you a cast-iron guarantee that I will be a champion of social justice and social emancipation—a champion of the poor, the dispossessed and the disadvantaged in our nation. I will redress the imbalance between the powerful and the weak, between the rich and the poor, between the satisfied and the hungry" (Odinga, 2007: 7). To make the point clear, his campaign T-shirts in 2007 espoused that he was the "People's President."

In Zambia, Sata likewise viewed himself as the people's liberator, proclaiming "Zambia needs a redeemer, Zambians want Moses to redeem [them] and I am the redeemer of Zambia!" (cited in Chellah, 2006: 3). However, who exactly he was redeeming them from shifted over time. In 2006, he used a highly xenophobic discourse targeted at Asian engagement in the Zambian economy. He decried Chinese and Indian ownership of the region's copper mines and that most of Lusaka's shops were owned by Chinese and South Asians (Wines, 2006). Re-labeling foreign business owners "foreign infestors," he vowed to deport them if elected into office. In subsequent campaigns, he toned down this rhetoric and claimed that he welcomed responsible foreign investors as long as they did not bring their own laborers (Kachali and Chilemba, 2008). Instead, more vitriol was reserved for the shortcomings of the MMD's growth strategy, which had led to impressive macroeconomic growth in the 2000s but done little to address inequality, creating neocolonial circumstances. In a 2011 rally in Lusaka, he chastised Zambians by saying, "You liberated yourselves from Europeans, how can you fail to liberate yourselves from [MMD president] Rupiah? There is no water in schools and there are pit latrines. How can you use pit latrines after 47 years of independence?" (cited in Sishuwa, 2011: 69).

Malema has adopted the most divisive approach. The EFF manifesto states: "Our decision is to fight for the economic emancipation of the people of South Africa, Africa and the world. Economic Freedom Fighters (EFF) locate the struggle for economic emancipation within the long resistance of South Africans to racist colonial and imperialist, political, economic, and social domination."[4] Relatedly, he has often equated elitism with race. Even highly competent white South Africans with liberation credentials have been criticized by *Juju* for being appointed to bureaucratic positions that should have instead gone to "an African child" (cited in Vincent, 2011: 7). By extension, the people Malema claims to represent are specifically poor, black South Africans, as evident from his 2014 campaign rally when he stated: "You must give the ANC a wake-up call. *Black people* your time is now. Political freedom without economic freedom is an incomplete freedom" (cited in Harding, 2014, emphasis added). To emphasize his calling, he proclaimed himself the "Son of the People."

Eclectic Economic Ideologies and the Centrality of Urban Concerns

Like their neopopulist counterparts in Latin America (see Roberts, 1995), African leaders who have employed populist strategies tend to adhere to eclectic economic ideologies, reinforcing Weyland's (2001) contention that populism cannot be defined in terms of economic strategy alone. Unlike the projects embarked on by Rawlings or Sankara in the 1980s, there is not a clear delineation of populist economic interventions. Instead, most of these leaders fused norms from both the left and right ideological spectrum. Economic diversification and reductions in taxes were combined with advocacy for social protection policies and government support for public services. Wade shied away from explicit claims about state intervention and at the time of his 2000 campaign, his party was associated with having at least in theory an economically liberal bent. By contrast, the minerals-based economies of Southern Africa have inspired more rhetoric about government intervention. For instance, Sata promised to increase the royalty rates on foreign mining companies in the Copperbelt if he was elected. Malema's 2014 campaign promises revolved around seven pillars, including expropriation of South Africa's land (from mostly white farmers) without compensation for redistribution; nationalization of mines, banks, and other strategic sections without compensation; and massive protected industrial development.[5]

A common thread across all of these populist strategies has been a more concerted focus on the priorities of the urban poor, especially employment but also upgrading slum housing and providing services such as sanitation, electricity, and water. For instance, Wade vowed to end the forced urban housing removals that had been commonplace under the PS regime by either relocating people into better housing or compensating them if they had to be moved elsewhere (see Resnick, 2014). Upon accepting the ODM's nomination as president, Odinga promised to rectify Kenya's "economic apartheid" by ensuring his supporters jobs and highlighting the unacceptably large share of urbanites living in informal settlements, stating: "Sixty percent of Nairobi residents live in informal settlements because of government mismanagement. We want to improve the economic power of the people. We want a social movement" (cited in Odula, 2007). Sata's main campaign slogan, used consistently across the 2006, 2008, and 2011 elections, was "lower taxes, more jobs, and more money in your pockets." This message directly attacked the MMD's poor record on employment creation and the high prices for food and services consumed by the poor. Upgrading rather than demolishing shanty housing, providing a clean water supply, and ceasing harassment of street vendors constituted other key promises. The EFF manifesto likewise promised to provide houses, sanitation, millions of sustainable jobs, and a minimum wage to reduce wage inequalities that are the legacy of apartheid.[6]

Ascriptive Identity Appeals in Rural Areas

Notably, aside from Malema's commitment to land expropriation, the promises made above are not especially relevant to the needs of the rural poor. Increased access to farming inputs, better rural infrastructure, improved agricultural research and extension, and off-farm opportunities were rarely heard in these campaigns. In the case of Zambia, one observer even noted, "His [Sata's] political vision is in town alone, talking about making flyover bridges, sweeping the markets, etc. Coming to issues that affect the rural multitudes, he has nothing to offer or talk about. Ask him about agricultural policies and you will get nothing from him" (Daka, 2008: 5). The challenge, however, in Africa is that rural populations are still numerically critical for winning presidential elections.

Thus, a common feature of many of these populist strategies was a combination of populist strategies to mobilize the urban poor with ascriptive identity appeals to particular ethnic or religious groups in rural areas. In 2006 and 2008, for instance, Sata's rural campaigns were predominantly located in Luapula and Northern provinces where his fellow Bemba co-ethnics are geographically concentrated. In 2011, Sata expanded to Western Province and promised to restore the sovereignty of the kingdom of the Barotse ethno-linguistic group (see also Cheeseman and Larmer, 2015). In Senegal, Wade drew on his strong ties with one of the country's four Sufi brotherhoods, the Mourides, which historically have commanded strong voting allegiances among rural constituencies. Kenya's electoral rules in 2007, which required that a candidate win a plurality of votes nationally and 25 percent of the votes in five of the country's then eight provinces, meant that Odinga needed a multi-ethnic alliance. His own ethnic group, the Luo, were predominantly concentrated in Nyanza province. As such, he mobilized a "Pentagon Alliance" that involved five other politicians who represented sizable minority ethnic groups and could present a sizable counterbalance to the Kikuyu, who were Kibaki's co-ethnics. Malema likewise drew on his Pedi ethnicity, often using the SePedi language to address even urban rallies, such as his concluding one in Pretoria in 2014. After urban Gauteng, Limpopo Province, where the Pedi are concentrated and where the population is almost 90 percent rural, was where the EFF won the most parliamentary seats in those elections.

Of course, this ethno-populism is certainly not uncommon elsewhere, particularly Latin America (see Madrid, 2008). But it is definitely a much more pronounced factor in the African context where ethnic and religious diversity often have important consequences in the political sphere. As in other regions, the feasibility of combining populist strategies with ascriptive appeals is due to the emphasis on marginalization. Feelings of exclusion and grievances over inequality among the urban poor have been complemented by perceptions among certain ethnic and religious groups of having been sidelined in the political sphere. Sata alluded to the exclusion of Bembas by MMD leaders, Odinga suggested that inter-provincial economic disparities had prevailed under Kikuyu leadership, and Wade capitalized on growing disenchantment by the Mourides of being sidelined by the PS regime.

CONCLUSIONS

By elaborating on the features of populism over different eras of post-independence Africa, this chapter illustrates which characteristics are shared across the different cases in an effort to illustrate the importance of adopting a cumulative approach to defining populism in the region. The populism both of the 1980s and of the 2000s was precipitated by disappointment with democratic experiments and the emergence of a corrupt elite that appeared detached from the poor masses. As shown in Table 5.1, anti-elitist discourse has therefore been a prominent feature in both eras. However, the people's

Table 5.1 Comparing eras of populist leaders in Africa.

Characteristics	1980s Populism	2000–2015 Populism
Charismatic leadership	Yes, leaders are genuine outsiders who enter politics through military	Yes, leaders are longstanding insiders who enter politics by forming new parties
Unmediated ties to the masses through socio-cultural performances	Metaphors, use of vernacular, foster messianic image, publicly eschewing political traditions	Theatrical antics and clothing, speaking in vernacular, quick wit and metaphors, eschew intellectualism
Anti-elitist discourse?	Yes	Yes
Pure People	Rural peasants, unemployed, women, youth	Urban poor, co-ethnics, youth
Corrupt Elite	Traditional chiefs, civil servants and professionals, "parasitic classes," post-independence leaders, colonial powers	Leaders of democratic transitions, politically powerful ethnic/religious/racial groups, international donors, foreign investors
General Will	A social revolution	Greater access to the economic "pie" through creating more jobs, reducing taxes, reducing harassment of poor, and expanding social protection
Economic ideologies	State intervention, import substitution industrialization, rural collectivization	Economic diversification, state intervention, nationalization

revolutions of the 1980s were generally driven by outsiders, particularly military leaders, who often had the latitude to implement radical plans for restructuring society and who sidelined existing bureaucratic administrative structures in favor of new grassroots structures ostensibly aimed at facilitating popular participation. Though concerned with the poor in general, they gave special weight to the plight of peasants in rural areas, to reforming patriarchal norms, and to confronting traditional authorities. There were clear similarities across their economic policies, which were firmly nationalist and interventionist, and which were influenced by the prevalence of dependency theory at the time. By contrast, the economic ideologies of more contemporary leaders have been highly variegated, their main constituency has been the (young) urban poor, and they have often courted traditional authorities where it helps to gain votes among particular ethnic and religious groups in rural areas.

The analysis presented here is useful not only for delineating how the notion of populism has changed over time in Africa but also for emphasizing that a cumulative approach identifies a narrower subset of cases that simultaneously satisfies the

FIG. 5.1 Applying populist conceptualisms to African cases.

conditions of all three definitions of populism discussed in the introduction. Indeed, the three conceptual approaches share many complementarities. However, Figure 5.1 highlights that each approach on its own may also result in classifying a broader set of cases as populism than the alternative approaches would suggest.

More specifically, Weyland's (2001; this volume) conceptualization of populism as predominantly about personalistic leadership around plebiscitarian ties with a majority of citizens certainly fits many of the leaders discussed here. But while it may be sufficient for identifying populism in Latin America, North America, or Europe, where programmatic parties are well-institutionalized, the relative newness of democracy in Africa and the absence of mediating organizations means that many parties are essentially synonymous with their leaders (see Lindberg, 2007). Many African parties are solely defined by their leader's personality and they are unafraid of bypassing established rules and bureaucratic structures for their own benefit once in office. A non-exhaustive list of examples of individuals who created their own parties, relied on unmediated ties to citizens in campaigns, and then tried to circumvent constitutional laws includes the late Bingu wa Mutharika of Malawi, Andry Rajoelina of Madagascar, and Yayi Boni of Benin. In other words, political strategy is too broad a definition in the African context to provide analytical precision on its own.

There is an elective affinity between the political strategy and the ideological approach advocated by Mudde (this volume). The ideological approach is helpful for distinguishing episodes of genuine populism from those where charismatic leaders simply try to mobilize voters based on promises of valence goods that appeal to a wide array of constituencies. But the ideological approach can also span efforts by political leaders to use exclusionary discourse that identifies a smaller set of the citizenry as the "pure people." In these circumstances, "purity" has been defined in ethnic, racial, or religious terms rather than constituting "purity" in a moral sense of being uncorrupted. As a result, it can include cases in Africa that do not necessarily rely on Weyland's notion of the principal power capability, whereby mobilizing the most people (i.e. most votes) possible is prioritized. Instead, such cases have depended on courting just a slice of the population who align with a leader's own ascriptive identity. In addition, the examples of such exclusionary ideological discourse include leaders who lack the direct form of intermediation that Weyland stresses. Instead, leaders such as Bédié and Mugabe attempted to mobilize through decades-old political parties (e.g. PDCI and ZANU-PF) with deep roots in communities in Côte d'Ivoire and Zimbabwe, respectively.

The overlap between the political strategy and ideological approaches in the African cases is reinforced through socio-cultural performances. Among the leaders discussed in this chapter, the way in which direct ties were pursued typically involved creating a strong affinity with the underclass through the social-cultural practices Ostiguy (this volume) discusses. Performances related to language, song, dance, and other theatrics were in abundance to win over poor voters. Sometimes these have been about "flaunting the low" and have been quite vulgar, even inciting violence and praising anti-intellectualism. But in other instances, these have simply involved clever, innovative techniques that help craft the image of a "common man" who can relate to his people. These leaders though only benefit from crafting their image as a "common man" if they are indeed purposely creating a Manichean contrast with an unresponsive and distant elite. The message of their populist enterprise is therefore disseminated more effectively through performative acts that are dramatic enough to attract media attention and large campaign rallies.

Importantly, these same characteristics that classify a leader as populist can create false expectations and a new cycle of disillusionment. Sankara's violent overthrow, Wade's ouster in Senegal's 2012 elections, and the slow implosion of the PF in the wake of Sata's death in 2014, are all suggestive in this regard. Indeed, while populism offers a means of mobilizing new constituencies, especially for opposition parties, its sustainability is often short-lived once charismatic leaders come to office. On the one hand, leaders with strong direct ties to the rural or urban poor need to widen their policies to the broader populace to gain a national foothold, and they rarely achieve the ambitious economic reforms they initially promised in order to rectify inequality and injustice. This winds up alienating the leaders' core supporters. On the other hand, as observed elsewhere (e.g. Weyland, 2001; Mudde and Rovira Kaltwasser, 2012), populist leaders in Africa have exhibited a certain intolerance for independent institutions, civil liberties, and internal dissent within their parties. Consequently, the lines between the pure people and the corrupt elite inevitably become blurred, confusing whose general will is in fact actually being pursued.

NOTES

1 Of the forty-eight countries that existed in the region at the time, only sixteen had not experienced a successful coup attempt by 1984 (see Goldsworthy, 1986).
2 See EFF website at http://www.economicfreedomfighters.org/eff-wants-to-wear-domestic-worker-uniforms-to-parliament/.
3 Cited in Findley (2015).
4 See http://www.economicfreedomfighters.org/documents/economic-freedom-fighters-founding-manifesto.
5 Ibid.
6 Ibid.

References

African Development Bank (AfDB). 2011. "The middle of the pyramid: dynamics of the middle class in Africa," market brief. Tunis: AfDB.

Barr, R. 2009. "Populists, outsiders, and anti-establishment politics," *Party Politics*, 15(29): 29–48.

Boone, C. 2003. *Political Topographies of the African State: Territorial Authority and Institutional Choice*. New York: Cambridge University Press.

Boone, C. 2009. "Electoral populism where property rights are weak: land politics in contemporary sub-Saharan Africa," *Comparative Politics*, 41/2(1): 183–201.

Boone, C. 2014. *Property and Political Order: Land Rights and the Structure of Conflict in Africa*. Cambridge: Cambridge University Press.

Bosire, B. 2007. "Raila Odinga, Kenya's mercurial political ogre," *Agence France Presse*, December 24.

Bratton, M. and N. van de Walle. 1997. *Democratic Experiments in Africa: Regime Transitions in Comparative Perspective*. New York: Cambridge University Press.

Breuillac, B. 2000. "Portrait: Le lievre Abdoulaye Wade, ou la ténacité récompensée," *Le Monde*, March 22.

Carbone, G. 2005. "'Populism' visits Africa: the case of Yoweri Museveni and No-party democracy in Uganda," working paper no. 73. Crisis States Programme. London: LSE.

Chazan, N., P. Lewis, R. Mortimer, D. Rothchild, and S. John Stedman. 1999. *Politics and Society in Contemporary Africa*, 3rd edn. Boulder: Lynne Rienner Publishers.

Cheeseman, N. and M. Larmer. 2015. "Ethnopopulism in Africa: opposition mobilization in diverse and unequal societies," *Democratization*, 22(1): 22–50.

Chellah, G. 2006. "I am Zambia's redeemer—Sata," *The Post*, June 15: 3.

Daka, H. 2008. "Editorial," *Times of Zambia*. September 29: 5.

Demmers, J., A. E. Fernández, and B. Hogenboom, eds. 2001. *Miraculous Metamorphoses: The Neoliberalization of Latin American Populism*. New York: Palgrave Macmillan.

Diaw, A. and M. Diouf. 1998. "The Senegalese opposition and its quest for power," in A. O. Olukoshi (ed.), *The Politics of Opposition in Contemporary Africa*. Uppsala: Nordiska Afrikainstitutet, 113–43.

Diouf, M. 1996. "Urban youth and Senegalese politics: Dakar 1988–1994," *Public Culture*, 8: 225–49.

Findlay, S. 2015. "Is Julius Malema the new Nelson Mandela?," *Maclean's*, May 11. http://www.macleans.ca/politics/worldpolitics/is-julius-malema-the-new-nelson-mandela/, accessed October, 2015.

Foucher, V. 2007. "'Blue marches': public performance and political turnover in Senegal," in J. Strauss and D. C. O'Brien (eds), *Staging Politics: Power and Performance in Asia and Africa*. New York: I.B. Tauris, 111–31.

Gerring, J. 2012. *Social Science Methodology: A Unified Framework*, 2nd edn. New York: Cambridge University Press.

Goldsworthy, D. 1986. "Armies and politics in civilian regimes," in S. Baynham (ed.), *Military Power and Politics in Black Africa*. London and Sydney: Croom Helm, 97–128.

Harding, A. 2014. "Julius Malema strikes a chord in South Africa townships," May 2. BBC News. http://www.bbc.com/news/world-africa-27260177, accessed June, 2014.

Harsch, E. 2014. *Thomas Sankara: An African Revolutionary*. Athens: Ohio University Press.

Kachali, L. and P. Chilemba. 2008. "If you loved Levy, vote for me—Sata," *The Post*, September 18: 1, 4.

Laclau, E. 2005. *On Populist Reason*. London: Verso.

Lindberg, S. 2007. "Institutionalization of party systems? Stability and fluidity among legislative parties in Africa's democracies," *Government and Opposition*, 42(2): 215–14.

Madrid, R. L. 2008. "The rise of ethnopopulism in Latin America," *World Politics*, 60(3): 475–508.

Martin, G. 1987. "Ideology and praxis in Thomas Sankara's populist revolution of 4 August 1983 in Burkina Faso," *Issue: A Journal of Opinion*, 15: 77–90.

Mouzelis, N. 1985. "On the concept of populism: populist and clientelist modes of incorporation in semiperipheral polities," *Politics and Society*, 14(3): 329–48.

Mudde, C. 2004. "The populist zeitgeist," *Government and Opposition*, 39(3): 541–63.

Mudde, C. and C. Rovira Kaltwasser. 2012. "Populism and (liberal) democracy: a framework for analysis," in C. Mudde and C. Rovira Kaltwasser (eds), *Populism in Europe and the Americas: Threat or Corrective for Democracy?* New York: Cambridge University Press, 1–26.

Mudde, C. and C. Rovira Kaltwasser. 2013. "Exclusionary vs. inclusionary populism: comparing contemporary Europe and Latin America," *Government and Opposition*, 48(2): 147–74.

Ndlovu-Gatsheni, S. 2009. "Making sense of Mugabeism in local and global politics: 'So Blair, keep your England and let me keep my Zimbabwe'," *Third World Quarterly*, 30(6): 1139–58.

Nugent, P. 2004. *Africa since Independence*. New York: Palgrave Macmillan.

Odinga, R. 2007. *Leadership Themes 2007*. Nairobi: The Raila Odinga Centre.

Odula, T. 2007. "Kenya opposition kicks off campaign, says 3 supporters shot," *Associated Press*, October 7.

Onishi, N. 2002. "Senegalese loner works to build Africa, his way," *New York Times*, April 10. http://www.nytimes.com/2002/04/10/world/senegalese-loner-works-to-build-africa-his-way.html.

Ravallion, M., S. Chen, and P. Sangraula. 2007. "New evidence on the urbanization of global poverty," *Population and Development Review*, 33(4): 667–701.

Resnick, D. 2014. *Urban Poverty and Party Populism in African Democracies*. New York: Cambridge University Press.

Resnick, D. 2015. "Varieties of African populism in comparative perspective," in C. de la Torre (ed.), *The Promise and Perils of Populism*. Lexington: University of Kentucky Press, 317–48.

Resnick, D. and D. Casale. 2014. "Young populations in young democracies: generational voting behavior in sub-Saharan Africa," *Democratization*: 1172–94.

Roberts, K. M. 1995. "Neoliberalism and the transformation of populism in Latin America: the Peruvian case," *World Politics*, 48(1): 82–116.

Roberts, K. M. 2007. "Latin America's populist revival," *SAIS Review*, XXVII(1): 3–15.

Roberts, K. M. 2015. "Populism, political mobilization, and crises of political representation," in C. de la Torre (ed.), *The Promise and Perils of Populism*. Lexington: University of Kentucky Press, 140–58.

Rothchild, D. and E. Gyimah-Boadi. 1989. "Populism in Ghana and Burkina Faso," *Current History*, 88(538): 221–44.

Schatzberg, M. 2001. *Political Legitimacy in Middle Africa: Father, Family, Food*. Bloomington: Indiana University Press.

Sishuwa, S. wa. 2011. The Making of an African Populist: Explaining the Rise of Michael Sata, 2001–2006. MSc dissertation, Oxford University.

Skinner, E. P. 1988. "Sankara and the Burkinabe revolution: charisma and power, local and external dimensions," *The Journal of Modern African Studies*, 26(3): 437–55.

Tripp, A. 2010. *Museveni's Uganda: Paradoxes of Power in a Hybrid Regime*. Boulder: Lynne Rienner Publishers.

van de Walle, N. 2003. "Presidentialism and clientelism in Africa's emerging party systems," *Journal of Modern African Studies*, 41(2): 297–321.

Vincent, L. 2011. "Seducing the people: populism and the challenge to democracy in South Africa," *Journal of Contemporary African Studies*, 29(1): 1–14.

Weyland, Kurt. 2001. "Clarifying a contested concept: populism in the study of Latin American politics," *Comparative Politics*, 34(1): 1–22.

Weyland, K. 2012. "Populism in the age of neoliberalism," in M. Conniff (ed.), *Populism in Latin America*, 2nd edn. Tuscaloosa: University of Alabama Press, 201–22.

Wines, M. 2006. "Strong challenge to Zambia's president," *The New York Times*, September 29. http://www.nytimes.com/2006/09/29/world/africa/29zambia.html?_r=0, accessed March, 2008.

World Bank. 2009. *World Development Report 2009: Reshaping Economic Geography*. Washington, DC: International Bank for Reconstruction and Development.

Young, C. 1982. *Ideology and Development in Africa*. New Haven: Yale University Press.

....

CHAPTER 6

POPULISM IN AUSTRALIA
AND NEW ZEALAND

....

BENJAMIN MOFFITT

Is there a distinctly antipodean populism?[1] While much scholarly attention has been paid to populism in Europe and the Americas, little work comparatively has been done on populism in Australia and New Zealand, which at first glance makes this a difficult question to answer. Indeed, while Pauline Hanson in Australia and Winston Peters in New Zealand may be recognisable names in the literature on populism, less attention has been paid to other prominent cases of populism in the antipodes. More so, there has been very little comparison of populism in the two countries,[2] and no attempt to ascertain whether there is a distinct "antipodean populism"—and what the features of this regional subtype might be. This chapter takes up this task, arguing that there is indeed a distinct antipodean populism. Drawing together contemporary examples of populism within Australia and New Zealand, it delineates antipodean populism's distinctive features, and argues that antipodean populism does not precisely resemble its usual comparator subtypes—Western European or North American populism—but rather should be seen as located between the two, mixing the general ethno-exclusivism and nativist sentiment of European populism with the more rural and protectionist aspects of North American populism.

The chapter proceeds as follows. It first outlines why Ostiguy's notion of populism as a cultural-relational performative style is most useful for understanding populism in the antipodes. Second, it provides an overview of populism in Australia and New Zealand, presenting a short discussion of populism's historical context before summarizing the key contemporary cases in each country. It then explains the institutional and political factors that have both hindered and helped populism in Australia and New Zealand's different political systems. The third section of the chapter draws together the Australian and New Zealand cases to put forward a case for understanding antipodean populism as a distinct regional subtype of populism, with a specific focus on the settler colonial status of Australia and New Zealand as well as the strong protectionist and productionist element of populism in the region. The chapter then closes by locating antipodean populism in the wider comparative literature on populism, and issuing a challenge to comparative scholars to take the region into account in future.

ANTIPODEAN POPULISM: STYLE OR IDEOLOGY?

What definition of populism is most useful and suitable for understanding populism in Australia and New Zealand? Of the definitions laid out in the opening chapters of this Handbook, it is Ostiguy's conception of populism as a performative style that revolves around the flaunting of the "low" that makes most sense in this regional context. Why this approach over the other approaches? First, Weyland's strategic approach remains highly specific to the Latin American context, and thus has limited "travelability"—something Weyland himself specifies in his chapter in this Handbook. This leaves us with the choice between Mudde's ideological approach and Ostiguy's cultural-relational performative approach. While both travel relatively well across contexts, it is the case that Ostiguy's travels *better* when considering populism in Australia and New Zealand.[3] Mudde's ideological approach was developed primarily to identify populist *parties* (Mudde, 2007)—something that makes a lot of sense in the European context—whereas Ostiguy's position is more flexible and can identify a number of political actors, whether individuals (such as leaders) or collectives (such as parties or movements), which makes it more useful for genuinely comparative analysis. This is important as while Mudde's approach might be able to identify the "usual suspects" of populist party politics in Australia and New Zealand, it cannot account for populism *within* the major parties. For example, while there are figures in the Australian Liberal Party who clearly espouse a populist ideology as per Mudde's definition, it makes little sense to call the Liberal Party itself a "populist party." Relatedly, individual leaders tend to hold more sway in populist politics in Australia and New Zealand than the populist parties themselves, which tend to fall into the category of what McDonnell (2013) has labeled "personal parties"—making a focus on the leader (and the role of representation, which is stressed by Ostiguy) more appropriate. Another main strength of Ostiguy's approach over Mudde's approach is that it sees populism as an ordinal category rather than as a binary category. In other words, one can be *more* or *less* populist in Ostiguy's eyes, whereas for Mudde, one "is" or "is not" populist. This is particularly important in the Australian and New Zealand context, given that populism has been relatively "mainstreamed" and diffused within these countries' political systems, with otherwise ostensibly "non-populist" actors adopting a populist performative style that relies on the flaunting of the "low." A binary approach can make no sense of such appropriations of populism, whereas an ordinal approach can. Finally, Ostiguy's focus on the exaltation of the "true" or "authentic" people is far more appropriate than the notion of the "pure" people of Mudde's definition when it comes to antipodean populism. Taken together, Ostiguy's focus on the performative dimensions of populism—accounting not only for the "content" of what is said by populists, but *how* it is stylistically delivered—provides a very useful approach for understanding populism in Australia and New Zealand.

POPULISM IN AUSTRALIA

There is a relatively long history of populism in Australia. Stokes (2000) traces forms of agrarian populism in rural Australia from the mid-nineteenth century onwards, with such early populists supporting colonial independence, and later rallying against the evils of the cities, which were seen as centers of vice and inequity. He also identifies populism in the anti-banking rhetoric that was common during the economic depressions of the 1890s and 1930s, as well as the appeal to the "forgotten people" by Prime Minister Robert Menzies in the 1940s. However, it is Joh Bjelke-Petersen who stands as the patron saint when it comes to understanding contemporary Australian populism. Earning the epithet "the Hillbilly Dictator" (Whitton, 2001), Bjelke-Petersen was Premier of the state of Queensland from 1968 until 1987. Known for his gerrymandering, corruption, constant threats of libel towards the press, and his politicization of the Queensland Police Force and public service, it has been argued that under Bjelke-Petersen's rule, "Queensland came as close to an authoritarian state as could be imagined within the democratic Australian federation" (Costar, 2005: online). However, his authoritarianism was balanced with a populist appeal to the low, with his communication style seemingly constructed to connect with "ordinary people"— it was full of rambling, awkward pauses and grammatical mistakes, all of which curiously seemed to disappear when he was on the international stage (Wear, 2002: 216). Bjelke-Petersen's downfall came with his ill-fated "Joh for Prime Minister" campaign in 1987, which failed to extend his Queensland-centric views (or popularity) federally.

Indeed, Queensland has since proven to be the cradle of contemporary Australian populism: Australia's most prominent populists have not only hailed from Queensland, but it has also been the state where populists have tended to receive the greatest electoral support. There have been a number of explanations offered for this. Wear (2000) argues that demographic factors (low levels of education, low numbers of non-English speaking migrants) as well as contextual factors (low media diversity, the most decentralized population of any Australian state) have provided a "congenial environment" (2000: 37) for populism in Queensland. Yet there are likely cultural explanations as well, such as the notion of "Queensland exceptionalism." Like other regional populist "hotspots" around the world, such as Northern Italy and Western Canada, Queensland has imagined itself (and is often imagined) as somehow special and different compared to the rest of the country. Rundle (2014) argues that the factors of this exceptionalism— provincialism, a strong agricultural and farming sector, suspicion of the southern states, and a deep cultural and religious conservatism—have driven its populism. The idea here is that "the things that came out of Queensland could come from nowhere else in the country" (Rundle, 2014: 33).

This includes Australia's most important contemporary populist figures. The best known of these is Pauline Hanson, whose One Nation Party enjoyed success in the late 1990s and reemerged as an influential political force in 2016. However, two of the more recent prominent populist figures in Australian politics—Bob Katter and Clive Palmer—have a more direct link to Queensland's populist forebearer, Bjelke-Petersen. Katter served as a minister in Bjelke-Petersen's government, and Palmer briefly worked as "Sir Joh's" press secretary (additionally, the one-time leader of the Queensland state branch of Palmer's United Party was Bjelke-Petersen's son, John). I outline each of these figures below.

Hanson is a familiar name in the populist literature. Leader of One Nation, a radical right populist party, Hanson achieved rapid fame in 1996 with a maiden speech in Parliament in which she claimed that Australia was being "swamped by Asians" (Hanson, 1996: 3861) and argued virulently against both multiculturalism and indigenous rights. Distinctive for her quavering voice, clipped suburban Queensland accent, her tendency to make controversial statements and her claim to be close to "the people" due to her time owning a fish-and-chip shop, Hanson became a constant fixture in the Australian media. Hanson's rise was precipitous, with One Nation capturing almost a quarter of the vote in the 1998 Queensland state election and approximately 8.4 percent in the 1998 federal election. However, her fall from grace was equally precipitous—the combination of a shoddy party structure, media attacks, unfavorable preferencing from other parties, and the "mainstreaming" of a number of her policies and discourse by Prime Minister John Howard (Mondon, 2013; Wear, 2008) saw Hanson fail to be re-elected in 2001. Despite unsuccessfully running for office throughout the 2000s, Hanson was a relatively constant presence in Australian public life, and sought to soften her public image through appearances on breakfast television and reality television shows such as *The Celebrity Apprentice* and *Dancing With The Stars*, and even going so far as to appear in a advertisement for a donut chain, which is perhaps the clearest "anti-high" performance one could imagine. However, she made a rather stunning and surprising return to political power in the 2016 federal election, when she was elected to the Senate after campaigning on an anti-Islam platform, with three other One Nation senators joining her.

Bob Katter, former National MP and now leader of the eponymous Katter's Australian Party, represents the rural side of Australian populism. A self-styled "maverick," Katter has been a long-lasting presence in Australian politics, having been in the Queensland Parliament since 1974, before moving to Federal Parliament in 1993, where he has remained since. He gained particular prominence following the 2010 federal election as one of the four independent MPs whose votes helped decide who would form a minority government. Katter's ideological position mixes economic protectionism—particularly for agricultural industries—with social conservatism, while stylistically, he is known for politically incorrect outbursts, particularly against homosexuals (once claiming that there were no homosexuals in his electorate), as well as the occasional argument against "little slanty-eyed ideologues who persecute ordinary, average Australians" (in Marks, 2013: 70), feminists, and environmentalists, all while defending what he calls the "Australian race" (Katter, 2012). His performative appeal to the low has made him a media favorite: he is never without his ever-present cowboy hat reminding us of his ties to the land; he is prone to making outrageous statements (to the extent that a book of his outlandish quotes has been released [Marks, 2013]); and his predilection for media stunts has seen him drive a ride-on lawnmower and burst into song in his press conferences.

Clive Palmer is the most recent prominent populist to emerge in the Australian political landscape. One of Australia's richest businessmen, Palmer formed the Palmer United Party (PUP) in 2013, not long after cancelling his lifetime membership of the Queensland Liberal National Party over a bitter preselection stoush. Unlike Hanson and Katter, Palmer's populism is neither anti-immigrant nor rural, but rather explicitly anti-major party. As Watson (2014: 26) notes of Palmer's party in the 2013 federal election: "while xenophobia certainly emerged after the election, prior to the election PUP had put forward an eclectic mix of policies which did not explicitly pursue the anti-immigrant or anti-Aboriginal vote. Rather it was the populist strand which dominated the rhetoric in the lead-up to the election: that professional politicians were too busy blaming each other and fighting, and Australia needed a party to 'bring people together,' provide leadership and grow the economy." In the 2013 federal election, PUP attracted approximately 5.5 percent of the vote, with Palmer being elected as an MP and three of his senators being elected to the Upper House—a success that commentators have put down to large amounts of funding from Palmer and a strong protest vote (King, 2015), given that Palmer's policies were ideologically all over the place, representing a mix of the two major parties (with a dose of pro-refugee policies) rather than anything particularly innovative (see Kefford and McDonnell, 2016). However, after the election, PUP ostensibly collapsed. Two of his highest profile senators—Jacqui Lambie[4] and Glenn Lazarus—quit to form their own parties, the party's polling dropped off, and in the 2016 federal election, Palmer did not recontest his seat and PUP did not even come close to winning any seats in either house of parliament (Lambie, however, was returned to the Senate in 2016 with her own personal party, the Jacqui Lambie Network). The party was disbanded in May 2017. Stylistically, Palmer is known for bizarre media appearances, which have included making music videos in which he "twerks" and dresses up in a rabbit onesie, his claims to be building a replica of the Titanic, and interviews full of unsubstantiated attacks on the Australian political and media classes.

Although these figures are all populist, they stress different elements of the "low" laid out by Ostiguy. To illustrate: Hanson, Katter, Palmer, and Lambie all certainly fall into the personalist aspect of the *politico-cultural low*, with claims to be close to "the people" and a distaste for proceduralism. However, their use of the two aspects of the *socio-cultural low* differs—while Hanson is clearly nativist, Katter and Lambie's use of nativism is less uniform (despite the former's talk of the Australian "race"), and Palmer's nativism is moderate to the extent he speaks about "ordinary Australians," but with few racial or ethic undertones. The other social-cultural dimension of the low outlined by Ostiguy—the way in which they appear "un-proper"—is also different from a performative standpoint. While Hanson, Lambie, and Katter's appeal here is linked to their politically incorrect coarseness, Palmer's is linked to his jocular sense of being uninhibited and unafraid to take on those in power.

When it comes to concrete political outcomes, what is striking about Australian populists like Hanson, Katter, Palmer, and Lambie is that although they tend to be quite prominent political actors—both because of their outsized media profiles and their tendency to hold crucial votes in a tightly contested parliamentary system—the fact remains that they have had little electoral success *overall*. Indeed, apart from the example of Bjelke-Peterson, populist actors and parties have not enjoyed anything approaching the sustained electoral success of their European counterparts. There are three main reasons for this: the party system, the electoral system, and the "mainstreaming" of populism in Australia.

First, Australia has a strongly institutionalized two-party system (Strangio and Dyrenfurth, 2009). Although the system is far more open to minor parties than the American party system, Australian politics is ultimately dominated by the Australian Labor Party and the Liberal-National Coalition. More so, these parties usually govern with a parliamentary majority: minority governments are so rare that the 2010 Labor minority government was the first in over seventy years. This situation makes it difficult for populist challengers (often running in minor parties or as independents) to "break through."

Second, the electoral design of Australia's bicameral system presents challenges for minor parties or independents. The Lower House (the House of Representatives) is comprised of Members of Parliament voted on the basis of single-member constituencies, thus making it difficult for minor party candidates to gain a majority, with preferences generally flowing to major parties. This makes Hanson, Katter, and Palmer's success in being elected to the Lower House even more remarkable, and reflects their high public profile and level of local support. The Upper House (the Senate) has been more conducive to minor party success, which has sometimes been of benefit to populists (as in the case of Hanson and Lambie's elections to the Senate in 2016). As the Senate is a "house of review," it is not uncommon for voters to vote for a smaller party or to register a "protest vote" in the Senate (Ghazarian, 2012). Senators are also elected on the basis of states, meaning that politicians with a strong state-based agenda or profile—which, as seen above, has been central to Australian populism—are more likely to be elected.

The third reason for the relative lack of electoral success of populists in Australia is somewhat paradoxical: populism is "mainstreamed" in contemporary Australian politics (Mondon, 2013; Sawer and Laycock, 2009; Snow and Moffitt, 2012), meaning that populist parties now have a hard time distinguishing themselves from the major parties. Certain issues—particularly around immigration and cultural identity—that were previously "owned" by populists have been successfully appropriated by the major parties. Central to this "mainstreaming" of populism was former Prime Minister John Howard, who adopted a watered-down version of Hanson's populism as well as implementing a number of her policies (Wear, 2008). Mondon (2013: 116) has demonstrated that Howard's key achievement in this regard was combining Hanson's anti-immigration stance with anti-elitist notions of mateship and egalitarianism: "Howard bravely attacked both the 'noisy' privileged minorities to restore 'egalitarianism', and those refugee 'queue jumpers' who took advantage of Australian generosity." The legacy of Howard in this regard is hard to refute: anti-immigrant sentiment, particularly located around the figure of the asylum seeker, is now reflected in the increasingly hardline policies of both major parties to the extent that it no longer has much political purchase for populist actors in Australian. Indeed, Wear (2008: 631) argues that "Howard's use of permanent populism was successful in banishing alternative populist movements" at the time. As a result, populist actors have moved onto other targets: Hanson and Lambie now focus their attack on Islam, Katter focuses on rural issues, and Palmer in fact advocates fairer treatment of asylum seekers.

A less acknowledged, but equally important element of the "mainstreaming" of populism in Australian politics is that the major parties are (and have been) home to a number of controversial populist figures. All of the main populist actors noted above—Hanson, Katter, Palmer, and Lambie—were once members of the Coalition, while controversial figures like (former) Liberal Senator Cory Bernardi, Nationals MP George Christensen (both of whom have publicly aligned themselves with Dutch populist Geert Wilders), and Deputy Prime Minister Barnaby Joyce clearly embody the populist style as laid out by Ostiguy. In this regard, the Coalition functions somewhat like the US Republican Party—it is able to accommodate and tolerate right populists *within* the party, without it necessarily making sense to call the party itself a "populist party."

Taken together, these three factors have meant that although there are a number of populist parties on the electoral market—as well as populist actors within the major parties—there is no widespread *populist movement*, or even a particular party that looks to establish a more permanent populist opposition to the major parties in Australia. As Tiffen (2011: 67) puts it, "in Australia now, populism is a style rather than an institutionalised movement"—an insight that not only adds credence to utilizing Ostiguy's definition of populism for understanding the Australian context, but also captures the mainstreamed status of populism in contemporary Australia.

POPULISM IN NEW ZEALAND

Like Australia, New Zealand has quite a long history of populism. In his review of populist leadership in New Zealand, Gustafson (2006) identifies populism in the rhetoric of Prime Ministers "King Dick" Seddon and Michael Joseph Savage, both of whom were in office during economic depressions in the early half of the twentieth century, as well as in the discourse of leaders of smaller parties during this period. In the latter half of the century, he identifies Prime Minister Rob Muldoon as "demonstrably and sometimes violently anti-elitist and anti-intellectual and suspicious of the bureaucracy" (Gustafson, 2006: 56–7), and argues that Bob Jones's New Zealand Party, Bruce Beetham and the Social Credit Party, and Jim Anderton's NewLabour Party each offered different variants of populism from the 1970s until the early 1990s. As in Australia, populism has thus found a home in both major and minor parties throughout New Zealand's political history.

Yet a striking difference between Australia and New Zealand is that while Australia may have a number of prominent contemporary populist figures, New Zealand has very few. Indeed, one singular populist figure has loomed large in New Zealand politics since 1993: Winston Peters, leader of New Zealand First. In comparison to the relative lack of electoral success of Australian populists, Peters's success and political longevity is remarkable: since the establishment of NZ First in 1993, Peters has held the positions of Deputy Prime Minister and Treasurer (1996–1998) and Minister of Foreign Affairs (2005–2008), while NZ First has formed governments with both major political parties, entering into coalition government with the National Party from 1996 to 1998 and providing confidence and supply to the Labour Party from 2005 to 2008.

Like his Australian populist brethren, Peters was originally a member of the major conservative party in his country—the National Party—first entering Parliament in 1978. While Peters held a number of Cabinet positions in National governments, he increasingly spoke out against the party, eventually resigning in 1993 and setting up NZ First. While the bedrock of Peters's populism has been a critique of privatization, neoliberalism, and globalization, this has been combined with a hardline stance on immigration, welfare chauvinism, and attacks on what he calls the "Māori industry." Like Hanson, Asian immigration and investment has also been a constant target of Peters, with claims that New Zealand is "being dragged into the status of an Asian colony" (in New Zealand Press Association, 2005: online). Yet also like Hanson, Peters shifted to targeting Muslims as well as Asian immigrants post-9/11. Peters's attacks against pro-Māori policies and the Treaty of Waitangi settlement process is complicated by the fact that Peters himself is of Māori heritage.

Despite the fact that his rhetoric is often as pointedly populist as that of Hanson or Katter, Peters is arguably a smoother and more effective political operator than any of the Australian populists described earlier. He rails against the usual suspects—"the elite," immigrants, "cultural Marxists," and "Smart Alec, arrogant, quiche eating, chardonnay drinking, pinky finger pointing" (Peters, 2002: online) journalists—and has made numerous politically incorrect comments throughout his career, among them telling racist jokes about Chinese people, calling an opponent an "illiterate woodwork teacher" (Peters in Magone, 2012: online), and crudely asking Prime Minister John Key "why don't the curtains match the carpet?" (Peters in Trevett, 2015: online) in Parliament in reference to the Prime Minster dyeing his hair. All of these clearly place Peters on the low. Despite these outbursts, Peters has nonetheless been able to present NZ First as a long-lasting credible party whose profile goes beyond the usual right populist agenda, to also including the protection of the elderly, the introduction of compulsory superannuation, and advocating lower taxation. This has led to some debate in the literature about where to fit NZ First on the ideological spectrum. While some put the party on the radical right (Betz and Johnson, 2004; Johnson et al., 2005; Miller, 1998), others claim that it fits much closer to the center, with Denemark and Bowler (2002: 51) arguing that it is a "populist-cum-nationalist centre party" and Kaiser (2008) simply labeling it as a center party. Norris (2005: 70) gets at this tension when highlighting the difference between NZ First and other radical right parties: "New Zealand First can be seen as more moderate than some of the other parties under comparison, for example in their policies on health care, unemployment, and the environment, and yet they can also be regarded as part of the radical right family through their strong emphases on economic and cultural nationalism" (although we should note that economic and cultural nationalism are by no means the exclusive domain of the right).

The broader confusion about how to characterize Peters and NZ First stems from a few possible sources. First, Peters was a long-serving National Party MP from the late 1970s onwards, meaning that he has an ostensibly "credible" backstory and background in politics, and thus lacks the "outsider" credentials so often ascribed to populists. Relatedly, Peters's time as Deputy Prime Minister and Treasurer has reinforced his perceived position as someone in the alleged "mainstream" of New Zealand politics, as has the fact that NZ First has formed governments with both major parties. Yet populists' participation in government does not automatically take them out of the "populist" category, as the work of Albertazzi and McDonnell (2015) has shown. Third, NZ First's mix of policies traditionally associated with both left and right can sometimes make it hard to place them accurately on the ideological spectrum. As the experience of the Nordic countries has shown, however, there is no incongruity in populists combining fervent anti-immigrant sentiment of the right with welfare or health policies more traditionally associated with the left (Jungar and Jupskås, 2014). In short, while Peters's position on the left-right spectrum is somewhat debated, his position on the high-low spectrum is decidedly more certain: Peters is a populist. He combines a politico-cultural appeal to personalism with strong socio-cultural nativism, yet sells it in a smoother package than his Australian populist brethren: his tone is not outrageous, particularly coarse, or "warm," but is rather direct and politically incorrect, with his lack of "properness" coming from a tendency to go "straight for the jugular" in a sardonic and exasperated manner.

What factors can explain the sustained success of Peters and NZ First as opposed to Australian populists' relative lack of success? First, the institutional context of the New Zealand electoral system has undoubtedly helped Peters. Prior to 1994, New Zealand had a first-past-the-post (FPTP) system, which favored an entrenched two-party system and made it very difficult for minor parties to make an electoral impact. This was made even more challenging by the fact that New Zealand has a unicameral legislature, meaning that unlike in Australia there was no "house of review" for protest votes. However, in 1994 New Zealand introduced a mixed member proportional (MMP) system, which combines an electorate vote for a local representative with a party vote that operates on a plurality system. This shift has created an environment more favorable to minor parties (Barker and McLeay, 2000), and it is little coincidence that the 1996 election—the first to be held using the new electoral system—still remains NZ First's best electoral result, with 13.35 percent of the vote. Indeed, since the shift to MMP, no government has been able to form on its own, but instead has relied on support from minor parties, demonstrating that the electoral system change has somewhat weakened the hegemony of the major parties.

Peters's success has also possibly been helped along by the fact that New Zealand's political landscape might be said to be comparatively less "populist" overall than Australia's, meaning he has less "populist competition" from the major parties. This was particularly the case throughout the 2000s, when the progressive Labour government led by Helen Clark provided plenty of fuel for right populists: as Johnson et al. (2005) point out, while Hanson was edged out by a government that was also populist and conservative, Peters was able to position himself *against* a government that was his "opposite" in terms of style and (arguably) ideology. However, this situation has somewhat changed since the National Party took government in 2008, with National being accused of copying NZ First's policies (Davison, 2014)—a familiar charge to anyone who watched the relationship between One Nation and the Australian Coalition government just over a decade earlier.

Overall, unlike in Australia, where a number of populist parties have sprung up and then imploded or slid into irrelevance over the past two decades, New Zealand has a remarkably resilient populist party in NZ First. Apart from its embarrassing showing in the 2008 election, where it lost all of its seats, NZ First has proven itself to be *the* populist party in New Zealand for an extended period, usually placing third or fourth in national elections over the past two decades. As such, there has been little space for other populist contenders to emerge. This may even extend to NZ First blocking the "anti-politics" or "anti-system" vote: despite the large profile (and even larger financial backing) of internet mogul Kim Dotcom, his Internet Party and Mana Movement Coalition received a paltry 1.42 percent of the vote in the 2014 elections, while other "anti-system" parties are either electorally insignificant or have disbanded over NZ First's lifetime. As such, while NZ First's eulogy has been written many times over, it would be unwise to write it off permanently, as Peters and his party have proven themselves a consistent fixture of New Zealand politics over the past two decades.

Is There A Distinctly Antipodean Populism?

Having laid out the coordinates of Australian and New Zealand populism, we can now turn to the question at hand: given that we often talk about "European populism" or "Latin American populism" as distinct, regionally bounded phenomena, is it possible to speak similarly of a distinct antipodean populism as a regional subtype? The answer is a qualified yes. Although populism in Australia and New Zealand is implicitly often seen as most similar to that of radical right populists in Europe (e.g. Betz and Johnson, 2004; Curran, 2004; Deangelis, 2003), it has its own distinct features that actually place it somewhere *between* the radical right populism of Europe and the more rural-based populisms of North America. Drawing together the discussion above, I now outline the distinct features of antipodean populism.

Antipodean Populism Is Primarily Exclusive

Firstly, contemporary antipodean populism is primarily "exclusive," to use the terminology introduced by Mudde and Rovira Kaltwasser (2013), and *generally* manifests on the right of the ideological spectrum (although as can be seen above, this ideological position is not always straightforward).[5] This means that populists in Australia and New Zealand primarily seek to exclude "others" along material, political, and symbolic dimensions. In the antipodes, this tends to be ideologically expressed through a mix of economic protectionism and social conservatism. Rather than bringing new actors into their conception of "the people," antipodean populists tend to seek instead to *protect* the already existing wealth, political rights, and status of "the people" against alleged usurpers. However, who "the people" are—and who they are opposed to—is both similar and different in a number of ways to their European and North American populist counterparts, as explained in the sections below.

Antipodean Populism Has a Producerist (and Often Rural) Notion of "the People," Which Is Generally Coded as White

Antipodean populism's notion of "the people" is not that of the "pure people" as proffered by Mudde, but rather is of an "authentic" people who have been forgotten or unrepresented by those at the top (as per Ostiguy's definition). These notions of authenticity are tied strongly to producerism, with a particular focus on agriculture and rural living. Although Australia and New Zealand are amongst the most highly urbanized countries in the world, the bush and the land still hold a mythical position in each country's national identity, while agriculture and the primary industries play a large role in Australia and New Zealand's economies. Indeed, Wear (2014) has made note of the rural flavor of Australian populism, noting that one of the most prominent populist protests of recent years—the so-called "Convoy of No Confidence"—was premised on an urban/rural divide: of the demonstrators, she notes that "it was clear that many of them felt that they were defending groups of ordinary, largely rural people, whose way of life was under threat. Old political themes emerged: a struggle between country and city, alienation, and lack of status and security for rural people" (Wear, 2014: 60). However, given that producerism is the driving force behind the notion of "the people" in antipodean populism, "the people" can also include small business owners and manual laborers, particularly those working in the smaller cities and suburban regions of Australia and New Zealand. Those who make decisions that affect "the people" in a deleterious way (major parties, bureaucrats), ignore their plight (the media, "greenies," inner-city "latte-sippers")—all subsumed under "the elite"—or allegedly "scrounge off" their hard-earned profits (welfare recipients, indigenous people, immigrants) are seen as enemies of "the people."

More so, while the rhetoric may not be as strong as the sometimes outward racism of European radical right populists, there is also an inherent understanding that "the people"—the hardworking people of the land and suburbs—are an inherently mono-cultural (or sometimes in the case of New Zealand, bicultural) group. This is coded in the rural/urban divide, whereby the cities are seen as multicultural and the country as white, as well as in the focus on producerism, where farmers and manual laborers are inherently imagined as white. This is hardly ever explicitly stated, but rather comes in statements about "mainstream" or "ordinary" Australians and New Zealanders that characterize antipodean populism, and is played upon to different degrees by antipodean populists depending on their use of the nativist component of the social-cultural low.

Antipodean Populism Is Set against a Triple Enemy: "The Elite," the Immigrant Other, and Indigenous People

So who are *not* "mainstream" Australians and New Zealanders? That is, who do antip-odean populists set "the people" against? The first group is the obvious enemy of "the people" within populism—"the elite." As can be seen above, this is a flexible signifier that can include anyone from the usual populist targets—bankers, financiers, bureaucrats, academics, the media, politicians from the major parties—to simply those who live in urban centers and are thus perceived as "soft" and "out of touch" from the lives of "ordi-nary" Australians and New Zealanders. These groups are often linked with globaliza-tion, whether due to their business/political ties or their cosmopolitanism, and this is perceived as both an economic as well as a cultural threat. Interestingly, however, prom-inent concerns about global or transnational forces—such as the UN or G20, or on the other end, conspiracy theories about the New World Order and so forth—that charac-terize elements of European and American populism are not a major feature of popu-lism in the region.

The second group "the people" is opposed to is the figure of the immigrant Other. In the late 1990s, Asian immigration was seen as the most prominent threat to Australia and New Zealand by populists, with both Hanson and Peters stoking fears about "Asian invasion" and alleging that the demography of their respective countries were chang-ing at an alarming rate. Following the terrorist attacks of 9/11, this anti-Asianism was taken over by a targeting of not just Muslims, but Middle Eastern immigrants in gen-eral. This was particularly the case in Australia, where panic about "the folk demon of the Middle Eastern/Muslim 'other'" (Poynting, 2006: 89) hit a boiling point during the 2005 Cronulla riots. This figure has arguably continued to be the primary targeted "Other" of populists in the region ever since 2001, with Peters raising concern about

Islam's "militant underbelly" (in Taylor and Harvey, 2005: online) in the New Zealand suburbs, and Hanson turning her focus to Islam—indeed, in her maiden speech to the Senate in 2016, Hanson echoed her 1996 claim of Australia being "swamped by Asians" by claiming that Australia was now being "swamped by Muslims" (Hanson, 2016: 937). The outlier here is Palmer, whose views on immigration are more progressive than either of the major Australian parties.

The third group targeted is where antipodean populists truly differ from their European counterparts: the indigenous people of Australia (Aboriginal Australians and Torres Strait Islanders) and New Zealand (the Māori people). A number of populists in the antipodes have displayed strong antipathy towards government assistance and programs of any kind for indigenous peoples, with Hanson and Peters both arguing that such programs are forms of "reverse racism" and "preferential treatment" that discriminate against non-native Australians and New Zealanders. Indeed, as Haeg (2006) has shown, there are similarities in the language used by Peters and Hanson in their arguments against the "Aboriginal industry" in Australia and the "Treaty Grievance Industry" in New Zealand. Bjelke-Petersen demonstrated similar contempt for indigenous rights. However, this situation seems to be changing in the Australian case: Katter has shown great passion for indigenous rights, particularly around Native Title; Palmer has made arguments about ending indigenous disadvantage; while Lambie has supported the creation of dedicated indigenous seats in the Australian Parliament and has claimed she has indigenous heritage. However, heritage does not necessarily equal empathy—as noted, while Peters is of Māori heritage, he has been one of New Zealand's most prominent critics of Māori "special treatment." Overall, the fraught history that each country has as a settler colonial state with often violent and bloody relations with their indigenous peoples means that these issues are likely to continue to play a part in antipodean populism well into the future.

Antipodean Populism Is Informed by Australia and New Zealand's Status as Settler Colonial States and as Geographically Isolated Islands

If Australia and New Zealand's history of being settler colonial states both informs and distinguishes antipodean populism from other regional subtypes, then we must also take account of the important fact that both are geographically isolated island countries. This is key to understanding the anxiety about "invasion" that has formed the basis for populist attacks on the Other—particularly the Asian Other and the figure of the asylum seeker—in the antipodes. In the first case, Australia and New Zealand's position as "Western" Commonwealth countries in an otherwise "Asian-Pacific" region has seen both countries periodically grapple with their cultural identity, and the result has been that anti-Asianism (particularly Sinophobia) has been an unfortunate mainstay of both countries' histories (Ip, 2003; Walker, 1999) in an attempt to construct national identity on the basis of ethnic in-groups and out-groups. In the second case, Australia's near-pathological obsession with "boat people" is a reflection of the fact that control of its maritime border is a permanent concern of contemporary Australian politics (Burke, 2008). While this tendency is much less pronounced in New Zealand—probably because of it being even more isolated than Australia, having a smaller coastline, and a generally less toxic debate on immigration—concern about asylum seekers arriving by boat remains (see Gulliver, 2015; Guy and Williamson, 2012).

Antipodean Populism Is "Mainstream"

Populism is relatively "mainstream" in the antipodes. This "mainstreaming" has taken several forms. As shown above, the major parties in Australia and New Zealand have proven to be accepting "homes" of populists, meaning that populists have been less likely to have to work outside the major parties to accomplish their goals. More importantly, populist style, discourse, and favored issues have been "owned" by the mainstream parties—particularly in Australia—meaning that there is less political space upon which populists can capitalize. More broadly, there is a strong undercurrent of anti-elitism in both Australian and New Zealand culture: anti-intellectualism is widespread in both countries (Sawer and Hindess, 2004; Simmons, 2007), politicians are widely disparaged (Burchell and Leigh, 2002), and both countries suffer from the "tall poppy syndrome," where high achievers or the ambitious are "cut down to size." As such, there is a widespread cynicism about those on the "high" of Ostiguy's approach. While this "inherent" anti-elitism (and thus the appeal of the low) may mean that citizens are possibly more predisposed to supporting populists, it also means that political actors across the political spectrum are more adept at utilizing populism as a cultural-relational style to garner political support, thus making it difficult for the "obvious" populist actors outside the major parties to differentiate themselves.

Conclusions

Having laid out the features of antipodean populism, it is clear that although it shares many features with both Western European and North American populism, it also has its own distinct attributes. For example, like the majority of European and American populists, populism in the antipodes is broadly "exclusive"—and beyond that, is generally located on the right side of the ideological spectrum. However, while figures like Hanson and Peters broadly fit the mold of the anti-immigrant radical right populists of Western Europe, recent Australian populists like Palmer and Katter are of a more moderate tack, and thus do not map so closely onto the prototypical radical right populist model. In these cases, we can confidently claim that their position on the high-low dimension (that is, their position as populists on the low) is more important than their position on the ideological spectrum.

Like North American populists, antipodean populists also share a producerist notion of "the people." However, unlike some recent North American variants of populism (such as the Tea Party and the Reform Party in Canada), antipodean populism is resolutely not aligned with neoliberalism. Protectionism runs strongly through the platforms of the majority of populist actors presented in this chapter, and this often sets up a clear difference between the economic policies of the major parties and populist challengers in Australia and New Zealand. Overseas investment—particularly in property—is viewed with particular suspicion, and Hanson and Katter go so far as to call for the return of tariffs.

Antipodean populism's antipathy towards "the elite" as well as the immigrant Other is also familiar to watchers of North American or European populism. This is particularly the case when it comes to the targeting of the conflated Middle Eastern/Muslim Other in the post-9/11 context. However, the targeting of Asian immigrants in the late 1990s may be less familiar, and speaks very much to the importance of taking geography into account when analysing the construction of "the people" and their Other in populism in the region. The same can be said about the importance of Australia and New Zealand's history as settler colonial states, and the influence this continues to have on contemporary populism in the antipodes. As Johnson et al. (2005: 90) have noted, populists in Australia and New Zealand "have to address ongoing tensions between indigenous peoples and colonial-settlers," as well as deal with the fact that these societies are immigrant nations, which "makes their politics of identity particularly complex when it comes to constructing both national identity and the neglected 'people' they claim to represent" (2005: 90–1). In this regard, antipodean populism has more in common with populism in the other settler colonial societies—particularly Canada—than Western European populism.

Finally, the "mainstream" status of populism in the antipodes looks much like the environment for populism in the United States. It is no coincidence that Ostiguy's approach to populism as a socio-cultural style is used in both this chapter and Lowndes's chapter on American populism: it resonates closely with political cultures in which appeals to "the low" have become increasingly common, where strong leadership and "ballsiness" is celebrated, and where there is clear polarization between the urban and the rural areas. While this tendency may be less pronounced in New Zealand than Australia due to the necessity of compromise and negotiation in an MMP system, the political system remains strongly adversarial (Bale and Roberts, 2002), and populism is generally seen as an "acceptable" form of politics.

It is perhaps this last point that has made antipodean populism somewhat difficult to study in comparative perspective over the past two decades. While populist actors (and their particular parties) are relatively easy to identify and compare in the European context, it is less clear in the antipodes. While there are some obvious cases—those figures whom I have profiled in this chapter—the fact that populism has essentially been mainstreamed by major parties in both countries makes things somewhat more blurry. Yet this is not a reason to avoid examining populism in the antipodes. Rather, it speaks to the necessity of utilizing an ordinal concept of populism instead of a binary one, given that it is only the former that captures the richness of what is happening to populism in the antipodes. Indeed, Australia and New Zealand provide important lessons for those interested in what happens when populism is "normalized," when populist performances are common, and how populists grapple with both the legacy of settler colonial violence as well as a clear multicultural future.

While it is likely that Europe and the Americas will remain the central focus for those who study populism—an understandable situation that I have elsewhere referred to as the "Atlantic bias" of the populist literature (Moffitt, 2015)—it is also important that comparativists set their sights beyond the "usual suspects" and take into account populism in the less studied regions of Africa (Resnick, 2014), Asia (Mizuno and Phongpaichit, 2009), and of course, the antipodes. This chapter has aimed to facilitate this task. It has profiled the central populist actors in Australia and New Zealand, explained the factors for populist success and failure in these countries, and demonstrated that a socio-cultural performative approach to populism is most useful for understanding populism in the antipodes. More so, it has argued that antipodean populism is the same as neither North American nor Western European populism, but should rather be seen as a distinct regional subtype. Having laid out these features, it is hoped that more comparativists take up the challenge to bring the antipodes into their comparative study of populism: there is clearly much to be gained from doing so.

NOTES

1 Thanks to Olivier Jutel and Michael Gaskin for their helpful advice on New Zealand politics, and Pierre Ostiguy, Cristóbal Rovira Kaltwasser, and Paul Taggart for their detailed comments on this chapter.
2 Exceptions include Denemark and Bowler (2002) and Johnson et al. (2005).
3 I have made a consonant argument for a stylistic/performative view of populism as the definition with the most "travelability" (Moffitt, 2016; Moffitt and Tormey, 2014).
4 Lambie has also built a large media profile as a populist figure. She has combined a strong Tasmanian regional identity and advocacy for veterans with attacks on Islam (under the auspices of being "anti-Halal") and on the major parties. Stylistically, she is known for being tough, blunt, and plainspoken (most notoriously claiming that she was looking for love with someone who was "well-hung" and with "a package between their legs" on a radio interview), with a talent for garnering media attention similar to her former party leader, Palmer.
5 While it is beyond the limits of this article to explore why contemporary populism tends to appear on the right rather than the left in the Antipodes, the reasons are likely similar to those for the relative lack of left populism in Europe (Mudde and Rovira Kaltwasser, 2013) and the United States (Kazin, 1998). More so, the main center-left parties in each country (the Australian Labor Party and New Zealand Labour Party) have been relatively successful in maintaining some elements of populist style and discourse, and their historical links to the unions have likely buffered suggestions that they are aligned with "the elite" enough to help stem populist demand on the left.

REFERENCES

Albertazzi, D. and D. McDonnell. 2015. *Populists in Power*. Abingdon and New York: Routledge.

Bale, T. and N. S. Roberts. 2002. "Plus ça change …? Anti-party sentiment and electoral system change: a New Zealand case study," *Commonwealth and Comparative Politics*, 40(2): 1–20.

Barker, F. and E. McLeay. 2000. "How much change? An analysis of the initial impact of proportional representation on the New Zealand parliamentary party system," *Party Politics*, 6(2): 131–54.

Betz, H.-G. and C. Johnson. 2004. "Against the current—stemming the tide: the nostalgic ideology of the contemporary radical populist right," *Journal of Political Ideologies*, 9(3): 311–27.

Burchell, D. and A. Leigh (eds). 2002. *The Prince's New Clothes: Why Do Australians Dislike Their Politicians?* Sydney: UNSW Press.

Burke, A. 2008. *Fear of Security: Australia's Invasion Anxiety*. Port Melbourne: Cambridge University Press.

Costar, B. 2005. "Sir Joh, our home-grown banana republican," *The Age*, April 25. http://www.theage.com.au/news/Opinion/Sir-Joh-our-homegrown-banana-republican/2005/04/24/1114281449030.html, accessed March 20, 2015.

Curran, G. 2004. "Mainstreaming populist discourse: the race-conscious legacy of neo-populist parties in Australia and Italy," *Patterns of Prejudice*, 38(1): 37–55.

Davison, I. 2014. "Conservatives butt heads with NZ First over lookalike policies," *New Zealand Herald*, July 19. http://www.nzherald.co.nz/nz/news/article.cfm?c_id=1&objectid=11295872, accessed July 3, 2015.

Deangelis, R. A. 2003. "A rising tide for Jean–Marie, Jörg, & Pauline? Xenophobic populism in comparative perspective," *Australian Journal of Politics and History*, 49(1): 75–92.

Denemark, D. and S. Bowler. 2002. "Minor parties and protest votes in Australia and New Zealand: locating populist politics," *Electoral Studies*, 21(1): 47–67.

Ghazarian, Z. 2012. "The changing type of minor party elected to Parliament: the case of the Australian Senate from 1949 to 2010," *Australian Journal of Political Science*, 47(3): 441–54.

Gulliver, A. 2015. "People-smuggling boat 'credible risk and threat' to NZ," June 2. http://www.stuff.co.nz/national/69027808/peoplesmuggling-boat-credible-risk-and-threat-to-nz, accessed July 2, 2015.

Gustafson, B. 2006. "Populist roots of political leadership in New Zealand," in R. Miller and M. Mintrom (eds), *Political Leadership in New Zealand*. Auckland: Auckland University Press, 51–69.

Guy, N. and M. Williamson. 2012. "Exercise Barrier shows New Zealand's readiness for mass arrivals," *New Zealand Government Press Release*, June 19. http://www.beehive.govt.nz/release/exercise-barrier-shows-new-zealand%E2%80%99s-readiness-mass-arrivals, accessed July 15, 2015.

Haeg, G. C. 2006. "Neo-populist party emergence in Australia, Canada, and New Zealand," PhD thesis, Department of Political Science, University of Oklahoma.

Hanson, P. 1996. "Australia, House of Representatives, Parliamentary Debates (Hansard)," September 10: 3859–62.

Hanson, P. 2016. "Australia, Senate, Parliamentary Debates (Hansard)," September 14: 937–41.

Ip, M. 2003. "Chinese immigrants and transnationals in New Zealand: a fortress opened," in L. J. C. Ma and C. Cartier (eds), *The Chinese Diaspora: Space, Place, Mobility, and Identity*. Lanham: Rowman and Littlefield Publishers, 339–58.

Johnson, C., S. Patten, and H.-G. Betz. 2005. "Identitarian politics and populism in Canada and the Antipodes," in J. Rydgren (ed.), *Movements of Exclusion: Radical Right-Wing Populism in the Western World*. Hauppauge: Nova Science Publishers, 85–100.

Jungar, A.-C. and A. R. Jupskås. 2014. "Populist radical right parties in the Nordic region: a new and distinct party family?" *Scandinavian Political Studies*, 37(3): 215–38.

Kaiser, A. 2008. "Parliamentary opposition in Westminster democracies: Britain, Canada, Australia and New Zealand," *The Journal of Legislative Studies*, 14(1–2): 20–45.

Katter, B. 2012. *An Incredible Race of People: A Passionate History of Australia*. Sydney: Pier 9.

Kazin, M. 1998. *The Populist Persuasion: An American History*, 2nd edn. Ithaca: Cornell University Press.

Kefford, G. and D. McDonnell. 2016. "Ballots and billions: Clive Palmer's personal party," *Australian Journal of Political Science*, 51(2): 183–97.

King, T. 2015. "The advent of two new micro parties: the Palmer United party and Katter's Australia Party," in C. Johnson, J. Wanna, and H.-A. Lee (eds), *Abbott's Gambit: The 2013 Australian Federal Election*. Canberra: ANU Press: 293–310.

Magone, P. 2012. "Peters booted out for 'illiterate' Brownlee insult," March 1. http://www.stuff.co.nz/national/politics/6507688/Peters-booted-out-for-illiterate-Brownlee-insult, accessed July 21, 2015.

Marks, R. (ed.). 2013. *Kattertonia: The Wit and Wisdom of Bob Katter*. Collingwood: Black Inc.

McDonnell, D. 2013. "Silvio Berlusconi's personal parties: from Forza Italia to the Popolo Della Libertà," *Political Studies*, 61(S1): 217–33.

Miller, R. 1998. "New Zealand First," in H.-G. Betz and S. Immersfall. (eds), *The New Politics of the Right: Neo-Populist Parties and Movements in Established Democracies*. Basingstoke and London: Macmillan, 203–11.

Mizuno, K. and P. Phongpaichit (eds). 2009. *Populism in Asia*. Singapore: NUS Press.

Moffitt, B. 2015. "Contemporary Populism & 'The People' in the Asia-Pacific: Thaksin Shinawatra & Pauline Hanson," in C. de la Torre (ed.), *The Promise and Perils of Populism: Global Perspectives*. Lexington: University of Kentucky Press, 293–316.

Moffitt, B. 2016. *The Global Rise of Populism: Performance, Political Style, and Representation*. Stanford: Stanford University Press.

Moffitt, B. and S. Tormey. 2014. "Rethinking populism: politics, mediatisation and political style," *Political Studies*, 62(2): 381–97.

Mondon, A. 2013. *The Mainstreaming of the Extreme Right in France and Australia: A Populist Hegemony?* Farnham: Ashgate.

Mudde, C. 2007. *Populist Radical Rights Parties in Europe*. Cambridge: Cambridge University Press.

Mudde, C. and C. Rovira Kaltwasser. 2013. "Exclusionary vs. inclusionary populism: comparing contemporary Europe and Latin America," *Government and Opposition*, 48(2): 147–74.

New Zealand Press Association. 2005. "Winston Peters' memorable quotes," *The Age*, October 18. http://www.theage.com.au/news/world/winston-peters-memorable-quotes/2005/10/18/1129401225653.html, accessed July 7, 2015.

Norris, P. 2005. *Radical Right: Voters and Parties in the Electoral Market*. New York: Cambridge University Press.

Peters, W. 2002. "A House Divided—Winston Peters Speech," *Scoop: Independent News*, July 25. http://www.scoop.co.nz/stories/PA0207/S00673/a-house-divided-winston-peters-speech.htm, accessed July 7, 2015.

Poynting, S. 2006. "What caused the Cronulla riot?" *Race and Class*, 48(1): 85–92.

Resnick, D. 2014. *Urban Poverty and Party Populism in African Democracies*. New York: Cambridge University Press.

Rundle, G. 2014. "Clivosaurus: the politics of Clive Palmer," *Quarterly Essay*, 56.

Sawer, M. and B. Hindess (eds). 2004. *Us and Them: Anti-Elitism in Australia*. Perth: API Network.

Sawer, M. and D. Laycock. 2009. "Down with elites and up with inequality: market populism in Australia and Canada," *Commonwealth and Comparative Politics*, 47(2): 133–50.

Simmons, L. (ed.). 2007. *Speaking Truth to Power: Public Intellectuals Rethink New Zealand*. Auckland: Auckland University Press.

Snow, D. and B. Moffitt. 2012. "Straddling the divide: mainstream populism and conservatism in Howard's Australia and Harper's Canada," *Commonwealth and Comparative Politics*, 50(3): 271–92.

Stokes, G. 2000. "One Nation and Australian populism," in M. Leach, G. Stokes, and I. Ward (eds), *The Rise and Fall of One Nation*. St Lucia: University of Queensland Press, 23–41.

Strangio, P. and N. Dyrenfurth (eds). 2009. *Confusion: The Making of the Australian Two-Party System*. Carlton: Melbourne University Press.

Taylor, K. and C. Harvey. 2005. "Peters warns of Muslim serpents," *NZ Herald*, July 29. http://www.nzherald.co.nz/nz/news/article.cfm?c_id=1&objectid=10338138, accessed July 10, 2015.

Tiffen, R. 2011. "We, the populists," *Griffith Review*, 31: 66–74.

Trevett, C. 2015. "Winston Peters: John Key's 'curtains don't match the carpet,'" *NZ Herald*, February 11. http://www.nzherald.co.nz/nz/news/article.cfm?c_id=1&objectid=11400333, accessed July 10, 2015.

Walker, D. 1999. *Anxious Nation: Australia and the Rise of Asia 1850–1939*. St Lucia: University of Queensland Press.

Watson, I. 2014. "Are the PUPs Pauline's progeny? Populism and political alienation among Australian voters," paper presented at Murray Goot *Festschrift*, Macquarie University, Sydney, December 2.

Wear, R. 2000. "One Nation and the Queensland Right," in M. Leach, G. Stokes, and I. Ward (eds), *The Rise and Fall of One Nation*. St Lucia: University of Queensland Press, 57–72.

Wear, R. 2002. *Johannes Bjelke-Petersen: The Lord's Premier*. St Lucia: University of Queensland Press.

Wear, R. 2008. "Permanent populism: the Howard government 1996–2007," *Australian Journal of Political Science*, 43(4): 617–34.

Wear, R. 2014. "Astroturf and populism in Australia: the convoy of no confidence," *Australian Journal of Political Science*, 49(1): 54–67.

Whitton, E. 2001. *The Hillbilly Dictator*, 2nd edn. Sydney: ABC Books.

CHAPTER 7

....

POPULISM IN CENTRAL AND EASTERN EUROPE

....

BEN STANLEY

"DEMOCRACY is a form of government, not a steam bath of popular feelings" (Dahrendorf, 2005: 13). Heretical as these words seemed at a revolutionary moment, they lurked in the minds of the new political elite at the beginning of the democratic transition in Central and Eastern Europe. Many of those who set about transforming the political and economic systems of these states had directly participated in the revolutions that brought about the downfall of communism, and were acutely conscious of the destructive potential of an excess of popular mobilization. There was, of course, an initial period of optimism, goodwill, and consent for liberal-democratic and capitalist reforms, but a backlash against the technocratic elites of transition was inevitable once the public began to experience the hardships of transition.

At first, the politics of populism was associated primarily with the fear that unscrupulous demagogues would seek to exploit the dissatisfaction of the masses with the painful outcomes of transition reforms, resulting in the emergence of ideologically radical populist challengers. However, in the context of new and volatile party systems, populism offered political entrepreneurs a means to aggregate support from a variety of groups who had different reasons to be discontented with mainstream political elites, avoiding the need to articulate a distinct, consistent, or even coherent political program. In the first section of this chapter, I outline two theories of radical and centrist supply-side populism that flow from these initial observations. According to the radical theory, populism in Central and Eastern Europe would consist in a backlash against the liberal politics of post-communist transition and the elites responsible for implementing these reforms. According to the centrist theory, populists would largely exploit dissatisfaction with corrupt and incompetent leaders, rather than rejecting the politics of transition.

The rest of the chapter consists in testing these theories against the evidence to date. My main argument is that empirical evidence clearly supports *both* radical and centrist theories of supply-side populism. Drawing on the work of country specialists and comparative studies of populist party ideology, I identify the key populist players in the ten countries of Central and Eastern Europe[1] where democratization and party-system building proceeded relatively uninterrupted over the twenty-five years since the end of communism, classifying them according to whether they were radical or centrist populists. Using primary analysis of expert opinion surveys, I find that the two main subsets of populist parties have provided distinct and persisting elements of the ideological landscape of Central and Eastern Europe, even if there has been significant turnover of parties themselves.

However, it is important not to overstate the extent to which populism has shaped the nascent party systems of the region. Examining the electoral strengths of these parties, I argue that while populism played an important role in defining ideological choices, in most countries of the region non-populist parties remained dominant both electorally and in terms of government formation, and there was no general rise in populism over the period, but significant country-level variation.

Populist Ideology
as Entrepreneurial Strategy

In recent years, discussion of populism has largely devolved into two competing sets of theories: those which define it as a political style, and those which define it as an ideology. The following analysis is rooted firmly in the latter, and in particular in the literature on populism as a "thin ideology" (Mudde, 2004; Stanley, 2008; see also Mudde in this book). There are two reasons why the ideological approach is more fruitful for the empirical investigation of CEE populism. Firstly, "political style" approaches to populism focus on how politicians conduct themselves in communicating a message, but not necessarily on the substance of that message itself. The unconventional character of the populist style is often conflated with demagoguery, so that populism is understood and evaluated negatively against the benchmarks of "respectable" political behavior, "reasonable" visions and principles, and "realistic" policy. The populist style is thereby understood to incorporate all elements of political life in a liberal democracy that fail to achieve these benchmarks. This is particularly problematic in the context of CEE transition, where any refusal to abide by the dry, pragmatic, and technocratic canon of political norms and conduct often sufficed to attract the epithet of populist.

Secondly, in the relatively unstructured party systems of CEE, political entrepreneurs had clear incentives to create populist ideologies in the search for electoral support, rather than simply rely on a particular mode of political appeal. Both ideologies and styles can be strategic choices, but ideology goes beyond that: it gives shape not only to how people *experience* politics but also to how they *conceive* of politics. The purpose of an ideology is to simplify the complex world of politics, aggregating and mobilizing cohorts of voters around shared understandings of how the political world operates, and how it ought to operate. In circumstances where social cleavages were inchoate and voters' perceptions of their own interests uncertain, voters looked to politicians not only to reflect their views, interests, and values, but also to structure them. Some politicians opted for more complex "thick ideologies" and identified with the interests of distinct social groups. However, the top-down nature of transition reforms and the multiple resentments and uncertainties generated by those reforms gave others the opportunity to create simple and compelling narratives of blame, solidarity, and moral solace. Populism's conceptual structure is ideal for the articulation of such narratives, and its simple, easily communicable message about politics made it an attractive entrepreneurial strategy for politicians aiming to make an immediate impact upon a politically fluid and relatively unsophisticated electorate.

RADICAL OR CENTRIST? TWO THEORIES OF POST-COMMUNIST POPULISM

Radical Populism: Responses to the Politics of Transition and Globalization

The expectation that populism would be an important feature of post-communist politics stemmed from the observation that transition to democracy was largely a political project designed and implemented by political elites. If bottom-up popular protest had played a significant role in the downfall of communism, the contours of the new democracies would be shaped at the top. However, to say that a reaction by the people against political elites was likely to occur does not imply much about the nature of that reaction. According to one theoretical approach to populism as a practical political ideology, to achieve concrete political goals populism must be combined with "thicker" ideologies which fill out its limited set of concepts with a fuller set of principles and policies.

The prevalence of radical right-wing forms of populism in Western Europe initially encouraged scholars of Central and Eastern European party politics to focus their attention on the potential for this kind of populism to emerge in the region. The collapse of communist state structures and one-party systems was thought to be conducive to the resurgence of "age-old antagonisms, ethnic racisms, and historic rivalries" (Hockenos, 1993: 4) which parties of the populist radical right could readily exploit. A deterioration in economic conditions would exacerbate tensions between ethnic groups, leading parties to articulate political appeals that focused not only on the identity politics of ethnic nationalism but also on "financial nationalism" (Johnson and Barnes, 2014) and welfare chauvinism.

The theory of populism as one pole of a nascent political divide in Central and Eastern Europe is consistent with broader theories of the relationship between populism and the political mainstream. Kriesi and his collaborators (Kriesi et al., 2006; 2008) placed the growth of the Western European populist radical right in the context of an emergent

"integration versus demarcation" cleavage, arguing that the social changes of globalization generated distinct cohorts of relative "winners," who benefited from economic,
cultural, and political openness, and relative "losers," who were exposed to greater risk.
Mainstream political parties were expected to formulate "integrationist" programs for
winners, combining open markets, cultural liberalism, and support for supranational
political integration. Radical and populist challengers of left and right would articulate
the "demarcationist" demands of losers, offering to protect the national economy from
global competition, preserve national cultural identity and values, and oppose supranational political integration.[2]

The prevailing model of post-communist transition to democracy required the creation of a fully functioning capitalist economy, the building of liberal-democratic institutions, and the establishment and protection of the rights of the individual. As this model
was imitative of globalization processes in Western Europe, it was logical to expect
that it would exert a similar impact on social divides and their politicization by elites.
Kitschelt (1992: 16) argued that the clash of interests between relative winners and losers
of transition would lead to the alignment of the main axis of competition between parties which offered pro-market, cosmopolitan, and internationalist policies, and parties
which offered particularist, interventionist, and anti-integrationist policies. Since integration with international institutions—in particular, the European Union—was one of
the key elements of the orthodox model of post-communist transition, radical populists
would also have an incentive to articulate Euroskeptic appeals, thereby differentiating
themselves from mainstream acceptance of integration.

Centrist Populism: Competence, Probity, and Newness

The theory of radical populism assumes that Central and Eastern European party politics will become more ideologically structured over time, and that populism will play an
important role in the coalescence of this structure. In contrast, the "centrist populism"
theory is founded in the contention that Central and Eastern European party politics
is, and to a large extent will remain, ideologically "hollowed out" in comparison to its
Western European counterpart, with parties competing over claims to competence and
moral probity rather than distinct policy platforms. Here, the "thick ideological" content of populist parties' appeals is minimal or non-existent, to the extent that the parties
appear—whether by design or by omission—to be more moderate and "centrist."

This theory takes the legacies of communist rule for party-system building as
a point of departure. The legacy of a hegemonic communist party system hindered
the development and institutionalization of ideologically differentiated and electorally distinctive political parties after the end of communism, with the vast majority of
parties in the region built from the top down by political elites, possessing only loose
organizational structures, a restricted membership base, and often a rather indistinct
ideological profile (Kopecký, 1995; van Biezen, 2005). The obligatory nature of political
participation under communism, and the omnipresence of an official and increasingly

moribund ideology inculcated an attitude of political cynicism among the citizens of communist regimes. In the post-communist era this could be expected to foster strong anti-ideological and anti-party sentiments, and encourage an "us versus them" narrative of political competition. In such circumstances, politics would be rooted not in opposition to the content of a dominant ideological position taken by establishment parties, but in opposition to the dominance of establishment parties per se (Mishler and Rose, 1997; Rose, 1995). Furthermore, the pathologies of communist-era economies, the lack of developed civil societies under communism, and, in some cases, the prevalence of informal rules and norms led to corruption becoming a significant problem for the newly democratized post-communist states (Karklins, 2005). In these circumstances, the fight against corruption could assume sufficient salience to serve as a substitute for the "thick" ideologies with which populism has tended to combine in Western Europe.

According to the theory of centrist populism, these legacies created a potentially fertile opportunity structure for populism at the center of the party system. Parties which had not yet been tainted by participation in government (or, at an earlier stage, the negotiation of transition from communism) could appeal to the people against allegedly corrupt and incompetent mainstream elites. These parties would emphasize the need to reform political institutions and create new channels for democratic expression, tackle corruption, replace inefficient and incompetent elites, and offer new political actors the opportunity to govern. Such aims did not require these parties to espouse a clear and consistent set of programmatic principles. They could oppose the institutional status quo without offering the radical right's ethnic nationalism and civic illiberalism, and seek to mitigate the social costs of transition while not sharing the radical left's opposition to capitalism (Hanley and Sikk, 2014: 2).

This is not to suggest that these parties would *necessarily* lack thick-ideological commitments or principles. As Učeň (2007: 47) notes, the centrism of these parties might derive from ideological inconsistency rather than intentional moderation, with aggregate policy stances comprising a mixture of apparently contradictory proposals (such as left-wing and right-wing economic policies). Yet their distinguishing feature would be a pragmatic approach to the thick-ideological aspects of their appeal, and the foregrounding of qualities such as competence, probity, and newness.

Contesting Liberal Democracy: Radical Populism from the Fringes to the Mainstream

The diverse literature on radical populism in the region yields a relatively straightforward narrative. During the first decade of transition, the typical radical populist party was a "purifier" fighting a lone and mostly unsuccessful battle against an allegedly corrupt, collusive post-communist establishment, on behalf of an ordinary people bearing the brunt of the upheavals of transition. Yet although disenchantment with the outcomes of transition and mainstream political elites persisted, radical populists who maintained a narrow focus on the hardships of transition tended to have limited electoral appeal. In some countries, radical populism remained at the margins or disappeared entirely; in others, mainstream parties built on the anti-establishment rhetoric of these parties to develop a radical critique of liberal democracy which had wider appeal.

Against the Hardships of Transition: Radical Populism in the 1990s

As predicted by the theory of radical populism, numerous parties of the radical right emerged in response to the immediate hardships of transition, combining a populist appeal with ethnic nationalism, authoritarianism, financial nationalism, and welfare chauvinism. However, contrary to the theory, the first wave of radical populists did not succeed in anchoring one pole of their party systems. Instead, they largely suffered the same problems experienced by many of their mainstream counterparts, being short-lived, poorly organized, faction-ridden, and lacking in influence.

Only three populist radical right parties emerged in the early 1990s and persisted into the second decade of transition. The most successful of these was the Greater Romania Party (*Partidul România Mare*, PRM), which gained a fifth of the vote at the turn of the millennium. PRM's program combined glorification of national interests and values with anti-semitic, anti-Roma, and anti-Hungarian rhetoric, and with a nativist-chauvinist economic program; and it emphasized the need to stand up for the interests of "our people" against foreign financial organizations, foreign governments, and the domestic elites which collaborate with them (Smrčková, 2012: 214). This is the populist radical right policy platform in a nutshell, and it was echoed in the political appeal of the other two long-lasting populist radical right parties: the Slovak National Party (*Slovenská národná strana*, SNS) (Učeň, 2007: 52) and the Slovenian National Party (*Slovenska nacionalna stranka*, SNS) (Krašovec, 2012: 273–4). Both of these parties oscillated between ethnocentric irredentism and the glorification of violence and more pragmatic expressions of exclusionist nationalism.

Most of the first wave of radical right populist parties failed to consolidate and broaden their support. The most prominent example was the Association for the Republic—the Republican Party of Czechoslovakia (*Sdruženi pro republiku—Republikánska strana Československa*, SPR-RSČ), which was set up in 1989, first won parliamentary representation in 1992, and remained in parliament until 1998, after which it fragmented. Party leader Miroslav Sládek achieved particular notoriety for the provocative and demagogic manner in which he attacked a post-communist elite establishment comprising communists and elements of the anti-communist dissident intelligentsia, whose seizure of power had allegedly prevented a genuine post-communist revolution (Hanley, 2012: 74). The Hungarian Truth and Life Party (*Magyar Igazság és*

Élet Pártja, MIÉP), which placed particular emphasis on the "non-Hungarian" character of the domestic establishment of former communists and "Jewish elites" (Vratislav Havlik, 2012: 146), entered the Hungarian party system in 1998, but failed to make a lasting impression.

Other populist radical right parties of the 1990s were either "flash" parties which had a brief impact on the party system, or ephemeral minor parties which had none. Examples of the former include the Estonian National Independence Party (*Eesti Rahvusliku Sõltumatuse Partei*, ERSP), which emerged from the radical wing of the anti-communist dissident movement and played an important role in the first few years of Estonia's reclamation of statehood and transition to democracy, but faded thereafter, and the Bulgarian National Radical Party (*Bălgarska nacionalna radikalna partija*, BNRP) (Mudde, 2007: 305–6). Examples of the latter include the Latvian For Fatherland and Freedom (*Tēvzemei un Brīvībai*, TB) party, the Romanian National Unity Party (*Partidul de Uniune Naţională a Românilor*, PUNR), and the Slovenian National Right (*Slovenska nacionalna desnica*, SND) (Mudde, 2007: 306–7).

There were far fewer examples of radical left-wing populism. The only prominent case during the early 1990s was the Union of the Workers of Slovakia (*Združenie robotníkov Slovenska*, ZRS), a radical left party which split from the moderate Party of the Democratic Left (*Strana demokratickej ľavice*, SDĽ) in 1994. Rather than appeal to a distinct class, ZRS instead attacked the elite as an egoistic coterie that placed its own interests above those of the losers of transition. The involvement of the ZRS in the controversial 1994–1998 coalition government significantly impaired its ability to attack the governing elite, and it did not return to parliament (Deegan-Krause and Haughton, 2009: 830).

Against the Liberal Establishment: Radical Populism in the 2000s

The second decade of transition saw the emergence of a new wave of radical populists who benefited from the "transition fatigue" of the electorate and their disenchantment with mainstream parties. On the right, the League of Polish Families (*Liga Polskich Rodzin*, LPR) succeeded where its predecessors in Poland had failed, harnessing the considerable potential of Catholic-nationalist movements to a political critique of enforced Westernization and its impact on Polish traditions (Liga Polskich Rodzin, 2006: 5–6). In Bulgaria, the National Union Attack (*Natsionalen Sayuz Ataka*, ATAKA) party emerged just prior to the 2005 election, appealing to a homogeneous and unified ethnic Bulgarian people against ethnic Turks and Roma (Smilov, 2008: 17). Ethnic exclusionism was also the leitmotif of Movement for a Better Hungary (*Jobbik Magyarországért Mozgalom*, Jobbik), which rose to become the third largest party in the Hungarian parliament by 2010.

The Syrian refugee crisis in the summer of 2014 and the prospect of imposed quotas for resettling immigrants provided a new outlet for radical populist parties to give vent to nativism and xenophobia. The issue of immigration, a staple of the Western European radical right political discourse for many years, was previously of low salience in CEE politics and thus of limited potential for populist exploitation. However, in the wake of the Syria crisis, parties which emphasized their opposition to immigration immediately reaped benefits: the Kukiz Movement (*Kukiz'15*) entered the Polish parliament in 2015 as the third largest party in part as a result of its implacable opposition to refugee quotas. The strongly Euroskeptic Czech Dawn of Direct Democracy (*Úsvit přímé demokracie*, ÚSVIT) also took up the refugee issue.

On the radical left, Poland's Self Defence (*Samoobrona Rzeczpospolitej Polskiej*, SRP) party exploited rising public discontent with the politics and politicians of transition to enter parliament as the third largest party in 2001. SRP's ideological appeal emphasized opposition to economic liberalism and the need to ensure a more equitable redistribution of the fruits of economic growth, combining this with attacks on the transition elite, international finance, and the institutions of the European Union, all of which were held culpable for the parlous economic circumstances in which transition losers found themselves. However, radical left populists remained significantly less common than their right-wing counterparts. The relative absence of left-wing populism reflected the compatibility of nationalist, traditionalist, and authoritarian attitudes with anti-market economic stances. Right-wing populists were able to articulate this combination of ideological views without difficulty, whereas populists who laid claim to a left-wing identity had to be more careful in associating themselves with non-progressive political currents.

The only party to make a success of left-wing populism was the Slovak Direction–Social Democracy (*Smer–sociálna demokracia*, Smer-SD—commonly known as SMER). Founded in 1999, SMER initially avoided taking ideological sides, arguing that it was standing up for a general public which had been "abandoned and mistreated by the elite" during the first decade of transition (Učeň, 2007: 57). However, after a disappointing performance in the 2002 elections, the party opted to make more explicit its commitment to the social democratic principles it had tended to side with previously, positioning itself as a socially sensitive alternative to the governing center-right bloc (Spáč, 2012: 246). However, after the party's victory in the 2006 election, SMER undertook another shift in its profile, maintaining its identification with the left, but departing from its populist rhetoric. Rather than a radical left-wing populist party SMER is perhaps better viewed as a centrist populist party which undertook a leftward shift.

While radical left-wing populism disappeared, radical right-wing populism persisted and thrived after being taken up by formerly mainstream parties. The participation of LPR in the short-lived "populist coalition" that governed in Poland during 2006 and 2007 stimulated a turn to the right on the part of its senior coalition partner, the post-Solidarity party Law and Justice (*Prawo i Sprawiedliwość*, PiS). While PiS was considered part of the political mainstream after its emergence in 2001, its leadership had contested the legitimacy of transition elites since the early 1990s. During its term in office, PiS increasingly outbid its coalition partners for populist rhetoric and sought to outflank LPR to the right, resulting in the ejection of the latter from the party system. In Hungary,

Fidesz—Hungarian Civic Alliance (*Fidesz—Magyar Polgári Szövetség*, Fidesz) underwent a similar shift. In parliament since the beginning of transition, for much of that period Fidesz was regarded as a party of the establishment. However, after losing power in 2002, the party embarked on an increasingly radical shift in programmatic priorities and rhetoric, competing with Jobbik on the terrain of ethnic nationalism while openly rejecting liberal constitutionalism. On regaining power in 2010, Fidesz used its supermajority in the Hungarian parliament to promulgate a new constitution and implement a series of controversial reforms to the media, electoral system, and state institutions.

The success of parties such as PiS and Fidesz pointed to a dynamic not initially envisaged by the theory of radical populism: the radicalization of mainstream parties. While radical populists largely failed to consolidate their positions in post-communist party systems, they nevertheless cleared a path for parties which had previously been more moderate in character and which were seen by the electorate as more credible and trustworthy. In this manner, radical populism remained an important element of many party systems in the region, despite the churn of radical populist parties.

Anti-Elitism for Moderates: The Rise of Centrist Populism

The theory of centrist populism was based on the expectation that populists would be best placed to exploit the dissatisfaction of voters with the corruption and incompetence of incumbent elites. As such, it is not surprising that this form of populism became much more significant in the second decade of transition, after the rotation of parties in successive elections provided justification for the argument that "they have had their turn." Yet while radical populism was the dominant form in the region during the 1990s, several parties provided a foretaste of centrist populism during this decade.

Moderate, but Mostly Marginal: Centrist Populism in the 1990s

By far the most prominent and successful centrist populist party of the first decade of transition was the People's Party—Movement for a Democratic Slovakia (*Ľudová strana—Hnutie za demokratické Slovensko*, ĽS-HZDS or HZDS). HZDS's policy platform was rather ambiguous, and the nature of its populism was quite unusual in that the party emerged from the founding elite of the Slovak Republic. In this sense, it is something of an anomaly with respect to the theory of centrist populism, which holds that such parties should emerge in response to the inadequacies of the political mainstream. While other centrist populist parties presented themselves as new alternatives to an outmoded elite, HZDS depicted itself as a party of the people against a "grand coalition" of forces conspiring to remove it from power (2012: 242).

After a controversial full term in office between 1994 and 1998, the party reacted to attempts to isolate it politically by repositioning itself as a "normal" party. HZDS's departure from populism coincided with its decline as a force in Slovak politics, but not with the disappearance of Slovak centrist populism. The upheaval in the Slovak party system between 1998 and 2002 led to the emergence of new centrist populist parties, albeit ones much less prominent and successful than their predecessor. The Party of Civic Understanding (*Strana občianskeho porozumenia*, SOP) emerged as a reaction to the polarization of Slovak politics, criticizing all political elites for their corruption and inability to compromise. However, after joining the coalition government in 1998, SOP soon moderated its attacks on the elite (Deegan-Krause and Haughton, 2009: 830). The Alliance of the New Citizen (*Aliancia Nového Občana*, ANO) combined a center-right economic profile with criticism of an increasing gap between the people and the self-interested elite (Spáč, 2012: 245). As with SOP, the populist appeal of this party did not last beyond its first election, after which it concentrated on developing its liberal appeal (Deegan-Krause and Haughton, 2009: 832).

Elsewhere, centrist parties were peripheral. Učeň (2007: 59) notes two cases in Latvia, Movement for Latvia (*Tautas Kustība Latvijai*, TKL) and the Democratic Party "Saimnieks" (*Demokrātiskā Partija "Saimnieks"*, DPS), both of which expressed moderate populist opposition to neoliberalism. Other examples include the Bulgarian Business Block (*Balgarski Biznes Blok*, BBB) (Cholova, 2012: 76–7) and the mysterious Party X (*Partia X*) in Poland.

"They Have Had their Turn": Centrist Populists and the Politics of Newness in the 2000s

Centrist populism became a much more prominent feature of Central and East European party systems in the second decade of transition. After several elections, electorates in the region were increasingly disenchanted with established parties, which were perceived to have failed to deal with numerous deficiencies of post-communist governance, most notably corruption. Centrist populism was also a relatively "cost-free" way for new parties to make an electoral impact: while attacking the elite from a distinct thick-ideological position restricted the electoral potential of new parties, centrist populists could appeal to a range of voters purely on the basis of their dissatisfaction with the elite, rather than with reference to the specific nature of that dissatisfaction.

This was certainly the case in Bulgaria, where the emerging cleavage crumbled with the return in 2001 of the former king of Bulgaria, Simeon II, who formed the National Movement Simeon II (*Natsionalno Dvizhenie Simeon Vtori*, NDSV). NDSV's campaign was based on downplaying cleavages among the people while attacking the political elite for corruption and incompetence (Cholova, 2012: 77). However, once in power it continued to implement the liberal-orthodox transition model and departed from its populist attacks on the previous elite (Smilov, 2008: 17), leading to a slow decline and eventual exit from the party system in 2009. It was replaced by Citizens for European Development of Bulgaria (*Grazhdani za Evropeysko Razvitie na Balgariya*, GERB), which came to power in 2009 with a similar political appeal that combined the explicit eschewal of ideological differences and cleavages with an emphasis on anti-corruption (Smilov, 2008: 19).

The Baltic States also saw the emergence of centrist populist parties. Res Publica (*Erakond Res Publica*, RP) gained a quarter of the votes in the 2003 Estonian parliamentary elections by presenting itself as a "purifying bridge" that spanned the existing cleavages, promoting greater public participation in the political process instead of the closed, centralized methods of decision making associated with the political establishment (Balcere, 2012: 57; Učeň, 2007: 59). Once in power, RP struggled with the problem of how to retain its claim to purity. As it failed to realize its vision of a new politics, its popularity waned, and it was unable to revive its former anti-establishment appeal, moving toward a more traditional center-right ideological position and dropping its populist rhetoric. In Latvia, the New Era Party (*Jaunais laiks*, JL) emerged just prior to the 2002 parliamentary election in the context of widespread dissatisfaction with constant political upheaval and scandals over the privatization of state enterprises. Combining a center-right emphasis on neoliberalism and conservatism with an uncompromisingly populist critique of the incompetence and moral turpitude of the mainstream governing parties, JL overturned the existing configuration of parties, gaining nearly a quarter of the votes and becoming the largest party in parliament (Balcere, 2012: 58). In contrast to its Estonian counterpart, JL remained highly critical of the political establishment while in power (Učeň, 2007: 59–60). Lithuania also saw the emergence of centrist populism as a response to profound public dissatisfaction with the social democratic and conservative parties that competed for power during the 1990s. The Labour Party (*Darbo Partija*, DP) eschewed identification with particular ideological options, rejecting what it saw as old-fashioned ways of doing politics and attacking elite corruption and incompetence (Učeň, 2007: 58). In the 2004 election campaign, it became the largest party, and remained a significant element of the Lithuanian party system thereafter.

The focus on competence, probity, and newness helps to explain the significant turnover of centrist populist parties. Indeed, the theory of centrist populism implies this kind of party churn. As Haughton and Deegan-Krause (2015: 15) note, centrist populists help fuel the expectation that politicians will be corrupt and incompetent, which makes it even more difficult for those parties to escape the same kind of scrutiny. When centrist populists became part of the establishment—whether as parties of opposition or parties of power—it is increasingly difficult for them to act as if they remained outside it.

This was illustrated by the further wave of centrist populism with the onset of the 2008 economic crisis and the rise of illiberal democracy in the region at the start of the third decade of post-communist democracy. These parties maintained the focus of their predecessors on the corruption and incompetence of political elites—some of whom had come to power themselves as a result of populist appeals—but also exploited a more general lack of confidence in the institutions of post-communist democracy amid Europe-wide economic and political crisis, emphasizing the need for institutional reform as well as elite replacement.

In Romania, the People's Party—Dan Diaconescu (*Partidul Poporului—Dan Diaconescu*, PP-DD) gained third place in the 2012 parliamentary elections by seeking to stand up for the interests of the people who had suffered the negative impact of the economic crisis, and call to account the elite which was held responsible for engendering the crisis (Smrčková, 2012: 207). In the Czech Republic, the re-emergence of populism in 2010 disrupted the hitherto stabilising party system. In the parliamentary elections of that year, Public Affairs (*Věci veřejné*, VV) entered parliament on a platform which rejected the politics of left and right and advocated counteracting the influence of entrenched elites through the use of instruments of direct democracy and the recall of elected politicians. After joining a coalition government—in spite of its professed opposition to all established political parties—the party experienced internal ructions and failed to return to parliament at the 2013 elections (Vlastimil Havlik, 2012: 111–12). Ordinary People and Independent Personalities (*Obyčajní Ľudia a nezávislé osobnosti*, OĽaNO) also broke through in 2010. While formally a party, OĽaNO purported to create a platform for non-partisans who could not run independently, positing itself as the "representative and defender of ordinary people" against the clientelistic and corrupt elite (Spáč, 2012: 238).

The Hungarian case offered an intriguing variant on centrist populism with the emergence of Politics Can Be Different (*Lehet Más a Politika*, LMP) in 2010. Like other centrist populist parties, LMP rejected the prevailing political style and the established political parties (Vratislav Havlik, 2012: 143). However, while populists typically criticize liberal constitutionalism as a set of restraints on the expression of the popular will, LMP emphasized the importance of these restraints as a system of checks and balances on authoritarian governments. To counteract the influence of unaccountable elites, LMP advocated giving ordinary people greater input into candidate selection and increasing the capacity of the state to regulate the influence of economic oligarchs on party politics (Vratislav Havlik, 2012: 150–1).

POPULIST PARTIES AND THE STRUCTURE
OF POLITICAL COMPETITION

The foregoing discussion suggests that there is empirical support for both the radical and centrist theories of populism. These findings, which draw on a largely qualitative secondary literature, can be corroborated by analysis of data on the ideological placement of parties and the creation of schematic maps of populist party attitudes. First,

I map populist and non-populist parties in the two-dimensional "integration versus demarcation" issue space, one dimension of which consists of attitudes to the economy, and the other of non-economic attitudes pertaining to democratic freedoms and rights.[3] Second, I map these parties according to their positions on the "non-economic" dimension and the stance they take on European integration.[4] This mapping makes it possible to evaluate the extent to which parties designated in the literature as radical and centrist populist conformed to those categories, and to identify the ideological relationships between populist and non-populist parties.

The most useful source of data for this purpose is the Chapel Hill Expert Survey (Bakker et al., 2015), which has included Central and Eastern European countries since 2002. This dataset provides information on party positions for all countries of interest, and for most parties identified in the preceding section. While this limits the analysis to 2002 and after, the four data points covered by the dataset are sufficient to illustrate the persistence of certain patterns characteristic of the two types of populist party discussed in the preceding sections, and to illustrate how those parties relate to broader tendencies.

The placements of populist and non-populist parties in the integration-demarcation issue space are plotted in Figure 7.1. Two conclusions can be drawn from this distribution. First, cumulated expert opinion about party placements largely bears out the qualitative distinctions between radical right-wing populists and centrist populists. While there is some overlap, the majority of the radical right-wing parties were more culturally conservative than centrist populists. They were also somewhat more economically interventionist, although the difference in this respect is less clear.

Second, the distinction between radical right-wing and centrist populist parties persisted over time, while the distribution of non-populist parties changed. In 2002, the majority of both populist and non-populist parties were either demarcationist or integrationist in character, with few parties holding a combination of left-wing economic ideas and progressive views on democracy and human rights, or a combination of right-wing economic ideas and conservative views on democracy and human rights. By 2014, non-populist parties were more ideologically diverse overall, with no clear relationship between economic and non-economic positions. However, as the trend lines show, the populist parties consistently fitted the expected integration-demarcation line of competition. Radical right-wing populists remained strongly demarcationist, while centrist populists largely retained their moderate positions. The two main subsets of populist parties persisted in spite of a changing ideological landscape.

Figure 7.2 shows the placement of parties in the issue space created by the intersection of attitudes toward European integration and non-economic attitudes. The placement of populist parties in Figure 7.2 illustrates the differences between radical right-wing populist parties and centrist populist parties. In almost all cases, centrist populists were at least moderately in favor of EU integration, and in some cases very much in favor. The trend lines show that the relationship between non-economic attitudes and attitudes to

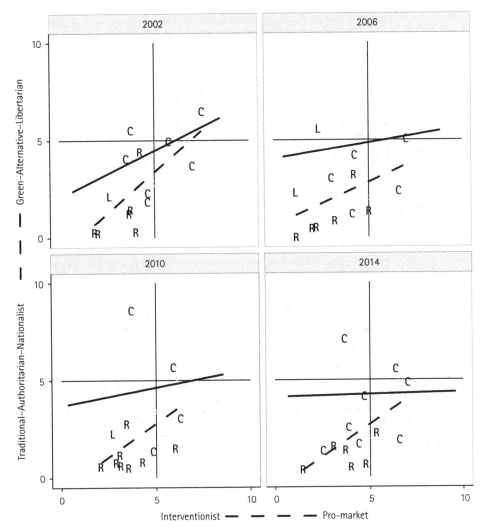

FIG. 7.1 Placement of parties in integration-demarcation issue space, by year. Author's own work, based on data taken from the Chapel Hill Expert Survey Trend File 1999–2014 (Bakker et al., 2015). Each of the letters and points corresponds to single political party. "L" refers to left-wing populists; "R" refers to right-wing populists; "C" refers to centrist populists, and the grey points identify non-populist parties. The continuous trend line shows the trend for non-populist parties, while the dashed trend line shows the trend for populist parties. Plots were generated using the ggplot2 package for the R programming language (Wickham, 2010).

EU integration was driven by the demarcationist and anti-EU attitudes of radical populist parties. While populists with culturally conservative attitudes were more likely to be opposed to EU integration, non-populist parties with similar cultural attitudes were more likely to be in favor of integration. Consistent with the two theories outlined above, the distinction between radical and centrist populists persisted throughout the period of interest, with radical populists remaining considerably more likely to combine

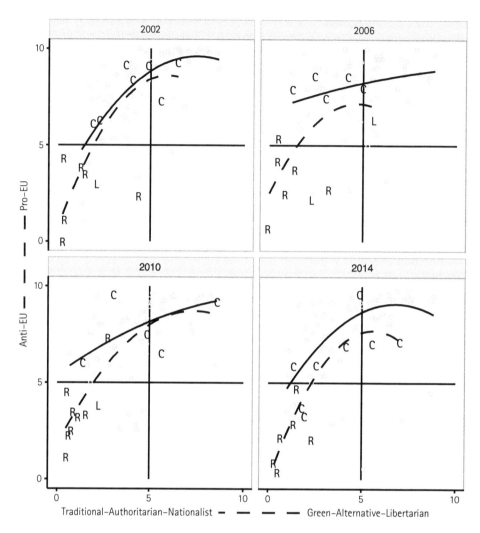

FIG. 7.2 Placement of parties in non-economic/EU issue space, by year. Author's own work, based on data taken from the Chapel Hill Expert Survey Trend File 1999–2014 (Bakker et al., 2015). Each of the letters and points corresponds to single political party. "L" refers to left-wing populists; "R" refers to right-wing populists; "C" refers to centrist populists, and the grey points identify non-populist parties. Quadratic trend lines were calculated using robust regression to minimize the influence of outliers. The continuous trend line shows the trend for non-populist parties, while the dashed trend line shows the trend for populist parties only. Plots were generated using the ggplot2 package for the R programming language (Wickham, 2010).

Euroskeptic and non-economic attitudes. Notably, with one exception, the few cases of left-wing populism that occurred were also consistent with this pattern, suggesting that there were fewer actual differences between the nominal designations of "left-wing" and "right-wing" populist parties than the labels might suggest.

THE ELECTORAL STRENGTH OF POPULIST PARTIES: VOTE SHARE AND PARTICIPATION IN GOVERNMENT

The empirical evidence shows that both the theory of radical populism and the theory of centrist populism were correct, with numerous examples of parties which corresponded to one or the other of these types. Populist parties played an important role in defining ideological choices, particularly during the second decade of post-communist democracy. However, an analysis of the electoral strength of these parties shows that in most countries of the region non-populist parties remained dominant both electorally and in terms of government formation. There was no general rise in populism over the period, but significant country-level variation.

Figure 7.3 shows the share of the vote obtained by populist and non-populist parties from the first post-communist elections onward. Populist parties are disaggregated by type, and those which subsequently participated in government are highlighted in bold. At almost every election, non-populist parties received a majority of the vote; the exceptions were Bulgaria in 2009 and Hungary in 2010 and 2014. There was no evidence of the rising electoral importance of populism across the region as a whole. Instead, there was significant differentiation between countries.

Slovenia stood out for a persistently low level of support for populists, declining from 10 percent in 1991 to only 2.2 percent in 2014. No populist party held power at any point during that period. Several countries saw moderate or fluctuating levels of support for populist parties. In Czech Republic, populism disappeared from the party system at the end of the 1990s, only to reappear at the start of the third post-communist decade, with populist parties gaining nearly 30 percent of the vote in 2014 and centrist populist parties gaining power. In Estonia, low levels of support for radical right-wing populists in the 1990s were followed by a breakthrough for centrist populism in 2003, but populism disappeared from the Estonian party system thereafter. In Latvia, centrist populist parties gained the support of a significant minority between 1995 and 2006, and entered government in 2002. In Lithuania, centrist populists gained power in 2000, and remained a significant presence, if one for which support fluctuated, while in Romania the radical right remained a constant presence throughout, but with diminishing support in recent years.

Four countries stand out as ones in which populism was particularly important, although the ways in which populism was important were different in each case. In Slovakia, populists remained a constant presence in the party system, with centrist, radical right, and left-wing populist parties each participating in government over the first quarter-century of post-communist democracy. Support for these parties fluctuated, but populism remained a well-established element of the party-political landscape. Support for populist parties also persisted throughout in Bulgaria, but here

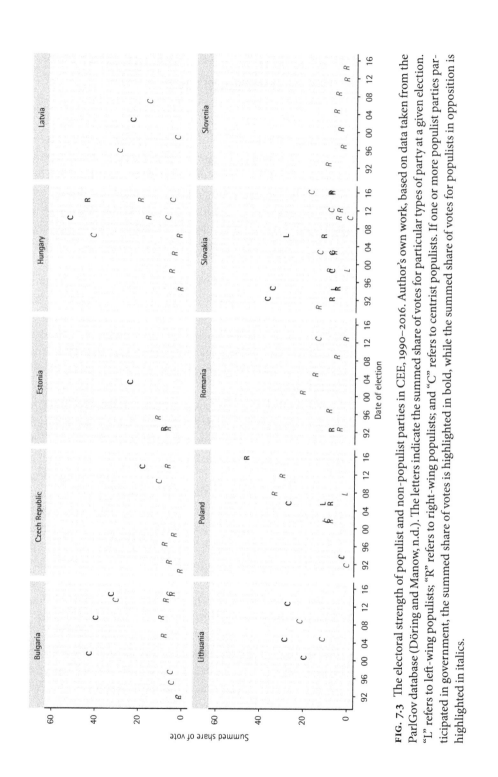

FIG. 7.3 The electoral strength of populist and non-populist parties in CEE, 1990–2016. Author's own work, based on data taken from the ParlGov database (Döring and Manow, n.d.). The letters indicate the summed share of votes for particular types of party at a given election. "L" refers to left-wing populists; "R" refers to right-wing populists; and "C" refers to centrist populists. If one or more populist parties participated in government, the summed share of votes is highlighted in bold, while the summed share of votes for populists in opposition is highlighted in italics.

centrist populist parties clearly dominated, supporting and forming governments from 2001 onwards, while radical right populists remained of minor importance. Conversely, centrist and left-wing populism was crowded out in Poland by the rise of radical right-wing populism, which became a central element of the party system by 2011 and was crucial to the rotation of governments. In Hungary, meanwhile, populist parties dominated the party system from 2010 onwards, holding power but also participating in opposition.

CONCLUSIONS

By the latter half of the second post-communist decade, the majority of Central and Eastern European countries had turned themselves into functioning—if far from flawless—liberal democratic states. However, events in the region prompted some concern about the emergence of democratic "backsliding," prompted by the return of numerous unresolved problems of transition and exacerbated by the lifting of the conditionality imposed by the EU accession process. One observer wrote pessimistically of the rise of populism in CEE, observing that "[g]overnments, political parties and political movements from Poland, Slovakia, Hungary, Romania, Bulgaria and Slovenia to the Baltic states have declared that they represent the true voice of the common people against the corrupt elites" (Bugaric, 2008: 192).

Yet while the rise of populism was clearly discernible in some of these countries, the threat of radical populism should not be overstated. As I have argued in this chapter, populism in Central and Eastern Europe was not purely radical in nature: no single dominant type of populism emerged in Central and Eastern Europe after the fall of communism. On the one hand, as in Western Europe, most radical populism was right-wing. As the quantitative analysis of populist party ideology showed, there was a distinct set of parties with an ideological profile that combined strongly authoritarian, traditionalist, and nativist attitudes with opposition to capitalism and European integration. However, while this remained the dominant type of populism found in Western European party systems, Central and Eastern Europe gave rise to a new subtype of populist party: the centrist populist party.

Centrist populism was marked by moderate or eclectic attitudes on political issues, a reluctance or refusal to be defined in accordance with traditional ideological dimensions, and above all an emphasis on the corruption and incompetence of established elites. Its emergence in Central and Eastern Europe was aided by the relative openness of the weakly consolidated party systems of the region. Centrist populists exploited the constant churn of parties in the region, profiting from the impatience of voters with incumbents and low levels of party identification and loyalty. However, in the absence of a broader programmatic appeal, centrist populists who gained office were particularly vulnerable to the perennial problem of populist parties: how to remain credible and relevant as an anti-establishment force after taking power. These parties often fell victim to the same public scepticism they had sought to cultivate when attacking established parties.

The emergence of centrist populists, and the relative weakness of radical right populism in most countries of the region, suggested that there was significant potential for populism to remain a relatively benign instrument for effecting the turnover of political elites, rather than a force for concerted opposition to the key tenets of liberal democracy. A counter-argument can easily be made: the ease with which parties moved from the mainstream to the radical right—Fidesz in Hungary and PiS in Poland being the prime examples—illustrated that the liberal democratic order remained vulnerable to a resurgence of radical populism, potentially to be stimulated by a deepening of the immigration crisis and declining faith in the governance capacities of EU institutions.

Nevertheless, as my analysis of the electoral strength of populist parties has shown, the relative weakness of populists in most countries of the region remained a strong argument against overly broad predictions of the regional rise of populism. While populism was a *significant* electoral force, it was *decisive* only in a minority of cases. Even in countries where populist parties enjoyed greater success, the strength of populism tended to fluctuate rather than accumulate, with populist parties remaining subject to the normal laws of party competition. Only in Hungary did populist parties succeed in amassing sufficient power to make changes to the political system that could not easily be overturned by competing parties.

The case of Central and Eastern Europe demonstrates that populism is not necessarily a vehicle for expressing anti-liberal sentiments. While many parties at the extremes of the dominant dimensions of political competition are populist, not all populist parties are at the extremes. Populism may emerge where political elites are resented for being remote and inattentive to the will of the people, or unwilling to tackle significant problems such as corruption. As much as they chafe at the restrictions that a liberal-democratic political system imposes upon the volition of political actors and the people they represent, not every populist is a sworn enemy of that system.

NOTES

1 These countries are Bulgaria, Czech Republic, Estonia, Hungary, Latvia, Lithuania, Poland, Romania, Slovakia, and Slovenia.
2 Hooghe et al. (2002: 968) found that while centrist and moderately left- or right-wing parties tended to be in favor of European integration, parties both of the radical right and the radical left were more likely to be opposed to it.
3 This composite dimension of non-economic issues is commonly referred to in the literature on party placement as the GAL-TAN dimension, where "GAL" stands for "Green-Alternative-Libertarian," and "TAN" stands for "Traditionalist-Authoritarian-Nationalist."
4 A similar mapping of economic attitudes and attitudes to European integration showed no clear pattern.

REFERENCES

Bakker, Ryan et al. 2015. "1999–2014 Chapel Hill expert survey trend file," *chesdata.eu*.

Balcere, Ilze. 2012. "Baltic Countries," in Vlastimil Havlik and Aneta Pinkova (eds), *Populist Political Parties in East-Central Europe*. Brno: MUNI Press, 39–71.

Bugaric, Bojan. 2008. "Populism, liberal democracy, and the rule of law in Central and Eastern Europe," *Communist and Post-Communist Studies*, 41(2): 191–203.

Cholova, Blagovesta. 2012. "Bulgaria," in Vlastimil Havlik and Aneta Pinkova (eds), *Populist Political Parties in East-Central Europe*. Brno: MUNI Press, 73–96.

Dahrendorf, Ralf. 2005. *Reflections on the Revolution in Europe*. New Brunswick: Transaction Publishers.

Deegan-Krause, Kevin and Tim Haughton. 2009. "Toward a more useful conceptualization of populism: types and degrees of populist appeals in the case of Slovakia," *Politics and Policy*, 37: 821–41.

Döring, Holger and Philip Manow. 2017. "Parliaments and Governments Database (ParlGov): Information on Parties, Elections and Cabinets in Modern Democracies. Development Version." http://dev.parlgov.org.

Hanley, Seán and Allan Sikk. 2014. "Economy, corruption or floating voters? Explaining the breakthroughs of anti-establishment reform parties in Eastern Europe," *Party Politics*: 1–12.

Haughton, Tim, and Kevin Deegan-Krause. 2015. "Hurricane season: systems of instability in Central and East European party politics," *East European Politics and Societies*: 0888325414566072.

Havlik, Vlastimil. 2012. "Czech Republic," in Vlastimil Havlik and Aneta Pinkova (eds), *Populist Political Parties in East-Central Europe*. Brno: MUNI Press, 97–134.

Havlik, Vratislav. 2012. "Hungary," in Vlastimil Havlik and Aneta Pinkova (eds), *Populist Political Parties in East-Central Europe*. Brno: MUNI Press, 135–61.

Hockenos, Paul. 1993. *Free to Hate*. London: Routledge.

Hooghe, Liesbet, Gary Marks, and Carole J. Wilson. 2002. "Does left/right structure party positions on European integration?," *Comparative Political Studies*, 35(8): 965–89.

Johnson, Juliet and Andrew Barnes. 2014. "Financial nationalism and its international enablers: the Hungarian experience," *Review of International Political Economy*, 22(3): 1–35.

Karklins, Rasma. 2005. *The System Made Me Do It: Corruption in Post-Communist Societies*. London: M.E. Sharpe.

Kitschelt, Herbert. 1992. "The formation of party systems in East Central Europe," *Politics and Society*, 20(1): 7–50.

Kopecký, Petr. 1995. "Developing party organizations in East-Central Europe: what type of party is likely to emerge?," *Party Politics*, 1(4): 515–34.

Krašovec, Alenka. 2012. "Slovenia," in Vlastimil Havlik and Aneta Pinkova (eds), *Populist Political Parties in East-Central Europe*. Brno: MUNI Press, 259–84.

Kriesi, Hanspeter et al. 2006. "Globalization and the transformation of the national political space: six European countries compared," *European Journal of Political Research*, 45(6): 921–56.

Kriesi, Hanspeter et al. 2008. *West European Politics in the Age of Globalization*, 1st edn. Cambridge: Cambridge University Press.

Liga Polskich Rodzin. 2006. "Skrót Programu Gospodarczego," in Inka Słodkowska and Magdalena Dolbakowska (eds), *Wybory 2005: Partie I Ich Programy*. Warsaw.

Mishler, William and Richard Rose. 1997. "Trust, distrust and skepticism: popular evalua-tions of civil and political institutions in post-communist societies," *The Journal of Politics*, 59(2): 418–51.

Mudde, Cas. 2004. "The populist zeitgeist," *Government and Opposition*, 39(4): 542–63.

Mudde, Cas. 2007. *Populist Radical Right Parties in Europe*. New York: Cambridge University Press.

Rose, Richard. 1995. "Mobilizing demobilized voters in post-communist societies," *Party Politics*, 1(4): 549–63.

Smilov, Daniel. 2008. "Bulgaria," in Grigorij Mesežnikov, Oľga Gyárfášová, and Daniel Smilov (eds), *Populism in Europe and the Americas: Threat or Corrective for Democracy?* Bratislava: Institute for Public Affairs, 13–35.

Smrčková, Markéta. 2012. "Romania," in Vlastimil Havlik and Aneta Pinkova (eds), *Populist Political Parties in East-Central Europe*. Brno: MUNI Press, 199–226.

Spáč, Peter. 2012. "Slovakia," in Vlastimil Havlik and Aneta Pinkova (eds), *Populist Political Parties in East-Central Europe*. Brno: MUNI Press, 227–58.

Stanley, Ben. 2008. "The thin ideology of populism," *Journal of Political Ideologies*, 13(1): 95–110.

Učeň, Peter. 2007. "Parties, populism, and anti-establishment politics in East Central Europe," *SAIS Review*, 27(1): 49–62.

van Biezen, Ingrid. 2005. "On the theory and practice of party formation and adaptation in new democracies," *European Journal of Political Research*, 44(1): 147–74.

Wickham, Hadley. 2010. *Ggplot2: Elegant Graphics for Data Analysis*. New York: Springer.

CHAPTER 8

POPULISM IN EAST ASIA

OLLI HELLMANN

INTRODUCTION

WHEN one peruses the academic literature on electoral politics in East Asia, one gets the quick impression that populist politicians and parties are everywhere: from the established democracy of Japan (Kabashima and Steel, 2007; Otake, 2009; Uchiyama, 2010) to the consolidated "third wave" democracies in industrialized South Korea and Taiwan (Shyu, 2008; Kimura, 2009; Matsumoto, 2009), to the developing democratic regimes in the Philippines, Thailand, and Indonesia (Hedman, 2001; De Castro, 2007; Pasuk and Baker, 2008; Okamoto, 2009). However, the problem with these empirical documentations of populism is that they are rarely ever based on established definitions of populism—and when they are, either definitions are applied in a rather lax manner or different definitions are combined to create incoherent analytical frameworks.

To address these conceptual shortcomings in the existing literature, the following chapter will employ the *ideological* approach to populism and provide a rigorous survey of populism in East Asia based on the following definition: "a thin-centered ideology that considers society to be ultimately separated into two homogeneous and antagonistic camps, 'the pure people' versus 'the corrupt elite,' and which argues that politics should be an expression of the *volonté générale* (general will) of the people" (Mudde, 2004: 543). The picture that emerges from this exercise is quite different: populist politicians and parties are, contrary to what a review of the existing literature suggests, an extremely rare species in East Asian democracies.

The chapter will offer an explanation for the dearth of populism in East Asia that is based on the more general argument that populism, as a thin ideology, rarely works on its own; rather, populist politicians tend to combine populism with other ideologies. This is because populism "can by itself offer neither complex nor comprehensive answers to the political questions that societies generate" (Mudde and Rovira Kaltwasser, 2013a: 498; also see Mudde in this volume). As the discussion will show, the ideological space in East Asia is highly distinctive, compared to the two regions that have received the most

attention in populism research: Latin America and Europe. First, the left-right divide in
East Asia is not structured by Marxist class theory, meaning that politicians do not have
access to a ready-to-use framework to describe the "people vs elite" divide in class terms.
Second, East Asian societies have not witnessed a shift towards post-material value orientations, as a result of which there is no room for populist politicians to position themselves as "defenders" of traditional values.

Moreover, the distinctiveness of the ideological space also helps explain why the
very few cases of populism that *have* emerged in East Asia in recent years do not easily
fall into categories of populism that were developed in Latin American and European
contexts: because broader reference frameworks (Marxism, globalization as a threat
to local culture) are not available, East Asian populists have had to draw heavily on
distinct narratives that only gain meaning within a country-specific context. This has
resulted in three highly distinctive types of populism: Joseph Estrada's *movie hero* populism, Thaksin Shinawatra's *agrarian* populism, and Prabowo Subianto's *nationalist*
populism.

More generally then, the argument that is advanced by this chapter is that the ideological space is an important contextual variable that shapes the opportunities and
constraints for populist politicians to establish themselves as significant players in the
electoral market.

Why Most Cases
of "Populism" Collapse

A review of the relevant academic literature shows that much of the existing work on
"populism" in East Asia shares an emphasis on the politician's status as an "outsider"
or "maverick."[1] Typically, studies proceed by describing how politicians construct their
outsider or maverick image through expertly crafted narrative scripts and visual cues,
arguing that this allows "populist" politicians to set themselves apart from the political establishment. For example, in the case of Japan, Otake (2009: 212) discusses how
Junichiro Koizumi—prime minister between 2001 and 2006—engaged in "theatrical
politics," playing "the role of hero in a drama that [was] carefully conceived and performed," and which presented Koizumi as "a traditional samurai" who bravely took on
vested interests within his own party. In Indonesia, Mietzner (2015: 2–3) makes the case
for how Joko Widodo (popularly known as Jokowi)—who rose from furniture maker to
Governor of Jakarta and Indonesian President—"offered his humility, politeness, and
hard work ethics as a counternarrative to the arrogance, hostility and self-indulgence of
the political establishment." Similarly, in the Philippines, Thompson (2010) highlights
how rags-to-riches stories feature prominently in the campaign messages of "populist"
politicians, as this makes them stand out against oligarchs and political dynasties who
otherwise dominate the electoral contest.

"Outsider" or "maverick" status, however, does not equal "populism"—at least if the ideological definition of populism is applied. As discussed in much detail elsewhere (Mudde in this volume; Rovira Kaltwasser, 2014; Mudde and Rovira Kaltwasser, 2013a; Stanley, 2008; Abts and Rummens, 2007), the ideological approach requires three key boxes to be ticked in order for the "populist" label to be attached to a particular politician. First, for a politician to be classified as populist, he or she must regularly make reference to "the people," using moral terms to describe the people as "pure." Second, the politician must pit the pure people against a "corrupt elite," with "corruption" again defined in moral terms—that is, as an impairment of virtue and moral principles. Third, the politician's message must be based on the belief that nothing should constrain "the will of the (pure) people." Populists therefore oppose the institutions of representative democracy, which they portray as being controlled by political elites who are out of touch with the people. Instead, populists cultivate a direct relationship with their followers, claiming to embody Jean-Jacques Rousseau's idea of the *volonté générale*. Practically, this often translates into putting forward alternative processes for political decision-making—processes that circumvent the institutions of interest mediation that have been hijacked by elite interests.

Of these different boxes, "populist" politicians in East Asia at best meet the procedural requirement. For example, studies of Japanese "populism" bring out how Prime Minister Koizumi bypassed his own political party—the Liberal Democratic Party (LDP), which he depicted as being strangled by "forces of resistance" against his political and economic reform program—by taking a top-down approach to decision-making and breaking with informally institutionalized norms (e.g. Uchiyama, 2010: 12–16). Indonesian President Jokowi, on the other hand, created a unique "participatory, people-centered leadership style" (von Lübke, 2014) by introducing the practice of *blusukan*—an approach to politics that centered around impromptu visits to local markets or neighborhoods aimed at discussing citizens' concerns directly and openly. Other examples of "populist" politicians who applied new thinking to the process of politics include Taiwanese President Chen Shui-bian, who—after being elected in 2000—established a nonpartisan "government of the people" and relied on direct democratic mechanisms for policy making (Matsumoto, 2009), and South Korean President Roh Moo-hyun, who rode to victory in the 2002 elections on the back of an online movement of "netizens" (Kim, 2008).

However, although often advocating a more direct style of politics that circumvents core institutions of representative democracy (such as political parties and parliaments), so-called "populists" generally fail to make a moral distinction between "the people" and "the elite." Specifically, this distinction does not emerge because "populists" either do not identify an enemy of "the people" or because they identify very narrowly defined enemies, rather than making a blanket critique of "the elite" as a homogenous group. Examples of the former include Jokowi, who has stayed away from polarizing rhetoric and anti-elite sentiments, and is described by Mietzner (2015: 26) as a "polite populist," not recognizing that anti-elitism is a key element of the ideological definition of populism. Likewise, rags-to-riches "populists" in the Philippines and other parts of Southeast

Asia have also refrained from attacking the elite. Instead, they cultivate a "friend of the poor" image around the themes of "benevolence" and "compassion"—for example, by giving away money and houses on popular TV shows.[2]

"Populists" in Northeast Asia, on the other hand, *do* identify an enemy of "the people"; however, in violation of the ideological definition of populism, they do not treat "the elite" as a homogeneous group. Instead, they single out particular actors within the political system whom they perceive to be working against the interests of "the people." Scholars of "populism" in Northeast Asia—seemingly unaware of the ideological definition of populism—acknowledge this themselves when they say that "populist" politicians "do not deliver *general* critique of existing political actors and structures, but *specific* critique against *specific* actors and structures" (Lindgren, 2015: 585; emphasis in the original). For example, Koizumi portrayed "pork barrel" politicians and bureaucrats as the "bad guys," diagnosing that the particularistic dealings of these groups had been undermining Japan's economic performance and the "the people's" well-being (Uchiyama, 2010). Chen Shui-bian aimed his attacks against the dominant *Kuomintang* (KMT), based on the argument that the party had, for decades, been ruling the country as part of the Chinese mainland, thereby ignoring the voice of the Taiwanese majority of "the people" (Matsumoto, 2009). Roh Moo-hyun, who capitalized on strong anti-American sentiment among the electorate, did not—unlike populists in Latin America, such as Hugo Chávez—engage in a paranoid style of politics that pictured South Korea as a colonial outpost of American interests; instead, he put forward a rather sober analysis of why US-Korean relations required re-negotiation (Kimura, 2009).

To sum up, it can be said that, in many cases, politicians whom the academic literature on East Asian "populism" has classified as "populist" are better described as outsiders or mavericks with a novel approach to politics. Crucially, most existing work on East Asian "populism" is not based on a rigorous application of the ideological definition of populism, which requires that populist politicians make a moral distinction between two homogeneous groups: "the people" and "the elite." However, this is not say that the region has been completely devoid of populist politicians. After filtering the empirical evidence through the conceptual framework of the ideological approach, we are left with three significant cases of populism. It is to these true cases of populism that we turn next.

THREE RARE CASES OF POPULISM

Despite placing heavy emphasis on the moral distinction between "the people" and "the elite" as a key definitional element of populism, the ideological approach argues that this distinction tends to make for a poor mobilizational tool in elections. The reason is that the concepts of "the people" and "the elite" are incredibly thin, and do thus not allow politicians to construct complex arguments regarding the solution of social problems. As a result, populist politicians will commonly have to borrow from other ideologies to add an additional dimension to the exclusively moral definition of these two key concepts. In fact, the ideological approach to populism considers this additional dimension so important that it identifies different subtypes of populism based on the question of which particular secondary feature populists employ to draw a more elaborate distinction between "the people" and "the elite." The two most common sub-types are *socioeconomic* (or *inclusionary*) populism, which uses a class-based interpretation of society in order to distinguish the people and the elite, and *xenophobic* (or *exclusionary*) populism, which defines the people on the basis of nativism, primarily attacking the elite for putting the interests of ethnic minorities over those of the "native" majority (Mudde and Rovira Kaltwasser, 2013a; 2013b). While socioeconomic populism is the dominant sub-type of populism in Latin America, xenophobic populism is the most widely used label to classify populist parties in Europe.

However, reflecting what Moffitt calls the "Atlantic bias" (2015: 293), these populism sub-types are somewhat difficult to apply to East Asia. Specifically, the three relevant cases of populism that we are left with after the careful sifting in the previous section do not easily fall into either the socioeconomic or the xenophobic category. Rather, we are confronted with a case of *movie hero* populism in the Philippines (Joseph Estrada), a case of *agrarian* populism in Thailand (Thaksin Shinawatra), and a case of *nationalist* populism in Indonesia (Prabowo Subianto).

Estrada's "Movie Hero" Populism

Joseph Estrada first came to prominence as a movie actor. Estrada's most famous role was that of a Robin Hood-like character who regularly breaks the law for the greater good—a role that Estrada played in countless movies in the 1970s. At the same time, Estrada embarked on a political career that saw him serve as mayor of San Juan (a city in the Metro Manila region), as a member of the Senate, and as vice-president of the Philippines, and which culminated in Estrada winning the 1998 presidential election. After being ousted by a military coup in 2001 and running for the presidency again in 2010 (albeit this time unsuccessfully), Estrada was elected mayor of Manila in 2013.

As a politician, Estrada developed an incredibly thin version of populism, based exclusively on his popular movie roles, to draw a clear distinction between "the morally upright people" and "the corrupt elite." For one, his cinematic Robin Hood image allowed Estrada to portray himself as a benefactor of the poor—captured, for example, in the tag lines "Erap for the poor" (*Erap para sa mahirap*) in 1998 and "With Erap there is prosperity" (*Kung may Erap, may ginhawa*) in 2010. Estrada further cultivated this portrayal with a "down with the people" campaign style, which saw him share meals with urban slum residents and tour poverty-stricken areas in a *Jeepney*—the most popular means of public transport for the poor. Moreover, not only did Estrada's cinema past allow him to paint himself as "someone from the edges of the elite who prefers the company of the poor," but his movie roles also led to a public image of "someone exposing elite oppression and hypocrisy" (Rocamora, 2009: 45). This provided Estrada with an opportunity to set himself apart from the political establishment—dominated by powerful dynastic clans and their local electoral machines—and attack the oligarchical elite for ignoring the common people.

Finally, Estrada used his previous movie roles as "a down-trodden hero struggling for his rights against corrupt elites" (Thompson, 2010: 259) to construct an alternative style of politics. For example, during his time in the presidential office, Estrada projected himself:

> as a savvy president who governed through personal connections, cut across bureau-cratic red tape, showed disdain for formality, and resorted to sophisticated and street-smart cunning. Thus, he presented himself as a populist president who did not need a ruling party and who simply relied on his popularity among the impoverished masses. (De Castro, 2007: 942)

In office, Estrada tried to further cement his reputation as a friend of the poor through policies and executive actions. For example, during his presidency, Estrada implemented an extensive poverty-reduction program that was designed to deliver a range of public services and interventions to the poor (the *Lingap Para sa Mahihirap* program). Similarly, as mayor of Manila, Estrada rolled out free public health care and a public housing program to the city's poorest families. However, it should be noted that the independent assessment of Estrada's pro-poor policies has been rather negative. For instance, Balisacan (2001) concludes that the *Lingap* program was largely used in a pork-barrel fashion to reward other politicians for their support.

To sum up, Joseph Estrada constructed a populist message by relying on his background as a movie actor to tap into "a familiar trope in Philippine society and cinema—that of the outlaw/criminal/rebel" (Hedman, 2001: 41). The result was an unusually thin version of populism that defined "the people" and "the elite" only in moral terms; it did not borrow from ideological frameworks or political discourses to provide a more specific definition of these two homogeneous groups.

Thaksin's Agrarian Populism

In Thailand, Thaksin Shinawatra, on the other hand, embodied an unusual case of agrarian populism. Generally speaking, agrarian populism distinguishes itself from other sub-types of populism by describing the peasantry as "biologically and morally the most healthy people," while industrialists and urban economic interests are depicted as a threat to the peasantry's virtues and authenticity. The case of Thaksin is unusual in the sense that the ideological approach to populism deems agrarian populism to be "a dying breed that merely inspires some rural social movements in the developing world" (Mudde and Rovira Kaltwasser, 2013a: 495). However, it was precisely such a rural social movement that had generated a national discourse that allowed Thaksin to develop his agrarian brand of populism.

In the beginning, the movement's protest activity—primarily aimed against new land and forest management policies as well as a major dam building project, all of which had fueled deep insecurities among the peasantry regarding access to land, water, and forest resources—remained fragmented and localized. It was only in 1995, when different local groups came together to form the Assembly of the Poor, that the movement assumed a national character. In 1997, the Assembly launched a massive march on Bangkok, which would turn into a three-month long "occupation" of the government district. This event gave the Assembly unprecedented media attention and allowed for concrete local griev-ances to be synthesized into a broader narrative account of how distinct "cultures" and "ways of life" in the countryside were being destroyed by urban-driven "development" (Missingham, 2003). The most visible element of the movement's message was the "Village of the Poor," which—by symbolically bringing the "rural village" into the heart of the city—"highlighted the destructive relationship between the city and the coun-tryside, symbolizing a rural village in crisis, threatened by the industrial development and environmental exploitation on which the economic prosperity of the city depends" (Missingham, 2002: 1662).

Overall, the Assembly of the Poor thus actively contributed towards the emergence of a political discourse that displayed all the key features of agrarian populism. In this dis-course, "rural Thailand was pictured, at least in its ideal form, as a repository of positive social values being lost in the scramble towards urban modernity, these values including respect for traditional authorities such as local Buddhist monks, as well as the extended family village community" (Glassman, 2010: 1302).

Initially, Thaksin—a self-made telecommunications mogul who had first entered pol-itics in 1994 as a candidate for the *Palang Dharma* Party (PDP)—paid little attention to this discourse.[3] Then, after launching his own political vehicle in 1998, the *Thai Rak Thai* (TRT) party, Thaksin positioned himself as a capable manager of the state and the econ-omy. Above all, he appealed to business interests, promising to rescue the Thai economy from the 1997 Asian financial crisis by, in particular, modernizing the bureaucracy and the political system.

However, subsequently, Thaksin decided to broaden his electoral appeal, when, shortly before the 2001 election, he was tried on corruption charges. More specifically, to secure popular support in the face of the impending trial, Thaksin "copied and pasted" some of the demands of the Assembly of the Poor directly into the TRT campaign plat-form, including ideas for a moratorium on rural debt, a village development fund, and a public health care scheme. And yet, although these policy proposals were framed in the Assembly's "vocabulary about strengthening communities and building recov-ery from the grassroots," Thaksin's strategic adjustment did not constitute a qualitative shift towards populism. As Pasuk and Baker (2012: 86) point out, Thaksin's main focus remained on "transforming Thailand in the interests of business." What is more, after the TRT won the 2001 election in a landslide, Thaksin moved to suppress rural protest and the organizations behind it.[4] Thaksin openly declared that he wanted *kan muang nin*—quiet or calm politics. The state, according to Thaksin, was to be managed like a business enterprise, following "a top-down strategic approach to policy management"

(McCargo and Ukrist, 2005: 177) without much input from below. The contrast to the populist belief that citizens possess the ability to make the laws could not have been more striking.

It was only during the run-up to the 2005 election that Thaksin went through the radical transformation to become a populist politician. This sudden shift can be explained by the fact that, over his first term as prime minister, Thaksin had made bitter enemies in both society and the political system. To begin with, through his political reform program and his personal popularity among the rural poor, Thaksin antagonized the core institutions of Thailand's "network monarchy"—that is, the king, the bureaucracy, and the military.[5] Moreover, the business sector had grown increasingly alienated from the government, accusing Thaksin of benefitting a small circle of cronies in the economic policy domain. Finally, due to Thaksin's increasingly authoritarian style of governing, the NGO community had also taken on a more hostile tone. So, again, as before the 2001 elections, Thaksin sought to bolster his position by mobilizing popular support. Yet, this time, the adjustments to the electoral strategy were more dramatic, as Thaksin discarded the pro-business language and reinvented himself through the "immoral city vs traditional countryside" discourse outlined previously. Of major importance for the discussion here, Thaksin thereafter displayed the three key elements of the ideological definition of populism.

First, Thaksin made a more conscious effort to portray himself as one of "the people," with "the people" being treated synonymously with "the peasantry"—in particular, from the northeast of Thailand, a region that has a long history of revolting against the imposition of Bangkok control. This effort is vividly summarized by Pasuk and Baker (2012: 88):

> His public appearance and speech underwent a makeover in this period. He shed his business suit in favour of shirtsleeves with buttons open at the neck, sometimes all down to his waist, and his hair lightly tousled. He stopped littering his speeches with English to denote internationalism and modernity, and instead used dialect and earthy humour. He stopped quoting Bill Gates and similar international figures, instead often mentioning his own family and sex life.

To further enhance this new image, the TRT campaign team actively sought "opportunities for Thaksin to be photographed in homely situations—emerging from a village bath-house in a common man's lower cloth; transported on a village tractor; riding a motorbike down a dusty village street; accepting flowers from toothless old ladies." Moreover, the TRT replaced its logo—"Think new, act new"—with a new one: "The heart of TRT is the people." Finally, these rhetorical frames were backed up with new policy proposals aimed at eradicating poverty in the countryside—including, for example, an extension of the village development fund, new cheap loan schemes, professional training schemes, and cheaper school fees.

Second, having come under attack from urban-based interests—the "network monarchy," the business community, and middle-class-led NGOs—Thaksin suddenly found himself in a good position from which to compose an image of himself as an "enemy" of Thailand's political elite. Thus, with the 2005 elections approaching, "Thaksin now constantly distinguished himself from an old guard of top bureaucrats, politicians and intellectuals who he claimed had never 'worked for the people'" (ibid.).

Third, based on this distinction between the people and the elite, Thaksin launched a crusade against the institutions of representative democracy, arguing that these often got in the way of "working for the people"; instead, Thaksin made the case that a powerful executive would deliver the people greater benefit. And in true populist style, "Thaksin offered himself as the vehicle through which the wishes of the people could be translated into action on the part of the government" (Pasuk and Baker, 2008: 69). In particular, this took the form of "mobile cabinet meetings," which were designed for local voters to present petitions to the government and for the government to publicly pledge support to rural communities.

Having outlined Thaksin's agrarian populism in some detail, it needs to be added that this was an experiment with a very short life span. After winning the 2005 election—with an even larger margin than the 2001 election—Thaksin was forcefully kicked out of office by a military coup in September 2006 while attending a United Nations meeting in New York. From "exile," Thaksin re-launched the TRT as the *Pheu Thai* Party, putting his sister Yingluck in charge. However, although winning the 2011 election, *Pheu Thai* eventually suffered the same fate as the TRT: in May 2014, Yingluck was impeached from office and, two weeks later, the military took over the government by a coup d'état.[6]

Prabowo's Nationalist Populism

While Thaksin is a textbook case of agrarian populism, Prabowo Subianto's take on populism is more difficult to classify. As highlighted by various observers of Indonesian politics, Prabowo copied heavily from Hugo Chávez when developing his populist campaign message (e.g. Aspinall, 2015; Mietzner, 2015). Seen through the lens of the ideological approach to populism, Chávez's populist style can be described as a particular brand of socio-economic (or inclusionary) populism that uses the ideology of *Americanismo* (i.e. pan-national Latin American identity) to draw a moral distinction between "the common people" and "foreign powers that are interlinked with the local oligarchy" (Mudde and Rovira Kaltwasser, 2013b: 164). Like Chávez, Prabowo identified foreign interests as the enemy of "the people"; however, unlike Chávez, he defined "the people" in ethnic terms. Prabowo's populism was, thus, similar to the xenophobic (or exclusionary) populism of European radical right-wing parties, characterized by strong nationalist tones, yet proposed policies that were aimed at fostering the *inclusion* of the poor in economic life rather than *excluding* certain groups of the population from economic life. In other words, Prabowo's nationalist populism sits somewhere between the two sub-types of socio-economic and xenophobic populism.

Similar to Thaksin, Prabowo's populist message only crystallized over time. According to Mietzner (2015: 21), it was only after Prabowo—who had pursued a successful military career under Suharto's New Order regime (1966–1998)—was denied nomination as the presidential candidate of the former regime party, Golkar, in 2004 that "he began the process of transforming himself into a maverick populist." Specifically, after establishing his own political party, the Great Indonesian Movement (*Gerakan Indonesia Raya*, Gerindra), Prabowo looked to carve out a niche in the electoral market by developing an ultra-nationalist demagogy that set himself apart from other politicians. To do so, Prabowo appropriated symbols and signifiers from Indonesia's anti-colonial movement—in particular, by modeling himself on Indonesia's founding father and first president, Sukarno. In the run-up to the 2014 presidential election, this communicative strategy reached its peak: Prabowo dressed in a Sukarno-style safari suit and mimicked Sukarno's signature oratory, using mid-century vintage microphones when delivering speeches. Campaign rallies resembled military parades, saturated with nationalistic symbols and references to Prabowo's highly decorated career as a soldier. For example, Prabowo often made a dramatic arrival by helicopter and inspected paramilitary troops on horseback.

In addition, Prabowo pinpointed an enemy of "the Indonesian people." As Aspinall (2015: 15) explains, "[t]he basic line was simple, and one that has been a staple of Indonesian nationalism since the Dutch period: Indonesia was a country blessed by great natural riches that were being sucked out by foreigners." Moreover, Prabowo condemned Indonesia's political and economic establishment in blanket terms, accusing "the elite" of acting as stooges of foreign interests and impoverishing the Indonesian people through their self-serving behavior. Based on this clear distinction between "the people" and "the elite," Prabowo put forward a program of economic nationalism that was aimed at—for example—achieving national self reliance in food production and re-negotiating contracts with foreign companies in the natural resource sector.

Finally, as is characteristic of populist politicians, Prabowo showed open disdain for the political process. In particular, keeping in line with the nationalistic theme of his campaign, Prabowo argued that political reforms implemented since the end of the Suharto regime had produced a democratic system that was "too liberal" and too closely based on the Western conception of democracy. Instead, Prabowo argued that a "benign authoritarian regime" would be more "suitable" for Indonesians. Specifically, Prabowo called for a return to the original 1945 constitution, which stipulated an executive-heavy political system that did not put significant constraints on the president's authority.

Unlike Estrada and Thaksin, Prabowo had—at the time of writing—never won the top executive post. In 2009, the election law prevented Prabowo from running in the presidential election, due to the fact that Prabowo's party, Gerindra, had failed to win the required number of parliamentary seats to field a candidate. In 2014, Prabowo was narrowly defeated by the aforementioned Jokowi (47 vs 53 percent). However, Gerindra emerged from the 2014 parliamentary elections as Indonesia's third largest party, thus securing Prabowo's position as one of Indonesia's most influential political actors in the medium term.

Explaining the Dearth (and Death) of Populism in East Asia

So far, this chapter has shown two things. First, when the ideological definition of populism is strictly applied, most cases of East Asian "populism" identified by the existing academic literature break down. The reason is that these so-called "populists" fail to tick one of the key definitional boxes of populism: instead of pitting a *homogeneous* "elite" against "the people," East Asian pseudo-populists either identify *specific* actors as enemies or refrain from using antagonistic language altogether. Second, the discussion has demonstrated that the few cases of populism that make it through the screening process do not easily fall into the dominant sub-types of populism that have emerged out of the study of Latin American and European electoral politics in recent years. Rather, what we are left with is an unusual case of "movie hero" populism (Estrada), a rare case of agrarian populism (Thaksin), and a case of nationalist populism (Prabowo) that displays characteristics of both the socio-economic and the xenophobic sub-types of populism.

The following sub-section will explore these findings through the lens of "discursive institutionalism." Broadly speaking, discursive institutionalism argues that for a discourse to be successful in persuading its audiences it must be based on forms of ideas (for example, narratives, frames, collective memories, images) that are relevant to the institutionalized ideational frameworks used by these audiences to make sense of the world around them. As succinctly summarized by Schmidt (2008: 313):

> A successful discourse "gets it right" in terms of a given "meaning context" according to a given "logic of communication." This suggests not only that the ideas in the discourse must "make sense" within a particular ideational setting but also that the discourse itself will be patterned in certain ways, following rules and expressing ideas that are socially constructed and historically transmitted.

One aspect of East Asia as an ideational setting that is frequently highlighted by scholars is the distinctiveness of the ideological space compared to other geographical regions. To begin with, although research has shown that citizens in East Asia recognize and use the left-right divide as a means to express their political identity (e.g. Jou, 2010), there is considerable evidence that the left-right divide is structured not by Marxist class theory and economic controversies over the role of the state, but instead by political controversies that are specific to East Asian societies (e.g. Dalton, 2006; Shin and Jhee, 2005). This, to a large extent, has to do with the fact that, historically, the political Left in East Asia has not been given much space to develop organizationally (e.g. Hewison and Rodan, 1994): socialist and communist organizations, which typically first emerged as anti-colonial movements in the 1920s and 1930s, only enjoyed a brief period of relative openness after the end of World War II; with the arrival of the Cold War, they were violently repressed. What is more, US-backed authoritarian regimes achieved—compared to other parts of the developing world—remarkable capitalist development, which greatly reduced the appeal of socialism. In this context of a struggling and oppressed Left, it was generally middle-class movements that pushed for democratization in the 1980s and 1990s rather than labor movements, as, for example, in Latin America.

In short, the social dimension of class is largely muted in East Asia. Consequently, a populist discourse that draws a class-based distinction between the economically marginalized "people" and the wealthy "elite" would convey very little meaning to voters. Or to put it in the terminology of discursive institutionalism, socio-economic populism would not "make sense" within the particular ideational setting that is East Asia, as class-based controversies are not a prominent theme in the ideological framework of target audiences. Instead, as outlined earlier, politicians aiming to mobilize voters of lower socio-economic status tend to find that cultivating a "friend of the poor" image is a more efficient electoral strategy than engaging in antagonistic class-based rhetoric. However, following the ideological approach to populism, this excludes these politicians from being classified as "populist."

Moreover, not only are socialist/capitalist controversies marginal in structuring politics in East Asia, but post-material issues, which play an important part in dividing European electorates, are also less salient. This is particularly notable for societies in Northeast Asia, which despite having achieved levels of economic development comparable to Western Europe, lag behind in terms of the development of post-material value orientations. At least this is according to Welzel's *emancipative values index* (EVI), which has been designed as an improvement on previous measures of post-material attitudes, based on people's views on two dimensions: (1) freedom of choice and (2) equality of opportunities (2013: 67). Welzel himself places societies in Northeast Asia in the culture zone of the "Sinic East," highlighting that there exist significant differences in the development of post-material values compared to the "West." How to interpret these differences, however, is subject to a fierce academic debate: while some scholars argue that "Asian" culture, with its emphasis on values such as communitarianism, conflict avoidance, and respect for hierarchy, is incompatible with post-material interests and individualistic self-expression (e.g. Bomhoff and Gu, 2012; Pye, 1985), others have argued that value orientations in Asia are indeed moving in the direction predicted by Inglehart's theory of "culture shift" (Inglehart, 1990)—in other words, increasing material security allows people to focus on post-material concerns for happiness (e.g. Welzel, 2012; Wang, 2007).

For our purposes here, this debate is tangential; what matters is that post-material values are not very common in the industrialized democracies of Northeast Asia. Unlike in Europe, the ideational setting does therefore not provide fertile ground for a xenophobic (or right-wing) populist discourse pitting "the common people" against an "elite" that promotes universal paradigms and global integration at the expense of the cultural traditions and popular values of "the heartland." Certainly, outsider and maverick politicians in Northeast Asia have repeatedly incorporated symbols of national identity into their campaign messages—examples include Junichiro Koizumi visiting the controversial Yasukuni shrine and Roh Moo-hyun fanning the dispute with Japan over the Dodko islands. However, they have done so without identifying a homogeneous "elite" that is threatening to displace traditional values with their own post-material agenda. Instead, values of national identity continue to be firmly entrenched in the dominant culture, leaving little opportunity for populist politicians to position themselves as defenders of these values.

To sum up the discussion so far, the ideational setting in East Asia militates against the emergence of the two main sub-types of populism: socioeconomic and xenophobic populism. This is because voters do generally not attach much relevance to class-based analyses of society nor do they feel that traditional belief systems are under threat. Populism has only emerged in cases where politicians were able to construct a distinction between "the people" and "the elite" based on country-specific discourses: Estrada played on the popular Robin Hood theme in Filipino cinema to develop his brand of "movie hero" populism, Thaksin's agrarian populism fed off the "immoral city vs traditional countryside" conflict that had arisen in Thailand in the mid-1990s, and Prabowo borrowed narrative elements from Indonesia's anti-colonial struggle to paint himself as "the people's" heroic protector against foreign exploitation. In other words, real cases of populism have only sprung up where individual politicians succeeded in weaving their outsider image into existing "people vs elite" narratives. Cases of East Asian populism have thus been the product of politicians' personal characteristics and local ideational frameworks.

Ultimately, however, all three populist projects were marked by failure: while Prabowo—at the time of writing—had been unsuccessful in winning the top executive post, both Estrada and Thaksin were removed from power through military coups. The primary cause for failure has been the same in all three cases: populism clashed with a different discourse of political representation—namely, that of "good governance." Similar to the East Asian variants of populism, the "good governance" discourse "avoids direct class-based appeals and claims instead to act in the interest of the nation as a whole" (Thompson, 2010: 156). Essentially, the "good governance" discourse embraces a rational, technocratic conception of politics, defining "good politics" as "the clean politics of issues, transparency, and accountability" (Schaffer, 2002: 27). Across Southeast Asia, this discourse has repeatedly been invoked to mobilize mass support against populism's moral view of politics (see Rodan, 2012).

For example, in the case of Indonesia, a number of analysts conclude that Prabowo lost the 2014 presidential election because his "confrontational textbook" populism was a less efficient strategy for gathering votes than Jokowi's "pragmatic and technocratic" program for "improving government effectiveness" (Mietzner, 2015; also see Aspinall, 2015).

In the Philippines, Estrada won the 1998 presidential election in a landslide. Yet, once in office, he became increasingly worn down by the contradictions between his "movie hero" populism and the "good governance" discourse. As Rocamora (2009: 55–6) explains, Estrada's populism required him to carry his "culture hero" persona into the presidential office. The "good governance" discourse, however, postulates a very different understanding of "performance" in office. Hence, in January, 2001, as stories of booze-fueled "midnight cabinet" meetings, evidence of economic mismanagement, and allegations of corruption and cronyism mounted to suggest that Estrada was not an able president, massive street demonstrations—the so-called People Power 2 campaign—erupted in Manila, which, in turn, led parts of the military to withdraw their support for the government, leaving Estrada no other option but to resign.

In Thailand, as outlined earlier, Thaksin had—through his sheer popularity and his political reform program—antagonized the core institutions of the "network monarchy." These actors, in an attempt to undermine Thaksin's agrarian populism, began to deploy a counter-narrative that depicted the rural regions not as "centres of traditional community, social simplicity and moral rectitude," but as "socially backward, steeped in illegal activity, dominated by local mafia-like political bosses and using their democratic majorities in parliament to flout basic principles of 'good governance' through cronyist practices" (Glassman, 2010: 1302; also see Callahan, 2005). In September 2006, conservative forces drew on this rational "good governance" discourse to justify a military coup against Thaksin, arguing that "Thaksin's legitimacy based on elections was void because votes were secured dishonestly by direct vote buying or by populist lures"—electoral strategies that were made possible "because the rural electorate was still uneducated and naïve" (Pasuk and Baker, 2012: 91). Subsequently, key players of the "network monarchy" employed a similar good governance discourse to remove Yingluck from office on charges of corruption and mismanagement.

In short, a comparison between East Asia and those regions that have been the main focus of existing populism research (Europe, Latin America) helps to make the argument that the ideological space is an important contextual factor that shapes both the characteristics and the success of populism.

CONCLUSION

This chapter has shown that—contrary to what existing accounts in the literature claim—populist politicians are a very rare breed in the democracies of East Asia. At least that is the conclusion one has to draw when applying the ideological definition of populism. As has been demonstrated, most cases of "populism" in East Asia do not stand up to rigorous conceptual scrutiny, as politicians fail to tick one of the key elements of the ideological definition of corruption—that is, the requirement for politicians to draw a moral distinction between two homogeneous groups: "the people" and "the elite."

Through the analytical lens of discursive institutionalism, it has been argued that politicians struggle to draw a populist "people vs elite" distinction because East Asia provides a very distinct ideational setting compared to those geographical regions that have been the focus of populism research. Specifically, the ideational setting in East Asia does not provide broader frameworks that would allow politicians to construct "the people" and "the elite" in ways that are meaningful to target audiences. For one, unlike in Latin America, for example, the social dimension of class is largely muted in political discourses, thus precluding politicians from defining "the people" and "the elite" in socioeconomic terms. Moreover, the shift towards post-material values is not as pronounced as in European societies, which means that there is less space for populist politicians to brand themselves as the embodiment of more traditional values.

In the absence of such broader ideational frameworks, true cases of populism have only emerged where politicians were able to extract definitions of "the people" and "the elite" out of country-specific narratives and collective memories: in the Philippines, Estrada's "movie hero" populism has been making reference to popular cinematic representations of the outlaw; in Thailand, Thaksin's agrarian populism piggybacked on a public discourse that set the "moral countryside" against the "immoral city"; in Indonesia, Prabowo defined "the people" and "the elite" mainly in ethnic terms, drawing similarities between Dutch colonialism and modern global capitalism.

The small number of genuine populists in East Asia does not mean, however, that scholars of East Asian politics cannot contribute to more general debates on populism. For one, studying negative cases in more detail can help better understand the contextual conditions under which populism emerges. Moreover, East Asia experts can further advance our knowledge of how populists may provoke a polarization of the political discourse and undermine democratic consolidation.

Notes

1 Barr (2009) defines an outsider as "someone who gains political prominence not through or in association with an established, competitive party, but as a political independent or in association with new or newly competitive parties," while a maverick "is a politician who rises to prominence within an established competitive party but then either abandons his affiliation to compete as an independent or in association with an outsider party, radically reshapes his party."

2 Two typical examples of this type of politician are Manuel "Manny" Villar (Philippines) and Wiranto (Indonesia). The 2010 TV campaign ad for Villar—who, according to *Forbes* magazine, is among the ten richest Filipinos and outspent other candidates in the presidential election by a huge margin—demonstrates the "friend of the poor" image perfectly. The ad featured a short song, performed by children in one of Manila's shanty towns: "Have you ever swum in a sea of garbage? / Have you ever spent Christmas in the street? / That's our question. / Are you one of us? / Did you know that he can send you to school? / That he can help us get a job? / That his plan is a house for everyone?" Investing into a similar brand message, Wiranto—who had a distinguished military career under the Suharto regime and whose family is one of Indonesia's wealthiest—appeared several times on the TV show *Mewudjukan Mimpi* ("Realizing Dreams") in the run-up to the 2014 election. The show is loosely based on the reality TV program *Secret Millionaire* and featured Wiranto going undercover in poor communities to help common people in need, such as pedicab drivers and street vendors.

3 Much of the following discussion draws from Pasuk and Baker's (2008; 2009; 2012) work on Thaksin.

4 It needs to be pointed out that the proposed pro-poor policies were only one reason for the TRT's resounding electoral victory. Importantly, Thaksin—partly because of his sheer wealth—was able to attract large numbers of established politicians and their political machines into the newly formed party. Moreover, the only viable contender party, the Democrat Party, suffered from a massive public image problem, as it was widely viewed as having "collaborated" with the International Monetary Fund (IMF) in the implementation of an unpopular rescue package during the 1997 financial crisis.

5 On the concept of "network monarchy," see McCargo (2005).

6 First, on May 7, the Constitutional Court ruled that Yingluck and members of her cabinet had abused their authority when they transferred a national security council official in 2011, thereby paving the way for one of Yingluck's relatives to become the national police chief. Then, one day later, the anti-corruption commission voted to impeach Yingluck over accusations that she had failed to suspend the government's rice-subsidy program despite being aware that it was hemorrhaging money.

References

Abts, K. and S. Rummens. 2007. "Populism versus democracy," *Political Studies*, 55(2): 405–24.

Aspinall, E. 2015. "Oligarchic populism: Prabowo Subianto's challenge to Indonesian democracy," *Indonesia*, 99(1): 1–28.

Balisacan, A. M. 2001. "Did the Estrada administration benefit the poor?," in Amando Doronila (ed.), *Between Fires: Fifteen Perspectives on the Estrada Crisis*. Manila, Anvil, 98–112.

Barr, R. R. 2009. "Populists, outsiders and anti-establishment politics," *Party Politics*, 15(1): 29–48.

Bomhoff, E. J. and M. M.-L. Gu. 2012. "East Asia remains different: a comment on the index of 'self-expression values' by Inglehart and Welzel," *Journal of Cross-Cultural Psychology*, 43(3): 373–83.

Calahan, W. A. 2005. "The discourse of vote buying and political reform in Thailand," *Pacific Affairs*, 78(1): 95–113.

Dalton, R. J. 2006. "Social modernization and the end of ideology debate: patterns of ideological polarization," *Japanese Journal of Political Science*, 7(1): 1–22.

De Castro, R. C. 2007. "The 1997 Asian financial crisis and the revival of populism/neo-populism in 21st century Philippine politics," *Asian Survey*, 47(6): 930–51.

Glassman, J. 2010. "'The provinces elect governments, Bangkok overthrows them': urbanity, class and post-democracy in Thailand," *Urban Studies*, 47(6): 1301–23.

Hedman, E.-L. E. 2001. "The spectre of populism in Philippine politics and society: artista, masa, Eraption!," *South East Asia Research*, 9(1): 5–44.

Hewison, K. and G. Rodan. 1994. "The decline of the left in South East Asia," *Socialist Register*, 30: 235–62.

Inglehart, R. 1990. *Culture Shift in Advanced Industrial Society*. Princeton: Princeton University Press.

Jou, W. 2010. "The heuristic value of the left-right schema in East Asia," *International Political Science Review*, 31(3): 366–94.

Kabashima, I. and G. Steel. 2007. "How Junichiro Koizumi seized the leadership of Japan's Liberal Democratic Party," *Japanese Journal of Political Science*, 8(1): 95–114.

Kim, Y. 2008. "Digital populism in South Korea? Internet culture and the trouble with direct participation," *KEI Academic Paper Series*, 8(3).

Kimura, K. 2009. "A populist with obsolete ideas: the failure of Roh Moo-hyun," in K. Mizuno and P. Pasuk (eds), *Populism in Asia*. Singapore: NUS Press, 167–80.

Lindgren, P. Y. 2015. "Developing Japanese populism research through readings of European populist radical right studies: populism as an ideological concept, classifications of politicians and explanations for political success," *Japanese Journal of Political Science*, 16(4): 574–92.

McCargo, D. 2005. "Network monarchy and legitimacy crises in Thailand," *The Pacific Review*, 18(4): 499–519.

McCargo, D. and P. Ukrist. 2005. *The Thaksinization of Thailand*. Copenhagen: NIAS Press.

Matsumoto, M. 2009. "Populism and nationalism in Taiwan: the rise and decline of Chen Shui-bian," in K. Mizuno and P. Pasuk (eds), *Populism in Asia*. Singapore: NUS Press, 181–201.

Mietzner, M. 2015. *Reinventing Asian Populism: Jokowi's Rise, Democracy, and Political Contestation in Indonesia*. Honolulu: East-West Center.

Missingham, B. 2002. "The village of the poor confronts the state: a geography of protest in the assembly of the poor," *Urban Studies*, 39(9): 1647–63.

Missingham, B. 2003. "Forging solidarity and identity in the assembly of the poor: from local struggles to a national social movement in Thailand," *Asian Studies Review*, 27(3): 317–40.

Moffitt, B. 2015. "Contemporary populism and 'the people' in the Asia-Pacific region: Thaksin Shinawatra and Pauline Hanson," in C. de la Torre (ed.), *The Promise and Perils of Populism: Global Perspectives*. Lexington: The University Press of Kentucky, 293–316.

Mudde, C. 2004. "The populist zeitgeist," *Government and Opposition*, 39(4): 542–63.

Mudde, C. and C. Rovira Kaltwasser. 2013a. "Populism," in M. Freeden, L. T. Sargent and M. Stears (eds), *The Oxford Handbook of Political Ideologies*. Oxford: Oxford University Press, 493–512.

Mudde, C. and C. Rovira Kaltwasser. 2013b. "Exclusionary vs. inclusionary populism: comparing contemporary Europe and Latin America," *Government and Opposition*, 48(2): 147–74.

Okamoto, M. 2009. "Populism under decentralisation in post-Suharto Indonesia," in K. Mizuno and P. Pasuk (eds), *Populism in Asia*. Singapore: NUS Press, 144–66.

Otake, H. 2009. "Neoliberal populism in Japanese politics: a study of prime minister Koizumi in comparison with president Reagan," in K. Mizuno and P. Pasuk (eds), *Populism in Asia*. Singapore: NUS Press, 202–16.

Pasuk, P. and C. Baker. 2008. "Thaksin's populism," *Journal of Contemporary Asia*, 38(1): 62–83.

Pasuk, P. and C. Baker. 2009. *Thaksin*. 2nd edn. Chiang Mai: Silkworm Books.

Pasuk, P. and C. Baker. 2012. "Populist challenge to the establishment: Thaksin Shinawatra and the transformation of Thai politics," in R. Robison (ed.), *Routledge Handbook of Southeast Asian Politics*. Abingdon: Routledge, 83–96.

Pye, L. 1985. *Asian Power and Politics: The Cultural Dimensions of Authority*. Cambridge: Harvard University Press.

Rocamora, J. 2009. "Estrada and the populist temptation in the Philippines," in K. Mizuno and P. Pasuk (eds), *Populism in Asia*. Singapore: NUS Press, 41–65.

Rodan, G. 2012. "Competing ideologies of political representation in Southeast Asia," *Third World Quarterly*, 33(2): 311–32.

Rovira Kaltwasser, C. 2014. "Latin American populism. Some conceptual and normative lessons," *Constellations*, 21(4): 494–504.

Schaffer, F. C. 2002. "Disciplinary reactions: alienation and the reform of vote buying in the Philippines," paper prepared for annual meeting of the American Political Science Association, Boston, August 29–September 1.

Schmidt, V. A. 2008. "Discursive institutionalism: the explanatory power of ideas and discourse," *Annual Review of Political Science*, 11: 303–26.

Shin, D. C. and B.-K. Jhee. 2005. "How does democratic regime change affect mass political ideology? A case study of South Korea in comparative perspective," *International Political Science Review*, 26(4): 381–96.

Shyu, H. 2008. "Populism in Taiwan: the rise of a populist-democratic culture in a democratising society," *Asian Journal of Political Science*, 16(2): 130–50.

Stanley, B. 2008. "The thin ideology of populism," *Journal of Political Ideologies*, 13(1): 95–110.

Thompson, M. R. 2010. "Reformism vs. populism in the Philippines," *Journal of Democracy*, 21(4): 154–68.

Uchiyama, Y. 2010. *Koizumi and Japanese Politics: Reform Strategies and Leadership Style*. Abingdon and New York: Routledge.

Von Lübke, C. 2014. "Maverick mayor to presidential hopeful: Jokowi's record in public office justifies his strong public image," *Inside Indonesia*, 115 [available online at: http://www.insideindonesia.org/current-edition/maverick-mayor-to-presidential-hopeful; last accessed: May 27, 2014].

Wang, Z. 2007. "Postmodern values in seven Confucian societies: political consequences of changing world views," *Japanese Journal of Political Science*, 8(3): 341–59.

Welzel, C. 2012. "The myth of Asian exceptionalism: response to Bomhoff and Gu," *Journal of Cross-Cultural Psychology*, 43(7): 1039–54.

Welzel, C. 2013. *Freedom Rising: Human Empowerment and the Quest for Emancipation*. New York: Cambridge University Press.

CHAPTER 9

....

POPULISM IN INDIA

....

CHRISTOPHE JAFFRELOT AND LOUISE TILLIN

INDIA's experiment with populism has been intense and paradoxical. The world's largest democracy is very familiar with this "ism," usually associated with authoritarian, personalized brands of politics. Not only has the country tried all kinds of populisms, but populists have also been in office over many years. Some of India's largest political personalities have been populist in their political strategy and vocabulary. Indira Gandhi, daughter of India's first Prime Minister Jawaharlal Nehru, was the first to hone a populist strategy to secure power in New Delhi relying upon heavily personalized appeals to a largely rural electorate, seeking to circumvent the power of older party bosses in the 1960s and 1970s. The national political leader who may be seen as the closest imitator of her populist style comes from the different tradition of Hindu nationalism: the BJP leader Narendra Modi who swept to power in 2014. Both in different ways saturated the public sphere with images of their person and governed in a way that sought both to embody the "people," variously depicted, and to reach directly to them over the heads of political intermediaries.

In common parlance, the term populism in India—as elsewhere—is often employed more expansively to denote the fiscally irresponsible distribution of subsidies and sops to a variety of social classes and interest groups. Yet this usage typically elides significant distinctions between short-term attempts to achieve electoral "popularity" by a variety of different types of political leader, on the one hand, and a more singular strategy and style of leadership, on the other. Populism is an "elusive and protean" notion (Ionescu and Gellner, 1969: 1) that requires some definition.

In this chapter, we identify a category of political leadership in India characterized by direct, personalized appeals to "the people" by leaders who deploy particular cultural registers to secure and maintain political power by circumventing intermediaries and neutralizing institutions. In doing so, we recognize that populism consists both of a distinctive form of political strategy (Weyland, this volume) and a politics conducted within a political cultural register grounded in a "plebeian grammar" (Ostiguy, this volume). This grammar must have a resonance with popular beliefs; it consists of more than a top-down political strategy (see also Wyatt, 2013). Most of the forms that populism has taken in India correspond to what Mudde (this volume) proposes as an ideological definition hinged around a moral claim to the authenticity and purity of the masses as opposed to a corrupt elite (with both people and the elite defined differently according to the context). Or, as Edward Shils (1956: 98) put it: "Populism identifies the will of the people with justice and morality." Yet it is in the combination of ideology and political strategy that populism takes concrete shape. Our definition of populism thus constitutes a somewhat less expansive category than some of the handful of existing academic accounts of populism in India which include all political appeals which distinguish between the "people," variously defined, and an "elite" (see, for instance, Subramanian, 2007).

In India, most political parties claim that they are "from the people, for the people and by the people," as evident from their own names where one often finds the word "people" itself: "Lok," Janata, or Jan. But populism did not appear along with the democratic system codified by India's 1950 Constitution. In the 1950s, Nehru and his fellow Congressmen presided over a parliamentary system where power was not heavily personalized and where institutions mattered—as much as local bosses who were key figures of a typically clientelistic dispensation. Things changed in the 1960s, primarily because of the political strategy of Indira Gandhi, whose version of populism took a left-leaning, socialist hue. But other variants of populism crystallized at the same time in which the people were defined on the basis of other criteria, their sense of belonging either to the peasantry (the true India) or to Hinduism (the original India).

In this chapter we identify three principal strains of populism in India's political history. The first is that of the 1960s and 1970s, in which period Indira Gandhi relied on personalized appeals to the rural poor over the heads of traditional bosses within the Congress Party to win elections. Outside the Congress Party, Charan Singh developed an agrarian form of populism that located virtue among the peasantry rather than the corrupt, urban establishment. A second strand of populism arose within Hindu nationalism, in which the people have been defined as Hindu and are to be protected from a minority-appeasing "pseudo-secular" establishment. Yet not all Hindu nationalist politicians have depended on populist strategies. Indeed the main Hindu nationalist party, the Bharatiya Janata Party (BJP), is one of India's better institutionalized political parties, although in the 1970s it moved towards deployment of more populist strategies around socio-economic themes (discussed in more detail in Jaffrelot, 2002). The populist leader par excellence within the Hindu Nationalist political tradition has been Narendra Modi, former Chief Minister of the state of Gujarat, who became Prime Minister of India in 2014. Modi as leader has sidelined the BJP party organization, appealed directly to the Indian public through sophisticated use of technology including simulcast speeches by 3D holograms of himself, and fostered a state of permanent political mobilization that seeks to bypass intermediaries. A third strand of populism is located within cultural regionalist politics in Andhra Pradesh and Tamil Nadu in which regional language and culture have been used to define the "people" in particular regional settings against corrupt political elites located in the alien, Sanskritic culture of northern India. In both states, film-stars-turned-politicians claimed special affinity with the people and while in office deployed personalized styles of leadership that bypassed institutional structures. The term populism may also be extended to describe some of the political leaders who have risen to represent lower and middle castes in parts of northern India, such as Lalu Prasad Yadav of the Rashtriya Janata Dal in Bihar.

THE 1960S: TWO TYPES
OF ANTI-ESTABLISHMENT POLITICS

In the 1960s, several leaders of South Asia, including Mrs Bandaranaike and Zulfikar Ali Bhutto, fulfilled the criteria of populism mentioned above. But Indira Gandhi probably went the furthest. While Bandaranaike and Bhutto either created a party or took over power in a rather recent party, Mrs Gandhi broke the older Congress Party and de-institutionalized the new political machine she had created for herself. She thereby succeeded in emancipating herself from the existing establishment and from the party bosses—who were known as the Syndicate—in the name of socialism, soon after becoming Prime Minister of India in 1966.

Indira Gandhi broke with the old Congress style during the mid-term elections she called in 1971. In these elections she sought to short-circuit the power of entrenched party bosses by presenting her socio-economic program directly to the people. In a broadcast to the nation, she declared in December 1970 that:

> The challenge posed by the present critical situation can be met only by the proper and effective implementation of our secular and socialist policies and programmes through democratic processes. Time will not wait for us. Millions who demand food, shelter and jobs are pressing for action. Power in a democracy resides in the people. That is why we have decided to go to the people and seek a fresh mandate from them. (Cited in Awana, 1988: 200)

The electoral campaign of 1971 illustrated well Indira Gandhi's new style of politics. Before the party split in 1969 the Congress had combined a socialist-like discourse at the top and conservative practices at the local level where notables ensured the party's electoral success. After 1969 most of these notables sided with the non-Indira wing of the old Congress Party (Congress (O)) because of affinities with the Syndicate bosses or because of the fears raised by Indira Gandhi's policies. Therefore Mrs Gandhi could not rely on the "vote banks" of the old party bosses, which she had anyway criticized as status quo-ist. She played a leading role in the election campaign. Her rallying cry, characteristically personal and demagogic—and expressive of the populist turn under her leadership—was:

> Some say let us get rid of Indira Gandhi (Indira Hatao)
> I say let us get rid of poverty (Garibi Hatao).

The party's manifesto projected the party as an agent of progress and the opposition parties (the Congress (O), the Jana Sangh, and the Swatantra party) clubbed together in a Grand Alliance as reactionary forces. But these forces were not very well defined sociologically. The manifesto simply argued that the Grand Alliance was "backed by vested interest" (Zaidi, 1972–3: 117). The vagueness of this rhetoric reflected the social ambivalence of Indira Gandhi herself. She did not sever her links from the establishment, including the business milieu, and while she used a socialist rhetoric, she did not go on to implement major social reforms—and therefore, remained a populist.

Besides a discursively socialist form of populism, India saw an agrarian form of populism in this period that claimed to be more in tune with the deep reality of society because it spoke for the true people who were not only poor (or anti-establishment), but also rooted in land. Charan Singh began his political career within the Congress Party, but left to form his own Bharatiya Kranti Dal (Indian Revolutionary Party) in 1967 and then Bharatiya Lok Dal (Indian People's Party) in 1974. He was briefly to be Prime Minister in late 1979 during the Janata government elected following the Emergency but his government collapsed and saw the return of Congress to power in 1980. Charan Singh forged a political appeal based on an eagerness to protect the peasants against merchants, the money lenders, and urban dwellers at large.

Charan Singh sought to reorient India's priorities from urban industrial development towards agriculture. In order to implement a rural oriented economic policy, he argued that the administration had to be filled up with sons of farmers because only an official who understood and thought like a peasant could effectively solve the problems of the peasant (Singh, 1986: 203). Charan Singh was a populist not only because he challenged the establishment (that was urban) in the name of the true people (who were rural), but also because he claimed to speak in the name of all these people. However, in reality, he largely represented the elite of the peasantry, those dominant castes who owned land and who exploited the landless peasants. He tried hard not to acknowledge the inner differentiation of the peasantry that was based both on class and caste. Ultimately he wanted to subsume caste into a new peasant identity.

In spite of his selective defence of the rural folk, Charan Singh systematically attempted to project himself as the spokesman for village India, against the city-based and parasitic elite. In that sense, the establishment he targeted was different from the one against whom Indira Gandhi tried to mobilize the plebeians. His discourse spelled out a village-centred-egalitarian agenda, which dictated his political strategy: "For creating an egalitarian society the reins of power of the country should lie in the hands of the 80 percent of the population; uneducated and poor, which lives in the villages" (Rawat, 1985: chap. 6). He was eager to protect the peasants against the merchants, the money lenders and the urban dwellers at large. As early as 1939 he showed a sharp awareness of the latent conflicts between rural and urban India that resulted in his demand to reserve 50 percent of government jobs for peasants in the framework of a policy of positive discrimination, challenging the hitherto caste-based schemes adopted in India:

In our country the classes whose scions dominate the public services are either those which have been raised to unexampled prominence and importance by the Britisher, e.g. the money-lender, the big *zamindar* or *taluqdar* [landlord], the *arhatia* or the trader, or those which have been, so to say, actually called into being by him—the *vakil* [advocate], the doctor, the contractor. These classes have, in subordinate cooperation with the foreigner, exploited the masses in all kinds of manner during these last two hundred years. The views and interests of these classes, on the whole, are, therefore, manifestly opposed to those of the masses. The social philosophy of a member of the non-agricultural, urban classes is entirely different from that of a person belonging to the agricultural rural classes. (Charan Singh, 1986: 203)

For Charan Singh, Nehru epitomized this elitist urban-oriented approach of Indian society:

This supreme city dweller administrator had no knowledge whatsoever about life conditions of the millions of helpless Indians who live in the villages of India. He, who had only knowledge of the western principles of economy learnt in the Oxbridge university education system, was given the charges of administering the growth of the country. He got carried away towards these ready-made theories and concepts, which promised comparatively higher national production. He had imagined that by a public ownership of the industries the country could get a high level of production. (Ravat, chap. 6)

In his populist discourse, Charan Singh presented the village community as forming a harmonious whole. He claimed that a village "was always a stronger moral unit than a factory. The sense of the community was a vital thing among the peasantry, providing a natural foundation for collaboration or co-operative action" (Singh, 1964: 270). Like Gandhi—from whom he explicitly drew his inspiration—he completely ignored the deep social contradictions and class antagonisms between landowners, tenants, share-croppers, and laborers and dwelled instead on consensual processes of conflict resolution. Charan Singh's *kisan* politics declined even before he died in 1987, but in the 1970s it was a major political repertoire that precipitated the demise of Congress clientelism and competed with Indira Gandhi's populism.

POPULISM AND HINDU NATIONALISM: ATTEMPTS TO REDEFINE THE "PEOPLE" AS HINDUS

The populist repertoires of Indira Gandhi and Charan Singh crystallized in the 1960s with a strong socio-economic overtone. Both tried to mobilize the people, beyond caste and class, against what they called "the establishment." Another variant of populism arose subsequently: the Hindutva version which sat further towards the right of the political spectrum. Hindu nationalism has what Ostiguy (this volume) would consider both "low" and "high" elements, but here we focus more on the "low."

Hindu nationalism (known as the Hindutva movement in India) became a full-fledged ideology in the 1920s after V. D. Savarkar wrote *Hindutva, who is a Hindu*, a book in which he claimed that the Indian nation is coterminous with the Hindu major-ity. Certainly, religious minorities (Muslims and Christians) can practice their rituals privately, but in the public sphere, they must pay allegiance to Hindu symbols of iden-tity. In this case, the populist equation is different because the Hindus become "the peo-ple" and not the poor or the peasants. Their enemies are not the establishment defined in socio-economic terms but an establishment defined in cultural terms, a group made of English-speaking, Westernized—uprooted—elites who defend secularism at the expense of the authentic, Hindu identity of the nation. Like other populisms of the right wing, they complain about the appeasement of Muslim minorities by "pseudo-secular" Congress governments. This variant of Indian populism also saw the blurring of inner divisions: Hindu nationalists seek to downplay caste and class divisions among Hindus. As a result, the Hindu nationalist movement has never attracted Dalits (ex-Untouchables) in large numbers, but low-caste Hindus have in more recent years rallied around it in greater numbers, especially after parties supported by the movement nomi-nated candidates from that milieu.

In the political realm, Hindu nationalists were represented by the Bharatiya Janata Party (BJP) (Indian People's Party), which has been, since 1980, the political "front" of the Rashtriya Swayamsevak Sangh (RSS), the mother organization of the Hindu nation-alist movement. For decades, they failed to capture the imagination of the majority Hindu community in spite of attempts to mobilize it by manipulating sacred symbols and issues such as cow slaughter. In the 1980s, they tried to capitalize on the Ayodhya issue, in a slightly more successful manner. The city of Ayodhya is considered by Hindus to be the birthplace of Lord Ram. Organizations within the Sangh Parivar (the family of Hindu nationalist organizations) demanded the construction of a Hindu temple to Lord Ram on the site of the Babri Masjid (mosque). This issue came to prominence when taken up as a rallying cry by party president, L. K. Advani, a clear indication that pop-ulism can only work when it is embodied in an individual figure. In 1990, L. K. Advani became a major crowd puller of India during his Rath Yatra (chariot tour) of India. Two years later, the Babri Masjid was pulled down by Hindu nationalist "volunteers." This marked the apogee of political polarization around Hindu nationalism and violence between Hindu and Muslim communities, as can be seen in Figure 9.1.

It has been Narendra Modi, however, who most powerfully refined and embodied a repertoire of Hindutva populism as political strategy, first in his state of Gujarat and then at the national level. In Gujarat, Narendra Modi re-arranged the politics of the BJP in particular and that of Hindu nationalism in general around his person. In 2002 he pro-jected himself as the protector of the Hindus in the wake of Hindu-Muslim violence in Gujarat of a scale unprecedented since Partition. Upwards of one thousand Muslims are estimated to have died in these riots that followed the burning of a train carriage carrying

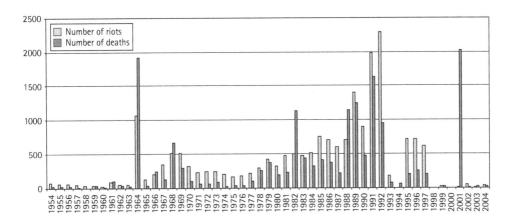

FIG. 9.1 Communal riots in post-independence India.

Source: C. Jaffrelot. 2011. "The Muslims of India", in C. Jaffrelot (ed.), *India since 1950: Society, Politics, Economy and Culture*. New Delhi: Yatra Books.

Hindu nationalist volunteers back from Ayodhya. Following the riots, Modi launched an election campaign loaded with Hindu nationalist overtones. His Gaurav Yatra (Pride procession) left from the Bhathiji Maharaj Temple in Phagval (Kheda district) and instantly met with great popular success. One of the slogans of Modi's campaign cast him as the Hindu hriday samrat (King of Hindus' hearts), a title that had until then been accorded to the nativist Shiv Sena leader, Bal Thackeray (*Indian Express*, 2013).

Having consolidated his hold on power in Gujarat through religious polarization, Modi began to place more emphasis on his record on economic growth and development. Gujarat's strong economic performance pre-dated Modi's time in office, but he claimed personal responsibility for its relative success. He projected himself as someone who was able to "get things done." His centralized and personalized style of administration, personally intervening to get investments moving or land allocated to favored projects, was quite consistent with a populist electoral strategy that sought to side-line intermediaries. This image and political platform was also central to his subsequent bid for the prime ministership in 2014.

His style of election campaigning is distinctive and led to the pioneering use of technology to reach ever wider audiences. During the state's 2007 election campaign Purshottam Rupala, the BJP state president in Gujarat, admitted that his party had a one-point program: Modi (Shah, 2007). Narendra Modi himself was the chief campaigner. Five years later, during the 2012 Gujarat state elections, he again took his caravan for a cavalcade throughout the state before Congress even started to hold meetings. His Swami Vivekananda Yuva Vikas Yatra (Youth Development March) involved a total of 135 rallies. But touring the state was physically demanding, time-consuming, and not sufficient to saturate the public space. As early as 2007 therefore Modi turned to more sophisticated modes of communication, pioneering a "hi-tech" populism that defined his campaign strategy for the prime ministership in 2014. This campaign was unique in itself for the attention it lavished on a prime ministerial candidate when in previous elections parties had often not even projected a clear candidate for the top role.

In addition to hiring the services of an American PR company, Narendra Modi explored new modes of communication using the latest technologies in 2007. Having three laptops—one in his office, one at home, and one for travelling—he allegedly spent several hours a day reading the 200–250 e-mails he received every day from citizens of Gujarat, and responding to a proportion of them personally. Modi's 2007 election campaign not only used this channel—the internet—but also the mobile phone, Gujaratis being very well equipped compared to the rest of India (14 out of 52 million inhabitant Gujaratis had a cell phone in 2007). Such phones enabled Modi to send thousands of SMS and MMS to potential voters as well as party cadres.

In the 2012 state elections, he also initiated a TV channel, NaMo. More importantly, he held a series of virtual meetings: Modi's hologram appeared on stage in 3D simultaneously in different locations to deliver his speeches to massive audiences which were sometimes mesmerized. While Modi continued with more conventional outreach too— so much so that he addressed 125 rallies in the first fifteen days of December 2012, or ten meetings a day (Dave, 2012)—his use of the 3D technique revealed his awareness of the exceptional power of images in politics (and in Indian civilization). He held 132 holographic shows during the election campaign in order to communicate directly with a huge number of citizens (Nair, 2012). Strikingly, the last leader to use technology so effectively in projecting herself to the people was Indira Gandhi, who has been described as India's first "televisual" leader (see Mehta, 2008). This underlines the importance of political communications in the construction and maintenance of populist modes of leadership.

Beyond the medium of communication, Modi has also paid close attention to his dress. His image and sartorial style also reflect the significance of the socio-cultural dimensions of populist appeals (see also Ostiguy, introduction). In his biography of Modi, Nilanjan Mukhopadhyay devotes one full chapter to what is known in Gujarat as "the Modi kurta." This long shirt has only one distinctive feature: its short sleeves. Modi told Mukhopadhyay that when he was an itinerant RSS worker, he had little time to wash his clothes, which is why he decided to cut his sleeves in half. After becoming a public figure, he had his style of kurta designed by an Ahmedabad-based tailor, Jade Blue. By 2004, the "Modi kurta" was so popular that this company asked Modi for permission to sell it under that name. Narendra Modi concluded: "it was part of my simplicity and has become a fashion for the outside world today" (Mukhopadhyay, 2013: 281). During the 2014 general elections, Modi altered his dress in different regions to suggest an affinity with other regional cultures.

Certainly, this making of a brand reflects a form of narcissism, but it also reveals a specific sense of communication: the Gujarati citizens will think about their Chief Minister not only when they see his picture on a wall (or on their child's school bag), but also when they see someone wearing "his" kurta. More importantly, still: they can wear it themselves and *look like* him. This is what happened, almost literally, in 2007 when the BJP distributed masks of Narendra Modi. His supporters canvassed while wearing a mask of him as if hundreds and even thousands of Modis were campaigning together. Sympathizers started to do the same and repeated the trick in the 2012 election campaign, as if to say: we are all Narendra Modi. This technique of mass communication suggests that a more sophisticated style of populism is taking shape when Modi invites his supporters to identify with him by wearing the same shirt and masking their face with his—suggesting that he is ubiquitous.

Narendra Modi has saturated the public sphere by introducing a state of quasi-permanent, or recurrent, mobilization. The organization of events mobilizing Gujarati society was not confined to election campaigns. Instead, Modi sought to keep society in a state of constant mobilization. A permanent state of mobilization is costly, but an investment from which Narendra Modi has derived political dividends. The Sadbhavana Mission is a case in point. In September 2011, Modi embarked on a new kind of program aiming at promoting social harmony against all forms of social division based on caste and religion, including vote bank politics. It consisted in visiting all districts in Gujarat and fasting one day in each of them in order to promote a new mind-set of "social harmony." Given the packed diary of the Chief Minister, this program could not be achieved in one fell swoop, so had three legs, the last of which ended a few months before the 2012 state elections. The newspapers of Gujarat trumpeted the achievements and the numbers reached through such a campaign. A couple of them, published as banner headlines, are worth citing: "New Record: Above 15 lakh citizens Personally Met the Chief Minister," "A Heartfelt Thanks to all Six Crore Gujaratis who Were Part of 36 Sadbhavana Fasts." The latter suggests that even those who did not take part in the movement were part of it. In that sense it was an all-encompassing, total mobilization during which Narendra Modi was in direct contact with society as a whole. Indeed, "unanimism"—ideas of collective consciousness and collective emotion—is an important aspect of political populism.

The last pillar of Modi's populism, honed in Gujarat but now projected on a national stage by Modi as Prime Minister, accords with what Ostiguy describes as the "political cultural." This is a style of leadership that is characterized as strong and personalized, and able to take tough decisions by bypassing existing institutions. Above all, it is a deeply personalized conception of political power which hinges on the character of the leader more than on formal rules or institutionally mediated authority. While the BJP has a reputation for having one of the more well-organized, penetrative party organizations aided by the organizational network of the Sangh Parivar, Modi's elevation as leader superseded these party networks (Jaffrelot, 2015). His projection as leader relied on direct, less mediated appeals to a wider public. On becoming Prime Minister, Modi has strengthened the role of the Prime Minister's Office (PMO) over other departments, and exercised control over the appointment of senior bureaucrats, whom he in turn has used to rein in his own ministers.

As Prime Minister, Narendra Modi has made his broader populist repertoire more sophisticated—and more difficult to detect since it is perfectly normal for the head of the executive to claim to represent the whole nation. Still, he has persisted with techniques he had explored in Gujarat. He has continued to saturate the public space by his omnipresence in the media. This achievement was due to the organization of mass movements like the International Yoga Day or the Swachh Bharat Abhiyan (Clean India Mission), a campaign requesting every Indian to clean their country—not to say anything about the orchestration of the press coverage of his many visits to foreign countries. But the effectiveness of his populist repertoire was also due to his routinized use of the radio to relate directly to "his" people. While Indira Gandhi had used All India Radio at the time of elections campaigns, Modi has initiated a monthly address to the citizens called "Maan ki baat" (the conversation of the month), a modus operandi that allows him to sidestep more combative questioning by interviewers.

Besides, Modi has continued to use religion in order to blur social distinctions based on caste and class and promote an undifferentiated Hindu, ethnic whole. He celebrated his electoral victory in 2014 from his constituency, Varanasi—the sacred place of the Hindus par excellence—by staging traditional rituals. Similarly, many of his official trips abroad have been marked by visits to Hindu temples through which the Prime Minister related to a certain section of the Indian diaspora. Thus while the agenda of government in New Delhi is inevitably more complex than for the chief minister of a state, Modi as Prime Minister has continued to project a populist style and grammar of leadership.

The Hindu nationalist variant of populism poses a threat to India's democracy because of its exclusivist overtone. Majoritarianism, here, means that the largest ethnic group is bound to govern the country and that minorities may end up as second-class citizens. This is evident from the decline of Muslims in every power center (including the lower house of parliament where for the first time in the history of India the ruling party, the BJP, has no Muslim MP). Like Israel, India appears more like an ethnic democracy where the majority community imposes its lifestyle. Some BJP-ruled states like Maharashtra and Haryana, for instance, banned beef from markets and restaurants in 2015.

REGIONAL NATIONALISM AND "WELFARE POPULISM": FILM-STARS-TURNED-POLITICIANS IN SOUTHERN INDIA

In southern India, a third strand of populism has crystallized in which regional language and culture has formed the basis of appeals to the people within specific regional settings defined against national political elites and the "alien" Sanskritic, Hindi-speaking culture of northern India. This style of populism was incubated in Tamil Nadu within the Dravidian movement from the 1950s onwards, but found its fullest expression with the rise of Tamil film-star-turned-politician M. G. Ramachandran or MGR, whose party won elections for the first time in 1977, and who dominated Tamil politics until his death in 1987. His successor, also a film actress, Jayalalithaa honed her own brand, adding a gendered dimension to her claims of victimization, as well as promises of protection (Spary, 2007). At a similar time in neighboring Andhra Pradesh another film-star-turned-politician, N. T. Rama Rao or NTR, established the Telugu Desam Party to contest against the Congress Party. What is significant about both these Tamil and Telugu variants of populism of the 1970s, and 1980s is that they combined the cultivation of rustic, home-spun regional identities pitched against alien, corrupt national political elites (often in the Congress Party); charismatic, personalized leadership—with prominent film-stars in both states—who claimed special affinity with the people; and attempts to consolidate broad social coalitions through collapsing social divisions under the umbrella of overarching regional identities. Both also focused on promoting the provision of welfare programs for the poor as a central part of their political platforms. It is significant that both variants emerged as rivals to the Indira Gandhi-led Congress Party. They demonstrated some parallels with her politics, although rather than adopting the rhetoric of the left they used rustic appeals to regional identities to establish a connection with the plebeian.

As with the forms of populism discussed above at the national level, these regional forms of populism also struggled to submerge inequalities within the social coalitions they sought to hold together. But over time, as authors including Arun Swamy (1998) and Narendra Subramanian (1999) have documented in the case of Tamil Nadu, they gave rise to reasonably stable patterns of party competition in which parties have built competitively populist platforms on the basis of which they rotate in power. These forms of party competition have had some positive effects on the provision of welfare, encouraging greater stability in the delivery of welfare programs and a progressive expansion of the pool of beneficiaries. However, the southern models have also been criticized for failing to address deeper structural problems in regional economies, and using populist platforms to hold together popular coalitions in contexts of rising inequality and processes of accumulation that rely on close relationships between political elites and dominant classes (see, for instance, Pandian, 1992).

Tamil Nadu in the 1970s and 1980s

The Tamil variants of populism have a long pedigree within a political context that from the early twentieth century has been heavily infused by a sense of Dravidian identity that makes Tamil-speaking southern India distinct from the Sanskritic cultures and languages of the north. The first regional Tamil political party, the Dravida Munnetra Kazhagam (DMK), was formed in 1949, as an offshoot of the older Dravidian Movement. While in its early incarnation it deployed the idea of Tamils as a distinct cultural nation, oppressed by north Indian outsiders, it did not develop an explicitly populist repertoire (see summary in Wyatt, 2013). The literature on Tamil politics has identified two subsequent modes of populism in Tamil Nadu that have come to define the broad contours of political competition in the state. Swamy (1998) and Subramanian (1999), in their separate analyses, argue that the DMK and the Anna DMK (ADMK, later All-India DMK or

AIADMK), which broke away from the DMK in 1972, relied upon two competing forms of populism. The DMK developed a form of what Swamy calls "empowerment populism" and Subramanian describes as "assertive populism" in which "the people" were identified as the middle strata—groups that had been ignored by the Congress Party—and were oppressed by a narrow elite. The DMK focused on promoting upward mobility and affirmative action for these middling groups, including—significantly in the mid-1960s—campaigning against the imposition of Hindi (a north Indian language) as a national language. The party first defeated the Congress Party to form the state government in the 1967 state elections at the height of the anti-Hindi movement. As Subramanian describes, over time Tamil political identity developed a popular appeal more through its association with "plebeian" cultural modes than as an anti-outsider platform. It was associated with non-Sanskritic cultural traditions that were strongest among intermediate and lower castes; with those who spoke Tamil more than English; and was opposed to national political elites who sought the imposition of Hindi as a national language (Subramanian, 1999: 49).

Yet it is during what Swamy calls the "protection populism," and Subramanian the "paternalistic populism," of the period that followed the formation of the ADMK under film-star-turned-politician MGR's leadership that the fuller version of populism took root in the south. The ADMK's appeal—especially under MGR—was made more directly to the poorer and less educated sections of Tamil society rather than upwardly mobile middling groups, though it was still encompassed within a broader appeal to Tamil identity shared with the DMK. One of the programs MGR is most remembered for is the "noon meals scheme" for school-children, the early precursor to today's national mid-day meals program. Swamy describes the ADMK strategy as a form of "sandwich coalition" in which a Tamil elite presented themselves as the protectors of the poor, in contrast to the intermediate groups at the heart of the DMK's social coalition. As Arun Swamy describes succinctly, MGR's political persona drew heavily on his on-screen persona:

> In general, three recurring themes in MGR movies have been seen as politically significant: MGR as crusader against tyranny; MGR as champion of the poor—often combined with the first through a Robin Hood-style social bandit role—and MGR as the protector of women ... One additional theme, however, that is seldom commented on is the frequency with which MGR is depicted *not* as a member of the working class himself, but as a member of the natural aristocracy to whom common folk look for leadership against usurpers. (Swamy, 1998: 135)

In the 1990s and 2000s, populist strategies in Tamil Nadu came under challenge including from caste-based parties which sought to mobilize groups that had been left behind by the Dravidian parties. The AIADMK also struggled to adjust after MGR's death as Jayalalithaa took over as leader (Wyatt, 2013: 370). As Wyatt (2013) writes, the rise of another film actor, Vijayakanth, into electoral politics in 2005 renewed interest in "paternalist populism" and a new generation of goods were offered to the electorate by both the DMK and AIADMK, focusing more on consumer durables including free food mixers/grinders, color TVs, as well as free rice for the very poor via the Public Distribution System, increased pension payments, and a new health insurance scheme. More recently, the AIADMK leadership have adopted a new form of populist appeal which has combined an emphasis on strong leadership protecting the vulnerable with a more technocratic edge focused on good governance designed to appeal to the middle classes, alongside an anti-elitism directed at the degeneracy and corruption associated with the extended family of DMK leader Karunanidhi (Wyatt, 2013).

Andhra Pradesh in the 1980s: The NTR Phenomenon

The rise of a brand of regional populism in neighboring Andhra Pradesh stemmed from different roots than that in Tamil Nadu. There was no longer term equivalent of the Dravidian movement in Andhra. Rather, a new regional party—the Telugu Desam Party (TDP)—was founded on the eve of state elections in 1983 under the leadership of the well-known local film-star N. T. Rama Rao—colloquially known as NTR. NTR, a household name throughout the state, proclaimed himself the prospective savior of the Telugu-speaking people from the corrupt and interfering rule of a Congress Party which had ruled the state for nearly thirty years, and increasingly appeared to treat Andhra Pradesh as its fiefdom with weak leaders repeatedly imposed by the center. In framing his appeal to the public against Congress, NTR—like MGR—used the rich symbolism of a film career spanning more than three hundred movies in which he most often played mythological roles of "gods and goodness" (Naidu, 1984: 130).

The symbolism of the campaign was as important as the content of campaign promises, as numerous observers recalled. Wearing a saffron robe, NTR travelled during the election campaign in a car dressed up to look like a chariot (Kohli, 1988: 998). By recalling mythological figures along with more local saints and rulers, the TDP's campaign materials sought to project an appeal that straddled caste and class, and projected a benevolent attitude towards the poor under the watchful eye of NTR (Naidu, 1984: 135). These were held together by reference to Telugu identity and pride. The party also promised free school meals and subsidized rice, following in MGR's shoes, to appeal to the poor. But it was above all NTR's personality that held the party's campaign together: "It was his charisma that dominated the election scene, rendering most of the organised political parties irrelevant" (Reddy, 1989: 286).

Like other populist leaders, NTR was not focused on building institutional capacity within either the TDP or the state government. He towered over the TDP, and developed a personalized style of leadership in office that was compared at the time to Indira Gandhi's. This triggered substantial dissent within the party and an inconsistent approach to governance whereby flagship policies such as free school meals and subsidized rice were introduced and withdrawn at numerous junctures; and social and political violence increased (see Kohli, 1988).

CONCLUSION

In this chapter we have shown that populism has taken numerous forms in India from the 1960s onwards as an earlier pattern of well-institutionalized Congress Party rule came under strain. The shift towards a more personalized style of leadership within the Congress Party under Indira Gandhi, who relied on a socialist discourse to craft new direct political appeals to the rural peasantry over the heads of her party, marked a major turning point. But populist strategies were also to develop outside, and against the Congress, from the agrarian populism of Charan Singh in north India to the regional, vernacular populisms of film-stars-turned-politicians MGR and NTR in southern India. From the right, there are some populist strands within the politics of Hindu nationalism, most visible in the rise of Narendra Modi first as Chief Minister of Gujarat and latterly as Prime Minister of India. All of these forms of populism share the deployment of a "plebeian grammar" (Ostiguy, this volume) by a leader who projects themselves simultaneously as one of the people and as their protector. All project themselves against an alien, degenerate, or exploitative "other" although their identification of both the people and their other differs considerably across the variants of populism delineated in this chapter. Most seek to downplay or gloss over social differentiation to craft the broadest possible social coalitions. For agrarian populists, the image of the "kisan" (peasant farmer) elided rural inequalities particularly between large and small farmers, and landless labor; for Hindu nationalists, the assertion of a primary Hindu identity glosses over caste differences; and for regional populists of southern India, cultural identity has been used as a capacious umbrella to relate to the "authentic" people. Yet all these forms of populist mobilization within Indian democracy have been vulnerable to the mobilization of other facets of identity or alternative definitions of the people by competing political entrepreneurs.

The discussion in this chapter is not exhaustive, yet it has sought to be judicious in its application of the term populism, a term which is often loosely used in India. Some of the forms of populism under discussion here, notably the regional populisms of the south, have stood alongside the development of social welfare programs and benevolent state patronage. Yet populism need not rely upon the distribution of material resources. Rather it is primarily a relational and often highly personalized style of leadership that frequently circumvents institutions to privilege a direct connection between a leader and the people, variously defined.

In fact, we can learn from India that populism has different faces, in spite of one common denominator. While it systematically relies on the concentration of power in the hands of one (wo)man who relates directly to the people, short-circuiting the regional and local notables of any clientelistic arrangement, the dominant repertoire may be either pro-poor or ethno-religious. That said, populist leaders may also combine these genres in order to be more effective: Indira Gandhi tended to blend both types in the 1980s and Narendra Modi also played upon his plebeian background—he is the first low-caste Prime Minister of India. All of this shows that India offers a rich source of inspiration to the students of populism.

REFERENCES

Awana, Ram Singh. 1988. *Pressure Politics in Congress Party: A Study of the Congress Forum for Socialist Action*. New Delhi: Northern Book Centre.

Dave, Kapil. 2012. "Unsure 3D effect will work, Narenda Modi to hit the road," *The Times of India*, November 25.

Indian Express. 2013. "Sena refuses to bestow Hindu Hriday Samrat title to Modi," *The Indian Express*, July 13, 2013. See http://www.indianexpress.com/ news/sena- refuses-to-bestow-hindu- hridaysamrat-title-on-modi/ 1141340/. Last accessed November 8, 2013.

Ionescu, Ghita and Ernest Gellner (eds). 1969. *Populism: Its Meanings and National Characteristics*. London: Weidenfeld and Nicolson.

Jaffrelot, Christophe. 2002. "A specific party-building strategy: the Jana Sangh and the RSS network," in *Parties and Party Politics in India*. New Delhi: Oxford University Press, 114–57.

Jaffrelot, Christophe. 2015. "The Modi-centric BJP 2014 election campaign: new techniques and old tactics," *Contemporary South Asia*, 23(2): 151–66.

Kohli, Atul. 1988. "The NTR phenomenon in Andhra Pradesh: political change in a South Indian state," *Asian Survey*, 28(10): 991–1017.

Mehta, Nalin. 2008. *India on Television: How Satellite News Channels Have Changed the Way We Think and Act*. New Delhi: Harper Collins.

Mukhopadhyay, Nilanjan. 2013. *Narendra Modi: The Man, the Times*. Chennai: Tranquebar Press.

Naidu, Ratna. 1984. "Symbolic imagery used by the Telugu Desam in Andhra elections (1983)," in George Mathew (ed.), *Shift in Indian Politics: 1983 Elections in Andhra Pradesh and Karnataka*. New Delhi: Concept Publishing Company, 129–39.

Nair, Avinash. 2012. "And they were 26: Modi scripts his 'victory sequel' in 3D now," *The Times of India*, December 3.

Pandian, M. S. S. 1992. *The Image Trap: MG Ramachandran in Film and Politics*. New Delhi: Sage Publications.

Rawat, Gyanendra (ed.). 1985. *Chaudhuri Charan Singh: Sukti aur Vichar*, Hindi. New Delhi: Kisan Trust.

Reddy, G. Ram. 1989. "The politics of accommodation: caste, class and dominance in Andhra Pradesh," in Francine Frankel and M. S. A. Rao (eds), *Dominance and State Power in Modern India: Decline of a Social Order*, Vol. 1. New Delhi: Oxford University Press, 272–323.

Shah, Rajiv. 2007. "Modi only mascot for BJP: Rupala," *The Times of India*, November 5.

Shils, Edward. 1956. *The Torment of Secrecy*. Melbourne: Heinemann.

Singh, Charan. 1964. *India's Poverty and Its Solution*, 2nd rev. edn. Bombay: Asia Publishing House.

Singh, Charan. 1986. *Land Reforms in U.P. and the Kulaks*. New Delhi: Vikas Publishing House Pvt.

Spary, Carole. 2007. "Female political leadership in India," *Commonwealth and Comparative Politics*, 45(3): 253–77.

Subramanian, Narendra. 1999. *Ethnicity and Populist Mobilisation: Political Parties, Citizens and Democracy in South India*. New Delhi: Oxford University Press.

Subramanian, Narendra. 2007. "Populism in India," *SAIS Review of International Affairs*, 27(1): 81–91.

Swamy, Arun. 1998. "Parties, Political Identities and the Absence of Mass Political Violence in South India," in Amrita Basu and Atul Kohli (eds), *Community Conflicts and the State in India*. New Delhi: Oxford University Press, 108–49.

Wyatt, Andrew. 2013. "Populism and politics in contemporary Tamil Nadu," *Contemporary South Asia*, 21(4): 365–81.

Zaidi, A. Moin (ed.). 1972–3. *Annual Register of Indian Political Parties*, vol. 1. New Delhi: Orientalia.

CHAPTER 10

POPULISM IN LATIN AMERICA

CARLOS DE LA TORRE

LATIN America is the land of populism.[1] From the 1930s and 1940s until the present, populist leaders have dominated the region's political landscapes. Mass politics emerged with populist challenges to the rule of elites who used fraud to remain in power. The struggle for free and open elections, and for the incorporation of those excluded from politics, is associated with the names of the leaders of the first wave of populism: Juan and Eva Perón in Argentina, Getulio Vargas in Brazil, Victor Raúl Haya de la Torre in Perú, or José María Velasco Ibarra in Ecuador. Populist movements and governments produced deep lasting political loyalties and cleavages. Like their classical predecessors, radical populists such as Hugo Chávez in Venezuela, Evo Morales in Bolivia, and Rafael Correa in Ecuador polarized their polities and the academic community into those who regarded them as democratic innovators, and those who considered them a threat to democracy.

This chapter explains the commonalities and differences between the different subtypes of Latin American populism: classical, neoliberal, and radical. It examines why these different manifestations of populism emerged, and their democratizing and inclusionary promises while seeking power. Then it analyzes their impact on democracy after gaining office. Whereas populists seeking power promised to include the excluded, once in power populists attacked the institutions of liberal democracy, grabbed power, aimed to control social movements and civil society, and clashed with the privately owned media. The next section analyzes the mechanisms used by populist leaders to forge links with their followers: populist organizations, clientelism, the mass media, and discourse. Subsequently I explain why populism continues to reappear in some countries, whereas in others it is either confined to the margins of the political system or not present.

Before proceeding, and because populism is such a contested category, I will explain how I use this category. Borrowing from strategic and discursive-ideological approaches, I understand populism as a Manichaean discourse that divides politics and society as the struggle between two irreconcilable and antagonistic camps: the people and the oligarchy or the power block. Under populism a leader claims to embody the unitary will of the people in their struggle for liberation. Populism produces strong popular identities and is a strategy of top-down mobilization that clashes with the autonomous demands of social movement organizations. However, populist glorification of common people and their attacks on elites could open spaces for common people to press for their agendas. The tension between top-down mobilization and autonomous mobilization from below is characteristic of populist episodes.

Classical Populism

In Latin America populism emerged in the 1930s and 1940s with the crisis of the oligarchical social order that combined liberal-inspired constitutions (division of powers, and elections) with patrimonial practices and values in predominantly rural societies. These estate-based societies had relations of domination and subordination characterized by unequal reciprocity. Institutional and everyday practices of domination excluded the majority of the population from politics and from the public sphere, which were kept in the hands of elites.

Processes of urbanization, industrialization, and a generalized crisis of paternal authority allowed populist leaders to emerge. Classical populist leaders of the 1930s and 1940s such as Juan Perón and José María Velasco Ibarra fought against electoral fraud, expanded the franchise, and were exalted as the embodiment of the nation's true, uncorrupted traditions and values against those of foreign-oriented elites. In more economically developed nations such as Argentina, Brazil, and Mexico, populist presidents pursued nationalist and redistributive social policies that coincided with the period of import substitution industrialization (ISI). Populism also emerged in agrarian contexts. In Bolivia, Ecuador, and Peru, populism was not linked to industrialization, even though, as in the industrializing republics, it led to the political inclusion of previously excluded electors.

In some countries populist leaders built enduring political organizations, such as Peru's APRA (Alianza Popular Revolucionaria Americana), Bolivia's Movimiento Nacionalista Revolucionario (Nationalist Revolutionary Movement, MNR), and Argentina's Peronist party. In other countries such as Ecuador, populist leaders did not create or institutionalize formal parties, and electoral coalitions were assembled for different electoral contests. Kenneth Roberts (2006) explained these different approaches to institution building in terms of the levels of polarization and confrontation provoked by different populist experiences. In some cases, such as Argentina and Peru, the polarized construction of politics ended in a total and fundamental struggle or cleavage between "the people" and "the oligarchy." To sustain conflict with the elite, leaders needed to organize followers in political parties and in civil society organizations. In other experiences, such as that of Velasco Ibarra in Ecuador, there was political but not social polarization. The level of confrontation was not as intense, and Velasco Ibarra did not feel impelled to create formal political and social organizations.

Populist leaders exalted workers as the soul of their nations while simultaneously repressing and co-opting existing labor groups. Social historians have shown how workers strategically used populist political openings to press for autonomous demands against specific bosses and elites. The labor historian Joel Wolfe (1994) described a form of workers' populism under Vargas. Similarly, Daniel James (1988) showed how Argentine workers used the Peronist opening and discourse to attack the symbols of their exclusion from the public sphere and to demand their recognition as workers and citizens. Perón extended the notion of democracy from political rights to include workers' participation in the social and economic life of the nation.

Latin American populists were famous for turning the stigmas of the poor into virtues. In the 1930s and 1940s the elites of Buenos Aires referred to the internal migrants using the term "cabecita negra" to refer to "the subject's dark skin and black hair" (Milanesio, 2010: 55). They called them "black Peronists," or "greasers"—evoking not only the dirt and oil on workers' overalls, but all that is cheap or of bad taste. Juan and his wife Eva Perón transformed the stigmas of these terms. Eva, for instance, used "the term grasita to affectionately refer to the poor" (Milanesio, 2010: 57).

The democratic credentials of classical populists lies in their struggles for open and free elections, and their demands to incorporate the excluded. Peronism expanded the franchise, and voter turnout during Perón's first government grew from 18 to 50 percent of the population. In 1951, under Perón, women won the right to vote, and 64 percent of women voted for the Peronist ticket (Plotkin, 2003: 165). "During Perón's terms in office the share of the national GDP represented by wages increased from 37 to 47 per cent, while real wages increased by 40 per cent between 1946 and 1949" (Plotkin, 2010: 273).

Latin American populists privileged notions of democracy based on the aesthetic and liturgical incorporation of common people in mass rallies more than the institutionalization of popular participation through the rule of law. This explains why the heyday of Latin American populism was associated with moments of collective action such as 17 October 1945 when crowds took over streets and plazas to show their support for Colonel Juan Perón, who claimed to be the embodiment of their will. However, as critics of populism have been arguing for a long time, mobilization and participation in mass rallies did not entail autonomy (Germani, 1971). Populist redemption was based on the authoritarian appropriation of the people's will. Because populist politicians claimed to embody the people, and the people's will was not given institutional channels to express itself, populist regimes replaced rational deliberation with plebiscitary acclamation. Moreover, due to their Manichean discourse and the resulting polarization of political and social cleavages, populist moments resembled situations of war. The foes and friends of populism saw each other as enemies and not as democratic rivals who seek negotiations and agreements.

One of the principal legacies of classical populism was its deep ambivalence toward liberal democracy. That is, classical populism was democratizing to the extent that previously excluded groups were brought into the political system; at the same time, however, populist leaders refused to accept the constraints and limitations of liberal constitutional principles that served to constrain state power, guarantee the political autonomy of civil society, and assure pluralism (Peruzzotti, 2008). After winning his first democratic election in 1946 Perón said: "we have given the people the opportunity to choose, in the cleanest election in the history of Argentina, between us and our opponents. The people have elected us, so the problem is resolved. What we want is now done in the Republic of Argentina" (Peruzzotti, 2008: 109).

Neoliberal Populism

Differently from classical populism, which brought marginalized people into the political community, neoliberal populism took place in the 1990s in nations where most had the right to vote and were already organized by political parties. Leaders such as Carlos Menem in Argentina and Alberto Fujimori in Peru were elected after the failure of import substitution industrialization led to economic catastrophes, as inflation reached levels of 30 to 50 percent per month. They blamed traditional politicians, arguing that they had appropriated the people's sovereignty and led their countries into economic chaos. Some neoliberal populists like Fujimori and Fernando Collor de Mello in Brazil ran as political outsiders. Others like Menem got to power against the wishes of their party's leadership, and Abdalá Bucaram in Ecuador used his personalistic party to challenge the political establishment.

Political parties and elites were portrayed not only as out of touch with the needs and desires of the electorate, but also as enemies of "the people." Fujimori and Bucaram were elected as symbols of the rejection of traditional white political elites. In January, 1990, when Fujimori appeared as the third contestant in opinion polls, the candidate of a coalition of right-wing forces, the internationally acclaimed novelist Mario Vargas Llosa was asked to give his opinion about Fujimori. He replied, "But nobody knows that *chinito* (little China man)." The next day Fujimori opened a major rally in a Lima shantytown with the phrase, "Here we are, the *chinitos* and the *cholitos*" [poor mestizos]. In this fashion, the election became a confrontation between the white elite (*blanquitos* and *pitucos*) and the non-white common people: *chinitos* and *cholitos* (Degregori, 1991: 115). Fujimori, like many Peruvians of indigenous background, was the son of immigrants who had to struggle with "deficient" Spanish, and was discriminated against by traditional white elites. Hence the allure of his simple slogan: "a president like you."

Similarly, after Ecuador's former right-wing president, León Febres Cordero, stated in 1996 that the voters for Bucaram were a "bunch of prostitutes and thieves," Bucaram transformed the meaning of these insults used to describe his base of support by saying that the only prostitutes and thieves were the members of the Ecuadorian oligarchy. During his presidential campaigns and short six-month term in office Bucaram claimed to embody the authentic values, cultures, and aspirations of the poor against those of foreign-oriented elites.

Fernando Collor cultivated the image of a young and energetic political outsider, a messiah acting above and beyond the interests of workers' unions or employers' associations. His mission was to destroy the privileges of inefficient bureaucrats, the *marajás*, to bring redemption to his followers. In the 1989 presidential campaign, Menem projected the image of a winner who has triumphed in two mythologized arenas of social mobility: sports and show business. That is why a few months after becoming president he declared, "I am the president of the nation and I play soccer with Maradona. What else can I ask in life?" (Novaro and Palerm, 1996: 213).

Illustrating how populism lacks an ideology and can be either right or left-wing, once in power these leaders abandoned the nationalist and statist policies of their classical predecessors. They shrank the size of the state and opened their economies. In many instances they privatized what their populist predecessors had nationalized. Draconian shock treatments brought inflation down in Argentina and Peru. In Argentina it "fell from 3,079 percent to 8 percent between 1989 and 1994, while in Peru it declined from 7,650 percent to under 40 percent between 1990 and 1993" (Weyland, 1999: 188).

Neoliberal populists met with differing degrees of success in exercising and holding onto power. Abdalá Bucaram in Ecuador lasted scarcely six months; lacking an institutional base, he was removed by the Congress on the dubious legal grounds that he was mentally incapable of governing. Fernando Collor in Brazil similarly had a weak support base in the legislature and could not survive corruption scandals. By contrast, Carlos Menem and Alberto Fujimori were both reelected to second terms. Their success was explained by how they had lowered hyperinflation and the fact that the privatization of state-owned enterprises gave them funds to pursue patronage and clientelism. Ultimately, the Fujimori regime collapsed under the weight of scandals related to corruption and electoral fraud (he is currently serving time in a Peruvian prison for his involvement in corruption and human rights abuses). Menem's quest for a third term was ruled unconstitutional.

Neoliberal populist leaders had a variety of effects on democratization in their respective countries. Under Menem, the transformation of Perónist identity from an antagonistic opposition between the people and the oligarchy into a more amorphous and less confrontational version with broader appeal made neoliberal populism, in Kurt Weyland's (2001: 16) words, "more representative than classical populism and more compatible with liberal democracy." In Fujimori's Peru liberal democratic institutions were attacked and destroyed. Fujimori "denounced members of Congress as 'unproductive charlatans,' Congress as a 'large, heavy, thick-skinned pachyderm,' and judges as 'jackals.' Fujimori belittled not only existing political parties, but also the concept of parties; they were '*palabrería*' (all talk and no action)" (McClintock, 2013: 223).

RADICAL POPULISM

The extensive bibliography on the turn to the left and the rebirth of radical populism in Latin America agrees that the emergence of the governments of Hugo Chávez, Evo Morales, and Rafael Correa was explained by three endogenous factors (Weyland,

Madrid, and Hunter, 2010; Levitsky and Roberts, 2011; de la Torre and Arnson, 2013). The first was a crisis of political representation. Traditional political parties and the institutional framework of democracy were in crisis. Parties were perceived as instruments of local and foreign elites that implemented neoliberal policies that increased social inequality. These leaders rose to power with platforms that promised to wipe away corrupt politicians and traditional parties, to experiment with participatory forms of democracy, and to implement policies to redistribute income.

Radical populists brought back the old leftist utopias of socialism and revolution, but with a new twist. Instead of violence, these leaders advocated for the revolutionary role of constituent power. Yet similarly to the old left, they disdained constituted power. Constituent power was understood as a revolutionary force that ought to be permanently activated to found again from scratch all the corrupt political institutions that had served the interests of foreign powers and local elites. They were elected with the promise to convene constitutional assemblies that, with the participation of social movements and common citizens, were tasked to draft new constitutions. These new constitutions expanded citizens' rights while simultaneously concentrating power in the executive.

The second cause that explains the rebirth of radical populism in Latin America was widespread popular resistance to neoliberalism. On February 27, 1989, the Venezuelan Caracazo—a massive insurrection against the hike in the price of gasoline—took place. "Many cities were paralyzed by the multitudes who blocked roads and looted thousands of commercial establishments" (López Maya and Panzarelli, 2013: 224). This rebellion conveyed elite nightmares of a savage and uncivilized rabble that invaded the centers of civility. These constructions of the poor as the rabble and as the antithesis to reason and civilized behavior allowed or justified the state's fierce and brutal repression, which ended in at least four hundred deaths. Hugo Chávez, who led a failed coup in 1992, was elected in 1998 with the promise to get rid of neoliberalism and the cartel of corrupt politicians.

Between 1997 and 2005 the three elected presidents of Ecuador—Abdalá Bucaram (1996–1997), Jamil Mahuad (1998–2000), and Lucio Gutiérrez (2003–2005)—were deposed in events where social movements and citizens occupied public spaces to protest against neoliberalism and political corruption. Sociologist León Zamosc (2013: 265) interpreted these uprisings as instances of popular impeachment that applied "the ultimate accountability sanction for a president: removal from office." Rafael Correa, a college professor who never belonged to a political party, was elected in 2006 with a platform to reverse neoliberalism, convene a constituent assembly, and revive national sovereignty.

From 2000 to 2003 Bolivia underwent a cycle of protest and political turmoil that resulted in the collapse of the party system established in 1985, and of the neoliberal economic model. Coalitions of rural and urban indigenous organizations, coca growers, and middle-class sectors fought against water privatization, increasing taxation, the forced eradication of coca leaves, and the surrender of gas reserves to multinational interests. Democratic legitimacy was understood to lie in crowd action where the people directly expressed its sovereignty. The state increasingly relied on repression, in turn radicalizing protestors. In the end, President Gonzalo Sánchez de Losada was forced to leave Bolivia and was succeeded by his vice president Carlos Mesa. Insurgents refused to take power, and "Morales supported a constitutional exit from the crisis in 2003" (Postero, 2010: 14). The insurgents accomplished their goals of getting rid of the neoliberal model, and defending Bolivia's national resources.

A third cause was that citizens perceived that politicians and neoliberal elites had surrendered national sovereignty to the International Monetary Fund, the World Bank, and the US government. Venezuela had changed its pro–third world foreign policy, and become an advocate of neoliberal reform and free trade. In a desperate move to stop hyperinflation in 2000 Ecuador had given up its national currency the Sucre for the US dollar. Bolivia had undergone social strife and human rights abuses as the military unsuccessfully followed US policies of forceful eradication of coca leaf production. Radical populists promised to bring back the interest of the nation state, and to build a multipolar world. They had anti-globalization and anti–United States postures at the core of their foreign policy rhetoric and strategies.

Despite important differences, the governments of Hugo Chávez–Nicolás Maduro in Venezuela, Evo Morales in Bolivia, and Rafael Correa in Ecuador represent a new and distinct phase of radical populism in the region (de la Torre and Arnson, 2013). First, these leaders engaged in permanent political campaigns, using the convening of frequent elections to displace older elites, rally supporters, and consolidate their hegemony. Second, these leaders claimed to be the embodiment of superior forms of democracy that would solve the participatory and representative deficits of liberal democracy, and fulfill the democratizing goal of promoting equality and social justice. For Correa, for example, the essence of democratic citizenship resided in the socio-economic sphere and depended on state policies to advance social justice. For Chávez and Maduro, advancing democracy depended on replacing the unresponsive institutions of liberal democracy with new forms of direct, participatory democracy. And for Morales democracy meant replacing and/or complementing liberal institutions with forms of indigenous communal democracy designed to enhance indigenous participation.

Third, constituent assemblies drafted new constitutions in all three countries to "refound" the nation. The goal was to establish a different kind of democracy, based on elections, but also on a new constitutional order that concentrates power in the hands of the president. Majoritarian mobilization led by a personalistic leader took precedence over the checks and balances and respect for basic civil rights inherent in liberal democracy. Mechanisms of horizontal accountability by other branches of government and an independent press have been replaced by a variant of vertical accountability involving frequent elections, referendums, and plebiscites.

Fourth, in emphasizing substantive democracy, all three regimes relied on state intervention in the economy in the name of distributing wealth and reducing poverty and inequality. Although this statist, redistributionist aspect of populism is not new, governments in Venezuela, Bolivia, and Ecuador were rich in hydrocarbons and reaped huge benefits from the commodity boom of the 2000s that sent oil and natural gas prices to record levels. As a result of enhanced revenues, public investment and social spending skyrocketed and poverty rates and, to a lesser extent, inequality fell when the prices of oil and other commodities were high (Lusting, 2009). Populist social programs had the advantage of rapidly targeting the poor; such programs served to boost the popularity of presidents and functioned as a visible instrument for maintaining power. At the same time, however, they suffered from major flaws in design. Social programs were haphazard and politicized, lacking in efficiency, transparency, and institutionalization. Because they were tied to the persona of the president—who distributed benefits primarily to his or her political supporters rather than on the basis of universal, objective criteria—programs were unlikely to survive beyond the mandate of a particular government. The fiscal foundation of social programs, especially those that rely so heavily on oil and other windfall commodity rents, were unsustainable in the long run (Weyland, 2006). Falling prices of oil led to a dramatic increase of poverty in Venezuela. In 2015 the level of poverty was 45 percent, three points higher that it was when Chávez was first elected in 1998 (Arenas, 2016).

Despite similarities, there are important differences in how these governments were linked with social movements. Evo Morales came to power at the peak of indigenous-led popular protest against neoliberalism and pacted democracy. His party was the political instrument of strong social movements. Participation in Bolivia was to a large extent grounded in communitarian traditions where all participate and deliberate until a decision is made. Leaders at all levels were accountable to their social base. Participation under Morales was more bottom-up, and organizations of the subaltern had the capacity to force the government to reverse policies (Crabtree, 2013).

Differently from Morales, who came to power at the peak of a cycle of protest, Correa was elected when the indigenous movement entered into a crisis, temporarily losing its capacity to engage in sustained collective action. The Ecuadorian opposition did not have the resources to engage in acts of collective defiance against Correa's administration, nor were the stakes perceived to be as high as in Bolivia or Venezuela. Coupled with Correa's technocratic leadership style, his government did not organize the subaltern beyond elections, and has not promoted mechanisms of participatory democracy at the local and community levels (de la Torre, 2013).

The relative weakness of social movements and the exclusion of the informal sector from corporatist organizations during the reign of the two party system known as *Punto fijo* democracy allowed Chávez to create organizations of the subaltern from the top down. The opposition had the organizational strength and the perception that the stakes were serious enough to use collective action to defy and even to try to topple Chávez. The government responded by further organizing popular sectors. Even though organizations of the subaltern were created from the top down, citizens used these organizations to try to push for their autonomous agendas.

The populist view of a homogeneous and inherently virtuous people contributed to the creation of authoritarian governments in Venezuela and Ecuador. Chávez claimed to be the embodiment of the Venezuelan people: "This is not about Hugo Chávez, this about a people" (Zúquete, 2008: 100). Because his mission was to redeem his people from oppression he could say: "I demand absolute loyalty to me. I am not an individual, I am the people" (Gómez Calcaño and Arenas, 2013: 20). Similarly, after winning his second presidential election in 2009 Rafael Correa asserted, "Ecuador voted for itself." He portrayed his struggle on behalf of the poor and the nation as heroic: "We defeated the representatives of the most reactionary sectors of the oligarchy, corrupt bankers, and the media that defend the past." He claimed that his revolution "is irreversible, and nobody would stop it." "We are ready to risk our lives to bring change" (de la Torre, 2012: 256–7).

Chávez did not face political rivals but the oligarchy defined as the enemies of the people, "those self-serving elites who work against the homeland" (Zúquete, 2008: 105). He confronted the oligarchy using a polarizing discourse. He called traditional politicians imbeciles, squalid ones, and little Yankees. He referred to the owners of the media as the "four horsemen of the Apocalypse." Similarly Rafael Correa faced a long list of enemies to his government, his people, and his nation. The list included traditional politicians, the owners of the privately owned media, journalists, the leadership of autonomous social movements, the infantile left, and almost anybody who questioned his policies.

The populist category of the people does not necessarily need to be imagined as one, and does not necessarily lead to the creation of an authoritarian government. In Bolivia, who can speak on behalf of the Bolivian people is contested between powerful social movements and Evo Morales, who at times has tried to embody the will of a unitary people. The Constitution of 2009 declared Bolivia a plurinational and communitarian state. The MAS did not use exclusionary ethnic appeals; on the contrary they constructed the notion of the people as multiethnic and plural (Madrid, 2012). Yet at times Evo Morales has attempted to be the only voice of the people. When indigenous people from the lowlands challenged his policies of mineral extraction they were depicted as manipulated by foreign NGOs, and as not truly indigenous. Morales's regime attempted to impose a hegemonic vision of indigeneity as loyalty to his government. But because of the power of social movements Morales has not been able to impose visions of the people-as-one. In contemporary Bolivia, according to anthropologist Nancy Postero (2015: 422), we are witnessing an "ongoing struggle to define who counts as el pueblo boliviano, and what that means for Bolivian democracy."

Leaders and Followers: How Are They Linked, Organized, and Mobilized?

Researchers have distinguished four linkages between leaders and followers in the three subtypes of populism discussed in this chapter: populist organization, clientelism, the mass media—particularly television—and populist discourse. Populist organizations are based on low levels of institutionalization (Hawkins, 2008). Leaders set their agendas and strategies, and it is difficult to build identities that differ from the image of the people as constructed by leaders. Even though populists actively organized supporters within their movements, these organizations are based on insularity, as they do not promote solidarity with similar organizations in civil society. Populist organizations do not value pluralism because they adopt the idea of the popular as an undifferentiated fusion of "the romantic notion of the people—folk—with the Marxian idea of class ... transforming the people into a unified, homogeneous entity" (Avritzer, 2002: 72). Hence the people can only be organized under organizations that are loyal to the leaders. Yet sometimes, common people use populist organizations, the openings of the political system under populism, and the rhetorical claims that they are the true nation to present their own demands.

Populist organizations created by Chávez's government such as Bolivarian Circles, Communal Councils, Urban Land Committees, and Technical Water Roundtables illustrate the tension between the autonomous organizations of the subaltern and their subordination to a charismatic leader. In order to promote the revolutionary process, President Chávez encouraged the formation of Bolivarian Circles in June, 2001. These were "small groups of seven to fifteen people ... intended to study the ideology of Bolivarianism, discuss local issues and defend the revolution" (Raby, 2006: 188). In their heyday, Bolivarian Circles boasted approximately 2.2 million members and had an active role in the massive demonstrations rescuing President Chávez when he was temporarily removed from office in an April, 2002, coup d'état. Kirk Hawkins and David Hansen (2006: 127) showed that mobilization of the Bolivarian Circles was not necessarily based in the "kind of autonomy that democracy requires." Their study demonstrated that even though Bolivarian Circles did constitute forms of participation for poor people, they often worked as clientelar networks to transfer resources to neighborhoods where the president had supporters.

Communal Councils were conceived as institutions to promote popular power and were seen as the foundation for the future establishment of a socialist direct and pyramidal democracy. Critics and supporters of the Bolivarian Revolution agree that communal Councils so far have faced the same problems as the Bolivarian Circles, namely the persistence of clientelism in the exchange of social services for political support, and a charismatic style of rule that neutralizes or prevents autonomous grassroots inputs (Wilpert, 2007: 195–204).

Bolivarian Circles and Communal Councils may have experienced problems of autonomy because they were created from above. Other institutions such as the Urban Land Committees and Technical Water Roundtables, for example, accepted more autonomous grassroots inputs. The government gave squatter settlements collective titles to land on which precarious self-built dwellings were situated. Through this process, "the community forms an urban land committee to administer its new collective property and to undertake and demand support for material improvement such as water, sewerage and electricity services or road paving" (Raby, 2006: 188–9). Similarly, local water committees "arrange the distribution of water between neighboring communities which share the same water mains" (Raby, 2006: 189). Nevertheless, Urban Land and Water Committees lacked autonomy from the charismatic leader, as Chávez was the guiding force for these institutions (García, 2007).

Populist parties and movements are organized through formal bureaucratic party networks and clientelist and informal networks that distribute resources, information, and jobs to the poor. The first round of studies on political clientelism showed that the poor were not irrational masses that voted for populist demagogic candidates. The poor voted instrumentally for the candidate with the best capacity to deliver goods and serv-ices (Menéndez Carrión, 1986).

The poor in Latin America live under conditions of material and legal deprivation, and in environments of dire violence and insecurity. Because their constitutionally prescribed civil rights are not always respected, the poor rely on politicians and their networks of brokers to have access to a bed in a public hospital, or a job. Brokers are the intermediaries between politicians and poor people. They hoard information and resources and are connected to wider networks and cliques of politicians and state offi-cials. Formal bureaucratic rules work together with personalist cliques and networks of friends who dispense "favors," including corruption.

Because the poor can choose to leave a broker and join a different network, brokers' positions are unstable, and the poor cannot be seen as a manipulated and captive vot-ing base. The poor can exit a network, they can also choose to not vote as the broker requested, or might feel compelled to repay a favor to the broker. The unreliable nature of political support gives certain advantages to the poor. For the system of exchanges to work, politicians have to deliver at least some resources.

Like other political parties, populists exchange services for votes. But in addition to offering material rewards, populist exchanges go together with a discourse that portrays common people as the essence of the nation. In addition to exchanging material goods for votes, populist networks also generate political identities (Auyero, 2001). The resil-ience of Peronism among the poor, for example, was partially explained by the informal and clientelist networks of the Peronist Party, which in addition to delivering material resources to the poor recreated political and cultural identities (Auyero, 2001; Levistky, 2001).

Latin American populists were media innovators. Eva Perón used the radio to com-municate directly with her followers, transforming politics into a melodrama where she staged her love to the poor.

> Her scenarios never changed and her characters were stereotyped by the same adjec-tives: Perón was always "glorious," the people "marvelous," the oligarchy *egoísta y vende patria* [selfish and corrupt], and she was a "humble" or "weak" woman, "burn-ing her life for them" so that social justice could be achieved, *cueste lo que cueste y caiga quien caiga* [at whatever cost and regardless of consequences]. (Navarro, 1982: 59)

Television became one of the main venues used by populists to win elections, and to govern. Populists creatively blended exposure on television with traditional mechanisms of vote gathering, like mass rallies and clientelist networks. Some like Carlos Menem were innovators. Following the example of Pope John Paul II, he visited common peo-ple in their neighborhoods in his *menemovil*. His image had more in common with a "religious leader or a show business celebrity, than with a typical politician campaigning" (Novaro and Palermo, 1996: 207). Like Menem, Abdalá Bucaram used the media to rep-resent his government as a televised show. With constant media exposure, Menem and

Bucaram attempted to construct their personas as central political events. They used sports and popular culture to demonstrate that they were like the common man, and to simultaneously show that they were superior because they triumphed in these nonpolitical arenas. Menem played soccer with Maradona, and Bucaram sang and danced on television. While Menem was successful in using television to help him to secure his rule, Bucaram failed because upper- and middle-class publics read his performances as an eruption of vulgarity in the presidential palace (de la Torre, 2010).

Hugo Chávez and Rafael Correa developed weekly television programs where they informed citizens about their governmental projects and policies, set the news agenda for the week, and simultaneously entertained the public by singing and mocking their political enemies. Like other populists, they had conflict with the privately owned media closing and censoring critical media venues. Fujimori used corruption to silence journalists and to create tabloids that supported his government (McClintock, 2013). Chávez and Correa were convinced that the media were the main tool used by the opposition, and that they have a big role in forging hegemony (Waisbord, 2013). They formed state-owned media venues. In nations without traditions of public media, these venues functioned as tools of government propaganda in the hands of the executive. They created laws and state institutions to control what the private media could publish, and to sanction the infractions of journalists and media owners. As a result, journalists and media owners self-censored their publications, and the quality of debates in the public sphere deteriorated.

Post-structuralists argue that discourse is "the primary terrain within which the social is constituted" (Laclau, 2005: 49). Scholars who do not accept the epistemological and ontological assumptions of their post-structuralist peers also consider discourse as one of the defining traits of populism. They claim that this particular way of framing social reality produces antagonistic conflict between groups, and constitutes identities. Populism constructs the struggle between the people and the oligarchy as an ethical and moral confrontation between good and evil, redemption and downfall. The term "the people," however, is profoundly vague and elastic. In order to disentangle its ambiguities it is important to start with Laclau's (2005: 48) observation that the people "as operating in populist discourses is never a primary datum but a construct—populist discourse does not simply *express* some kind of original popular identity; it actually *constitutes* the latter." What needs to be researched is: Who is excluded and included in these discursive constructs? Who has created these categories? And, what are the levels of social and or political polarization produced by populist discourse?

Populist rhetoric in Latin America historically constructed the people as urban and mestizo (ethnically and culturally mixed folk) who had an antagonistic relationship with the oligarchy. The exaltation of poor and mestizo as the essence of the nation repelled elites who were terrified by populist challenges. The populist creation of a virtuous and mestizo nation, however, excluded those of indigenous and African descent. In order to belong to the people and to the nation, indigenous and Afro-descendants were encouraged to adopt national-mestizo values, to reject their cultural specificity, and to whiten themselves.

During the 1952 Bolivian revolution, for example, the "Indian was erased in favor of a mestizo identity," and languages of class tried to conceal ethnicity (Canessa, 2006: 245).

Due to the strength of indigenous organizations the discursive elaborations of who belongs to the people changed. Evo Morales and his party Movimiento al Socialismo replaced "the mestizo as the iconic citizen with the indígena" (Canessa, 2006: 255). Morales's success is explained, in part, by his ability to articulate anxieties provoked by globalization while presenting indigenous people as the essence of the nation. Raúl Madrid (2012) uses the term ethnopopulism to explain the success of Morales's strategies in using populist and inclusionary ethnic appeals. The confrontation was between those who have struggled to defend Bolivia's natural resources—indigenous people—and the oligarchy that has transferred them to imperialist and foreign powers (Canessa, 2006).

The degree of social and political polarization produced by populist discourse allows for a differentiation between experiences. In some cases, such as in Chavismo as well as in the classical populist experience of Peronism, the Manichean construction of politics ends in a total and fundamental struggle between the people, as a social and political category, and the oligarchy. Chavez's nationalism, anti-imperialism, positive glorifications of *el pueblo* as *el soberano*, and his use of mass meetings and mobilization, are similar to the already mentioned classical populist experience. But most important is that his movement politicized economic, cultural, and ethnic cleavages. In other cases, for instance Alberto Fujimori in the 1990s in Peru or Velasco Ibarra in Ecuador in the 1940s, the terms *pueblo* and *oligarquía* had political but not necessarily social contents. Political polarization did not lead to social polarization. Finally, there are mixed cases, such as Abdalá Bucaram's and Lucio Gutiérrez's elections and short administrations in Ecuador. Despite their attempts to bring traditional elites abroad into their neoliberal project, their personas brought political, social, and even cultural polarization. All of their actions, words, and performances were read through class lines and were portrayed by the upper and middle class as the embodiment of the culture of the rabble.

Populism cannot be reduced to the words, actions, and strategies of leaders. The autonomous expectations, cultures, and discourses of followers are equally important in understanding the populist bond. In order to comprehend the appeal of populism, serious attention should be paid to the words, communications, and conversations between leaders and followers as they occur during political rallies. Populist narratives empowered common people who have to endure humiliations in their daily lives. Populist leaders have symbolically dignified the poor and the non-white who are portrayed by elites and the media as the rabble, the embodiment of barbarism.

WHY DOES POPULISM REAPPEAR IN SOME NATIONS AND NOT IN OTHERS?

Whereas populist leaders of different ideologies keep on reappearing in Argentina, Bolivia, Brazil, Ecuador, Peru, and Venezuela, in Chile, Uruguay, Colombia, and Costa Rica populist leaders did not get to power. When populism emerged in the latter nations, such as with Jorge Eliecer Gaitán in Colombia in the 1930s and 1940s, he did not win the

1946 presidential election, was assassinated in 1948, and a wave of violence erupted in the aftermath (Braun, 1985). The most common explanations for the absence of populism in some nations of Latin America are strong party systems and functioning liberal democracies upholding the rule of law.

Populism, as Kenneth Roberts (2015: 147–8) argues, is the result of a crisis of political representation. It first emerged when excluded people without partisan loyalty were enfranchised for the first time. In some countries, like in Colombia and Uruguay, traditional political parties incorporated the previously excluded. However, in most countries, like Argentina, Brazil, Bolivia, Venezuela, Mexico, and Peru, "new labor-based populist parties and political movements arose in opposition to the oligarchical political establishment reconfiguring party systems around an elite/popular sociopolitical cleavage." In Ecuador populism emerged with Velasco Ibarra in the 1930s and 1940s but he did not organize followers in stable parties or organizations of civil society.

A second crisis of political representation was produced by political systems such as Venezuela's two parties system, when it became unresponsive and unaccountable in the 1990s. Hugo Chávez rebelled against closed, self-interested, and self-reproducing cartel parties. A third scenario for a crises of political representation, according to Roberts (2015: 149), occurs when "political representation and political competition tend to become highly personalized, voters support and identify with leaders rather than party organizations or platforms, and the axes of political competition are likewise drawn between rival personalities who claim to better represent the true interests of the people." Under these conditions a series of populist leaders, political outsiders, and personalist leaders as in Ecuador or Peru emerged and rose to power.

Another hypothesis to explain the attraction of populism has focused on the particular form of political incorporation in Latin America: one based on weak citizenship rights and strong rhetorical appeals to, and mobilization of, *el pueblo* (de la Torre, 2010: 124–5). In Latin America, there is a duality between the official recognition of rights in constitutions and the rhetoric of state officials and the weak implementation of these same rights in everyday life. The rule of law is tenuous at best; at worst, the law appears to serve only the interests of the powerful few. A vast social science literature has explored these "deficits" in the quality of democracy in Latin America, the truncated nature of citizenship, and the difficulties of democratic deepening once democracy's electoral dimensions have been established. Not all forms of legal, political, or socio-economic exclusion give rise to populism. But in the absence or discrediting of mechanisms of political mediation and institutions of representation, populist interventions that give name to and politicize people's daily experiences of marginalization and humiliation remain a constant possibility. As Kirk Hawkins argues (2010: 149), "a Manichaean discourse denouncing elite conspiracies and celebrating the eventual triumph of the popular will speaks to a real underlying problem of democratic failure in which the vast majority of citizens are poorly served by a dysfunctional or even predatory state." Nations where citizens perceive that the rule of law protects them from the state and the powerful, such as Uruguay, Chile, and Costa Rica, are free of populism.

Populism occurred in three distinct historical waves, and as Rovira Kaltwasser (2015) argues we have to account for its mechanisms of diffusion and emulation. Perón and Chávez purposefully aimed to export their models of political transformation and their ideologies not only to Latin America, but also to the world at large, generously funding politicians and social movements. The current wave of radical populism was influenced by Chávez's script of political transformation. Without denying the importance of endogenous factors it is evident that Chávez's model was emulated and adapted in Ecuador and Bolivia where leaders conveyed constitutional assemblies, concentrated power in the executive, enacted laws to regulate the content of what the privately owned media could publish, regulated NGOs, and co-opted independent social movements. These self-described Bolivarian nations also claimed to be implementing policies to reach a different form of development based on the ideology of socialism in the twenty-first century, and forged the Bolivarian Alliance of the Peoples as an alternative to US-led free trade agreements.

CONCLUSIONS

Populism is based on the discursive antagonistic confrontation between the people and the power block. Latin American populists shared understandings of democracy as mass action on behalf of a leader constructed as the incarnation of democratic ideals, more than in the institutionalization of democracy through the rule of law. Populism is not tied to specific social and economic conditions, and might arise in nations with fragile institutions, and where the rule of law is weak. In nations where the poor have to endure humiliations by the rich and by state officials, the populist temptation to transform stigmas into sources of dignity and pride is always present.

Classical populism represented the first incorporation of previously excluded people into the national community. It was based on the exaltation of common people as the embodiment of true and uncorrupted national traditions and values against foreign-oriented elites. In the more developed nations such as Mexico, Argentina, and Brazil it built or co-opted labor organizations, and followed nationalist and redistributive social policies that coincided with import substitution industrialization. In more agrarian-based societies it was not linked to policies of industrialization, but represented the political inclusion of previously excluded electors. Populists expanded the franchise, and through mass rallies and demonstration gave a symbolic sense of inclusion and dignity to the poor and the marginalized. In many nations it built long-lasting organizations that created strong political loyalties.

Neoliberal populists used discourses against political parties portraying them as oligarchic cliques that have illegally appropriated the people's sovereignty. Differently from classical populist experiences where political schism led to social polarization, these movements and regimes were confined to political divisions. In some cases, such as Fujimori's Peru, neoliberal populism led to the destruction of previously existing political systems. Similarly to classical populism it included previously excluded people, this time those who made a living in the informal sector and were not part of working- or middle-class organizations. As with classical populism it led to the renewal of economic elites, as business people without social recognition sought to be accepted as equals by well-established elites. Even though in their rhetoric they focused on the values of common people portrayed as the essence of the nation, their policies abandoned nationalism, pursued the opening of their economies to international markets, and reduced the size of the state.

Radical populists of the twenty-first century are similar to classical populists in their politicization of social and economic exclusions. As in some classical populist experiences, political and social polarizations coincided. Similarly to neoliberal populists, they portrayed traditional political parties as the source of their country's ills, and contributed to the collapse of party systems. They linked neoliberal economic policies directly with liberal politics, practices, and values. As a result the evils of "the long night of neoliberalism," as Correa liked to say, were intimately tied to the failures of liberal democracy. Their nationalist and statist policies were similar to those of their classical predecessors. In mineral-rich nations such as Venezuela, Ecuador, and Bolivia, they reversed neoliberal policies, and implemented nationalist and redistributive policies based on mineral resources rent. Yet they kept policies of their neoliberal populist cousins that targeted the poor who make a living in the informal sector.

Radical populists of the twenty-first century differed in their leadership styles and in the type of relationship between leaders and social movement organizations. Rafael Correa, Hugo Chávez, and Nicolás Maduro resorted to a leadership style based on unity and command from above where the leader appears to be the condensation of diverse demands made from below. These leaders claimed to embody the demands of diverse constituencies, and to directly represent the sovereignty of the people. Evo Morales followed a different leadership strategy. He pursued convergence and persuasion, allowing more autonomy to his grassroots constituency (French, 2009: 367). Chávez, Maduro, and Correa followed top-down strategies of mobilization, and co-opted previously existing social movement organizations. Morales built his leadership on a network of autonomous movement organizations. It remains to be seen whether these organizations will keep their autonomy, or if they will be included and co-opted into corporatist structures like the ones built by the MNR in the 1950s. Like previous populists, they promised better democratic arrangements to improve on the failures of participation and representation in liberal democratic regimes. Yet, as in previous populism, popular organizations were subordinated to the will of leaders, and atmospheres of political confrontation and polarization were created. In Venezuela and Ecuador authoritarian tendencies prevailed. In Bolivia the strength of social movements and the inclusion of indigenous people might mitigate Morales's authoritarian temptations.

As with the previous waves, radical populism was unstable. Its nationalism, anti-imperialism, and redistribution rested on the high prices of commodities. These were hyper-personalistic regimes, and as Chávez's death illustrated, charisma could not be transferred to a hand-picked successor. Yet despite these vulnerabilities, radical popu-lism had strong ideological appeals. In a world dominated by neoliberalism, and with increasing inequalities, it promised social justice, and the democratization of society via the transformative power of constituent power. Yet, its views of the people as one, of rivals as enemies, and of popular sovereignty as one and undivided led to the creation of authoritarian governments.

NOTE

1   I thank Paul Taggart, Cristóbal Rovira Kaltwasser, Pierre Ostiguy, Sebastían Barros, and the other participants in the workshop on Comparative Populism World Wide, at the Catholic University of Chile, Santiago, July 4 and 5, 2014, for their comments on a previous version of this chapter.

REFERENCES

Arenas, Nelly. 2016. "El chavismo sin Chávez: la deriva de un populismo sin carisma," *Nueva Sociedad*, 261: 13–22.

Auyero, Javier. 2001. *Poor People's Politics*. Durham: Duke University Press.

Avritzer, Leonardo. 2002. *Democracy and the Public Sphere in Latin America*. Princeton: Princeton University Press.

Braun, Herbert. 1985. *The Assassination of Gaitán: Public Life and Urban Violence in Colombia*. Madison: University of Wisconsin Press.

Canessa, Andrew. 2006. "Todos somos indígenas: toward a new language of national political identity," *Bulletin of Latin American Research*, 25(2): 241–63.

Crabtree, John. 2013. "From the MNR to the MAS: populism, parties, the state, and social movements in Bolivia since 1952," in Carlos de la Torre and Cynthia Arnson (eds), *Populism of the Twenty First Century*. Baltimore and Washington, DC: Johns Hopkins University Press and Woodrow Wilson Center Press, 269–95.

Degregori, Carlos Iván. 1991. "El aprendiz de brujo y el curandero chino," in Carlos Iván Degregori, Carlos Iván and Romeo Grompone (eds), *Demonios y redentores en el nuevo Perú*. Lima: IEP, 71–137.

de la Torre, Carlos. 2010. *Populist Seduction in Latin America*, 2nd edn. Athens: Ohio University Press.

de la Torre, Carlos. 2012. "Correa un populista del siglo XXI," in Isidoro Cheresky (ed.), *¿Qué Democracia en América Latina?* Buenos Aires: CLACSO Prometeo, 251–81.

de la Torre, Carlos. 2013. "El Tecnopopulismo de Rafael Correa. ¿Es compatible el carisma con la tecnocracia?," *Latin American Research Review*, 48(1): 24–43.

de la Torre, Carlos and Cynthia Arnson. 2013. "Introduction: the evolution of Latin American populism and the debates over its meanings," in Carlos de la Torre and Cynthia Arnson (eds), *Latin American Populism in the Twenty-First Century*. Baltimore and Washington, DC: Johns Hopkins University Press and Woodrow Wilson Center Press, 1–37.

French, John. 2009. "Understanding the politics of Latin America's plural lefts (Chavez/Lula): social democracy, populism and convergence on the path to a post-neoliberal world," *Third World Quarterly*, 30(2): 249–70.

García Guadilla, María Pilar. 2007. "Ciudadanía y autonomía en las organizaciones sociales bolivarianas: los Comités de Tierra Urbana como movimientos sociales," *Cuadernos del CENDES*, 24(6): 47–73.

Germani, Gino. 1971. *Política y sociedad en una epoca de transición*. Buenos Aires: Editorial Paidos.

Gómez Calcaño, Luis and Nancy Arenas. 2013. "El populismo chavista: autoritarismo electoral para amigos y enemigos," *Cuadernos del CENDES*, 82: 17–34.

Hawkins, Kirk. 2008. "La organización populista. Los Cículos Bolivarianos en Venezuela," in Carlos de la Torre and Enrique Peruzzotti (eds), *El retorno del Pueblo*. Quito: FLACSO, 125–60.

Hawkins, Kirk. 2010. *Venezuela's Chavism and Populism in Comparative Perspective*. Cambridge: Cambridge University Press.

Hawkins, Kirk and David Hansen. 2006. "Dependent civil society: the Círculos Bolivarianos in Venezuela," *Latin American Research Review*, 41(1): 102–32.

James, Daniel. 1988. *Resistance and Integration. Peronism and the Argentine Working Class 1946-1976*. Cambridge: Cambridge University Press.

Laclau, Ernesto. 2005. "Populism: what's in a name?," in Francisco Panizza (ed.), *Populism and the Mirror of Democracy*. London: Verso, 32–55.

Levitsky, Steven. 2001. "An 'organized disorganization': informal organisation and the persistance of local party structures in Argentine Peronism," *Journal of Latin American Studies*, 33: 29–65.

Levitsky, Steven and Kenneth Roberts (eds). 2011. *The Resurgence of the Latin American Left*. Baltimore: Johns Hopkins University Press.

López Maya, Margarita and Alexandra Panzarelli. 2013. "Populism, rentierism, and socialism in the twenty-first century: the case of Venezuela," in Carlos de la Torre and Cynthia Arnson (eds), *Latin American Populism in the Twenty-First Century*. Baltimore and Washington, DC: Johns Hopkins University Press and Woodrow Wilson Center Press, 239–69.

Lustig, Nora. 2009. "Poverty, inequality, and the New Left in Latin America," *Woodrow Wilson Center Update on the Americas*, October. http://www.wilsoncenter.org/sites/default/files/LAP_090716_LustigBulletinENG_1.pdf.

Madrid, Raúl. 2012. *The Rise of Ethnic Politics in Latin America*. Cambridge: Cambridge University Press.

McClintock, Cynthia. 2013. "Populism in Peru: from APRA to Ollanta Humala," in Carlos de la Torre and Cynthia Arnson (eds), *Latin American Populism in the Twenty-First Century*. Baltimore and Washington, DC: Johns Hopkins University Press and Woodrow Wilson Center Press, 203–39.

Menéndez-Carrión, Amparo. 1986. *La conquista del voto*. Quito: Corporación Editora Nacional.

Milanesio, Natalia. 2010. "Peronists and Cabecitas: stereotypes and anxieties at the peak of social change," in Matthew B. Karush and Oscar Chamosa (eds), *The New Cultural History of Peronism*. Durham: Duke University Press, 53–85.

Navarro, Marysa. 1982. "Evitas's charismatic leadership," in Michael Conniff (ed.), *Latin American Populism in Comparative Perspective*. Albuquerque: University of New Mexico Press, 47–67.

Novaro, Marcos and Vicente Palermo. 1996. *Política y poder en el gobierno de Menem*. Buenos Aires: FLACSO and Norma.

Peruzzotti, Enrique. 2008. "Populismo y representación democrática," in Carlos de la Torrre and Enrique Peruzzotti (eds), *El Retorno del Pueblo*. Quito: FLACSO, 97–125.

Plotkin, Martin. 2003. *Mañana es San Perón: A Cultural History of Peron's Argentina*. Wilmington: Scholarly Resources.

Plotkin, Martin. 2010. "Final reflections," in Matthew B. Karush and Oscar Chamosa (eds), *The New Cultural History of Peronism*. Durham: Duke University Press, 271–87.

Postero, Nancy. 2010. "Morales's MAS government building indigenous popular hegemony in Bolivia," *Latin American Perspectives*, 37(3): 18–34.

Postero, Nancy. 2015. "El pueblo Boliviano de composición plural: a look at plurinationalism in Bolivia," in Carlos de la Torre (ed.), *The Promise and Perils of Populism*. Lexington: University Press of Kentucky, 398–431.

Raby, D. L. 2006. *Democracy and Revolution: Latin America and Socialism Today*. London: Pluto Press.

Roberts, Kenneth. 2006. "Populism, political conflict, and grass-roots organization in Latin America," *Comparative Politics*, 38(2): 127–48.

Roberts, Kenneth. 2015. "Populism, political mobilizations, and crises of political representation," in Carlos de la Torre (ed.), *The Promise and Perils of Populism*. Lexington: University Press of Kentucky, 140–59.

Rovira Kaltwasser, Cristóbal. 2015. "Explaining the emergence of populism in Europe and the Americas," in Carlos de la Torre (ed.), *The Promise and Perils of Populism*. Lexington: University Press of Kentucky, 189–231.

Waisbord, Silvio. 2013. *Vox Populista: Medios, periodismo, democracia*. Buenos Aires: Gedisa.

Weyland, Kurt. 1999. "Populism in the age of neoliberalism," in Michael L. Conniff (ed.), *Populism in Latin America*. Tucaloosa: University of Alabama Press, 172–91.

Weyland, Kurt. 2001. "Clarifying a contested concept," *Comparative Politics*, 34(1): 1–22.

Weyland, Kurt. 2006. "The rise of Latin America's two lefts: insights from rentier state theory," *Comparative Politics*, 41(2): 145–64.

Weyland, Kurt, Raúl Madrid, and Wendy Hunter (eds). 2010. *Leftist Governments in Latin America: Successes and Shortcomings*. Cambridge: Cambridge University Press.

Wilpert, Gregory. 2007. *Changing Venezuela by Taking Power: The History and Policies of the Chávez Government*. London: Verso.

Wolfe, Joel. 1994. "'Father of the poor' or 'mother of the rich'? Getúlio Vargas, industrial workers, and constructions of class, gender, and populism in São Paulo, 1930–1954," *Radical History Review*, 58(80): 80–112.

Zamosc, León. 2013. "Popular impeachments: Ecuador in comparative perspective," in Mario Sznajder, Luis Roniger, and Carlos Forment (eds), *Shifting Frontiers of Citizenship: The Latin American Experience*. Leiden-Boston: Brill, 237–67.

Zúquete, José Pedro. 2008. "The missionary politics of Hugo Chávez," *Latin American Politics and Society*, 50(1): 91–122.

CHAPTER 11

....

POPULISM IN
THE POST-SOVIET STATES

....

LUKE MARCH

ALTHOUGH the term populism is used in analysis of the former Soviet Union (FSU), it has not received sustained academic attention. One reason is that several studies focus on post-communist countries generally, thereby conflating non-Soviet East Central Europe (ECE) and the post-Soviet states (e.g. Mudde, 2001; Tismaneanu, 2001). A second reason is the prevalence of case studies rather than comparative analyses. A third is the understandable problems of empirical research in many countries in the region, not least the more authoritarian countries of Central Asia.

A closer look at the region reveals that the term is ubiquitous, much as in Western Europe, which looks like evidence of a similar populist zeitgeist. However, employing the more discriminatory ideological definition of populism allows us to discount the majority of such instances. In fact, particularly compared with the supposed "populist backlash" in ECE (Rupnik, 2007), clear and sustained instances of populism are a distinct rarity.

This chapter focuses on the content and context of post-Soviet populism. The focus is on the twelve non-EU post-Soviet states, i.e. Armenia, Azerbaijan, Belarus, Georgia, Kazakhstan, Kyrgyzstan, Moldova, Russia, Tajikistan, Turkmenistan, Ukraine, and Uzbekistan. The Baltic states (Estonia, Latvia, Lithuania) will be mentioned but are also covered in Ben Stanley's chapter in this volume. Because of Russia's size and role as a norm-maker for the region, it naturally receives the most analysis. On closer inspection, it will become apparent that, although ECE and the FSU share some common Leninist legacies, the demand side for populism is more complex in the latter, and it does not represent an equally propitious "breeding ground" for populist backlash. However, it is the supply side that is most problematic. The "democratic transition" has seen the consolidation of authoritarian tendencies across the FSU, with competitive authoritarianism increasingly giving way to outright authoritarian regimes. Without a minimal level of pluralism, such as that existing in "imperfect" democracies in Eastern Europe and Latin America, it is extremely difficult to develop genuine and stable populist forces.

Therefore, populism is usually confined to the margins of the political systems in the FSU. Where it has become more relevant and prevalent, it has usually been in cases of regime breakdown or elite infighting where pluralism has got an outlet. Yet, in most of these cases, populist mobilization is temporary, as former populists become post-populist authoritarians whose populist rhetoric appears increasingly insubstantial. However, generally, elites manage to consolidate and *anti*-populist leaders (such as Vladimir Putin) have become the rule. Such leaders may employ some populist rhetoric, but their fundamental impulse is elitist. They co-opt, mimic, or simply oppress social mobilization, making stability their watchword and regarding genuine populism as a dangerous threat to their rule.

The chapter proceeds as follows. The first section highlights how using discourse-related definitions of populism is insufficiently discriminatory, since many actors use populist discourse sporadically, and argues that the ideological definition of populism is far more effective. The second section shows how there are strong incentives for populism in the FSU (especially the Leninist ideological heritage and socio-economic conditions), but that the absence of pluralism and democracy in much of the region acts as a strong retardant. Further, the third section highlights how the dominant form of leadership in the region is anti-populist elitism. Such leadership is clientelistic and fundamentally opposed to populist mobilization. The fourth section focuses on some exceptions: "mobilizational presidents" who have emerged in periods of regime break-down and/or popular mobilization, but who have generally been unable to maintain their populist policies. The fifth section highlights the presence of populism in party systems, stressing that populist parties have struggled to endure in conditions generally inimical to pluralism. This section is followed by the conclusion.

DEFINITIONS: VERNACULAR POPULISM VS IDEOLOGICAL POPULISM

Prima facie, almost every political force in the FSU is populist. Bale et al. note the "vernacular" use of populism by media and political actors world-wide, whereby populism is applied randomly to seemingly unrelated actors in a pejorative way (Bale, van Kessel, and Taggart, 2011). The FSU is little different: "populism" is similarly a catch-all insult for "irresponsible" political opponents. Former Ukrainian President Viktor Yanukovych provided an archetypal example, describing all his national-liberal opponents as populists: "Total populism and a pack of lies—that is their essence" (quoted in Kuzio, 2010: 9).

Problematically, much of the academic study of populism in the FSU either employs variants of the vernacular definition (e.g. Korguniuk, 2010); fails to define the term at all (e.g. Shekhovtsov, 2013); or uses idiosyncratic definitions (e.g. including anti-Americanism) (Kuzio, 2010). One common usage describes higher social spending as "social populism" (Kuzio, 2010). Similarly, hydrocarbon-rich states in the region (e.g.

Russia and Turkmenistan) have been described as being governed by "petro-populism," defined as "the excessive use of natural resource revenues to buy political support" (Matsen, Natvik, and Torvik, 2014: 1). But there is no necessary connection between populism and expansionary economic policies, as neoliberal populisms in Latin America and ECE demonstrate. The result of such diverse definitions is the vast exaggeration of instances of populism in the FSU.

This chapter utilizes the ideological definition of populism as expounded in the introduction (see also Mudde's chapter in this volume). The chief advantages of the ideological approach are that it is parsimonious, minimal, and comparative, and is the only definition to focus on the core (rather than peripheral or instrumental) features of a populist. I will also use Stijn Van Kessel's useful method of relating the ideological definition to discourse-related definitions (Van Kessel, 2014). At a higher level of abstraction, populism is a "descriptor," a rhetorical strategy used sporadically by any political actor. At a lower level of abstraction, populism is a "classifier"; parties can be classified as populist when populism is a core and consistent ideological component. Van Kessel argues that since post-communist EU countries are characterized by widespread dissatisfaction, corruption, and new parties, the extension of "populist discourse" used in a "fleeting sense" by many actors is very high, but the occurrence of genuinely ideological populist actors is much rarer. We will see that this applies to the FSU too: using the ideological definition helps distinguish more consistent populists (for example, Yulia Tymoshenko) from those who occasionally employ demotic rhetoric (e.g. Vladimir Putin), and helps decide whether actors are truly populist, borderline populist, or essentially non-populist (cf. Stanley, this volume). But before we look at the specifics of these "populists," we will examine the environment and political opportunity structures that condition the context within which they operate.

CONTEXT: FROM LENIN, PERÓN, TO PUTIN?

At first glance, the post-Soviet environment indicates every reason to expect a similar "populist backlash" to that which has allegedly affected ECE over the last decade, not least because of fundamental similarities in the still-persistent communist legacy. On closer look, there are as many differences as similarities. Nevertheless, let us take the similarities first.

Perhaps most relevant is the way in which communism provided a ready ideological-lexical arsenal for populism. The ideas of the nineteenth-century Russian revolutionary peasant populists (the *narodniki*) informed Marxism-Leninism's radical rejection of constitutional limits on the state and assertion of the revolutionary potential of the peasantry (Clarke, 2002). David Brandenburger even argues that Stalin was an "authoritarian populist" because he presided over a Soviet populism designed to mobilize society "on the mass level" and formed a new national identity from a non-proletarian past (Brandenberger, 2010). Moreover, because Marxist-Leninists saw proletarian interests as universal, it was simple to elide distinctions between proletariat and people in "popular fronts" and "people's democracies." Nikita Khrushchev's 1961 formulation of the "all-people's state" arguably indicated that proletarianism had become populism.

However, seeing the Soviet Union as "socialist in form, populist in content" is vastly overstated, because to the end the Party tried to "lead and guide" popular interests and control popular mobilization. Nevertheless, when divested of its Marxist-Leninist ideological underpinning and Party control, the communist lexicon provides handy additions to the populist rhetorical canon, such as a core commitment to popular sovereignty, the Cult of Personality, anti-bureaucratism, and Manichean conspirology (the awareness of "wreckers," "enemies," and "fifth columnists"). Communist discourses, mentalities, and practices have deeply embedded themselves in post-communist politics, particularly where there are continuities between the elites and security services (Wilson, 2005).

The post-Leninist socio-economic landscape also appears to provide propitious conditions, with significant parallels to the drivers for Latin American populism. Populism is recurrent in countries with "deep structural inequalities," "weak institutional channels to process social conflicts," "where people are economically and legally poor" and "discourses of democracy are used to silence and exclude" (de la Torre, 2010: xv). Both Latin America and post-communist countries share such conditions. Relative to Western Europe, post-communist systems exhibit an ideological "vacuum": they are low trust societies, with greater social stratification, less stable party systems, and in general less institutionalized and more personalized political landscapes (Tismaneanu, 1996). The lack of historically entrenched parties (with the exception of those emerging from the former ruling regimes) mirrors the absence in much of Latin America of "mass-bureaucratic" parties with stable institutionalized links to social movements, classes, and organizations such as trade unions (Levitsky, 2001). In Latin America, this absence allowed "mass populist" parties to flourish, with charismatic leaders at the head of loosely institutionalized social movements. In post-communist countries, the absence of strong intermediary institutions has also exacerbated the elite-driven nature of democratic "transition." When the elites are either ex-communists, endemically corrupt, or both, this has fostered an anti-elite discourse of "revolution betrayed," with the post-Leninist ideological vacuum engendering the reassertion of dormant authoritarian political-cultural motifs (Mudde, 2001; Rupnik, 2007). In other words, "communism's collectivist and egalitarian promises have risen again in the form of new salvation fantasies that attempt to synthesize far-left and far-right radical visions" (Tismaneanu, 2014: 63).

In this context, the FSU looks a still more propitious "breeding ground" for populism than post-communist ECE, especially compared with countries (e.g. the Czech Republic) whose relative prosperity, stability, and structured party systems have (generally) limited the success of populist parties therein. FSU countries are generally still poorer, more stratified, and more corrupt. For example, Georgia is the only FSU state less corrupt than ECE countries such as Croatia, Hungary, and Romania (Transparency International, 2015). Moreover, the FSU countries have still weaker liberal traditions, more unstable intermediary democratic institutions, and still more dominant elite-led political systems. Most FSU countries (the Baltic States excepted) emerged from "patrimonial communist" regimes, i.e. communist systems that developed in largely pre-industrial, pre-democratic environments, which therefore have more residual legitimacy than those systems imposed by force in more developed countries in ECE and the Baltics (Kitschelt et al., 1999). This has led to fluid and informal socio-political institutions being the norm, along with "patrimonial" rather than "rational-legal" forms of authority (Stewart et al., 2012). Patrimonialism results in weak to non-existent party systems and "patronal presidential" forms of governance, i.e. where presidents act as the fulcrum of rent-seeking elites (Hale, 2005). In many cases, the formal and informal powers of such patronal presidents surpass those of the Latin American presidentialist "delegative democracies."

Conversely, there are key features of the FSU landscape, both on the demand and supply side, which on closer view actually retard the prospects for populism relative to ECE or Latin America. The main obstacle is the ambiguous status of democracy, pluralism, and civil society in the region. In the FSU, only the Baltic States are stable democracies. Moldova, Ukraine, and Georgia are examples of "feckless pluralism," with weak, corrupt states, but "significant amounts of political freedom, regular elections, and alternation of power between genuinely different political groupings" (Carothers, 2002: 11). Armenia, Azerbaijan, and Kyrgyzstan (although the latter is increasingly pluralist) are "dominant-power" countries where elite dominance limits pluralism and prevents the rotation of power. The other Central Asian states, Belarus, and now arguably Russia are outright authoritarian states with virtual leaders-for-life and emasculated civil societies. Indicatively, Freedom House scores confirm that between 2000 and 2015 the Baltic States were Free; Armenia, Moldova, Georgia, and Ukraine were Partly Free (Ukraine was briefly classed Free in 2010); Kyrgyzstan oscillated between Unfree and Partly Free; and Belarus had moved from Partly Free to Unfree by 2000, while Azerbaijan and Russia followed by 2005. The rest were emphatically Unfree during this period. Conversely, all East Central European and Latin American Countries were either Free or Partly Free (Freedom House, 2015).

The reasons for these varied regime trajectories are complex and beyond the scope of this contribution. What is relevant to note is that the parlous status of pluralism and democracy in the region limits populism. Populism needs a modicum of both to flourish. It has an ambiguous relationship to democracy and can be semi-democratic and semi-authoritarian with little respect for liberal-democratic niceties (de la Torre, 2010: 216). As such it is can be a democratic pathology or a democratic illiberalism that leads to authoritarianism. But it is still an ideology *of democracy*, whose emergence is *internal* to democratic politics as democracy's "shadow," illustrating the gap "between haloed democracy and the grubby business of politics" (Canovan, 1999: 12; cf. Arditi, 2004). Similarly, populism is both a descriptive and proscriptive ideology with an explicitly mobilizational aim, i.e. it "arises from a dissatisfaction with existing politics but also as an attempt to fix its representational failures" (Beasley-Murray, 2010: 27). For some, of course, populism *is* mobilization (Jansen, 2011). See also Aslanidis's chapter dealing with social movements in this volume.

In fragile democracies, populism's illiberalism can lead to competitive authoritarianism. However, such regimes maintain pluralist elements, as well as a mobilizational impetus, as populists continue to combat incumbent elites and appeal to supporters through plebiscitarian mechanisms (Levitsky and Loxton, 2013). Yet if an authoritarian regime fully loses populist mobilizational elements, then it becomes simply authoritarian. Above all, if an authoritarian polity has no concept of demos, and power is legitimated solely via authority, populism cannot take root. In practice, though, this apparently neat heuristic distinction is harder to concretize. Even resolutely authoritarian regimes in the FSU pay homage to democracy and popular sovereignty (e.g. ruling parties in Tajikistan, Kazakhstan, and Uzbekistan have all been called variants of "People's Democratic Party"). Yet closer inspection of elements that repress popular mobilization reveal the fictive quality of these regimes' lip-service to populist themes. They have multifaceted controls over unsanctioned activity (e.g. fines on political protest, banning of labor unions, and state media control). There is thus simply no prospect of a genuinely popular populist movement getting any significant executive or legislative power in such countries.

More detailed examination of the landscape of the region reveals further obstacles to the development of populist forces. First, public commitment to democracy is at best ambiguous. Publics have often favored order, stability, and economic growth over democracy, and significant nostalgia for the Soviet system has persisted (de Waal et al., 2013). The ECE discourse of a "stolen revolution" has far less traction where the population does not regard there as having been any revolution to steal, or where they regard the elites as guarantors of stability. In contexts where popular majorities consider democracy neither "haloed" nor even a special priority, and if the Leninist political-cultural tradition leads them to consider that political grubbiness is an inevitable part of politics, then populism cannot attract as a redemptive force that can bring "true democracy" back. Put another way, the persistence of communist-era authoritarian and collective norms needn't necessarily lead to new forms of radical populist mobilization rather than acquiescence in the status quo, particularly since post-Soviet elites like Russia's have actively tried to demobilize their populations (Krastev, 2006).

Second, whereas EU integration has become a focal point for populist mobilization in Europe, West and East, it plays little such role in the FSU (apart from the Baltics, already EU members since 2004). Certainly, the EU factor has become a contested subject element in those FSU states (Ukraine, Moldova, and Georgia) that are members of the Eastern "neighborhood," not least during Ukraine's Euromaidan of 2013–14. Nevertheless, the majority of the electorate and elites support EU accession, while remaining outside the EU removes the salience of issues which so exercise populists elsewhere (e.g. immigration, the "profligacy" of the EU, its primacy over many domestic laws). Indicatively, the Ukrainian radical right party "Svoboda" supports EU membership and the pro-EU Euromaidan movement (Shekhovtsov and Umland, 2014). Conversely, the populist radical right Liberal-Democratic Party of Russia occasionally criticizes the EU over discrete matters (e.g. for its Ukraine policy, or for its support for an independent Kosovo), but has no developed ideological critique of the EU, nor prioritizes attacking it over the West in general. Indeed, there was no mention of the EU in the party's 2016 electoral program.

The final relevant point is that, relative to Latin America and even ECE, the ability for populist actors to mobilize civil society and social movements is extremely circumscribed. Latin American populist movements have often relied on organized social movements (e.g. labor or indigenous movements). Post-communist social movements are far weaker, but those in the FSU weakest of all. Some form of *narodnik* agrarian populism might have re-emerged in Eastern Europe (Mudde, 2001). However, this has been impossible in countries where (unlike e.g. in Poland) an independent peasantry did not survive Stalin. Peasant parties (e.g. in Ukraine, Russia, and Kazakhstan) were marginal creatures of the former collective farm lobby and the Soviet *nomenklatura*. The only temporarily successful example was the Democratic Agarian Party of Moldova, a post-communist "successor party" which governed from 1994 to 1998 before collapsing. Nor (again unlike in Poland) are FSU populist parties able to use religious organizations as a mobilizational or ideological ally—the Orthodox Churches and official Muslim councils invariably gravitate towards the authorities. Similarly, organized labor is weak and depoliticized. Political parties are generally elite creations with little or no social roots. Even two decades after "democratization" in the most pluralist countries, "poor party infrastructure, unclear ideological foundations, political agendas driven by personal interest, and lack of reification resulted in weak party institutionalization" (Mierzejewski-Voznyak, 2014). Underpinning this de-institutionalization is that even the more pluralist FSU countries remain rife with patrimonialism. Patrimonialism resembles populism in linking personalist leaders to loosely organized followers, but is based on hierarchical patron-client relations that limit mass mobilization and thus tend towards oligarchy, not populism (Roberts, 2006). Overall, even the more pluralist FSU countries face an environment much more inhospitable to populism than at first glance.

THE RULE: ANTI-POPULIST ELITISTS

Before discussing the genuine populists, it is worth analysing the dominant model of leadership in the region. Patronal presidentialism is ascendant, which often utilizes quasi-populist rhetoric and is seen by some as populist. However, its primary impetus is authoritarian, patrimonial, and hence anti-populist. Patronal presidents' primary function is to act as patrons of elite factions and their privileges; accordingly they promote elite equilibrium, and aim to minimize and manipulate electoral uncertainties. They do adopt demotic rhetoric, particularly while building authority or facing elite unrest. For example, all the Central Asian presidents regularly invoke anti-corruption rhetoric and periodically purge errant members of their elite. They often ostensibly laud popular sovereignty (e.g. former President

Niyazov of Turkmenistan invoked "the people," "citizens of the Motherland," and described himself as "son of the Turkmen people") (Akbarzadeh, 1999). They may even introduce plebiscitarian elements (e.g. the Kazakhstani and Uzbekistani presidents held popular referendums to extend their rule). However, such people-centrism co-exists with multiple invocations to elite authority. For instance, Niyazov was not just son, but father: *Turkmenbashi* (Head of Turkmens). His core ideology invoked *Vatan* (Motherland). Love of the Motherland, not coincidentally, demanded loyalty to Turkmenbashi.

Vladimir Putin of Russia is the president most often seen as having populist elements (e.g. Hill and Gaddy, 2013: 137–42). Most notably, Casula argues that Putin's authority relies on "*populism from above*, a populism that is not oppositional but systemic" (Casula, 2013, 10). This populism involves introducing a "dividing line to the split between the people and the institutional system: between 'bad institutions,' which are not responsive; and 'good institutions' [i.e. the president] that side with the people." Other sources note Putin's "telepopulism" (his unmediated communication with voters via the state-controlled media, including at marathon press conferences) (Judah, 2013).

Yet Putin's "populist" tone most accurately characterizes his early presidency in 2000–2003, when he was still building authority amongst the political elites and conducting a purge of disloyal "oligarchs," rather than the post-2003 period when his regime was increasingly consolidated. Moreover, his "populism" is outweighed by elitism. Ivan Krastev notes that similarities between Putin and genuine populists like Hugo Chávez resulted from their anti-pluralism: both saw the elite and people as homogeneous entities and denied the heterogeneity advocated by pluralism (Krastev, 2006). However, each drew divergent political conclusions: Chávez sought to mobilize the people against the elite, whereas patronal presidents like Putin are elitists who deeply abhor "people's power" and seek to marginalize and depoliticize it however possible.

For instance, the Kremlin's "sovereign democracy" doctrine, promoted in 2005–2008 but still evident in Russia's ideological inclinations, was no invocation to *popular* sovereignty, but argued that (following Carl Schmitt) democracy emerges from the reason of enlightened elites; true sovereignty entails the state's independence from domestic and foreign policy interference. Particularly since the "Colored Revolutions" of 2003–2005 in Georgia, Ukraine, and Kyrgyzstan, the Russian elite has developed a "militant anti-revolutionism" and aversion to the "populist egalitarianism and communist nostalgia of those below" (Krastev, 2006: 57, 60). This has meant that Russia is at the forefront of anti-populist efforts at home and abroad. Domestically, the authorities have developed a panoply of "ersatz populist" GONGOs (Government-Organized NGOs) such as the Popular Front and the Nashi youth movement whose aim has been to direct social mobilization towards regime goals (Blank, 2008). Regionally, Russia has exported its anti-populist policies for the perusal of other FSU elites (e.g. in Belarus, Kazakhstan, and Uzbekistan). Russia has become a "'resister state'—one which actively seeks to halt or contain the spread of democracy in order to preserve its own autocratic political system" (Ambrosio, 2007: 233).

THE EXCEPTIONS:
MOBILIZATIONAL PRESIDENTS

There are a few exceptions to the patronal presidential rule: times when politicians have managed to use populism to connect with mass mobilization and bring themselves to power. Roberts notes how mass constituencies are useful for populists as political counterweights and instruments for waging sociopolitical conflict. Absent these, populists tend not to fundamentally challenge elites (Roberts, 2006). In the FSU, the aforementioned constraints on civil society have meant that populist mobilization has not sustained itself, and populist presidents have either fallen from power or transformed into more conventional semi-authoritarian or patronal presidents. The common environment for such mobilizational populism is greater mass/elite pluralism, where political competition cannot be completely contained within regime circles presided over by a patronal president. For this reason, it is more prevalent in the more pluralist states (e.g. Ukraine, Georgia, and to a lesser extent Moldova and Armenia), to periods before full regime consolidation (e.g. Russia and Belarus in the 1990s), and to periods of temporary regime breakdown (the Colored Revolutions of the mid-2000s).

The first heyday of populism was the insurgency phase of anti-communist politics in 1989–1993. During transition from the communist system, national-populist leaders such as Boris Yeltsin (Russia), Zviad Gamsakhurdia (Georgia), and Abulfaz Elchibey (Azerbaijan) headed broad pro-sovereignty "popular fronts" combating the communist *nomenklatura*. Not all anti-communist leaders (e.g. Leonid Kravchuk [Ukraine] and Levon Ter-Petrosyan [Armenia]) were consistently ideologically populist, but Zviad Gamsakhurdia of Georgia and Boris Yeltsin of Russia largely fit the definition, combining "people-centrism" (forming new popular identities separate from the Communist Party); "anti-elitism" (focusing on the corruption of the communist bureaucracy and conducting personal crusades to undermine communist power); and "popular sovereignty" (prioritizing democracy, sovereignty, and independence for their national republics). Moreover, such leaders were "populist" in stylistic and organizational terms, being perceived as charismatic, identifying the popular movement with themselves personally, and disdaining liberal checks on their power. As Yeltsin once claimed, Russians do not like to obey "any kind of previously established regimentation of behaviour. We are a casual sort of people and rules cut us like a knife" (cited in Colton, 1995: 146). Of course, these politicians were also nationalist, and in Gamsakhurdia's case his slogan "Georgia for Georgians" was perceived as increasingly taking on an ethnically exclusivist element, and helped prompt his removal from power in 1992. In most other cases, populism did not last. The anti-communist populist movements split after the demise of the Communist Party and the new leaders had to rule in concert with old elites. In Boris Yeltsin's case, the populist phase ended with the instauration of a new super-presidential constitution approved by referendum in December, 1993. Despite his increasing authoritarianism thereafter, some populist elements continued to the end of his rule (for example, his refusal to join a political party).

Alyaksandr Lukashenka of Belarus was the most consistently populist president in the FSU in the 1990s (e.g. Matsuzato, 2004). He was a surprise presidential victor as an independent "outsider" candidate in 1994. Without a notable elite pedigree (his background was in construction and collective farming), he used his post-1993 position as chair of the anti-corruption committee of the Belarusian parliament to burnish his image as an anti-corruption crusader who was unafraid of accusing the highest state officials of embezzlement. His winning political platform was a populist campaign with slogans such as "defeat the mafia."

In office, the populist elements continued. Lukashenka promoted strongly plebiscitarian rule, using referenda for deciding important political questions such as the national symbols (1995), the composition of parliament (1996), and extending his own presidential term (2004). Like Yeltsin but unlike other FSU presidents, he has continued to invoke the principle of direct connection with the people by not joining a pro-presidential party. But whereas Yeltsin allowed such parties to form and tolerated party-based opposition, Lukashenka gradually eviscerated the parliament so that it has become largely comprised of independents. At the same time, populist elements have been key to his ideological discourse. Terms such as "people" [*narod*], denoting a homogeneous moral community, "popular," and "to give the choice to the people" are used "excessively to give citizens the impression that they are actively participating in social, economic, and political life" (Goujon, 1999: 664). Accompanying the people-centrism is an anti-elitism, whereby elites are attacked as obstacles to the central actors in politics, "the leader and the people" (Matsuzato, 2004: 237–8). Lukashenka also speaks *trasyanka*, a mixed Belarusian-Russian countryside language, which burnishes his "People's President" image, especially when "he wants to emphasize his concern for the day-to-day problems of the public" (Goujon, 1999: 668).

The persistence of populism in Belarus is explained by its specific context. In other FSU countries, such persistent anti-elitism would upset the elite balance of power maintained by patronal presidencies and destabilize the whole regime. However, Lukashenka has repressed any significant development of elite clans. To this end, he has directly mobilized the masses, "trying to provoke their anti-elite emotions and attack the elites from above and below" (Matsuzato, 2004: 237–8). Belarusian political culture (with its paternalism and absence of ethnic or regional divisions) and Belarus's compact geography has facilitated the relatively uncontested demand for a single leader who can restore Soviet-era conceptions of social and economic justice.

This implies that the persistence of populism has been more structural than ideological. Indeed, after the early 2000s, Lukashenka cannot be called a genuine populist. While undoubtedly retaining some demotic, quasi-populist rhetoric, he is now a standard FSU authoritarian patronal president. When faced with deteriorating relations with Russia, Colored Revolutions, and the constitutional end to his own presidential term, he resorted increasingly to standard forms of oppression (including regular incarceration of his main electoral opponents). Belarus had become unfree by 2000 and the more authoritarian elements of Lukashenka's rule came increasingly to the fore. Indeed, such elements had always been present in his "Father of the Nation" image (he is often unofficially referred to as бацька [*bats'ka*, "daddy"]).

The second major phase of populist mobilization was the Colored Revolutions of 2003–2005 in Georgia, Ukraine, and Kyrgyzstan. These were less genuine revolutions than "regime cycles" caused by elite infighting after the delegitimization of incumbent patronal presidents (e.g. Hale, 2005). In turn, these regime cycles opened up space for populist mobilization against incumbent elites. For example, the major beneficiary of Georgia's 2003 Rose Revolution was Mikheil Saakashvili, an opposition ideological populist who had built extra-parliamentary links with the urban poor and excoriated establishment corruption (Jones, 2006). Moreover, Saakashvili frequently exhibited discursive populism, with an oratorical style that was "quite emotional, hot-tempered and populist" (Ghia Nodia, cited in Holley, 2004); he "refashioned himself as a populist: kissing babies and raising pensions in television broadcasts that are half infomercial, half fireside chat" (Vaisman, 2008). However, his populism diminished in office. Whilst remaining strongly nationalist and pursuing anti-corruption policies, his Manichean rhetoric was largely directed at Russia, and his strategic aims (however flawed in practice due to increasing authoritarianism) involved Europeanization, civic nationalism, and institution-building. Saakashvili should therefore be seen as populist prior to 2003 and a marginal populist in office from 2003–2012. The "Georgian Dream" coalition, which removed him in 2012, was emphatically non-populist, trying to overcome his centralizing policies through more moderate, incremental domestic and foreign policies.

Ukraine's 2004 Orange Revolution had similar populist elements, as encapsulated by its unofficial anthem, GreenJolly's *Razom nas bahato, nas ne podolaty* ("Together we are many, we cannot be defeated"). The Orange coalition, headed by Viktor Yushchenko and Yulia Tymoshenko, articulated virulent anti-elite rhetoric such as "bandit authorities" and "bandits to jail" (Kuzio, 2010). However, while Tymoshenko can be seen as a consistent populist, Yushchenko largely dropped his anti-elite rhetoric as president.

Similar populist elements can be seen in Kyrgyzstan's Tulip Revolution (2005), Russia's abortive "Snow Revolution" of 2011, and Ukraine's Euromaidan of 2014. In the first case, protests were initially very uncoordinated, and only later coalesced enough to unseat the incumbent president. In Russia in 2011, the relatively greater visibility of the protests compared with previous attempts is attributable to an increased populist emphasis on uniting the discordant opposition against the ruling regime of "swindlers and thieves." In the latter, populist elements were visible in groups to the right and left, and even in the anti-Maidan reaction (with the creation of "People's Republics" in the separatist East). These cases indicate that when elites split, populist ideologies and discourses can swiftly gain traction even in formerly authoritarian regimes. However, in all cases, the anti-elite demonstrations were largely leaderless and even anti-leader, divorced from political parties and social movements. Therefore, populism was largely inchoate and transient.

THE EXCEPTIONS: POPULISM IN
THE PARTY SYSTEM

Picking out true ideological populists in FSU party systems is difficult, because populist rhetoric is spread across the party system. Indeed, Ukraine is typical in that all major parties have some populist elements (Kuzio, 2010). The sheer marginality of most opposition parties virtually compels them to resort to extra-parliamentary mobilization and quasi-populist anti-elite rhetoric. Nevertheless, there are some more stable and long-lasting ideological populists, who span the political spectrum, albeit even these are at best marginally populist.

On the right, the most stellar example is the misnamed Liberal-Democratic Party of Russia, headed by the maverick Vladimir Zhirinovskii, which has been a persistent, albeit increasingly marginal actor. In ideological terms, although the party was initially seen as an authentically fascistoid organization, it has developed a clearer "populist radical right" image, stressing (formally at least) some commitment to democratic and constitutional procedures. At the same time, its anti-establishment rhetoric remains unabashed: Zhirinovskii is prone to lengthy diatribes that denounce all other parties as "swindlers and thieves" (March, 2012). Its people-centrism is strongly ethnic: Zhirinovskii was one of the first to popularize the chauvinist slogan "Russia for the Russians" and the LDPR seeks to defend the (ethnic) Russian people against the "genocide" and "ethnocide" inflicted on it since the collapse of the USSR. However, while the LDPR's populism is clear in ideological terms, like other Russian "managed opposition" parties that are *de facto* Kremlin-controlled, its radicalism is largely rhetorical and "self-limiting" (March, 2012). It attacks the elite only in vague terms, supports Vladimir Putin and has no capacity to enact its radical program, thereby directing popular protest to regime goals. Overall, the LDPR's "populist bluster" conceals a "lack of *real* extremism" (Wilson, 2005: 205).

A more independent right-wing populist has recently emerged in the shape of Aleksei Naval'nyi, who turned the campaign against "swindlers and thieves" into the major opposition slogan in 2010–2011 and ran a strong second for the 2013 Moscow Mayoral elections. Naval'nyi's increased profile is based partly on distinctive on-line anti-corruption campaigns. However, he has got most traction through a "populist re-ordering" of the Putin regime's ideology (Lassila, 2016). Previous (especially liberal-democratic) opposition figures have been unable to articulate a convincing ideological basis for opposing Putin. However, Naval'nyi challenges the regime in its own terms by portraying it as unable to uphold its core values (people, patriotism, and the rule of law) and thereby opening up a chasm between "us and them." Naval'nyi's ability to use the Kremlin's own values against it means that he is potentially a highly dangerous anti-regime opponent; accordingly the authorities have swiftly squashed his potential by legal repression (house arrest, suspended sentences, and depriving registration to his Progress Party).

In Ukraine, a partially analogous party to the LDPR is Svoboda (Freedom), which made its national breakthrough with 10.4 percent in the 2012 parliamentary elections. The party originated in the ultra-nationalist Social-National Party of Ukraine, but since 2004 has sought to present itself as a more moderate force, ending its direct paramilitary links. It is debatable whether Svoboda is still an extremist, racist, or fascist organization which retains anti-Semitic sentiments, especially in an allegedly hidden "unofficial" program (Olszański, 2011). Certainly it increasingly resembles European populist parties' anti-corruption anti-elitism, focus on a charismatic leader, and social solidarity (Kuzio, 2010: 3). Nevertheless, the party is at best marginally populist. Its core programmatic identity remains "ultra-nationalist," emphasizing "blood-and-soil" ethnic nationalism, and appealing more to the historically informed grievances of (Western) ethnic Ukrainians than to the "moral people," with its electoral base largely confined to western Ukraine, especially Galicia (Rudling, 2013; Shekhovtsov, 2013).

Svoboda's vote fell back to 4.7 percent in 2014 and it was surpassed by the Radical Party of Oleh Lyashko, an offshoot of the centrist populist Fatherland party. Lyashko (who came third in the 2014 presidential elections) represents a less ideological, but more incendiary, macho, and media-astute populism akin to a "radio shock jock" (e.g. Kozloff, 2015). He supports a folksy, peasant-based populism focusing on anti-corruption and higher taxes on the oligarchs, as well as more dubious policies such as support for the ultra-nationalist Azov battalion fighting the Eastern separatists and vigilantism. His approach has gained added traction in Ukraine's fraught post-2014 environment, albeit he might struggle in the future because the prevalence of populist rhetoric muddies divisions between populists and the establishment.

A feature of the post-Soviet landscape is that radical left-wing quasi-populist forces have been as prevalent (perhaps more so) than those of the right. This is unsurprising, since across Europe, the post-Soviet radical left has become more populist, acting no longer as the vanguard of a (now diminished) proletariat but as the *vox populi* (e.g. March, 2011). Whereas many left-wing parties retain a strong socialist ideological core, there are other social populists whose populism has become a more systematic element of their ideological appeal.

In the FSU, Soviet welfarist traditions mean that the appeal of social populism is potentially enhanced. Certainly, many communist parties have sought new forms of legitimacy, and therefore their ideologies have become more eclectic, nationalistic, and populist, without as yet fully supplanting their communist ideology. This has gone furthest in the Communist Party of the Russian Federation (KPRF), which since 1993 has promoted a "state patriotic" ideology that has downplayed Marxist-Leninism in favor of a catch-all oppositional appeal, seeking to mobilize broad oppositional strata in a "national-liberation" struggle against the "anti-popular" liberal-oligarchic elite (e.g. March, 2002). Nevertheless, as the party has lost popularity (particularly since 2003), it has been reduced to its ideological core and has undergone re-traditionalization, becoming both more Stalinist and politically conformist. Like the LDPR, it inveighs against the bureaucratic elite and Putin's United Russia party, while avoiding more trenchant anti-system critique.

Other FSU communist parties have also dabbled with populism. For example, the Communist Party of Ukraine, while remaining more Marxist-Leninist than the KPRF, nevertheless developed amorphous East Slavic nationalism over time. Concomitantly, its electoral appeals focused ever more on a vague social populism, including slogans such as "return the country to the people" and "the corrupt belong in prison" (ignoring its own oligarchic connections) (Rafalsky and Onyshkiv, 2012). Similarly, the Party of Communists of the Republic of Moldova (which governed Moldova from 2001 to 2009) has a populist streak. Whilst this was much downplayed in government, the party has since re-radicalized in opposition, with parliamentary boycotts and extra-parliamentary "civil disobedience" mobilization. The party has denounced official corruption, "oligarchs," and "[economic] criminals in power," while aiming to defend Orthodox "moral values" against Western intrusions (Socor, 2013). However, once again, all of the above parties are at most *marginally populist*: their main ideological nucleus continues to be Marxism-Leninism and European socialism.

More consistently populist have been a plethora of (usually small and evanescent) non-communist social populists (e.g. the former Moldovan Patria-Rodina bloc). Relative to the communists, these parties have been more obviously creations of a few dominant leaders, less programmatic, and far more single-issue: their principal raison d'être has been to accuse the mainstream left of "selling out," and they have adopted an emotional, non-ideological defence of some of the cherished ideals of "pure" socialism. An archetypal example was Ukraine's Progressive Socialist Party, a 1995 split from the increasingly social-democratic Socialist Party of Ukraine. Leader Nataliya Vitrenko was another regime "scarecrow" like Zhirinovskii and got the nickname "Zhirinovsky in a skirt" because of her faux-firebrand quarrelsomeness (e.g. Wilson, 2005). She saw herself as Ukraine's only "true Marxist" and outlined a nostalgic anti-Western platform, accusing the IMF of colonizing Ukraine and promising to expel all foreign advisers. Although the party performed strongly in 1998–1999 (with 11 percent in the 1999 presidential elections), it was backed by the presidential administration to reduce the Communist/SPU vote. Thereafter, the authorities lost interest and the party dropped permanently from parliament after 2002.

Such social populist parties can combine leftist welfare rhetoric with more marked "rightist" nationalist, ethno-centric, or even xenophobic policies (the most notorious example arguably being Slobodan Milošević's Serbian Socialist Party). In Russia, a partially analogous actor was the Russian Motherland (*Rodina*) bloc. In 2003, Motherland ran on a left-nationalist platform that combined "protest populism" and "identity populism," epitomized by proposals to expropriate wealth from Russia's oligarchs and to restore popular control over the authorities, gaining 9 percent of the vote (Laruelle, 2006). Motherland eventually co-founded the more consistently leftist Just Russia party in 2006, campaigning as "the party of working people" on a "social justice" platform directed against bureaucratic corruption (March, 2009). Just Russia veered between radical quasi-communist rhetoric and a social-democratic image, finally joining the Socialist International in January, 2008. Nevertheless, the social-democratic core is still overlain with a strong focus on Russian identity politics and a populist anti-elite animus (using the slogan "swindlers and thieves" in 2011, despite being a creature of the presidential administration).

It is natural that there is elective affinity between populism and radical fringe parties. But Peter Učeň has argued that ECE has seen a large number of "centrist" populists: these are anti-elite and anti-corruption, not radical but pragmatic and technocratic (Učeň, 2007). The prevalence of anti-elite sentiment even amongst "moderate" FSU parties makes centrist populism arguably the default political position. Nevertheless, a convincing case could be made for Yulia Tymoshenko's Fatherland (*Batkivshchyna*) party (earlier the Yulia Tymoshenko bloc) being a genuine centrist populist party. This party is ideologically eclectic and personalist. From 2003 to 2007, it developed the idea of "solidarism" as a "third-way" between capitalism and socialism (Kuzio, 2010). Virulent anti-elite rhetoric was a consistent part of Tymoshenko's appeal, as she sought to draw on the anti-elite heritage of the Orange Revolution. Symptomatically, the party lost much of its support after Tymoshenko's politically motivated imprisonment in 2011–2014.

CONCLUSION

On the face of it, there is a proliferation of populism in the post-Soviet space, enabled by a highly fertile breeding ground. However, using the more restrictive ideological definition of populism shows that although populist themes are abundant in political rhetoric, actors with populism as a consistent ideological feature are very few. Populist rhetoric can clearly flourish in an environment influenced by Manichean ideological and cultural traditions, fluid institutional structures, and severe socio-economic problems. But more consistent, developed ideological populism is limited to a handful of executives, and a paltry few political parties, generally at the political margins.

Some of the same reasons permitting the flourishing of fleeting populist rhetoric also inhibit the emergence of ideological populism, above all the weakness of political parties and social movements that might foster social mobilization and sustain populism as an ideology with greater programmatic content. Most of the ideological populist executives and political parties examined here have struggled to maintain consistent positions over time, let alone populist ones. In short, that the ideological definition fails to identify many cases of ideological populism is logical in an environment where the majority of political actors do not espouse clear ideologies at all.

However, the major reason for the poor performance of populism across the region is that the socio-political environment has permitted the re-emergence of authoritarian patronal presidentialism with very little scope for pluralism and hence sustained populist appeals. Such patronal presidents have co-opted demotic rhetoric, but sought to limit genuine populism both domestically and internationally. Where populism has gained a foothold, it is generally in political systems which have the most sustained traditions of elite and public pluralism (especially Ukraine, Moldova, and Georgia), or is a diminished residue in political systems that were more pluralist in the 1990s than now (e.g. Belarus and Russia). Above all, it can temporarily re-emerge in conditions of temporary elite breakdown, even in formerly authoritarian states. However, even in the more pluralist states, patrimonial legacies limit populism. Moreover, populism is far more a feature of opposition parties and campaigns than it is of executive power. The twin pressures of dominant authoritarian/clientelistic elites and weak societal plural-ism/mobilization mean that populism's ability to sustain itself in office is far poorer even than in more developed democratic systems. Whereas populism can play a great role in redeeming democracy, without a modicum of democracy in the first place, it is difficult to see how it can even start.

REFERENCES

Akbarzadeh, S. 1999. "National identity and political legitimacy in Turkmenistan," *Nationalities Papers*, 27(2): 271–90.

Ambrosio, T. 2007. "Insulating Russia from a Colour Revolution: how the Kremlin resists regional democratic trends," *Democratization*, 14(2): 232–52.

Arditi, B. 2004. "Populism as a spectre of democracy: a response to Canovan," *Political Studies*, 52(1): 135–43.

Bale, T., S. van Kessel, and Taggart, P. 2011. "Thrown around with abandon? Popular under-standings of populism as conveyed by the print media: a UK case study," *Acta Politica*, 46(2): 111–31.

Beasley-Murray, J. 2010. *Posthegemony: Political Theory and Latin America*. Minneapolis: University of Minnesota Press.

Blank, S. 2008. "The Putin succession and its implications for Russian politics," *Post-Soviet Affairs*, 24(3): 231–62.

Brandenberger, D. 2010. "Stalin's populism and the accidental creation of Russian national identity," *Nationalities Papers*, 38(5): 723–39.

Canovan, M. 1999. "Trust the people! Populism and the two faces of democracy," *Political Studies*, 47(1): 2–16.

Carothers, T. 2002. "The end of the transition paradigm," *Journal of Democracy*, 13(1): 5–21.

Casula, P. 2013. "Sovereign democracy, populism, and depoliticization in Russia: power and discourse during Putin's first presidency," *Problems of Post-Communism*, 60(3): 3–15.

Clarke, S. 2002. "Was Lenin a Marxist? The populist roots of Marxism-Leninism," in W. Bonefeld and S. Tischler (eds), *What Is to Be Done? Leninism, Anti-Leninist Marxism and the Question of Revolution Today*. Aldershot: Ashgate, 44–75.

Colton, T. J. 1995. "Superpresidentialism and Russia's backward state," *Post-Soviet Affairs*, 11(2): 144–8.

de la Torre, C. 2010. *Populist Seduction in Latin America*. Athens: Ohio University Press.

de Waal, T., M. Lipman, L. Gudkov, and L. Bakradze. 2013. *The Stalin Puzzle: Deciphering Post-Soviet Public Opinion*. Washington, DC: Carnegie Endowment for International Peace.

Goujon, A. 1999. "Language, nationalism, and populism in Belarus," *Nationalities Papers*, 27(4): 661–77.

Hale, H. E. 2005. "Regime cycles: democracy, autocracy, and revolution in post-Soviet Eurasia," *World Politics*, 58(1): 133–65.

Hill, F. and C. G. Gaddy. 2013. *Mr. Putin Operative in the Kremlin.* Washington, DC: Brookings Institution Press.

Jansen, R. S. 2011. "Populist mobilization: a new theoretical approach to populism," *Sociological Theory*, 29(2): 75–96.

Jones, S. F. 2006. "The Rose Revolution: a revolution without revolutionaries?," *Cambridge Review of International Affairs*, 19(1): 33–48.

Judah, B. 2013. *Fragile Empire: How Russia Fell in and out of Love with Vladimir Putin.* New Haven and London: Yale University Press.

Kitschelt, H., Z. Mansfeldova, R. Markowski, and G. Toka. 1999. *Post-Communist Party Systems: Competition, Representation, and Inter-Party Cooperation.* Cambridge: Cambridge University Press.

Korguniuk, Yu. 2010. "Populist tactics and populist rhetoric in political parties of post-Soviet Russia," *Sociedade e Cultura*, 2(13): 233–45.

Kozloff, N. 2015. "Welcome to Ukraine: wild west of populist politics," *The Huffington Post*, May 3. http://www.huffingtonpost.com/nikolas-kozloff/welcome-to-ukraine-wild-w_b_6820930.html.

Krastev, I. 2006. "Democracy's 'doubles,'" *Journal of Democracy*, 17(2): 52–62.

Kuzio, T. 2010. "Populism in Ukraine in a comparative European context," *Problems of Post-Communism*, 57(6): 3–18.

Laruelle, M. 2006. "Rodina: les mouvances nationalists Russes du loyalisme à l'opposition," CERI-Sciences Po. www.ceri-sciencespo.com/archive/mai06/artml.pdf.

Lassila, J. 2016. "Aleksei Naval'nyi and populist re-ordering of Putin's stability," *Europe-Asia Studies*, 68(1): 118–37.

Levitsky, S. 2001. "Organization and labor-based party adaptation: the transformation of Argentine Peronism in comparative perspective," *World Politics*, 54(1): 27–56.

Levitsky, S. and J. Loxton. 2013. "Populism and competitive authoritarianism in the Andes," *Democratization*, 20(1): 107–36.

March, L. 2002. *The Communist Party in Post-Soviet Russia.* Manchester: Manchester University Press.

March, L. 2009. "Managing opposition in a hybrid regime: Just Russia and parastatal opposition," *Slavic Review*, 68(3): 504–27.

March, L. 2011. *Radical Left Parties in Europe.* London: Routledge.

March, L. 2012. "The Russian Duma 'opposition': no drama out of crisis?," *East European Politics*, 28(3): 241–55.

Matsen, E., G. J. Natvikand, and R. Torvik. 2014. "Petro populism." CAMP Working Paper Series: Norwegian Business School.

Matsuzato, K. 2004. "A populist island in an ocean of clan politics: the Lukashenka regime as an exception among CIS countries," *Europe-Asia Studies*, 56(2): 235–61.

Mierzejewski-Voznyak, M. G. 2014. "Party politics after the Colour Revolutions: party institutionalisation and democratisation in Ukraine and Georgia," *East European Politics*, 30(1): 86–104.

Mudde, C. 2001. "In the name of the peasantry, the proletariat, and the people: populisms in Eastern Europe," *East European Politics and Societies*, 15(1): 33–53.

Olszański, T. 2011. "Svoboda party—the new phenomenon on the Ukrainian right-wing scene," *OSW*, July 5. http://www.osw.waw.pl/en/publikacje/osw-commentary/2011-07-05/svoboda-party-new-phenomenon-ukrainian-right-wing-scene.

Rafalsky, D. and Yu. Onyshkiv. 2012. "Communists' populist rhetoric does not match their actions," *Kyiv Post*, July 26. http://www.kyivpost.com/article/content/politics/communists-populist-rhetoric-does-not-match-their--310528.html?flavour=mobile.

Roberts, K. M. 2006. "Populism, political conflict, and grass-roots organization in Latin America," *Comparative Politics*, 38(2): 127–48.

Rudling, P. A. 2013. "The return of the Ukrainian far right: the case of VO Svoboda," in R. Wodak and J. E. Richardson (eds), *Analyzing Fascist Discourse: European Fascism in Talk and Text*. London: Routledge, 228–55.

Rupnik, J. 2007. "From democracy fatigue to populist backlash," *Journal of Democracy*, 18(4): 17–25.

Shekhovtsov, A. 2013. "From para-militarism to radical right-wing populism: the rise of the Ukrainian far-right party Svoboda," in R. Wodak, M. Khosravinik, and B. Mral (eds), *Right-Wing Populism in Europe Politics and Discourse*. London: Bloomsbury, 249–66.

Shekhovtsov, A. and A. Umland. 2014, "Ukraine's radical right," *Journal of Democracy*, 25(3): 58–63.

Socor, V. 2013. "Russia and the Moldovan communists' Red October (part one)," *The Jamestown Foundation*, October 3. http://www.jamestown.org/single/?tx_ttnews%5Btt_news%5D=41446&no_cache=1.

Stewart, S., M. Klein, A. Schmitz, and H.-H. Schroder (eds). 2012. *Presidents, Oligarchs and Bureaucrats Forms of Rule in the Post-Soviet Space*. Farnham: Ashgate.

Tismaneanu, V. 1996. "The Leninist debris or waiting for Perón," *East European Politics and Societies*, 10(3): 504–35.

Tismaneanu, V. 2001. "Hypotheses on populism: the politics of charismatic protest," *East European Politics and Societies*, 15(1): 10–17.

Tismaneanu, V. 2014. "The moving ruins," *Journal of Democracy*, 25(1): 59–70.

Učeň, P. 2007. "Parties, populism, and anti-establishment politics in East Central Europe," *SAIS Review*, 27(1): 49–62.

Vaisman, D. 2008. "Saakashvili's gambit," *Prospect Magazine*. January 20. http://www.prospect-magazine.co.uk/magazine/saakashvilisgambit.

Van Kessel, S. 2014. "The populist cat-dog: applying the concept of populism to contemporary European party systems," *Journal of Political Ideologies*, 19(1): 99–118.

Wilson, A. 2005. *Virtual Politics: Faking Democracy in the Post-Soviet World*. New Haven: Yale University Press.

CHAPTER 12

....

POPULISM IN
THE UNITED STATES

....

JOSEPH LOWNDES

INTRODUCTION

POPULISM in the United States today retains the features and contradictions of the late nineteenth-century movement which gave the term its name—the broad coalition of farmers and workers who came together in a variety of political and economic forma-tions that culminated in the People's Party. Nineteenth-century Populism has been the subject of continual historical argument, a debate that concerns the nature of US pop-ulism in the contemporary moment. Historian Richard Hofstadter depicted the move-ment as a provincial, moralistic form of agrarianism that was marked by xenophobia and a hatred of cities and cosmopolitanism (Hofstadter, 1955). Lawrence Goodwyn, on the other hand, saw populism as a revolt that created a culture of participatory democ-racy in its economic challenge to concentrated capital (Goodwyn, 1976). More recently, Charles Postel has argued that the small farmers and laborers at the movement's core were progressive modernizers committed to opening up the market that they might bet-ter participate in it (Postel, 2007). Indeed, populism in the United States has been as intellectually confusing as it has politically generative precisely because it encompasses all of these elements.

While populist ire is typically aimed at wealthy elites, populists tend to prefer the lan-guage of popular sovereignty to class, blurring distinctions in a broad definition of *the people*. As Berlet and Lyons have argued, the representative figure of *the people* in the US since the Jacksonian era of the 1830s has been the virtuous, independent producer (Berlet and Lyons, 2000). Politically, Andrew Jackson's Democratic party coalition was made up of farmers, emergent industrial wage workers, and slave owners, all depicted as the "producing classes" of society. "Producers" understood themselves in contrast to those seen as the idle rich above, such as bankers, and to people of color. The discursive link between whiteness and independence can be traced over time in contrast to those seen as parasitic on the body politic: black slaves, Chinese laborers, "welfare queens," Latino immigrants, and others, marking off the white citizen as the bearer of republican virtue.

A RECENT HISTORY OF US POPULISM

While populism has had various iterations in the United States, it can be roughly divided between left-wing and right-wing variants according to how each defines the principal foe of the people: for left populists it is economic elites; for right populists it is non-white others and by extension the state itself. The left variant is more properly associated with the nineteenth-century People's Party, populist politics in the southern region of the United States in the early twentieth century, and finally elements of Franklin Delano Roosevelt's New Deal. The most famous figure of southern populism is Huey Long, the Louisiana Governor and US Senator during the Great Depression. Under the slogan "Every Man a King," Long, an authoritarian figure more reminiscent of Latin American populism, pioneered a program called Share the Wealth aimed at curtailing the wealth of the very rich and redistributing it to the "little man." Prior to his assassination in 1935, Long was considering a third party presidential run (White, 2006).

Since the mid-twentieth century populism has been a far more potent force on the right. This is the case, I argue, because for most of US history whiteness and masculinity defined the contours of the political imaginary of those who promoted visions of producerism and popular sovereignty. These identity positions came under severe challenge in the 1960s and 1970s as social movements aimed at white racism, patriarchy, and homophobia rocked US society and made demands on the state. Opportunities thus opened for the generation of a right populism that demonized the state as opposed to the wealthy (Self, 2013).

In the midst of the social conflicts of the 1960s the arch-segregationist Alabama Governor George Wallace ran for president in 1968 on a third party ticket. Although Wallace was a former New Deal Democrat who emerged from a tradition of left-leaning southern populism, he forged a racist and antistatist politics that attacked "pointy-headed bureaucrats" and social meddlers in rants against school integration, welfare, crime, and civil rights protest. Such themes proved popular not just in the white South, but also among white working- and middle-class voters in the Northeast, Midwest, and West (Carter, 1996). The 1968 Republican presidential nominee Richard Nixon saw the political potential of Wallace's populist rhetoric, and began using the terms *Silent Majority*, *Forgotten Americans*, and *Middle America* to describe an aggrieved white majority squeezed by both the unruly, dependent poor below and government elites above (Lowndes, 2008).

This populist political identity was revived in Ronald Reagan's 1980 presidential campaign through his simultaneous demonization of government and "welfare queens." Reagan and other conservative populists also argued that the liberal state's intrusion into the traditional realm of family (through abortion, moral permissiveness, and women's rights) was of a piece with its intrusions into the natural functions of the market.

However, populism did not entirely comfortably exist within the Republican Party. Reagan's successor George H. W. Bush conveyed the image of a more privileged elite committed to the central role of the US in building a cosmopolitan "new world order" which helped nurture a renewed populism outside the party. In 1992 former Nixon speechwriter and columnist Pat Buchanan ran a campaign that railed against the idea of the US as an empire, attacked banks and big business, courted labor through protectionism and opposition to immigration, and excoriated feminism, gays and lesbians, and multiculturalism. "Pitchfork Pat's" campaign to spark a populist insurrection could not be achieved, but Buchanan gave an infamous keynote address at the 1992 Republican Convention, calling for a "cultural war" for the "soul of America." The 1992 presidential election cycle saw the emergence of an independent candidate who evinced populist frustration with the political establishment in general terms: business tycoon Ross Perot. Running against both George H. W. Bush and Democrat Bill Clinton, Perot campaigned against Washington insiders, describing this elite group as "a political nobility that is immune to the people's will," a contemporary version of "the British aristocracy we drove out in our Revolution" (Wilentz, 1993). Perot polled well among middle-class voters with some college education, and received 19 percent of the popular vote in that election. His United We Stand Party ran again in 1996, but was rent by infighting and lack of sustained organization. Clinton, who won that election and was re-elected in 1996, was dogged throughout by populist attacks from the right on the issues of gays in the military, national health care, and ultimately his own sexual behavior.

From the Great Recession of 2008 came a movement initially aimed at federal mortgage lenders, and overweening state power more generally opened the possibility for new articulations of right-wing populism from a group that could nurture a sense of angry outsiderness. The Tea Party movement was brought into being by anti-government rage through protests against anti-recessionary spending, most of which were organized by FreedomWorks and Americans For Prosperity—corporate-funded organizations—and given ample coverage on the conservative cable television network Fox News. The nascent movement solidified over the summer of 2009, through the public spectacle of protests at town hall meetings across the country where elected officials at public fora discussed federal health care reform legislation (Williamson, Skocpol, and Coggin, 2013; Zernike, 2010).

The Tea Party movement attacked increased state spending on infrastructure, loans to failing banks and automobile companies, and health care reform. Tea Party leaders described the movement as driven first and foremost by a concern to stave off encroaching state power over the lives of individuals. The mission statement of the Tea Party Patriots, the largest network of the Tea Party organizations, states: "The impetus for the Tea Party movement is excessive government spending and taxation. Our mission is to attract, educate, organize, and mobilize our fellow citizens to secure public policy consistent with our three core values of Fiscal Responsibility, Constitutionally Limited Government, and Free Markets" (Tea Party Patriots, 2011). FreedomWorks says in its mission statement that it "fights for lower taxes, less government and more economic freedom for all Americans" (FreedomWorks, 2011). Similarly, Tea Party Express advertises on its website that its aim is to "speak out against the out-of-control spending, higher taxes, bailouts, and growth in the size and power of government!" (Tea Party Express, 2011). The movement has pushed Republicans in Congress past their comfort zone to radically reduce spending on programs for the poor as well as on middle-class entitlements such as Medicare and Social Security.

Although the main thrust of US populism from the 1960s onward was rightward, there were populist phenomena on the left. Jesse Jackson's presidential campaigns in 1984 and 1988 sought to revive an older economic language of populism and link it to emergent struggles for racial equality. These campaigns drew from a legacy of black exclusion and protest politics from outside the system, and extended it to include marginalized rural whites and Latinos as well. Jackson sought to overcome the racial divide that had fragmented left populism, but was unable to create the conditions for a sustainable movement beyond the Democratic primaries and outside his self-presentation as the embodiment of the movement.

Left populism emerged again, like the Tea Party movement, in the wake of the 2008 recession, in the form of Occupy Wall Street (Gould-Wartofsky, 2015). The moment it engaged in an extralegal direct action in the heart of New York's financial district, Occupy Wall Street enacted a notion of the people in antagonistic relationship with elites. It performed the rage felt by millions of Americans about the economic and political wreckage wrought by the financial sector producing a constituent moment—the 99 percent. The occupation symbolically broke out of the business-as-usual, incremental reform politics that typify progressivism today, offering instead a protest that indicts not just Wall Street but both major parties for the crisis. The militancy of the occupation inevitably resulted in police violence early on, which served to underscore the drama of the action and the conviction of the actors involved, while metaphorically playing out the brutality of the system being protected. Through social media Occupy Wall Street created its own compelling and easily digestible spectacle, and, like the Tea Party, Occupy Wall Street announced itself through antagonism. Yet while Tea Partiers aggressively confronted representatives of state power at health care town halls and at the US capitol, Occupiers performed the role of recipients of state violence.

Occupy Wall Street's claim to populism was greatly enhanced by the "99 percent" meme, helping it skirt a major difficulty for the left since the 1960s: nationalism. The post-1960s left opposed US imperialism abroad and racism at home, opening up space on the right to lay popular claim to American patriotism. But the 99 percent could be viewed in a patriotic light: a national identification insofar as it demands changes in the US political system, yet vague enough to include both the citizen and the noncitizen immigrant. And by identifying Wall Street as the enemy in an era of neoliberalism, the 99 percent could also stand for humanity across borders in alliance against a common global foe.

The anti-authoritarian orientation of many of the first Occupiers contributed not only to Occupy Wall Street's militancy but also to a horizontal, egalitarian, and creative style of protest, which made clear its autonomy from the institutions that currently run politics—including progressive institutions such as unions and other inside-the-beltway groups. For Occupy Wall Street, the people was rendered in public space in a performance of democratic experience. The general assembly model, which let any participant speak, the insistence on consensus decision-making, and the human amplifier model of enunciation enacted a Rousseauian fantasy that there could be unanimity.

Like the Tea Party, Occupy Wall Street was in some sense a short-lived movement. But its brevity may be attributed to diametrically opposed reasons. While the Tea Party followed up its initial autonomous political action with incorporation into the structures of existing conservative organizations, Occupy travelled in the opposite direction. At the beginning, the direct democratic ethos of Occupy Wall Street and its refusal to make concrete demands was an enormous strength, as it allowed a broad range of people to see themselves within the 99 percent. Over time, however, the organizational structure (or lack thereof), along with the geographic model of holding free space, made it virtually impossible for Occupy to assert any specific program.

The Paradox of the Unpresentable Other

The populist politics of the contemporary right articulate the "flaunting of the low," in Ostiguy's terms. As such, this populism has been that of "an antagonistic appropriation for political purposes of an 'unpresentable Other,'" produced in relation to progressive liberalism, particularly in regard to the black freedom struggle in the United States. This Other is thrust into the political realm in disruptive ways—as a poke in the eye to liberal proceduralism, bipartisan compromise, state bureaucracy, and "political correctness."

However, this figure of the outsider, or "unpresentable Other," is presented as the true "national self," the "true people." As Ostiguy puts it, "The 'Other' is in fact not an 'Other,' but rather the 'truest' Self of the nation, of 'the people.'" In the (lower case "r") republican logic that has always shaped US populism, this figure of the "Other" is contrasted to what are seen as unruly and dependent elements below, and controlling elites above. Ostiguy describes this as the populist facing a three-way coalition of resented minority, a government that supports that minority's interest, and powerful international forces. Of the three, international or global forces have been the least intense rhetorically in the US, which may have something to do with the global reach of US power itself. But it is present nevertheless in anti-communism, anti-Islam, and anti-UN discourse.

However, this relational positioning of the populist between minorities below and government elites above fundamentally shapes the politics of the low. In this sense then I would modify Ostiguy's notion. Right-wing populism in the US is indeed folksy, colorful, self-consciously crude, and corporeally demonstrative. But because of the history of slavery and white supremacy in the US, within the co-constitutive cultural production

of whiteness and blackness, this populism often emphasizes a republican figure of autonomy that is sharply defined against elements seen as low or uncontrolled. American
populism dwells ambivalently in the discursive lineage of the classical/grotesque binary
as it has always been couched in beliefs in Enlightenment ideals of progress, and in celebration more of bourgeois understandings of the production of wealth than the redistribution thereof. As historian Michael Kazin has argued, "Through populism, Americans
have been able to protest social and economic inequalities without calling the entire
system into question ... To maintain that most citizens—whatever their occupation
or income—are moral, hardworking people denies the rigorous categories of Marxism
and the condescension of the traditional Right" (Kazin, 1995). Populist identity thus distinguishes itself against those seen as exploitive elites above and parasitic dependents
below, which are depicted as imprudent, excessive, wasteful, and indolent.

George Wallace often spoke about the "average citizen" and "the common man"
in order to claim a majoritarian bloc in the American electorate; yet he claimed that
these people were not represented by their political leaders. Rather, he said that his
Americans were the outsiders, the scorned, those who were distant from centers of
power. Yet in order for Wallace supporters to see themselves as average citizens, their
enemies had to be cast as the real outsiders; not people with whom they simply had
political disagreements, but parasites on the national body. In other words, in order to
make his outsiders insiders, Wallace rhetorically connected the liberal center to those
he described as unproductive and decadent. Thus as his rhetoric evolved, he invoked
bureaucrats, "permissive" judges, the decadent ultra-wealthy, protesters, rioters, welfare
recipients, and criminals alike as threats to the nation to establish a fundamental unity
among the groups he claimed to represent (Lowndes, 2008). This particular populist
logic was embraced by Nixon afterwards. As Nixon speechwriter Pat Buchanan put it,
"We were the vanguard of Middle America and they were the liberal elite. It's a schism
that's cultural, political, social, emotional. When we came in 1968, they dominated all
American society—the media, the Supreme Court, the bureaucracy, the foundations.
They left us with our cities burning, and inflation going, our students rioting on campus" (White, 1973).

By 1980, Reagan shepherded right-wing populism to the center of US politics as a
leader who could stand as a homology for *Middle America*. He conveyed the image of a
political outsider who would fight against the corruption and overreach of government.
He presented himself as an innocent—someone who lived and governed by quotidian
truths available to anyone. At the end of his time in office he referred to what was now
called the "Reagan Revolution" as simply "common sense."

Jesse Jackson's campaigns on the left expressed the unpresentable other by bestow-
ing dignity on the labor of those whose work is largely unseen. "We work every day," he
would tell crowds, in the cadence of the Black church:

> and we are still poor. We pick up your garbage; we work every day. We drive your
> cars, we take care of your children, we empty your bedpans, we sweep your apart-
> ments; we work every day. We cook your food, and we don't have time to cook our

own. We change your hospital beds and wipe your fevered brow, and we can't afford
to lie in that bed when we get sick. We work every day. (*The Nation*, 1988)

Yet the outsiders he sought to represent—coal miners in Appalachia, African Americans
in urban slums, migrant workers in agricultural production—did not have the same
claims to the "truest Self" of the nation because they did not fit the historic figure of the
American producer—the white, male skilled laborer.

In sympathetic portraits, the Tea Party has been described as a spontaneous people's
movement that has come together to wrest power from corrupt elites, "triggered by the
growing sense that politics has become a cozy game for insiders, and that the interests
of most Americans are ignored" (Reynolds, 2010). The very name "Tea Party" was taken
from the 1773 direct action by American colonists against British taxation. The popular
Tea Party icon of the Gadsden Flag, also from the American Revolution, depicts a coiled
rattlesnake over the caption "Don't Tread on Me."

Occupy Wall Street also sought to speak on behalf of the unpresentable other—to use
the power of anonymity to represent those who were at once excluded and yet the true
people. The phrase "We are the 99 percent" was given shape by a Tumblr site early on,
where an unknown blogger decided that a way to demonstrate the effects of the recession on everyday people was to "[g]et a bunch of people to submit their pictures with a
hand-written sign explaining how these harsh financial times have been affecting them,
have them identify themselves as the '99 percent', and then write 'occupywallst.org' at
the end" (Weinstein, 2011). Less than a month later, the blog was getting more than 100
pictures a day from a broad heterogeneity of figures: faces from across the phenotypic
spectrum identifying as nurses, war veterans, couples in their 50s, students, doctors.
The faces were generally accompanied by hand-written testimonies describing challenging medical conditions, untenable financial situations, being forced out of work,
or school, or their homes. The very diversity of posts displays a chain of equivalents in
what Ernesto Laclau calls an empty signifier (Laclau, 1996). As Priscilla Grim, one of the
Tumblr site editors, told *Mother Jones Magazine*, "I submitted one of the first photos on
the site, and I chose to obscure my face because I did not want to be recognized. I saw it
as a way to anonymize myself: I am only one of many."

PERFORMANCE OF THE LOW

Political enunciations of the people are always performative utterances, to use
J. L. Austin's term, an assertion from the outside meant to act on the political realm generally. Political theorist Jason Frank calls these "constituent moments." "The people," he
writes, "have been the central authorizing fiction in post-revolutionary American political culture and the figure that reveals its underlying contingency, its persistent exposure
to transformative contestation and change" (Frank, 2010). Similarly, political theorist
Jacques Ranciere argues that politics does not take place between constituted groups

within a regime, but rather by the actions of a "part with no part" or the struggle of unrecognized elements who, in the name of the people, aim to redefine the terms of the political realm (Ranciere, 1998; 2010). The part with no part does not refer to the poor, or other excluded or disenfranchised groups, because by their very exclusion these groups are already made intelligible by the extant political realm. It is rather the emergence of a new set of demands, a new notion of the people with previously unarticulated identifications and interests.

Populist movements have impact at moments when powerful institutions can be convincingly cast as corrupt or parasitic on the body politic. It is then when the rhetoric of *the people* has more resonance, it is then that myths of the latent power that reside in *the people* become more powerful. Such performances can focus on the leader as the identificatory figure through which people see themselves. Alternatively, they can be performances of *the people* themselves.

In distinctions drawn between the productive and the unproductive through producerism, populism draws on a dominant structuring of Western thought on questions of both the polity and the autonomous political subject, and Greek and Roman taxonomies of high and low. Indeed, the Roman term from which the adjective "classical" is drawn was originally meant to distinguish the taxpaying citizen from the proletarian. In his famous study of the carnivalesque, semiotician Mikhail Bakhtin argued that the classical body was produced in contrast to a grotesque body marked by impurity, heterogeneity, physical needs, and pleasures of the lower bodily stratum (Bakhtin, 2009). Populism traverses this line even as it defends it—depending on the disruptive, rageful articulation of race and gender truths repressed by "politically correct" liberalism even as it claims to stand for law and order, hard work, piety, and responsible citizenship.

Fueled simultaneously by resentment and the pleasure of transgression, the populist right has, since the 1960s, drawn on a performative image of the outsider. This dynamic is not solely one of populism: in his study of culturally liminal figures, anthropologist Victor Turner highlights the role of the jester as a privileged arbiter of a kind of *communitas* against the reigning stratifications of a given social and political structure (Turner, 1969). But outsider identity is key to the populist politics of the low.

Wallace accepted invitations to speak at elite institutions such as Harvard and Yale, where long-haired, bearded students were sure to shout him down. Wallace would provoke them, knowing that such confrontations would play well to those who would see the students as spoiled, foul-mouthed children of privilege. Wallace played up this role of anti-establishment trickster, describing himself as a poor Southerner and even purposely mispronouncing words (Lowndes, 2008). This helped craft an image as someone whose authority was gleaned from his very distance from the centers of power.

In 1992 Pat Buchanan, one of the rhetorical architects of the Silent Majority, fashioned himself as a scrappy working-class Irish American outsider on the campaign trail to Bush's wealthy WASP New England pedigree. He repeatedly attacked George H. W. Bush's manhood, and his class background. In an insurgent gesture anticipating the Tea Party, he repeatedly called Bush "King George" (Decker, 1992).

Tea Partiers asserted their political authority by naming themselves by reference to the illegal direct action that preceded the American Revolution, the Boston Tea Party. In rallies that featured Revolutionary era iconography and dress, Tea Partiers identified as both rebels and regime-founders. Such gestures provided a language and set of practices through which agents could see themselves as an aggrieved people, as a Rancierean part with no part.

Donald Trump, adored by supporters as a disruptive teller of unvarnished truths, watched his poll numbers rise with each outrageous statement—be it about Latin American immigrants, Muslims, women, or his political opponents. Yet again, this performance of the low was also loaded with its own visceral sense of abjection. "Disgusting" is perhaps his most common term of disparagement, whether talking about breastfeeding, terrorism, or protests. Similarly, Trump often employs metaphors of bodily weakness or lack of control. Referring to Democratic candidate Martin O'Malley's response to black demonstrators, Trump said, "he apologized like a little baby, like a disgusting, little, weak, pathetic baby." Extending the description to the national body he went on, "[a]nd that's the problem with our country" (Johnson, 2015).

TRANSGRESSION

In the right-wing context of US populism rage against government officials on behalf of an aggrieved majority is a well-developed pleasure, and one that evinces not only a "return of the repressed," but what psychoanalytic theorist Melanie Klein called projective identification. In other words, the violent rhetoric of populism depends on the notion that you are responding to threats of violence. Ostiguy discusses what he calls a "combative pleasure principle," expressed in the sociocultural dimension of populism. This transgression can be rhetoric that provides fantasies of violence, or an outsider's playful mockery.

George Wallace promised retribution against demonstrators and rioters, and as noted, in his rallies supporters and opponents would often be encouraged to clash. When Wallace campaigned, his aides would often set up rallies in venues that were too small to hold his audiences, almost ensuring that violence would erupt (Jones, 1966). These riveting expressions of mostly symbolic violence helped shape the identity of modern US populism—as they at once held the allure of transgressing the norms of respectable political behavior, and a return of what was felt to be repressed by a liberal power structure that right-wing populists saw as scolding, condescending, and coercive.

In one illustrative example, singer Merle Haggard made country and western music both nationally popular and part of right-wing populist identity with his 1968 song, "Okie from Muscogee." The song champions hard-working, modest "squares" who eschew drugs, keep their hair short, and do not demonstrate. As he sings, "[f]ootball's still the roughest thing on campus, and the kids here still respect the college dean." This paean to decency in opposition to "rough" behavior was followed by a popular 1969 single, "The Fightin' Side of Me," in which Haggard openly threatened violence against anti-war demonstrators on behalf of his country.

The normally staid Richard Nixon sought to secure populist credentials by courting working-class whites whom he called "hardhats" through just such appeals to aggression. In May of 1970, immediately after the widely reported savage clubbing of anti-war demonstrators in New York City's financial district by construction workers, Nixon—who praised "silent," law-abiding citizens—invited the head of the construction union to a ceremony in the Oval Office where he posed for photographs in a hard hat.

A number of films in the 1970s and 1980s evinced this populist transgression as well. Clint Eastwoood's popular "Dirty Harry" movies for example featured a police officer in San Francisco who faces a city falling into violent degeneracy, but who is constrained by a liberal city bureaucracy that panders to criminals. Taking justice into his own hands, "Dirty Harry" Callahan blows away gangsters, rapists, and hold-up men with his enormous Magnum pistol, indulging fantasies of both racial vengeance and immediate justice. In 1985 President Reagan taunted Congress by quoting Dirty Harry from the film *Sudden Impact*. "I have my veto pen drawn and ready for any tax increase that Congress might even think of sending up. And I have only one thing to say to the tax increasers. Go ahead—make my day." In the film, Dirty Harry has his gun trained on a black robber who has a knife at the throat of a white waitress when he utters those words.

A notorious commercial produced by the Buchanan campaign in 1992 showed slow-moving images of a film depicting gay black men in chains, criticizing Bush for allowing the National Endowment for the Arts to fund such art. "It's tasteless, and it's going to hurt Pat Buchanan," said one consultant for Bush. "If Pat wants to be the leader of the conservative movement, this is suicidal," said another. "It's like throwing acid around." Buchanan made the most of the transgression. On the campaign he would tell audiences, "I'd clean house at the NEA.... If I am elected, the place would be shut down, padlocked and fumigated" (Kurtz, 1992).

As McCain's vice presidential candidate in the race against Barack Obama in 2008, Sarah Palin whipped up crowds by telling them that Obama was "palling around with terrorists," to which audience members would respond with shouts of "kill him!" and "Off with his head!" "Mama Grizzly," as she began calling herself, built a subsequent political career as a figure of populist aggression for the Tea Party, going as far as to place targeted districts for Tea Party candidates in a rifle's crosshairs on her political action committee website.

Transgressive rage was foundational for the Tea Party, which became a viable social movement in the summer of 2009 when members began showing up at "town hall meetings" across the country organized by members of Congress to discuss federal health care legislation. Disruptions at these events were turned into tumultuous spectacles where members of Congress were shouted down, taunted by crowds, and hanged in effigy. Fistfights were frequent, some resulting in hospitalization. And demonstrators often openly carried firearms. Conservative media encouraged this response, as did newly formed Tea Party organizations. "Become a part of the mob!" was an exhortation on a banner of the Web site of talk show host Sean Hannity (Zernike, 2010). This phenomenon intensified during protests in Washington DC the following March. While walking to the Capitol, Representatives André Carson of Indiana, Emanuel Cleaver II of Missouri, and John Lewis of Georgia, all black, were subject to racial epithets and spitting by Tea Partiers who were there to protest the passage of federal health care reform (Pear, 2011).

The 2016 presidential campaign of Donald Trump was marked by violence in his rhetoric, at his rallies, and among white nationalists more generally. Negative comments about Latino immigrants and Muslims drew people to his rallies, where physical assaults on black and Latino protesters were common. His rhetoric also inspired attacks, including two men severely beating and urinating on a homeless Latino man in Boston, one of whom said afterward, "Donald Trump was right; all these illegals need to be deported." Far from denouncing the assault, Trump said when asked about it, "I will say that people who are following me are very passionate. They love this country and they want this country to be great again. They are passionate" (Walker, 2015).

The relationship between transgressive rage and racism is complex. As Ostiguy points out, populism expresses repressed desires (Ostiguy, this volume). Right-wing populism in the US, as we have discussed, was conceived principally in opposition to the black freedom struggle of the 1960s, but also in opposition to changing politics of gender and family. The representative figure of populism was an aggrieved white man displaced from his centrality in politics, the workplace, and the home. The moral force of what came to be called identity politics forbade this figure from expressions of racism, chauvinism, etc. This explains the extraordinary popularity of the phrase "politically correct." This term, originally used in debates among Communists and Socialists in the 1930s in relation to proximity to the "party line," became a chiding in-joke among leftists in the 1970s over the use of racist or sexist language. In the 1990s the term was picked up by the right as a way of demonstrating the authoritarianism of feminists, anti-racists, and liberals in general. Within this logic, any opposition to expressions of racism, misogyny, or homophobia is an act of repression—indeed of repressed truths.

THE POLITICAL-CULTURAL
AND THE IMMEDIACY OF REPRESENTATION

Populist discourse assumes a homogeneous notion of the people and their right to self-rule. Ostiguy correctly connects the low to the fantasy of politics as direct and personal as opposed to remote and institutional. Populism has an egalitarian as well as an intolerant legacy, but even populist movements driven by democratic impulses have ultimately foundered on their excessive concern for homogeneity. Political actors who employ populist language deemphasize differences among the group on whose behalf they claim to speak, depicting group members as wholly equivalent with each other, and utterly different than those outside the collective identity. Moreover, populist leaders claim an immediate identification between themselves and those they represent. As tribunes of the people, they are meant to translate popular will directly into governance. The actual content of popular sovereignty is not distinct. What is crucial is that the people see themselves reflected in those who speak in their behalf. Wallace's campaign slogan "Stand Up for America" was just this sort of claim.

Nixon's famous "Vietnamization" speech, wherein he first invoked the silent majority, was initially met with strong criticism from television commentators. Nixon, who had always believed that the press, Congress, courts, and protesters stood between him and the vast majority of Americans, reacted angrily, as did his staff. Vice President Spiro Agnew denounced what he called "instant analysis," claiming that the president had a right to speak to the people without interference of "a small band of network commentators and self-appointed analysts, the majority of whom expressed in one way or another their hostility to what he had to say." He went on to suggest that "the networks be made to be more responsive to the views of the nation." Nixon speechwriter William Safire later wrote, "Many of us felt strongly that no unelected personality clothed in the garb of network objectivity should be interposed between the elected leader in the 'bully pulpit' and the people" (Safire, 1975). The president's populist showdown with the press began the era of what political scientist Stephen Skowronek has called "the plebiscitary presidency," in which presidents regularly appeal to the public "over the heads of the elites of the Washington establishment, hoping to use their public standing to compel that establishment into following their lead" (Skowronek, 1993). Indeed, the very notion of a silent majority implies that they do not speak for themselves and must thus be spoken for.

The populist notion that presidents should wield direct power over and against the Courts and Congress can be traced to Andrew Jackson in the American case, but had special resonance for the populist right of the late twentieth century. Decisiveness by a leader indulges the populist fantasy that a decision has been made on behalf of the people by its representative without mediation through or compromise with other forces and institutions. Although leaders, presidents in particular, can easily overreach in the authority they believe they have been granted, after 9/11 George W. Bush would enhance his sole decision-making power as president, going as far as to employ a radical Constitutional interpretation of executive power called "the unitary executive," which holds that executive authority cannot be abridged by Congress or the courts. And Bush was impatient with criticism of his administration on either domestic or foreign policy matters. As he once said to journalists in response to waning confidence in his Secretary of Defense Donald Rumsfeld, "I hear the voices, and I read the front page, and I know the speculation. But I'm the decider, and I decide what is best" (Henry and Starr, 2006).

The immediacy of populist politics can be expressed through deep identification with a leader, and the decisiveness of that leader. But it can also nurture fantasies of direct political participation of the people as such. This, of course, is the flip side of the populist feeling of being an outsider, of feeling powerless. Hence the moniker "Tea Party," a reference to direct political action aimed at the British government to demonstrate lack of representation.

Today, the economic gap between the very wealthy and everyone else is more vast than at any time in US history. This gap is a political one as well. The last four decades have seen a wholesale shift of what were formerly public functions into private hands. Meanwhile the absence of campaign finance regulations gives ever greater influence to corporations and billionaires. Large sectors of the US population are falling out of the middle class, and awash in debt. New forms of populism may continue to emerge as public trust in institutions continues to decline, and popular power continues its rapid erosion. New enunciations of *the people* in contrast to anti-democratic rule may become more common. Yet articulating hegemonic versions of the people will probably continue to prove elusive in a time of both increasing inequality and shifting racial demographics.

Right-wing populism draws on rage and resentment in an affective way as we saw in the Trump campaign expressing what Elizabeth Anker has called "orgies of feeling"—the generation of intense emotional states that displace "ordinary experiences of political powerlessness" (Anker, 2014). Trump may in this way indicate a shift in US populism. The Trump brand is primarily associated with enormous wealth and luxury, not modesty and hard work. While Wallace bestowed dignity on those working people he sought to represent and Buchanan saw himself as a working-class representative of labor, Trump talks not like a worker but like an owner. This echoes Mitt Romney's Republican presidential campaign in 2012 wherein the candidate used the producerist language of "makers and takers" in such a way as to assign almost half of the US population to the parasitic category. This trend gives perverse evidence, perhaps, of neoliberalism's total absorption into American political culture today.

Yet what did Trump offer besides a promise to build a wall around the US and purge it of immigrants? In an era that has seen the long-term decline of economic security and standing in the world, disgust and self-defeat express perhaps an even more intense "politics of the low," a deep belief in the national weakness that Trump continually talked about on the campaign trail, even titling his most recent book *Crippled America* (Trump, 2015). Sounding a kind of lament of the end of producerism, Trump regularly said on the campaign trail, "We don't make anything anymore."

If populism on the right now expresses melancholia, perhaps on the left it expresses mourning. The public response to the killing of African Americans by law enforcement has erupted with sharp militancy since 2014. This movement, sometimes referred to as Black Lives Matter, mobilized massive street demonstrations and direct actions in cities across the United States, and confronted national political candidates. The movement, which had queer women and men at the forefront, was a radical departure from the representative figures of producerist populism in the US historically, in terms of race, gender, sexuality, and class position. This broadened representation of who constitutes the people, forged in sharp conflict with both the state and the US racial order, may open new vistas of populist identification beyond this particular set of issues to broader counterhegemonic concerns over poverty, state violence, and political powerlessness.

CONCLUSION

Populist phenomena in the United States differ from those elsewhere in two distinct respects—one institutional, the other historical. Institutionally, the constitutional frame of US politics constrains and fragments political expression. Indeed, where populism demands popular sovereignty and unmediated representation of the people, the Constitution separates governance between three branches of government, breaks up representation over time and space (staggered elections, overlapping electoral units), divides sovereignty between the national government and the states, and filters popular political expression into two great parties. Thus there are, one the one hand, no durable "populist" parties as one finds in Europe, nor the possibility of populist majoritarian control of government as one finds in Latin America. Rather, populism in the United States is expressed in the discourse of political candidates to a greater or lesser degree, and within social movements, or as Laura Grattan has argued, in extra-institutional formations such as economic cooperatives (Grattan, 2016). It is perhaps better then to analyze not what populism is but what populism does.

To say that populism occupies no formal space in the US political system is not to diminish its power, however, and this leads to its second distinguishing feature. As Michael Kazin described it, US populism is a "mode of persuasion." This mode can be quite powerful because it invokes *the people*—which in the US context is the greatest form of legitimation. This notion of the people is rooted in republicanism—which has been an authorizing form of political discourse since the founding.

For this reason US populism remains open politically, because authorizing definitions of the people cannot be given in advance. Populist movements emerge at moments when powerful institutions can be convincingly cast as corrupt or parasitic on the body politic. It is then that myths of the latent authority that resides in the people become more powerful. Legible articulations of the people draw on prior framings of peoplehood, which bear the traces of race, gender, class, etc. But each new enunciation of the people creates newly rendered political identities.

This then is the tension at the heart of US populism—at moments of populist upheaval, the boundaries around *the people* can be fluid and unstable. Yet the intelligibility of populist claims require an idea of the people that can credibly be narrated within identifiable logics. In the United States, this logic has employed the binary of producer and parasite—one that is often rendered in raced and gendered associations, yet need not be. Its expressions can be egalitarian and inclusive, or hierarchical and exclusive, or some of both.

To the degree that populism is a mode of persuasion, future research should focus on how persuasion happens. Populist political identifications occur as subjectification—a coming into being of new identities. We must better understand the ways in which this happens, which necessitates analyses of political culture. Recent work in affect theory can help us understand how new media shape political passions. Political theory that attends to genre can offer insights into how actors become situated within political narratives. Lived categories such as race, gender, and sexuality must be examined not merely as political variables but as fundamental features in the production of populist identities. In other words, the study of populism should push researchers to widen the horizons of what constitutes the political, and therefore what constitutes notions of *the people.*

REFERENCES

Anker, Elizabeth R. 2014. *Orgies of Feeling: Melodrama and the Politics of Freedom.* Durham: Duke University Press.

Bahktin, Mikhail. 2009. *Rabelais and His World.* Bloomington: Indiana University Press.

Berlet, Chip and Matthew N. Lyons. 2000. *Right-Wing Populism in America: Too Close for Comfort.* New York: Guilford Press.

Carter, Dan T. 1996. *The Politics of Rage: George Wallace, the Origins of the New Conservatism, and the Transformation of American Politics.* New York: Simon and Schuster.

Decker, Cathleen. 1992. "Buchanan shows confidence in attacking Bush," *Los Angeles Times,* February 14.

Frank, Jason. 2010. *Constituent Moments: Enacting the People in Postrevolutionary America.* Durham: Duke University Press.

FreedomWorks. "Our Mission," FreedomWorks website. www.freedomworks.org/about/our-mission, accessed May 24, 2011.

Goodwyn, Lawrence. 1976. *Democratic Promise: The Populist Movement in America.* New York: Oxford University Press.

Gould-Wartofsky, Michael A. 2015. *The Occupiers: The Making of the 99 Percent Movement.* New York: Oxford University Press.

Grattan, Laura. 2016. *Populism's Power: Radical Grassroots Democracy in America.* New York: Oxford University Press.

Henry, Ed and Barbara Starr. 2006. "Bush: 'I'm the decider' on Rumsfeld: defense secretary: changes in military meet resistance," CNN.com, April 18. http://www.cnn.com/2006/POLITICS/04/18/rumsfeld/, last accessed December 15, 2015.

Hofstadter, Richard. 1955. *The Age of Reform: From Bryan to FDR.* New York: Knopf.

Johnson, Miles. 2015. "Trump blasts O'Malley: 'disgusting, little, weak, pathetic baby,'" *Mother Jones Magazine,* August 21.

Jones, Bill. 1966. *The Wallace Story.* Northport: American Southern Publishing.

Kazin, Michael. 1995. *The Populist Persuasion: An American History.* New York: Basic Books.

Kurtz, Howard. 1992. "The man behind Buchanan's daring anti-Bush ad," *Washington Post,* March 22.

Laclau, Ernesto. 1996. *Emancipation(s).* London: Verso Press.

Lowndes, Joseph E. 2008. *From the New Deal to the New Right: The Southern Origins of Modern Conservatism.* New Haven: Yale University Press.

Nation editors. 1988. "For Jesse Jackson and his campaign," *The Nation,* April 16.

Pear, Robert. 2011. "Spitting and slurs directed at lawmakers," *Prescriptions* (blog), *New York Times,* March 20, accessed May 24, 2011: http://prescriptions.blogs.nytimes.com/2010/03/20/spitting-and-slurs-directed-at-lawmakers/.

Postel, Charles. 2007. *The Populist Vision*. New York: Oxford University Press.

Ranciere, Jacques. 1998. *Disagreement: Politics and Philosophy*, trans. Julie Rose. Minneapolis: University of Minnesota Press.

Ranciere, Jacques. 2015. *Dissensus: Politics and Aesthetics*, trans. Steven Corcoran. New York: Bloomsbury Academic.

Reynolds, Glenn Harlan. 2010. "At issue: is the tea party the next great awakening?," *CQ Researcher*, 20(11): 257.

Safire, William. 1975. *Before the Fall: An Inside View of the Pre-Watergate White House*. Garden City: Doubleday.

Self, Robert. 2012. *All in the Family: The Realignment of American Democracy since the 1960s*. New York: Hill and Wang.

Skowronek, Stephen. 1993. *The Politics Presidents Make*. Cambridge: Harvard University Press.

Tea Party Patriots. "Tea Party Patriots mission statement and core values." www.teapartypatriots.org/mission.aspx, accessed May 24, 2011.

TeaPartyExpress.org. www.teapartyexpress.org/contribute/, accessed May 24, 2011.

Trump, Donald J. 2015. *Crippled America: How to Make America Great Again*. New York: Threshold Publishing.

Turner, Victor. 1969. *The Ritual Process: Structure and Anti-structure*. Chicago: Aldine Publishing.

Walker, Adrian. 2015. "'Passionate' Trump fans behind homeless man's beating?," *Boston Globe*, August 21.

Warren, Donald. 1976. *The Radical Center: Middle Americans and the Politics of Alienation*. South Bend: Notre Dame University Press.

Weinstein, Adam. 2011. "'We are the 99 percent' creators revealed," *Mother Jones Magazine*, October 7.

White, Richard D., Jr. 2006. *Kingfish: The Reign of Huey P. Long*. New York: Random House.

White, Theodore. 1973. *The Making of the President, 1972*. New York: Atheneum.

Wilentz, Sean. 1993. "Pox populi," *The New Republic*, August 8.

Williamson V., T. Skocpol, and J. Coggin. 2011. "The Tea Party and the remaking of Republican conservatism," *Perspectives on Politics*, 9(1): 25–43.

Zernike, Kate. 2010. *Boiling Mad: Inside Tea Party America*. New York: Times Books.

CHAPTER 13

....

POPULISM
IN WESTERN EUROPE

....

PAUL TAGGART

In their 1969 volume on populism Ghita Ionescu and Ernest Gellner argued that there was a specter of populism haunting the world (Ionescu and Gellner, 1969).[1] As with this volume, they therefore surveyed populism across the world. They had chapters on North America, Latin America, Russia, and Eastern Europe. They did not include Western Europe. Today not including Western Europe in a consideration of populism would be almost unthinkable. The proliferation of parties, mainly on the radical right end of the ideological spectrum, has become one of the key features of contemporary Western European party politics (Betz, 1994; von Beyme, 1988; Kitschelt, 1995; Ignazi, 2003; Carter, 2005; Norris, 2005; Mudde, 2007). And for some populism has become almost synonymous with its Western European form.

Populism in contemporary Western Europe is manifested in the form of a multitude of political parties. Often these parties have been insurgent forces but with the passage of time some of these have moved into being established parts of their respective party systems. The contemporary phenomenon is not a new one, with its origins as far back as the early 1970s in Denmark and France.[2] But there has been, in recent decades, a growing trend in terms of rising support and a growing heterogeneity in the forms of these forces. There has also been a coming in from the cold as some of these parties have been included in governments such as in Austria, Greece, Italy, and Switzerland (Heinisch, 2003; Albertazzi and McDonnell, 2015; Aslanidis and Rovira Kaltwasser, 2016) or their support has been vital to survival of governments, such as in the Netherlands and Denmark, leading some to ask if they have entered the mainstream (Akkerman et al., 2016).

Populist parties in Western Europe now exist as new and old, as insurgent and government and as left- and right-wing parties. This chapter argues that we need to understand this diverse group in terms of their populism and in terms of their ideology as a whole, and that the understanding of this collective group of parties allows us also to understand the changes in contemporary Western European politics in general.

Populist parties in Western Europe are here being defined in ideological terms with a broad adherence to the approach advocated by Mudde (this volume). This means we are considering political parties whose approach sets them in an antagonistic relationship to elites, with the parties fetishizing the purity of the people as an undifferentiated mass and contrasting this with the nature of the elite and the establishment as tainted, unrepresentative, and indeed often corrupt. But, although the approach is largely ideological, I would also suggest that there is real purchase in seeing the populism in contemporary Western Europe in Ostiguy's (this volume) terms as being framed in the terms of "low" politics. This chapter argues that the issue basis of populism needs to be differentiated but that the totality of populism can only be discerned in terms of surveying the range of issue basis. And what unifies that range of issue basis is the way in which they are framed in low politics terms.

This description of the populism of these political parties is very abstract. In practice political parties do not articulate these positions per se but express these broader sentiments in terms of positions and issues that are more tangible and more focused around issues that mobilize voters and citizens. There is a variety in terms of the issues that Western European parties focus upon but that variety can obscure the underlying similarity that can be identified if we focus upon their populism. Specifically this chapter suggests that there are four issues that are touchstones for contemporary Western European populism. They are immigration, regionalism, corruption, and European integration. The chapter will consider each in turn.

The reason for focusing on each of these issues is not to provide a cumulative comprehensive picture of all the populist parties but rather it is to illustrate how populism emerges in diverse forms and to show that this diversity can be understood partly in terms of its underlying populism.

It is a common assertion of populist studies that populism is characterized by its thin-centered nature (Taggart, 2000; Stanley, 2008; Mudde, 2004). This means that populism attaches to other ideologies. It is also a reflection of the chameleonic nature of populism that means that it is fundamentally colored by its environment. The nature of populism, the issues it focuses on, and what it celebrates as "low" politics derive from the context. This is why populism is particularly given to variation and makes it difficult to integrate the studies of populism from very different contexts. But its thin-centered nature is what means that in contrasting contexts, even within Western Europe, it emerges with different issue bases. Teun Pauwels (2014) argues that the thin-centered nature means that populism should be categorized, in Western Europe, according to the type of ideology to which it is adjacent (neo-liberal, social or national). However, the focus here on issues deliberately eschews such an approach as ideologies are more static and less fluid than issues. Issues can be, and are, framed differently, constructed with different emphases, and subject to change according to differences in the political environment.

In this chapter I use the range of cases of populist parties in contemporary Western Europe to illustrate the themes and issues used by populist parties. The chapter is not designed to be a comprehensive survey of the cases but rather uses the cases illustratively and somewhat selectively. In many of these cases, the parties can and have been analysed in other terms—as regional (De Winter and Tursan, 2003), as radical right (e.g. Mudde, 2007), as anti-immigrant parties (e.g. Van der Brug, Fennema, and Tillie, 2005) or as Euroskeptical parties (e.g. Szczerbiak and Taggart, 2008). Such categorizations are not incorrect and not unhelpful. But what I am suggesting here is that the parties can be understood also as populist parties and that populism in Western Europe can only be fully understood if we consider the range of populist forces.

What underlies the four issue foci of these parties is that these issues are framed in populist terms. The issues themselves are not inherently populist. For the immigration issue, the emphasis is on the people as a homogeneous entity. Furthermore the people embody wisdom and virtue and, by implication, these attributes are diluted and dulled when the homogeneity of the people is undermined by immigration and particularly when that immigration is the function of an elite-driven project to create multicul-turalism. Those parties that load on regionalism are using a meshing of a "heartland" (Taggart, 2000) based on a sub-national community with a wider critique of central state politics. Neatly embodied in calls for devolution or independence are the virtuous people and the national elites that deny them access to that virtue. Where corruption is the driver it draws a fundamental aspect of populism, in its distaste for politics and the sneaking suspicion that politics as an activity inherently corrupts the virtue of the ordi-nary people. An antipathy towards the European Union presses the populist buttons of remote complex detached political institutions par excellence.

In effect what we see is a populist politicization of the issues involved. This means that the issues are appropriated by populist actors but also that the issues act as vehicles for mobilizing a sort of latent populist possibility. By using these issues and by building an agenda, and then support of them, these parties bring the issues into wider contention. This then forces other actors in the party systems to react to them. The importance of populism often lies in the reactions that it engenders in others.

The idea of focusing on issues is not to see these parties as single-issue parties.[3] It is also not to argue that the issues are mutually exclusive. Indeed, they are very often mutually reinforcing. It is also not to see the issue focus of the parties as immutable. In fact, if any-thing we can see a tendency for those issues to change in terms of how they are framed; we often see the parties emerging with one particular focus but as they come to develop longevity they tend to broaden out their focus and sometimes shift in terms of what their primary emphasis is. Identifying the four issues that the parties focus on is a way of put-ting into relief the context of West European politics that shapes the manifestation of their populism. But it shows that the relief is uneven: that different polities and the differ-ent patterns of competition within them push some issues further forward than others.

The Populist Politics of Immigration

The focus on immigration is the clearest and most widespread of the four different issues. Indeed there has been an almost universal tendency to treat the parties that focus on this issue as being synonymous with populist parties in Western Europe. This is, in part, defensible. The cluster of populist parties that focus on immigration as a primary issue have been researched as populist radical right parties (Betz, 1993; Taggart, 1995; Mudde, 2007) and as anti-immigration parties (Van der Brug, Fennema, and Tillie, 2000; 2005; Art, 2011) but less often as populist parties.

The identification of populism with immigration is down largely to the prominence, longevity, and success of the French National Front. The party was formed and mobilized largely around the issue of opposition to immigration (Hainsworth and Mitchell, 2000). Central to its identity was the focus on the nature of French society and the defence of that against the alleged challenge of immigration. The party has been through many internal conflicts and fluctuating electoral fortunes, with the party entering the second round of the French presidential election in 2002, and, more recently, with the succession of Marine Le Pen to the leadership of her father's party. She has significantly changed the party in an attempt to de-demonize it but there is still a strong emphasis on French national identity, opposition to immigration, and a policy of national preference designed to oppose multiculturalism (Shields, 2013). In many senses, the party can be seen as a trail blazer for populist parties primarily focusing on immigration and its sustained presence in European politics has served as a flag-bearer for populist parties with immigration at the top of their agenda.

From the rise of the French National Front, there have been a series of high profile populist parties that emphasize immigration and fit clearly into the category of the radical right. The entry of Jorg Haider's Freedom Party into government in coalition with the Christian Democrats in Austria marked for many a high-water mark for this party but it has proved able, even without Haider, to maintain a significant section of the vote in Austria over the years.

In recent years the Netherlands has come from being a case with a very little populism to one that is a well-spring of populism (see van Kessel, 2011). The most prominent case is that of Geert Wilders who has come to represent the face of Dutch populism in contemporary Europe. But Wilders's success and prominence is built on the development of other forms of populism in the Netherlands. The most important of these is the List Pim Fortuyn. Pim Fortuyn was a politician who started to raise the issue of Islamic immigration as a challenge for Dutch society and social values with his party List Pim Fortuyn (Van Holsteyn and Irwin, 2003; Akkerman, 2005). Fortuyn was a gay sociology professor and so hardly what we would consider a "poster boy" for the extreme right. Indeed, Fortuyn's critique of Islamic immigration was that it was at odds with the social liberalism of Dutch society. So, in some senses, Fortuyn was defending a pluralist inclusive version of a tolerant society against what he saw as a non-pluralist and exclusionary version of Islam. Fortuyn was assassinated in 2002 and although his party won the subsequent election, the party imploded without his leadership. It was onto this agenda and on this constituency that Wilders then started to build his base with his Freedom Party (Vossen, 2011). It is clear that Wilders has certainly moved Dutch populism to a position that is more clearly on the extreme right but it is still the case that elements of his position reflect the defence of liberalism.

In Nordic countries we have clear cases of early populist mobilization not around immigration but around a more diffuse attack on the welfare state and taxation, only using immigration as a sub-text. This was the case with the Progress Parties in Norway and Denmark and with New Democracy in Sweden (Taggart, 1995). In Denmark the Progress Party has evolved into the Danish People's Party. In Sweden, New Democracy faded and was succeeded by the Sweden Democrats who have performed electorally more successfully (Erlingsson et al., 2014). And in Finland the Finns (formerly the True Finns) have become a significant presence, developing out of the Rural Party (Arter, 2010). Populist parties in the Nordic region have now emerged to champion the politics of immigration (Jungar and Jupskås, 2014). It is not coincidental that, with the politicization of immigration in recent years, earlier forms of populist mobilization which did not champion immigration, such as New Democracy in Sweden, have now faded and been superseded by new anti-immigration populist parties such as Sweden Democrats.

The focus on immigration has led many to characterize West European populism as right-wing. Indeed, in this context (and in contrast to Central and East Europe) populism is seen as synonymous with right-wing populism. There is no doubt that the vast majority of these parties are on the right. However, it is important to bear in mind that there are significant variations in what sort of position these parties take on the right. On the economy, the parties vary considerably between economic protectionism and free-market policies. And there is even evidence to suggest that there are important forms of West European populism that can be considered as either on the left, or, at least, not unequivocally on the right, even where immigration is a primary issue.

To say that there is a group of populist parties focusing on immigration is not to say the same thing concerns them. In fact, what we see is that immigration means different things to different parties (Mudde, 2013: 8). The politics of immigration is framed differently in different states. We can also see that some of the variety comes as immigration has been re-framed in European politics by new challenges. The emergence of Islamophobia has offered a new set of demons for populists and a powerful mobilizing tool for populists in some countries like the Netherlands and France. It is also important to note that there are populist parties in Europe, like the Five Star Movement in Italy or Podemos in Spain, that have no concern with immigration politics. What this variety shows is that there is nothing necessary about the equation of populism and immigration politics in contemporary Europe. It demonstrates how the issue is a carrier for deeper concerns about politics and that where the issue is salient in the politics of the country there may be successful populist actors that channel their frustrations through the politics of immigration.

THE IDENTITY POLITICS OF POPULISM
AND THE ROLE OF REGIONALISM

The issue of identity is a broad topic in contemporary European politics. The politics of identity has many different contemporary manifestations. But in terms of populism the politics of identity, in certain cases, fuses with the assertion of sub-national identities. The cases of parties asserting different identities against larger national identities and structures are becoming more common. The cases of the Flemish Block in Belgium and the Northern Leagues in Italy exemplify this fusing of sub-national identity politics with populism. They do not represent all the cases as we may also look to the Lega de Ticinesi in Switzerland as another similar case; but the Belgian and the Italian cases offer us emblematic cases with some contrasting facets. The rejection of central state structures and the assertion of regional identities is not enough to characterize these as populist actors. There has been a proliferation of regional movements and parties. The populist cases only exist as a sub-set of this group. Taking both Mudde (this volume) and Ostiguy (this volume) as our guide, the regionalist forces that frame their demands for regional autonomy in the ideological terms of the rejection of the elite and the wider rejection of the rules of the game, and in the cultural terms of asserting low politics, are those that we consider populist. Indeed it may even be possible to analyse these cases more in terms of being a reactive response to rejection of the core state structures and less as a bottom-up assertion of regional identities. The rise of regionalist parties has thrown up many cases of parties that assert regional identity but broadly do so without rejecting the wider political game. We should here note that the vernacular usage of populism (Bale, van Kessel, and Taggart, 2011) has often characterized regionalist parties such as the Scottish Nationalist Party in the UK as populist but this does not square with the tighter academic definitions of populism as they conform to more social democratic models of politics. Of course, there is a natural tendency to see parties that reject central structures in favor of devolving or seeking independence as inherently rejectionist. But I would suggest that there is a key difference between those parties that use sub-regional identities as a way of framing a wider rejection of politics and those parties that reject political structures because of their assertion of alternative identities. The former represents a populist form of mobilizing identity but there are other ways in which these identities can be framed. Looking at the Flemish Block and the Northern League we can see that both parties' discourses feed on the difficulties of the central state. In the case of the Flemish Block this critique resonates in a state already composed of a profoundly divided society in Belgium based on historical, linguistic, and cultural identities in terms of Wallonia and Flanders (Lucardie, Akkerman, and Pauwels, 2016). Largely as a consequence of this, the nature of politics and the functioning of the central states has faced profound difficulties in recent years as perhaps exemplified in the challenge of forming coalition governments that have both to span an ideological range and also to do so in a way that spans the Flemish-Walloon divide. The parallel for the Flemish block with the Northern League is that the Northern League represents a development that reflects the profound transformation of Italian politics in the early 1990s with the collapse of the party system in the wake of corruption scandals. The failure of central Italian politics is also twinned, in the case of the Northern League, with a critique of the regional disparity between the (in the eyes of the Northern League) industrious North of Italy and the feckless, corruption-ridden South. This critique is embodied in calls for greater autonomy for the North to free itself from the ineffective Italian state and from the need to support the South. There is a key difference between the Flemish and Italian cases. In the case of Flanders the assertion of a regional identity represents an established historical identity. In the case of the Northern League, regional identity has been constructed and crystallized around the invention of Padania as a new entity (Giordano, 2000). What this demonstrates is just how the identity can, in an extreme case, become almost invented in order to act as a weapon to beat up on the real object of fury—the established political system.

There is a sense in which other Western European populist parties that are not primarily regionalist parties can be seen to have adopted forms of regional identity. The Left Party in Germany has moved a long way from its origins as a regional party representing the former East Germany but it still has a residual element that sees regional identity as important (Hough, Koß, and Olsen, 2007).

For populists, the politics of regional identity have served as a vehicle for the expression of a more diffuse frustration with the wider functioning of politics in general. We need to be careful to not see all politics of regional identity as populist. The overwhelming majority of regionalist parties are not, in fact, populist. But where the assertion of regional identity is combined with the wider rejection of the functioning of politics we can identify a distinct populist politics.

THE POPULIST POLITICS OF CORRUPTION

There is very often a link between populists and a view of the world that focuses on the corrupt nature of politics. For some commentators, the focus on corruption is due to populism's tendency to moralism (Mény, 1996). For others it is linked to the Manichaeism of populism (Hawkins, 2010). It features in Mudde's (2004: 543) definition in the form of a belief in a "corrupt elite." But to see it as a consequence of other aspects of populism, or as simply a leitmotif, misses the point that an emphasis on corruption can be traced to a fundamental feature of populism and this is the view of politics. Central to populist thinking is a fundamental ambivalence about the very activity and process of politics. Although seeing politics as necessary, populism implicitly views corruption as an almost endemic and inevitable consequence of politics.

Strict definitions of corruption focus on the use of public office for private gain (Nye, 1967). But, more broadly understood, and in a way that is much more amenable to the understanding of populism, corruption entails a process of deterioration. It implies a loss of purity. In this sense, populism has a strong theme of antagonism to the process of politics which it sees as inherently corrupting (Taggart, 2000). It is this which explains both the characterization by populists of elites as corrupt(ed) and also therefore the antagonism between them and the pure uncorrupted people whom they are supposed to be representing.

The corruption that Western European populists in practice focus on is two-fold. First there is the corruption of the elites themselves. Politicians and establishment figures of various types are taken to be detached from those they are supposed to represent and, by implication, to be in politics for less than honorable motives. This sort of critique is both fostered by and feeds populism when there are explosions of interest. For example, the scandal about the expenses of UK MPs in 2009 represented one such moment where a whole political class was seen to be tainted by charges that public money had been misused for private gain.

The second way that corruption manifests itself for Western European populists is, in practice, the most frequent form. This is where the institutions are seen as corrupting. The critique is very often, therefore, of the failure of political parties. For parties like the Freedom Party in Austria, much of their initial success was based on the appeal of their critique of the collusion between the major parties and their tendency to act together in ways that placed them at a distance from the constituencies of citizens, making the established political parties such objects of scorn (Heinisch, 2003; Fallend, 2004). The Austrian case with its consociational aspects, of course, particularly lends itself to the idea of parties divorced from their constituencies, but this critique of the corrupting nature of parties is widespread.

The observation of the failure of established parties runs throughout all of the populist parties in Western Europe. However, in states that have consociational structures, there is a greater emphasis on this critique. We can see the strong vein of criticism in the Wilders' Freedom Party in the Netherlands and the Flemish Block in Belgium. But it is by no means confined to these states as it has been a significant mobilizing issue for a number of parties (Ivarsflaten, 2008). The issue of institutional corruption has been a leitmotif of most Western European populists. But it is with the emergence of Beppe Grillo's Five Star Movement in Italy that we can see the clearest articulation of a charge of corruption. The link here is made specifically with the elite and their relationship to the Mafia.

In Grillo's Five Star Movement we have one of the few examples of a party mobilizing explicitly on the issue of opposition to corruption (Bordignon and Ceccarini, 2013; Lanzone and Woods, 2015; Conti and Memoli, 2015). And more recently the emergence of Podemos in Spain also reflects a focus on the corruption of "la caste" (Kioupkiolis, 2016). We can even see the Greek SYRIZA party in this light. Of course, the dire economic crisis and the imposition of austerity made the circumstances special for SYRIZA to come to power advocating hostility to the settlement and the actors that had imposed this on Greece, but still pervasive in the discourse was a sense of confronting a powerful "establishment" (Stavrakakis and Katsambekis, 2014: 128–31).

In practice, what we can observe is that there is often an elision between the charges of elite corruption and institutional corruption in the populist discourse in Western Europe. Although there is something inherently Manichaean in populism's tendency to see the world as divided between the two forces of the people and the elites, between the good and the bad, it is striking that in Western Europe, the discourse has generally shied away from dismissing politicians (as the elite) as inherently evil or bad. More often the discourse is framed in terms of the politicians *becoming* unrepresentative and divorced from the concerns of their electoral constituency. Once again, this illustrates a fundamental ambivalence towards the processes and institutions of politics from the populists.

THE POPULIST POLITICS OF EUROPEAN INTEGRATION AND EUROSKEPTICISM

The issue of opposition to the European Union is nothing new. And it is not a new phenomenon for populist parties in Europe. For parties motivated by their opposition to domestic elites, portrayed as disconnected from the concerns of their citizens and corrupted by the process of politics, the distant and complex architecture of the EU makes it a natural extension for such sentiments. Taking pot shots at national capitals is easy. But taking pot shots at those in Brussels has been even easier. Populist parties in Europe have nearly always had opposition to the EU as part of their ideological weaponry. But, in reality, this remained a minor component of their appeal.

Two developments have increased the importance of Euroskepticism to West European populists. The first is the increasing politicization of the European issue as a facet of domestic politics. The roots of this lie in the collapse of the so-called permissive consensus after the process of ratifying the Maastricht Treaty in 1992. The permissive consensus held that European integration was essentially an elite-driven process and that elites proceeded on the basis that there was a broad social consensus in favor of integration. The process of ratifying the Maastricht Treaty had the effect of dispelling the idea that the EU was an uncontested project.

The second occurrence that increased the politicization of the issue of the EU has been a series of crises kicked off by the economic crisis and particularly the crisis of the Euro that has unfolded since 2009. Unsurprisingly the unsettling of politics that has occurred in times of austerity has increased many divisions within states but it has also had a particular effect in undermining European solidarity where EU member-states like Germany are seen to bail out other member-states such as Greece, Ireland, Spain, and Portugal for the sake of ensuring the survival of the Euro. The paradox is therefore that Euroskepticism emerges in those donor states where a common sentiment may be frustration at providing the means and it also emerges in recipient states where the conditions of the bail-out are perceived as overly austere. At both extremes, populist parties advocating hostility towards aspects of European integration have not only emerged but prospered electorally. The subsequent crises of the refugee crisis and the trauma of the UK's Brexit decision have overlaid issues of immigration and legitimacy on top of the profound economic travails of the EU.

It comes then as no surprise that we see the emergence of populist parties whose primary issue base has been Euroskepticism. The most prominent example of this is the United Kingdom Independence Party (UKIP) (Ford and Goodwin, 2014). The party has emerged and developed as a party committed to British withdrawal from the EU and is seen by many to have played a key role in facilitating the referendum that gave rise to the Brexit decision. In a sense this has not been surprising as the UK has had one of the highest levels of public opposition to the EU among all the member states. But it has meant that the party has in fact often been analysed only as a Euroskeptic party, whereas, as the party has developed, it has developed a broader issue base with a very strong emphasis on the issue of immigration (Usherwood, 2016). Its critique of politics is not restricted to the EU and the position of the party as a critic of the political class makes it far more useful to think of the party as a populist party with a Euroskeptic agenda rather than as simply a Euroskeptical party.

The United Kingdom has a peculiarly hostile position to the European Union and yet in other countries with a very different relationship to the EU, populist parties with a primary issue focus on Europe have emerged. Germany lies at the heart of the EU project and has strong support for the EU among its population. It is striking then that a Euroskeptic party has emerged in the form of the Alternative for Germany, a party that advocates withdrawal from the Euro. While this is clearly not as extreme as advocating withdrawal from the EU, the very fact that a party in the most un-Euroskeptical state questions the legitimacy of a key component of the European project shows that Euroskepticism is not the sole preserve of the UK. As the Alternative for Germany has developed, and indeed won significant support in elections, it has broadened its base. The confluence of anti-Euro sentiment combined with the politics of immigration in the wake of the refugee crisis proved a powerful cocktail in generating support for this new party, with commentators sharing the idea that "finally" it constituted a right-wing populist party for Germany (Berbuir et al., 2015; Arzheimer, 2015).

The issue of Euroskepticism has been a hardy perennial for populist parties in Western Europe. While UKIP and the Alternative for Germany are relatively recent phenomena, the issue of Europe has always been on the agenda of populist forces—even if it has been rather low down. The French National Front has always maintained a hostile position as the EU has been seen to compromise national identity. The reason for the common advocacy of Euroskepticism by populists lies in the nature of the integration process itself: a project of elites that is, at best, complex and remote and, at worst, democratically deficient is too easy a target for populists. It is not a coincidence that it is hard to think of a contemporary West European populist party that does not exhibit a degree of Euroskepticism. For very few it is the primary focus but for almost all it is one part of their armory of issues.

Populism in Western Europe

Using the themes discussed above to examine populism in Western Europe allows us to see a diverse set of issues. But, as will have been clear, the issues often intersect for the populist parties: immigration is often linked to European integration and regionalism is often linked with corruption. Most populist parties in contemporary Western

Europe do focus on most of the four issues (albeit in different ways). These issues serve as a sort of issue palate that parties select from and then emphasize one issue over the others.

The analysis above assumes that for populist parties there is often one primary issue that the party focuses on. This issue will often be the initial rationale for mobilization (e.g. Europe for UKIP, regionalism for the Northern League, immigration for the National Front) but it is clear that all these parties over time develop fuller policy agendas that tend to circulate around the other issues. There is a clear sense in which the early lives of the parties have been superseded by a broadening of their agenda such that it allows us to discern the populism that underlies them. This is not simply instrumentalism on the part of the parties but is rather part of a natural process of both the development of the parties and a reaction to the changing nature of the political context in which they find themselves.

There is also the phenomenon of parties switching their primary issue focus. We can see this clearly in the case of the transformation of the French National Front that has occurred with the change of leadership from Jean-Marie Le Pen to his daughter Marine Le Pen. The attempt has been made to shift the party away from an over-emphasis on immigration in order to de-demonize it (Shields, 2013). Concomitantly the issue of Euroskepticism has increased in importance. This assumes a central instrumentalism in terms of the parties themselves. But this is not to suggest that parties necessarily cynically pick up issues to increase their popularity; it is to suggest that the changing emphasis of the parties on certain issues is indicative of widespread change in the issue agenda.

There is nothing inherent in the issues that make them populist. Certainly there are issues that seem to lend themselves to populist mobilization but this is a function of the nature of Western European society and politics more than a function of populism. The collective issue portfolio of contemporary Western European populists provides a way into understanding Western European societies and politics. This means that, if we are to have a long-term perspective, then it is certainly possible that, as the nature of society and politics in Western Europe changes, so will the issue base. We can already see this in evidence as Islam was not an issue for the populist parties in the 1970s and 1980s but emerged as a key driver for populist parties in the late 1990s and 2000s (Betz and Meret, 2009), as it increased in salience both nationally and internationally.

CONCLUSION

This chapter has argued that populism in contemporary Western Europe needs to be understood comprehensively—that we need to consider all the elements of populism together. The four issue areas that we have used to look at populism, taken at their broadest meaning, constitute attacks on the core pillars of contemporary Western Europe. Together then they tell us about Western Europe as well as about populism there. That issues of identity—be it ethnic (immigration), regional (European), or national (minority nationalism)—and of corruption have political purchase tells us about how West European politics are changing. They are not immutable and unchangeable but their mutations and changes tell us about the dynamics of politics in contemporary Western Europe.

The focus on immigration and opposition to both the general principle of multiculturalism and the specific phenomenon of Islamic immigration constitutes a challenge to the diversification of Western European societies and it is an attack on the pluralism of the post-war settlement (see Mudde and Rovira Kaltwasser, 2012). Whether this attack is justified or not is an irrelevance to us here. What is relevant is that this attack has real resonance and has found significant electoral support. It has had implications for both the positions of major parties (Bale, 2003) and the policy process itself.

The issue of corruption feeds into and from a wider discourse about democratic disconnect. What is striking about Western Europe is that the discourse of corruption in this context is not so much about the illegality of corruption as about the discourses of moral decline and particularly about the institutional effects on politics. Whereas in other parts of the world such as India, China, and Latin America (Hawkins, 2010), the terminology of corruption is more explicit and more salient, the sort of corruption that is focused on in Western Europe is more moral than financial and more political than economic. In a sense this can be read as a consequence of the strength of democratic politics in Western Europe. Politics in this part of the world, as an activity, is rarely seen as criminal but is very often perceived as unethical and as unrepresentative. It is upon this diffuse but pervasive sentiment that populism in Western Europe builds.

Regionalism and the politics of identity constitute an attack on the power and authority of the central nation-states in Western European. It is common to talk of the attack on the nation-state from above and below but, in the case of populism, where regionalism is significant, the attack is more on the state as the institution of power. The challenge of populism in Western Europe is more against the sort of politics that the nation-state embodies than against the nation-state itself.

The ubiquity of Euroskepticism in Western European populism is a testimony to the difficulty of constructing an integrated Europe. A complex, opaque, and distant political architecture has fed the populist distrust of the political institutions in general. But the ubiquity of Euroskepticism among populists is also a consequence of the elite-driven nature of the European project for its first four decades. For member-states the consensus that existed between particularly the center-left and center-right major parties fed the idea that European integration was the result of political collusion. And where elites are unified a populist critique will often prosper. The populist politics of Euroskepticism are therefore a critique of what the European Union has become but also how it became this way.

For Kriesi and his co-authors (Kriesi, 2014; Kriesi et al., 2006; Kriesi et al., 2008), the cleavage lines of contemporary Europe have been transformed with an economic and cultural cleavage becoming ascendant. Populism in this context mobilizes globalization "losers" against globalization "winners" through the defence of the nation-state and national community. The focus on European integration is therefore linked to larger globalizing tendencies. However, it is important to stress that we need to take account of the role of powerful domestic political structures in shaping the context into which populists emerge and in determining the sorts of issues that they will mobilize their discontent around. Identifying these issues is therefore another way of highlighting fundamental fault-lines within politics in contemporary Western Europe.

What is also striking about three out of the four issues is the way in which the same issue can be mobilized in either a left-wing or a right-wing form. The issue of regionalism or minority nationalism can potentially be used by the left and right. There are minority nationalist parties that have adopted a social democratic agenda and there are those that have taken a more conservative focus. This may be partly a function of whether ethnic or civic nationalism is adopted (Keating, 2004), but whatever the differentiation, it is the outcome that minority nationalist forces are located on very different parts of the left-right spectrum. Hostility to their respective central states may unite these parties but much divides them.

Euroskepticism is a position that has always been taken up by the right and the left, and more at the poles than towards the center (Taggart, 1998). The project of European integration can be demonized as a project of rich capitalists as much as a project of regulatory state-loving idealists. And both arguments exist. Even among populist Euroskeptics on the right there are very different versions of critique as exemplified by the libertarian, free-trading UKIPers as against the protectionist nationalists in France's Front National.

The critique of corruption and the focus on unrepresentative elites and an embedded "establishment" can also be drawn with different connotations. On the left, the elite can be vilified for its wealth and links to finance and corporate power centers (March and Keith, 2016). For the right, the elite can be attacked for being unrepresentative of "ordinary people" and as being cosmopolitan and out of touch. Using Ostiguy's terms both sides will implicitly attack elites for being "high" and disconnected from the virtuous "low." The composition of those elites may vary on either side but there is quite a similarity in the discourse used by both sides.

Populism and its popularity are an indicator of either structural problems or legitimacy issues for a Europe that is socially and politically pluralist, state-centered, and integrated. We need to take disparate elements of populist politics together if we are to understand populist politics in Western Europe. But we also need to reflect on the fact that the criticisms that they make go to the heart of some of the key issues of contemporary Europe today—and that these criticisms have significant electoral currency. Populism, love it or loathe it, may be an important barometer of the health of politics in the contexts in which it arises.

NOTES

1 The author would like to thank Cristóbal Rovira Kaltwasser and Neil Dooley for their comments on drafts of this chapter.
2 There were populists in Western Europe before the 1970s; one of the best cases is that of the Poujadists in France in the 1950s.
3 Indeed there is something of a consensus in the literature on these parties that rejects the single-issue party label. See Fennema (1997); Mudde (1999); Erlingsson et al. (2014).

REFERENCES

Akkerman, T., 2005. "Anti-immigration parties and the defence of liberal values: the exceptional case of the List Pim Fortuyn," *Journal of Political Ideologies*, 10(3): 337–54.

Akkerman, T., S. L. de Lange, and M. Rooduijn (eds). 2016. *Radical Right-Wing Populist Parties in Western Europe: Into the Mainstream?* London: Routledge.

Albertazzi, D. and D. McDonnell. 2015. *Populists in Power*. London: Routledge.

Art, D. 2011. *Inside the Radical Right: The Development of Anti-Immigrant Parties in Western Europe*. Cambridge: Cambridge University Press.

Arter, D. 2010. "The breakthrough of another West European populist radical right party? The case of the True Finns," *Government and Opposition*, 45(4): 484–504.

Arzheimer, K. 2015. "The AfD: finally a successful right-wing populist Eurosceptic party for Germany?," *West European Politics*, 38(3): 535–56.

Aslanidis, P. and C. Rovira Kaltwasser. 2016. "Dealing with populists in government: the SYRIZA-ANEL coalition in Greece," *Democratization*, 23(6): 1077–91.

Bale, T. 2003. "Cinderella and her ugly sisters: the mainstream and extreme right in Europe's bipolarising party systems," *West European Politics*, 26(3): 67–90.

Bale, T., S. van Kessel, and P. Taggart. 2011. "Thrown around with abandon? Popular understandings of populism as conveyed by the print media: a UK case study," *Acta Politica*, 46(2): 111–31.

Berbuir, N., M. Lewandowsky, and J. Siri. 2015. "The AfD and its sympathisers: finally a right-wing populist movement in Germany?," *German Politics*, 24(2): 154–78.

Betz, H. G. 1993. "The new politics of resentment: radical right-wing populist parties in Western Europe," *Comparative Politics*, 25(4): 413–27.

Betz, H. G. 1994. *Radicalism and Right-Wing Populism in Western Europe*. New York: St. Martin's Press.

Betz, H. G., and S. Meret. 2009. "Revisiting Lepanto: the political mobilization against Islam in contemporary Western Europe," *Patterns of Prejudice*, 43(3–4): 313–34.

Beyme, K. von (ed.). 1988. *Right-wing Extremism in Western Europe*. London: Frank Cass.

Bordignon, F. and L. Ceccarini. 2013. "Five stars and a cricket: Beppe Grillo shakes Italian politics," *South European Society and Politics*, 18(4): 427–49.

Carter, E. 2005. *The Extreme Right in Western Europe: Success or Failure?* Manchester: Manchester University Press.

Conti, N. and V. Memoli. 2015. "The emergence of a new party in the Italian party system: rise and fortunes of the Five Star Movement," *West European Politics*, 38(3): 516–34.

De Winter, L. and H. Tursan (eds). 2003. *Regionalist Parties in Western Europe*. London: Routledge.

Erlingsson, G. Ó., K. Vernby, and R. Öhrvall. 2014. "The single-issue party thesis and the Sweden Democrats," *Acta Politica*, 49(1): 196–216.

Fallend, F. 2004. "Are right-wing populism and government participation incompatible? The case of the Freedom Party of Austria," *Representation*, 40(2): 115–30.

Fennema, M. 1997. "Some conceptual issues and problems in the comparison of anti-immigrant parties in Western Europe," *Party Politics*, 3(4): 473–92.

Ford, R. and M. J. Goodwin. 2014. *Revolt on the Right: Explaining Support for the Radical Right in Britain*. London: Routledge.

Giordano, B. 2000. "Italian regionalism or 'Padanian' nationalism—the political project of the Lega Nord in Italian politics," *Political Geography*, 19(4): 445–71.

Hainsworth, P. (ed.). 2000. *The Politics of the Extreme Right: From the Margins to the Mainstream*. London: Pinter.

Hainsworth, P. and P. Mitchell. 2000. "France: the Front National from crossroads to crossroads?," *Parliamentary Affairs*, 53(3): 443–56.

Hawkins, K. A. 2010. *Venezuela's Chavismo and Populism in Comparative Perspective*. Cambridge: Cambridge University Press.

Heinisch, R. 2003. "Success in opposition—failure in government: explaining the performance of right-wing populist parties in public office," *West European Politics*, 26(3): 91–130.

Kitschelt, H. (in collaboration with A. J. McGann). 1995. *The Radical Right in Western Europe: A Comparative Analysis*. Ann Arbor: University of Michigan Press.

Hough, D., M. Koß, and J. Olsen. 2007. *The Left Party in Contemporary German Politics*. Basingstoke: Palgrave Macmillan.

Ignazi, P. 2003. *Extreme Right Parties in Western Europe*. New York: Oxford University Press.

Ionescu, G. and E. Gellner (eds). 1969. *Populism: Its Meanings and National Characteristics*. London: Weidenfeld and Nicolson.

Ivarsflaten, E. 2008. "What unites right-wing populists in Western Europe? Re-examining grievance mobilization models in seven successful cases," *Comparative Political Studies*, 41(1): 3–23.

Jungar, A. C. and A. R. Jupskås. 2014. "Populist radical right parties in the Nordic region: a new and distinct party family?," *Scandinavian Political Studies*, 37(3): 215–38.

Keating, M. 2004. "European integration and the nationalities question," *Politics and Society*, 32(3): 367–88.

Kioupkiolis, A. 2016. "Podemos: the ambiguous promises of left-wing populism in contemporary Spain," *Journal of Political Ideologies*, 21(2): 99–120.

Kriesi, H. 2014. "The populist challenge," *West European Politics*, 37(2): 361–78.

Kriesi, H., E. Grande, R. Lachat, M. Dolezal, S. Bornschier, and T. Frey. 2006. "Globalization and the transformation of the national political space: six European countries compared," *European Journal of Political Research*, 45(6): 921–56.

Kriesi, H., E. Grande, R. Lachat, M. Dolezal, S. Bornschier, and T. Frey. 2008. *West European Politics in the Age of Globalization*. Cambridge: Cambridge University Press.

Lanzone, L. and D. Woods. 2015. "Riding the populist web: contextualizing the Five Star Movement (M5S) in Italy," *Politics and Governance*, 3(2): 54–64.

Lucardie, P., T. Akkerman, and T. Pauewels. 2016. "It is still a long way from Madou Square to Law Street," in T. Akkerman, S. de Lange, and M. Rooduijn (eds), *Radical Right-Wing Populist Parties in Western Europe: Into the Mainstream?* London: Routledge.

March, L. and D. Keith (eds). 2016. *Europe's Radical Left: From Marginality to the Mainstream?* London: Rowman and Littlefield.

Mény, Y. 1996. "Politics, corruption and democracy: the 1995 Stein Rokkan lecture," *European Journal of Political Research*, 30(2): 111–23.

Mudde, C. 2004. "The populist zeitgeist," *Government and Opposition*, 39(4): 542–63.

Mudde, C. 2007. *Populist Radical Right Parties in Europe*. Cambridge: Cambridge University Press.

Mudde, C. 2013. "Three decades of populist radical right parties in Western Europe: so what?," *European Journal of Political Research*, 52(1): 1–19.

Mudde, C. and C. Rovira Kaltwasser. 2012. "Populism and (liberal) democracy: a framework for analysis," in C. Mudde and C. Rovira Kaltwasser (eds), *Populism in Europe and the Americas: Threat or Corrective for Democracy?* Cambridge: Cambridge University Press.

Norris, P. 2005. *Radical Right: Voters and Parties in the Electoral Market*. Cambridge: Cambridge University Press.

Nye, J. S. 1967. "Corruption and political development: a cost-benefit analysis," *The American Political Science Review*, 61(2): 417–27.

Pauwels, T. 2014. *Populism in Western Europe—Comparing Belgium, Germany and the Netherlands*. London: Routledge.

Shields, J. 2013. "Marine Le Pen and the 'new' FN: a change of style or of substance?," *Parliamentary Affairs*, 66(1): 179–96.

Stanley, B. 2008. "The thin ideology of populism," *Journal of Political Ideologies*, 13(1): 95–110.

Stavrakakis, Y. and G. Katsambekis. 2014. "Left-wing populism in the European periphery: the case of SYRIZA," *Journal of Political Ideologies*, 19(2): 119–42.

Szczerbiak, A. and P. Taggart. 2008. *Opposing Europe? The Comparative Party Politics of Euroscepticism*, 2 vols. Oxford: Oxford University Press.

Taggart, P. 1995. "New populist parties in Western Europe," *West European Politics*, 18(1): 34–51.

Taggart, P. 1998. "A touchstone of dissent: Euroscepticism in contemporary Western European party systems," *European Journal of Political Research*, 33(3): 363–88.

Taggart, P. 2000. *Populism*. Buckingham: Open University Press.

Usherwood, S. 2016. "The UK Independence Party: the dimensions of mainstreaming," in T. Akkerman, S. L. de Lange, and M. Rooduijn (eds), *Radical Right-Wing Populist Parties in Western Europe*. London: Routledge.

Van der Brug, W., M. Fennema, and J. Tillie. 2000. "Anti-immigrant parties in Europe: ideological or protest vote?," *European Journal of Political Research*, 37(1): 77–102.

Van der Brug, W., M. Fennema, and J. Tillie. 2005. "Why some anti-immigrant parties fail and others succeed: a two-step model of aggregate electoral support," *Comparative Political Studies*, 38(5): 537–73.

Van Holsteyn, J. and G. Irwin. 2003. "Never a dull moment: Pim Fortuyn and the Dutch parliamentary election of 2002," *West European Politics*, 26(2): 41–66.

Van Kessel, S. 2011. "Explaining the electoral performance of populist parties: the Netherlands as a case study," *Perspectives on European Politics and Society*, 12(1): 68–88.

Vossen, K. 2011. "Classifying Wilders: the ideological development of Geert Wilders and his Party for Freedom," *Politics*, 31(3): 179–89.

PART III

ISSUES

CHAPTER 14

POPULISM AND ITS CAUSES

KIRK A. HAWKINS, MADELEINE READ,
AND TEUN PAUWELS

INTRODUCTION

OVER the last two decades the literature on populism has proliferated. While most studies have focused on the conceptualization, measurement, and consequences of populism, a number have theorized about its causes. This latter group continues a long tradition that began in the 1950s and 1960s with the earliest studies of populism in Europe and the Americas, which sought to understand why populist forces emerged and succeeded electorally (Germani, 1978; Ionescu and Gellner, 1969; Di Tella, 1965; Shils, 1956).

Causal arguments in these last two decades draw from a few basic and familiar mechanisms. These highlight the rational, material side of populist party appeals and their simultaneous connection to emotionally laden political identities. But these arguments fall short in three important ways. First, they fail to explain populism's universal, cross-regional characteristics. Current studies focus on regional varieties of populism (radical right populism in Europe, or radical left populism in Latin America) rather than on populism per se (cf. Conniff, 2012; de la Torre and Arnson, 2013; Kriesi and Pappas, 2015; Mudde, 2007). The resulting theories are oriented more towards the manifest, ideological dimension of these parties and their sociological functions than their populist rhetoric.

Second, scholars have given little attention to the causes of populism at the individual level. Existing research typically focuses on the aggregate level, with an emphasis on structural changes and institutional barriers to entry (e.g., Albertazzi and McDonnell, 2008; Hawkins, 2010). This research says little about the mentality of populist voters or the cognitive processes that lead people to join populist forces. Only a few studies use survey data to explore the nature of populist attitudes (Akkerman, Mudde, and Zaslove, 2014; Spruyt, Keppens, and Van Droogenbroek, 2016), and almost none use experiments to test the framing mechanisms behind the activation of these attitudes (Bos, Van Der Brug, and De Vreese, 2013).

Finally, scholars trying to explain populism's causes have given surprisingly little attention to the role of populist ideas. While theoretically or philosophically oriented work has given pride of place to the ideational nature of populism (Arditi, 2007; Canovan, 1981; Laclau, 2005; Panizza, 2005), empirically oriented studies that agree with these definitions have tended to ignore the substance of populism in favor of its ideological correlates. These studies say little about the circumstances under which populist ideas in their own right would be appealing to voters or where these ideas come from.

In this chapter, we outline and critique these theories while offering a more promising direction of theorizing at both the aggregate and individual levels. This theory is not an amalgam of previous arguments, although it draws from their insights. Rather, it builds on the ideational definition championed by many of the contributors to this handbook, which sees populism as *a Manichaean discourse or a thin-centered ideology that posits a struggle between the will of the common people and a conspiring elite* (see, for instance, Mudde's chapter in this volume). We argue that this definition also speaks to populism's causes. Instead of being a purely material response to interests, populism is a normative response to perceived crises of democratic legitimacy. As such, it has an ideational dimension that goes beyond the narrowly conceived ideologies of Downsian accounts. Likewise, the existence of these democratic norms and the resonance of a popular identity suggests that these attitudes are not simply invented by politicians to fill a gap in the citizens' psyche, but constitute a pre-existing set of beliefs that can be activated and framed under certain contexts.

In what follows, we outline the two strains of causal theorizing that dominate the literature on populism. We then present our own ideational argument and offer a series of hypotheses for testing this argument against the others. In the conclusion, we point out areas of further research with an emphasis on individual-level testing.

EXISTING ARGUMENTS

In many of the studies of populism reviewed for this chapter, arguments are laid out in terms of their temporally ultimate causes: modernization, globalization, or electoral laws. This reflects a covering-law approach to explanation, which aims for law-like correlations. In this review, however, we approach theory in terms of causal arguments (cf. Elster, 1989; Hempel, 1965). Rather than categorize existing arguments in terms of their independent variables, we categorize them in terms of their causal mechanisms and use their independent variables for second-order classification.

Taking a cue from Rydgren's (2007) review of the literature on radical right populism in Europe, we identify two broad causal mechanisms in the populism literature: (1) a Durkheimian "mass society" thesis that revolves around threats to culture and feelings of identity loss and (2) a Downsian "economic" thesis based on spatial and materialist conceptions of political representation. Although there are important variations within each group (usually in terms of the independent variable that starts the process), the theories within them depend on similar arguments about how human beings and societies operate.

MASS SOCIETY THESIS

Mass society theory represents an attempt to grapple with a complex question: what holds a society together, and how has that changed with the advent of modernity? Durkheim (1997) and later authors (Arendt, 1973; Kornhauser, 2013) claimed that society was constituted by solidarity between individuals, arguing that certain values and norms—a "collective consciousness"—form a moral glue that results in social integration. Industrialization, however, fundamentally changes the way individuals interact with each other and the institutions with which they are familiar. By restructuring the division of labor, it creates a society in which social relations are increasingly mediated by the state. Society becomes atomized as power shifts away from local units, like the church or the family, and toward large, impersonal, bureaucratic institutions. During the transition, mass society may be characterized by what Durkheim called *anomie*— disconnection and normlessness.

Durkheim did not address populism directly, but several branches of populism theory appropriate his mass society thesis. Most of these argue that populism is predicated on the weakness or absence of mass-based civil society, especially organized labor or traditional religion (Lubbers and Scheepers, 2000; Roberts, 1995; Vilas, 1992). For example, structural changes to the way labor is handled—either as a result of the initial phases of modernization or later as a result of globalization—produce a splintered and atomized workforce; without powerful unions to reinforce a new sense of class identity, individuals find themselves powerless to mobilize. Discontent grows and grievances fester without redress. Especially when party identification is also weak, as in many Latin American countries with frail party systems, this fragmentation and the inability to organize autonomously drive individuals to a search for some other source of identity.

According to this argument, citizens find that identity in populist politics. Populist appeals cut across class and ideology, offering a broad, "popular" identity that proclaims the previously marginalized masses the true sovereign. This popular identity is constituted positively, by reference to the supposed moral superiority of the common people, but also negatively, by positing a history of exploitation at the hands of a corrupt elite. Charismatic leaders (which most of the literature understands in a Weberian way, as leaders perceived as having exceptional or even quasi-divine attributes) play an especially important role in articulating this identity, positioning themselves on the periphery of mainstream politics and stepping in to offer themselves as the embodiment of the popular will. In this way, the collective consciousness is reconstituted. But the process is fragile: charismatic leaders may prove incompetent or unfaithful to their popular mandate, and the economic policies that undergird their coalitions may ultimately be unsustainable. Indeed, some scholars question whether a popular identity can ever serve as a stable, long-term basis for social cohesion (Di Tella, 1965; Di Tella, 1997; Ianni, 1975; Weffort, 1978).

Outside of Latin America, there has been little empirical support for the mass society argument and thus few studies make use of it today, especially in Europe (Lubbers and Scheepers, 2000; Rydgren, 2007). However, there are two important variations found in all regions. One of these is the discursive framework of Laclau (1977; 2005). Because Laclau approaches populism from a Marxist perspective, he is largely untroubled by the negative consequences of *anomie*. His concern is not that capitalist industrialization leaves the masses bereft of norms and identity; rather, it is that industrialization creates multiple new identities that compete with the proletarian or working class identity that would spark the transition to socialism and radical democracy. In contrast to classical Marxist theorizing, Laclau argues that the creation of this identity requires political action. This is best accomplished through a populist movement led by a charismatic leader. By positing an identity of "the people," populist movements create the functional equivalent of a working class identity that is capable of overcoming differences and uniting citizens against a capitalist elite. The charismatic leader is an essential component of this process because he or she provides a physical referent, an "empty signifier," into which otherwise diverse citizens can read their individual interests.

Another important variation of mass society theory comes from media studies of populism. These argue that new media technologies take advantage of or even reinforce the cognitive weaknesses and emotional vulnerability of the masses, thus making them easy prey for populist demagoguery. Older versions of this theory are found in Latin American studies of populism, which talk about the capacity of new media—radio or television—to foster a personalized connection between politicians and their audiences (Conniff, 1999; Skidmore, 1993). Its newer versions are prevalent in Europe, where scholars argue that a process of increased competition and commercialization has made the media a powerful mobilizing device for populist leaders. As news media compete over readers and viewers, they tend to focus more on entertainment, simplifications, personalization, spectacular events, and scandals. Populist parties can adapt themselves easily to this "media logic," as they are often led by personalized leaders whose provocative language is more interesting for (tabloid) media than boring, mainstream speeches (Mazzoleni, 2008). Both arguments hark back to older notions of urban masses as "the crowd": a vast segment of citizens that is emotionally vulnerable and easily swayed by powerful images and demagoguery (Le Bon, 1960).[1]

Economic Thesis

In contrast to Durkheim's sociological approach, Downs (1957) applied rational-choice theory from neoclassical economics to the study of democratic politics, arguing that voters and politicians are, in essence, materially self-interested decision-makers. All of them make choices most likely to maximize their self-interest under conditions of uncertainty. In particular, politicians respond to the voters' challenges of uncertainty and costly information by providing packages of positions ("ideologies") marketed by parties. Both voters and politicians are strategic, taking into account the ways that others' behavior narrows their options. Consequently, the interaction of voters and politicians can be modeled spatially, with parties under majoritarian electoral rules likely to adopt the centrist ideological position of the median voter.

Like Durkheim, Downs was not immediately concerned with populism (although other rational-choice theorists were; see Riker (1982)). But most current studies of populism draw at least implicitly from an economic logic. Some theorists in this set, such as Betz (1994), stray into Durkheimian territory by arguing that the transition from industry to post-industry has fragmented society, but their overarching claims still assume that politicians and citizens are essentially instrumental decision-makers maximizing their material self-interest, rather than cognitively vulnerable masses acting on a subconscious need for identity or a sense of belonging. Specifically, arguments tend to fall into two narrower categories, which interpret populism as either (1) a medium-term failure of established parties to respond to the demands of their electorate in the face of socioeconomic change, or (2) a long-term reaction to problems of corruption and weak governance. A third set of factors (3), which often crops up in iterations of the first two, addresses the role of party organization and electoral rules in creating space for new populist parties. In the following, we briefly explain these three types of arguments.

Medium-Term Structural Change

In what has come to be known as the *globalization losers* thesis, Betz (1994) was among the first to argue that changes to labor in the wake of globalization bode ill for some sectors of society. In an age of post-industrialism, defined by the decline of the industrial sector and the burgeoning of the service sector, workers need to be flexible, professional, and entrepreneurial to stay afloat socially and economically. Those who are not—the unemployed, the underemployed, the unskilled, and those whose jobs are threatened by advancing technology—are the "losers" of globalization. Because they feel inadequately represented by traditional mainstream parties, which have implemented the market-oriented policies undergirding globalization, these individuals turn instead to populist parties of the left and right.

Betz's theory has been widely cited in the European literature, especially on radical right populism (Kitschelt, 1994; Kriesi et al., 2012; Mudde, 2007). More recent versions of this argument focus also on the impact of European Union institutions, which are seen as denying their member states the ability to adopt heterodox economic policies (the complaint of left populists) or to defend national culture from immigration and heavy-handed regulation (the complaint of right populists). Indirect evidence for the argument has been provided by studies finding that right-wing populist parties are supported by lower-educated voters (Ivarsflaten and Stubager, 2013). While these arguments are helpful in making sense of an expanding repertoire of populist issues in the region, however, the key point of all of these theories is essentially the same: populist parties are a response to the electoral space created by a changing electorate and an unresponsive party system.[2]

Failures of Democratic Governance

While this medium-term argument seems to explain the recent emergence of populist forces in contemporary Europe, it struggles to account for the long-term presence of populism in the Americas, especially Latin America. Here, populism is not a recent phenomenon at all (Kazin, 1998; Conniff, 2012). While it is important to note the negative cases—that is, countries with long or frequent episodes in which populism does not resurface—the fact remains that populism has made periodic appearances in much of Latin America, the United States, and Canada for decades.

The most common explanation for this pattern is that populism is a response to long-term problems of weak democratic governance, especially corruption. Political corruption is defined here as an act by political officials that violates legal or social norms for private or particularistic gains (Gerring and Thacker, 2004). In most countries, corruption is a long-term problem associated with critical junctures in the process of state-building (Acemoglu and Robinson, 2013; Acemoglu, Johnson, and Robinson, 2001). Where corruption is widespread, citizens feel unfairly treated by authorities and are persistently dissatisfied with the functioning of democracy (Kriesi, 2014). Drawing on a qualitative comparative analysis, Hanley and Sikk (2014) find that corruption is one of the most crucial conditions in the pathways towards the success of anti-establishment parties in Central Europe, a concept that comes close to populism. Similarly, Hawkins (2010) finds that corruption and weak rule of law are associated with aggregate-level populism, while de la Torre (2010) argues that populism is rooted in the deep inequalities and injustice created by the legacy of colonialism in Latin America.

An older *relative deprivation* argument alternatively theorizes the rise of populism as the result of a gap between expectations on the part of the people and delivery on the part of elites. A variety of problems could arouse popular expectations. Di Tella (1965; 1997) argued that people in countries on the periphery of wealthier, more developed regions (as Latin America is on the periphery of the United States or Eastern Europe on that of Western Europe) see the prosperity of their neighbors and want it for themselves; more recently, Panizza and Miorelli (2009) argue that democratization produces high-flown, revolutionary ideals that crumble when reality produces flimsy democratic institutions and a weak and arbitrary rule of law. Either way, individuals are disappointed by the lackluster performance of democratic institutions and become disenchanted with traditional parties (Kriesi, 2014: 374). Populist parties, frequently led by candidates who cast themselves as political outsiders, become the natural recourse for the disadvantaged.

Institutions and the Electoral Space

The economic approach to populism concerns itself not only with the material demands of voters but also with politicians' strategies to address these demands (the political "supply"). While few studies go so far as to produce formal spatial analyses of populist competition, a key aspect of these arguments is the attempt to identify institutions or other mechanisms that shape this strategic environment. Admittedly, many of these arguments apply to both mainstream and populist parties, but because they circulate frequently in populism research, they are worth mentioning. Furthermore, some of these institutional elements, such as internal party organization, may have a special impact on populist parties.

One factor often invoked to explain the rise of (radical right) populist parties is the openness of the electoral system (Carter, 2005; Golder, 2003; Norris, 2005; van Kessel, 2015). Systems based on proportional representation with relatively low electoral thresholds should benefit the populist challengers, whereas majoritarian systems present newcomers with a higher threshold.

A more general way of approaching the supply of parties is through the electoral opportunity structure, or the interactions among mainstream parties within the electoral arena. A high level of electoral volatility combined with a large space in the electoral arena (i.e. mainstream parties ignoring issues which voters find important) is generally beneficial for populist parties. Immigration is such an issue on which mainstream parties originally did not position themselves too strongly, explaining why national populists could exploit this niche (Pellikaan, Van der Meer, and De Lange, 2003). However, when populists face competition from a large mainstream competitor with similar party positions and more chances to affect policy, they will have fewer chances to emerge (Van der Brug, Fennema, and Tillie, 2005).

The electoral opportunity structure depends not only on the electoral system, which helps shape the number of parties and thus their capacity to converge on the median voter, but also on the organizational capacities of party leaders. Traditional parties controlled by tenured national executive committees may prove unwilling to adapt their message, especially if it requires admitting new leadership into the party to make the message of change credible; the lack of flexibility can hasten the decline or even the collapse of the traditional party system (Morgan, 2011; Seawright, 2012). In contrast, many populist parties are new party-movements under the personalistic control of a charismatic leader. These parties are more flexible with their ideological positions and able to promote popular candidates. Charisma by itself, however, may not be enough for populist parties to succeed. Populist parties are more likely to persist when charismatic leaders are able to recruit competent party personnel, organize campaigns professionally, and keep the party united. Such parties gradually become perceived as competent, united, and trustworthy, making them credible alternatives to established parties over time (de Lange and Art, 2011; Pauwels, 2014).

CRITIQUING THE TWO STRANDS

These two strands of theorizing about populism—the Durkheimian and the Downsian—each have important strengths that are to some degree complementary. Durkheimian mass society theory pays more attention to the rich variety of normative motivations that undergird politics. It especially highlights the emotional role that political identity plays in the lives of citizens and how these identities depend on a complex web of social interactions. This is an important corrective to economic approaches, which rely on a narrow set of assumptions about the materially self-interested motivations of citizens and political elites.

Likewise, the Downsian economic argument captures the capacity of citizens and politicians for rational, introspective behavior. It better grasps the material concerns of citizens and how these shape their choices about parties. This model of decision-making is more clearly political, allowing us to take into account the impact of party organization, electoral institutions, and the configuration of the party system on the competitiveness of populist forces.

Nevertheless, each strand leaves a number of anomalies unresolved. While mass society theory offers a tempting explanation for older waves of populism, it struggles to explain the persistence of populism in contemporary politics. Today's movements are not a direct response to problems of incipient modernization, and most of them reaffirm political identities created in earlier processes of mass incorporation and nationalism. While media studies offer an intriguing reformulation of the theory for the contemporary environment in much of Europe, it seems clear that changes in media cannot fully explain most variation in populist forces in other regions, such as the Americas or the UK, where tabloid media are an older phenomenon that varies little with waves of populism. As the media are a mirror of society, it is probably more fruitful to see them as an intervening, rather than independent, variable (Mazzoleni, 2008).

While the Durkheimian approach struggles with the historical pattern of populism, the Downsian one struggles with populism's geographical variation. Each set of structural factors (losers from globalization, chronic problems of democratic governance) works in its own region, but not in the other—Western Europe versus Latin America and Central and Eastern Europe. These theories do not offer a logic that unifies populism across these regions, other than a general sense of deprivation (for a similar critique, see Mudde (2007: 203–5)). Likewise, it seems clear that the institutional constraints mentioned by theorists have a widely varying impact on the strategic situation that parties confront. With minoritarian populist forces in Western Europe, these institutions do an admirable job of explaining variation in populist party success. For example, differences in electoral rules explain why populist parties had a hard time gaining a foothold in the UK's first-past-the-post electoral system until UKIP was successful in the proportional contest of European elections. And the FN in France made its breakthrough after a short-lived change from majoritarian to proportional rules in 1986 (Ivarsflaten and Gudrandsen, 2014). However, electorally powerful populist forces in Latin America and Central and Eastern Europe were able to win office and change their constitutions despite a host of institutional constraints. This suggests that electoral rules and other institutional constraints may not matter much once populism garners overwhelming support (Hawkins, 2016; Rovira Kaltwasser and Taggart, 2016).

A second weakness of these two theories is their failure to address populism at the individual level. Ecological fallacies abound. Few mass society theories of populism test their theories at the individual level with surveys, interviews, or experiments. They find rough aggregate-level associations between structural change and the emergence of populists, but they never show if voters for populist parties feel some kind of *anomie* and whether the populist leader and his movement fill this void with a populist identity. Economic approaches to populism do better, providing survey data that links occupational status and issue positions of individual voters to the ideological appeals of their parties (Bornschier and Kriesi, 2012; Ivarsflaten, 2008; Oesch, 2008; Van der Brug, Fennema, and Tillie, 2005). But these studies fail to gauge populist attitudes per se and whether these somehow interact with issue positions to determine vote. Furthermore, as with economic theories more generally, they assume a highly simplified cognitive process in which issue positions and other ideas are constantly at the forefront of voters' and politicians' calculations.

The most serious weakness of these two theories, however, is their failure to grapple with populism's ideas. If we think that populist forces are primarily distinguished by their ideas—a Manichaean discourse that posits a cosmic struggle between the putative "will of the people" and a conspiring elite—it is because we think these ideas matter. That is, we think that politicians' decisions to create these types of parties and movements, and voters' decisions to support them, are driven by their appreciation of the populist message. People do not support populist forces merely because the discourse fulfills a certain social function or coincides with other ideologies.

The literature on populism increasingly demonstrates that populist ideas exist and have a significant impact on behavior. Numerous studies now measure the populist rhetoric of political elites through textual analysis, and they show that ideologically dissimilar politicians across very different regions—Hugo Chávez or Viktor Orban, Alexis Tsipras or Geert Wilders—have a similar discourse manifesting key features of populism (Armony and Armony, 2005; Jagers and Walgrave, 2007; Hawkins, 2009; Rooduijn and Pauwels, 2011). Furthermore, this elite rhetoric seems to match elite behavior. Although political scientists now discount the tendency of economists to identify populism with short-sighted economic policies (cf. Dornbusch and Edwards, 1991; Roberts, 1995; Weyland, 1999), studies increasingly show that populist parties and movements are associated with declines in liberal democracy (Hawkins and Ruth, 2015; Huber and Schimpf, 2015; Levitsky and Loxton, 2013; Mudde and Rovira Kaltwasser, 2012).

Much the same can be said for populism at the level of ordinary citizens. Studies of mass populist ideas are still rare, but a growing survey-based literature shows that populist attitudes are common, exist at similar levels across different regions, and correlate predictably with key political and demographic indicators (Akkerman, Mudde, and Zaslove, 2014; Hawkins, Riding, and Mudde, 2012; Hawkins and Rovira Kaltwasser, 2014). Importantly, these studies find that individuals with these attitudes are much more likely to vote for populist parties and candidates.

Mass society theories fail to say why these populist ideas offer a special response to the lack of political identity among citizens, or why easily duped voters would naturally gravitate towards a populist message. It is true that a popular identity is one potential way of reconstituting a collective consciousness in modern, democratic society, but reconstituting one's identity around a charismatic leader is only one way of building this political identity, and many charismatic leaders do not use a populist message. Also, it is not obvious why a popular identity has to assume a Manichaean form that presumes a knowing evil in opposition to the people; this identity could just as easily be formed positively, as in pluralist discourses that describe an inclusive political collective built around the citizenry proper (Hawkins, 2009; Ochoa Espejo, 2011; O'Donnell, 1979; Plattner, 2010).

Likewise, Downsian arguments explain the success of populist parties primarily in terms of their issue positions, not their populist discourse. While these issue positions clearly matter (there is a reason why voters prefer left populists in some countries and right populists in others), they are not inherently linked to a Manichaean approach to politics that romanticizes the common people and vilifies a political elite. Integrating populist ideas into a purely rational-choice approach is difficult because it requires tapping into democratic norms that lie outside the bounds of material self-interest.

An Ideational Theory of Populism

How can we make sense of these findings, especially cross-regional findings concerning the prevalence and impact of populist ideas at the mass level, while acknowledging the strengths of existing theories? Can we do so in a way that is more amenable to individual-level analysis?

To create a more general theory of populism, we start at the individual level with the recognition that populism represents a distinct set or type of ideas. Although broadly shared, these ideas are not consciously articulated like traditional ideologies and thus coexist with them. They operate much more like a set of attitudes, a discursive frame, or a trait than they do a set of issue positions.

Consequently, we think the next move is to see populism as a set of attitudes that must be *activated*. Current political psychology suggests that the operation of attitudes is often complicated. Many personality traits, such as authoritarian personality or the Big Five traits, exist as latent dispositions that are only activated by context (Feldman and Stenner, 1997; Mondak et al., 2010; Stenner, 2005; Hetherington and Weiler, 2009). Likewise, frames must coincide with an objective context in order to be accepted and repeated by citizens (Chong and Druckman, 2007; Fiske, 1992). Populist ideas behave in much the same way, as a disposition that generally lies latent. These ideas may be widespread among individuals, but they coexist with other discourses and must be activated through a context of actual material conditions and linguistic cues.

To determine what context activates this disposition, we turn again to the content of populist ideas. Specifically, given the populist argument that the popular will has been subverted by a conspiring elite, we suggest that populist ideas are sensibly activated when policy failures can be traced to systematic malfeasance by traditional politicians. In its most serious form, this malfeasance manifests itself as widespread corruption (in the objective sense of politicians' abuse of public office for private gain), which prevails in much of the developing world where populist forces are more frequent and dominant. But it also occurs in lesser forms when political elites collude for practical or ideological reasons to keep issues off the public agenda. This latter form is more common in developed countries where outright corruption is rare but the advantages of incumbency help shelter elites from popular concerns, or where globalization and international commitments constrain the decisions of party leaders, producing gaps in democratic representation (Katz and Mair, 1995; Mair, 2011).

How does this activation take place? While populism requires a suitable context to make it sensible, the interpretation of that context is not automatic. Here we think the Durkheimian and Downsian arguments agree, and are correct, in arguing that citizens live in a world of incomplete information that is often difficult to interpret. It may be unclear what caused the latest economic downturn or who is implicated in a corruption scandal. Hence, populism depends on a supply of politicians who articulate the populist message. These politicians provide the specific populist frames that facilitate the interpretive step. Their populist message has to perform several functions, such as ascribing problems to knowing agents rather than impersonal forces and referencing an in-group identity that causes citizens to think beyond their particular interests. But when connected to a sensible context, this message catalyzes the activation of populist attitudes.

The Downsian approach also provides a key insight concerning the coordination problems that beset political mobilization. Not only do citizens live in a world of incomplete information, but they have to pursue their objectives through collective action that is not automatic. Hence, it is essential for politicians to offer a rhetorical frame and an organizational framework. Even after citizens interpret the causes of their political problems through a populist lens, they lack solutions in the form of a credible, organized alternative capable of staffing the government. Mobilization is rendered especially problematic by the populist argument against professional political insiders and in favor of broad, enthusiastic participation by citizens, as well as the need that populism creates for politicians to demonstrate their divorce from the elite and their connection to the people. While smaller, institutionalized associations (such as parties) can provide these mobilizational resources, majoritarian populist forces often assume the form of a movement, or a non-hierarchical network of activists, that multiplies the challenges to collective action. This may be one of the reasons why successful movements often have charismatic leaders. By serving as an "empty signifier" into which participants can read their individual wills, a charismatic leader provides a focal point for collective action.

Finally, populist forces (including both the citizens and the politicians who constitute them) have to take into account formal institutions and the opportunities and constraints these impose on electoral competition. If traditional parties can reformulate
their programmatic appeal to address unmet needs, or if electoral rules and other institutions make it difficult to register and run new parties, populist forces are less likely to
mobilize. But what the Durkheimian perspective suggests (and we agree) is that these
institutions and spatial dynamics matter only at the margins. When the context for populist mobilization is strongest—for example, in an environment of widespread corruption and major policy failures—the broad social consensus that underlies institutions
may simply vanish. Populist voters are not just disappointed, but angry, and when large
numbers of voters feel this anger and direct it at the current political system, they have
the electoral strength and the motivation to smash it. Formal institutions and competing parties in a traditional Downsian space only become constraints when the conditions for populism are weakly developed.

We think this ideational theory offers a more complete picture of populist activation
and success. It not only addresses the impact of populist ideas, but resolves some of the
anomalies in the existing strands of the populism literature. The first anomaly is the fact
that populism is surprisingly prevalent across different countries and regions and has
not vanished even in this post-modern era. We think this is because populism is rooted
in a belief in democracy, especially popular sovereignty (Arditi, 2007; Canovan, 1999;
Panizza, 2005). It seems likely to have emerged long before the classic populist movements of the late nineteenth century in the United States and Russia, accompanying
instead the emergence of mass democracy in countries such as France and the United
States in the late eighteenth and early nineteenth centuries. We should see populist attitudes and movements today in any country where democracy is widely embraced—it
is a "pathological normalcy" (Mudde, 2010). According to this perspective, it is not the
recent emergence of populism in Western Europe that is surprising, but the lack of populist forces in the decades after World War II;[3] the frequent appearance of "third party"
populist movements like we see in the United States is probably the norm.

Second, an ideational theory of populism helps make sense of what we consider the
"puzzle of populism": the fact that populist attitudes are widespread across countries
today, but successful populist parties and movements are rare (cf. Conniff, 1982; 2012).
Populism is not a traditional ideology or conscious set of issue positions, and we should
not assume that it is always active in citizens' and politicians' minds. While a few people
may always see the world through a populist lens, most of us require a combination of
context, framing, and mobilizational resources to arouse our populist sentiments and
put them into action.

A third anomaly is that populism is not strongly correlated with policy crises. For
example, while some scholars and much of the public associates the emergence of populist forces with economic recession, not every downturn prompts the emergence of
populists. Certainly, the Great Recession has not prompted a uniform wave of populism across Western Europe (Kriesi and Pappas, 2015). One reason is that many policy
failures take place without a background of systematic elite collusion. This helps explain

why successful populist movements have only emerged in response to the economic crisis in Southern Europe, mostly strongly in Greece and Italy and less so in Spain, and why similar economic crises did not produce populist movements in countries such as Ireland and Iceland.[4] In these North Atlantic countries, elite collusion in the form of patronage, clientelism, and corruption scandals was much less widespread.

Fourth—and this may appear to contradict the previous point—populism does not perfectly correlate with corruption, either. Less-radical populist forces appear and even win office in a number of countries with strong governance, such as Norway, Switzerland, Austria, and the Netherlands. The answer is that populism requires a background of elite collusion, but this collusion can assume other forms that are less severe than the rampant corruption found in most developing countries. Even the best-functioning democracies are likely to provide some type of collusion, given the ever-present challenge of competing with incumbent politicians and established party leadership. That said, in countries with better governance and more responsible parties, populist parties tend to be more moderate.

Finally, not all populist forces are the same. Recognizing that populist ideas can vary in their intensity, and that this intensity sometimes reflects a strong, widespread demand for democratic change, helps us anticipate that institutions and other barriers to entry may not always provide a meaningful check on radical populist movements. These barriers matter more in advanced industrial democracies, where the demand for populism is generally more moderate.

CONCLUSION AND FUTURE DIRECTIONS FOR RESEARCH

Despite the proliferation of populism research, we still lack an understanding of the causes of populism, especially at the individual level. Most studies trying to explain populist success draw on two sets of causal arguments: Durkheimian mass society theory or Downsian rational choice theory. While these arguments have their merits, neither acknowledges the importance of populist ideas—and both thereby miss the mark. At its heart, populism is a response to perceived normative failures of democratic government. The populist message matters because it interprets failures of governance as something larger, as a violation of democratic norms of citizenship. Most citizens and politicians in democracy have internalized a set of values that predisposes them to adopt populist interpretations of events—if the events are serious enough and can be credibly connected to this political rhetoric, and if the message is combined with a set of issue positions or an ideology that coincides with their beliefs. Thus, populism constitutes part of the ideational mix that influences political behavior.

Older strands of theorizing still provide crucial insights that flesh out the ideational approach. For instance, the Downsian argument that citizens vote for parties addressing their material interests explains the particular ideological flavor of the voters' populism, whether on the left or the right. But this argument cannot explain why these flavors are populist. Populism is a way of making ideological claims more extreme, but it is also a specific normative argument that resonates under a particular set of circumstances. Recognizing the impact of populist ideas requires adding another dimension to the standard Downsian space.

Likewise, mass society theories help us think more about the role of identity and affect in understanding political behavior, as well as the ways that these interact with institutions to create a web of social relationships. But these arguments tend to disregard the substance of the populist argument with its particular claims to fairness, equality before the law, agency, and the notion of a popular will. In the contemporary era, at least, populism pronounces a familiar argument that is already embedded in democracy (Canovan, 1999).

The ideational theory we offer suggests a number of possible directions for further research. The most interesting and potentially fruitful one is survey research at the micro-level of individual voters. Scholars should study the impact of contextual factors on populist attitudes. Time-series cross-national research exists for individual regions or specific types of populist parties (e.g. Arzheimer, 2009), but not for populist parties in general across regions. Moreover, the success of populist parties depends on supply-side factors that are difficult to control for. A first suggestion would therefore be to include a measurement of populist attitudes in cross-national surveys and explore what contextual factors activate these attitudes. Drawing on the ideational theory, we can think of several factors likely to interact with populist attitudes, including perceived corruption, assessments of government performance, quality of representation, and ideological or issue positions. It would be especially interesting to compare these effects in countries where contextual factors are strong with those in countries in which they are weak, and to consider countries where there are already strong populist parties to see if populist attitudes undergird their support.

A second area of research at the micro-level is survey research to examine where populist attitudes come from. Although populist attitudes may be widespread across countries, they vary within populations, and it is not clear what causes this variation. Are populist attitudes the product of short-term events such as repeated crises and corruption scandals, or of heritable traits and long-term forces of socialization such as education? Do they mark stages of life, or of historically specific cohorts? Although there is tentative research here suggesting the role of personality (Bakker, Rooduijn, and Schumacher, 2015), further study is needed, especially studies that connect to populist attitudes per se and not just behavioral outcomes.

A third area of research is experimental (laboratory, field, or survey-based). Experiments are an especially useful way of studying the impact of populist framing. It should be possible to test to what extent framing issues in a populist way—by emphasizing that *the people* support an issue against *a conspiring elite*—has an impact on agreeing with the issue. Social psychology has long demonstrated the impact of conformism (Asch, 1955), so this mechanism might also help populists find support for specific policies. The effect of populist frames might also depend on the issue itself (contested or valence) or characteristics of voters (such as levels of education). This kind of research has limitations with regard to external validity, yet it would provide insights into the mechanisms of populist persuasion.

Finally, of course, work remains to be done at the macro-level. We need aggregate, national-level studies that juxtapose the strength of populist parties with the kinds of causal factors we have mentioned here, such as corruption, economic crisis, and globalization. And more of this work should be cross-regional to distinguish populism from its ideological flavors.

NOTES

1 In contrast, some media studies see journalists as gatekeepers who can provide certain issues and parties with more or less visibility. For example, it has been argued that the limited and negative coverage on the German NPD fueled its demise, whereas the Austrian FPÖ profited from more (favorable) coverage in tabloid newspapers (Art, 2007). This gatekeeper argument relies on causal mechanisms different from mass society theory and is more compatible with the economic approach.

2 A version of this argument has also appeared in the Latin American literature. In studying the recent breakdown of party systems in Latin America, Roberts (2015) argues that the willingness of traditional leftist parties to support neoliberal reforms created programmatic space for left-populist challengers.

3 A common assumption in the literature is that Europe experienced very little populism between the end of World War II and the 1980s (e.g., Albertazzi and McDonnell, 2008; Betz, 1994; Mudde, 2007). While we share this view, it is important to note that there is little systematic historical evidence to substantiate it—a gap in the literature that future research should address.

4 Despite a low corruption index, O'Malley and FitzGibbon (2015) argue that elite collusion is also present in Ireland. However, they argue that populism is already a common feature among established parties, making it more difficult for a populist challenger to emerge.

REFERENCES

Acemoglu, Daron and James Robinson. 2013. *Why Nations Fail: The Origins of Power, Prosperity, and Poverty*. New York: Crown Business.

Acemoglu, Daron, Simon Johnson, and James A. Robinson. 2001. "Reversal of fortune: geography and institutions in the making of the modern world income distribution," *National Bureau of Economic Research Working Paper Series*, No. 8460. http://www.nber.org/papers/w8460.

Akkerman, Agnes, Cas Mudde, and Andrej Zaslove. 2014. "How populist are the people? Measuring populist attitudes in voters," *Comparative Political Studies*, 47(9): 1324–53.

Albertazzi, Daniele and Duncan McDonnell (eds). 2008. *Twenty-First Century Populism: The Spectre of Western European Democracy*, 1st edn. Basingstoke: Palgrave Macmillan.

Arditi, Benjamín. 2007. *Politics on the Edges of Liberalism: Difference, Populism, Revolution, Agitation*. Edinburgh: Edinburgh University Press.

Arendt, Hannah. 1973. *The Origins of Totalitarianism*. New York: Houghton Mifflin Harcourt.

Armony, Ariel C. and Victor Armony. 2005. "Indictments, myths, and citizen mobilization in Argentina: a discourse analysis," *Latin American Politics and Society*, 47(4): 27–54.

Art, David. 2007. "Reacting to the radical right: lessons from Germany and Austria," *Party Politics*, 13(3): 331–49.

Arzheimer, Kai. 2009. "Contextual factors and the extreme right vote in Western Europe, 1980–2002," *American Journal of Political Science*, 53(2): 259–75.

Asch, Solomon E. 1955. "Opinions and social pressure," *Scientific American*, 193(5): 31–5.

Bakker, Bert N., Matthijs Rooduijn, and Gijs Schumacher. 2015. "The psychological roots of populist voting: evidence from the United States, the Netherlands and Germany," *European Journal of Political Research*, 55(2): 302–20. doi: 10.1111/1475-6765.12121.

Betz, Hans-Georg. 1994. *Radical Right-Wing Populism in Western Europe*. New York: St. Martins Press.

Bornschier, Simon and Hanspeter Kriesi. 2012. "The populist right, the working class, and the changing face of class politics," in Jens Rydgren (ed.), *Class Politics and the Radical Right*. London: Routledge, 10–30.

Bos, Linda, Wouter Van Der Brug, and Claes H. De Vreese. 2013. "An experimental test of the impact of style and rhetoric on the perception of right-wing populist and mainstream party leaders," *Acta Politica*, 48(2): 192–208.

Canovan, Margaret. 1981. *Populism*. New York: Harcourt Brace Jovanovich.

Canovan, Margaret. 1999. "Trust the people! Populism and the two faces of democracy," *Political Studies*, 47(1): 2–16.

Carter, Elisabeth. 2005. *The Extreme Right in Western Europe*. Manchester: Manchester University Press.

Chong, Dennis and James N. Druckman. 2007. "Framing theory," *Annual Review of Political Science*, 10(1): 103–26.

Conniff, Michael L. (ed.). 1982. *Latin American Populism in Comparative Perspective*. Albuquerque: University of New Mexico Press.

Conniff, Michael L. 1999. *Populism in Latin America*. Tuscaloosa: University of Alabama Press.

Conniff, Michael L. 2012. *Populism in Latin America*, 2nd edn. Tuscaloosa: University of Alabama Press.

de la Torre, Carlos. 2010. *Populist Seduction in Latin America*, 2nd edn. Athens: Ohio University Press.

de la Torre, Carlos and Cynthia J. Arnson (eds). 2013. *Populism of the Twenty-First Century*. Washington, DC: Woodrow Wilson Center Press.

de Lange, Sarah L. and David Art. 2011. "Fortuyn versus Wilders: an agency-based approach to radical right party building," *West European Politics*, 34(6): 1229–49.

Di Tella, Torcuato S. 1965. "Populism and reform in Latin America," in Claudio Véliz (ed.), *Obstacles to Change in Latin America*. London: Oxford University Press, 47–74.

Di Tella, Torcuato S. 1997. "Populism into the twenty-first century," *Government and Opposition*, 32(2): 187–200.

Dornbusch, Rudiger and Sebastian Edwards (eds). 1991. *The Macroeconomics of Populism in Latin America*. Chicago: University of Chicago Press.

Downs, Anthony. 1957. *An Economic Theory of Democracy*. New York: HarperCollins Publishers.

Durkheim, Emile. 1997. *The Division of Labor in Society*, tr. W. D. Halls. New York: The Free Press.

Elster, Jon. 1989. *Nuts and Bolts for the Social Sciences*. New York: Cambridge University Press.

Feldman, Stanley and Karen Stenner. 1997. "Perceived threat and authoritarianism," *Political Psychology*, 18(4): 741–70.

Fiske, Alan P. 1992. "The four elementary forms of sociality: framework for a unified theory of social relations," *Psychological Review*, 99(4): 689–723. doi: 10.1037/0033-295X.99.4.689.

Germani, Gino. 1978. *Authoritarianism, Fascism, and National Populism*. New Brunswick: Transaction Publishers.

Gerring, John and Strom C. Thacker. 2004. "Political institutions and corruption: the role of unitarism and parliamentarism," *British Journal of Political Science*, 34(2): 295–330.

Golder, Matt. 2003. "Explaining variation in the success of extreme right parties in Western Europe," *Comparative Political Studies*, 36(4): 432–66.

Hanley, Seán and Sikk Allan. 2014. "Economy, corruption or floating voters? Explaining the breakthroughs of anti-establishment reform parties in eastern Europe," *Party Politics*, 22(4): 522–33.

Hawkins, Kirk A. 2009. "Is Chávez populist? Measuring populist discourse in comparative perspective," *Comparative Political Studies*, 42(8): 1040–67.

Hawkins, Kirk A. 2010. *Venezuela's Chavismo and Populism in Comparative Perspective*. Cambridge: Cambridge University Press.

Hawkins, Kirk A. 2016. "Responding to radical populism: Chavismo in Venezuela," *Democratization*, 23(2): 242–62.

Hawkins, Kirk A. and Cristóbal Rovira Kaltwasser. 2014. "The populist specter in contemporary Chile," in *XXXII Congress of the Latin American Studies Association*. Chicago.

Hawkins, Kirk A. and Saskia Ruth. 2015. "The impact of populism on liberal democracy," in *8° Congreso de La Asociación Latinoamericana de Ciencia Política*. Lima.

Hawkins, Kirk A., Scott Riding, and Cas Mudde. 2012. "Measuring populist attitudes," *Working Paper Series on Political Concepts*, ECPR Committee on Concepts and Methods.

Hempel, Carl. 1965. *Aspects of Scientific Explanation and Other Essays in the Philosophy of Science*. New York: The Free Press.

Hetherington, Marc J. and Jonathan D. Weiler. 2009. *Authoritarianism and Polarization in American Politics*. Cambridge: Cambridge University Press.

Huber, Robert A. and Christian H. Schimpf. 2015. "Friend or foe? Testing the influence of populism on democratic quality in Latin America," *Political Studies*, 64(4): 872–89.

Ianni, Octávio. 1975. *La formación del Estado populista en América Latina*. Mexico, DF: Ediciones Era.

Ionescu, Ghiţa and Ernest Gellner (eds). 1969. *Populism: Its Meanings and National Characteristics*. London: Weidenfeld and Nicolson.

Ivarsflaten, Elisabeth. 2008. "What unites right-wing populists in Western Europe? Re-examining grievance mobilization models in seven successful cases," *Comparative Political Studies*, 41(1): 3–23.

Ivarsflaten, Elisabeth and Frøy Gudrandsen. 2014. "The populist radical right in Western Europe," in *Europa Regional Surveys of the World*. London: Routledge.

Ivarsflaten, Elisabeth and Rune Stubager. 2013. "Voting for the populist radical right in Europe: the role of education," in Jens Rydgren (ed.), *Class Politics and the Radical Right*. New York: Routledge.

Jagers, Jan and Stefaan Walgrave. 2007. "Populism as political communication style: an empir-
    ical study of political parties' discourse in Belgium," *European Journal of Political Research*,
    46(3): 319–45.
Katz, Richard S. and Peter Mair. 1995. "Changing models of party organization and party
    democracy: the emergence of the Cartel Party," *Party Politics*, 1(1): 5–28.
Kazin, Michael. 1998. *The Populist Persuasion: An American History*. Ithaca: Cornell
    University Press.
Kitschelt, Herbert. 1994. *The Transformation of European Social Democracy*. Cambridge:
    Cambridge University Press.
Kornhauser, William. 2013. *Politics of Mass Society*. New York: Routledge.
Kriesi, Hanspeter. 2014. "The populist challenge," *West European Politics*, 37(2): 361–78.
Kriesi, Hanspeter and Takis S. Pappas, eds. 2015. *European Populism in the Shadow of the Great
    Recession*. Colchester: ECPR Press.
Kriesi, Hanspeter, Edgar Grande, Martin Dolezal, Marc Helbling, Dominic Höglinger,
    Swen Hutter, and Bruno Wüest. 2012. *Political Conflict in Western Europe*. Cambridge and
    New York: Cambridge University Press.
Laclau, Ernesto. 1977. *Politics and Ideology in Marxist Theory: Capitalism, Fascism, Populism*.
    London: New Left Books.
Laclau, Ernesto. 2005. *On Populist Reason*. London: Verso Books.
Le Bon, Gustave. 1960. *The Crowd: A Study of the Popular Mind*. New York: Viking Press.
Levitsky, Steven and James Loxton. 2013. "Populism and competitive authoritarianism in the
    Andes," *Democratization*, 20(1): 107–36.
Lubbers, Marcel and Peer Scheepers. 2000. "Individual and contextual characteristics of the
    German extreme right-wing vote in the 1990s: a test of complementary theories," *European
    Journal of Political Research*, 38(1): 63–94.
Mair, Peter. 2011. "Bini Smaghi vs. the parties: representative government and institutional
    constraints," EUI Working Papers 2011/22. Robert Schuman Centre for Advanced Studies,
    European Union Democracy Observatory. http://hdl.handle.net/1814/16354.
Mazzoleni, Gianpietro. 2008. "Populism and the media," in Daniele Albertazzi and Duncan
    McDonnell (eds), *Twenty-First Century Populism: The Spectre of Western European
    Democracy*. Basingstoke: Palgrave Macmillan, 49–64.
Mondak, Jeffery J., Matthew V. Hibbing, Damarys Canache, Mitchell A. Seligson, and
    Mary R. Anderson. 2010. "Personality and civic engagement: an integrative framework
    for the study of trait effects on political behavior," *American Political Science Review*,
    104(1): 85–110.
Morgan, Jana. 2011. *Bankrupt Representation and Party System Collapse*. University Park: Penn
    State University Press.
Mudde, Cas. 2007. *Populist Radical Right Parties in Europe*. Cambridge: Cambridge
    University Press.
Mudde, Cas. 2010. "The populist radical right: a pathological normalcy," *West European
    Politics*, 33(6): 1167–86.
Mudde, Cas and Cristobal Rovira Kaltwasser (eds). 2012. *Populism in Europe and the
    Americas: Threat or Corrective to Democracy?* Cambridge: Cambridge University Press.
Norris, Pippa. 2005. *Radical Right: Voters and Parties in the Electoral Market*.
    Cambridge: Cambridge University Press.

Ochoa Espejo, Paulina. 2011. *The Time of Popular Sovereignty: Process and the Democratic State*. University Park: Penn State Press.

O'Donnell, Guillermo. 1979. "Tensions in the bureaucratic-authoritarian state and the question of democracy," in David Collier (ed.), *The New Authoritarianism in Latin America*. Princeton: Princeton University Press, 285–318.

Oesch, Daniel. 2008. "Explaining workers' support for right-wing populist parties in Western Europe: evidence from Austria, Belgium, France, Norway, and Switzerland," *International Political Science Review/Revue Internationale de Science Politique*, 29(3): 349–73.

O'Malley, Eoin and John FitzGibbon. 2015. "Everywhere and nowhere: populism and the puzzling non-reaction to Ireland's crises," in Hanspeter Kriesi and Takis Pappas (eds), *European Populism in the Shadow of the Great Recession*. Colchester: ECPR Press, 287–300.

Panizza, Francisco (ed.). 2005. *Populism and the Mirror of Democracy*. London: Verso Books.

Panizza, Francisco and Romina Miorelli. 2009. "Populism and democracy in Latin America," *Ethics and International Affairs*, 23(1): 39–46.

Pauwels, Teun. 2014. *Populism in Western Europe: Comparing Belgium, Germany and The Netherlands*. New York: Routledge.

Pellikaan, Huib, Tom Van der Meer, and Sarah De Lange. 2003. "The road from a depoliticized to a centrifugal democracy," *Acta Politica*, 38(1): 23–49.

Plattner, Marc F. 2010. "Populism, pluralism, and liberal democracy," *Journal of Democracy*, 21(1): 81–92.

Riker, William H. 1982. *Liberalism Against Populism: A Confrontation Between the Theory of Democracy and the Theory of Social Choice*. Prospect Heights: Waveland Press.

Roberts, Kenneth M. 1995. "Neoliberalism and the transformation of populism in Latin America: the Peruvian case," *World Politics*, 48(1): 82–116.

Roberts, Kenneth M. 2015. *Changing Course in Latin America: Party Systems in the Neoliberal Era*. Cambridge: Cambridge University Press.

Rooduijn, Matthijs and Teun Pauwels. 2011. "Measuring populism: comparing two methods of content analysis," *West European Politics*, 34(6): 1272–83.

Rovira Kaltwasser, Cristóbal and Paul Taggart. 2016. "Dealing with populists in government: a framework for analysis," *Democratization*, 23(2): 201–20.

Rydgren, Jens. 2007. "The sociology of the radical right," *Annual Review of Sociology*, 33: 241–62.

Seawright, Jason. 2012. *Party-System Collapse: The Roots of Crisis in Peru and Venezuela*. Stanford: Stanford University Press.

Shils, Edward. 1956. *The Torment of Secrecy: The Background and Consequences of American Security Policies*. Glencoe: Free Press.

Skidmore, Thomas E., ed. 1993. *Television, Politics, and the Transition to Democracy in Latin America*. Washington, DC: Woodrow Wilson Center Press.

Spruyt, Bram, Gil Keppens, and Filip Van Droogenbroek. 2016. "Who supports populism and what attracts people to it?," *Political Research Quarterly*, 69(2): 335–46.

Stenner, Karen. 2005. *The Authoritarian Dynamic*. Cambridge: Cambridge University Press.

Van der Brug, Wouter, Meindert Fennema, and Jean Tillie. 2005. "Why some anti-immigrant parties fail and others succeed: a two-step model of aggregate electoral support," *Comparative Political Studies*, 38(5): 537–73.

van Kessel, Stijn. 2015. *Populist Parties in Europe: Agents of Discontent?* New York: Palgrave Macmillan.

Vilas, Carlos M. 1992. "Latin American populism: a structural approach," *Science and Society*, 56(4): 389–420.

Weffort, Francisco C. 1978. *O Populismo Na Política Brasileira*. Coleção Estudos Brasileiros, v. 25. Rio de Janeiro: Paz e Terra.

Weyland, Kurt. 1999. "Neoliberal populism in Latin America and Eastern Europe," *Comparative Politics*, 31(4): 379–401.

....

CHAPTER 15

POPULISM
AND POLITICAL PARTIES

....

KENNETH M. ROBERTS

THE study of populism and political parties has often been conducted along separate tracks that occasionally connect but never truly intertwine and enrich each other as they might, or more importantly, should. Both "topics" have been defined by a distinctive set of seminal studies, canonical literatures, and paradigmatic rivalries, but these remain relatively impervious to intellectual developments in the other field, even after "populist parties" became a widely (albeit loosely) used analytical category in several different regions of the world. Populist politics, however, can hardly be understood in isolation from party politics. In part, that is due to the basic reality—better put, a central paradox—that populist leaders and movements invariably create some type of political party to serve as an electoral vehicle in formal democratic arenas, even where they owe their rise to and stake their legitimacy on a civic rejection of established representative institutions (see Taggart, 2002: 113–14). More fundamentally, perhaps, this paradox suggests that any explanation for the rise of populism must inevitably address the inauthenticity or deficiencies in mainstream party–based modes of political representation for which populism claims to offer a corrective (see Peruzzotti, 2013). The study of populism, therefore—despite its challenges to the intermediary institutions of representative democracy, and its attendant claims to offer more "direct" forms of democratic empowerment of mass constituencies—must be firmly situated in the larger domain of political representation, and it is necessarily intertwined with the study of party politics.

As the aforementioned paradox suggests, populism is often, to paraphrase Schumpeter, a force of "creative destruction" for national party systems (Roberts, 2013: 40). On one hand, political space for populism is opened by the failure of established parties to effectively represent salient interests or sentiments in the body politic. Populism thrives where mainstream parties are in crisis, or at least where they exclude or ignore major currents of opinion that are denied institutionalized channels of expression. The rise of populist alternatives thus helps to crystallize such failures of representation, weaken or supplant traditional party organizations, and, in extreme cases, accelerate the demise of the old order. On the other hand, populism can provide at least a partial corrective for representational deficiencies by offering citizens new leaders, parties, or plebiscitary channels that articulate the preferences and promote the political incorporation of previously excluded or alienated sectors. At a minimum, therefore, the rise of a populist alternative adds a new contender to any national democratic arena; at a maximum, it can sweep aside traditional party organizations and fundamentally reconfigure the basic outlines of democratic representation and contestation.

This chapter is organized around these two basic dimensions of the relationship between parties and populism. Drawing from the theoretical literature on parties and political representation, it begins with an analysis of the representational deficiencies that are conducive to the rise of populist challengers, giving special attention to the recent European and Latin American experiences. It then explores the construction of populist parties and their transformative effects on national party systems. It concludes with an argument for a more explicit and thorough integration of the study of populism and political parties as interconnected components of contemporary democratic representation.

Before proceeding, it is necessary to locate this chapter within the broader conceptual debates about the meaning and extension of populism as a political phenomenon. Although I have often employed a restrictive conceptualization similar to that proposed by Kurt Weyland in his contribution to this volume, associating populism with the appropriation of popular subjectivity by a dominant personality (see, for example, Roberts, 2015), in order to speak to the steadily proliferating literature on populist parties and movements in different world regions I rely here on Mudde's less restrictive ideological approach. Implicitly or explicitly, much of the emerging literature understands populism as the ideological construction of antagonistic elite and popular blocs, assuming that invocations of "the people" can be made by mass movements as well as dominant personalities, and that intermediary organizations—parties in particular—are routinely constructed (from the top-down or the bottom-up) to provide institutional expression for such invocations. Since the theoretical questions addressed in this chapter regarding anti-elite and anti-establishment politics are germane to this larger audience, I opt here for conceptual extension and inclusiveness, recognizing—as Weyland suggests—that tradeoffs exist when a common label is applied to political phenomena that share discursive traits in common, but otherwise vary widely in their organizational forms and patterns of socio-political mobilization.

Party Politics and Representational Deficiencies: The Origins of Populist Challengers

Although populism has been defined in myriad ways, virtually all conceptualizations consider some sort of anti-establishment appeal to mass constituencies to lie at the heart of the political phenomenon. Populism is, in short, the quintessential expression of anti-elite and anti-establishment politics. Needless to say, who or what constitutes "the establishment" is both variable and historically constructed, but in democratic settings it nearly always includes mainstream party organizations. The rise of populism, therefore, poses an intrinsic challenge to mainstream party organizations and their control over the electoral marketplace. Either populist currents emerge within a mainstream party and challenge traditional leadership structures—the US Republican Party in recent times being an especially telling case (Skocpol and Williamson, 2013)—or, more typically, they emerge outside and against traditional parties and promise "the people" a more authentic mode of political representation.

Such challenges to mainstream parties are not necessarily commonplace. Indeed, some of the leading theoretical work on political parties and party systems suggests that outsider challenges to established party systems should be few and far between. The seminal sociological account of the origins of party systems by Lipset and Rokkan (1967: 50), for example, suggests that modern party systems are grounded in deep historical socio-political cleavages that "freeze" competitive alignments in place once universal suffrage is achieved and the electorate has been fully mobilized into rival partisan camps. Likewise, Bartolini and Mair (1990) find that established parties grounded in deep social cleavages can close the electoral marketplace to newcomers. The rational choice approach of Aldrich (2011: 44–50) pays little attention to the structuring of political alignments by social cleavages, but suggests that both elite political entrepreneurs and rank-and-file voters have incentives to stick with established party organizations— the former to exploit name-brand loyalties and economies of scale that address collective action problems in the process of electoral mobilization, and the latter to provide information short-cuts in the act of voting. Other influential work emphasizes the tendency for regular electoral competition to "habituate" voters and thus forge stable partisan identities (Converse, 1969), or the socializing effects of family and social networks that nurture durable partisan loyalties (Zuckerman, Dasović, and Fitzgerald, 2007).

Under what conditions, then, do these systemic reproductive mechanisms break down or weaken, leaving a significant number of citizens available for anti-establishment electoral mobilization by populist outsiders? As Laclau (2005: 137) states, a "crisis of representation" is "at the root of any populist, anti-institutional outburst," and recent research on Latin America has explored the nature of such crises and how they are related to the breakdown of traditional parties and the rise of populist challengers (Mainwaring, Bejarano, and Pizarro, 2006; Morgan, 2011; Lupu, 2016). At the most basic level, a crisis of representation indicates that large numbers of citizens do not identify with, or have confidence in, the intermediary institutions—political parties in particular—that claim to link society to the state and articulate societal interests in public policy-making arenas. Needless to say, such lack of identification or trust does not lead inevitably to a strengthening of populist alternatives; citizens who do not identify with existing parties may simply opt out of democratic participation, or they may cast uninspired votes for traditional parties out of some combination of civic duty, habituation, or the absence of perceived alternatives. A crisis could be said to exist, however, when large blocs of these citizens become amenable to political mobilization by extra-systemic actors who claim to offer more responsive or authentic forms of interest representation, and particularly when such actors use their "outsider" status and opposition to establishment institutions as a primary basis of appeal. A crisis of representation, therefore, threatens established parties' control over the electoral marketplace; indeed, it poses a basic challenge to the reproduction of the party system itself, exposing the system to highly disruptive or trans-formative forces. The comparative historical record suggests at least four different types of representational deficiencies that could produce such a crisis and leave mainstream parties vulnerable to populist challenges. These deficiencies are not mutually exclusive; where they overlap or reinforce each other, the vulnerability of established parties is mag-nified, and the potential for populist challenges is sure to increase.

Political Exclusion and the Initial Process of Mass Political Incorporation

Oligarchic patterns of political domination, even where they are organized competi-tively among rival factions of a ruling elite, necessarily suffer from the representational deficiency of excluding large numbers of people. The initial process of mass political incorporation following extended periods of oligarchic or exclusionary rule, therefore, involves the enfranchisement and political mobilization of large blocs of voters who have weak or non-existent ties to established party organizations—a set of conditions that are highly conducive to the rise of populism. Notably, such conditions are logically prior to the type of systemic "freezing" that Lipset and Rokkan famously described in the European context, which followed the extension of the suffrage to working classes that were in the process of being politically mobilized by labor unions and labor-based parties of the left. Universal suffrage and lower-class political mobilization outside of Europe, however, often had a different effect. In particular, populism thrived in much of Latin America during the middle of the twentieth century, when the combination of industrialization and suffrage reforms gave the vote to emerging urban working and middle classes who had few ties to the traditional oligarchic parties of landed and com-mercial elites (Collier and Collier, 1991).

Rather than entering class-based parties of the left, with the notable exception of Chile, these urban popular sectors were often mobilized politically by populist figures and the socially heterogeneous, ideologically eclectic parties that they founded. In that sense, populism was Latin America's political analogue to social democracy, promis-ing political inclusion, vigorous state intervention, and redistributive social reforms to working- and lower-class groups. Social and political citizenship rights were not simply aimed at getting a seat at the table for previously excluded groups, however, as populist discourse was openly hostile to a political establishment shaped by oligarchic forms of domination and exclusion. Populism thrived, therefore, when oligarchic forms of rule—in both their partisan and patrimonial authoritarian variants—weakened and lost their capacity to enforce political exclusion as the Great Depression of the 1930s undermined commodity export-based economies and encouraged a spurt of import-substituting industrialization. This historical timing helped to account for the ancillary features that are typically associated with classical forms of populism in Latin America, including its assertive nationalism, its promotion of state-led industrialization, its multi-class urban-industrial social constituencies, and its trade union organizational base tied to corporatist patterns of interest intermediation (Conniff, 2012).

Initial processes of mass political incorporation in other parts of the developing world during the so-called "third wave" of democratization (Huntington, 1991) at the end of the twentieth century have also been conducive to populism, although the very different world historical timing has attached different ancillary properties to these new expressions of populism. The populist movement led by Thaksin Shinawatra in Thailand is a case in point (Hewison, 2010), and opposition figures in emerging African democracies have also started to employ populist appeals to the urban poor (Resnick, 2012; 2014). By definition, however, initial incorporation can only occur once in any democratic setting; the most prominent populist movements in recent times, therefore, have not entailed the initial incorporation of mass constituencies, but rather their mobilization in opposition to political establishments that they previously supported during earlier periods of democratic incorporation. As such, contemporary forms of populism are more likely when incorporation gives way to disillusionment and detachment—in Lipset and Rokkan's terms, to the "thawing" of party systems of varying degrees of "frozenness" or consolidation. Such disillusionment and thawing leave mass constituencies available for political mobilization by anti-establishment outsiders. This mobilization is associated with three other sets of representational deficiencies that can generate crises in party systems: namely, organizational cartelization, performance failures, and programmatic convergence.

Organizational Cartelization

Lipset and Rokkan's freezing metaphor rests on the assumption that party systems are grounded in deep social cleavages that structure and align voters' partisan identities and electoral competition. Such cleavages are alleged to anchor voters in rival partisan camps that represent distinct social constituencies with alternative programmatic preferences, thus limiting individual voter mobility, reducing electoral volatility, and closing the electoral marketplace to new partisan contenders (Bartolini and Mair, 1990). Recent European scholarship, however, has highlighted some of the potential downsides of such frozen representation. In particular, Katz and Mair (1995) have argued that the social embeddedness of established parties can progressively wither over time as they alternate in public office and become entrenched in state institutions. Party organizations may become increasingly professionalized and dependent on state resources, eroding their grassroots membership branches and linkages to social actors. That is especially the case when social cleavages based on class and religion have themselves weakened and become more fluid as a result of social mobility, the expansion of middle classes, universal welfare states, and societal secularization (Franklin, Mackie, and Valen, 1992). Consequently, as Schmitter (2001) states, "parties are not what they once were"; rather than represent and politically integrate diverse societal interests, they allow representational functions to be assumed by a wide range of civic and social actors, while rival party organizations collude to share state resources and monopolize access to public institutions (Katz and Mair, 1995; see also Dalton and Wattenberg, 2000). Established parties may even come to resemble a closed and powerful political cartel that shares in the spoils of public office and excludes alternative voices from effective representation.

As Mair (1995: 106) puts it, states can become "an institutionalized structure of support, sustaining insiders while excluding outsiders," such that parties "are absorbed by the state" and "become semi-state agencies." Although such forms of cartelization and "partyarchy" (Coppedge, 1994) are predicated on the exclusion of outsiders, they can become highly susceptible to outsider challenges in the electoral arena. Simply put, voters may come to see established parties as protectors of an elite political caste that serves its own narrow self-interests rather than looking out for—or "representing"—the broader interests of society. Evidence of political corruption, naturally, only reinforces societal perceptions of parties as self-serving cartels rather than authentic representatives of societal interests. Under conditions of cartelization, as Mair states (1997: 117–18), the "rallying cry" of outsiders which "seems particularly effective for mobilizing support" is the demand to "break the mould" of established politics. Such anti-establishment appeals are the linchpin of populist movements of varying persuasions, and they are often reinforced by other representational deficiencies outlined below.

Performance Failures

Voters are more likely to identify with or have confidence in parties that perform reasonably well in public office—that is, parties that are responsible, effective, and capable of "getting things done." Not surprisingly, then, incumbent parties typically bear the brunt of the political costs generated by severe economic crises or corruption scandals, which often produce retrospective anti-incumbent voting patterns (Remmer, 1991). Indeed, prolonged economic crises or chronic corruption may culminate in sequential patterns of anti-incumbent voting that weaken a succession of established parties, undermining a party system at-large (Roberts, 2014: 53). Systemic performance failures of these types are especially conducive to the rise of populist outsiders; they loosen voter attachments to the political establishment across a wide range of parties, and allow populist figures to appeal for support from a heterogeneous but previously disconnected bloc of alienated voters with a plethora of grievances against the status quo. In Laclauian terms, the promise of ill-defined "change" in a context of systemic failure is perhaps the ultimate example of the populist construction of an "empty signifier" that welds together disparate strands of anti-establishment discontent (Laclau, 2005: 69–71).

It is hardly surprising, then, that chronic corruption or severe and prolonged economic crises often play a major role in the institutional weakening of established party systems and the rise of new populist challengers. Italy's massive corruption scandal in the early 1990s was integral to the demise of that country's post–World War II party system, inadvertently setting the stage for the political ascent of the maverick outsider Silvio Berlusconi. Similarly in Venezuela, a generalized belief that corrupt politicians had squandered the country's oil wealth not only created disillusionment with established parties, but arguably exacerbated the political costs of a deepening economic crisis in the 1990s (Romero, 1997). In Latin America, massive performance failures undergirded the rise of such disparate populist outsiders as Alberto Fujimori in Peru, Hugo Chávez in Venezuela, and Rafael Correa in Ecuador, all of whom capitalized on popular discontent with traditional parties that had been discredited by corruption and repeated economic crises. More recently, the prolonged period of economic recession and austerity in Europe triggered by the 2008 global financial crisis spawned the rise of new leaders or movements in Greece, Spain, and Italy who appealed to a disaffected "people" while challenging mainstream party organizations.

In addition to imposing the direct political costs of performance failures on mainstream party organizations, economic crises typically narrow the range of viable policy options. Indeed, they generate powerful market-based pressures on any ruling party, no matter its ideological persuasion, to adopt unpopular austerity and adjustment measures that can exacerbate material hardships, at least in the short term. Crisis situations are thus conducive to an especially acute form of the final type of representational deficiency that is conducive to the rise of populism—the programmatic convergence of mainstream party organizations that largely cease to offer the electorate a meaningful range of policy alternatives.

Programmatic Convergence

Although political parties often cultivate clientelistic and personalistic (or charismatic) linkages to societal constituencies (see Kitschelt, 2000), programmatic linkages based on alternative policy platforms and preferences are integral to any conception of democratic representation and competition. The articulation of policy alternatives has historically been a primary function of political parties, and the programmatic expression of the social blocs or cleavages that undergird the most stable forms of partisan representation. Although policy orientations are not exclusive foundations for the partisan "brands" that help to secure voter loyalties, they are integral to many forms of stable partisanship (Aldrich, 2011; Sniderman and Stiglitz, 2012; Lupu, 2016).

Programmatic linkages, however, require that rival parties articulate meaningfully different policy platforms, campaign for public office on the basis of such differentiated proposals, and make a good faith effort to implement their platform when elected into office, even when changing political or economic circumstances mandate adaptations or compromise. Programmatic linkages are necessarily difficult to sustain when major parties converge around a narrow set of policy choices that do not allow voters to differentiate among rival party organizations. The failure of mainstream parties to effectively articulate and represent policy preferences that are salient to a significant portion of the electorate is, therefore, a widely recognized source of new party formation—and the resultant "thawing" of "frozen" party systems—in established democracies (Kitschelt, 1988; Hug, 2001). Although such policy preferences are often assumed to be located along programmatic dimensions that are "new" and orthogonal to the conventional left-right economic policy-making spectrum—such as preferences related to environmental or other post-materialist values, or foreign immigration—the same logic can account for new party challenges that emerge when the left-right spectrum itself has been compressed by the convergence of mainstream parties, leaving vacant political space on the left and/or right poles of a given party system. As stated by Rovira Kaltwasser (2015: 198), "when the mainstream political forces become too similar, they provide a fertile ground for the rise of populism."

Indeed, new populist parties or movements often emerge to articulate these orthogonal issue dimensions or challenge programmatic convergence in mainstream party systems. In Europe, right-wing nationalist parties with an anti-establishment populist discourse have emerged or strengthened in recent years by articulating anti-immigrant and anti-European integration stands that found limited expression in mainstream party organizations (Mudde, 2007; Berezin, 2009; Art, 2011). In so doing, they have triggered new forms of democratic contestation along issue dimensions that were previously ignored or suppressed, forcing mainstream parties to take stands on issues that often lay outside their comfort zones.

In the recent Latin American experience, the rise of populist leaders and movements has been associated less with the articulation of new issue dimensions than with challenges to programmatic convergence on the left-right spectrum during periods of economic crisis and market-based structural adjustment. The collapse of state-led development models in the debt crisis and hyperinflationary spirals of the 1980s led to the adoption of austerity and market liberalization policies throughout the region. Where such policies were adopted by conservative, pro-business leaders or parties and a major party of the left remained in opposition, societal resistance to market orthodoxy could be channeled by the leftist party in ways that stabilized party system competition and closed political space for emerging populist contenders. Where structural adjustment was imposed by center-left or labor-based populist parties that traditionally supported statist and redistributive policies, however, programmatic convergence left party systems without an institutionalized channel for societal opposition to market liberalism. Such patterns of reform often left a sequel of mass social protest (Silva, 2009), party system demise, and forms of electoral protest that empowered emerging left-populist outsiders, including Hugo Chávez in Venezuela, Rafael Correa in Ecuador, and the movement-party led by Evo Morales in Bolivia (Roberts, 2014). In these cases, then, the populist backlash against programmatic convergence—what Lupu (2016) characterizes as "brand dilution"—culminated in an outflanking to the left of established party systems.

A similar dynamic can be seen in the recent European experience, where the post-2008 economic crisis led to the adoption of painful austerity measures by historic Socialist parties in a number of countries, followed by widespread social protest. In Greece, Spain,

Italy, and Hungary, the convergence of mainstream parties around austerity platforms was followed by the emergence or strengthening of anti-establishment contenders who deployed a populist discourse, while representing a wide range of ideological dispositions. In contrast to Latin America, where societal resistance to market orthodoxy combined with indigenous movements to push populism toward the left pole in the post-adjustment era, conflicts related to immigration and nationalism in Europe created the potential for anti-establishment and anti-austerity populist appeals to emerge on the right as well as the left flank of mainstream party systems. Economic crises, then, not only impose the direct political costs of retrospective, anti-incumbent vote shifts on ruling parties, but may also de-align party systems programmatically by forcing mainstream parties to converge on a narrow set of policy options. Where these options do not fully represent the distribution of societal preferences, party systems can easily be outflanked by emerging populist contenders that are located more closely to one or another ideological pole.

In comparative perspective, the strengthening of both left- and right-wing variants of populism in Western Europe in recent times surely reflects the erosion of the distinctive party system attributes that historically differentiated the region's politics from those in other parts of the world—namely, their deep roots in class cleavages and the well-defined programmatic structuring of partisan competition (Bartolini and Mair, 1990). These two attributes were antithetical to the political logic of populism, which typically aims to draw support from heterogeneous social bases and eschews strict ideological definition. As these distinctive attributes weaken, however, European politics more closely resembles the loosely structured and de-aligned patterns of competition found in regions like Latin America, where diverse strands of opposition to the establishment find expression through populist leaders and movements (Laclau, 2005).

To summarize, populism thrives in contexts of representational failures or deficiencies, when mainstream political parties have lost control of the electoral marketplace due to the mobilization of previously unincorporated mass constituencies, organizational cartelization, performance failures, or programmatic convergence and electoral outflanking. In these contexts, large blocs of voters are amenable to anti-establishment forms of political mobilization. Populism, therefore, is an inherently contestatory political phenomenon that challenges mainstream party organizations and representative institutions. It provides an alternative to such institutions, but rarely, if ever, does populism present an alternative to representation per se. Instead, as explained below, populism generates alternative vehicles for representation which typically assume partisan forms. As such, populism transforms and reconfigures national party systems, more than it displaces them.

POPULISM, PARTY BUILDING, AND PARTY SYSTEM TRANSFORMATION

In Laclauian terms, populism entails the dichotomic and "antagonistic division of the social field," whereby "a set of particular identities or interests tend to regroup themselves as equivalential differences around one of the poles of the dichotomy" (Laclau, 2005: 19, 137). Such regrouping does not always or necessarily take place around a party organization; for Laclau, a dominant personality or popular movement can construct the antagonistic frontier that demarcates popular forces—or "the people"—from establishment elites. Historically, many populist phenomena had their origins in such non-partisan forms of political articulation. Regrouping around dominant personalities has been especially prevalent in Latin America, where the logic of presidentialism allows for the capture of executive office—even by political outsiders—in the absence of partisan intermediation. In Ecuador, for example, José María Velasco Ibarra was elected to the presidency five times in the middle of the twentieth century at the head of loosely organized socio-political coalitions without ever establishing a meaningful party vehicle (Sosa, 2012). Velasco Ibarra famously stated that if given a balcony from which to address the masses, he would make himself president; party organization was superfluous to his ambitions. More recently, Rafael Correa captured the presidency of Ecuador in 2006 without even bothering to sponsor an accompanying list of legislative co-partisans, for the express purpose of accentuating his independence from Ecuador's political class and his singular capacity to represent "the people."

In neighboring Peru, Alberto Fujimori notoriously registered under a new party label for every election cycle in which he stood for office, with only the most minimal (and transferable) forms of organization attached to these labels (Roberts, 2006a: 93–6). Although Argentine Peronism eventually spawned a highly competitive and resilient (if weakly institutionalized) party organization, it initially identified as a movement much more than a party organization and relied on trade unions rather than party branches to mobilize support. Perón quickly dissolved the labor-based party that supported his initial presidential campaign, and thereafter adopted consistent measures to keep his movement's partisan appendages weak and subordinate to his personal authority. As McGuire (1997: 14–15) argues, Perón neither wanted nor needed to build a major party, as he "did not want to provide potential rivals with an organizational base" and "tried to establish a direct relationship with his followers unmediated by party organization."

Although some scholars make such plebiscitarian constructions of direct, unmediated relationships between a leader and mass constituencies a definitional attribute of populism (see, for example, Weyland, 2001; Barr, 2009), Laclau's formulation and other discursive and ideational approaches allow for social movements to construct the antagonistic frontier from the bottom-up (see Rovira Kaltwasser, 2014: 496, 502). In recent times, protest movements in strikingly diverse national settings have employed a populist discourse to evoke "the people" and challenge entrenched political and economic elites, transcending narrow class or sectoral claims to weld together varied strands of discontent that do not—initially, at least—find expression in a party organization. Paradigmatic examples include the massive uprising of Bolivian indigenous and popular movements that toppled two presidents in 2003 and 2005 (Madrid, 2008; 2012), the Occupy Wall Street Movement in the US, and the anti-austerity protest movement of the *indignados* in Spain (della Porta, 2015: 96–102).

Party organization, therefore, is clearly not a precondition for the populist construction of an antagonistic frontier between the people and establishment elites. Nevertheless, the logic of populism aims at the construction of a counter-hegemonic force that not only contests, but also displaces established elites; populism, in short, has a vocation for power that cannot be satiated by policy concessions targeted to its particularistic strands. As such, powerful political pressures exist for populist forces to transition from the domain of socio-political protest to institutional arenas where elections are contested, governments are constituted, and public policies are designed and implemented. These pressures routinely induce both populist leaders and mass movements to construct party organizations in order to enhance their leverage in formal regime institutions, even where populist forces ultimately seek to displace and reconfigure such institutions. Indeed, the rationale for party organization among populist leaders and movements largely conforms to the theoretical insights derived by Aldrich (2011: 27–64) from non-populist settings: political entrepreneurs build party organizations to address collective action problems in the process of electoral mobilization and social coordination problems in governing and policy-making arenas.

Pressures for party building are especially pronounced in Europe, where parliamentary institutions preclude strictly plebiscitarian paths to executive office. Short of a popular insurrection that sweeps aside parliamentary institutions, a populist figure such as Rafael Correa could not be elected prime minister without partisan support in the legislative branch. Not surprisingly, then, until the recent wave of anti-austerity—and largely left-leaning—protest movements, populism in Europe has typically assumed partisan forms and routinely engaged in electoral contestation. It has, moreover, been most prevalent on the right side of the political spectrum, where nativist and nationalist forces have mobilized opposition to foreign immigration, Islamic influences, and European integration, as well as domestic political elites who are alleged to have tolerated such multi-cultural distortions of the national identity (Mudde, 2007; Berezin, 2009; Art, 2011; Mudde and Rovira Kaltwasser, 2012). As Mudde (2007: 267–8) explains, some of these parties have movement origins and many are organized around dominant personalities, with relatively "simple structures and few members." Nevertheless, they are characterized by "strict internal hierarchies" and "demand a high level of internal discipline" of the few members they recruit.

The right-wing positioning of these parties is attributable to their stands on nationalist and cultural issues, as they are not defined by ideological commitments to market orthodoxy; though some have neoliberal or anti-taxation roots, they are increasingly inclined toward forms of "welfare chauvinism" that defend generous national welfare states against the costs of caring for immigrant populations (Mudde, 2007; Art, 2011: 17–18). Paradoxically, given their own chauvinist and illiberal tendencies (Pappas, 2014; Kriesi, 2014), they also claim to defend Western liberal values against cultural imports—Islam in particular—that they see as being hostile to women's rights and individual liberties. Populist radical right parties have thus politicized issue dimensions that are largely orthogonal to the traditional left-right axis of competition based on statist and free-market programmatic positions—along the lines of Hug's (2001) model of new party formation—even if immigration and cultural integration issues are neither new to democratic politics nor the exclusive domain of radical right parties (see Mudde, 2013: 11–12). As Art (2011: 19–24) suggests, these radical right parties gained a stronger foothold in France, Flanders, Austria, and Italy, where historically strong nationalist sub-cultures or movements and the absence of strict post-war *cordons sanitaires* allowed nascent parties to attract activists with higher levels of education and political experience. Only the National Front in France built a mass party organization, however, and populist radical right parties remained relatively minor actors on the national political stage through the first decade of the twenty-first century. Despite being, in electoral terms, "the most successful new European party family since the end of the Second World War" (Mudde, 2013: 4), populist radical right parties had only modest effects on the competitive dynamics of party systems, the shape of public opinion, and the content of public policy. The political mainstream may have moved in their direction, but that shift was a product of larger societal forces at work, and not simply the "pull" of the radical right itself (see Mudde, 2013).

Nevertheless, as Kriesi (2008) argues, long-term patterns of party system de-alignment related to structural changes like post-industrialism, globalization, and European integration allowed right-wing nationalist and populist parties to appeal to less educated and working-class sectors of the European population that were often on the losing end of structural transformations. Political opportunity structures arguably became more even more favorable when these long-term patterns of de-alignment were reinforced by a series of more conjunctural factors, including the political costs of the post-2008 financial crisis, the convergence of mainstream parties on painful austerity measures, and the surge in immigration to Europe from troubled regions of Africa and the Middle East. This combination of factors weakened the hold of mainstream parties over the electorate and created potential bases of social support for the anti-establishment and welfare chauvinist appeals of populist radical right parties.

The post-2008 crisis, however, also fostered the rise of new protest movements and left-populist parties in parts of Southern Europe. As in Latin America, the adoption of orthodox austerity and adjustment measures by traditional center-left parties in power during the early stages of the regional crisis led to widespread social protest that quickly translated into forms of electoral protest against established party systems. Much of this electoral protest was channeled by new populist or left-populist parties, such as PODEMOS in Spain and the Five Star Movement in Italy, or previously marginal radical left parties like SYRIZA in Greece and the Left Bloc in Portugal (della Porta, 2015; Kriesi, 2014; Stavrakakis, 2014; Stavrakakis and Katsambekis, 2014). Although these parties were not necessarily organic expressions of mass protest movements like Bolivia's *Movimiento al Socialismo* (MAS), they clearly drew upon the energy and organizational networks of these movements to nurture their growth in the electoral arena.

The political fallout from the European crisis, therefore, has spawned or strengthened populist forces on both the right and left flanks of traditional party systems, posing the most serious challenge to Lipset and Rokkan's (1967) "frozen" party systems that the region has seen in modern times. To be sure, although left- and right-wing variants

of populism may both find fertile soil for growth in the representational crises produced by economic hardships and party system de-alignment, they offer radically different correctives to these representational deficiencies. As stated by Kriesi (2014: 362),
"Populism's meaning varies with the understanding given to 'the people,' i.e. to the idealized conception of the community (the 'heartland') to which it applies" (see also de la
Torre, 2015). Right-wing populists in Europe conceive of "the people" in cultural and
national terms that are highly exclusionary toward cultural minorities. Left-wing populism, by contrast, is more inclined to conceptualize the community in class terms that
are broadly inclusive of subaltern groups, defining "the other" as political and economic
elites that are the domestic embodiment of transnational market and power relations.
Both variants, however, converge in their opposition to mainstream party organizations
and in their claims to offer more authentic forms of popular representation.

In the recent Latin American experience, such populist challenges have thoroughly
transformed traditional party systems in a number of countries. Even charismatic populist figures who were able to win presidential elections with minimal forms of party
organization, such as Chávez in Venezuela and Correa in Ecuador, found it necessary
to engage in serious party building efforts in order to govern effectively and implement
major political and economic reforms. That is especially the case where populist leaders pursued redistributive social and economic policies that challenged traditional elites
(see Roberts, 2006b). Although conservative populist figures like the earlier Velasco
Ibarra in Ecuador and Fujimori in Peru tried to govern without the backing of a major
party organization, relying instead on the support of elite business, technocratic, and
military networks, their political fates demonstrated the institutional fragility of such
personalized leadership patterns; Velasco Ibarra was repeatedly toppled by military coups and failed to complete four of his five presidential terms in office, while the
Fujimori regime imploded at the beginning of its third term when efforts to bribe con-
gressional support triggered a major corruption scandal. In the absence of significant
efforts to build a party organization or mobilize grassroots constituencies, both leaders
bequeathed legacies of "serial populism," with the cyclical ascendance of one independent personality or populist figure after another (Roberts, 2014). By contrast, Chávez and
Correa—committed from the outside to challenge established elites by re-founding
regime institutions and contesting neoliberal development models—built new parties
to provide organizational support as they convoked constituent assemblies, elected new
legislatures with majoritarian support, asserted state control over extractive industries
that generated major export revenues, and implemented ambitious social programs
and redistributive reforms (Conaghan, 2011; López Maya, 2011; Hawkins, 2010). In so
doing, they reconfigured national party systems around a central socio-political cleavage between a dominant left populist party and center-right opposition forces that
remained politically fragmented (Ecuador) or loosely organized in a broad electoral
front (Venezuela).

Although the parties founded by Chávez and Correa were surely instruments of their
personal authority, they nevertheless demonstrated how state office and resources could
be used for organization-building purposes. As McGuire (1997: 23–4) argues, however,

following much the same logic as Shefter's classic analysis (1994), even stronger parties may develop when they are founded in opposition and forced to rely on their organizational strength to challenge entrenched power and compensate for the lack of state resources. This was surely the case of APRA in Peru, which legendary populist figure Victor Raul Haya de la Torre built into a highly disciplined mass party organization during extended periods of state repression and opposition in the middle of the twentieth century. The Bolivian case is also instructive, as the political leadership and organizational networks of the MAS were directly spawned by indigenous, peasant, labor, and community-based movements that emerged to challenge established elites and their neoliberal economic model in the 1990s and early 2000s (Madrid, 2008; 2012). The MAS, therefore, is a paradigmatic "movement party" (Kitschelt, 2006), with more extensive grassroots networks that retain a greater capacity for autonomous collective action than is typically found in populist parties built from the top-down by charismatic leaders (see Anria, 2013; Crabtree, 2013).

Whether organized from the top-down or the bottom-up, populist mobilization has repeatedly reconstituted national party systems and reconfigured their cleavage alignments in Latin America. That was the case during the region's first wave of labor-based populism during the early stages of industrialization in the middle of the twentieth century (Collier and Collier, 1991; de la Torre and Arnson, 2013), and it remains the case during the second great wave of populist mobilization that followed in the wake of market-based structural adjustment in the 1980s and 1990s. Even with the passing of Hugo Chávez from the political scene, populist/anti-populist cleavages are sure to remain a central axis of political contestation in many countries, including Venezuela. Populist parties are prominent and recurring features on the region's political landscape, and they are likely to remain so as long as heterogeneous popular constituencies can be mobilized against the exclusionary tendencies of traditional representative institutions.

Conclusion

As a political phenomenon, populism cannot be understood in isolation from the study of party politics. Populist mobilization emerges and thrives when established party systems are incapable of offering effective representation to the plurality of interests that are found in modern societies. At its most basic level, therefore, populism offers a corrective to deficient representation, and is best located within the representational sphere of democratic politics, even when it trumpets its hostility to established representative institutions.

The challenge for scholarship on populism and party politics is thus two-fold. First, it is essential to conceptualize and theoretically explain the representational deficiencies that create favorable political opportunity structures for populist appeals, especially in countries that have long had relatively well-institutionalized party systems. The rise of populism is not especially surprising during the initial stage of mass political incorporation, but it is more unexpected—and thus more theoretically interesting—where popular constituencies have long been attached to mainstream party organizations. This chapter identifies several different institutional contexts where significant blocs of voters are likely to detach themselves from such parties and become receptive to anti-establishment populist appeals: namely, contexts of organizational cartelization, performance failures, and programmatic convergence. Much work remains to be done, however, to identify the causal mechanisms that link such contexts to populist mobilization, to explore cross-national and cross-regional patterns of variation, and to explain the micro-analytic foundations of such changes in voting behavior.

Second, what types of correctives do populist parties offer to the representational deficiencies of mainstream parties? Beyond offering voters a new or alternative electoral vehicle, do populist parties politicize new issue dimensions or expand the range of policy alternatives? Do they offer distinctive patterns of organization or opportunities to supplement representative channels with new modes of popular participation? To which excluded societal interests and preferences do they give voice, and how do they weld them together into a coherent political project? Where such projects achieve majoritarian status, how do they reconcile the hegemonic temptations of popular sovereignty with the minority rights and institutional checks and balances of liberal democratic governance? Finally, how do populist parties' linkages to their social bases change when they gain access to public office and make a transition from oppositional or protest politics to policy-making and governance? The answers to these questions largely determine what kinds of representation populist parties offer to their social bases, and how they differ from the mainstream parties they seek to displace.

References

Aldrich, John A. 2011. *Why Parties? A Second Look*, 2nd edn. Chicago: University of Chicago Press.

Anria, Santiago. 2013. "Social movements, party organization, and populism: insights from the Bolivian MAS," *Latin American Politics and Society*, 55(3): 19–46.

Art, David. 2011. *Inside the Radical Right: The Development of Anti-Immigrant Parties in Western Europe*. New York: Cambridge University Press.

Barr, Robert R. 2009. "Populists, outsiders and anti-establishment politics," *Party Politics*, 15(1): 29–48.

Bartolini, Stefano and Peter Mair. 1990. *Identity, Competition, and Electoral Availability: The Stabilisation of European Electorates 1885–1985*. Cambridge: Cambridge University Press.

Berezin, Mabel. 2009. *Illiberal Politics in Neoliberal Times: Culture, Security and Populism in a New Europe*. New York: Cambridge University Press.

Collier, Ruth Berins and David Collier. 1991. *Shaping the Political Arena: Critical Junctures, the Labor Movement, and Regime Dynamics in Latin America*. Princeton: Princeton University Press.

Conaghan, Catherine. 2011. "Ecuador: Rafael Correa and the Citizens' Revolution," in Steven Levitsky and Kenneth M. Roberts (eds), *The Resurgence of the Latin American Left*. Baltimore: Johns Hopkins University Press, 260–82.

Conniff, Michael L. (ed.). 2012. *Populism in Latin America*, 2nd edn. Tuscaloosa: University of Alabama Press.

Converse, Philip E. 1969. "Of time and partisan stability," *Comparative Political Studies*, 2(2): 139–71.

Coppedge, Michael. 1994. *Strong Parties and Lame Ducks: Presidential Partyarchy and Factionalism in Venezuela*. Stanford: Stanford University Press.

Crabtree, John. 2013. "From the MNR to the MAS: populism, parties, the state, and social movements in Bolivia since 1952," in Carlos de la Torre and Cynthia J. Arnson (eds), *Latin American Populism in the Twenty-First Century*. Washington, DC: Woodrow Wilson Center Press.

Dalton, Russell J. and Martin P. Wattenberg (eds). 2000. *Parties Without Partisans: Political Change in Advanced Industrial Democracies*. Oxford: Oxford University Press.

de la Torre, Carlos. 2015. "Power to the people? Populism, insurrections, and democratization," in Carlos de la Torren (ed.), *The Promise and Perils of Populism: Global Perspectives*. Lexington: University of Kentucky Press, 1–28.

de la Torre, Carlos and Cynthia J. Arnson (eds). 2013. *Latin American Populism in the Twenty-First Century*. Washington, DC: Woodrow Wilson Center Press.

della Porta, Donatella. 2015. *Social Movements in Times of Austerity: Bringing Capitalism Back In*. Cambridge: Polity Press.

Franklin, Mark N., Thomas T. Mackie, and Henry Valen, et al. 1992. *Electoral Change: Responses to Evolving Social and Attitudinal Structures in Western Countries*. Cambridge: Cambridge University Press.

Hawkins, Kirk. 2010. *Venezuela's Chavismo and Populism in Comparative Perspective*. New York: Cambridge University Press.

Hewison, Kevin. 2010. "Thaksin Shinawatra and the reshaping of Thai politics," *Contemporary Politics*, 16(2): 119–33.

Hug, Simon. 2001. *Altering Party Systems: Strategic Behavior and the Emergence of New Political Parties in Western Democracies*. Ann Arbor: University of Michigan Press.

Huntington, Samuel P. 1991. *The Third Wave: Democratization in the Late Twentieth Century*. Norman: University of Oklahoma Press.

Katz, Richard S. and Peter Mair. 1995. "Changing models of party organization and party democracy: the emergence of the Cartel Party," *Party Politics*, 1(1): 5–31.

Kitschelt, Herbert. 1988. "Left-libertarian parties: explaining innovation in competitive party systems," *World Politics*, 40(2): 194–234.

Kitschelt, Herbert P. 2000. "Linkages between citizens and politicians in democratic politics," *Comparative Political Studies*, 33(6/7): 845–79.

Kitschelt, Herbert P. 2006. "Movement parties," in Richard S. Katz and William Crotty (eds), *Handbook of Party Politics*. London: Sage Publications, 278–90.

Kriesi, Hanspeter. 2008. "Contexts of party mobilization," in Hanspeter Kriesi, Edgar Grande, Romain Lachat, Martin Dolezal, Simon Bornschier, and Timotheos Frey (eds), *West European Politics in the Age of Globalization*. New York: Cambridge University Press, 23–52.

Kriesi, Hanspeter. 2014. "The populist challenge," *West European Politics*, 37(2): 361–78.

Laclau, Ernesto. 2005. *On Populist Reason*. London: Verso.

Lipset, Seymour Martin and Stein Rokkan. 1967. "Cleavage structures, party systems, and voter alignments: an introduction," in Seymour Martin Lipset and Stein Rokkan (eds), *Party Systems and Voter Alignments: Cross-National Perspectives*. New York: Free Press, 1–64.

López Maya, Margarita. 2011. "Venezuela: Hugo Chávez and the populist left," in Steven Levitsky and Kenneth M. Roberts (eds), *The Resurgence of the Latin American Left*. Baltimore: Johns Hopkins University Press, 213–38.

Lupu, Noam. 2016. *Party Brands in Crisis: Partisanship, Brand Dilution, and the Breakdown of Political Parties in Latin America*. New York: Cambridge University Press.

Madrid, Raúl L. 2008. "The rise of ethnopopulism in Bolivia," *World Politics*, 60(3): 475–508.

Madrid, Raúl L. 2012. *The Rise of Ethnic Politics in Latin America*. New York: Cambridge University Press.

Mainwaring, Scott, Ana María Bejarano, and Eduardo Pizarro (eds). 2006. *The Crisis of Democratic Representation in the Andes*. Stanford: Stanford University Press.

Mair, Peter. 2005. *Party System Change: Approaches and Interpretations*. Oxford: Clarendon Press.

McGuire, James W. 1997. *Peronism without Perón: Unions, Parties, and Democracy in Argentina*. Stanford: Stanford University Press.

Morgan, Jana. 2011. *Bankrupt Representation and Party System Collapse*. University Park: Pennsylvania State University Press.

Mudde, Cas. 2007. *Populist Radical Right Parties in Europe*. Cambridge: Cambridge University Press.

Mudde, Cas. 2013. "Three decades of populist radical right parties in Western Europe: so what?," *European Journal of Political Research*, 52: 1–19.

Mudde, Cas and Cristóbal Rovira Kaltwasser. 2012. "Populism and (liberal) democracy: a framework for analysis," in Cas Mudde and Cristóbal Rovira Kaltwasser (eds), *Populism in Europe and the Americas: Threat or Corrective to Democracy?* Cambridge: Cambridge University Press.

Pappas, Takis S. 2014. "Populist democracies: post-authoritarian Greece and post-Communist Hungary," *Government and Opposition*, 49(1): 1–23.

Peruzzotti, Enrique. 2013. "Populism in democratic times: populism, representative democracy, and the debate on democratic deepening," in Carlos de la Torre and Cynthia J. Arnson (eds), *Latin American Populism in the Twenty-First Century*. Washington, DC: Woodrow Wilson Center Press, 61–84.

Remmer, Karen L. 1991. "The political impact of economic crises in Latin America in the 1980s," *American Political Science Review*, 85(3): 777–800.

Resnick, Danielle. 2012. "Opposition parties and the urban poor in African democracies," *Comparative Political Studies*, 45(11): 1351–78.

Resnick, Danielle. 2014. *Urban Poverty and Party Populism in African Democracies*. New York: Cambridge University Press.

Roberts, Kenneth M. 2006a. "Do parties matter? Lessons from the Fujimori experience," in Julio Carrión (ed.), *The Fujimori Legacy: The Rise of Electoral Authoritarianism in Peru*. University Park: Pennsylvania State University Press, 81–101.

Roberts, Kenneth M. 2006b. "Populism, political conflict, and grass-roots organization in Latin America," *Comparative Politics*, 38(2): 127–48.

Roberts, Kenneth M. 2013. "Parties and populism in Latin America," in Carlos de la Torre and Cynthia Arnson (eds), *Latin American Populism in the Twenty-First Century*. Washington, DC: Woodrow Wilson Center Press, 37–60.

Roberts, Kenneth M. 2014. *Changing Course: Party Systems in Latin America's Neoliberal Era*. New York: Cambridge University Press.

Roberts, Kenneth M. 2015. "Populism, political mobilizations, and crises of political representation," in Carlos de la Torre (ed.), *The Promise and Perils of Populism: Global Perspectives*.
Lexington: University of Kentucky Press, 140–58.

Romero, Aníbal. 1997. "Rearranging the deck chairs on the Titanic: the agony of democracy in
Venezuela," *Latin American Research Review*, 32(1): 3–36.

Rovira Kaltwasser, Cristóbal. 2014. "Latin American populism: some conceptual and normative lessons," *Constellations*, 21(4): 494–504.

Rovira Kaltwasser, Cristóbal. 2015. "Explaining the emergence of populism in Europe and the
Americas," in Carlos de la Torre (ed.), *The Promise and Perils of Populism: Global Perspectives*.
Lexington: University of Kentucky Press, 189–227.

Schmitter, Philippe C. 2001. "Parties are not what they once were," in Larry Diamond and
Richard Gunther (eds), *Political Parties and Democracy*. Baltimore: Johns Hopkins
University Press, 67–89.

Shefter, Martin. 1994. *Political Parties and the State*. Princeton: Princeton University Press.

Silva, Eduardo. 2009. *Challenging Neoliberalism in Latin America*. New York: Cambridge
University Press.

Skocpol, Theda and Vanessa Williamson. 2013. *The Tea Party and the Remaking of Republican
Conservatism*. New York: Oxford University Press.

Sniderman, Paul M. and Edward Stiglitz. 2012. *The Reputational Premium: A Theory of Party
Identification and Policy Reasoning*. Princeton: Princeton University Press.

Sosa, Ximena. 2012. "Populism in Ecuador: from José M. Velasco Ibarra to Rafael Correa,"
in Michael L. Conniff, ed. *Populism in Latin America*, 2nd edn. Tuscaloosa: University of
Alabama Press, 159–83.

Stavrakakis, Yannis. 2014. "The return of 'the people': populism and anti-populism in the
shadow of the European crisis," *Constellations*, 21(4): 505–17.

Stavrakakis, Yannis and Giorgos Katsambekis. 2014. "Left-wing populism in the European
periphery: the case of SYRIZA," *Journal of Political Ideologies*, 19(2): 119–42.

Taggart, Paul. 2002. *Populism*. Buckingham: Open University Press.

Weyland, Kurt. 2001. "Clarifying a contested concept: populism in the study of Latin American
politics," *Comparative Politics*, 34(1): 1–22.

Zuckerman, Alan S., Josip Dasović, and Jennifer Fitzgerald. 2007. *Partisan Families: The
Social Logic of Bounded Partisanship in Germany and Britain*. New York: Cambridge
University Press.

CHAPTER 16

....

POPULISM
AND SOCIAL MOVEMENTS

....

PARIS ASLANIDIS

INTRODUCTION

....

THE word "populism" conjures images of outsider politicians lambasting corrupt establishments and glorifying the sovereignty of a "noble people" in a struggle to win presidential offices or seats in legislative chambers. Yet the top-down perspective that locates the phenomenon squarely within institutionalized party systems is only one side of the story. This chapter explores the equally interesting aspect of bottom-up populism, forged outside established political institutions in a grassroots fashion, instigated by anonymous political entrepreneurs and substantiated through protests and social movements.

The study of populist leaders such as Hugo Chávez and Alberto Fujimori, Huey Long and George Wallace, or the Le Pens, Geert Wilders, and Nigel Farage has over the years informed a rich literature. In contrast, populist episodes of social mobilization since the Great Revolutions have fallen between the cracks. Luddites and Chartists of the nineteenth century, Latin American movements against austerity in the late twentieth century, Tea Partiers, Occupiers, the various flavors of European *indignados*, or the activists of the Umbrella Revolution fail to draw significant scholarly attention. Populist social movements remain a conspicuously under-researched phenomenon. This is then the first aim of this chapter: to restore balance by establishing that populism is not the exclusive domain of political parties and their leaders.

Emphasizing the distinct nature of top-down and bottom-up populism does not preclude a rich area of interaction between the two parts. While the relationship is arguably bidirectional, the idea explored here is that party system populism occasionally emerges as a corollary of its bottom-up incarnation, a correlation that political scientists often overlook. Unpacking the multifaceted circumstances transforming grassroots populism into an institutionalized force is the second aim of the chapter.

The third point taken up is the evaluation of populism vis-à-vis democracy. Populist mobilization has been commonly criticized as undermining important pillars of liberal democracy, yet its potential role as a driver of democratization passes relatively unnoticed. It will be argued that investigating cases where grassroots populism exhibits democratizing effects carries the potential to inform this wider normative debate.

Lastly, it is argued that studying social movements under the framework of populism opens up the prospect of productive cross-fertilization between political scientists and social movement theorists. Both camps can benefit from a previously unexplored analytical overlap to exchange conceptual ingredients, enrich their methodological toolboxes, and incorporate untapped empirical cases, thus extending the scope and improving the validity of their research findings. Brokering this interdisciplinary partnership is the overarching aim of the chapter.

The Logic of Populist Mobilization

While blending mainstream social movement studies with populism theory remained outside his purview, Ernesto Laclau pioneered the comprehensive exploration of populism as a movement (Laclau, 1977; 2005a; 2005b). Conceptualizing populism as the discourse of a progressive political project, he offered a blueprint of how populist fronts assemble at the grassroots through the discursive collection of distinct social "particularities" under a single framework. His ideas have been influential mainly with scholars of the Essex school (Stavrakakis, 2004; Panizza, 2005) and even political formations of the radical left such as PODEMOS in Spain and SYRIZA in Greece (Iglesias, 2015).

Despite Laclau's originality in outlining the various stages of development in populist mobilization, the resulting framework contains significant limitations (Arato, 2013; Aslanidis, 2016a; Rovira Kaltwasser, 2012; Stavrakakis, 2004). A crucial impediment is his often obscure post-Marxist language. Aiming at the leftist intelligentsia rather than the scholarly mainstream, Laclau used esoteric neologisms and cryptic formalizations that made his corpus difficult to access and rendered it easily dismissible as inordinately abstract (Mudde and Rovira Kaltwasser, 2012). Nevertheless, translating this jargon into standard social movement terminology can furnish a relatively straightforward theory of populist mobilization that serves our integrative analytical purposes, reintroducing him to mainstream populism theorists while also making his work accessible for social movement scholars. This is undertaken in the remainder of this section, where theoretical arguments are supported by empirical evidence from particular episodes of grassroots populism.

Analytically, populist mobilization should be expected to utilize the same discursive appeals employed by electoral populism. Drawing elements from the ideational approach (see Mudde this volume), populist social movements can be seen as non-institutional collective mobilization along a catch-all political platform of grievances that divides society between an overwhelming majority of "pure people" and a "corrupt elite," demanding the restoration of popular sovereignty in the name of the former (Aslanidis, 2016b). Populist movements differ from other types of mobilization in two main respects: (1) they claim to represent a social whole rather than the interests of particular social strata as, for instance, with working-class movements or LGBTQ rights movements, and (2) they generally refrain from negotiating narrow policy concessions from the state, as they seek a wholesale reform of the political regime to restore the sovereignty of the people. Seeing it from the vantage point of the psychology of emotions, populism mobilizes felt injustice (Demertzis, 2006), building momentum upon the conviction that individuals invested with political authority are deliberately falling short of serving the needs of the people they were supposed to represent. This cause can be taken up by a standard, hierarchical political organization, leading to electoral (party system) populism, or it can assume the form of a grassroots, non-institutional collectivity, producing a populist social movement.

How does populist mobilization come about? The bottom-up process that Laclau outlines begins modestly, with the existence of disparate *grievances* in a given population. Grievances—objective, relative, or simply constructed—are the generic constitutive matter of mobilized discontent (Laraña et al., 1994). "Not In My Back Yard" (NIMBY) protests, to use a familiar example, such as when citizens react against a regional authority's decision to install a waste disposal facility or construct a new highway in their locality, are elementary examples of collectively expressed disaffection with authority. According to Laclau (2005b), isolated protest events may never become politically significant on their own, yet they carry the potential to kick-start a process of populist mobilization when the state—for various reasons—begins failing to address them in a proper manner. Laclau seems to refer almost exclusively to the mobilizing capacity of material grievances, but social scientists, especially after the onset of the so-called New Social Movements, have established that post-materialist values are equally important mobilizing factors (Inglehart, 1977; Kriesi et al., 1995; Melucci, 1988).

Grievances therefore supply a necessary backdrop but do not constitute sufficient factors, being generally ubiquitous and unable to automatically generate mobilization (Dalton, van Sickle, and Weldon, 2010; Klandermans and van Stekelenburg, 2013; Kriesi et al., 1995). Economic malaise, a surge in anti-immigration sentiment, or the general discomfort from globalization, can potentially provide a substrate for populist agitation, but aggrieved populations do not take to the streets in a deterministic fashion. A simplistic grievance-based causal framework cannot resolve why the activists of PEGIDA successfully mobilized German anti-immigrant feelings in late 2014 and not earlier (or later), or why Occupy Wall Street emerged well after the United States had largely absorbed the major shockwaves of the Great Recession, or why Israel's J14 movement influenced scores of relatively affluent middle-class citizens in a democratic country largely untouched by the economic crisis.

This is where political opportunity and agency weigh in. Grievances remain latent until they become subject to a process of strategic interpretation by politically savvy movement entrepreneurs who sense a ripe moment for their agenda (Snow et al., 1986). Expressed grievances, or "demands" in Laclauian terminology, are not genuinely

political until someone articulates them in a way that infuses them with political importance, cultivating an appetite for action. It takes the expertise of the populist entrepre-
neur to animate a stage fraught with discontent into a full-fledged populist movement.
This requirement explains part of the observed variation in populist mobilization across
empirical settings. For instance, debt-ridden Latin American countries of the 1980s and
1990s faced more or less similar social problems, but only a subset experienced the rise
of populist movements (Silva, 2009; Walton and Seddon, 1994). *Solidarność*, a grassroots populist movement (Canovan, 2005; Laclau, 2005a), emerged in 1980 Poland to
contest a decades-old, Soviet-backed communist regime, but the activists of Leipzig's
Monday demonstrations in East Germany conceived their populist frame only in 1989
(Pfaff, 2006), even though the whole communist bloc endured comparable hardships.
More recently, countries of the Eurozone periphery were collectively seen as the main
victims of the Great Recession in the continent, earning the acronym of the PIIGS, yet
while suffering populations in Portugal, Greece, and Spain gave birth to the large populist wave of the European *indignados*, citizens in Ireland and Italy, as well as Cyprus,
remained fairly quiescent (Aslanidis, 2016b).

The tight interconnections between political opportunity, agency, and the availability of resources, frustrate attempts at disaggregating causal processes. The fact that
our dependent variable, populism, manifests itself in degrees rather than clear-cut
instances complicates classificatory exercises even further. Laclau's causal suggestion
in this regard is that authority, in its normal capacity, maintains control by tackling
sporadic and isolated demands on a case-by-case basis, appeasing some while post-
poning the handling of others. This situation, where no significant bloc of demands
has yet surfaced, is governed by the "logic of difference" (Laclau, 2005a; 2005b) and
populism fails to materialize. However, in those rarer cases where the state fails to
mitigate a concurrent set of grievances, aggrieved groups can gradually coalesce
to compose a front in the form of an "equivalential chain" of demands. When this
mobilization adopts the distinct nature of populist logic, grievances are discursively
aggregated and collectively articulated as outcomes of an underlying social division
between "people" and "elites."

Laclau's implicit assertion that populism affects only pre-existing civil society groups
and associations overemphasizes the mesomobilization aspect (Gerhards and Rucht,
1992) of populist activism—its coordinating and integrating capacity—revealing
Laclau's distaste for methodological individualism, a side-effect of a paradigm that
decries class reductionism but stops short of reaching out to the individual actor.
Nevertheless, populist discourse is also powerful at the micro level, able to mobilize
non-affiliated individuals by activating a myriad of untapped *personal* grievances, eventually nudging us to join a populist movement or support a populist party (Akkerman,
Mudde, and Zaslove, 2014; Hawkins, Rovira Kaltwasser, and Andreadis, 2016; Spruyt,
Keppens, and Van Droogenbroeck, 2016).

Archival evidence from populist movements such as Occupy Wall Street is telling
in this respect. Occupy's manifesto includes a checklist of a total of twenty-three separate grievances ranging from excessive student debt, workplace discrimination, and

colonialism, to animal torture. Occupy activists, wary of excluding untapped disaffec-
tions of the "99 percent" potentially compatible with their populist project, hastened
to add a special footnote to the list declaring it "not all-inclusive" (Occupy Wall Street,
2011). Similarly colorful were the issues raised by the Brazilian protesters of the V for
Vinegar movement in June, 2013: "[t]ransportation, infrastructure, health, education,
housing, women-gay-indigenous-black-citizen rights, corruption, political reform
(parties, elections, congress), justice, security, environment, specific legislation, energy
(nuclear, hydro, oil), and violence" (Holston, 2014: 889) were all on their agenda.

This attests that populism essentially fulfills an aggregative function as a "mode of
articulation" of social grievances (Laclau, 2005a; 2005b). It can be seen as a "flexible way
of animating political support" (Jansen, 2015: 161) that works by shifting the interpretative perspective of a problematic situation to allow for the recruitment of disaffected
social groups or individuals under the encompassing banner of "the people," with "elites"
as the perpetrators of injustice. Around the same time Occupy Wall Street was protest-
ing against rising inequality in American society, the Greek *indignados* were mobilizing
against austerity, the *Geração à Rasca* against the bleak prospects of Portuguese youth,
and the J14 against unaffordable housing in Israel. Yet their activists employed the same
populist themes and claimed to take part in the same global struggle (Aslanidis, 2016b).
An important conclusion follows: nothing entirely peculiar should be expected of populist grievances. The single prerequisite of eligibility is a discursive rapport with the formal structure of populist discourse—a certain flexibility allowing them to fit the mold of
the central Manichean divide that conditions populist rhetoric. It is not therefore in the
actual content of demands that we find populism, Laclau (2005b) instructs, but in the
way they are articulated or, to put it better, in the way they are *framed*.

IDENTITY POLITICS: POPULISM AS
A COLLECTIVE ACTION FRAME

To better integrate the issues raised so far we must turn to the microsociological study
of social movements and examine the considerable mobilizing potential of populist discourse by appreciating it as a *collective action frame* (Aslanidis, 2016a; 2016b;
Caiani and della Porta, 2011; Jagers and Walgrave, 2007; Tsatsanis, 2011). Frame theory, a major strand in social movement scholarship, harks back to Erving Goffman,
and his seminal *Frame Analysis* (1974) that informed research in various scientific
fields. In the mid-1980s Goffman's ideas were taken up by David Snow and his associates with the aim of reducing the unfruitful dependence upon structural causal
explanations for social mobilization, shifting the focus to the significance of strategic
constructions of meaning by activists at the micro level (Benford and Snow, 2000;
Snow et al., 1986; Snow and Benford, 1992). The core concept of the theory, the *frame*,
refers to discursive "schemata of interpretation" (Goffman, 1974: 21) that suggest

a specific vantage point for assessing the predicament, a purposeful snapshot of what is taking place "out there," broadcast by movement entrepreneurs in order to reach potential audiences and recruit them to their cause.

Collective action frames aim at triggering a cognitive process that transforms discontent into action. They cherry-pick information and imagery to "interpret people's life situations, including such emotions as the anger and fear they may feel, by articulating them as grievances against an unjust system or enemy" (Williams, 2013: 2), empowering audiences to seek change through mobilization. According to this constructivist perspective, mobilizing grievances should be "seen neither as naturally occurring sentiments nor as arising automatically from specifiable material conditions, but as the result of interactively based interpretation or signifying work" (Snow, 2013: 1).

Grassroots movements depend heavily on the framing and organizational expertise of their leading activists. Even though much is said about the spontaneity of populist mobilization, a closer look invariably points to the existence of a core group of individuals or pre-existing organizations that command disproportionate leverage over framing and other tactics. To take again the example of the populist Great Recession movements in 2011, field research on Occupy Wall Street (Gould-Wartofksy, 2015; Graeber, 2013), the Portuguese (Accornero and Ramos Pinto, 2015), Spanish (Castells, 2012; Gerbaudo, 2012), and Greek *indignados* (Aslanidis, 2016b), as well as the Israeli J14 (Alimi, 2012; Rosenhek and Shalev, 2014), reveals a considerable element of leadership by dedicated individuals who—to varying degrees—retained control of important facets of the movements' activity. Leadership structures were also pivotal for the Egyptian Revolution that preceded them, with individuals such as Wael Ghonim and activist groups such as the April 6 Youth Movement and the youth wing of the Muslim Brotherhood contributing crucially to bringing thousands of people to Tahrir square (Gerbaudo, 2012; Ghonim, 2012; Gunning and Baron, 2014).

Students of populism should readily acknowledge the analytical congruence between populist discourse and the use of framing tactics. The populist frame offers a diagnosis of reality as problematic due to the usurpation of sovereign authority by "elites," suggesting that the "people" should mobilize to reclaim what is rightfully theirs. "Banks got bailed out, we got sold out" was the narrative of Occupy (Gould-Wartofksy, 2015). We will not submit to becoming "products in the hands of politicians and bankers," cried the Spanish *indignados* (Castells, 2012). The Greeks similarly resolved "not [to] leave the squares, until all those who led us here are gone: governments, the Troika, Banks, Memoranda, and all those who take advantage of us" (Aslanidis, 2016b). Contrary to other adversarial frames, blame rests not with abstract socioeconomic forces, policy miscalculations, innocent mishaps, or a swing of the balance of power between equally legitimate political ideas. The all-encompassing and morally legitimizing primacy of popular sovereignty is invoked to lay blame upon specific actors in their various incarnations.

The pattern points to another important dimension: the existence of a resonant *collective identity* for movement participants (Melucci, 1988; Polletta and Jasper, 2001). Constructing collective identities is a crucial function of social movement entrepreneurship and populism constitutes an exemplary case of identity mobilization under the inclusive banner of "the people." As Canovan (1982: 551) explains, populists master "calculatedly vague notions of 'the people'" in order to "blur established political divisions," using the "chameleonic" quality of their rhetoric (Taggart, 2000) to build broad social alliances. The capacity of the popular subjectivity and its antithesis—the "elites"—to serve as "empty signifiers" (Laclau, 2005a: 40; 2005b: 69), or simply, flexible symbolic labels, explains the adaptability of the populist frame across diverse societies and political systems. Populist activists act as "identity entrepreneurs" (Eder, 2003; Huddy, 2013), exploiting the symbolic power of these labels to align their meaning with strategic needs, simplifying political struggle into a clear dichotomy and maximizing political mobilization on the side of the "we." Occupy's motto, "We Are the 99 Percent," epitomizes this aspect of populist discourse (Calhoun, 2013).

FROM BARRICADES TO BALLOTS: POPULIST FRAMES AS PUBLIC GOODS

Grassroots and electoral populism are quite distinct phenomena but populist contention can potentially navigate the porous intersection, shifting its weight "from barricades to ballots" (McAdam and Tarrow, 2010). Despite considerable gray zones and overlaps, it is useful to distinguish three main ways that populist movements can inform party system politics: (1) a new political organization may spring up from the ranks of the populist movement; (2) the movement may associate (partly or as a whole) with existing political parties that sympathize with the populist cause; (3) the populist identity may be co-opted by a political party exogenous to the movement. This section provides several empirical examples pertaining to these ideal types but also stresses the convoluted nature of this transformation.

Clear-cut cases of the first type are rather rare. A famous one is the US People's Party that rose to prominence as the institutional aftermath of the populist Farmers' Alliance and their Knights of Labor allies (Postel, 2007). In Bolivia, it was the grassroots populist movements active in the Water and Gas Wars that forced President Gonzalo Sánchez de Lozada to flee the country, ushering a "movement populist" to power (Levitsky and Loxton, 2013) in the figure of Evo Morales, the leader of both the *cocaleros* and MAS (Collins, 2014). In more recent episodes, the leftist populist PODEMOS can be seen as the (belated) institutional follow-up of the Spanish *indignados*, where several of its founding members were involved (Iglesias, 2015) and the same could be said for the radical right-wing populist Independent Greeks who regularly claim origin in the Greek *indignados* and dutifully uphold the movement's legacy (Aslanidis and Marantzidis, 2016). However, both of these cases also contain an element of strategic co-optation. The Italian Five Star Movement is a more contentious case, since the mobilization that preceded the party was largely a personal affair of Beppe Grillo rather than a typical social movement (Tronconi, 2015).

Discerning instances of the second type requires extensive research that is seldom available. Here, the political party can benefit from the movement's vigor and adopt some of its populist themes without wholly surrendering to populist discourse. The Tea Party in the United States achieved great popularity among Republican voters from 2008 onwards, influencing the outcome of the 2010 midterm elections (Bailey, Mummolo, and Noel, 2012) and steering the discourse of the party towards a new direction (Van Dyke and Meyer, 2014), paving the way for radical candidates such as Ted Cruz and Donald Trump in the 2016 GOP primaries (Skocpol, 2016). The J14 movement in Israel, where several high-profile activists joined the ticket of the Labor party (Craig, 2015), also seems to fit the description.

Occasionally, this second type accommodates a bidirectionality of influence between populist movements and existing political parties. The role of Muslim Brotherhood cadres during the Egyptian Revolution is a case in point (Gunning and Baron, 2014), and so is the involvement of members of the Communist Party and the radical Left Bloc in the Que se Lixe a Troika movement in Portugal (Accornero and Ramos Pinto, 2015). In some instances, populism is a salient characteristic on both sides. The surge in support for the Alternative for Germany party is due to an opportune public discourse about immigration produced by the populist frames of the PEGIDA movement and its agenda setting effects (Häusler, 2016), and researchers have observed a significant exchange of human resources between movement and party (Dostal, 2015). The case of SYRIZA also fits here. The party's young leader, Alexis Tsipras, rose to prominence during a severe European economic crisis that had Greece at its epicenter, siding openly with the grievances of the Greek *indignados* with whom a number of his party's cadres had been covertly active (Aslanidis and Marantzidis, 2016). Watering down his radical leftist rhetoric to make room for the populist framing forged in the squares, Tsipras eventually won power in 2015, forming a government with the Independent Greeks mentioned above (Aslanidis and Rovira Kaltwasser, 2016).

The most intriguing type is the third one. The bottom-up construction of a recalcitrant and morally superior popular identity that captures the hearts and minds of the citizenry is a prized commodity—the crown jewel of populist entrepreneurship. However, the same moment a collective identity grips the consciousness of the public, it slips away from the hands of its creators, turning into a public good (Friedman and McAdam, 1992). In Laclau's (2005a; 2005b) words, the collective identity of "the people" becomes a "floating signifier" at the disposal of actors creative enough to put it to work. Grassroots activists may struggle hard laying the symbolic groundwork and cultivating a vibrant populist movement only to see its vigor co-opted by a political party with no stake in the original mobilization (Collins, 2014; de la Torre, 2013; Levitsky and Loxton, 2013). Politicians, sensing opportunity, seize the momentum by piggybacking on successful popular identities, ironing out potential wrinkles of their narrative to credibly claim to embody the emergent will of "the people," promising to drive a wedge into politics as usual and achieve redemption by capturing state power.

In India, the grassroots activists of the regional populist social movement of the Uttarakhand *jan andolan* managed to construct a resonant and inclusive popular identity in 1994, masterfully overcoming ethno-linguistic and social divides, but their political goals materialized only after being co-opted by the now ruling Bharatiya Janata Party (Kumar, 2011). In Israel, Yair Lapid, a former news anchor, formed the Yesh Atid party in April, 2012, to repackage the populist cause of the J14 for the Israeli middle and upper-middle class, winning a considerable share of the vote in the next elections (Craig, 2015). But the most famous example in this theme is Ecuador. Rafael Correa appropriated a popular collective identity that had been built at the grassroots right before he inaugurated a populist presidential campaign against the *partidocracia*, which brought him to power in 2007 (Collins, 2014).

The case of Hugo Chávez is more complex. In *We Created Chávez*, Ciccariello-Maher (2013) recounts the story of the various movements and grassroots organizations that crafted and established a resonant populist frame for a recalcitrant Venezuelan *pueblo* many years prior to and even after the crucial 1989 populist *Caracazo* when, under the slogan "The People Are Fed Up," thousands of citizens rioted against the government of Carlos Andrés Pérez. The convoluted nature of this bottom-up populist backdrop and the different levels of support given to Chávez's MBR-200 does not allow easy judgment on whether the latter spearheaded the grassroots movements or co-opted their identity. In any case, the people's struggle foreshadowed Hugo Chávez's bellicose populist language and Manichean political project, paving the way for a "Bolivarian Revolution" that eventually dethroned the representatives of *puntofijismo* and installed him in the seat of power until his death (Hawkins, 2010).

To be sure, the three ideal types delineated above do not exhaust the possible political outcomes of grassroots populism. Time and again, populist movements have waxed and waned without transforming into a sustainable political party. Occupy Wall Street and the Portuguese *Geração à Rasca* are telling examples, and so are the nineteenth-century movement of the Russian *narodniki* and the 2013 Gezi Park protests in Turkey. Political appropriation attempts may also fail for several reasons: the ambitious actor may not manage to credibly pass as "one of us," she may enter the scene when the momentum is already lost, or may yield to competition by more qualified players. Frequently though, as proven by several empirical examples, a political organization will skillfully manage to ride the wave into the higher echelons of power.

At the same time, failed attempts at reaping immediate political benefits do not necessarily signal the political irrelevance of grassroots populist episodes. Once it establishes itself, the sheen of "the people" will rarely dull. The great symbolic value of successful populist brand names such as the "*indignados*," "Occupy," or "The 99 Percent" depreciates very slowly, if at all. Populist identities remain latent, "in abeyance" (Taylor, 1989), awaiting political reactivation, bound to inspire and inspire again (Kazin, 1995), sparing activists of the need to reinvent the wheel. Fertile political opportunities such as an economic crisis, a sudden disaster, or a high-profile case of corruption, can re-render the popular identity relevant, infusing it with salience and threatening to discompose mainstream politics.

Moreover, successful populist movements may heavily influence political discourse even before they start enjoying direct institutional representation, effecting a general shift in the national political agenda. The J14 in Israel and Occupy Wall Street in the United States emerged forcefully only to gradually disappear within the second half of 2011, but they both managed to spark heated debates around wealth inequality in their societies (Calhoun, 2013; Rosenhek and Shalev, 2014). In Israel, the government was forced to appoint a committee of experts to deal with the demands of the protesters and partially adopted its guidelines. In the United States, President Obama welcomed and incorporated elements of this discourse in its early stages. Bernie Sanders later centered his 2016 Democratic primaries campaign upon the populist message emanating from Occupy (Kazin, 2016).

Populism and Transnational Waves of Protest

Collective action frames do not travel exclusively along the temporal dimension, bounded by national political cultures. They can also cross borders, occasionally giving rise to transnational cycles of contention (Tarrow, 2011). Surprisingly rapid distributions of collective action frames have been observed among geographically distinct movements when activists adapt best practices used elsewhere to their own causes. Social movement scholars have coined the term "master frame" (Snow and Benford, 1992) to denote their special nature. Due to its flexible and adaptable nature, the populist frame has served as a potent master frame for transnational mobilization in several cases. Apart from the movements of the Great Recession in the West, the Latin American anti-austerity wave of mobilization that preceded the "left turn" in the region, and the movements collectively known as the Arab Spring are two further protest waves that warrant mention due to the predominantly populist nature of their discourse.

The southern part of the American continent has served as a hotbed of grassroots mobilization throughout the decades. During the last quarter of the previous century, citizens of several Latin American countries mobilized under the banner of "the people" to protest IMF-inspired austerity and free market reforms, invariably accusing international financial institutions and their purported "domestic lackeys" of violating or betraying national sovereignty in service of dark ulterior motives. As Walton and Seddon (1994: 94) have argued, such spontaneous "austerity protests" are:

> not inherently ideological, nor "political" in the narrow sense, but represent in effect social movements in opposition to what is perceived as the illegitimate

dismantling of a historically negotiated contract between state and people; such movements are, however, political in a broader sense—with their central concern for social justice and "the moral economy," they constitute a distinctive form of populist movement.

The link between Latin American anti-austerity movements and the rise of oppositional party system actors that claimed to represent them has been emphasized by Silva (2009), who understands this phenomenon as the rational outcome of a "Polanyian backlash" against imposed reforms. Almeida (2010) suggests the term "social movement partyism" to describe the process by which mass popular reaction paves the way for collaboration with (or co-optation by) politicians who "aspire to establish a constituency on issues with widespread public opinion support that eventuates in greater electoral power in future elections" (Almeida, 2010: 177).

The transnational dimension of populist mobilization is also exemplified by the Arab Spring. This wave of protest manifested a distinctive "people-power" element, constituting a historical novelty in invoking popular sovereignty for grassroots contention in the Arab world (Abulof, 2015; Chalcraft, 2016; De Smet, 2016; Zartman, 2015). The Tunisian uprising, the wave's progenitor, triggered the reproduction of an iconic populist master frame that reverberated among millions in Egypt, Syria, and other countries of the Middle East and North Africa, famously epitomized in the phrase "al-sha'ab yurid isqat an-nizam" ["the people want the overthrow of the regime"]. This slogan accentuated the immense significance of the idea of popular sovereignty, of a *general will* that transformed "a passive 'population' into an active 'people'" (De Smet, 2016: 140) with a particular sense of collective agency against what was perceived as a handful of corrupt, incompetent, and unaccountable elites.

Gunning and Baron (2014) emphasize how crucial for the success of the Egyptian Revolution was the fact that protesters internalized an inclusive collective action frame that set aside intramural differences in face of the common enemy. The silent majority of Egyptians managed to reconstruct and re-enact peoplehood (Sadiki, 2015) by reaching a tacit agreement "on who the victims were (the people) and who was responsible for these wrongs (the regime)" (Gunning and Baron, 2014: 191). Activists consciously refrained from expressing grievances associated with cross-cutting cleavages of class, ethnicity, ideology, or religion. As De Smet (2016: 139) observes, the populist framing of the movement instilled a Manichean identity divide of being either "with *al-sha'b* (the people) or with *al-nitham* (the regime)."

The protests reached exceptional levels of support exactly because of this "inclusivity of demands, this funneling into a set of pared-down core demands, beyond ideological divisions" (Gunning and Baron, 2014: 191). Wael Ghonim, the activist behind the Facebook call for the inaugurating protest at Tahrir square, describes how he strategically aimed at constructing a catch-all popular identity: "I deliberately included poverty, corruption, and unemployment in the title," he claimed, "because we needed to have everyone join forces: workers, human rights activists, government employees, and others who had grown tired of the regime's policies. If the invitation to take to the streets had been based solely on human rights, then only a certain segment of Egyptian society would have participated" (Ghonim, 2012: 136–7).

The *gros mots* that social scientists usually employ can never fully qualify a political phenomenon, and the Arab Spring was certainly not a working-class or middle-class cycle of protest, neither was it a collection of nationalist or religious movements. The activists knew that any sectional framing would fail to provide the necessary inclusive identity to topple their oppressive regimes. On the contrary, as Chalcraft (2016) notes, they had to confront leaders who were themselves champions of nationalist anti-colonial uprisings. A different type of symbolic subject was needed. The mobilizing subjectivity had to be framed not as a nation rising against colonial powers, but as a sovereign people demanding its deserved access to political decision making. Ghonim (2012) summarized this populist zeitgeist in the title of his memoirs: *Revolution 2.0: The Power of People is Greater than the People in Power*. There lay the major innovation of the Arab protest wave: an "on-the-spot and unpredetermined constitution of the people as a rights-bearing, activist, diverse, demanding, and sovereign subject" (Chalcraft, 2016: 8).

The Arab Spring triggered monumental political transformations. While in hindsight they were not all benign, their outbreak spurred enthusiasm around the world, planting the seed for fresh contentious episodes. The populist identity framing and the innovative protest repertoires crafted on the Northern African shores soon cascaded across the Mediterranean to Southern Europe, inspiring further mobilization in a much different setting. The European *indignados* adopted—and adapted—the discursive and repertorial toolkit of the Arab Spring to spawn populist movements expressing a multitude of social grievances simmering since the onset of the Euro crisis (Aslanidis, 2016b; Gerbaudo, 2012). The wave began with the *Geração à Rasca* in Portugal, moving on to the Spanish *indignados*, and finally spreading to the squares of major Greek cities by late May. In July, the cycle unexpectedly expanded to Israel, where the J14 movement protested against the local "tycoons" for two months, under the rallying cry "ha'am doresh tzedek chevrati" ["the people demand social justice"], carefully navigating the traditionally contentious domestic political landscape to avoid activating existing cleavages of religion, class, and ethnicity (Rosenhek and Shalev, 2014). Occupy Wall Street took the US by storm in the fall, reinvigorating the global dynamics of the cycle (Gould-Wartofksy, 2015). The populist wave of the Great Recession dissipated after 2011, but the master frame resurfaced in various incarnations across countries and regions in the following years. In Turkey's Gezi Park protests in the summer of 2013, the Bulgarian and Bosnian protest wave of 2013–2014, the Ukrainian Euromaidan, Brazil's V for Vinegar movement, and Hong Kong's Umbrella Revolution, populism provided a conveniently loose symbolic scaffolding for the local movements' discursive arsenal, with protesters taking over central city squares to uphold the democratic sovereignty of the people against ruling elites perceived as unaccountable, treacherous, or otherwise unwelcome.

POPULIST SOCIAL MOVEMENTS
AND DEMOCRATIZATION

Populist mobilization is regularly implicated for the erosion of liberal democracy (Urbinati, 2014). However, populism does not deterministically lead to negative outcomes for democratic politics (Mudde and Rovira Kaltwasser, 2012). Its study in a predominantly normative rather than analytical fashion and its increasing abuse in the hands of politicians and journalists are relegating populism to little more than a political smear word, endangering its usefulness for applied political science (Aslanidis, 2016a; Fukuyama, 2016). Craig Calhoun (2012), in the introduction to his *Roots of Radicalism*, strongly criticizes elitist interpretations of populist mobilization, accusing analysts of being "tone-deaf" to populist politics and their positive repercussions for societies. Yet, valorizing populism as inherently progressive is equally unsound. Moving from a phenomenological exploration to a value-judgment of populist mobilization requires considerable caution and, as a rule, empirical observations should drive our appraisals, rather than an outright adoption of a valenced position.

As a starting point, the fundamental question of whether populist social movements constitute a threat or a corrective for democracy must surely remain open-ended (de la Torre, 2015). Iconic analysts of Western liberalism acknowledge that populist mobilizations are "neither inherently bad nor inherently good" (Fukuyama, 2016). Similar to populist political parties (Mudde and Rovira Kaltwasser, 2012), bottom-up populism can contribute to positive outcomes for societies but also negative ones. The answer will always depend on the type of society one holds as a yardstick, but reducing all populisms to opportunistic vehicles in the hands of politically savvy entrepreneurs misses the point.

At the same time, a direct causal relationship with the quality of democracy is hard to substantiate, since populism does not deterministically translate into a specific policy orientation affecting democratic institutions. The populist identification of social movements can analytically overlap with other useful classifications (e.g. anti-austerity, conservative, anti-communist, libertarian, democratic, or anti-neoliberal), since it mainly refers to the identity framing of the movement rather than its ideological prerogatives, the specific content of grievances it represents, or the general macro-causal dimensions that condition it. The analyst must recognize the interplay of several accompanying factors before assigning disproportionate primacy to the frequently overstated causal effects of populist framing on democratic quality.

Germany provides a good example of the indeterminacy of populist discourse. In the 1989/90 *Montagsdemonstrationen*, "the people" in Leipzig gathered every Monday in the thousands to protest against an oppressive regime, chanting "Wir sind das Volk" to assert the unquestionable authority of a movement that grew to become "a populist rebellion" (Pfaff, 2006: 263–4). As Pfaff (2006: 264) explains in his monograph, "a populist protest identity gave the movement its radical edge," allowing activists to declare "themselves the authentic people that had the right to be seen and heard" and bridge lines that divided the population, linking a large set of diverse grievances into a coherent framework. The successful populist frame contributed to the fall of the Berlin Wall and the unification of Germany, and then laid dormant for twenty-five years. In 2014, the same populist frame was again put to work, by the same "people," in the same squares, Monday after Monday, this time tweaked by the political activists of PEGIDA to express grievances against immigrants and foreign cultures (Dostal, 2015).

The German case attests that populist social mobilization is certainly not inimical to democratization. As Tilly (2004: 13) maintains, social movements can consolidate wide social alliances to "assert popular sovereignty" by challenging the notion that "sovereignty and its accumulated wisdom lie in the legislature," even in established democracies. Populist mobilization, under circumstances, can contribute to the further democratization of a certain polity by empowering previously unrepresented social groups and forcing democratically elected governments to address overlooked social problems.

In perhaps the first comprehensive exploration of this phenomenon, Calhoun (1982) describes how populist movements of early nineteenth-century Britain, from the Luddites to those involved in the Peterloo Massacre, struggled against political oppression to safeguard their rights, achieve the extension of suffrage, and reform parliamentary representation (see also Wiles, 1969). Later in the same century, numerous populist movements in the United States gave voice to grievances of excluded segments of the population (Formisano, 2008), culminating with the formation of the People's Party of America (Postel, 2007). The populist movements of the Great Recession, from the European *indignados* to Occupy Wall Street, also exhibited considerable democratizing effects (de la Torre, 2015), leading to a re-politicization of important issues such as the accountability of representation, wealth inequality, and debt forgiveness that, in the eyes of many, had been unduly placed under the authority of technocratic governance, to the detriment of transparency and democratic responsiveness.

Populist social movements can also escape the confines of liberal democracies and function as important drivers for democratizing oppressive regimes. Della Porta (2014: 111) draws interesting comparisons between Eastern European transition movements and the Arab Spring, pointing to the construction of the identity of "the people" as a "broad and inclusive definition of the 'us'" and the diagnosis of the "corruption of the political class" as the main framing elements in both instances. In Hong Kong, the 2014 Umbrella Revolution echoed populist frames of the 1989 Chinese Democracy Movement (Zuo and Benford, 1995) in a rare effort to unsettle the daily affairs of the single-party state. However, these positive cases should not overstate the thesis. Populism does not equal democratization in the same way that social movements do not necessarily equal democratization (Payne, 2000; Tilly, 2004). But they do carry the potential of nudging authoritarian regimes over the edge, opening public space to more benign alternatives. And even episodic populist encounters in established democracies can serve a positive role, providing intermediate myths for societies, fomenting make-believe in the supremacy of popular sovereignty and the potentiality of reclaiming power, and nourishing democratic capital for the next generation of political personnel. When institutional politics lose their capacity to stir democratic sentiment, populist grassroots movements stand out as fountainheads of the faith that "keeps the church going," as Canovan (1999) would affirm. Rather than being mocked and dismissed by elitist appraisals, their contribution to the struggle over symbolic competition for democratic meaning-making should be taken seriously.

CONCLUSION

In the *Communist Manifesto*, Marx and Engels famously proclaimed all movements prior to the proletarian one to have been "movements of minorities, or in the interest of minorities." In contrast, the proletarian movement was supposedly "the self-conscious, independent movement of the immense majority, in the interest of the immense majority." This was, of course, a blatant exaggeration. Nowhere did the proletarians comprise immense majorities since they excluded large social groups by definition. The populist movement seems to fit Marx and Engels's inclusive aspirations much better. Populists uphold the majoritarian view of democracy, arguing that power-holding elites should always yield to the primacy of the overwhelming majority of the people over any other source of political legitimacy. They diagnose severe injustice in how current affairs are run and masterfully weave together a criticism of the existing regime with an evocation of the voice of the people to collect disparate grievances under a common political cause. Owing to its Manichean nature, those who accept its diagnosis will tend to evaluate populism positively; those who do not will tend to discredit it.

Weaving together concepts and mechanisms from populism and social movement studies, this study has presented a framework for analysis to argue that political firebrands can employ the same populist frame to animate both streets and legislatures. Despite the two-fold nature of populist politics, the bottom-up form has so far been insufficiently problematized, earning unreasonably low attention relative to its frequency and significance in the global political arena. Restricting populism to a rigidly top-down phenomenon (Roberts, 2015) loses a lot analytically. Apart from producing an ad hoc conceptual paradox, to overlook the production of collective action frames and identities by populist social movements is to render developments in our party systems inexplicable. We cannot begin to understand the Democratic and Republican primaries of 2016 if we do not study Occupy Wall Street and the Tea Party. We are unable to grasp the meteoric rise of SYRIZA and PODEMOS if we do not examine the dynamics unleashed by the mobilization of Greek and Spanish *indignados* in 2011. We cannot fathom Latin America's "left turn" if we don't shift our gaze to the popular subjectivities brought to life in the streets of Caracas, Buenos Aires, La Paz, and Quito. And we cannot adequately appreciate any of the previous if we fail to discern the overarching significance of the populist framing of social grievances that runs through them all.

Given their recurring appearance, should we expect populist movements to remain relevant in the future? In repressive regimes, populism has shown great capacity in overcoming debilitating cleavages among the population, bringing together disparate social groups against authoritarian rule and demolishing the wall of fear that keeps these societies quiescent. Democratic activists all over the world are taking note of the tactics of their predecessors in the Arab Spring, the Umbrella Revolution, and elsewhere, and are eager to spread their own populist frames through social media and other platforms of mass communication whenever censors lower their guard.

But populist movements will remain relevant in democratic contexts alike. Long before the Great Recession, Klaus Eder (2003) observed a transformation in the dynamics of social action from issue mobilization to identity mobilization and stressed the increasing salience of discursive politics in the form of "language games" competing over symbolic hegemony. The routine of "merely" defending interests on the left and right, he posits, has been taken up by professional actors; narrow interests cannot credibly instigate grassroots action anymore. Identity claims are what is left, "based on the logic of boundary marking, of socially categorizing the other and identifying the common-ness inside of these boundaries" (Eder, 2003: 64).

The ability to translate the dull mobilization of single issues into broad and colorful struggles over identity is one element that testifies to the increasing relevance of populist mobilization. A second, even more important, element is added from a different perspective that sees populism as representing a widely felt disaffection with institutional politics in the developed world. Ivan Krastev (2014) has interpreted the "disruption of democracy" brought about by the recent cycle of grassroots populist movements as a rational reaction of a technologically empowered citizenry. According to this reading, the democratic middle class is revolting against a growing perception that politicians are unable to make promises they can keep and inspire their voters. Instead of proclaiming their unequivocal determination to improve society, politicians are increasingly alluding to their powerlessness. Populism will therefore continue to express a widespread suspicion that elections have become irrelevant, losing their celebrated capacity in "mobilizing the passive and pacifying the outraged" (Krastev, 2014: 38) for the welfare of democracy.

Populist mobilization stands at the pivot point of these secular transformations. In a globalizing world where old cleavages are constantly losing ground and party systems are being rendered unable to function as channels for the expression of popular demands (Kriesi et al., 2012), populist movements have become the default bottom-up challengers (Mair, 2002). Nothing sounds more vigorous today than the quest for the restoration of popular sovereignty, lost or never attained owing to unlawful, power-yielding elite minorities. The public space is being recast as "a space for populist claims" (Eder, 2003: 62). A little more than a decade later, Mudde's (2004) claim of an emerging populist zeitgeist has become a truism.

REFERENCES

Abulof, U. 2015. "'The people want(s) to bring down the regime'—(positive) nationalism as the Arab Spring's revolution," *Nations and Nationalism*, 21(4): 658–80.

Accornero, G. and P. Ramos Pinto. 2015. "'Mild mannered'? Protest and mobilisation in Portugal under austerity, 2010–2013," *West European Politics*, 38(3): 491–515.

Akkerman, A., C. Mudde, and A. Zaslove. 2014. "How populist are the people? Measuring populist attitudes in voters," *Comparative Political Studies*, 47(9): 1324–53.

Alimi, E. Y. 2012. "'Occupy Israel': a tale of startling success and hopeful failure," *Social Movement Studies*, 11(3–4): 402–7.

Almeida, P. 2010. "Social movement partyism: collective action and oppositional political parties," in N. Van Dyke and J. McCammon (eds), *Strategic Alliances: Coalition Building and Social Movements*. Minneapolis: University of Minnesota Press, 170–98.

Arato, A. 2013. "Political theology and populism," *Social Research*, 80(1): 143–72.

Aslanidis, P. 2016a. "Is populism an ideology? A refutation and a new perspective," *Political Studies*, 64(IS): 88–104.

Aslanidis, P. 2016b. "Populist social movements of the great recession," *Mobilization: An International Quarterly*, 21(3): 301–21.

Aslanidis, P. and N. Marantzidis. 2016. "The impact of the Greek indignados on Greek politics," *Southeastern Europe*, 40(2): 125–57.

Aslanidis, P. and C. Rovira Kaltwasser. 2016. "Dealing with populists in government: the SYRIZA-ANEL coalition in Greece," *Democratization*, 23(6): 1077–91.

Bailey, M. A., J. Mummolo, and H. Noel. 2012. "Tea Party influence: a story of activists and elites," *American Politics Research*, 40(5): 769–804.

Caiani, M. and D. della Porta. 2011. "The elitist populism of the extreme right: a frame analysis of extreme right-wing discourses in Italy and Germany," *Acta Politica*, 46(2): 180–202.

Calhoun, C. 1982. *The Question of Class Struggle: Social Foundations of Popular Radicalism during the Industrial Revolution*. Chicago: University of Chicago Press.

Calhoun, C. 2012. *The Roots of Radicalism: Tradition, the Public Sphere, and Early Nineteenth-Century Social Movements*. Chicago: University of Chicago Press.

Calhoun, C. 2013. "Occupy Wall Street in perspective," *The British Journal of Sociology*, 64(1): 26–38.

Canovan, M. 1982. "Two strategies for the study of populism," *Political Studies*, 30(4): 544–52.

Canovan, M. 1999. "Trust the people! Populism and the two faces of democracy," *Political Studies*, 47(1): 2–16.

Canovan, M. 2005. *The People*. Cambridge: Polity Press.

Castells, M. 2012. *Networks of Outrage and Hope: Social Movements in the Internet Age*. Cambridge: Polity Press.

Chalcraft, J. 2016. "The Arab uprisings of 2011 in historical perspective," in A. Ghazal and J. Hanssen (eds), *The Oxford Handbook of Contemporary Middle-Eastern and North African History*. doi: 10.1093/oxfordhb/9780199672530.013.13.

Ciccariello-Maher, G. 2013. *We Created Chávez: A People's History of the Venezuelan Revolution*. Durham: Duke University Press.

Collins, J. N. 2014. "New left experiences in Bolivia and Ecuador and the challenge to theories of populism," *Journal of Latin American Studies*, 46(1): 59–86.

Craig, Alan. 2015. "The Israel tent protests," in L. Sadiki (ed.), *Routledge Handbook of the Arab Spring: Rethinking Democratization*. New York: Routledge, 538–46.

Dalton, R., A. van Sickle, and S. Weldon. 2010. "The individual–institutional nexus of protest behaviour," *British Journal of Political Science*, 40(1): 51–73.

de la Torre, C. 2013. "In the name of the people: democratization, popular organizations, and populism in Venezuela, Bolivia, and Ecuador," *European Review of Latin American and Caribbean Studies*, 93: 27–48.

de la Torre, C. 2015. "Introduction: power to the people? Populism, insurrections, democratization," in C. de la Torre (ed.), *The Promise and Perils of Populism: Global Perspectives*. Lexington: University Press of Kentucky, 1–28.

De Smet, B. 2016. "In want of the people. Tahrir as a revolutionary reconstitution of the Egyptian national-popular subject," in S. J. Holliday and P. Leach (eds), *Political Identities and Popular Uprisings in the Middle East*. London: Rowman and Littlefield, 137–56.

della Porta, D. 2014. *Mobilizing for Democracy: Comparing 1989 and 2011*. Oxford: Oxford University Press.

Demertzis, N. 2006. "Emotions and populism," in S. Clarke, P. Hoggett, and S. Thompson (eds), *Emotion, Politics and Society*. New York: Palgrave Macmillan, 103–22.

Dostal, J. M. 2015. "The Pegida movement and German political culture: is right-wing populism here to stay?," *The Political Quarterly*, 86(4): 523–31.

Eder, K. 2003. "Identity mobilization and democracy: an ambivalent relationship," in P. Ibarra (ed.), *Social Movements and Democracy*. Basingstoke: Palgrave Macmillan, 61–80.

Formisano, R. P. 2008. *For the People: American Populist Movements from the Revolution to the 1850s*. Chapel Hill: University of North Carolina Press.

Friedman, D. and D. McAdam. 1992. "Collective identity and activism: networks, choices, and the life of a social movement," in A. D. Morris and C. M. Mueller (eds), *Frontiers in Social Movement Theory*. New Haven: Yale University Press, 156–73.

Fukuyama, F. 2016. "American political decay or renewal? The meaning of the 2016 election," *Foreign Affairs*, 95(4): 58–68.

Gerbaudo, P. 2012. *Tweets and the Streets: Social Media and Contemporary Activism*. London: Pluto Press.

Gerhards, J. and D. Rucht. 1992. "Mesomobilization: organizing and framing in two protest campaigns in West Germany," *American Journal of Sociology*, 98(3): 555–96.

Ghonim, W. 2012. *Revolution 2.0: The Power of People is Greater than the People in Power*. Boston: Houghton Mifflin Harcourt.

Goffman, E. 1974. *Frame Analysis: An Essay on the Organization of Experience*. Boston: Northeastern University Press.

Gould-Wartofsky, M. A. 2015. *The Occupiers: The Making of the 99 Percent Movement*. Oxford: Oxford University Press.

Graeber, D. 2013. *The Democracy Project: a History, a Crisis, a Movement*. New York: Spiegel and Grau.

Gunning, J. and I. Z. Baron. 2014. *Why Occupy a Square: People, Protests and Movements in the Egyptian Revolution*. Oxford: Oxford University Press.

Häusler, A. (ed.). 2016. *Die Alternative für Deutschland: Programmatik, Entwicklung und politische Verortung*. Wiesbaden: Springer VS.

Hawkins, K. A. 2010. *Venezuela's Chavismo and Populism in Comparative Perspective*. Cambridge: Cambridge University Press.

Hawkins, K. A., C. Rovira Kaltwasser, and I. Andreadis. 2016. "The activation of populist attitudes: evidence from contemporary Chile and Greece," paper prepared for the Team Populism January Conference: The Causes of Populism, January 28–30, Provo, Utah.

Holston, J. 2014. "'Come to the street!': urban protest, Brazil 2013," *Anthropological Quarterly*, 87(3): 887–900.

Huddy, L. 2013. "From group identity to political cohesion and commitment," in L. Huddy, D. O. Sears, and J. S. Levy (eds), *The Oxford Handbook of Political Psychology*, 2nd edn. Oxford: Oxford University Press, 737–73.

Iglesias, P. 2015. "Understanding Podemos," *New Left Review*, 93(May-June): 7–22.

Inglehart, R. 1977. *The Silent Revolution: Changing Values and Political Styles among Western Publics*. Princeton: Princeton University Press.

Jagers, J. and S. Walgrave. 2007. "Populism as political communication style: an empirical study of political parties' discourse in Belgium," *European Journal of Political Research*, 46(3): 319–45.

Jansen, R. S. 2015. "Populist mobilization: a new theoretical approach to populism," in C. de la Torre (ed.), *The Promise and Perils of Populism: Global Perspectives*. Kentucky: University Press of Kentucky, 159–88.

Kazin, M. 1995. *The Populist Persuasion: An American History*. New York: Basic Books.

Kazin, M. 2016. "Occupy the party," *Dissent*, 63(2): 4.

Klandermans, B. and J. van Stekelenburg. 2013. "Social movements and the dynamics of collective action," in L. Huddy, D. O. Sears, and J. S. Levy (eds), *The Oxford Handbook of Political Psychology*, 2nd edn. Oxford: Oxford University Press, 774–811.

Krastev, I. 2014. *Democracy Disrupted: The Global Politics of Protest*. Philadelphia: University of Pennsylvania Press.

Kriesi, H., E. Grande, M. Dolezal, M. Helbling, S. Hutter, D. Höglinger, and B. Wüest. 2012. *Political Conflict in Western Europe*. Cambridge: Cambridge University Press.

Kriesi, H., R. Koopmans, J. W. Duyvendak, and M. G. Giugni. 1995. *New Social Movements in Western Europe: A Comparative Analysis*. Minneapolis: University of Minnesota Press.

Kumar, A. 2011. *The Making of a Small State: Populist Social Mobilisation and the Hindi Press in the Uttarakhand Movement*. New Delhi: Orient Blackswan.

Laclau, E. 1977. *Politics and Ideology in Marxist Theory: Capitalism-Fascism-Populism*. London: Verso.

Laclau, E. 2005a. *On Populist Reason*. London: Verso.

Laclau, E. 2005b. "Populism: what's in a name?," in F. Panizza (ed.), *Populism and the Mirror of Democracy*. London: Verso, 32–49.

Laraña, E., H. Johnston, and J. R. Gusfield. 1994. *New Social Movements: From Ideology to Identity*. Philadelphia: Temple University Press.

Levitsky, S. and J. Loxton. 2013. "Populism and competitive authoritarianism in the Andes," *Democratization*, 20(1): 107–36.

Mair, P. 2002. "Populist democracy vs party democracy," in Y. Mény and Y. Surel (eds), *Democracies and the Populist Challenge*. Basingstoke: Palgrave Macmillan, 81–98.

McAdam, D. and S. Tarrow. 2010. "Ballots and barricades: on the reciprocal relationship between elections and social movements," *Perspectives on Politics*, 8(2): 529–42.

Melucci, A. 1988. "Getting involved: identity and mobilization in social movements," in B. Klandermans, H. Kriesi, and S. Tarrow (eds), *From Structure to Action: Comparing Social Movement Research Across Cultures*. Greenwich: JAI Press Inc., 329–48.

Mudde, C. 2004. "The populist zeitgeist," *Government and Opposition*, 39(4): 542–63.

Mudde, C. and C. Rovira Kaltwasser. 2012. "Populism and (liberal) democracy: a framework for analysis," in C. Mudde and C. Rovira Kaltwasser (eds), *Populism in Europe and the Americas: Threat or Corrective for Democracy?* Cambridge: Cambridge University Press, 1–26.

Occupy Wall Street. 2011. *Declaration of the occupation of New York City.* http://occupywall-street.net/learn, accessed May 19, 2016.

Panizza, Francisco (ed.). 2005. *Populism and the Mirror of Democracy.* London: Verso.

Payne, L. A. 2000. *Uncivil Movements: The Armed Right Wing and Democracy in Latin America.* Baltimore: Johns Hopkins University Press.

Pfaff, S. 2006. *Exit-Voice Dynamics and the Collapse of East Germany: The Crisis of Leninism and the Revolution of 1989.* Durham: Duke University Press.

Polletta, F. and J. M. Jasper. 2001. "Collective identity and social movements," *Annual Review of Sociology,* 27: 283–305.

Postel, C. 2007. *The Populist Vision.* Oxford: Oxford University Press.

Roberts, K. M. 2015. "Populism, social movements, and popular subjectivity," in D. Della Porta and M. Diani (eds), *The Oxford Handbook of Social Movements.* Oxford: Oxford University Press, 681–95.

Rosenhek, Z. and M. Shalev. 2014. "The political economy of Israel's 'social justice' protests: a class and generational analysis," *Contemporary Social Science: Journal of the Academy of Social Sciences,* 9(1): 31–48.

Rovira Kaltwasser, C. 2012. "The ambivalence of populism: threat and corrective for democracy," *Democratization,* 19(2): 184–208.

Sadiki, L. 2015. "Unruliness through space and time: reconstructing 'peoplehood' in the Arab Spring," in L. Sadiki (ed.), *Routledge Handbook of the Arab Spring: Rethinking Democratization.* New York: Routledge, 1–13.

Silva, E. 2009. *Challenging Neoliberalism in Latin America.* Cambridge: Cambridge University Press.

Skocpol, T. 2016. "Who owns the GOP?," *Dissent,* 63(2): 142–8.

Snow, D. A. 2013. "Framing and social movements," in D. A. Snow, D. della Porta, B. Klandermans, and D. McAdam (eds), *The Wiley Blackwell Encyclopedia of Social and Political Movements.* Malden, MA: Wiley-Blackwell.

Snow, D. A. and R. D. Benford. 1992. "Master frames and cycles of protest," in A. Morris and C. M. Mueller (eds), *Frontiers in Social Movement Theory.* New Haven: Yale University Press, 133–55.

Snow, D. A., E. B. Rochford, S. K. Worden, and R. D. Benford. 1986. "Frame alignment processes, micromobilization, and movement participation," *American Sociological Review,* 51(4): 464–81.

Spruyt, B., G. Keppens, and F. Van Droogenbroeck. 2016. "*Who* supports populism and *what* attracts people to it?," *Political Research Quarterly,* 69(2): 335–46.

Stavrakakis, Y. 2004. "Antinomies of formalism: Laclau's theory of populism and the lessons from religious populism in Greece," *Journal of Political Ideologies,* 9(3): 253–67.

Taggart, P. 2000. *Populism.* Buckingham: Open University Press.

Tarrow, S. 2011. *Power in Movement: Social Movements and Contentious Politics,* rev. 3rd edn. Cambridge: Cambridge University Press.

Taylor, V. 1989. "Social movement continuity: the women's movement in abeyance," *American Sociological Review,* 54(5): 761–75.

Tilly, C. 2004. *Social Movements, 1768–2004.* Boulder: Paradigm Publishers.

Tronconi, F. (ed.). 2015. *Beppe Grillo's Five Star Movement: Organisation, Communication and Ideology.* Farnham: Ashgate.

Tsatsanis, E. 2011. "Hellenism under siege: the national-populist logic of antiglobalization rhet-oric in Greece," *Journal of Political Ideologies*, 16(1): 11–31.

Urbinati, Nadia. 2014. *Democracy Disfigured: Opinion, Truth, and the People*. Cambridge: Harvard University Press.

Van Dyke, N. and D. S. Meyer (eds). 2014. *Understanding the Tea Party Movement*. Farnham: Ashgate.

Walton, J. and D. Seddon. 1994. *Free Markets and Food Riots: The Politics of Global Adjustment*. Cambridge: Blackwell Publishers.

Wiles, P. 1969. "A syndrome, not a doctrine: some elementary theses on populism," in G. Ionescu and E. Gellner (eds), *Populism: Its Meanings and National Characteristics*. London: Weidenfeld and Nicolson, 166–79.

Williams, R. S. 2013. "Culture and social movements," in D. A. Snow, D. della Porta, B. Klandermans, and D. McAdam (eds), *The Wiley Blackwell Encyclopedia of Social and Political Movements*. Malden: Wiley-Blackwell, 312–17.

Zartman, W. (ed.). 2015. *Arab Spring: Negotiating in the Shadow of the Intifadat*. Athens: University of Georgia Press.

Zuo, J. and R. D. Benford. 1995. "Mobilization processes and the 1989 Chinese democracy movement," *The Sociological Quarterly*, 36(1): 131–56.

CHAPTER 17

....

POPULISM
AND TECHNOCRACY

....

CHRISTOPHER BICKERTON AND CARLO
INVERNIZZI ACCETTI

INTRODUCTION

POPULISM has recently been attracting a lot of scholarly attention but one feature of the discussion has gone without much comment at all. By and large, populism has been treated as a *stand-alone* phenomenon; that is, in isolation from other politically salient features of the contexts in which it has emerged. This is reflected in the fact that most contributions to the literature on this topic consist in attempts at identifying an "essence" of populism, and thereby distinguish it from other contiguous concepts, such as "democracy," "popular sovereignty," and "plebiscitarianism" (Müller, 2013; Taggart, 2000; Urbinati, 2014). While this is certainly an important endeavor from a conceptual point of view, it has lent a certain taxonomical quality to the literature on populism, which may at times give the impression of getting bogged down by definitional quarrels.

This chapter approaches the study of populism from a different perspective. Instead of searching for its "essence," we propose to look at it *relationally*; that is, from the point of view of its relationship with another very salient political phenomenon present in almost all the contexts in which populism has emerged: the call for a transfer of political power to actors and institutions drawing legitimacy from their technical competence and administrative expertise, which we shall refer to as "technocracy" (Fischer, 1990; Valbruzzi and McDonnell, 2014; Dargent, 2015; Habermas, 2015).

Populism and technocracy have been treated, by some observers, as correlative and related to one another. Jan-Werner Müller, for instance, has recently suggested that they are "mirror images of each other." "Technocracy" he writes "holds that there is only one correct policy solution; populism holds that there is only one authentic will of the people … In a sense, therefore, both are curiously apolitical. For neither technocrats nor populists is there any need for democratic debate" (Müller, 2016). This depiction is reminiscent of a characterization already proposed by Vivienne Schmidt of populism as a form of "politics without policy" and technocracy as "policy without politics" (Schmidt, 2006). Indeed, some recent commentators have even gone as far as to suggest that in many advanced western democracies the old opposition between left and right is increasingly being replaced by a new structuring opposition between populism and technocracy (Freeland, 2010; Ferguson, 2015).

By looking at this relationship between populism and technocracy far more systematically, we hope to shed light on the meaning of populism itself and to identify some broader dynamics at work in contemporary democratic regimes. To fulfill this double purpose, the chapter will proceed as follows. We begin by noting that although populism and technocracy are more often than not treated as conceptual opposites, there are also some important affinities and complementarities between them. At the most abstract level, this can be observed in their shared hostility to two key features of modern democratic politics: political mediation and procedural legitimacy. Since these two features have been historically embodied in the institution of political parties, our first key claim is that populism and technocracy can be understood as parallel critiques of a specific political form, which we refer to as party democracy. In substantive terms, this account of populism echoes the ideological approach proposed by Cas Mudde in this volume. However, the stress on situating populism within a wider discursive framework that includes seemingly different concepts such as technocracy is part of an attempt to think about populism in more relational terms, which is central to the chapter of Pierre Ostiguy in this volume.

In the second part of the chapter we examine what this insight can teach us concerning the reasons for the emergence of populism and technocracy as organizing poles of contemporary politics. The argument advanced is that long-term structural transformations in the nature of party democracy provide grounds for an explanation of the contemporary emergence of both populism and technocracy as salient features of contemporary politics. This leads to the conclusion that far from being political opposites (or even correctives) for one another, populism and technocracy can only be understood—and therefore tackled—*together*, as parallel expressions of the same underlying set of phenomena.

POPULISM AND TECHNOCRACY: OPPOSITES OR COMPLEMENTS?

The most common way of understanding the relationship between populism and technocracy is to treat them as opposites. Indeed, this opposition is often taken as a starting point in defining the two terms themselves. For instance, Laclau's definition of populism as a way of structuring politics in terms of an opposition between the "people" and its "other" only assumes its full significance when it is set against what he describes as the "administrative" or "technocratic" way of dealing with social demands as "individual problems to be solved" (Laclau, 2005: 79). Similarly, in his discussion of the literature on technocracy, Miguel Centeno has observed that "[p]erhaps the only term as loosely defined as 'technocracy' is its opposite, populism" (1993: 331).

The idea that populism and technocracy are opposites has its roots in several recurrent features of the way in which the two terms are ordinarily employed. At the level of concrete political discourse, these labels are rarely used approvingly, or to describe oneself, but rather as *terms of abuse*, to describe one's political opponents. So-called "populists" therefore routinely chastise their political opponents for being "technocrats" and vice versa.[1] Consequently, in political and academic commentary, populism and technocracy are routinely interpreted as *reactions* to one other. Whereas technocratic bodies such as independent central banks and inter-governmental regulatory agencies are usually justified as "bulwarks" against the threat of populism (Majone, 1994; Scharpf, 1999; Rosanvallon, 2008), the rise of populism is frequently described as a response to the growing technocratization of public life.[2]

Without denying these important dimensions of opposition between populism and technocracy, on closer inspection we can also observe a more complex relationship. For instance, it is striking to note that both labels are often used to describe the *same* political phenomena. In his seminal analysis of the British "New Labour" party, Peter Mair argued that the latter could only be properly understood by taking account of how it managed to "combine" both populist and technocratic elements, citing as evidence a statement by the former Lord Chancellor, Lord Falconer, according to which "the depoliticizing of key decision-making is a vital element in bringing power closer to the people" (Mair, 2006). Similarly, in a study of Barack Obama's rhetorical style as a campaigner, David Bromwich observed that he tended to adopt two different tones depending on his audience: the folksy "populist" tone when speaking to those he considered ordinary people, and the more elevated "technocratic" tone that he used when speaking to policy professionals (Bromwich, 2010).

A convergence of populist and technocratic features is also evident in other recent and contemporary political figures, such as former French President Nicolas Sarkozy and former Italian Prime Minister Silvio Berlusconi. Both presented themselves as the direct interlocutors of the people whilst also adopting a managerial view of political action—as was pointed out by Pierre Musso, who coined the term "*Sarkoberlusconisme*" to capture this distinctive blend of populist and technocratic elements (Musso, 2008). Finally, Carlos de la Torre has recently described Ecuador's Rafael Correa as a "technocratic populist" (de la Torre, 2013). Although his analysis remains wedded to the idea of an underlying antagonism between populism and technocracy, de la Torre's overarching thesis clearly points in the direction of the possibility of a convergence, or at least complementarity, between populism and technocracy. In an interview with a newspaper, the exiled former Thai Prime Minister, Thaksin Shinawatra, gave an account of himself that combined his well-documented "populist chutzpah" with a less visible and more technocratic side. Asked whether he had still been governing Thailand indirectly through his sister and other figures, he answered that his role was that of a "benevolent advisor," of a teacher. "Even in the cabinet, within my prime ministership," he recounted, "I read books and I gave lectures to the cabinet before starting the agenda" (Peel, 2016).

What none of the above authors has yet really brought into focus, however, is what *enables* this coexistence of populist and technocratic elements in the same political figures. In order to get a grip on this, we start by focusing on two abstract conceptual affinities between populism and technocracy, before moving on to spell out how these play out in practice. As befits the common terrain between two concepts that are usually employed as terms of abuse, the categories we will be focusing on here are not "positive" features of either populism or technocracy, but characteristics of what they generally oppose. The affinities between populism and technocracy therefore begin to emerge when we consider what they both stand against.

The first key concept in this respect is *political mediation*. Derived from the Latin meaning "to be or to divide in the middle," mediation was originally a term used in Christian theology, referring to the position of a prophet as a mediator between God and the world. Whilst mediation is still popularly understood as referring to the pacification of disputes by the positioning of a third party "in the middle," in political philosophy it refers specifically to concrete social and institutional forms that exist "in between" the state and the individual. Thus, instead of there being any single or pure relationship between the individual and the state, mediated politics is characterized by the existence of intermediary institutions that collect individual preferences and recast them as the will of a corporate body. From medieval and early modern "estates" through to the factions that competed with one another in the early periods of parliamentarism, individual wills have related to the state in this mediated fashion. Indeed, in a sense, it is only through this mediation that the relationship between the state and civil society is realized.[3]

On most accounts of populism, we can see its hostility to this idea of mediation. In his vindication on populist discourse, for instance, Laclau is scathing of mediation. According to him, the concept is inextricably tied to a "totalizing Hegelian metaphysics" where all forms of social division are "rationally sublated" into a higher unit that both preserves and overcomes them (Laclau, 2005: 93). For Laclau, the choice is only between a politicized and populist "logic of equivalence," where social demands are bundled into one single opposition between the people and the elite, and a depoliticized and technocratic "logic of difference" where individual demands are treated on a case-by-case basis by the state (Laclau, 2005; Bickerton and Invernizzi-Accetti, 2015: 6–10). Similarly, in his account of the "political core" of neopopulism, Weyland highlights the way the intermediary institutions of civil society are bypassed. In his words, neopopulists enjoy "an adversarial relationship to much of organized civil society" and neopopulist leaders seek "an unmediated connection to the masses" (1996: 15).

Other accounts of populism concur in their view of populism's hostility to the idea of mediation. For Mény and Surel, populism needs to be understood as a challenge to the idea of popular will mediated through the institutional apparatus of the liberal state (Mény and Surel, 2001). In place of checks and balances, constitutional courts, and

other key features of a mediated political life, populism asserts the vitality of "the people" and the "demos." Tellingly, in a recent account of Spain's PODEMOS movement,
Pablo Iglesias argued that the Spanish population was "not representable within the traditional left-right categories" and that "our objective of identifying a new 'we' ... initially
came together around the signifier 'Pablo Iglesias'" (Iglesias, 2015: 17).

Accounts of technocracy concur in this critique of political mediation. From the
perspective of technocrats, writes Centeno, political mediation appears as a source of
inefficiency and corruption: in short, as "rent-seeking" (1993: 313). One way of framing the idea of mediation is in the language of the whole and the parts. Mediated politics functions as a struggle between the parts, each of which lays claim to some idea of
the common good. The parts are thus not dissolved into the whole, as Laclau suggests,
but rather the struggle between them is formalized at the level of political society itself.
Technocracy, in contrast, seeks to do away with the parts in the name of the whole. As
Centeno puts it, "a technocrat's task is to assure that the higher rationality of [the] whole
is protected from the undue influence of particular interests." Technocracy, as a result,
"cannot take opposition or popular participation into account" (1993: 313). In contrast,
the idea of mediation implies a role either for political opposition or—at the very least—
for the representation of different interests at the level of political society. In his study
of technocratic government in Italy, Culpepper conceptualizes Mario Monti's time as
prime minister from 2011 to 2013 as a time of "unmediated democracy" and observes
that this technocratic form of rule "appears to stand in the same relation to elected governments as populist governments," namely in a relationship of antagonism to parliamentary parties and their role as mediating bodies in politics.[4]

The second key conceptual category that both populism and technocracy are opposed
to is *procedural legitimacy*. This is the idea that legitimacy is not imported into politics
from outside the political system in the form of some pre-political conception of "truth"
or "justice." Rather, legitimacy emerges from the procedures themselves. This introduces a degree of arbitrariness to political life, where a struggle between what is morally "right" or "wrong" gives way to competition between social groups whose outlooks
are morally equivalent but substantially at odds with one another. Madison's famous
words about all government resting upon "opinion" are followed by an account of the
necessarily subjective and social nature of political truth. In his words, "the reason of
man, like man himself, is timid and cautious, when left alone; and acquires firmness and
confidence in proportion to the number with which it is associated" (Hamilton et al.,
2003: 246). The legitimacy of a position is thus erected not upon a moral principle but
upon the strength of support that can be won for it.

The attachment of populism to a reified conception of the "people" clearly challenges
procedural conceptions of legitimacy, by attributing all the moral authority to "the people." Political truth, embodied in the popular will, is thus prior to and outside of procedural rules. Moreover, such rules are often associated with the corruption of the political
establishment, implying that popular sources of legitimacy may be opposed to procedural ones. In the same way that "the people" as a category is taken out of political life,
so does technocracy remove the "right policy" from political competition. From the

perspective of technocracy, legitimacy resides in the expertise and knowledge of technocrats and it is to be shielded from the partisanship associated with political competition. As Centeno explains, "technocratic legitimacy is based on the appeal of scientific knowledge. This claim accompanies an implicit, and often explicit, rejection of 'politics' as inefficient and possibly corruptive" (1993: 313). "A politicians' state," he argues, "is an 'empty vessel' into which their constituencies pour their needs and aspirations" whereas "the technocrat sees the state as embodying a unit that is greater than the mere sum of its parts."

At the most abstract level, we can therefore say that the complementarity between populism and technocracy can be observed in their shared rejection of two key political categories: political mediation and procedural legitimacy. If we now ask in what ways these two categories have taken form concretely in political life, we can say that the modern expression of these principles is to be found in the regime known as *party democracy*. This emerges if we look into some of the key features of the way in which this political form has been traditionally understood.

First of all, parties have always been understood as "mediating bodies," whose function is to link society to the state. Various metaphors have been used to capture this in the literature, including parties as "transmission belts" (Sartori, 1976), "bridges" (Muirhead and Rosenblum, 2006), and "conduits" (White and Ypi, 2010). They have been routinely described as "crystallizing," "coagulating," "synthesizing," and "moulding" social divisions (Duverger, 1954). Historically, parties are said to have taken up this function in the transition from parliamentarism to mass politics. Earlier forms of representation based on a more limited franchise were mediated by rigid institutions such as estates or by the fluidity of factionalism. As the masses entered politics, factions developed into parties and estates became a relic of the medieval and early modern past. With the move towards universal suffrage, and owing to the dynamics of industrialization and nationalism, political parties therefore became the key mediating institution of modern political life (Maier, 1981; Manin, 1997; Lipset and Rokkan, 1967).

A second key feature of political parties and the conception of democracy they are tied to is a procedural understanding of political legitimacy. As argued above, this refers to the idea of legitimacy being internal to the political procedures themselves (cf. also Urbinati and Saffon, 2013). In party democracy, legitimacy is based on the principles of freedom and equality that are realized through parliamentary deliberation and decision-making rules that are either majoritarian or more consociational depending on the country in question. What is "right" does not precede political competition and deliberation. Whether it be in the ability to secure firm majorities, as in a British "first-past-the-post" system, or the ability to hold together a coalition of parties in many proportional systems, legitimacy derives above all from the ability to secure the political authority needed to govern effectively. No pre-political moral content is to be found in party democracy and one might say that in this political regime, political truth is inherently relative and to be found on whatever side is able to legitimately secure a hold on power (Kelsen, 2013).

In so far as populism and technocracy converge in their critique of both mediation and procedural legitimacy, we can therefore say that they converge on a critique of party democracy as a historically specific political regime that has these two principles at its very core. It should come as no surprise, therefore, that both populism and technocracy regularly target political parties and the procedures of party democracy as the key culprits of everything they take to be amiss in contemporary politics. This is clearly visible in Latin America, where several of the most prominent political figures of the past few decades—from Peru's Alberto Fujimori and Argentina's Carlo's Menem, up to Venezuela's Hugo Chávez and Ecuador's Rafael Correa—employed the concept of *partidocracia* to qualify the features of existing regimes they stood most vehemently against (Levitsky and Cameron, 2003; Gratius, 2007; Conniff, 2012). The same term has also been employed by several European protest movements such as Italy's Lega Nord and France's Front National (Albertazzi and McDonnell, 2008), although more recently the term that appears to be most frequently used to pour scorn on the political system as a whole by populist politicians such as Pablo Iglesias and Beppe Grillo is *la casta* (Rizzo and Stella, 2010; Rivero, 2014).

Similar condemnations of political parties as institutions, and of the mechanisms and dynamics of party politics more generally, can also be observed—although perhaps in somewhat less colorful or evocative forms—within the remit of contemporary technocratic discourse. In the same book in which they make a case for an "adequate balancing of technocracy and democracy," for instance, the former European Commissioner and Italian Prime Minister Mario Monti and currently France's Minister of Defense Sylvie Goulard consistently equate political parties with all the features they find most troublesome of democracy itself: "short-termism," "demagoguery," "rent-seeking," and the systematic pursuit of "private interests" at the expense of the common good (Monti and Goulard, 2012). Similarly, in his book on *Technocracy and Democracy in Latin America*, Eduardo Dargent develops a justificatory theory of "technocratic autonomy" which rests in a large part on the claim that technocrats are likely to display a much higher degree of policy expertise than party politicians, since they are not bogged down by "squabbles for office and power," and can therefore focus more directly on the substance of the policy issues at stake (Dargent, 2015). This confirms that party democracy is usually the implicit—if not the explicit—target of critique against which both populists and technocrats construct their political identity and legitimacy.

The Crisis of Party Democracy and its Consequences

What is to be gained for our understanding of populism by bringing out this element of its relationship with technocracy? Beyond the intrinsic value of conceptual clarification, what we have here is a strong lead for an analysis of the underlying causes of the emergence of populism and technocracy as structuring poles of contemporary politics. If a key feature of these two concepts is that they are both predicated on an underlying critique of party democracy, then it seems reasonable to expect that at least part of the explanation for their contemporary rise to prominence is to be found in transformations occurring at the level of the nature or structure of party democracy itself. In the remaining part of this chapter we shall therefore pursue this lead as a way of bringing out more fully the potential benefits of studying populism in conjunction with technocracy.

A recurrent theme in the recent literature on party democracy is that political parties are somehow in "crisis" (Ignazi, 1996; Dalton and Wattenberg, 2001; Daalder, 2002; Whiteley, 2010; Delwit, 2011; Mair, 2013; 2014). Although the claim itself is not new, inasmuch as the effectiveness—and indeed the very existence—of political parties has always been an object of contestation (Ostrogorski, 1993; Schmitt, 1985), several long-term structural developments have contributed to making this into a particularly pressing concern at the present time. Three developments in particular have attracted sustained attention: the overarching sociological process of *individualization*, which is thought to erode the traditional social bases of party identification, while at the same time furnishing individuals with both the interest and the means to engage in alternative forms of political participation (Giddens, 1991; Beck and Gernsheim, 2002; Gauja, 2015); the rise of *new media* as alternative vectors of political information and socialization, which undercuts many of the traditional functions political parties were historically assumed to perform (Mazzoleni and Schulz, 1999; Graber, 2003; Kriesi et al., 2013); and the impact of *globalization*, which challenges the national parties' capacity to address many of the most important problems of present-day societies (Held, 1995; Bickerton, 2012; Kriesi et al., 2013).

In response to these long-term structural developments, political parties have adopted coping strategies that in many ways run against their capacity to function as effective mediators between society and the state (Crouch, 2000; Papadopoulos, 2013). In particular, several commentators have pointed out that political parties have been progressively loosing their foothold in society, and seeking to draw sustenance from the state. This is a theme that has been developed in particular by Richard Katz and Peter Mair in terms of the concept of "cartelization" of political parties. The key idea is that political parties have attempted to respond to the underlying structural causes of their present crisis by adopting collusive strategies, which restrict the scope of political competition, thereby diminishing the cost of electoral defeat, and therefore enabling them to survive even in the face of severely declining social support (Katz and Mair, 1995; 2009).

To be sure, several aspects of this "cartelization" hypothesis have also been challenged by commentators (Koole, 1996; Kitschelt, 2000; Krowel, 2012). Most of these criticisms have centered on the question of whether the ideal-typical model of intra-party organization Katz and Mair associate with the notion of a "cartel party" is so different from other models of party organization that had previously been put forward in the literature on party transformation in the second half of the twentieth century, such as Kircheimer's "catch-all party" (1967) and Panebianco's "electoral-professional party" (1980). From the point of view of the set of questions under consideration here, however, this issue is not central. What all the most important theories of party transformation over the past few decades seem to have in common, beyond terminological differences, is the claim that parties have increasingly become more akin to professionalized "political enterprises," dominated by their interest in the pursuit or maintenance of power. As a consequence, they have developed a set of common interests that are not necessarily aligned with those of the constituencies they are supposed to represent, and which form the basis for power-sharing agreements that insulate them against the threat of social disaffection or electoral defeat (on this point, see also Detterbeck, 2015).

What we are interested in exploring here is the light this can shed on the parallel emergence of populism and technocracy as structuring poles of contemporary politics, independently of whether this transformation is best described as a process of "cartel-ization," or in terms of the emergence of "catch-all" or "electoral-professional" parties. From this point of view, Katz and Mair's seminal discussion of party "cartelization" offers a number of additional insights that are not as frequently discussed in the contemporary literature on party democracy, but which nonetheless appear highly relevant to the present discussion.

The first such insight concerns the political conditions for the effective realization of a party cartel. In this respect, Katz and Mair point out that, in order to enter into the kinds of collusive agreements that allow them to insulate each other from the potential costs of social disaffection and electoral defeat, parties first need to overcome—or at least neutralize—the grounds for their previous ideological and programmatic opposition to each other. The simplest way of doing this is to remove politically contentious issues from the domain over which party politicians are required to make decisions. The expectation is therefore that the process of party cartelization should go hand-in-hand with a broader process of depoliticization, characterized by the progressive relegation of contentious policy issues outside the remit of partisan politics, and into the hands of "neutral" or "independent" bodies, such as central banks and other "expert" authorities.

The point here is that these kinds of organizations cannot by definition draw their legitimacy from their capacity to adequately represent social demands. Instead, the claim is that they offer more "competent" and "effective" policy management compared to the parties themselves. For this reason, Katz and Mair suggest that party cartelization is likely to be accompanied by an increased reliance on a "technocratic" discourse of legitimation, which puts more emphasis on the expertise and problem-solving skills of policy-makers, at the expense their representative capacity. "With the development of the cartel party," they write, "the goals of politics become self-referential, professional and technocratic, and what substantive inter-party competition remains becomes focused on the efficient management of the polity" (2009: 755).

The other key insight Katz and Mair draw from their analysis of the process of cartelization concerns the conditions for the emergence of new political parties or electoral forces within the framework of an electoral system marked by strong cartelization. The point here is that since power-sharing agreements between mainstream parties have the effect of mounting high barriers to entry for new or prospective contenders, the only way of penetrating a cartelized electoral market is by denouncing the cartel itself. In this, political outsiders can draw on the wide pool of popular resentment that is likely to be generated by the process of cartelization, since as we have seen this implies that political parties—and therefore the political system as a whole—must become less directly responsive to the demands of their electoral constituencies. A new vertical axis of political opposition between "society" and the "state" (or the "people" and the "elite") is therefore likely to be superimposed on the more traditional horizontal division between "left" and "right."

As we have seen, these are amongst the most important ingredients for the emergence of a "populist" discourse of contestation: the attack against intermediary bodies and established procedures in the name of a direct appeal to the sovereign authority of the people's will. For this reason, Katz and Mair suggest that the recent rise of populist protest movements and parties can also be seen as a direct consequence of the process of cartelization of political parties. "The growing incorporation of parties within the state, their increasingly shared purpose and identity and the ever more visible gap that separates them from the wider society have contributed to provoking a degree of popular mistrust and disaffection that is without precedent in the postwar experiences of long-established democracies." Thus, "cartelization has clearly contributed to the rise of populist anti-system parties that appeal directly to public perceptions that the mainstream parties are indifferent to the desires of ordinary citizens" (2009: 759–60).

Taking these two insights together, we obtain the idea that the present crisis of party democracy—manifested most immediately in the set of processes Katz and Mair seek to capture through the notion of party "cartelization"—has been directly implicated in two parallel developments that are extremely pertinent to our present analysis: on one hand, a growing "technocratization" of politics, as mainstream parties seek to insulate themselves from the costs of social disaffection and electoral defeat by entering into collusive agreements that require them to justify policy outcomes in terms of their administrative competence and technical expertise; on the other hand, a "populist" backlash, as prospective contenders find it increasingly difficult to penetrate the space of electoral competition and therefore resort to denouncing the conditions that keep the cartel in place by tapping into the widespread popular resentment generated by the perception that political parties are becoming increasingly unresponsive to social demands. From this perspective, populism and technocracy therefore appear as parallel symptoms of the ongoing crisis of party democracy. Of course, this is not to suggest that this is the only possible explanation. Populism and technocracy are complex political phenomena and they are bound to be the result of a multitude of overlapping social and political processes. There may certainly be other explanatory variables—from more macro- and more micro-analyses—that ought to be taken into account to provide a more complete picture. For the purposes of this chapter, we have sought to identify how transformations occurring at the level of the nature and structure of party democracy provide *one* dimension of the explanation for the rise of populism and technocracy as structuring poles of contemporary democratic politics. The focus on this explanatory variable was motivated by the recognition that populism and technocracy are both predicated on a common critique of party democracy, which suggests that these three phenomena—populism, technocracy, and party democracy—ought to be studied in conjunction with one another. Although this line of explanation still depends on the idea that populism is a *reaction* against the growing technocratization of contemporary politics—and therefore that the two remain in an important sense opposed to one another—it also has the merit of bringing out why populism and technocracy have emerged simultaneously, and indeed in conjunction with one another, over the course of the past few decades. It therefore confirms and deepens the claim made in the first part of this chapter, showing that it would be a mistake to treat populism and technocracy exclusively as opposites of one another. Rather, what we have attempted to bring out through the analysis above is that these two phenomena also display an important element of complementarity, inasmuch as they both emerge from an underlying crisis of party democracy, while also converging on its critique. The notion of party democracy therefore emerges as the implicit *trait d'union* between populism and technocracy, suggesting they can ultimately be seen as two sides of the same coin—that coin being the contemporary critique and therefore crisis of party democracy.

CONCLUSION

This chapter has pursued a relational approach to the study of populism, focusing in particular on its relationship with technocracy, and what the latter can teach us about populism itself. The conclusion reached is that—although populism and technocracy are usually understood as political opposites—they also share an important element of complementarity, which consists in the fact that they both emerge from an underlying crisis and converge on an overarching critique of party democracy. As well as providing the basis for what we call here a "relational" approach, this argument about populism and technocracy suggests that scholarly work focused on examining the root causes of the contemporary "populist moment" should expand its scope of investigation. Rather than focusing purely and narrowly on populism proper, a wider study of the crisis of party democracy promises to shed light on the causes of populism and the other associated developments—such as the rise of technocracy—that have common roots.

Our conclusion is also of practical relevance, inasmuch as it challenges commonly held views about how to address concerns raised by the contemporary rise of populism and the growing technocratization of politics. Relying on the assumption that these are straightforwardly opposite developments, several contemporary commentators have suggested that they could perhaps be made to function as antidotes—or at least correctives—for one another. In his book *On Populist Reason*, Ernesto Laclau presents populism as a way of countering the depoliticization inherent in the "administrative" or "technocratic" way of dealing with social demands as individual problems to be solved (Laclau, 2005). Conversely, in his treatise on *Democratic Legitimacy*, Pierre Rosanvallon has suggested that a transfer of political power to "independent authorities" drawing their legitimacy from their "impartiality" vis-à-vis social conflicts may provide a bulwark against the "simplifications" and "reifications" of democratic legitimacy he takes to be inherent in all forms of populism (Rosanvallon, 2011).

These recommendations rely on the assumption that populism is to be understood as a sort of "hypertrophy" of popular sovereignty, whereas technocracy would consist in a way of "limiting" it or controlling it from outside. It follows that "party democracy" must be situated somewhere in between these two extremes. From this perspective, it seems plausible to suggest that populism and technocracy can function as correctives for one another, akin to a search for balance between the pull of two opposite extremes. What we have outlined in this chapter is a different conceptual topography, in which populism and technocracy are not situated on opposite sides of party democracy in the manner of a spectrum. Rather, they appear as parallel symptoms of its underlying crisis, as well as vectors of its critique. From this it follows that populism and technocracy cannot function as correctives for one another, since any increase in one or the other is likely to reinforce the underlying set of developments from which they both stem. A more adequate conclusion would be that any attempt at countering either populism or technocracy must necessarily address them *together*, as two sides of the same coin, with the strong implication that our attention should turn to the crisis of party democracy itself rather than to two of its symptoms.

NOTES

1   For instance, Marine Le Pen's electoral manifesto for the European parliamentary elections of 2014 stated that: "the submission of French democracy to the European technocracy … is a crime that symbolizes all our current representatives' contempt for the very idea of democracy" (Front National, 2014). Almost by way of response, in their joint political pamphlet entitled *Democracy in Europe*, the former European Commissioner Mario Monti and the former Member of the European Parliament Sylvie Goulard state that: "Irrespective of what the populists say, the task of government is not to blindly follow the people's passions … It is not through a demonization of expertise, but through a correct combination of technocracy and democracy that public policy can achieve a better temporal pertinence" (Monti and Goulard, 2012).

2   Commenting on the run-up to a previous round of European elections, for instance, Mark Leonard described the EU as "the ultimate technocratic project," suggesting that as that project has matured, "its very success as a bureaucratic phenomenon fuelled a populist backlash at the national level" (Leonard, 2011).

3   This is for instance how Hegel understands the role of estates. In his words, "the proper significance of the Estates is that it is through them that the state enters into the subjective consciousness of the people, and that the people begins to participate in the state" (1991: 342).

4   Culpepper goes on to say that the two phenomena are "mirror images" of one another: "populist parties are anti-elite movements whose simple solutions make them popular with the public until they run into the world of complex problems. Unmediated democratic governments are elite non-movements whose ability to cope with complex problems means that parties and the public are willing to turn to them until crisis abates" (2014: 1268). What populist governments and unmediated forms of rule such as Monti's do have in common is

their antagonistic relationship to party democracy. As Culpepper observed, Monti's government relied in part on support of parties in parliament and in part on public opinion but it preferred to ground itself in the language of necessity rather than accept the legitimacy of the "parts" of the Italian political economy.

References

Albertazzi, D. and D. McDonnell. 2008. *Twenty-First Century Populism: The Spectre of Western European Democracy.* London: Palgrave Macmillan.

Barr, R. 2003. "The persistence of neopopulism in Peru? From Fujimori to Toledo," *Third World Quarterly,* 24(6): 1161–78.

Beck, U. and E. Gernsheim. 2002. *Individualization: Institutionalized Individualism and its Social and Political Consequences.* London: Sage.

Bickerton, C. J. 2012. *European Integration: From Nation-States to Member States.* Oxford: Oxford University Press.

Bickerton, C. J. and C. Invernizzi-Accetti. 2013. "Italy: populism vs. technocracy?," *Le Monde Diplomatique,* March.

Bickerton, C. J. and C. Invernizzi-Accetti. 2017. "Populism and technocracy: opposites or complements?," *Critical Review of International Social and Political Philosophy,* 20(2): 186–206.

Bordignon, F. and L. Ceccarini. 2013. "Five Stars and a cricket. Beppe Grillo shakes Italian politics," *South European Society and Politics,* 18(4): 427–49.

Bromwich, D. 2010. "The Fastidious President," *London Review of Books,* 32(22): 3–6.

Canovan, M. 1981. *Populism.* New York: Harcourt Brace Jovanovich.

Carrión, J. F. (ed.). 2006. *The Fujimori Legacy: The Rise of Electoral Authoritarianism.* University Park: Pennsylvania State University Press.

Centeno, M. A. 1993. "The new Leviathan: the dynamics and limits of technocracy," *Theory and Society,* 22/3: 307–35.

Centeno, M. A. 1999. *Democracy within Reason: Technocratic Revolution in Mexico.* Pennsylvania State University Press: Pennsylvania.

Centeno M. A. and P. Silva (eds). 1998. *The Politics of Expertise in Latin America.* London: Macmillan.

Collier, D. and J. Gerring (eds). 2009. *Concepts and Method in Social Science: The Tradition of Giovanni Sartori.* London: Routledge.

Conniff, M. (ed.) 2012. *Populism in Latin America.* Tuscaloosa: University of Alabama Press.

Crouch, C. 2000. *Post-Democracy.* London: Polity.

Culpepper, P. D. 2014. "The political economy of unmediated democracy: Italian austerity under Mario Monti," *West European Politics,* 37(6): 1264–81.

Daalder, H. 2002. "Parties: denied, dismissed or redundant? A critique," in Richard Gunther, José Ramon Montero, and Juan Linz (eds), *Political Parties: Old Concepts and New Challenges.* Oxford: Oxford University Press.

Dalton, R. J. and M. Wattenberg (eds). 2001. *Parties without Partisans.* New York: Oxford University Press.

Dargent, E. 2015. *Technocracy and Democracy in Latin America: The Experts Running Government.* Cambridge: Cambridge University Press.

de la Torre, C. 2013. "Technocratic populism in Ecuador," *Journal of Democracy,* 24(3): 33–46.

Delwit, P. 2011. "Still in decline? Party membership in Europe," in E. Van Haute (ed.), *Party Membership in Europe.* Brussels: Editions de l'Université de Bruxelles.

Detterbeck, K. 2005. "Cartel parties in Western Europe," *Party Politics*, 11(2): 173–91.

Duverger, M. 1954. *Political Parties: Their Organization and Activity in the Modern State.* New York: Wiley.

Fabbrini, S. and M. Lazar. 2013. "Still a difficult democracy? Italy between populist challenges and institutional weakness," *Contemporary Italian Politics*, 5(2): 106–12.

Fella, S. and C. Ruzza. 2013. "Populism and the fall of the centre-right in Italy: the end of the Berlusconi model or a new beginning?," *Journal of Contemporary European Studies*, 21(1): 38–52.

Ferguson, N. 2015. "The nasty Greek outcomes that democracy precludes," *Financial Times*. https://www.ft.com/content/48df30c2-2182-11e5-ab0f-6bb9974f25d0.

Fischer, F. 1990. *Technocracy and the Politics of Expertise*. London: Sage.

Freeland, C. 2010. "Forget left and right: the real divide is technocrats versus populists," *Reuters*. http://blogs.reuters.com/chrystia-freeland/2010/11/05/forget-left-and-right-the-real-divide-is-technocrats-versus-populists/.

Gauja, A. 2015. "The individualisation of party politics: the impact of changing internal decision-making processes on policy development and citizen engagement," *British Journal of Politics and International Relations*, 17(1): 89–105.

Giddens, A. 1991. *Modernity and Self-Identity: Self and Society in the Late Modern Age.* Cambridge: Polity.

Gidron, N. and B. Bonkowski. 2013. "Varieties of populism: literature review and research agenda," Weatherland Center for International Affairs, Working Paper Series, 13(0004).

Graber, D. 2003. *Media Power in Politics*. New York: CQ Press.

Gratius, S. 2007. "The third wave of populism in Latin Ametica," FRIDE working paper no. 7.

Grillo, B. and G. Casaleggio. 2011. *Siamo in Guerra: per una nuova politica.* Milano: Chiarelettere.

Habermas, J. 2015. *The Lure of Technocracy*. Cambridge: Polity.

Hameiri, S. and K. Jayasuriya. 2011. "Regulatory regionalism and the dynamics of territorial politics: the case of the Asia-Pacific region," *Political Studies*, 59(1): 20–37.

Hamilton, A., J. Madison, and J. Jay. 2003 [1788]. *The Federalist, with Letters of "Brutus."* Cambridge: Cambridge University Press.

Held, D. 1995. *Democracy and the Global Order: From the Modern State to Cosmopolitan Governance*. Stanford: Stanford University Press.

Iglesias, P. 2015. "Understanding Podemos," *New Left Review*, 93: 7–22.

Ignazi, P. 1996. "The crisis of parties and the rise of new political parties," *Party Politics*, 2(4): 549–66.

Katz, R. and P. Mair. 1995. "Changing models of party organization and democracy: the emergence of the cartel party," *Party Politics*, 1(1): 5–28.

Katz, R. and P. Mair. 2009. "The cartel party thesis: a restatement," *Perspectives on Politics*, 7(4): 753–66.

Kazin, M. 1998. *The Populist Persuasion: An American History.* Ithaca: Cornell University Press.

Kelsen, H. 2013. *The Essence and Value of Democracy.* Lanham: Rowman and Littlefield.

Kitschelt, H. 2000. "Citizens, politicians and party cartelization: political representation and state failure in post-industrial democracies," *European Journal of Political Research*, 37(2): 149–79.

Koole, R. 1996. "Cadre, catch-all or cartel? A comment on the notion of the cartel party," *Party Politics*, 2(4): 507–34.

Kriesi, H. 2014. "The populist challenge," *West European Politics*, 37(2): 361–78.

Kriesi, H., D. Bochsler, J. Matthes, S. Lavenex, M. Bühlmann, and F. Esser. 2013. *Democracy in the Age of Globalization and Mediatization.* Basingstoke: Palgrave Macmillan.

Kriesi, H., E. Grande, M. Dolezal, M. Helblin, P. Statham, and H.-J. Trenz. 2012. *Political Conflict in Western Europe.* Cambridge: Cambridge University Press.

Krowel, A. 2012. *Party Transformations in European Democracies.* New York: State University of New York Press.

Laclau, E. 2005. *On Populist Reason.* London: Verso.

Lanzone, M. E. 2014. "The 'post-modern' populism in Italy: the case of the Five Star Movement," *Research in Political Sociology,* 22: 53–78.

Leonard, M. 2011. *Four scenarios for the reinvention of Europe,* European Council of Foreign Relations, London. http://www.ecfr.eu/page/-/ECFR43_REINVENTION_OF_EUROPE_ESSAY_AW1.pdf.

Levitsky, S. 1999. "Fujimori and post-party politics in Peru," *Journal of Democracy,* 10(3): 78–92.

Levitsky, S. and M. A. Cameron. 2003. "Democracy without parties? Political parties and regime change in Fujimori's Peru," *Latin American Politics and Society,* 45(3): 1–33.

Levitsky, S. and J. Loxton. 2012. "Populism and competitive authoritarianism: the case of Fujimori's Peru," in Mudde and Rovira Kaltwasser (eds), *Populism in Europe and the Americas: Threat or Corrective for Democracy?* Cambridge: Cambridge University Press.

Lipset, M. and S. Rokkan. 1967. *Party Systems and Voter Alignments: Cross-national Perspectives.* New York: Free Press.

Maier, C. 1981. "Fictitious bonds ... of wealth and law: on the theory and practice of interest representation," in S. Berger (ed.), *Organizing Interests in Western Europe.* New York: Cambridge University Press.

Mair, P. 2006. "Ruling the void?: the hollowing of western democracy," *New Left Review,* 42. London: Verso.

Mair, P. 2014. "Populist democracy vs. party democracy," in Ingrid van Biezen (ed.), *On Parties, Party Systems and Democracy: Selected Writings of Peter Mair.* Exeter: ECPR Press.

Majone, G. 1994. "The rise of the regulatory state in Europe," *West European Politics,* 17(3): 77–101.

Manin, B. 1997. *The Principles of Representative Government.* Cambridge: Cambridge University Press.

Marcussen, M. 2005. "Central banks on the move," *Journal of European Public Policy,* 12(5): 903–25.

Mazzoleni, G. and W. Schulz. 1999. "Mediatization of politics: a challenge for democracy?," *Political Communication,* 16(3): 247–61.

Mény, Y. and Y. Surel. 2001. *Democracies and the Populist Challenge.* London: Palgrave Macmillan.

Monti, M. and S. Goulard. 2012. *De la Démocratie en Europe.* Paris: Flammarion.

Muirhead, R. and N. Rosenblum. 2006. "Political liberalism vs. 'the great game of politics': the politics of political liberalism," *Prespectives on Politics,* 4(1): 99–108.

Müller, J.-W. 2013. "We the people: on populism and democracy," lecture, Institute for Human Sciences of the University of Vienna. http://www.iwm.at/events/event/iwm-lecture-in-human-sciences-we-the-people-on-populism-and-democracy-i/.

Müller, J.-W. 2016. *What Is Populism?* Philadelphia: University of Pennsylvania Press.

Musso, P. 2008. *Le sarkoberlusconisme.* Paris: Editions de l'Aube.

O'Donnell, G. 1994. "Delegative democracy," *Journal of Democracy,* 5(1): 55–69.

Ostrogorski, M. 1993 [1903]. *La Démocratie et les Partis Politiques.* Paris: Calmann-Lévy.

Papadopoulos, Y. 2013. *Democracy in Crisis*. London: Routledge.

Peel, M. 2016. "Lunch with the FT: Thaksin Shinawatra," *Financial Times*, March 12/13.

Rivero, J. 2014. *Conversacion con Pablo Iglesias*. Madrid: Turpial.

Rizzo, S. and G. A. Stella. 2010. *La casta: così i politici Italiani sono diventati intoccabili*. Milano: Rizzoli.

Rosanvallon, P. 2008. *Counter-Democracy: Politics in an Age of Distrust*. Cambridge: Cambridge University Press.

Rosanvallon, P. 2011. *Democratic Legitimacy*. Princeton: Princeton University Press.

Sartori, G. 1976. *Parties and Party Systems: A Framework for Analysis*. Cambridge: Cambridge University Press.

Scharpf, F. 1999. *Governing Europe: Effective and Democratic?* Oxford: Oxford University Press.

Schmidt, V. 2006. *Democracy in Europe: The EU and National Polities*. Oxford: Oxford University Press.

Schmitt, C. 1985 [1923]. *The Critics of Parliamentary Democracy*. Cambridge: MIT Press.

Taggart, P. 2000. *Populism*. London: Open University Press.

Urbinati, N. 2014. *Democracy Disfigured*. Cambridge: Harvard University Press.

Urbinati, N. and M. P. Saffron. 2013. "Procedural democracy, the bulwark of equal liberty," *Political Theory*, 41(3): 441–81.

Valbruzzi, M. and D. McDonnell. 2014. "Defining and classifying technocrat-led and technocratic governments," *European Journal of Political Research*, 53(4): 654–71.

Van Biezen, I. and M. S. Michael. 2008. "Democratic theorists and party scholars: why they don't talk to each other, and why they should," *Perspectives on Politics*, 1: 21–35.

Weyland, K. 1996. "Neopopulism and neoliberalism in Latin America: unexpected affinities," *Studies in Comparative Institutional Development*, 31(3): 3–31.

Weyland, K. 2001. "Clarifying a contested concept: populism in the study of Latin American politics," *Comparative Politics*, 34(1): 1–22.

White, J. and L. Ypi. 2010. "Rethinking the modern prince: partisanship and the democratic ethos," *Political Studies*, 58(1): 809–28.

Whiteley, P. 2010. "Is the party over? The decline of party activism and membership across the democratic world," *Party Politics*, 17(1): 21–44.

CHAPTER 18

POPULISM AND NATIONALISM

BENJAMIN DE CLEEN

INTRODUCTION

THIS chapter disentangles the concepts of populism and nationalism and uses that theoretical clarification to shed light on the different ways in which populism and nationalism have been articulated in populist politics. Populism and nationalism have been closely related, both empirically and conceptually. Many of the most prominent instances of populist politics have been nationalist—including the populist radical right and most of the Latin American populisms—and nationalisms have often had a populist component. Moreover, both populism and nationalism revolve around the sovereignty of "the people." On top of that, the nation-state remains the dominant context for democratic political representation so that populism usually operates within a national context (even if nation-states' actual decision-making power has decreased significantly).

All this has contributed to a partial conflation of populism with nationalism. In Gellner and Ionescu's seminal volume on populism, Stewart (1969: 183) goes as far as to call populism "a kind of nationalism." A more recent example is the argument—based on analyses of the populist radical right—that "the people" in populism refers to "ethnos rather than demos" (Akkerman, 2003: 151) or both ethnos and demos (e.g. Jansen, 2011; Taguieff, 1997: 15). Including elements of nationalism in definitions of populism hinders the application of the concept to other (non-nationalist) forms of populism. And even when looking specifically at politics that are both nationalist and populist, our understanding still depends on a clear conceptual distinction between the two concepts.

Much valuable work has been done on how populism and nationalism come together in particular movements and parties. But explicit conceptual reflections on the relation between populism and nationalism that could strengthen such empirical analyses have been surprisingly uncommon (but see Canovan, 2005; Hermet, 1997; Mény and Surel, 2000: 204–14; Stavrakakis, 2005).

The key move in this chapter is to distinguish populism and nationalism as distinctive discourses and then look at how they have been articulated in different kinds of populist politics.[1] The theoretical backbone for this endeavor is the post-structuralist and post-Marxist discourse theory formulated by Laclau and Mouffe (2001/1985) and further developed by the so-called Essex school (see Glynos and Howarth, 2007). Discourse theory approaches politics as the discursive struggle for hegemony, whereby hegemony is understood as the (always partial and temporary) fixation of meaning (Torfing, 1999: 36–8). In studying political projects' attempts to fix meaning and make their views prevail, discourse theory studies how they produce a structure of meaning through the *articulation* of existing discursive elements.

In the context of discourse theory, with its focus on how meaning comes about through meaning relations between signifiers, *articulation* refers to bringing together discursive elements in a particular way to construct a more or less original structure of meaning. Each politics is necessarily tied in to existing and more encompassing structures of meaning, by drawing on, reproducing, altering, and contesting those discourses. In this fashion, political projects are always connected to political history and to the broader political context within which they operate. The agency of political projects lies in the fact that articulations are contingent relations of "no necessary correspondence" (Laclau, 1990: 35) and that the process of articulation changes the meaning of that which it articulates (Laclau and Mouffe, 2001: 105, 113–14).

The chapter starts by disentangling the concepts of nationalism and populism. These definitions are then used to discuss the different ways in which nationalism and populism have been articulated in populist politics. This discussion starts with a brief section on how, because of the predominantly national organization of political representation, most populist politics operate within a national context. After this reflection on the nation as context for populist politics, the focus shifts to the articulation of populism and actual nationalist politics that revolve around the identity, interests, and sovereignty of the nation. The chapter zooms in on two main kinds of articulation: the articulation of populism with exclusionary nationalist demands, and its articulation with demands for the sovereignty of the nation as against larger state structures, colonizing forces, and supra-national political bodies. A final section of the chapter reflects on the possibilities of a transnational populism that supersedes the boundaries of the nation-state and constructs a transnational people.

NATIONALISM

Theoretical confusion between populism and nationalism can mainly be found in work on the former. Despite considerable conceptual debate on nationalism, overlap with populism is not one of nationalism's major conceptual problems. Let me therefore start by defining nationalism and then move on to define populism in a way that distinguishes it clearly from nationalism.

344 BENJAMIN DE CLEEN

Nationalism is a discourse structured around the nodal point[2] nation, envisaged as a limited and sovereign community that exists through time and is tied to a certain space, and that is constructed through an in/out (member/non-member) opposition between the nation and its outgroups.

The constructionist theorization of nationalism as a discourse that constructs the nation (e.g. Bhabha, 1990; Day and Thompson, 2004: 13–17; Jenkins and Sofos, 1996: 11; Sutherland, 2005: 186) implies a move away from the search for the essence of the nation—what defines national belonging—towards the identification of the particularities of how nationalism discursively constructs the nation.

The starting point for a discursive definition of nationalism is the signifier "the nation." This does not mean that nationalists exclusively use the word "nation." They also refer to "the people" (*das Volk, el pueblo*), for example. What matters is that nationalism is structured around a group constructed in a particular nationalist way. The nation is the "organising principle" (Greenfeld, 1992: 7) that makes all different nationalisms nationalist, or in discourse-theoretical terms, the nodal point around which nationalist discourse is structured (see Sutherland, 2005: 186). In nationalism, other signifiers such as state, land, freedom, democracy, and culture acquire meaning in relation to the signifier nation (see Freeden, 1998: 755).

Nationalism, like racism and sexism, divides the human species in exclusive groups (Balibar, 1989: 9–10). It is helpful to think about the structure of nationalist discourse in spatial terms; this will also help to distinguish it from populism (Dyrberg, 2003; 2006). Nationalist discourse is structured around an in/out relation, with the "in" consisting of the members of the nation and the "out" of different types of non-members. As the in/out construction of group identity is not exclusive to nationalism, we need to identify the particular manner in which nationalism constructs "in" and "out" (see Day and Thompson, 2004: 102–3). Here we can turn to Anderson's (2006) idea of the nation as a "imagined community." Although Anderson was concerned "in an anthropological spirit" (2006: 6) with how the members of a nation imagine themselves as a community, his analysis of how the nation is imagined is very helpful to an understanding of how nationalism discursively constructs the nation.

Firstly, the nation is constructed as *limited*: nationalism is first and foremost a representation of the world as made up of distinct nations (Anderson, 2006: 7; Vincent, 2002: 10). Indeed, the nation can only be constructed through the distinction between one nation and other nations, and between members of the nation and non-members. Secondly, the nation is constructed as a *community*. Whereas to Anderson, community means that the members of the nation actually feel as if they belong together, what matters from a discursive perspective is the discursive construction of the nation as an organic community that all members of the nation are considered to be part of. Thirdly, the nation is constructed as *sovereign*: it has the rights to take decisions independently and without interference. This becomes most evident in demands for an independent state. However, it is not the state but the nation that serves as the nodal point of nationalism: the state's legitimacy depends on its representation of the sovereign nation (see Jenkins and Sofos, 1996). Shared time (a shared past, present, and future) and space (a shared territory with borders and certain characteristics)—and the shared language, customs, etc. that follow from this—serve to differentiate ingroup from outgroup, to obscure the (historical) contingency of the nation, as well as to provide legitimacy for the nation's sovereignty over a territory (Freeden, 1998: 752; Wodak et al., 2009: 26).

Populism (and Why It Is Not Nationalism)

Populism is a discourse centered around the nodal points "the people" and "the elite," in which the meaning of "the people" and "the elite" is constructed through a down/up antagonism between "the people" as a large powerless group and "the elite" as a small and illegitimately powerful group. Populists claim to represent "the people" against a (some) illegitimate "elite," and construct their political demands as representing the will of "the people" (for similar definitions see Laclau, 2005a; 2005b; Stavrakakis, 2004; Stavrakakis and Katsambekis, 2014).

This is not the place for a detailed discussion of the various conceptualizations of populism (see the opening chapters of this handbook). The key point here is that, more so than other approaches, a discourse-theoretical definition focuses on how populism discursively constructs "the people" through an antagonism between "the people" and "the elite." This goes against the tendency to take for granted (to a more or lesser extent) the existence of the category "the people" in definitions of populism as a political communication or performance style that speaks about and/or appeals to "the people" (Jagers and Walgrave, 2003; Kazin, 1995; Moffitt and Tormey, 2014). It also highlights more explicitly the construction of "the people" than conceptualizations of populism as a set of ideas—a (thin) ideology—about what role the people and the elite should play in politics (e.g. Canovan, 2002; Mudde, 2007 and this volume; Stanley, 2008). This move away from ideology and towards how populists discursively construct and claim to represent "the people" allows taking into account more thoroughly the crucial *strategic* dimensions of populism (see Stavrakakis and Katsambekis, 2014). Parties and movements can turn to populism as a strategy to acquire power, even when they were originally not populist, and they do not necessarily remain populist once they are in power. Finally, populism is not necessarily opposed to the existence of an elite per se, but against a current and illegitimate elite that they want to replace as power holders that *do* represent the people.

This discourse-theoretical definition does strongly resemble the thin ideology definition developed by Mudde (this volume) and others in its "minimal" character. It too focuses on the distinction between "the people" and "the elite" and on the populist claim to represent "the people," and keeps all other characteristics of particular populist politics out. With its focus on the down/up dimension, the definition proposed here also shares Ostiguy's (this volume) identification of the "low" as central to populism. And through its attention to populism's strategic dimensions, it bears some resemblance to Weyland's (this volume) definition of populism as a political strategy. But it is less focused on personalistic leadership and attaches more importance to discourse than Weyland with his focus on "deeds" rather than "words."

Laclau's discourse-theoretical work on populism (1977; 2005a; 2005b) obviously served as a major inspiration. However, in his recent work Laclau treats "populism [a]s the royal road to understanding something about the ontological constitution of the political as such" (2005a: 67). Populism thus becomes a synonym for politics, and the question becomes how to distinguish the two concepts (see Stavrakakis, 2004: 263). My aim is not to reveal something about the nature of politics as such, but to use the concept of populism to further understanding of a particular kind of politics (see Stavrakakis, 2005; Stavrakakis and Katsambekis, 2014).

Populist politics are organized according to a particular political logic. Logics, Glynos and Howarth (2007: 136) argue, are "constructed and named by the analyst" in order to identify and understand the "rules or grammar of [a] practice under study." To look at populism as a political logic implies identifying how populism interpellates and mobilizes subjects, how it formulates its demands, how it contests existing regimes or underpins power relations (Glynos, 2008: 278). By looking at populism through the prism of logics, our understanding of populism is "formalized": the focus shifts from the contents of populism—what are the demands formulated by populist parties, what is their ideology— to *how* it formulates "those contents—whatever those contents are" (Laclau, 2005b: 33).

The question becomes what is *specific* about how populists formulate their demands. Populism revolves around the antagonistic relation between "the people" and "the elite." Populists bring together different demands and identities in what Laclau and Mouffe (2001) call a "chain of equivalence" that is symbolized by the signifier "the people." What groups different demands and identities together in such a chain—what makes them "equivalent"—is not something positive they have in common, but that they are all frustrated and endangered by "the elite" (see Laclau, 2005a; 2005b; Stavrakakis and Katsambekis, 2014). Populists mobilize and simultaneously stimulate or reinforce dissatisfaction with "the elite" for its (real and/or perceived) frustrating or endangering of a number of demands, interests, or identities (see Stanley, 2008: 98).

In spatial terms, populism is structured around a vertical, down/up axis that refers to power, status and hierarchical position (Dyrberg, 2003; Laclau, 1977; Ostiguy, 2009 and this volume). This down/up structure differentiates populism from other discourses that also revolve around the signifier "the people" but construct "the people" in a different fashion, such as democracy (the people-as-demos), and, most relevant to this chapter, nationalism (the people-as-nation) (Canovan, 2005; Mény and Surel, 2000: 177–222). Populist rhetoric often refers to these down/up identities with the words "the people" and "the elite" but also uses a range of other labels. What is crucial is that populists claim to speak for "the ordinary people," "the little man," "the common man," "the man in the street" as a down-group, and reject "the establishment," "the political caste," "the ruling" as an up-group for not representing "the people" and for endangering its interests.

The demands located in "the people" and the reasons for treating "the elite" as illegitimate vary widely across the variety of populisms: (radical) right or left, agrarian, nationalist, fascist, democratic or authoritarian, progressive or conservative (Jansen, 2011: 82; Taguieff, 1997: 8–10). The definition of populism developed here only aims to grasp the specifically populist dimension of populist parties' politics (and the specifically populist meaning of "the people" in their rhetoric). To study the diversity of populist politics we need to treat the specificity of particular populist politics as the result of the articulation of (a shared) populism with a diverse range of other discourses.

THE ARTICULATION OF POPULISM AND NATIONALISM IN POPULIST POLITICS

The remainder of this chapter discusses how certain populist politics have articulated populism with nationalism.[3] It studies how the nodal points of populism (the people-as-underdog and "the elite") and nationalism (the (people-as-)nation) acquire meaning through the articulation of populism and nationalism with their respective down/up and in/out structure. Looking at the relation between populism and nationalism from a discourse-theoretical perspective it becomes clear that: (1) political projects that articulate nationalism and populism draw on broader and more encompassing structures of meaning; (2) the articulation of nationalism and populism produces a particular structure of meaning in which a multi-layered meaning of "the people" (as underdog and as nation) plays a central role; (3) the resulting structure of meaning will look different depending on the *kind* of nationalism populism is articulated with (e.g. exclusive or inclusive, ethnic or civic); and (4) the resulting structure of meaning will look different depending on what *other* discourses are articulated with the populist-nationalist structure of meaning (e.g. conservatism or socialism).

Populism and the Nation-State

As a consequence of the predominantly national organization of political representation, most populist politics operate within a national context (but not all, as we will see in the section on transnational populism below). They therefore tend to define the people-as-underdog on a national level, even when nationalism does not play a structural role in their political projects.

Nationalism-as-discourse is not limited to what are usually considered "nationalist" politics: radical right politics and sub-state nationalist demands for a sovereign state. It also covers the (more implicit or banal) nationalism that underlies and reproduces existing nation-states and that can also be found in societal spheres from culture to sports (see Billig, 1995). Nationalism is so hegemonic and is so firmly sedimented in our political institutions that most contemporary politics function within a national context, and thus reproduce the tenets of nationalist discourse to at least some extent. Whereas decision-making power has shifted increasingly to supra-national political levels (and to non-elected actors), the nation-state remains the principal context in which citizens' are represented, political parties operate, elections are held, and public debate and contestation is organized. Notwithstanding far-reaching supra-national integration in Europe, for example, Europeans are still mainly represented democratically as members of nation-states. Even the European Parliament is an aggregate of politicians belonging to national parties and elected on a national level.

Populist actors too, and certainly populist *parties*, are usually organized on the level of the nation-state. So, when populists claim to represent the people-as-underdog and demand that politics follow the will of this people-as-underdog, this people-as-underdog is usually, almost by default, defined on the level of the nation-state—whether these parties are nationalist or not. This becomes even clearer when populists enter national governments and especially when their leaders take up function as presidents or as prime ministers and come to represent the nation and the nation-state.

"The elite" also often refers to certain powerful groups within the nation: national politicians, but also intellectuals and artists. But it is, as we will see, much more common for populists to construct an antagonism between the (nationally defined) people-as-underdog and non-national elites. In some cases, the nation in its entirety even comes to be identified as the underdog in opposition to an international or foreign elite.

Populism and Nationalist Demands and Identities

My interest in this chapter is mainly in the articulation of populism and more explicitly nationalist politics that formulate demands about the identity, interests, and sovereignty of the nation. A first group of nationalist demands that has prominently been articulated with populism revolves around the exclusion of certain groups of people from the nation, from the nation-state and from political decision-making power. A second group of nationalist demands that has been formulated in populist terms is about the sovereignty of the nation and its right to its own nation-state, as against larger state structures, colonizing forces, and supra-national political bodies. A final section of this chapter asks whether populism can function beyond the national context. It looks at the possibility of the construction of a people-as-underdog that supersedes national boundaries.

THE ARTICULATION OF EXCLUSIONARY NATIONALISM AND POPULISM

Some of the most significant examples of populist politics have revolved around an exclusionary nationalist rejection of ethnic-cultural diversity. Populist radical right (PRR) parties such as the French Front National (National Front), the Austrian Freiheitliche

Partei Österreichs (Freedom Party of Austria), and the Belgian Vlaams Belang (Flemish Interest) are the prime examples here. But similar articulations of populism and exclusionary nationalism can be found in less radical and even mainstream populist right-wing rhetoric.

The rise of PRR parties was an important trigger for the renewed interest in the concept of populism in Europe. In some cases, these parties have even simply been labeled populist. This misses the point, however, for these parties cannot be understood through the notion of populism alone. Nor even is populism the most important element of their politics. At the core of these parties' projects is not populism but a radical right politics. And the very core of radical right politics is an exclusionary ethnic-cultural nationalism (also labeled nativism) (Mudde, 2007; Rydgren, 2005; 2007).[4] This chapter follows Mudde's (2007) preference for the term populist radical right (and not radical right populist or national-populist, for example). This stresses that PRR parties are a particular and historically specific manifestation of an older and more encompassing radical right tradition. It makes clear that there were and are radical right parties that are not populist (see Mény and Surel, 2000: 12; Mudde, 2007: 24), that PRR parties are first and foremost radical right parties, but equally that populism is vital to our understanding of these parties.

The People-as-Underdog and the Exclusionary Definition of the Nation

That the nodal points of populism acquire meaning through the articulation with exclusionary nationalism becomes clear, firstly, in the fact that the people-as-underdog is a sub-group of the ethnic-culturally defined nation. When PRR parties and other populist exclusionary nationalists claim to speak for the people-as-underdog, they only refer to (what they consider to be) members of the nation and exclude all others. Migrants and their descendants (including those who are national citizens) that in socioeconomic terms might be close to the "ordinary people" for whom they claim to speak are excluded from the category of the people-as-underdog (see Caiani and della Porta, 2011; Laclau, 2005a: 196–8).

Simultaneously, the people-as-underdog is pitted *against* migrants and other national(ist) outgroups. Indeed, PRR politics interpellate ordinary people primarily (but not exclusively) *as* an underdog using exclusionary nationalist arguments. "Ordinary people," it is argued, are the prime victims of multicultural society. They live in poor urban areas with high immigration rates that suffer from "immigrant crime" or "Roma crime." They have lower education rates and lose their jobs to immigrants, or have their already low pensions threatened by the cost of providing asylum to refugees. The socio-economic dimension does play a crucial role here, but is subordinate to and used in the service of nationalism.

The articulation of populism and exclusionary nationalism thus serves to legitimate exclusionary nationalist demands as the representation of the will of the people-as-underdog. This allows PRR parties to fend off criticisms that their exclusionary nationalism is undemocratic and even to claim the signifier democracy. By presenting themselves as the voice of the people-as-underdog and by legitimizing their exclusionary nationalist demands as the will of the (silent) majority, the signifier democracy is turned against the liberal democratic rights of people of foreign descent (see De Cleen and Carpentier, 2011; Mudde and Rovira Kaltwasser, 2012b; Rydgren, 2007).

Against the Multiculturalist and Multicultural Elite

The populist signifier "the elite" too acquires meaning through the articulation with exclusionary nationalism. The PRR's main argument for calling the elite illegitimate is a nationalist one. One of the central claims of these parties has been that the political elite has furthered the rights of foreigners and immigrants to the detriment of the interests of its own nation (Mudde, 2007). "The elite" is argued to not represent and betray "the people" (as both nation and underdog) because of its positions on immigration and multicultural society. This argument is not limited to the political elite, but is also used to criticise artists, intellectuals, journalists, and academics. "The party of the people" that says things as they are, "dares" to speak "unpleasant truths" about multicultural society, and "says what you [the ordinary citizen] think" is opposed to a "politically correct elite" that lives in an "ivory tower."

This "ivory tower" has a socio-economic dimension, but here too this is used to support nationalist arguments. The PRR systematically points to how the political establishment favors foreigners—for example through welfare allocations—and disadvantages and "betrays" its "own" ordinary people. In parallel to the claim that its anti-migration stance represents "what ordinary people think" because it is the ordinary members of the nation who suffer most from multicultural society, the elite's privileged socio-economic status serves to explain why they are so far removed from ordinary people's concerns and fears. They do not live in the neighborhoods that suffer from high immigration. They do not lose their jobs due to immigration. Across all of these arguments against the elite, the nationalist distinction between the nation and its outsides serves as the main explanatory framework, not the socio-economic distinctions within the nation. The ideological dominance of nationalism over any socio-economic concerns also shows in the fact that in contrast to the political elite, the national economic elite is usually not considered to be part of an illegitimate "elite" (except when they speak out against the PRR and thus "support the political elite"). Indeed, national economic elites have often been treated as central to national prosperity.

Whereas exclusionary nationalist populists define the people-as-underdog as a subgroup of the nation, "the elite" includes members of the nation but can also include different kinds of national outgroups. It is helpful here to distinguish between multiculturalism as an ideology and the *multicultural* reality of ethnically and culturally diverse societies.

The *multiculturalist* "elite" members of the ethnic-culturally defined nation still belong to the ethnic-cultural national community defined in an essentialist way. This shows the ideological dominance of nationalism over populism in PRR politics: elite members of the nation remain part of the nation, even when they betray the interests of the nation and their allegiance to the nation is questioned. As part of their rejection of *multicultural* society, exclusionary nationalists have also fiercely rejected members of the elite of the nation-state that are *not* part of the nation. Jews have been prominently rejected as a foreign and cosmopolitan elite that undermines the nation from within the nation-state, but similar arguments have also been used against Muslims and other people of foreign descent. These groups are criticized as foreign even when they are national citizens because for exclusionary nationalists national citizenship does not imply ethnic-cultural belonging. Beyond these "foreign" elites on the level of the nation-state, populists have also fiercely criticized the leaders of other countries and supranational organizations as illegitimate elites, for their multiculturalist and globalist policies, for their breaches of the nation's sovereignty over its state, and for their sheer membership of an international, cosmopolitan elite (see the section on "Populism and the Sovereignty of the Nation over its State").

Populism and Exclusion: Conceptual Clarifications

Before moving on to discussing other articulations of populism and nationalism, let me make two more conceptual reflections about populism that are strongly related to discussions about the PRR and its articulation of populism and exclusionary nationalism.

Some authors have suggested that populism has a *double* vertical structure: upwards between "the people" and "the elite," and downwards between "the (good) people" and foreigners, drug dealers, and other outgroups (Abts and Rummens, 2007: 14; Mény and Surel, 2002: 12). However, the distinction between "the people" and foreigners is a nationalist in/out distinction, not a populist down/up distinction. The in/out distinction between the nation and its outsides does sometimes have a vertical dimension in the sense of racial, national, or cultural superiority. But this is subordinate to the in/out distinction, and of a different nature than the populist distinction between powerless and powerful. The distinction between "the good people" and criminals and other deviants is not a matter of populism either, but part of an authoritarian worldview that excludes and punishes people who deviate from the norm. Populists do not necessarily further authoritarian policies regarding drugs or crime, as certain forms of left-wing populism show. Populists on the right have often presented their authoritarian demands as being what ordinary people want, but this does not make those authoritarian demands inherent to populism.

The conceptual disentanglement of populism and nationalism and the focus on the articulation of the two also helps clarify the distinction between *exclusionary* (or *exclusive*) and *inclusionary* (or *inclusive*) populism. These notions usually refer to the inclusion or exclusion of specific social classes, of specific ethnically and culturally defined groups, as well as of "the elite" (e.g. Jagers and Walgrave, 2007; Mudde and Rovira Kaltwasser, 2012a). However, if only the down/up antagonism between the people-as-underdog and the elite is inherent to populism, then the exclusion of specific socio-economic or ethnic-cultural (or other) groups is not a matter of populism per se. It is the result of the articulation of populism with other discourses (socialism or nationalism for example). Mudde and Rovira Kaltwasser's (2012a) comparison of European and Latin American populism shows that (the most prominently European) exclusionary populisms are exclusionary mainly because of their exclusionary nationalism, with the PRR as the clearest example. The (most prominently Latin American) inclusionary populisms are mainly situated on the left, and are inclusionary due to their focus on equality and on strengthening the political participation of lower classes and excluded groups (e.g. the poor and indigenous groups). Latin American populisms such as those of Chávez in Venezuela and of Morales in Bolivia (Mudde and Rovira Kaltwasser, 2012a), as well as recent European left-wing populist movements like SYRIZA and PODEMOS (Stavrakakis and Katsambekis, 2014: 213; Stavrakakis, 2015) are examples here. As these illustrations clearly show, the articulation of populism with nationalism does not *necessarily* lead to exclusionary populism. But when populism is exclusionary it *is* usually because it is articulated with exclusionary nationalism.

What clouds this distinction is that both inclusionary left-wing populists and exclusionary (right-wing) nationalist populists, according to Mudde and Rovira Kaltwasser (2012a: 165), "exclude" "the elite." This would make populisms inherently exclusionary, at least partly, even the ones they label inclusionary populisms. The question is whether it is very helpful to label both the exclusion of national outgroups (or the exclusion of religious minorities or LGBT populations for that matter) *and* the populist exclusion of "the elite" a matter of "exclusion." Antagonistic seems a better term for the relation between people-as-underdog and "elite" in populism. The antagonism between the people-as-underdog and "the elite" does symbolically exclude "the elite" from the definition of the people-as-underdog. But in contrast to exclusionary nationalism's exclusion of certain groups of people from political participation (political exclusion) and from access to state resources (material exclusion) because of their ethnic-cultural background, the antagonism between the people-as-underdog and the elite does not *in itself* exclude "the elite" from the demos and from access to state resources (see Filc, 2010 and Mudde and Rovira Kaltwasser, 2012a on the material, political, and symbolic dimension of inclusion/exclusion).

Certain forms of populism do indeed threaten certain (formerly) powerful groups with exclusion. But this is not inherent to the populist antagonism between the people-as-underdog and "the elite." It is only through the articulation with other discourses that populism becomes exclusionary in the political and material sense. This is not to say that there are no questions to be asked about the (liberal) democratic character of populism per se (e.g. Arditi, 2007; Mény and Surel, 2002; Mudde and Rovira Kaltwasser, 2012b). But it does mean that the potential populist threat to democracy is of a different character than the exclusionary nationalist threat to democracy.

Populism and the Sovereignty of the Nation over its State

Let me now turn to a second set of nationalist demands that have frequently been formulated in populist terms: demands for the autonomy, independence, and sovereignty of nations over their territory. Here too, the populist signifiers "the people" and "the elite" acquire meaning through their articulation with nationalism. The people-as-underdog becomes equated with the nation (see Laclau, 2005a: 196–8), and "the elite" is opposed to the nation and its interests.

The articulation between populism and demands for national self- determination has a long history (Canovan, 2005: 45; Hermet, 1997). Hermet (1997; also 2001) argues that, since the eighteenth century, long before the term populism even existed, struggles for national autonomy have been frequently articulated with populism. This was especially so in ethnic-cultural nationalisms that legitimated their claims for autonomy and sovereignty by locating an authentic national identity in the ordinary people, and opposing this to the bourgeois culture of liberal and cosmopolitan elites that were disconnected from national culture. The fact that ethnic-cultural nationalisms tend to refer to "the people" (*Volk* in German) rather than to "nation" captures this nationalist-populist articulation, with "the people" referring both to the ordinary people/classes and to the ethnic-culturally defined national group (Hermet, 1997; Rémi-Giraud, 1996).

This articulation could be found in German nationalism, as well as in Eastern and Central European ethnic-cultural nationalist movements striving for autonomy from large empires (e.g. Croatia and Czechoslovakia from the Austro-Hungarian empire, Poland and the Baltic states from Russia), and have been used ever since by nationalist movements and parties all over the world. This includes sub-state nationalisms that strive for autonomy or independence from (what they consider) multi-national states (e.g. Flemish nationalism in Belgium, Scottish nationalism in the UK), and movements that strive to become independent from colonizing powers and occupying forces in Africa, Asia, and elsewhere.[5]

Such populist-nationalist arguments are not limited to the struggles of "nations without states" either. A very similar articulation of nationalism and populism also structures the resistance against supra-national politics by nationalists in established nation-states. Here too, the interests of the people-as-underdog and the interests of the nation are equated and opposed to the interests of supra-national elites. The populist-nationalist argument used to *fight for* popular-national sovereignty from larger state structures or foreign rulers is used here to *resist* the shift of political power to supra-national bodies, or to reclaim power, as the case of Brexit illustrates.

On the elite end of this populist-nationalist antagonism there are both national and foreign elites. The former are the national elites that "collaborate" with multinational states that go against the interest of the own nation (e.g. the Flemish political elite in Belgium) or collaborate with colonizing forces (e.g. the national elites working with the

British and the French in their many former colonies), and the national elites that fail to defend the nation's interest on a supra-national level or "collaborate" with such forces on a national level (e.g. the national politicians "collaborating" with the European institutions). These national elites remain part of the nation, however, through their ethnic-cultural identity.

This is not the case for foreign elites. Foreign elites are the elites of the dominant nation in multinational states (e.g. the Francophone political elite in Belgium), the colonizers, and the non-national elites that use supra-national politics to go against the sovereignty of the nation. In the racist and exclusionary nationalist politics discussed above, this populist-nationalist articulation is also used to exclude minorities as "enemies within" of both the people-as-underdog and of the nation. An example is the anti-Semitic rhetoric about the Jews as a cosmopolitan and alien elite governing the country (also through their ties with Jews around the world).

Populist political movements and parties on both the left and the right have constructed such popular-national versus elitist-supra-national antagonisms. On the left, this articulation of popular and national interests has been most prominent in the resistance against neoliberal policies "imposed" by supra-national or foreign elites (in collaboration with national elites) and going against national sovereignty. This becomes clear in left-wing populist-nationalist resistance against the United States, the International Monetary Fund, and the World Bank in Venezuela, Argentina, Bolivia, and other Latin American countries under left-wing rule (Rovira Kaltwasser, 2014a: 207–8; 2014b). Parties such as SYRIZA (Greece) and PODEMOS (Spain) have used a similar articulation to reject austerity measures "imposed" by European and other supra-national institutions in the wake of the financial crisis that started in the late 2000s (see Stavrakakis and Katsambekis, 2014; Stavrakakis, 2015; also March, 2011). In some cases, this populist-nationalist resistance against policies imposed by supra-national European institutions has also led to fierce criticisms of individual European countries (mainly Germany) as *foreign* powers, including even parallels to the Nazi occupation of Greece. Although focused on the socio-economic interests of the people-as-underdog and the nation, left-wing populist-nationalist articulations also appeal to national (cultural) identity as well as to for example "the pride" of the nation in (its attempts at) re-establishing national sovereignty over economic policy (see Halikiopoulou et al., 2012).

Matters of national cultural identity have been far more prominent on the right, where they have often been central in the resistance against foreign and supra-national (as well as national) elites. For example, in populist right-wing politics—in its radical and less radical forms—the antagonism has mainly revolved around the defence of the popular-national against multiculturalist and globalist policies imposed "from above" that threaten the identity, culture, and economic interests of the nation. In Europe, especially European institutions are accused of undermining national identity and interests through lenient migration policies as well as through furthering European integration and globalization. Economic issues do play an important role here, but whereas on the left this is a matter of opposing neoliberalism, on the right the struggle is not at root one between opposing economic models. It is mainly globalization, the free movement of workers, and the loss of national (economic and other) decision-making power per se that is resisted. Indeed, the populist right has also defended the free market economy in nationalist-populist terms. In the US, the Tea Party as well as Donald Trump and other right-wing Republicans, for example, have opposed all kinds of (national and) international government interventions as well as NGOs as elitist attacks on American identity (Rovira Kaltwasser, 2014a: 208). Moral and ethical demands too have been formulated in populist-nationalist terms. The Tea Party and other populist (radical) right actors have opposed foreign and supra-national elites for their cosmopolitanism and for imposing progressive ("liberal" in the US sense of the term) measures regarding issues such as gay rights, gender relations, and abortion.

Transnational Populism?

The prominence and strength of the articulations between nationalism and populism leads to the question of whether populism is necessarily nationalist, or at least national.[6] Or to put it differently: is a transnational populism possible? So far, there has been very little true conceptual reflection on what could be called transnational populism (but see for example Gerbaudo, 2014; Pelfini, 2014). Theoretically, populism is certainly not necessarily national or nationalist. All that is needed to speak of transnational populism is a politics that discursively constructs and claims to represent a transnational people-as-underdog. However, whereas populism has frequently opposed a nationally defined people-as-underdog to supra-national and international *elites*, the construction of a transnational *people-as-underdog* has been far less common and straightforward.

There are two dimensions to transnational populism, the second more profoundly transnational than the first. A first dimension is the international cooperation between nationally organized populist parties and movements. Examples are the cooperation between left-wing populist leaders in Latin America (concretized for example in the foundation of the Bank of the South as an alternative to the World Bank and the International Monetary Fund), and the (difficult and partial) formation of political groups in the European Parliament by PRR parties. This is perhaps best labeled *inter-national* rather than *transnational* populism: it is more about the *inter*-national ties *between* nationally organized populisms (that revolve around nationally defined people-as-underdogs) than about a truly *trans*-national politics *across* national contexts. A truly transnational populism is more profoundly transnational in that it constructs a transnational people-as-underdog as a political subject that *supersedes* the boundaries of the nation-state, rather than merely *linking up* national people-as-underdogs. In a reflection on "global populism," Pelfini (2014: 199) speaks of the Occupy Movement and the *indignados* as "transnational connections of protests, cyberpolitics, and mass mobilizations, claiming for more democracy and against international financial agents" (see also Gerbaudo, 2014; Husted, 2015). The Occupy Movement's claim to represent the "99 percent" against the "1 percent" does indeed have the potential to serve as a transnational populist claim to represent a transnational people-as-underdog (but this has largely remained a potential).

The distinction between international and transnational populism is a matter of degree: international populisms do create a transnational people-as-underdog, and transnational populisms bring together nationally organized political actors and nationally defined people-as-underdogs. Let me look at these two arguments in some more detail.

When populisms in different countries revolve around similar antagonisms between the people-as-underdog and the same international, transnational, and foreign elites (and similar national elites), the similarities and shared interests between nationally defined people-as-underdogs are accentuated and a transnational people is constructed *to some extent*. This is true even without actual cooperation between organizations, but is of course strengthened when nationally organized populists work together. The transnational people-as-underdog can have a socioeconomic basis, as when left-wing populisms oppose similar national economic and political elites and the same transnational (the IMF, the World Bank, the European Union, or even "neoliberalism") and foreign (e.g. the US government) elites. The collaboration between left-wing Latin American populists is a case in point here. But even when "the people" is defined as underdog on the basis of ethnic-culturally nationalist arguments, a transnational people-as-underdog does appear to some extent. For example, PRR parties across Europe have constructed an antagonism between ordinary people who resist multiculturalism and cherish their national identity, and national and European elites that are undermining national identity through lenient integration and migration policies. Especially when these parties actually cooperate on a European level, and certainly when their European political representatives speak for the entire political group (and thus for all the nations and people-as-underdogs the group claims to represent) a claim towards the representation of a transnational people-as-underdog is made.

To different degrees, what appears through the international collaboration between populists is a sort of *meta*-populism. A populist chain of equivalence between populisms is constructed: different populisms with their specificities are brought together through the opposition to common international, transnational, or foreign elites (and to similar national elites). Laclau's remark that the articulation of demands and identities in a chain of equivalence does not eliminate the particularity of each of the articulated demands—that articulation "can weaken, but not domesticate differences" (Laclau, 2005a: 79)—is helpful here. It allows us to understand how the construction of an international or even transnational populism (with a transnational people against a transnational elite) is not in contradiction with the continued existence of nationally organized populisms (with nationally defined peoples against national and transnational elites). Indeed, in the case of international cooperation between strongly national*ist* populisms, it is exactly the shared demands for national particularity of all the different national(ist) populisms in opposition to the same elites that are said to threaten these national particularities that will make up the meta-populist chain of equivalence. At the same time, of course, the exclusionary nationalist character of PRR parties also limits their cooperation and the construction of a truly transnational people-as-underdog.

This is a tension that other populist movements suffer from less, so that a truly transnational populism (with a truly transnational people-as-underdog) is more likely to come from elsewhere than from exclusionary nationalists. The left seems the most obvious candidate here. International socialist and communist collaborations like the Communist International with their appeals for "Workers of the World" to unite are an obvious reference. But whereas the proletariat does indeed transcend the boundaries of the nation-state, the focus on class struggle hindered the development of a broader populist chain of equivalence symbolized by the people-as-underdog. And despite the internationalist rhetoric, the national focus of the participating parties and movements often stood in the way of a truly transnational politics (March, 2011: 149–66).

Indeed, even for populisms that are not nationalist or to whom nationalism is but one demand among many, the nation-state remains crucial. In a world in which political representation is still strongly organized on the level of nation-states, the construction of a transnational populism almost inevitably depends on nationally organized movements; and therefore on the interpellation of nationally defined people-as-underdogs (and also, but less so, on nationally defined elites). With no political institutions directly representing a transnational demos it is not easy to construct and claim to represent a transnational people-as-underdog (see Gerbaudo, 2014; Pelfini, 2014: 208). This is especially true for political parties. For political movements that do not strive to operate and claim power within existing democratic political institutions, it might be easier to construct a more truly transnational people-as-underdog beyond the context of national democracies, with forms of representation that go beyond the party political and traditional democratic institutions. But this raises questions as to how they are going to use that representational claim to yield actual influence on decision-making, be it via political institutions or perhaps otherwise.

A number of attempts at forging a European-wide left-wing project are interesting in this respect, as some of them are built around populist demands for the "democratization" of European institutions (see March, 2011: 155–66). For example, Yannis Varoufakis (former Greek Finance Minister in the SYRIZA government that entered power in 2015) has urged that it is only through the "democratization" of what he considers the thoroughly undemocratic European institutions that left-wing forces would ever stand a chance against "those people in Brussels." To this end, in 2015, he founded the "pan-European platform" (called DiEM25, Democracy in Europe Movement 2025) with a strong transnational character, a "coalition of citizens," not a "coalition of parties," with the idea "not to replicate national politics" (Varoufakis and Sakalis, 2015). A crucial question, for our purposes here, is whether the representation of citizens would still be supranational (indirect, via national representation) or truly transnational. Would citizens be represented as national citizens or as European citizens, or as some combination of both? Next to such attempts at "democratizing" existing supra-national structures, transnational populist politics can also aim to create new spaces for politics. Such spaces can range from the very local to the regional and the global, can be overlapping, and can compete with each other and with existing political institutions on different levels.

International and transnational populisms, we have seen, can continue to simultaneously construct a nationally defined people-as-underdog. But there is more. International or transnational populist resistance against a shared foreign or transnational elite has often gone hand in hand with the construction of a pan-national or regional identity. Such pan-nationalist identities, in fact, show strong similarities with nationalism as they too are based on shared territory and history, and constructed through the opposition to outgroups. What we see here is the articulation of pan-nationalism or regionalism and populism. The pan-Americanism associated with Chávez's Bolivarianismo, for example, constructs a Latin American identity, mainly in opposition to the "imperialist" US and international financial institutions as foreign elites (Mudde and Rovira Kaltwasser, 2012a: 162). And in Europe, not only do different PRR parties share a strong and exclusionary nationalism, but many of these parties simultaneously present themselves as defenders of European identity and civilization against immigration and "Islamization" (through new Islamic immigrants and existing Muslim populations). This is articulated with a populist rejection of the European elites "promoting" immigration and "furthering" Islamization. International and transnational populism, it appears, is not necessarily incongruous with the thorough articulation between populism and nationalism. And it points to the articulation of populism with politics that revolve around logics very similar to nationalism, only on a larger scale.

CONCLUSION

This chapter started with a reflection on the conceptual confusion resulting from the many empirical and conceptual ties between populism and nationalism. Throughout the chapter it has become clear that populism and nationalism have been strongly articulated indeed. The chapter has provided insight into the various articulations of populism and nationalism by distinguishing between populist politics and nationalist politics as revolving, respectively, around the claim to represent the people-as-underdog, constructed through a down/up antagonism between the people-as-underdog and the elite, and the claim to represent the nation, constructed through the in/out distinction between the nation and its outgroups. It is through this clear conceptual distinction that the intricate and complex conceptual and empirical relations between populism and nationalism can be grasped.

Clearly distinguishing populism and nationalism as distinct discourses might also help us to critically evaluate contemporary debates about populism and uses of the notion of populism. By focusing attention on the populist dimension of populist forms of exclusionary nationalism, the actual roots of the democratic problems posed by such politics are missed. Moreover, this has given populism a worse name than it deserves. Quite some of the contemporary critiques of populism are actually critiques of (exclusionary) nationalism. These critiques denounce populism not only for the potential threats of populism per se to liberal democracy, but also for sins that are not in fact populist (but are "committed" by some populists). Because the populist logic can be used to articulate a wide range of political demands—from racist and exclusionary demands to demands for workers' rights and for the democratization of democratic as well as undemocratic political systems—the populist character of a particular politics is insufficient not only as a basis for understanding that politics but also for evaluating it.

Whilst the use of the notion of populism in politics and journalism will come and go with the ebbs and flows of political debate, the concept of populism promises to retain its value for political analysis (even if it will certainly ebb and flow along with political reality). The concept of populism is crucial for understanding our political reality, but only if we use it to grasp one particular aspect of that political reality, and refrain from imprecision and from overloading the concept with more and broader meanings than it can bear. By looking at populism and nationalism as distinct but often closely articulated discourses, this chapter, I hope, has contributed to further strengthening the concept of populism for academic usage. A clearer distinction between populism and nationalism (and other concepts) certainly would not harm the quality of political debate either, but I do not hold very high hopes for that to happen.

NOTES

1   This chapter first defines nationalism and populism and then discusses the articulations of the two, but the conceptual distinction between nationalism and populism is actually originally the result of an iterative back-and-forth process between theory and empirical analysis in an analysis of populist radical right politics in Belgium (see De Cleen, 2009; De Cleen and Carpentier, 2010; De Cleen, 2013; 2015).

2   Nodal points are the "privileged discursive points that partially fix meaning within signifying chains" (Torfing, 1999: 98) and around which other signifiers within the discourse acquire their meaning (Laclau and Mouffe, 2001: 112).

3   This discourse-theoretical focus on the articulation of populism and nationalism is not very far removed from the view of populism as a "thin ideology" that is combined with full ideologies such as conservatism or socialism.

4   Next to nationalism and populism, the other central ideological components of PRR politics are authoritarianism (Mudde, 2007; Rydgren, 2007) and conservatism (Betz and Johnson, 2004; Taggart, 2004).

5   The categories of sub-state nationalism and decolonization struggle partly overlap, of course, with nationalist struggles for independence being waged in the name of ethnic groups for part of much larger colonial territories. Moreover, sub-state nationalist parties have sometimes labeled as colonizers (the elite of) the "multinational" state they contest.

6   I would like to thank Benjamin Moffitt for valuable input on the idea of transnational populism.

References

Abts, Koen and Stefan Rummens. 2007. "Populism versus democracy," *Political Studies*, 55(2): 405–24.

Akkerman, Tjitske. 2003. "Populism and democracy: challenge or pathology?," *Acta Politica*, 38: 147–59.

Anderson, Benedict. 2006. *Imagined Communities: Reflections on the Origin and Spread of Nationalism*, rev. and ext. edn. London: Verso.

Arditi, Benjamin. 2007. *Politics on the Edges of Liberalism: Difference, Populism, Revolution, Agitation*. Edinburgh: Edinburgh University Press.

Balibar, Etienne. 1989. "Racism as universalism," *New political science*, 8(1–2): 9–22.

Betz, Hans-Georg and Carol Johnson. 2004. "Against the current—stemming the tide: the nostalgic ideology of the contemporary radical populist right," *Journal of Political Ideologies*, 9(3): 311–27.

Bhabha, Homi K. (ed.). 1990. *Nation and Narration*. London: Routledge.

Billig, Michael. 1995. *Banal Nationalism*. London: Sage.

Caiani, Manuela and Donatella della Porta. 2011. "The elitist populism of the extreme right: a frame analysis of extreme right-wing discourses in Italy and Germany," *Acta Politica*, 46(2): 180–202.

Canovan, Margaret. 2002. "Taking politics to the people: populism as the ideology of democracy," in Yves Mény and Yves Surel (eds), *Democracies and the Populist Challenge*. Basingstoke: Palgrave Macmillan, 25–44.

Canovan, Margaret. 2005. *The People*. Cambridge: Polity Press.

Carpentier, Nico and Benjamin De Cleen. 2007. "Bringing discourse theory into media studies," *Journal of Language and Politics*, 6(2): 265–93.

Day, Graham and Andrew Thompson. 2004. *Theorizing Nationalism*. Basingstoke and New York: Palgrave Macmillan.

De Cleen, Benjamin. 2009. "Popular music against extreme right populism," *International Journal of Cultural Studies*, 12(6): 577–95.

De Cleen, Benjamin. 2013. "The Vlaams Blok/Belang versus the Flemish city theatres: an analysis of populist radical right rhetoric about culture," in Majid Khosravinik, Birgitte Mral, and Ruth Wodak (eds), *Right-Wing Populism in Europe: Politics and Discourse*. London: Bloomsbury Academic, 209–22.

De Cleen, Benjamin. 2015. "'Flemish friends, let us separate!': the discursive struggle for Flemish nationalist civil society in the media," *Javnost—The Public*, 22(1): 37–54.

De Cleen, Benjamin and Nico Carpentier. 2010. "Contesting extreme right populism through popular culture: the Vlaams Belang and the 0110 concerts in Belgium," *Social Semiotics*, 20(2): 175–96.

Dyrberg, Torben Bech. 2003. "Right/left in context of new political frontiers: what's radical politics today?," *Journal of Language and Politics*, 2(2): 339–42.

Dyrberg, Torben Bech. 2006. "Radical and plural democracy: in defence of right/left and public reason," in Lars Tønder and Lasse Thomassen (eds), *Radical Democracy: Politics between Abundance and Lack*. Manchester: Manchester University Press, 167–84.

Filc, Dani. 2010. *The Political Right in Israel: Different Faces of Jewish Populism*. London: Routledge.

Freeden, Michael. 1998. "Is nationalism a distinct ideology?," *Political Studies*, 46(4): 748–65.

Gerbaudo, Paulo. 2014. "The 'movements of the squares' and the contested resurgence of the 'sovereign people' in contemporary protest culture," Working paper available at SSRN: http://ssrn.com/abstract=2439359.

Glynos, Jason. 2008. "Ideological fantasy at work," *Journal of Political Ideologies*, 13(3): 275–96.

Glynos, Jason and David Howarth. 2007. *Logics of Critical Explanation in Social and Political Theory*. London and New York: Routledge.

Greenfeld, Liah. 1992. *Nationalism: Five Roads to Modernity*. Cambridge: Harvard University Press.

Halikiopoulou, Daphne, Kyriaki Nanou, and Sofia Vasilopoulou. 2012. "The paradox of nationalism: the common denominator of radical right and radical left Euroscepticism," *European Journal of Political Research*, 51(4): 504–39.

Hermet, Guy. 1997. "Populisme et nationalisme," *Vingtième Siècle, Revue d'Histoire*, 56(1): 34–47.

Hermet, Guy. 2001. *Les populismes dans le monde*. Paris: Fayard.

Husted, Emil. 2015. "From participation to amplification: exploring Occupy Wall Street's transition into an online populist movement," in Julie Uldam and Anne Vestergaard (eds), *Civic Engagement and Social Media*. Basingstoke: Palgrave Macmillan, 153–73.

Jagers, Jan and Stefaan Walgrave. 2007. "Populism as political communication style: an empirical study of political parties' discourse in Belgium," *European Journal of Political Research*, 46(3): 319–45.

Jansen, Robert S. 2011. "Populist mobilization: a new theoretical approach to populism," *Sociological Theory*, 29(2): 75–96.

Jenkins, Brian and Spiros A. Sofos. 1996. "Nation and nationalism in contemporary Europe: a theoretical perspective," in Brian Jenkins and Spiros A. Sofos (eds), *Nation and Identity in Contemporary Europe*. London and New York: Routledge, 9–32.

Kazin, Michael. 1995. *The Populist Persuasion*. Ithaca and London: Cornell University Press.

Laclau, Ernesto. 1977. *Politics and Ideology in Marxist Theory: Capitalism, Fascism, Populism*. London: New Left Books.

Laclau, Ernesto. 1990. *New Reflections on the Revolution of Our Time*. London: Verso.

Laclau, Ernesto. 2005a. *On Populist Reason*. London: Verso.

Laclau, Ernesto. 2005b. "Populism: what's in a name?," in Francisco Panizza (ed.), *Populism and the Mirror of Democracy*. London: Verso, 32–49.

Laclau, Ernesto and Chantal Mouffe. 2001. *Hegemony and Socialist Strategy*, 2nd edn. London: Verso.

March, Luke. 2011. *Radical Left Parties in Europe*. London: Routledge.

Mény, Yves and Yves Surel. 2000. *Par le peuple, pour le peuple: le populisme et les démocraties*. Paris: Fayard, 2000.

Mény, Yves and Yves Surel (eds). 2002. *Democracies and the Populist Challenge*. Houndmills: Palgrave Macmillan.

Moffitt, Benjamin and Simon Tormey. 2014. "Rethinking populism: politics, mediatisation and political style," *Political Studies*, 62: 381–97.

Mudde, Cas. 2007. *Populist Radical Right Parties in Europe*. Cambridge: Cambridge University Press.

Mudde, Cas and Cristóbal Rovira Kaltwasser. 2012a. "Exclusionary vs. inclusionary populism: comparing contemporary Europe and Latin America," *Government and Opposition*, 48(2): 147–74.

Mudde, Cas and Cristóbal Rovira Kaltwasser (eds). 2012b. *Populism in Europe and the Americas: Threat or Corrective to Democracy?* New York: Cambridge University Press.

Ostiguy, Pierre. 2009. "The high-low political divide: rethinking populism and anti-populism," Kellogg Institute Committee on Concepts and Methods Working Paper Series 360. http://nd.edu/~kellogg/publications/workingpapers/WPS/360.pdf.

Pelfini, Alejandro. 2014. "Megatrend global populism? From South America to the Occupy movement," in Alexander Lenger and Florian Schumacher (eds), *Understanding the Dynamics of Global Inequality*. New York: Springer, 199–221.

Rémi-Giraud, Sylvianne and Pierre Rétat (eds). 1996. *Les mots de la nation*. Lyon: Presses Universitaires de Lyon.

Rovira Kaltwasser, Cristóbal. 2014a. "Explaining the emergence of populism in Europe and the Americas," in Carlos de la Torre (ed.), *The Promise and Perils of Populism: Global Perspectives*. Lexington: University Press of Kentucky, 189–228.

Rovira Kaltwasser, Cristóbal. 2014b. "Latin American populism: some conceptual and normative lessons," *Constellations*, 21(4): 494–504.

Rydgren, Jens. 2005. "Is extreme right-wing populism contagious? Explaining the emergence of a new party family," *European Journal of Political Research*, 44(3): 413–37.

Rydgren, Jens. 2007. "The sociology of the radical right," *Annual Review of Sociology*, 33: 241–62.

Segal, Daniel A. and Richard Handler. 2006. "Cultural approaches to nationalism," in Gerard Delanty and Krishan Kumar (eds), *The Sage Handbook of Nations and Nationalism*. London, Thousand Oaks, and New Delhi: Sage, 57–65.

Stanley, Ben. 2008. "The thin ideology of populism," *Journal of Political Ideologies*, 13(1): 95–110.

Stavrakakis, Yannis. 2004. "Antinomies of formalism: Laclau's theory of populism and the lessons from religious populism in Greece," *Journal of Political Ideologies*, 9(3): 253–67.

Stavrakakis, Yannis. 2005. "Religion and populism in contemporary Greece," in Franciso Panizza (ed.), *Populism and the Mirror of Democracy*. London: Verso, 224–49.

Stavrakakis, Yannis. 2015. "Populism in power: Syriza's challenge to Europe," *Juncture*, 21(4): 273–80.

Stavrakakis, Yannis and Giorgios Katsambekis. 2014. "Left-wing populism in the European periphery: the case of Syriza," *Journal of Political Ideologies*, 19(2): 119–42.

Stewart, Angus. 1969. "The social roots," in Ghita Ionescu and Ernest Gellner (eds), *Populism: Its Meanings and National Characteristics*. London: Weidenfeld and Nicholson, 180–95.

Sutherland, Claire. 2005. "Nation-building through discourse theory," *Nations and Nationalism*, 11(2): 185–202.

Taggart, Paul. 2004. "Populism and representative politics in contemporary Europe," *Journal of Political Ideologies*, 9(3): 269–88.

Taguieff, Pierre-André. 1997. "Le populisme et la science politique du mirage conceptuel aux vrais problèmes," *Vingtième Siècle, Revue d'Histoire*, 56: 4–33.

Torfing, Jakob. 1999. *New Theories of Discourse: Laclau, Mouffe and Žižek*. Oxford: Blackwell.

Varoufakis, Yannis and Alex Sakalis. 2015. "'One very simple, but radical, idea: to democratise Europe': an interview with Yanis Varoufakis," *Open Democracy*, October 25. https://www.opendemocracy.net/can-europe-make-it/yanis-varoufakis-alex-sakalis/one-very-simple-but-radical-idea-to-democratise-eur.

Vincent, Andrew. 2002. *Nationalism and Particularity*. Cambridge: Cambridge University Press.

Wodak, Ruth, Rudolf de Cillia, Martin Reisigl, and Karin Liebhart. 2009. *The Discursive Construction of National Identity*, 2nd edn. Edinburgh: Edinburgh University Press.

CHAPTER 19

....

POPULISM AND FASCISM

....

ROGER EATWELL

INTRODUCTION

....

OF all the major "-isms," fascism and populism are the most elusive.[1] This is partly because they have rarely been used as terms of self-reference, which creates a major problem in identifying cases on which to build models. Moreover, the terms are often used pejoratively: thus "populists" are denounced as "demagogic" and/or "unprincipled," "fascists" as "authoritarian" and/or "racist," and so on. As a result, many academics have been unwilling to discern either a populist or fascist "family" of parties/regimes, or have seen them primarily in terms of stylistic features, such as the fascist paramilitary party and the near-ubiquitous populist charismatic leader (Eatwell, 2017).

Attempts to identify generic forms have typically taken socio-psychological and socio-economic approaches. An influential interpretation of the US populist tradition claims that it exhibits a "paranoid style" based on anger, exaggeration, and fear of elite conspiracies (Hofstadter, 1964). However, supporters of the People's Party at the turn of the twentieth century were largely correct in attributing sweeping powers to their plutocratic enemies, while growing inequalities in the new millennium have similarly raised legitimate fears. A common interpretation of contemporary populism in established democracies has identified its core supporters as the "losers of modernization" (Betz and Immerfall, 1998). Certainly Donald Trump's 2016 American presidential campaign gathered some support from this enraged group, but supporters of the Tea Party were characterized by their social normality and tendency to come from higher income groups (Skocpol and Williamson, 2013) and Trump's constituency was not simply "angry white men." Thus even in one country, populism should not be reduced to pathologies and/or specific social groups.

A common Marxisant approach, which has influenced others, has identified an economically and politically threatened middle class as fascism's core supporters (Lipset, 1960). However, in Germany, where the empirical evidence is best as a result of extensive elections before Adolf Hitler became Chancellor, the Nazis' vote was relatively young and broad-based. Supporters of this catchall *Volkspartei* were attracted by economic and welfare policies targeted at different socio-economic groups, as well as affective nationalist and quasi-religious motivations. Thus the common claim that early Peronism in Argentina was not fascist because its support was based on the working class (Germani, 1978) employs out-dated comparative historical sociology.

Similarly structural-development theories provide weak grounds on which to base models. Fascism has been seen as a form of "developmental dictatorship" in which the agricultural elite comes together with a new industrial one to control rising working-class power, but the main inter-war fascist movements in Europe emerged in countries with very different levels of economic development. Germany's Gross Domestic Product was second globally to the US, whereas Romania was a largely rural economy. Moreover, the developmental approach diverts attention from the fact that the rise of fascism differed in important ways across countries. In Italy Fascism took off electorally in the rural parts of the more industrialized north, whereas in Hungary it was more urban-based. Furthermore, the developmental approach does not explain the specificity of fascist authoritarianism, which was notably different to pre-war autocracies and other forms which emerged after 1918 in countries such as Portugal (though these often adapted aspects of fascism, especially its style, in an attempt to appear dynamic and popular).

There has been a growing willingness in recent decades to identify a generic fascist ideology (Eatwell, 1992; 2013a), where ideology is understood as a map of the inter-relationship of key conceptual features (Freeden, 1996). One influential approach holds that fascism is a form a palingenetic (rebirth) ultra-nationalism, though it confusingly adds "populist" to this Weberian ideal type (Griffin, 1991: 26). There has been a similar ideological "turn" in populist studies, though with greater emphasis placed on variations such as left- and right-wing economic differences and weaker party organization in Latin America compared to Europe (Mudde and Rovira Kaltwasser, 2012; Taggart, 2000). This approach views populism as a "thin" ideology, which can combine with other ideologies to produce very different visions.

The main focus of this chapter is the neglected question of how to differentiate fascism from populism in terms of ideology. Broadly in line with Mudde's approach in this volume, I hold that populism is a thin ideology combining three discourses: (1) the unique defence of the *plain people* (though not necessarily an ethnically or morally pure one); (2) hostility to corrupt and *self-serving elites* who deprive the people of their legitimate voice (though distinctions may be made between elites); and (3) the goal of producing a social and political system which allows the *popular will* to prevail (for example, through referendums). However, it is also important to consider praxis. Populists tend to rouse the people by a variety of rhetorical and stylistic devices, including authoritarian charismatic leaders, Manichean demonization, slipperiness on policy issues, and the use of popular language. These can both pose threats to liberal democracy and help to integrate people who feel divorced from the "system," as populism in practice can be Janus-faced.

I hold that fascism is a syncretic, utopian ideology that combines three different discourses. These are: (1) the forging of a *holistic nation* in order to survive internal and external threats (though its geopolitical vision does not necessarily involve expansion); (2) the need for a dynamic new elite to foster a communal and martial *new man* (devoid of bourgeois individualism); and (3) the creation of a neither capitalist nor communist *third way authoritarian state* (which involves government for, but not by, the people). Again, it is important to consider praxis in movements that can openly embrace the "big lie," including playing down radicalism and stressing anti-Marxism in pursuit of Establishment support. The fascist style borrowed from populism, though the paramilitarism of inter-war parties was not typical of populism. After 1945, fascism became a pariah, which led keepers of the flame to adopt abeyance tactics. These included entryism into other parties and propaganda which sought to hide fascist influences, a combination which can be seen in the French National Front (FN) with its varying mix of esoteric propaganda and largely populist tropes.

In the first two sections that follow, I expand on these different conceptualizations, discussing "foundational" examples of populism and fascism in Europe and the US. The triadic matrices derived from these cases are then applied in a third section to select case studies about which there has been notable classificatory debate in Latin America, the US, and Europe.

It is important to stress that this does not imply an immutable, essentialist approach to either fascism or populism, as there has been diachronic and synchronic variation both nationally and transnationally. It is also important to note reflexive hybridity (Eatwell, 2014), in which movements and regimes have consciously borrowed aspects from others—especially at times when ideologies seem in the ascendant, as fascism was in the inter-war era and populism has been more recently. Indeed, the common neat distinction in turn-of-the-millennium Europe between an old, declining fascist-inspired right and a rising, new populist radical right (Ignazi, 2003; Mudde, 2007) fails to bring out important similarities in some cases.

CONCEPTUALIZING FOUNDATIONAL POPULISM

Although the term "populist" can be traced back to *populares* (courting the people) Senators in Ancient Rome, the first political movements emerged during the late nineteenth century. However, some of the movements that have been portrayed as progenitors of modern populism did not develop a truly populist ideology. It was only with the coming of Boulangism in France and the American People's Party, which was also known as the Populist Party, that the foundational forms of populism can fully be discerned. In particular, it was during this era that terms such as "people" and "popular sovereignty" became a major part of the vocabulary of insurgent political movements that courted mass support among an expanding electorate by claiming that they uniquely embodied their interests (which in turn reinforced fears among liberals as well as conservatives about the rise of the irrational and/or socialistic masses).

The Russian *narodniks* (going to the people) are often seen as the first populist movement. The goal of these urban intellectuals was the creation of a new order based on mythologized peasant institutions and values, which were contrasted with growing capitalist individualism and materialism. However, these proselytizing outsiders soon found that the rural people were not only illiterate, but also deeply attached to the Orthodox Church and autocratic Tsarist regime (though its aristocratic elite was seen as distant from the people). As a result, many *narodniks* turned to forms of vanguard socialism.

Another commonly identified early form of populism—and for some, a seminal precursor of Nazism (Mosse, 1981)—is the German *Völkisch* movement (*Volk* can connote people, nation, race, and folk). Its most important strand was an anti-modern, Romantic celebration of traditional rural life, which was at odds with the syncretic modernist side of fascism. It celebrated a transcendental conception of the deep-rooted, ethnic nature of the German nation. *Völkisch* thought held that the soul was determined by landscape, which meant that Jews were seen as aliens who were arid progenitors of internationalist liberal rationalism (and later communism). It was largely a top-down movement that lacked populism's emphasis on people power or fascist mass organization, though it could be anti-elitist in its attacks on capitalism and Jews.

A pioneering political party that is often seen as populist is Karl Lueger's Austrian Christian Social Party, an early example of the attempt to stem the rise of socialism through a mixture of nationalism and reform. It undoubtedly demonstrated aspects of what were to become associated with the populist style, such as using popular language and targeting enemies. However, the party differed from populism in major ways, especially its deferential attitude towards the Austro-Hungarian monarchy, the nobility, and Catholic Church. Moreover, whilst Hitler was influenced by Lueger (Hamann, 2010; Hitler, 1969: 51ff.), this was mainly in the context of style, as he rightly saw that the party's targeting of Jews was linked to a conservative defence of the established order.

The Plain People

Boulangism and the People's Party clearly exhibit the thin ideological triadic matrix set out in the Introduction. Although Boulanger did not term himself "populist," he borrowed from Abraham Lincoln's Gettysburg Address when he called for government "by the people, for the people, and which would help the people to realize their wishes of the ordinary man" (the term "populism" entered the French language during the 1920s in relation to a group of writers who expressed sympathy for ordinary people). The US People's Party played on the Jacksonian democratic ideal which combined the celebration of a strong presidency with emphasis on widening ordinary white-males' participation in politics. In this vein, the 1892 Omaha Platform stated that it sought "to restore the government of the Republic to the hands of the 'plain people.'"

Boulangism marked a major step in the shift away from an "open" conception of the people. Boulangism was the first movement to exploit growing hostility towards new immigrants from countries such as Belgium who were seeking work in rapidly indus-trializing areas. Although American Populism has frequently been seen as "nativist," it did not exhibit the hostility of the earlier "Know Nothings" (a name coined because of the party's desire for secrecy) to all immigrants who did not derive from the found-ing fathers' individualist and productive Protestant stock. Indeed, many recent immi-grants were active within the People's Party in key states such as Kansas (Nugent, 2013). Nevertheless, the Omaha Platform sought to close the door to illiterate "pauper and criminal classes," such as "coolies" from Asia, who were seen as threatening wages and not capable of being assimilated into a people characterized by democratic rights and values.

The Boulangist movement appealed across the political spectrum. Its campaign embraced advanced media, though the message was often simple. Influenced by American practice, Boulangists distributed large numbers of leaflets and used the new medium of photography. These often featured the dashing General Boulanger, and his promise to secure national revenge against Germany following France's humiliating 1870 defeat. The Populist Party was more bottom up, building on earlier local campaigns. Its leader, Thomas Watson, called for the largely un-enfranchised poor blacks and whites to unite against elites—though as initial electoral momentum waned during the 1890s, he turned on blacks and other minorities. American populism's conception of the people was based less on the imagined community of the nation than on personal experience of rural and small town communities. Whereas Boulangism was especially strong among the working class in cities, the Populists made fewer inroads into urban areas in spite of attempts to form alliances with the working class, which reflected a pluralist appreciation that America was highly diverse socio-economically as well as ethnically. The Populists attracted more support among women, helped by their hostility to the demon alcohol, but in most states women could not vote and in general Populists did not press for female suffrage.

Self-Serving Elites

Populist prohibitionism was linked to a wider evangelism to save the American people from being abused by the Devil incarnate. At the heart of this Populist demonology lay a new plutocratic elite, "unprecedented in the history of mankind," who had corruptly bought off the main parties and owned much of the press and even judges. Boulangism was similarly hostile to the rich "exploiters" of the people and the corrupt and weak poli-ticians whom it claimed populated parliament, an accusation made more plausible by a series of financial scandals implicating politicians. Although Boulangism was cautious about using aggressive anti-semitism nationally as some leading members were Jewish, "fools' socialism" which identified capitalism with Jewish elites was beginning to dem-onstrate a strong appeal across the political spectrum in French politics. This was based on the alleged Jewish dominance of finance and predilection for conspiracies against their "host" nation (claims which played on earlier Catholic tropes).

Boulangism was vague about how to control the economic elites who threatened the people, though anti-semites favored the expulsion of aliens and there were widespread calls to curb foreign business interests. Its first program, published in 1888, dealt only in vague statements about economic policy, such as the need for protection of "industry, commerce and agriculture" at a time of depression. Although there were notably different factions in the movement, there tended to be agreement that greater state intervention was needed to secure more benefits for the people. In contrast, the US Populists had far more specific economic plans, including graduated income tax, and state control of banking and the railroads, sectors whose plutocrats were seen as leading exploiters of core Populist supporters (Kazin, 1998)—though like most Boulangists they did not challenge private ownership generally.

The Popular Will

Populists believed that political change was crucial to making the people's voice heard. Rather than replacing the US Constitution, the Populists sought to make the system less elitist and corrupt, including use of the "initiative and referendum" which would bypass representatives and the interests behind them, and limiting the presidential office to one term. Boulangists publicly called for a constituent assembly and referendums to establish a more democratic regime, including a directly elected strong president. Their main target was the Parliamentary regime based on what were seen as corrupt and weak parties. However, there was some tension between those influenced by pluralist Republican ideas and those who sought more to create a system in which the people's general will was embodied in a leader who was not constrained by liberal rights (a tension which remained central to populist practice). Certainly the charismatic Boulanger's rhetoric was highly personalized, using slogans such as "Boulanger is the people," and popular language rather than elite political cant.

Boulanger's lack of a detailed program and political inexperience led both Bonapartists and Monarchists to fund him lavishly, believing he could be used to restore their dynasties (Irvine, 1988). Whilst Boulanger specifically denied the charge, the claim that he sought to establish a dictatorship was widely made against him, and at times his rhetoric seemed more authoritarian than democratic. This charge was later made by academics who saw him as a key harbinger of a fascist style of politics.

CONCEPTUALIZING FOUNDATIONAL FASCISM

Some have argued that fascist ideology had clearly emerged by 1914, especially in France (Sternhell, 1994). Certainly the term "national socialism" can be found before 1914—not least in the writings of the former Boulangist, Maurice Barrès, though his cult of the "land and the dead" owed more to the right than the left. However, it was only after the impact of World War I, communist revolutions across Europe followed by right-wing counter-revolution, and the onset of post-war economic instability that fascism began to take on a clear form (though as fascism lasted only briefly as a rising force, its quest for a new order lacks the body of serious texts possessed by other full ideologies).

Benito Mussolini founded the first fascist movement in 1919. The term *fasci* (alliance or union in a political context) had previously been used by both left- and right-wing groups, and was etymologically linked to the Roman *fasces*, a symbol of unity and authority. Fascists sought to forge a new Italian nation, led by an "aristocracy of the trenches" which would synthesize left- and right-wing policies in a new authoritarian state. Adolf Hitler's German National Socialist Party (NSDAP) emerged from the German Workers' Party, also founded in 1919. It did not refer to itself as fascist, but was influenced by Fascism (other forms of fascism often did not acknowledge Italian, or later German influence, as they sought to stress national roots).[2] However, Nazism differed in several ways, including its rabid racism and the more totalitarian regime that it established after 1933. There were also notable differences compared to the Hungarian Arrow Cross, which lacked a charismatic leader, and a fourth major manifestation of fascism, the Romanian Iron Guard, which did not seek territorial expansion (Payne, 1995). Nevertheless, they can all be fitted into the triadic matrix outlined in the Introduction.

The Holistic Nation

Fascists held the nation had a specific character which required its own state, and whose interests should be prioritized. They sometimes used "people" and "nation" inconsistently or as synonyms, a reflection of the fact that these terms are complex and elusive. The problem of understanding their use is compounded by the fact that some key words, especially *Volk*, are ambiguous. However, at the heart of fascist thought lay a key distinction. Most fascists claimed that they did not seek dictatorship, as they sought the support of the people. Certainly fascists like Mussolini and Nazi Propaganda Minister, Josef Goebbels, took a major interest in academic and professional ideas about how to influence public opinion and were willing to moderate policy at times and employ emotive and stylistic devices to build support. Nevertheless, fascists did not believe that the people had democratic rights, or that they were capable of ruling. As the Iron Guard's leader Corneliu Codreanu, wrote: who within the "nation is capable of understanding, able to intuit, its codes and laws? The people? The crowd? It's too much to ask of them." Only a vanguard was seen as capable of forging a new nation, which linked the past, present, and future to secure prosperity and survive internal and external threats. For fascists, the nation was both a real and imagined concept, a *Volksgemeinschaft* blending old and new. It was real as it was founded on traits identified among mythologized ancestors; it was imagined in the sense that a great task lay ahead.

During World War I Mussolini came to see nationalism as the dynamic motivating myth, a concept he took from the crowd psychologist Gustave Le Bon (who was influenced by Boulangism) and the syndicalist theorist Georges Sorel, who before the Great War saw the revolutionary general strike as the key myth. The Fascist cult of *Romanità*, which harked back to the glories of ancient Rome, was used to unite conservative and radical nationalists, and as an exemplar of an imperial past in order to help build popular support for a new empire. Other forms of fascist nationalism similarly used history to shape both identity and build support. The Falange leader proclaimed a "unity of destiny in the universal," which was used to help reject the breakaway claims of the Basques and others from a Spain which could rediscover its greatness. The Arrow Cross, which sought the restitution of Hungary's pre-war boundaries, portrayed the nation as holding a special place in mediating between east and west, bridging cultures. Unusually, its nationalism was less holistic, claiming in its propaganda that it would give rights to many of its ethnic minorities which remained (though not to Jews and Roma, who suffered a murderous fate after the Nazis set up the Arrow Cross in a puppet regime).

For the Nazis, the nation was based on a *Volksgeist* with deep cultural and blood roots, a belief reinforced by the rise of German racial science after the late nineteenth century in fields such as eugenics (which had strong links with the influential American eugenics movement, greatly admired by Hitler). This form of genetic racism, and especially the Holocaust, is a key reason why some scholars have sought to distinguish it from fascism. However, fascism was clearly racist in its belief that it had the right to rule over lesser peoples, and went on to introduce its own Nuremberg-style anti-semitic laws in the late 1930s. Moreover, many Nazi leaders did not share Hitler's obsession with "blood" and Jewish conspiracies, though Jews were at the heart of their various demonologies (capitalism, communism, and liberalism). As a result, all sought to make Germany "Jew free" with forced emigration, including to Palestine, the preferred route before the war (Eatwell, 2013b).

Whilst fascists in many countries did not seek territorial expansion, the need for *spazio vitale / Lebensraum* (living space) was central to Fascist and Nazi nationalism. This was underpinned by the growth of geopolitical thought, which portrayed the world as divided into natural spheres that needed to be controlled by great powers like Britain. The US's westward expansion and the Monroe Doctrine have been neglected influences, with Hitler talking of the Volga as "our Mississippi." Changes in the balance of power furthered this form of thinking, and reinforced views about the need for a new man. After Japan's defeat of Russia in 1905, a leading Italian nationalist intellectual, Enrico Corradini, wrote revealingly of the need to create a Bushido-type ethic to help fight future wars. Within Germany, the desire to prevent the Soviet Union expanding was merged by the Nazis into a crusade against Bolshevism. Looking into the future, Alfred Rosenberg, whose *The Myth of the Twentieth Century* (1930) is second only to Hitler's *Mein Kampf* in the Nazi best-seller list (though probably read even less), wrote of the need to guard against the coming hatred of the "Black races and bastards, led by the fanatical spirit of Muhammed." (Whilst the Nazis and Fascists dabbled in pro-Muslim politics, this reflected an attempt to de-stabilize British and French colonial interests rather than a belief in ideological symbiosis of the sort implied by those who at the turn of the new millennium wrote of the rise of "Islamofascism.")

The New Man

The fascist "new man" referred in the first place to an elite. Prior to 1914, elite theorists like Robert Michels and Vilfredo Pareto influenced the development of Mussolini's socialism, but war was crucial to his forming the Fascist movement (initially the term "party" was eschewed, as it could connote democratic divisions). After 1918 he called on a young "trenchocracy" to launch a new paramilitary and electoral movement. Hitler, who associated communist revolution with Jews, wrote in *Mein Kampf* (1925) that the "mob" needed a leader to make them understand a great alternative "idea." During the early 1920s he came to believe that he was destined to be the historic Führer, though he realized—like Mussolini—that an understanding with the Establishment was necessary to achieve power. The leader of the Spanish Falange, José Primo de Rivera, looked directly to the army to renovate the dictatorship his father had led during the 1920s and which exhibited an early form of "reflexive hybridity" with fashionable Fascism, including borrowing its emphasis on dynamic leadership.

The fascist conception of the new man also encompassed the masses. Central to fascist thinking was decadence, a point of contact with the right generally (helping to bring authoritarian conservatives into electorally successful fascisms). A revealing insight into the concept is given by Barrès, when he quipped that on the tombstone of the bourgeoisie should be carved: "Born a man, died a grocer" (perhaps "accountant" would be today's *mot juste*?) For conservatives, the task was to restore traditional values, which was an important aspect of fascist attitudes towards women. Roles such as motherhood and running the home were celebrated, accompanied by rewards for large families—though space was accorded for women to be active in fascist organizations, a mix which helps explain the Nazis' strong electoral appeal to women by the time they came to power (de Grazia, 1993; Stephenson, 2001). A sense of the idealized male, and fascism's syncretic style of thought, can be gained from Mussolini's claim: "From beneath the ruins of liberal, socialist, and democratic doctrines, Fascism extracts those elements which are still vital … Man is integral, he is political, he is economic, he is religious, he is saint, he is warrior" (Mussolini, 1935: 25–6 and 59). Contrary to those who portray fascism as a "political religion" (Gentile, 1996), it sought a syncretic mix recognizing the economic and martial as well as the spiritual side of the new man. There were also notable differences in this context concerning how the "new man" was to be created. For example, after World War II, the former leader of the Iron Guard, Horia Sima, argued that Fascism sought to educate people through the state, whereas the Guard's deeply religious first leader, Codreanu, spoke directly to people's "souls."

There were differences too among fascists over violence. Fascism is often associated with the nihilist sentiment "When I hear the word 'culture,' I reach for my gun," which is often misattributed to the leading Nazi, Hermann Göring. In fact it comes from a play written in 1933 by the Nazi intellectual Hanns Johst and a better translation is: "When I hear the term (German High) Culture, I remove the safety catch from my Browning." It points more to an attack on traditional, elitist views of culture and is a celebration of activism rather than mindless violence. Turning to Italy, no major Fascist theorist held that violence had a significant long-term role in domestic politics (Gregor, 2005), though in both Italy and Germany, paramilitary parties were viewed as channels both for disseminating propaganda and through which the new elite could be nurtured. In Germany during the Great Depression, the Stormtroopers were further seen as means of organizing local work schemes which would impress others.

Nevertheless, in the aftermath of a brutalizing war, many activists saw violence in terms of catharsis and male bonding. Violent clashes with the left in turn provided a stream of martyrs, celebrated in quasi-religious ceremonies which were part of the fascist style. Violence too was seen as a way of impressing conservative elites, who feared that the democratic state could not contain the rising left. After coming to power, the paramilitary side of fascism was linked to preparing the new man for military expansion. Giovanni Papini, a leading nationalist writer and later Fascist intellectual, had seen this need before World War I when he contemptuously wrote: "Italy in 1860 was made up of shit, dragged kicking and screaming into a new state by a daring elite, and shit it has remained for the last fifty years." Even young children engaged in forms of military training in order to harden the nation.

The Third Way Authoritarian State

Although communism and fascism constitute the basis of the "totalitarian" model, Fascism in some ways bore more resemblance to the less ideological and mobilizing "authoritarian" regime model (Linz, 2000; cf. Roberts, 2006)—though these were not necessarily less oppressive and violent, as the Spanish Franco dictatorship demonstrates. In the early years, not all Fascists sought a single party, highly centralized and pervasive state. Even after the banning of left-wing parties, some dissent was possible and the Catholic Church remained a major independent power center, which was accorded formal recognition by the 1929 Concordat and Lateran Pacts that regularized church–state relations for the first time since the unification of Italy. Business and large landowners too continued to exercise significant independent power. Moreover, there was nothing like the Nazi terror and concentration camp system for opponents of the regime (Wachsmann, 2015), though the threat of repression was pervasive. In 1943 there was even a widespread outbreak of strikes.

Opponents of Fascism coined the term "totalitarianism" in the early 1920s in order to point to its anti-pluralist and mass-mobilizing trajectory. It was quickly adopted by Fascist intellectuals, who argued that such a state could achieve goals unattainable by the divided and weak major democracies. The philosopher king of Fascism, Giovanni Gentile, wrote of the need for an "ethical state" to teach core values to the new man, unlike the liberal state with its relativist distinction between private and public spheres.

Although the extent of Fascist penetration of civil society and the support it engendered remains a matter of dispute, the Fascist state certainly adopted an aestheticized and pervasive face very different from the classic liberal model.

The Nazis did not speak of "totalitarianism," though some used terms such as "total war" and early Nazis frequently talked about the need for a new state. Some, like the economist Goffried Feder, envisaged a form of corporatist order including a representative "House of the People" and "Central Council." However, the reality of the Nazi state after 1933 was amorphous, even chaotic, reinforced by the fact that for six of its twelve years' life Germany was engaged in fighting a world war, which helped lead to a process of "cumulative radicalization," especially in relation to Jewish policy (plans for extermination gradually developed after it became impossible to make Germany "Jew free" following the outbreak of war in 1939 and the conquest of territory containing large numbers of Jews). Much of the senior bureaucracy of the Weimar regime was retained, as it was impossible to purge more than a relatively small number. However, this ran in tandem with a burgeoning party bureaucracy, which owed its loyalty to Hitler rather than any lingering concept of a *Rechsstaat*.

Hitler had made clear in *Mein Kampf* that the great leader was not constrained by a "body, which decides anything by the majority." He ruled through a court of acolytes, who were transfixed by his coterie charisma. The Führer's power was reinforced by the way in which his centripetal charisma had attracted a broad swathe of voters to the Nazis after 1930, and the god-like cultic charismatic aura that was later developed around him by party and state propaganda. Mussolini too exhibited strong charismatic traits, though he was less important to Fascist voting and was overthrown by his own party in 1943 (subsequently creating, under Nazi tutelage, the chaotic Salò Republic which sought a return to Fascism's radical 1919 roots). Nevertheless, a charismatic leader is not a defining characteristic of fascism. Georges Valois, the founder of the French Faisceau, was widely seen as lacking personal presence, as was the Arrow Cross leader, Ferenc Szálasi—though both had strong senses of mission to create a new socio-economic order.

It has frequently been argued that fascism lacked a clear economic policy. There were certainly differences among the early Fascists, who included some who sought a strong state to defend economic liberalism against the left and whom Mussolini welcomed as part of a policy to assuage Establishment fears. However, both the syndicalists and conservative nationalists within the party agreed on the need for greater production to underpin both social unity and future wars (an important reason why some syndicalists turned to fascism was their belief that egalitarian socialism lacked a work ethic and sought to redistribute rather than create wealth). A broad area of further agreement was the need to create some form of "syndicate" or "Corporation," which was intended to unite management and workers and promote national goals. Although the resulting reality of the "Corporate State" was a business-dominated and largely uncoordinated form of social Catholicism, there was undoubtedly a desire among many Fascists to create a new socio-economic order involving state intervention and the provision of extensive welfare benefits for workers.

Whilst Hitler argued for the primacy of politics over economics, this meant a rejection of the materialist conception of human nature, not of policy per se. The Nazis after 1928 developed a panoply of economic programs, which were crucial to attracting support in sectors such as agriculture (including a "blood and soil" proto-ecological strand). A key figure in this policy development was Gregor Strasser, who advocated a stridently anti-capitalist line even though this conflicted with Hitler's strategy of courting business support. After coming to power, the Nazis proceeded to develop a third way economy to achieve full employment and social harmony. Although they accepted the right to private property and held entrepreneurship in high regard, they believed that government regulation of and involvement in business was vital to make it work in the national interest and secure a "social dividend" for everyone (Barkai, 1990). The third way also involved cultural as well as bureaucratic apparatuses, especially the way in which the Strength through Joy organization (which was modeled on the Italian Dopolavoro) offered a "beautification of the factories" program to help remove worker alienation, as well as concrete benefits such as the Volkswagen car and cheap holidays with pay. In 1939 the largest hotel in the world was being built on the island of Rügen to provide mass holidays. These economic policies, rather than the appeal of a putative political religion, are crucial to understanding the widespread support that Nazism enjoyed by the late 1930s.

Externally, fascists believed that the international form of capitalism that had emerged in the nineteenth century did not necessarily work in the national interest (a view often linked to a belief that finance was Jewish dominated). In the German case, the devastating external impact of the 1929 Wall Street crash was seen as self-evident proof. Fascists sought a more autarchic economy, which in the Italian and German cases was linked to geopolitical ambitions. Especially after the outbreak of World War II, Nazi thinkers began to develop the idea of a co-ordinated core European economy, led by Germany—though in part this was a mask for German domination and exploitation of national economies. Indeed, in the post-war era many fascists used the slogan "Europe a Nation," though for many this new Europe was to be founded on the basis of a federation of fascist nations rather than the liberal state and internationalized political economy which was to become mandatory for membership of the European Union (EU).

CLASSIFICATORY CONUNDRUMS

There have been major debates among academics about whether various movements and regimes should be labeled populist or fascist. In the following section a series of select case studies will be used to help expand on previous conceptualizations of populism and fascism, highlighting issues about variation, hybridity, and esoteric agendas noted briefly in the Introduction.

Latin America

Latin America has seen a large number of movements and regimes which have been termed populist, of which the most interesting in the context of discussions about fascism is Argentinian Peronism.

Juan Perón came to prominence after the 1943 military takeover in Argentina and by 1946 the charismatic Colonel had been elected president, serving a further two terms as president during the 1950s–1970s. While on a visit to Europe before the war, Perón had undoubtedly been impressed by Fascism, especially its attempts to integrate the working class into the nation and improve its welfare. As a result, some have seen early manifestations of Peronism as an example of a "local fascist ideology" (Spektorowski, 2001: 530). On the other hand—and more commonly—Peronism has been seen as an archetypal form of Latin American populism (Mudde and Rovira Kaltwasser, 2012: 3)

Those who place Peronism in the populist camp cite several factors. Ideologically, there were strong indigenous strands to Peronism, especially the pre-liberal *caudillista* tradition, social Catholicism, and inter-war populist Argentinian politicians who railed against the idle and exploitative rich, a rhetoric which very much characterized Peronism. The form of *nacionalismo* that developed in the inter-war era was a hybridization of Fascism and Catholicism, which was notably different to the Italian model (Finchelstein, 2010)—although it shared its early lack of domestic racial theory and had affinities with the Iron Guard in its overt religiosity. Politically, Perón saw the dangers of truly totalitarian power and he sought to balance state control with genuine inclusionary working class participation in the system. However, this did not involve joining any Peronist mass organization. Moreover, Congress continued to include non-Peronists and strikes remained legal (much to the consternation of business elites, as they rose notably in number after 1946). Some have also pointed to Eva Perón's encouragement of female political activity and the centrality of the Evita myth, which had developed even before her early death, as very different to male-dominated fascism—Mussolini's wife was largely hidden from the public and Hitler was "married" to the German people.

However, Eva Perón wrote at the beginning of her autobiography that: "All that I am, all that I have, all that I think and all that I feel, belongs to Perón," which is perfectly consistent with seeing Perón as the great "new man." Although Peronism did not feature a specific "new man" rhetoric, it denounced bourgeois decadence and sought national renewal through a new elite which was not part of the oligarchic classes who had traditionally ruled Argentina. It sought to unite the nation around "three flags" involving social justice, economic development, and political sovereignty. The emphasis on social justice in particular was notably different to Francoism, which exerted a contemporary attraction in more right-wing circles in Latin America. A key institution was corporatism, which sought mainly to control the unions, though there were linked socio-economic benefits for workers. At the same time, nationalization was used to threaten the owning classes. Whilst non-left-wing parties remained legal and some dissent was possible, Perón supported the hounding and sometimes violent suppression of troublesome opponents. In many respects the regime was similar to the illiberal democratic aspect of the early period of Fascist rule, minus the paramilitary party. Although later Peronism was to fall under the influence of neoliberalism, its early years illustrate the spell which ascendant fascism cast well beyond Europe. Whilst it never developed the totalitarian side that came to characterize the major fascist regimes especially in Germany, Peronism bore enough similarities to refute the claims of those who have argued that fascism was solely a European-epochal movement (Nolte, 1965).

The US

Another major center of populism has been the US, though in this case debates linked to fascism focus on personalities rather than movements or regimes—especially the Louisiana politician, Huey Long, "Radio Priest" Father Coughlin, and the campaign and subsequent Presidency of Donald Trump.

Following the brief flowering of the People's Party, the next major populist wave to emerge in the US was during the inter-war era (Brinkley, 1983; Kazin, 1998). Long and Coughlin rose to prominence at a time of a growing *Zeitgeist* that admired strong leadership. This was reflected in Mussolini's picture appearing on the front cover of *Time* magazine as early as 1923, while Studebaker sold a "Dictator" car from 1927 to 1937 (the word became tainted mainly after the rise of Hitler and Stalin's terror). While state governor, Long undoubtedly developed a clientelistic and oppressive political machine, though this was not dissimilar to machine politics in similarly corrupt areas. One notable difference compared to other leading politicians in the south at the time was that Long did this without systematically playing the race card. Indeed, some of his reforms helped poor blacks as well as whites (though few had the vote, which he did not challenge). Had he ever become president he would have extended, perhaps even abused, the Oval Office's powers as he saw the New Deal as insufficiently radical and President Roosevelt too close to corporate interests. However, at the time of his assassination in 1935 his "Every Man a King" platform was built on opposition to rich business elites and the need for the redistribution of wealth to the people, rather than proposals for any form of dictatorship.

Unlike Long, Coughlin made little effort to develop a mass organization through his popular radio broadcasts. He initially too focused on anti-elite and often ill-defined socio-economic campaigns, preaching that he sought to help the ordinary man. However, by the late 1930s Coughlin became more overtly anti-semitic, claiming that Jewish interests were conspiring to bring the US into an unnecessary European war. This was accompanied by favorable comments about General Franco's fight in the Spanish Civil War against communism, the Nazis' achievement of full employment, and their expansion of the welfare state. Nevertheless, Coughlin's beliefs were located within social Catholicism rather than holistic, let alone aggressive, nationalism. Like Long, he believed that only stronger federal government could curb dangerous elites and help the plain man, though it was a federal government that would remain democratic, not dictatorial. The truly fascist inter-war US groups, like William Pelley's Silver Legion, never attracted more than a fringe following even among German and Italian Americans.

Donald Trump, an egocentric rich businessman, was also frequently labeled "fascist" during the 2016 presidential election. His "Make America Great Again" slogan was seen as clearly fitting into the influential model of fascism which holds that it centers around ultra-nationalism (Reid Ross, 2016). He was accused of a "boasting disrespect for the niceties of democratic culture that he claims … has produced national weakness and incompetence" (Kagan, 2016). He was charged with being racist following statements such as the need to ban Muslim immigration and build a wall to keep out Mexicans. He was labeled misogynist and sexist on account of repeated public comments and a bragging leaked videotape. Whilst Trump talked about embodying the views of plain people, he did not seek to empower them so much as induce a belief in his authoritarian leadership. He appealed especially to less-educated whites who felt politically neglected, whose economic position had absolutely or relatively declined and who were alienated by post-1960s cultural changes.

Nevertheless whilst Trump held that America was sick, he lacked an ideological commitment to forge a new holistic nation in a country characterized by patriotic individualism. His exclusionary views on immigrants were more nativist than racist in the sense of believing in hierarchies, though he attracted a clearly racist fringe. Like the early US Populists, he accepted that many ethnic minorities could be part of the American melting pot. In the economic sphere, Trump's attacks on globalization and the role of the state focused more on restricting trade than developing a third way attack on capitalism, though he erratically and often vaguely supported forms of welfare not typical of Republicans. Trump fits more clearly into the populist matrix and especially the populist strong-man style (though this has not been a characteristic of American populism in recent decades, especially in the Tea Party). After winning the California primary, he claimed that the election was not "about Republican or Democrat," but about "who runs this country, the special interests or the people." Trump's defence of the neglected common man and attacks on a corrupt political class and business elites (including threatening action against Apple and Ford for "exporting" American jobs and Pfizer for evading taxes) were very much part of foundational populist ideology. His demagogic slipperiness on issues was also part of the typical populist style. His tendency to provocation, not least through extensive new media usage, was designed to attract free media attention and build on the celebrity status he derived from the television program, *The Apprentice*. Indeed, it is important to note the way in which this showcasing of his business skills and financial independence meant that Trump fitted into a growing form of Western technocratic politics which is suspicious of the "masses." This trend is often contrasted to populism, as it typically involves rule by expert elites (though there had been a strand of admiration for non-political technocrats in populism dating back to the nineteenth century).

Nevertheless Trump's aggressive rhetoric, including threats to journalists, judges, and Hillary Clinton, and claims about conspiracies against him raised legitimate fears that he might abuse presidential powers. His campaign, including open admiration for Russian President Vladimir Putin, raised the specter of a more illiberal form of majoritarian democracy which would bypass US checks and balances (that had not prevented past liberal infringements, such as the McCarthyite witch-hunts). However, this did not make him a potential fascist dictator, though his demagogic and dishonest rhetoric broke liberal shibboleths and the boundaries of mainstream discourse—even challenging the legitimacy of the democratic process—which could have longer term consequences in a country where voters increasingly rely on one-sided media representations.

Europe

For a long period after 1945 it seemed that sustained major fascist and populist movements were dead in democratic Europe. However, starting in the 1970s "new" forms of "populist radical right" parties (Ignazi, 2003; Mudde, 2007) began to emerge. In some cases there was clearly no connection to the fascist tradition, but the Front National (FN) in France illustrates the issue of esoteric agendas and hybridity, while the Golden Dawn in Greece illustrates that electoral forms similar to foundational fascism can still emerge.

The formation of the FN in 1972 was influenced by the strategy of the post-war Italian Social Movement (MSI), which sought to bring together fascists who looked to the "social" Salò Republic for inspiration and more conservative nationalists in a party that would both court electoral support and build a new cadre organization (Rydgren, 2002). The man chosen as leader was Jean-Marie Le Pen, a charismatic, authoritarian ex-paratrooper who had been active in a variety of non-fascist right-wing groups. His language in the 1970s was classically populist, claiming that the people was being ignored by a "gang of four" mainstream parties and advocating a Sixth Republic based on a stronger presidency and greater use of referendums to ensure the people's voice was heard. The FN later turned its fire on a variety of issues which were initially ignored by the mainstream, including: the threats posed by immigrants to French identity; law and order, which was related to immigration; the European Union which was allegedly undermining French democracy; and US-led globalization which was threatening French employment and workers' rights.

In 2002, Le Pen made the run-off ballot for the French presidency, but a "Republican front" against his allegedly partly hidden extremist views meant that he won just 17.8 percent of the vote. One alleged influence on his party has been the *Nouvelle Droite*, an elitist intellectual group that sought to rehabilitate and sanitize aspects of fascist ideology (Bar-On, 2007; Mammone, 2015). Its use of the term "differencialism" rather than "race," arguing that peoples had a right to difference and that Islam in particular could not be assimilated into European cultures, has undoubtedly been a widely influential form of exclusionary argument. However, this re-branding was accompanied by Le Pen on occasion using a language which seemed aimed at reassuring hardcore extremists rather than broadening the party's appeal, most notoriously when he spoke of the Holocaust as

a "detail" of history (although another explanation is his taste for provocative and politically incorrect statements).

After his daughter succeeded him in 2011, the party sought to broaden its appeal
including specifically pursuing the female vote, dropping its homophobia, and purging
party literature of references to former extreme right politicians and thinkers. Marine
Le Pen sought to "de-demonize" the FN, openly adopting the term "populist" which
many had previously seen as implying watering down extremist ideology, and promising to "return government to the French people." In 2015 her party expelled Jean-Marie
over continued provocative and anti-semitic references. However, this does not prove
that the party has become more mainstream, as many have claimed. Internationally,
it seeks the collapse of the EU and closer links with Russia (which has provided the
party with loans). Domestically, the FN has pursued a complex mix, adopting more
left-wing policies on issues such as welfare and state action and right-wing policies
linked to immigration, especially developing a more radical discourse about the threat
from Islam. Indeed, the FN frequently adopts a "neither left nor right" line. Although
it is important to distinguish between reflexive hybridity and elements of policy overlap, there remain echoes of fascist ideology in this archetypally "new," "populist radical
right party."

Some have portrayed the Greek Golden Dawn as part of a growing wave of post-
2008 recession populist parties (Kuper, 2015), and its program certainly states that
"power comes from the people." However, it clearly fits into the fascist matrix. It
claims a heritage stretching back to ancient Sparta, which was ruled by a king with
"elements of socialism and nationalism," and which heroically led the Greek defence
against the invading Persians. It celebrates the inter-war Ioannis Metaxas dictatorship, which was influenced by aspects of fascist policy and style, though it resisted
Italian territorial demands. Golden Dawn defends the 1967–1974 military Junta for
suppressing communism and laying the foundations for economic growth, only for
this to be destroyed by clientelistic and kleptocratic mainstream parties after the
return of elections. It argues that contemporary democracy stems not from Greece
but from the English parliamentary system, and is manipulated by elites including
the mass media (Golden Dawn, like the FN, extensively uses new media). It seeks an
ethnically pure Greater Greece and supports the creation of an authoritarian regime.
This would end the decadence that has left society in "ruins" and pursue a third way
economic policy divorced from EU control ("neither communist internationalism"
nor "universalism-liberalism"). Externally it supports a "geopolitical shift to Russia."
At the street level, Golden Dawn supporters sometimes sport fascist symbols, and
engage in violent attacks on immigrants and others (though it is also victim of attacks
from the extreme left), which has led to criminal charges. However its leader, the
notably uncharismatic Nikolaos Michalokiakos who has been involved in far right
politics for decades, denies that he or his "popular association" are fascist. He claims
the party logo is a traditional Greek meander, not the relatively similar Nazi swastika
(Vasilopoulou and Halikopoulou, 2015). Fascism still remains a "truth which dare
not speak its name."

CONCLUSION

This chapter has not attempted to theorize the rise of populism and fascism—though the stress on fascist ideological syncretism points to the dangers of largely mono-causal explanations which do not recognize its ability to exploit economic grievances, a sense of loss of community, and the appeal of its longer term visions. Nor does this chapter systematically attempt to assess the argument that populist parties may offer a useful safety valve for discontent in contemporary democracies—though it should be clear that this has to be weighed against dangerous traits such as egocentric leaders, Manichean demonization, and loss of faith in a liberal system based on representative government, compromise, and legal rights.

Instead, the main purpose has been to conceptualize what I have termed "foundational" populist and fascist ideologies, as these constitute the key to the classification of later manifestations in a way that contextual and epochal aspects, like anti-communism and street violence, do not. Although populism in practice has at times degenerated into forms of authoritarian leader-oriented and exclusionary politics, it requires a broader ideological package to metamorphosize into fascism. Whilst many have made "genuine populism" central to their definition of fascist ideology (Griffin, 1991: 26; 1998: 36), this was not the case with foundational fascism. The main point of contact in practice has been a strategic use of aspects of populist discourse and style in an attempt to boost support—partly linked to the fact that the fascist view of man has encouraged manipulation by charismatic leaders and the use of populist language, though neither are necessary defining features of fascism.

When employing these matrices it is important to remember two caveats noted in passing above. Firstly, foundational fascist propaganda stressed national rather than transnational influences and often played down radicalism in an attempt to broaden support. As fascism has been a pariah since the war, few outside an alienated fringe have been willing openly to situate themselves within its ideological matrices. Indeed, any major new form of fascism today is likely to be dressed in new habits, including a more populist rhetoric concerning the people's will, and an anti-fascist rhetoric through the demonization of "Islamofascism." Old-style, single paramilitary-party fascist states could be replaced by a new syncretic form of illiberal democracy, especially when strong leaders gain power and can manipulate the media, intimidate opposition, and deploy other tactics to achieve their ideological goals. Secondly, it is important to re-iterate the possibility of esoteric and exoteric agendas. Before he became leader of the British National Party (BNP), Nick Griffin wrote that populism, "which starts with thoughts of trimming policies, avoiding holding election rallies in areas which might cause Asian riots, sneering at skinheads and acquiescing in the Holohoax lie," was the "kiss of death" for the BNP. However, he later sought to "modernize" the BNP along the lines of the FN in a quest to break out of the fascist electoral ghetto (Eatwell, 2004). Revealing in this context is a special edition on populism of the French extreme right magazine *Le*

Choc du Mois in November, 2006, which reflected a growing willingness to adopt the previously despised term—partly to help hide other ideological influences and pursue an electoral road which seemed far more promising than a generation before, following growing disillusionment with elites and concern about issues such as immigration and adverse economic change.

Nevertheless, by way of final conclusion it is important to re-emphasize the major ideological differences, which lie at the core of foundational populism and fascism. Unlike fascism, populism is a form of democracy, albeit not liberal democracy. It is inconceivable that a populist could espouse the Hitlerjugend slogan: "You are nothing, your nation (*Volk*) is everything." Near the end of the war, Mussolini made a comment which is revealing about both his egocentrism and the centrality of the new man project to fascism: "It isn't fascism that has ruined Italians, it's Italians who have ruined fascism.... It's this great mass of contaminated and sick slaves who go from lethargy to desperation who have failed." Populists can hold that the people may exhibit failings, even be "demoralized" by their exploitation, as the Omaha Program claimed. But they cannot hold that an authoritarian new elite is required to foster a "new man" in order to achieve radical change.

NOTES

1   I am grateful to the editors, James Eatwell, Craig Fowlie, and Marta Lorimer, for their most helpful comments on the first draft.
2   In keeping with common Anglophone practice, this chapter uses capital "F" for the specifically Italian variant, and "f" to refer to generic fascism.

REFERENCES

Barkai, Avraham. 1990. *Nazi Economics: Ideology, Theory and Policy*. New Haven: Yale University Press.

Bar-On, Tamir. 2007. *Where Have all the Fascists Gone?* Aldershot: Ashgate.

Betz, Hans-Georg and S. Immerfall (eds). 1998. *The New Politics of the Right*. New York: St Martin's Press.

Brinkley, Alan. 1983. *Voices of Protest: Huey Long, Father Coughlin and the Great Depression*. New York: Vintage Books.

De Grazia, Victoria. 1993. *How Fascism Ruled Women: Italy, 1922–1945*. Berkeley: University of California Press.

Eatwell, Roger. 1992. "Towards a new model of generic fascism," *Journal of Theoretical Politics*, 4: 161–94.

Eatwell, Roger. 2004. "The extreme right in Britain: the long road to 'modernization,'" in R. Eatwell and C. Mudde (eds), *Western Democracies and the New Extreme Right Challenge*. London: Routledge, 62–79.

Eatwell, Roger. 2013a. "Fascism," in M. Freeden, L. T. Sargent, and M. Stears (eds), *The Oxford Handbook of Political Ideologies*. Oxford: Oxford University Press, 474–92.

Eatwell, Roger. 2013b. "Fascism and racism," in J. Breuilly (ed.), *The Oxford Handbook of the History of Nationalism*. Oxford: Oxford University Press, 573–91.

Eatwell, Roger. 2014. "The nature of 'generic fascism': complexity and reflexive hybridity," in A. Costa Pinto and A. Kallis (eds), *Rethinking Fascism and Dictatorship in Europe*. Basingstoke: Palgrave Macmillan, 67–86.

Eatwell, Roger. 2017. "Charisma and the radical right," in J. Rydgren (ed.), *The Oxford Handbook of the Radical Right*. Oxford: Oxford University Press, in press.

Finchelstein, Federico. 2010. *Translatlantic Fascism. Ideology, Violence, and the Sacred in Argentina and Italy, 1919–1945*. Durham: Duke University Press.

Freeden, Michael. 1996. *Ideologies and Political Theory: A Conceptual Approach*. New York: Oxford University Press.

Gentile, Emilio. 1996. *The Sacralization of Politics in Fascist Italy*. Cambridge: Harvard University Press.

Germani, Gino. 1978. *Authoritarianism, Fascism and National Populism*. New Jersey: Transaction Books.

Gregor, A. James. 2005. *Mussolini's Intellectuals: Fascist Social and Political Thought*. Princeton: Princeton University Press.

Griffin, Roger. 1991. *The Nature of Fascism*. London: Pinter.

Griffin, Roger (ed.). 1998. *International Fascism: Theories, Causes and the New Consensus*. London: Arnold.

Hamann, Brigitte. 2010. *Hitler in Vienna*. London: Tauris Parke.

Hitler, Adolf. 1969 [1925]. *Mein Kampf*. London: Hutchinson.

Hofstadter, Richard. 1964. *The Paranoid Style In American Politics and Other Essays*. Cambridge: Harvard University Press.

Ignazi, Piero. 2003. *Extreme Right Parties in Western Europe*. Oxford: Oxford University Press.

Irvine, William D. 1998. *The Boulanger Affair Reconsidered: Royalism, Boulangism, and the Origins of the Radical Right in France*. Oxford: Oxford University Press.

Kagan, Robert. 2016. "This is how fascism comes to America," *Washington Post*, May 18.

Kazin, Michael. 1998. *The Populist Persuasion: An American History*. Ithaca: Cornell University Press.

Kuper, Simon. 2015. "Populism: what happens next?," *Financial Times Magazine*, January 9.

Linz, Juan J. 2000. *Totalitarian and Authoritarian Regimes*. Boulder: Lynne Rienner.

Lipset, Seymour Martin. 1960. *Political Man: The Social Bases of Politics*. New York: Doubleday and Company.

Mammone, Andrea. 2015. *Transnational Neo-Fascism in France and Italy*. Cambridge: Cambridge University Press.

Mosse, George L. 1981. *The Crisis of German Ideology: Intellectual Origins of the Third Reich*. New York: Shocken Books.

Mudde, Cas. 2007. *Populist Radical Right Parties in Europe*. Cambridge: Cambridge University Press.

Mudde, Cas and Cristóbal Rovira Kaltwasser (eds). 2012. *Populism in Europe and the Americas: Threat or Corrective for Democracy?* Cambridge: Cambridge University Press.

Mussolini, Benito. 1935. *Fascism: Doctrine and Institutions*. Rome: Ardita.

Nolte, Ernst. 1965. *Three Faces of Fascism*. New York: Holt, Rinehart, and Winston.

Nugent, Walter. 2013. *The Tolerant Populists: Kansas Populism and Nativism*. Chicago: University of Chicago Press.

Payne, Stanley. 1995. *A History of Fascism, 1914–1945*. Madison: University of Wisconsin Press.

Reid Ross, Alexander. 2016. *Trumpism*. https://itsgoingdown.org/wp-content/uploads/2016/06/trumpism.pdf.

Roberts, David. 2006. *The Totalitarian Experiment in Twentieth-Century Europe*. New York: Routledge.

Rydgren, Jens. 2002. *Political Protest and Ethno-Nationalist Mobilization: The Case of the French Front National*. Stockholm: University of Stockholm.

Skocpol, Theda and Vanessa Williamson. 2013. *The Tea Party and the Remaking of Republican Conservatism*. New York: Oxford University Press.

Spektorowski, Alberto. 2001. "The fascist and populist syndromes in the Argentine revolution of the right," in S. Larsen (ed.), *Fascism outside Europe*. Boulder: Social Science Monographs, 529–60.

Stephenson, Jill. 2001. *Women in Nazi Germany*. London: Routledge.

Sternhell, Zeev (with Mario Sznader and Maia Asheri). 1994. *The Birth of Fascist Ideology*. Princeton: Princeton University Press.

Taggart, Paul. 2000. *Populism*. Buckingham: Open University Press.

Wachsmann, Nikolaus. 2015. *KL: A History of the Nazi Concentration Camps*. New York: Farrar, Straus, and Giroux.

Vasilopoulou, Sofia and Daphne Halikopoulou. 2015. *The Golden Dawn's "National Solution": Explaining the Rise of the Far Right in Greece*. New York: Palgrave Macmillan.

··

CHAPTER 20

POPULISM
AND FOREIGN POLICY

··

BERTJAN VERBEEK AND ANDREJ ZASLOVE

INTRODUCTION

RESEARCH on populism tends to focus on populists' impact on their country's domestic politics, particularly because researchers tend to emphasize the anti-elitist motivation of both populist politicians and their supporters. This is puzzling, as in today's globalized world, politics is less and less an exclusively domestic sphere. Indeed, the distinction between the domestic and the foreign has become less clear: domestic events spill over into the international context, while international events affect domestic affairs. Recent examples suggest that populism studies should take this into account: Hugo Chávez's populism contained a substantive dose of anti-Americanism (Hakim, 2006; Roberts, 2012). The proposed changes in their respective political systems by the Polish populist government led by Law and Justice (PiS) and by the Hungarian FIDESZ government have provoked responses from the European Union (EU) (Berendt, 2016; Sedelmeier, 2014). Developments such as these point to the need to take a closer look at the relationship between populism and foreign policy. Curiously, to date, few studies of this relationship exist.[1] In this chapter, we seek to identify this link between populism and foreign policy.

This contribution offers the three following claims: (1) (developments in) international relations can have a major impact on domestic politics, helping us understand the variation in the rise and strength of populism across time and countries; (2) populist parties do not pursue identical foreign policies despite their shared distinction between the corrupt elite and the pure people: the variation in their foreign policy preferences can be understood via the specific ideology populism as a thin-centered ideology attaches itself to; and (3) populism may impact the foreign policies of states, thus affecting the relations between states. In making these claims, we seek to combine insights from comparative politics (CP) and international relations (IR).

In this contribution, we exclusively focus on populism as a thin-centered ideology (see Mudde's contribution in this volume); this approach allows us to identify clearly the core characteristics of populism while it also permits us to theorize the substantive policy positions that populist parties may take vis-à-vis foreign policy issues. This means that, although all populist parties will cast their positions in terms of the pure people versus the corrupt elite, they may differ regarding their foreign policy positions, depending on the thin-centered ideology to which they have attached themselves. The evidence from this chapter suggests that there may be up to four different types of populist parties/movements. We categorize these four different types according to their attaching ideologies.

Importantly, conceiving of populism as a thin-centered ideology will help us make a useful distinction between the often conflated concepts of populism and nationalism. We will present our argument by drawing from empirical studies of populism in European, Latin American, North American, and Australasian countries. Before we embark on our journey, however, we need to clarify two additional concepts central to this chapter: foreign policy and nationalism.

Foreign Policy

Foreign policy is a common, yet much debated concept. In general, it refers to the intentions and actions of an actor directed at the actor's external world (Neack et al., 1995: 18). In most cases, the actor is regarded to be a sovereign state (Neack, 2008: 9), but this perspective raises all types of problems. For one, various entities are not a sovereign state formally but are commonly regarded as conducting foreign policy: a sovereign without a state such as the Holy See; a government that has not been universally recognized as the legitimate representative of a sovereign state, such as Taiwan; *de facto* state(let)s that have not been recognized at all, such as Puntland or Kurdistan; subnational entities with diplomatic competencies, such as Flanders and the Walloon Region in Belgium; or supranational entities with such competencies, such as the European Union. Here we assume foreign policy to be a property of a representative of a sovereign state because international diplomacy is still conducted predominantly by sovereign states and because populist parties manifest themselves within sovereign states.

The notion of foreign suggests that a distinction can be made between the domestic and international spheres (Kaarbo et al., 2013: 2–4; Neack et al., 1995: 6–7; White, 1989: 5); traditionally, foreign policy was about the physical security of the state and its inhabitants, limiting the main foreign policy domain to defence and assuming that the state's other external behavior (e.g. trade, cultural ties, etc.) were subordinated to traditional security concerns. Although this ordering has always been debated, it has come under serious attack because of the end of the Cold War, the advent of globalization, and the rise of regional organizations. The end of the Cold War has made traditional security less salient and has made room for what is now called humanitarian intervention; globalization effectively has turned trade, finance, migration, and the environment into highly salient foreign policy issues that are subject to pressures from various affected domestic actors; regionalization, especially within the EU, has increased the number of actors involved in foreign policy and has forced member states to coordinate (and adjust) their foreign policy with other member states (Hill, 2003; Verbeek and Van der Vleuten, 2008: 358–62).

In this chapter, we contend that in the contemporary world, foreign policy, although still mainly the act of a sovereign state, encompasses many different policy domains and that it is the product of many actors (domestic as well as international) that feel affected by events in the outside world (Verbeek and Zaslove, 2015a: 531–2). Hence, populist parties can be expected to develop an interest in many different policy domains that currently could be considered as the object of a state's foreign policy. In addition, in regional organizations such as the EU, populist parties may (in)directly affect the EU's foreign policy through their membership in the European Parliament or through their member state's governments.

Nationalism

In the process of linking populism with foreign policy, it is tempting to equate populist foreign policy with nationalist foreign policy. This requires us to discuss the concept of nationalism as it pertains to populism (see also De Cleen's contribution in this volume). Two important issues often cloud the relationship between populism and nationalism: first, populism and nationalism are both thin-centered ideologies (Freeden, 1998; Mudde, 2004). Thus, they cannot stand alone, and they must each attach themselves to other ideologies. Second, and in part related to the first point, populism and nationalism often (but do not have to) appear together. Thus, for example, the defining characteristics of the populist radical right (PRR) are both populism and an exclusive form of nationalism, i.e. nativism (De Cleen, this volume; Mudde, 2007), or what De Cleen refers to as "an exclusionary ethnic-cultural nationalism" (De Cleen, this volume).

If we further consider the core characteristics of nationalism, we see that nationalism often reflects populist premises because of nationalism's emphasis on the nation, mirroring the populists' will of the people. Conversely, if we turn to populism, we see that populism often manifests itself within a nation-state and often links the people with the nation. For example, nationalism is a defining characteristic of the populist radical right, which uses a nativist-nationalist discourse to mobilize anti-immigration sentiments (De Cleen, this volume; Mudde, 2007). In addition, the success and the failure of a populist party may be determined by the ability of the populist party to appeal to the national culture of a nation. A prime example was the ability of Dutch populist Pim Fortuyn in the early 2000s to succeed where other Dutch radical right parties had previously failed (i.e., the *Centrumpartij*, the *Centrumpartij'86*, and the *Centrumdemocraten*) (Mudde and van Holsteyn, 2000; Rydgren and Van Holsteyn, 2005). Fortuyn framed his populism as the protection of traditional Dutch liberalism. This allowed him to juxtapose traditional Dutch liberal values to the presumed illiberalism of Islam (Akkerman,

2005). This appeal to the notion of Dutch liberal sentiments (and his ability to contextu-alize it in Dutch national culture) proved crucial for the legitimization, and the success, of his party (*Lijst Pim Fortuyn*) (Akkerman, 2005). At the same time, populist move-ments need not necessarily be nationalist: they may emphasize the tension between peo-ple and elites without hammering on the question of national identity; examples include PODEMOS in Spain and *Movimento Cinque Stelle* (M5S) in Italy.

In essence, therefore, even if populism and nationalism often appear in a single move-ment, the key difference between populism and nationalism is the distinction between the people and the elite, which is inherent to populism but need not be present in nationalism (cf. De Cleen, this volume). It is possible to conceive of an elitist national-ism, while an elitist populism is an oxymoron. To be sure, it could be argued that popu-list leaders may emerge from the political elite or the political establishment (i.e., Geert Wilders in the Netherlands, see Vossen, 2011) or that they may attract voters with elitist attitudes (Akkerman et al., 2014), but in order for the party to be considered populist it must employ a people-oriented anti-elite discourse.

Throughout our discussion of the relationship between populism and foreign policy, we therefore need to be cautious and avoid automatically equating the two. This requires us to argue more specifically which items of foreign policy are salient to populists. Describing their foreign policy attitudes as nationalist would be too one-dimensional and miss the importance of preserving the pure people as the point of departure for any policy, including foreign policy.

THE IMPACT OF INTERNATIONAL POLITICS ON POPULISM

International relations (IR) and comparative politics (CP) have developed largely as separate research fields within political science. Although this has produced fruit-ful theory building and empirical research within each area, their separation has also resulted in mutual neglect. At the same time, it has repeatedly been argued that domestic politics and international relations are often interrelated. In IR, this has led to the sub-discipline of comparative foreign policy analysis, which seeks to account for international outcomes by examining domestic level ("second image") explana-tions (Hudson, 2005). Similarly, IR scholars have engaged with the question of how processes at the level of the international system may impact domestic politics ("sec-ond image reversed") (Gourevitch, 1978). This attention to the international-national nexus has been adopted by some comparativists (see esp. Almond, 1989) and has always been present in the work of comparative historians such as Charles Tilly (esp. Tilly and Ardant, 1975) who focused on the strong relationship between war and state building. Our contribution seeks to build on these traditions by focusing on how changes in the international political and economic systems create the conditions for changes in party competition in various countries and for hindering or favoring the rise of populism. In doing so, we will discuss the impact of structural changes in international relations on domestic political systems.

Focusing on the link between international and domestic politics allows us to examine attempts by foreign actors to influence the domestic politics of countries in which populism thrives. Indeed, there is plenty of evidence that foreign actors seek to influence domestic developments in countries where populism is strong, especially when these parties participate in government coalitions. This may lead to a lack of trust or even shaming and ridiculing behavior, e.g. when the Berlusconi government in Italy and the Orban government in Hungary were perceived to threaten political stability (Kington, 2011; Sedelmeier, 2014); it may even lead to sanctions, as when the EU took measures against Austria when the Austrian Freedom Party (FPÖ) joined the Austrian government (Merlingen et al., 2001). Because of lack of space, we here limit ourselves to the general impact of international developments on the rise of populism.[2]

Within the European context, building on the discussion of radical right-wing parties, interest in populism enjoyed a growth spurt in the early 1990s (Betz, 1994; Taggart, 1995). Not coincidentally, this surge coincided with three major international transformations: the end of the Cold War; the advent of (or, depending on one's view, a new spurt in) globalization; and the intensification of the European integration process. As a matter of fact, studies of earlier expressions of populism had already suggested that its rise and success were related to a specific international context; for example, the American Populist Movement was partly a response by agricultural producers who reacted to the steady downfall in prices into a depression in 1893. This downfall itself was partially caused by increased international competition thanks to the opening of the Suez Canal and the advent of steam transportation (Hofstadter, 1969: 14–16). Populism's popularity among the urban middle classes in Latin America in the twentieth century, and possibly all Latin American politics, cannot be understood without taking into account the impact of economic transformations and the attempt to incorporate the disenfranchised masses. Populist parties often attempted to accomplish this where other parties had failed; this was the case, for example, for Peronism in Argentina (Jansen, 2015; Roberts, 2015).

European integration spurred populist resentment in the Netherlands as early as the 1950s and 1960s when groups of farmers mobilized against the perceived threat of the European Common Agricultural Policy, which found its political expression in a fairly successful farmers' party, the *Boerenpartij* (1966–1981) (Vossen, 2004). In this chapter, we will focus on populism's popularity as a subject of academic research since the late 1980s and the early 1990s, when globalization is often said to have taken off (Strange, 1988) and when the European integration process began to accelerate due to the adoption of the Single European Act in 1984, which envisioned a common market by 1992 as a European response to increased international economic competition from Asia and the Americas (Moravcsik, 1991).

The End of the Cold War

The end of the Cold War restructured many Western political systems, particularly in terms of the legitimacy of different political discourses, thus redefining the political space for electoral competition. Most importantly, it left the radical left bereft of much of its ideological credentials and suggested that liberal democracy was not only the only game in town but that it was here to stay (Fukuyama, 1989). As much as this was celebrated in many circles, it soon became evident that political parties had now lost their main adversary. Consequently, the imperfections of these parties' governments, which had widely been accepted as part of a necessary political stability in times of Communist threat, could now become the focal point of political debate, legitimizing the populist perspective of the elites as the enemy of the honest people. This contributed to the end of the traditional dominance of specific parties in countries such as Austria, Italy, Japan, Mexico, the Netherlands, and Sweden. These deeper and more immediate changes acted to transform old political parties (e.g. social democrats moving towards the Third Way) and to create opportunities for new political parties to emerge, particularly populist parties. The effect was not limited to Western European parties. In Latin America, radical left ideologies no longer enjoyed the same appeal as before the fall of communism, with the exception of Cuba. In Central and Eastern Europe, where few parties chose to rally behind the radical left banner, the new era caused dormant domestic issues, which had remained frozen because of Cold War restrictions, to resurface and become part of the political discourse. This was particularly true for old irredentist claims regarding territory and national identity that had not been touched since the Interbellum, especially in Hungary, Slovakia, Romania, and (the former Republic of) Yugoslavia.

Indeed, it is not a coincidence that when democracy becomes the only game in town, political differentiation will be founded on the fundamental questions underlying democracy: Who belongs to the demos and is the demos properly represented by the elite? The salience of these questions was to be reinforced by globalization and regional integration. These developments opened up a new space for populist actors. This is not to argue that populism was nonexistent before the end of the Cold War: there are numerous examples such as Poujadism in France and Peronism in Argentina. The argument is rather that the post-Cold War era created a ripe set of opportunity structures for the rise of populism.

Globalization

Globalization might best be captured as the disembedding of social relations from territory (Scholte, 2005). Politically, the end of the Cold War removed the territorial lid on the spread of political discourse that had already been partly lifted by technological advances that had made cross-border communication more difficult to control in the 1980s, particularly satellite television and the fax machine. Substantively, democracy, coupled with ideas about the rule of law, human rights, and economic liberalism, emerged as the dominant global discourse that set the boundaries on everyday politics. Relatively speaking, economic and financial globalization has meant that producers and financial investors face fewer restrictions in moving production and investment to places where the conditions are best for delivering their products and services anywhere on the globe. These developments have created (relative) winners and (relative) losers in societies all over the world in terms of job security, wages, social benefits, etc. (Frieden and Rogowski, 1996).

Politically, this has had three consequences for domestic politics. First, the differentiated patterns of winners and losers of globalization ensured that the salience of traditional left-right cleavages was reduced: globalization split the working class and created new social strata (Kriesi et al., 2008; 2012). It opened the door for left-wing populism to establish the notion of the global economy as the common man's new enemy. Second, globalization made it more difficult for national governments to promote their citizens' welfare: producers hopped between countries in search of the lowest production costs; currency crises in the 1990s (ERM crises 1992; Asian financial crisis 1998–1999) brought home the message that governments wanting to profit from global financial markets needed to surrender their freedom regarding monetary policy (Rodrik, 2000). This meant that it was harder for a country to build and defend a welfare state. Thus, some states turned to regional bodies to try to institutionalize social rights, in a regional block, within the context of globalization. The European Union is an extreme example of this pattern (Ross, 2006). A consequence of this shift has been a decrease in voters' trust in national governments to deliver goods and services, spurring an interest in local governance and decentralization. In addition, it created an opportunity for political actors to mobilize voters against the transnational elite (be they managers of transnational corporations, financial speculators, or civil servants employed by international organizations). Third, globalization has put identity firmly on the political agenda, creating an environment in which the global, the national, and the local compete for loyalty, producing a debate on citizens' identity. Whereas some manage to combine different identity pressures, others rally around a geographically narrowed identity. This offers fertile ground for those trying to locate the true people; hence, the territorial component (often national or local) attached to such efforts. All in all, globalization has produced a politically powerful sentiment: a feeling that the global economy produces new victims and villains, renders governments less powerful, and requires a new anchor in terms of identity. It is therefore no surprise that globalization has functioned both as an opportunity structure and as material for the mobilization of left- and right-wing populism (e.g. Halikiopoulou et al., 2012; Harmsen, 2010; Mudde, 2007; Taggart, 1998; Vasilopoulou, 2011).

Regional Integration

Regional integration can be defined as a process in which national governments durably coordinate policies by being prepared to bear the short- and mid-term policy adjustment costs resulting from such coordination. Regional integration can remain strictly inter-governmental, but it can also involve the creation of a wider political-administrative system in which states pool their sovereignty (Keohane and Hoffmann, 1991) and accept a supranational legal system to ensure compliance. Through regional integration, often following existing trade patterns, states sought to strengthen their reduced steering capacity resulting from globalization. By opening up the economies of their region, yet tightening their borders within the wider global economy, states could profit from glob-alization and recapture some policy capacity. At the same time, such policy coordina-tion meant that some groups in their own societies would bear the adjustment costs and that some steering capacity had to be transferred to the newly created regional level (cf. Scholte, 2005). Many regional integration schemes were reinforced or newly founded after the Cold War. The European integration project has developed the furthest in this regard, and it now involves regional integration that can be characterized as suprana-tional in its economic and monetary dimensions.

This Janus-faced characteristic of regional integration has posed difficulties for national political parties, especially within the EU. First, it reinforces the debate over the proper locus of identity. Second, it opens up a debate regarding who belongs to the regional integration scheme and who does not. Third, it adds to the existing debate of winning or losing from globalization. Finally, it makes room for political parties that would assess the advantage of integration in terms of its consequences for the locality they seek to represent (e.g. Catalonia, Flanders, *Padania*). Together, these difficulties set the stage for populist parties that thrive on issues of inclusion and exclusion.

All in all, the end of the Cold War, globalization, and regional integration have thus changed the context in which day-to-day politics is currently played. They have con-tributed to the weakening of established parties and to the reduction of trust in national governments. International politics has thus contributed to a fundamentally different type of domestic politics. All these international developments thus create the condi-tions for a possible demand for populist parties and subsequently for these parties' for-eign policy positions.

Is There a Populist Foreign Policy?

As noted, the rise of populist parties follows important international developments: globalization, the end of the Cold War, and growth of regional organizations such as the EU. This brings populist parties, like all parties, to a fork in the road: because so many domestic issues now encompass international dimensions, populists have to take position in what Hanspeter Kriesi and his colleagues have defined as the new demarcation-integration cleavage (Kriesi et al., 2008; 2012). Kriesi and his colleagues argue that the traditional Rokkanian cleavages have been superseded by the demar-cation-integration cleavage. As a result, voters increasingly align along the degree to which they support open or closed societies, regarding both the economic and the cultural dimension. This potential realignment subsequently forces parties to take positions on both the cultural and economic dimensions of an increasingly internationalized environment, which often boil down to decisions regarding open or closed economic or cultural borders. All parties thus have to take issue with the contrast between a more cosmopolitan outlook, emphasizing multiculturalism, and a more parochial outlook, emphasizing closed cultural and economic borders. In a sense, populist parties face a more difficult challenge than traditional parties because these international developments force them to define more explicitly who constitutes the pure people. In doing so, the attached ideology becomes important in determining the foreign policy of the populist party in question. Depending on their specific thin-centered ideology, populist parties may be expected to take a more open or protectionist view on trade and finance. However, a similar issue arises when looking at the cultural dimension: some populist parties, i.e., populist radical right parties, constrict the pure people to a cultural unit confined within a nation state. Other populist parties have a notion of the people that is not necessarily restricted to a territorial unit such as the nation state: left-wing populists identify with the exploited. Thus, as Mudde and Rovira Kaltwasser (2013) note, left-wing populism tends to be inclusionary while right-wing populism tends to be exclusionary. Mudde and Rovira Kaltwasser (2013) base these conclusions on a comparison between left-wing populists in Latin America and right-wing populists in Europe. However, more recently, left-wing populists in Europe such as SYRIZA and PODEMOS also demonstrate that populists do not have to be exclusionary, given that both parties have a broader and more plural notion of the people (Kioupkiolis, 2016; Stavrakakis and Katsambekis, 2014).

We do not expect populist parties to take identical foreign policy positions. Rather, we expect them to differ in their foreign policy preferences because they will differ in their assessment of the impact that the international environment will have on their own understanding of who the pure people are. Below, we will discuss the foreign policy outlook of different populist parties on the basis of the demarcation-integration cleavage (Kriesi et al., 2008; 2012). This theoretical discussion is based on the most commonly cited populist parties in the literature, which can be categorized in the following way.

1. The radical right takes a nativist approach to the pure people. It includes the Italian Northern League (after the mid-1990s), the French National Front, the Austrian Freedom Party, the Danish People's Party, the Swiss People's Party, Jobbik in Hungary, the Party for Freedom in the Netherlands, and One Nation in Australia.
2. The market liberal creed locates the pure people in the honest, hardworking citizens who are endangered by the elite-run state. It encompasses Berlusconi's Go Italy!, the Belgian List Dedecker, the Dutch List Pim Fortuyn,[3] Peruvian president Alberto Fujimori in the 1990s, and the Liberal Party in Australia under John Howard.
3. The regionalists limit the pure people as historically belonging to a clear, smaller territorial unit. They are represented by the Italian Northern League and the Belgian Flemish Interest.[4]

4. Left-wing populism sees the pure people as a specific social category not necessarily hemmed in by national borders. It incorporates Germany's The Left, Greece's SYRIZA, the Dutch Socialist Party, Spain's PODEMOS, and Latin American parties led by leaders such as Chávez in Venezuela, Morales in Bolivia, and Correa in Ecuador.[5]

Below, we will describe how these four populist types take positions on four issue domains that have become salient issues of foreign policy since 1990. We expect them to determine their positions on the basis of their conception of the pure people and their attaching ideology: their general attitude towards international politics, their position regarding global finance and trade, their position on transborder migration, and finally their stand on regional integration.

General Outlook on International Politics

It might be tempting to argue that all populists will be anti-cosmopolitan. However, this is not the case. In fact, it would be a mistake to simply equate populism with nationalism, isolationism, and protectionism. Because the concept of the pure people may or may not refer to a group residing within the borders of a sovereign state, populists may or may not be internationalist in orientation. Left-wing populists refer to the exploited generally, which can induce them not to ignore the internationalist solidarity dimension of foreign policy, e.g. in terms of supporting development aid and global policies that protect workers (via, for example, organizations such as the International Labour Organization).

In Latin America this left-wing internationalism takes on a specific angle: left-wing populists such as Morales define the pure people by encompassing indigenous people and by excluding from their identity any links with the old (European) colonizing powers or the newer imperialism of the United States. Chávez, on the other hand, associated the people with the Bolivarian revolutionary movement and the elites with serving American interests (Thies, 2014: esp. 11–13). This has resulted in an internationalist foreign policy of a specific type that is aimed at uniting Latin American countries against the United States, the international institutions the US built, the global economic policies the US espouses, and those countries in the region that remain close to the US. The Organization of American States (OAS) was viewed by Ecuador's Rafael Correa as American-controlled, and its assessment of Ecuador's civil rights situation prompted him to support the construction of rival international organizations (de la Torre and Ortiz Lemos, 2016: 2). The Bolivarian Alliance of the Americas (ALBA) is thus meant to serve as an institution to counter American power in the region (and to mobilize domestic support) and has even resulted in a closer relation between alliance members and the People's Republic of China (Ellis, 2014: 49; Hawkins, 2016: 4–5). Similarly, Chávez created new regional institutions; for instance, the Spanish-language cable channel *TeleSUR* and a regional development bank, the *Banco Sur* (Hawkins, 2016: 14).

Anti-Americanism can also be observed in populist parties such as Jobbik in Hungary, which seeks to establish strong ties with Russia and Iran. More mainstream and governmental parties such as FIDESZ pursue a softer line, but clearly deviate from the overall more pro-Atlantic attitude of the EU (Nagy et al., 2013: 235).

Likewise, populists who borrow from market liberalism tend to favor market economies because they consider the market economy to be beneficial to the people as they define the people (this is the case for populist parties in Australia and Canada): the elite, through state bureaucracy and support of special interest groups, prevented the people from reaping the fruits of a true market economy (Sawer and Laycock, 2009). Hence, there is relative sympathy towards economic multilateralism in parties such as Go Italy! in Italy; in neoliberal populists in Peru under Fujimori, Brazil under Collor, and Argentina under Menem; and in so-called market populists in Australia (Howard) and Canada (Harper) (Sawer and Laycock, 2009; Verbeek and Zaslove, 2015b; Wear, 2008; Weyland, 1999). Nevertheless, such multilateralism was also easily put aside once the national interest seemed to be at stake: Berlusconi's governments never hesitated in defying western criticism and in concluding bilateral agreements, for example, with Libya (Verbeek and Zaslove, 2015b). Importantly, economic multilateralism is not always paralleled in other domains: Australia under Howard grew increasingly critical of the UN human rights system, especially the role of NGOs in that system, when the UN started monitoring Australian refugee policies (Sawer and Laycock, 2009: 146; Wear, 2008: 626–7).

The condemnation of the powerful state and the desire to protect the pure people need not go hand in hand with an internationalist outlook: the Tea Party in the US shows that populists may also decide that protectionism and even isolationism can be put forward as the proper foreign policy (Mead, 2011). This isolationist streak is also present in several populist parties that generally tend to oppose or be critical of military missions abroad, such as the Italian Northern League (Verbeek and Zaslove, 2015b). The attitude towards development aid depends on how the aid's effects on the pure people are assessed: the Dutch Party for Freedom (PVV) calls for a reduction in development aid (*Partij voor de Vrijheid*, 2010). However, the Italian Northern League argues that is it necessary to help people in their country of origin: this prevents migrants from coming to Europe and coincides with their claim of protecting their own pure people, i.e. *Padanians* and/or Italians. The infamous phrase of the party is *aiutiamo i popoli a casa loro* (Let's help the people in their own country; *Lega Nord*, 2014).

Importantly, the end of the Cold War opened old diplomatic wounds dating back to the World Wars I and II that had remained hidden under the cloak of communism and East-West confrontation. The democratic transitions in Central and Eastern Europe allowed populist parties, in both the East and West, to play the nationalist card (Weyland, 1999: 383). The Austrian FPÖ used accession to the EU to demand that the Czech government repeal the so-called Beneš Decrees and that the Slovenian government repeal the so-called AVNOJ Mandates; demands that were meant to cater to the grievances of ethnic Germans who were expelled from these countries after 1945

Table 20.1 Expected positions of populist parties on salient foreign policy issues.

	Populist Radical Right	Populist Market Liberal	Populist Regionalist	Populist Left-Wing
General attitude	Isolationist—opposed to multilateral deployment of the military	Economic cosmopolitan—open to multilateralism	Undefined—foreign policy should serve the region	Social cosmopolitan—international arrangements to protect the weak and to counter the existing hegemony
Regional (including European) integration	Opposed to Europeanization	In favor of open market	Depending on how the EU affects their goals for more autonomy	Critical of Europeanization, but more willing to engage with international organizations than the PRR
Trade and finance	Protectionist	Open	Depending on whether globalization serves prosperity in the region	Protectionist because of labor displacement
Transborder migration	Opposed	Not necessarily opposed	Unclear	Not necessarily opposed

(Heinisch, 2003: 106–7). Hungary's *Jobbik* openly seeks to redraw the map of Europe and to incorporate the old territories Hungary lost in the Treaty of Trianon in 1923 (Nagy et al., 2013: 234).

In sum, there is not a single populist foreign policy. Rather, we see a range of positions across populist types (see Table 20.1), ranging from isolationist policies to more open positions regarding cosmopolitanism or even a type of social cosmopolitanism. The differences among these positions depend in part on the relation between populism and the attaching ideology. Thus, the populist radical right tends to be more isolationist; the market liberals tend to be more open regarding cosmopolitanism and/or the market; and left-wing populists tend to have a more social cosmopolitan orientation, while favoring economic protection.

Transborder Migration

Currently, when we think of populism—in particular, European populism—migration is the first issue that comes to mind. There is no question that empirically immigration can be linked with populism, but it is linked with a specific type of populism: the populist radical right. Studies demonstrate that migration is one of the issues that matters most to populist radical right parties and their supporters (Ivarsflaten, 2008; Mudde, 2007; Van der Brug et al., 2005). Moreover, if one issue can be said to have prompted policy-making over the past thirty years, it would be migration. To be sure, it is difficult to trace the tangible effect of the populist radical right on immigration policy. Some scholars are sceptical of the impact of the radical right on immigration policies (Mudde, 2013), while others encourage us to also look to the role played by mainstream parties (Bale, 2008; Odmalm and Bale, 2015). On the surface, it does appear that migration policies in Western Europe have become stricter in the last decade. Although it might not be possible to trace the direct impact of the PRR on immigration, the PRR is part and parcel of the politicization of immigration.

One might wonder whether migration is a foreign policy issue. If a state's foreign policy is about maintaining sovereign control over its territory, its migration policies regulate the size and nature of its population. Moreover, states have created various arrangements to address the transborder movement of individuals: states have acknowledged the rights of refugees via international treaties and are bound by them, and in economic integration schemes, states regulate foreigners' access to the labor market. Migration policies thus belong to the core business of a state's foreign policy. Consequently, populist parties that agitate against migration are attempting to affect a country's foreign policy.

We can see the tangible influence of such parties on multilateral and bilateral policies: early on in Germany, for example, the rise of the *Republikaner* and violent attacks on migrants had an influence on German immigration policy as well as on the German government's move to change European asylum law (Verbeek and Zaslove, 2015a). In the 2000s, the Italian government under Berlusconi struck bilateral agreements with Libya to limit migration (Verbeek and Zaslove, 2015b). To be sure, the changing discourse surrounding migration has also led to the securitization of immigration and the European borders. Sometimes this can be attributed to populists' participation in government (or their support of a government); for instance, in Denmark. In other cases, the link is indirect: the rising popularity of populist radical right parties has often permitted mainstream parties to become stricter on migration (Bale, 2003) not only in Europe but also in Australia, where the Howard government had to respond to the challenge of One Nation (Wear, 2008), and in the United Kingdom, where quarrels over migration seem to have spurred the Brexit group (Taub, 2016). Recently, these dynamics have played out within the context of the EU's external policies: populists and the populist radical right have contributed to the discussion concerning Schengen (closing borders) in countries such as Denmark and France, while the European responses to the migration streams that began to emerge in Europe in 2015 have been influenced by radical opposition to migrants (for example, demonstrations in Germany by *PEGIDA* and protests against asylum centers in the Netherlands). Populist radical right parties in Central and Eastern Europe have influenced state reactions to the migration crisis, leading several governments (e.g. Hungary and Slovakia) to refuse to take in Islamic refugees. Countries such as Poland and Hungary have become sceptical of EU asylum policies, particularly burden sharing.

However, linking immigration with populism refers to a specific type of populist party. Thus, left-wing populist parties in Europe tend to be less anti-immigrant. Some parties, such as the Left Party in Germany and the Dutch Socialist Party, have at times made critical remarks regarding migration or have engaged in actions that could be interpreted as anti-immigrant (Furlong, 2005; Trouw, 2012); however, migration is not a core theme for these populist left-wing parties. This is even clearer for other populist left-wing parties such as PODEMOS in Spain or SYRIZA in Greece (Kioupkiolis, 2016; Stavrakakis and Katsambekis, 2014). In this regard, left-wing populist parties in Europe resemble left-wing parties in Latin America. Of course, in Latin America, migration is not as important an issue as it is in Europe. Importantly, Mudde and Rovira Kaltwasser (2013) argue that in Latin America, populists focus on economic issues and inclusion, while in Europe, (radical right) populists focus on culture and exclusion. Market liberal populist parties do not fully display the expected pattern: Berlusconi's Go Italy! (until it joined a coalition with the Northern League in 2000) was not particulary concerned with immigration, owing in part to the fact that it was a populist liberal and not a populist radical right party (Zaslove, 2011). Yet, under populist and liberal Prime Minister John Howard Australia adopted strong policies to counter migration.

Again, we see a range of positions rather than a single perspective regarding foreign policy (cf. Table 20.1): the most distinct is the populist radical right, which embraces opposition to migration as its core position. For the other populist creeds, this is less clear. Both market liberal and regional populists do not necessarily oppose migration, although more often than not they are also sceptical of it. A clear example of the latter is the Northern League. In the early 1990s, when it was more of a regional populist than a populist radical right party, it was sceptical of migration but was not outright anti-immigrant (Zaslove, 2011). Finally, left-wing populists often do not oppose migration. Or, in cases in which left-wing populist parties are critical of immigration, they tend to be milder than the populist radical right, often linking their claims with labor market issues rather than with cultural exclusion.

Trade and Finance

Populist parties will also take a different stance on economic issues depending on their attaching ideology. However, unlike migration, there tends to be more overlap between radical left and radical right populist movements with regard to the economy. Radical left and radical right populist movements both tend to oppose economic globalization (March, 2007; Mudde, 2007). In addition, populist radical left parties such as the Left Party in Germany, the Socialist Party in the Netherlands, and SYRIZA in Greece are also critical of EU integration, often linking the EU with neoliberalism and with the process of marketization. However, unlike with the populist radical right, there tends to be a willingness among the populist radical left to have a more constructive engagement with the EU (*Die Linke*, 2011; *Socialistische Partij*, 2012; Stavrakakis and Katsambekis, 2014). In Latin America, populist left parties oppose neoliberalism. Populist left-wing parties have been particularly successful in states that possess natural resources, taking advantage of their wealth (and a certain degree of economic independence) to oppose the neoliberal reforms. The populist left in countries such as Venezuela, Bolivia, and Ecuador have used the monies received from natural resources to promise an alternative politics, an anti-austerity left-wing politics (Weyland, 2009).

If we return to our broader notion of foreign policy, we see that the discourse of populist parties could potentially play an important role in influencing foreign policy. The real effects are, however, more difficult to tangibly determine. Populist radical right parties such as the Dutch Party for Freedom, the Italian Northern League, and the Austrian Freedom Party appear on the surface to have affected EU integration policies via their impact on public opinion and the government coalitions of which they were part. However, in the end, their tangible influence is often not as significant as one might expect (for Italy, see Verbeek and Zaslove, 2015b). In contrast, left-wing populists such as SYRIZA in Greece, even while in power, were not able to push for an alternative to austerity measures. Perhaps oil-rich countries such as Venezuela have been more successful in steering their own course; for example, Chávez sought to forge an alliance of Latin American countries, seeking "to realize the Bolivarian Dream—the unification of Latin American countries under a single government that excluded the United States" (Hawkins, 2016: 255). Chávez attempted to create an alternative or even a counter hegemonic movement through his ALBA organization and already existing organizations such as Mercosur (Hawkins, 2016).

In sum, we again see various patterns (cf. Table 20.1): unsurprisingly, the PRR tends to be protectionist, while populist liberals favor an open economy. For regionalists, it is somewhat different: their position depends on whether they see globalization as a threat. A perfect example is the Northern League. In the early 1990s it was more in favor of open borders, while in the later 1990s it began to demand more protectionist policies (Zaslove, 2011). Finally, the populist left's protectionism is in part based on fear of labor displacement and its opposition to neoliberalism and globalization.

Regional Integration

It is often assumed that populists oppose regional integration. However, in reality, the views of populists towards regional integration can vary, while their tangible influence on regional integration is also uncertain. For example, we would expect populists to oppose MERCOSUR and the EU. This is in part true: populist radical right parties tend to be sceptical of EU integration on several fronts. They oppose the EU with regard to migration, they are often sceptical of economic integration and the loss of sovereignty and question the democratic legitimacy of the EU, while also opposing the bureaucratization of domestic politics (Liang, 2007b; Mudde, 2007). Indeed, Wilders's PVV has called for the Netherlands to leave the EU (*Partij voor de Vrijheid*, 2012; *NRC Handelsblad*, 2016), while Nigel Farage's UKIP was influential in the victory of the Brexit referendum in 2016. This is also true for right-wing populist parties in Central and

Eastern Europe: FIDESZ in Hungary and PiS in Poland can be viewed as parties that are sceptical of the EU (Ágh, 2015). In addition, Berlusconi's party Go Italy! demonstrated a high degree of scepticism towards EU integration, even though when push came to shove, the Berlusconi government complied with the EU and ratified the important measures (Verbeek and Zaslove, 2015b; Zaslove, 2011).

However, at the same time, it should be noted that the PRR has not always opposed European integration. In the late 1980s and the early 1990s, many PRR parties were in favor of European integration. For many PRR parties, the 1992 Maastricht Treaty was a turning point towards a more Euroskeptic position (Mudde, 2007). Still, this does not mean that all populist radical right parties oppose all aspects of the EU. PRR parties often see the advantage of the EU. Thus, the Italian Northern League called on the EU to invoke trade barriers against low-cost Chinese imports (Woods, 2009; Zaslove, 2011). Moreover, a number of PRR parties have attempted to facilitate a closer working relationship, focusing, for example, on controlling immigration, opposing terrorism and Islam, advocating for policies that support the family, and supporting a more social Europe (Liang, 2007b: 14), while more recently, several populist radical right parties have begun to collaborate in the European Parliament, forming the *Europe of Nations and Freedom* group (Paris and Holehouse, 2015; http://www.enfgroup-ep.eu/).

The picture regarding left-wing populism is similarly blurred. In Latin America, left-wing populists tend to be more sceptical of the market economy, but, at the same time, as noted above, they have also tried to work together to forge regional blocks that oppose neoliberalism. In Europe, the positions of left-wing populists are also ambiguous. Although they often perceive the EU to be linked with neoliberalism, parties such as PODEMOS and even SYRIZA do not necessarily oppose the EU and regional integration; instead, they seek to propose an alternative EU.

If we turn to regional integration, we encounter patterns similar to those above (cf. Table 20.1). The populist radical right in most cases opposes regionalization. Populist liberals tend to favor regional integration insofar as it facilitates an open economy. The populist left tends to be critical of regional integration, although less so than the populist radical right. In some cases, i.e. in Latin America, there may even be attempts to forge counter hegemonic international alliances and institutions using international organizations. With regard to the populist regionalists, their position depends again on how regional integration affects their goal for regional autonomy.

Conclusion

The relationship between populism and foreign policy is dynamic: the changing nature of foreign policy, particularly after the Cold War, has created new opportunities for the rise of populist parties. Consequently, populist parties have had to develop their own foreign policies. The distinguishing feature of populist parties is the moral people/elite distinction. Determining a consistent populist foreign policy across all populist parties is difficult, however, given that it is the attaching ideology that often determines the specific foreign policy positions of the parties. Here, we have distinguished between four such populist variations: populist radical right; populist market liberal; populist regionalist; and populist left-wing. Still, they all judge foreign policy in terms of its effects on the elite-people juxtaposition. After all, this is what makes them a populist party. In some cases, this is manifested in the isolationist policy of the populist radical right, which entertains a narrow notion of the people; in other cases, it can take on the solidaristic internationalist cloak of the populist left parties, which seek to project a more encompassing notion of a people. In sum, international politics matters to populism, but the way it plays out differs across states and ideologies. Although all countries discussed here faced the triple challenge of the end of the Cold War, the advent of globalization, and the growth of regional organizations, populist parties have responded in different ways. We maintain that this variation is mainly caused by the thin-centered ideology of populism: it needs to seek an ideological bedfellow, the choice of which steers their position regarding international challenges and hence their foreign policy positions.

However, another plausible explanation presents itself, one that originates from populism's basic distinction between the elite and the pure people: the prevailing international challenges offer an opportunity for populists to redefine or expand the notion of the corrupt elite; for example, the populist radical right tends to view the European elites in Brussels as their enemies, which influences their opposition to EU integration, financial open borders, and migration (insofar as these policy dimensions are often linked with EU integration). For the populist liberals, the elite is something else: the bureaucratic politician. If we turn to the populist regionalists, the elite is less obvious. It can be the dominant political parties, or it can be the bureaucrats in Brussels. For the populist left parties, the elites can be politicians within the state, but they can also be transnational financial elites or leaders of other countries who push for globalization. In sum, it appears that international events, through the need to formulate a foreign policy, may induce populists to rethink their notion of the elite, and hence the threat to the pure people.

The study of populism and foreign policy is an emerging field. It will require more empirical research on the effect of international politics on the fortunes of populists as well as the foreign policies these parties pursue. Here, we set out to delineate four different possible types of populist foreign policy. If we want to understand populists' successes and failures in pursuing specific foreign policies, we need to incorporate the impact of domestic political systems (cf. Kaarbo, 2012), as well as the dynamics of coalition politics (Verbeek and Zaslove, 2015b) and possibly agenda setting. Implementing this research agenda might bring comparative politics and international relations closer together.

NOTES

1 Exceptions are: Liang, 2007a; Verbeek and Zaslove, 2015a; 2015b; Chryssogelos, 2010.
2 See, for more information, the special issue edited by Taggart and Rovira Kaltwasser (2016) devoted to international and national responses to populists in government.

3   The List Pim Fortuyn is a difficult case to classify. Given its strong anti-Islam position, it is often classified as a populist radical right party.

4   The Northern League and the Flemish Interest are classified as populist, regionalist, and radical right. The Northern League, in particular, evolved in the mid-1990s from a populist regionalist to a populist radical right party.

5   That leaves some mavericks that are more difficult to classify, such as Italy's Five Star Movement and America's (Republican) Tea Party.

REFERENCES

Ágh, A. 2015. "Radical party system changes in five East-Central European states: Eurosceptic and populist parties on the move in the 2010s," *Baltic Journal of Political Science*, 4(1): 23–48.

Akkerman, A., C. Mudde, and A. Zaslove. 2014. "How populist are the people? Measuring populist attitudes in voters," *Comparative Political Studies*, 47(9): 1324–53.

Akkerman, T. 2005. "Anti-immigration parties and the defence of liberal values: the exceptional case of the List Pim Fortuyn," *Journal of Political Ideologies*, 10(3): 337–54.

Almond, G. A. 1989. "The international–national connection," *British Journal of Political Science*, 19(2): 237–59.

Bale, T. 2003. "Cinderella and her ugly sisters: the mainstream and extreme right in Europe's bipolarising party systems," *West European Politics*, 26(3): 67–90.

Bale, T. 2008. "Turning round the telescope: centre-right parties and immigration and integration policy in Europe," *Journal of European Public Policy*, 15(3): 315–30.

Berendt, J. 2016. "E.U. accuses Polish government of undermining democracy," *The New York Times*, April 13.

Betz, H. G. 1994. *Radical right-wing populism in Western Europe*. New York: St. Martin's Press.

Chryssogelos, A. S. 2010. "Undermining the west from within: European populists, the US and Russia," *European View*, 9(2): 267–77.

de la Torre, C. and A. Ortiz Lemos. 2016. "Populist polarization and the slow death of democracy in Ecuador," *Democratization*, 23(2): 221–41.

Die Linke. 2011. "Programme of the *Die Linke* Party." http://en.die-linke.de/die-linke/documents/party-programme/, English version accessed July 8, 2016.

Ellis, R. E. 2014. "Latin America's foreign policy as the region engages China," *Security and Defense Studies Review*, 15(1): 41–59.

Freeden, M. 1998. "Is nationalism a distinct ideology?," *Political Studies*, 46(4): 748–65.

Frieden, J. A. and R. Rogowski. 1996. "The impact of the international economy on national policies: an analytical overview," in H. Milner and R. O. Keohane (eds), *Internationalization and Domestic Politics*. Cambridge: Cambridge University Press, 25–47.

Fukuyama, F. 1989. "The end of history?," *The National Interest*, 16: 3–18.

Furlong, R. 2005. "New German left gains momentum," *BBC News*, May 8.

Gourevitch, P. 1978. "The second image reversed: the international sources of domestic politics," *International Organization*, 19(4): 881–912.

Hakim, P. 2006. "Is Washington losing Latin America?," *Foreign Affairs*, 85(1): 39–53.

Halikiopoulou, D., K. Nanou, and S. Vasilopoulou. 2012. "The paradox of nationalism: the common denominator of radical right and radical left euroscepticism," *European Journal of Political Research*, 51(4): 504–39.

Harmsen, R. 2010. "Concluding comment: on understanding the relationship between populism and Euroscepticism," *Perspectives on European Politics and Society*, 11(3): 333–41.

Hawkins, K. A. 2016. "Responding to radical populism: Chavismo in Venezuela," *Democratization*, 23(2): 242–62.

Heinisch, R. 2003. "Success in opposition—failure in government: explaining the performance of right-wing populist parties in public office," *West European Politics*, 26(3): 91–130.

Hill, C. 2003. *The Changing Politics of Foreign Policy*. Houndmills: Palgrave Macmillan.

Hofstadter, R. 1969. "North America," in G. Ionescu and E. Gellner (eds), *Populism: Its Meanings and National Characteristics*. London: Weidenfeld and Nicolson, 9–27.

Hudson, V. M. 2005. "Foreign policy analysis: actor-specific theory and the ground of international relations," *Foreign Policy Analysis*, 1(1): 1–30.

Ivarsflaten, E. 2008. "What unites right-wing populists in Western Europe? Re-examining grievance mobilization models in seven successful cases," *Comparative Political Studies*, 41(1): 3–23.

Jansen, R. S. 2015. "Populist mobilization: a new theoretical approach to populism," in Carlos de la Torre (ed.), *The Promise and Perils of Populism: Global Perspectives*. Lexington: University Press of Kentucky, 159–88.

Kaarbo, J. 2012. *Coalition Politics and Cabinet Decision Making: A Comparative Analysis of Foreign Policy Choices*. Ann Arbor: University of Michigan Press.

Kaarbo, J., J. S. Lantis, and R. K. Beasley. 2013. "The analysis of foreign policy in comparative perspective," in J. Kaarbo, J. S. Lantis, and R. K. Beasley (eds), *Foreign Policy in Comparative Perspective*, 2nd edn. Los Angeles: Sage, 1–26.

Keohane, R. O. and S. Hoffmann. 1991. "Institutional change in Europe in the 1980s," in S. Hoffman and R. O. Keohane (eds), *The New European Community: Decisionmaking and Institutional Change*. Boulder: Westview, 1–39.

Kington, T. 2011. "Merkozy smirk at EU crisis summit boosts Berlusconi," *The Guardian*, October 24.

Kioupkiolis, A. 2016. "Podemos: the ambiguous promises of left-wing populism in contemporary Spain," *Journal of Political Ideologies*, 21(2): 99–120.

Kriesi, H., E. Grande, M. Dolezal, M. Helbling, D. Höglinger, S. Hutter, and B. Wüest. 2012. *Political Conflict in Western Europe*. Cambridge: Cambridge University Press.

Kriesi, H., E. Grande, R. Lachat, M. Dolezal, S. Bornschier, and T. Frey. 2008. *West European Politics in the Age of Globalization*. Cambridge: Cambridge University Press.

Lega Nord. 2014. http://www.leganord.org/sostienici/185-eventi/referendum-2014, accessed July 7, 2016.

Liang, C. S. (ed.). 2007a. *Europe for the Europeans: The Foreign and Security Policy of the Populist Radical Right*. Aldershot: Ashgate, 2007.

Liang, C. S. 2007b. "Europe for the Europeans: the foreign and security policy of the populist radical right," in C. S. Liang (ed.), *Europe for the Europeans: The Foreign and Security Policy of the Populist Radical Right*. Aldershot: Ashgate, 1–32.

March, L. 2007. "From vanguard of the proletariat to *vox populi*: left-populism as a 'shadow' of contemporary socialism," *SAIS Review of International Affairs*, 27(1): 63–77.

Mead, W. R. 2011. "The Tea Party and American foreign policy," *Foreign Affairs*, 90(2): 28–44.

Merlingen, M., C. Mudde, and U. Sedelmeier. 2001. "The right and the righteous? European norms, domestic politics and the sanctions against Austria," *Journal of Common Market Studies*, 39(1): 59–77.

Moravcsik, A. 1991. "Negotiating the Single European Act: national interests and conventional statecraft in the European Community," *International Organization*, 45(1): 19–56.

Mudde, C. 2004. "The populist zeitgeist," *Government and Opposition*, 39(4): 542–63.

Mudde, C. 2007. *Populist Radical Right Parties in Europe*. Cambridge: Cambridge University Press.

Mudde, C. 2013. "Three decades of populist radical right parties in Western Europe: so what?," *European Journal of Political Research*, 52(1): 1–19.

Mudde, C. and C. Rovira Kaltwasser. 2013. "Exclusionary vs. inclusionary populism: comparing contemporary Europe and Latin America," *Government and Opposition*, 48(2): 147–74.

Mudde, C. and J. van Holsteyn. 2000. "The Netherlands: explaining the limited success of the extreme right," in P. Hainsworth (ed.), *The Politics of the Extreme Right: From the Margins to the Mainstream*. London and New York: Pinter, 144–71.

Nagy, A. B., T. Boros, and Z. Vasali. 2013. "More radical than the radicals: the Jobbik Party in international comparison," in R. Melzer and S. Serafin (eds), *Right-Wing Extremism in Europe: Country Analyses, Counter-Strategies and Labor-Market Oriented Exit Strategies*. Berlin: Friedrich Ebert Stiftung, 229–54.

Neack, L. 2008. *The New Foreign Policy: Power Seeking in a Globalized Era*. Plymouth: Rowman and Littlefield.

Neack, L., J. A. K. Hey, and P. J. Haney. 1995. "Generational change in foreign policy analysis," in L. Neack, J. A. K. Hey, and P. J. Haney (eds), *Foreign Policy Analysis: Continuity and Change in Its Second Generation*. Englewood Cliffs: Prentice Hall, 1–16.

NRC Handelsblad. 2016. "Komt er ooit een Nexit?," June 16.

Odmalm, P. and T. Bale. 2015. "Immigration into the mainstream: conflicting ideological streams, strategic reasoning and party competition," *Acta Politica*, 50(4): 365–78.

Paris, S. H. and M. Holehouse. 2015. "Marine Le Pen forms far-right group in European Parliament," *The Telegraph*, June 16.

Partij voor de Vrijheid. 2010. "De agenda van hoop en optimisme. Een tijd om te kiezen: PVV 2010–2015," Documentatiecentrum Nederlandse Politieke Partijen: http://pubnpp.eldoc.ub.rug.nl/root/verkiezingsprogramma/TK/pvv2010/, accessed August 12, 2016.

Partij voor de Vrijheid. 2012. "Hún Brussel, óns Nederland: Verkiezingsprogramma 2012–2017," Documentatiecentrum Nederlandse Politieke Partijen: http://pubnpp.eldoc.ub.rug.nl/root/verkiezingsprogramma/TK/pvv2012/, accessed August 12, 2016.

Roberts, K. M. 2012. "Populism and democracy in Venezuela under Hugo Chávez," in C. Mudde and C. Rovira Kaltwasser (eds), *Populism in Europe and the Americas: Threat or Corrective for Democracy?* Cambridge: Cambridge University Press, 136–59.

Roberts, K. M. 2015. "Populism, political mobilizations, and crisis of political representation," in C. de la Torre (ed.), *The Promise and Perils of Populism: Global Perspectives*. Lexington: University Press of Kentucky, 140–58.

Rodrik, D. 2000. "Governance of economic globalization," in J. S. Nye and J. D. Donahue (eds), *Governance in a Globalizing World*. Washington: Brookings, 347–65.

Ross, G. 2006. "The European Union and the future of European politics," in M. Kesselman and J. Krieger (eds), *European Politics in Transition*. Boston: Houghton Mifflin Company, 37–132.

Rovira Kaltwasser, C. and P. Taggart (eds). 2016. "Dealing with populists in government," *Democratization*, 23(2), special issue.

Rydgren, J. and J. van Holsteyn. 2005. "Holland and Pim Fortuyn: a deviant case or the beginning of something new?," in J. Rydgren (ed.), *Movements of Exclusion: Radical Right-Wing Populism in the Western World*. New York: Nova Science Publishers, 41–59.

Sawer, M. and D. Laycock. 2009. "Down with elites and up with inequality: market populism in Australia and Canada," *Commonwealth and Comparative Politics*, 47(2): 133–50.

Scholte, J. A. 2005. *Globalization: A Critical Introduction*. Houndmills: Palgrave Macmillan.

Sedelmeier, U. 2014. "Anchoring democracy from above? The European Union and democratic backsliding in Hungary and Romania after accession," *Journal of Common Market Studies*, 52(1): 105–21.

Socialistische Partij. 2012. "Nieuw vertrouwen: Verkiezingsprogramma SP 2013–2017," Documentatiecentrum Nederlandse Politieke Partijen, accessed August 12, 2016.

Stavrakakis, Y. and G. Katsambekis. 2014. "Left-wing populism in the European periphery: the case of SYRIZA," *Journal of Political Ideologies*, 19(2): 119–42.

Strange, S. 1988. *State and Markets: An Introduction to International Political Economy*. London: Pinter.

Taggart, P. 1995. "New populist parties in Western Europe," *West European Politics*, 18(1): 34–51.

Taggart, P. 1998. "A touchstone of dissent: Euroscepticism in contemporary Western European party systems," *European Journal of Political Research*, 33(3): 363–88.

Taub, A. 2016. "A lesson from 'Brexit': on immigration, feelings trump facts," *The New York Times*, June 27.

Thies, C. G. 2014. "Role theory and foreign policy analysis in Latin America," *Foreign Policy Analysis*, on-line publication. doi: 10.1111/fpa.12072.

Tilly, C. and G. Ardant (eds). 1975. *The Formation of National States in Western Europe*. Princeton: Princeton University Press.

Trouw. 2012. "SP begon in 2005 al meldpunt Oost-Europeanen," February 14.

Van der Brug, W., M. Fennema, and J. Tillie. 2005. "Why some anti-immigrant parties fail and others succeed: a two-step model of aggregate electoral support," *Comparative Political Studies*, 38(5): 537–73.

Vasilopoulou, S. 2011. "European integration and the radical right: three patterns of opposition," *Government and Opposition*, 46(2): 223–44.

Verbeek, B. and A. van der Vleuten. 2008. "The domesticization of the foreign policy of the Netherlands (1989–2007): the paradoxical result of Europeanization and internationalization," *Acta Politica*, 43(2): 357–77.

Verbeek, B. and A. Zaslove. 2015a. "The counter forces of European integration: nationalism, populism and EU foreign policy," in K. E. Jørgensen, A. K. Aarstad, E. Drieskens, K. Laatikainen, and B. Tonra (eds), *The SAGE Handbook of European Foreign Policy*. London: Sage, 530–44.

Verbeek, B. and A. Zaslove. 2015b. "The impact of populist radical right parties on foreign policy: the Northern League as a junior coalition partner in the Berlusconi governments," *European Political Science Review*, 7(4): 525–46.

Vossen, K. 2004. "De andere jaren zestig. De opkomst van de Boerenpartij (1963–1967)," *Jaarboek Documentatiecentrum Nederlandse Politieke Partijen 2004*. DNPP, 245–66.

Vossen, K. 2011. "Classifying Wilders: the ideological development of Geert Wilders and his Party for Freedom," *Politics*, 31(3): 179–89.

Wear, R. 2008. "Permanent populism: the Howard government 1996–2007," *Australian Journal of Political Science*, 43(4): 617–34.

Weyland, K. 1999. "Neoliberal populism in Latin America and Eastern Europe," *Comparative Politics*, 31(4): 379–401.

Weyland, K. 2009. "The rise of Latin America's two lefts: insights from rentier state theory," *Comparative Politics*, 41(2): 145–64.

White, B. 1989. "Analysing foreign policy: problems and approaches," in M. Clarke and B. White (eds), *Understanding Foreign Policy: The Foreign Policy Systems Approach*. Aldershot: Edward Elgar, 1–26.

Woods, D. 2009. "Pockets of resistance to globalization: the case of the Lega Nord," *Patterns of Prejudice*, 43(2): 161–77.

Zaslove, A. 2011. *The Re-Invention of the European Radical Right: Populism, Regionalism, and the Italian Lega Nord*. Montreal: McGill-Queen's Press.

CHAPTER 21

....

POPULISM
AND IDENTIFICATION

....

FRANCISCO PANIZZA

INTRODUCTION

....

MOST definitions of populism make references to the people, so this may be as good as any entry point for understanding populist identities. The argument I would like to develop in this chapter is that populism is a mode of political identification that constructs and gives meaning to "the people" as a political actor (Laclau, 2005b: 153; Reyes, 2005: 100). But, simple as it looks, this claim raises some very difficult questions: Who are the people? Who *constructs* the people? How can the people be *constructed*? Moreover, the notion of *the people* is central to most political lexicons and not exclusive to populist discourse. To start answering these questions it must first be made clear that by *constructing* the people it is not meant here that the people are a work of fiction or that its identity is conjured out of nothing but that the people as a political identity is central to the understanding of populism, although not all references to the people are necessarily populist in nature.

In a book appropriately titled *Inventing the People: The Rise of Popular Sovereignty in England and America*, Edmund S. Morgan (1988) recalls Lincoln's dedication to "government of the people, by the people, and for the people," only to note that all governments are of the people, that all profess to be for the people, and that none can literally be by the people. Morgan's book is not about populism but, as the title suggests, about what he calls the fiction that replaced the divine right of kings, the notion of the sovereign people. As he put it: "The people are the governed; they are also, at least fictionally, the governors, at once subjects and rulers. How such a contradiction could win acceptance among a governing elite as well as among the many whom they governed is logically puzzling but historical explicable" (1988: 38).

The gap between what governments profess to be and what they cannot be (by the people) brings us a step closer to our subject of study, the populist mode of identification.

To get even closer we need another historian, a historian of American's populism. In his book *The Populist Persuasion: An American History*, Michael Kazin (1995) argues that what he calls the populist persuasion is available to any political actor operating in a politico-discursive field in which the notion of the sovereignty of the people and its inevitable corollary, the conflict between the powerful and the powerless, are core elements of its political imaginary. Kazin further notes that when tracing the history of populism in the US, he does not contend that his subjects were populists, in the way they were unionists or socialists, Protestants or Catholics, liberal Democrats or conservative Republicans. Rather, his premise is "that politicians employ populism as a flexible mode of persuasion" (1995: 3).

In what follows, I discuss the populist mode of identification as a specific form of constructing the identity of the people as a political actor. This chapter critically adopts a discursive approach to populism represented among others by the works of Ernesto Laclau, as well as the socio-cultural approach of Pierre Ostiguy, in order to show how populist identities are created and how populist interventions shape politics differently in different political contexts. By defining populism as a mode of political identification I seek to incorporate into mainstream analyses of populism the rich tradition of post-structuralist discursive analysis of populism. I borrow from it the notion of the complex, relational, and incomplete nature of identities and of the equally incomplete nature of the institutions that underpin them. This allows me to question the binary classification of political actors as either being populists or not, and to introduce the notion of populist interventions as a political appeal to be used alongside other political appeals. The notions of incomplete and permanently dislocated institutions and of populist interventions are then used to question the necessary rupturist nature of populism and to show how it can be used in highly institutionalized political settings to change the boundaries of what is sayable and hence doable in a given political order.

The rest of this chapter is structured as follows. The next two sections introduce the concept of political identities and relate it to the populist mode of identification. The fourth section looks at the relations of identification between populist leaders and the people. The fifth section analyses the socio-cultural roots of the populist mode of identification and introduces the concept of populist interventions. The sixth section challenges the argument that the populist mode of identification can only be effective at times of institutional crisis to show that populist interventions can and do have a significant political impact in highly institutionalized political systems. The chapter concludes that while usually regarded as the product of crises of political representation, populism can be the cause as much as the outcome of said crises.

Political Identities

Political identities are part of social imaginaries, that is "of the ways in which people imagine their social existence, how they fit together with others, how things go on between them and their fellows, the expectations that are normally met and the deeper norma-tive images that underlie these expectations" (Taylor, 2002: 106). One of post-struc-turalism's contributions to the understanding of political identities is the argument that identities are complex, relational, and incomplete. William Connolly (2002: 204) defines identity as "a set of interlocking elements in strife and tension, a set periodi-cally scrambled, reorganized, blocked and gridlocked by contingencies from within and without." Social actors' overlapping and partially contradictory identities are only relatively fixed and naturalized by their grounding in a given social order as workers, parents, women, youths, bosses, etc. For example, the identity of someone who may be a gay female boss is, at a personal level, what Connolly (ibid.) refers to as the inter-locking elements in strife and tension that are part of every identity, be it personal or collective.

Social identities are relational because the social identity of, say, a worker is constructed in terms of the network of social relations that both links and differentiates a worker from other workers, employers, the state, and the unions, among many other social actors. Employment law, company regulations, and working practices sediment workers' identi-ties and "put them in their place" within the framework of a wider institutional context. Social (and personal) identities are incomplete because they can never fulfill the telos of subjective identification. Borrowing from psychoanalytic theory, post-structuralism defines identity in terms of its inability to achieve completion or as an absent fullness (a constitutive *lack*) (Laclau, 2005b: 85) and argues that a *lack* is a feature of any structure or system (Legget, 2016). As Yannis Stavrakakis (2001) put it, identity, at both the per-sonal and political levels, is only the name of what we desire but can never fully obtain: if I need to identify with something or someone it is because I do not have a full identity in the first place. From this insight it follows that identities, as well as the institutions that sediment them, are never fully structured and are always already dislocated. As incom-pleteness is constitutive of both the structure and the subject, the construction of any identity—or the linking together of previously heterogeneous identities into a common project—is always contingent and precarious (Glynos and Howarth, 2007). Dislocated and incomplete structures make possible the activation of contingent forms of subjectiv-ity and alternative forms of identification, characteristic of political agency (Panizza and Miorelli, 2013).

Collective identities are socially constructed but not all social identities are neces-sarily political in nature. Political identities require the rediscovery of the contingent nature of social objectivity that makes possible the de-sedimentation of social identi-ties. An identity is political to the extent that it publicly contests the norms of a par-ticular practice or systems of practices in the name of a principle or ideal (Glynos and Howard, 2007). Motherhood as a social identity is constructed by traditional notions of what it means to be a mother in a certain society, grounded on religious beliefs, social costumes, and the power relations of patriarchal society. But it remains largely confined to the private realm of family relations until and unless it is politicized by discourses that put into question its place in the social order. Which identities become politicized and the nature of their politicization is contingent on the agent's identification with a political appeal grounded in the lived experiences of their political and socio-cultural life (Ostiguy, this volume). Within the context of the military regime of Argentina in the 1970s, motherhood became politicized as a mother's right to know what had happened to her "disappeared" sons and daughters, as demanded by the organization Mothers of Plaza de Mayo. In the context of welfare cuts in the advanced industrial democracies of the twenty-first century, motherhood may became politicized in terms of demands for free childcare for working mothers.

THE POPULIST MODE OF IDENTIFICATION

Modes of political identification are the material and symbolic practices that constitute and sustain complex, conflictive, and permanently dislocated identity claims (Stavrakavakis, 1999). Identificatory practices give meaning to our lives. They define who we are and what we want, how we perceive ourselves and how we position ourselves in relation to others (Panizza, 2016). They involve the construction of differences and of antagonisms and the drawing of political frontiers between "insiders" and "outsiders" (Howarth, 2000). They are politico-discursive by nature on the condition that we do not equate discourse with just words. The notion of discourse used in this chapter includes both semantic and material practices that together constitute a more or less coherent framework for what can be said and done in a given society (Torfin, 1999: 300).

As societies became more complex and social identities more fluid in the late twentieth century and early twenty-first century, the politicization of hitherto sedimented social identities has led to the rise of so-called identity politics, usually in the form of social movements that make political demands based on gender, ethnic, religious, cultural, or other identity claims (Flesher Fominaya, 2010). As a mode of political identification, populism can be construed as an expression of identity politics. For example, right-wing European populist movements are said to defend the interests and culture of the "native" white population (Mudde, 2009). But at a certain level of analysis populism is the antithesis of identity politics. Social movements' identity politics are based on the politics of differences that assert the distinct and differential nature of identity groups within a certain political community. Identity-based social movements are thus part of a complex network of social actors that advance discrete political demands within the institutional context of pluralist political institutions.

In contrast, the populist mode of identification aims at constructing a single, homogeneous identity (de la Torre, 2013), the identity of the people. It is based on the politics of equivalence that simplifies the political space into two antagonistic camps within the context of majoritarian politics (Laclau, 2005b: 73). As Legget (2016: 122) put it, the logic of equivalence draws dispersed elements (agents, ideas, practices, demands) into a discourse by reinforcing what they have in common (their "equivalence" or sameness). This commonality can only be articulated in *antagonism* to a particular *other*. It highlights an "us and them" boundary, such as "workers vs bosses," "local people vs immigrants," "the people vs the oligarchy," "the nation vs the colonizers." The identity of the group is thus established against an *other* as its constitutive outside. But the *other* also represents a threat to the full identity of the group (e.g. "the immigrants are threatening to destroy our native cultural identity"; "we cannot become a true nation because we are being oppressed by an imperial power"). This is why in the rather opaque formulation of post-structuralism, the *other* is both the condition of possibility and of impossibility of a full identity (Laclau, 2005b).

Populist leaders often articulate at political level demands expressed by social move-ments at a social level. For example, Juan Pablo Ferrero (2014) shows the crucial role played by social movements in the emergence of Kirchnerismo as a form of radical left-populism in Argentina in the first decade of the twenty-first century. Ferrero's work maps how the practices of resistance to free market reforms by grassroots organiza-tions in the late 1990s and early 2000s created the conditions for new issues to become politically significant, enacting a political dynamic that contributed to create a new, contingent, *we*. The identification of a constitutive outside (neoliberalism) by the anti-neoliberal political appeal of Néstor Kirchner in the 2003 election (Panizza, 2016) pro-vided the external point of unity necessary for the activated but loose social identities to become a unified political identity: Kirchnerismo.

The identity of the people as a political actor requires the perfomative drawing of an internal frontier of exclusion within society (Barros, 2006; Casullo, 2016). The popu-list "people" is something less than the totality of the members of the community: it is a partial component that nevertheless aspires to be conceived as the only legitimate totality (Laclau, 2005b: 81). Laclau argues that in the process of constitution of populist identities, disparate grievances and demands crystallize around certain common sym-bols, which he calls nodal points or floating signifiers that bind demands together by attaching a plurality of meanings to the same signifier. The more extended the chain, the less a signifier will refer to its original content, potentially becoming in Laclau's linguis-tic-inspired theoretical formulation an empty signifier (a signifier without a signified, or a name without a concept). As Laclau (2005b: 96) put it, "the semantic role of these sig-nifiers is not to express any positive content but to function *as the name* of a full identity which is constitutively absent" (emphasis added).

"The people" is the defining signifier of populism. It can be defined as a process of nam-ing that retroactively determines who are "the people" (Reyes, 2005: 106). As a signifier, it acquires its full meaning by reference to what it is not: "the British people," "ordinary folks," "the white working class," "the 99 percent," as the name of the people in different political contexts. The European Union, "the establishment," "corrupt politicians," "the oligarchy," "neoliberalism," "the caste," "the 1 percent," as the name of the *other*. It is only by politically overcoming the other that the promise of a full popular identity ("we the people") can be fulfilled, a promise that can never fully materialize (Glynnos and Howarth, 2007: 150).

For example, in the British 2016 referendum on the European Union (EU), the EU was presented by the *Brexit* campaign as having taken away from the British people their sovereign right to control the country's borders and pass their own laws. As the *Leave* campaign put it, when Britain leaves the European Union *we* (the British people) "will have our country back." But once the *Leavers* have their country back by opting out of the EU, it is difficult to imagine the *we* of the British people as signifying a single, sover-eign, unified identity in light of the country's political, social, and regional divisions, not to speak of the divide between the majority that voted out and the significant minority that supported remain and the constraints on sovereignty imposed by globalization. In short, for the Leave campaign, Brexit was conceived as a moment of supreme plenitude for the British people ("having our country back") but, rephrasing Stravakakis's (2001) definition of identity, it was only the name of what Leave voters desire but can never fully obtain.

While relations of antagonism can be formulated in purely logical terms as constituted by chains of equivalences, populist identities cannot be understood as purely logical constructions and "the people" as a signifier can never be totally "empty." As noted above, an identity is political to the extent that its holders publicly contest the norms of a particular practice or systems of practices in the name of a principle or ideal. Populist identities are always grounded in some kind of lived experiences and normative claims that are not reducible to a formal logic. In the populist mode of identification, the signifier *the people* refers to the people both as an underdog (the plebs) and as the holder of sovereignty (the demos). It refers to an oppressed or excluded part of the political community whose claims as a legitimate member of the demos are being denied by the political establishment. As the work of Kazin (1995) about the changing political incarnations of populist identities in the US shows, the gap between the plebs and the demos always makes reference to a rich semantic field of rights, justice, culture, nationhood, and sovereignty that are part of the populist mode of identification.

While the populist mode of identification is not a pure logic it is not an ideology either, not even a thin one (Mudde, 2009; Moffit and Tormey, 2014). Ideologies are complex ideational constructs. While there may be no final agreement about what is meant by democracy or by liberalism, they share a conceptual core (Freeden, 1996) that makes reference to a recognized intellectual genealogy, a cannon of principles and a body of thought, even if the precise meaning of these principles remains essentially contested (Gallie, 1956). In contrast, there is not such a cannon or genealogy in populism, which is an external attribution frequently contested by the very same actors that are characterized as such. The name of the people as a floating signifier gives the populist mode of identification an extraordinary ideological malleability. In Europe, populism has been associated to the left-wing politics of SYRIZA in Greece and PODEMOS in Spain and to the right-wing politics of the National Front in France and the Freedom Party in Austria. In Latin America, populism has been neoliberal in Argentina under Menem and antineoliberal under Néstor and Cristina Kirchner. It has been articulated to indigenous identities in Bolivia under Evo Morales (Madrid, 2008) and to the white working class in right-wing European populism (Mudde, 2009).

THE POPULIST LEADER

Scholars of populism argue that the identification between the leader and the people is central to populism (Weyland, 2001 and this volume; Frajman, 2014). As Casullo (2016: 7) put it:

populist leaders use discourse to transform existing "objective" social problems into political demands, to forge chains of solidarity between the disparate social groups that form their coalition, and to lay out collective repertoires for political action. They cannot simply give commands; they must at the very least keep the fiction that they speak *for* the people. Therefore, they have to talk to their followers in a way that inspires and persuades them.

But there is no clarity about why and how identification between the leader and the people takes place. For some scholars, populist leaders are plebiscitarian opportunists who seek to win quasi-direct, unmediated mass support from a broad cross-section of a people. Identification is said to be top-down, as the leader seeks the mobilization of mass constituencies that lack the capacity for autonomous political expression and delegate their sovereignty to the personalistic leader (Weyland, 2001 and this volume; Roberts, 2013). This characterization of the process of identification fails to explain why the people are receptive to top-down manipulation or how populist movements can survive the demise of their leaders; it also fails to account for the powerful sense of agency that characterizes the constitution of populist identities, as expressed in the intensity of political participation and in the activation of formerly politically passive agents that characterizes populist politics.

In answering critics of populism's perceived top-down personalist bias Laclau (2006: 60) argues that political leadership is central not only to populism but also to many other political practices that are part of democratic politics, and that accusing populism's personalist leadership of being anti-democratic reveals an ideological bias. While attacks on populism's personalism may indeed include an element of political bias, arguably relations of identification between the leader and the people under populism are of a different nature to those in different political traditions. As Arditi (2004: 143) notes, the centrality of the leaders and their direct rapport with the "common man" transform populist leaders into something akin to infallible sovereigns, in that their decisions are unquestionable because they are theirs. The argument is further elaborated by Abts and Rummens (2007) in terms of the populist assumptions that (1) the will of the people is considered to be transparent and immediately accessible to those willing to listen to the *vox populi*, and (2) that the transparency of the will of the people is possible because populism conceptualizes the people as a homogeneous unity. As they put it: "This means that the citizens, as a political community, constitute a homogeneous political body with a singular will, the *volonté générale*. Importantly, the substantial identity of all members of the political community *also encompasses the identity of rulers and subjects*" (2007: 415; emphasis added).

Arguably, both Laclau's and Abts and Rummens's notions of populist leadership are problematic. Laclau's (2005a) claim that the name of the leader is the only possible surface of inscription for populist identification betrays a notion of populism that exists in a political, socio-cultural, and institutional vacuum. The issue at stake is not to dispute the centrality of the leader in the constitution of populist identities but the political context in which the leadership operates. In terms of the relation between the leader and the people there is a significant difference between the type of identification that takes place when the leader is addressing the multitude in the street and the identification between the leader and the people that takes place when the leader is the head of a political movement with complex representational structures or is head of government.

If identities are complex, relational, and incomplete, processes of identification involve more than just an unmediated relationship between the leader and the plebs. Grassroots popular organizations, political movements, and other political actors play an important role in identificatory practices, including those characteristic of populism, particularly in a democratic environment. The presence of strong grassroots popular organizations or of an equally strong liberal democratic tradition in which populist leaders operate makes a significant difference in the relations of identification between the leader and the people (Panizza, 2005b). Active popular movements and a populist leadership that is constrained by democratic institutions and principles mean that the person/name of the leader can never monopolize popular identification and thus can never fully close the chasm between the plebs and the demos. Under these conditions, popular movements and political institutions retain significant degrees of political autonomy that prevent the constitution of a homogeneous popular identity crystallized in the figure of the leader.

If Laclau's account of the populist leadership needs to take into account the politico-institutional framework in which identification takes place, Abts and Rummens's argument about the homogeneous identity of rulers and subjects does not fully consider the nature of the relations of identification between the leader and the people. If Abts and Rummens are right about the encompassing identity of rulers and subjects under populism, the identification between an homogeneous people and their leader would not only restore the king's head (Foucault, 1980) but remerge the king's two bodies (Kantorowicz, 1957). However, Abts and Rummens's argument is based either on the assumption that the people are passive receptors of the populist leader's appeal or on the belief that identification is a transparent, encompassing, direct relationship rather than the name of what we desire and can never fully obtain.

Paraphrasing and modifying Alejandro Groppo's (2006) definition, populist identification takes place in the out-of-joint space between the leader's attempt at constituting the imaginary unity of the people and the final impossibility of controlling the people's reactions to this attempt. Perhaps a way of understanding this relationship is to think of identification not so much in terms of the metaphor of the leader's name as a blank canvas on which popular identities are inscribed but as a two-way echo, whose reception is distorted and unhinged by the static noises of pre-existing modes of identification, by competing identity claims, and by the transiency of desires and affections. In this process, the people are not passive receptors of this echo but actively involved in the production of messages that the leader must in turn reinterpret and redirect in an attempt to maintain the unity of the people. Thus the relation between the people and the leader is not necessarily one in which the people are passive receptors of the populist discourse of the *beloved leader* but one in which the leader's persona acts as a floating signifier to which a multiplicity of meanings can be attributed, and the leader makes his/her impact felt as much with his/her presence as a charismatic orator as with his/her absences, silences, and ambiguities. In practical terms, this means that the leader's power to impose a political discourse with a univocal meaning on what is effectively a highly diverse public can be severely constrained by the audience's multiple interpretations of the leader's discourse which are then transformed into new demands. As a result, the leader must often limit himself or herself to arbitrate between different politico-ideological re-enunciations of his/her own discourse, leaning alternatively in favor of one or the other without ever making a final adjudication.

The comparison between the populist appeals of Hugo Chávez in Venezuela and Evo Morales in Bolivia illustrates the range of alternatives, from the top down to the bottom up, that can shape relations of identification between the leader and the people. The differences in the direction of the two leaders' appeals are marked in the case of Chávez by his military origins and by his leadership of a populist movement that was constructed mainly (but not only) from the state.[1] Morales, in contrast, built up his leadership bottom-up from a social movement (the "Cocaleros") (Harten, 2011). But Morales was not a complete outsider to the political system. He was elected to Congress in 1995 before heading a mass and political diverse street protest movement in the early 2000s against the governments of the time (the so-called "gas" and "water" wars) and was first elected president in 2005 as the leader of the Movimiento Al Socialismo (MAS), a party both active in parliament and with a strong bottom-up grassroots culture (Philip and Panizza, 2011). While Chávez's (and particularly his successor Nicolas Maduro's) appeal became increasingly top-down, centralizing, and authoritarian (Corrales, 2015), Morales negotiated the 2009 constitution with the opposition and his at times fractious relations with the grassroots political movements that support his presidency (Crabtree, 2013) illustrate how populist leaders, far from being modern-day absolute sovereigns reigning over a homogeneous people, are often *bricoleurs* who face the never-ending task of reconstituting the identity of a fractured people.

THE POPULIST GAZE

How is identification achieved? Populist leaders appeal to those who feel politically excluded by having no voice in the political system (the plebs) and making them feel recognized as holders of sovereignty (the demos). Identification with the plebs is often achieved by the leader's adopting, turning upside down, and putting into public discourse socio-cultural elements that are considered as markers of inferiority by the dominant culture. As Pierre Ostiguy (this volume, p. 73) puts it: "Populism is characterized by a particular form of political relationship between political leaders and social basis, one established and articulated through 'low' appeals which resonate and receive positive reception within particular sectors of society for socio-cultural, historical reasons." By "flaunting the low" the leader transgresses the rules of public discourse. Populist leaders position themselves outside the political and cultural establishment and in the same process turn markers of exclusion of the plebs into attributes of the demos. As Carlos de la Torre (2000) noted in relation to the Ecuadorian former presidential candidate, Abdala "El Loco" ("The Madman") Bucaram, by consciously embodying the dress, language, and mannerisms of the common people who were despised by the elites and their middle-class imitators, Bucaram attracted the vote of those who saw in him a mirror of their own popular selves and the elevation of their own culture to the public realm.

As an element of the populist mode of identification, flaunting the low can be a crucial element in distinguishing between populist and non-populist imaginings of the people. To this purpose, it may be useful to recall Žižek's (1989) psychoanalytically-inspired distinction between imaginary and symbolic identification: imaginary identification is identification with the image in which we appear likable to ourselves and symbolic identification is identification with the place from where we are being observed. Drawing on this distinction, Žižek makes an important observation: the trait on the basis of which we identify with someone is by no means necessarily a glamorous feature. The corollary to this remark is that the trait-of-identification can also be a certain failure, weakness, or guilt of the other, so that by pointing out the failure we can unwittingly reinforce the identification (1989: 106).

The 2016 presidential primary election in the US offers an example of this trait of imaginary identification. In his highly transgressive speeches the Republican party contender, Donald Trump, was a serial offender not only of his political adversaries but of women (he called Fox News anchor Megyn Kelly "a bimbo" and suggested that her aggressive questioning was related to the fact that she was menstruating),[2] disabled people (he mocked a disabled reporter),[3] Mexican immigrants (calling them rapists and drug dealers), and members of his own party (calling his rival Senator Ted Cruz a "pussy").[4] Commentators were surprised when Trump's approval ratings did not fall but rather went up after his outrageous remarks, without considering what Oscar Reyes (2005) calls populism's "solidarity of the dirty secret;" that is, the populist leader's readiness to say in public what his audience secretly identified with but felt guilty about. For some within his audience, the ability to tell the truth unencumbered by political calculations, patterns of human decency, or political correctness was more important than the traditional tropes of Republican conservatism, such as fiscal rectitude, free trade, and strong Christian beliefs. Asked by Ryan Lizza, a reporter from the New Yorker, what attracted her to Trump, Joanna Patterson, a deeply religious Pentecostal Christian, replied that it was his [i.e. Trump's] forthrightness more than any particular issue. "We like raw truth," Patterson said. "Tells us what we need."[5]

But the populist mode of identification is not just about the leader's holding a mirror to the plebs as they appear likable to themselves, warts and all. It is about the elevation of the plebs to the position of the demos, the holders of sovereignty. This is why populist identification also requires a political narrative that includes what Margaret Canovan (1999: 2) calls the emancipatory promise of populism, a promise that once the enemy of the people is overcome through political struggle, the people and the demos will be at one both socio-culturally and politically.

In Bolivia Evo Morales's inaugural address of his first presidency, on 22 January 2006, offers a particularly powerful narrative of emancipation that combines the denuncia-tion of socio-cultural exclusion with a rhetoric of emancipation. In the excerpt below, Morales alludes to Bolivia's history of socio-cultural (and political) discrimination:

> This morning (…) I have seen with much joy some brothers and sisters singing in the historic Plaza Murillo, as well as in Plaza San Francisco, when forty or fifty years ago we didn't have the right to enter Plaza San Francisco and Plaza Murillo. Forty or fifty years ago our ancestors didn't even have the right to walk in the sideways. This is our history, our memory.[6]

While not explicit in his description of the situation, the reason why the "brothers and sisters" (i.e. fellow indigenous people) were not allowed to walk in the sideways of La Paz's historic squares was because their ethnic features, forms of dressing, and other socio-cultural traits marked them as not "proper" for sharing a public space.

Immediately afterwards, Morales's speech elaborates a narrative of political emancipation:

> Bolivia looks like South Africa. Threatened, condemned to extinction, we [Bolivia's indigenous people] are here. I want to tell you that there are still remnants of these people that are enemies of the indigenous people[.] [W]e want to live in equality of conditions with them, and this is why we are here to change our history[.] [T]his indigenous movement is nobody's concession, nothing has been gifted to us, it is the consciousness of my people, of our people. (ibid.)

In short, transgressive socio-cultural elements ("the flaunting of the low") cannot be separated from populism's political dimension (the politics of antagonism) in the making of populist identities. As Ostiguy argues in this volume, the flaunting of the low incorporates in a subjective, identity-centered, and socially connected way the notion of antagonism. This means that low cultural appeals without an antagonistic dimension are not enough per se to construct the populist people, as has been the case of the "low politics" of patronage and clientelism characteristic of many Latin American countries or, in a very different political key, by the former president of Uruguay José "Pepe" Mujica flaunting the low in terms of his lifestyle and popular language but remaining firmly within the realm of non-populist, pluralist politics in Uruguay (Panizza, 2013).

Again with reference to the 2016 US presidential primaries, Trump's low culture appeal and outsider status trounced the Republican party establishment's candidate Jeb Bush's high culture and sense of political entitlement. As Trump put it, he loved the poorly educated (and the poorly educated loved him in turn).[7] Throughout the cam-paign Trump combined the flaunting of the low with attacks on the political establish-ment to draw a dividing line between the people and the establishment other.[8] In the Democratic party's presidential primary, senator Bernie Sanders also set up political

dividing lines that can be characterized as populist. Not dissimilar to Trump's, his political contest with his primaries' rival, Hillary Clinton, was framed in terms of the people against the establishment (to which Sanders accused Clinton of belonging).[9] But
the political divide in Sanders's discourse was defined in terms of the gap in wealth and
power rather than on socio-cultural grounds: "America today is the wealthiest country
in the history of the world," he told his audience, "but most people don't *know* that, most
people don't *feel* that, most people don't *see* that—because almost all the wealth rests in
the hands of a tiny few."[10]

The comparison between Trump and Sanders brings to light the question of who *is*
a populist? According to some measures, Sanders's populist appeal was more radical
than Trump's: he called for a "political revolution" against the "billionaires and oligarchs" who had hijacked the country's political system,[11] while Trump promised just
a "better deal" for the American people. And yet, a more comprehensive view of the
populist mode of identification that brings together its socio-cultural and political
dimensions makes Trump look more like the real thing. Trump was a true outsider
to the political system and to the Republican party. Sarah Pailin's endorsement of his
candidacy captured his condition as the representative of the politics of anti-politics that is a quasi-contingent element of populism: "He is from the private sector,
not a politician. Can I get a Hallelujah?" she crowed.[12] His contempt for the party
establishment was reciprocated by the venom that was directed against him by the
Republican establishment, with former presidential candidate Mitt Rommey calling
him "a phony" and "a fraud" and claiming that Trump posed a fundamental threat
to American democracy.[13] In contrast, Sanders ran as an anti-establishment candidate but not as an anti-party, anti-politics, one. He was not a political outsider, as he
had twenty-five years of service in the Senate and a longer history of political activism. Sure, there were the markers of authenticity in Sanders's political persona that
contributed to differentiate him from archetypical politicians. Commentators noted
Sanders's gruffness, his didacticism, and indifference to appearances. But authenticity is not the same as flaunting the low. Trump flaunted his wealth and his political style was firmly low culture. Sanders did not engage in culture wars: his focus
was firmly on attacking a corrupt political and financial establishment, a traditional
trope of radical left politics.

A way of solving the question of who is and who is not a populist is to reject the
terms in which it is posed. Populism is neither a categorical divide nor an encompassing identity. Politicians use populist appeals in combination with other modes
of political identification. That is why I have argued elsewhere (Panizza, 2013) that it
makes more sense to talk about "populist interventions" rather than about populist
actors or regimes. To understand what is meant by *interventions* it is important to
recall Kazin's observation that throughout American history so-called populist politicians employed populism as a flexible mode of persuasion. As he put it (1995: 6): "populism, of course, was not the sole element in their rhetoric but its significance is,
I think, impossible to deny."

POPULIST INTERVENTIONS
AND THE MAINSTREAMING OF POPULISM

The questioning of populism as an all-or-nothing category and the introduction of the notion of populist interventions is related to the issue of whether the populist mode of identification can only be effective at times of institutional crises and whether populism is always, necessarily, a discourse of rupture with the political order. For some scholars there is no populist identity without a populist rupture. Thus, in Laclau's (2005b) characterization, demands that are addressed by the institutional order are regarded as being dealt with by the realm of administration. In adopting Ranciere's inspired distinction between the realm of the political and the realm of administration, Laclau is failing to fully take into account the incompleteness of both identities and of the social order in which identities are grounded. Any demand, no matter how specific, is grounded on some kind of identity claim: what *I am* determines *what I want*. Demands being addressed by institutional means can be, and often are, intensely political, creating antagonisms *within* the institutional structure. Struggles for their fulfilment involve processes of hegemonic construction and challenges to the limits of the political order in so far as we understand institutional orders not as fully constituted totalities but as the articulation of a plurality of partially constituted social, economic, political, ethnic, regional, gender, etc. institutional networks.

What I am arguing is for the deconstruction of what Norval (2006) calls heroic conceptions of political agency, in which processes of identification only take place in those rare occasions when decisions are taken and new paths are opened up. Norval argues that more often than not identification will take the form of a multitude of different practices, which, when taken together, make possible a different way of looking at things. While dislocation constitutes the condition of possibility for processes of identification, dislocations do not need to follow "a great event," as social orders are always already dislocated. Processes of de-identification and re-identification, the redrawing of political frontiers and the contestation of the norms of a particular institution also take place within a given institutional order and not just outside it. In relatively highly institutionalized political orders, they can take the form of an accumulation of populist interventions concerning questions such as the mass influx of immigrants or episodes of corruption that when politicized by populist entrepreneurs make possible a different way of looking at things by allowing the recognition of the discontinuous within the continuous (ibid.).

Acting within the confines of the institutional order, populist interventions redraw the boundaries of political debate by redefining what is sayable and hence doable in a given political order. The issue of immigration is among the ones that best illustrate how populist interventions have changed the boundaries of the political debate in Europe with significant policy implications. The discursive change was achieved through a two-way process: on the one hand, some populist leaders have sought to partially "de-toxify" populism by articulating it within traditional liberal democratic and civilizational values, such as the legacy of the Enlightenment and the defence of gay and women's rights against the threat posed by Islamic fundamentalism. Socio-cultural elements are central to this strategy that is aimed at drawing a dividing line between a civilized West and uncivilized, un-integrated, and un-reconcilable other. For instance, the late Dutch populist leader Pim Fortuyn claimed that Islam was a "backward culture" and argued that he had no desire to go through the emancipation of women and homosexuals all over again (Bedell, 2016). The former Italian prime minister Silvio Berlusconi stated that we should be "conscious of the superiority of our civilizations" and the Danish populist leader Pia Kjaersgaard told parliament that September the 11th was not the start of the clash of civilizations as "a clash would indicate that there are two civilisations," when there is "only one civilisation, and that's ours" (Fekete, 2006: 8–9).

On the other hand, in an attempt to neutralize the appeal of populism, center-right and center-left parties mainstreamed populist discourse (Mudde, 2004) on immigration with the effect of enacting a radical change in the boundaries of public discourse and legitimizing anti-immigration legislation. A political genealogy of the discourse on immigration in Britain allows one to appreciate the boundary-shifting process resulting from the mainstreaming of populist interventions and its impact on the political system.

In the 2005 British general election campaign immigration was at the margins of the electoral debate. However, during the campaign, the Conservative Party published an outdoor poster, which in imitation handwriting stated: "It's not racist to impose limits on immigration" below which was written in type-faced capitals: "ARE YOU THINKING WHAT WE ARE THINKING? (Signed) CONSERVATIVE." The poster was notable as much for what it said as for what it alluded to. The handwritten message made it appear to be written by a private individual brought to the public domain by the Conservative type-faced signature. It suggested that speaking openly about immigration was unsayable in the public debate of the time, as it had still strong racist connotations going far back to the Conservative politician Enoch Powell's famous April 1968 "Rivers of Blood" speech.[14] What is unthinkable is unsayable but in this case what was thinkable was still (almost) unsayable. The not-so-secret message was captured by a defaced poster on which was scribbled: "Yes it is—You Tory SCUM!" and another in which the word "RACISTS" was written above the "CONSERVATIVE" signature.[15]

Ten years later, in the 2015 electoral campaign, immigration had moved from the margins to the center of the electoral debate to the extent that it was, according to certain polls, the main issue for the electors. The Labour Party, which when in government had opened the doors to unlimited immigration from the European Union's then-new Eastern European member states, now had "Control of Immigration" as one of its six core pledges written in stone in an ill-fated publicity stunt.[16] Nigel Farage, the leader of the anti-immigration, anti-European Union populist party United Kingdom Independence Party (UKIP), captured the nature of the shift and took credit for it when he addressed his party's Conference. After defining immigration as "the biggest single issue facing this country" and accusing the establishment of closing down the immigration debate for twenty years he called for an open debate and pointedly noted: "Because when we believe something—we don't go 'are you thinking what we're thinking.' We say it loud."[17]

Populist interventions in highly institutionalized political systems are not just an adaptive strategy but can lead to populist ruptures (Norval's discontinuous within the continuous). Just a year later, in June 2016, in the referendum campaign about whether the UK should leave the European Union the *Leave* campaign articulated the themes of immigration and sovereignty to constitute a political antagonism with the EU that culminated in *Brexit*, the most radical political rupture in modern British history. The *Brexit* campaign bound together the populist mode of identification's political and socio-cultural dimensions. While the *Remain* campaign sought to appeal to citizens' self-interest by arguing that they would be economically worse off by voting to leave, *Leave* voters cast their choice in terms of rights and identity: the right of the sovereign British people not to be ruled by Brussels and to control the country's borders. When the *Remain* campaign drew on the opinion of experts to back up their arguments about an impending economic doom, the *Leave* campaign used the experts' opinion as a weapon against *Remain* by claiming that "the people of this country have had enough of experts."[18] While *Remain* won in highly cosmopolitan London, *Leave* got some of its highest winning margins in rural areas and small towns and villages that had been bypassed by globalized cosmopolitanism and had among the lowest rates of immigration.[19]

Similar examples of detoxification and mainstreaming could be found elsewhere in Europe in the aftermath of the Great Recession and the mass influx of immigrants in 2015–2016. In France, Nicolas Sarkozy, who in 2016 was seeking his party's nomination for president in 2017, sought to appropriate and outdo some of the ideas of the leader of the populist National Front (FN) Marie Le Pen on immigration, security, and Islam. For example, as part of this strategy, he called for the locking up of anyone suspected of radicalization even if they had committed no crime, to which Le Pen reacted by arguing for the protection of the rule of law.[20] The articulation of populist interventions to mainstream center-right and center-left political appeals had the predictable effect of legitimizing populist discourse, thus further blurring the dividing line between populism and non-populist identification. As Gilbert Collard, then one of Le Pen's parliamentarians, said, "If you look at our whole diagnosis of society's ills you can hate us, but everyone knows that our ideas are being taken up and reproduced by everyone else."[21]

Conclusions

This chapter has been an attempt to engage different understandings of populism and show how the populist mode of identification relates to them. In quoting Kazin's (1995) definition of populism as a "flexible mode of persuasion," I have sought to suggest that populism can be regarded as a political strategy (Weyland, 2001 and this volume) without implying that it is necessarily top-down or indicative of the people's lack of agency or mobilization autonomy. Following Laclau, I have argued that populism follows the political logic of equivalence but that it cannot be reduced to a pure logical form. I have further argued that it incorporates ideas and values but is not an ideology (Hawkins, Riding, and Mudde, 2012); that it includes a transgressive socio-cultural dimension (the flaunting of the low) but that populism's socio-cultural dimension requires the construction of political antagonisms and not just the leader's adoption of common folks' culture and mannerisms (Ostiguy, this volume); that it is performative (Moffit and Tormey, 2014) on condition that we understand performative as denoting both some kind of discursive performance and that the populist mode of identification does not truly or falsely *describe* the people but performatively (Austin, 1975) *creates* the people.

I have used the post-structuralist notion of identities as complex, relational, and incomplete to analyse relations of identification between populist leaders and the people. My analysis has attempted to show that populism's alleged imagining of the people, as a homogeneous political body with a transparent will immediately accessible to the (populist) leader, and Laclau's conception of the name of the leader as a blank canvas (an empty signifier) for the people's imaginary identification, convey a fundamental misunderstanding of what is at stake in processes of political identification. Both conceptions assume that the people have no previous history, culture, or identity and that identification with the name of the leader is a transparent, totalizing, direct relationship rather than the name of what we desire and can never fully obtain. I have also sought to show that the top-down or bottom-up nature of the populist mode of identification is contingent on the strength of alternative modes of political identification, resulting from practices of political organization and mobilization and depending on the nature of the political institutions that sediment and support identities.

Pierre Ostiguy's socio-cultural approach to populism ("the flaunting of the low") has influenced my understanding of how populist identification is achieved. More specifically, it contributed to the understanding that populism's imaginary identification of the people (Žižek, 1989) is not an identification with the sanitized visions of the good people that are part of the symbolic order but rather with transgressive socio-cultural traits that are considered by the dominant culture as crude, unrefined, or even unspeakable ("the solidarity of the dirty secret").

I have used the concept of populist interventions to argue for an ordinal rather than binary classification of populist identities. The concept of populist interventions is also useful for understanding the ubiquity and the impact of populism in contemporary politics. I have deployed it for analysing how populist interventions have contributed to the redrawing of the boundaries of political discourse in highly institutionalized political systems through processes of de-toxification and the mainstreaming of political appeals. Last but not least, the notion of populist interventions is a useful conceptual lens for understanding the relations between populism and crises of representation. It has been argued that the rise of populist politics is the product of crises of representation but the direction of causality between the two is less than straightforward (Laclau, 2005b: 137; Panizza, 2005a; Roberts, 2013). By looking at the political impact of populist interventions within highly institutionalized political systems I have shown that it is possible to argue that populism can be the cause as much as the outcome of crises of representation. Once regarded as a symptom of political backwardness, populism may not be synonymous with politics (Laclau, 2005b) but is certainly a dimension of politics.

Notes

1 I am not claiming that Chávez's appeal was exclusively top-down; no political appeal ever is under democracy. For a bottom-up history of Chavismo, see Fernández (2010).
2 http://www.nydailynews.com/news/politics/trump-calls-fox-news-anchor-megyn-kelly-bimbo-article-1.2512993; http://www.theguardian.com/us-news/2015/aug/09/megyn-kelly-donald-trump-winner-republican-debate.
3 http://edition.cnn.com/videos/tv/2015/11/26/donald-trump-mocks-reporter-with-disability-berman-sot-ac.cnn.
4 https://www.youtube.com/watch?v=C6QeqoYgQxw; https://www.youtube.com/watch?v=UHcD5-TGHvY.
5 Ryan Lizza. 2016. "Faceoff. The duel. Insiders loathe them; voters love them. Who will decide the future of the GOP?," *The New Yorker*, January 25. http://www.newyorker.com/magazine/faceoff, accessed October 17, 2016.
6 http://www.beersandpolitics.com/discursos/evo-morales/toma-de-posesion/138.
7 http://www.rollingstone.com/politics/news/watch-trump-brag-about-uneducated-voters-the-hispanics-20160224.
8 "We are just tired of the actions of the government nowadays. The simple people pretty much has been forgotten." Ryan Lizza. 2016. "Faceoff. The duel. The Trump and Cruz campaigns embody opposite views of politics and the future of the GOP," *The New Yorker*, February 1.
9 "It is just too late for establishment politics and establishment economics." "We do not represent the interests of the billionaire class Wall Street, or corporate America." John Cassidy, "Bernie Sanders just changed the Democratic Party," *The New Yorker*, February 2.
10 Margaret Talbot. 2015. "Profiles. The populist prophet," *The New Yorker*, October 12.
11 http://newpol.org/content/bernie-sanders-calls-political-revolution-against-billionaires-campaign-needs-build-independ.
12 http://www.nytimes.com/2016/01/21/us/politics/sarah-palin-endorsement-speech-donald-trump.html?action=click&contentCollection=Politics&module=RelatedCoverage&region=Marginalia&pgtype=article.
13 http://www.wsj.com/articles/mitt-romney-to-attack-donald-trump-as-a-fraud-1457021229.
14 https://www.youtube.com/watch?v=mw4vMZDItQ.
15 https://edwardcain.files.wordpress.com/2015/03/are-you-thinking-what-were-thinking.jpg.
16 http://www.independent.co.uk/incoming/article10221945.ece/alternates/w620/labour-ed-miliband-stone-v2.jpg.
17 http://blogs.spectator.co.uk/coffeehouse/2013/09/nigel-farages-speech-full-text-and-audio/.
18 https://www.ft.com/content/3be49734-29cb-11e6-83e4-abc22d5d108c.

19   https://www.theguardian.com/news/datablog/2016/jun/24/the-areas-and-demographics-where-the-brexit-vote-was-won, accessed October 17, 2016.

20   "'The nation state is back': Front National's Marine Le Pen rides on global mood," *The Guardian*, September 18, 2016. https://www.theguardian.com/world/2016/sep/18/nation-state-marine-le-pen-global-mood-france-brexit-trump-front-national.

21   Ibid.

REFERENCES

Abts, Koen and Stefan Rummens. 2007. "Populism versus democracy," *Political Studies*, 55(2): 405–24.

Arditi, Benjamín. 2004. "Populism as a spectre of democracy: a response to Canovan," *Political Studies*, 52(1): 135–43.

Austin, John L. 1975. *How To Do Things with Words*, ed. J. O. Urmson and M. Sbisa. New York: Oxford University Press.

Barros, Sebastián. 2006. "Inclusión radical y conflicto en la constitución del pueblo populista," *Revista Confines*, 2/3: 65–73.

Bedell, Geraldine. 2006. "To face the facts beyond the veil," *The Guardian*, October 28. https://www.theguardian.com/books/2006/oct/29/biography.islam.

Canovan, Margaret. 1999. "Trust the people! Populism and the two faces of democracy," *Political Studies*, 47(1): 2–16.

Casullo, María Esperanza. 2016. "Looking forward, looking backward: making sense of the differences between Latin American and European populisms," submitted to the panel "The Relational Approach to Populism," 112th annual meeting of the American Political Science Association, Philadelphia, September 1–4.

Connolly, William E. 2002. *Identity/Difference: Democratic Negotiations of Political Paradox*. Minneapolis and London: University of Minneapolis Press.

Corrales, Javier. 2015. "Autocratic legalism in Venezuela," *Journal of Democracy*, 26(2): 37–51.

Crabtree, John. 2013. "From the MNR to the MAS: populism, parties, the state and social movements in Bolivia since 1952," in Carlos de la Torre and Cynthia J. Arson (eds), *Latin American Populisms in the Twenty-First Century*. Washington, DC: Woodrow Wilson Center Press, 269–93.

de la Torre, Carlos. 2000. *Populist Seduction in Latin America: The Ecuadorian Experience*. Athens: Ohio University Press.

de la Torre, Carlos. 2013. "Technocratic populism in Ecuador," *Journal of Democracy*, 24(3): 33–46.

Fekete, Liz. 2006. "Enlightened fundamentalism? Immigration, feminism and the right," *Race and Class*, 48(2): 1–22.

Fernandes, Sujhata. 2010. *Who Can Stop The Drums? Urban Social Movements in Chávez's Venezuela*. Durham and London: Duke University Press.

Ferrero, Juan Pablo. 2014. *Democracy Against Neoliberalism in Argentina and Brazil: A Move to the Left*. New York: Palgrave Macmillan.

Flesher, Fominaya. 2010. "Collective identities in social movements: central concepts and debates," *Sociology Compass*, 4(6): 393–404.

Foucault, Michel. 1980. *Power/Knowledge: Selected Interviews and Other Writings 1972–77*, edited by Colin Gordon. New York: Pantheon.

Frajman, Eduardo. 2014. "Broadcasting populist leadership: Hugo Chávez and *Aló Presidente*," *Journal of Latin American Studies*, 46(3): 501–23.

Freeden, Michael. 1996. *Ideologies and Political Theory*. Oxford: Clarendon Press.

Hawkins, Kirk, Scott Riding, and Cass Mudde. 2012. "Measuring populist attitudes," Committee on Concepts and Methods Working Paper No. 55. www.concepts-methods.org.

Gallie, Walter B. 1955–1955. "Essentially contested concepts," *Proceedings of the Aristotelian Society*, 56: 167–98.

Glynos, Jason and David Howarth. 2007. *Logics of Critical Explanation in Social and Political Theory*. London and New York: Routledge.

Gropppo, Alejandro. 2006. "People and politics: a post-structuralist approach to Latin American populism," paper prepared for delivery at the 2006 meeting of the Latin American Studies Association, San Juan, Puerto Rico, 15–18 March.

Harten, Sven. 2011. *The Rise of Evo Morales and the MAS*. London: Zed Books.

Howarth, David. 2000. *Discourse*. Buckingham: Oxford University Press.

Kantorowicz, Ernst H. 1957. *The King's Two Bodies: A Study in Mediaeval Political Theology*. Princeton: Princeton University Press.

Kazin, Michael. 1995. *The Populist Persuasion: An American History*, 2nd edn. Ithaca: Cornell University Press.

Laclau, Ernesto. 2005a. "Populism: what's in a name?," in Francisco Panizza (ed.), *Populism and the Mirror of Democracy*. London: Verso, 32–49.

Laclau, Ernesto. 2005b. *On Populist Reason*. London: Verso.

Laclau, Ernesto. 2006. "La deriva populista y la Centro Izquierda Latinoamericana," *Nueva Sociedad*, 205: 56–61.

Legget, Will. 2016. *Politics and Social Theory: The Inescapable Social, the Irreducible Political*. London: Palgrave Macmillan.

Madrid, Raúl. 2008. "The rise of ethnopopulism in Latin America," *World Politics*, 60(3): 475–508.

Moffitt, Benjamin and Simon Tormey. 2014. "Rethinking populism: politics, mediatisation and political style," *Political Studies*, 62(2): 381–97.

Morgan, Edward S. 1998. *Inventing the People: The Rise of Popular Sovereignty in England and America*. New York and London: W. W. Norton and Company.

Mudde, Cas. 2004. "The populist zeitgeist," *Government and Opposition*, 39(3): 541–63.

Mudde, Cas. 2009. "Populist right parties in Europe redux," *Political Studies Review*, 7(3): 330–7.

Norval, Aletta J. 2006. "Democratic identification: a Wittgensteinian approach," *Political Theory*, 34(2): 229–5.

Panizza, Francisco. 2005a. "Introduction: populism and the mirror of democracy," in Francisco Panizza (ed.), *Populism and the Mirror of Democracy*. London: Verso, 1–31.

Panizza, Francisco. 2005b. "Unarmed utopia revisited: the resurgence of left of centre politics in Latin America," *Political Studies*, 53(4): 716–34.

Panizza, Francisco. 2013. "What do we mean when we talk about populism?," in Carlos de la Torre and Cynthia J. Arson (eds), *Latin American Populism in the Twenty-First Century*. Baltimore: John Hopkins University Press, 85–115.

Panizza, Francisco. 2016. "Populism, social democracy and the tale of the 'two lefts' in Latin America," in Anthony Petros Spanakos and Francisco Panizza (eds), *Conceptualising Comparative Politics*. New York and London: Routledge, 192–214.

Panizza, Francisco and Romina Miorelli. 2013. "Taking discourse seriously: discursive institutionalism and post-structuralist discourse theory," *Political Studies*, 61(2): 501–18.

Philip, George and Francisco Panizza. 2011. *The Triumph of Politics: The Return of the Left in Venezuela, Bolivia and Ecuador*. Cambridge: Polity.

Reyes, Oscar. 2005. "Skinhead conservatism: a failed populist project," in Francisco Panizza (ed.), *Populism and the Mirror of Democracy*. London: Verso, 99–117.

Roberts, Kenneth M. 2013. "Parties and populism in Latin America," in Carlos de la Torre and Cynthia J. Arson (eds), *Latin American Populisms in the Twenty-First Century*. Washington, DC: Woodrow Wilson Center *Press*, 37–60.

Stavrakakis, Yannis. 1999. *Lacan and the Political*. London and New York: Routledge, 1999.

Stavrakakis, Yannis. 2001. "Identity, political," in Paul. B. Clarke and Joe Foweraker (eds), *Encyclopaedia of Democratic Thought*. London and New York: Routledge, 333–7.

Taylor, Charles. 2002. "Modern social imaginaries," *Public Culture*, 14(1): 91–124.

Torfing, Jacob. 1999. *New Theories of Discourse: Laclau, Mouffe and Žižek*. Oxford and Malden: Blackwell Publishers.

Weyland, Kurt. 2001. "Clarifying a contested concept: populism in the study of Latin American politics," *Comparative Politics*, 3(1): 1–22.

Žižek, Slavoj. 1989. *The Sublime Object of Ideology*. London: Verso.

CHAPTER 22

....

POPULISM AND GENDER

....

SAHAR ABI-HASSAN

THE theoretical and empirical study of populism encompasses a wide variety of research that ranges from regionally based studies to inquiry into the varieties of populism along political, economic, and ideological lines. However, while populism has been extensively explored in different contexts, its relationship with gender issues remains largely understudied. On one hand, focus has been almost entirely on male leadership, despite the presence of a significant number of female populist leaders (Eva Perón in Argentina, Pia Kjœrsgaard in Denmark, Marine Le Pen in France, to mention a few). In this sense, studies of populism have generally overlooked the way in which populist discourse frames female populist leadership. On the other hand, definitions of populism that focus primarily on procedural aspects ignore the substantive and symbolic elements that emerge from a populist gendered discourse. For instance, in some countries populist politics can be associated with the expansion of political rights for women. However, is this an instance of a gendered dimension specific to populism or is it conditioned by the sociopolitical context, which gets appropriated by populism either opportunistically or ideologically?

To date, only few studies have made a comprehensive contribution to our understanding of the relationship between gender and populism. On one hand, an edited volume by Karen Kampwirth focuses on the historical evolution of gender issues throughout various populist moments in Latin America. In her study Kampwirth (2010) maps gender issues onto three phases of populism: classical populism, neopopulism, and radical populism. On the other hand, a special number of the *Journal of Patterns of Prejudice* covers a variety of studies of populism and gender issues as they mainly pertain to radical-right parties in Europe (Spierings and Zaslove, 2015b).

In their extensive, but divergent, contribution towards our understanding of gender and populism, these studies make evident the difficulty in finding common patterns in the treatment of gender issues across different populist moments. In the case of Latin America where a significant number of populist leaders have emerged, Kampwirth (2010) finds that throughout the three historical populist periods, the treatment of gender issues has been mainly opportunistic with the aim to recruit a greater number of supporters and activists to advance the populist cause. While this is also the case in European countries, the relationship between gender and populism, especially in Western Europe, is greatly shaped by the advances in human rights and gender equality made throughout the region (Mudde and Rovira Kaltwasser, 2015). This generates a wide variety of gender treatments across European countries.

Using an ideational definition of populism, this article explores the varieties of populism in its relation to gender. For decades now, populism has been one of the most debated concepts in the discipline. It has been applied to both left-wing leaders such as Hugo Chávez in Venezuela and right-wing parties such as the Austrian Freedom Party (FPÖ) in Europe. It can be a politics of opposition or government, it is found in Europe as much as in Latin America, and it can be an advocate for the underclass as much as it promotes the exclusion of minorities (Mudde and Rovira Kaltwasser, 2013).

Definitional divergence in the study of populism can be mainly attributed to its emergence in different times and contexts. This has produced a series of incongruous and even opposite definitions that span the economic, political, social, and discursive domains based on different political movements, parties, ideologies, and leaders. According to Canovan (1982), the basis for the vagueness in the definition of populism is the intent of scholars to cast either a wide-ranging normative definition, or one empirically based. The first approach attempts to bring all possible cases under one "theoretical roof." The second is more "phenomenological," collecting cases and following a descriptive mode to build a theory of populism (Canovan, 1982: 545). This has led to a "tradeoff between comprehensiveness and clarity" (Canovan, 1982: 548), where the first is very diffuse to provide substantive information, and the latter is too narrow to be applicable to all cases.

More recently, scholars have converged on a definition of populism that is mainly based on political attributes, either institutional or ideational (Abts and Rummens, 2007; Arditi, 2004; Barr, 2009; Brett, 2013; de la Torre, 2013; Hawkins, 2010; Laclau, 2005a; Mudde and Rovira Kaltwasser, 2012; Panizza, 2005; Weyland, 2001). Specifically, this contribution follows the definition of populism as a "thin-centered ideology, that considers society to be ultimately separated into two homogeneous and antagonistic groups, 'the pure people' and 'the corrupt elite,' and which argues that politics should be an expression of the *volonté générale* (general will) of the people" (Mudde and Rovira Kaltwasser, 2012: 8; see also Mudde's contribution in this volume). This definition contains necessary and sufficient attributes to make populism a worldwide phenomenon. More importantly, it provides two thresholds against which to study the relationship between populism and gender.

First, as a "thin-centered ideology," it makes the populist contents of each case relative to its socio-political and economic context (Mudde and Rovira Kaltwasser, 2011), hence context-specific. As such, we can expect to find clear distinctions between the gender dimension that emerges from the populist radical-right in Europe and the left-wing populists in Latin America. Second, populism has one clear manifestation that remains constant regardless of socioeconomic structures or the power position it operates from: the moral distinction between the "the pure people" and the "corrupt elite"

(Mudde, 2004; Mudde and Rovira Kaltwasser, 2013: 151). This makes gender an almost unnecessary or even irrelevant category for the construction of "the people" and the "other" (Mudde and Rovira Kaltwasser, 2015).

Within this framework, it becomes evident that an important component of any analysis of populist politics is the context in which it emerges. Markedly, there are manifestations of right- and left-wing populism in Europe as well as right- and left-wing populism in Latin America, despite the difficulty in placing them on a specific point of the political spectrum. However, a clear regional divide between the dominance of left populists in Latin America and radical right populism in Europe steers this contribution to focus on these two salient varieties of populism across these two regions. Through a generalized discussion and references to specific examples in Europe and Latin America, this article identifies three major topics at the intersection of gender and populism: populist supporters, populist gendered representation, and the subordination of personal (gender) identity in populist discourse.

As an issue-based phenomenon, gender politics is contrary to the more flexible open-ended nature of populist politics (Weyland, 2010). This leads one to question the extent to which populism opens a space for the treatment of gender issues. Hence the following framing questions: is there a specific gender dimension inherent to populist politics? Is the populist support base gendered as well? How and why? Has this changed overtime? What are the particular gendered features of populist representation? How does the issue of gender interact with the primacy of personalization in populist discourse and subsequent policies? Answering these questions will help provide a comprehensive analysis of the relationship between gender and populism, as the latter has come to occupy an important place in the politics of Latin America and Europe.

SETTING THE CONTEXT: GENDER ISSUES AND POPULISM IN LATIN AMERICA AND EUROPE

The earliest manifestation of gender issues in modern times emerged from the demand of women to be included in the political process. Although struggles for female enfranchisement started as early as the mid-nineteenth century, it was not until the 1920s that mobilizations in the United States and Britain were able to secure the right to vote for women (Osborne, 2001). Known as the first wave of feminism, this movement struggled to create a space for women in politics. Markedly, these movements took place in democratic countries that already had a wide platform for political participation. For instance, in Britain securing the right to vote was part of the progressive movement towards a consolidated parliamentary democracy that had began two centuries before. In the United States the anti-slavery movement of the nineteenth century served as the underpinning framework for the emergence of the Suffragists movement, culminating in the Nineteenth Amendment in 1920 (Osborne, 2001).[1]

The struggles of this first wave of feminism helped lay the foundation for the expansion of public and legal rights for women. However, in neither of these advanced democracies was this accompanied by populist politics. The advent of populism in Britain and Europe in general is a relatively recent phenomenon, and in the United States, where we find populism's earliest manifestation, it was mainly focused on the rights of agricultural workers (Goodwyn, 1978).[2]

In less advanced democracies, the right to vote also became a subject of debate and struggle. In Latin America, a wide variety of movements emerged, working within and in opposition to their current governments to secure the right to vote (Jaquette, 2009). These struggles in Latin America coincided with the emergence of classical populism, where charismatic leaders appropriated female suffrage as an issue of the nation and the "people" (Kampwirth, 2010). For instance, between the 1920s and 1940s, the leadership of Juan Domingo Perón in Argentina, Getulio Vargas in Brazil, and Lázaro Cardenas in Mexico, among others, found an ally in women as their fight originated from a disadvantaged position in politics as well; they too were political outsiders.

Having won the suffrage battle, women's movements in the United States and Europe began to shift towards issues of welfare and employment. Notwithstanding some important advances, World War II and its legacies dramatically slowed down the organized struggle to expand women's rights (Osborne, 2001). It was not until the late 1950s and beginning of the 1960s that women's movements gained momentum again in the developed world. For instance, in Europe, the post-war initiative to unite the continent created the space to debate and address gender issues. In what is known as the second wave of feminism, the scope of gender issues expanded to include the treatment of women in the workplace, protections for mothers and the provision of childcare, and even questions of gender equality (Osborne, 2001: 25).

Despite its heavy emphasis on economic unity and limited political integration, the European Union played an important role in promoting progressive agendas, such as gender equality, at the national and local levels (Kantola, 2010). As a civic project conceived on universal values (Risse, 2010), the EU established a normative basis for the type of gender relations to be promoted in its member states. Early integration efforts shaped the political framework in Europe and with it the treatment of gender issues, leaving little room for radical movements to emerge. However, the challenges of the late twentieth and early twenty-first century—globalization, immigration, and integration—created the space for radical populist parties to become legitimate political actors (Berezin, 2009). Accelerated integration efforts, especially with the ratification of the Maastricht Treaty in 1992, served as a catalyst for originally fringe parties to challenge the politics of post-war compromise and champion populist politics in their opposition to greater European integration (Taggart, 1998).

While Western Europe's relationship with radical movements is shaped by European integration and Euroskepticism, the manifestation of populism in other regions was greatly shaped by (a lack of) democratization processes. For instance, in Latin America, the second wave of feminism coincided with the end of classical populism, the emergence of military dictatorships in the 1960s–1970s, followed by a wave of democratization in the 1980s and 1990s.

Despite the instability experienced throughout the region, the incorporation of women into the labor force and the expansion of government services promoted in previous decades allowed for the creation of more gender-conscious policies (Kampwirth, 2010: 3). However, this was greatly constrained due to the lack of a true democratic framework (Jaquette, 2009). It was not until the democratization wave of the 1980s–1990s that we begin to see gender equality initiatives, such as reforming discriminatory family and labor laws, criminalizing violence against women, and introducing gender parity laws for legislative elections (Jaquette, 2009).

Coinciding with contradictory developments around the world, from the emergence of right-wing radicalism to religious fundamentalism to processes of democratization, women's movements beginning in the 1990s coincided with a clear and widespread manifestation of populist politics throughout Europe and Latin America. While in Latin America populism has had a constant presence, the emergence of democratic processes and institutions in what is known as the third wave of democratization brought a renewed form of populist politics (Kampwirth, 2010). Almost simultaneously, Europe saw the expansion and strengthening of a variety of populist parties mainly dominated by the radical right (PRR). Aligned with populism's generalized sense of disenfranchisement, some of the major issues championed by third-wave feminists included social security reform, women's health, and voter registration (Osborne, 2001).

In Europe, advances in gender equality make it increasingly difficult to reconcile this with the radical discourse and policy preferences of right-wing populists. As such, we see how the originally conservative stance towards gender issues (family values and traditional gender roles) shifts towards a more liberal view that ranges from the acceptance of women into the labor force to defense of women's equality and same-sex marriage (Akkerman, 2015).[3] However, through their anti-immigration discourse, PRR parties re-crafted their position towards gender issues. For instance, they frame the use of veils and the treatment of women in Islam as a threat to the modern societies of Europe (Andreassen and Lettinga, 2012). Moreover, debates about immigration have also shifted towards family migration and integration. Within this context, populist radical right parties portray the position of women in immigrant families as a sign of backwardness in the treatment of women (Mudde and Rovira Kaltwasser, 2015)

Through these two issues, populist radical right parties have adapted their conservative discourse to mirror changes in society, finding a new enemy: the backwardness of Islam and its treatment of women (Akkerman, 2015). From this, it becomes evident that PRR parties in Europe can be placed on a continuum rather than a specific point when it comes to their treatment of gender issues. Overall, "populist radical-right parties have adapted their conservative views to the liberal and democratic contexts of Western European countries" (Akkerman, 2015: 56); this applies to gender issues as well.

In Latin America, the infusion of populist politics with neoliberal ideas in the 1990s complicated the relationship between gender and populism. While the era of classical populism focused mainly on voting rights and the introduction of women to public life, the new populism had to deal with the commitments of the first wave (legal and public rights) in addition to the issues brought forward by the second wave of feminism: reproductive rights (sexuality issues), gender equality, and responses to violence against women (Kampwirth, 2010: 4–5). Moreover, changes in the political economy of the region made this most recent wave of populism greatly reliant on personalistic politics to compensate for the leaders' reduced ability to implement patronage. But overall, populists in Latin America have consistently remained engaged with gender issues through the welfare state and the redistributive perspective that has characterized them throughout different periods.

Gender struggles have been widely divergent in their timing and outcomes across the world. Yet, a fundamental attribute equal to all is the constructed inferior position of women within social and political frameworks. Theoretically, in populist terms, this makes the position of women in society analogous to the populist category of the "underdog." However, can this assertion withstand an empirical analysis? Does the position of women serve as a basic ingredient in the emergence of a populist logic? Moreover, do gender issues become more notorious when populist women rise to a leadership position?

As the issues presented and discussed by women's movements evolved, the responses of governments changed as well. However, it appears that no particular response or solution emanates from populist politics per se, neither on the right nor left as they dominate in Europe and Latin America, respectively.

Gender and Populist Supporters

One consistent trend found in electoral behavior studies in Europe and Latin America is that women are more likely to support left-wing candidates/parties and men are more likely to support right-wing candidates/parties (Ingelhart and Norris, 2000). So, does this gender bias hold for supporters of populist leaders and parties? There is substantial evidence behind the notion that the composition of the population that votes for populist parties and leaders is only a more extreme version of the composition of mainstream parties' voters (Harteveld, Van Der Brug, Dahlberg, and Kokkonen, 2015; Spierings and Zaslove, 2015a). For instance, in Europe, support for radical right parties tends to be dominated by white-male blue-collar workers, consistently similar to the patterns of support for mainstream right parties (Harteveld et al., 2015). In Latin America, starting with the suffragist movement, women have consistently made up an important portion of populist leaders' support base (Kampwirth, 2010).

This gender gap is strikingly marked when it comes to the support base of populist radical right parties in Europe. Although Latin America exhibits a similar gender gap in political participation in general, left-wing populism is not particularly prone to this pattern, or at least it has not been sufficiently explored (Desposato and Norrander, 2009).

According to Betz (1994: 142–6), "gender remains one of the most consistent predictors of support for radical right-wing populist parties in Western democracies." Consistent with this claim, Harteveld et al. (2015) provide an overview of the gender gap in Western and Eastern European countries, using the 2009 European Election Studies (EES). On average, they find that support for PRR parties in seventeen European countries is 2.32 among men and 2.00 among women (on a 0–10 scale). However, their work also shows this gap to be more significant in some countries than others. For instance, in France and Austria, the gap is insignificant at a 5 percent level, where in Denmark the gap stands close to the average, at 34 percent (Harteveld et al., 2015).

Specifically looking at the gender gap in Denmark, the People's Party's (DFP) conservative ideology towards welfare and multiculturalism combined with Euroskepticism puts it in a unique position to capture a wide spectrum of voters (Southwell and Lindgren, 2013: 129). A fluctuation in its support rates between 1995 and 2000 shows that the DFP has filled a void by catering to voters concerned with both political and economic issues (Meret, 2015). This divergence between Denmark, and France and Austria (countries that also have successful PRR parties, FN and FPÖ, respectively) reduces the strength of the argument of a relationship between the voting gender gap and PRR parties' success.

Controlling for socio-structural factors such as age and religion increases this gap. However, adding indicators such as work, class, and education has the opposite effect, reducing the gap by 11 percent (Harteveld et al., 2015). Hence, socio-structural factors partially explain the difference in male versus female vote. Discontent cannot explain the gap either, as both men and women exhibit the same levels of discontent. Harteveld et al. (2015) argue that while women and men do have different characteristics and political attitudes, this is only a limited explanation for the gender gap.

Instead, Harteveld et al. (2015) find that men and women also attach different considerations in their evaluation of PRR parties, which would explain why women show greater apprehension in voting for them. Hence, women are not necessarily less likely to be dissatisfied with the working of democracy or to have more attenuated negative feelings towards immigration; it is that their discontent does not strongly translate into support for PRR candidates (Harteveld et al., 2015: 129).

In sum, the evidence supporting the gender gap as a strong predictor of PRR parties' success in Europe appears to be mixed. Cultural values and beliefs seem to provide only limited explanations. Where the gender gap has been one of the most puzzling features of support for the radical right in Europe, the relationship between gender and populism certainly extends beyond the voting booth.

Populism, Gender, and Political Representation

One of the most enduring features of populist politics is the establishment of a "strong symbolic relation between the leader and his/her followers" (Meret, 2015: 82). This process falls within the realm of political representation and as such is greatly shaped by the institutional and sociocultural context in which populism emerges. However, in order to understand how this personalistic feature of populism shapes its relationship with gender, first it is necessary to understand how political representation is conceptualized in general.

In her seminal work, Hanna Pitkin (1967) categorizes political representation into formal, descriptive, substantive, and symbolic representation. Formal representation is defined through the rules allowing representatives to act and constituents to hold them accountable. Pitkin (1967) argues that this form of representation impacts the extent to which the diversity of elected officials mirrors the composition of society, known as descriptive representation.

Moreover, both formal and descriptive representations, in time, shape substantive representation defined by the actions of political representatives and their responsiveness to their constituents' concerns. Ultimately, the previous three forms of political representation shape symbolic representation or the emotional responses of people towards their elected officials (Pitkin, 1967). Through these four categories of representation—formal, descriptive, substantive, and symbolic—Pitkin (1967) presents an integrated model of political representation in which all forms feed into each other for a context-specific model of representation (Schwindt-Bayer, 2010).

Through Pitkin's model of representation, it becomes evident that each specific socio-political context is highly influential on the form of politics in general, and populist politics in this specific contribution. For instance, the ability of female populist leaders to become viable political representatives and the gender-related discourse and policies that emanate from populism could generally be traced back to each context specific dynamic model of representation. This leads to the following questions: Are there inherent features to populism that increase (decrease) female representation in political institutions (formal and descriptive representation)? Is the presence of female populist leaders more conducive to a departure from pre-existing attitudes towards gender issues and the implementation of gender conscious policies (substantive representation)? Finally, are there gender-driven differences in the emotional responses generated by populist leaders (symbolic representation)?

Gendered Representation in Populist Politics

Historically, populism in Latin America was instrumental for overhauling political institutions with the aim of expanding the rights of previously disenfranchised sectors of the population; to an extent this included women (Panizza, 2005). Starting with the right to vote, populist leaders in Latin America understood the value of incorporating women into the political space as a way of expanding their support base. One of the earliest examples of this is the Peronist party in Argentina. Through the right to vote and extensive changes in party structure, women were consolidated as the newest political class (Grammático, 2010), which served as a stepping-stone for future efforts to expand the political rights of women.

More recently, during the presidency of Carlos Menem, implementation of the gender parity law in 1991 was a progressive move towards changing the composition of the legislature and increasing the number of women in the cabinet. Later on, during the presidency of Néstor Kirchner (2003–2007), women began to occupy decision-making roles, such as the Ministries of Economy and Production, of Defense, and of Social Development (Kohen, 2009: 90). Finally in 2007, the election of Cristina Fernández de Kirchner (Néstor Kirchner's wife) to the presidency can be interpreted as the most recent achievement in the struggle for gender equality.

Constitutional reforms have also served as an opportunity for expanding the role of women in formal political representation. For instance, through the Constituent Assembly elections in Bolivia, "gender parity was adopted as a principle and imposed on party lists" (Rousseau, 2010: 156). In addition to being headed by a woman, the Bolivian Constituent Assembly resulted in 34 percent female representation in the assembly; this was even higher for Morales's party—MAS (47 percent). Also guided by the new constitution, Morales's government initiated a process to register undocumented citizens, especially indigenous women who did not posses proper identification and hence could not vote (Rousseau, 2010: 153). In Venezuela, the Constituent Assembly process also achieved proportional participation between female and male delegates (Espina and Rakowski, 2010).

These efforts have allowed women to enjoy some of the civil and political rights already enjoyed by men, translating formal and descriptive representation into substantive representation. For instance, the assembly process in Bolivia translated into important advances for gender struggles, such as the separation of the state from the Catholic Church, and the establishment of sexual and reproductive rights as constitutional rights (Rousseau, 2010).

Likewise, in Venezuela gender-oriented laws established by the 1999 Constitution expanded female involvement not just in politics, but also in community work (Fernandes, 2010). According to Fernandes (2010: 203), "increasing the presence of women in local communities and assemblies has created new forms of democratic participation that challenge gender roles." This is especially accentuated in their involvement in health and educational programs (Espina and Rakowski, 2010: 189).

However, even in instances where women have become powerful political agents, their ability to represent women on women's issues has remained limited to activities or policies sanctioned as "adequate" for women (Schwindt-Bayer, 2010). For instance, the institutional structure of the Peronist party allowed women more participation; this is evident in the creation of the *División de Trabajo y Asistencia de la Mujer* (Women's

Welfare and Labor Division) as part of the Ministry of labor, or the formation of the *Partido Peronista Fememino* (Feminine Peronist Party) in 1949 (Grammático, 2010: 123). Yet, the activities reserved for female participants were mainly in the areas of education, health, and food, areas usually framed as feminine. This has remained the case even in light of recent presidential appointments (Kohen, 2009).

Moreover, in Bolivia the main concerns of feminist groups greatly diverged from the priorities of women's organizations and female leaders closely allied with President Morales (women in indigenous and peasant organizations). As such, Morales's government has maintained at best an ambiguous relationship with feminist groups (Rousseau, 2010; 2011). On one hand, Morales changed the political framework to allow greater female participation in politics. On the other hand, women in power tend to associate their role in politics with an extension of their "maternal duties," which greatly diverges from the commitment of feminist movements towards greater gender equality (Rousseau, 2010: 158).

Even in Western Europe, where the advancement of gender policies stands ahead of Latin America, it exhibits similar patterns in the translation of female representation onto gender-conscious policies (substantive representation). However, it is worth noting that Europe's experience with populism has been somewhat different, primarily in two dimensions. First, the right-to-vote element present in Latin American is absent due to the more recent emergence and consolidation of populist parties in Europe. Second, because the most successful populists have been radical right-wing parties, their policy focus is not on extending political participation or social services but on who should be included in the provision of existing ones. Nevertheless, the presence of notable female populist leaders such Pia Kjœrsgaard in Denmark and Marine Le Pen in France are perfect examples of the ambiguous relationship between populism and female representation.

Female Populist Leaders

Populist leadership has been mostly associated with strong charismatic leaders who give voice to those disenfranchised by their political system. In their roles of "speaking for the people," as argued by Paul Taggart, "populism requires the most extraordinary individuals to lead the most ordinary people" (2000: 1). These necessary extraordinary qualities are usually associated with "predominantly masculine attributes" (Meret, 2015: 83); in a way, this seems to be antithetical to populist female leadership. So, how do female leaders and populist supporters resolve this contradiction?

When it comes to female leadership, it is no secret that women have had to "reconcile the traditional values of their specific context (sexual difference) with their presence in the public and political sphere" (Kofman, 1998: 102). As such, the style of populist female leaders is also a reflection of the contradiction between social traditional values and public life.

For instance, in Denmark, the leadership of Pia Kjœrsgaard is seen as a perfect balance between a "rigid and domineering" public image counterbalanced by a private image of a "simple, unpretentious family woman and mother" (Meret, 2015: 93). As the first female to launch a party in Denmark—the Danish People's Party (DFP)—and the first to lead a populist party in Western Europe, Kjœrsgaard is portrayed as the mother of the nation, and is often called *mama Pia* (Meret, 2015). According to Meret (2015: 96), Kjœrsgaard's "status of caring mother, housewife and social worker are deliberately seen in opposition to the professionalized, educated, political elite and particularly to current Danish female politicians who have an academic background, a political career and little direct experience in the Danish labor market." This makes evident that while the centralizing and disciplined nature of Kjœrsgaard's leadership allows her a position in the public sphere, gender continues to be a defining feature of her leadership.

As such, formal and descriptive representation in these cases has not always translated into substantive representation (Kohen, 2009). For instance, in Argentina, despite having a woman president, over half of the female population still does not receive any sort of labor benefits (Pautassi, 2005). Regardless of their developed (or developing) nature, in these examples, the incorporation of women into politics and the labor force has not entirely translated into a change in the balance of home responsibilities among genders—in many instances, women are still expected to fulfill the role of primary caregivers even after being incorporated into public life.

Especially in Latin America, gender struggles have also been weakened by the divide between those who consider themselves feminists and fight for gender-oriented policies, and those who use gender policies to fight for the leader or party (Craske, 1999). For instance, during the Venezuelan 1999 National Assembly process, the incorporation of female delegates was mainly driven by partisan affiliation rather than a true commitment to gender issues (Espina and Rakowski, 2010).

Beyond their newfound role as supporters and relevant political actors in populism, women have also served as activists, especially supporting the expansion of social services, a staple policy of Latin American populist leaders. This can be read as an instance of the emotional responses generated by populist representation.

In Argentina, motherhood became the Peronists' go-to discourse to recruit women in their fight towards the development of "national greatness" (Di Liscia, 1999). Motherhood was appropriated as a militant subject position. Qualities such as self-abnegation, sacrifice, and selflessness, seen as motherhood virtues, were widely associated with the populist category of the "people" (Grammático, 2010: 128). Women's role as mothers became complementary to their position as working-class women, which made them part of the people and hence Peronist (populist).

The media have also contributed towards "reinforcing stereotypical gender qualities and attributes" by constructing an association between masculinity and rational thinking or objectivity, and femininity and emotional feeling or social empathy. According to Susi Meret (2015: 87–8), both female and male populist leaders strategically conflate the two to "create an image that people can identify with." This maps onto the way in which populist leaders have utilized (and continue to utilize) a public/private dichotomy to frame women's role in politics.

From this, it is evident that contextual features and partisan attachment are the main predictors of the patterns of gendered representation in populist politics, rather than a true commitment to gender struggles. Even with the implementation of gender-oriented policies and radical institutional reforms, the place for gender has always been either secondary or framed within the leader/party's ideology.

A striking feature of women's involvement as leaders and activists in the establishment of a populist agenda is the challenge it poses to the vertical structures of power in populism. However, in many cases, the leader's direct appeal to women brings them into the political sphere, a sphere that is directly managed by the leader (e.g. Hugo Chávez in Venezuela: Fernandes, 2010; Pia Kjœrsgaard in Denmark: Meret, 2015). This speaks to the ability of populist politics to mediate the primacy of personalistic politics with the claim to represent the will of the "people." In the following sections, the chapter explores this dynamic as it mediates the relationship between gender and populism.

The Subordination of Personal Identity: Feminist versus Feminine in Populist Discourse and Policies

In the discourse theory tradition, Laclau (2005b: 39) argues that "the construction of an enemy" or opposition to the status quo is not enough to stabilize the heterogeneity of people's demand. The articulation of a populist logic requires the identification of an anchor or agent (an empty signifier) that embodies the homogenization of disparate demands; a concept or name that without losing its own specificity, stands as a universal representation for all other demands to which it is seen as equivalent (Laclau, 2005a; 2005b; Panizza, 2005). As argued by Eco (1995: 15), in populist politics:

> individuals as individuals have no rights, and the "people" is conceived as a quality, a monolithic entity expressing the Common Will. Since no large quantity of human beings can have a common will, the Leader pretends to be their interpreter. Having lost their power of delegation, citizens do not act; they are only called on to play the role of the People.

This particular dimension of populism makes it prone to subvert any issues that do not emanate from the leader or the party. This is especially evident in Latin American populism, where despite its many contributions towards the inclusion of women, it did so to the extent that it served the leader/party's ideals.

For instance, the discourse of the Peronists in Argentina, as well as other modern-day populists such as Chávez in Venezuela and Morales in Bolivia, stems from class and ethnic cleavages. As such, the participation of women in the political process is encouraged as long as it supports social services, and advances their redistributive goals in general. The primary mechanism to achieve this is by extending the feminine role attributed to women in the private sphere to the public sphere (Kampwirth, 2010; Mudde and Rovira Kaltwasser, 2015). Hence, feminine attributes (motherhood, abnegation, sacrifice) in the political space are encouraged, while feminist struggles of individualism and autonomy are discouraged and seen as elitist or bourgeois distractions (Craske, 1999).

In Argentina, the Peronist party embraced motherhood as one of the most important ways in which women could commit to the state and the development of the nation (Di Liscia, 1999). Through the extension of motherhood as necessary for the protection of the nation, populist politics in Argentina blurred the line between women's private work at home and their public contribution in society as guardians of the values promoted by populism (Grammático, 2010). This bestows upon women an important role in educating future generations in the ideological content attached to populism.

A similar discourse emerges in Bolivia, although its gender dimension is strongly associated with the struggle of indigenous women and the restoration of their values to the community (Rousseau, 2010: 154): Morales highlights the "negative impact of colonialism on gender relations," presenting "machismo" as a foreign discourse. However, this does not necessarily incorporate all gender struggles. The priorities of many feminist groups (advocating for women's individual rights and autonomy) are subverted under the definition of womanhood advanced by those closely associated with the regime.

Morales's populist discourse advocates for the inclusion of women in all aspects of society based on gender complementarity, through the incorporation of indigenous culture and community values (Rousseau, 2010: 154). As such, the incorporation of peasant indigenous women into the political process established a close relation between women's role in politics and their role as mothers of the community. While this has certainly been beneficial to women's struggles in Bolivia, through the adoption of gender parity laws and the establishment of legal grounds for gender equality in the 2009 constitution (Rousseau, 2010: 155), indigenous women's issues have come to dominate all dimensions of the gender struggle in Bolivia (Monasterios, 2007: 33). According to Rousseau (2010: 157), this is not an indication of a natural opposition of populist politics towards feminist struggles but is consistent with ethnic and class cleavage dynamics within Bolivian society.

In Venezuela, again women's rights are articulated through feminine attributes, and the extent to which they serve the populist ideal. In the last decade and a half, political loyalties moved to the forefront at the expense of women's issues and struggles. Despite the inclusion of feminist elements in the 1999 Constitution and an increase in female representation in the legislature, these were presented as a commitment to Chávez's "revolution" and not to women's issues (Espina and Rakowski, 2010); indeed, any instance where women's issues did not conform to Chávez's populist agenda it was portrayed as elitist. For example, women are encouraged to work and participate in the political process to fulfill their role as mothers of the community, and not ideals of personal development and independence.

Although in populist terms, feminists continue to be constructed as the elite, Chávez's particular brand of populism appropriates feminism as an instrument of empowerment within a revolutionary context. As such, while populism has the potential to undertake feminist issues due to the excluded nature of the group, its antagonistic nature is too keen on portraying feminists as elitist, overly educated people who do not fit the construction of a real woman in populist terms (Kampwirth, 2010: 14).

Moreover, Latin American populism has consistently drawn on the figure of the father, "a strong leader with whom people could identify above all in emotional terms" (Stein, 1980:11 cited in Kampwirth, 2010: 12), which turns citizens into children. This creates an analogy between the "party" or the state and the family. It provides an extension for the work of women in the house to their work outside and their dedication towards the populist cause (Plotkin, 2003: xii, 178). As such, women's position as outsiders makes them the perfect subject to spread the word about populist reforms (Kampwirth, 2010: 15).

In Europe, the nature of the dominant populist parties frames gender issues through the domains of family relations, immigration, and integration. Considering the differential advancement towards gender equality in European countries, radical right parties' discourse and policies tend to have a broader range (from conservative to flexible conservative) than left-wing populism in Latin America (Akkerman, 2015). For instance, in France one of the primary features of the populist radical right is the correlation between gender issues and the composition of society. Gender issues are only instrumental to more pressing concerns such as the transmission of values, the demarcation of national borders, and how society reproduces and functions (Kofman, 1998: 129) in an increasingly multicultural and borderless region.

According to Kofman (1998: 97), in France gender issues have figured prominently as an important link between the family and the nation. The gender relations of immigrant groups are constructed as a threat to the nation. This is compounded by the fact that immigrant groups in France have tended to have a higher birth rate than the indigenous population. As such, sexual differences are used to construct racial boundaries (Kofman, 1998: 97). This elevates the role of women and their reproductive function to something essential for the preservation of the local population (Kofman, 1998: 93). Their responsibility towards the public is underpinned by something as private as motherhood and nurture, again sanctioning women's feminine role as part of the political process.

Populist radical right parties in other Western European as well as Eastern European countries have appropriated gender-equality discourse to justify their positions against the integration of immigrants into society. Most radical right parties address this contradiction by framing "gender as a universal value that Muslim women do not possess, which leads to a reconfiguration of gender equality as a marker of cultural boundaries" (Andreassen and Lettinga, 2012: 31–2). Xenophobic discourse and anti-immigration policies are reframed through gender and human rights (de Lange and Mügge, 2015: 65), to make it "potentially respectable and a politically legitimate anti-immigration position" (Meret and Siim, 2013: 83).

In Denmark, discourse about gender equality occupies a significant place for the Danish People's Party (DFP) as it uses this to frame its position on assimilation and anti-immigration agendas (Hans-Goerg Betz and Meret, 2009). In its 2009 party program, the DFP dedicates a whole chapter to the issue of gender equality, where it emphasizes total support for equality between the sexes (Meret and Siim, 2013: 85). This indicates that populist radical right parties acknowledge the importance of gender issues, at least in traditionally liberal democracies such as Denmark and Norway (Akkerman and Hagelund, 2007). In Austria, the Austrian Freedom Party's (FPÖ) latest program also showcases their commitment to gender equality and equality of roles within the family, at work and in society in general. According to Meret and Siim (2013: 88), this contrasts with the "traditional-conservative approach to family values and family policies" and their exclusionary discourse towards immigrants, especially Muslim immigrants.

The disposition of populists—across regions and political ideologies—towards greater gender equality contrasted with an attachment to traditional cultural values and the feminization of women's role in society appears to be the only feature possibly characteristic of the relationship between gender and populism. However, until further inquiry is undertaken, it is not possible to know if this relationship is a constant in populism or something inherent to the treatment of gender, regardless of the framing political logic (populist or mainstream).

CONCLUSION

As suggested by Mudde and Rovira Kaltwasser (2015), differences within the category of the "people" are all secondary to the categorical distinction between the "us" versus "them." Yet, populists do not operate in an ideological vacuum. As a "thin-centered ideology" populism is framed by each specific sociopolitical context in which it emerges. Hence, the treatment of gender issues within populist politics remains consistent with contextual features.

While the appearance of similar patterns in all cases would point to a gender dimension of populist politics, this review suggests that consistency across regions is more an instance of the treatment of gender issues in general, rather than a specific relation between gender and populism. From the previous analysis, it is possible to see that populist leaders embrace gender issues as an extension of their political struggle to the extent to which it serves the specific ideas they attach to it. In this sense, the cultural and historic-political context is key to understanding the relationship between populism and gender. This is not an altogether a striking finding, considering that populism in its various manifestations takes on each county's particular socio-economic and political struggles and salient ideologies.

Another important finding that also seems to manifest cross-regionally is the divide between embracing femininity as consistent with populist ideals. In all manifestations of populism, old and new, left- or right-wing, European or Latin American, leaders and parties consistently advocate for gender equality and sympathize with gender struggles, while maintaining a rather traditional-conservative approach to societal dynamics (family, work, political participation, etc.).

This contradiction in the treatment of gender issues becomes evident through Pitkin's integrated model of political representation (Schwindt-Bayer, 2010). On one hand, through formal changes to the institutional political framework, populism, especially in Latin America, expanded the role of women in the political process. However, as these changes were mainly driven by the need to recruit supporters and activists, it failed to fully enhance the role of women in politics specifically and society in general. As such, feminist movements that advocate for women's individual rights and autonomy are constructed as corrupt and elitist. This seems to be antithetical to the populist claim of elevating those who have been previously disfranchised by the political system. However, one explanation for this is that feminist movements tend to embrace intellectualist and progressive ideals that go against the general idea of "the people." In this sense, the populace must be conceived as those who adhere to traditional beliefs and values, and where anything that could be conceived as foreign must be rejected.

On the other hand, formal and descriptive representation does not always translate into substantive representation. Populist leaders in both regions consistently frame the role of women in politics as an extension of their gender role in the home, even when they occupy high political offices. This consistency is striking considering the wide spectrum that outlines populist movements across the world. The discipline would greatly benefit from future research into the macro- and micro-dynamics of feminine versus feminist struggles within populist politics.

This modest inquiry makes evident that the treatment of gender issues in populism is highly contextualized. While populist dynamics such as antagonistic and anti-establishment politics are consistently found throughout regions and ideological positions, the political and policy outcomes associated with gender issues are diverse. Moreover, even when similar discourses and policy outcomes are found across countries and regions, this seems to be an instance of the parallel progression in the treatment of gender issues in general, and not of populist politics per se.

While this analysis provides a comprehensive overview of the relationship between gender and populism, and argues for a weak relationship between the two, the availability of theory in populism and gender studies begs for more empirical studies into the determinants of this relationship.

NOTES

1 The Nineteenth Amendment gave women the right to vote by making it illegal to be "denied or abridged by the United States or by any States on account of sex" (The Constitution of the United States).
2 In the US, the National Farmers Alliance and Industrial Union served as a base for the agrarian revolt and the establishment of the People's Party in 1892, which led the first populist movement (Goodwyn, 1978).

3   This is exemplified by the liberal discourse of the PVV in Netherlands, which defends same-sex marriage, contrasted by the conservative stance of parties such as FIDEZ in Hungary.

REFERENCES

Abts, K. and S. Rummens. 2007. "Populism versus democracy," *Political Studies*, 55(2): 405–24.

Akkerman, T. 2015. "Gender and the radical-right in Western Europe: a comparative analysis of policy agendas," *Patterns of Prejudice*, 49(1–2): 37–60.

Akkerman, T. and A. Hagelund. 2007. "'Women and children first!' Anti-immigration parties and gender in Norway and the Netherlands," *Patterns of Prejudice*, 41(2): 197–214.

Andreassen, R. and D. Lettinga. 2012. "Veiled debates: gender and gender equality in European national narratives," in S. Rosenberg and B. Sauer (eds), *Politics, Religion and Gender: Framing and Regulating the Veil*. London and New York: Routledge, 17–36.

Arditi, B. 2004. "Populism as a spectre of democracy: a response to Canovan," *Political Studies*, 52(1): 135–43.

Barr, R. R. 2009. "Populists, outsiders, and anti-establishment politics," *Party Politics*, 15(1): 29–48.

Berezin, M. 2009. *Illiberal Politics in Neoliberal Times: Culture, Security and Populism in the New Europe*. Cambridge: Cambridge University Press.

Betz, H.-G. 1994. *Radical Right-wing Populism in Western Europe*. New York: St Martin's Press.

Betz, H.-G. and S. Meret. 2009. "Revisting Lepanto: the political mobilization against Islam in contemporary Western Europe," *Patterns of Prejudice*, 43(3–4): 313–34.

Brett, W. 2013. "What's an elite to do? The threat of populism from left, right and centre," *The Political Quarterly*, 84(3): 410–13.

Canovan, M. 1982. "Two strategies for the study of populism," *Political Studies*, 30(4): 544–52.

Craske, N. 1999. *Women and Politics in Latin America*. New Brunswick: Rutgers University Press.

de Lange, S. L. and L. M. Mügge. 2015. "Gender and right-wing populism in the Low Countries: ideological variations across parties and time," *Patterns of Prejudice*, 49(1–2): 61–80.

de la Torre, C. 2013. "In the name of the people: democratization, popular organizations, and populism in Venezuela, Bolivia, and Ecuador," *European Review of Latin American and Caribbean Studies*, 95: 27–48.

Desposato, S. and B. Norrander. 2009. "The gender gap in Latin America: contextual and individual influences on gender and political participation," *British Journal of Political Science*, 39(1): 141–62.

Di Liscia, M. H. 1999. "Ser madre es un deber (maternidad en los gobierons Peronistas)," in D. Villa (ed.), *Historia y género: seis estudios sobre la condición femenina*. Buenos Aires: Biblos, 33–51.

Eco, U. 1995. "Ur-Fascism," *The New York Review of Books*, 42(11): 12–15.

Espina, G. and C. A. Rakowski. 2010. "Waking women up? Hugo Chávez, populism, and Venezuela's 'popular women'," in Kampwirth (ed.), *Gender and Populism in Latin America: Passionate Politics*. University Park: Pennsylvania State University Press, 180–201.

Fernandes, S. 2010. "Gender, popular participation, and the state in Chávez's Venezuela," in K. Kampwirth (ed.), *Gender and Populism in Latin America: Passionate Politics*. University Park: Pennsylvania State University Press, 202–20.

Goodwyn, L. 1978. *The Populist Moment: A Short History of the Agrarian Revolt in America.* Oxford: Oxford University Press.

Grammático, K. 2010. "Populist continuities in 'revolutionary' Peronism: a comparative analysis of the gender discourses of the first Peronism (1946–1955) and the Montoneros," in K. Kampwirth (ed.), *Gender and Populism in Latin America.* University Park: Pennsylvania State University Press, 122–39.

Harteveld, E., W. Van Der Brug, S. Dahlberg, and A. Kokkonen. 2015. "The gender gap in populist radical-right voting: examining the demand side in Western and Eastern Europe," *Patterns of Prejudice,* 49(1–2): 103–34.

Hawkins, K. A. 2010. *Venezuela's Chavismo and Populism in Comparative Perspective.* New York: Cambridge University Press.

Ingelhart, R. and P. Norris. 2000. "The developmental theory of the gender gap: women's and men's voting behavior in global perspective," *International Political Science Review,* 21(4): 441–63.

Jaquette, J. S. 2009. "Introduction," in J. S. Jaquette (ed.), *Feminist Agenda and Democracy in Latin America.* Durham and London: Duke University Press, 1–18.

Kampwirth, K. 2010. "Introduction," in K. Kampwirth (ed.), *Gender and Populism in Latin America.* University Park: Pennsylvania State University Press, 1–23.

Kantola, J. 2010. *Gender and the European Union.* New York: Palgrave Macmillan.

Kofman, E. 1998. "When society was simple: gender and ethnic divisions and the far and new right in France," in N. Charles and H. Hintjens (eds), *Gender, Ethnicity and Political Ideologies.* London and New York: Routledge, 91–106.

Kohen, B. 2009. "The effectiveness of legal strategies in Argentina," in J. S. Jaquette (ed.), *Feminist Agendas and Democracy in Latin America.* Durham and London: Duke University Press, 83–112.

Laclau, E. 2005a. *On Populist Reason.* London and New York: Verso.

Laclau, E. 2005b. "Populism: what's in a name?," in F. Panizza (ed.), *Populism and the Mirror of Democracy.* London and New York: Verso, 32–50.

Meret, S. 2015. "Charismatic female leadership and gender: Pia Kjærsgaard and the Danish People's Party," *Patterns of Prejudice,* 49(1–2): 81–102.

Meret, S. and B. Siim. 2013. "Gender, populism and politics of belonging: discourses of right-wing populist parties in Denmark, Norway and Austria," in B. Siim and M. Mokre (eds), *Negotiating Gender and Diversity in an Emergent European Public Sphere.* New York: Palgrave Macmillan, 78–96.

Monasterios, K. 2007. "Bolivian women's organizations in the MAS era," *NACLA Report on the Americas,* 40(2): 33–7.

Mudde, C. 2004. "The populist zeitgeist," *Government and Opposition,* 39(4): 542–63.

Mudde, C. and C. Rovira Kaltwasser. 2011. "Voice of the peoples: populism in Europe and Latin America compared," Helen Kellogg Institute for International Studies, Working Paper #378, 1–47.

Mudde, C. and C. Rovira Kaltwasser. 2012. "Populism and (liberal) democracy: a framework for analysis," in C. Mudde and C. Rovira Kaltwasser (eds), *Populism in Europe and the Americas: Threat or Corrective for Democracy?* New York: Cambridge University Press, 1–26.

Mudde, C. and C. Rovira Kaltwasser. 2013. "Exclusionary vs inclusionary populism: comparing contemporary Europe and Latin America," *Government and Opposition,* 48(2): 147–74.

Mudde, C. and C. Rovira Kaltwasser. 2015. "Vox populi or vox masculini? Populism and gender in Northern Europe and South America," *Patterns of Prejudice,* 49(1–2): 16–36.

Osborne, S. 2001. *Feminism*. Harpenden, UK: Pocket Essentials.

Panizza, F. 2005. "Introduction: populism and the mirror of democracy," in F. Panizza (ed.), *Populism and the Mirror of Democracy*. London and New York: Verso, 1–31.

Pautassi, L. 2005. "El derecho de las mujeres a la salud," *Informe sobre género y derechos humanos: vigencia y respoto de los derechos de las mujeres in Argentina*. Buenos Aires: Biblos, 93–168.

Pitkin, H. 1967. *The Concept of Representation*. Berkeley: University of California Press.

Plotkin, M. B. 2003. *Mañana es San Perón: A Cultural History of Perón's Argentina*. Wilmington: Scholarly Resources.

Risse, T. 2010. *A Community of Europeans? Transnational Identities and Public Spheres*. Ithaca: Cornell University Press.

Rousseau, S. 2010. "Populism from above, populism from below: gender politics under Alberto Fujimori and Evo Morales," in K. Kampwirth (ed.), *Gender and Populism in Latin America: Passionate Politics*. University Park: Pennsylvania State University Press, 140–61.

Rousseau, S. 2011. "Indigenous and feminist movements at the constituent assembly in Bolivia: locating the representation of indigenous women," *Latin American Research Review*, 46(2): 6–28.

Schwindt-Bayer, L. A. 2010. *Political Power and Women's Representation in Latin America*. Oxford: Oxford University Press.

Southwell, P. and E. Lindgren. 2013. "The rise of neo-populist parties in Scandinavia: a Danish case study," *Review of European Studies*, 5(5): 128–35.

Spierings, N. and A. Zaslove. 2015a. "Gendering the vote for populist radical-right parties," *Patterns of Prejudice*, 49(1–2): 135–62.

Spierings, N. and A. Zaslove. 2015b. "Special issue: gender and populist radical right politics," *Patterns of Prejudice*, 49(1–2): 1–173.

Stein, S. 2010. *Populism in Peru: The Emergence of the Masses and the Politics of Social Control*. Madison: University of Madison Press.

Taggart, P. 1998. "A touchstone of dissent: Euroskepticism in contemporary Western European party systems," *European Journal of Political Research*, 33(3): 363–88.

Taggart, P. 2000. *Populism (Concepts in the Social Sciences)*. Buckingham: Open University Press.

Weyland, K. 2001. "Clarifying a contested concept: populism in the study of Latin American politics," *Comparative Politics*, 34(1): 1–22.

Weyland, K. 2010. "Foreword," in K. Kampwirth (ed.), *Gender and Populism in Latin America*. University Park: Pennsylvania State University Press, vi–xii.

CHAPTER 23

POPULISM AND RELIGION

JOSÉ PEDRO ZÚQUETE

"THE relationship between populism and religion hits you in the eye," declared a scholar of populism (Zanatta, 2014). Even though that is indeed the case, the study of the specific relationship between the phenomenon of populism and religion has not made significant inroads but remains a neglected area of research (Mudde, 2015: 446). In terms of an ideological definition of populism, which is followed in this chapter, there is almost unanimity about the core elements of the phenomenon, or its minimal conceptual center. In short, populism identifies politics with the will of the people and anchors the political world in the vertical opposition between two homogeneous, fundamentally antagonistic groups that are judged differently: the *people*, who are exalted, and the *elite*, who are condemned (Woods, 2014: 3–5). This struggle is gauged on a good-evil spectrum, and it is common practice of populism scholars to resort to the religious-originated word "Manichaeism"—in reference to the ancient religious movement whose radical worldview divided the world into the diametrically conflicting principles of Light and Darkness (Hutter, 2006: 1142–4)—to describe the centrality of such dualism in the populist worldview (Hermet, 2007: 81; Hawkins, 2010: 5; de la Torre, 2015: 9).

With this "populist minimum" (Abromeit et al., 2016: xiii) in mind, the connection between populism and religion must be viewed as part of a subtype of populism (de la Torre and Arnson, 2013b: 375; Rovira Kaltwasser, 2015: 216). Operationalized by religious or political actors and related constituencies, *religious populism* is a form of populism that shares its conceptual center but reproduces it in a specific religious key or fashion (Apahideanu, 2014: 77). Religious populism is two-dimensional, and only by looking at both sides of this subtype of populism will it be possible to achieve a comprehensive view of its role in contemporary societies. One of its dimensions is *overtly* religious, in the sense that it is shaped by religion understood in a narrow sense of a relationship with a divine sphere. Often, but not necessarily, tied with traditional organized religions, this manifestation of religious populism proclaims to be following, or fulfilling, the will and plans of the Almighty—with whom the groups feel, and believe, that they have a privileged relationship. In sum, these populists are doing God's work here on earth against its Godless enemies. The other dimension of religious populism is *covertly* religious, speaking to the sacralization of politics in modern-day societies. It is shaped by religion in a broader sense, centered above all on the experience of the sacred and the function that it fulfills by setting the group, with its this-worldly secular mission, apart as an absolute and transcendent force that will fundamentally change mundane everyday evil politics. Although they should be kept distinct, these two sides of religious populism intertwine and cross-pollinate. What is more, in some radical cases (exceptions) the special relationship with a higher divine power emerges also in proclamations from the covertly religious side of religious populism.

The following sections explore the dual dimension of religious populism—in terms of both the politicization of religion and the sacralization of politics—and then, in tune with the importance given to an empirical-deductive model in the study of populism (Moffitt and Tormey, 2014: 390; Woods, 2014: 7–9), the last part of the text gives a more detailed empirical account of early twenty-first-century examples of religious populisms, in Europe, with the French *Front National* under the leadership of Jean-Marie Le Pen, and in Latin America, with the Bolivarian Revolution of Venezuela's President Hugo Chávez.

Religious Populism (I)—Populism and the Politicization of Religion

For the most part, studies on religious populist groups or movements that openly profess a transcendent interpretation of human reality (which may involve a relationship with the supernatural) have interpreted them through the lens of the concept of the "politicization of religion," which refers to the ways in which, in old and present times—both in moderate and extreme forms (Linz, 2004: 111–12)—traditional religion serves to legitimize a social order, a particular regime, or a political community against destructive forces. In the case of religious populism, it means that a revealed and scriptural religion is used to sanctify a cause. These populists' worldview obeys the dictates of holy books or teachings—which they believe are divinely inspired—and, in their conflict against the putative enemies of the people, they often refer to these sacred texts and words (assuming a position of interpreters), in order to justify their role, actions, and wider goals. The way that this kind of religious populism manifests itself is not exclusive to any religious tradition, and crosses doctrinal differences and denominational divides.

Christianity

The first historical example of religious populism corresponds to what is usually pointed to in the literature as the first populist movement: the US-based People's Party of the 1890s. Protestant evangelicalism was the master-frame though which this grassroots populist wave of mostly farmers and workers from the Deep South and Western states saw the main economic and political questions of its time. Their work was to reignite the lost connection with America's God-given inalienable rights, freedoms, and values that were under assault by the elites (mostly plutocrats, the political establishment, and basically every holder of power, including traditional clergy) who had iniquitously built an unjust, oppressive, and unmoral society. In this manner, "as their religious ideals shaped the way Populists understood themselves and their movement, they wove their political and economic reforms into a grand cosmic narrative pitting the forces of God and democracy against those of Satan and tyranny." Further, "[a]s they did so these patterns of thought energized the movement with a sacred, even apocalyptic sense of urgency" (Creech, 2006: xviii–xix). This is why the Populist writers and orators aligned themselves with prophetic tradition and "again and again ... call down the judgment of God—and the Almighty's designs for the American nation—against worldly transgressors who made their fortunes unjustly and used their power to keep the plain people enslaved" (Wiliams and Alexander, 1994: 7). Through political action Populists—addressing a constituency that understood religious language—vowed to restore the country toward the course bestowed upon America by God. As the twentieth century approached, the American populist orator and former Civil War hero James B. Weaver wondered, "[M]ay we not reverently believe that the struggle of the oppressed people of our day, to reinvest themselves of their lands, their money and their highways, is from heaven also?" (Wiliams and Alexander, 1994: 8).

Plainly, the politicization of religious discourse follows a wide geography, and its scope has not diminished in the purportedly secular contemporary world. In the 1990s and into the 2000s, in Europe, Greece witnessed the articulation of a populist discourse by the patriarch of the Greek Orthodox Church. This politicization of religious discourse was tied to the defense of Greece's national identity—rooted in Hellenism and Orthodoxy—against evil forces, and the enemies of the "blessed people of God." In typical populist fashion, the Archbishop Christodoulos (1998–2008) split society in two conflicting camps and distinguished "between 'us', the forces of Go(o)d (the *people* as represented by the *Church* under *God*) and 'them' (an *atheist, modernizing, intellectualist* and *repressive* government)"; in a speech to those who wanted to undermine the traditional foundations of Greece, he warned, "You are losing your time ... the People of God are not following you ... you do not express the people" (Stavrakakis, 2005: 242–3, 241). Religious populism also seems to have taken root in post-Cold War Poland, through the activities of the Roman Catholic priest Father Tadeusz Rydzyk and his media network. In particular, Rydzyk's radio station *Radio Maryja* (Mary, as in Virgin Mary)—whose main audience consists of elderly, rural Poles—promotes, and is the epitome of, a certain version of Polish Catholicism as an "ideology of struggle" (Porter-Szucs, 2011: 271). Its worldview divides the world between the faithful (the good but excluded, thwarted people) and their diabolical enemies—the enemies of both God and Man, and true forces of Satan—sometimes perceived and articulated in a conspiratorial manner, with traces of anti-Semitism and anti-masonry. Hell-bent on destroying the nation and its Church, these satanic forces have infiltrated and taken control of the country's (and the Church's) institutions. The Vatican and the Polish Episcopate have repeatedly reproached this politicized religious discourse (Buzalka, 2005; Stępińska, Lipiński, Hess, and Piontek, 2016).

Another variation of religious populisms is that they can also emerge from within a larger secular populist movement. Such is the case with Teavangelicalism (Brody, 2012), which arose from the first US right-wing populist movement of the twenty-first century, the Tea Party (which from the beginning had enjoyed the strong support of evangelical Protestants). In the Teavangelicals' rationale for involvement in political action, social issues are part of the mobilization, but a "biblical" defense of small government and fiscal conservatism—grounded in a "moral" interpretation of the economy—is also a significant part of this newfound political engagement. The ever-expanding government, which is being transformed into an oppressive super state, is viewed by Teavangelicals as a fundamental contradiction to the moral outlook of the biblical scriptures and as a threat to all Americans. Big government facilitates the rule of the few over the many, gives unlimited power to a power-grabbing minority, and eventually leads to the oppression that is widely condemned in the Bible. The case for a constitutionally limited government is framed within this defense of freedom (which is a God-given principle) against despotism and, ultimately, enslavement. As argued by Jonathan Wakefield, the author of *Saving America: A Christian Perspective of the Tea Party Movement*, even government's spending, which is spiraling out of control, is part of this process of enslavement of Americans and future generations to a preordained life of slavery to pay taxes in order to pay down uncontrollable debt. The New Testament teaching, from the Gospel of Matthew, that "No man can serve two masters"—which Teavangelicalism sees as a choice between the government under an earthly king vs the government under the one and only True God—is a driving force behind much evangelical activism within the Tea Party movement. As a consequence, the Teavangelical political horizons are large: internal narratives often claim that the goal is restoring America to its Judeo-Christian roots, which makes its political activism oriented toward a wider reformation of society, rather than tiny, cosmetic changes incapable of reversing America's decline. It is not surprising that references to an "awakening," as a revitalized approximation between the people and God (against the nefarious political, economic, and cultural elites) are also present in Teavangelical circles. This of course also means that, in the Teavangelical viewpoint, tea partiers must also engage, decisively, at the level of culture—which is the arena in which ideas circulate and spirituality is formed—pushing back the left-wing control of popular culture and of the entertainment industry (Wakefield, 2013).

Finally, and also within secular political formations, dynamics of politicization of religion may also emerge in which Christianity (or more precisely Christendom) is used essentially as a marker of identity and not necessarily as a matter of faith, or religious observance. This happened, for instance, in the first quarter of the twenty-first century when many European right-wing populist movements invoked their attachment to a "Christian Identity of Europe" as a way of distinguishing the good, native people and its age-old culture from a dangerous and threatening Other (the specter of the "Islamization" of the continent). In *this* case cultural belonging, rather than belief, is the defining factor in the invocation of religion (Marzouki et al., 2016).

Islam

The struggle of the "oppressed people"—even if interpreted differently in diverse religious contexts and informed by different goals—is unvaryingly invoked by other religious populists to justify their actions as an accomplishment of, and in line with, what they recognize as the divine. A case in point is the rise of Islamism—as an "extreme politicization of traditional religion" (Payne, 2008: 31). A major starting point for Islamic religious populism was the politicization of Shi'ism following the 1979 Iranian Revolution, when the Ayatollah Ruhollah Khomeni, as an interpreter of the religious tradition, proclaimed that the revolutionary cause was for the "dispossessed" against the traditional elites (Halliday, 1982–3; Alamdari, 1999: 32). The religious interpretation of events—coupled with messianism and the belief in the return of the hidden Imam—is also present in the subsequent presidency of Mahmood Ahmadinejad (2005–2013). As a "man of the people," Ahmadinejad vowed a "return to the ideals" of the Islamic revolution, often in opposition to the ruling clergy, and certainly merits inclusion under the subtype of religious populism (Dorraj, 2014: 134–40).

Still within the vast realm of political Islam, Global Jihad has also been analyzed as a "contemporary form of religious populism." It has constructed a narrative in which the *Umma*, the Islamic supernation, has been defiled by *jahiliyyah* society. The term *jahiliyyah* referred originally to the paganism of pre-Islamic Arabia but is "attributed to modern secular nation-states, Western-dominated global culture, and the elites who run both." It is "the duty of the faithful to rise up and wage jihad to repel the 'great *kufr*' (literally, unbelief) and restore the holy geography of believers" (Yates, 2007: 129–30). Even if more work is needed to distill the populist frames that emerge, in all different contexts, from Islamism (so that they are not lost in the religious magma), in the landscape of religious populism this has been certainly the most extreme, and violent, expression of the need, felt by religious populists of all times, to harmonize the secular and the transcendental worlds.

Lastly, it should be added that in contemporary Muslim-majority societies, such populist mobilization of the umma, as a sort of proxy for "the people," against the malignant elites, can be confined to the borders of the nation-state, and may or may not involve—at least openly—the call for the establishment of a state based on Islamic law. This twenty-first-century "new Islamic populism"—in places such as Egypt, Turkey, and to a less extent in Indonesia—coalesces under an homogeneous and marginalized umma a wide range of socio-economic and cultural dispossessed groups against a political/social order deemed unjust and immoral, and may wage its combat, with success or not, within democratic politics (Hadiz, 2016).

Judaism

Within the tradition of Judaism, the ultra-orthodox Israeli political party Shas (or Guards of the Torah) may also be included under the scope of religious populism, which calls into question—or at least is an exception to—the assertion that religious parties are not usually considered populists (Hawkins, 2010: 40). Advocate of the Sephardic population of Israel and of a state run by Jewish religious law, Shas is simultaneously viewed as a "complete populist party" because of its anti-elitism (especially against the Ashkenazis), and its appeals to the oppressed social classes, as well as the rejection of a myriad of Others, such as African immigrants, Palestinians, and Israelis of Russian origin (Weiss and Tenenboim-Weinblatt, 2016).

It is important that scholarship look beyond the three Abrahamic religions and determine the development or not of religious populisms in other cultural and religious environments. Hindutva in India (Frykenberg, 2008) or Sinhalese Buddhist nationalism in Sri Lanka (Berkwitz, 2008), for example, may provide rich avenues for research, owing to the fact that, as indicated, a tell-tale indicator of a *possible* presence of religious populism is the politicization of a religious discourse and mindset.

RELIGIOUS POPULISM (II)—POPULISM AND THE SACRALIZATION OF POLITICS

If these religious populisms described above are rooted in a phenomenological, narrow definition that is couched in terms of a relationship with a transcendent being, force, or spirits, the second manifestation of religious populisms in the modern world is tied with a functional, expansive understanding that is expressed through a relationship with the sacred, and the holy, which in this case involves a process of sacralization of politics, that happens when politics acquires a transcendent nature. It is no longer a mundane, limited affair, but is viewed and experienced as a tool for total change, anchored in myths, rites, and symbols that galvanize group solidarity and give ultimate meaning to the life and destiny of communities.

The sacralization of politics is a modern Western phenomenon, and cannot be detached from the inexorable forward march of the rationalization of human life, the replacement of mystery by calculation, the advent of a demystified society, and the overall independence of politics from traditional, established, religion. This gradual secularization was powerfully explained by Max Weber in his early twentieth-century philosophy of history. In the world of politics, however, and almost since the beginning of the secularization process, this "spiritual vacuum" has been periodically filled with movements that aimed to create heaven on earth and confer spiritual guidance and meaning on the human condition. Many authors—from the French Revolution onward—have described what the historian Jacob Talmon called the "political messianism" of such movements. Raymond Aron, as a perceptive observer of twentieth-century politics, saw these "millenarian politics"—which could have had a positive role in "calm and happy eras" but not in times of crisis—as a type of politics that "endow an objective ... with absolute value, or again that confuse a society in history, actual or to be created, with the ideal society that would fulfill human politics" (1978: 239). The attention, especially by historians and sociologists, given to the politico-religious dimensions of the mass ideologies of the twentieth century—mostly fascism, communism, and Nazism—led to their conceptualization as political religions (Gentile, 2006). They featured a strong level of member commitment that was akin to religious faith, a community dimension, and an ultimate goal of attaining salvation not outside but within the world, representing, as a consequence, the transfer of the sacred from the religious sphere into the political realm. Exemplified in these total ideologies, the sacralization of the political constituted thus a "metamorphosis of the sacred in modern times" (Sironneau, 1982: 576). This transference of the sacred was not just a feature of totalitarian regimes. Robert Bellah in particular noted how such a "religious" dimension operated within a twentieth-century representative democracy. Nevertheless, the concept of political religion, with some exceptions (Zúquete, 2007; Augusteijn, Dassen, and Janse, 2013), has been detached from the age of democracy and viewed essentially as a "companion" to totalitarianism, such as Marxism-Leninism, National Socialism, and Italian Fascism (Gregor, 2012: 281–2).

The metamorphosis of the sacred—and its manifestations in politics—should, however, be seen in a more expansive way, because, as argued by sociologist of religion Peter L. Berger, modernity does not necessarily secularize but pluralizes: "Modern man may have lost the one enchanted garden in which his ancestors dwelled, but instead he confronts a veritable emporium of such gardens, among which he must make a choice" (2011: 136). It is in this sense that this second dimension of religious populism offers one of such "enchanted gardens" available to modern man. It constitutes, and provides, an intimate relationship with the sacred: the people is transfigured and consecrated, its enemies combated as the embodiment of evil on earth, and politics is interpreted, experienced, and felt like a transcendental cause. It is important to bear in mind, therefore, that in contemporary times "we should not ignore the possibility of another sense of transcendence, that of reaching beyond the limits of what actually exists, beyond the now and the identification of the real with the actual" (Calhoun, 2012: 359). The sacralized politics of religious re-enchants, therefore, the political landscape.

No wonder that, and to a greater extent than in relation to other parties and movements, scholars on populism, or at least a fair number of them, have noted populism's affinity with religion not in terms of essence but in terms of *resemblance*. This second dimension of religious populism is, therefore, acknowledged, almost as self-evident, through analogical thinking, in terms of "looking like" religion (Paul, 2013: 26). In his debunking of American populism, Richard Hofstadter noticed the "tendency of our politics" to "secularize a religiously derived view of the world, to deal with political issues in Christian imagery, and to color them with the dark symbology of a certain side of Christian tradition" (1996: xi). Because in the framework of populisms politics is an all-consuming cause, grounded in the vital opposition between the elites and the people—which tends to be elevated as an absolute force for good in society against the corrupt and the polluted embodied in the others—the political world is viewed, felt, and experienced as a binary opposition between the sacred (the cause, the leadership, the people) and the profane (those who are opposed to it). This bifurcation lends such righteousness to the political combat, infused by a good-vs-evil imagery and rhetoric, that politics detaches itself from the "normal" and holds instead the promise of the extraordinary. It should be no surprise that populists "still believe in the univocal opposition between the truth and the false" (Godin, 2012: 17)—the sacred is, after all, also understood as what is "unquestionable" (Moore and Myerhoff, 1977: 20).

References to the "quasi-religious imagery," "semi-religious overtones," or "almost religious significance" of populist politics—in which "the political becomes moral, even religious"—are recurrent in the description of populist movements (de la Torre, 2000: 15; Taggart, 2002: 78; Canovan, 2002: 29). Similarly, allusions to their salvationist character permeate the literature. Scholars state that populism constitutes a "political journey of redemption" (Panizza, 2013: 114), or a "redemptive crusade" (de la Torre and Arnson, 2013b: 353), and while populists "preach impending doom, they also offer salvation" (Albertazzi and McDonnell, 2008: 5), because an "appeal to a purifying or salvationist rupture" (Taguieff, 2007: 48) with the status quo is one of the defining features of populist mobilization. Similarly, the use of religious language, at least in a fair number of empirical cases, has not gone unnoticed in the analysis of populisms.

Populist appeals are also sometimes presented through religious arguments, images, metaphors, and parables (de la Torre, 2015: 10). This characteristic could be included in the categorization of populism as a "low" way of politics: by using a popular, common—and culturally specific—religious vocabulary, populist actors distinguish themselves from the polished, rationalist—and cosmopolitan—politically correct way of doing politics of politicians located on the "high" end of politics (Ostiguy, this volume). In this way, the invocation of the religious is not only a way of distinction *from* but also of transgression *against* the established ways of mainstream political behavior. This, of course, is connected with the importance of "markers of identity"—adding to the populist actor a perceived authenticity—in the populist mode of identification (Panizza, 2013: 91–4). Ultimately, and to compound the analogical approach to the study of populism and religion, scholarship focuses on the need—grounded on empirical cases—to add symbolic depth to the study of populism. Therefore, "[i]f populism offers more than economic rewards, we need to know more about the symbolic dimensions of populist interactions" (de la Torre and Arnson, 2013b: 374). In this case, this means to enrich the understanding of the role played in it by the "experiencing of the sacred," or the cultural dimensions of religion.

Furthermore, the "promise of the extraordinary" entailed by populism—a popular empowerment that may lead, at a minimum, to a substitution/renovation of the political elites, or, more broadly, to a refoundation of the political system (Roberts, 2015: 142)—is centered on an expansive view of political action as a holistic tool. Such "popular foundings," although infrequent, are not "strange" to democracy, but are part of its history (Kalyvas, 2008: 7). Moreover, political theorists have paid attention to this place of the redemptive in modern politics. The political philosopher Michael Oakeshott saw it as the unfolding of a totalizing "politics of faith," in which "perfection, or salvation, is something to be achieved in this world: man is redeemable in history," against which stood the "politics of skepticism" that offers a piecemeal approach to politics, where governing is detached from the pursuit of human perfection (1996: 23, 31). Drawing from Oakeshott's analysis, Margaret Canovan offers an interpretation of the phenomenon that has become prevalent in the theory of populism. Canovan specifically connected populist politics—the promise of a better world through action by the transcendent sovereign people—with a specific face of democracy that is less rational and more emotional, and boasts a strong component of faith, that operates along the horizons of redemption rather than the boundaries of pragmatism, or democracy's other face. Within this tension between the mundane (routine politics) and the extraordinary (redemptive politics), populism dwells (1999: 11; 2005: 89–90).

Claims that the sacred has entered into the political realm, albeit in a secularized disguise—and that religious populisms are a manifestation of it—are contested and ignite skepticism. The religious flavor, and visions of change and hope, the argument goes, is not unique to populism. Accordingly, this argument continues, "populist movements are not the only ones that adopt a political style based on the idea of redemption. Every political party in campaign makes promises of redemption. Does this automatically transform them into populist parties? I doubt it." Therefore, "there must be something more" than a seeming religious commitment to such a redemptive promise (Prud'Homme, 2001: 54–5). The fact that the relationship between populism and religion has, for the most part, been lightly approached—focusing mostly on remarks on religious vocabulary, or imagery—probably contributes to the skepticism and demands for details on the "something more" that supposedly makes such a relationship distinct from other non-populist actors.

In order to overcome the resistance and tighten the analytical grip on religious populism—and with the exception of political philosophy, political science has for the most part downplayed sacralized frameworks prioritizing instrumental and materialistic explanations—scholarship must deal with this issue in a non-fragmentary manner. Instead, by focusing on empirical reality, it must deduce, isolate, and highlight the essential features of the sacralization of politics in these modern political movements. This ideological/discursive approach—aiming at capturing the self-understanding of these groups (how they see themselves and perceive their role, looking at their internal dynamics rather than imposing an external view)—must then systematically reveal the different manifestations of religious dynamics and how they interact, thereby showing a sacred and coherent discourse that is intrinsic to those movements and illuminating the salvation discourse that unites and supports a populist discourse. In short, this empirical/deductive approach should reveal religious populisms as political religions that are characterized by a dynamic interaction between charismatic leadership, a narrative of salvation, ritual, and the creation of a moral community that sees itself with the collective *mission* of fighting conspiratorial enemies, redeeming the nation from its alleged crisis. These features together constitute an ideal type that has been categorized as missionary politics (Zúquete, 2013). This analytical investigation helps to reevaluate the belief that political religions, because of the coming of age of a society that was now "in the clutches of modernity," were so obviously frail that they were on their way out of the world (Burrin, 1997: 342); untethered from the past (and in this way no longer viewed as relics from the totalitarian behemoth ideologies of the twentieth century), political religions are viewed as still relevant in twenty-first-century democratic politics.

Even though all populisms share a conceptual center, they are not all alike; nor do they develop with the same intensity, display the same fervor, or share the same overriding claims. This realization of different degrees of populism is at the basis of divisions of populism, between those that are "hard" or "polarized," and a "soft," "serial," and less radical version (de la Torre and Arnson, 2013a; Roberts, 2013). Some scholars have phrased this division as that between "complete" and "empty" populism (Jagers and Walgrave, 2007). This means that in regard to religious populism, there should be no sweeping generalizations. Not all religious populisms exhibit the full scale of characteristics that bring them close to the ideal type; it is the empirical analysis that will show the intensity and the extent to which such a nonmaterial dimension (the frame of the sacralization) is carried by each group, and, which is more unusual, if such an accomplishment is complete (and therefore quasi-replicates the ideal type). At the same time, as the literature repeatedly points out, the emergence and development of populism is conditioned by a number of cultural, political, and social factors. Different contexts generate different possibilities for populism's success and, consequently, also affect the development of full-fledged religious populisms. While strong institutional settings (consolidated party systems able to channel social claims, inclusive political representation) may be constraining, weak institutions (an ineffective State, a disarrayed party-system, low political representation) seem to facilitate the path for a populist challenge to the status quo. The same reasoning applies to the impact of political culture (its meaning systems and cultural variables), on populist mobilization (or de-mobilization) across different geographies (Pasquino, 2008: 21–7; Roberts, 2015).

THE ELEMENTS OF SACRALIZED POLITICS AND POLITICIZED RELIGION

With this in mind, attention now turns to two contemporary seminal demonstrations of religious populism—political religions in their own right—which have emerged and developed in regions where, certainly in recent decades, populism has been the strongest, and that have already been the focus of cross-regional comparison: Latin America and Europe (Mudde and Rovira Kaltwasser, 2013). These examples show that, in radical cases of populism, there may be present elements both of a sacralized politics *and* of a politicized religion, in the sense of a worldview based on an ecclesiastical or scriptural tradition. This means that the separation between the sacralization of politics and the politicization of religion, in the case of *some* populist actors, may not be clear-cut, but involves a syncretic dimension.

Leaving aside institutional contexts, it can be argued that, particularly in relation to religious populism, the cultural/religious ground plays a crucial part in these movements' mobilizing potency—this cultural resonance facilitates both the articulation of the religious populist message and its reception. The role of religion in Latin America has always been palpable, and one of the main factors why populism has there a *tierra electa* is attributed to the permanence and vigor of a "holistic imaginary" that is deeply rooted in the "spiritual and normative structures of Christianity" (Zanatta, 2008: 40–1). Conversely, Europe, at least Western Europe, which is viewed as "the odd man out" (Clark, 2012: 193), or the only example where the secularization thesis still holds, has also witnessed the development of a prototypical example of religious populism. In this case, the cultural/religious breeding ground is connected to what has been dubbed the "second disenchantment of the world," or the crumbling of the total ideologies and their great epic identity-giving narratives, creating an emptiness (a crisis of meaning) which has been filled by promises of security (a framework of meaning) and of moral and spiritual renaissance (Lecoeur, 2003: 173–92). Therefore, these empirical illustrations—the French radical right party *Front National* (FN), under the leadership of its founder, Jean-Marie Le Pen (1972–2011), and Hugo Chávez's left-wing Bolivarian revolution in Venezuela (1999–2013)—although diverging in their geography, ideology, and level of political power (political opposition, in the case of Le Pen, statecraft, in the case of Chávez), constitute nevertheless quintessential examples of missionary politics by displaying a sacred framework—a discursive/ideological construction—that upholds, and contributes to, the formation and mobilization of their collective identities. In summary, these political religions are built on three major sacred pillars: charismatic leadership, a moral community, and a mission of salvation.

Charismatic Leadership

Although *charismatic leadership* is not usually viewed as belonging to the definition of populism—but is instead viewed as an important facilitator (Hawkins, 2010: 42; Rovira Kaltwasser, 2015: 193)—it is certainly a prominent attribute of ideal typical examples of religious populisms. These movements have internal narratives that give the leader a messianic status and invest him with a sacred authority. There is what is called an "industry," made up of the words and actions of the leader and the work of close collaborators (a coterie), as well as of the follower's beliefs, that constructs the image of the leader as a missionizing figure of historical proportions.

There are six key images attached to the leader:

1. The first is the leader as the *Prophet*. The leaders are men ahead of their times. In the story that each of these movements tell, different events are constantly interpreted as evidence of the leader's clairvoyance. Above all, the leader-as-prophet receives praise both for stating the hard truths and for a tireless commitment, by the use of the "word," to exposing and shattering the lies of the dominant official

paradigm that is promoted by the elites, who are the enemies of the people. To use James C. Scott's terminology, prophecy gives voice to the "hidden transcript" about the "real" problems that affect societies, while defiling the "public transcript" (1990: 221–2). The prophetic nature of the leaders is enhanced by the manner in which, in the eyes of militants, they shatter the false vision put forth by the dominant groups and embody the voices currently under domination, or that have been under such domination.

2. The second image is that of the leader as the *Moral Archetype*. The narratives of these movements have portrayed their respective leaders as exemplary figures. This, of course, has long been seen as part of the arsenal of true leadership. In the nineteenth century, the Victorian social theorist Walter Bagehot expressed his belief that "men are guided by type, not by argument." It was a matter of "commonplace" that "it is the life of teachers which is catching, not their tenets" (1874: 59). In these contemporary cases, the power of the leader's example emanates both from his personal qualities and from his life achievements.

3. The leader is also the *Martyr*. The internal scripts of these movements share the dominant theme of the leader's self-sacrifice for the cause. Each forfeited self-interest, well-being, and even health for the sake of the mission. Their biographies serve as evidence of their martyrdom. Furthermore, these leaders alluded to the possibility of being assassinated. Personal affliction enhances the missionizing image of the leader as a heroic and stoic figure who goes through pain and tribulation for the fulfillment of the mission.

4. The leader *is* the *People*. The movements portray the leaders as personifications of the "common man," with everyday qualities, attitudes, and lifestyles. They embody the radical anti-elitism of the movements they lead. Their character and behavior is at the opposite end of the self-serving and aloof elites that the rank-and-file despises. The leaders, because they *are* from the people, have a direct, spontaneous, intuitive, unmediated link to what the people *really think*, no matter how deceitful the propaganda from the establishment and the media of the powerful. This demotic dimension is crucial for their strategy of self-legitimation as saviors of the community.

5. In a similar vein, the leader is also the *Party*. The political parties have served to preserve the primacy of the leader as well as the personal attachment between the followers and the leader. The fact that each leader was present at the time of creation of the parties (they are the founders) is one more factor that explained the highly personalized nature of each organization. They are seen as the products of the leader's commitment and vision: the leader has a natural sense of entitlement to decide about its structure and decision-making process.

6. This entails that, above all, the leader is the *Missionary*. The central narrative produced by the Le Pen and Chávez industries consisted in the sacralization of their respective leaders as savior-like figures driven by a sense of mission to save the community. This overriding theme confirms the principle that, as stated

by Robert C. Tucker, in the vein of Max Weber, "charismatic leadership is spe-cifically salvationist or messianic in nature ... and herein lies its distinctiveness" (1968: 743). However, the missionizing dynamic is not merely connected with a simple proclamation of the leader's mission. "Formulas for salvation" (1968: 751) are necessary but not sufficient. The mission must gain strength from the leader's capacity to embody the mission and to transmit the urgency of the times (the turning point) to the followers. At a deeper level it deals with the issue of authenticity. The sense of a personal mission is common in the biographies of these leaders. Le Pen never failed to mention his youth adoption as a "pupil of the nation" by the French State: "I felt that I had a particular role in life, of being more French than the others" (Zúquete, 2007: 81). In jail, after the failed coup to over-throw the Venezuelan government, Chávez wrote a letter to a friend, in which he said, "I don't want nothing more to myself than to be with the dreams and hopes of my people and the immense compromise that I now feel on my shoulders. I feel, dear friend, that a force stronger than me is dragging me as in a hurricane. I don't feel that I belong to myself, I feel that all this exceeds me. I don't have per-sonal aspirations" (Garrido, 2002: 91). Dynamics of "before" and "after" abound in the description of the impact of the leadership in people's lives. For example: "We were like those little animals, caged, who receive in their mouth the daily food; we had lost the capacity of being, of defending ourselves and of fighting for what was ours ... Until Chávez came" (Roz, 2003: 52). Le Pen was one of such men of destiny. In times of decadence and turbulence, "everytime Le Pen speaks about France, about its past, about its future, he emerges as the one who holds the baton of French civilization, as the holder of the flame, that French flame that comes from faraway and which we do not have the right to let fade. His first ambi-tion, regardless of his own personal destiny, is to remain faithful to this duty" (Daoudal, 2002: 21).

The leaders are the personification of the cause. Howard Gardner's conclusion that a crucial aspect of leadership as a narrative is a set of "stories of identity" is confirmed. These leaders, both by themselves, and through their respective disciples, in their inter-action with followers, constantly generate such stories: "about themselves and their groups, about where they were coming from and where they were headed, about what was to be feared, struggled against, and dreamed about" (1995: 14). But the extent to which each leader personifies the narrative (the story) is crucial, otherwise the efficacy is undermined and, ultimately, fades. The manner that the leader carries out the mission is therefore of great importance in the development of charismatic dynamics (Willner, 1984: 58–9). The leader's incarnation of the spirit and substance of the mission boosts the trustworthiness from, and within, the community: followers are more likely to accept shifts in strategy or policy because they *trust* that the leader, who *knows* what is best for the community, would *never* do anything to harm the community. This echoes the break with the rational order characteristic of Weber's definition of charismatic domination: "It is written ... But I say unto you" (1958: 250).

A Moral Community

At the same time, the ingrained narrative of "chosenness" and "election" attributed to the people (who are the heroic, true patriots), in addition to making it the embodiment of Good in the struggle against Evil (those "others" who oppose the people, constitute its nemesis, and are often involved in conspiracies against it), transforms its activists into a *moral community*. Elevated into a sacred entity, this community is separated from the surrounding, profane corruption through the dynamics of a political theology composed of myths, rites, and symbols. Historical figures are the avatars of the essence of the respective communities. In the case of the FN, the figures of Clovis and, especially, Joan of Arc are sacred national references, eternal symbols of France's greatness, independence, and sovereignty. The Bolivarian revolution took to new heights the worship of Simón Bolívar. He is a living spirit and the guide for revolutionary activism. There is a permanent analogy between the times of the liberator and the time of Chávez: it is the same continuous struggle to liberate Venezuela from the clutch of oligarchy. In each case, the association between the *holiness* of past figures and the messianic leaders of the present is further reinforced by a comprehensive ritualism, in the form of processions and rallies in the sacred places, or sanctuaries, of the movements. These moments of worship serve also to objectify the communal nature of charismatic leadership, which is rooted in group ecstasy and effervescence (Lindholm, 1990; Tiryakian, 1995). Ritualism gives visibility to the nonmaterial values that are at the core of the charismatic bond and that transform the community of followers into a moral community, united by feelings of love, brotherhood, idealism, and righteousness. Through ritualization this moral community *is* experienced; it helps to foster a sense of collectivity as a chosen people and plays a crucial role in legitimizing its soteriological dimensions. Importantly, cultural sociology has undoubtedly advanced the understanding of the role of symbolism and ritualism—in terms of fused performances between leaders and crowds—in the struggle for political power (Alexander, 2011).

A Mission of Salvation

All of this is connected with the view of politics as *salvation* that runs throughout the discursive frames (both verbal and symbolic) of these political religions. The twin notions of a sacred history and sacred place are complemented by a third, equally important, notion: sacred time. There is an eschatological myth at the root of their worldview (Tudor, 1972: 92). Not only must the rejection of the present lead to its abolishment; their political activity culminates in a "society to come" that is visualized as a new age of plenty. There is a "fullness of time" (Talmon, 1962: 130) that, nevertheless, is not religious in the sense of being miraculous or dependent on a supernatural entity. The millenarianism of these movements was political: this complete reversal of affairs and the coming into being of the new order happens *within* the world. The evil present will give way to a redemptive future.

At the same time the internal dynamics of these movements confirm to an extent the assertion that, in extreme cases, the secular dimension of religious populism also postulates a "special relationship" with the divine. In the fulfilling of this mission, Le Pen often gave the impression that his group basked in God's favor: "As stated in the holy gospel," he said, "'Unless the Lord watches over the city, the watchmen stand guard in vain.'" Sometimes ambiguously, other times openly, Le Pen stressed his belief that a supernatural agency would help the group in their quest for the salvation of France. As noted by Le Pen, "History, in its intimacy, is not a simple succession of causes and effects but an abrupt apparition of founding events," of what he calls "hours of destiny ... those manifestations of Providence." Using an expression made famous by John Paul II, the Front National founder invited his countrymen to "cross the threshold of hope," adding, "we are not alone. The people of France have begun their liberation and Providence supports us in its invincible arm." But "having God on their side" is not an invitation to passivity. "Providence may act no matter how weak is the spirit of resistance. But [Providence], as we know it, only helps those who help themselves," he proclaimed to his followers (Zúquete, 2007: 88–91). In the case of the FN, it was the community, integrated and revitalized by the party, which sooner or later would lead to the renewal of values and to a moral rebirth, putting an end to the materialism and individualism—the forces of disintegration—that have corrupted eternal France. "The enemy is in you," claimed Le Pen in a speech. "It was within the souls of the French that deformation occurred. It is in the bottom of your hearts, families, divorces, churches, schools, newspapers, courts, books ... in all the false ideas and negative thoughts ... it is within ourselves that the evil that weakens France, the Nation, the State, lies, and it is within ourselves that their survival can be found" (2001). And since evil is everywhere, the success of the FN will inevitably bring with it cleansing, and, from an ontological viewpoint, the purging of evil, conquered by good. Such is the fate of the political millenarianism of the party.

This dynamic is even clearer in the case of the Bolivarian revolution. The "Socialism for the twenty-first century," in its final version, corresponded to the myth of the Final Kingdom. It is the leader who in fact announced it: The Bolivarian revolution would continue until "the kingdom announced by Christ becomes a reality: the kingdom of equality, the kingdom of justice. This is our struggle." This kingdom would encompass the entire world: "[W]e cannot allow the world to come to an end ... if we sacrifice for the country, only then we will save ourselves and next save the world" (2005: 721–2). Although the intensity of the millennial visions varies in each group, the overall picture is that of a community that is in between ages—at the threshold of both worlds, warning about evil's imminent victory, while provoking the totalistic reaction that will vanquish it, and open the luminous door of a redeemed future.

The politics of salvation of these movements is a reflection of the eschatological myth that integrates reality in a coherent whole, that does not separate the past from the future, and that explains the role and the meaning of the community in history. For that reason, politics must seek a total transformation, expunging evil (injustice, inequality, exclusion, oppression, decadence, and so forth), and giving an answer to the problem of existence itself (Garcia-Pelayo, 1964: 192–3; Sironneau, 2000: 63–4). "It is rare that in its very newness, the messianic reign does not appeal from the *present* to a distant, unknown, forgotten or unconscious *past*, in order to found its plan for the *future*," wrote Henri Desroche in his *Sociology of Hope* (1979: 91–2). The centrality that the times of Joan of Arc, or Bolívar, have in the expectations, and ritual celebrations, of the "world to come" within these prophetic-soteriological populist movements indeed confirm this rarity. These political religions, however, are always contingent and provisional; they are not a once-and-for-always entity but are in fact necessarily limited in time. They are also dependent upon factors that range from changes in leadership (old age, death), to an abatement of the sense of crisis that fueled their dynamics, making the political religion wither in time, narrowing to only a small circle of true believers.

Conclusion—The Search for Reenchantment in Politics

The work on the religious subtype of populism must extend beyond its main focus of Western Christendom, as well as beyond the parameters of liberal democracies, and into other hybrid regimes. The focus is still overwhelmingly Western-centric. And in regard to that, the rise of religious populism (in its first, explicit, religious dimension) is a counterforce to the vision of Western modernity as ruled by formal rationality, and conceptualized as a place of disenchantment. Religious populist movements serve to re-enchant the world and display the belief that human and divine agency are interrelated. Similarly, the proliferation of religious populism (in its second, implicit, dimension) provides an alternative to the widespread "disenchantment of politics" in modern democratic societies at the time of ebbing of mass-based parties, which are declining in party membership, as well as the growth in political disaffection and the domination of governments by bureaucratic and technocratic classes. After the "gradual elimination of politics as an instrument of this-worldly salvation" rooted in big projects and visions of a better world (Van Kersbergen, 2010: 41), religious populisms tend (to varying degrees) to suffuse the political sphere with a religious zest as well as zeal, prophesying a vision of politics as a tool for the foundation of a new society.

Certainly, the admonition against the consequences of a "mechanical age" has been made before in history. "Only the material, the immediately practical, not the divine and spiritual, is important to us," observed Thomas Carlyle (1869: 333). But even acknowledging that political activism can manifest itself through other venues (such as in social movements), the fact is that apathy toward traditional politics and traditional means of representation seems to have become a modern condition. This "discrediting" of conventional politics and downgrading of political parties has also been blamed for the rise of populisms rooted in enchanted frameworks of redemption (Mastropaolo, 2008: 40). If politics as usual is synonymous with a bureaucratic and technocratic affair, populism is not "normal politics" (Moffitt and Tormey, 2014: 393). Populism—and this comes to the fore exemplarily in religious populisms—connects with a dimension of imagination, wonder, and mythology that extends way above the cold view of politics as management and administration (Oudenampsen, 2010: 20; Augusteijn, Dassen, and Janse, 2013: 258). In order to capture the success of populist appeals in democratic politics, it is *also* necessary take into account what has been called "the central role played by passions" (Mouffe, 2005: 69) in the formation and mobilization of collective political identities. Hence, the call to reinvigorate democratic life by "giving democracy a new lease on life, a new force, and a new passion"—it is needed because "the word 'democracy' has turned soft" (Touraine, 1997: 190). This is the case even if there is a recurrent warning about going too far into the "faith and redemption" direction in modern politics, and the inherent dangers posed by "political theologies" (Arato, 2015: 50), as well as the need to find a necessary equilibrium between instrumental politics and politics as enthusiasm (Ezrahi, 2002: 181).

Altogether, the most important observation to emerge from this overview of the articulation of populist appeals in modern politics is that it is necessary to focus on populist constituencies—not only on their material demands, but, and this is crucial in capturing the mobilizing power of religious populisms of all sorts, on the non-material, cultural-religious, and symbolic matrix and its popular expectations, desires, and transcendent hopes for a more fulfilling existence. Such an approach contributes directly to the twenty-first-century study of politics and religion and their nexus: there is a repeat encounter, with many intersections, between the two fields, instead of a clash.

REFERENCES

Abromeit, John, Bridget Maria Chesterton, Gary Marotta, and York Norman (eds). 2016. *Transformations of Populism in Europe and the Americas: History and Recent Tendencies.* London: Bloomsbury.

Alamdari, Kazem. 1999. "Who holds the power in Iran? Transition from populism to clientelism," *CIRA Bulletin,* 15(1): 31–4.

Albertazzi, Daniele and Duncan McDonnell. 2008. "Introduction: the sceptre and the spectre," in Danielle Albertazzi and Duncan McDonnell (eds), *Twenty-First Century Populism: The Spectre of Western European Democracy.* New York: Palgrave Macmillan, 1–11.

Alexander, Jeffrey. 2011. *Performance and Power.* Malden: Polity Press.

Apahideanu, Ionut. 2014. "Religious populism: the coup de grâce to secularisation theories," *South-East European Journal of Political Science,* II (1, 2): 71–100.

Arato, Andrew. 2015. "Political theology and populism," in Carlos de la Torre (ed.), *The Promise and Perils of Populism: Global Perspectives.* Lexington: University Press of Kentucky, 31–58.

Aron, Raymond. 1978. "History and politics," in Miriam Bernheim Conant (ed. and trans.), *Politics and History: Selected Essays by Raymond Aron.* New York: The Free Press, 237–48.

Augusteijn, Joost, Patrick Dassen, and Maartje Janse. 2013. *Political Religion Beyond Totalitarianism: The Sacralization of Politics in the Age of Democracy.* New York: Palgrave Macmillan.

Bagehot, Walter. 1872. *Physics and Politics,* reprint. Charleston: BiblioBazaar.

Berger, Peter L. 2011. *Adventures of an Accidental Sociologist: How to Explain the World without Becoming a Bore*. Amherst: Prometheus Books.

Berkwitz, Stephen C. 2008. "Resisting the global in Buddhist nationalism: Venerable Soma's discourse of decline and reform," *The Journal of Asian Studies*, 67(1): 73–106.

Brody, David. 2012. *The Teavangelicals: The Inside Story of How the Evangelicals and the Tea Party are Taking Back America*. Grand Rapids: Zondervan.

Burrin, Philippe. 1997. "Political religion: the relevance of a concept," *History and Memory*, 9(2): 321–49.

Buzalka, Juraj. 2005. "Religious populism? Some reflections on politics in post-socialist South-East Poland," *Slovak Foreign Policy Affairs*, 6(1): 75–84.

Calhoun, Craig. 2012. "Time, world, secularism," in Philip S. Gorski, David Kyuman Kim, John Torpey, and Jonathan VanAntwerpen (eds), *The Post-Secular in Question: Religion in Contemporary Society*. New York: New York University Press, 335–65.

Canovan, Margaret. 1999. "Trust the people! Populism and the two faces of democracy," *Political Studies*, 47(1): 2–16.

Canovan, Margaret. 2002. "Taking politics to the people: populism as the ideology of democracy," in Yves Mény and Yves Surel (eds), *Democracies and the Populist Challenge*. London: Palgrave Macmillan, 25–44.

Canovan, Margaret. 2005. *The People*. Cambridge: Polity Press.

Carlyle, Thomas. 1869. *Critical and Miscellaneous Essays: Collected and Republished*, Vol. 2. London: Chapman and Hall.

Casanova, José. 2011. "Religions, secularizations and modernities," *European Journal of Sociology*, 52(3): 425–45.

Chávez, Hugo. 2005. "Selección de discursos del presidente de la República Bolivariana de Venezuela, Tomo VII." Caracas: Ediciones de la Presidencia de la República: 721–2.

Clark, J. C. D. 2012. "Secularization and modernization: the failure of a 'grand narrative,'" *The Historical Journal*, 55(1): 161–94.

Creech, Joe. 2006. *Righteous Indignation: Religion and the Populist Revolution*. Urbana: University of Illinois Press.

Daoudal, Yves. 2002. *La face cachée de Le Pen*. Paris: Éditions Godefroy de Bouillon.

Davie, Grace. 2010. "Resacralization," in Bryan S. Turner (ed.), *The New Blackwell Companion to the Sociology of Religion*. Malden: Wiley-Blackwell, 160–77.

de la Torre, Carlos. 2000. *Populist Seduction in Latin America*. Athens: Ohio University Press.

de la Torre, Carlos. 2015. "Introduction: power to the people? Populism, insurrections, democratization," in Carlos de la Torre (ed.), *The Promise and Perils of Populism: Global Perspectives*. Lexington: University Press of Kentucky, 1–28.

de la Torre, Carlos and Cythia J. Arnson. 2013a. "Introduction: the evolution of Latin American populism and the debates over its meaning," in Carlos de la Torre and Cythia J. Arnson (eds), *Latin American Populism in the Twenty-First Century*. Baltimore: Johns Hopkins University Press, 1–35.

de la Torre, Carlos and Cythia J. Arnson. 2013b. "Conclusion: the meaning and future of Latin American populism," in Carlos de la Torre and Cythia J. Arnson (eds), *Latin American Populism in the Twenty-First Century*. Baltimore: Johns Hopkins University Press, 351–76.

Desroche, Henri. 1979. *The Sociology of Hope*, trans. Carol Martin-Sperry. London: Routledge and Kegan Paul.

Dorraj, Manochehr. 2014. "Iranian populism: its vicissitudes and political impact," in Dwayne Woods and Barbara Wejnert (eds), *The Many Faces of Populism: Current Perspectives*. Bingley: Emerald Books, 127–42.

Ezrahi, Yaron. 2002. "Political style and political theory—totalitarian democracy revisited. Comments on George L. Mosse paper," in Yehoshua Arieli and Nathan Rotenstreich (eds), *Totalitarian Democracy and After*. London: Frank Cass, 177–82.

Frykenberg, Robert E. 2008. "Hindutva as a political religion: an historical perspective," in Roger Griffin, Robert Mallett, and John Tortorice (eds), *The Sacred in Twentieth-Century Politics: Essays in Honour of Professor Stanley G. Payne*. New York: Palgrave Macmillan, 178–220.

Garcia-Pelayo, Manuel. 1964. *Mitos y simbolos politicos*. Madrid: Taurus.

Gardner, Howard. 1995. *Leading Minds: An Anatomy of Leadership*. New York: Basic Books.

Garrido, Alberto. 2002. *El otro Chávez: testimonio de Herma Marksman*. Mérida: Producciones Karol.

Gentile, Emilio. 2006. *Politics As Religion*. Princeton: Princeton University Press.

Godin, Christian. 2012. "Qu'est-ce que le populisme?," *Cités*, 49(1): 11–25.

Gregor, A. James. 2012. *Totalitarianism and Political Religion: An Intellectual History*. Palo Alto: Stanford University Press.

Hadiz, Vedi R. 2016. *Islamic Populism in Indonesia and the Middle East*. Cambridge: Cambridge University Press.

Halliday, Fred. 1982–3. "The Iranian revolution: uneven development and religious populism," *Journal of International Affairs*, 36(2): 187–207.

Hawkins, Kirk A. 2010. *Venezuela's Chavismo and Populism in Comparative Perspective*. New York: Cambridge University Press.

Hermet, Guy. 2007. "Populisme et nationalisme," in Jean-Pierre Rioux (ed.), *Les populismes*. Paris: Éditions Perrin, 61–83.

Hofstadter, Richard. 1996. *The Paranoid Style in American Politics and Other Essays*. Cambridge: Harvard University Press.

Hutter, Manfred. 2006. "Manichaeism," in Kocku von Stuckrad (ed.), *The Brill Dictionary of Religion*, Vol. 2. Leiden: Brill, 1142–4.

Jagers, Jan and Stefaan Walgrave. 2007. "Populism as political communication style: an empirical study of political parties' discourse in Belgium," *European Journal of Political Research*, 46(3): 319–45.

Kalyvas, Andreas. 2008. *Democracy and the Politics of the Extraordinary: Max Weber, Carl Schmitt, and Hannah Arendt*. New York: Cambridge University Press.

Kersbergen, Kees van. 2010. "Quasi-messianism and the disenchantment of politics," *Politics and Religion*, 3: 28–54.

Le Pen, Jean-Marie. 2001. "21ème fête des Bleau-Blanc-Rouge," September 23. http://www.frontnational.com/doc_interventions_detail.php?id_inter=15, accessed July 21, 2005.

Lecoeur, Erwan. 2003. *Un néo-populisme à la française: trente ans de Front national*. Paris: Éditions La Découverte.

Lindholm, Charles. 1990. *Charisma*. Cambridge: Basil Blackwell.

Linz, Juan J. 2004. "The religious use of politics and/or the political use of religion: ersatz ideology versus ersatz religion," in Hans Meier (ed.), *Totalitarianism and Political Religions: Concepts for the Comparison of Dictatorships*, trans. Jodi Bruhn. New York: Routledge, 107–25.

Marzouki, Nadia, Duncan McDonnell, and Olivier Roy (eds). 2016. *Saving the People: How Populists Hijack Religion*. London: C. Hurst and Co.

Mastropaolo, Alfio. 2008. "Politics against democracy: party withdrawal and populist breakthrough," in Danielle Albertazzi and Duncan McDonnell (eds), *Twenty-First Century Populism: The Spectre of Western European Democracy*. New York: Palgrave Macmillan, 30–48.

Moffitt, Benjamin and Simon Tormey. 2014. "Rethinking populism: politics, mediatisation and political style," *Political Studies*, 62: 381–97.

Moore, Sally F. and Barbara G. Myerhoff. 1977. "Introduction: secular ritual, forms and meanings," in Sally F. Moore and Barbara Myerhoff (eds), *Secular Ritual*. Amsterdam: Van Gorcum, 3–24.

Mouffe, Chantal. 2005. "The 'end of politics' and the challenge of right-wing populism," in Francisco Panizza (ed.), *Populism and the Mirror of Democracy*. London: Verso, 50–71.

Mudde, Cas. 2015. "Conclusion: some further thoughts on populism," in Carlos de la Torre (ed.), *The Promise and Perils of Populism: Global Perspectives*. Lexington: University Press of Kentucky, 431–51.

Mudde, Cas and Cristóbal Rovira Kaltwasser. 2013. "Exclusionary vs. inclusionary populism: comparing contemporary Europe and Latin America," *Government and Opposition*, 48(2): 147–74.

Oudenampsen, Merijn. 2010. "Speaking to the imagination," *Open*, 20: 6–20.

Panizza, Francisco. 2013. "What do we mean when we talk about populism?," in Carlos de la Torre and Cythia J. Arnson (eds), *Latin American Populism in the Twenty-First Century*. Baltimore: Johns Hopkins University Press, 85–115.

Pasquino, Gianfranco. 2008. "Populism and democracy," in Danielle Albertazzi and Duncan McDonnell (eds), *Twenty-First Century Populism: The Spectre of Western European Democracy*. New York: Palgrave Macmillan, 15–29.

Paul, Herman. 2013. "Religion and politics: in search of resemblances," in Joost Augusteijn, Patrick Dassen, and Maartje Janse (eds), *Political Religion Beyond Totalitarianism: The Sacralization of Politics in the Age of Democracy*. New York: Palgrave Macmillan, 15–32.

Payne, Stanley F. 2008. "On the heuristic value of the concept of political religion and its application," in Roger Griffin, Robert Mallett, and John Tortorice (eds), *The Sacred in Twentieth-Century Politics: Essays in Honour of Professor Stanley G. Payne*. New York: Palgrave Macmillan, 21–35.

Porter-Szucs, Brian. 2011. *Faith and Fatherland: Catholicism, Modernity, and Poland*. New York: Oxford University Press.

Prud'Homme, Jean-François. 2001. "Un concepto evasivo: el populismo en la ciencia política," in Guy Hermet, Soledad Loaeza, and Jean-François Prud'Homme (eds), *Del populismo de los antiguos al populismo de los modernos*. México City: El Colegio de México, 35–63.

Roberts, Kenneth M. 2013. "Parties and populism in Latin America," in Carlos de la Torre and Cythia J. Arnson (eds), *Latin American Populism in the Twenty-First Century*. Baltimore: Johns Hopkins University Press, 37–60.

Roberts, Kenneth, M. 2015. "Populism, political mobilizations, and crisis of political representation," in Carlos de la Torre (ed.), *The Promise and Perils of Populism: Global Perspectives*. Lexington: University Press of Kentucky, 140–58.

Rovira Kaltwasser, Cristóbal. 2015. "Explaining the emergence of populism in Europe and the Americas," in Carlos de la Torre (ed.), *The Promise and Perils of Populism: Global Perspectives.* Lexington: University Press of Kentucky, 189–227.

Roz, José Sant. 2003. *Bolívar y Chávez.* Merida: Fuerza Bolivariana de la Universidad de Los Andes.

Scott, James C. 1990. *Domination and the Arts of Resistance: Hidden Transcripts.* New Haven: Yale University Press.

Sironneau, Jean-Pierre. 1982. *Sécularisation et religions politiques.* Paris: Mouton Éditeur.

Sironneau, Jean-Pierre. 2000. *Métamorphoses du mythe et de la croyance.* Paris: L'Harmattan.

Stavrakakis, Yannis. 2005. "Religion and populism in contemporary Greece," in Francisco Panizza (ed.), *Populism and the Mirror of Democracy.* London: Verso, 224–49.

Stępińska, Agnieszka, Artur Lipiński, Agnieszka Hess, and Dorota Piontek. 2016. "Research on populist political communication in Poland," in Toril Aalberg et al. (eds), *Populist Political Communication in Europe: A Cross-National Analysis of XX European Countries.* London: Routledge, 311–25.

Taggart, Paul. 2002. "Populism and the pathology of representative politics," in Yves Mény and Yves Surel (eds), *Democracies and the Populist Challenge.* New York: Palgrave Macmillan, 62–80.

Taguieff, Pierre-André. 2007. "Le populisme et la science politique," in Jean-Pierre Rioux (ed.), *Les populismes.* Paris: Éditions Perrin, 17–59.

Talmon, Yonina. 1962. "Pursuit of the millennium: the relation between religious and social change," *Archives Européennes de Sociologie,* 3(1): 125–48.

Tiryakian, Edward A. 1995. "Collective effervescence, social change and charisma: Durkheim, Weber and 1989," *International Sociology,* 10(3): 269–81.

Touraine, Alain. 1997. *What is Democracy?,* trans. David Macey. Boulder: Westview Press.

Tucker, Robert C. 1968. "The theory of charismatic leadership," *Daedalus,* 97(3): 731–56.

Tudor, Henry. 1972. *Political Myth.* London: Macmillan.

Wakefield, Jonathan. 2013. *Saving America: A Christian Perspective of the Tea Party Movement.* Houston: Crossover.

Weber, Max. 1958. *The Protestant Ethic and the Spirit of Capitalism.* New York: Scribner.

Weiss, Naama and Keren Tenenboim-Weinblatt. 2016. "Israel: right-wing populism and beyond," in Toril Aalberg et al. (eds), *Populist Political Communication in Europe: A Cross-National Analysis of XX European Countries.* London: Routledge, 207–20.

Williams, Rhys and Susan M. Alexander. 1994. "Religious rhetoric in American populism: civil religion as movement ideology," *Journal for the Scientific Study of Religion,* 33(1): 1–15.

Willner, Ann Ruth. 1984. *The Spellbinders: Charismatic Political Leadership.* New Haven: Yale University Press.

Woods, Dwayne. 2014. "The many faces of populism: diverse but not disparate," in Dwayne Woods and Barbara Wejnert (eds), *The Many Faces of Populism: Current Perspectives.* Bingley: Emerald Books, 1–25.

Yates, Joshua J. 2007. "The resurgence of jihad and the specter of religious populism," *SAIS Review of International Affairs,* 27(1): 127–44.

Zanatta, Loris. 2008. "El populismo, entre religión y política: sobre las raíces históricas del anti-liberalismo en América Latina," *Estudios Interdisciplinarios de América Latina y el Caribe,* 19(2): 29–45.

Zanatta, Loris. 2014. "La relación entre populismo y religión salta a la vista," *La Voz*, July 10. http://www.lavoz.com.ar/ciudad-equis/la-relacion-entre-populismo-y-religion-salta-la-vista, accessed October 1, 2015.

Zúquete, José Pedro. 2007. *Missionary Politics in Contemporary Europe*. Syracuse: Syracuse University Press.

Zúquete, José Pedro. 2008. "The missionary politics of Hugo Chávez," *Latin American Politics and Society*, 50(1): 91–121.

Zúquete, José Pedro. 2013. "On top of the volcano: missionary politics in the twenty-first century," *Politics, Religion and Ideology*, 14(4): 507–21.

CHAPTER 24

POPULISM AND THE MEDIA

LUCA MANUCCI

INTRODUCTION

POPULISM is a globally successful political discourse: to praise the virtues of the people while pillorying the elites for their greed and corruption seems to be an effective way to frame the political debate and obtain good results in elections.[1] Populism is here understood as an ideology—or worldview—articulated discursively by political and media actors. The Manichean opposition between the pure people and the corrupt elites lies at the core of the populist ideology, while the second pillar is represented by the claim for unrestricted popular sovereignty.[2] The presence of populism is often linked to certain socio-economic and political conditions such as low credibility of mainstream parties and scandals of corruption. In the last decade, however, growing attention has been devoted to the role played by the media as a supply-side factor for the success of populism.[3] This chapter aims at summarizing theories and results present in the relevant literature, while advancing a more sophisticated framework for analysis.

A burgeoning strand of literature links the diffusion and success of populist discourses to the process of mediatization of politics (Mazzoleni, 2008; Ellinas, 2010; Esser and Strömbäck, 2014). In other words, the commercial logic driving tabloid newspapers and television channels is considered to be a key trigger for the ambitions of populist actors seeking media exposure. Indeed, populist discourses are considered to fit the media-logic by providing controversial and newsworthy content, thus incrementing the visibility of politicians articulating populist discourses vis-à-vis mainstream politicians. As is clarified in the following sections, however, the convergence between populist messages and media-logic has not been proven so far, and further empirical research is needed.

A second strand of literature considers the effects of populist messages diffused by the media as a threat to the quality of democracy (Blumler and Gurevitch, 1995; Mutz and Reeves, 2005; Mazzoleni, 2014). In particular, it has been argued that the media privilege conflict and negativity, which in turn foster political alienation and cynicism, thus providing a fertile ground for populist messages. Once again, the theoretical assumptions presented in literature should be substantiated by further empirical research. Future studies would make a valuable contribution insofar as they take into consideration different degrees of media freedom and independence.

A third strand of literature focuses on the possibility for political actors to articulate populist discourses and convey them directly to the public via Web tools such as online social media (Canovan, 2002; Meyer, 2002; Fortunati, 2005). Once again populist discourses, because of their alleged emotional tone and simplistic content, are supposed to fit the logic of online communication, granting a comparative advantage to populists vis-à-vis old-style political actors. Further empirical research is also needed in this field. What appears to be certain is that mediatization 2.0 is radically changing political communication while re-defining the link between representatives and citizens.[4] It is quickly becoming impossible to imagine any political discourse without online tools for communication.

The main contribution of this chapter consists in proposing to consider the relationship between populist actors and the media not as a battle between two opposing logics, but rather as an integrated process of content production involving both political and media actors, and traditional as well as new media. In fact the relationship between populist discourses and the media is structured as a circular and multifaceted process involving different communication outlets and actors. In particular, this integrated approach has the advantage of explaining how populist discourses are generated and through which channels they reach different audiences without taking a normative position on the supremacy of the media sphere over politics or vice versa. The idea is that the media sphere and the political realm are intertwined to the point that they constitute an integrated system for the production of user-friendly political news.

The main precondition for advancing the research about the relationship between populist discourses and media outlets consists in adopting a clear understanding of populism and a subsequent operationalization. Despite a large number of alternative definitions of populism in the relevant literature, it is possible to observe a growing consensus towards an ideological and discursive approach (Mudde and Rovira Kaltwasser, 2012). In other words, populism is conceived as an ideology—or a worldview—articulated discursively (Hawkins, 2010). It implies that populism should be conceptualized not only as a binary concept, but also as a gradual phenomenon. At an empirical level, one can then decide where to draw the dividing line between populist and non-populist actors. What really matters is who sends what type of populist messages, how often, through which channels, and under which circumstances.

The discursive approach has two main advantages. First: it allows one to measure populism beyond its electoral dimension. Second: it fits the study of populism in a cross-cultural perspective. Holding constant the way populism is measured in discourses and media outlets, it becomes possible to highlight not only media factors, but also socio-economic, cultural, and political opportunity structures for the presence of populism in different countries and eras. This chapter contextualizes and problematizes the existing theories about media and populism and the empirical findings available, while suggesting possible directions for future research. The aim is to follow Mazzoleni's advice (2003: 2): "A full understanding of the populist phenomenon cannot be achieved without studying mass communication perspectives and media-related dynamics, especially not without using a comparative approach."

The next section explores the literature on mediatization of politics and the implications for the diffusion of populist messages, and subsequently it is argued that the existing empirical research has not so far confirmed the theoretical expectations. The fourth section presents the debate concerning the impact of mediatized populist messages on the quality of democracy, proposing to consider different levels of media freedom as a decisive variable. The fifth section introduces the role of new media in diffusing populist messages directly to the public. The sixth section relies on the critical literature review previously elaborated in order to formulate an integrated framework of analysis for the diffusion of populist discourses which goes beyond the existing literature on the process of mediatization of politics. Finally, directions for future research are presented and discussed in the conclusion.

MEDIATIZATION OF POLITICS

The relationship between populism and the media has been observed mainly through the lens of the concept of the mediatization of politics.[5] Studies using this concept generally consider the media as an erosive force threatening and transforming the political sphere, since the media system is supposed to grant visibility and good reporting mainly to political actors answering to criteria such as newsworthiness and marketability. In this scenario, populism is seen as the typology of political discourse which best suits the commercial logic driving the media, and this grants to political actors articulating a populist discourse a competitive advantage compared to mainstream politicians. The main problem concerning this strand of literature is that the expected convergence between media-logic and populism is based on the alleged presence of stylistic elements associated with populist discourses which have not yet been tested empirically: e.g. colloquial and emotional language, controversial content, black and white rhetoric, dramatization, spectacularization, personalization.

Mediatization refers to a long-term process of convergence between media-logic[6] and political-logic. On the one hand, the media distance themselves from the political power and become more and more marketized: commercial media organizations thus have an interest in adjusting their content to the interests of the public in order to attract advertisers (Mazzoleni, 2008), thus privileging populist actors. On the other hand, political actors—in order to gain visibility and attract voters—need to strategically adapt to the logic followed by the media. This process is also called self-mediatization.[7] Figures 24.1 and 24.2 illustrate this process.

The "marketization" of the media-logic is the by-product of the third phase of mediatization, which began around the mid-1990s and is characterized by media abundance,

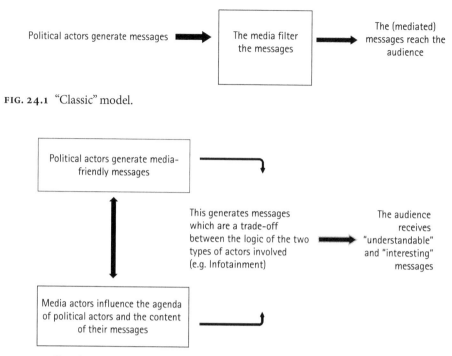

FIG. 24.1 "Classic" model.

FIG. 24.2 "Mediatization of politics" model.

ubiquity, and fragmentation (Blumler and Kavanagh, 1999). Compared to previous stages of mediatization, political communication is now shaped by a growing space for extreme voices, new political challengers, and an anti-elitist agenda pushed by news media. Since many media outlets have to compete for advertising revenue, they place more emphasis on sensational and superficial news and focus more on personalities than on policies (Ellinas, 2010), thus propagating populist discourses.

As a result, *infotainment* has become a central feature of contemporary mass media, blurring the boundaries between information and entertainment.[8] Political debates are therefore increasingly framed as a competition opposing prominent personalities rather than between different policies or ideologies, while human interest stories become more and more relevant.[9] In turn, political actors organize events and adopt styles which push the media to grant them visibility. Once again populist actors, considering their charisma combined with the controversial messages they deliver in a flamboyant style, are supposed to be the undisputed protagonists of talk shows, news broadcasting, and media attention in general (Mazzoleni et al., 2003).

Among the different media outlets, the best allies of populist politicians are supposedly commercial television channels and tabloid newspapers. Indeed, they are supposed to act in complicity with populist political actors, while up-market newspapers are considered as "paladins" of the status quo (Mazzoleni, 2003: 8). Since commercial media need to "sell" political issues, they have to make the political process understandable and interesting for the audience. Indeed, populist discourses—with their anti-elitist touch and focus on ordinary citizens—are supposed to resonate with the ideas of the general public.

Mény and Surel (2000: 126) noticed that populist actors feed the media with "provocative and fiery statements, and (…) violent attacks on their opponents," therefore having a significant advantage in gaining media attention. Nigel Farage, for example, regularly feeds the media exactly with the type of populist discourses they find controversial and newsworthy: about the decision of the United Kingdom to leave the European Union, Farage said that "[t]he ordinary people have ignored all the threats that have come from big business and big politics and it has been a huge and amazing exercise in democracy."[10]

Thaksin Shinawatra in Thailand and Pauline Hanson in Australia are other excellent examples of how populism can resonate with the media-logic. Thaksin Shinawatra, tycoon turned politician, was the Prime Minister of Thailand between 2001 and 2006. Among other things, Shinawatra had his own television show (*Backstage Show: The Prime Minister*), where he was usually portrayed as being in touch with common people and speaking the local dialect instead of English. Moreover, he had a radio program (*Premier Thaksin Talks with the People*) in which he appeared "as easily reachable, relatable, and identifiable by 'the people,' especially when chatting about his personal life or taking questions from the audience" (Moffitt, 2014: 300). Pauline Hanson, Australian politician and leader of the far right party *One Nation*, has also proven to master perfectly this kind of role. In particular, she appeared in the media "as one of 'the people' through her affectless voice and plain-spoken vocabulary, and depicted herself as 'salt-of-the earth' by continually referring to her time at her fish-and-chips shop" (Moffitt, 2014: 301).

Despite many empirical examples which allow one to inductively develop theories about the relationship between populist discourses and commercial media, these theories have not been substantiated by comparative studies. For example, the idea that the media circulate populist discourses because of purely commercial reasons has been questioned. As Hallin and Mancini have claimed (2004: 27), the media might decide to spread populist messages—implementing what they call "political parallelism"— because they actually back the political line of populist actors. Moreover, the media can generate populist discourses by themselves and not only spread or block the populist messages generated by political actors (for example Mazzoleni, 2014; Krämer, 2014).

All in all, the space that the media provide to populist political actors is probably a combination of their self-mediatization skills (Meyer, 2002), willingness by the media to lend them visibility, and political opportunity structures which open or close the space for political parties articulating a populist discourse. In this regard, political scientists should learn from scholars in communication studies that the media can play an active role in creating and diffusing populist messages, and they do not simply decide how much space to give to different political actors and how to report their statements. On the other hand, media scientists should learn from scholars in political science that populist discourses are not all the same, and they can be articulated by political actors in power or in opposition, who control the media system or not, and ultimately that the media system is composed of institutions which are embedded in a broader socio-economic and institutional context.

The next section presents the results produced by the existing empirical research, highlighting the following key ideas: how they lack a uniform understanding of populism, how they often confuse two levels of populist discourses (content and style), and how they do not confirm any of the theoretical expectations generated by the existing literature.

EMPIRICAL RESULTS VS THEORETICAL EXPECTATIONS

As mentioned above, populist discourses are often expected to find more space in the media compared to other discourses given their stylistic features and rhetoric, which make them attractive to media outlets interested in generating controversies in order to attract their audience. The first obstacle that empirical studies have to face when testing the hypotheses linked to the literature on mediatization of politics is the way in which populism is defined and operationalized.

Indeed, the studies presented in this section are not fully comparable precisely because they lack a common framework for analysis and their results derive from different definitions and operationalizations. As mentioned above, the best approach to analyzing the relationship between populism and the media consists in understanding populism as an ideology or worldview articulated discursively. Moreover, populist ideas (the ideological *content*) can be expressed in different ways (or *styles*). The two dimensions should be distinguished in order to separate the populist content from the stylistic elements which are associated to those contents: the tone, the rhetoric strategies, the emotional elements of the language pertain to a different layer of the discourse.

Unfortunately, relevant studies about populist discourses often confuse the two dimensions. For example, Jagers and Walgrave (2007) defined populism as a political communication style; Cranmer (2011) also relies on the notion of populism as a communication style; Bos, van der Burg, and de Vreese (2011) distinguish between substantive aspects of populists' rhetoric (people-centrism and anti-elitism) and populist-style elements[11] but take the latter for granted instead of empirically testing their presence.

A second aspect to be considered, apart from the lack of conceptual consistency, is the contradiction between theoretical expectations and empirical findings. Looking at the role of the media in spreading and legitimizing populist messages, both Akkerman (2011) and Rooduijn (2013) have investigated whether debates in tabloids show pro-populist positions when compared with quality newspapers, but the expected complicity between tabloids and populist messages was not confirmed. Bos and Brants (2014) came to similar conclusions, while Bos, van der Burg, and de Vreese (2010) found that the two types of media outlet give the same prominence to populist and non-populist actors.

Focusing on the importance of gaining media visibility in order to obtain electoral success, Plasser and Ulram (2003), Biorcio (2003), Birnenbaum and Villa (2003), and Hellström et al. (2010), found that the role of the media was paramount in determining the electoral success of the Austrian Freedom Party in Austria, the Lega Nord in Italy, the Front National in France, and the Swedish Democrats in Sweden. However, this seems to constitute evidence of the importance of the role of the media system vis-à-vis political parties, rather than indicating a privileged relationship between media and populist actors. In fact, every new party in the political arena needs media attention.

A possible explanation could be offered by the studies conducted by Walgrave and Swert (2004) and Boomgaarden and Vliegenthart (2007) suggesting that right-wing populist parties in Belgium were successful mainly because the media extensively covered issues such as immigration and crime, which were the core issues of those same right-wing populist parties. In other words, populist parties might be successful because they are able to set the agenda, or because they are able to exploit the media agenda for electoral purposes.

Another strand of literature investigated the self-mediatization of political actors, and explained the success of populist parties by making reference to their supposed emotional tone. However, the few studies going in this direction operationalized populism in different ways and therefore their measurements are not fully comparable.[12] Moreover, it remains unclear whether populist messages are in fact more emotional than non-populist ones: this should constitute another direction for future empirical research.

All in all, there is a wide gap between a vast array of theoretical expectations and their empirical validation. Available empirical studies seem to generally contradict the expectations about the role of the media in spreading and backing populist messages. Moreover, many aspects have not yet been tested empirically. The difficulty in obtaining relevant empirical results can be linked to three main factors: (1) the lack of a common understanding of populism which is an essential precondition for a consistent and comparative test of existing theories; (2) the different approaches used in measuring populism, since even authors adopting the same understanding of populism use different measurement techniques; and (3) cross-cultural and longitudinal studies are very limited since they are time-consuming and often expensive.

EFFECTS OF MEDIATIZATION ON DEMOCRACY

Another second strand of literature, strictly linked to the idea of mediatization of politics, describes the impact of populist discourses on the quality of democracy as extremely negative. Apart from the lack of a common framework for analysis, when analysing the impact of populism on democratic quality researchers often fail to address two elements: first, populist actors and mass media could enhance the chain of accountability through a rigorous scrutiny of the actions of politicians; second, populist discourses constitute a threat for the quality of democracy according to the degree of control that populist actors can exercise over the media system.

From a liberal perspective, populism is deemed a threat for democracy (Rovira Kaltwasser, 2012). In a similar vein, populist discourses are considered as satisfying the audience's taste by giving space to conflict, drama, triviality, and negativity. In turn, these elements foster political alienation (Blumler and Gurevitch, 1995), and cynicism and disillusionment (Coleman and Blumler, 2009), both of which—according to Mazzoleni and Schulz (1999)—provide a fertile ground for the messages of populist outsiders. Several authors describe the effects of this vicious circle as *video-malaise* (Robinson, 1976; Mutz and Reeves, 2005). Mazzoleni (2008: 51) maintains that "the public cynicism of particular media outlets and certain campaigns against political corruption, government misdeeds and controversial policies, may be held responsible for the diffusion of political discontent and even anti-political attitudes among the citizenry." Dalton (2004), on the other hand, showed that negative reporting on the media is growing over time, and this can constitute an advantage for anti-establishment parties.

Although these expectations are legitimate, they have been discarded by Avery (2009) who shows that those with low levels of political trust do not become less trusting following new media exposure, while Norris (2011) claims that exposure to political news can even increase favorable predisposition towards civic activity.

Another media-driven advantage for populism is related to the fact that the media increasingly privilege personal aspects at the expense of policies, emphasize short, controversial and simplistic sentences instead of providing a real debate based on argumentation, and give space to political actors according to their mediagenic presentation (Mazzoleni, 2014: 43–4). Therefore, politicians with a background in show business are supposed to exploit their personal charisma to articulate a populist message in order to be perceived as "one of the people" in opposition to the corrupt elites. This is more likely to happen in a context in which the media system is not completely free.

A case-study in this sense is Joseph "Erap" Ejercito Estrada. He used his popularity as an actor to gain the presidency of the Philippines in 1998, until his impeachment in 2001 (Headman, 2001). Also the former Italian Prime Minister Silvio Berlusconi established a strong link with his audience thanks to uncommon communication skills, perhaps sharpened during his years as a singer on cruise ships. However, his success was at least partly due also to his position as media tycoon. For example, in 2002 Berlusconi criticized the behavior of some journalists and TV stars, and this led to the removal from the air of three journalists critical towards Berlusconi himself.[13]

In even less free media markets—such as in the case of Latin American countries—it is quite common to observe populist political leaders taking control of the media to create a strong bond and influence public opinion. Boas (2005) found strong evidence that TV was a key element for the election of both Fernando Collor in Brazil in 1989 and Alberto Fujimori in Peru in 2000. This corroborates Waisbord's description of the populist vision of the role of the media in Latin America: "strengthening the media power of the President, bolstering community media, and exercising tighter control of the press through legislation and judicial decisions" (2012: 508).

All in all, researchers should not dismiss the impact of populist discourses on the quality of democracy as inherently negative. In contexts characterized by a high degree of freedom of the media system, the process of mediatization of politics is supposed to favor populism by generating alienation and cynicism, which in turn are exploited by actors articulating a populist message. However, the link between media and populist actors might force policy-makers to be more responsive to public opinion, especially when the media act as watchdog of the political system. In this case, populist discourses might constitute a corrective for democracy and the media might play a decisive role in lending them relevance.

On the other hand, in contexts characterized by a low degree of freedom of the media system, populist political actors can take control of the media system to silence the opposition and influence public opinion. However, if the media system is not completely free, this constitutes a problem per se, and whether populist or non-populist actors take advantage of the situation is not particularly relevant. Moreover, since populism is often confused with radical right-wing populism, researchers should consider the possibility for populist discourses to be inclusive and not only exclusive towards minorities and other social groups.[14]

In conclusion, when assessing the impact of the process of mediatization of politics and its convergence towards populist messages, it is important to evaluate on a case-by-case basis and to consider different media and political cultures both across countries and over time. Even more importantly, one must consider the fact that the political process does not entirely take place in the media or in traditional media.

POPULISM AND NEW MEDIA

New media play a pivotal role in the politics.[15] Social networks such as Facebook and Twitter are said to have contributed to mobilization in favor of Arab World upheavals,[16] while the Occupy Wall Street movement forced the mainstream media to follow and adapt to its online communication. Many cyber-optimists, indeed, consider new media as a way to bypass the gatekeeping role of traditional media (Canovan, 2002; Fortunati, 2005) and to implement a virtual version of the Athenian direct democratic system (Meyer, 2002).

In particular, social media are often said to represent a perfect channel for the diffusion of populist messages: first, populist actors often accuse the traditional media system of being controlled by the mainstream political elites, and therefore they consider the new social media as the only neutral and independent arena; second, populist actors build their credibility on their links with ordinary people and advocate unrestricted popular sovereignty, hence the possibility of communicating directly with their electorate can reinforce their image of being approachable people; third, social media are more informal and favor a type of communication close to colloquial language, based on emotions rather than on reasoning, this being close to a populist discursive style. For all these reasons, populist actors are expected to mobilize voters via social media more easily than mainstream actors, thus enhancing their electoral performance.

Once again, these theoretical expectations should be substantiated by empirical research. In fact, it needs to be tested empirically as to whether populist messages are more often associated with a private dimension of politicians' lives compared to non-populist messages. In fact, a politician can post cats' pictures on Instagram without articulating a populist message. Or, vice versa, one can spread populist messages while not sharing personal details via Facebook. As mentioned in the sections above, moreover, it should be tested empirically whether populist actors use a certain type of language (stylistic dimension) compared to mainstream actors, and whether or not populist actors tend to privilege the private side of politics.

Moreover, what constitutes the natural link between populist discourses and social media is often neglected: the possibilities to implement direct and participative democracy. In particular, researchers should focus on the possibility of achieving the populist ideal of bottom-up participation and legitimization of power through new media and online tools. Two interesting cases in this regard are constituted by the Five Star Movement (5SM) in Italy, and PODEMOS in Spain.

PODEMOS, a left-wing party articulating a populist discourse based on social equality and basic income, proposes an effective combination of online and offline tools to implement direct democracy and redefine the idea of sovereignty. This allows the electorate to access and question the representatives, formulate, discuss, and vote on proposals, and select the candidates. However, the paramount role of the leader Pablo Iglesias seems to show that the role of bottom-up participatory elements is almost irrelevant when compared to the top-down hierarchic structure.[17]

Similarly the 5SM attributes to the Web an almost utopic role and proposes practices of participative, digital, and direct democracy. The official voice of the party is expressed through the blog of Beppe Grillo,[18] leader of the movement and former comedian. Moreover the party relies on online voting for the selection of candidates and impromptu issues, provides the possibility of online discussions through the Meetup platform,[19] and recently introduced *Rousseau*, a Website that allows the activists—among other things—to vote draft laws, conduct fund raising, share information about the legislative actions of the party, and learn about the bureaucratic functioning of the legislative mechanisms.

However, according to its "non-statute"[20] the 5SM's logo and name are property of Beppe Grillo, while the movement's headquarters are located in Grillo's blog. Moreover, the procedures of online voting seem to be of a plebiscitarian nature rather than the expression of real deliberation. Fabio Bordignon and Luigi Ceccarini (2014: 62) observed a striking discrepancy between the movement's ideals of direct democracy and its vertical structure: "In spite of insistence on the 'shared' nature of the political action carried out by the M5S, its organization is strongly conditioned by Grillo's 'ownership' of the brand name, which gives him considerable room for manoeuvre in making decisions and in managing internal dissent." Recent studies also proved that the majority of the posts removed from the blog contained criticisms of Beppe Grillo (Mosca, Vaccari, and Valeriani, 2015). Hence, one can claim that the Web tools for bottom-up participation exist, but this does not mean that every populist movement will implement them properly, or that the public is ready to use them.

To sum up, future research should address four main issues: first, to what extent and for which reasons political actors articulating a populist discourse make different uses of social media compared to other political actors; second, the impact of political and media cultures in determining the relationship between populist actors and social media; third, the impact of social media in determining the electoral success of populist vis-à-vis non-populist political actors; fourth, to what extent parties articulating a populist discourse implement online tools for direct and participative democracy compared to mainstream political parties.

Rethinking the Relationship between Media and Populism

The process of mediatization of politics should be analyzed for its dynamic and interactive elements, thus avoiding the idea that political actors must surrender to the media-logic, or the other way around. In fact, researchers should rather investigate to what extent the two logics interact and overlap, and under which political, institutional, and cultural conditions one plays a more prominent role than the other. Cross-country and cross-media analysis on a longitudinal level should be implemented. Moreover, growing attention should be devoted to the impact of new media, which could either strengthen or weaken the role of traditional media and their effects on the political sphere.

Building on the critical literature review presented above, this section advances two main arguments. First, the opposition between media and political logic should be overcome in favor of a more integrated understanding of the relationship between political and media actors. Second, the impact of the media on the success of populist actors should not be overstated, but rather re-considered according to new empirical studies both on the stylistic elements of populist discourses and the "political parallelism" of the media system.

Political Communication as an Ecosystem

Most of the studies about the process of mediatization of politics portray the media as an almighty industry able to set the agenda of political actors as well as to determine their electoral success. The debate focused mainly on the adaptation of political actors to the so-called media-logic, but much less has been said about the adaptation of the media to the so-called political-logic. It has been argued, in fact, that the media-logic does not fully define and control the political system (Van Aelst et al., 2014) and the growing role of social media seems to reinforce the independence of political actors vis-à-vis the media system.

Media actors and politicians adapted to each other to the point that the two logics are almost indistinguishable. Therefore, it is possible to understand political communication as a field of production of messages where the boundaries between different actors and their respective roles are not only blurred, but ultimately unnecessary.

The goals of media and political elites are quite similar: they both need to attract an audience, in one case in order to generate advertising and in the other to obtain electoral support. Political messages need to adapt to the media logic in order to gain visibility, and the media need to adapt to the political logic in order to have fresh political news to broadcast. Researchers should now determine under which conditions mediatization favours populist rather than mainstream actors. Moreover, future research should investigate to what degree the two logics are still separate, or if it is rather possible to claim that media and political actors symbiotically follow the same logic in order to generate messages which are at the same time attractive for advertisers and electors.

Figure 24.3 conveys precisely the idea that the possible interactions between media and political actors are manifold and can be understood as a constant flux of different combinations of those interactions, each following political or media logic in different proportions, while the way these interactions are combined can fit different empirical situations.

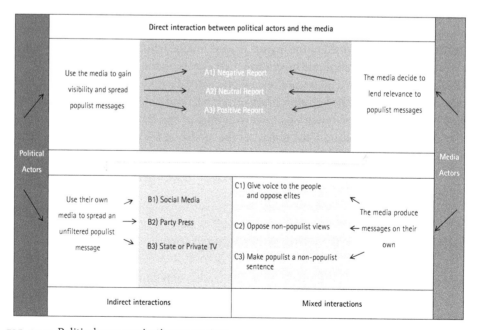

FIG. 24.3 Political communication ecosystem.

1. *Direct interactions* occur when political actors formulate their messages in the form of press conferences, press releases, party events, and interviews, relying on the media system to spread their message. This kind of interaction can create three different outcomes according to the type of reaction by the media: legitimization or stigmatization of the political actor in the case of positive or negative reports, preservation of the status quo in the case of a neutral report. This is the type of interaction that, so far, has been studied more in-depth, and populist discourses are expected to find space in commercial media more easily than others, even though it remains unclear whether this increases the credibility of politicians articulating a populist discourse, and to what extent populist messages receive positive reports compared to non-populist ones.

2. *Indirect interactions* between media and political actors, in turn, occur when political actors rely on their own media channels: social media and Web 2.0, party press, and state or private TV and radio. Through these channels, political actors can articulate a populist message bypassing several functions of traditional journalism such as framing and agenda-setting. These messages, although "indirect," are very often reported by mass media in a second stage. This type of interaction is receiving growing attention, probably because the diffusion of social media makes it more frequent and relevant, while before it produced rather atypical combinations such as public and private TV companies at the service of dictators and tycoons. Indirect interactions via social media might increase the success of politicians articulating a populist message, since they can rely on unmediated and direct links with the audience.

3. *Mixed interactions* concern media-originated populist messages. As mentioned above, it would be reductive to think of media actors only as filters for other actors' messages. In particular, mass media can give voice to the "man in the street" and act as a spokesman of the common people as opposed to the elite. In a similar vein, mass media can decide to oppose non-populist[21] views expressed by political actors. Finally, mass media can transform a non-populist political actor's statement into a populist one. In all three scenarios, these messages might or might not be followed by a reaction from political and media actors, therefore they are labelled as "mixed." These types of interactions are by far less studied, and it is still unclear how often they occur empirically, although they are theoretically plausible.

To sum up, *media actors* can report[22] populist messages in a more or less positive way (1), and future research should analyze to what extent and for which reasons different types of media outlet report different types of populist messages. On the other hand, media actors can also articulate a populist discourse on their own (3). For example, they can transform the non-populist communication of any political actor into a populist message, or they could counter a non-populist argumentation with a populist message.

On the other hand, *political actors* can try to exploit the media in order to obtain visibility, and will eventually receive different types of coverage (1). It would be interesting to observe whether the media report in different ways populist messages when they are originated by mainstream compared to niche (or extreme) parties. Alternatively, political actors can spread unfiltered and unmediated messages directly to their audience (2). It might be valuable to assess to what extent populist compared to non-populist political actors rely on this type of communication.

Proposing three possible types of interactions (direct, indirect, and mixed) does not imply that other types are impossible or that one excludes the other. For example, messages belonging to type (2) can be filtered and re-proposed by the media, who frame them and give positive, negative, or neutral coverages (1). Moreover, it is possible to hypothesize that when the media spread messages of type (3), they are also more prone to offer positive coverages to populist messages on type (1). In general, the idea is that the possible relationships between media and political actors are circular and can exist in different combinations. Moreover, not only journalists and politicians can articulate populist messages, but also other actors such as religious leaders, celebrities, members of NGOs, institutional actors, as well as ordinary people.

"Speaking Populist" Means Being a Media Darling?

To conceive the process of mediatization of politics as one *integrated ecosystem for user-friendly content production* implies discarding the idea that the mass media are the main arbitrators of the electoral contest. In fact, media and political logics can largely overlap, and there are no strong reasons to think that politicians articulating a populist discourse are the main beneficiaries of the process of mediatization of politics. First, it is unclear whether populist messages are characterized by a peculiar style which resonates with the media logic, granting them more media exposure. Second, the media might decide to spread populist messages (implementing "political parallelism") because they actually back the political line of populist actors (Hallin and Mancini, 2004: 27).

The fact that populist actors benefit from the process of mediatization of politics[23] is a cliché deriving from several theoretical assumptions about the nature of populist discourses which should be tested empirically. In particular, actors articulating populist discourses are considered to be newsworthy because they are seen to have charisma, to express simple concepts with an understandable language, and to rely on emotions and generate conflict. In other words, they are portrayed as adopting a mediagenic style, and therefore to be media darlings (Mazzoleni, 2014: 9). In turn, this grants them visibility and credibility, improving their electoral chances.

Mazzoleni maintained that "the media simply cannot ignore what is newsworthy, and clearly newsworthy are the politicians who defy the existing order, with their abrasive language, public protests, and emotive issues" (2003: 6–7). However, it remains unclear to what extent a populist message is more emotional, abrasive, or simplistic compared to non-populist ones. Moreover, it is unclear to what extent different media outlets give space to messages featuring those stylistic elements compared to others.

These should represent key research questions driving future research on the topic. On the one hand it is plausible to imagine that populist messages are expressed through a pattern of peculiar stylistic elements, but it would be wrong to claim a priori that using a simple language or making a reference to emotional and private aspects are "populist" stylistic elements.

The alleged "charisma" of populist actors should also be tested, since it corroborates the idea that media privilege populist actors because of their charisma. First of all, it would be preferable to think in terms of discourses or messages, and not of actors. However, even if the unit of analysis is constituted by individual and collective actors, political parties articulating a populist message do not necessarily have a strong leader[24] or a charismatic one.[25] Several authors (for example, Taggart, 1995; Eatwell, 2005; Kitschelt, 2007; Pappas, 2013) have claimed that populist parties often rely on charismatic leaders because they have limited political programs and weak party organization, but these are not necessarily features of "populist parties."[26]

Moreover, since the leaders of populist parties need to get media attention, they are supposed to adopt an extraordinary behavior and a recognizable style in their messages. For example, Mazzoleni describes populist leaders as exploiters of free advertising, "by generating controversy or staging bullying events" (2003: 15). Indeed, Beppe Grillo—Italian former comedian turned politician—swam the 2.8 km of the strait of Messina showing that a normal man can achieve exceptional results. This could constitute a good example of a "populist" actor staging a spectacular (hence newsworthy) event, but it should be tested whether performing symbolic actions is exclusively part of the populist discursive repertoire.[27]

Finally, it might be the case that the introduction of social media reduced the importance of traditional media. This might lead political actors, and in particular populist actors, to abandon their abrasive and controversial language or to stop staging spectacular events in order to reach the spotlight, since they can establish a direct contact with their audience. In a similar vein the importance for a political party of relying on the newsworthiness of a charismatic leader might be reduced by the possibility for political actors to spread populist messages through social media. In this case it would be necessary to study how different political actors communicate online and how the idea of charisma can be altered once applied to Web communication.

CONCLUSIONS

The relationship between populism and the media represents a central aspect of many contemporary democracies. In virtually every society it is possible to observe the circulation of populist discourses, and in every modern state the media play a central role in mediating political content and acting as a filter between citizens and political elites. Scholars from both political science and media studies are trying to determine to what extent the process of mediatization of politics is determining the increasing success of populist discourses, but with mixed and contradictory results so far. The conclusions of this chapter aim at highlighting three directions for future research.

The main obstacle is represented by the lack of a uniform and shared framework for the analysis of populist discourses, and it is probably linked to the multidisciplinary nature of this field of study. A minimal definition of populism as ideology articulated discursively would provide a perfect starting point if it were adopted by both media and political scientists. Once this definitional uniformity is achieved, future research should proceed through two steps. First, it should be assessed whether populist messages are associated to any particular stylistic feature compared to non-populist ones, such as emotional and private elements. The second step consists in assessing whether these messages find more space in down-market media compared to up-market ones. Finally, if populist messages actually feature peculiar stylistic elements and find more space in commercial media, it should be tested whether this happens because populism is more marketable or because those media back the political line of the actors articulating populist messages. Moreover, it should be assessed to what extent these mechanisms change across countries with different levels of mediatization of politics, as well as different media and political cultures.

In parallel, at the micro-level the impact of political communication on individuals, and the influence of populist messages on voting behavior compared to non-populist messages should be studied. At the meso-level, research should be conducted to see which parties rely on populist discourses and how often; moreover, it should be assessed as to how these parties are portrayed by different media outlets and the impact of the media in determining the electoral success of populist compared to non-populist parties. At the macro-level, it would be valuable to analyze the correlation between different levels of mediatization and the electoral performance of parties articulating populist messages, and how these vary according to different political and media cultures in different countries and over time.

Furthermore, studying the diffusion of populist discourses without considering the role of social media would result in only a partial and superficial analysis. As discussed above, political messages are already produced within a highly integrated system composed of political and media actors, whose logics are increasingly overlapping. In this context, the growing importance of social media might definitely blur the distinction between political and media actors, and introduce the role of user-generated contents in the political debate. Additionally, political parties can now establish a direct link with the electorates, bypassing the traditional role of the media and broadcasting their own content. In this way, populist discourses might become even more effective, since they reach the audience without being mediated by journalists, and this might increase the credibility of political actors articulating populist discourses. Finally, it should be investigated to what extent different types of online media constitute a favorable arena for the diffusion of populist discourses compared to different types of traditional media.

Conversely, it is crucial also to understand the different use that populist and non-populist actors make of social media. We might investigate the type of interaction that populist politicians establish online with their electorate compared to mainstream politicians. In addition, it would be extremely valuable to assess to what extent populist political movements implement online tools for direct and participative democracy compared to other movements and parties, and how these differences correlate with the electoral performance of actors articulating a populist discourse.

Empirical observations seem to suggest that populist actors are more interested in interacting online with their constituency (or their followers). This means that in order to establish a direct connection with the "man in the street," politicians have to become extremely media-savvy, either personally or by embedding in their staff more and more journalists, technicians, IT experts, and (social) media strategists. For example, Italian Prime Minister Matteo Renzi discussed national reforms via *Twitter* through the hashtag #Matteorisponde (Matteo Answers), and Donald Trump—who defined himself as "the Ernest Hemingway of 140 characters"—constantly interacted online with his supporters, thus saturating the public debate with his presence.

Not only is the role of politicians more and more influenced by the possibility of diffusing self-generated messages, but also political journalism is experiencing a deep transformation linked to technical and social evolutions. It should be investigated to what extent old and new media are responsible for the diffusion of populist messages, and whether this is a strategic choice linked to economic or ideological reasons, or whether the growing success of populist movements forces the media system to "follow the news." On the other hand, it might be the case that mainstream media actually constitute an obstacle for the diffusion of populist messages, since they privilege executive and government actors which are seen as reliable and relevant. Moreover it should be investigated to what extent, in the age of online social networks, the traditional media are able to preserve their traditional role of framing and agenda setting.

In conclusion, media and political scientists with the help of political psychologists should develop a common frame for the analysis of populist discourses, based on the distinction between populism as an ideology and populism as a discourse, which consequently should lead to an investigation of the stylistic elements linked to populism compared to other political discourses. Moreover, political communication should be understood as a highly integrated ecosystem for the production of user-friendly content, thus overcoming the fictitious opposition between media- and political-logic. Finally, longitudinal and cross-country studies should be implemented in order to expand the analysis to different types of media and political cultures. All in all, this field of research still remains largely unexplored although it plays a crucial role in analyzing the impact of media and political populism on contemporary democracies.

NOTES

1   Framing is here understood as an activity of selection of some aspects of a perceived reality in order to make them more salient in a communicating text, while excluding others in order to downplay them. In other words, I follow the definition provided by Robert Entman (1993).

2 According to the strand of literature which defines populism in its ideational and discursive dimension (for example, Mudde, 2004; Albertazzi and McDonnell, 2008; Hawkins, 2010).

3 To be fair, this has been for slightly more than a decade. The importance of the media as a supply-side factor has been emphasized, among others, by Mazzoleni, Stewart, and Horsfield (2003); Bos, van der Brug, and de Vreese (2011).

4 I define mediatization 2.0 as the process of bi-directional political communication between politicians and citizens taking place on social media, websites, and blogs, in which both types of actors—representatives and represented—are at the same time producers and consumers (hence *prosumers*) of political content.

5 Many authors use the term in a similar way (for example, Cook, 2005; Strömbäck, 2008; Esser, 2013; Schulz, 2014).

6 The concept of media-logic was introduced by Altheide and Snow (1979).

7 The concept of self-mediatization was introduced by Meyer (2002). Strömbäck (2008: 238) argues that no political actor can "ignore the media or can afford not to adapt to its logic." In a similar vein, Esser (2013: 162) maintains that through self-mediatization politicians engage "in a process of self-initiated stage-management and media-friendly packaging."

8 Gunther and Mughan (2000: 430) introduced the term infotainment. It is a portmanteau of information and entertainment.

9 Among others, Webb and Poguntke (2005) observed the process of presidentialization of politics, based on increasing personalization of the political debate.

10 C. Engineer, June 24, 2016, "'It should be our independence day': Farage calls for national holiday in honour of Brexit," *Express*, online version. http://www.express.co.uk/news/politics/682969/nigel-farage-independence-day-brexit, accessed in July, 2016.

11 Bos, van der Burg, and de Vreese (2011: 187) include among the populist-style elements references to a situation of crisis, dramatization, simplicity and clarity, "friend vs foe" rhetoric, and simple and strong language.

12 Some of the studies belonging to this strand of literature are: Jagers and Walgrave, 2007; Cranmer, 2011; Bos, van der Burg, and de Vreese, 2010; 2011; Ruzza and Fella, 2011; Bos and Brants, 2014.

13 This episode was labeled by Italian newspapers as "Bulgarian Edict."

14 The right-wing and ethnocentric version of populism remains largely dominant in Europe, while in Latin America its left-wing character is much more common.

15 Interestingly, the increased use of social media is even changing the nature of political scandals. By blurring the boundaries between public and private spheres, political scandals are no longer necessarily linked to corruption or other illegal activities but they can often be traced to personal missteps. For example, in 2015 during the campaign for the Federal election in Canada, twelve politicians were dropped by their respective parties for saying something inappropriate or bizarre on social media. This phenomenon can be contextualized in a general process of "privatization" of the political experience, in the case of both politicians (who bypass the party organization and show to the public their "private" dimension) and citizens (who are no longer loyal to a single party and tend to have opinions which transcend partisan divisions).

16 Tufekci and Wilson (2012), for example, discuss the role of social media in the Egyptian protests.

17 PODEMOS co-founder Juan Carlos Monedero resigned after criticizing the party's strategy. Among other things, he stated that PODEMOS "no longer has the time to meet with the small circles, because it is more important to get one minute of TV airtime or to do something that adds to the collective strategy." Francesco Manetto, El Pais, April 30, 2015: *Podemos co-founder criticizes mainstream drift in his own party*. Online version, accessed last in April, 2016: http://elpais.com/elpais/2015/04/30/inenglish/1430403454_148415.html.

18 Until April, 2016, when it was replaced by a blog of the movement itself: http://www.ilblog-dellestelle.it/.

19 As of April, 2016 there are 169,624 members divided among 1302 groups all over the world. Data provided by the official website of the Meetup groups for Beppe Grillo: http://www.meetup.com/topics/beppegrillo/.

20 It is possible to download it, in Italian, from the official website of the movement (accessed last in May, 2015): https://s3-eu-west-1.amazonaws.com/materiali-bg/Regolamento-Movimento-5-Stelle.pdf.

21 The category "non-populist" can include technocratic messages, but also explicitly anti-populist ones.

22 They can also decide not to report populist messages if they prefer not to lend them visibility. Indeed, certain political actors articulating a populist discourse might even be excluded and stigmatized by the media system, e.g. extreme right-wing parties in Germany (Art, 2006). Moreover, according to Ellinas (2010: 30), "the media can alter the parameters of partisan competition by granting or denying access to political newcomers. While mainstream party competition structures the opportunities available to new contestants, access to the media grants them the resources necessary to capitalize on these opportunities."

23 For example, Plasser and Ulram argue that "mass media provide a necessary and permanent soundboard for neo-populism" (2003: 40).

24 See, for example, the *Pirate Partei* in Germany, as well as other Pirate Party experiences all over Europe.

25 See, for example, Alberto Fujimori, former Peruvian President.

26 Some of them have a really organized structure and clear program, since they have been present in the national and international political arena for decades. On the other hand, mainstream parties might show a low degree of internal organization and a rather limited political program.

27 The Canadian Prime Minister Justin Trudeau (to mention just one case) also performed several activities that portray him as "one of the people," but if they are not combined with anti-elitist messages they should not be considered as evidence of populism.

REFERENCES

Akkerman, T. 2011. "Friend or foe? Right-wing populism and the popular press in Britain and the Netherlands," *Journalism*, 12(8): 931–45.

Altheide, D. L. and R. P. Snow. 1979. *Media Logic*. Beverly Hills: Sage.

Art, D. 2006. *The Politics of the Nazi Past in Germany and Austria*. New York: Cambridge University Press.

Avery, J. M. 2009. "Videomalaise or virtuous circle?," *The International Journal of Press/Politics*, 14(4): 410–33.

Biorcio, R. 2003. "The Lega Nord and the Italian media system," in G. Mazzoleni, J. Stewart, and B. Horsfield (eds), *The Media and Neo-Populism: A Contemporary Comparative Analysis*. London: Praeger, 71–95.

Birnenbaum, G. and M. Villa. 2003. "The media and neo-populism in France," in G. Mazzoleni, J. Stewart, and B. Horsfield (eds), *The Media and Neo-Populism: A Contemporary Comparative Analysis*. London: Praeger, 45–70.

Blumler, J. G. and M. Gurevitch. 1995. *The Crisis of Public Communication*. London and New York: Routledge.

Blumler, J. G. and D. Kanavagh. 1999. "The third age of political communication: influences and features," *Political Communication*, 16(3): 209–30.

Boas, T. C. 2005. "Television and neopopulism in Latin America: media effects in Brazil and Peru," *Latin American Research Review*, 40(2): 27–49.

Boomgaarden, H. G. and R. Vliegenthart. 2007. "Explaining the rise of anti-immigrant parties: the role of news media content," *Electoral Studies*, 26(2): 404–17.

Bordignon, F. and L. Ceccarini. 2014. "Protest and project, leader and party: normalization of the Five Star Movement," *Contemporary Italian Politics*, 6(1): 54–72.

Bos, L. and K. Brants. 2014. "Populist rhetoric in politics and media: a longitudinal study of the Netherlands," *European Journal of Communication*, 29(6): 703–19.

Bos, L., W. van der Burg, and C. H. de Vreese. 2010. "Media coverage of right-wing populist leaders," *Communications*, 35(2): 141–63.

Bos, L., W. van der Burg, and C. H. de Vreese. 2011. "How the media shape perceptions of right-wing populist leaders," *Political Communication*, 28(2): 182–206.

Canovan, M. 2002. "Taking politics to the people: populism as the ideology of democracy," in Y. Mény and Y. Surel (eds), *Democracies and the Populist Challenge*. New York: Palgrave Macmillan, 5–44.

Coleman, S. and J. G. Blumler. 2009. *The Internet and Democratic Citizenship: Theory, Practice and Policy*. New York: Cambridge University Press.

Cook, T. E. 2005. *Governing with the News: The News Media as a Political Institution*, 2nd edn. Chicago: University of Chicago Press.

Cranmer, M. 2011. "Populist communication and publicity: an empirical study of contextual differences in Switzerland," *Swiss Political Science Review*, 17(3): 286–307.

Dalton, R. J. 2004. *Democratic Challenges, Democratic Choices: The Erosion of Political Support in Advanced Industrial Democracies*. Washington, DC: CQ Press.

Eatwell, R. 2005. "Charisma and the revival of the European extreme right," in J. Rydgren (ed.), *Movements of Exclusion: Radical Right-Wing Populism in the Western World*. New York: Nova Science, 101–20.

Ellinas, A. 2010. *The Media and the Far Right in Western Europe: Playing the Nationalist Card*. New York: Cambridge University Press.

Entman, R. M. 1993. "Framing: toward clarification of a fractured paradigm," *Journal of Communication*, 43(4): 51–8.

Esser, F. 2013. "Mediatization as a challenge: media logic vs political logic," in H. Kriesi, D. Bochsler, J. Matthes, S. Lavenex, M. Bühlmann, and F. Esser (eds), *Democracy in the Age of Globalization and Mediatization*. Basingstoke: Palgrave Macmillan, 155–76.

Esser, F. and J. Strömbäck (eds). 2014. *Mediatization of Politics: Understanding the Transformation of Western Democracies*. Basingstoke: Palgrave Macmillan.

Fortunati, L. 2005. "Mediatization of the net and internetization of the mass media," *International Communication Gazette*, 67(1): 27–44.

Gunther, R. and A. Mughan (eds). 2000. *Democracy and the Media: A Comparative Perspective.* Cambridge: Cambridge University Press.

Hallin, D. C. and P. Mancini. 2004. *Comparing Media Systems: Three Models of Media and Politics.* Cambridge: Cambridge University Press.

Hawkins, K. 2010. *Venezuela's Chavismo and Populism in Comparative Perspective.* Cambridge: Cambridge University Press.

Hedman, E-L. 2001. "The spectre of populism in Philippine politics and society: artista, masa, Eraption!," *South East Asia Research*, 9(1): 5–44.

Hellström, A., T. Nilsson, and P. Stoltz. 2012. "Nationalism vs. nationalism: the challenge of the Sweden Democrats in the Swedish public debate," *Government and Opposition*, 47(2): 186–205.

Jagers, J. and S. Walgrave. 2007. "Populism as political communication style: an empirical study of political parties' discourse in Belgium," *European Journal of Political Research*, 46(3): 319–45.

Kitschelt, H. 2007. "Growth and persistence of the radical right in postindustrial democracies: advances and challenges in comparative research," *West European Politics*, 30(5): 1176–1206.

Krämer, B. 2014. "Media populism: a conceptual clarification and some theses on its effects," *Communication Theory*, 24(1): 42–60.

Mazzoleni, G. 2003. "The media and the growth of neo-populism in contemporary democracies," in G. Mazzoleni, J. Stewart, and B. Horsfield (eds), *The Media and Neo-populism: A Contemporary Comparative Analysis*. London: Praeger, 1–20.

Mazzoleni, G. 2008. "Populism and the media," in D. Albertazzi, and D. McDonnell (eds), *Twenty-First Century Populism: The Spectre of Western European Democracy*. Basingstoke and New York: Palgrave Macmillan, 49–64.

Mazzoleni, G. 2014. "Mediatization and political populism," in F. Esser and J. Strömbäck (eds), *Mediatization of Politics: Understanding the Transformation of Western Democracies*. Basingstoke: Palgrave Macmillan, 42–56.

Mazzoleni, G. and W. Schulz. 1999. "Mediatization of politics: a challenge for democracy?," *Political Communication*, 16(3): 247–61.

Mazzoleni, G., J. Stewart, and B. Horsfield (eds). 2003. *The Media and Neo-populism: A Contemporary Comparative Analysis*. Westport: Praeger.

Mény, Y. and Y. Surel. 2000. *Par le peuple, pour le peuple: le populisme et les démocraties.* Paris: Fayard.

Meyer, T. 2002. *Media Democracy: How the Media Colonize Politics.* Cambridge: Polity Press.

Moffitt, B. 2014. "Contemporary populism and 'the people' in the Asia-Pacific: Thaksin Shinawatra and Pauline Hanson," in C. de la Torre (ed.), *The Promise and Perils of Populism: Global Perspectives*. Lexington: University Press of Kentucky, 293–316.

Mosca, L., C. Vaccari, and A. Valeriani. 2015. "An internet-fuelled party? The Movimento 5 Stelle and the Web," in F. Tronconi (ed.), *Beppe Grillo's Five Star Movement: Organization, Communication and Ideology*. Farnham: Ashgate, 127–51.

Mudde, C. and C. Rovira Kaltwasser (eds). 2012. *Populism in Europe and the Americas: Threat or Corrective for Democracy?* Cambridge: Cambridge University Press.

Mutz, D. M. and D. Reeves. 2005. "The new videomalaise: effects of televised incivility on political trust," *The American Political Science Review*, 99(1): 1–15.

Norris, P. 2011. *Democratic Deficit: Critical Citizens Revisited.* Cambridge: Cambridge University Press.

Pappas, T. S. 2013. "Populist democracies: post-authoritarian Greece and post-Communist Hungary," *Government and Opposition*, 49(1): 1–23.

Plasser, F. and P. A. Ulram. 2003. "Striking a responsive chord: mass media and right-wing populism in Austria," in G. Mazzoleni, J. Stewart, and B. Horsfield (eds), *The Media and Neo-Populism: A Contemporary Comparative Analysis*. London: Praeger, 21–43.

Robinson, M. J. 1976. "Public affairs television and the growth of political malaise: the case of the 'selling of the Pentagon,'" *American Political Science Review*, 70(2): 409–32.

Rooduijn, M. 2013. "The mesmerising message: the diffusion of populism in public debates in Western European media," *Political Studies*, 62(4): 726–44.

Rovira Kaltwasser, Cristóbal, 2012. "The ambivalence of populism: threat and corrective for democracy," *Democratization*, 19(2): 184–208.

Schulz, W. 2014. "Mediatization and new media," in F. Esser and J. Strömbäck (eds), *Mediatization of Politics: Understanding the Transformation of Western Democracies*. Basingstoke: Palgrave Macmillan, 57–73.

Strömbäck, J. 2008. "Four phases of mediatization: an analysis of the mediatization of politics," *International Journal of Press/Politics*, 13(3): 228–46.

Taggart, P. 1995. "New populist parties in Western Europe," *West European Politic*, 18(1): 34–51.

Tufekci, Z. and C. Wilson. 2012. "Social media and the decision to participate in political protest: observations from Tahrir Square," *Journal of Communication*, 62(2): 363–79.

Van Aelst, P., G. Thesen, S. Walgrave, and R. Vliegenthart. 2014. "Mediatization and political agenda-setting: changing issue priorities?," in F. Esser and J. Strömbäck (eds), *Mediatization of Politics: Understanding the Transformation of Western Democracies*. Basingstoke: Palgrave Macmillan, 200–20.

Waisbord, S. 2012. "Democracy, journalism, and Latin American populism," *Journalism*, 14(4): 504–21.

Walgrave, S. and K. de Swert. 2004. "The making of the (issues of the) Vlaams Blok," *Political Communication*, 21(4): 479–500.

Webb, P. and T. Poguntke. 2005. "The presidentialization of contemporary democratic politics: evidence, causes, and consequences," in T. Poguntke and P. Webb (eds), *The Presidentialization of Politics: A Comparative Study of Modern Democracies*. Oxford: Oxford University Press, 335–56.

CHAPTER 25

POPULISM AND THE QUESTION OF HOW TO RESPOND TO IT

CRISTÓBAL ROVIRA KALTWASSER

DESPITE the fact that populist leaders and parties are making headlines across the globe, there is almost no research on the question of how to respond to populist forces.[1] Part of the problem lies in the use of the term as a battle cry. Academics and pundits alike usually employ the concept of populism to denote all sorts of distasteful political behaviors. While there are good reasons to worry about authoritarianism, economic mismanagement, opportunism, and racism, we should not confuse these phenomena with populism. Nevertheless, the constant misuse of the term is only part of the problem. Another is the absence of agreement on how to think about the relationship between populism and democracy. Although it is true that most scholars are inclined to consider populism a danger for democracy, some academics argue that populism should be seen as something positive for democracy. No wonder, then, that little work focuses on how to respond to populism.

This chapter aims to start filling this research gap by developing a framework for analysis that maps the actors that can try to deal with populism and what type of responses they can muster. Empirical illustrations from Europe and the Americas are given to show why some approaches seem to be more prevalent than others. However, it is worth indicating that coping with populism is a complex endeavor, so there is no one-size-fits-all approach. To better understand this complexity, the very first step consists in shedding light on the ambivalent relationship between populism and democracy. Without clarity on the ways in which populist forces can have both negative and positive effects on the democratic regime, it is impossible to identify the approaches that existing democracies should try to develop when responding to populism. Fortunately, recent research has generated new insights that help to provide conceptual clarity and form the basis of new empirical analyses (e.g. Hawkins, 2016b; Houle and Kenny, 2016; Huber and Schimpf, 2016; Mudde and Rovira Kaltwasser, 2012; Rovira Kaltwasser, 2012).

The rest of this contribution is divided into five sections. In the next section, the difficult relationship between populism and democracy is explained. This helps us to understand that populism can have positive and negative influences on the democratic regime, and therefore one should avoid overreacting to the challenge posed by populist forces. After this, an overview of the different actors that at the domestic and external levels can cope with populism is presented and empirical illustrations are given. Subsequently, different responses to the rise of populism are discussed and some empirical illustrations are also provided. The next section depicts a common and problematic phenomenon that occurs when trying to respond to populism, namely "fighting fire with fire." As will be explained, this consists in responding to populism by employing moral categories that end up strengthening populist forces and can lead to the formation of a populism vs anti-populism cleavage that is orthogonal to the left vs right conflict that normally structures the party system. Lastly, the chapter concludes by summarizing the main ideas that have been developed and by presenting some avenues for future research on the question of how to respond to populism.

POPULISM VS DEMOCRACY: UNDERSTANDING THE CHALLENGE

No discussion of populism can proceed without first acknowledging its diverse definitions, an ambiguity that hampers the study of and accumulation of knowledge about the phenomenon in question. Although this continues to be a problem, we should not exaggerate its magnitude. First, with growing academic interest and research on populism, scholars are increasingly dedicating effort to providing clear conceptualizations. Additionally, the number of definitions is not necessarily growing. The three conceptual approaches in ascendency in political science literature are those presented at the beginning of this Handbook. Moreover, despite the differences between these three definitions, they have significant overlap. Not by chance, there is vast agreement in the political science literature that cases such as Chavismo in Venezuela, the National Front in France, and Victor Orbán's FIDESZ in Hungary should be seen as examples of populism.

This notwithstanding, and as I have explained in detail elsewhere (Mudde and Rovira Kaltwasser, 2013; 2017; Rovira Kaltwasser, 2014a), the so-called ideational approach has a number of advantages for the study of populism. As a consequence, in line with the contribution of Mudde presented in this volume, populism is conceived of as a moral discourse, which by pitting "the pure people" against "the corrupt elite" defends the idea that popular sovereignty should be respected by all means. In other words, populism can be understood as a worldview whereby the establishment is seen as a dishonest entity and the people are depicted as a virtuous community that has ultimate political authority. By emphasizing that populism is above all a set of ideas, this definition permits us to understand an important aspect: while it is true that political ideas are promoted by agents (be they leaders, parties, or movements), they also exist and last because living persons and groups believe in them. This means that the study of populism and the question of how to respond to it must pay attention not only to the supply of populist ideas, but also to the demand for them. I will come back to this point later.

As with any other discourse or ideology, populism is not necessarily harmless. There are ongoing debates over the impact of ideologies such as nationalism, (neo)liberalism, or socialism on democratic regimes: how should we analyze the relationship between populism and democracy? At an abstract level, there is little doubt that populism contains a strong democratic urge: it promotes the idea that the ultimate political authority is vested in "the people" and not in divine powers or unelected bodies composed of experts (Rovira Kaltwasser, 2014b). Nevertheless, given that the conceptualization of "the people" advanced by populism is characterized by its moral nature, it hurts the odds of establishing a cooperative dialogue and reaching agreements. "The people" are seen as good, honest, and pure, while "the elite" is portrayed as corrupt, fraudulent, and tainted. In effect, populism is inclined to develop a monolithic understanding of who "the people" are, according to which it is possible to identify a fixed and unified will of the people, but there is no space for thinking of popular sovereignty as a dynamic and open-ended process (Ochoa Espejo, 2015).

This peculiar understanding of "the people" vis-à-vis "the elite" that is inherent to populism helps us to grasp its difficult relationship with democracy. As mentioned, populism favors the notion of self-government by the people and thus has a strong democratic impetus. However, democracy today—at least in the Western world—means above all *liberal* democracy: a complex institutional setting that not only gives power to the people by permitting the periodic holding of free and fair elections, but also limits people's power by building an array of unelected bodies, such as central banks, (constitutional) courts, and supranational institutions that are in charge of providing public goods. Not by coincidence, populist actors and constituencies are prone to criticize these unelected bodies for their undemocratic character and alleged tendency to prioritize the interests of powerful minorities.

For instance, the UK Independence Party (UKIP) has been marked by a strong populist discourse against the European Union and it played a key role in the results of the 2016 "Brexit" referendum, in which a slight majority of the UK's population voted in favor of withdrawing from the European Union. In a similar vein, leftist populist forces in Latin America came to power in countries such as Bolivia (Evo Morales), Ecuador (Rafael Correa), and Venezuela (Hugo Chávez) by claiming that the existing constitutions had been drafted to protect the interests of "the elite" and calling for constituent assemblies in charge of modifying constitutional settings to allegedly better give voice to and respect the interests of "the people."

Does this mean that all forms of populism should be seen as dangerous? Not necessarily. On the one hand, populist actors are able to represent certain constituencies, who are of the opinion that their ideas and interests are not being (properly) addressed by the establishment. As Hans-Peter Kriesi (2014) has rightly noted, the more the established political parties have problems working as intermediaries between the citizens and public policy, the higher the odds that populist forces will come to the fore. Seen in this light, populism can indeed play a positive role for democracy: it can help to articulate the demands of different social groups who feel abandoned. On the other hand, the rise of a populist discourse puts liberal democracy under stress because it can eventually lead to the destruction of the so-called checks and balances, the circumvention of minority rights, and the movement toward a plebiscitary form of politics. There is probably no better example of this type of negative effect on liberal democracy than Venezuela since the end of 1990s, where the coming into power of Hugo Chávez first and Nicolás Maduro later has led to a gradual transformation of the political regime into competitive authoritarianism (Hawkins, 2016a; Mainwaring, 2012).

Nevertheless, it would be wrong to assume a priori that populism works as a threat to or as a corrective for democracy. The question about the impact of populism on liberal democracy should be answered empirically; fortunately, a new wave of studies is taking this approach (e.g. Hawkins, 2016b; Houle and Kenny, 2016; Huber and Schimpf, 2016; Mudde and Rovira Kaltwasser, 2012; Rovira Kaltwasser, 2012). Despite the fact that there is little consensus about the negative and positive effects that populism has on the liberal democratic regime, there is no doubt that the very rise of populist forces puts liberal democracy under stress. The reason for this is simple: by politicizing issues that intentionally or unintentionally are not being addressed by established political elites, populist forces develop a moral language that not only hinders the reaching of agreements but also promotes reforms that can potentially lead to the erosion of the liberal democratic regime. As a consequence, it is important to ask ourselves how to deal with the rise of populism. To answer this question, in the next two sections the actors that can respond to populism and the type of responses they can advance are mapped.

ACTORS: WHO RESPONDS?

Comparative politics literature has highlighted that the emergence and survival of democracy hinges upon the role of both domestic and external actors. In fact, the pioneering work of O'Donnell, Schmitter, and Whitehead (1986) argued that the fall of authoritarian regimes is usually triggered by two forces: on one side, pressures from below against the status quo and divisions within the ruling elite, and from the other, changes at the international level and pressures from foreign governments and institutions. At the same time, those who study the consolidation of democratic regimes have also emphasized that one should take into consideration the role of both domestic and external actors (Linz and Stephan, 1996; Stoner and McFaul, 2013).

This observation should be borne in mind when examining the actors that, at the domestic and external level, respond to the challenge that populism poses to liberal democracy. First of all, populist forces are inclined to develop a discourse that combines the moral critique of the establishment with certain forms of nationalism (see also De Cleen, in this volume). To define the boundaries of "the people" populists normally refer to nationalist markers and symbols. Therefore, they are prone to attacking actors at the national level who are depicted as members of "the establishment." For instance, new populist formations that have emerged in Southern Europe as a result of the Great Recession (e.g. the Five Star Movement in Italy, PODEMOS in Spain, and SYRIZA in Greece) speak about the existence of a "political caste," i.e. a group of untouchable individuals who rule the country and make deals behind closed doors for their own benefit. In addition, the populist discourse has a tendency to be hostile to foreign actors who allegedly work together with national elites to circumvent the will of "the people." For example, the populist Tea Party claims that the US liberal establishment works in partnership with foreign governments sympathetic to its cosmopolitan vision with the aim of limiting people's power and empowering the United Nations (Formisano, 2012).

Given that populism has a difficult relationship with domestic and external actors, these actors usually respond to the rise of populist forces. In the following paragraphs the most relevant actors at the domestic level and external level are depicted and some empirical illustrations of their approaches toward populist forces are presented (see Figure 25.1). It will be shown that actors not only oppose but also cooperate with populist forces. Whether attacking or collaborating is better for dealing with the populist challenge is an empirical question that cannot be answered a priori, so the framework presented in this contribution should be seen as an invitation for undertaking empirical research on this topic.

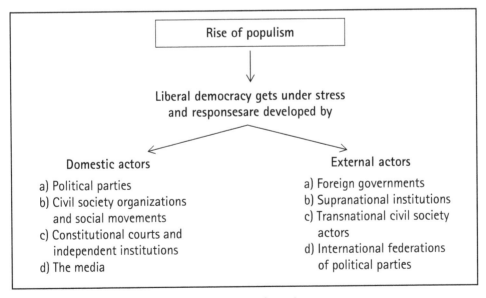

FIG. 25.1 Actors that normally respond to the rise of populism.

Domestic Actors

Political Parties

Modern democracy hinges upon the existence of political parties, which are in charge of representing the ideas and interests of society through the development of policy programs. While it is true that programmatic representation is not the only linkage mechanism between political elites and the citizenry (Kitschelt, 2000; Morgan, 2011), it is the one most affected by the rise of populism. After all, populist forces politicize certain topics that are uncomfortable for the political establishment, forcing it to take action which can range from adapting political programs to ignoring the demands put forward by populists. In effect, a growing number of scholars are studying the extent to which the emergence of populist radical right parties in Western Europe is leading to a transformation of the policies advanced by mainstream political parties (e.g. Akkermann, 2012; Alonso and da Fonseca, 2012; Bale et al., 2010; de Lange, 2012).

Civil Society Organizations and Social Movements

Political parties are not the only agents that articulate the preferences of the citizenry. Civil society organizations and social movements also help to give voice to different groups. As a consequence, they can support or oppose populist forces. For instance, Art (2007) has shown that in Germany civil society organizations are very hostile to the emergence of populist radical right forces due to the singular culture of remembrance of the country. By contrast, the rise of Evo Morales in Bolivia and his populist party "Movement toward Socialism" cannot be explained without taking into account the support of several civil society organizations and a strong social movement with a leftist agenda focused on the integration of the indigenous population and the development of a post-neoliberal development agenda (Anria, 2013).

Constitutional Courts and Independent Institutions

Liberal democracy is characterized by the nurturing of various bodies that are neither directly elected nor controlled by the demos. These unelected institutions have been gaining increasing power as they are seen not only as an effective mechanism to enhance the separation of powers (Vibert, 2007), but also as a new source of democratic legitimacy due to their capacity to foster processes of impartial decision-making (Rosanvallon, 2011). Populist constituencies and leaders are highly skeptical of these types of unelected bodies, which, depending on their strength and actual autonomy, can play an important role in defending the rule of law and enhancing horizontal accountability. In effect, while the constitutional court seriously limited the maneuvering room of the populist government headed by the Kaczyński twins in Poland between 2006 and 2007 (Stanley, 2016), Rafael Correa's populist administration in Ecuador has been able to bypass unelected bodies by convening a constituent assembly to reform the constitution of the country and packing the most important unelected institutions with individuals loyal to himself (de la Torre and Ortíz Lemos, 2016).

The Media

The public sphere plays an important role in democracy as it permits the airing of differ-ent arguments and standpoints, which in turn influence the political decision-making process. However, the quality of the public debate is related to the performance of the media system, its political autonomy, and level of marketization. Depending on the cir-cumstances, media outlets can opt to ostracize populist actors or establish implicit alli-ances with them and endorse their political agenda (see e.g. Manucci's contribution to this volume). This is in fact the case in the US, where a well-established complex of con-servative media outlets has served as platform for the populist Tea Party (Skopol and Williamson, 2012). By contrast, contemporary leftist populist leaders in Latin America are aware of the opposition they experience from established media outlets and so have spared no effort in erecting a new media model that places the state at the center to pro-mote the ideas of "the people" and attack the views of "the elite" (Waisbord, 2011).

External Actors

Foreign Governments

One of the main targets of the discourse advanced by populist forces is foreign govern-ments, which allegedly work together with the national establishment to impose meas-ures against the will of the people. This is particularly true for populist actors in power, who often claim that they cannot govern adequately because of foreign governments' pressures. Take for instance the case of the government coalition between two popu-list parties (SYRIZA and ANEL) in Greece, which maintain—not without reason—that economic austerity has been imposed not only by Northern but also by Southern and Eastern European administrations (Aslanidis and Rovira Kaltwasser, 2016). Nevertheless, populist actors both in power and in opposition can try to establish alli-ances with foreign governments that share their views in order to develop an interna-tional shield of support. There is probably no better example of this than Hugo Chávez's administration in Venezuela (1998–2013), which leveraged the wealth derived from high oil prices to win the support of various Latin American governments (Hawkins, 2016a).

Supranational Institutions

Another key target of the discourse advanced by populist constituencies and leaders is supranational institutions, which they usually depict as undemocratic bodies that seek to bypass the popular will and intentionally or not destroy what Paul Taggart (2000) has called "the heartland"—a version of the past that celebrates an uncomplicated and non-political territory of imagination from which populists draw their own vision of their unified and ordinary constituency. This type of critique has become quite evident in Europe, where populist forces of different political stripes are becoming increasingly Euroskeptic (Szczerbiak and Taggart, 2008) to the point that populist formations as diverse as the French National Front and the Italian Five Star Movement argue in favor of withdrawing from the European Union. Something similar has been occurring in the Americas, where the involvement of the Organization of American States in the assessment of the state of democracy in countries governed by populist leaders has sparked political conflict at the international level (Perina, 2015).

Transnational Civil Society Actors

Transnational think tanks, NGOs, and advocacy networks can play a significant role in responding to the moral discourse developed by populist forces. Because many of them monitor the state of democracy across the globe, it is common for them to criticize the ideas defended by populists in opposition and the policies promoted by populists in power. The work of these transnational civil society actors influences the image and thus legitimacy of populist forces at the global level, since it can call the attention of the international community to populist attacks on the liberal democratic regime. For instance, Amnesty International and Human Rights Watch have often provided evidence of measures undertaken by leftist populist presidents in Latin American that seriously limit basic democratic guarantees, such as freedom of expression and the right of political leaders to compete for votes.

International Federations of Political Parties

Although it is true that political parties work mainly at the national level, it is also important to consider that they can cooperate at the international level. This is particularly relevant in the case of Europe, where the existence of the European Union and European Parliament favors the development of alliances between political parties with similar beliefs and projects. So far, the attempts to create a European federation of political parties that share the populist set of ideas have failed. However, mainstream parties usually work together in the European Parliament and they can mobilize opposition to some of their members if they feel that populist forces are putting the liberal democratic regime at risk. For instance, the decision of the Austrian Christian Democratic Party (ÖVP) to form a government coalition with the populist radical right at the beginning of the 2000s sparked a major debate within parties across Europe. Special pressure was exercised by the European People's Party (EPP), the umbrella party of Christian Democratic parties in the European Parliament, over the new elected Chancellor, who committed to respecting the rule of law and supporting the EU (Fallend and Heinisch, 2016). By contrast, although FIDESZ is a member of the EPP, the latter has voiced no major criticism of the situation in Hungary since the coming into power of Viktor Orbán's FIDESZ in 2010 and the much debated constitutional reform undertaken by his administration (Batory, 2016).

RESPONSES: WHICH STRATEGIES ARE AVAILABLE?

The domestic and external actors discussed above can employ different strategies to cope with populist forces. Despite the existence of very diverse strategies, all of them are related to the very notion of "militant democracy": the idea that democratic regimes need to protect themselves from political actors committed to the erosion of democracy (Löwenstein, 1937; Capoccia 2013). While a reasonable notion, it brings to the fore the paradox of democratic self-destruction (Müller, 2012). On the one hand, democracy is characterized by permitting public contestation and political participation with the aim of warranting the periodic holding of free and fair elections. On the other hand, permitting public contestation and political participation can allow the rise of political forces that might seek to destroy the democratic regime. Militant democracy tries to solve this paradox by establishing (legal) mechanisms to fight against those actors who seek to damage democracy and the most common device consists in party bans. However, by fighting their enemies, governments might end up becoming like their enemies and thus damaging democracy (Kirshner, 2014).

The paradox of democratic self-destruction is particularly challenging when it comes to responding to populist forces, which—as noted above—are not against democracy per se, but rather against *liberal* democracy. Remember that populists neither argue that elections should be proscribed nor are inclined to disrespect the results of elections.[2] What they claim is that unelected bodies that are intrinsic to the liberal democratic regime have a tendency to run amok and thus protect the interests of (powerful) minorities instead of defending the popular will. Seen in this light, one could maintain that populist actors and constituencies favor vertical accountability at the cost of horizontal accountability. By contrast, those who are at odds with populism normally prefer to invest in horizontal rather than in vertical accountability. To paraphrase the terminology advanced by Dan Slater (2013), the political conflict that emerges here has less to do with consolidating democracy vis-à-vis collapsing into authoritarianism and much more to do with the tension between populist vis-à-vis oligarchic modes of politics.

As a consequence, fighting populist forces with "hard" measures (e.g. banning them or cancelling the political rights of their leaders) is particularly problematic, because populists normally do have some right in claiming that it is crucial to "control the controllers" and prevent elites from disempowering the many (Rovira Kaltwasser, 2014b). Despite all the reasonable criticism against leftist populist leaders in Latin America for their involvement in the deterioration of the "checks and balances," there is little doubt that their coming into power is connected to their capacity to represent large swaths of the population who were excluded and have been governed by an unresponsive establishment. At the same time, the growing Euroskepticism of left-wing and right-wing populist parties in Europe closely related to the elitist nature of the European Union and the pressure that the latter exerts on political parties to act responsibly rather than responsively (Mair, 2009).

That being said, a useful starting point for thinking about the strategies for dealing with populism is the work of Giovanni Capoccia (2005), which is focused on the approaches employed by different actors for coping with extremism in inter-war Europe. Although this work is not centered on populism per se, it has a great deal to offer because it considers the paradox of democratic self-destruction. Capoccia maintains that responses to extremism need to find a difficult balance between limiting the use of discriminatory measures to avoid making the democratic regime increasingly

Table 25.1 Approaches that can be used for dealing
with populist forces.

Nature of the reactions	Time range of the reactions	
	Short term	Long term
Repressive	militancy	purge
Accommodative	incorporation	education

The distinctions presented in this table are based on the work of
Capoccia (2005: 49).

illiberal and fighting against intolerant forces that might end up provoking the collapse of democracy. This difficult balance can be summarized in Table 25.1, which presents a typology of reactions according to their political nature (repression vs accommodation) and their time range (short term vs long term).

Militancy

In line with Löwenstein's work (1937), this approach alludes to the implementation of measures, mostly of a legal nature, which attempt to limit the civil and political rights of certain actors because their ideas and activities are defined as harmful to the survival of the democratic system. The most common strategy within the militant democracy approach consists in banning political parties and it has been used from time to time in Europe (see e.g. Bale, 2007), but to deal with extremist parties that are not necessarily populist. Although Peronism was proscribed in Argentina in the 1950s and 1960s, leading to what Guillermo O'Donnell (1973) called an "impossible game" (i.e. no government was able to create a stable political coalition), in contemporary Latin America there is almost no debate on banning populist forces. This is probably related to the fact that these forces normally have a democratic discourse and moreover they usually obtain a significant amount of votes. Therefore, banning them could generate major political turmoil and suspicions about the legitimacy of this strategy.[3]

Incorporation

To use the language of Linz (1978: 29), this approach seeks to convert semi-loyal into loyal political actors. In other words, the idea is to bring into the democratic system the more tolerant activists and constituencies of an existing populist formation, thereby fostering the division of the latter into moderates and radicals. The most common incorporation consists in cooperating with populist parties by generating an electoral alliance with them as opposed to ostracizing populist parties, which occurs when established actors systematically rule out cooperation with populist forces. According to various scholars, the cooperation of mainstream right parties with populist radical right parties in Europe hinges mainly on two factors: the level of programmatic proximity between the two and the electoral strength of populist parties (e.g. van Spanje, 2010; de Lange, 2012). In the case of both the US and Latin America, cooperation between populist forces and other actors occurs from time to time. While in the US there is a long tradition of incorporating some leaders (and policies) of populist movements into mainstream parties (Formisano, 2012), in Latin America some populist forces have been able to cooperate with social movements and leftist parties (Silva, 2009).

Purge

With the partial exception of regime transitions, this type of approach does not often come to the fore because it involves prosecuting the architects and administrators (including state officials and bureaucrats) of anti-democratic activities connected with the previous regime. This approach involves hard measures (such as imprisonment) and soft measures (such as job loss). Given that in Latin America various populist forces have been able to conquer the executive branch, they have sometimes been prosecuted afterwards, particularly when there is enough evidence of democratic backsliding during their time in office (e.g. the case of Alberto Fujimori in Peru). By contrast, the formation of governing alliances with populist radical parties in Europe has not led to the purge approach, since there are no evident signs that these governments have fostered democratic erosion.[4] However, it is also worth indicating that the purge approach can be used by populist forces in power against their opponents. It is not a coincidence that populist actors such as Chávez in Venezuela, Correa in Ecuador, Morales in Bolivia, and Orbán in Hungary have introduced significant constitutional reforms that have helped them to get rid of their opponents (Taggart and Rovira Kaltwasser, 2016).

Education

This approach seeks to strengthen democratic beliefs by, for instance, developing forms of civic education through the creation of new school curricula, designing programs aimed at integrating activists who want to abandon extremist parties, and giving state funding to organizations interested in promoting tolerance and democratic attitudes. There is little research on these types of strategies when it comes to dealing with populist forces, since most of the existing studies tend to focus on the supply side rather than the demand side of populism. However, as noted at the beginning of this contribution, populism is a set of ideas present at the mass level (Akkerman, Mudde, and Zaslove, 2014; Spruyt, Keepens, and van Droogenbroeck, 2016), thus researchers should devote more attention to the factors that explain why certain constituencies rely on the populist worldview to make political decisions such as voting. It would also be important to analyze the effectiveness of civic education and similar strategies at curbing the proliferation of populist attitudes at the mass level. Nevertheless, this is an area of research that it is still in its infancy.

FIGHTING FIRE WITH FIRE

Regardless of who the actors are that most commonly react to the rise of populism and the types of response they employ, the struggle between populism and anti-populism can become visceral. When this happens, liberal democracy runs the risk of damaging itself. Given that this is a damaging, difficult to escape scenario, every effort should be made to avoid it. This situation occurs when actors respond to populism by employing moral categories that end up giving more validity and visibility to the discourse advanced by populist forces. Treating populist followers and leaders as silly only reinforces their victimizing self-image. Taken to an extreme, the (over)use of moral categories can foster the formation of a true populism vs anti-populism cleavage, which crosscuts other cleavages, such as the classic left vs right distinction, that normally structure the political game (on this topic, see also Ostiguy, in this volume). However, to better understand why "fighting fire with fire" is poisonous for liberal democracy, it is important to examine the factors leading to the rise of populism.

Whether one likes it or not, populists around the world are posing legitimate questions about the current state of liberal democracy. Many citizens are angry at the establishment and feel betrayed by mainstream political forces. To a great extent, this can be explained by the growing influence of unelected bodies and the concurrently declining power of politicians. Although elected leaders can make important decisions, their maneuvering rooming is increasingly limited by unelected institutions, which in theory are autonomous and contribute to the provision of public goods. Nevertheless, under certain circumstances unelected bodies can run amok and favor the interests of powerful minorities (Dahl, 1989). Consider the inability of the European Union to tame capital to generate social peace. As Wolfgang Streeck (2014) has pointed out, even though the deregulation and liberalization of financial markets promoted by the European Union is one of the main causes of the Great Recession, the European Union has imposed austerity measures rather than forcing the financial industry to assume a significant part of the costs of the Great Recession.

At the same time, politicians are reluctant to accept that they are not almighty. Despite the fact that they have adopted measures such as economic liberalization, they have limited capacity to counter the unintended consequences of those measures. This problem is linked to the tension between responsiveness and responsibility that democratic regimes are increasingly experiencing. Whereas responsiveness refers to the obligation of leaders and parties to respond to the demands of voters in order to win elections and stay in power, responsibility alludes to the necessity for those same leaders and parties to think about the long-term needs of the electorate, which often are not articulated as concrete proposals, and consider the claims made by international markets, foreign governments, and global institutions (Bardi, Bartolini, and Trechsel, 2014; Mair, 2009). The more leaders and parties act responsibly, the higher the chance that voters will become irritated and channel their anger by supporting populist forces, which not baselessly will criticize "the establishment" for trampling the popular will.

In addition, politicians are inclined to use the growing influence of unelected bodies to depoliticize contested political issues, such as economic liberalization. In this way, they have implemented reforms with limited popular support without making enough effort to justify them to the electorate. Moreover, the very implementation of these types of reform by both leftist and rightist forces gives ground for suspicion of increasing programmatic convergence between mainstream political parties and thus the belief that there are few if any differences within "the establishment." This produces in the voting public disappointment and frustration, which is fueled by populist leaders and parties that help to give voice to voters' negative attitudes towards the current state of affairs. Not by coincidence, various forms of populism are on the rise around the globe, each proposing solutions to whatever problems seem most pressing to its particular voting public.

Therefore, it would be wrong to assume that populism appears out of nowhere. Its emergence can be explained to a great extent by the sense in the electorate that the ideas and interests of "the people" are not being taken into consideration. One should bear this in mind when it comes to thinking about how to respond to populism. Forgetting it may lead to "fighting fire with fire." By this I mean that those who are worried about the rise of populist forces opt to disqualify them and present them as irrational individuals who are driven by emotional cues and are incapable of understanding the complexity of the contemporary world. There is a long tradition of portraying populism as a "disease" or "pathology" (Arditi, 2004). According to this view, populist forces are a dangerous anomaly that should be eradicated. Despite valid concerns over the emergence of populism, framing it in medical terms is anything but helpful.

After all, populism is not something external to democracy. Populist actors and constituencies can articulate their worldview due to the very existence of the two dimensions of democracy identified by Robert Dahl (1971): public contestation and political participation. Without them, the development of populist forces is extremely difficult, because whoever governs will tilt the rules of the game in their own favor and seriously limit the emergence of competitors. Conceiving of populism as something internal to democracy has important consequences. To begin with, populist forces do not misrepresent "the people" but rather offer an alternative and usually polemic opinion about the demands of the voting public. Moreover, those who support populist leaders and parties have important reasons to interpret their political reality through the lens of populism. As Hawkins, Read, and Pauwels indicate in this volume, the decision of individual voters to back populist forces should be thought of as a normative response to perceived crises of democratic legitimacy.

Instead of portraying populists as foolish actors, we should reflect on the fact that they are able to give voice to constituencies who do not feel represented. Populists are real experts in politicizing issues that deliberately or not have been ignored by the establishment. Their moral language is a powerful mechanism to mobilize certain segments of the electorate. But policy-makers and scholars need to avoid "fighting fire with fire": portraying ourselves as the good and smart guys fighting against the bad and stupid fellas. As difficult as it is, the best way to cope with populist actors and supporters lies in engaging in an honest dialogue with them. This dialogue should strive not only to better understand the issues that are being politicized by populists, but also to consider how to address these issues within the liberal democratic framework.

A paradigmatic example of how democracies can damage themselves by "fighting fire with fire" can be found in Venezuela. There is little doubt that the coming into power of Hugo Chávez in 1998 was the result of a major crisis of democratic representation produced by a highly clientelist two-party system that was increasing unable to channel the ideas and interests of the Venezuelan electorate (Hawkins, 2011; Morgan, 2011). Under these circumstances, Chavismo became a hegemonic political force which, by employing the moral categories that are inherent to populism, was able to mobilize and get the support of large swaths of the population. After an initial phase of shock and accommodation, actors at the domestic and external level exercised increasing pressure over Chavismo by using a moral rhetoric that fostered polarization and hindered dialogue (Cannon, 2014). This approach facilitated the emergence and consolidation of a political cleavage between populism and anti-populism that has probably come to stay. Not by chance, the death of Chávez in March, 2013, did not spell the end of Chavismo. Nicolás Maduro was elected in April, 2013, as president of the country and the opposition has constructed an umbrella organization (the so-called Democratic Unity Roundtable) that has few points in common beyond its disapproval of the Chavista project.

Another possible example of a democratic regime that seems to be "fighting fire with fire" is Greece after the Great Recession. Although this case is quite recent and thus more uncertain, it looks as if it is gradually sliding into a similar scenario (Aslanidis and Pappas, 2015). In 2015 the country experienced two general elections that permitted the formation of an unthinkable coalition between two populist parties: on the one hand, SYRIZA is a leftist populist party characterized by its inclusionary discourse, and on the other hand, ANEL is a populist radical right party marked by its exclusionary rhetoric (Aslanidis and Rovira Kaltwasser, 2016). Therefore, the commonality between these two parties has little to do with their programmatic positions and much more with their populism, which provides a shared understanding of who should be blamed for the problems Greece is facing today. At the same time, the reactions of domestic and external actors to the SYRIZA-ANEL government facilitated the formation of a populism vs anti-populism cleavage. Pressure from the so-called Troika (the European Commission, the European Central Bank, and the International Monetary Fund) to enact painful austerity reforms in one way or another was music to the ears of populist followers and leaders: rhetoric reached the point that one minister of the SYRIZA-ANEL government accused the country's creditors of "terrorism." In turn, various domestic actors have begun using moral categories to present themselves as "the good" ones, although they share responsibility for the country's difficulties (Pappas, 2013).

CONCLUSION

Populist forces have been becoming increasing influential across the globe. Given that they maintain a difficult relationship with the liberal democratic regime, scholars and policy-makers should reflect on how to respond to the populist challenge. In this contribution I have developed a framework for analysis that identifies the actors that at the domestic and external levels can try to respond to populism and what strategies they have at their disposal. Moreover, I have argued that "fighting fire with fire" is anything but beneficial for liberal democracy. Depicting populists as "the bad ones" and their opponents as "the good ones" fosters political polarization and can eventually lead to the formation of a populism vs anti-populism cleavage, making building stable political coalitions and reaching agreements between government and opposition extremely difficult, if not impossible.

Liberal democrats should certainly worry about the rise of populism. However, they need also to better understand what circumstances facilitate the activation of populist sentiments across the population. This means that the way ahead lies in identifying the anxieties of the voting public with the aim of trying to find a better balance between responsiveness and responsibility. Of course, this should lead to engagement in a critical and difficult dialogue with populist forces in order to show why the solutions they propose are usually not adequate while acknowledging that the problems they detect are real. At the end of the day, populist forces are right in claiming that ultimate political authority is derived from "the people" and not from divine powers or the expertise contained in unelected bodies. Opposing that idea means denying the essence of democracy. Yet populists are mistaken in maintaining that there is such a thing as a unified, self-evident popular will that should be respected at any cost. Therefore, responding to populism in a liberal democratic fashion entails the difficult process of discovering, framing, and redefining not only "we, the people" but also what "we, the people" aspire to.

NOTES

1   The arguments developed here are related to those of the special issue of *Democratization* on "Dealing with Populists in Government" that I have edited with Paul Taggart (see Rovira Kalwasser and Taggart, 2016) and the book that I have recently published with Cas Mudde (see Mudde and Rovira Kaltwasser, 2017). For helpful comments on previous versions of this contribution, I would like to thank Paul Taggart. Moreover, I would like to acknowledge support from the Chilean National Fund for Scientific and Technological Development (FONDECYT project 1140101), the Chilean Millennium Science Initiative (project NS130008), and the Center for Social Conflict and Cohesion Studies (COES, CONICYT/ FONDAP/15130009).

2   Take, for instance, the very balanced analysis provided by Hawkins (2016b) on Chavismo, in which he maintains that despite the existence of an uneven playing field in Venezuela and thus an increasing proximity to a competitive authoritarian regime, those who support Chavismo have allowed the opposition to win.

3   An alternative explanation for this has been suggested recently by Müller (2016), who argues that militant democracy might be a non-option for countries where there is no wide consensus on the relevance of supporting *liberal* democratic institutions. According to him, "[…] any country where the most powerful actors can agree on what genuine threats to democracy are (irrespective of whether these threats emanate from the right or the left, or from religious or secular ideologies) probably has such a strong democratic consensus that challenges to democracy will fail by themselves. Conversely, in highly polarized and unstable policies, characterized by deep moral disagreement, militant democracy might

make some sense, but the very facts of polarization and disagreement probably prevent the creation of a militant democracy. Everyone might be too concerned about the abuse of party bans for partisan purposes, for instance, to agree to have such measures available."

4 The only exception is probably the current administration of Orbán's FIDESZ in Hungary (Batory, 2016).

References

Akkerman, Agnes, Cas Mudde, and Andrej Zaslove. 2014. "How populist are the people? Measuring populist attitudes in voters," *Comparative Political Studies*, 47(9): 1324–53.

Akkermann, Tjitske. 2012. "The impact of radical right parties in government: a comparative analysis of immigration and integration policies in nine countries (1996–2010)," *West European Politics*, 35(3): 511–29.

Alonso, Sonia and Saro Claro da Fonseca. 2012. "Immigration, left and right," *Party Politics*, 18(6): 865–84.

Anria, Santiago. 2013. "Social movements, party organization, and populism: insights from the Bolivian MAS," *Latin American Politics and Society*, 55(3): 16–46.

Arditi, Benjamin. 2004. "Populism as a spectre of democracy: a response to Canovan," *Political Studies*, 52(1): 135–43.

Art, David. 2007. "Reacting to the radical right. Lessons from Germany and Austria," *Party Politics*, 13(3): 331–49.

Aslanidis, Paris and Cristóbal Rovira Kaltwasser. 2016. "Dealing with populists in government: the SYRIZA-ANEL coalition in Greece," *Democratization*, 23(6): 1077–91.

Bale, Tim. 2007. "Are bans on political parties bound to turn out badly? A comparative investigation of three 'intolerant' democracies: Turkey, Spain, and Belgium," *Comparative European Politics*, 5(2): 141–57.

Bale, Tim, Christoffer Green-Pedersen, André Krouwel, Kurt Richard Luther, and Nick Sitter. 2010. "If you can't beat them, join them? Explaining social democratic responses to the challenge from the populist radical right in Western Europe," *Political Studies*, 58(3): 410–26.

Bardi, Luciano, Stefano Bartolini, and Alexander H. Trechsel. 2014. "Responsive and responsible? The role of parties in twenty-first century politics," *West European Politics*, 37(2): 235–52.

Batory, Agnes. 2016. "Populists in government? Hungary's 'system of national cooperation,'" *Democratization*, 23(2): 263–82.

Cannon, Barry. 2014. "As clear as MUD: characteristics, objectives, and strategies of the opposition in Bolivarian Venezuela," *Latin American Politics and Society*, 56(4): 49–70.

Capoccia, Giovanni. 2005. *Defending Democracy: Reactions to Extremism in Interwar Europe*. Baltimore: Johns Hopkins University Press.

Capoccia, Giovanni. 2013. "Militant democracy: the institutional bases of democratic self-preservation," *Annual Review of Law and Social Science*, 9: 207–26.

Dahl, Robert. 1971. *Polyarchy: Participation and Opposition*. New Haven: Yale University Press.

Dahl, Robert. 1989. *Democracy and Its Critics*. New Haven: Yale University Press.

de la Torre, Carlos and Andrés Ortíz Lemos. 2016. "Populist polarization and the slow death of democracy in Ecuador," *Democratization*, 23(2): 221–41.

de Lange, Sarah Leah. 2012. "New alliances: why mainstream parties govern with radical right-wing populist parties," *Political Studies*, 60(4): 899–918.

Fallend, Franz and Reinhard Heinisch. 2016. "Collaboration as successful strategy against right-wing populism? The case of the centre-right coalition in Austria, 2000–2007," *Democratization*, 23(2): 324–44.

Formisano, Ronald. 2012. *The Tea Party: A Brief History*. Baltimore: The Johns Hopkins University Press.

Hawkins, Kirk A. 2011. *Venezuela's Chavismo and Populism in Comparative Perspective*. New York: Cambridge University Press.

Hawkins, Kirk A. 2016a. "Responding to radical populism: Chavismo in Venezuela," *Democratization*, 23(2): 242–62.

Hawkins, Kirk A. 2016b. "Chavismo, liberal democracy, and radical democracy," *Annual Review of Political Science*, 19: 311–29.

Houle, Christian and Paul D. Kenny. 2016. "The political and economic consequences of populist rule in Latin America," *Government and Opposition*, online. doi: http://dx.doi.org/10.1017/gov.2016.25.

Huber, Robert A. and Christian H. Schimpf. 2016. "Friend or foe? Testing the influence of populism on democratic quality in Latin America," *Political Studies*, 64(4): 872–89.

Kirshner, Alexander S. 2014. *A Theory of Militant Democracy: The Ethics of Combating Political Extremism*. New Haven: Yale University Press.

Kitschelt, Herbert. 2000. "Linkages Between Citizens and Politicians in Democratic Polities," *Comparative Political Studies*, 33(6–7): 845–79.

Kriesi, Hanspeter. 2014. "The populist challenge," *West European Politics*, 37(2): 361–78.

Linz, Juan. 1978. *The Breakdown of Democratic Regimes: Crisis, Breakdown and Reequilibration: An Introduction*. Baltimore: The Johns Hopkins University Press.

Linz, Juan and Alfred Stepan. 1996. *Problems of Democratic Transition and Consolidation: Southern Europe, South America, and Post-Communist Europe*. Baltimore: The Johns Hopkins University Press.

Lowenstein, Karl. 1937. "Militant democracy and fundamental rights, I," *The American Political Science Review*, 31(3): 417–32.

Mainwaring, Scott. 2012. "From representative democracy to participatory competitive authoritarianism: Hugo Chávez and Venezuelan politics," *Perspectives on Politics*, 10(4): 955–67.

Mair, Peter. 2009. "Representative versus responsible government," *MPIfG Working Paper*, 9/8: 1–19.

Morgan, Jana. 2011. *Bankrupt Representation and Party System Collapse*. University Park: Penn State University Press.

Mudde, Cas and Cristóbal Rovira Kaltwasser (eds). 2012. *Populism in Europe and the Americas: Threat or Corrective for Democracy?*, Cambridge: Cambridge University Press, 2012.

Mudde, Cas and Cristóbal Rovira Kaltwasser. 2013. "Populism," in Michael Freeden, Lyman Tower Sargent, and Marc Stears (eds), *The Oxford Handbook of Political Ideologies*. Oxford: Oxford University Press, 493–512.

Mudde, Cas and Cristóbal Rovira Kaltwasser. 2017. *Populism: A Very Short Introduction*. New York: Oxford University Press.

Müller, Jan-Werner. 2012. "Militant democracy," in Michel Rosenfeld and András Sajó, *The Oxford Handbook of Comparative Constitutional Law*. Oxford: Oxford University Press, 1253–69.

Müller, Jan-Werner. 2016. "Protecting popular self-government from the people? New normative perspectives on militant democracy," *Annual Review of Political Science*, 19: 249–65.

Ochoa Espejo, Paulina. 2015. "Power to whom? 'The people' between procedure and populism," in Carlos de la Torre (ed.), *The Promise and Perils of Populism: Global Perspectives*. Lexington: Kentucky University Press, 59–90.

O'Donnell, Guillermo. 1973. *Modernization and Bureaucratic-Authoritarianism: Studies in South American Politics*. Berkeley: Institute of International Studies, University of California.

O'Donnell, Guillermo, Philippe C. Schmitter, and Laurence Whitehead (eds). 1986. *Transitions from Authoritarian Rule: Southern Europe*, Vol. 1. Baltimore: The Johns Hopkins University Press.

Pappas, Takis. 2013. "Why Greece failed," *Journal of Democracy*, 24(2): 31–45.

Pappas, Takis and Paris Aslanidis. 2015. "Greek populism: a political drama in five acts," in Hanspeter Kriesi and Takis Pappas (eds), *European Populism in the Shadow of the Great Recession*. Colchester: ECPR Press, 181–96.

Perina, Rubén. 2015. *The Organization of American States as the Advocate and Guardian of Democracy: An Insider's Critical Assessment of its Role in Promoting and Defending Democracy*. Maryland: University Press of America.

Rosanvallon, Pierre. 2011. *Democratic Legitimacy: Impartiality, Reflexivity, Proximity*. Princeton: Princeton University Press.

Rovira Kaltwasser, Cristóbal. 2012. "The ambivalence of populism: threat and corrective for democracy," *Democratization*, 19(2): 184–208.

Rovira Kaltwasser, Cristóbal. 2014a. "Latin American populism: some conceptual and normative lessons," *Constellations*, 21(4): 494–504.

Rovira Kaltwasser, Cristóbal. 2014b. "The responses of populism to Dahl's democratic dilemmas," *Political Studies*, 62(3): 470–87.

Rovira Kaltwasser, Cristóbal and Paul Taggart. 2016. "Dealing with populists in government: a framework for analysis," *Democratization*, 23(2): 201–20.

Silva, Eduardo. 2009. *Challenging Neoliberalism in Latin America*. New York: Cambridge University Press.

Skocpol, Theda and Vanessa Williamson. 2012. *The Tea Party and the Remaking of Republican Conservatism*. Oxford: Oxford University Press.

Slater, Dan. 2013. "Democratic careening," *World Politics*, 65(4): 729–63.

Spruyt, Bramn, Gil Keepens, and Filip van Droogenbroeck. 2016. "Who supports populism and what attracts people to it?," *Political Research Quarterly*, 69(2): 335–46.

Stanley, Ben. 2016. "Confrontation by default and confrontation by design: strategic and institutional responses to Poland's populist coalition government," *Democratization*, 23(2): 263–82.

Stavrakakis, Yannis and Giorgos Katsambekis. 2014. "Left-wing populism in the European periphery: the case of SYRIZA," *Journal of Political Ideologies*, 19(2): 119–42.

Stoner, Kathryn and Michael McFaul (eds). 2013. *Transitions to Democracy: A Comparative Perspective*. Baltimore: The Johns Hopkins University Press.

Streeck, Wolfgang. 2014. *Buying Time: The Delayed Crisis of Democratic Capitalism*. London: Verso.

Szczerbiak, Alex and Paul Taggart (eds). 2008. *Opposing Europe? The Comparative Party Politics of Euroscepticism*. Oxford: Oxford University Press

Taggart, Paul. 2000. *Populism*. Buckingham: Open University Press.

Taggart, Paul and Cristóbal Rovira Kaltwasser. 2016. "Dealing with populists in government: some comparative conclusions," *Democratization*, 23(2): 345–65.

van Spanje, Joost. 2010. "Parties beyond the pale: why some political parties are ostracized by their competitors while others are not," *Comparative European Politics*, 8(3): 354–83.

Vibert, Frank. 2007. *The Rise of the Unelected: Democracy and the New Separation of Powers*. Cambridge: Cambridge University Press.

Waisbord, Silvio. 2011. "Between support and confrontation: civic society, media reform, and populism in Latin America," *Communication, Culture and Critique*, 4(1): 97–117.

PART IV

NORMATIVE
DEBATES

....

CHAPTER 26

POPULISM AND THE HISTORY
OF POPULAR SOVEREIGNTY

....

DUNCAN KELLY

INTRODUCTION

....

WORK on populism in political theory tends to react to upsurges in populist politics in the real world, though in practice, neither political theory nor overtly populist parties are very clear about what populism is or how to analyze it. This is hardly accidental. Populism always claims to speak for "the people," but precisely who "the people" are is never clear, because that is always the subject of political argument. In order to explain instances of populism, political theory usually provides potted genealogies of modern populism in order to frame an account of populist responses to contemporary crises. Unsurprisingly, therefore, studies of the subject have tended to come in waves, during which populism has seemed coterminous with the structural transformations affecting the modern, particularly liberal state. This has been especially true from the later 1970s onwards. Since then, the specter of a populist charge that modern politics has become little more than administered or "managed democracy" after the Cold War, for example, provides one powerful way of accounting for the myriad ways in which populism has helped transform modern political language into a battleground, pitching "the people" against "political elites." Similarly, one might register the magnitude of populist temptations in practice, by examining how those once on the radical left, after cultivating forms of structuralist Marxism to criticize the state in the 1970s, have since come to align their anti-capitalism with very public forms of cultural conservatism (cf. Wolin, 2008: 27, 156; Fraenkel, 1997: 66, 74, 83). Populism cuts across both theory and practice, and left and right, because it has no fixed ideological weight. And by reacting to crises and producing a certain, often explicitly emotive and typically aggressive or angry style of political engagement rather than resting on clearly defined social philosophies, it seems like populism is an aberration from conventional histories of political theory.

Still more recently, populism has been described not only as a form of anti-politics, a response to structural crises that connect its avowedly left (progressive) and right (ethnic) variants, but also as a political style intent on displacing foundational democratic commitments to political equality, with the search for new (and necessarily exclusive) forms of political unity instead (Urbinati, 1998: 110). The roots of these renewed attempts to unify, through populist language, particular segments of the citizens in a political community into a discrete political unity (one that it is often alleged has been forgotten by a mainstream political elite, whether because of race, gender, class, economic precarity, and so forth) has certainly sharpened in the aftermath of the welfare-state crises that belabored large democracies in the middle of the 1970s (see Purdy, 2016). Then there was the production of a worried report by the Trilateral Commission on *The Future of Democracy* and a series of panics about ungovernability, inflation, and unemployment. But its more determinate contemporary impact lies in the caching out of those stresses in the wake of the more recent global financial crisis from 2007 to 2008 (see Crozier, Huntington, and Watanuki, 1975; Streeck, 2013; Runciman, 2014). The dramatic rise in studies of populism since then, whether historical or theoretical, runs in parallel to the rise of anti-austerity parties in parts of the European left like PODEMOS or SYRIZA, or Tea Party radicalism and Donald Trump's presidential campaign on the right in the US. It also perceives the rise of authoritarian populisms in Hungary or Turkey, as being equally bound up with reflections on the causes of this global crisis and its implications. These populist movements in turn attempt to apportion blame for the unintended consequences (from mass migration and civil war to unemployment or automation) of major recent geopolitical entanglements and perceived threats to national security, particularly those that come through Africa and the Middle East. From these divergent interests, two different styles of populist reasoning about "the people" seem to emerge, particularly in America. One sees a political as well as a corporate elite whose sectional interests threaten the shared civic values that unite a diverse people within a nation. Think Bernie Sanders. Another aligns in more pointed fashion a critique of these avowedly "sinister" interests (though without reference to the Benthamite origins of such a term) to a more ethnically and culturally limited account of who "the people" really are. Think Donald Trump (Kazin, 2016).

Yet despite the huge levels of political complexity that are alluded to in such discussions of populist theory and practice, the structural direction of causality remains the same, and the nature of populist success routinely relies upon a series of simplifications to explain cause and effect. Reflections upon populism surge when populism seems most prevalent politically, and populism tends towards political prevalence at key moments of state crisis and uncertainty, however vaguely both are defined. This interconnection is often obscured by discussions of whether populism constitutes an ideology, but does provoke the sense that different styles of populism exist between nations and continents. The most obvious instance of this is an historical claim about the different character of American, Latin American, and European populisms. My claim in this chapter is more simple, namely that populism is always one possible response to the crises of modern democratic politics, but because modern democratic politics is premised upon claims about the history of popular sovereignty, the history of modern populism and the history of modern popular sovereignty are coterminous. This is a claim that undercuts the idea that we need to search for the roots of populism as an ideology, or that certain sorts of populism are necessarily more prevalent in certain regions, though does accept that certain styles of populism are more effective in certain national contexts of course. It simply seeks instead to reorient contemporary political theory, particularly in Europe and America, towards a shared history of popular sovereignty in order to recalibrate the longer-term foundations behind the different short-run judgments that routinely abound in the scholarly literature about populism.

Nevertheless, the modern political origins of the term do lie in the growth of a formally Populist Party in North America. As Michael Kazin has written, this means that we should probably distinguish between the Populism of the short-lived American party, and any notable political "style" of populism in the round, based on its capacity to persuade and its basis in some sort of opposition between an ill-defined notion of the people and an equally loose account of an elite who stand opposed to them (Kazin, 2007: 12–13, 39–40; Lasch, 1998: 531–2). Yet even though this latter opposition has long been crucial to discussions of populism in political theory, the former is actually part and parcel of a wider discourse about the origins of a distinctively modern American science of politics. The connections between these two areas, however, have in this context been relatively underexplored, so this chapter also considers them together. By so doing, one central claim is that modern American discussions of populism and the rise of a distinctively American science of politics are equally part of longer-standing debates about the nature of popular sovereignty. More importantly still, these discussions of popular sovereignty were transatlantic from the beginning, receiving their high point in the wake of the European revolutions of 1848 and registering a huge impact upon American political theory. The point of my attempt at an intellectual reconstruction of this relationship between political theory and populism is to show both that arguments about populism are actually part and parcel of mainstream histories of popular sovereignty, and that the distinction between a singularly American style of populism set against European populisms is simply false, a red herring for contemporary political theory. Similarly, the idea of a distinctive and exceptionalist science of American politics free from European influence, and vice versa, is another red herring. The relationship between populism and political theory is better located alongside more general histories of popular sovereignty and representative government. This provides the necessary background to understand how these histories are routinely reconstructed, reinterpreted, or memorialized to meet the demands of the contemporary moment.

THE POPULIST MOMENT

In his coruscating polemic from 1948, Richard Hofstadter famously declared the leading figure of the American Populist Party, William Jennings Bryan, to have a "torpor of the mind," with no real ideas of his own save the thought that all social problems were reducible to moral ones. From his pen, however, a moral language of reform signaled the necessary direction in which American populism could travel. Bryan built on the hope that Ignatius Donnelly had outlined in 1892, at the founding convention of the Populist Party in Omaha, to return political power from the government to "the plain people." Yet Bryan's so-called "Cross of Gold" speech at the Democratic Party convention in Chicago in early July, 1896, allied to his "detachment of intellectuality" would, according to Hofstadter, eventually be his undoing. Even as he was rapidly vaulted into position as both Democratic Presidential candidate, and later Woodrow Wilson's Secretary of State for War, many worried about the shape of his own understanding of what he was actually arguing for, save that current political elites didn't provide it (Hofstadter, 1962: 188ff., 191, 197). Many people still worry about what, if anything, lies beneath populist rage.

The moralizing strand behind political Populism and its compromise during the 1890s with Democratic Party politics was nevertheless both novel and banal. Later historical reconstruction has often tried to connect Populism with wider political tendencies, from Jacksonian democracy to New Deal liberalism, in order to give it greater intellectual ballast (Hicks, 1931). Yet the agrarian language of Jeffersonian liberalism that lay behind modern Populism had long been familiar terrain for the Democratic Party in America, and was simply rejuvenated in the electoral competition of the 1890s (Goodwyn, 1978). Populism wasn't new, even in its infancy, but those who later revived its history in response to contemporary political crises in the early 1930s (John Hicks), the later 1940s (Richard Hofstadter), or again in the 1960s and 1970s (Lawrence Goodwyn) continued to reconstruct the contexts of this moment in order to signal connections between past history and present politics, and perhaps to reflect upon the renewed possibility of third-party populism in America.

Nonetheless, Bryan's language did galvanize a party around some particular elements crucial to popular politics, most obviously (though there was hardly unity on the subject) the idea of bimetallism, whereupon a free silver currency might float against gold. This could offer a more egalitarian and farmer-friendly currency policy for the government than the golden "cross" upon which national as well as individual self-reliance was likely to be pilloried in his view if a gold standard was maintained (Kazin, 2007: 43, 45; for the speech, see "Official Proceedings of the Democratic National Convention, 1896": 224–34; and on Bryan specifically, Kazin, 2007b; cf. Ware, 2006, 74ff., who shows how close Bryan came to winning). In Bryan's hands, Populism become something analogous to an updated producerist ideology, predicated upon a claim about the "average" American before Americans routinely became "averaged" through surveys and censuses, and defined by a Christian moral language though not a Christian moral fundamentalism (Igo, 2008). It built explicitly on long-standing domestic discourses of Americanism, as well as retrofitted arguments about the ethics of work and organization derived from utopian socialism in Europe and ideas of the cooperative commonwealth from Saint Simon to Edward Bellamy and Henry George, which would subsequently return anew in debates about the New Deal on both liberal left and "America First" right (Guarneri, 1991: 394; Rossinow, 2008: 18ff.; Brinkley, 1995: 59, 144–5; Kazin, 2016).

The moral language through which a political community could be unified remained its principal focus, while languages of labor, production, national control, and anti-trust as well as anti-monopoly gained at least a foothold, if only for a short while. As a third party Populism quickly aligned with the gradual transition from a Southern to a Northern political force in Democratic Party politics, but what might have looked to be an original update of American agrarianism or progressivism, and its attempt to connect property ownership to citizenship and political education that could be continuously updated in new forms of cooperation, had some unusual results. Ideas about the national ownership of wealth became a means of avoiding both socialism and private monopoly, as private wealth was rendered artificial and plutocratic, while socialism as a language of cooperation was re-described as un-American in its statist interventionism, or so it seemed (Hofstadter, 1962: 194; Kazin, 2007a: 32–3, 39ff.; Ritter, 2010). Populism was incorporated into mainstream Democratic politics almost entirely, even if today it is more readily associated with the GOP.

Yet as the legacy of European utopian socialism in American contexts showed, there had for some time been a transatlantic conversation, both in theory and in practice, about the relationship between modern ideas of populism and the practice of modern politics based on the will of the people, or popular sovereignty. And this recognition challenges the idea that there was a domestic, one might even say nativist and straightforwardly exceptionalist American science of politics in this regard in the nineteenth century through which populism could be explained. We might agree with Dorothy Ross's powerful claim that in the origins of American social and political science we see continued attempts to naturalize American historical development and construct "models of the world that embody the values and follow the logic of the national ideology of American exceptionalism" (Ross, 1991: 38ff., 471; cf. Fries, 1973: 391–404). But those values and the attempt to naturalize them were part and parcel of a transatlantic conversation, largely about liberalism and democracy in fact, as much as it was developed by home-grown public moralists like Bryan (see Adcock, 2014). Indeed when Hofstadter was writing about Bryan in 1948, other American historians were reconsidering the legacy and memory of the revolutions of 1848 in Europe for the development of American political science, the American Civil War, and indeed American politics more broadly. Here the complicated entanglement of transatlantic ideas about popular sovereignty matters hugely, and has significant implications for how we connect the history of populist politics, as part of those debates, to contemporary political theories of populism.

Popular Sovereignty and the Legacies of 1848

The centenary of 1848 led some intellectual historians, notably Merle Curti and Carl Wittke, to appraise this conversation for themselves in ways different from

Hofstadter. Wittke focused attention on the German '48ers in the United States, emigrants who reconsidered some of the basic principles of American democracy. One of Wittke's characters, about whom he wrote a biography (which Curti reviewed positively), was the so-called "philosophical tailor," Wilhelm Weitling, a crucial figure in both the history of pre-Marxian communism and 1850s New York radicalism (see Wittke, 1948: 718ff., 724ff.; Wittke, 1950: 150ff., and ch. 9; this and the following section borrow from Kelly, 2016a: 115–32). Curti's social history of ideas by contrast focused attention on Lajos Kossuth, who came to New York in 1851 and was greatly feted. Indeed, the significance of the Hungarian revolt of 1848 to both Northern and Southern thinkers engaged in struggles over the Union was profound (Curti, 1949: esp. 211ff.). Penned as a short centennial essay on the American memory of 1848, "The Impact of the Revolutions of 1848 on American Thought" repeated themes Curti had earlier explored in 1935, noting the connections between John C. Calhoun's *Disquisition on Government* (Calhoun, 1851), which expounded the compact theory of Union, and Calhoun's awareness of attempts to foster a German confederacy, which he believed ought not to be an homogenized federation, not least because the German states were so various.

On May 28, 1848, Calhoun had written to Baron Friedrich von Gerolt, the Prussian minister-resident to Washington who had asked Calhoun's advice on how best to structure a German constitution, then under discussion in the Frankfurt Diet. "If France has taken the lead in pulling down the old government," Calhoun said, "it is reserved for Germany, if I do not mistake, to lead the more glorious task of constructing the new on true principles" (Curti, 1935: 478). Calhoun's own *Disquisition*, which was already being written in 1848, was grounded upon a distinction between a federal compact and a national one. The federal compact stressed the priority of the states in making (and perhaps unmaking), as well as monitoring the activities of any federal government over a nationality, even if grounded in the sovereign power of an American people that transcended the states (Calhoun, 1851: 113, 130ff., 162, 300ff.). For Calhoun, watching the German situation was less an opportunity to learn than a chance to teach what he had learned from older American debates he helped to initiate. These stretched back at least to the Virginia and Kentucky Resolutions of 1798, the nullification controversy of the late 1820s and early 1830s, and aligned with similar controversies that ranged compact theorists like Virginia's Beverley Tucker against nationalists like Joseph Story of the US Supreme Court (see O'Brien, 2004: 807, 824–33, 849–62, 921–37). Nonetheless, events in Germany suggested, even to as un-cosmopolitan a thinker as Calhoun, that American differences over interpreting the American Constitution could not be dissevered from contemporary European experience and thought. Populism was just as much part of this shared heritage, because it was part of the history of popular sovereignty.

Some historians, notably Timothy Roberts, have gone so far as to claim that a divided American response to the bloody revolutions of 1848 helped to create the Civil War (Roberts, 2009: 20). He notes how both North and South were perturbed by the developments in Paris, where revolutionary violence had given rise to demands that politics be restructured not merely by the abolition of monarchy (a demand Americans found congenial), but by altering social and class relations (alarming to almost all Americans). By contrast, Hungarians were thought of as the "Americans of Europe," and the charismatic Kossuth venerated as a symbol of how to assert national self-determination and destroy monarchical oppression by means of a national movement that was natural and organic, rather than artificially scripted and imposed. That had been the French way since the 1790s. Still, even Kossuth was controversial. His criticism of the Pope, the Jesuits, and the Hapsburg monarchy alarmed American Catholics, while his desire for an Anglo-American alliance annoyed the Irish. The Whigs in the South especially feared that Kossuth's popularity would push their natural voters towards the Democrats. Clearly, transatlantic connections could also have a major impact upon local and national party politics (Holt, 1999: 696ff., 717, 747; cf. Morrison, 2003: 111–32). Nonetheless the citizens of Little Rock, Arkansas, probably embodied the views of most Americans when they gave money to support the Hungarian nationalists as a way of expressing solidarity with those who resisted monarchical absolutism, something Americans had done generations earlier. Peoples could be unified through opposition to elites, and construct a common international heritage that way too.

The idea that practice should govern theory, not theory practice, was an old one, asserted during the American Revolution and passionately reasserted during the French Revolution when many Americans took the side of Edmund Burke (Roberts, 2005: 271ff.). The idea would be powerfully restated in the mid-twentieth century by émigrés like Hannah Arendt (1965: 42ff.) and Leo Strauss (1953). In the 1850s, however, one of the idea's most powerful advocates was George Bancroft in his multivolume *History of the United States*. There he contrasted the contemporary "crisis" in Europe, which "foreboded the struggles of generations," with the United States, where "the influences of time were molded by the creative force of reason, sentiment and nature." True to this, the American Revolution had been accomplished "with such benign tranquility, that even conservatism hesitated to censure," and had "substituted the irresponsible authority of a sovereign, [for] a dependent government emanating from the concord of opinion" (Bancroft, 1859–75: 12).

That such a sentiment would reconnect with later émigré narratives of the German origins of modern American political science is not so surprising, given that Bancroft was powerfully immersed in German Romantic scholarship. European and American debates about popular sovereignty continued through him. He had studied philology and theology at Göttingen with the conservative historian Arnold Heeren, whose scholarship explained how contemporary conditions in Germany might be understood through reflection upon the history of civilizations from ancient Greece onwards (Carr, 2012: 10, 17ff., 45, 48). Bancroft translated much of Heeren's work for an American audience, and particularly drew upon Heeren's double claim that the idea of a constitution was a background structure for the history of political theories, and that in post-revolutionary Europe what was needed was a return to either monarchies or republics, rather than republican monarchies or monarchical republics. Unclear, even confusing, to Heeren was the question of sovereignty. Was it really the case that "sovereignty" as absolute power might be either active or "dormant," as Rousseau had proposed (Heeren, 1836: 194; more recently, see Tuck, 2016)? If so, then to resolve the confusion—and this idea Bancroft supported—was less a focus on the "form" of the state (either as "machine" or "organism") and more a consideration of its "spirit" (Heeren, 1836: 196ff.). Implicitly though not necessarily, adopting such a view was to be partisan in the American debate over whether states were the arbiters of the federal compact or, instead, the sovereign people, whose views might be represented by a Supreme Court and whose unified "spirit" might make unconscionable the idea of a secession that would damage the integrity of the Union. The question of who constituted the people, so crucial to the theory and practice of populism in general, was the principal question in debates over popular sovereignty throughout the nineteenth century out of which modern populism emerged.

In part this was because the 1848 revolutions in Europe, which had made so much of making nations, had equally made Americans more aware of the issue of nationality. For some, American nationality had been long accomplished, perhaps by 1750, probably by 1776, but certainly by 1789. For others, this was a process only fortunately unaccomplished, since they believed that the American Union had never been a nation and ought not to be. For a minority, though one that would succeed in creating the Confederate States of America, the Union was blocking the healthy accomplishment of real nationalities, grounded in social experience and embodying the "spirit" which Heeren and other German thinkers had deemed indispensable. The ambiguous character of the people could find unification in debates about nationality, slavery, and popular sovereignty around the American Civil War.

A case in point was William Henry Trescot of South Carolina. He was a close student of American foreign policy who would later serve in the American embassy in London and be Assistant Secretary of State, and who was convinced that the events of 1848 required that policy to change (Trescot, 1849; Quigley, 2012). In 1850, however, he was thinking through the implications of the Mexican War, the Wilmot Proviso, and Henry Clay's bill that would lead, eventually, to the Compromise of 1850. Trescot was clear that this immediate "crisis," this "sectional jealousy" between North and South, had existed ever since the "formation of the government" and that the only reasonable course that might achieve Southern prosperity was "the formation of an independent nation" (Trescot, 1850: 7, 17; O'Brien, 2010: 82ff., 323–8). The "dissolution of the Union," he wrote, "is almost a historical necessity." A new state had to be formed, so that the Southern political economy might be free to structure itself unhindered (Trescot, 1850: 19; see too Bensel, 1990: 92ff.). But absorbing the territories annexed from Mexico, a process that quickened the controversy over race and slavery, had forced questions of legitimacy and popular sovereignty onto the political agenda in a new and complex fashion. Trescot's analysis was, nonetheless, relatively straightforward, though most arguments turned on the question of whether slavery or anti-slavery was part of the mental and cultural inheritance of the American people, and were part of a wider discourse about the place of religion in motivating political change (Voss-Hubbard, 1995: 159–84; Sehat, 2011: ch. 4). This debate did not go unnoticed abroad, especially in cultures where state formation and nationality was an urgent issue. When Southerners began to talk seriously of secession, Italian newspapers took bets on the dissolution of the union (Roberts, 2005: 274).

But the curious fact is that, both in the South and in the middle-class worlds of Europe, particularly in Hungary, those who pushed for change usually claimed themselves to be defensive patriots, rather than radicals or revolutionaries.

Political language was fluid. One could defend nationality and be for the Union, whether as a Northerner or a Southern Unionist. Or one could defend nationality, as Trescot did, and still be for secession. One could even be for secession without subscribing to the new principles of a historicist nationalism, and point to the resonant words of the Declaration of Independence, which nowhere mentioned nations. In the 1848 election (the first to take place in all states on the same day), the matter of "popular sovereignty," which had been raised by the Wilmot Proviso, was equally intermittent. The Democrats favored the idea, while the Whigs were carefully silent (Howe, 2007: 833; Childers, 2011: 48–70). Older ideas were still available, those which had worked during the American Revolution, the debate over the Constitution, and the quarrels between the Jeffersonians and the Federalists, ideas that stretched back to the Stuarts and the Glorious Revolution, deployed an earlier "patriot royalist" idiom (Nelson, 2011: 570ff.; Manin, 1994: 27–62). But there were also new ideas. For although the presumption of American exceptionalism was not, in itself, new, in the late eighteenth century Americans had thought themselves better than others. Such self-regard had then rested on the belief that Americans, as it turned out, were better at exercising those natural rights which all men were supposed to exercise. Yet by 1850, in the hands of Trescot and others, exceptionalism had come to mean something different. Americans (or Southerners) were now exceptional, because their social and economic experience was different and such a difference mandated unique political forms and values. Strictly, the idea of natural rights was now irrelevant and more overtly "populist" forms of reasoning took their place, constructing a vision of government as the servant of a self-constituted "people." As Abel P. Upshur had observed in the Virginia Constitutional Convention of 1829–1830, "*There are no original principles in Government at all … existing in the nature of things, to which Government must of necessity conform, in order to be either legitimate or philosophical. The principles of Government are those principles only, which the people who form the Government, choose to adopt and apply to themselves*" (quoted in O'Brien, 2004: 803). Even abolitionists were not immune to this logic. Wendell Phillips worried about the problem of coercing the South towards closer union, while others saw in secession a threat to established and conservative interests (Frederickson, 1968: 56ff.). There was no shared moral ground, in part because historicism said there could not be, and each side of the debate tried to capture the language of the people and the trajectory of popular sovereignty in order to justify itself.

So the mood did shift between 1848 and the early 1850s. The European revolutions had failed and reaction had taken hold, particularly under Louis Bonaparte, and Americans were less willing self-consciously to align with the idea of European revolution. As Daniel Howe has explained, American commercial and financial imperatives prompted a desire for European stability, not revolution, in the aftermath of war with Mexico (Howe, 2007: 795). (For one thing, European stability meant a greater demand for American cotton.) Arguably, Bonaparte's 1851 coup in Paris strengthened the forces for Union and weakened those who, earlier, had met in Nashville in 1850 to consider whether secession was a viable option. It became impolitic to associate secession with revolution, but the intellectual legitimacy and political practicality of dissociating secession from revolution was not self-evident. Many Northerners claimed it could not be done, while many Southerners suggested that it could (Roberts, 2005: 273–4, 276, 280ff.). If the lesson of the first French Revolution had been that revolution led to reigns of terror, the lessons of the 1830 and 1848 European revolutions were that revolutions led to reaction, and the tyranny created by reaction was always worse than the gains achieved by revolutionary fervor (Rohrs, 1994: 359–77). This thought lasted into the 1860s and then beyond the Civil War, and by 1865, revolution had become "anathema to many Northerners." It became important for them to stress that the war had not been a revolutionary event, that what had been striking about American political development had been its evenness, and that the war, as Orestes Brownson insisted, had not been about humanitarianism or even "the realization of liberty," but instead "the realization of the true idea of the state." In a postwar world it made sense to be at ease with such amorality and be content to observe the "twilight of humanitarianism" (Frederickson, 1968: ch. 12, esp. 187, 192ff.). But each of these populist constructions of a people were part and parcel of a wider argument about popular sovereignty and state unification, and they had been motivated by debates around particular moments of crisis—founding, revolution, civil war, and union.

POPULAR SOVEREIGNTY AND MODERN POLITICAL SCIENCE

If one lasting legacy of the 1848 revolutions in Europe was the development of a series of populist contests over nationality and popular sovereignty in both Europe and America, it is unsurprising that the origins of modern American political science have been thought to have their roots in the transmission of European political theory. As the nineteenth century developed, in fact, such arguments came to look more like manifest destiny. The relationships between space, time, and process that are the heart of popular sovereignty were given new form in this intermingling of transatlantic languages, as the various permutations of domestic electoral time merged with longer-term histories of popular sovereignty and representative government as historically inevitable, part of a shared liberal, even civilizational heritage, out of which populist attempts to simplify and clarify who constitutes "the people" would develop in both Europe and America.

Francis Lieber is habitually claimed to have been the first American political scientist, even before he became Professor of History and Political Science at New York's Columbia College in 1857 (Gunnell, 2006: 481). (His title, when he had been at South Carolina College, had been Professor of History and Political Economy.) As the emigré author of numerous discussions of the natural outgrowth of "national" sentiment during the American founding era, Lieber put American constitutionalism into a wider inter-national (his hyphenation was purposeful) and developmental narrative about the shape of modern politics predicated upon free trade and an account of democracy just as much beholden to its status as providential fact as had been that of his friend and correspondent, Alexis de Tocqueville. His ambivalent position on African-American slavery remained exactly that, just as the proposed unification of the people into a single unit by Populists and populists alike was based on racial exclusion, particularly in America though equally often just as clearly in the rest of the world (Lieber, 1868: 12, 18, 22). Constructing the people has always been an exercise in exclusion as much as inclusion, and populism simply amplifies this general issue in popular sovereignty.

The "constitution" itself "makes our [the American] polity a National Representative Republic," he said, meaning that a sense of nationality is determined by its constitutional and territorial framework (Lieber, 1868: 1, 17; cf. Curti, 1941: 275ff.). Feeling himself a part of this developing process, during the Civil War he reasoned out the implications of his standpoint for defining the laws of war between civilized states, enemy combatants, and guerillas in producing, very famously, his comment on *General Orders 100* and its "enthusiasm for fierce measures," as his most recent historian has put it (Witt, 2012: 181, 186, 232). This connects him back to another theorist of cosmopolitan nationalism formed in the revolutionary decade of the 1840s with whom he is regularly bracketed, Johan Kaspar Bluntschli, and who was another pioneering theorist of the rise of a certain sort of national popular sovereignty that could be judged at the bar of humanity itself (Giladi, 2012: 81–116).

In Lieber's hands, this led to a radical political intervention whose impact still lingers. He pushed for a more rooted, grounded, and radically national solution to the constitutional problems of federalism, union, and secession, understood from the perspective of what he saw as latent tendencies towards nationalization within the American "race." In fact, he argued, no other entity than the "United States collectively" had "ever been sovereign," so that the secessionist debates of 1860–1861 had literally made no sense (Lieber, 1881b: 98ff., 108). This would consolidate and entrench a nationalist and statist framework for understanding the American Union and, as Ross and others have suggested, helped lay the foundations of modern American political science as putatively exceptionalist. Not the smallest part of his radicalism was that Lieber welcomed the Civil War because it could bring forth the humanity of the American people and propel them into the ranks of higher forms of civilization, where leading nations should be judged (Lieber, 1838–9: 686). Lieber's logic was congenial to his colleague and correspondent Bluntschli.

Bluntschli was the doctoral supervisor of Herbert Baxter Adams, who in turn at Johns Hopkins became the unloved tutor of Woodrow Wilson. Alongside Lorenz von Stein, Bluntschli had influenced Wilson's theory of the separation between politics and administration. Wilson (1898, chs 7–8; for detail, see Rosser, 2010: 551ff.; Thompson, 2008: 119ff.) devoted two massive chapters to governmental reform in Germany and Switzerland in his book *The State*, and both were matters extensively considered by Bluntschli. And Bluntschli was also a figure, alongside Lieber, who developed arguments about international law and the laws of war between civilized, cosmopolitan states, arguments that would in turn also frame discussion of who was, or was not, part of an international as much as a domestic political community.

This link between Bluntschli and Lieber is discernible through *General Orders 100* (Lieber, 1881c: 245–74). As Lieber wrote to Bluntschli on April 16, and then again on June 2, 1866, upon receipt of the latter's text on laws of war, *"the national polity is the normal type of modern government"* and German nationalism as it had come to be defined in 1848 had been derailed by the doctrine of "state sovereignty," which had rendered constitutional monarchies illegitimate. Until the common purpose of establishing national polities was achieved, the future of both Europe and America remained in peril (Perry, 1882: 362, 365; also Giladi, 2012: 16–21). Thus, clarifying the relations between combatants and partisans on the battlefield had a wider purpose, and served as a proxy for articulating a broader theory of international relations based on the self-identification of the people with the nation. But equally like Lieber, Bluntschli was also an anti-Napoleonic writer concerned to develop a liberal theory of national, popular sovereignty in post-revolutionary Europe that could be distinguished from the French (Lieber, 1881a: 385; 1859: 394–7, 404). Furthermore, Lieber, Bluntschli, and most nineteenth-century political and legal theorists clearly presumed that because the state was the site of politics and war, it was therefore the focus for a law of nations. Both domestic and international politics required a reconceptualization of "the people" who were its subject matter, and of course European and American international law tended to apply a skewed measure of "civilization" as the standard upon which peoples would in turn be judged (see Rodogno, 2016).

Educated in post-revolutionary Europe, Bluntschli attended Bartold Niebuhr's lectures at the University of Bonn, where he was also tutored by Karl von Savigny, and so became deeply influenced by two of the chief sponsors of Romantic historicism. He worked first in Zurich, writing the brief that exiled Wilhelm Weitling by convincing "the court that Weitling's brand of communism meant revolution, guerilla warfare, and social chaos" (see Wittke, 1950: 80). He was then appointed to the Ludwig-Maximilian University of Munich in 1848, where he made his reputation as a political scientist, international lawyer, and theorist of war. His 1866 treatise *The Modern Laws of War of Civilized States* [*Das Moderne Kriegsrecht der Civilisierten Staaten*] was published in both French and German, and used by both sides during the Franco-Prussian War (see Bluntschli, 1874). At the same time, Bluntschli was revising the standard narrative of the rise of the modern nation state, seen through the lens of the history of political thought in German-speaking Europe, America, and beyond. Like Lieber later in America, this interest had arisen because he had also been compelled to take a stand on the issue of civil war, in his case the *Sonderbundkrieg* in his native Switzerland, a struggle that erupted briefly between Protestant and Catholic cantons in 1847. Later he felt compelled to elaborate a theory of the state that could explain the Europe-wide revolutionary zeal for national self-determination evident in its wake during 1848 and after (in general, see Lerner, 2012; Bluntschli, 1865: 304–41).

For that to work, on Bluntschli's scheme so-called "civilized" nation states and the international system they were part of were motivated by the "highest political idea" of liberalism, which was "not nationality, but humanity." True politics, Bluntschli wrote, was thus always "liberal" in essence, and his liberal concept of the state had a "psychological character" (Bluntschli, 1876: 601, 605ff.). With that in mind, a host of nineteenth-century boundary issues could be conceptually as well as practically controlled. These included the boundaries of the international, of the civilized, and of race and of honor, all comprehended within the framework of an updated international law based on a liberal vision of popular sovereignty as national sovereignty (Koskenniemi, 2004: ch. 3). What Bluntschli and Lieber principally show about the mid-century development of American political science, however, is the way in which very wide-ranging intellectual foundations for thinking about the nature of the modern federal nation state in the aftermath of the American and French Revolutions primarily, and the revolutions of 1848 secondarily, could be encompassed by a state-led and nationally focused narrative, again providing a statist foundation for popular sovereignty. He was already well aware of the populist challenges that could result from crises to this state form, having long thought of radical socialism in precisely such terms.

When publishing his three-volume *Lehre vom modernen Staat*, beginning in 1852, Bluntschli separated the concept of the state as law (*Staatsrecht*), from the normative dimensions of its forward-looking agency (*Politik*), and re-combined them to form a general theory of the state (*Allgemeine Staatslehre*). This was his way of reconciling the twin dimensions of *Iustitia* and *Salus Populi* as the foundations of the modern state, as it moved and was directed by its particular personality. In Bluntschli's formulation, that personality was given material rather than artificial form through the figure of the constitutional monarch, a figure transposable in the American case on to the figure of the president.

Both Bluntschli and Lieber suggested that national self-determination was natural, but the process of civilization and national self-development was uneven, so that while civilization developed towards the good ends of humanity there were bound to be tensions both within and between nations along this cosmopolitan path. Theirs was a nationally grounded, if highly unequal, form of cosmopolitan liberalism, but they meant by cosmopolitanism a form of statist inter-nationalism. For both, partisans and populist threats could come in the form of Communist renegades or anti-Unionist Confederates in states ravaged by civil war. Similarly, both recognized the wider dangers posed to democratic republics by demagoguery and modern political parties, which was why they supported indirect (or representative) democracy as one of the principled achievements of European modernity. This in turn was something the American Revolution had usefully found a constitutional form to embody (Bluntschli, 1876: 382). Populism in any of these forms threatened the unity of the people under their nationally conceived visions of popular sovereignty, but they recognized also that populist challenges were part and parcel of that normal, or natural history in any case. So in order to buttress social cohesion and constitutional order, what both proposed was a state that was a federal union, one that was less than a Hobbesian perfect (artificial) unity, but more than mere concord. As Bluntschli put it, a "union is always imperfect when it is merely personal," but a "higher unity is to be found in the so-called Real Union, which is related to Federation, as Personal Union is to Confederation" (Bluntschli, 1901: 271–2). That concern with federal union, explicit in its anti-Hobbesianism, also served another purpose.

For Bluntschli, the intellectual origins of the modern state could not be sought in Hobbes, because the genealogy of sovereignty Hobbes was part of led directly towards Rousseau, and then the French revolutionary terror (Bluntschli, 1876: 601). In fact, according to Bluntschli's narrative, the French Revolution was the counter-revolution of modernity, whose source in Hobbes made sense given that he was often thought of as the counter-revolutionary theorist of seventeenth-century absolutism. If the French model of sovereignty from Rousseau was not the model to follow, therefore, Bluntschli's own counter-narrative located the origins of the modern European state in the reforms of Frederick II of Prussia (Bluntschli, 1876: 547). So both Bluntschli and Lieber sought an alternative model of federal nationalism in Europe, one that avoided the problem of sovereignty that had afflicted European discourse since Hobbes (Bluntschli, 1901: 301ff., 107). And looking beyond Europe, both Bluntschli and Lieber alighted, very early, on the theme of American exceptionalism but worked to combine it within this cyclical story, such that combined claims of nationality and humanity were achieved in an American science of politics that was already part of the history of modern representative government (Bluntschli, 1901: 509).

According to these early founders, a modern American science of politics appeared in a world governed by a new principle, nationality, which was set within a cosmopolitanism of nations (Bluntschli, 1901: 482). This form of representative democratic nationalism was then embodied in the mid-century experience of American political development, whose transatlantic connections between 1848 and the Civil War were preoccupied with exploring the claims of inter-nationalist or cosmopolitan humanity, as they were advanced or vitiated by revolution. After the Civil War, matters changed. What had been both cosmopolitan and inter-national became more preoccupied with what was more obviously domestic. What came to be "exceptional" in terms of the development of American political science was therefore a rejection of an earlier, and perhaps more radical, commitment to "humanitarian democracy." Both were liberal visions, both were statist and nationalist, but one presumed to locate the United States within the framework of cosmopolitan humanity, the other simply affirmed the historical uniqueness of the American state. For example, the hyperbolic-sounding formulations of Orestes Brownson suggested that after the Civil War a fear of "Jacobin democracy" seemed to require the construction of a new, Lieber-like model of territorial democracy, one that could avoid the problems of traditional theories of sovereignty. The construction of such a model, however, necessarily "thwarted the drive for 'humanitarian democracy'" that the American model seemed initially to promise (Frederickson, 1968: 190, 198). Now, just as then, accounts of cosmopolitanism that revert back to this older idiom of humanitarian democracy wish to uphold avowedly liberal claims. But equally now, just as then, the question of who constitutes the people in a national or indeed a cosmopolitan perspective remains the crucial question, and the contrast between the people and a ruling elite, one that was at the heart of American Populism, was in turn part of this wider history of popular sovereignty. It has remained absolutely critical to it.

POPULAR SOVEREIGNTY AND POPULISM

Nineteenth-century theories of popular sovereignty, then, were primarily concerned with the connections between nationality and the indirect sovereignty of modern representative government. In this they were the logical heirs to claims about the national foundations of popular sovereignty that were elaborated by Sieyès during the brief decade of his major political writing around the French Revolution. Bluntschli in fact develops Sieyès's anti-Jacobin theory of constituent power and complex political representation, but simultaneously proposes to reintroduce it into the nineteenth century as popular sovereignty governed by the principles of peaceful federation that follow on from a revised principle of nationality (Kelly, 2016b: 270–96). He sought, that is, to reintroduce a peace that had been shattered by the French Revolution, and render it less susceptible to the fanaticism of political extremes. Furthermore, he tried to explain unity in the modern state as the result of a process of deliberation rather than the imposition of a general will. In its tentative ways, this clearly mapped onto the fluid legal and cartographic boundaries of sovereign territories in central Europe in the nineteenth century (Weichlein, 2005). In fact, Bluntschli might even constitute an unacknowledged foundation for contemporary democratic theory in its attempt to reconnect popular sovereignty with indirect forms of deliberative and federal politics, through which populist appeals to sovereign statehood might come to be rejected (Manin, 1987: 346ff.). But as Harold Laski suggested when writing about the theory and practice of popular sovereignty after the Great War, "certainly the history of popular sovereignty will teach its students that the announcement of its desirability in nowise coincides with the attainment of its substance" (Laski, 1919: 215). Representative government has never been able to insulate itself from structural crises, and its deeply ambiguous quality renders it permanently susceptible to populist challenge and critique, because populism is really just another term of art that structures certain explanations about the limits to modern politics.

Modern political theorists have recently tried to develop new arguments about the apparent resurgence of populism over the past forty years, seeking to explain something that might connect the rise of authoritarian right-wing political protest from the UKIP in Britain and the Front National in France, to the American Tea Party or Hungarian authoritarian constitutionalism. They have done so by constructing a vision of populism as the anti-democratic shadow, or illiberal mirror, of modern representative democracy; it's ever-present dark side almost (Müller, 2013; 2016; Webb and Bale, 2014: 961–2, 967). Political scientists have also, though less often, examined radical left party political criticisms of national representative government under the heading of populism, grounded in what they call the "demand side" contexts of poor macroeconomic performance more than the "supply side" failures of party politics itself (March and Rommerskirchen, 2015: 40–1, 48). Left and right forms of populism remain here, but both are responses to perceived as well as real structural failures. To that extent, though, this simply means that populism is just one sort of response to the ongoing tendencies towards crisis or disaffection in modern representative government, no more and no less. In fact, in the minds of voters such criticisms often coalesce even when the questions posed to them are not explicitly about either economic performance or party politics, such as in the recent British referendum that by a margin of 52 percent to 48 percent voted for what has become known as "Brexit." After the referendum, however, it seems clear that although disaffection with some ideas about what the European Union does or doesn't lie behind many who decided to vote leave, for others too, rather more conventional forms of disaffection in a country still hugely divided upon class and economic lines across and between its various regions played a more obvious role. And although many writers move quickly to distinguish American Populism from other forms of lower-case populism in Europe and elsewhere, the relationship between populism and the inequalities that are inscribed into the basic logic of representation that underpins modern democracy means that it is both easy to exaggerate the novelties of modern populism on the one hand, and difficult to explain how populism might constitute something more than just another form of the reactionary rhetoric on the other (Hirschman, 1998). As part and parcel of popular sovereignty and representative government, populism is but one critical strand of that history, which exploits the fundamental tension between "the people" and the so-called "elite" who rule in their name.

In the early 1890s, the Populist Party stood against rich Eastern "elites" in America, claiming the desirability as well as the necessity of the referendum and popular initiative in politics (Rooduign, 2014: 580; cf. Johnson, 2012: 2). Yet the moral valence of a "pure" people set against a "corrupt" elite offers a most basic conceptual framework, explaining the normative "thinness" of populism considered as political ideology (Mudde, 2004: 543; in general, Mudde, 2007). Indeed, the tense relationship between mass and elite has been a long-standing refrain in debates about democracy from the ancient Greeks onwards (Ober, 1998). In the ancient world, for example, the demagogue might technically be neutral while still remaining part of an elite, with popular sovereignty filtered through procedural rotation between different sorts of office holding. As the practice of its democratic politics changed, however, this reconciliation quickly morphed into an opposition between the responsible statesman versus the partial and typically populist demagogue, which has in turn structured much modern political thinking that opposes prudence with rabble-rousing. In this worldview, populism is inherently demagogic and negative towards whatever existing rulers have to say (cf. Finley, 1962: 3–24; Lane, 2012: 197–200).

But whether demagogues, populists, or demagogic populists are in charge, the idea that politics in any moderately complex system just concerns the circulation of particular elites was clearly generalized by the time of the later nineteenth century amid the rise of mass democracy. This was also a period dominated by so-called elite theories of democracy. At this point, elite theories were designed not so much to defend a classical vision of democracy against contemporary politics, one that seemed somewhat ideal-ized, grounded upon the pure will of a homogeneous people (Schumpeter, 1942); nor were they designed to criticize contemporary elites in the name of some other vision of "the people." Instead they aimed to support a general claim about politics particu-larly, and organizational life more broadly, such that problems of coordination and organization lead to the formation of elites or oligarchies which tend naturally to repro-duce themselves. On this reading, populist demagogues, responsible statesmen, or socialist revolutionaries are part of the same basic structure as anyone else, elites seek-ing after power or coming to power because that's how organizational life works (see Femia, 2001). Elite theorists of democracy claimed to offer truths about human nature and competition, but they were most explicitly developed as part of a wider critique of Marxism, which at this point was re-described precisely as another instance of populist demagoguery. Curiously though, during the 1890s when Marxism was a dramatically powerful political force scarcely touched by the political charge of the elite theorists, the scientific status of its economic theory had been critically weakened by them, particu-larly because elite theory had aligned itself with new, marginalist theories of value and utility as well as optimal distribution. This led them to focus intensely on the impossi-bilities of collectivist planning amid the complexity of understanding intersubjective, as opposed to individual preferences and wants, and the impossibility of freedom without organization, and thus without elites. Writers such as Vilfredo Pareto had been develop-ing the two arguments in tandem for several years, alongside modern economists like Carl Menger and Léon Walras. They would be refined and updated by Austrian econo-mists like Ludwig von Mises and Friedrich Hayek through the twentieth century (see Tuck, 1993: 75ff.).

Yet the interplay of ideas was certainly complex. For while elite theorists chal-lenged Marxism as a valid economic theory of value and utility, both elite theory and Marxism in their turn challenged particular versions of modern populism on left and right respectively—so much so that towards the end of the nineteenth century, anti-Marxism, positive Populism, and thereafter more generally populist styles of political theory seemed to coalesce independently around a shared critique of various, pejora-tively "wrong" kinds of "elite." Whether monopolies, trusts and cartels, big businesses, or some notion of a political class the pattern repeated itself. Elitism was part of the basic structure, or hidden logic, governing populism itself, even while populism offered the promise of bypassing an apparently obstructive (because indirect) form of representa-tive politics, claiming to be able to superimpose the demos above politicians and their own special interests, and to create "the people" as the one true elite (Urbinati, 1998: 113, 119). However, where American Populism pitted agrarian producers against financial or landed elites, favoring a search for the average American and a critique of big gov-ernment, modern populism (whether in the form of a support for paternalistic leaders as has occurred in many Latin American countries, or as part of a strategy by political parties and trades unions in continental Europe) offers the possibility of widening the scope of the people versus elites into a much broader, and potentially infinite space. (For the American story, see Fine, 1964: 133, 234, 301ff., 309; and on the opposition between agrarianism and trade unionism in American and European thought, see Kloppenberg, 1986: 218.)

By this time, Marxism had, of course, in its theory of the dictatorship of the proletariat in the aftermath of 1848 literally re-described an ancient model of politics into a modern idiom, making itself almost populist *avant la lettre*. What else was the dictatorship of the proletariat after all, if not rule by the poor majority, and what else was that if not an attempt to re-describe a particular class in universal terms, who were both the subject of politics and the only hope of its future realization in the realm of true freedom? So Marxist and socialist politics retained a profound emotional sense of hope and possibility by universalizing the proletariat and promising to overcome elitism into the future, but it did so just as the economic theory upon which it was based had been undercut and on the basis that the true elite was really the mass of the people. Furthermore, its attempt to relocate the dictatorship of the proletariat into a hitherto unspecified time and space in the future would become the subject of major criticism in the early twentieth century, particularly in the work of Carl Schmitt. His alternative, anti-Marxist genealogy of the idea of dictatorship and its relationship to liberal models of popular sovereignty created yet another political possibility, one which saw the challenge of modern politics as investing the people with a quasi-mystical force as the foundation of political legitimacy, but who, nevertheless, were given political form only when they were represented by political elites who could claim to speak in their name (Kelly, 2017: 217–44).

Many of these forms of political theory effectively invest a modern, secular idea of "the people" with the same sort of mystical force that was drawn from traditional political theology, conjuring them up through ideas of representation and the politically symbolic, but giving them voice only through the figure of a representative sovereign ruler (Kantorowicz, 2012; Lefort, 1988). The once mystical body of the sovereign king is transposed into the newly sovereign body of the people, the real force of political decision remains with the sovereign political ruler, and the real hope for political equality is pressed into the realm of the future. Yet because the history of populisms is also a part and parcel of such complex histories and re-descriptions of modern popular sovereignty, some radical theorists have recently attempted to divest the theological from the people in order (metaphorically) to liberate them. They suggest that populism, broadly understood, is simply the attempt to define "the people," and that is precisely what the concept of the political refers to (Laclau, 2007; for criticism, Arato, 2013: 153, 156–7; also Colliot-Thélène, 2011: 131, 135). Populism on this reading simply is the political. Others, by contrast, suggest that the real power of these mystical, even mythical origins of the collective construction of the people comes from the overwhelming challenge they pose to those who wish to reconstruct popular sovereignty under modern democracies as the pursuit of rational deliberation that relies upon an adherence to abstract constitutional principles of equality and right. They do so to try and prompt the development of a powerful and progressive mythology on the left, which might take the place of those posited by the authoritarian right (cf. Canovan, 2003: 93–4, 137–8; Habermas, 1997: 95ff., 464–5, 470). But such binaries and the mythologies that so often lie behind these discussions of populism in political theory cannot be resolved at the level of normative speculation alone, for there must be some reckoning with the historical record of the ways in which these values that shape our contemporary political choices have been constructed through the development of modern democratic politics and popular sovereignty. Only this can shape the quality of our current demands and gauge the possibility of them really enacting change, a central question that lies behind many contemporary debates about "realism" in political theory (cf. Williams, 2007: 9, 82–3, 92–3; Dunn, 1979: 81, 84, 90, 98–9; Rossi and Sleat, 2014: 689–701; Diamond, 1995: 42–3, 55, 62, 351).

One might thus posit the claim that it is precisely the responsive character of populism, whether from right or left, that helps to rouse "the people" from their slumbers and enact their sovereignty under conditions of state crisis or political uncertainty, before returning to their drowsy state once more as their rulers cycle through the usual procedures and practices of modern politics (cf. Tuck, 2016). If so, that makes populism a mainstream component part of modern political life, and thus makes discussions of populism more interesting, because more directly related to historical discussions in political theory about the relationship between the people, sovereignty, and political economy. That thought might also provide a longer-term perspective on the way that such clear members of plutocratic elites as Donald Trump, for example, can successfully run a presidential campaign casting themselves as somehow independent of whatever shadowy "elite" the political elite is taken to consist of, and provide more scope for comparing this to the sort of left-wing "populism" pursued by Bernie Sanders. The power of money in modern American politics has had many such perverse and disorienting representation effects, but both responses are two of the possible outcomes of longer-term structural crises faced by the American state since the 1970s at least (Gilens, 2013; Mayer, 2016).

Unsurprisingly, the one area around which Trump and Sanders supporters have routinely been aligned is a shared sense of disenchantment directed towards the promises of global free trade from those who have been ill-treated by it (Gilman, 2016). Education levels are routinely discussed at this point, to differentiate supporters and critics, and not only in the US, but also in Britain around Brexit, but these debates obfuscate deeper and more structural political problems (Runciman, 2016). All that this really means here, though, is that populism is one possible response to the general political consequences of modern representative government based on popular sovereignty in a world of economic competition, and that has an even longer history. It might be possible to see populism as its ever-present, darker shadow, but that is simply also to say that it is part and parcel of mainstream political theory across Europe and America, attempting to engage in its own forms of political and ideological simplifications, just like any other political theory. For instance, populism suggests a clear and present "people," when the reality is anything but; expresses a desire for procedural and institutional action on their behalf, when the possibility is anything but clear; and opposes a corrupt elite to the apparent purity of the people, when neither the idea of a ruling political class in charge of a singular entity called the state, nor the existence of a pure and homogeneous people, is obvious at all. (On these populist "simplifications," see Rosanvallon, 2011; Müller, 2014.) For political theory, populism is both a political style geared towards simplification and expressive engagement, but therefore also a political problem, because in practice flirting with populist styles, particularly in times of crisis, is hardly exceptional (Moffit and Tormey, 2014: 387, 393). If it is simply a recognizable style and tactic for any politician under the right circumstances, it would mean populism is neither more nor less than part and parcel of the mainstream theory and practice of modern representative democracy and popular sovereignty in all its messy, historical complexity. That is all this chapter has tried to show.

REFERENCES

Adcock, R. 2014. *Liberalism and the Emergence of American Political Science: A Transatlantic Tale*. Oxford: Oxford University Press.

Arato, A. 2013. "Political theology and populism," *Social Research*, 80(1): 143–72.

Arendt, H. 1965. *On Revolution*. New York: Viking.

Bancroft, G. 1859–75. *History of the United States: From the Discovery of the Continent*, Vol. 4. Boston: Little Brown.

Bensel, R. F. 1990. *Yankee Leviathan: The Origins of Central State Authority in America, 1859–1877*. Cambridge: Cambridge University Press.

Bluntschli, J. K. 1865. "Die Schweiz," in J. K. Bluntschli and K. Brater (eds), *Deutsches Staats-Wörterbuch*, Vol. 9. Stuttgart and Leipzig: n.p., 304–41.

Bluntschli, J. K. 1874 [1866]. *The Modern Laws of War of Civilized States*, 2nd edn. Nordlingen: C. H. Beck.

Bluntschli, J. K. 1876. *Lehre vom modernen Staat*, Vol. 3. Stuttgart: J. G. Cotta.

Bluntschli, J. K. 1901. *The Theory of the State* [1885] 3rd edn, trans. from the 6th German edn. Oxford: Clarendon Press.

Brinkley, A. 1995. *The End of Reform*. New York: Vintage.

Calhoun, J. C. 1851. *Disquisition on Government*, ed. R. Crallé. Columbia: S. C. Johnston.

Canovan, M. 2003. *The People*. Oxford: Polity.

Carr, N. 2012. "Romanticism and modernity in American historical narrative, 1830–1920," PhD diss., University of Cambridge.

Childers, C. 2011. "Interpreting popular sovereignty: a historiographical essay," *Civil War History*, 57: 48–70.

Colliot-Thélène, C. 2011. *La démocratie sans «demos»*. Paris: PUF.

Crozier, M., S. Huntington, and J. Watanuki [The Trilateral Commission]. 1975. *The Crisis of Democracy*. New York: New York University Press.

Curti, M. 1935. "John C. Calhoun and the unification of Germany," *American Historical Review*, 40: 476–8.

Curti, M. 1941. "Francis Lieber and nationalism," *Huntington Library Quarterly*, 4: 263–92.

Curti, M. 1949. "The impact of the revolutions of 1848 on American thought," *Proceedings of the American Philosophical Society*, 93: 209–15.

Diamond, C. 1995. *The Realistic Spirit*. Cambridge: MIT Press.

Dunn, J. 1979. *Political Obligation in Historical Perspective*. Cambridge: Cambridge University Press.

Femia, J. 2001. *Against the Masses*. Oxford: Oxford University Press.

Fine, S. 1964. *Laissez-Faire and the General Welfare State*. Ann Arbor: University of Michigan Press.

Finley, M. 1962. "Athenian demagogues," *Past and Present*, 21: 3–24.

Fraenkel, B. 1997. "Confronting neoliberal regimes," *New Left Review*, I/226: 57–92.

Frederickson, G. M. 1968. *The Inner Civil War: Northern Intellectuals and the Crisis of the Union*. New York: Harper and Row.

Fries, S. 1973. "*Staatstheorie* and the new American science of politics," *Journal of the History of Ideas*, 34: 391–404.

Giladi, R. 2012. "A different sense of humanity: occupation in Francis Lieber's code," *International Review of the Red Cross*, 94: 81–116.

Gilens, M. 2013. *Affluence and Influence*. Princeton: Princeton University Press.

Gilman, N. 2016. "Technoglobalism and its discontents," *The American Interest*, 12(2).

Goodwyn, L. 1978. *The Populist Moment*. Oxford: Oxford University Press.

Guarneri, C. 1991. *The Utopian Alternative: Fourierism in Nineteenth-Century America*. Ithaca: Cornell University Press.

Gunnell, J. 2006. "The founding of the American Political Science Association: discipline, profession, political theory, and politics," *American Political Science Review*, 100: 479–86.

Habermas, J. 1997. *Between Facts and Norms*. Oxford: Polity.

Heeren, A. 1836 [1821]. *Historical Treatises … on the Rise, Progress, and Practical Influence of Political Theories, and on the Preservation of Monarchical Principles in Modern Europe*, trans. George Bancroft. Oxford: D. A. Talboys.

Hicks, J. D. 1931. *The Populist Revolt*. Minneapolis: University of Minneapolis Press.

Hirschman, A. 1998. *The Rhetoric of Reaction*. Cambridge: Harvard University Press.

Hofstadter, R. 1962 [1948]. *The American Political Tradition*. London: Jonathan Cape.

Holt, M. 1999. *The Rise and Fall of the American Whig Party: Jacksonian Politics and the Onset of the Civil War*. Oxford: Oxford University Press.

Howe, D. W. 2007. *What Hath God Wrought: The Transformation of America, 1815–1848*. Oxford: Oxford University Press.

Igo, S. 2008. *The Averaged American*. Cambridge: Harvard University Press.

Johnson, S. 2012. "When populism is sound," *New York Times*, March 15: 2.

Kantorowicz, E. 2012. *The King's Two Bodies*. Princeton: Princeton University Press.

Kazin, M. S. 2007a. *The Populist Persuasion*. Ithaca: Cornell University Press.

Kazin, M. S. 2007b. *A Godly Hero*. New York: Anchor.

Kazin, M. S. 2016. "Trump and American populism," *Foreign Affairs*, June 10.

Kelly, D. 2016a. "Popular sovereignty as state theory in nineteenth-century Europe," in Q. Skinner and R. Bourke (eds), *Popular Sovereignty in Historical Perspective*. Cambridge: Cambridge University Press, 270–96.

Kelly, D. 2016b. "Nationalism and cosmopolitan humanity in mid-nineteenth-century American political science," in J. Isaac, M. O'Brien, J. Ratner-Rosenhagen, and J. T. Kloppenberg (eds), *The Worlds of US Intellectual History*. Oxford: Oxford University Press, 115–32.

Kelly, D. 2017. "Carl Schmitt's political theory of dictatorship," in J. Meierhenrich and O. Simons (eds), *The Oxford Handbook of Carl Schmitt*. Oxford: Oxford University Press, 217–44.

Kloppenberg, J. T. 1986. *Uncertain Victory*. Oxford: Oxford University Press.

Koskenniemi, M. 2004. *The Gentle Civilizer of Nations: The Rise and Fall of International Law, 1870–1960*. Cambridge: Cambridge University Press.

Laclau, E. 2007. *On Populist Reason*. London: Verso.

Lane, M. 2012. "The origin of the statesman-demagogue distinction in and after ancient Athens," *Journal of the History of Ideas*, 73(2): 179–200.

Lasch, C. 1998. s.v. "Populism," in R. W. Fox and J. T. Kloppenberg (eds), *A Companion to American Thought*. Oxford: Blackwell, 531–2.

Laski, H. J. 1919. "The theory of popular sovereignty: I," *Michigan Law Review*, 17(3): 201–15.

Lefort, C. 1988. "The permanence of the theologico-political," in *Democracy and Political Theory*, trans. D. Macey. Oxford: Polity, 213–55.

Lerner, M. 2012. *A Laboratory of Liberty: The Transformation of Political Culture in Republican Switzerland, 1750–1848*. Leiden: Brill.

Lieber, F. 1838–9. *Manual of Political Ethics*, Vol. 2. Boston: Charles C. Little and James Brown.

Lieber, F. 1859. *On Civil Liberty and Self-Government*. Philadelphia: J. B. Lippincott.

Lieber, F. 1868. *Fragments of Political Science on Nationalism and Inter-Nationalism*. New York: Charles Scribner.

Lieber, F. 1881a [1849]. "Anglican and Gallic liberty," in D. C. Gilman (ed.), *Miscellaneous Writings of Francis Lieber*, Vol. 2. Philadelphia: J. B. Lippincott, 371–88.

Lieber, F. 1881b [1861]. "What is our Constitution?" in D. C. Gilman (ed.), *Miscellaneous Writings of Francis Lieber*, Vol. 2. Philadelphia: J. B. Lippincott, 89–123.

Lieber, F. 1881c [1863]. "Instructions for armies in the field: general orders No. 100," in D. C. Gilman (ed.), *Miscellaneous Writings of Francis Lieber*, Vol. 2. Philadelphia: J. B. Lippincott, 245–74.

Manin, B. 1987. "On legitimacy and political deliberation," *Political Theory*, 15(3): 338–68.

Manin, B. 1994. "Checks, balances and boundaries: the separation of powers in the constitutional debate of 1787," in B. Fontana (ed.), *The Invention of the Modern Republic*. Cambridge: Cambridge University Press, 27–62.

March, L. and C. Rommerskirchen. 2015. "Out of left field: explaining the variable electoral success of European radical left parties," *Party Politics*, 21(1): 40–53.

Mayer, J. 2016. *Dark Money*. New York: Doubleday.

Moffit, B. and S. Tormey. 2014. "Rethinking populism," *Political Studies*, 62: 381–97.

Morrison, M. A. 2003. "American reaction to European revolutions, 1848–1852: sectionalism, memory and the revolutionary heritage," *Civil War History*, 49: 111–32.

Mudde, C. 2004. "The populist zeitgeist," *Government and Opposition*, 39(4): 542–63.

Mudde, C. 2007. *Populist Radical Right Parties in Europe*. Cambridge: Cambridge University Press.

Müller, J-W. 2013. "Defending democracy within the EU," *Journal of Democracy*, 24(2): 138–49.

Müller, J-W. 2014. "The people must be extracted from within the people," *Constellations*, 21(4): 483–93.

Müller, J-W. 2016. *What is Populism?* Pennsylvania: University of Pennsylvania Press.

Nelson, E. 2011. "Patriot royalism: the Stuart monarchy in American political thought, 1769–1775," *William and Mary Quarterly*, 68: 533–72.

O'Brien, M. 2004. *Conjectures of Order: Intellectual Life and the American South, 1810–1860*, Vol. 2. Chapel Hill: University of North Carolina Press.

O'Brien, M. 2010. *Intellectual Life and the American South, 1810–1860*. Chapel Hill: University of North Carolina Press.

Ober, J. 1998. *Mass and Elite in Democratic Athens*. Princeton: Princeton University Press.

"Official Proceedings of the Democratic National Convention held in Chicago, Ill., July 7–11, 1896." 1896. Logansport: Wilson, Humphreys, and Co.

Perry, T. S. 1882. *The Life and Letters of Francis Lieber*. Boston: James R. Osgood and Co.

Purdy, J. 2016. "Populism's two paths," *The Nation*, October 31.

Quigley, P. 2012. *Shifting Grounds: Nationalism and the American South, 1848–1865*. Oxford: Oxford University Press.

Ritter, G. 2010. *Goldbugs and Greenbacks: The Antimonopoly Tradition and the Politics of Finance in America, 1865–1896*. Cambridge: Cambridge University Press.

Roberts, T. M. 2005. "'Revolutions have become the bloody toy of the multitude': European revolutions, the South, and the crisis of 1850," *Journal of the Early Republic*, 25: 259–83.

Roberts, T. M. 2009. *Distant Revolutions: 1848 and the Challenge to American Exceptionalism*. Charlottesville: University of Virginia Press.

Rodogno, D. 2016. "European legal doctrines on intervention and the status of the Ottoman Empire in the 'Family of Nations' throughout the nineteenth century," *Journal of the History of International Law*, 18: 5–41.

Rohrs, R. C. 1994. "American critics of the French revolution of 1848," *Journal of the Early Republic*, 14: 359–77.

Rooduign, M. 2014. "The nucleus of populism: in search of the lowest common denominator," *Government and Opposition*, 49(4): 573–99.

Rosanvallon, P. 2011. "Penser le populisme," *La vie des idees*, January 27. http://www.laviedesidees.fr/Penser-le-populisme.html.

Ross, D. 1991. *The Origins of American Social Science*. Cambridge: Cambridge University Press.

Rosser, C. 2010. "Woodrow Wilson's administrative thought and German political theory," *Public Administration Review*, 70: 547–56.

Rossi, E. and M. Sleat. 2014. "Realism in normative political theory," *Philosophy Compass*, 9/10: 689–701.

Rossinow, D. 2008. *Visions of Progress*. Philadelphia: Penn University Press.

Runciman, D. 2014. *The Confidence Trap*. Princeton: Princeton University Press.

Runciman, D. 2016. "How the education gap is tearing politics apart," *The Guardian*, October 5.

Schumpeter, J. A. 1942. *Capitalism, Socialism and Democracy*. London: Routledge.

Sehat, D. 2011. *The Myth of American Religious Freedom*. Oxford: Oxford University Press.

Strauss, L. 1953. *Natural Right and History*. Chicago: University of Chicago Press.

Streeck, W. 2013. *Buying Time*. London: Verso.

Thompson, J. A. 2008. "Woodrow Wilson and a world governed by evolving law," *Journal of Policy History*, 20(1): 113–25.

Trescot, W. H. 1849. *A Few Thoughts on the Foreign Policy of the United States*. Charleston: John Russell.

Trescot, W. H. 1850. *The Position and Course of the South*. Charleston: Walker and James.

Tuck, R. 1993. "The contribution of history," in P. Pettit and R. Goodin (eds), *A Companion to Contemporary Political Philosophy*. Oxford: Blackwell, 72–89.

Tuck, R. 2016. *The Sleeping Sovereign*. Cambridge: Cambridge University Press.

Urbinati, N. 1998. "Democracy and populism," *Constellations*, 5(1): 110–24.

Voss-Hubbard, M. 1995. "The political culture of emancipation: morality, politics, and the state in Garrisonian abolitionism, 1854–1863," *Journal of American Studies*, 29: 159–84.

Ware, A. 2006. *The Democratic Party Heads North, 1877–1962*. Cambridge: Cambridge University Press.

Webb, P. and T. Bale. 2014. "Why do Tories defect to UKIP? Conservative Party members and the temptations of the radical right," *Political Studies*, 62: 961–70.

Weichlein, S. 2005. "Europa und der Föderalismus: zur Begriffsgeschichte politischer Ordnungsmodelle," *Historisches Jahrbuch*, 125: 133–52.

Williams, B. 2007. *In the Beginning was the Deed*, ed. G. Hawthorn. Princeton: Princeton University Press.

Wilson, W. 1898. *The State*. Boston: Rockwell.

Witt, J. F. 2012. *Lincoln's Code*. New York: Free Press.

Wittke, C. 1948. "The German Forty-Eighters in America: a centennial appraisal," *American Historical Review*, 53: 711–25.

Wittke, C. 1950. *The Utopian Communist: A Biography of Wilhelm Weitling, Nineteenth-Century Reformer*. Baton Rouge: Louisiana State University Press.

Wolin, S. S. 2008. *Democracy Inc*. Princeton: Princeton University Press.

CHAPTER 27

··

POPULISM AND HEGEMONY

··

YANNIS STAVRAKAKIS

INTRODUCTION

How can theories of hegemony advance our understanding of populist politics?[1] The concept of hegemony has a long pedigree within political research and especially within its Marxist and post-Marxist variants. Here, the work of the Italian Marxist Antonio Gramsci immediately springs to mind. And yet, Gramsci has not engaged explicitly in an analysis of populism *tout court*, although, as we shall see, many of his ideas have inspired contemporary theorization. It was the recasting of the theory of hegemony by Laclau and Mouffe, a project initiated in the 1970s and 1980s, that provided and consolidated this explicit link between hegemony and populism. Against the background of Gramsci's work, this chapter draws on the work of Laclau, Mouffe, and other relevant theoretical resources in order to illuminate the matrices and patterns shaping and animating populist discourse and accounting for its (variable) hegemonic potential. We focus on populist articulatory practices as political interventions emerging and operating within a broader socio-symbolic as well as psycho-social terrain that influences their formation, stimulates their construction, and—at the same time—limits their scope.

From this point of view, a hegemonic perspective highlights the representational (and affective) mechanisms through which: (1) failures of established identifications and hegemonic orders can trigger a crisis of representation allowing populist and other actors to put forward alternative narrations of the crisis and of their proposed solutions; (2) "the people" comes to function as a discursive point of reference articulating the distinct political orientation of such populist actors; and (3) the ensuing articulation comes to rely on an antagonistic staging of the socio-political field along an us/them axis. The crucial implication of the theoretical perspective advanced here involves the need to take into account the broader hegemonic terrain of populist/anti-populist antagonisms in order to effectively identify and inquire into the political performance and hegemonic effects of populist movements. Needless to say, far from being a mere speculative exercise, an emphasis on the dialectic between hegemony and populism can facilitate a more comprehensive analysis of populist discourse and its implications. A series of empirical examples will thus be used to illustrate its analytical impact.

CONCEPTUAL FRAMEWORKS: GRAMSCI, MOUFFE, LACLAU

Gramsci has never provided a clear definition of "hegemony," but his work is renowned for utilizing the concept "to mean the formation and organization of consent" (Ives, 2004: 3), although the relationship between consent and coercion is far from neglected.[2] In Judith Butler's words:

> hegemony emphasizes the ways in which power operates to form our everyday understanding of social relations, and to orchestrate the ways in which we consent to (and reproduce) those tacit and covert relations of power. Power is not stable or static, but is remade at various junctures within everyday life; it constitutes our tenuous sense of common sense, and is ensconced as the prevailing epistemes of a culture. (Butler in Butler, Laclau and Zizek, 2000: 14)

Here, language and social construction play a crucial role. In fact, Gramsci's initial exposure to the concept of hegemony was through the field of linguistics, where the concept "was used to describe how a given population would adopt a particular linguistic form ... from another group of people." Crucially, the mechanisms involved in this adoption were related not to coercion, but "to cultural prestige as well as economic, political, social and at times even military power" (Ives, 2004: 47). In this sense, Gramsci's references to "language" imply a whole "specific conception of the world" (Gramsci, 1971: 323). Language and hegemonic politics are intimately related:

> Every time the question of language surfaces, in one way or another, it means that a series of other problems are coming to the fore: the formation and enlargement of the governing class, the need to establish more intimate and secure relationships between the governing groups and the national popular mass, in other words to reorganize cultural hegemony. (Gramsci, 1985: 183–4)[3]

With its emphasis on linguistic representation, Gramsci's work will function as a crucial inspiration for the development of Laclau and Mouffe's "discourse theory." Indeed, "hegemony" constitutes a central concept already from Laclau's early work (Laclau, 1977: 131) and has preoccupied Mouffe very early on as the publication of her edited collection *Gramsci and Marxist Theory* demonstrates (Mouffe, 1979). Later on, its genealogy within Marxist theory and its subsequent post-Marxist recasting will occupy most of Laclau and Mouffe's *opus magnum*, characteristically entitled *Hegemony and Socialist Strategy* (Laclau and Mouffe, 1985; 2001). Last but not least, it will retain its privileged position up until the publication of Laclau's last major *solo* work, *On Populist Reason* (Laclau, 2005).

This take on hegemony has arguably moved beyond the remnants of class reductionism still implicit in Gramsci's work—for example, "his insistence that hegemonic subjects are necessarily constituted on the plane of the fundamental classes" as well as "his postulate that, with the exception of interregna constituted by organic crises, every social formation structures itself around a single hegemonic centre" (Laclau and Mouffe, 2001: 137–8)—to highlight the importance of the field of representation in accounting for the construction and (partial/temporary) sedimentation of political subjectivity, social objectivity, and hegemonic orders.[4] Representation is here conceptualized in terms of discursive articulation, revealing a social constructionist understanding of social reality; and yet, this is a constructionism that knows its limits, recasting articulatory practices as fragile interventions under constant threat from two angles: (1) from the ultimate impossibility of the field of the symbolic (prevalent in representational structures) to capture an always escaping real (Lacan); (2) from the realization that any such (futile) attempt to symbolize the real involves an irreducible *pluralization* to the extent that different agents are bound to arrive at different such symbolizations which, lacking any universal common ground, end up *antagonizing* each other.

In that sense, Laclau and Mouffe's stress on discourse and representation only makes sense against an ontological horizon of negativity. What they call "hegemony" comprises both (1) the Sisyphean choreography between the articulation of new political representations and the obstacles they encounter from within (from their inherent inability to fully capture the real, to represent the unrepresentable)[5] and from without (from other antagonistic representations); and (2) the transient crystallization of such representations in the short term and—more rarely—in the long term.[6] What needs to be stressed here is that the antithetical poles involved in such a choreography are locked into a symbiotic relationship: "The fullness of society is an impossible object which successive contingent contents try to impersonate" ad infinitum (Laclau in Butler, Laclau, and Zizek, 2000: 79). For example, *dislocation* and *antagonism*, two concepts central in Laclau's theorization, what threatens our discursive representations, is also what stimulates their constant *articulation*: "It is because hegemony supposes the incomplete and open character of the social, that it can take place only in a field dominated by articulatory practices" (Laclau and Mouffe, 2001: 134).

Populism as Articulatory Practice: The Antagonistic Production of Empty Signifiers

Laclau and Mouffe's post-Marxist hegemony theory has exerted tremendous influence from the 1980s onwards in a variety of fields.[7] And yet, it is populism that repeatedly emerges as the ground on which this approach has been initially conceived and to which it inevitably returns. It is clear, for example, that it was the experience of Argentinian Peronism that has triggered Laclau's theoretical trajectory and his embrace of hegemony theory. In a 1988 interview he explains how the Peronist rupture has made redundant any reference to a standard Marxist interpretation of political life and how political activism in Buenos Aires in the 1960s prepared his embrace of Althusser, Lacan, Derrida, and others (Laclau, 1990: 198–200). Indeed, populism has thus emerged as the type of politics marking the interruption of any sense of normal unfolding (conceptualized either in Marxist terms or within the scope of the modernization paradigm), as the type of hegemonic politics par excellence, given that hegemony—as we have seen—is precisely what designates the negative dialectic between dislocation and articulation:

> For Germani, "populism" stems from the uneven integration of the masses into the political system and the delays in the transition from a traditional to an industrial society. His whole model of interpretation is based on an extremely simplistic version of the "modernization and development" theories. For me, on the other hand, "populism" is the permanent expression of the fact that, in the final instance, a society always fails in its efforts to constitute itself as an objective order. (Laclau, 1990: 201)

Hegemony thus denotes the mechanisms constantly (re)negotiating this failure: "No social fullness is achievable except through hegemony"; and yet, by relying on representation, hegemony is revealed as "nothing more than the investment, in a partial object, of a fullness which will always evade us because it is purely mythical" (Laclau, 2005: 116). Echoing Gramsci's interest in the "national-popular" dimension, such a mythical hegemony—within democratic societies—invariably involves "constructing a popular identity out of a plurality of democratic demands" (Laclau, 2005: 95). This *radical construction through articulation* is arguably what populism performs. Within such a broad framework, populism is linked to articulations claiming to express popular interests and identities. This is why Laclau's first criterion in identifying a discourse as populist is the extent to which it privileges as its main point of reference "the people," which—in Laclau's jargon—comes to operate as a "nodal point" or an "empty signifier."

To the extent that such articulations never take place in a political vacuum, populism research stands to benefit from focusing on the complex and antagonistic language games developed around such claims: games involving recognition and idealization, rejection and demonization. Both these attitudes can take a variety of forms as the history of populist politics reveals. Recognition can proceed from an emancipatory embrace of egalitarian demands, but idealization can also stem from a reduction of the popular to the ethnic core of the nation. Likewise, rejection can involve distrust of the particular ways in which popular demands are formulated and of the agents (movements, parties, or leaders) putting them forward or a deeper rejection of popular sovereignty itself as the foundation of democracy. As a result, both populist and anti-populist discourses can acquire progressive and regressive, democratic and anti-democratic forms.

Needless to say, the identity and consistency of each camp relies on its antagonism towards the other; as we know from Saussure, identity is impossible to formulate without difference. The meaning of a particular unit within a system of signification can only arise via its differentiation from other elements within the same system: "in language there are only differences" (Saussure, 1959: 120; also see Connolly, 1991: ix). This is a point deeply marking Laclau's theory: "linguistic identities are exclusively relational"; a point indeed recognized as the "very principle involved in the constitution of all social identity" (Laclau, 1990: 207). Thus the ascription of the pejorative label "populist" to a political adversary is very often a construction of anti-populist discourse utilized to dignify, through differentiation, its own purity; in an inversely analogous way, populist forces often denounce the tyrannical powers of their enemies that allegedly ignore or even repress popular will in order to highlight, through difference, their own commitment to truly represent it.

Even more crucially, the role of the identity/difference dialectic is paramount in the differential identification of populist discourse put forward by Laclau and the Essex School and influences the theorization of the aforementioned "empty signifier." How does Laclau define the "empty signifier"? Through a typical differential dialectic between negativity and positivity, lack and fullness. As we have already seen, "the fullness and universality of society is unachievable," and yet "its need does not disappear"; this is exactly what constitutes the terrain of hegemony. In fact, the need for fullness "will always show itself through the presence of its absence" (Laclau, 1996: 53). This is precisely where Laclau's category of the empty signifier becomes relevant:

> In a situation of radical disorder "order" is present as that which is absent; it becomes an empty signifier, as the signifier of this absence. In this sense, various political forces can compete in their efforts to present their particular objectives as those which carry out the filling of that lack. To hegemonize something is exactly to carry out this filling function. (Laclau, 1996: 44)

Laclau suggests, moreover, that signifiers other than "order"—signifiers like "unity," "revolution," "justice," "change," "happiness," etc.—can function in a similar way: "Any term which, in a certain political context becomes the signifier of the lack, plays the same role. Politics is possible because the constitutive impossibility of society can only represent itself through the production of empty signifiers" (Laclau, 1996: 44). In conditions of increasing inequality, exclusion, and failed representation, the "people" can function as such an empty signifier, expressing the need to address the perceived lack in equal rights, inclusion, and representation, calling forth a political subject in need of restoring its lost power/sovereignty and claiming the representation of its true will against an anti-popular/anti-populist power bloc that has allegedly hijacked it.

The meteoric rise of SYRIZA in contemporary Greek politics, its elevation from a political outsider (attracting a mere 4.6 percent of the vote in the 2009 elections) to a party of government (getting 36.34 percent in the January, 2015, elections and almost replicating this result in September, 2015) provides a suitable example. The prevailing characteristics of the party's hegemonic discourse involved (1) putting forward an antagonistic representation of the socio-political field along an us/them dichotomy—indeed "*either us or them*" was a much utilized slogan in the 2012 elections reproduced in SYRIZA posters and party leaflets; and (2) elevating "the people" to the position of the privileged signifier, the nodal point, representing the "us" camp in a sufficiently flexible (tendentially empty) manner allowing diverse groups and subjects hit by the crisis to identify themselves with this position (Stavrakakis and Katsambekis, 2014). Needless to say, this populist articulation became the target of a variety of anti-populist discourses within the political and media spheres that singled out populism itself—a synecdoche of political evil projected onto SYRIZA—as the source of the crisis and of the inability to effectively deal with it (Stavrakakis, 2014a).

At any rate, it seems impossible to effectively study populism without examining anti-populism as well, without taking into account their mutual constitution: both the reliance of populist discourse on attributing the source of social grievances and exclusions to an "enemy of the people" as well as the construction of the "dangerous populist" by anti-populist discourses as the demagogue who capitalizes on such grievances in an irresponsible and ultimately anti-democratic way.

In addition, especially given Gramsci's well-known interest in the role of intellectuals in securing social hegemony by functioning in a traditional or "organic" manner, justifying "the way a given society is organized" or supporting the agents of radical change (Ives, 2004: 76–7), populism research would greatly benefit from a reflexive assessment of its own involvement in the antagonistic language games between populism and anti-populism. For example, Annie Collovald (2004) has persuasively shown how French academics (mostly Pierre-Andre Tagguieff) have been instrumental in associating the extreme right in France with populism, an association which may not be as "natural" as it seems (Stavrakakis and Katsambekis, 2014). The work of intellectuals such as Gino Germani in Latin America (see, for example, Germani, 1962; 1978) and Nikiforos Diamandouros in Greece (see Diamandouros, 1994) has also advanced analytical models drawing on modernization theories that have more or less inspired and shaped anti-populism in the broader public sphere in their respective contexts.[8] One can probably trace the anti-populist matrix of such academic discourse back to the work of Richard Hofstadter on the American populism of the 1890s (Hofstadter, 1955). Indeed, in Hofstadter's account, the populist imaginary is denounced as backward-looking, provincialist, and nativist, even as conspiratorial, irrational, and anti-semitic. A lot of stereotypes plaguing debates around populism emanate from Hofstadter's work. No matter whether withdrawn by Hofstadter himself following an avalanche of academic criticism (see Collins, 1989, for a summary of the debate), these stereotypes still dominate public discussion and need to be seriously highlighted and reflexively discussed in future research on populism. What also needs to be discussed is the inverse situation: in Argentina, for example, academic work on populism which avoids the demonization characteristic of Hofstadter's argument, in fact the contributions by Laclau and Mouffe, have been directly embraced by the populist governments of the Kirchners as well as by other similar governments in Latin America, instituting a politico-theoretical choreography at the antipodes of the one we have been analysing up to now. In addition, the same scenario is now played out in the European field. PODEMOS, for example, has been openly adopting a "populist" strategy with one of its most prominent leaders co-authoring a relevant book with Chantal Mouffe (Errejon and Mouffe, 2015).[9]

EQUIVALENCE VS DIFFERENCE: DISCURSIVE INFRASTRUCTURES OF POPULISM

Now, to move to Laclau's second criterion in identifying populist discourse, the ensuing choreography between populism and anti-populism highlights the operation of two distinct political logics. Arguably all political systems have to rely on popular incorporation to stabilize themselves. Perhaps popular legitimation acquires importance because the ruling elite can exchange its concessions to previously excluded groups for their voluntary participation in an army based on universal conscription which is deemed necessary for the defence of the community—an ancient Greek city-state, for example— from external enemies. The expansion of democratic and social rights in Europe and the US was also aided by the existence of an enemy camp (the Soviet bloc) espousing an ostensibly egalitarian rhetoric. When, however, such an external pressure is missing or recedes from the horizon and the balance of power is less favorable to egalitarian demands, when for example an economic crisis makes it impossible to sustain a previously hegemonic model of incorporation (be it the welfare state or, perhaps, a corporatist or clientelist structure), then popular demands are frustrated and the conditions for a populist rupture start coalescing.

Drawing on the linguistic work of the founder of modern (structuralist) linguistics Ferdinand de Saussure and especially on the distinction he introduces between the *paradigmatic* and *syntagmatic* poles of language, as well as on the Jakobsonian concepts of metaphor and metonymy, Laclau and Mouffe have elaborated *equivalence* and *difference* as two distinct logics through which the representation of social space is formed and legitimation is offered and/or demanded:

> We, thus, see that the logic of equivalence is a logic of the simplification of political space, while the logic of difference is a logic of its expansion and increasing complexity. Taking a comparative example from linguistics, we could say that the logic of difference tends to expand the syntagmatic pole of language, the number of positions that can enter into a relation of combination and hence of continuity with one another; while the logic of equivalence expands the paradigmatic pole—that is, the elements that can be substituted for one another—thereby reducing the number of positions which can possibly be combined. (Laclau and Mouffe, 2001: 130)

In social life both these logics continuously overlap. Diverse social actors, identities, or demands obviously occupy "differential positions within the discourses that constitute the social fabric. In that sense they are all, strictly speaking, particularities." If such demands can be addressed within the existing institutional structure, then they cannot escape their own particularity and end up reproducing hierarchical relations of domination implicit all along in the practice of articulating a demand towards an authority, simultaneously winning certain—sometimes important—concessions. When, however, these identities feel the limits imposed in their development by a power structure frustrating their demands (especially in times of crisis destabilizing the reproduction of an existing economic, social, and political order), social antagonisms can emerge creating internal frontiers on the basis of the "dichotomization of the social space" (Laclau in Butler, Laclau, and Zizek, 2000: 77) within a social fabric previously represented in terms of continuity.

Thus a new representation emerges, splitting the social field by paratactically grouping differences, temporarily reducing their multiplicity into a single polarity: "Vis-a-vis oppressive forces, for instance, a set of particularities establish relations of equivalence between themselves" (Laclau and Mouffe, 2001: xiii). It becomes clear that apart from claiming to represent the popular will, apart that is to say from ascribing a privileged position to "the people," which now—as we have seen in the previous section—functions as a nodal point, an empty signifier, populism presupposes a privileging of the logic of equivalence over that of difference. This is the second criterion put forward by Laclau: the process through which populist discourse is articulated typically involves the establishment of linkages between a series of initially heterogeneous unsatisfied demands, which enter into relations of equivalence, thus forming a collective identity around "the people" and the leadership representing them. The equivalential linkage sublimating heterogeneity is achieved through the opposition towards a common enemy (the power bloc, the establishment) accused of frustrating the satisfaction of these demands in the first place.

To return to our previous example, the way SYRIZA's typically populist discourse managed to become hegemonic in the Greek context clearly involved the construction of linkages between a series of heterogeneous demands resulting from the failure of the established party system to deal with the Greek crisis. Indeed SYRIZA was probably the only party to engage from the beginning with the demands of various protest groups severely hit by the economic downturn (such as the Greek *indignants* engaging in Square occupations) and even meet them out in the streets, providing a unifying vessel for their political representation. It is in these encounters that a chain of equivalences started to be formed between different groups and demands through a shared opposition towards European and Greek political structures (the so-called external and internal *troika*), identified as an indifferent and brutal "establishment" imposing draconian austerity measures (Stavrakakis and Katsambekis, 2014; also see Pappas, 2014: 86).

Last but not least, the resulting populist discursive articulation can acquire a hegemonic appeal through processes of affective investment through which discursive *form* acquires its hegemonic *force* (Laclau, 2004: 326). Indeed, Gramsci was already aware of the importance of affectivity, of the fact that "words and propaganda" are never enough "to cause the broad masses to rise up, or to determine the necessary and sufficient conditions for the foundation of a new order of things" (Gramsci, 1978: 36):

> If the relationship between intellectuals and people-nation, between the leaders and the led, the rulers and the ruled, is provided by an organic cohesion in which feeling-passion becomes understanding and thence knowledge (not mechanically but in a way that is alive), then and only then is the relationship one of representation. Only then does there take place the exchange of individual elements between governed and governing, between led and leaders, and one achieves the life of the whole which alone is the social force, one creates the "historical bloc." (Gramsci, 2000: 350)[10]

By linking equivalence and difference with broader mechanisms of signification (Saussure's syntagmatic and paradigmatic axes) and affective investment, Laclau and Mouffe highlight a set of socio-symbolic as well as psycho-social *infrastructures* making possible, even overdetermining, the articulation and hegemonic success of discourses like populism. Such infrastructures—prefiguring the shape (not the content) and the articulatory patterns human sociality can take as well as highlighting the importance of their affective investment—have been observed in many human societies, even in so-called primitive ones. In dialogue with Laclau, Slavoj Zizek reminds us of the way Claude Levi-Strauss has described the two dominant representations of the social field encountered in the two distinct groups to be found in Winnebago, one of the Great Lake tribes. Drawing on Paul Radin's work—which he subsequently relates to similar anthropological findings from other communities—Levi-Strauss describes thus the social structure of Winnebago: "We know that the Winnebago were formerly divided into two moieties, called, respectively, *wangeregi*, or 'those who are above', and *manegi*, or 'those who are on earth' (hereafter, for greater convenience, we shall call the latter 'those who are below')" (Levi-Strauss, 1963: 133). Now, what is of interest, is that when asked to draw on a piece of paper (or on sand) the spatial arrangement of his or her village, members of the two different subgroups produced very different illustrations along differential/equivalential lines:

> Both perceive the village as a circle, but for one subgroup there is within this circle another circle of central houses, so that we have two concentric circles; while for the other subgroup the circle is split into two by a clear dividing line. In other words, a member of the first subgroup (let us call it "conservative-corporatist") perceives the ground plan of the village as a ring of houses more or less symmetrically disposed around the central temple; whereas a member of the second ("revolutionary-antagonistic") subgroup perceives his or her village as two distinct heaps of houses separated by an invisible frontier. (Zizek in Butler, Laclau, and Zizek, 2000: 112)

Throughout history, signifiers like "the people" invariably function as markers of the internal division of every political community between part and whole, between the few and the many, those governing and those governed, those inside and those outside, those above and those below. This division seems to traverse the development of

European if not global societies from Greek and Roman antiquity up until modernity, setting the stage for a passionate and often bitter political antagonism arguably between two distinct historical blocs: a populist and an anti-populist one.

What makes things even more troubling, however, is the fact that the frontier between these two blocs is continuously displaced without ever disappearing. If the populist moment continuously reappears—especially where it was not supposed to—this must be seen as a clear indication of the limitations processes of democratization encounter in their continuous attempts to lift exclusions, to incorporate the marginalized, to expand the scope of political and economic equality. Indeed, inclusion and exclusion are here revealed as mutually dependent. Every democratic advance is bound to involve institutional sedimentations involving their own exclusions and thus leading to further struggle:

> My understanding of the view of hegemony established by Ernesto Laclau and Chantal Mouffe in *Hegemony and Socialist Strategy* (1985) is that democratic polities are constituted through exclusions that return to haunt the polities predicated upon their absence. That haunting becomes politically effective precisely in so far as the return of the excluded forces an expansion and rearticulation of the basic premises of democracy itself. (Butler in Butler, Laclau, and Zizek, 2000: 12)

Besides, we know already from Michels about the oligarchic tendencies implicit in political organization: even the most dynamic egalitarian forces often "undergo a gradual transformation, adopting the aristocratic spirit, and in many cases also the aristocratic forms, against which at the outset they struggled so fiercely," instituting thus a cruel game without end (Michels, 1966: 371). This play of largely unintended consequences poses a grave risk especially when, due to the post-democratic mutation of established party systems (Crouch, 2004), due to the "hollowing of democracy" in Peter Mair's terms (Mair, 2013), the only political forces claiming to represent popular demands and grievances belong to the extreme right and explicitly prioritize hierarchical, anti-democratic political orientations.[11]

If, on the one hand, and due to the irreducible impurity of every relation of representation, even genuine popular grievances and demands can end up being represented by exclusionary forces or becoming hostages of oligarchic institutional dynamics, on the other hand, attempts to establish hierarchical modes of domination are also inescapably destabilized by a democratic *excess*, which is bound to fuel "populist" calls for inclusion, by the reappearance and continuous insistence of what Breaugh has called "the plebeian experience" (Breaugh, 2013). Since antiquity, we have lived in unequal societies; and yet, all attempts to legitimize oligarchic rule invariably result in the generation of a democratic *supplement*,[12] precisely to the extent that political stability and legitimization require the organization of consent, that is to say *hegemony*. As Rancière observes, "there are people who govern because they are the eldest, the highest-born, the richest, or the most learned." And yet this aristocratic "power of the best" cannot be legitimized "except via the power of equals": "There is no service that is carried out, no knowledge that is imparted, no authority that is established without the master having, however little, to speak 'equal to equal' with the one he commands or instructs." If, as we have seen, even egalitarian/inclusive types of populism can ultimately introduce new exclusions, at the same time, inegalitarian claims for domination can only function thanks to their implicit reliance on a set of egalitarian relations: "It is this intrication of equality in inequality that the democratic scandal makes manifest in order to make it the basis of public power" (Rancière, 2007: 47–8). It is the same intrication, the same mutual dependence, that installs the populism/anti-populism divide as a more or less irreducible characteristic of political societies.

DEBATING CRISIS: THE DUAL CHARACTER OF DISLOCATION

We have seen how, by shedding light on the operation of discursive practices, Laclau and Mouffe's theory of hegemony can account for the emergence and hegemonic appeal of populist discourses. To the extent that, as it has been already argued, such practices only make sense against the background of a negative ontology, we now need to explain the distinct way in which Laclau and the Essex School at large have theorized this aspect as well within the general background established by Gramsci. This theorization is very much related to a rubric quite common in populism research, the relation between populism and crisis (see, in this respect, Taggart, 2000: 66; Roberts, 1995; Moffitt and Tormey, 2014: 391–2). Obviously, this is something not restricted exclusively to populism but applicable to all hegemonic interventions; due to the ultimate impossibility of social closure and the constitutive incompleteness of identity, " 'Hegemony' will be not the majestic unfolding of an identity but the response to a crisis" (Laclau in Butler, Laclau, and Zizek, 2000: 7). Interestingly enough, already from his early work, Laclau had linked such crises to the emergence of populism: "the emergence of populism is historically linked to a crisis of the dominant ideological discourse which is in turn part of a more general social crisis" (Laclau, 1977: 175).

It is obvious that, in this respect also, Laclau's position is, once more, heavily indebted to the work of Gramsci. In the latter's argument, we can observe the confluence between the two etymological origins of "crisis" as both a *critical conjuncture* (emanating from ancient Greek medical discourse) and a *final judgment* (originating from the juridical field) in a bid to account for political crises, crises of political meaning and orientation, beyond economic reductionism. As Gramsci, who had captured before anybody else the representational/discursive dimension of crises (Hay, 1999: 335), points out, "It may be ruled out that immediate economic crises of themselves produce fundamental historical events; they can simply create a terrain more favourable to the dissemination of certain modes of thought, and certain ways of posing and resolving questions involving the entire subsequent development of national life" (Gramsci, 1971: 184). Indeed Gramsci's take manages to combine the problematics of crisis, representation, hegemony, and mobilization, to which we shall return:

> [T]he crisis of the ruling class's hegemony … occurs either because the ruling class has failed in some major political undertaking for which it has requested, or forcibly extracted, the consent of the broad masses … or because huge masses … have passed suddenly from a state of political passivity to a certain activity, and put forward demands which taken together, albeit not organically formulated, add up to a revolution. A "crisis of authority" is spoken of: this is precisely the crisis of hegemony, or general crisis of the State. (Gramsci, 1971: 210)

Last but not least, Gramsci highlights the ambivalent and largely open character of the outcomes of crisis, formulating the oft-quoted phrase that crisis "consists precisely in the fact that the old is dying and the new cannot be born" (Gramsci, 1971: 276; also see Koselleck, 1988: 127).

More recently, within the field of political science, many of the aforementioned characteristics of crisis have been rigorously restated and further developed by Colin Hay. Hay is right when, partly drawing on Koselleck, he locates within "crisis" the cohabitation of two distinct dimensions, that of *objective* contradiction leading a given system into a phase of instability with unpredictable consequences and that of *subjective* intervention which signifies and represents this instability in particular ways. While objectivist conceptions of crisis tend to obscure this dual and ambiguous character, Hay attempts to underline it by clearly distinguishing systemic contradictions or *failures*, that is to say condensations of such contradictions, and *crises* understood as decisive interventions on behalf of a variety of competing social actors through which these contradictions are identified, highlighted, and meaningfully represented, that is to say socially constructed and mediated (Hay, 1995: 68; 1999: 323).

In the most recent populism literature two orientations seem to occupy center-stage. The most orthodox approach, cogently restated recently by Kenneth Roberts (Roberts, 2015), highlights the multiple ways in which a crisis—indeed a crisis of representation—operates to trigger populist mobilization. Questioning the externality between crisis as trigger (cause) and populism (effect), Moffitt places emphasis on the performative construction of crisis by populist discourse itself (Moffitt 2015: 190). By conceptualizing—as we have seen—hegemonic struggles within a terrain of negativity, Laclau manages to link an understanding of crisis as triggering mechanism with an awareness of the constructed character of populist performances of crisis. This is made possible through his theorization of "dislocation." This category denotes the (inherent) limit of social objectivity, the moment of failure that ruptures our established reality and opens up an antagonistic play between competing discursive articulations struggling to impose a new hegemony (Laclau, 1990). Thus, Laclau will accept the gap between "failure" and "crisis" in Hay's schema, between triggering backgrounds (Roberts) and populist performative constructions (Moffitt); however, he will also register and conceptualize the continuous encounters between them, highlighting the inherent link between the two dimensions.

Indeed it is Laclau's highlighting of the dual character of dislocation (disruptive as well as performatively constructive, objective as well as subjective) that manages to link the two orientations we have encountered: a dislocation, the failure of a sedimented system of representation, is presupposed as a triggering mechanism for new populist (and other) discursive constructions uniquely narrating its characteristics and offering distinct solutions. And yet, far from being determined by the "objectivity" of the dislocatory situation, these new articulations (populist or other) involve *radical construction*: "the construction of the 'people' is a radical one—one which constitutes social agents as such, and does not express a previously given unity of the group" (Laclau, 2005: 118). The "people" is always something retroactively constructed, an *empty signifier* that needs to be invoked, a performative call incarnated in a proper name that (partially) creates what it is supposed to be expressing (a sovereign collective identity):

> If I refer to a set of social grievances, to widespread injustice, and attribute its source to the "oligarchy," for instance, I am performing two interlinked operations: on the one hand, I am constituting the "people" by finding the common identity of a set of social claims in their opposition to the oligarchy; on the other, the enemy ceases to be purely circumstantial and acquires more global dimensions.... [W]e are dealing not with a conceptual operation of finding an abstract common feature underlying all social grievances, but with a performative operation constituting the chain as such. (Laclau, 2005: 97)

Dislocations associated with the 2008 sub-prime collapse should thus be located at the basis of popular mobilizations culminating in Occupy Wall Street in the US. As it has been substantiated in a series of expert and activist interviews conducted within the scope of the POPULISMUS project, the exact mechanism involved here is consistent with the model previously discussed. Thus, as Bruce Robbins comments, economic failure was quickly translated into a crisis of trust towards financial institutions and the banking sector and, eventually, into a crisis of representation, following the political decision to support the banking system in a manner that for some seemed scandalous (Bruce Robbins, interview, New York, October 21, 2014). According to Ritchie Savage, economic dislocations have shaken the hegemonic "symbolic order," creating space for the development of antagonistic discourses from the left and the right, including *Occupy* and the *Tea Party* (Ritchie Savage, interview, New York, October 22, 2014). Within this context, OWS activists managed to articulate a discourse that attracted international attention on the basis of dividing society into two camps in a distinctly proto-populist way: the 99%, the people, against the 1%, the establishment of the super-rich controlling the economy and the established party system. Empty signifiers like "99%" and "We the people" managed thus to capture the dual *crisis of representation* affecting the US both at the economic and the political level in a way that facilitated the identification of many different segments of the population and created media-buzz (Pablo Benson, interview, New York, October 19, 2014). Once more, what permitted the articulation of previously unconnected and even antithetical demands and subject positions was the antagonistic profile of this discourse that created a chain of equivalences on the basis of opposing a common adversary. As illustrated in a well-known slogan of the period: "All our grievances are connected" (see Figure 27.1).

And yet, the OWS mobilization did not take the full step from horizontalism to verticalism, from what political philosopher Simon Critchley has termed "politics of presentation," based on the immediate physical presence in the "squares," to the "politics of representation," to the symbolically mediated intervention in the formal institutions of representative democracy (Simon Critchley, interview, New York, October 18, 2014). It is perhaps here one can locate one of the reasons for the limited political effect of OWS as well as one of the differences with similar developments in Southern Europe (mainly Greece and, to a lesser extent, Spain) where, under conditions of severe economic and social dislocation, the ensuing crisis of representation was constructed in dichotomic

FIG. 27.1 Flowchart of the declaration of the Occupation of NYC. Illustration by Rachel Schragis, 2011, based on text by the Call to Action Working Group of the Zuccotti Park general assembly, drawn in Zuccotti park through a crowd-sourced research process.

terms by populist actors that, having incorporated most of the energy of the "squares" (the Spanish and the Greek *indignados*), took the crucial step of acquiring a party form and contesting a series of elections with quite significant results. In the Greek case, for example, dramatic societal dislocations were performatively constructed both as a "humanitarian crisis" and a "crisis of democracy." It was only against this dual background that voters massively dis-identified with the established political system and became increasingly attracted by the blame attribution at the kernel of SYRIZA's discourse, which (as we have already seen) purported to represent their grievances and demands—as well as their dignity—against the common enemy that frustrated their satisfaction.

This is where commentators influenced by theorists like Gilles Deleuze and Antonio Negri, who reject hegemony altogether as a suitable theoretical and analytical matrix for understanding contemporary politics, seem to get it wrong. For example, in a book characteristically entitled *Gramsci is Dead*, Richard Day purports to overturn "the hegemony of hegemony" (Day, 2005) by focusing on what he calls "the Newest Social Movements," mainly radical groups "operating *non-hegemonically* rather than *counter-hegemonically*" (Day, 2005: 8). However, what the "fate" of OWS shows is that an exclusive theoretical as well as political stress of autonomy (horizontality) is never enough, although verticality alone makes no sense either as the trajectory and the limitations of the SYRIZA experiment have demonstrated:[13]

> the horizontal dimension of autonomy will be incapable, left to itself, of bringing about long-term historical change if it is not complemented by the vertical dimension of "hegemony"—that is, a radical transformation of the state. Autonomy left to itself leads, sooner or later, to the exhaustion and the dispersion of the movements of protest. But hegemony not accompanied by mass action at the level of civil society leads to a bureaucratism that will be easily colonized by the corporative power of the forces of the status quo. To advance both in the directions of autonomy and hegemony is the real challenge to those who aim for a democratic future. (Laclau, 2014: 9)

In these cases, as in many others (for example, in Latin America), the importance of economic and social dislocations in triggering a crisis of representation and, subsequently, the formation of populist alternatives is evident. The emergence of populist movements cannot be properly interpreted if one does not place them within the context of such failures of social reproduction and the resulting crisis of representation. In addition, the antagonistic type of politicization put forward by populist political actors seems to construct and perform the crisis in a particular (confrontational) way in an—often explosive and unpredictable—bid to represent marginalized popular demands. Last but not least, this is bound to create anti-populist reactions. Especially in times of crisis, when ruling elites fail to deal with economic frustration and social dislocation, allowing thus systemic inconsistencies to develop into a deep crisis of representation, calls for political radicalization—whether justified or not—are often and summarily denounced as "populist."

Conclusion

We have seen how, by radicalizing the Gramscian moment, the post-structuralist take on hegemony developed by Ernesto Laclau and Chantal Mouffe has managed to introduce a series of conceptual innovations forming a distinct approach to populism. Laclau's theorization of dislocation as a condition of both possibility (a triggering mechanism generating antithetical performative narratives) and impossibility (a limit) of discursive production allows a novel take on the relationship between crisis and populism under a radical constructionist perspective. Moving from the negative ontology marking hegemonic politics and populism into an assessment of populism as articulatory practice, we have also highlighted the two criteria put forward by Laclau for the differential identification of populist discourse: (1) the operation of the "people" as an empty signifier, a nodal point shaping a particular discursive ensemble; (2) the reliance on discursive infrastructures (the logic of equivalence and its affective investment) imposing a dichotomic representation of society and power relations along an us/them axis.

In both respects difference and antagonism play a crucial role in the formation and hegemonic potential of populist discourse. An empty signifier only makes sense against the background of deep societal grievances, of experiences of social lack (widening inequality, failure of representation, etc.), drawing its appeal from an often mythical promise to radically redress them. At the same time, the effective construction of a populist equivalential chain relies on the populist narration of such dislocations: blame attribution and the construction of an enemy are crucial here. And yet, populism is never alone in operating like that, that is to say hegemonically/counter-hegemonically. And thus, in advancing further its scope, a hegemony perspective needs to highlight the importance of studying populism together with anti-populism, focusing on their mutual constitution on both the symbolic and the affective plane, within a negative ontological framework placing dislocatory limits on both of them and constantly redrawing their frontiers.

Notes

1   Part of this chapter draws on research conducted within the context of the "POPULISMUS: Populist Discourse and Democracy" research project (2014–15). POPULISMUS has been implemented at the School of Political Sciences of the Aristotle University of Thessaloniki within the framework of the Operational Program "Education and Lifelong Learning" (Action "ARISTEIA II") and was co-funded by the European Union (European Social Fund) and Greek national funds (project no. 3217). More information is accessible from the POPULISMUS Observatory: http://www.populismus.gr. Many thanks are due to my co-researchers Alexandros Kioupkiolis, Giorgos Katsambekis, Thomas Siomos, and Nikos Nikisianis, as well as to Ioanna Garefi for her technical support.

2   In fact, it has been argued that one of Gramsci's most important contributions has been precisely the illumination of the highly complex relationships between coercion and consent in democratic capitalist societies: "He was continually perceptive about how the possibility or threat of coercion and subtle uses of it are often integral to shaping and organizing consent" (Ives, 2004: 64).

3   Also see Carlucci, 2013: 3; Ives, 2004: 82. We are following Carlucci's modification of the English translation.

4   In Ives's reading, Laclau and Mouffe seem to overstate Gramsci's ultimate reliance on a reductionist logic.

5   In Laclau's words: "The representation of the unrepresentable constitutes the terms of the paradox within which hegemony is constructed ... we are dealing with an object which is at the same time impossible and necessary" (Laclau, 2000: 66).

6   In the first case, Laclau talks about "myths"; in the second about "imaginary horizons" (Laclau, 1990: 61–7).

7   Cultural studies is an important case in point (Lash, 2007: 58, 68) as even the most vitriolic critics of Laclau have conceded (Beasley-Murray, 2010: 15).

8   No wonder that, in the September, 2015, Greek elections, Diamandouros figured as a prominent candidate in the electoral list of the new anti-populist *River* party (Ποτάμι).

9   For a more comprehensive discussion of this double hermeneutic challenge to theories of populism, see POPULISMUS, 2015: 30–2. If PODEMOS has been openly inspired by the Laclau and Mouffe version of hegemony theory, the alleged connection between SYRIZA cadres and the Essex School has been severely overstated.

10 In potentially hegemonic populist movements and parties, this affective investment is often crystallized in charismatic bonds and relations. For the ways in which SYRIZA's discursive strategies have cultivated such a bond in its first six months in government, see Stavrakakis, 2015.

11 This is made possible by translating demands for equality in nationalist and exclusionary terms, by making membership of an exclusive ethic in-group a condition for the pursuit of equality at the expense of out-groups, in other words "by exploiting a relationship of inequality" (Rosanvallon, 2013: 147–8). Here extreme right-wing populism reproduces traditional strategies (originating from the nineteenth century) "pitting a definition of equality as homogeneity, based on xenophobia and defense of the nation" (Rosanvallon, 2013: 87).

12 This concept is used here partly because of its Derridean connotations.

13 During the last few years, theories of so-called "post-hegemony" have also disputed the relevance of "hegemony" as a conceptual vehicle capable of illuminating contemporary politics (Lash, 2007; Beasley-Murray, 2010). For a critical discussion of such arguments see Stavrakakis, 2014b.

References

Beasley-Murray, Jon. 2010. *Posthegemony*. Minneapolis: University of Minnesota Press.
Breaugh, Martin. 2013. *The Plebeian Experience*. New York: Columbia University Press.
Butler, Judith, Ernesto Laclau, and Slavoj Zizek. 2000. *Contingency, Hegemony, Universality*. London: Verso.
Carlucci, Alessandro. 2013. *Gramsci and Languages*. Leiden: Brill.

Collins, Robert. 1989. "The originality trap: Richard Hofstadter on populism," *The Journal of American History*, 76(1): 150–67.

Collovald, Annie. 2004. *Le "Populisme du FN": un dangeroux contresens*. Broissieux: Éditions du Croquant.

Connolly, William. 1991. *Identity/Difference: Democratic Negotiations of Political Paradox*. Ithaca: Cornell University Press.

Crouch, Colin. 2004. *Post-Democracy*. Cambridge: Polity.

Day, Richard. 2005. *Gramsci is Dead: Anarchist Currents in the Newest Social Movements*. London: Pluto Press.

Diamandouros, Nikiforos. 1994. "Cultural dualism and political change in post-authoritarian Greece," working paper no. 50. Madrid: Instituto Juan March.

Errejon, Inigo and Chantal Mouffe. 2015. *Construir pueblo*. Madrid: Icaria.

Germani, Gino. 1962. *Politica y sociedad en una epoca de transicion*. Buenos Aires: Paidos.

Germani, Gino. 1978. *Authoritarianism, Fascism, and National Populism*. New Brunswick: Transaction.

Gramsci, Antonio. 1971. *Selections from the Prison Notebooks of Antonio Gramsci*. London: Lawrence and Wishart.

Gramsci, Antonio. 1978. *Selections from Political Writings (1921–1926)*. London: Lawrence and Wishart.

Gramsci, Antonio. 1985. *Selections from Cultural Writings*. London: Lawrence and Wishart.

Gramsci, Antonio. 2000. *The Gramsci Reader: Selected Writings, 1916–1935*. New York: New York University Press.

Hay, Colin. 1995. "Narratives of the new right and constructions of crisis," *Rethinking Marxism*, 8(2): 60–76.

Hay, Colin. 1999. "Crisis and the structural transformation of the state," *British Journal of Politics and International Relations*, 1(3): 317–44.

Hofstadter, Richard. 1955. "The folklore of populism," in *The Age of Reform*. New York: Vintage Books.

Ives, Peter. 2004. *Language and Hegemony in Gramsci*. London: Pluto Press.

Koselleck, Reinhardt. 1988. *Critique and Crisis: Enlightenment and the Pathogenesis of Modern Society*. Cambridge: MIT Press.

Laclau, Ernesto. 1977. *Politics and Ideology in Marxist Theory: Capitalism, Fascism, Populism*. London: New Left Books.

Laclau, Ernesto. 1990. *New Reflections on the Revolution of our Time*. London: Verso.

Laclau, Ernesto. 1996. *Emancipation(s)*. London: Verso.

Laclau, Ernesto. 2004. "Glimpsing the future," in Simon Critchley and Oliver Marchart (eds), *Laclau: A Critical Reader*. New York: Routledge.

Laclau, Ernesto. 2005. *On Populist Reason*. London: Verso.

Laclau, Ernesto and Chantal Mouffe. [1985] 2001. *Hegemony and Socialist Strategy*. London: Verso.

Lash, Scott. 2007. "Power after hegemony: cultural studies in mutation?," *Theory, Culture and Society*, 24(3): 55–78.

Levi-Strauss, Claude. 1963. *Structural Anthropology*. New York: Basic Books.

Mair, Peter. 2013. *Ruling the Void: The Hollowing of Western Democracy*. London: Verso.

Michels, Robert. 1966. *Political Parties*. New York: The Free Press.

Moffitt, Benjamin. 2015. "How to perform crisis: a model for understanding the key role of crisis in contemporary populism," *Government and Opposition*, 50(2): 189–217.

Moffitt, Benjamin and Simon Tormey. 2014. "Rethinking populism: politics, mediatisation and political style," *Political Studies*, 64: 381–97.

Mouffe, Chantal. 1979. *Gramsci and Marxist Theory*. London: Routledge and Kegan Paul.

Pappas, Takis. 2014. *Populism and Crisis Politics in Greece*. Abingdon: Palgrave Macmillan.

POPULISMUS. 2015. "Background paper," *Populism and Democracy* international conference, Thessaloniki, June 26–8. http://www.populismus.gr/wp-content/uploads/2015/06/POPULISMUS-background-paper.pdf.

Rancière, Jacques. 2007. *The Hatred of Democracy*. London: Verso.

Roberts, Kenneth. 1995. "Neoliberalism and the transformation of populism in Latin America: the Peruvian case," *World Politics*, 48(1): 82–116.

Roberts, Kenneth. 2015. "Populism, political mobilizations, and crises of political representation," in Carlos de la Torre (ed.), *The Promise and Perils of Populism*. Lexington: University Press of Kentucky, 140–58.

Rosanvallon, Pierre. 2013. *The Society of Equals*. Cambridge: Cambridge University Press.

de Saussure, Ferdinand. 1959. *Course in General Linguistics*. New York: Philosophical Library.

Stavrakakis, Yannis. 2004. "Antinomies of formalism: Laclau's theory of populism and the lessons from religious populism in Greece," *Journal of Political Ideologies*, 9(3): 253–67.

Stavrakakis, Yannis. 2014a. "The return of 'the people': populism and anti-populism in the shadow of the European crisis," *Constellations*, 21(4): 505–17.

Stavrakakis, Yannis. 2014b. "Hegemony or post-hegemony? Discourse, representation and the revenge(s) of the real," in Alexandros Kioupkiolis and Giorgos Katsambekis (eds), *Radical Democracy and Collective Movements Today: The Biopolitics of the Multitude Versus the Hegemony of the People*. Farnham: Ashgate, 111–32.

Stavrakakis, Yannis. 2015. "Populism in power: SYRIZA's challenge to Europe," *Juncture*, 21(4): 273–80.

Stavrakakis, Yannis and Giorgos Katsambekis. 2014. "Left-wing populism in the European periphery: the case of SYRIZA," *Journal of Political Ideologies*, 19(2): 127–9.

Taggart, Paul. 2000. *Populism*. Buckingham: Open University Press.

....

CHAPTER 28

POPULISM AS A THREAT
TO LIBERAL DEMOCRACY

....

STEFAN RUMMENS

THE precise nature of the relation between populism and liberal democracy is a matter of ongoing contestation. According to some, populism should be branded as a dangerous *threat*. Because of its illiberal and authoritarian tendencies, populism is at odds with some of the core values of our liberal democratic regime and should therefore be consistently opposed (Urbinati, 1998; Levitsky and Loxton, 2012; Albertazzi and Mueller, 2013). According to others, however, populism has a much more ambiguous relationship with liberal democracy. Although it can indeed constitute a threat to a certain extent, it can also operate as a wholesome *corrective* (Taguieff, 1995; Arditi, 2003; Mudde and Rovira Kaltwasser, 2012b). Because of its ability to give a voice to unheeded concerns or to mobilize hitherto excluded groups, populism has, for instance, the potential of making the democratic process more inclusive (Laclau, 2005). In a similar vein, populism is said to operate as a redemptive force which provides some counterweight to the unavoidably elitist and pragmatic character of liberal democratic politics and which, thus, reminds us of the democratic possibilities inherent in our political system (Canovan, 1999).

In this contribution, I revisit this ongoing debate by focusing on the different ways in which populism and liberal democracy conceptualize the *demos*. Although both traditions are committed to the idea of popular sovereignty, they mean very different things when they talk about "the people." For populism, the people should be understood as a homogeneous community with a shared collective identity. For liberal democracy, in contrast, the people should be understood as an irreducible plurality, consisting of free and equal citizens. This difference is crucial and has many implications for the way in which both traditions understand, for instance, the importance of individual rights or the role of oppositional dynamics as part of the democratic process.

As I will argue, a full appreciation of these different understandings of the *demos* provides support for the position—which I already defended in earlier work together with Koen Abts—that populism and liberal democracy embody antagonistic and irreconcilable understandings of the concept of democracy (Abts and Rummens, 2007). If this analysis is correct, the suggestion that populism might have beneficial effects turns out to be misguided. Sure enough, there is a relevant sense in which populism operates as a *symptom*, signaling an underlying malfunctioning of our liberal democratic system. Nevertheless, because of its deeply problematic understanding of the concept of popular sovereignty, populism can never itself function as the remedial *corrective*. Instead, it should be considered an important *threat* to democracy, which ought to be countered by actions aiming to remedy both the symptom and the underlying problem.

The Co-Originality of Liberalism and Democracy

In order to analyse the relation between populism and liberal democracy, I propose to first have a closer look at liberal democracy itself. In the debate on populism, many authors start from the assumption that liberal democracy is a paradoxical regime. Here, the central reference is the work of Chantal Mouffe (2000), who has repeatedly argued that liberalism and democracy form distinct ideological traditions which are, in fact, incompatible. For her, liberal democracy is based on the contingent combination of a liberal and a democratic "pillar," whereby the paradoxical tensions between the universalistic logic of the liberal pillar and the majoritarian logic of the democratic pillar can never be fully eliminated.

This understanding of liberal democracy has, in turn, given rise to an analysis of populism which identifies populism with the democratic pillar of this paradoxical combination (Canovan, 1999; Mény and Surel, 2002; Mouffe, 2005; Mudde and Rovira Kaltwasser, 2012a). On this highly popular view, populism does not mark a break with the logic of liberal democracy but rather represents one of its constitutive components. Not surprisingly, this analysis also supports the view that populism can be both a threat and a corrective to liberal democracy. The idea here is that we need to preserve the proper balance between the two pillars. So, in circumstances where the liberal pillar has become too dominant, a rise of populism can reinvigorate our democratic system by "bringing back the disruptive noise of the people" (Arditi, 2003: 26–7). At the same time, of course, we should make sure not to tip the balance too much in favor of populism as that would threaten to undermine the liberal safeguards which form the other constitutive pillar of our political regime.

From the point of view of political philosophy more generally, the widespread acceptance, in the populism debate, of the idea that liberal democracy is a paradoxical regime is rather surprising. In fact, the leading scholars of contemporary American, German, and French political philosophy—John Rawls (1996; 1998), Jürgen Habermas (1996), and Claude Lefort (1988)—have all argued at length in favor of the exact opposite point of view. Each of them has insisted, in his own unique way, that liberal democracy should not be seen as some kind of paradoxical mixture. Although we can, of course, distinguish between the liberal and the democratic *dimensions* of liberal democracy—referring to the existence of individual liberty rights on the one hand and the presence of democratic procedures on the other—these dimensions should not be seen as independent and separable *pillars*. Liberal democracy should be understood, rather, as a coherent and autonomous political regime with its own independent logic and ideology. A proper understanding of this normative logic reveals that the liberal and democratic dimensions are not incompatible at all, but represent, rather, inseparable or "co-original" aspects of a regime which aims to preserve and protect human freedom. This claim of co-originality should, thereby, not be misunderstood as a historical or empirical claim. The histories of the liberal and the democratic traditions are to an important extent distinct whereby, in modern times, the former arguably pre-dates the latter. The point of the thesis of co-originality is, rather, a conceptual one. It means that liberal democracy is a normatively coherent regime and that the alleged pillars of "pure liberalism" and "pure democracy," when taken in isolation, in fact represent ideologies which are deeply at odds with liberal democracy's basic procedures and core values.

In the work of John Rawls (1996), for instance, the co-originality of liberalism and democracy already reveals itself in the liberal principle of legitimacy at the core of his theory of justice. This principle states that political power is only legitimate to the extent that it is exercised in accordance with "a political conception of justice that all citizens might be reasonably expected to endorse" (Rawls, 1996: 137). Rawls uses the method of the reflexive equilibrium to argue that such a conception of justice will necessarily contain, amongst other principles, a commitment to the full set of basic liberties typically associated with liberalism. At the same time, Rawls also emphasizes that his own a priori reconstruction of the content of the political conception of justice cannot simply be externally imposed on a democratic sovereign people. It is, in the end, up to the citizens themselves to determine, on the basis of a democratic process of public deliberation, the precise content of the political conception of justice which they are willing to endorse and use to settle the questions of justice that arise in their society (Rawls, 1996: 409–21).

Although Rawls explicitly endorses the co-originality of liberalism and democracy, it is also true that his work has always focused more on the liberal dimension of liberal democracy and that he has not provided us with an extensive analysis of the democratic process itself. In this regard, the work of both Habermas and Lefort is more relevant for our present purposes.

Jürgen Habermas (1996) is well known for his deliberative model of democracy. This model is committed to what he calls an intersubjective and communicative understanding of popular sovereignty. This means that the laws of the democratic state should be based on the will of the people and that the will of the people itself should be generated on the basis of actual processes of reasonable deliberation between free and equal citizens.

This approach is fundamentally different from both pure liberalism and pure democracy, which, according to Habermas, remain wedded to untenable subjectivistic conceptions of political legitimacy (Habermas, 1998: 239–52). Pure liberalism, on the one hand, focuses on individual citizens and understands the legitimacy of a regime in terms of the safeguards it provides for the prepolitical (natural) rights these citizens are supposed to enjoy. Pure democracy, on the other hand, focuses on the political community as a collective identity which forms a Subject writ large. This collective is supposed to have a common will, the *volonté générale*, which provides the ultimate source of political legitimacy. For Habermas, both of these traditions fail to appreciate the *intersubjective* nature of the political community. In contrast with pure democracy, deliberative democracy emphasizes that the *demos* should not be understood as a singular collective, but should properly be understood as a pluralistic community consisting of free and equal citizens with inalienable rights. In contrast with pure liberalism, deliberative democracy stresses, however, that these inalienable rights can never be prepolitical. Citizens enjoy their liberty rights only to the extent that they are granted these rights by the *demos* as the sovereign ruler.

According to the deliberative model, the liberal and the democratic aspects of liberal democracy are, thus, not incompatible but represent, rather, two co-original dimensions which mutually presuppose each other (Habermas, 1996: 118–31; 1998: 253–64). On the one hand, the realization of individual liberty rights presupposes a democratic process. The meaning of our fundamental freedoms (freedom of religion, freedom of expression, etc.) cannot be fixed in a timeless fashion, but is unavoidably subject to an ongoing interpretative process. Thereby, only the citizens themselves are able—on the basis of an inclusive process of democratic deliberation—to determine which interpretations do justice to their needs and concerns in an adequate and impartial manner. On the other hand, the democratic process also presupposes the existence of liberal rights. This holds on a pragmatic level in the sense that in a purely majoritarian regime without liberal safeguards, the current majority is likely to protect itself from future majorities by abolishing the democratic process itself. As Levitsky and Loxton (2012: 162), for instance, recognize, majority rule without liberty rights is unlikely to persist. This holds, however, also on a deeper theoretical or conceptual level (Rummens, 2006). Granting democratic rights of participation to all individual citizens indiscriminately only makes sense on the assumption that these citizens are indeed autonomous individuals who are capable of shaping their own lives both individually and collectively. It would be inconsistent to grant this autonomy and accept, at the same time, that it could subsequently be curtailed in the name of some illiberal ideology which contingently happens to be endorsed by the majority. As Habermas (1998: 259) has rightly emphasized, liberal rights should be seen not as constraints limiting the sovereign power of the people, but rather as the conditions of possibility of democratic rule in the first place.

When we turn to the work of Claude Lefort (1988), it should be noted, first, that there are important differences between his understanding of democracy and Habermas's deliberative model. Lefort objects, for instance, to a rationalistic and consensualistic conceptualization of democracy and emphasizes the central role of political conflict and, thus, the agonistic nature of the democratic process. In spite of these differences, however, there are also many crucial similarities which are relevant for our present purposes. Most importantly, Lefort also defends his own version of the thesis of co-originality (1988: 21–44, 165–82). For him, both our individual (liberal) and political (democratic) freedoms emerge in the transition from premodern to modern society. In premodern society, the final authority with regards to the organization of both our private and public lives resides with God as the supreme ruler. In the context of our modern and pluralistic societies, however, "the markers of certainty" are dissolved and the reference to a shared religious worldview and the shared recognition of a supreme divine ruler become inoperative. As a result, people are now confronted with their own freedom as the unavoidable task of deciding for themselves in both the private and the political sphere.

Modern democracy is the regime in which this new found freedom is protected, Lefort argues, on the basis of the fundamental liberty rights typically associated with liberalism. Lefort thereby argues—as does Habermas—that these rights should not be misunderstood as prepolitical or natural rights. Instead, they are political rights, installed and guaranteed by the democratic community of free and equal citizens itself. In order to characterize the nature of the democratic process in which this type of self-legislation takes place, Lefort (1988: 9–20) makes use of his famous metaphor of democracy as the regime in which the place of power remains empty. In contrast with absolute monarchy, where the figure of the king embodied the unity of the whole people in his own person, democracy is the regime in which power can no longer be embodied in one single figure. The fact that the place of power, in this sense, remains symbolically empty does not imply, of course, that power should not be exercised in a democracy. We have a parliament and a majority government which effectively make decisions on behalf of the people. The symbolical emptiness refers, rather, to the fact that the will of the majority should never be identified with the will of the people as a whole. In a democracy, no single party and no single politician can claim to embody or represent the will of the people as such. Although a majority provides temporary interpretations of the will of the people, these majority decisions are not endorsed by the remaining minority. Since the minority is, however, as much part of the people as the majority, the democratic process is an open-ended process in which the "will of the people" necessarily remains fragmented and elusive. This fragmentation is not problematic, however. It simply reflects the fact that a democratic society is a community consisting of an irreducible plurality of free and equal citizens with diverging views and opinions.

According to both Lefort and Habermas, the conceptualization of the *demos* as a unity-in-diversity uniquely characterizes liberal democracy and marks a decisive difference with both "pure democracy" and "pure liberalism." "Pure democracy," on the one hand, understands the democratic people in terms of a homogeneous body with a singular will, whereby, in the famous phrase of Rousseau, the minority is mistaken in its understanding of the *volonté générale* and can therefore be "forced to be free" by being subjected to the will of the majority. This collectivistic understanding of the *demos* is, thus, deeply at odds with the liberal democratic understanding of the *demos* as a pluralistic community of free and equal citizens. On the other hand, however, the plurality of the liberal democratic *demos* should also not be mistaken for the pure diversity characteristic of "pure liberalism." Society does not consist of a loose collection of atomized individuals born with a set of prepolitical natural rights. A democratic community is a genuine unity in the sense that its members are united by the democratic process itself as a process through which they jointly interpret, elaborate, and realize the basic rights they grant each other as free and equal citizens.

Populism as the Closure of the Empty Place of Power

The currently most widely endorsed conception of populism is undoubtedly the ideological conception as formulated, prominently, by Cas Mudde. He defines populism as:

> an ideology that considers society to be ultimately separated into two homogeneous and antagonistic groups, "the pure people" versus "the corrupt elite," and which argues that politics should be an expression of the volonté générale (general will) of the people. (Mudde, 2004: 543)

In line with an earlier suggestion by Margaret Canovan (2002: 32), populism should thereby be understood as a "thin-centred ideology" (Freeden, 1998: 750). Populism does not provide a comprehensive political ideology but focuses only on the way in which power should be organized and legitimized in a "democratic" society. As a thin-centered ideology populism can be complemented by additional ideologies which, amongst other things, explain how the identity of the homogeneous people should be understood. Right-wing populism generally understands this identity in ethno-cultural terms (our "own" people), whereas left-wing populism usually resorts to economic categories (e.g. the poor peasants or the working class).

The ideological definition of populism is able to account for two of the main characteristics often associated with populism: a specific (populist) mode of representation and a particular (populist) style of politics.

Benjamin Arditi, for instance, explains populism in terms of a *mode of representation*

> which rests on a crossover between "acting for others," the re-entry of authorization under the guise of *trust* for the leader, and a strong symbolic dimension that seeks to produce an effect of virtual immediacy, that is, an imaginary identification that suspends the distance between masses and authorities. (Arditi, 2003: 23)

The fact that the populist ideology relies on a homogeneous conception of the people indeed implies that populists are generally wary of complex mediated forms of representation. As Nadia Urbinati (1998) has explained, populism's view on representation can be understood on the basis of Carl Schmitt's conception of democracy which emphasizes the identity of the rulers and the ruled (Schmitt, 1988; 2008; Abts and Rummens, 2007: 415–19). The people as a community have a singular collective will which is understood and represented in an immediate manner by the populist leader who is "one of us," whom we identify with and whom we therefore trust to lead us well.

In a recent contribution, Benjamin Moffit and Simon Tormey (2014: 390–2) revive an older suggestion that populism should essentially be understood as a new *style of politics*. According to them, this style is basically characterized by three main elements: an appeal to the people, a reference to the threat of a possible breakdown of society as the result of a crisis situation, and the coarsening of political discourse. And indeed, the populist ideology as understood by Mudde implies that all political problems can be framed and reduced to the simple antagonistic opposition between "us," the good people, who are thwarted in their legitimate claims to power by an usurping "them." As a result, simplistic claims, the cultivation of a sense of crisis which threatens the true people, and a course dismissal of the counterclaims of the opponents can be expected.

Although the ideological conception of populism can account for the fact that populist parties generally endorse a populist mode of representation and make use of a populist style of politics, I believe that it would be conceptually misleading to actually identify populism with either of these two characteristics. The problem is that populist modes of representation as well as populist styles of politics are, to an important extent, endemic features of the new type of mediatized "audience democracy" which succeeded our more traditional "party democracy" already some decades ago (Manin, 1997; Mair, 2002).

Although an extensive analysis of this transition is beyond present purposes, it is important to remind ourselves of the fact that in the times of "party democracy" ideological dividing lines were relatively clear and rigid, voters were firmly embedded in an extensive network of ideological civil society organizations, and voter loyalty was high. In the new media democracy, in contrast, voters have emancipated themselves from these ideological networks and have become much more volatile. As a result, parties now have to address voters in a more "direct" and mediatized manner. Since well-established ideological divisions have lost much of their appeal, it has thereby become almost unavoidable for politicians to claim to represent "the people" (rather than some subsection of society) and to tell a story about the collective identity of the community they believe significant parts of the electorate might identify with. Thereby, parties will be generally prone to put forward charismatic leaders who are well adapted to the mediatized circumstances and able to appeal to the voters by virtue of their direct and trust-inspiring style of communication.

In other words, in the new "audience democracy," it is almost unavoidable that "populism," when understood merely in terms of a new mode of representation or a new style of politics, becomes a label which is applicable to some degree to *most if not all* political parties (Mazzoleni, 2008: 57; Arditi, 2003: 23; Moffitt and Tormey, 2014: 392–3). These conceptualizations of populism are, therefore, at risk of becoming uninformative in the sense of being unable to clearly discriminate between ordinary mainstream politics and populism as a much more specific and problematic phenomenon.

Here, the ideological conception of populism proves superior in the sense that it is much more selective. Sure enough, parties endorsing the populist ideology will generally prefer a populist mode of representation and use a populist style of politics to a larger extent than their competitors. In this sense, these traits are indeed significant markers of populism. Importantly, however, in the case of the true populists these traits are, at the same time, also firmly rooted in a specific ideological understanding of the nature of democratic legitimacy. For them, the reference to "the people" is more than merely a rhetorical gesture used to catch more voters. Instead, they take the idea of the true people as a kind of homogeneous collective and the idea of the *volonté générale* as the ultimate source of political authority very seriously.

On the ideological conception, populism is identified with the kind of pure democracy we have analysed in the previous section. In terms used by Habermas, this means that populism understands the people as a Subject writ large, i.e. a collective identity with a singular will. Populism thereby fails to recognize the intersubjective nature of democracy as a constructive process in which the will of the people reflects a discursive interpretation of the liberties all participants grant each other as free and equal citizens. Instead, populism believes that the will of the people is singular, that it can be captured and represented directly by the populist party and that it can be imposed on society as a whole even at the expense of the individual freedom of parts of the citizenry. In terms used by Lefort, populism should be seen as a failure to respect the emptiness of the place of power. Populism conjures up a collectivist image of the homogeneous identity of the people, the People-as-One, and takes this image as the sole reference for legitimate policy-making. This means that populist parties and leaders make an exclusive claim to represent and embody the will of the people and, thus, feel entitled to impose this will upon society at the expense of the ideological diversity which is constitutive of the liberal democratic regime.

As explained, populism as "pure democracy" does not represent a constitutive pillar of liberal democracy, but rather an ideology deeply at odds with its core values and procedures. With regards to the *liberal dimension* of liberal democracy, there seems to be widespread agreement in the literature that populism has illiberal tendencies (Mudde and Rovira Kaltwasser, 2012a: 21–2; Albertazzi and Mueller, 2013: 348–50). Precisely because it conceives of the people as a homogeneous unity, it considers all those individuals not conforming to its idea of the collective identity as outsiders with fewer entitlements. As a result, populism fosters the marginalization of specific groups of society and tends to undermine minority rights and protections. In a similar vein, populism has little patience with the ordinary constitutional checks and balances of liberal democracy. Because the people as a collective is recognized as the ultimate source of legitimacy, populism considers itself above those ordinary constraints and does not flinch from instrumentalizing the constitution as a means for promoting its own ends.

The antagonism between populism and liberal democracy is, however, not restricted—as the two-pillar model of populism claims—to the liberal dimension. The populist understanding of the democratic process is deeply incompatible with the *democratic dimension* of liberal democracy as well. The main characteristic of populism, in this regard, is that it generally refuses to recognize the democratic legitimacy of its opponents. Since the populist leader claims to solely represent the singular will of the people, other parties and politicians can only be branded as illegitimate usurpers distorting rather than representing the will of the people. This delegitimization of the opponent is well captured by a distinction introduced by Chantal Mouffe (2000: 98–105). In line with the work of Carl Schmitt, she emphasizes the importance of antagonistic oppositions as a defining characteristic of the political. Schmitt understood such an antagonism as a conflict between enemies who set out to destroy each other. Mouffe recognizes, however, that in a democratic context the struggle between opponents needs to be relativized. In a liberal democratic regime, the *antagonistic* struggle between enemies should therefore give way to an *agonistic* opposition between adversaries who recognize each other's legitimacy and who share a commitment to the core liberal democratic values of freedom and equality. The problem with populists, now, is that they do not share these core values and that they do not recognize other politicians as legitimate adversaries. For them the political struggle becomes once again an all or nothing affair in which their opponents appear as enemies who should, ideally, be cleared from the political stage.

In my view, the tendency of populists to delegitimize their opponents is underappreciated as both a defining trait of populism and a core aspect of the threat populism poses to democracy. It is precisely this delegitimization which explains the authoritarian tendencies of populism and which explains why populist politicians can easily develop into autocratic leaders.

Populism as a Threat and a Symptom, Not a Corrective

Although the populist ideology is incompatible with liberal democracy, there are exceptional circumstances under which populism can render it a great service. In situations where a liberal democratic regime is not yet in place, populism might provide the kind of revolutionary politics necessary to install it (Mudde and Rovira Kaltwasser, 2012a: 17). In this regard, it is telling that Ernesto Laclau (2005) uses the rise of *Solidarność* as one of his main examples in his important book on populism. For Laclau, populism uses "the people" as an empty signifier which can help to establish a chain of equivalences between a seemingly unrelated set of unfulfilled demands of the people. This chain establishes an antagonistic frontier between the people on the one hand and the regime that is challenged on the other.

In cases such as these, populism provides a revolutionary strategy which seems acceptable from a normative point of view. As long as a liberal democratic regime has not been established, the people can be strongly united in their opposition against an oppressive regime such as communism or military dictatorship. In this struggle, the regime constitutes a power structure which is not legitimate from a democratic perspective. The struggle is therefore an antagonistic rather than an agonistic one. The current political elite are indeed the enemy of the people and the goal of the populist uprising is to replace the current power structures with alternative, more democratic ones.

As soon as such a populist revolution has become successful, however, the situation changes drastically. If the goal is to install a truly (liberal) democratic regime, antagonism should be transformed into agonism. Although all liberal democrats should be united in their antagonistic struggles with the enemies of liberal democracy, the struggles liberal democrats have amongst themselves should be institutionalized as agonistic rather than antagonistic oppositions. This relativization of antagonism is something which Laclau is, however, incapable of conceptualizing within his own theoretical framework (Rummens, 2009). Here, Mouffe's work is markedly superior in the sense that she appreciates that this transformation is based on the shared commitment of all liberal democrats to the core values of freedom and equality as well as on the recognition by democratic adversaries of the fact that their opponents are legitimate representatives of the people as much as they are themselves.

Many authors, however, have a more positive view about the virtues of populism and argue that it can also have beneficial effects in the context of an established liberal democratic regime. Although they recognize that populism poses a certain *threat*, most notably for its illiberal tendencies, they believe that populism can also function as a wholesome *corrective* (Canovan, 1999; Arditi, 2003; Mudde and Rovira Kaltwasser, 2012a; 2012b). The main idea is that populism can make the democratic process more inclusive by giving voice to concerns that are currently not taken seriously in the political process or by mobilizing excluded sections of society. As mentioned, the beneficial nature of populism is thereby explained in terms of the two-pillar model: populism reinforces democratic dynamics in a context in which the democratic process has been stifled by an excess of liberal elitism.

On the ideological conception of populism, this understanding of the democratic potential of populism is deeply problematic because, as argued, populism is incompatible with both the liberal and the democratic dimensions of liberal democracy. In this respect, it is surprising that authors such as Mudde and Rovira Kaltwasser combine an endorsement of the ideological conception of populism with a defence of the two-pillar model as a justification for its alleged corrective potential (2012a: 8, 17). This combination is theoretically incoherent. Since the populist ideology implies a genuine commitment to the sovereign rule of the people as a homogeneous collective, it has an essentially exclusionary nature: it cannot accept those individuals who do not conform to its understanding of the collective identity as full members of society. As a consequence, populism cannot itself function as an inclusionary corrective for the malfunctions of liberal democracy.

Of course, the underlying idea that populists often give voice to concerns that are not adequately taken up in the democratic process is undoubtedly compelling. In my view, however, it is more correct to conclude from this observation that populism operates as a *symptom* which signals that something is going wrong in the representative process. The rise of right-wing populism in Europe testifies to smouldering but unheeded concerns amongst large parts of the electorate about the problems associated with the increasingly multicultural character of European societies. The rise of left-wing populism in

Latin America often signals widespread concerns about forms of economic deprivation or economic injustice which the political system fails to adequately address.

Although populism can fulfill crucial functions in *signaling* problems with our political system, I do not see how it could by itself also *correct* these problems (Taggart, 2002: 78–9). In line with their undemocratic ideology, populists generally advocate "solutions" for the underlying concerns of voters which would make the liberal democratic system worse off than it was before. When right-wing populist parties such as the French FN, the Dutch PVV, or the Belgian *Vlaams Belang* advocate measures that curtail the fundamental rights of Muslim citizens and asylum seekers, or when left-wing populists such as Hugo Chávez use authoritarian means to implement more leftist social policies, the alleged cure is much worse than the illness.

Dealing with Populism

Populism signals an underlying problem with our democratic system, but cannot itself provide the solution for this problem. The question, therefore, arises what an appropriate response to the rise of a populist party looks like from the perspective of liberal democracy. How should we deal with the populists themselves and how should we deal with the underlying problem?

In this regard, Koen Abts and I have defended what we call a concentric containment strategy for dealing with undemocratic political forces appearing in the context of an established liberal democracy (Rummens and Abts, 2010). The main idea of that strategy is that undemocratic forces should be relatively free to operate in the informal public sphere at the periphery of the democratic system, but that tolerance for these forces should decrease as they come closer to the actual centers of power where the decisions are being made. The underlying rationale is that political freedom is a core value of liberal democracy which implies that all voices, even the unpleasant and undemocratic ones, should be heard in the public debate because this is the only way in which all the possibly relevant concerns of voters can be detected. At the same time, individual liberty and equality are core values of liberal democracy. This means that forces which aim to deal with voters' concerns on the basis of solutions which are at odds with these values should not be given the opportunity to translate these solutions into actual legislation or policies.

With regards to the rise of populist parties and their undemocratic ideologies, this general guideline of decreasing tolerance translates into a two-fold strategy of exclusion and inclusion. In view of the fact that the populist ideology poses a *threat* to the democratic system, populist parties should, as much as possible, not be allowed to participate in government. In order to protect the core values of our liberal democratic system, a *cordon sanitaire* around these parties seems generally in order. This exclusionary attitude vis-à-vis the populist party itself should, however, be combined with an inclusionary openness towards the populist voters. Since populism is a *symptom* of an underlying problem, this problem should be addressed. The democratic parties should listen to the concerns of voters, deal with the issues, and try to win back the voters on the basis of solutions which—in contrast with the solutions proposed by the populist party—are in line with the core values of a modern-day pluralistic society.

In the literature, the strategy of a *cordon sanitaire* is often decried as an inappropriate "moralization" of politics (de Lange and Akkerman, 2012: 40–1; Mudde and Rovira Kaltwasser, 2012b: 213), whereby populist opponents are delegitimized on the basis of "moral" rather than "political" grounds. Chantal Mouffe (2005: 58), for instance, considers a *cordon* a distortion of the oppositional dynamics of democracy and suggests that populists should not be treated as "moral enemies" but, instead, as ordinary "political adversaries." This is a strange claim, however, which seems based on a false dichotomy: populists, in my view, are neither moral enemies nor political adversaries; they are, rather, political enemies. The *cordon* is not a moral strategy, but a political one aimed to protect the liberal democratic regime. Mouffe's suggestion that populists should thereby be treated as ordinary adversaries seems, furthermore, manifestly incompatible with her own distinction between agonism and antagonism. As explained, the difference between the two is that agonistic adversaries share a commitment to the core values of liberal democracy. To the extent that populists fail to share this normative framework, they should be treated as antagonistic enemies who should be kept from power (Rummens, 2009).

Another well-rehearsed argument against containment strategies is that they are believed to be ineffective when compared to more inclusionary strategies. Populist parties which are allowed to participate in government will supposedly be forced to compromise and to moderate their ideological position. This moderation is believed to both diminish the threat populism poses and undermine the populist party's appeal with the more uncompromising voters. This argument is, however, increasingly refuted by the empirical evidence available. On the one hand, there are indications that the two-fold strategy advocated here, combining a sustained exclusion of the populist party with a forceful attempt to provide populist voters with a democratic alternative, might actually prove successful (Capoccia, 2007; Art, 2011; Pauwels, 2011). On the other hand, it is becoming increasingly clear that populists who gain access to executive power positions are not inclined to deradicalize but instead try to push through the undemocratic reforms they promised their voters (Akkerman and Rooduijn, 2015). Daniele Albertazzi and Sean Mueller summarize their empirical findings on these issues nicely, when they state:

> where populists have accessed government, a subsequent erosion of liberal democratic principles has not been a mere accident but was constant, unrelenting and, most importantly, fully consistent with these parties' ideology. (Albertazzi and Mueller, 2013: 350)

Populism, it turns out, is not a minor or temporary threat that could easily be tamed by throwing the dog a bone. Liberal democrats should take the threat far more seriously and be consistent and unwavering in their defence of the core values that uphold an open and pluralistic society of free and equal citizens.

Technocracy and Populism
as Opposite Threats

If populism functions as a symptom of an underlying problem, the seemingly unstoppable wave of populist movements that we've seen emerging in recent decades in both Europe and Latin America should give us pause. The magnitude and persistence of the phenomenon might suggest that the problem goes beyond the fact that traditional parties occasionally fail to pick up on concerns that preoccupy some of the voters. It might indicate, instead, that liberal democracy is suffering from a deeper and more structural malaise.

In this regard, I agree with those authors who point a finger at the ongoing depoliticization of politics (Crouch, 2004; Mair, 2013; Mouffe, 2013). Particularly relevant seems to me the ongoing growth of technocratic governance networks gradually replacing more traditional forms of government (Rosenau and Czempiel, 1992; Bellamy and Palumbo, 2010). We have been witnessing, for some time now, a systematic displacement of power away from parliament and government towards more hybrid networks in which public and private stakeholders come together for the purpose of solving all kinds of societal coordination problems. This displacement of power does not merely occur at the national level but also has a clear vertical dimension. Thereby, national governments are increasingly confronted with policy constraints imposed upon them by supranational institutions and networks.

This displacement of power leads to a depoliticization of politics in two complementary ways. On the one hand, the new governance networks themselves are characterized by consensus-oriented forms of decision-making in which stakeholders try to come up with "efficient"—in practice often market-oriented—solutions. These decentralized networks are generally insulated from institutionalized forms of oppositional dynamics. As a result, they lack visibility and appear in the eyes of ordinary citizens as an anonymous force over which they have no electoral control but which nevertheless profoundly shapes their lives.

The traditional political institutions, on the other hand, remain committed to the game of a visibly staged political struggle between opposing parties. These institutions have, in reality, lost much of their grip on society. In this regard, Ivan Krastev (2012: 45) has argued that more and more people are living in a democracy without choice in which it is easier to change government than to change policies. In a similar vein, Vivien Schmidt (2013: 12) has pointed out the growing gap between politics and policies in the context of the European Union, where the European level has become increasingly powerful but has not been adequately politicized. As a result, the European level has become the level of (technocratic) policies without politics, whereas the member state level has become the level of (democratic) politics without policies.

Voters, however, are no fools. They increasingly realize that their national politicians have lost much of their power and that, as a result, they themselves have lost much of their electoral control over their own society. In these circumstances, it is not surprising that voters are more and more turning against the system and become receptive to the rhetoric of populist parties that promise to restore the power of the people. In the European context, populist resentment is not surprisingly increasingly directed against the European Union. But also in the Latin American context, as Mudde and Rovira Kaltwasser (2012b: 216–18) rightly point out, the success of populism should at least partly be understood as a reaction against the growing impact of (neoliberal) supranational institutions and trade agreements.

From the perspective of liberal democracy, technocratic governance and populism represent opposite but related threats (Bickerton and Invernizzi Accetti, 2015). In terms of Lefort's image of the empty place of power, populism operates, as we have seen, as an attempt of closure in which the fragmented and open conception of the people as a pluralistic society is being replaced by an imaginary conception of the people as a homogeneous unity. Here, the unity-in-diversity of the *demos* is reduced to a singular identity. Technocratic governance, on the other hand, could be seen as the disappearance of the place of power altogether. Because of the decentralized nature of our governance networks, power becomes elusive and invisible and citizens no longer know where to look in order to understand who is deciding what on behalf of whom. With the displacement of power away from parliament and government, there is no longer a visible stage with identifiable actors who act on behalf of the people and thereby provide a (fragmented) interpretation of the will of the people (Rummens, 2012). In the age of governance, the unity-in-diversity of the *demos* is increasingly reduced to a pure diversity of citizens who no longer dispose of the electoral means to represent themselves as a unified political community capable of shaping its own destiny (Lievens, 2015).

Populism and technocracy are not simply opposite threats; they also seem trapped in a mutually reinforcing dynamic with liberal democracy caught in the middle. Populists attempt to restore popular control over society in an age of technocratic depoliticization. Technocrats, in turn, perceive the rise of populism as proof of the chaotic nature of democracy and as an incentive to further insulate key policy decisions from the vagaries of an unpredictable electorate. In order to break out of this vicious circle and preserve liberal democracy in the long run as a regime in which free and equal citizens shape their own societies, we will need to find ways to curb the rise of the new technocratic governance regime. In an age, however, in which the technocratic network is encompassing the globe, the revitalization of politics can no longer simply be a national project. We will, one way or another, have to reinvent liberal democracy also at the supranational level. And that, to put it mildly, is no small order.

Conclusion

This contribution has investigated the relation between populism and liberal democracy. It has argued against the prominent two-pillar model, which analyses liberal democracy as a paradoxical regime consisting of two mutually incompatible pillars. It claims, in contrast, that the liberal and the democratic dimensions of liberal democracy are not incompatible, but rather co-original. Liberal democracy is a coherent regime which aims to protect human freedom both at an individual and a political level and which conceives of the *demos* as an irreducibly pluralistic community of free and equal citizens.

Liberal democracy, thus conceived, is deeply at odds with populism, which should be understood as an ideology which conceptualizes the will of the people in terms of the *volonté générale* of a homogeneous collectivity. On the liberal dimension, populism therefore tends to undermine the individual liberties of parts of the citizenry as well as to disregard constitutional checks and balances. On the democratic dimension, populism fails to recognize the democratic legitimacy of its political opponents and presents itself as the sole representative of the true people. Especially this latter characteristic is as yet insufficiently recognized as a defining trait of populism and should probably receive more attention in the empirical investigations into the detrimental effects of populist parties on the democratic system.

The antagonistic relation between populism and liberal democracy implies that populism can never operate as a corrective to the democratic system but presents, rather, both a threat and a symptom of an underlying problem. In response to the rise of a populist party, liberal democrats should therefore envisage strategies for dealing with both the threat itself and the underlying malfunction of the representative system. In this regard, Koen Abts and I defend a strategy of concentric containment which isolates populist parties behind a *cordon sanitaire*, but which at the same time aims to provide democratic alternatives to populist voters. The effectiveness of such a strategy as compared to alternative strategies is, and should be, a matter of ongoing empirical investigation.

In the final section, I have argued that technocracy should be understood as an alternative threat to liberal democracy which in many ways forms the mirroring opposite of populism. Since both of these threats are, moreover, caught in a mutually reinforcing dynamic, democracy seems at risk of being crushed in the middle. If we want to devise strategies for safeguarding liberal democracy as the regime which protects and preserves human freedom, a better understanding of these mechanisms, at both the conceptual and the empirical level, seems urgently needed.

References

Abts, K. and S. Rummens. 2007. "Populism versus democracy," *Political Studies*, 55(2): 405–24.
Akkerman, T. and M. Rooduijn. 2015. "Pariahs or partners? Inclusion and exclusion of radical right parties and the effects on their policy positions," *Political Studies*, 63(5): 1140–57.

Albertazzi, D. and S. Mueller. 2013. "Populism and liberal democracy: populists in government in Austria, Italy, Poland and Switzerland," *Government and Opposition*, 48(3): 343–71.

Arditi, B. 2003. "Populism, or, politics at the edges of democracy," *Contemporary Politics*, 9(1): 17–31.

Art, D. 2011. *Inside the Radical Right: The Development of Anti-Immigrant Parties in Western Europe*. Cambridge: Cambridge University Press.

Bellamy, R. and A. Palumbo (eds). 2010. *From Government to Governance*. Farnham: Ashgate.

Bickerton, C. and C. Invernizzi Accetti. 2017. "Populism and technocracy: opposites or complements?," *Critical Review of International Social and Political Philosophy*, 20(2): 186–206.

Canovan, M. 1999. "Trust the people! Populism and the two faces of democracy," *Political Studies*, 47(1): 2–16.

Canovan, M. 2002. "Taking politics to the people: populism as the ideology of democracy," in Y. Mény and Y. Surel (eds), *Democracies and the Populist Challenge*. New York: Palgrave Macmillan, 25–44.

Capoccia, G. 2007. *Defending Democracy: Reactions to Extremism in Interwar Europe*. Baltimore: John Hopkins University Press.

Crouch, C. 2004. *Post-Democracy*. Cambridge: Polity Press.

de Lange, S. L. and T. Akkerman. 2012. "Populist parties in Belgium: a case of hegemonic liberal democracy?," in C. Mudde and C. Rovira Kaltwasser (eds), *Populism in Europe and the Americas: Threat or Corrective for Democracy?* Cambridge: Cambridge University Press, 27–46.

Freeden, M. 1998. "Is nationalism a distinct ideology?," *Political Studies*, 46(4): 748–65.

Habermas, J. 1996. *Between Facts and Norms: Contributions to a Discourse Theory of Law and Democracy*, trans. W. Rehg. Cambridge: MIT Press.

Habermas, J. 1998. *The Inclusion of the Other: Studies in Political Theory*. Cambridge: MIT Press.

Krastev, I. 2012. "Europe's democracy paradox," *The American Interest*, 7(4): 41–7.

Laclau, E. 2005. *On Populist Reason*. London: Verso.

Lefort, C. 1988. *Democracy and Political Theory*. Cambridge: Polity Press.

Levitsky, S. and J. Loxton. 2012. "Populism and competitive authoritarianism: the case of Fujimori's Peru," in C. Mudde and C. Rovira Kaltwasser (eds), *Populism in Europe and the Americas: Threat or Corrective for Democracy?* Cambridge: Cambridge University Press, 160–81.

Lievens, M. 2015. "From government to governance: a symbolic mutation and its repercussions for democracy," *Political Studies*, 63(S1): 2–17.

Mair, P. 2002. "Populist democracy vs party democracy," in Y. Mény and Y. Surel (eds), *Democracies and the Populist Challenge*. New York: Palgrave Macmillan, 81–98.

Mair, P. 2013. *Ruling the Void: The Hollowing-Out of Western Democracy*. London: Verso.

Manin, B. 1997. *The Principles of Representative Government*. Cambridge: Cambridge University Press.

Mazzoleni, G. 2008. "Populism and the media," in D. Albertazzi and D. McDonnell (eds), *Twenty-First Century Populism: The Spectre of Western European Democracy*. Basingstoke: Palgrave Macmillan, 49–64.

Mény, Y. and Y. Surel. 2002. "The constitutive ambiguity of populism," in Y. Mény and Y. Surel, *Democracies and the Populist Challenge*. New York: Palgrave Macmillan, 1–21.

Moffitt, B. and S. Tormey. 2014. "Rethinking populism: politics, mediatisation and political style," *Political Studies*, 62(2): 381–97.

Mouffe, C. 2000. *The Democratic Paradox*. London: Verso.

Mouffe, C. 2005. "The 'end of politics' and the challenge of right-wing populism," in F. Panizza (ed.), *Populism and the Mirror of Democracy*. London: Verso, 50–71.

Mouffe, C. 2013. *Agonistics: Thinking the World Politically*. London: Verso.

Mudde, C. 2004. "The populist zeitgeist," *Government and Opposition*, 39(4): 541–63.

Mudde, C. and C. Rovira Kaltwasser. 2012a. "Populism and (liberal) democracy: a framework for analysis," in C. Mudde and C. Rovira Kaltwasser (eds), *Populism in Europe and the Americas: Threat or Corrective for Democracy?* Cambridge: Cambridge University Press, 1–26.

Mudde, C. and C. Rovira Kaltwasser. 2012b. "Populism: corrective *and* threat to democracy," in C. Mudde and C. Rovira Kaltwasser (eds), *Populism in Europe and the Americas: Threat or Corrective for Democracy?* Cambridge: Cambridge University Press, 205–22.

Pauwels, T. 2011. "Explaining the strange decline of the populist radical right Vlaams Belang in Belgium: the impact of permanent opposition," *Acta Politica*, 46(1): 60–82.

Rawls, J. 1996. *Political Liberalism, with a New Introduction and the "Reply to Habermas."* New York: Columbia University Press.

Rosenau, J. N. and E. Czempiel (eds). 1992. *Governance Without Government: Order and Change in World Politics*. Cambridge: Cambridge University Press.

Rummens, S. 2006. "Debate: the co-originality of private and public autonomy in deliberative democracy," *The Journal of Political Philosophy*, 14(4): 469–81.

Rummens, S. 2009. "Democracy as a non-hegemonic struggle: disambiguating Chantal Mouffe's agonistic model of politics," *Constellations*, 16(3): 377–91.

Rummens, S. 2012. "Staging deliberation: the role of representative institutions in the deliberative democratic process," *The Journal of Political Philosophy*, 20(1): 23–44.

Rummens, S. and K. Abts. 2010. "Defending democracy: the concentric containment of political extremism," *Political Studies*, 58(4): 649–65.

Schmidt, V. A. 2013. "Democracy and legitimacy in the European Union revisited: input, output *and* 'throughput,'" *Political Studies*, 61(1): 2–22.

Schmitt, C. 1988. *The Crisis of Parliamentary Democracy*. Cambridge: MIT Press.

Schmitt, C. 2008. *Constitutional Theory*. Durham and London: Duke University Press.

Taggart, P. 2002. "Populism and the pathology of representative politics," in Y. Mény and Y. Surel (eds), *Democracies and the Populist Challenge*. New York: Palgrave Macmillan, 62–80.

Taguieff, P. 1995. "Political science confronts populism: from a conceptual mirage to a real problem," *Telos*, 103: 9–43.

Urbinati, N. 1998. "Democracy and populism," *Constellations*, 5(1): 110–24.

CHAPTER 29

....

POPULISM AND
THE PRINCIPLE OF MAJORITY

....

NADIA URBINATI

INTEREST in the study of populism is strongest among scholars who see it as a problem.[1] Political theorists who have suggested that populism might have a positive role to play in a contemporary democracy are thus few. To this minority, populism's putative virtues include "folk democracy" versus institutionalized politics; the concerns of the large numbers ahead of the interests of the few; the lived experience of the local, the village, the neighborhood over an abstract, distant citizenship; and finally the consistent actualization of popular sovereignty as the substance of the whole over and above constitutional rules (Hofstadter, 1969; Canovan, 1999; Mudde, 2001; Mény and Surel, 2002). Populist political theorists emphasize also the political directness, sincerity, and transparency of ordinary people versus the indirection and opacity of representative institutions; they oppose the "purity" of political purpose of the many against the bargaining games played by the politicians, who are part of the few and the elite (Kazin, 1995; Canovan, 2002; Mudde, 2004); they praise decisiveness (and also decisionism) over parliamentary time-consuming compromises, procedural formalism, and institutional obfuscation; they use the language of the organic unity of the *populus* versus the artificial and abstract language of intellectuals and scholars; finally they stress the priority and homogeneity of the whole versus pluralism and conflict of interests.

None of these several qualities and characteristics has as yet converged on an undisputed definition; populism is, like other political categories, controversial and at times polemical, branded to accuse actual political movements or leaders—this explains the "repugnance with which the words 'populism' and 'populist' are uttered," particularly among European scholars (D'Eramo, 2013: 5). However, recent literature has enriched our knowledge of this phenomenon and, as this book testifies, it is now possible to have some convergence around definitions of populism in relation to at least its ideological character, its strategic mechanism, and its socio-cultural content (see the chapters by Mudde, Weyland, and Ostiguy).

Based on these novel investigations, in this chapter I adopt the distinction between *populism as a movement* of opinion (critical or oppositional) and *populism as a ruling power*, a perspective that allows us to face populism in its rhetorical style, its propaganda tropes, its contents, and finally its aims and achievements. This double condition mirrors the diarchic character of democracy, or citizens' equal right to participate both in the informal power of opinion-making *and* in the formal designation of lawmakers. Consent through opinion and consent through voting are the coordinates for judging populism in its meaning, functions, and possible consequences. This means that it is inaccurate to treat populism as the same as "popular movements," movements of protest, or "the popular" (Berlin et al., 1968).

Both populism as a movement and populism as a within-state power are parasitical on representative democracy (Arditi, 2008).[2] But while a certain populist rhetoric is to be detected in almost all parties (particularly when they radicalize their claims close to elections), populism as a ruling power has some recognizable characteristics that can sharply contrast with "practical democracy" and the procedural structures of ordinary politics, like hostility towards party pluralism, the principles of constitutional democracy, and the division of powers (Mény and Surel, 2002; Canovan, 2002). Hence, although ingrained in the ideology of the people and the language of democracy, populism as a ruling power tends to give life to governments that stretch the democratic rules toward an extreme majoritarianism (Bobbio, 1989; Taggart, 2000). This is the thesis holding together this chapter, whose subject is populism as a *within-state power* phenomenon.

The argument I propose originates from the assumption (which is a generalization from historical experiences) that a populist movement that succeeds in securing an electoral majority in a democratic society tends to move toward institutional forms that change, and even shatter, constitutional democracy for the sake of a further, more intense majority. Benjamin Arditi has written (2008) that because of its radical contestation of parliamentary politics, populism can be seen as representative democracy's "internal periphery." I have elsewhere isolated and analyzed some basic characteristics of this periphery, from the simplification of social interests and political polarization to Caesarism and the centrality of decision over deliberation (Urbinati, 2014: ch. 3). In what follows I intend to go to ground zero of populism's relationship to democracy, so to speak, where democracy takes root: the interpretation of the people and majority rule as the basic norms that qualify a democratic government. The pressing questions animating this chapter are the following: "How can we deny that populism is democratic or a form of democratic politics given that it does not question the golden rule of democracy and is actually a radical affirmation of it?" "What puts populism and democracy in tension although they rest on the same principle and claim to be government by the people?" The answers to these questions bring me to the following conclusion: when it seeks to implement its agenda through state power, populism enters a direct competition with constitutional democracy over the meaning and expression of the people; puts into question a party-democracy's conception of representation because it is impatient with the tension between pluralism of social interests and unity of the polity that electoral representation triggers and channels. Populism challenges political pluralism and party-democracy with a representation of the people as one and by merging the interests existing within society into a unified meaning that holds for the whole.

A Double Criterion of Evaluation

Since "we simply do not have anything like a *theory* of populism" (Müller, 2011), it is important I offer some preliminary clarifications on the usage of this term and on the relevance of the social context. On the first issue, I will *not* treat populism as the same as "popular movements," movements of protest, or "the popular." We may say that there is populist rhetoric but *not* yet populist power when the polarizing and anti-representative discourse is made up of a social movement that wants to be a constituency independent of elected officials, wants to resist becoming an elected entity, does not have nor want representative leaders who unify its several claims, and wants to keep elected officials or the government under the scrutiny of the public. This was the case, for instance, of popular movements of contestation and protest like the Girotondi in Italy in 2002, Occupy Wall Street in the United States in 2011, and Indignados in Spain in 2011.[3] Without an organizing narrative, the aspiration to win seats in the Parliament or the Congress and a leadership claiming its people to be the true expression of the people as a whole, a popular movement remains very much what it is: a sacrosanct democratic movement of opinion, protest, and contestation against a trend in society that betrays some basic principles, which society itself has promised to respect and fulfill (political equality in particular). On the other hand, there is populist rhetoric *and* populist power when a movement does not want to be a constituency independent of the elected officials but wants instead to conquer the representative institutions and win a majority in order to model society on its own ideology of the people. This is for instance the case of Hungary's Fidesz party that in 2012 won a supermajority of the seats in Parliament and used it to scrap the old Constitution by amending it continuously, entrenching its own political vision at the expense of opposition parties and an independent judiciary (Müller, 2015). Thus, populism is a *pars-pro-toto* project (Arato, 2013). This makes me argue that while a symptom of political and social malaise in a democratic society, populism can hardly be a cure.

As for the second issue (the relevance of the social context), it is important we understand that if populism can hardly become a theory it is also because of its social and historical embeddedness (Mény and Surel, 2002: pt 3). Positive and negative judgments on populism are context sensitive in the deepest sense. For instance, in the United States, where the term was coined in the age of post–Civil War industrial reconstruction and never brought to a regime change, populism developed along with political democratization and was, and still is, predictably met positively by historians and political theorists (Kazin, 1995). Born when the country was ruled by an elected notabilate representing the interests of an oligarchy (before universal suffrage was implemented), the Declaration of Independence and the Bill of Rights became extant conditions for a more democratized polity (Beaumont, 2014), and populism a collective movement against the domestic enemies of "the people" (Frank, 2010: 4–18) in the name of an alleged purity of the *origins* of popular government and its adulteration by the artificial complexity of civilization and the institutional organization of the state (Lasch, 1991). On the other hand, in some Latin American countries, "the land of populism" as Carlo de la Torre writes in his chapter, populism has been met with mixed feelings in relation to its historical phases; thus whether it was evaluated at the beginning of its career or at the pick of its fulfillment as a regime; as an opposition party mobilizing against an existing government or as a regime itself; and then also, as a regime in its consolidation stage or when it had to face succession in power (Weyland, 2001; Rovira Kaltwasser, 2012; Finchelstein, 2014; de la Torre, 2014). Like in the United States, also in Latin America populism emerged in the age of social modernization but much like fascism in Italy it governed the path towards modernity that used state power to both protect and empower its popular classes, repress dissent, and meanwhile implement social-welfare policies (Germani, 1978). Thus Ernesto Laclau described populism (and Peronism in particular) as a strategy of hegemonic rebalancing within the "power blocs" through the incorporation of the popular-democratic ideology of the masses within the ruling majority (Laclau, 1977; 2005a pt 2). Yet although populist leaders seeking power promised to include the excluded, "once in power" they "attacked the institutions of liberal democracy, grabbed power, aimed to control social movements and civil society, and clashed with the privately owned media" (de la Torre in this book, p. 195).

These several experiences and interpretations suggest we study populism as a political phenomenon that is dependent on the social conditions and class relations within a horizon that is already democratic or in the process of becoming democratic. They confirm, in some sense, Aristotle's theory of demagoguery (which I will analyze below) as a phenomenon developing within a constitutional government to be explained and judged with careful attention to the social and economic conditions in which it emerges and the impact it has on the institutional order. In this sense populism is not simply context sensitive but, more specifically, socially context sensitive.

Reference to the social context would seem to prove that populism plays a positive role not only in accelerating democratization in societies that are semi-democratic, but also in amending liberal democracies whenever social inequalities make the proclaimed political equality a mere figure of speech and institutions too remote from the people (Rovira Kaltwasser, 2012). Precisely because populism refuses to make the people a merely legal category that is not sensitive to the socio-economic condition of the majority, its emergence is taken to be evidence of its democratic inclusiveness.

Yet judgments about the democratic role of populism ask to be calibrated in relation not only to the social context and the hegemonic content unifying the people but also to the constitutional norms of democracy (i.e. separation of powers, rights protection, and thus the distinction between the majority rule and the rule of the majority). This double criterion of evaluation (social and normative) suggests caution in rushing to the identification of populism with democracy because they both rely on the people. It makes sense of the fact that populism might have more of a chance to play a democratizing role in those societies that are not yet fully democratic, in which "the people" is a *de facto* claimant of a sovereign power it does not yet have and that it claims with the strength of its social unity—in not yet democratic societies the claim for power may benefit from the unity of the claimant (this was for instance Sieyes's strategy). However, if we want to prove that populism is consistent with democracy (and moreover strengthens it in societies that are democratic) we have to resort to the normative criterion and ascertain whether it is satisfied by the populist interpretation of the people as a social whole.

In fact, the populist's goal is not so much that of claiming and monitoring the equal distribution of political and civil rights among equal citizens—it is not a constitutional goal—but that of evaluating the impact of civil rights on the unity of the people, which is its primary concern. Populism is "impatient of procedures" (Crick, 2005: 626) and norms and thus is primed to permanently contest the constitutional order of an existing democracy, because the people it refers to is not simply a legal and political unity made up of citizens endowed with equal political rights to participate, directly or indirectly, in the government of their country (Canovan, 1984; Panizza, 2005).

The double criterion—social and normative—suggests that the debate over the meaning of populism is in effect a debate over the interpretation of democracy and democratic citizenship. Yet in relation to this debate, starting with a sociological conception of the people (the people as an hegemonic social unity), as scholars who embrace a populist reading of democracy do, does not seem promising because the people as a social category may fit within several domains, so that we need in any case to clarify what kind of unity we adopt in order to qualify "the people." In a word, the people as a social category can be unified under different criteria—socio-economical, cultural, ethnical, national, religious, etc.[4]—yet none of them is sufficient to make a people a democratic actor, even if can create a corporate and homogeneous collective.

To tackle this problem, two lines of argument can be pursued: one that asks how "the people" as a social category evolved through history and under which typologies it can be grouped; and one that goes to the source of political legitimacy and interrogates the consistency of populism's people with democracy's political norms. As anticipated at the start, when we examine populism's view of the *political* identity of the people we see it does not have an independent conception of political authority. Populism is parasitic on democracy because democracy is the political regime and the form of politics in the name of which it claims its own legitimacy and challenges the legitimacy of existing majorities and constitutional democracies; moreover it is parasitic on representative democracy because it challenges it in the name of an exclusive and undivided representation of the people. Populism thus questions primarily the identification of democracy with pluralistic political representation and the constitutional limitation of the power of the majority, two conditions consistent with a vision of political autonomy that has the citizens and the rules of the game at its core. Hence, scholars have observed, representative democracy is the true target, as the populist critique of parliamentary politics translates into a call for an unmediated relation of the leader to the people en masse (Bobbio, 1989; Mudde and Rovira Kaltwasser, 2013). Understanding populism's relation to representative democracy (populism's true critical target) is thus my next step, before analyzing the populist interpretation of the majority principle.

The Representative Challenge

All populist movements, Yves Mèny and Yves Surel (2002) have argued, exhibit a strong reservation and even hostility to the mechanisms of representation, in the name of one collective affirmation of the will of the electors or the people under a leading figure. Yet they do not renounce representation to institute direct democracy.[5] To specify my earlier claim, populism is parasitical not so much on democracy but on representative democracy; it is *not* external to representative democracy but *does* compete with it about the meaning and use of representation as the way of claiming, affirming, and managing the will of the people. Populism's representative claim is the source of populism's radical contestation of parliamentary democracy. It may be useful at this point to recall the genesis of representation.

Representation was born in a confrontational environment. Its origins are to be found in the context of the medieval church and in the recurrent disputes over whether the pope or the council of bishops represented the unitary body of the Christians (Gierke, 1958: 61). It was born *both* as an institution for the containment and control of power (the chief of the church or the king) *and* as a means of unifying a large and diverse population. It flourished in the context of a social universe (made of subjects or believers) that was separated from the authority of the ruling power (whether secular or religious). These aspects together presumed an involvement of both the representative and the represented because the former, who was sometimes called "procurator" and "commissary," was supposed to speak or act for a specific group of people, who endowed him with the power of representing their interests in front of an authority, secular or religious, that was recognized as superior (Pitkin, 1967: ch. 4). Representation originated when a given community delegated some members to represent it before the pope or the court of the king, with powers to bind those who appointed them. This technique was then transferred to the context of the state. In the form of a synthesis, thus, unification (of the multitude) and subjection (of the represented to the decisions made by the chosen delegates) merged in the institution of representation.

Yet it was the institutionalization of elections by those "subjected" that injected a new factor of conflict and competition, and introduced the quest for accountability. Indeed, elections simultaneously separate and link citizens and government. They create a gap between state and society and at the same time allow them to communicate and even conflict, but never fuse. Hence, within eighteenth-century constitutional states, representation started becoming the terrain of an *unresolvable tension* between its traditional *unifying* and *subjecting* functions and the new ones that elections conferred upon it, namely, electors' *advocacy* of their *interests and claims* (whence the call for accountability). Thus, when the parliament became the place of representative politics, it fatally acquired the character of an agora of ideas that was primed to bring social dissension at the core of the state. The unifying element was entrenched in the constitutional moment, a grammar that would allow pluralism to emerge without disrupting effects and actually play a stability function. Carl Schmitt defined this as liberal representative politics. He argued (rightly) that political representation both exalts advocacy of interests and allows their temporary mediation in majority decisions, and then criticized it for transforming (and, in his mind, deforming) politics in an art of compromise that transfers to the state the norms and procedures that regulate social conflicts and their bargained resolutions. In giving populism a strong argument, Schmitt made clear that it is the unity of the sovereign that is at stake with electoral representation, not a broader or deeper participation by the citizens (Urbinati, 2011).

The state's relationship with civil society is the heart of electoral representation and the terrain of party politics. Among the functions that electoral representation plays, the following is most relevant to our case: it serves to channel social and ideological conflicts within the law-making institutions through party competition and in this way makes the sovereign visible through divisions and conflicts. Populism infiltrates the tension between parties and the state in order to overcome it. It thus opposes the unifying function of representation (Hobbes/Schmitt) against its compromissory bargaining as in parliamentary and party democracy (Mair, 2002: 88–92; Urbinati, 2006: chs 1 and 2).

Populism aims at a more direct identification of the represented with the representatives than free elections allow because it sees representation primarily as a strategy for embodying the whole people under a leader, rather than regulating the political dialectics among citizens' plural claims and advocacies. Populism wants to merge together material unification (ordinary politics) and formal unification (state politics) thus overcoming the merely normative reading of procedures and the constitution. In this important sense it is a break with representative democracy because it is impatient with the tension between pluralism and unity, material and formal aspects that electoral representation entails. The representative, Laclau writes (2005a: 157–8), must be an active agent who gives words and credibility to the represented unity, the actor of the homogenizing process who puts an end to the divisions of the electorate. The populist representative is in fact a leader who wants people's faith and emotional identification with no question of accountability; in the end, not even the political party he relies upon can check him, because it is usually made instrumental to the acquisition and the preservation of his power.

Within this context, elections are transformed into a plebiscite for celebrating the leader and result in a visual construction of the whole national body at the symbolic and institutional level. Similarly to the President in Schmitt's conception of representation as incorporation that makes visible the invisible sovereign, populism builds on a view of representation as a work of unity and identity construction in relation to which party pluralism and electoral competition are an obstacle. "The President, by contrast [to the fragmentation of parliamentary grouping] has the confidence of the entire people not mediated by the medium of a parliament splintered into parties. This confidence, rather, is directly united in his person" (Schmitt, 2008: 370). In a similar manner, populism uses representation as a hegemonic strategy that repels the liberal calls (of advocacy, control, monitoring, and a constant dialogue between society and politics) and narrows the distance between the elected leader and the electors so as to incorporate society within the state. In Margaret Canovan's words, "A vision of 'the people' as a united body implies impatience with party strife, and can encourage support for strong leadership where a charismatic individual is available to personify the interests of the nation" (Canovan, 1999: 5). The demagogical factor is a part of populism and the ideological construction of consent is its instrument.

DEMAGOGUERY AND A DENSE MAJORITY

Unification versus pluralism is the structural trope of populism in representative democracy as it was of ancient demagoguery in relation to direct democracy. The impact of their appeal to the people is of course different. Indeed, while populism's upheaval develops within the non-sovereign sphere of opinion (the world of ideology) and may very well remain so if it does not get the majority to govern, in ancient direct democracy demagogy had an immediate law-making impact. While aware of the crucial differences that elections bring to democracy, I use ancient analysis of demagoguery to explain populism's conflictual relationship to democracy and its cunning cooptation of majority rule to its power concentration plan (Lane, 2012; Ober, 1989: 106–7).

Aristotle is the author who offered the most precise characterization of demagoguery; his ideas are illuminating in understanding the nature and social dynamic of modern populism. First of all, he dropped Plato's identification of the demagogue with the tyrant and made the former part of the democratic style of politics; secondly, he proposed a distinction among demagogues and in this way emancipated demagoguery (and democracy) from total disdain. Aristotle thought that democracy can go through internal transformations from constitutional to unconstitutional, from majority to majoritarianism.

Aristotle thus listed examples of both "good" democracy (constitutional) and "bad" democracy (demagogical). Cleisthenes was the popular leader who, "after the fall of the tyranny," gave to the Athenians "a constitution more democratic than that of Solon." By contrast, Pisistratus, who "had the reputation of being a strong supporter of the common people," cunningly masked his intention to become a tyrant. He was a formidable demagogue who manipulated the bitterness of the recently enfranchised peasants to conquer political power with their support; in this way he "seized power" by "flattering the people" (Aristotle, 1998: 1304b1–10).

Clearly, in direct democracy demagoguery was a permanent possibility, although not in itself an exit from democracy and a regime in its own right. A disfigured demagogical democracy was still a democracy; and according to Aristotle, demagoguery was certainly the worst among the forms democracy could take because it exploited free speech by putting it at the service of unanimity or the appeal to the whole, rather than a free and frank expression of ideas and thus the appeal to a majority vote. Demagoguery could not exist without a leader because it was not simply the spontaneous horizontal mobilization of ordinary citizens. And it could not exist without the public either because the demagogue constructed his success in the assembly, drawing his audience from the public. We can say the same of populism which, when it aspires to power, cannot be headless and cannot impose the headless will on the people without people's assent and support.

Aristotle's analysis is pivotal for our argument also because it suggests we focus on the use that leaders make of their speaking abilities and democracy's political liberties in order not merely to win a majority vote but to overwhelm the opposition and make it feel a meaningless entity. As Nancy Rosenblum writes in describing what she calls "shadow holism", "invocation of a majority—actual or imagined—as if it were the whole people" translates easily into the "assumption that the cohesion of the whole has priority over the minority's claim" (Rosenblum 2008, 48–51). The majority treats minority views as an obstacle rather than a physiological component of the political game; on the other hand, the minority is seen from the perspective of the majority, not of the civil and political rights shared by all the citizens: "the concept of majority assumes the right of existence of a minority" (ibid., 51).

To complete his depiction of demagoguery, Aristotle reconstructed the social context and class divisions. "In democracies the principal cause of revolutions is the insolence of the demagogues; for they cause the owners of property to band together, partly by malicious prosecutions of individuals among them (for common fear brings together even the greatest enemies), and partly by setting on the common people against them as a class" (Aristotle, 1998: 1304b20–25).

Aristotle offers us a structural analysis of the social conditions and class relations that can facilitate the emergence of demagoguery (or populism). His generalization from Greece's and Athens's history wanted to be an interpretative frame for understanding some institutional and political transformations. Let us analyze them.

The crisis of social pluralism and the narrowing of the middle class are the two intertwined factors that accompanied that transformation. Polarization (well-off/the poor) and the erosion of the middle class were, and still are today, at the origin of political simplification and the polarization of political positions (Atkinson and Brandolini, 2011). We should recall that Aristotle takes the presence of a robust middle class to be the condition for any constitutional government (also of "good" democracy) and its disappearance or exhaustion because of economic crisis and the decline of general well-being as the condition for constitutional changes or even revolution. "And constitutions also undergo revolution when what are thought of as opposing sections of the state become equal to one another, for instance the rich and the people, and there is no middle class or only an extremely small one; for if either of the two sections becomes much the superior, the remainder is not willing to risk an encounter with its manifestly stronger opponent" (Aristotle, 1998: 1304b1–10).

The disappearance of social mediation and moderation translates into the end of moderation and mediation in political decisions. We should read moderation as a politics of compromise because this is what makes the numerical minority always part of the democratic game in a self-containing way. Until the opposition has the power to threaten the majority and thus be part of the bargaining game, a strong majority in the assembly or the parliament does not endanger political stability. Then, under certain conditions, demagoguery transfigures democracy even if it does not overturn it necessarily. As we shall see, this is the case with populism and the populist leader, which tend to grow in conditions of economic crisis and take advantage of social distress to exalt polarization and nurture in the winner of the political majority the temptation to use state power in a punitive way against the oppositions and the minorities, thus to break class compromise (or, as for Laclau, to rearrange the "formal" generality of *politeia* with a "true" one) (Laclau, 2005a: 169). This twist of majority rule for decision-making into the domination of the decision-maker (a given majority) explains the normative difference between constitutional democracy and populist democracy.

In comparison to the numerical majority of which democracy's process of decision-making consists, demagoguery reifies a given majority as it promotes policies that translate the interests of the winners immediately into law, with no patience for mediation and compromise or institutional checks and balances. Polarization helps this strategy. From majority rule as a procedure for making decisions in a climate of pluralism to the ruling power of a majority in a climate that sees pluralism as an obstacle to the making of swift and possibly uncontested decisions: this is the radical transformation of democracy from within that demagoguery (and populism) prompts.

Is demagoguery the tyrannical rule of the majority of the people? Not entirely according to Aristotle. Certainly, the demagogue needs the consent of the majority and uses speech to bring the assembly on his side and make it one thing with the opinion of the agora. Yet manipulation by means of speech is part of an open democratic competition; thus it is hard to make or achieve a clear-cut distinction between what is straight and what is twisted when freedom of speech dominates a political order. In a government based on *doxa*, distinguishing populism and democracy, populist rhetoric and party rhetoric, is hard. If majority rule works both in a pluralistic democracy and in a polarized or populist democracy how can we make a tenable distinction? Aristotle teaches us that although they rely on the majority, democracy and demagoguery are different. His suggestion can be applied to representative democracy and populism as well.

This should make us agree that to gain a large majority in a collective is still not the same as having democratic politics. The same argument can be found in Rousseau's *Social Contract*, which tells us that when *the will* and *the opinion* merge, the republic enjoys stronger legitimacy because the will of the assembly is so little contested (decisions are made with a large majority of votes) that all the people feel themselves one body politic *de iure* and *de facto*. It is not unanimity or a large majority per se that makes a democracy demagogical thus, but *the way* it is achieved.

We should recall that according to Rousseau when meeting in the assembly citizens should only vote not talk; this was meant to block manipulation and make each citizen follow his reason. Conviction by reason rather than by rhetorical persuasion was in his mind the safe condition for making the merging of *de iure* (general will) and of *de facto* (*l'opinion générale*) sovereignty a sign of political justice, rather than merely of numerical power and thus the domineering and in his mind illegitimate majority (the will of all). Yet Rousseau suggested that it is possible to achieve that unison both by reason and by rhetoric—demagoguery, as populism, is a permanent risk in a regime that, like democracy, is based on public speech and opinion-and-will formation. Taking away the right of free speech in the assembly as Rousseau recommends is no solution in a representative democracy, where public discussion is the unavoidable condition for forming, challenging, and changing majorities. Thus, once again, the problem is the meaning of people's unity, whether material (social sameness) or regulative (procedures and the constitution), that channels diversity of opinion and the majority/opposition divide in collective decision-making (Kelsen, 2013: ch. 6). The unification of the people under a leader and with negligible internal pluralism or with a radical simplification of classes that unify the two inimical camps is the source of the problem. Aristotle offers us some important suggestions on how to interpret the phenomenon of unification or, in Laclau's words, to create the hegemonic unity.

Recall that a good constitution is, in Aristotle's mind, an institutional arrangement that rests on a dynamic equilibrium between the two main social classes—the rich and the poor. Regardless of the form of government, this equilibrium is what makes a government moderate and the home of liberty. For social (and political) equilibrium to exist, a broad social medium is needed. In the case of democracy, this medium is primed to more easily persist so long as the very poor are few in number and the very rich feel safe although they are a numerical minority. Instead, problems arise through the uprooting of the middle and the radicalizing of the social poles: this is what demagoguery explodes and exploits. This is when majority rule can be pursued with an intensity that is unknown to a constitutional democracy. As we saw previously, the social context is an important condition to understand and judge populism. Yet, achieving an intense majority for doing what? Why is a more intense majority needed?

This question is relevant precisely because demagoguery is not identical to democracy even if, in Aristotle's reading, the poor or the workers (which populism like demagoguery claims to empower) are the majority in both cases. Why should the social numerical majority be in need at a certain point of a more intense political majority? Why is a simple majority of votes no longer enough? These questions suggest that, presumably, the particular actor of demagoguery is *not* the numerical majority alone or in itself. As majority is the norm of democratic decision-making, demagoguery occupies the "space" of the majority and appropriates the norm. Aristotle offered a social explanation of this phenomenon which highlighted class polarization and an increase in poverty: compromises that the poor were previously able to strike with the middle class and the rich become more difficult when a large number of impoverished people need a more interventionist policy on the part of the state. They need a policy that is more on their side in an unprecedented way (that raises taxes, for instance, and asks more from the wealthy few in a way unbearable to them) and this is primed to upset some among the well-off, who start "banding together" in order to better resist popular claims and protect their assets. Hence, it is not the presence of the multitude of the ordinary people (the non-wealthy) per se that explains the demagogical attack on constitutional democracy as contemporary populists claim.

What explains the assault on constitutional democracy is instead the *breakdown of social equilibrium*, which is primed to open the door to a politics of power concentration that erodes the impartiality of the law although not necessarily for the enactment of fairer policies. A radical social polarization and the over-empowerment of class interests are the premises of a more intense majority which demagoguery and populism exploit in order to build their power within the state. This dynamic was elucidated by Claude Lefort, who identified populism with the overturning of the non-foundational character of representative democracy as a process that reveals that power does not belong to anybody, neither to the politicians who exercise it nor to the people in whose name power is exercised. Constitutional democracy makes sure that no social or political actor embodies the will of the people, which must remain the permanent creation and recreation of the democratic process itself. In materializing the will of the people and condensing state power into a homogeneous actor, populism attempts to resolve the "paradox" of the "empty space" of politics by "determining who constitutes the people" (Lefort, 1988: 13–20).

This is the important difference with the democratic rule of majority, and the reason why democracy and demagoguery (or populism) are not the same, although they both make appeal to the people and the majority principle, and although they belong to the same genre. Economic crisis and the decline in the well-being of the many can make the numerical majority more ready to pass laws that induce "the owners of property to band together" in order to resist, for instance, tax increases that a more socially active state is required to enact by a larger impoverished population. This is the class factor at the origin of demagoguery and which demagoguery exploits in the name of the nation or the people as one. As European history shows with astonishing regularity, constitutional democracy risks a great deal if society becomes poorer and the welfare is under threat by internal crisis or/and immigration.[6]

Why call it demagoguery and not tyranny? As we saw with Pisistratus, Aristotle listed cases in which demagoguery can become a tyranny. Nonetheless, demagoguery operates within constitutional democracy, in which the assembly of freeborn citizens is the supreme organ and proposals must gain the majority of their votes to become laws. As long as the equilibrium among classes persists, the weapon of words seems to be not a worrisome strategy and moreover is a strategy still within the constitutional limits. Demagoguery represents in this sense a form of political language that is consonant with assembly politics, and thus democracy. Yet this "neutral" reading may easily end and, when this happens, a tyrant emerges.[7]

This is the paradox we want to consider: it is not the oligarchs or the few in their totality (as if they were one homogeneous class) per se that break with the rule and turn demagoguery into tyranny. It is a part of them, who understand that the time has arrived when they can, through the expediency of rhetoric and the exploitation of social duress, acquire more power and use the people's impoverishment and social distress to turn them against the very constitution, and first of all against those among the few who still uphold the equilibrium among classes and make the democratic constitution hold. The *third party* between the few and the many to which Aristotle referred in order to explain Pisistratus's tyranny is the key element to understand not merely the social condition for the demagogical victory but also the role of the individual leader (Lane, 2012). Social distress unleashes the immoderate desire for power among the few, who realize that the breakdown of social and political balance can be turned into a strategy of regime change, through which they can make decisions without consulting the opinion of the people.

The demagogue represents a new class within the class of the wealthy, those who think they can obtain more power or enjoy more privileges or rule without institutional constraints with the very support of the many. This is the moment in which they oppose the social condition against the presumed useless legal political equality with the support of the majority. They are "men ambitious of office by acting as popular leaders." They represent a split inside the class of the few and are able to gain the favor of the people to pass laws in their own favor and with the people's support (Aristotle, 1998: 1305a30–35; Przeworski, 1999)! Aristotle's scheme seems timeless. As Joseph M. Schwartz writes in his merciless analysis of the erosion of equality in modern democracy, few reformist theorists would have predicted at the end of the 1970s that "the right (particularly in the United Kingdom and the United States) would build a populist majoritarian politics in favor of deregulation, de-unionization, and welfare state cutbacks, particularly of means-tested programs" (Schwartz, 2009: 178). Other examples can be adduced to prove the success of populist parties and policies in contemporary European countries, which adopt at the same time a politics of privatization of social services and a nationalistic policy of closed borders against immigrants and refugees, that cut down taxes and narrow the public sectors, and by doing so gain the support of the lower classes and the higher classes alike.

Thus, like demagoguery and regardless of its cunning appeal to the "united body" of the people, the populist power is a movement that relies upon the studious usage of words, images, and the media in order to make the many converge toward politics that are not necessarily in their interests although they are so framed that they seem to be consistent with the will of the people as one homogeneous body. Polarization (which comes from the simplification of social pluralism through economic crisis) is indeed for the sake of a new unification of the people, and is a strategy an elite uses to claim and acquire more power in order to achieve some results that an open, pluralist, and articulated deliberation would not allow. All populist leaders claim that decisions need to be made quickly and deliberation or party contestation in parliament is a waste of time.

Partyless Democracy and a Populist Constitution

Clearly, populist policies are not merely the product of procedural majority. A larger majority is needed and claimed. The people's collectivity as a homogeneous whole, rather than an *ex post* result of counting of votes, seems to be, since Aristotle, one of the signs of a disfigured democracy, a democracy that is prone to host a demagogic or populist leadership. In a similar vein, Niccolò Machiavelli made a distinction that can be useful to expand our analysis of populist politics—that between *partisan-friends* and *partisan-enemies*, or party conflicts as articulations of different and seldom opposite interests (which are good as they veto temptations for unrestrained power) and factionalism (as the superimposition of one interest over the others, whether of the few or of the many).

Conflict, according to Machiavelli, is the oxygen to freedom so long as it is managed by the social classes or groups in a way that neither of them can use the other as a mere instrument (this is what the "buoni ordini" do). Conflict for what the political actors argue to be in an open competition good for the city is thus the prerequisite—a norm of freedom because it does not allow a zero-sum game among the two parts of society (Machiavelli, 1970: 16). As long as political pluralism and an open conflict persist or, to adapt this idea to our time, as long as elections are an open game and not a means that de facto advantages one part with the support of the majority, demagoguery is powerless although free to emerge.

It is thus not demagogic speech (or populist rhetoric) but rather its victory with large popular support that is the problem. Pluralism is a strategy to solve this problem without abolishing liberty. Party politics, thus, is both a way to channel participation and a way to make conflict and partisanship work in the service of liberty of all the citizens. In altering this dynamic equilibrium populism wants to make its representation of the people that the leader embodies into the whole people, while the opposition is no longer honored as partisan-friend but treated as partisan-enemy—in this sense Peter Mair has written that "populist democracy primarily tends towards partyless democracy" (2002: 89). When this happens, the institutional order starts working as a strategy that is doubtfully constitutional as it functions for the power of a part—the city becomes a city of two peoples, of which only one holds state power and uses it against the other and in order to retain power for as long as possible.

The divorce of institutions and virtue was the argument Machiavelli devised in order to explain the decline of the republic, and he flagged two things, in particular: first, that good rules produce the foreseen effects depending on the social and ethical conditions in which they operate; second, that a political system can change without its constitutional principles changing. In the case of ancient Rome, for instance, Augustus did not revoke its republican institutions, which however became futile and no longer able to make the empire qualify as a republic. The same institutions that made Rome a republic were able to mark its decline because the citizens were corrupt, that is, the social structure was changed and virtuous behavior became too onerous.

Elections may allow the emergence of ambitious orators. But it is not orators per se who define the change to demagoguery and it is not elections and majority rule that cause demagogy. Going back to the distinction I started with, applied to contemporary politics we may say that populism is not simply a popular movement that contests the establishment but a movement whose leader wants to conquer a supreme power in order to occupy the state and use its institutions *as if* they belonged to him and his "people", so as to distribute favors and posts and thus strengthen their constituency over time. Reaching power through mobilization, a populist leadership can consolidate and perpetuate it through patronage or clientelism. A democratic Machiavelli would say that in that case, it would not be the people sovereign "over the law" but the leaders who win people's consent to their plans. Political scientists call this "discriminatory legalism"— the idea that "everything for my friends; for my enemies, the law" (Weyland, 2013).

This is what populism may do when it succeeds in conquering consent and changing the procedures of constitutional democracy. Populist leaders or parties that have enough power are not content with simply winning a majority but want a more unbounded power and moreover to stay in power as long as possible; they "will seek to establish a new populist constitution—in both the sense of a new sociopolitical settlement and a new set of rules for the political game" (Müller, 2016: 62). This is what in some European countries is today happening with the emergence of strong populist leaders or nationalistic parties or institutional populism. Just to offer an example, the Hungarian Civil Alliance (Fidesz) won a supermajority of the seats in Parliament and since 2012 has used it to scrap the old Constitution, write a new one, and amend it continuously, entrenching its own political vision at the expense of opposition parties and an independent judiciary.

Although the focus on the populists' appeal to the many versus the few have dominated the literature on populism, it is however the relationship between populist governments and democratic institutions (constitution-remaking, in particular) that has to be deemed central although it has been largely overlooked.[8] Cas Mudde has argued that populist parties and politicians use or will use the constitution opportunistically if they are able to achieve the majority in parliament. He stressed their opportunistic claim to speak for "we the people," while operating in order to co-opt the constitutions by those who make the claim in the name of the people (Mudde, 2013). As we learned from Aristotle's structural analysis, by harnessing their policy preferences onto the constitution they are able to fuse their party platform into the will of the state. Clava Brodsky (2014) has thus proposed we give this opportunistic claim a more strategic character and proposed, convincingly, that within the state populism aims at creating a constitution of its own and finally a democratic regime that reflects closely the characteristics of its representation of the people: the populist constitution "is an entrenched Constitution, filled with policy points traditionally left to ordinary legislative processes. As such, the populist Constitution seeks to eliminate any distinction between constitutional and ordinary politics, so critical to the maintenance of a liberal democratic order" (Brodsky, 2014). It is one may say with more precision a denial of the constitution.

The Hungarian case can be used to argue that the collapse of the distinction between populism as a movement and populism as a ruling power corresponds to the collapse of the distinction between ordinary political and constitutional politics; it corresponds to the transformation of ordinary "changeable" policy into relatively immutable constitutional provisions. This change is for the sake of freezing the new majority into a permanent one, and thereby undermining the most basic of the democratic principles: majority rule within a political pluralistic environment in which any majority is presumed temporary and changeable. Populism in power makes democracy an extreme majoritarianism. Because constitution's revision "raises the question of the source of law or the people as 'popular sovereignty' in its most institutional concrete form" (Holmes and Sunstein, 1995: 276) it is thus unfortunate that the literature has largely overlooked populist constitution-remaking as transformation and reification of the democratic principle of majority rule into the domination of a majority.

To conclude, populism is cross-eyed politics because while it shares with democracy the two fundamental principles of the people and the majority, it does not offer the same answer when claiming to be government by the people. In order to see this tension we have to look not at populism as a movement of opposition (which is a sacrosanct expression of civil freedom) but at populism as a ruling power. In this chapter I situated populism within the domain of representative government and argued that it challenges pluri-party democracy in the name of a conception of the people that represents a part (no matter how large) as if it were the whole. The outcome is a politics of partial inclusion that justifies a discrimatatory use of state power against the minority. Populism in power is a majoritarianist regime.

Notes

1   Some statements of this chapter are derived from a previous work of mine, *Democracy Disfigured: Opinion, Truth and the People* (Harvard University Press, 2014), particularly pp. 138–40 and 189.
2   I take this definition of a parasite from Jacques Derrida (1988: 90): "The parasite then 'takes place.' And at the bottom, whatever violently 'takes place' or occupies a site is always *something* of a parasite. *Never quite* taking place is then part of its performance, or its success, as an event, or its 'taking place.'" Populism is a permanent possibility within representative democracy, and the "never taking place" refers to its being a permanent mobilizing possibility even when it is strong enough to manifest its power. If all the populist potentials were actualized it would replace representative democracy altogether and this would be a regime change (like what happened when fascism "took place").
3   OWS was a horizontal movement that refused leaders and representations, indirect procedures of any kind, and majority vote: it did not want to be represented and have leaders, it also refused vote counting and adopted the criterion of unanimity, "a 'leaderless,' 'structureless,' 'unorganized' phenomenon, which spontaneously came together in a general assembly" (Gould-Wartofsky, 2015: 8).
4   Paulina Ochoa (2011) proposed thus a Heraclitean versus static conception of the people so as to put forth an idea of "unity" as condition for the inclusion of diverse people.
5   Canovan (1981) argued that some populists do advocate plebiscitary democracy and in this sense direct democracy, which can figure as a sub-type of populism. Yet a plebiscite is a procedure to crow a leader and his politics not make an autonomous decision by the citizens directly. Napoleon held several plebiscites but was hardly an advocate of direct democracy; this was his comment on the plebiscite of 1802 that made him consul for life: "the plebiscite has the advantage of legalizing my extension of office and placing it on the highest possible basis" (Woloch, 2004: 33). De Gaulle held also some plebiscites which were democratic because they occurred within a constitutional and representative democracy frame but were not institutive of populism.
6   Adam Przeworski (1985: 207–21) made a similar argument in his comparative analysis of class conflicts, capitalism, and democratic stability (or uneasiness).

7 Both a negative and a neutral meaning of the term can be found in Moses Finley (1985: 38–75), who, writing in a time in which bad demagogues proliferated, was, however, more prone to stress the former one.

8 With the exception of Pierre Rosanvallon (2015: 174–9), who identifies a populist regime with "ultra-présidentialisme de type autoritaire" in which an "électoralisme majoritaire" rules.

REFERENCES

Arato, A. 2013. "Political theology and populism," *Social Research*, 80(1): 143–72.

Arditi, B. 2008. *Politics on the Edge of Liberalism: Difference, Populism, Revolution, Agitation.* Edinburgh: Edinburgh University Press.

Aristotle. 1998. *Politics*, trans. H. Rackham. Cambridge: Harvard University Press.

Atkinson, A. B. and A. Brandolini. 2011. "On the identification of the 'middle class,'" Society for the Study of Economic Inequality, Working Paper 217.

Beaumont, E. 2014. *The Civic Constitution: Civic Visions and Struggles in the Path toward Constitutional Democracy.* New York: Oxford University Press.

Berlin, I. et al. 1968. "To define populism," *Government and Opposition*, 3(2): 137–80.

Bobbio, N. 1989. *Democracy and Dictatorship: The Nature and Limits of State Power*, trans. P. Kennealy. Cambridge: Polity Press.

Brodsky, C. 2014. "Some of the people: populist constitution-making in Hungary," paper written for the colloquium "Interpretations of Democracy," Columbia University, Department of Political Science, Academic year 2013–14 (spring, 2014).

Canovan, M. 1981. *Populism.* New York: Harcourt Brace Jovanovich.

Canovan, M. 1984. "'People', politicians and populism," *Government and Opposition*, 19(3): 312–27. doi: 10.1111/j.1477-7053.1984.tb01048.x.

Canovan, M. 1999. "Trust the people! Populism and the two faces of democracy," *Political Studies*, 47(1): 2–16.

Canovan, M. 2002. "Taking politics to the people: populism as the ideology of democracy," in Y. Mény and Y. Surel (eds), *Democracies and the Populist Challenge.* Oxford: Palgrave Macmillan, 25–44.

Crick, B. 2005. "Populism, politics and democracy," *Democratization*, 12(5): 625–32.

de la Torre, C. 2014. "The people, democracy, and authoritarianism in Rafael Correa's Ecuador," *Constellations*, 21(3): 457–66.

D'Eramo, M. 2013. "Populism and the new oligarchy," tr. G. Elliott, *The New Left Review*, 82: 5–28.

Derrida, J. 1988. *Limited Inc.*, trans. S. Weber. Evanston: Northwestern University Press.

Finchelstein, F. 2014. *The Ideological Origins of the Dirty War: Fascism, Populism, and Dictatorship in Twentieth Century Argentina.* New York: Oxford University Press.

Finley, M. 1985. *Democracy Ancient and Modern*, 2nd edn. London: Hogarth Press.

Frank, J. 2010. *Constituent Moments: Enacting the People in Postrevolutionary America.* Durham: Duke University Press.

Germani, G. 1978. *Authoritarianism, Fascism, and National Populism.* New Brunswick: Transaction Books.

von Gierke, O. 1958. *Political Theories of the Middle Ages*, trans. F. W. Maitland. Cambridge: Cambridge University Press.

Gould-Wartofsky, M. A. 2015. *The Occupiers: The Making of The 99 Percent Movement*. New York: Oxford University Press.

Hofstadter, R. 1969. "North America," in G. Ionescu and E. Gellner (eds), *Populism: Its Meaning and National Characteristics*. London: Weidenfeld and Nicolson, 2–22.

Holmes, S. and C. Sunstein. 1995. "The politics of constitutional revision in Eastern Europe," in S. Levinson (ed.), *Responding to Imperfection: The Theory and Practice of Constitutional Amendment*. Princeton: Princeton University Press, 275–306.

Kazin, M. 1995. *The Populist Passion: An American History*. New York: Basic Books.

Kelsen, H. (2013). *The Essence and Value of Democracy*, 1st German edn, 1929, trans. B. Graf, ed. N. Urbinati and C. Invernizzi Accetti. Lanham: Rowman and Littlefield.

Laclau, E. 1977. *Politics and Ideology in Marxist Theory: Capitalism-Fascism-Populism*. London: NLB.

Laclau, E. 2005a. *On Populist Reason*. London: Verso.

Laclau, E. 2005b. "Populism: what's in a name?," in F. Panizza (ed.), *Populism and the Mirror of Democracy*. London: Verso, 32–49.

Lane, M. 2012. "The origins of the statesman: demagogue distinction in and after ancient Athens," *Journal of the History of Ideas*, 73(2): 179–200.

Lasch, C. 1991. *The True and Only Heaven: Progress and Its Critics*. New York: Norton.

Lefort, C. 1988. *Democracy and Political Theory*. Minneapolis: University of Minnesota Press.

Machiavelli, N. 1970. *Discourses*, Vol. 1, ed. B. Crick, trans. L. J. Walker. London: Penguin Books.

Mair, P. 2002. "Populist democracy vs. party democracy," in Y. Mény and Y. Surel (eds), *Democracies and the Populist Challenge*. Oxford: Palgrave Macmillan, 81–97.

Mény, Y. and Y. Surel. 2002. "The constitutive ambiguity of populism," in Y. Mény and Y. Surel (eds), *Democracies and the Populist Challenge*. Oxford: Palgrave Macmillan, 1–21.

Mudde, C. 2001. "In the name of the peasantry, the proletariat, and the people: populisms in Eastern Europe," *East European Politics and Societies*, 15(1): 33–53.

Mudde, C. 2004. "The populist zeitgeist," *Government and Opposition*: 541–63. doi: 10.1111/j.1477-7053.2004.00135.x.

Mudde, C. 2013. "Are populists friends or foes of constitutionalism?," The Foundation for Law, Justice and Society in association with the Centre for Socio-Legal Studies and Wolfson College, University of Oxford. http://www.fljs.org/sites/www.fljs.org/files/publications/Mudde_0.pdf.

Mudde, C. and C. Rovira Kaltwasser (eds). 2013. *Populism in Europe and the Americas: Threat or Corrective for Democracy?* New York: Cambridge University Press.

Müller, J.-W. 2011. "Getting a grip on populism," *Dissentmagazine.org*, 23 September. https://www.dissentmagazine.org/blog/getting-a-grip-on-populism.

Müller, J.-W. 2015. "Hungary: sorry for our prime minister," *The New York Review of Books*, 14 October.

Müller, J.-W. 2016. *What Is Populism?* Philadelphia: University of Pennsylvania Press.

Ober, J. 1989. *Masses and Elite in Democratic Athens*. Princeton: Princeton University Press.

Ochoa, P. E. 2011. *The Time of Popular Sovereignty: Process and the Democratic State*. University Park: Penn State University Press.

Panizza, F. 2005. "Introduction: populism and the mirror of democracy," in F. Panizza (ed.), *Populism and the Mirror of Democracy*. London: Verso, 1–31.

Pitkin, H. F. 1967. *The Concept of Representation*. Berkeley: University of California Press.

Przeworski, A. 1985. *Capitalism and Social Democracy*. Cambridge: Cambridge University Press.

Przeworski, A. 1999. "Minimalist conception of democracy: a defense," in I. Shapiro and C. Hacker-Cordón (eds), *Democracy's Value*. Cambridge: Cambridge University Press, 23–49.

Rosanvallon, P. 2015. *Le bon gouvernement*. Paris: Seuil.

Rosenblum, N. L. 2008. *On the Side of the Angels: An Appreciation of Parties and Partisanship*. Princeton: Princeton University Press.

Rovira Kaltwasser, C. 2012. "The ambivalence of populism: threat and corrective for democracy," *Democratization*, 19(2): 184–208.

Schmitt, C. 2008. *Constitutional Theory*, 1st edn 1928, trans. and ed. J. Seitzer, foreword by E. Kennedy. Durham: Duke University Press.

Schwartz, J. M. 2009. *The Future of Democratic Equality: Rebuilding Social Solidarity in a Fragmented America*. New York: Routledge.

Taggart, P. 2000. *Populism*. Philadelphia: Open University Press.

Urbinati, N. 2006. *Representative Democracy: Principles and Genealogy*. Chicago and London: University of Chicago Press.

Urbinati, N. 2011. "Representative democracy and its critics," in John Keane (ed.), *The Future of Representative Democracy*. Cambridge: Cambridge University Press, 23–49.

Urbinati, N. 2014. *Democracy Disfigured: Opinion, Truth and the People*. Cambridge: Harvard University Press.

Urbinati, N. 2015. "A revolt against intermediary bodies," *Constellations*, 22 (4): 477–86.

Weyland, Kurt. 2001. "Clarifying a contested concept: populism in the study of Latin American politics," *Comparative Politics*, 34(1): 1–22.

Weyland, Kurt. 2013. "The threat from the populist left," *Journal of Democracy*, 24(1): 18–32.

Woloch, I. 2004. "From consulate to empire: impetus and resistance," in P. Baehr and M. Richter (eds), *Dictatorship in History and Theory: Bonapartism, Caesarism, and Totalitarianism*. Hong Kong and New York: Lingnan University, Hong Kong, and The City University of New York, 29–52.

CHAPTER 30

···

POPULISM
AND CONSTITUTIONALISM

···

JAN-WERNER MÜLLER

POPULISM has proven a notoriously difficult concept to define.[1] Despite the great divergence of attempts to capture this political phenomenon, it is striking that many observers agree on one point: namely that, whatever else it is, populism is inherently hostile to mechanisms and, ultimately, values, commonly associated with constitutionalism: constraints on the will of the majority, checks and balances, protections for minorities, or, for that matter, fundamental rights as such (an illuminating exception is Rovira Kaltwasser, 2015). Populists are supposedly impatient with procedures and pre-structured political time; they are even said to be against "institutions" and "mediated representation" per se, preferring a direct, unmediated relationship between the personal leader and the people (Taggart, 2000; Weyland, 2001; de la Torre, 2015). Related to this supposed anti-institutionalism is the charge that populists dislike "representation" and opt for "direct democracy" (as exemplified by referenda) instead. Hence also the impression—widespread among political philosophers, social scientists, and at least a significant number of American legal theorists—that populism, despite some serious normative flaws, might under some circumstances act as a "corrective" to a liberal democracy which has become too remote from "the people" (Mudde and Rovira Kaltwasser, 2013). Or, in conceptually more sophisticated language: there is at least a tension between liberalism and democracy, and populism might somehow help the democratic side.

The tone of the previous paragraph might have given the (legal and normative) game away already: I believe that we have to regard many of the claims made about (and, to some extent, for) populism skeptically. Articulating this skepticism is made more difficult by the fact that commentators on populism hardly agree on terms and conditions for exchanging arguments about the phenomenon. To the extent that there is a meaningful debate about populism and constitutionalism in conjunction, it suffers from several unfortunate characteristics: first, the discussion, especially but not only in the US context, becomes conflated with the normative controversy about the merits of majoritarianism (and, conversely, judicial review) (Kramer, 2004); second, there is no clear, or even just discernible, distinction between *popular* constitutionalism, on the one hand, and *populist* constitutionalism, on the other (Brettschneider, 2006; 2015); and, third and most important: "populism" becomes a vague placeholder for "civic participation" or "social mobilization" (and, conversely, weakening of the power of judges and other elites): witness for instance constitutional scholar Elizabeth Beaumont writing "I take the liberty of using the terms civic and popular loosely and interchangeably as laymen's terms meaning largely ordinary people, citizens, or nonofficials" (Beaumont, 2014: 4; also Balkin, 1995; and, for an application of populism to a German constitutional context, Haltern, 1998). Or consider Tom Donnelly claiming that for all their differences, advocates of popular constitutionalism supposedly share a "populist sensibility"—which, in the end, comes down to nothing more than "a common belief that the American people (and their elected representatives) should play an ongoing role in shaping contemporary constitutional meaning" (Donnelly, 2012: 161–2). Or think of Mila Versteeg holding that a populist constitution is one whose content can be said to be in line with the values that large majorities of a country hold, irrespective of whether "the people themselves" are involved in constitution-making or constitution-changing (Versteeg, 2014).

Quite apart from the vagueness of the concepts used (or perhaps related to this vagueness), there is the fact that debates about populism and constitutionalism—especially in the US—quickly turn emotional: accusations of elitism and "demophobia" (if not hatred of democracy *tout court*) start to fly, theorists are suspected of having bad "attitudes toward the political energy of ordinary people," or, accused of promoting ochlocracy, if not crowd violence (Parker, 1993: 532).

Clearly, without a proper concept of populism no meaningful analysis of the relationship between populism and constitutionalism can proceed. Hence I shall first put forward a definition of populism as a distinct discursive phenomenon; in particular, I shall argue that, when we examine their rhetoric, we find that populists are not just anti-elitists; they are also necessarily anti-pluralists, when they advance what I call the *core populist claim*: that they and *only they* properly represent the authentic people (*pace* the view that populists are inherently against the principle of political representation). This definitional work is followed by three arguments about how populism can play out in practice as a distinct style of governance and as the imperative to build particular kinds of institutions (*pace* the view that populism is inherently anti-institutional). I shall then argue that populists might indeed write constitutions, but that such constitutions tend to violate certain core ideas of a *normative* understanding of constitutionalism (as well as, in fact, democracy more broadly): they do not function to enable and preserve pluralism; and they fall of short of properly protecting democracy-constitutive rights such as freedom of speech and free assembly. My particular (very brief) examples will be the Hungarian constitution in force since the beginning of 2012 and the three most important instances of recent populist constitutionalism in Latin America (Bolivia, Ecuador, and especially Venezuela—without claiming that these are all equally problematic from a normative point of view). I shall then try to distinguish an undesirable *populist* constitutionalism from a legitimate form of *popular* constitutionalism. I conclude that populists can write constitutions that do offer genuine constraints, but populism and normative constitutionalism—understood as pluralism-preserving and rights-guaranteeing—do *not* go together.

Just What Is Populism?

Even a cursory glance at contemporary political commentary on populism reveals widely divergent understandings of what populism might be. At least in Europe, populism is today generally associated with "irresponsible policies" or some form of "political pandering" (sometimes demagoguery and populism are used interchangeably). However, populism is also frequently identified with a particular class, especially the petty bourgeoisie. This can seem like a sociologically robust theory (classes are constructs, of course, but they can be empirically specified in fairly plausible ways). This class diagnosis often comes with a much more speculative account of social psychology: those espousing populist claims publicly and, in particular, those casting their ballot for populist parties, are said to be driven by "anxiety" or "fears" (of modernization, globalization, etc.) or—the feeling most frequently invoked in talking about populists—"resentment."[2]

None of these seemingly straightforward criteria is helpful for clearly identifying populism. The focus on particular socio-economic groups is empirically dubious, as has been shown in a number of studies (Priester, 2012); less obviously, it often results from a largely discredited set of assumptions from modernization theory. The concentration on political psychology is not necessarily misguided, but it is hard to see that certain emotions could only be found among populist politicians and their followers; and, once more, some of the psychological approaches are intimately tied to modernization theory (after all, people are said to experience resentment in reaction to modernization and then long to retain or return to a "pre-modern" world).

What, finally, about the notion of populism as a matter of false political promises? It is, of course, difficult to deny that some policies really can turn out to have been irresponsible: those deciding on such policies did not think hard enough; they failed to gather all the relevant information; or, most plausibly, their knowledge of the likely long-term consequences should have made them refrain from policies with only short-term electoral benefits for themselves. Such concerns are not just the product of some neoliberal fantasy world. But they do not serve to establish anything like a definition (or ideal type) of populism. There is in most cases no clear, uncontested line between responsibility and irresponsibility. Often enough, charges of "irresponsible populism" are themselves highly partisan, and it just so happens that the "irresponsible policies" denounced almost always benefit the worst-off.

So if all these perspectives and possible criteria are problematic, the question remains: what is populism? I suggest that populism is a particular *moralistic imagination of politics*, a way of perceiving the political world which opposes a morally pure and fully unified—but, I shall argue, ultimately fictional—people to small minorities, elites in particular, who are put outside the authentic people. Apart from this criticism of elites, there is an additional element of populist discourse, however: populists necessarily claim that they—and only they—properly represent the authentic, proper, and morally pure people.

Populists, then, are not just anti-elitists—criticism of elites (when populists are in opposition) is a necessary, but not a sufficient condition for populism. They also need to be anti-pluralists.[3] The claim to *exclusive* moral representation of the real or authentic people is at the core of populism. Political actors not committed to this claim, according to my understanding, are not populists. Put differently: no populism without a *pars-pro-toto* argument and a claim to exclusive representation, with both being primarily of a *moral*, as opposed to empirical, nature (Arato, 2013).

Most commonly, but not necessarily, "morality" is specified by populists with languages of work and corruption (which has led some observers to associate populism with an ideology of "producerism").[4] Populists pit the pure, innocent, always hard-working people against a corrupt elite who do not really work (other than to further their self-interest), and, in right-wing populism, also against the very bottom of society (those who also do not really work and instead live off others). Moreover, right-wing populists typically construe an "unhealthy coalition" between the elite that does not really belong and marginal groups that do not really belong either (think of the American Tea Party as a recent example).

Note that populists always perform a double exclusion: first, populists' political competitors and critics are inevitably condemned as part of the immoral, corrupt elite, or so populists say when running for office; once in government, they will not recognize anything like a legitimate opposition. And second: the populist logic also implies that whoever does not really support populist parties might not be part of the proper people at all: there are American citizens, and then there are what George C. Wallace, an arch-populist of the 1960s often viewed as a precursor of Donald Trump, always called "real Americans" (white, God-fearing, hard-working, gun-owning, etc.). Or think of Nigel Farage celebrating the Brexit vote by claiming that it had been a "victory for real people" (thus making the 48 percent of the British electorate who had opposed taking the UK out of the European Union in the June 2016 referendum somehow less than real—or, more precisely, questioning their status as members of the political community). Or consider a deeply revealing remark by Trump that went virtually unnoticed, given the frequency with which the New York billionaire has made scandalous statements. At a campaign rally in May 2016 Trump announced that "The only important thing is the unification of the people—because the other people don't mean anything."

Now, this moralist conception of politics advanced by populists clearly depends on some criterion for distinguishing the moral and the immoral, the pure and the corrupt. It does not have to be "work." If work turns out to be indeterminate, ethnic markers can readily come to the rescue. It is a mistake to think that populism will always turn out to be a form of nationalism. In fact, critics of populism make it too easy for themselves, if they assume that populism is just nationalism or even some form of ethnic chauvinism.

One has to recognize that in many cases they appear to be operating with an under-standing of the common good that can seem close to epistemic conceptions of democracy. Populists can and often do rely on the notion that there is a distinct common good, that the people can discern *and* will it, and that a politician or a party (or, less plausibly, a movement) could unambiguously implement such a conception of the common good as policy—in other words, they conjure up something like an imperative mandate, based on a monist conception of the people and what the people supposedly say (Urbinati, 2014). Moreover, this emphasis on one common good, clearly comprehensible to common sense, and capable of being articulated as one correct policy which then can be collectively willed, at least partly explains why populism is so often associated with the idea of an over-simplification of policy challenges: witness, for instance, Ralf Dahrendorf—who no doubt echoed a wide-spread impression among liberals—claiming that "populism is simple, democracy is complex" (Dahrendorf, 2003).

It is crucial to recognize that the imperative mandate aimed at realizing the common good is derived from what the populists construe as "the real people." "The people's will" which populists claim they will just faithfully execute—in that sense denying their own role as leaders and also any real political responsibility—is a fiction. There is no single political will, let alone a single political opinion, in a modern, complex, pluralist—in short, enormously messy—democracy. Populists put words into the mouth of what is after all their own creation: the fiction of the homogeneous, always righteous people. And then they say, like Trump did at the Republican Party Convention in July 2016, "I am your voice."

It is furthermore important to understand that populists do not have to be against the idea of representation as such; rather, they can positively endorse a particular version of it. Put simply: populists are fine with representation, as long as the right representatives represent the right people who are making the right judgment and consequently willing the right thing, so to speak. Some populists demand more referenda, to be sure—but only as a means to confirm what they already take the morally pure people to think; not because they wish for the people to participate continuously in politics, or because they want at least some ordinary people to have a say in government (as proposals for selecting representatives by lot, for instance, would suggest). Populists view the people as essentially passive, once the proper popular will aimed at the proper common good has been ascertained; and, in theory—and in practice—that particular will can be ascertained without any popular participation whatsoever, if one properly understands the correct symbolic identity of the real, morally pure people.

Now, how can the claim to exclusive moral representation go together with the reality of populists actually being in opposition, or, even if in power, not obtaining 100 percent of the vote? Populists exhibit a clear pattern of how to deal with this problem. One strategy is to deny that the people in their empirical totality as voting citizens actually are the real people, and that an election outcome on the basis of regular procedures is the closest approximation we have to the "popular will." Ultimately, "the people" can become something like a fictional entity outside any existing democratic or, even more generally, legal procedures, a supposedly homogeneous body the invocation of which can be played off against actual election results (and other legal niceties) in democracies. It is not an accident that Richard Nixon's famous (or infamous) notion of a "silent majority" has had such a career among populists: if the majority were not silent, it would already have a government that truly represents the people. If the populist politician fails at the polls, it is not because he in fact doesn't represent the majority at all, but because the majority has not yet dared to speak. In other words, populists are not necessarily against political institutions per se, as some accounts of the phenomenon have suggested, but at least as long as they are in opposition, they will always invoke an un-institutionalized people "out there"—in existential opposition to the popular will, as it has manifested itself in actual voting or even opinion polls.

Such a fictional—one might even say: mystical—notion of "the people" is not without precedent in the history of political thought. Theorists like Baldus held a conception, analogous to the theory of the king's two bodies, according to which there was the empirical, ever-changing people as a group of individuals on the one hand—and, on the other, the eternal *populus* as a *corpus mysticum* (Kantorowicz, 1997: 209): the *corpus mysticum* had corporational character signifying a fictitious or juristic (collective) person; hence it was used synonymously with *corpus fictum, corpus imaginatum, corpus repraesentatum*. Just as there was always a possibility of distinguishing the king body politic from the king body natural, so the people body politic (what Baldus called *hominum collectio in unum corpus mysticum*) and the people as represented and mediated via institutions could be separated. And just as it was not a paradox, then, for the opponents of Charles I to "fight the king to defend the king," populists can fight legitimately elected elites to defend the true people (ibid.: 21–3).

More recently, the people as an existential reality was played off by Carl Schmitt against merely liberal representation of voters in parliament (Schmitt, 1993). This distinction infamously served as a bridge from democracy to non-democracy: Mussolini, so Schmitt held, was a genuine incarnation of democracy; philosophers like Giovanni Gentile also claimed that fascism could be a more faithful realization of democratic ideals (Gentile, 1927/8). Conversely, an opponent of Schmitt such as Hans Kelsen would insist that the will of parliament is not and in fact can never be *the* popular will—since *the* popular will is in fact impossible to discern: all we can ever verify are election outcomes; everything else (in particular some conception of an organic unity of "the people" from which some interest above parties could be inferred), according to Kelsen, amounts to a "metapolitical illusion" (Kelsen, 1981: 22). Put differently: Schmitt thought that a political body (individual or collective) could make the body of the people as a whole visible. Kelsen thought the latter would always necessarily remain invisible and hence unknowable.

Let me summarize: populism is a distinctly moral way to imagine the political world and always involves a claim to exclusive moral representation. Of course, virtually all political actors make what Michael Saward has called "the representative claim" (Saward, 2006). What distinguishes democratic politicians from populists is that the former make them like hypotheses—claims to be representative, in Saward's conception—which can be empirically disproven on the basis of the empirical results of regular procedures and institutions like elections (ibid.: 298). Populists, on the other hand, will persist with their representative claim no matter what; since their claim is of a moral, not an empirical nature, it cannot be disproven. Moreover, when in opposition, populists are bound to cast doubt on the institutions which produce the "morally wrong" outcomes. Hence they might indeed be seen as the "enemies of institutions"—but not institutions in general; rather, they become the enemies of mechanisms of representation which fail to vindicate their claim to excusive moral representation (or they replace what they see as one flawed institution with what they see as a proper one—think of Rafael Correa replacing Congress in Ecuador with the National Assembly, for instance [de la Torre, 2010]).

POPULISM IN POWER:
THREE CHARACTERISTICS

Conventional wisdom has it that populist parties are primarily protest parties and that protest cannot govern, since one cannot protest against oneself (and, once political actors have become an elite in power, it becomes impossible—which is to say: self-contradictory—for them to perpetuate an anti-elitist stance). While populist parties do indeed in one sense necessarily protest against elites, this does not mean that populism in government will become self-contradictory. First of all, all failures of populists in government can still be blamed on elites acting behind the scenes, whether at home or—more likely—abroad (or, sometimes, they can fault coalition partners and the compromises and constraints they impose [Albertazzi and McDonnell, 2015]). Many populist victors continue to behave like victims. Second, populists in power are likely to govern according to the populist logic which holds that populists are the only morally legitimate representatives of the people and that, furthermore, only some of the people are actually the real, authentic people—and hence deserving of support and, ultimately, good government. This logic can manifest itself in three distinct ways: colonization of the state; mass clientelism as well as discriminatory legalism; and, finally, repression of civil society.

First, populists tend to colonize or "occupy" the state. Such a strategy to consolidate or even perpetuate power is not exclusive to populists, of course. What is particular about populists is that they can undertake such colonization openly and with the back-up of their core moral representative claim. Why, populists might ask indignantly, should the people not take possession of their state through their only rightful representatives? Why should those who obstruct the genuine popular will in the name of civil service neutrality, for instance, not be purged?

Second, populists tend to engage in what political scientists call mass clientelism: the exchange of material and immaterial favors by elites for mass political support. Again, such conduct is not exclusive to populists: many parties reward their clientele for turning up at the voting booths; some observers might even say that, from a realist perspective, mass clientelism and democracy are more or less the same thing (Fukuyama,

2014). What—once more—makes populists distinctive is that they can engage in such practices openly and with public moral justifications: after all, for them, only some people are really the people and hence deserving of the support of what is rightfully their state. In the same vein, only some of the people will enjoy the full protection of the laws; others who do not belong to the people or even actively work against the people should be treated appropriately. This is what political scientists call "discriminatory legalism" (put simply: the idea of "everything for my friends; for my enemies, the law" [Weyland, 2013]).

State colonization, mass clientelism, and discriminatory legalism are phenomena that can be found in many historical situations (Priester, 2012; Mazzuca, 2013). In populist regimes, however, we can find all three—*and* a kind of moral surplus: such practices can at least potentially be avowed and justified. It is state colonization, mass clientelism, and discriminatory legalism with, so to speak, a clean moral conscience.

There is one further element of populist statecraft that is worth mentioning. Populists in power tend to be harsh (to say the least) with non-governmental organizations that criticize them. Again, harassing or even suppressing civil society is not a practice exclusive to populists. But for them opposition from within civil society creates a particular moral and symbolic problem: it potentially undermines their right to exclusive moral representation. Hence it becomes crucial to claim (or even supposedly "prove") that civil society isn't civil society at all, and that what can seem like popular opposition has nothing to do with the proper people. This explains why rulers like Vladimir Putin in Russia and Viktor Orbán in Hungary have gone out of their way to try to discredit NGOs as being controlled by outside powers (and declare them as "foreign agents"). In a sense, they try to make the unified (and passive) people in whose name they had been speaking all along a reality on the ground: by silencing or discrediting those who refuse Putin and Orbán's representative claim (and, sometimes, by giving them every incentive to leave the country and thereby to separate themselves from the pure, true people).

Above all, then, populism in power will mean the dominance of political actors who, even in the face of persistent opposition, speak in the name of the whole (and essentially claim: *l'état, c'est nous*, with the proviso that this particular "we" constitutes the only legitimate representative of the people)—with the consequence that opposition will be not just a matter being a particular, partisan part of the people, but literally being apart—from the people (Arato, 2013: 150). And this is a great irony, because populism in power always brings about or at least reinforces, or offers another variety of, what it most opposes and what it habitually tends to accuse established elites of: exclusion and the usurpation of the state (Priester, 2012: 20). What corrupt elites supposedly do, populists will also end up doing, only with a clear justification and a clean conscience.

POPULIST CONSTITUTIONALISM ...

I have spent some time on the characteristics of populist regimes in order to make a point plausible which perhaps should have been obvious all along: populists are not generally "against institutions" (in fact, there is no politics without institutions for anyone available anyway—which is not say that any particular institution, such as the state, is somehow historically inevitable). Populists are only against specific institutions—namely those which, in their view, fail to produce the morally (as opposed to empirically) correct political outcomes. But this form of "anti-institutionalism" is only articulated when populists are in opposition. Populists in power will be fine with institutions—which is to say: *their* institutions.

Those populists who have enough power will seek to establish a new, populist constitution—in the sense of both a new socio-political settlement and a new set of rules for the political game (what some scholars of constitutionalism have called the "operating manual"). It is tempting to think that in terms of such an "operating manual," populists will seek a system that allows for the expression of an unconstrained popular will, or will somehow reinforce the direct, institutionally unmediated relationship between a leader and the proper *pueblo*. Populists are, after all, often deemed to be heirs of the Jacobins (and, consciously or un-consciously, students of Rousseau).

Yet, here again, things are not so simple. The claim for an unconstrained popular will is plausible for populists when they are in opposition—after all, they want to play an authentic expression of the *populus* as un-institutionalized, non-proceduralized *corpus mysticum* off against the actual results of an existing political system. In such circumstances, it is also plausible for them to say that the *vox populi* is one (and fully unified)—and that checks and balances, divisions of power, etc. prevent the singular, homogeneous will of the singular, homogeneous people from emerging clearly.

Yet, when in power, populists will in all likelihood be much less skeptical about constitutionalism as a means of creating constraints on what they interpret to be the popular will—except that the popular will (never given empirically, but to be construed morally) has first to be ascertained by populists, then constitutionalized, and then constrained constitutionally. Or, picking up a distinction recently elaborated by Martin Loughlin: positive constitutionalism is followed by negative constitutionalism (Loughlin, 2015). Populists will seek to perpetuate what they regard as the proper image of the morally pure people (the proper constitutional identity, if you will) and, if possible, constitutionalize policies which they find to conform to that image of the people (Jacobsohn, 2010). Hence, populist constitutionalism will not necessarily privilege popular participation or allow for more avenues to express whatever might be construed as a general will; and nor will they try somehow to "constitutionalize the charisma" of a popular leader, in the way Bruce Ackerman has suggested (Ackerman, 2015). It is not even clear that populist constitutions will reflect widely held values more accurately (but then again, as Mila Versteeg has shown, few constitutions do, while "populist constitutions are most likely to be found among nations that do not uphold their constitutional promises in practice" [Versteeg, 2014: 1168]).[5]

Apart from these features—which are explained yet again by the underlying moral claims of populism—there is a more mundane goal that constitutions might achieve for populists: they can help to keep populists in power. Of course, one might say that even this goal still has a moral dimension related to the underlying populist imagination: as the only legitimate representatives of the people, populists should perpetually be in office. And if the perpetuation of power becomes the aim, then there's also the possibility that populists treat the constitution as a mere façade, as Giovanni Sartori once put it, while operating quite differently behind the façade (Sartori, 1962). They might even openly sacrifice their own constitution, if it no longer serves that purpose. Here the Jacobins really are an appropriate example. As Dan Edelstein has argued, their concern was much less with a faithful expression of the general will than historians have tended to assume (Edelstein, 2009). They worried about corruptions of the general will and put their hope in the realization of a form of natural right independent of people's actual wills (and attendant frailties) altogether. When their own constitution—and the elections it enabled—threatened to remove the Jacobins from power, they did not hesitate effectively to suspend the constitution and unleash terror against those deemed *hors la loi*.

Not all examples of populist constitutionalism are as dramatic (let alone terroristic) as this. A recent example is the constitution—officially named "Fundamental Law"—of Hungary, which came into effect at the beginning of 2012. The constitution had been preceded by a non-binding "national consultation" to which, according to the government, about 920,000 citizens responded (Uitz, 2015: 286). The outcomes of that consultation could be freely interpreted by the constitution-makers so as to fit their general conception that the 2010 parliamentary elections had resulted in a "revolution at the voting booths," because the winning party had received a two-thirds majority in parliament. This "revolution" had supposedly yielded an imperative mandate to establish what the government termed a new "national system of cooperation"—and to write a new constitution. The preamble of the document, or "National Avowal," ended up constitutionalizing a very particular image of the Hungarian people as a nation committed to survival in a hostile world, as good Christians, and as an ethnic group that can be clearly distinguished from minorities living with the proper Hungarians. In some of the institutional provisions—especially in the Amendments and the Transitional Provisions (which de facto had constitutional status)—the perpetuation of populists in power was clearly the goal (ibid.). Age limitations and qualifications for judges were introduced so as to remove professionals not in line with the governing populist party (discriminatory constitutionalism, one might say); the competences and structure of the constitutional court (the crucial check on government power before the introduction of the "Fundamental Law") were re-engineered; and the terms of office-holders chosen by the governing party were made unusually long (nine years in many cases), with a view, it seems, to constrain future governments in line with a supposed popular will. As Renáta Uitz has put it, the constitution-drafters displayed "open political discretion in selecting veto players for the new constitutional regime" (ibid.: 292).

The Hungarian Fundamental Law, while supposedly inspired by the views expressed in the national consultation, was never put to a referendum. By contrast, a number of new constitutions in Latin America have been created by elected constituent assemblies and were eventually made subject to a popular vote. Venezuela, Ecuador, and Bolivia are the well-known examples of what sympathetic observers, such as Roberto Viciano

Pastor and Rubén Martínez Dalmau, have called *nuevo constitucionalismo latinoameri-cano*.[6] Older constitutions were effectively bypassed in the process of forming a constituent assembly, and then replaced by documents which were supposed to perpetuate the founding popular will (or "constituting will," *la voluntad constituyente*). That founding "popular will" was decisively shaped by populists, though: Hugo Chávez, for instance, controlled the way "his" constituent assembly was elected, and ensured that a majority of 60 percent for his party at the polls translated into more than 90 percent of the seats in the constituent assembly.

Effectively, the ideal of populist constitutionalism was invoked to strengthen the executive and weaken horizontal accountability (diminishing the power of the judiciary and/or staffing judicial offices with partisan actors).[7] The new constitutions thus helped decisively in the populist project of "occupying the state," as the shift to a new constitution justified the replacement of existing office holders (Landau, 2013: 213). In general, elections were made less free and fair, parliaments and political parties weakened, and the media more easily controlled by executives.

There is no doubt that the experiments in constitutionalism in Latin America were "more democratic" than the case of Hungary in that they introduced mechanisms, such as recall, that facilitated the participation of actual citizens (as opposed to just invoking, Schmitt-style, a symbolic substance of *el pueblo*). Moreover, unlike in the case of Hungary, the introduction of new rights went together with actual advances in socio-political inclusion of previously marginalized and discriminated groups. However, while normatively not equally problematic, important parallels in what makes populist constitutionalism so perilous for democracy remain: the manipulative construction of *la voluntad constituyente*, the contention that only a part of the people is the real people (often now at least symbolically privileging indigenous communities at the expense of mestizos, or making the "hidden majority" the only authentic people [Stavrakakis et al., 2016]); the exception detail and rigidity of the new constitutions; and the tendency further to develop constitutions in order to keep populists in power (most visible in the reign of Nicolás Maduro).[8]

... AND POPULAR CONSTITUTIONALISM

It might seem that the implications of the analysis so far must be profoundly conservative: politics should be confined to an interaction of official political institutions; whatever these institutions produce by way of empirical outcomes must be legitimate; and claims *about, for*, let alone *by* the people are prohibited. But this would be a misunderstanding. In a democracy, anybody can launch a representative claim and see whether a particular constituency is responsive to the claim; any group of what Ackerman has called "mobilized outsiders" can seek to transform a constitution (Ackerman, 2015). In fact, one might even say that democracy is precisely designed to multiply such claims: the conduct of official representatives should be contestable; and the contestation may involve the argument that the representatives fail to represent—which may mean that they fail to act for their constituents, or that, more symbolically, they become unfaith-ful to them (Garsten, 2009). However, such contestation is different from attempts to speak in the name of the people as a whole—and efforts to morally de-legitimate all those who in turn contest that claim (which is to say: those who contest their involun-tary inclusion in a "We the People"; such resisters to populism are effectively saying: "not in our name"). Street protest, online petitions, etc.—these all have genuinely democratic meaning, but they lack proper democratic form (Möllers, 2008: 33–4).

And yet: what about those struggling in the name of "people power" in various parts of the world? To take a recent example: the demonstrators against the Mubarak regime on Tahrir Square used expressions such as "One hand," "One society," and "One demand."[9] Should they be lectured at and be told that, unfortunately, they had failed properly to understand democracy and were fated to misconstrue constitutionalism?

The analysis presented here does not in any way exclude claims about exclusions, so to speak. Anyone can criticize existing procedures, fault them for moral blind spots, and propose criteria and means for further inclusion. What is problematic is not the crit-icism that present arrangements have failed, but that the critic and only the critic can counterfactually speak for "the people." What is problematic is also the assumption—prevalent, but neither empirically nor normatively justified—by many radical demo-crats that *only* the *pars-pro-toto* claim can achieve anything truly worthwhile for the previously excluded, and that everything else will amount to mere administration or incorporation into existing systems (Laclau, 2005). It is almost a cliché to point out that many constitutions have evolved because of struggles for inclusion and because "citizen interpreters" of the constitution have sought to redeem previously unrealized moral claims contained in the constitution, or radically changed existing forms of polit-ical pluralism (Frank, 2010). The not so trivial point is that those fighting for inclusion have rarely claimed "We and only we are the people"; on the contrary, they have usually claimed "We are *also* the people" (with attendant claims of "we *also* represent the peo-ple"). Constitutions with democratic principles allow for an open-ended contestation of what those principles might mean in any given period; as said above, democracy is designed to multiply, but also in the end empirically to test, claims to representation (Garsten, 2009). Of course, there is no guarantee that such contestation will actually happen, or that struggles for inclusion will be successful (or that struggles will be about inclusion in the first place—as opposed to struggles against the constitutional order as such; and, of course, struggles might also happen for *exclusion*).

Constitutions can ideally facilitate what one might call a *chain of claim-making for inclusion*. An initial "We the People" neither entirely disappears inside the regu-lar political process nor stays as an actual, empirical, unified agent—a kind of macro-subject—outside the constituted order. Instead, who are "We the People" remains an open question, one which democracy in many ways is *about*. As Claude Lefort once put it, "democracy inaugurates the experience of an ungraspable, uncontrollable society in which the people will be said to be sovereign, of course, but whose identity will constantly be open to question, whose identity will remain forever latent" (Lefort, 1988: 304). It is actually populists who break off the chain of claim-making by asserting that "the people" can now be firmly and conclusively identified—and that the people is now actual, and no longer latent.[10] It is a kind of final claim. In that sense, populists de facto want a kind of closure (including and especially constitutional *closure*), quite unlike those who, by arguing for inclusion, should be committed to the idea of further inclusion, or, put differently, a continuation of the chain of claim-making. Arguably, the American Tea Party is a prime example for advocating this kind of constitutional closure.

What, then, about the shouts heard on Tahrir Square, or, going back a quarter century, the emphatic chanting of "We are the People" on the streets of East Germany in the fall of 1989? This slogan is entirely legitimate in the face of a regime that claims exclusively to represent the people—but in fact shuts large parts of the people out politically. One could go further and argue that what prima facie might seem like an arch-populist slogan was in fact an anti-populist claim: the regime pretends exclusively to represent the people and their well-considered long-term interest (or so a standard justification of the "leading role" of state socialist parties went)—but in fact *das Volk* are something else and want something else. In non-democracies "We are the People" is a justified revolutionary claim, not a populist one; it can even lead to fleeting moments of "popular charisma" (Hassanzadeh, 2015). And in populist regimes that stretch the limits of representative democracy, but still retain some respect for procedure (and empirical reality, for that matter), even a seemingly small contestation of the populist regime can have enormous repercussions. Think of the single "standing man" on Taksim Square in the wake of the crackdown on the Gezi Park protesters (who was eventually joined by many standing men and women). A silent witness, a reminder of Atatürk's values (he stood facing Atatürk's statue)—but also a living, standing reproach against the government's claim to represent all upright Turks without remainder.[11]

When a particular claim is democratic and when it is populist will not always be a clear-cut, obvious matter. For instance, in Egypt, there was a period between the initial protests on Tahrir Square and the fraught constitution-making process where it was not always easy to discern which was which—certainly one cannot tell simply by checking whether "the people" are somehow being invoked. But during 2012 and 2013 it became clear that the Muslim Brotherhood was trying to create a populist, partisan constitution which defined their image of the pure people and put in place constraints inspired by their particular understanding of what constitutes a good Egyptian (Halmai, 2013).

Conclusion

Are populism and constitutionalism necessarily in contradiction? I have argued that the picture is far more complicated than clichéd invocations of Rousseau and the general will, or simple schemas that put populism on the side of democracy and constitutionalism on the side of liberalism, would suggest. It is crucial to understand populism's anti-pluralist core moral claim to distinguish between the discourse of populists in opposition—where they indeed see the authentic popular will as being obstructed—and populists in power crafting constitutions that are intended to reflect their image of the people (and seek to perpetuate populists in power). In particular, such constitutions might put constraints in place that will preserve the product of a highly partisan constitution-making process, all in the name of remaining faithful to a supposed authentic "founding will."

Note that my analysis has not depended on taking a particular stance on the question whether there ever is such a thing as constituent power. However, it has depended on a notion that democracy must be pluralist—without thereby committing to the view that pluralism is itself anything like a first-order value (along the lines of: more diversity is always better); it has also depended on an understanding of constitutions as pluralism-enabling and pluralism-preserving devices (this is not their only function, to be sure; but in the context discussed here, it is indeed crucial). Democracy has to be pluralist because, as Lefort argued most famously, in a democracy the people rule—and yet the place of power must remain empty. No political actor can claim fully and without remainder to represent or even incarnate the people—instead, all we have is a shared political stage (as specified in a constitution) on which various actors can launch representative claims; and these claims always have to be understood as provisional, fallible, and self-limiting (Lefort, 1988; Ochoa Espejo, 2015). Democracy, as Lefort also never tired of emphasizing, is institutionalized uncertainty (with the institutionalization being provided by a constitution). Populists, on the other hand, promise certainty and, as some of the examples discussed here show, will not hesitate to use constitutions to make their image of the people and what they regard as the morally right policies as certain as possible. What they destroy in the process, though, is proper constitutionalism—and, ultimately, democracy itself.

NOTES

1   This piece draws on Müller, 2014; Müller, 2015a; Müller, 2015b; Müller, 2016a; and especially Müller, 2016b. I thank audiences at the Social Science Research Center, NYU Law School, and ELTE for occasions to discuss the arguments put forward in this chapter. I am especially grateful to Mattias Kumm, Cristóbal Rovira Kaltwasser, and Paulina Ochoa Espejo for very helpful feedback.
2   The very notion of resentment tends to import a legacy of cultural pessimism and questionable assumptions about mass psychology into contemporary public discourse.
3   I am indebted to Cristóbal Rovira Kaltwasser for discussions on this point. Rovira Kaltwasser also stresses the anti-pluralism of populists, but locates it mainly in the image of a homogeneous people; my argument is that populists promote such an image and, furthermore, oppose a pluralism of representative claims.
4   Producerism cannot be purely economic—it is a moral concept valorizing the producers. Think of Georges Sorel.
5   One of Versteeg's other astounding results in her global comparison of the "popularity" of constitutions is that "popular referendums do not produce more populist constitutions" in her sense of constitutions reflecting values wide-spread in the population (Versteeg, 2014: 1170).

6   To be sure, there are important variations among these cases; Venezuela conforms most clearly to the pattern suggested here. Also, my claim is not that all that is contained in these constitutions is automatically tainted with populism in my understanding of the term: think in particular of the elements relating to indigenous people and the environment (such as the rights for nature in the Ecuadorian constitution), which, I believe, can be analyzed quite apart from any populist template. At the same time, the declaration of the Bolivian state as plurinational cannot automatically be considered evidence that the constitution enables the preservation of pluralism.

7   There was also the attempt in formulating a "committed constitution" (as part of a *constitucionalismo comprometido*) to include new fundamental rights (such as a "right to the good life" and environmental rights), and to strengthen the role of civil society actors in constitutional politics (though both remained more at the level of aspiration).

8   Which is not to say that long periods in power automatically indicate the triumph of populism—the question is not just about factual alternation of power, but whether those in power accept the idea of a legitimate opposition.

9   There were also more creative demands, such as "The people want a president who does not dye his hair!" (Achcar, 2013: 1).

10 Of course, the firmness is not an empirical one. One can move *hors du peuple* by ceasing to be moral in the manner prescribed by populists. It is harder to see how one can join the people proper.

11 The standing man was the performance artist Erdem Gündüz.

REFERENCES

Achcar, Gilbert. 2013. *The People Want: A Radical Exploration of the Arab Uprising.* Berkeley: University of California Press.

Ackerman, Bruce. 2015. "Three paths to constitutionalism—and the crisis of the European Union," *British Journal of Political Science*, 45: 705–14.

Albertazzi, Daniele and Duncan McDonnell. 2015. *Populists in Power.* New York: Routledge.

Arato, Andrew. 2013. "Political theology and populism," *Social Research*, 80: 143–72.

Balkin, J. M. 1995. "Populism and progressivism as constitutional categories," *Yale Law Journal*, 104: 1935–91.

Beaumont, Elizabeth. 2014. *The Civic Constitution: Civic Visions and Struggles in the Path toward Constitutional Democracy.* New York: Oxford University Press.

Brettschneider, Corey. 2006. "Popular constitutionalism and the case for judicial review," *Political Theory*, 34: 516–21.

Brettschneider, Corey. 2015. "Popular constitutionalism contra populism," *Constitutional Commentary*, 30: 81–8.

Dahrendorf, Ralf. 2003. "Acht Anmerkungen zum Populismus *Transit*," *Europäische Revue*, 25: 156–63.

de la Torre, Carlos. 2010. *Populist Seduction in Latin America.* Athens: Ohio University Press.

de la Torre, Carlos. 2015. "Introduction: power to the people? Populism, insurrections, democratization," in Carlos de la Torre (ed.), *The Promise and Perils of Populism.* Lexington: University of Kentucky Press, 1–30.

Donnelly, Tom. 2012. "Making popular constitutionalism work," *Wisconsin Law Review*, 159: 159–94.

Edelstein, Dan. 2009. *The Terror of Natural Right: Republicanism, the Cult of Nature, and the French Revolution*. Chicago: University of Chicago Press.

Frank, Jason. 2010. *Constituent Moments: Enacting the People in Postrevolutionary America*. Durham: Duke University Press.

Fukuyama, Francis. 2014. *Political Order and Political Decay*. New York: FSG.

Garsten, Bryan. "Representative government and popular sovereignty," in Ian Shapiro, Susan C. Stokes, Elisabeth Jean Wood, and Alexander S. Kirshner (eds), *Political Representation*. New York: Cambridge University Press, 90–110.

Gentile, Giovanni. 1927. "The philosophic basis of Fascism," *Foreign Affairs*, 6: 290–304.

Halmai, Gábor Halmai. 2013. "Guys with guns versus guys with reports: Egyptian and Hungarian comparisons," 15 July 2013. http://www.verfassungsblog.de/de/egypt-hungary-halmai-constitution-coup, last accessed 13 November 2013.

Haltern, Ulrich. 1998. *Verfassungsgerichtsbarkeit, Demokratie und Mißtrauen: Das Bundesverfassungsgericht in einer Verfassungstheorie zwischen Populismus und Progressivismus*. Berlin: Duncker and Humblot.

Hassanzadeh, Navid. 2015. "On the question of authority in the Arab Spring," *European Journal of Political Theory*, first published online: February 27: 1–20.

Jacobsohn, Gary J. 2010. *Constitutional Identity*. Cambridge: Harvard University Press.

Kantorowicz, Ernst H. 1997 [1957]. *The King's Two Bodies: A Study in Medieval Political Theology*. Princeton: Princeton University Press.

Kelsen, Hans. 1981 [1929]. *Vom Wesen und Wert der Demokratie*. Aalen: Scientia.

Kramer, Larry. 2004. *The People Themselves*. New York: Oxford University Press.

Laclau, Ernesto. 2005. *On Populist Reason*. London: Verso.

Landau, David. 2013. "Abusive constitutionalism," *University of California Davis Law Review*, 47: 189–260.

Lefort, Claude. 1988. *Democracy and Political Theory*, trans. David Macey. Minneapolis: University of Minnesota Press.

Loughlin, Martin. 2015. "The constitutional imagination," *Modern Law Review*, 78: 1–25.

Mazzuca, Sebastián L. 2013. "The rise of rentier populism," *Journal of Democracy*, 24: 108–22.

Möllers, Christoph. 2008. *Demokratie: Zumutungen und Versprechen*. Berlin: Wagenbach.

Mudde, Cas and Cristóbal Rovira Kaltwasser (eds). 2013. *Populism in Europe and the Americas: Threat or Corrective for Democracy?* New York: Cambridge University Press.

Müller, Jan-Werner. 2014. "'The people must be extracted from within the people': Reflections on Populism," *Constellations*, 21: 483–93.

Müller, Jan-Werner. 2015a. "Parsing populism," *Juncture*, 22: 80–9.

Müller, Jan-Werner. 2015b. "Populista alkotmányosság: fogalmilag kizárt?," *Fundamentum*, 2–3: 41–9.

Müller, Jan-Werner. 2016a. "Trump, Erdoğan, Farage: the attractions of populism for politicians, the dangers for democracy," *The Guardian*, 2 September 2016.

Müller, Jan-Werner. 2016b. *What is Populism?* Philadelphia: University of Pennsylvania Press.

Ochoa-Espejo, Paulina. 2015. "Power to whom? The people between procedure and populism," in Carlos de la Torre (ed.), *The Promise and Perils of Populism: Global Perspectives*. Lexington: University Press of Kentucky, 59–90.

Parker, Richard D. 1993. "'Here the people rule': a constitutional populist manifesto," *Valparaiso University Law Review*, 27: 531–84.

Priester, Karin. 2012. *Rechter und linker Populismus: Annäherung an ein Chamäleon*. Frankfurt/Main: Campus.

Rovira Kaltwasser, Cristóbal. 2015. "Populism vs. Constitutionalism?," FLJS policy brief. http://www.fljs.org/sites/www.fljs.org/files/publications/Kaltwasser.pdf, last accessed 16 June 2015.

Sartori, Giovanni. 1962. "Constitutionalism: a preliminary discussion," *American Political Science Review*, 56: 853–64.

Saward, Michael. 2006. "The representative claim," *Contemporary Political Theory*, 5: 297–318.

Schmitt, Carl. 1993. *Verfassungslehre*. Berlin: Duncker and Humblot.

Stavrakakis, Yannis et al. 2016. "Contemporary left-wing populism in Latin America: leadership, horizontalism, and postdemocracy in Chávez's Venezuela," *Latin American Politics and Society*, 58: 51–76.

Taggart, Paul. 2000. *Populism*. Philadelphia: Open University Press.

Uitz, Renáta. 2015. "Can you tell when an illiberal democracy is in the making? An appeal to comparative constitutional scholarship from Hungary," *International Journal of Constitutional Law*, 13: 279–300.

Urbinati, Nadia. 2014. *Democracy Disfigured: Opinion, Truth, and the People*. Cambridge: Harvard University Press.

Versteeg, Mila. 2014. "Unpopular constitutionalism," *Indiana Law Journal*, 89: 1133–90.

Weyland, Kurt. 2001. "Clarifying a contested concept: populism in the study of Latin American politics," *Comparative Politics*, 34: 1–22.

Weyland, Kurt. 2013. "The threat from the populist left," *Journal of Democracy*, 24: 18–32.

....

CHAPTER 31

POPULISM AND THE IDEA OF THE PEOPLE

....

PAULINA OCHOA ESPEJO

WHO are the people in populist politics? Some imagine that populism creates a people through grassroots movements wresting power from elites. Others see the people as thoughtless masses organized by an authoritarian populist leader. Yet despite these differences, most who think about populism tend to put the term "the people" in scare quotes. When supporters or detractors of populism talk about "the people," they seem to deny that the people is what populists claim it is, or that the people can rule. But democracy also requires a people: does denying that "the people" of populism can rule also mean denying the legitimacy of democracy? Making clear what we mean when we say "the people" is crucial to understanding both populism *and* democracy. How does the people emerge as a unified body (if it can ever do so)? How can a people decide? Who gets to speak for the people? How does it legitimize rule? These are central questions of democratic theory, which are often ignored in the literature on populism. Yet, unless we examine these questions, we cannot properly understand what defines populism, nor whether it is good or bad for democracy. Without addressing these questions, the scare quotes around "the people" are a form either of intellectual neglect or of ideological hand-waving.

In this chapter, I show that scholars' definitions and judgments of populism depend on how they conceive of the people and its role in a contemporary democratic order. Whether a scholar advocates one definition of populism over another depends on how she thinks about "the people." Their view of the people, in turn, depends on normative views about democracy, representation, constitutional government, individual rights, political solidarity, and the nature and scope of the common good. Populism is internal to democracy (Arditi, 2007), hence how one thinks about populism always hinges on how one thinks about the legitimacy and value of democratic politics.

To reach this conclusion, the first section of the chapter describes "the problem of the people" in democratic theory. This problem, which becomes evident during populist episodes, is that democratic legitimacy rests on the idea of a unified people; yet the people are always indeterminate. The second section analyzes the terms of a long-standing debate generated by that problem. The debate concerns the nature and function of a unified people. On the one hand, there is the view, often espoused by populists, that the people can rule themselves only if they unify by mobilizing and participating in politics. On the other hand, there is the rival view that any actual group or historically recorded struggle will be a partial and incomplete version of the people; hence we cannot say what exactly is the people's will, nor can we invoke that will without undermining the rights of individuals and minorities. On this view, the people is not an actual group of individuals, but rather an ideal reference to guide legislation. For the first view, which is held by populists among others, democratic politics are only legitimate if they follow the people's will, both as a constitutional ground and also as a revolutionary force. For the second view, which is held by liberal constitutionalists and others, talking about "the people" as if it were a substantial entity in the real world endangers the practices and institutions of representative democracy. In recent years, this debate has been mediated by a view of the "people as process," which sees the people as sufficiently unified to act so that it can function as the ground and limit of the constitutional order, but open and complex enough to escape the appropriation of its will by any one person or group.

The third section of the chapter shows how this debate in democratic theory illuminates the main debate about populism in political science. I draw illustrations from the conceptual part of this Handbook to show that how an author categorizes populism depends on their normative views regarding the role of the people in a democracy. These views determine an author's position on how populism differs from democracy, whether it is dangerous or desirable, and what to do about populist movements.

With this conclusion in hand, the last section proposes an account of populism that draws from the "people as process." On this view, if a consistent account of democratic legitimacy requires that we see the people as an unfinished process, then no one can claim to fully represent it. The invocation of the people is a way of limiting a democrat's claims. Populism differs from democracy in that populists claim to speak with the true voice of the real people, and thus their position is *unlimitable*. This view thus makes clear why populists betray the ideals of democracy they themselves claim to endorse.

"The Problem of the People" in Democratic Theory

The concept of populism depends on an older and deeper debate on the role of the people in a democracy. This debate has gone hand in hand with democracy and democratic theory since antiquity (Bourke and Skinner, 2016), but it became somewhat muted in the mid-twentieth century, when the main concern of those who studied liberal democracy was to contrast it with other major forms of political organization, such as fascism and socialism. However, since the end of the Cold War, political science has renewed its emphasis on self-reflection about democratic politics and has made a new effort to revise "hidden premises and unexplored assumptions" in democratic theory (Dahl, 1989: 3). In the last few decades, this renewed debate on the nature of the people and its limits in democratic theory has led political science to reconsider many assumptions regarding democratic legitimacy and, thus, the role that populism plays in a democratic regime.

The wider question put by this debate is this: by definition, in a democracy the people rules. Yet who are the people? And what does it mean for them to rule? Answering these questions is a necessary step to determine whether we can realize the principles that animate democracy, or, in other words, whether democracy can be legitimate (in the philosophical, not in the sociological sense). So, to explain: there is wide agreement that, in principle, democracy is a legitimate form of government because it offers equal freedom to all. But is it possible to realize in practice the values of freedom and equality contained in this guiding principle? Intuitively, the answer is that to realize equal individual autonomy, all should have a say in the making of important political decisions that affect them. But to say that "all" should have a say is not to say much—not unless we know who exactly are these "all." Who comprises the people? As the many examples of populist politics constantly remind us, this is not something that is settled once and for all. In fact, one of the most contentious issues in current democratic politics is deciding who should count as a citizen, and who gets to make decisions about membership and inclusion. Clearly, not "all" have an equal right of political participation in today's sovereign states: for example, children and the mentally disabled do not get the right to vote. More controversially, the foreign-born and the children of migrants are also in a gray zone of political participation. So the question of democratic legitimacy eventually leads to the question of what are the appropriate criteria for determining who should be enfranchised.

It might seem that this is a legal question, and that it should therefore be answered according to law. But this opens up the question of the legitimacy of current legislation about the criteria for enfranchisement.[1] When it comes to deciding on the people's boundaries, the decision must be prior to law, because in a democracy the people are not simply the electorate, they are also *the sovereign*. The modern theory of popular sovereignty distinguishes between the powers of the government, on the one hand, and the people as the ground of authority in the state, on the other. The people are the authority that constitutes the state, and thus they are logically prior to the law.[2] Another way to understand the question of logical priority is to ask: Why are the lawmakers and politicians the appropriate arbiters of these decisions? Is the law the ultimate ground of legitimacy in democratic politics? This question on the ultimate deciding authority arises when reflecting on any critical issue that may precipitate a constitutional crisis, but it is particularly urgent when it comes to rights of citizenship and political membership. If we want to know who belongs to the people, we cannot simply assume that laws of exclusion are legitimate and move on, because the ground of the laws' legitimacy is itself the people. Take the example of slavery in the nineteenth-century United States: slaves were legally excluded from the democratic political community, but, morally, neither slaves nor their supporters could have been expected to comply with the law in this respect. This gave rise to a civil war and the re-structuring of the political community, which then legally included former slaves. As the example illustrates, when it comes to the legitimacy of criteria for political inclusion, the law cannot be the ultimate standard for judging these criteria.

Who, then, has the ultimate authority to determine the people's limits? To answer this, we could make an abstract moral inquiry into the right criteria of inclusion (López-Guerra, 2014). However, as with all hard ethical questions, there is bound to be profound disagreement on any answer: no one philosophical view can settle the point in politics. So, when making such foundational decisions in a democracy, it should be a higher authority that decides on the question, and in a democracy it is the sovereign people who have the final say. However, as should by now be clear, asking the people to determine the limits of the people does not make sense. This is what political philosophers call "the boundary problem" (Whelan, 1983; Abizadeh, 2008).

The boundary problem is that it is impossible to define democratically who precisely the people are: if we need an election to delimit the *demos*, how do we choose the electors? We would need a people to determine who are the people, to determine who are the people and so on, ad infinitum. Defining an electoral people leads to a problem of self-reference, and eventually to a series of logical paradoxes. In the self-reflective discussions of the grounds of democracy in the 1990s and early 2000s, these paradoxes emerged as the central concern of democratic theory, and they remain central to this day. These paradoxes have been also been called "the problem of the unit" (Dahl, 1989), "the paradox of founding" (Dahl, 1990; Connolly, 1995), "the democratic paradox" (Mouffe, 2000), "the paradox of popular sovereignty" (Yack, 2001), "the paradox of democratic legitimacy" (Benhabib, 2006), "the paradox of politics" (Honig, 2007), and "the problem of constituting the demos" (Goodin, 2007).

Democratically determining the limits of a democratic people, then, seems impossible. This puts democracy in a tight spot, because it makes democratic legitimacy incoherent. If the principle of equality is democracy's justificatory ground (Buchanan, 2002; Christiano, 2008; Dahl, 1989), then equality requires that all those individuals ruled democratically have a right to participate in creating and transforming the basic institutions that rule them, because otherwise they would not be treated equally. Yet this commitment is incompatible with a second democratic commitment: popular rule. According to the first commitment, all individuals should be allowed to participate in creating institutions of rule. According to the second, the people is a basic institution of rule. The commitments are incompatible because a democratic decision to create the people generates an infinite regress. Hence, it seems that democracy is incoherent. This is what I have called elsewhere "the problem of popular indeterminacy" (Ochoa Espejo, 2011).

If popular indeterminacy is indeed inevitable, then appealing to the popular will to determine the legitimacy of the state seems futile. For this reason, since early modernity, many have held that democracy should not be interpreted in terms of self-rule or collective autonomy: democracy is not what we would ideally want it to be; rather, it is mostly what it *can* be. If the people are indeed indeterminate, then it seems that we should not expect to have a rational decision on what is generally good for the collective, and we cannot expect rational agreement on its terms (Riker, 1988). So, for many citizens and scholars, what we call "democracy" is in fact representative government: a type of institutional arrangement where rulers are voted into office, but make decisions independently of those whom they govern (Manin, 1997). "The people," then, is not the ruling sovereign, but instead an ideal reference, which is used to guide legislation at a constitutive level: the sovereign people is a "sleeping sovereign," as Tuck (2016) has put it. While in electoral politics, "the people" is simply a term of art to describe the result of party contests. What we know as "democracy" should not be considered as equivalent to popular rule, but rather as an institutional arrangement by which some individual or group acquires the power to make policy after winning a competitive election (Schumpeter, 1942; Przeworski, 1999).

This minimal view of democracy seems to accurately describe what goes on in contemporary representative regimes. However, it cannot deal with a problem it creates. Can minimal democracy uphold democracy's justificatory grounds? If it was not the people, but rather an elite, who established electoral institutions with no hope of finding the common good; and if it is the elites who govern in the name of the others, then why would these others accept the institutional arrangement? This is a particularly disturbing question when the arrangement is not itself transparent or stable, or when it creates the ground for political disagreement. Any such disagreement undermines the arrangement's legitimacy, and it is particularly disruptive when individuals disagree on fundamentals, such as the rightful powers of institutions, or the limits of the *demos*. If we cannot say that the people rules (where "the people" is understood broadly, so as to admit of *any* widely held definition), then democrats have good reasons to denounce the rules of the democratic game as an imposition by unaccountable elites.

Faced with these difficulties, it seems that "the people" is indeed merely an ideological tool, one used to rally populations and give a veneer of legitimacy to the state. On this view, "the people" is used to make enough individuals believe that the order is legitimate because it represents them in some way, and to provide some cosmetic unity to stabilize a political order. This view holds that the scare-quoted "people" functions as a symbolic reference invoked through myths and rites, a reference which politicians often shore up by associating it with an ethnic group or the ethnic nation (Yack, 2012; Smith, 2004). Yet while the ethinic nation provides the desired pre-political unity, it cannot explain or justify exclusion among individuals who would otherwise be equals without appealing to inherited privilege (specifically, to bloodlines). National exclusion thus eventually undermines the justifying principles of democracy. So, as Margaret Canovan put it, to sustain a political order on this basis, "it would appear that voters need to swallow the democratic equivalent of Plato's 'noble lie,' whilst not believing it to the point that they attempt to act on it" (Canovan, 2002: 42). Moreover, the people as myth poses an even harder question for democrats: if "the people" is just an idea to superficially unify a group so as to guarantee the state's stability, then why should we prefer democracy over other forms of unaccountable rule propped up by the idea of the nation, which may prove more stable than electoral democracy?

This question underlay the late nineteenth-century critiques of parliamentary politics, which saw electoral democracy as incapable of governing in the age of the masses (Stanton, 2016). At the turn of the twentieth century, critics such as Carl Schmitt put forward a view of democracy where plebiscitary elections could lay down a claim to popular legitimacy grounded in a nation sharply defined, internally, by ethnicity, externally, by its enemies. This claim would then empower the people's leader who could govern decisively, without the trammels imposed by parliamentary politics and their constant wrangling (Schmitt, 1985: 2008). Those who are repulsed by this view, however, would have to offer a better defense of the institutions of liberal democracy than the one offered by the first wave of democratic theorists in the eighteenth and nineteenth centuries, and also better than the view of proponents of minimal democracy in the twentieth. Democrats must clarify which view of "the people" can sustain the legitimizing grounds of democracy despite popular indeterminacy. In the next section, I analyze how democratic theory has dealt with the problem in the last three decades, and what these debates tell us about populism.

The People as Process: Between Hypothetical and Historical Versions of the People

Populism is often defined and judged by how it refers to the people. But the conception of the people that populists and critics adopt in turn depends on prior views of what makes democracy legitimate. Thus, the two most important discussions about populism—first, how to define populism, and second, debating what is good or bad about populism—hinge on a deeper debate over the role of "the people" in democratic theory.

As we saw in the previous section, we cannot say that the people is "everybody" or "all," because the limits of the people are not settled prior to asking the question of who the people are. "The people" cannot be either the sum total of the citizenry, nor the full roster of the democratic electorate, because both those interpretations land you squarely in the logical paradoxes described above. Alert to these difficulties, democratic theorists tend to adopt one of two very different accounts of "the people." On the one hand, they acknowledge that "the people" cannot be unified, but they use the term "the people" as an abstract construction, which grounds the legitimacy of the democratic state through a constitution. This is what we could call a *hypothetical* account of the people: a view held by many liberals. On the other hand, there are theorists who also acknowledge that "the people" is indeterminate, but think of it as contingent political movements that surge from demands of actually existing groups of citizens who organize to claim their rights from the state, or to redress wrongs done to the poor, the vulnerable, or the oppressed. We could call this the *historical* account of the people, which is often espoused by populists and their supporters.

Which of these two accounts of the people should sustain democracy? Proponents of the historical view hold that rules and institutions in the state are insufficient for realizing democratic ideals. Legitimacy, they argue, arises from praxis: it requires actual political will and action. So "the people" comes into being when the disenfranchised, the excluded, or the oppressed struggle for inclusion into the political order and re-draw the map of representation and the composition of the governing classes. "The people" can be reconstructed retrospectively from the history of political struggles, and those who identify their cause with these struggles can say that when the dispossessed win, then "the people rules." However, critics of this historical account often hold that while the construction of real-world hegemonies and the historical battles in which they are embedded is important for democracy, this struggle cannot and should not be detached from the rational ideals of democracy, which are embedded in democratic institutions and the rule of law. On the hypothetical account, "the people" should always be an ideal reference which guarantees legitimate representative government, as well as individual rights and the rights of permanent minorities. "The people," on this account, is constructed using hypothetical free and equal individuals who act rationally to establish a form of government that protects the rights of all. From these assumptions, we can construct norms and principles embedded in representative institutions to legitimize the state democratically. The hypothetical account thus emphasizes the principles which guarantee that popular participation takes the proper course, and that majoritarian rule is not overtaken by leaders exercising power vertically, and that it does not undermine the rights of individuals or minorities (Meckstroth, 2015).

Note that it is not only self-avowed populists who accept the historical account of the people. Many democrats are also committed to it. In the United States, in particular, "the people" and "populism" are associated with grassroots organizations, and with the mobilization of ordinary folk who try to disrupt the established order so as to widen the reach of participatory politics (Grattan, 2015; Frank, 2010; Kazin, 1998). In other parts of the world, we also associate "the people" with political movements that seek new ideas to create equality, to share power horizontally, and to disrupt the power of elites through building political hegemonies (Errejón and Mouffe, 2015; Laclau, 2005). "The people" is often thought to emerge in struggles to give birth to political orders that do not yet exist, as happens, for example, during revolutions or wars of national liberation (Badiou, 2016). In this view, moreover, democratic political power is born from the solidarity that emerges through participation (Arendt, 1990; Wolin, 1994). So many equate the democratic people with actual individuals on the street, and with the strength of popular movements; they see these as the building blocks of emerging democracy. "The people" remains a "permanent principle of revolution" within established democratic orders (Butler, 2016).

We saw above, however, that any group that comes into being through political participation is indeterminate. The scattered group does not have a unified voice or the capacity to make decisions. So, the critics of the historical account would say, just because such movements claim to speak for "the people," does not mean that they have democratic legitimacy (Müller, 2016; Urbinati, 1998). Given the fact of indeterminacy, the movement's legitimacy cannot come from the idea of upholding equal freedom for all, or from any claim to an objective account of the common good which is assumed about "the people" in hypothetical accounts. The normative standards by which we judge mobilized groups must be external to the group itself. "The people" alone is not normative, oppression does not itself give direction to political morality, and thus our judgment of a political movement that claims to speak for the people cannot be detached from the justice or injustice of the cause they pursue. Moreover, due to their indeterminacy, these movements have a dangerous tendency to be taken over by representatives or leaders. When a leader draws her power from claiming to speak for the people without institutional constraints, it is only a short step to authoritarianism and encroachment on the rights of minorities (Urbinati, 1998). More controversially, when politically mobilized individuals realize that their group is indeterminate, there is a tendency in political movements to look for a substantive ground of popular unity in the form of a politicized national, religious, ethnic, or racial identity (Abts and Rummens, 2007). Rather than a vague "people," popular movements often become a racial, religious, or national "us" defined partially by the exclusion of a racially, religiously, or nationally different "them" (Mouffe, 2005). Thus, in any appeal to the historical "people" there is always a risk of turning to xenophobia and violent political exclusion (Yack, 2001; McKean, 2016).

In contrast, the hypothetical version of the people promises to solve these problems by creating a legal framework that protects the rights of individuals and minorities. In this view, "the people" is not a collection of individuals, but rather a normative guide that specifies the terms of cooperation within a legal order. This "people" as an abstraction has been a staple of democracy since Kant revised Rousseau's version of the Social Contract (Ochoa Espejo, 2014). In this account, "the people" remains solely the ground of the constitution. It is the people, after all, who charters the state and the constitution, and it is the ultimate judge in the legal order. However, this "We the People" is not an actual group of individuals. It is, rather, a normative guide to legislation (Holmes, 1995). According to it, lawmakers in a democracy should not pass laws that would not be approved by a group of rational individuals conceived in the abstract. For example, a law that legalizes slavery could never be agreed to by those who are to be enslaved. So we can safely say that the people could not possibly approve it; there is no need to poll the populace to find out what they think. "The people," then, is hypothetical: a counterfactual idealization that allows us to evaluate the legitimacy of legal norms.

This conceptualization of the people works well in theory. In practice, however, it is not so easy to find "the [hypothetical] people's voice." In any judgment about what rational individuals would agree to, there is always an element of subjective interpretation, which cannot be subsumed under universal norms. When the answer to a political question is not self-evidently correct (and few are), then the law or policy that eventually gets enacted will be the product of the decisions of *actual* politicians or judges, regardless of which counterfactual idealization test it has been subjected to. So, political decisions endorsed by the hypothetical "people" could understandably be seen as an imposition by the elites upon the rest of the population. Talking about the people in this sense might seem a way to assert that only those who actually rule have the right to represent the people. Moreover, "the people" as an ideal reference may work well when the boundaries of a political unit are settled and stable, but it cannot possibly tell you who precisely are the members of the group which is to be governed. An abstract people is universal, and for this reason it is in principle unbounded (Näsström, 2011; Abizadeh, 2008). So, in this respect, even the abstract hypothetical people remains indeterminate.

This indeterminacy has two immediate defects. First, a hypothetical people does not generate the internal solidarity required to get citizens to make personal sacrifices for the common good. Second, given that a hypothetical people cannot explain or justify exclusion, it is silent on how to create borders, jurisdictions, or demarcations, and it cannot legitimize the limits of a concrete political order. Hence, since no actual political order is universal, this view imposes one interpretation of universal political morality on others as if it were neutral and universal, and it dismisses actual local political struggles. The hypothetical people, according to its critics, is therefore "anti-political" (Stavrakakis, 2014; Rancière, 2007). Given this second defect, those who are committed to liberal democratic ideals and do not give "the people" more than a legal role must be able to respond to those concrete individuals who see themselves alienated from politics and who see the abstract terms of the legal order as an obstacle in their search for political autonomy. Elsewhere I call this second defect "constitutional paternalism": a charge to which a hypothetical view of the people cannot fully respond (Ochoa Espejo, 2011).

So, how to navigate between the abstract Scylla of the hypothetical account of the people and the concrete Charybdis of the historical account? In the last three decades, there has been mounting interest in a procedural view of democratic legitimacy. This view mediates between the "reason" of the hypothetical account, and the "will" of the historical account. "The people," on this procedural view, is not a collection of individuals, but a procedure of decision-making, by which individuals interact with each other mediated by legal institutions that channel popular demands and force representatives to adopt views and make decisions. In the long term, these procedures can be recognized as "the popular will" and, thus, we can eventually think of them as popular sovereignty (Habermas, 1998; Ackerman, 1991). This procedural view, then, integrates the hypothetical and the historical, or popular participatory accounts. Normative principles and institutions, according to proceduralism, are not settled once and for all. These can be revised over time through popular struggles in which people contest and re-interpret democratic principles and give new shape to the political communities that enact them (Benhabib, 2006). An examination of these historical trajectories (Rosanvallon, 2000; Morgan, 1988) shows how "the people" have been forged over time. Moreover, the people's trajectory could be seen as having normative content because the re-interpretation of institutions leads decisions towards inclusion, securing individual and collective rights over time and even expanding them across borders (Meckstroth, 2015; White and Ypi, forthcoming).

However, to complete this procedural view of democratic legitimacy, we must also revise the concept of "the people." The people, like institutions, must also be conceived dynamically. The people is not a determinate group of persons, but rather, the interplay of political movements and legal constraints itself. The people, then, is a series of events in which individuals participate, rather than a specific collection of individuals or a disembodied legal procedure (Ochoa Espejo, 2011). We recognize the people in those momentous events such as battles, elections, riots; but also in more mundane events that make politics everyday: the way we talk to neighbors about politics, or the local ways of practicing citizenship. All those events constitute a political trajectory over time that we call *the people*. This conception allows us to think of the people as unified, but open to the future. And the way to tell that politicians and citizens uphold such an open view is that they acknowledge that the people is not settled and stable; that the people is not homogeneous once and for all. The people does not have a unified voice, and it does not make final decisions. Those who invoke an open view of the people acknowledge that institutional norms can be amended; they acknowledge that the population will change composition in the future; they acknowledge that norms will be contested; they acknowledge that ethnicity, religion, and other forms of identity change over time. This processual view of the people is concrete enough to generate solidarity and even to come to power; but given that it sees the people as always changing and potentially unbound, it makes it less likely to generate exclusion and xenophobia, or to undermine the rights of minorities.

Now that we have in hand an account of the nature and function of "the people," we can use this account to examine the current debates in political science over the meaning and value of populism. We have just seen that any given view of "the people" depends on assumptions about the legitimacy and limits of democratic politics. Hence we should be able to work out how any conception of "populism" also depends on normative assumptions about the ideal workings of the democratic state.

"The People" in Categorizations of Populism

The most important academic debate on populism is on how to categorize it. What kind of a thing is populism? Is it a strategy of political organization? An ideology? A socio-cultural account (see Weyland, Mudde, and Ostiguy, this volume)? There is also an important discussion in political science on whether populism is good or bad for democracy. Is it a threat or a corrective (Rovira Kaltwasser, 2012: 14; Abts and Rummens, 2007; Müller, 2016; Urbinati, 1998)? It might seem that the normative debate follows in the footsteps of the conceptual debate. There is a common assumption that we cannot know whether something is good or bad unless we know what kind of a phenomenon it is. So it seems that the normative debates depend on the prior categorization and descriptive definition, which in turn depend on empirical observation (see Weyland, Mudde, Ostiguy, this volume).

However, categorizing does not come only from observation; it requires a good many theoretical assumptions. I argue here that how scholars categorize populism depends on their theoretical views and value judgments regarding "the people" and, more generally, their normative views on democracy. Among political scientists, there is a persistent belief that an ideal definition of populism can be independent from ideal views of democracy, and that therefore a definition of populism can be "normatively neutral" or free from normative biases (Rovira Kaltwasser, 2012). However, given that all accounts of populism and democracy depend on prior value judgments, this search for purely descriptive views is futile. Moreover, it creates an artificial gulf between theoretical and empirical work on populism. Indeed, I suggest that looking at the empirical literature on populism from the normative perspective allows us to better understand why the populist phenomenon occurs, to what extent it is an anomaly within democratic orders, and whether democracies can avoid it. These are all central questions in the empirical discussion of populism; hence, if I am right, this discussion would be greatly enriched if we approached it from a normative perspective. Moreover, examining empirical categorizations of populism from this normative perspective will help us better understand how both critics and sympathizers react (and how they should react) to populist movements.

How then does the discussion about democratic legitimacy and the concept of the people illuminate conceptual debates about populism? Within the empirical analysis of populism, there is a persistent debate on what exactly characterizes the phenomenon. In this volume alone, we find three important and conflicting conceptual accounts of populism: empirical scholars categorize populism as an ideology (Mudde, this volume), as a political strategy (Weyland, this volume), and as a "political style" of socioculturally constructing a political identity (Moffit and Tormey, 2014; Ostiguy, this volume). But populism can also be categorized as a "discourse" (Stavrakakis, this volume; Howarth, Stavrakakis, and Norval, 2000), a "logic" (Laclau, 2005), or a type of regime (Müller, 2016; Urbinati, this volume), and the list is not exhaustive. The ongoing discussion suggests that "populism" may just be one of those (few) concepts that are contested by their very nature, and the content of which is determined by the disagreement over its proper meaning and scope. This suggests that populism is "an essentially contested concept" (Gallie, 1956). But if so, then we must remember that all essentially contested concepts are embedded in normative debates.[3] Indeed, this is one of the most important features of such concepts. In the case of the concept of populism, I hold that the relevant normative debate is primarily on the nature and the role of the people in a democracy, the debate described in the previous section. To illustrate this point, in the rest of this section I examine a (non-exhaustive) list of categorizations of populism, showing how each depends on a specific conception of the people, which in turn depends on normative views on what makes democracy legitimate and desirable.

Populism as Ideology

Populism is often categorized as an ideology (Canovan, 1999; Mudde, 2004; Abts and Rummens, 2007; Stanley, 2008). This view has gained traction in recent years, due partly to Mudde's useful definition. According to Mudde, "populism is a thin-centred ideology that considers society to be ultimately separated into two homogeneous and antagonistic groups, 'the pure people' and 'the corrupt elite' and which argues that politics should be an expression of the volonté générale (general will) of the people" (Mudde, 2004: 543; Mudde and Rovira Kaltwasser, 2012: 8). This definition may at first seem purely descriptive: it describes a party's ideology. However, it is in fact normative, because the description is dependent on a prior, normative, view of the *demos* in a democracy.

But why should we see this as normative? After all, one of the main attractions of minimal definitions, such as this one, is that they do not seem to evaluate the phenomenon in advance, that is, they are mostly descriptive (Weyland, 2001). Yet, this view does not take into account that the description hinges on a contrast with other views, and the contrast presupposes an evaluation. Specifically, it presupposes that the populists' account of "the people" deviates from what "the people" ought to be in a democracy (according to the scholar who defines populism). In Mudde's view, the example we are discussing, a democratic people should be the totality of a country's plural electorate. We know this because he characterizes populism as one ideology among many within the democratic field, and he positively evaluates an expansive electorate, the ground of democracy (Mudde, 2004: 546, 554). But if one views populism primarily as a party ideology, one must also hold that in a democracy "the people" (which underpins the legitimacy of this type of rule) cannot be the people envisioned by the populists. Instead, the democratic people should be the totality of the electorate, which thus includes other parties, as well as the members of "the elite" that the populists eschew.

We can see this trait of Mudde's definition more clearly in Rovira Kaltwasser's use of this conceptualization. When inquiring whether populism is a "threat" or a "corrective" to democracy, he argues that populism is a threat, because it is an ideology holding that the people's will is unified and supreme, and thus curtailing democratic pluralism. Yet on the other hand, Rovira also holds that populism can set democracy back on its course, because it gives "voice to groups that do not feel represented by the elites" (Rovira Kaltwasser, 2012: 185, 192). Using Margaret Canovan's terms, he calls this the "redemptive side of populism" (192). However, it is clear that for a populist, somebody who holds that the people is unified and its will is supreme, democracy would be strengthened, not threatened, if a country enacted the people's will. So, the fact that Rovira Kaltwasser sees this as a threat shows that he holds that "the people" envisioned by populists is not the view that undergirds democratic legitimacy. Hence a minimal definition that categorizes populism as an ideology seems, at first, not to determine in advance whether populism is good or bad for democracy. Yet such a definition nevertheless contains a rule that determines that populism is in principle wrong (although its effects could somehow redeem the mischief it will inevitably cause). Rovira's definition therefore contains an ideal view of the *demos*, and hence a strong normative commitment in how populism relates to a standard model of democracy.

Populism as a Style of Performing Political Relations

Many have conceived of populism as a style (Knight, 1998; de la Torre, 2010) and a type of *performance* of political relations (Laclau, 2005; Howarth, Stavrakakis, and Norval, 2000). Here I discuss these categories together as "a style of performing political relations" because they both focus on the relations by which politics are enacted in public settings. I follow Moffitt and Tormey (2014) and Ostiguy (this volume), whose categorizations are clear, and also compatible in this respect. Moffit and Tormey describe a style as a "repertoire of political performances that are used to create political relations" (2014: 387). In their view, what distinguishes this political style from others, such as the "technocratic" or the "authoritarian," is that populists appeal to "the people" in their performance, they overplay the perception of a threat or crisis, and they do so with "bad manners" (2014: 382, 392). This last defining feature is the main characteristic of this style, which Ostiguy analyzes extensively. Ostiguy (this volume) emphasizes the construction of political relations through performance by "flaunting the low," where "the low" can be understood as the extreme of a scalar "high-low" axis perpendicular to the traditional view of politics as existing in a right-left continuum. The "low" is conceived as a sociocultural category, distinct from economic class.

On this view, "the people" of the populists is not a group that can be objectively described. Rather, the group is the *product* of political performances through which political leaders establish a relation with those who actively participate in the political process. So Moffit and Tormey explain, when a leader claims to speak for "the people," she does not speak for all citizens. In fact, "'the people' does not—and cannot, in reality—include all citizens within a given community." However, when populists claim to speak in the name of "the people," they are attempting "to bring a subject called 'the people' into being: they produce what they claim to represent" (2014: 389).

This view of the people as the *product* rather than a cause or condition of political relations is what Saward has termed "the representative claim" (Saward, 2006). The view seems to accurately describe how populists create political power. Moreover, it also seems to provide a normatively neutral hypothesis about how political movements and populist leaders unify a people when they claim to represent it. However, as in the previous case, the choice of conceptualization is not itself neutral: it reveals a normative choice, given the author's own conception of the people (which is different from the people-conception of the populists, which the author attempts to describe).

If you hold that the populists' "people" emerges from a political performance, where the relation "creates what it claims to represent," then it seems that your approach is not compatible with the most common conception of democratic legitimacy. To clarify: if "the people" is the outcome, rather than the ground of political representation, then popular sovereignty means (for all practical purposes) the actual sovereignty of the leaders who bring the people into being. This view of the people has been in circulation at least since Hobbes's *Leviathan*. For Hobbes, in a commonwealth there are only scattered individuals: the people don't exist as a body unless they are unified in the person of the sovereign who rules them and represents the state (Hobbes, 1991: ch. 16). But this also means that the people have little or no power without their representative, and that the person of the sovereign is above the law. If the people have no capacity to act, unless they are politically organized or legally sanctioned, then "the people" cannot reject the leader, representative, or movement, without destroying itself. The upshot, then, is that democracy conceived as a form of government that fosters individual or collective autonomy becomes impossible. This view further implies that although popular sovereignty is impossible, the need for order justifies the creation of political hegemonies and thus, the leader's (or claim-maker's) power. When this Hobbesian view of representation is applied to the politics of populism, we find similar arguments to Carl Schmitt's account of the role of the leader in a democracy, who creates the state by embodying it (Schmitt, 2008).[4]

Yet, as Hannah Pitkin wrote in her classical account of Hobbesian representation: "After reading this we feel that somehow we have been tricked" (Pitkin, 1967: 34). What happened to the representative as a steward of the people's interests? Here we can see that Ostiguy, as well as Moffitt and Tormey, may feel that they also have been tricked; because, unlike Hobbes, they do not fully subscribe to the account of political performance that they claim to endorse. This becomes clear when we see that rather than adhering to a purely performative account of political representation (where the people does not exist as a collective prior to the representation), they actually commit to a view of the people defined independently of representation in the political process. That is, they also hold that the people has some intrinsic traits that we can recognize independently of the process of representation. This is evident in the concept of "the low" or "bad manners." On this view of the people, the traits of the lower part of society are also the main traits of this style of building political relations. For this view, there is a society organized in cultural strata; a society, which is (logically) prior to the political construction of the people. If the people is not purely brought into being by representation, but also by references to the lower end of a stratified society, then we can see that for the populists "the people" is in fact equivalent to those who participate in the cultural "low-brow" (where "high-" and "low-brow" do not refer to social class, but to cultural distinction or "civilizatory" refinement). That is, in this account of populism, "the people" is not *just* a political construction brought about by the creation of political hegemonies. The people is also an actual stratum of society that can be found and located prior to populist organization. "The people" of the populists, on this account, is the lower sociocultural stratum: the bad-mannered, the uneducated (*pés descalços, descamisados, sans-culottes* ...). "The people" is thus created by an explicit exclusion of the cultural elites in the act of representation. This means that the people of populists does have a real substance, but it is incompatible with the view of democracy that promises equality for "all." So, if one holds with Ostiguy and others that populism is a particular style of building political relations that "flaunts the low" or has "bad manners," then they see the populist's "people" as the symbolic construction that seeks to represent an actually existing *section* of society. Populists hold that a democratic people should be the low-brow, and only them. Yet, the scholars who see populists as singling out only a *section* of society think that the democratic people ought to comprise *all* social strata, both "the low" and "the high."

Populism as Political Strategy

Kurt Weyland defines populism "as a political strategy through which a personalistic leader seeks or exercises government power based on direct, unmediated, uninstitutionalized support from large numbers of mostly unorganized followers" (Weyland, 2001: 14). This is a traditional way of conceiving of populism through the "methods and instruments of winning and exercising power" (2001: 12). Since classical antiquity this kind of political strategy has been associated with demagoguery. Like the classical account, this view focuses on the leader who steals the mantle of legitimacy by claiming to be the proper interpreter of the people's will. As Christopher Meckstroth puts it, the populist's claim to channel an already formed will which is prior to any political process is the "old populist trick through which calls to seize all power for 'the people' become the surest means of mastering them" (Meckstroth, 2015: 21).

For Weyland, the conception of "the people" does not seem to occupy an important place in the account of populism, given that what really matters is the organizational strategy rather than the politician's ideology or conceptual repertoire. However, this lack of emphasis on populists' idea of "the people" actually reveals a normative view of "the people" in democracy. Not the view that the leader espouses, but rather, that of the scholar who holds this definition of populism. For Weyland, regardless of what a political leader says in his discourses, what really matters is what he gets individuals to do in order to build up his power. In short, the focus is on individuals constituted as masses: a multitude which is mostly passive, and only produces political effects when leaders orchestrate individual actions. For Weyland, "the people" are "a *very* broad aggregate— ... amorphous, heterogeneous, and largely unorganized, they cannot exercise effective agency; collective action dilemmas preclude that" (this volume, 54). So in his view, "the people" in a democracy cannot be an independent collective actor.

Underlying this view of populism is Weyland's conception of "the people" as the substratum of a minimal conception of democracy (Przeworski, 1999). Here, the population is organized by leaders, or by representative institutions, and individual participation is reduced to the vote. The underlying assumption is that "the people" does not have a common will and popular sovereignty does not track the common good outside of representative institutions. We only have the competition for votes among politicians organized in political parties or relating directly to the masses. So the only purpose of referring to the idea of "the people" is to use it as a euphemism to talk about majorities or electoral victories. Adopting this view of populism as a political strategy implicitly endorses a view of democracy as a form of government that rejects collective autonomy as the basis of legitimacy, and which endorses electoral competition as its ground and goal.

So to conclude, as these three examples illustrate, categorizing populism requires a (logically) prior conception of the people in a democracy. This conception, in turn, illustrates the normative commitments that frame an author's view of democracy. The process of choosing a category itself introduces a normative judgment into any discussion of populism (although this normative judgment is often implicit); and the debate over the concept of populism reveals deeper disagreements over the value of democracy. Each view of the democratic people is tied to deeper normative views about individual rights, political solidarity, and the nature and scope of the common good. Making these commitments explicit matters, because they determine whether populism is seen as an anomalous (positive or negative) phenomenon, or simply business as usual in democratic politics. A scholar's view of the people, moreover, illuminates their views on what makes democracy legitimate and why populism may foster or challenge this legitimacy.

Self-Limitation as the Criterion for Distinguishing Populism from Democracy

With this conclusion in hand, I would like to offer a categorization of populism that corresponds to the conception of democratic legitimacy described in the second section. On this view, a consistent account of democratic legitimacy requires that we see the people as an unfinished process, which no one can claim to fully represent. A view of populism that corresponds to this open conception of the people is generally congruent with the categorization of the populism as an ideology in Mudde's definition. However, Mudde equivocates on the Rousseauvian "general will." Mudde uses "the general will" as equivalent to "whatever (the populists') people want." Yet, given that Rousseau's view of the people is normative (rather than a description of an actual state of affairs), one cannot use it to describe a populist's view, or to distinguish it from other democratic ideologies. What Mudde misses here is that an abstract reference to the people is necessary in any ideology that is compatible with democracy: all democratic views refer to the people as a collective and make some reference to the "will of the people" as the common good. So, rather than the Rousseuvian "general will," what distinguishes populism from other ideologies is the fact that a fraction of the people symbolically appropriates the whole (Müller, 2014). Populism is the only ideology that turns the people into a closed whole that they (and only they) represent. Populists are distinguishable not because they invoke the "general will," or the people's common good, but rather because they take their view as the only possible rendition of the people's will. In their view, membership in the people requires adhering to this exclusive idea of the common good at the exclusion of all others.

In practical politics, a test for determining whether a party's or a movement's view of "the people" is compatible with democratic legitimacy is seeing whether politicians or movements that invoke the people are *self-limited* (Ochoa Espejo, 2015). If they represent the people, but they consider the people to be open to change, then the movement or party will acknowledge the possibility of defeat and will be open to incorporate disagreement, or accept other views as legitimate contestants. In contrast, the view of the people that populists often adopt leads them to say that the people is *unlimitable*. Populists claim that the people is always right and, thus, complete and absolute. In their view, their being on the side of "the people" allows them to reject any limits on their claims. Their alleged embodiment of the will of the people means that their view is always right; it is always the supremely authoritative correct interpretation of the common good. Those who accept limitations, by contrast, may also appeal to the people, but they depict it as the framework that guarantees pluralism, and thus they also frame any particular cause as fallible, including their own. Self-limitation arises from openness: if the people can (and probably will) change, then any appeal to its will is also fallible, temporary, and incomplete.[5]

Thus, our reflections on the idea of "the people" can help us better define populism. If a consistent account of democracy requires that we see "the people" as a process, then, we can see democracy at work when those who invoke "the people" in political contests acknowledge its limited character. A self-limited conception of the people forces politicians to accept protections for minorities, and also to admit that they may not have considered all relevant interests in the past. This offers a clear contrast with "the people" without constraints that we find at the core of populism. The only limit to the people of populists is its opposition to an out-group. Thus, populism cannot see itself as one ideology among many options, but only as the true voice of the real people, both in opposition and in government.

This prior discussion on the nature of "the people" in a democracy can help us to more accurately categorize populism. See, for example, Müller (2016). The most useful conceptualizations of populism would be those that can clearly distinguish populist views from others, those that capture the whole range of phenomena in the "common sense" description of the term in the media and the press, but also, and perhaps most importantly, those that make clear why a democratic appeal to the people is possible and desirable, and how it differs from the appeals of populists.

Categorizing populism as ideology seems compatible with an open view of the people. Ideology may indeed be the *genus*, but populism's specific difference is not its appeal to "the general will" but rather its appeal to "the people's" closure. Populism is distinct from other ideologies because of how populists embrace the purported stability, coherence, and homogeneity of the collective. If we think of populism in these terms, we can even better capture what "common sense" conceives as populism. For example, common sense counts as populist the Trump campaign in the 2016 United States elections, which did not explicitly mention "the general will" and hardly ever mentioned "the people." But it did insist on the unlimited character of the claims that "the real America" stands for, and on the impossibility that the cause could experience defeat at the polls. It is not that populists invoke the people that distinguishes populism from other ideologies: it is *how* they invoke the people. For populists, the fact that they are on the side of the people means that they are always right. A democrat, by contrast, believes that he is on the side of the people, but the people can revise its decisions: the people's will is always open to change.

In conclusion, both populists *and* democrats must invoke the people when they offer a justification of their views, and when they give a normative grounding to the state. However, they differ on whether they conceive of "the people" as a historical fact, or as a hypothetical ideal for guiding legislation. When the normative account abstracts away from the real life experience of individuals, and their actual participation in politics, it strips democracy of its political strength. When the populist's historical account makes "the people" equivalent to one specific group within the state, it makes its claims *unlimitable*, and thus betrays the democratic ideals that the populists claim to endorse.

These normative accounts of the people, moreover, find their way into descriptions and categorizations of populism in the academic literature. When political scientists attempt to offer purely descriptive accounts of populism, they in fact frame the problem according to a prior idea of what a people should be, and thus they smuggle in their value judgments through the back door.

An account of the "people as process" provides an explicit normative ground to sustain democratic legitimacy, at the same time that it gives us tools to characterize populism by describing how populist practices stray from their democratic goals. However, this does not settle the question of *how* exactly to keep the people open to contestation and pluralism. If what allows us to talk about the people, without having to put the term in scare quotes, is accepting its changing nature, then we cannot rest satisfied with one final account of these terms. We still have to see whether the evolving practices of populism (both in power and in opposition) shift the framework of democracy itself. How a democratic people will change to resist the challenge is still an open question.

Notes

1 This is not to say that the legal question is easy to settle either. See for example Bosniak (2006) and Cohen (2009).

2 The terminology of "constituent power" and "constituted power" comes from Sieyès (2003: 136); he writes "[i]t would be ridiculous to suppose that the nation itself was bound by the formalities of the constitution to which it had subjected those it had mandated." For analysis, see Kalyvas (2005) and Pasquino (1998).

3 Gallie called these terms "appraisive" because they are embedded in discussions of value judgment. In political debates, speaking of "value judgments" often implies normative views. By "normative views," I mean claims that tell us what to do by providing a standard or norm. In politics, this is often an account of whether something is good or bad *for a specific purpose.*

4 This view, in turn, is very similar to Laclau's account of the construction of populist hegemony. He acknowledges the Hobbesian connection in *On Populist Reason* (2005: 100). For insightful critiques emphasizing this point, see Arditi (2010); McKean (2016).

5 This view of the people can also have its own problems, of course. For example, self-limitation is hard to espouse (candidates and political movements have a strategic disadvantage when they acknowledge their own limitations) and, also, the definition of the people is not itself democratically crafted. Like other liberal principles, it is a normative principle which is not internal to democracy. However, unlike other principles self-limitation can avoid the worst kinds of constitutional paternalism, and it can provide a clear criterion to distinguish populist views from others that are fully compatible with democratic governance.

References

Abizadeh, Arash. 2008. "Democratic theory and border coercion: no right to unilaterally control your own borders," *Political Theory*, 36(1): 37–65.

Abts, Koen and Stefan Rummens. 2007. "Populism versus democracy," *Political Studies*, 55: 405–24.

Ackerman, Bruce. 1991. *We the People: Foundations*, Vol. 1. Cambridge: Harvard University Press.

Arditi, Benjamin. 2007. *Politics on the Edges of Liberalism*. Edinburgh: Edinburgh University Press.

Arditi, Benjamin. 2010. "Populism is hegemony is politics? On Ernesto Laclau's *On Populist Reason*," *Constellations*, 17(3): 488–97.

Arendt, Hannah. 1990. *On Revolution*. New York: Penguin.

Badiou, Alain. 2016. "Twenty-four notes on the uses of the word people," in Alain Badiou (ed.), *What is a People?* New York: Columbia University Press, 21–31.

Benhabib, Seyla. 2006. *Another Cosmopolitanism: Hospitality, Sovereignty and Democratic Iterations*. Oxford: Oxford University Press.

Bosniak, Linda. 2006. *The Citizen and the Alien: Dilemmas of Contemporary Membership*. Princeton: Princeton University Press.

Bourke, Richard and Quentin Skinner (eds). 2016. *Popular Sovereignty in Historical Perspective*. Cambridge: Cambridge University Press.

Buchanan, Allen. 2002. "Political legitimacy and democracy," *Ethics*, 112(4): 689–719.

Butler, Judith. 2016. "'We the People': thoughts on freedom of assembly," in Alain Badiou (ed.), *What is a People?* New York: Columbia University Press, 49–64.

Canovan, Margaret. 1999. "Trust the people: populism and the two faces of democracy," *Political Studies*, XLVII: 2–16.

Canovan, Margaret. 2002. "Taking politics to the people: populism as the ideology of democracy," in Yves Mény and Yves Surel (eds), *Democracies and the Populist Challenge*. New York: Palgrave Macmillan, 25–42.

Christiano, Thomas. 2008. *The Constitution of Equality: Democratic Authority and Its Limits*. Oxford: Oxford University Press.

Cohen, Elizabeth. 2009. *Semi Citizenship in Democratic Politics*. Cambridge: Cambridge University Press.

Connolly, William E. 1995. *The Ethos of Pluralization*. Minneapolis: Minnesota University Press.

Dahl, Robert A. 1989. *Democracy and Its Critics*. New Haven: Yale University Press.

Dahl, Robert A. 1990. *After the Revolution? Authority in a Good Society*. New Haven: Yale University Press.

de la Torre, Carlos. 2010. *Populist Seduction in Latin America*. Athens: Ohio University Press.

Errejón, Iñigo and Chantal Mouffe. 2015. *Construir Pueblo*. Barcelona: Icaria.

Frank, Jason. 2010. *Constituent Moments: Enacting the People in Postrevolutionary America*. Durham and London: Duke University Press.

Gallie, Walter Bryce. 1956. "Essentially contested concepts," *Proceedings of the Aristotelian Society*, 56: 167–98.

Goodin, Robert. 2007. "Enfranchising all affected interests and its alternatives," *Philosophy and Public Affairs*, 35(1): 40–68.

Grattan, Laura. 2015. *The Populist Persuasion*. New York: Oxford University Press.

Habermas, Juergen. 1998. "Popular sovereignty as procedure," in *Between Facts and Norms: Contributions to a Discourse Theory of Law and Democracy*. Cambridge: MIT Press, 463–90.

Hobbes, Thomas. 1991. *Leviathan*, ed. Richard Tuck. Cambridge: Cambridge University Press.

Holmes, Stephen. 1995. *Passions and Constraint: On the Theory of Liberal Democracy*. Chicago: University of Chicago Press.

Honig, Bonnie. 2007. "Between decision and deliberation: political paradox in democratic theory," *The American Political Science Review*, 101(1): 1–18.

Howarth, David, Yannis Stavrakakis, and Aletta Norval. 2000. *Discourse Theory and Political Analysis*. Manchester: Manchester University Press.

Kalyvas, Andreas. 2005. "Popular sovereignty, democracy and constituent power," *Constellations*, 12(2): 223–44.

Kazin, Michael. 1998. *The Populist Persuasion*. New York: Cornell University Press.

Knight, Alan. 1998. "Populism and neo-populism in Latin America, especially Mexico," *Journal of Latin American Studies*, 30(2): 223–48.

Laclau, Ernesto. 2005. *On Populist Reason*. London: Verso.

López-Guerra, Claudio. 2014. *Democracy and Disenfranchisement: The Morality of Electoral Exclusions*. Oxford: Oxford University Press.

Manin, Bernard. 1997. *The Principles of Representative Government*. Cambridge: Cambridge University Press.

McKean, Benjamin. 2016. "Toward an inclusive populism? On the role of race and difference in Laclau's politics," *Political Theory*, 44: 797–820. doi: 10.1177/0090591716647771.

Meckstroth, Christopher. 2015. *The Struggle for Democracy: Paradoxes of Progress and the Politics of Change*. Oxford: Oxford University Press.

Moffit, Benjamin and Simon Tormey. 2014. "Rethinking populism: politics, mediatisation and political style," *Political Studies*, 62(2): 381–97.

Morgan, Edmund. 1988. *Inventing the People*. New York: W. W. Norton.

Mouffe, Chantal. 2000. *The Democratic Paradox*. London: Verso.

Mouffe, Chantal. 2005. *On the Political*. London and New York: Routledge.

Mudde, Cas. 2004. "The populist zeitgeist," *Government and Opposition*, 39(4): 542–63.

Mudde, Cas and Cristóbal Rovira Kaltwasser (eds). 2012. *Populism in Europe and the Americas: Threat or Corrective for Democracy?* Cambridge: Cambridge University Press.

Müller, Jan-Werner. 2014. "'The people must be extracted from within the people': reflections on populism," *Constellations*, 21(4): 483–93.

Müller, Jan-Werner. 2016. *What is Populism?* Philadelphia: University of Pennsylvania Press.

Näsström, Sofia. 2011. "The challenge of the all affected principle," *Political Studies*, 59(1): 116–34.

Ochoa Espejo, Paulina. 2011. *The Time of Popular Sovereignty: Process and the Democratic State*. University Park: Pennsylvania State University Press.

Ochoa Espejo, Paulina. 2014. "Popular sovereignty," in Michael T. Gibbons (ed.), *The Blackwell Encyclopedia of Political Thought*. London: Wiley, 2887.

Ochoa Espejo, Paulina. 2015. "Power to whom? The people between procedure and populism," in Carlos de la Torre (ed.), *The Promise and Perils of Populism*. Lexington: University Press of Kentucky, 59–90.

Pasquino, Pasquale. 1998. *Sieyès et l'invention de la constitution en France*. Paris: Odile Jacob.

Pitkin, Hannah. 1967. *The Concept of Representation*. Berkeley: University of California Press.

Przeworski, Adam. 1999. "Minimalist conception of democracy: a defense," in Ian Shapiro and Casiano Hacker-Cordón (eds), *Democracy's Value*. Cambridge: Cambridge University Press, 23–55.

Rancière, Jacques. 2007. *Hatred of Democracy*, trans. Steve Corcoran. London: Verso.

Riker, William H. 1988. *Liberalism against Populism: A Confrontation between the Theory of Democracy and the Theory of Social Choice*. Long Grove: Waveland.

Rosanvallon, Pierre. 2000. *La démocratie inachevée: histoire de la souveraineté du peuple en France*. Paris: Gallimard.

Rovira Kaltwasser, Cristóbal. 2012. "The ambivalence of populism: threat and corrective for democracy," *Democratization*, 19(2): 1–25.

Saward, Michael. 2006. "The representative claim," *Contemporary Political Theory*, 5(2): 297–318.

Schmitt, Carl. 1985. *The Crisis of Parliamentary Democracy*, trans. Ellen Kennedy. Cambridge: MIT Press.

Schmitt, Carl. 2008. *Constitutional Theory*, trans. Jeffrey Seltzer. Durham: Duke University Press.

Schumpeter, Joseph. 1942. *Capitalism, Socialism and Democracy*. New York: Harper Brothers.

Sieyès, Emmanuel Joseph. 2003. *Political Writings*, trans. Michael Sonenscher. Indianapolis: Hackett.

Smith, Rogers. 2004. *Stories of Peoplehood: The Politics and Morals of Political Membership*. Cambridge: Cambridge University Press.

Stanley, Ben. 2008. "The thin ideology of populism," *Journal of Political Ideologies*, 13(1): 95–110.

Stanton, Timothy. 2016. "Popular sovereignty in an age of mass democracy," in Richard Bourke and Quentin Skinner (eds), *Popular Sovereignty in Historical Perspective*. Cambridge: Cambridge University Press, 297–319.

Stavrakakis, Yannis. 2014. "The return of 'the people': populism and anti-populism in the shadow of the European crisis," *Constellations*, 21(4): 505–17.

Tuck, Richard. 2015. *The Sleeping Sovereign: The Invention of Modern Democracy*. New York: Cambridge University Press.

Urbinati, Nadia. 1998. "Democracy and populism," *Constellations*, 5(1): 110–24.

Weyland, Kurt. 2001. "Clarifying a contested concept: populism in the study of Latin American politics," *Comparative Politics*, 34(1): 1–22.

Whelan, Frederick G. 1983. "Democratic theory and the boundary problem," in J. R. Pennock and J. W. Chapman (eds), *Liberal Democracy*. New York: New York University Press, 13–47.

White, Jonathan and Lea Ypi. Forthcoming. "The politics of peoplehood," *Political Theory*. doi: 10.1177/0090591715608899.

Wolin, Sheldon. 1994. "Fugitive democracy," *Constellations*, 1(1): 11–25.

Yack, Bernard. 2001. "Popular sovereignty and nationalism," *Political Theory*, 29(4): 517–36.

Yack, Bernard. 2012. *Nationalism and the Moral Psychology of Community*. Chicago: University of Chicago Press.

CHAPTER 32

....

POPULISM AND PRAXIS

....

JASON FRANK

ANY theoretical inquiry into the contested meaning of populism leads to central and recurring dilemmas of democratic theory and democratic politics. This chapter will travel this path and argue that populism—conceived as a theoretical construct and a historical phenomenon—has political resources often unrecognized by either its liberal critics or its radical democratic admirers in contemporary democratic theory. Rather than focus on what James Morone has called populism's "democratic wish" (Morone, 1998)—its desire to transcend mediating institutions and return power to the purifying immediacy of popular voice—or insist on what Ernesto Laclau calls its "oppositional logic" (Laclau, 2005)—its efforts to construct from disparate grievances a popular subject ("the people") defined against the dominating power of a corrupt elite ("the few")— I will emphasize the institutional improvisations and formative praxis of populism, its robust but often unexamined experimentation with different forms of political cooperation and democratic enactment. This chapter approaches populism as an exemplary instance of radical democratic praxis and prefiguration.

This important aspect of populism's history has been systematically obfuscated by the influential theory of populism presented in the work of Carl Schmitt. Schmitt's focus on the centrality of popular identification to any theory of democracy has prevented populism's critics and admirers in democratic theory from engaging with the neglected elements I focus on here; it has captivated democratic theory with the admittedly difficult question of *who* the people are ("the boundary problem") and too often obscured the closely related question of *how* the people act ("the enactment problem") (Abizadeh, 2012; Frank, 2010; Honig, 2007; Nässtrom, 2007; Whelan, 1983). Rather than focusing on either political identity or institutional and practical form, democratic theories of populism should investigate the historical entanglement of these registers in the praxis of populist politics.

In the first section, I critique the Schmittian conception shared by populism's liberal critics and radical democratic admirers in contemporary democratic theory; in the second section, I briefly exemplify the kind of historical inquiry elicited by this theoretical critique. A return to the rough ground of populism's history—and I will focus on the nineteenth-century American case—might help disenthrall democratic theorists of the debilitating Schmittian picture, and, doing so, reorient the questions we ask about populism's relation to democratic politics: from the identity of the popular subject to its different repertoires of popular enactment. The hope is that this reorientation will encourage a democratic theory of populism less narrowly preoccupied with debates over populism's ends and more attentive to its inventive means, or, better, how the question of its ends has been historically entangled with questions surrounding the means envisioned to achieve them.

POPULISM: FROM IDENTITY TO PRAXIS

Who is the subject of populism? It is a familiar, if also vexing, question. Populism's appeal to the authority of a unitary popular will has long been denounced by liberal democratic theorists as a dangerous perversion of democracy, even a "proto-totalitarian logic" (Koem and Rummens, 2007: 414). Following the work of prominent critics like Robert Michels and Walter Lipmann, populism's appeal to "the people" has also been debunked as a delusional fantasy—a political metaphysics and a quasi-mysticism—by social scientists on both the class-analysis left (e.g. Bourdieu, 1990) and the rational-choice right (e.g. Riker, 1988). Even more sympathetic scholars tend to disagree about what distinguishes populism and its subject from other forms of politics. Indeed, there is little agreement on what category of analysis populism should be included under in the first place. Is it a form of party organization and electoral mobilization, or a social movement and example of contentious politics (Mudde and Rovira Kaltwasser, 2012)? Is it a style of political rhetoric—a "flexible mode of persuasion" (Kazin, 1998: 3)—or a coherent albeit "thin-centred" ideology (Mudde, 2004: 543)? Or is it "something more nearly resembling a mood or ... an ethos" (Goodwyn, 1976: x)? With all of this disagreement, it should not be surprising that one of the most influential contemporary theories of populism—Ernesto Laclau's—places indeterminacy or ambiguity at its very center, and argues that "populist reason" and its appeal to the authorizing power of "the people" is equivalent to the logic of the "empty signifier" (Laclau, 2005).

While many scholars of populism—historians, political scientists, and political theorists—emphasize its political and ideological flexibility, it is not completely "open." Populism is a discourse organized around a relatively clear set of normative commitments. Most obviously, populism emerges from—and is enabled by—a superordinate commitment to popular sovereignty, to the modern legitimating idea that the people are the ultimate ground of public authority (Morgan, 1989; Tuck, 2016). Populism shares this central reference with modern democracy itself, and in this sense Nadia Urbinati is right to note that populism's "character and claims are parasitic to democratic theory" (Urbinati, 1998: 116). However, the populist parasite cannot be so easily removed from the democratic host as Urbinati and other liberal democratic theorists would have us believe. Populism cannot be easily excised from democracy because it emerges from a familiar paradox internal to democracy's commitment to the authority of "We the People." I don't mean the supposedly paradoxical relationship between constitutionalism and democracy, or legality and legitimacy, but the more fundamental (as in, logically prior) paradox of democratic peoplehood itself. Bonnie Honig simply calls it the "paradox of politics" (Honig, 2007). "Determining who constitutes the people is an inescapable yet democratically unanswerable dilemma; it is not a question the people can procedurally decide because the very question subverts the premises of its resolution" (Frank, 2010: 2). In *Constituent Moments* I tracked the adventures of this paradox in post-revolutionary American political culture, but argued beyond that case that what Sophia Nässtrom has called the "legitimacy of the people" problem haunts all theories of democracy and continually vivifies democratic practice (Nässtrom, 2007). It does so because it opens up dilemmas of authorization not only in extraordinary moments of constitutional crisis but in the small dramas of authorization that mark the agonistic course of ordinary democratic speech and action.

Populism should be understood as a political manifestation of this underlying dilemma of democratic theory and practice, because this dilemma establishes the discursive condition of populism's defining claim to transcend the authorized but corrupted institutions of popular representation through a purifying appeal to unmediated popular voice. The defining claim of populism emerges from the democratic necessity and impossibility of the people speaking in their own name; it arises from the fact that the people's authority is based in a "continually reiterated but never fully realized reference to the sovereign people beyond representation, beyond the law, the spirit beyond the letter, the Word beyond the words" (Frank, 2010: 3). Populism's people—"the working man," "the forgotten man," "the silent majority," "the 99 percent"—is at once enacted through representational claims and forever pointing beyond the political and legal boundaries inscribed by those claims. The subject of populism is therefore neither the sovereign electorate determined by the constitutional rules of the game ("pre-existing legal rules for aggregating preferences") (Holmes, 1995: 148), nor an immanent "multitude" capable of formulating popular will altogether free from the vicissitudes of representational claims (Hardt and Negri, 2004). The parasite of populism takes place in the representational gap of authorization between these spheres. Indeed, some of the power of populist enactments and their central claims can be attributed to the political contest opened up by this gap in authorization, to its performative transfiguration of a given political context. Populism emerges as an event by exploiting this tension between the authorized representation of public authority and the enactment of popular power that proceeds without authorization. Populism is indeed parasitic on democracy, but this parasitism is what lends it the transformative and rejuvenating democratic power attributed to it by some of its best scholars in history and political theory (Kazin, 1998; Canovan, 1981; 2002).

In order to isolate the populist parasite from the democratic host, many democratic theorists reject populism's transformative potential beyond the existing rules of the game and instead emphasize populism's denial of pluralism, its rejection of the separation of powers, and similar affronts to liberal constitutionalism (e.g. Kirshner, 2010; Urbinati,

2014). Populism is said to adopt a "phantasmal image of the organic unity of the political community" as a way of legitimating the suspension of constitutional protections it presents as obstacles to the unified articulation of popular voice (Koen and Rummens, 2007: 414). But doesn't liberal constitutionalism also quietly rely on some image of "the people-as-one," to use Claude Lefort's term, even if that image usually goes underarticulated and unjustified in liberal democratic theory (Lefort, 1986)? Responding critically to the dangers of populism's appeal to the people's constituent power does not in itself adequately confront, much less resolve, the political paradox that underwrites or engenders that appeal. Liberals sometimes seem to worry about the "organic unity" of populism's people as a way of displacing their own inability to adequately conceptualize the formation of the subject of popular authorization. To take that problem seriously is to invite the parasite into your house, to see that it cannot be simply seen as "a degeneration of the democratic logic" (Urbinati, 1998).

What I have written about populism up to this point clearly resonates with key aspects of Ernesto Laclau's work, and with other radical democratic admirers of populism who nonetheless remain critical of the romanticism of the immanent and self-organizing multitude (which Laclau dismisses as a "metaphysical wish" and "a gift from heaven") (Laclau, 2005: 240). Laclau's longstanding interest in populism dates to his early Gramscian writings on Peronism in Argentina—his exploration of why there can be "both progressive and reactionary forms of Caesarism"—but this interest is given a fully articulated formal analysis more recently in *The Populist Reason* (Laclau, 1977; 2005). The "logic" of populism on this account—which Laclau takes to be "synonymous with the political" itself—is centered on "the formation of an internal antagonistic frontier separating the 'people' from power," and the unification of this people around a powerful symbol or ideal: the empty signifier (Laclau, 2005: 154). In Benjamin Arditi's sympathetic development of Laclau's argument, populism is an "internal periphery" that opens up within democratic institutions, as the people identify with a symbolic representation of popular power, the "virtual immediacy" of which constitutes a political authority or source of decision beyond established or legally authorized institutions of governance (parliamentary representation, political parties, courts, and so on) (Arditi, 2005). For both liberal critics and radical democratic admirers, populism is often defined by the antagonistic formation of a unifying political identity out of the conflicted social terrain of competing interests and demands. It organizes competing interests into a demand that claims to transcend interest and interest group politics altogether. Populism, on this account, is a political phenomenon centered around the constitution of an authorizing political subject, which critics and admirers understand primarily in terms of popular identification: a qualitative identification that necessarily precedes and transcends the quantitative aggregation of individual votes or the mediation of legal procedures.

This radical democratic affirmation of populism thus echoes liberal critics who worry that populist appeals to the regenerative and unified authority of the people's uncorrupted will entails a dangerous Caesarist rejection of pluralism, checks and balances, proceduralism, deliberation, and law. According to Urbinati, populism's polarization of politics into the "pure many" and the "corrupt few," its simplification of political debate into the Manichean opposition of good and evil, and its reliance on the politics of popular acclamation make representative democracy its "true and real target" (Urbinati, 2014: 133). What Urbinati and other liberals often object to most about populism is what Laclau and his radical democratic followers enthusiastically affirm: populism's logic of "polarization," which Urbinati claims makes it "less inclusive" than formal democratic citizenship. "Populism," she writes, "is a politics not of inclusion but primarily of exclusion" (Urbinati, 2014: 147). Populism converts opinion into the homogeneous popular acclamation that takes shape around the concentrated power of a single leader who alone is capable of giving form to the popular will. Urbinati insists that without "the presence of a leader or a centralized leadership ... a popular movement that has populist rhetoric (i.e. polarization and antirepresentative discourse) is not yet populism" (Urbinati, 2014: 129). "The search for a leader is one of populism's most specific characteristics," she claims, so the "personalization of politics is not an accident in populism, but rather its destiny" (Urbinati, 2014: 153, 156). It is only through the identification of the popular will with that of the Caesarist leader, on this account, that the people can be effectively reinstalled at the center of populist democracy and exercise its "limitless decisionism" (Urbinati, 2014: 152).

The problem with this familiar emphasis on populism's "virtual immediacy" (Arditi, 2005), its "impatience with procedures" (Crick, 2005), and its "attempt to achieve an immediate identity of governed and governing" (Urbinati, 1998: 116) is that it is more beholden to the political theory of Carl Schmitt than it is drawn from the diverse political histories of populism. In *The Crisis of Parliamentary Democracy* and elsewhere Schmitt offered a compelling account of democracy built around mechanisms of identification. The "abstract logic" of democracy, Schmitt writes, rests on "a series of identities" (between governed and governing, sovereign and subject, will and law, and so on) (Schmitt, 1992: 27). However, all of these identities are not a "palpable reality," but solely the effect of "a *recognition* of the identity. It is not a matter of something actually equal legally, politically, or sociologically, but rather of identifications," and a "distance always remains between real equality and the results of identification ... Everything depends on how the will of the people is formed" (Schmitt, 1992: 26–7). For Schmitt, the "Jacobin logic" of democracy—the ability of a minority or even a single leader to speak on behalf of popular will—always exists as a possibility because this symbolic identification is not encumbered by formal procedures, mediating institutions, or the tallying of votes, but instead relies on a vital rearticulation of the qualitative identification with popular will on which all of these secondary quantitative mediations rest: it brings the otherwise latent or presumed reliance on "the-people-as-one" into full articulation. Through (relatively) unmediated popular acclamation the will of the people emerges as a kind of self-evident and unchallenged presence, but one only sustained through the antagonistic and political line it draws between itself and its enemy. "An absolute human equality would be an equality understood only in terms of itself," Schmitt writes, "and without risk; it would be an equality without the necessary correlate of inequality ... an indifferent equality" (Schmitt, 1992: 12). The Schmittian approach to democracy is bluntly directed against the false and deadening mediations of the constitutional state—elections, parliamentary procedures—in favor of the enlivening immediacy of popular and oppositional identifications, or what he calls the "direct expression of democratic substance and power" (Schmitt, 1992: 17). This focus makes democracy compatible not only with populism but—notoriously—with dictatorship. This sets the stage for the essential role of the Caesarist leader to this conception of populism and democracy, and its devastating reduction of political speech and action to plebiscitary acclamation.

With this familiar picture now before us, it is worth asking: What does this picture of populism prevent us from seeing? Democratic theory's preoccupation with populism's extraordinary appeal to a popular symbolic authority beyond the mediating institutions of the state, and its debates over whether this appeal is restorative or destructive of democracy, is sustained by a captivating picture of populism that obscures some of its most important resources for democratic theorizing. This preoccupation retains a focus on *who* the authorizing people are—the affective power of identification—and distracts attention from *how* the people are institutionally embodied, how their power is collectively enacted and sustained. It remains focused first and foremost on the political subject, secondarily on its ends, and leaves its formative means largely uninterrogated and unexplored. It is revealing that the "logic" of populism is often referred to in contemporary democratic theory, but very rarely its formative praxis. Laclau, for example, emphasizes both at various moments in his work, but he invokes praxis primarily in the sense of the emergence of a collective subject through struggle and hegemonic articulation (especially in his earlier work with Chantal Mouffe). This formalist account offers few resources for thinking about the importance of practical habituation into certain orientations, dispositions, and capacities for radical democratic action and cooperative self-government, and how this formative praxis actively shapes the ends that radical democrats pursue. Laclau is interested primarily in how a plurality of different grievances and interests are articulated and transformed into a unifying popular "demand," but he spends little or no time on the shaping practical transformation of the spaces and institutions from which these demands and their subjects emerge. While radical democratic activists have sometimes stressed these issues, with a few important exceptions radical democratic theories of populism have usually neglected how the practices of popular enactment give concrete form to the popular subject and the ends it pursues (but see Coles, 2004; Grattan, 2016; Mantena, 2012; Phulwani, 2016). A brief return to the rough ground of populism's political history, and in particular its institutional improvisations and attentiveness to formative praxis, may loosen the hold of this theoretical picture and help reorient debates over populism's democratically robust or destructive qualities in contemporary democratic theory. The prevailing focus on the immediacy of symbolic identification above, below, and beyond institutions seems to force a choice between the positive political subject conceived primarily in terms of an electorate or the "democratic mysticism" of immediate expressions of popular will (Holmes, 1995: 148). It is an opposition that secures a highly suspect formulation of populist politics and prevents both liberal critics and radical democratic admirers from exploring the limitations of the theoretical model they share.

DESPERATE INVENTIONS
AND MOVEMENT CULTURE

The Farmers' Alliance, which Lawrence Goodwyn describes as the heart of American Populism's "movement culture," was born in rural Lampasas County, Texas, in 1877 (Goodwyn, 1976).[1] The first organizers proclaimed themselves the "Knights of Reliance," and while their initial efforts were short-lived—they disbanded after a year—the movement was revived in the mid-1880s with the emergence and rapid spread of hundreds of county alliances and suballiances throughout the American South. By the time the People's Party was founded in 1892, and the Minnesotan orator Ignatius Donnelly wrote the rousing preamble to its Omaha Platform, the Alliance had spread to forty-three states and territories. Hundreds of thousands of men and women participated in this interlacing network of alliances and suballiances over this period. In the words of the Platform, their goal was "to restore the government of the Republic to the hands of 'the plain people,' with which class it originated" (Pollack, 1967: 59). As Goodwyn summarizes, over these years "the farmers ... experimented in democratic forms in an effort to address the causes of the poverty of their lives. Gradually, they learned the strength of what they called 'cooperation and organization.' With growing confidence they learned a way to address their condition, and they also learned how to explain their way to others. It was a new democratic language, fashioned out of the old heritage, but straining to break free so as to give definition to liberating new conceptions about the social relations of man" (Goodwyn, 1976: xi). The farmers' experimentation with new democratic forms and their sustained collective effort to understand and act on the impoverished conditions of their lives—to generate cooperative democratic power outside the established institutions of governance—defines American Populism's radical democratic realism.

The impoverished conditions these farmers sought to collectively understand and combat were an effect of the social, economic, and cultural dislocations of the crop-lien system, which effected nothing less than a Polanyian "great transformation" in the organization of rural life in much of the American South and Midwest in the wake of Reconstruction (Polanyi, 1944). The crop-lien was a system of debt peonage through which independent landowning farmers became increasingly dependent upon creditors, furnishing agents, and merchants. Farmers relied on these creditors for the seed, equipment, and furnishings necessary for farm productivity, putting a lien on their eventual harvest. As Goodwyn explains, "once a farmer signed his first crop-lien he was in bondage to his merchant as long as he failed to pay out" (Goodwyn, 1976: 28). The terms of these loans, both in the interest charged and in the inflated cost of loaned equipment and furnishings, along with low commodity prices and the occasional drought, engendered a system of increasing indebtedness that over these decades culminated in dramatic increases in the seizure of debtor land by creditors. The crop-lien system converted millions of independent land-owning yeoman farmers into indebted tenants in the 1870s through the 1890s (Sanders, 1999). As the Arkansas populist editor

W. Scott Morgan wrote in 1889, the "tendencies toward centralization ... concentrate the wealth of the country into the hands of the few, the inevitable result of which is to establish a land aristocracy on the one hand, and a mass of dependent tenants on the other" (Tindall, 1976: 18). More than a way of organizing economic relations and exchange, the crop-lien was a "system that ordered life itself," creating an intricate economy of domination and dependence that wove the experience of humiliation and powerlessness into the daily life of millions of black and white American farmers; Goodwyn goes so far as to describe it as a "modified form of slavery" (Goodwyn, 1976: 25, 28).

The Alliance was created to understand and collectively organize against the far-reaching causes and consequences of this life-ordering system, including the political forces that sustained and enforced it. As W. L. Garvin and S. O. Daws wrote in their *History of the National Farmers' Alliance and Co-Operative Union of America*, the Alliance "was initially organized for the purpose of studying and investigating questions having direct reference to economic legislation"(Garvin and Daws, 1887: 87), but the initial *Declaration of Purposes of the National Farmers' Alliance and Cooperative Union*, written in 1887, also sought to identify the broader working of an impersonal system that led to the "concentration of wealth and power in the hands of a few, to the impoverishment and bondage of so many" (Garvin and Daws, 1887: 72–83). The alliances and suballiances that took shape over these years investigated and deliberated upon the workings of this system and the legal and political powers that sustained it; they developed cooperative economic organizations that might effectively combat or replace it, in the form of cooperative stores, commodity exchange pools, and lending agencies. Their experiments in building a "cooperative commonwealth" within the framework of increasingly industrialized capitalism grew out of their collective experience of having structural and impersonal forces practically undermine their republican ideals of independence and equality. The Alliance gave farmers a "place to think in," in Goodwyn's words, and a place to deliberate together by connecting their personal experience of impoverished dependence with the similar experiences of millions of others (Goodwyn, 1976). In doing so, the Alliance allowed its members to see the broader economic and political relevance of their personal tragedies, and to build a countervailing collective power on the basis of that shared realization. The Alliance offered sites, or what Sara M. Evans and Harry C. Boyte call "free spaces," where these farmers could learn to think and act politically outside of the vice grip of the two party system (Evans and Boyte, 1986; Boyte, 1989).

The Farmers' Alliance developed a class analysis of American politics and economy, and understood the central division around which they organized to be between the "producing classes" and "the moneyed interests." "There are two distinct and well-defined classes composing society," declared the editor of the *Louisiana Populist*, "the producing and the non-producing classes. Between these two is irrepressible conflict" (Mitchell, 1987: 81). The ideology of producerism which underwrote much of Populist social and political analysis had roots in Physiocratic economic theory as well as the Yeoman Ideal of Jeffersonian and Jacksonian republicanism, and it has played a powerful role in episodes of political radicalism since the time of the Revolution (Stock, 1997). The central idea of pruducerism was that the production of material goods by farmers and workers was the economic and moral basis of the social and political order. "On the products they created rested all else," Bruce Palmer explains: "society's laws, government, medium of exchange, the welfare of the entire social order" (Palmer, 1980: 3). Following this basic commitment, American populists believed there was "something radically wrong," as one Populist publicist put it, with an economic system "where those who work most get least, and those who work least get most" (Tindall, 1976). American Populists treated those who made money outside of production—in creating markets, exchange, banking—as parasitic on the productive capacities of the body politic. "Wealth belongs to him who creates it," as the Omaha Platform declared, "and every dollar taken from industry without an equivalent is robbery" (Pollack, 1967: 63). Intrinsic to this producerist ideology, beyond its economic theory, was a broader and more encompassing suspicion of abstraction and delegation. Just as wealth should remain in the hands of those who physically produced it, so personal independence, and that of one's surrounding community, should not be compromised by impersonal market forces or by political and economic decisions made by distant and unaccountable bureaucrats.

A central contradiction shaped the experience of millions of American farmers who supported Populism: their inherited republican and producerist ideals no longer corresponded to their practical experience living in a rapidly industrializing national economy; this contradiction led American Populists to argue that the basic terms of the social contract were being torn apart. Dorothy Ross has argued that this widely perceived contradiction between ideals and experience produced a crisis period in American liberalism, and in its hegemonic discourse of American exceptionalism, as Populists in the countryside and socialists in the cities came to reject the "irrelevance of the inherited political dialogue of the nation" and envision new forms of "cooperative commonwealth" (Ross, 1984). Envisioning a different and more cooperative form of democratic life than the vision offered by the Yeoman ideal was the Farmers' Alliance's response to this perceived crisis; their organized struggle against the crop-lien system produced not only an alternative vision of economic organization within the deep inequalities of America's first Gilded Age, but the outlines of an alternative practice of democratic citizenship. Focusing narrowly on the Alliance's economic motivations, or treating the vast network of alliances and suballiances of the "cooperative commonwealth" merely as institutional means for achieving larger economic, or narrowly electoral ends, neglects how the cooperative experiences facilitated by the Alliance shaped the ends they pursued. The "cooperative commonwealth" American Populists struggled for was practically enacted on a smaller scale within the ongoing cooperative activities of the Alliance itself. The political goals of the Farmers' Alliance were revised and reformed by the means these poor farmers experimented with to achieve them. Theodore Mitchell has demonstrated the centrality of political education—which he describes as a form of political "paideia": the formation of assertive and cooperative citizenship through practical activity—to Populist politics and self-understanding (Mitchell, 1987: 3–23). The importance of political education to Populism brings its complex entwinement of means and ends into clear view. "Out of crouching slaves," declared the *National Economist* in 1890, participation in the Alliance is "making daunt-less, intelligent citizens" (Mitchell, 1987: 93).

Political education and formative praxis was a guiding motivation of American populism from the very beginning of the movement. In his unpublished memoirs that give an account of the founding of the first Alliance in Lampasas County, for example, A. P. Hungate wrote that he and the other founders had originally organized to "more speedily educate ourselves in the science of free government," fearing that "the day is rapidly approaching when all the balance of labor's products will become concen-trated into the hands of a few, there to constitute a power that would enslave posterity" (Goodwyn, 1976: 33). These founders envisioned a self-created association that would create a countervailing democratic power to the bigness, progress, consolidation, and empire of the Gilded Age. Hungate described their alliance as "a grand social and politi-cal palace where liberty may dwell and justice be safely domiciled" (Goodwyn, 1976: 33). The central importance of education to American Populism has often been forgotten by liberal historians critical of the movement. Richard Hofstadter, to take only the best-known example, took Populism to be a terrible symptom of "anti-intellectualism" in American life and of the "paranoid style" of American politics (Hofstadter, 1962; 1967). It is worth remembering that "Knowledge is Power" was an Alliance slogan, and that when the People's Party was founded it was often referred to by contemporaries as the "reading party" and the "writing and talking party." Writing in the *Southern Mercury* in 1891, Evan Jones echoed a typical refrain when he wrote that "those who have combined by organized effort … dread us because they know that our organization is a school, and through its teachings the road to liberty will soon be available to the oppressed" (Mitchell, 1987: 47).

Populism's educational agenda had many components, including a vast lecturing network, hundreds of daily and weekly newspapers, inexpensive books and pamphlets, lending libraries, book clubs, and, of course, the meetings of alliances and suballiances themselves. All of these components were geared to increasing the individual and col-lective power farmers had over their own lives. In part, this cooperative process of self-education was about disseminating useful information—providing information about "business intelligence," for example, how liens and mortgages worked, or scientific and technological improvements in agricultural production, but also detailed discussions of political economy and political theory. Populist newspapers such as *The American Nonconformist, The Appeal to Reason, The Southern Mercury, The People's Party Paper,* and *The Progressive Farmer* were filled with articles on tax policy, commercial regula-tion, the financial and monetary system, but also on American history and political the-ory, cooking tips, and home economics. Readers of these newspapers were addressed as active participants in a collective struggle to take back control of their lives and restore the promise of a threatened democratic egalitarianism. Through reading these papers and through participating in the alliances, attending the lectures, and celebrating the movement in parades and fairs, these farmers came to see themselves as a part of a broader struggle. As Goodwyn writes, through these activities a new sense of political possibility took shape, even a "sweeping new sense of what politics was" (Goodwyn, 1976: 51).

The central term of American Populism, and the term that best describes the "new sense" of politics emerging from its democratic experimentalism, was cooperation. It was, as Evan Jones wrote, "the true principle on which the advancement of civilization depends" (Postel, 2009). Populists opposed cooperation to the "combination" and "consolidation" associated with growing monopolies of industrial capitalism, and also to the "competition" embraced by the right-wing social Darwinist theories that legitimated them. They also distinguished cooperation from communism and the abolition of private property. Cooperation was used in various ways by Populists, and applied to different regions of social life—in economic relations of production and distribution, for example, and in political relations of suballiance associations and ultimately in the People's Party—but across these different applications the term always emphasized practical reciprocity, egalitarian interdependence, and mutual responsibility. Cooperation was a way of understanding egalitarian relations of mutual support in public without fusing individuality into a single collective identity, or all self-interest into a common interest.

However, even more important than the term was the practical enactment of cooperation in the many associations set up under the rubric of the Alliance; Goodwyn is surely right to note that "the central educational tool of the Farmers Alliance was the cooperative experiment itself" (Goodwyn, 1976: 110). The many faces of this cooperative experiment engendered a practical understanding of the extent to which individual freedom and independence required common effort and coordination. The sense of equal reciprocity coupled with the power it engendered was often expressed by the Populists themselves. As the Alliance president Leonidis Polk declared in 1890, a central goal of the Alliance was to "educate in the mutual relations and reciprocal duties between each other, as brethren, as neighbors, as members of society" (Mitchell, 1987: 10). According to the *Declaration of Purposes of the National Farmers Alliance and Cooperative Union* the network of associations would "break up the habits of farmers, improve their social condition, increase their social pleasures, and strengthen their confidence in and friendship for each other" (Garvin and Daws, 1887: 76). More than a coherent ideology or ideal, cooperation was a multifaceted practice that shaped the Populist vision of the reformed democratic state for which they struggled. When traveling lecturers regularly referred to the Alliance as a "schoolroom," it was as much this cooperative experience to which they referred as it was the various lessons and information imparted. The democratic world envisioned by the alliances took shape through the democratic organization they participated in and cooperatively built.

In this sense, American Populism offers an important historical example of what some contemporary social theorists and activists call the world-building praxis of "prefigurative politics" or "prefigurative action" (Graeber, 2009). As Marianne Maeckelbergh writes, "prefigurative politics" enacts a "conflation of movement ends and means; it is an enactment of the ultimate values of an ideal society within the very means of struggle for that society" (Maeckelbergh, 2011: 302). The alliances were associations for coordinating popular power from below, they were practical sites of political subjectivization more than simply incubators of class consciousness, and this subjectivization is poorly understood in the simple terms of a qualitative identification with "the people" opposed to "the elites." Essential to the experience of nineteenth-century American Populism was what Elizabeth Sanders calls its "desperate inventions": their practical experimentation with building cooperative institutions that could enact and sustain popular authority over economic, cultural, and political life in the face of powerful opposing forces (Sanders, 1999). These desperate inventions and experiments in democratic enactment do not exemplify vital moments of popular identification so much as they do the hard work of creating alternative institutions to organize and sustain popular power in the face of a political and economic system geared to creating and reproducing radical inequalities of power and resources. As such, they must also be understood as formative sites of political subjectivization. The academic distinction between grassroots political organization, on the one hand, and the textured dimensions of political subject formation, on the other, is a heuristic abstraction. The experience of American Populism reveals the extent to which these registers of analysis were richly interconnected in practice, and conceptualized this way by the theorist activists of the movement. Democratic theorists could learn important lessons from their example.

Populism's practical cultivation of collective agency and demotic power is almost entirely missing from discussions of populism in contemporary democratic theory. Goodwyn's thick description of Populism's "movement culture" offers a powerful antidote to the formalism of many contemporary accounts. According to Goodwyn, Populism was:

> first and most centrally, a cooperative movement that imparted a sense of self-worth to individual people and that provided them with the instruments of self-education about the world they lived in. The movement gave them hope—a shared hope—that they were not impersonal victims of a gigantic industrial engine ruled by others but that they were, instead, people who could perform specific acts of self-determination. The movement taught its participants who they were and what their rights were and the people of the movement thereupon created its program and its strategy ... Populism was, at bottom, a movement of ordinary Americans to gain control over their own lives and futures. (Goodwyn, 1976: 196)

This chapter's focus on the importance of populism's forms of institutional experimentation need not replace the more familiar emphasis democratic theorists have placed on the political dilemmas of popular identity and "the boundary problem." Indeed, there are good reasons to see these issues as closely related. Political contestation around who the people are has been historically entangled with contestation around how the people act, how their will is represented, or institutionally embodied. A more detailed investigation by democratic theorists of populism as a historical phenomenon might lead to productive examinations of this important relationship—"the boundary problem" and "the enactment problem"—and away from the intransigent ideological oppositions that have long defined it.

NOTE

1 The following sketch of nineteenth-century American Populism necessarily overlooks significant divergences and disagreements within the movement based in geography, ideology, partisanship, and, perhaps most decisively, race. Goodwyn's book offers a lively account of these disagreements while also attempting—persuasively, in my view—to derive a broader conclusion about the central meaning of Populism's "movement culture." I have relied on his book in this account and in my presentation of the corrective it offers to approaches to populism in contemporary democratic theory.

REFERENCES

Abizadeh, A. 2012. "On the demos and its kin: nationalism, democracy, and the boundary problem," *American Political Science Review*, 106(4): 867–82.

Arditi, B. 2005. "Populism as an internal periphery of democratic politics," in F. Panizza (ed.), *Populism and the Mirror of Democracy*. London: Verso, 72–98.

Bourdieu, P. 1990. "The uses of the people," in *In Other Words: Essays Towards a Reflexive Sociology*. Palo Alto: Stanford University Press, 150–5.

Boyte, H. 1989. *Commonwealth: A Return to Citizen Politics*. New York: Free Press.

Canovan, M. 1981. *Populism*. New York: Harcourt Brace Jovanovich.

Canovan, M. 2002. "Taking politics to the people: populism as the ideology of democracy," in Y. Mény and Y. Surel (eds), *Democracies and the Populist Challenge*. New York: Palgrave Macmillan, 25–44.

Coles, R. 2004. "Moving democracy: industrial areas foundation social movements and the political arts of listening, traveling, and tabling," *Political Theory*, 32(5): 678–705.

Crick, B. 2005. "Populism, politics and democracy," *Democratization*, 12(5): 625–32.

Evans, S. M. and H. C. Boyte. 1986. *Free Spaces: The Sources of Democratic Change in America*. Chicago: University of Chicago Press.

Frank, J. 2010. *Constituent Moments: Enacting the People in Postrevolutionary America*. Durham: Duke University Press.

Garvin, W. L. and S. O. Daws. 1887. *History of the National Farmers' Alliance and Cooperative Union of America*. Jacksboro: J. N. Rogers and Company.

Goodwyn, L. 1976. *Democratic Promise: The Populist Moment in America*. New York: Oxford University Press.

Graeber, D. 2009. *Direct Action: An Ethnography*. New York: AK Press.

Grattan, L. 2016. *Populism's Power*. New York: Oxford University Press.

Hardt, M. and A. Negri. 2004. *Multitude: War and Democracy in the Age of Empire*. New York: Penguin Books.

Hofstadter, R. 1962. *Anti-Intellectualism in American Life*. New York: Vintage Books.

Hofstadter, R. 1967. *The Paranoid Style in American Politics and Other Essays.* New York: Vintage Books.

Holmes, S. 1995. *Passions and Constraint: On the Theory of Liberal Democracy.* Chicago: University of Chicago Press.

Honig, B. 2007. "Between deliberation and decision: political paradox in democratic theory," *American Political Science Review,* 101(1): 1–17.

Kazin, M. 1998. *The Populist Persuasion: An American History.* Ithaca: Cornell University Press.

Kirshner, A. 2010. "Proceduralism and popular threats to democracy," *Journal of Political Philosophy,* 18(4): 405–24.

Koen, A. and S. Rummens. 2007. "Populism versus democracy," *Political Studies,* 55(2): 405–24.

Laclau, E. 1977. "Towards a theory of populism," in *Politics and Ideology in Marxist Theory.* London: New Left Books, 143–98.

Laclau, E. 2005. *On Populist Reason.* London: Verso.

Lefort, C. 1986. "The image of the body and totalitarianism," in *The Political Forms of Modern Society: Bureaucracy, Democracy, Totalitarianism.* Cambridge: MIT Press, 292–306.

Maeckelbergh, M. 2011. "The road to democracy: the political legacy of '1968,'" *International Review of Social History,* 56(2): 301–32.

Mantena, K. 2012. "Another realism: the politics of Gandhian nonviolence," *American Political Science Review,* 106(2): 455–70.

Mitchell, T. R. 1987. *Political Education in the Southern Farmers' Alliance, 1887–1900.* Madison: University of Wisconsin Press.

Morgan, E. 1989. *Inventing the People: The Rise of Popular Sovereignty in England and America.* New York: W. W. Norton and Company.

Morone, J. A. 1998. *The Democratic Wish: Popular Participation and the Limits of American Government.* New Haven: Yale University Press.

Mudde, C. 2004. "The populist zeitgeist," *Government and Opposition,* 39(3): 541–63.

Mudde, C. and C. Rovira Kaltwasser (eds). 2012. *Populism in Europe and the Americas: Threat or Corrective for Democracy?* Cambridge: Cambridge University Press.

Nässtrom, S. 2007. "The legitimacy of the people," *Political Theory,* 35(5): 624–58.

Palmer, B. 1980. *"Man Over Money": The Southern Populist Critique of American Capitalism.* Chapel Hill: University of North Carolina Press.

Phulwani, V. 2016. "The poor man's Machiavelli: Saul Alinsky and the morality of power," *American Political Science Review,* 110(4): 863–75.

Polanyi, K. 1944. *The Great Transformation: The Political and Economic Origins of Our Time.* New York: Farrar and Rinehart.

Pollack, N. (ed.). 1967. *The Populist Mind.* New York: Bobbs-Merrill.

Riker, W. H. 1988. *Liberalism against Populism: A Confrontation Between the Theory of Democracy and the Theory of Social Choice.* Long Grove: Waveland.

Ross, D. 1984. "Liberalism," in J. P. Greene (ed.), *Encyclopedia of American Political History.* New York: Scribner, 750–63.

Sanders, E. 1999. *Roots of Reform: Farmers, Workers, and the American State, 1877–1917.* Chicago: University of Chicago Press.

Schmitt, C. 1992. *The Crisis of Parliamentary Democracy.* Cambridge: MIT Press.

Stock, C. M. 1997. *Rural Radicals: From Bacon's Rebellion to the Oklahoma City Bombing.* New York: Penguin.

Tindall, G. B. (ed.). 1976. *A Populist Reader: Selections from the Works of America's Populist Leaders.* Gloucester: Peter Smith.

Tuck, R. 2016. *The Sleeping Sovereign: How Democracy Became Possible in the Modern World.* Cambridge: Harvard University Press.

Urbinati, N. 1998. "Democracy and populism," *Constellations*, 5(1): 110–24.

Urbinati, N. 2014. *Democracy Disfigured: Opinion, Truth, and the People.* Cambridge: Harvard University Press.

Whelan, F. G. 1983. "Prologue: democratic theory and the boundary problem," in J. R. Pennock and J. Chapman (eds), *Nomos 25: Liberal Democracy.* New York: New York University Press, 13–42.

CHAPTER 33

POPULISM AND COSMOPOLITANISM

JAMES D. INGRAM

AT first blush, the relationship between populism and cosmopolitanism is simple: they are opposites, theoretical antitheses and political antagonists. A cosmopolitan is a citizen of the world, someone whose identity and loyalties transcend local belonging or national citizenship. A populist, conversely, is someone who puts "the people" first, defending its interests and promoting its values above all else. In academic and public discourse alike, various forms of anti-cosmopolitanism, from opposition to transnational organizations or global economic forces to more or less open xenophobia and even racism, are taken to be virtually definitive of populism. The most common examples, from France's Front National to the United Kingdom Independence Party to the American Tea Party, are parties and movements built around fear of and/or hostility to those who are not of "the people." Populism, like the nationalism, nativism, or communalism with which it is often identified, is defined by its rejection of the foreign, the different, or the global—in a word, the cosmopolitan.

If this picture corresponds to the most common uses of the two terms, it is nonetheless questionable in a number of respects. On one side, equating populism with anti-cosmopolitanism depends on identifying the populists' "people" with a particular, delimited community, defined not only territorially (usually though not always by a state), but also in terms of other exclusive, historically sedimented forms of commonality, such as language, culture, religion, or ethnicity. This amounts to reducing it to communalism. On the other side, equating cosmopolitanism with anti-populism depends on identifying it with interests and allegiances opposed to those of "the people." Most often, this amounts to reducing it to elitism. While these reductions are not without basis, both in the use of the terms and in underlying tendencies of the phenomena they designate, neither follows inevitably from the concept. Both reductions are complicated and even contradicted by important historical as well as contemporary examples.

The idea that there is an inherent and inevitable contradiction between populism and cosmopolitanism, then, rests on a hasty, overly cynical interpretation of both ideas, one that narrows populism to communitarian self-interest and self-aggrandizement, and cosmopolitanism to elite self-interest and self-aggrandizement. Such an interpretation overlooks important moments in the histories of both cosmopolitanism and populism, exceptional but promising cases where they overlapped and intersected. In this chapter I argue that the conventional interpretation of both phenomena is too cynical—in part by arguing that it is not *Cynic* enough. For if we return to cosmopolitan's origins in Greek antiquity, to Diogenes the Cynic, we find a mode of politics and ethics that cannot be subsumed into contemporary categories. To be sure, ancient Cynicism stands at a distance from what is regarded as properly political, then or now, but it introduces a difference into the discussion that goes some distance to rendering cosmopolitanism and populism compatible. This distance can be illuminating, since it points toward deeper limits and dangers as well as unexpected potentials within the two phenomena.

In this chapter I take a detour to the ancient world in order to complicate the usual associations of populism and cosmopolitanism. To be sure, populism is often anti-cosmopolitan and cosmopolitan is often anti-popular, and in the first two sections of this chapter I explore why. But there are good reasons for not simply presuming their incompatibility, let alone turning their negative affinity into a defining characteristic of either concept. Only by holding open the polyvalence and ambiguity of cosmopolitanism and populism can we distinguish between pathological and potentially salutary varieties of each. The salutary versions are particularly worth hanging onto today because they represent perhaps the only way democratic, egalitarian political movements can avoid being parochial and exclusionary, and universalistic, inclusionary political movements being elitist and anti-democratic. We arrive at the most useful conception of both populism and cosmopolitanism, I argue, by taking into account not only the tensions between them, but also the possibility of a cosmopolitan populism.

POPULIST ANTI-COSMOPOLITANISM

It is a commonplace of writing on populism that it is hard to pin down. Even when compared to the broad and contested ideologies understood to map out the coordinates of modern politics, populism is subject to such extreme variation as to be all but ungraspable. It tends to be located on the right of the political spectrum in Europe but the left in Latin America. In North America, meanwhile, some track it from the left in the late nineteenth century to the right in the twentieth—even, as in the interwar case of Social Credit and agrarian socialism on the Canadian prairies or the recent rise of the Tea Party and the Occupy movement, as sprouting simultaneously at both extremes. Added to this is the difficulty that populists seldom identify as such. With the notable exception of the American left, which continues to harken back to the late nineteenth-century People's Party as a rare instance of successful large-scale mobilization, the label "populist" tends to be pejorative, leading some observers to conclude that it "defines those who use it rather than those who are branded with it. As such, it is above all a useful hermeneutic

tool for identifying and characterizing those political parties that accuse their opponents of populism" (D'Eramo, 2013: 8).

In order to cut through this definitional thicket and avoid a merely additive empiri-
cism on one side and a skeptical nominalism on the other, I begin with an oft-cited definition, as minimal as it is useful, from Cas Mudde:

> In its original form, populism is a thin-centred ideology that considers society to be
> ultimately separated into two homogeneous and antagonistic groups, "the pure peo-
> ple" and "the corrupt elite," and which argues that politics should be an expression
> of the *volonté générale* (general will) of the people. (2013: 23; see also Mudde, this
> volume)

Mudde calls this ideology "thin-centred" because it is defined less by its content than by
its underlying logic of political identification and mobilization. Populism's substance is
then filled out with elements from other, more fully articulated ideologies, from nativism on the right to socialism on the left. Thus, although Mudde is mainly interested in
populism in its right-wing, nativist-xenophobic European variant, he joins Margaret
Canovan (2005: ch. 4) and Paul Taggart (2000: ch. 1), among others, in honing in on
two elements that seem to be common to all populisms, right and left, Old World and
New, historical and contemporary: an insistent reference to "the people," on one side,
and opposition to a hated "elite," on the other.

From this minimal definition different theories of populism typically go on to identify
specific aspects of its political rhetoric, style, or self-definition that they regard as distinguishing it from other political currents. Many focus on the pathologies, perversions,
or disfigurations populism introduces into liberal-democratic politics. Thus, Nadia
Urbinati, like Koen Abts and Stefan Rummens, regards populism as parasitic on representative democracy (Urbinati, 2014: ch. 3; Abts and Rummens, 2007). On this view,
populism rebels against liberal democracy's constitutional and representational mediations, which it seeks to overcome. This aspiration is incoherent, however, since modern democracy is necessarily mediated and representative. Likewise, at a higher level of
abstraction, Pierre Rosanvallon and Jan-Werner Müller see populism as a denial of the
pluralism and indeterminacy that for Claude Lefort are definitive of modern democracy (Rosanvallon, 2011; Müller, 2014: 483–93; Müller, 2016; Lefort, 1988). By claiming
to represent an uncorrupted and unified "people," populism seeks to incarnate identity,
power, and legitimacy; it tries, in Lefort's terms, to "fill the place of power." Since modern democracy depends on that place remaining empty, populism is essentially authoritarian and anti-democratic. If these accounts treat populism as inherently pathological,
however, for others it can also play a positive role. Canovan (1999) has argued that populism can introduce a "redemptive," participatory moment into representative politics,
helping to revitalize democratic life and overcome political alienation. Norberto Bobbio
(1987: 26–7) portrays populism as a warning sign, prodding the political class to address
institutional sclerosis, while Michael Kazin (1995) points to its contribution to mobilizing excluded and marginalized populations.

Rather than choose between these negative and positive aspects, we can better discern the deeper roots of populism's ostensible antagonism with cosmopolitanism by abstracting from them. Ernesto Laclau's work is helpful here because of its emphasis on populism's formal properties (2005: chs 6–8). Laclau seeks to isolate the "political logic" specific to populism, by which he means its way of constituting a political subject. Populism rests, he argues, on a rhetorical equivalence between two different but overlapping meanings of "the people": in Roman terms, the *populus*, or the whole of the population, and the *plebs*, the common, ordinary, or exploited, marginalized people. Populism is defined by the idea, at once an organizational principle and a rhetorical operation, that the *plebs*, the subordinate people, should be recognized and empowered as the *populus*, the legitimate or whole people, but is prevented from achieving this by an illegitimate elite or ruling class. By unifying all popular demands behind a particular demand and thereby constructing a popular hegemonic project, populism aims to unite "the people" and overcome the obstacles that prevent it from taking its legitimate place.[1]

While this view does not see populism like the first does, as negative and inherently antidemocratic, it nevertheless sees populism as coming into conflict with cosmopolitanism in two ways, both implied by the necessary particularity of populism's referent, "the people." First, the populist "people" always retains some trace of the particular identity that is meant to stand in for the people as a whole. For this reason the popular identity can never be universal or all-inclusive, and to this extent cosmopolitan. Instead, it must always and necessarily refer to some concrete identity. Second, populism has to sustain the popular identity it proposes by opposing some "other"—in the first instance elites who dominate, exploit, or otherwise betray "the people," but often outsiders who threaten them as well. The latter may take the form of actual outsiders, from the global business class to international organizations (the United Nations, the European Union), but it may also take the form of suspiciously "foreign" resident populations, from so-called middleman minorities (Jews in Europe, Chinese in Southeast Asia, South Asians in East Africa) to immigrants, guest-workers, refugees, or an underclass perceived as parasitic and alien. Populism's anti-elitism shades into anti-cosmopolitanism because the elites and outsiders, whether they are perceived as threatening "the people" from above or below, are identified by their distance from, and failure to be "of," "the people."

This account explains not only populism's tendency to oppose cosmopolitanism, but also its ambiguous profile on the left-right spectrum. The oscillation of populist claims depends on which "others" it emphasizes: the elites and imperialist or economic forces above or outside, or the perceived aliens within or below. A focus on elites, global economic forces, or imperialist oppressors pulls "the people" to the left; a focus on weaker groups, seen as corrupting, leaching off, or otherwise undermining the integral "people," pulls it to the right. Moreover, this bivalent logic also explains why populism is often Janus-faced: egalitarian, inclusive, liberal, and/or social-democratic when it comes to insiders, but fearful, hostile, exclusionary, and potentially aggressive toward outsiders, especially "internal-outsiders" present on the territory but not identified with the in-group. This latter tendency, referred to as "welfare chauvinism," is often associated with the Front National's *préférence nationale* for "real" Frenchmen and with other anti-immigrant parties, such as the otherwise liberal Dutch or Austrian Freedom Parties or the otherwise social-democratic Danish People's Party or Sweden Democrats (see e.g. Kitschelt, 1997). In both directions, against elites as well as outsiders, the people's tool and ally is the state (once it is reclaimed from its usurpers)—in the first instance in its redistributive guise, in the second in its repressive one. Thus, the populist identification with a narrowly defined people and against its internal and external enemies is supplemented by identification with the nation-state, so that populism resolves into belligerent nationalism.

While this formal logic shows why populism often goes along with exclusionary, nativist, communalist, and xenophobic politics, this should be understood as indicating a tendency rather than a necessity, let alone identifying a defining characteristic. While a popular identity may be narrowed by focusing on what distinguishes "the people" from outsiders, most scholars concur with Mudde that populism's primary and most characteristic tendency is to define "the people" against elites, foreign and domestic, rather than against vulnerable members of one's own population or foreigners. In Laclau's terms, the principal antagonism through which populism defines a people is vertical, not horizontal, and aims up, not down; populism is in the first instance directed against the elites who keep the *plebs* from becoming the *populus*. Indeed, in principle—as well as, as we shall see, in certain historical and contemporary instances—it has been possible to define "the people" in ways that escape a narrow identification with tribe, race, nation, or state. While it is important not to lose sight of the obstacles to this possibility, it should not be foreclosed by theoretical fiat. Before articulating this more positive prospect in the chapter's third section, we must first see what stands in the way of a populist-cosmopolitan rapprochement from the other side, that of cosmopolitanism.

COSMOPOLITAN ANTI-POPULISM

If we are accustomed to thinking of populism as invariably anti-cosmopolitan, there is an even longer tradition of the reverse. Indeed, cosmopolitanism was in a sense born of anti-populism. The term was famously coined by Diogenes of Sinope, known, on the basis of his bestial habits, as the Cynic (from *kynikos*: dog-like). Diogenes was a radical Socratic who took the priority of nature and reason over law and convention to such extremes as sleeping rough, eating raw meat without utensils, and defecating and pleasuring himself in public. According to Diogenes Laertes (6.63), the Cynic, notorious for his defiance of law and convention, was asked where he was from. To the hyper-political Greeks, that meant what city or *polis*. The appropriate answer would have been Sinope, even though he had been banished from his native city. Instead, Diogenes replied that he was a *kosmopolitēs*, a citizen of the cosmos, a universal citizen of no *polis* in particular. He was thereby, in his usual fashion, rejecting the artificiality of the *polis* and proclaiming his allegiance to the universal over the local and to nature over custom. And because the Greeks identified a city not with its territory but with its people, he was quite precisely rejecting identification with any "people," and thus any "populism."

Diogenes's gesture is worth dwelling on, for its echoes through the history of cosmopolitanism can help disclose some of the latter's possibilities. These possibilities are not themselves Cynic.[2] Instead, they represent different lines of thinking that can be traced back to Diogenes's original provocation. My interest in them here is in how they mark out possibilities that cover much of the terrain of subsequent cosmopolitanism.

First, commentators note that it would have been easy for Diogenes to pronounce himself an *apolitēs*, a man without a *polis*—a stateless person, in modern terms, and therefore, for the Greeks, an a- or unpolitical one (Sellars, 2007: 4). This would have been perfectly intelligible in view of his banishment from Sinope and his conspicuous indifference to the laws and customs of Athens and Corinth, where he lived (Baldry, 1965: 108ff.). The idea of a cosmopolitan as someone who is above or below politics, be it by choice or by circumstance, is a staple of discussions of cosmopolitanism. In one form it is what Rousseau had in mind when he denounced cosmopolitans as those who "boast that they love everyone, to have the right to love no one" (1997: 158): elites convinced that their enlightenment spares them the burden of specific political and even ethical duties. In another form this unpolitical cosmopolitanism corresponds to the *Lumpenproletariat*, according to Marx the "indefinite, disintegrated mass" whose lack of identity, affiliation, and purpose renders them useless or even dangerous to proletarian, and thus truly "popular," politics.[3] In either case, we could refer to this as an *exilic* cosmopolitanism.

Such forms of a- or unpolitical cosmopolitanism are still very much with us. They correspond to two opposite kinds of cosmopolitans proliferating in the contemporary world: on the one hand, global elites for whom politics and membership are strictly optional, a matter of convenience as they play localities off against each other in a search for things to consume and places to invest; on the other, "abject cosmopolitans" (Nyers, 2003), stateless people whom no political community wants, who subsist on sufferance and lack even the right to have rights. We should observe that these are precisely the figures we encountered in the last section as the two natural enemies of populism: deracinated elites above, who escape commonality with and responsibility to "the people," and threatening masses below, who have typically come from elsewhere and are neither integrated into the community nor, in the populists' eyes, contribute to it. In both cases, to be cosmopolitan is to be outside the community, and thus outside politics. To return to the historical case with which cosmopolitanism began, it is uncertain which of these Diogenes would have been taken for. If his way of life, poverty, and lack of rights suggest the abject, his sovereign self-assurance and reports that Alexander the Great praised him and paid him a call suggest the elite. What is clear, though, is his rejection of precisely what seems to bind them: their common status as unpolitical. For Diogenes specifically chooses to pronounce himself a *citizen* of the cosmos—a *political* identity (Moles, 1996).

A second possibility opened up by Diogenes's claim to be a citizen of the world softens his provocation. It affirms that the universal (nature or reason) is greater than and, depending on other considerations, can even trump the local (culture or politics), but reassures us that the two need not come into direct conflict. Such an approach was taken most notably by Stoicism—whence, with an admixture of Christianity and liberalism, it reaches us in the form of modern cosmopolitanism. In this form it can be regarded as the first universalistic fruit of philosophy, the idea that there is wisdom, guidance, and even identity beyond the city in which we find ourselves. With Socrates, Cicero, or Marcus Aurelius, Augustine, Luther, or even Jesus,[4] one can appeal to higher, transcendental values and even identity, yet submit to the legitimate political authorities. Just as Socrates defied the judgment of his fellow citizens yet felt bound to accept their verdict, this kind of cosmopolitan practices an art of separation, rendering unto God (Nature, Justice, Reason) the things that are theirs (truth, ethical fidelity), but unto Caesar (the Polis, the People) the things that are theirs (obedience, political loyalty). On this kind of *ethical* cosmopolitanism, we can be personally and philosophically universalist while practicing politics in the vernacular (see e.g. Appiah, 2006).

An approach of this kind has long been favored by those who want to defend cosmopolitanism against the charge that it is otherworldly or excessively demanding. It allows them to be cosmopolitans in ethics, as a matter of personal morality and even identity, without violating given obligations and affiliations. Thus, on Martha Nussbaum's Stoic-inspired account:

> We need not give up our special affections and identifications, whether ethnic or gender-based or religious. We need not think of them as superficial, and we may think of our identity as constituted partly by them.... But we should also work to make all human beings part of our community of dialogue and concern, base our political deliberations on that interlocking commonality, and give the circle that defines our humanity special attention and respect. (1996: 9)

Critics like David Miller, in contrast, dismiss cosmopolitanisms that wave aside hard choices as "platitudinous" (2002: 81). Politics, Miller insists with Rousseau and most populists, requires membership in and obligations to a particular community. Yet, to return once again to our original historical case, while these were no longer available to Diogenes in Sinope, he did not seek them elsewhere. Cast out of the community of his birth, he replaced it only with the cosmos—in practical terms, no community at all. Diogenes accepted that cosmopolitanism posed a hard choice, only to deliberately opt for the harder, perhaps impossible, alternative.

A third and final possibility that emerges from the Cynic's declaration of world citizenship tries to go beyond what critics see as the Stoics' weak bromides by turning more directly to politics. Against the apoliticism of the first alternative and the accommodation of the second, this third position views world citizenship not as a paradox or an ethical constraint on worldly life, but as a substantive political vision and project. A prototype of this approach can be found in the thought of Zeno of Citium, usually regarded as the first Stoic, a student of Diogenes's follower Crates. Zeno's book on politics, his *Republic* (*Politeia*), has been lost, but its general outlines have been gleaned from summaries and commentaries.[5] Zeno is said to have described a world without laws or communities, where everyone follows a single, natural law and shares everything in common—a philosophical utopia that makes none of the concessions to the irrational that Plato admitted even into his *Republic*. There is no record of Zeno's plans for realizing his dream; in practice, his cosmopolitanism may have closely resembled the second variety. But it adds to ethical cosmopolitanism the aspiration to a world that has overcome conflict, organized along rational lines—what we could call a *utopian cosmopolitanism*.

There have been many cosmopolitan utopias since Zeno's day, especially in the last two-and-half centuries, when the development of capitalism and imperialism on a global scale have made it possible to imagine the world becoming a single legal-political order—and to fear what might happen if it does not, or does so in the wrong way. The best known of these of course comes down to us from Immanuel Kant, but his vision of "perpetual peace" is only one in a long series of visions for overcoming war (see Johnson, 1987). Such designs for lawful universal order vary greatly in their details, from Kant's voluntary federation of peoples to world states, but one thing they have in common is that they would exclude at least the more toxic versions of populism. This is because in such worlds human rights would be respected and international law enforced; elites would be subject to the law and minorities protected by it. And even if these protections failed, those affected could simply move elsewhere under a universal right to asylum. Yet it seems unlikely that Diogenes would have welcomed such a cosmopolis in which to practice his cosmopolitanism, or joined Zeno in drawing one up. This is not because he, like Plato, Rousseau, or the populists, believed that politics is necessarily irrational, particularistic, and local. Rather, it is because, so far as we know, Diogenes never evinced any interest in prescribing anything, let alone a universal legal-political order, for anyone.[6]

If Diogenes's cosmopolitanism can be identified neither with transcending worldly politics nor with accommodating it nor with aspiring to transform it—three versions of cosmopolitanism that, as we have seen, continue to be associated with the idea in its exilic, ethical, and utopian guises—how should we understand his originary cosmopolitics? In the first instance it would consist in a radical Socratic attack on everything false, unjust, and unnatural, a politics of truth-telling or "fearless speech" (*parrhesia*), according to the slogan posthumously popularized by Michel Foucault (2001). The Cynic's "shameless cosmopolitanism," as Sara Gebh terms it (2013), would find practical expression in subjecting the community's identities and norms to radical universalistic critique with the aim of liberating the critic and, if only by example, others to live freely, rationally, and naturally. In these respects a Cynic cosmopolitanism could be, as Gebh argues, both critical and emancipatory. And yet, despite Diogenes's insistence, we might wonder about the extent to which it could be termed political. For although cosmopolitans adopting such a Cynic spirit can intervene into the life of the community, they do so principally if not exclusively negatively. The solidarity and cooperation required for any positive or constructive politics—let alone a "populism," which by definition identifies with some "people"—seem to be beyond them.

If populism's need to identify with a particular people tends to pull it in the direction of communalism and exclusion, then, an opposite tendency seems to stand between cosmopolitanism and not only populism but any kind of positive politics. If populism suffers from a dangerous excess of politics, understood as identification and solidarity, cosmopolitanism seems to suffer from the reverse: a resistance to politics as such—at least if we understand "politics" in conventional terms, as focused around a community and what it has or should have in common. Trapped in the moment of identification, populism seems enthralled to the pull of communalism; trapped in the moment of dis-identification and rebellion, cosmopolitanism seems permanently disposed to a sterile politics of negation. In my conclusion I will suggest that, in view of their opposite tendencies, it may be best to regard populism and cosmopolitanism as checks on one another's defects. But first I want to explore a more constructive possibility: a way of understanding populism not only as popular without being exclusionary, of advancing the interests of "the people" without doing so at the expense of outsiders, but also, beyond this, of being actively and indefinitely inclusive, and to that extent cosmopolitan.

Cosmopolitan Populism?

Historians remind us that populism thrived in certain corners of the ancient world, with the masses asserting their claim to be the true *demos* or *populus* and politicians eager to speak for them (e.g. Finley, 1983: esp. ch. 1). Mining this vein, we might locate the origins of populism with the *populares*, Senators of the late Roman Republic who, in contrast to the conservative *optimates*, claimed to speak for the plebs. For Cicero and most subsequent historians, the *populares* were dangerous demagogues who bribed their supporters with bread and circuses and undermined republican institutions. The fabled status of the best known of their number, Julius Caesar, as the Republic's gravedigger, if not its executioner, does nothing to enhance their reputation. But on a more democratic telling, the *populares* can be seen as taking up the slack from a declining Tribunate, the republican institution created in the wake of the Plebeian Secession of 494 BCE to give voice to the plebs (see Parenti, 2003). Far from being a threat that eventually overwhelmed the Republic, this continuous populist element within Rome's politics and institutions has been praised since at least Machiavelli as the source of its strength, freedom, and durability.

Ancient populism continues to be defended by those who take the side of democracy against oligarchic and aristocratic forms of republicanism (McCormick, 2001; Vatter, 2011). Of particular interest in the present context is the distance of this popular politics from the narrow-minded communalism usually identified with populism. To be sure, as the Roman games remind us, the plebeians may have left much to be desired from an ethical point of view. We should not expect of them the high-minded cosmopolitanism of Stoic aristocrats like Cicero, though we should remember that the latter's refinement rested on fiercely defended privileges. But it is worth observing that efforts to extend the scope of Roman citizenship were consistently the work of the *populares*. From a patrician perspective, this may have been a cynical ploy to increase the populists' base of support, but for the plebeians, allies were welcome where they could be found. Inclusion, the expansion of the circle not only of one's sympathies (which, the plebs might scoff, only aristocrats can afford) but of one's comrades, was a popular cause. This preference for inclusion may have been cynical in some respects, but it was also Cynic in content if not in inspiration, since it placed the natural commonality of human beings ahead of the traditions and interests of the polity as constituted.

A number of historians and theorists have tried to reconstitute a subterranean historical current of popular politics that is at once insurgent or insurrectionary and inclusionary. Thus Martin Breaugh (2013) writes of a tradition of "plebeian politics" that extends from the strike of the Roman plebs to the Ciompi Revolt in fourteenth-century Florence, the French Revolution's *sans-culottes*, the British Chartists, and the Paris Commune. Such groups were seldom defined in exclusive terms, and they were often remarkably open to diverse new recruits. From Spartacus via the Anabaptists and Levellers to the revolutionary ex-slaves of Haiti, who declared the Europeans who joined their revolt "black" and therefore full members of their nascent community,[7] such revolutionary popular movements did not espouse exclusionary conceptions of community because exclusions are precisely what they sought to overthrow. As a consequence, they did not define themselves against outsiders or those below them; instead, their popular identity was constructed against their oppressors and the restrictions the latter had imposed on them, in some cases extending their community of peers and comrades almost indefinitely.

These considerations point in at least two directions, both directly relevant to the idea of popular or populist cosmopolitanism. The first is the long tradition of cosmopolitanism-from-below, transnational solidarities that grow up among subaltern peoples in the shadows of world-spanning trade routes and empires. From Paul Gilroy's *Black Atlantic* (1993) to Robbie Shilliam's *Black Pacific* (2015), scholars have reconstructed a variety of "rooted," "subaltern," "peripheral," "discrepant," and "transgressive" cosmopolitanisms developed by marginalized or displaced people who build and maintain social, cultural, and political networks across national frontiers (see also Kurasawa, 2004; Gidwani, 2006). Often relying on performative accounts of action, according to which political actors bring new forms of political identity into being through their action, these studies show how those on the edges of national and state politics—migrants of various kinds, from refugees and displaced people to undocumented immigrants (*sans-papiers*), but also those on the margins of national culture and political representation, from ethnic, religious, and sexual minorities to indigenous peoples—create new transnational solidarities. While these cross-border networks and communities do not typically begin as political, in some cases they disrupt and transform political structures as well as structures of belonging (Baban and Rygiel, 2014; Little, 2015).

A second, more obviously political tradition of transnational subaltern solidarities is that of the great radical movements of the age of revolution, from the mid-eighteenth to the mid-twentieth century. Perry Anderson (2002) reminds us that during this period, universalism was generally regarded as wholly compatible with popular politics. As illustrated by the 1848 "Springtime of Nations" or the *Communist Manifesto*'s precisely contemporaneous call, "Workers of all countries, unite!," no contradiction was perceived between the liberation struggles of peoples of different nations. It is true that this fraternal solidarity among emancipatory struggles, which traversed liberal, social-democratic, communist, anarchist, anticolonial, labor, and other movements,[8] often went by the name "internationalism" rather than "cosmopolitanism"—a usage cemented by Antonio Gramsci, for whom the latter represented the false, reactionary universalism of the Church and the ruling classes. But during most of this period, the "populism" of radical political movements was not felt to contradict their universalism. To the contrary, it was understood as its basis.

All these examples show the possibility of a radical emancipatory politics that is at once emphatically popular and resolutely universalistic (Ingram, 2013). Probably the most original and influential theorization of such struggles for inclusion in our day is that undertaken by Jacques Rancière. For Rancière, the protagonist of these emancipatory struggles from below is a part of society that has no part or share within it—in the Roman terms Laclau applies to struggles for democratic hegemony, a *plebs* that is denied standing in the *populus* but insists on such standing all the same (Rancière, 1999: ch. 2). Since Rancière imagines this politics as always waged from the margins or the outside of the community, it is intrinsically democratic and egalitarian, emancipatory and inclusionary. More than espousing populism, however, Rancière may be best regarded as an *anti-anti-populist* (2007: 80; 2016). While he would never defend the nationalistic, racist, or xenophobic movements commonly termed populist, he denounces critics who blame their objectionable content on their connection to "the people." On his view, even if populism is not itself always innocent, attacks on it are almost invariably anti-popular and anti-democratic, elitist attempts to keep "the people" out of politics.

For his part, Laclau has criticized Rancière's affirmative characterization of populism, reproaching Rancière for obscuring populism's normative ambivalence (2005: 246–8). "The people," Laclau insists, can be defined in ways that are exclusionary and authoritarian as well as democratic and egalitarian. Moreover, as noted above, since a political subject always retains a trace of its empirical starting point, just as "the proletariat" continues to refer to industrial workers, "the people" always remains connected to some concrete and therefore restricted identity. No "people" is *only* inclusive, and its limits can always be turned against outsiders. The deeper root of the one-sidedness of Rancière's account of the populist-democratic "people," we might observe, is that it is entirely processual. It does not describe popular identities as such, only a particular moment in the process of people-making: the moment of an egalitarian demand for inclusion. As Ella Myers points out (2016: 60–2), Rancière's retellings of Rome's secession of the plebs never extend to the creation of the Tribunate or the rise of the *populares*, stopping long before the moment of institutionalization. Rancière describes only a people-in-the-making against exclusions, not the new people that results, which inevitably has exclusions of its own.

Should we infer from this that populism is cosmopolitan only during its insurrectional moment, as it rebels against the structures that exclude it and seeks allies and recruits for its cause? Can cosmopolitanism be popular only in opposition, when it is aligned with the excluded? Do the popular and the inclusive only coincide in the moment in which the "people" resists its exclusion, securing a foothold—which it will then inevitably use to exclude others? Such a conclusion seems at once too categorical and too cynical. If we look not to where Laclau and Rancière disagree but to their larger areas of agreement, we see that, for both them, populism is not simply opposed to universalism. For Laclau in particular, populist-democratic politics is always centrally concerned with universality: it is only by linking particular demands to some indefinitely inclusive symbol of commonality—what Laclau calls an "empty signifier"—that a "people" can be constructed in the first place (1996). Rather than simply equating the universal with given universals opposed to given particulars, on this account universals are always the result of ideological construction and contestation, a work of conflictual universalization—as is, by the same token and for the same reasons, any "people" (2006).

The lesson I draw from this, consistent with both Laclau and Rancière, is that we should not be content to be for or against "cosmopolitanism" or "populism," "the universal" or "the popular." Popular struggles are not by definition universalistic, let alone cosmopolitan, but neither are they perforce narrowly and exclusively nativist or communitarian—any more than cosmopolitanism or universalism is by definition antipopular. To the extent that "the universal" and "the people" are only ever the provisional results of an ongoing process of contestation, their compatibility or incompatibility in a given instance will depend on such things as their provenance, the ideologies and aims to which they are attached as well as those they oppose, and the struggles through which they develop. Moreover, the fact that the construction of universals as well as popular identities is contingent, a matter of choice as well as chance but never of necessity, means that such processes are open to judgment, deliberation, and criticism. By defining populism as always and everywhere xenophobic and cosmopolitanism as always and everywhere elitist, we deprive ourselves of any basis on which to judge or criticize either, since they stand convicted a priori.

The significance of this emerges when we consider contemporary examples. While the global justice or alter-globalization movement of the 1990s and 2000s is often regarded as a prime example of popular cosmopolitanism from below (de Sousa Santos, 2006; Murray, 2010), I propose to consider instead the more recent Occupy movement. It is, after all, hard to imagine a slogan more populist than "We Are the 99 Percent." Not only does it perform the quintessential populist maneuver of claiming to be a part of the people that should be the whole, it does so in explicit contrast to an enemy responsible for its woes: the 1 percent, parasitic financial-managerial elites who have corrupted politics and ruined the economy. But was Occupy cosmopolitan? While its component occupations were local in the sense that they were bound to particular sites, the movement was fiercely universalistic in its rhetoric and global in its consciousness. After beginning in a small park in lower Manhattan, within weeks there were sister protests in hundreds of cities around scores of countries. These occupations remained in close contact throughout and after the movement's brief efflorescence. Ideas and participants flowed freely from one site to another. None specified that they referred to the 99 percent of any particular country; the "people" to which they tried to give voice applied to every scale, from local to global, with no priority placed on the national (Pârvu, 2015: 266–8).

Peter Osborne went so far as to connect the movement to ancient Cynicism (2012: 15). He had in mind Occupy's rebellious, carnivalesque spirit and its refusal to formulate concrete demands, in which he heard echoes of Diogenes's provocations. But the movement's indifference to existing political structures, social conventions, and received notions of practicality, its insistence on universal procedural justice even at the price of operational stasis, its principled reluctance to eject individuals from the margins of society, including not only the homeless and non-conformists but criminals and the mentally ill—in all these respects Occupy recalled Diogenes at his most cosmopolitan, his most inclusive, and his most popular. These Cynic aspects were precisely what most exasperated Occupy's friendly critics, who reproached the movement for seeing itself as above normal democratic politics and thereby embracing its own irrelevance (e.g. Dean, 2013). Such critics can ask whether the movement should have been more populist or more cosmopolitan, more democratic or more universalistic, geared more toward effectiveness or toward principle, and even whether it might have been possible to do both at once. But they can do so only armed with conceptions of populism and cosmopolitanism that do not answer the question in advance.

CONCLUSION

My argument here has not been that the differences and tensions between populism and cosmopolitanism are unimportant or mistaken, nor is it that we should forget everything that divides them. Not only does populism's particularism run up against cosmopolitanism's universalism; populism's need to construct a "people" in opposition to enemies and obstacles tends to set it against precisely the figures most identified with cosmopolitanism. Moreover, more abstractly, populism's hyper-politicism, its need to identify—and identify *with*—a "people," comes into conflict not only with cosmopolitanism's tendency toward *dis*-identification, to reject or transcend particular communities and identities, but also with cosmopolitan's tendential a- or unpoliticalness. Yet despite these deep tensions between them, we should not simply view the two ideas as antitheses. There have been and continue to be more and less cosmopolitan, universalistic, and inclusive populisms, just as there have been and continue to be more and less popular, common, and inclusive cosmopolitanisms. It is important to recall this not only in order to avoid a distorted or one-sided view of either object, but also for practical purposes: by predetermining the nature of such multifarious phenomena, we deprive ourselves of tools for making ethical and political judgments.

Without opposing a crude anti-populism with an equally crude anti-anti-populism, I therefore conclude with a plea concerning the formulation and use of concepts. As

I noted in the first section, many scholars have followed conventional usage, first of all in Europe but increasingly also in the Americas to carve out a critical, pejorative, and even polemical conception of populism. By binding populism to democracy's demagogic, authoritarian, xenophobic, anti-pluralistic, and anti-constitutional aspects, they forge an uncomfortably tight link between "the people" and illiberal policies, cementing an opposition between liberalism and democracy that in many cases they do not intend.[9] And even where they concede that some degree of populism may be inevitable in democratic politics, this concession is of limited practical value unless we know how much populism may be welcomed, in what forms, and under what circumstances. A useful concept of populism would be one that allows us to say how much of what kind of populism is desirable and how much of what kind undesirable or dangerous, when, where, and why.

Rather than using a strictly negative understanding of populism for diagnostic purposes, then, to sniff out pathogens in the democratic body, a bivalent concept could allow us to distinguish between malignant and benign strains. Such an approach would allow us to put the tension between populism and cosmopolitanism to more fine-grained critical use: each concept can point out where the other becomes problematic, the point at which it succumbs to its destructive internal tendencies. Populism becomes anti-cosmopolitan as it becomes exclusionary and xenophobic, which it does when it seeks to secure the identity of "the people" from those outside (foreigners or aliens) or below (minorities or an underclass), rather than above. Cosmopolitanism becomes anti-populist when, defining itself against the local and the popular, it becomes elitist and anti-democratic. These two tendencies clearly indicate where populism becomes regressive and reactionary, and cosmopolitanism, haughty and anti-political. While these tendencies are widely observed, neither is necessary. As I have tried to show, there have been inclusive populisms and popular cosmopolitanisms. Even if these must be seen as outliers (in social-scientific terms) or utopian possibilities (in humanistic ones), they are possibilities worth keeping open and indeed fostering.

NOTES

The author wishes to thank Tamara Caraus, Sylwia Chrostowska, and John McGuire as well as Paulina Ochoa Espejo and Cristóbal Rovira Kaltwasser for their comments and suggestions.
1   Laclau is often criticized for failing to distinguish populist from other forms of democratic politics; indeed, he affirms that all democratic politics is populist to some degree. It should be noted, however, that this is a feature his theory shares with other leading studies of populism, which likewise depict it as a necessary aspect or "shadow" of democracy. See e.g. Canovan, 1999; Arditi, 2004: 135–43; Mény and Surel, 2000.
2   For a systematic working out of ancient Cynicism as a basis for thinking through cosmopolitanism, see McGuire, forthcoming.
3   Marx, 1990: 75. As Stallybrass points out (1990), Marx's *Lumpenproletariat* shares with the proletariat a withering of national and traditional bonds, and thus a kind of

cosmopolitanism. What makes it dangerous is its failure to replace these with a properly political, class-based identity, leaving it exposed to populist appeals like those of Louis-Napoleon Bonaparte.

4 While most of these figures articulate a roughly Stoic position that balances allegiance to the *kosmos* with that to the *polis*, Jesus of Nazareth is not infrequently read as articulating a more radical, possibly Cynic, indifference or antipathy to conventional political order. See Downing, 1992.

5 Since only fragmentary comments on Zeno's *Republic* remain, discussion of its content is speculative. See Baldry, 1959; Sellars, 2007.

6 If Diogenes's stance is indeed, as he seems to assert, political, it seems to be political in the anarchistic sense of Otanes, recounted by Herodotus and recalled by Rousseau and Hannah Arendt. Asked about his preferred political regime, Otanes declared that he would rather "neither rule nor be ruled" (*Histories*, 3.80.27).

7 While Buck-Morss, in the work that did more than any other to remind theorists and historians of the universal significance of the Haitian Revolution, regrets this declaration of universal "black" citizenship as a betrayal of the Revolution's universality (2009: 145–6), I suggest that we instead follow Nesbitt (2005) in seeing it as a prolongation of that universalism within an irreducibly political context: recognizing the need to draw frontiers, the Haitian revolutionaries drew them in a self-consciously *inclusionary* way.

8 Recall the story, oft retold in radical trade unionist circles, of how the members of the cosmopolitan Industrial Workers of the World came to be known as "Wobblies": "Legend assigns it to the lingual difficulties of a Chinese restaurant keeper with whom arrangements had been made during this strike to feed members passing through his town. When he tried to ask 'Are you IWW?' it is said to have come out: 'All loo eye wobble wobble?'" (Thompson and Bekken, 2006: 60). The point (lurking behind the now somewhat uncomfortable mockery of the immigrant's accent) is that the union defined itself by its inclusiveness and transcendence of particularistic identities.

9 A strictly critical conception of populism also has the peculiar consequence of forcing the author, who relies on conventional usage for the concept's negative valence, to declare certain parties or movements widely considered populist to be no such thing. In Müller's case (2016), this extends across much of the left side of the political field, including not only such present-day examples as Occupy, SYRIZA, PODEMOS, and Bernie Sanders's campaign for the 2016 US Democratic presidential nomination, but even the American People's Party itself.

REFERENCES

Abts, K. and S. Rummens. 2007. "Populism versus democracy," *Political Studies*, 55(2): 405–24.
Anderson, P. 2002. "Internationalism: a breviary," *New Left Review*, II(14): 5–25.
Appiah, K. A. 2006. *Cosmopolitanism: Ethics in a World of Strangers*. New York: Norton.
Arditi, B. 2004. "Populism as a spectre of democracy: a response to Canovan," *Political Studies*, 52(1): 135–43.
Baban, F. and K. Rygiel. 2014. "Snapshots from the margins: transgressive cosmopolitanisms in Europe," *European Journal of Social Theory*, 17(4): 461–78.
Baldry, H. C. 1959. "Zeno's ideal state," *Journal of Hellenic Studies*, 79: 3–15.
Baldry, H. C. 1965. *The Unity of Mankind in Greek Thought*. Cambridge: Cambridge University Press.

Bobbio, N. 1987. *The Future of Democracy*, trans. R. Griffin, ed. R. Bellamy. Cambridge: Polity.

Breaugh, M. 2013. *The Plebeian Experience: A Discontinuous History of Political Freedom*, trans. L. Lederhendler. New York: Columbia University Press.

Buck-Morss, S. 2009. *Hegel, Haiti, and Universal History*. Pittsburgh: University of Pittsburgh.

Canovan, M. 1999. "Trust the people! Populism and the two faces of democracy," *Political Studies*, 47(1): 2–16.

Canovan, M. 2005. *The People*. Cambridge: Polity.

de Sousa Santos, B. 2006. "Globalizations," *Theory Culture and Society*, 23(2): 393–9.

Dean, J. 2013. "Occupy Wall Street: after the anarchist moment," *Socialist Register*, 49: 52–62.

D'Eramo, M. 2013. "Populism and the new oligarchy," *New Left Review*, II(82): 5–28.

Downing, F. G. 1992. *Cynics and Christian Origins*. Edinburgh: T & T Clark.

Finley, M. 1981. *Politics in the Ancient World*. Cambridge: Cambridge University Press.

Foucault, M. 2001. *Fearless Speech*, ed. J. Pearson. New York: Semiotext(e).

Gebh, S. 2013. "Shameless cosmopolitanism: Diogenes the Cynic and the paradox of the cosmopolis," *History of Political Thought*, 2(1): 65–81.

Gidwani, V. K. 2006. "Subaltern cosmopolitanism as politics," *Antipode*, 38(1): 7–21.

Gilroy, P. 1993. *The Black Atlantic: Modernity and Double Consciousness*. Cambridge: Harvard University Press.

Ingram, J. D. 2013. *Radical Cosmopolitics: The Ethics and Politics of Democratic Universalism*. New York: Columbia University Press.

Johnson, J. T. 1987. *The Quest for Peace: Three Moral Traditions in Western Cultural History*. Princeton: Princeton University Press.

Kazin, M. 1995. *The Populist Persuasion: An American History*. New York: Basic Books.

Kitschelt, H. 1997. *The Radical Right in Western Europe: A Comparative Analysis*. Ann Arbor: University of Michigan Press.

Kurasawa, F. 2004. "A cosmopolitanism from below: alternative globalization and the creation of a solidarity without bounds," *European Journal of Sociology*, 45(2): 233–55.

Laclau, E. 1996. "Why do empty signifiers matter to politics?," in *Emancipation(s)*. London and New York: Verso.

Laclau, E. 2005. *On Populist Reason*. London and New York: Verso.

Laclau, E. 2006. "Why constructing a people is the main task of radical politics," *Critical Inquiry*, 32: 646–80.

Lefort, C. 1988. "The revolutionary terror," in *Democracy and Political Theory*, trans. D. Macey. Cambridge: Polity.

Little, A. 2015. "Performing the demos: towards a processive theory of global democracy," *Critical Review of International Social and Political Philosophy*, 18(6): 620–41.

Marx, K. 1990. *The Eighteenth Brumaire of Louis Bonaparte*, ed. C. P. Dutt. New York: International Publishers.

McCormick, J. P. 2001. "Machiavellian democracy: controlling elites with ferocious populism," *American Political Science Review*, 95(2): 297–313.

McGuire, J. forthcoming. *Friends of the Gods? Cosmopolitan Theory and Political Agency*. Leiden: Brill.

Mény, Y. and Y. Surel. 2000. *Par le peuple, pour le peuple: le populisme et les démocraties*. Paris: Fayard.

Miller, D. 2002. "Cosmopolitanism: a critique," *Critical Review of International Social and Political Philosophy*, 5(3): 80–5.

Moles, J. L. 1996. "Cynic cosmopolitanism," in R. B. Branham and M.-O. Goulet-Cazé (eds), *The Cynics: The Cynic Movement in Antiquity and its Legacy*. Berkeley: University of California Press.

Mudde, C. 2007. *Populist Radical Right Parties in Europe*. Cambridge: Cambridge University Press.

Müller, J.-W. 2014. "'The people must be extracted from within the people': reflections on populism," *Constellations*, 21(4): 483–93.

Müller, J.-W. 2016. *Populismus*. Berlin: Suhrkamp.

Murray, D. 2010. "Democratic insurrection: constructing the common in global resistance," *Millennium*, 39(2): 461–82.

Myers, E. 2016. "Presupposing equality: the trouble with Rancière's axiomatic approach," *Philosophy and Social Criticism*, 42(1): 45–69.

Nesbitt, N. 2005. "The idea of 1804," *Yale French Studies*, 107: 6–38.

Nussbaum, M. 1996. "Patriotism and cosmopolitanism," in J. Cohen (ed.), *For Love of Country? Debating the Limits of Patriotism*. Boston: Beacon.

Nyers, P. 2003. "Abject cosmopolitanism: the politics of protection in the anti-deportation movement," *Third World Quarterly*, 24(6): 1069–93.

Osborne, P. 2012. "Disguised as a dog: cynical Occupy?" *Radical Philosophy*, 174: 15–21.

Parenti, M. 2003. *The Assassination of Julius Caesar: A People's History of Ancient Rome*. New York: New Press.

Pârvu, C. A. 2015. "The logistics of dissent: prefigurative politics in Occupy Wall Street," in T. Caraus and C. A. Pârvu (eds), *Cosmopolitanism and the Legacies of Dissent*. New York: Routledge.

Rancière, J. 1999. *Disagreement*, trans. J. Rose. Minneapolis: University of Minnesota Press.

Rancière, J. 2007. *Hatred of Democracy*, trans. S. Concoran. London and New York: Verso.

Rancière, J. 2016. "The populism that is not to be found," in Rancière et al. (eds), *What Is a People?*, trans. J. Gladding. New York: Columbia University Press.

Rosanvallon, P. 2011. "Penser le populisme," http://www.laviedesidees.fr/Penser-le-populisme.html.

Rousseau, J.-J. 1997. "Geneva manuscript," in V. Gourevitch (ed. and trans.), *The Social Contract and Other Later Political Writings*. Cambridge: Cambridge University Press.

Sellars, J. 2007. "Stoic cosmopolitanism and Zeno's *Republic*," *History of Political Thought*, 28(1): 1–29.

Shilliam, R. 2015. *The Black Pacific: Anti-Colonial Struggles and Oceanic Connections*. London: Bloomsbury.

Stallybrass, P. 1990. "Marx and heterogeneity: thinking the lumpenproletariat," *Representations*, 31(1): 69–95.

Taggart, P. 2000. *Populism*. Birmingham: Open University Press.

Thompson, F. and J. Bekken. 2006. *The IWW: Its First 100 Years*. Cincinnati: IWW.

Urbinati, N. 2014. *Democracy Disfigured: Opinion, Truth, and the People*. Cambridge: Harvard University Press.

Vatter, M. 2011. "The quarrel between populism and republicanism: Machiavelli and the antinomies of plebeian politics," *Contemporary Political Theory*, 11(2): 242–63.

CHAPTER 34

··

POPULISM IN THE SOCIALIST IMAGINATION

··

KEVIN OLSON

A specter haunts socialism—the specter of the people. Socialism has always portrayed itself as an advocate of the people, a principled position promoting equality and empowering the disenfranchised against the predations of a democratic politics that only masks elite interests. These commitments are often filled with tensions in both theory and practice, however. In their efforts to forcefully criticize contemporary capitalism, socialists frequently adopt populist orientations that sound thin or perfunctory—political embraces of the people that are subsidiary to more deeply held socialist commitments. This ambivalence towards populism is, I believe, a tension that has been deeply structured into socialism since its founding.

Socialism was one of the most vital and innovative political movements of the nineteenth century, and it has matured into one of the organizational bases of modern government. Given its pivotal importance to world history, the development of socialism is a crucial episode in the archive of populism. More than any other set of political ideals, it has been imagined as a politics of the people, either through their direct action or through the leadership of a vanguard that organizes and directs their force. Similarly, a socialist society is envisioned as a radically egalitarian one: a society of the people in the purest sense, freed from distinctions of class, property, or privilege.

Central to these concerns are specific notions of political collectivity. Socialism's origins in the nineteenth century are reflected in its embrace of mass politics, characteristic of the problematics of the era. At times this consists of vague references to "the people" or "workers," but such casual usage is typically underpinned by more rigorous ideas. Socialists have tended to set aside universalist or undifferentiated conceptions of the people in favor of a politics of class. Yet the people do not disappear from view, primarily because of socialism's populist commitments. The result is an awkward set of identifications between the iconic socialist collective subject, the proletariat, and "the people" more broadly construed. This complex relation will be my focus here. While such notions of collectivity may be rigorous in certain ways, they are often fraught with internal tensions. Much of the conceptual richness and potential of socialism is driven by their energy.

I will trace these tensions through three moments of socialist innovation. (1) Karl Marx remains the classic point of reference for any such discussion. He is important not simply as *the* canonic writer of the socialist oeuvre, but more importantly for his hegemonic position as the deep thinker of socialism's formative years: the writer and political operative against whom all others were forced to justify their positions. (2) The Blanquists were radical socialists who departed notably from Marx's ideas, occasionally earning his admiration in the process. They marked out a distinctive brand of socialism that embraced populism more fully. A generation younger than Marx, they were principally active from the 1860s to 1890s. (3) A third strand competed hotly with Marxism at the end of the nineteenth century and has arguably displaced it today. "Social democracy" was so called because it advocated a fusion of democratic politics and socialism. It rearticulates socialist populism as a conception of economic justice in novel ways. My focus will be on Eduard Bernstein's formulation of these ideals in the late 1890s and their subsequent elaboration in Sweden during the 1920s–1940s.

The texts I will examine are largely ignored in the study of populism. With the exception of Marx, they are also given far too little attention for the important socialist alternatives they articulate. In the ensemble, these works provide a picture of shifting problematics and competing ideas. They reveal much about the relationship between socialism and populism, particularly about the senses in which socialism has been haunted by the people in fundamental, constitutive ways that have deeply shaped its development.

This is a story of tension and resolution. What begins as a tension between populism and socialism is partly resolved, I will claim, through confrontation with actually existing circumstances. The result is a fusion of the two that has the (as yet unrealized) potential to set aside socialism's ambivalence about the people.

AMBIGUITIES OF POPULISM

Let me begin with several interpretive notes about what it means to discern a populist orientation in socialism. Populism is an ambiguous idea. As a term of art in the study of politics, it typically indicates a political appeal to the people. Such appeals can be made in several senses, however. They can be made as an effort at political instrumentality, to propagate one's views or enhance one's political prospects. This can occur as a broad appeal to public opinion, as a means of consolidating electoral support within a representative system of government, or as a way to build a political movement (Laclau, 2005; Urbinati, 2014). Populism can also refer, however, to a more sincere commitment to participatory and inclusive politics. In these cases, the focus is more genuinely normative. Here populism tries to open politics more fully to the people, breaking down barriers to entry, criticizing the power of elites, and giving more equal weight to the views, opinions, and action of all. These strands of populism constitute a principled commitment to a politics of the people, rather than a form of political instrumentality (Canovan, 1999: 4–5).

Most frequently, the idea of populism tends simultaneously to invoke both principled commitments and political instrumentality, with no clear way of discerning between them. When an appeal to the people is described as "populist," its sincerity is not at all clear. Such an appeal could be made in a principled sense, but the very idea of populism tends to leave that possibility suspended in some degree of doubt. Deceit is always cloaked in sincerity, and an appeal to the people can be a facade for political instrumentality. Invoking the people is thus an ambiguous gesture with unclear intent. As a result, populism refers ambiguously to pure expressions of our normative ideal of democracy, *and* to cynical deployments of those ideals for other ends.

The question of who "the people" are is also a fraught topic. The people can indicate the majoritarian part of a binary opposition: the many or the masses, as opposed to the few or the elite (McCormick, 2011). It can designate an impoverished class fraction: the mass of the poor (Agamben, 1998: 176). Or it can indicate a more universalistic notion of society as a whole, one of potentially boundless inclusion. These, however, are just some of the possibilities.

Finally, the normative valence of the people can be imagined in many different ways (Olson, 2016). It can designate the democratic sovereign in the most idealized sense, an easily manipulated mass, or a dangerously undirectable crowd. In short, the people is a figment of our political imaginaries with a wide variety of normative connotations, and to say that a political position is "populist" does not specify what normative attitude is being expressed.

All of this is to say that populism is a highly ambiguous way of describing political thought and action. It can indicate the most cynical forms of political instrumentality or the most radically universalist and egalitarian commitments. It can invoke widely differing political collectivities: the masses, the poor, any citizen of a given jurisdiction, or any person without limit. To make matters even more confusing, these contrasting meanings are often intermixed, so that several are invoked at the same time. In short, populism is a complex cocktail of meaning and signification, an ambiguous phenomenon. That ambiguity is found in the ways the people are appealed to as justification and legitimation, the ways such appeals mix principled motives and political instrumentalities, the ways these characteristics are frequently combined in impure mixtures without clear intention by the people enacting them.

Many commentators have responded to this situation by trying to "get clear" about populism, either through some kind of stipulative definition that singles out its "core" manifestations (Laclau, 2005; Urbinati, 2014), or by generating typologies and classifactory schemes (Canovan, 1981). This attitude is unfortunate, because it seeks deliberately to eradicate one of the core characteristics of populism: its very ambiguity. I will take a rather different tack. Rather than attempting a distorting clarification of what populism really means, I will trace its various threads through several generations of socialist politics. Being interpretively aware of ambivalances, tensions, equivocations, and subtle shifts of meaning allows us to see in more vivid detail how socialism and populism have come together in the past. This in turn provides a basis for seeing how their combination can provide politics with new energy in the future.

AMBIVALENCE TOWARDS THE PEOPLE

Populism has a complicated career in the work of Karl Marx. On one hand, he was deeply involved in the concrete politics of his day and wrote in great detail about many of these events. A consistent theme of these works is a biting attack on elite power as a tool of popular immiseration and subordination. On the other hand, his well-known analysis of class is deployed in a series of ambiguous identifications with the people, creating subtle tensions within his work that are never fully resolved. The result is an ambivalent embrace of populism, one that is articulated within the conceptual appa-ratus of Marx's socialism and has an awkward relation with it.

In Marx's analysis, capitalism is a system of property relations that exercises a struc-turing influence on society. It incorporates people into a system of cooperation and shapes their political and economic interests:

> The great industry masses together in a single place a crowd of people unknown to each other. Competition divides their interests. But the maintenance of their wages, this common interest which they have against their employer, unites them in the same idea of resistance—combination…. In this struggle—a veritable civil war—are united and developed all the elements necessary for a future battle. Once arrived at that point, association takes a political character. (Marx, 1847 [1920]: 188)

Industrial capitalism is a form of governmentality that creates workers where once was an undifferentiated mass of people. It simultaneously fragments this group by placing its members in competition with one another. While this structural situation creates opposing interests, it also elicits a new kind of political macrosubject, a form of collec-tive association that unites workers across their divided interests.

Immediately following this, Marx reformulates the point somewhat more technically:

> The economic conditions have in the first place transformed the mass of the people of a country into wageworkers. The domination of capital has created for this mass of people a common situation with common interests. Thus this mass is already a class, as opposed to capital, but not yet for itself. In the struggle, of which we have only noted some phases, this mass unites, it is constituted as a class for itself. The interests which it defends are the interests of its class. But the struggle between class and class is a political struggle. (Marx, 1847 [1920]: 188–9)

The language in this passage is telling. "The mass of the people" indicates an undifferen-tiated multitude, seemingly without any particular character. However, they are already formed into a class—in some abstract sense—by prevailing economic conditions. Political struggle in turn exercises a constitutive influence on this virtual collectivity, transforming it into a self-aware movement, a "class for itself."

In this discussion, class-in-itself is a virtual collectivity that is predicted to exist based on a theorist's assessment of "material interests." Class-for-itself is an actually existing collectivity based on affective identification with a particular group. Thus we arrive at a complex, paradoxical notion of collectivity, one suspended in tension between a structural position and an actual identification. This distinction between *potentia* and *actualitas* is reminiscent of the conceptual moves underlying classical political theology: the idea that the king is sovereign in his political body even before his physical body occupies the throne, or that Adam was created with monarchical power even before he had subjects to govern (Kantorowicz, 1957: 273–336; Filmer, 1991: 144–5). In each of these cases, the potential for sovereignty and political unity is explained by invoking a theoretical construct whose existence is highly controversial. Similarly, Marx's claim that the decisive political cleavages of the era are matters of class begs some very important questions. It theoretically charges the interpretation of actual politics by hypothesizing that actual collective identifications will or should form along lines of class. This idea sits in awkward relation to populism, which typically involves more complicated and messy identifications.

Such tensions show up in Marx's reflections on the politics of his time. He was a scrupulous observer of the political scene around him. His accounts of these events tend to focus on the thrust and parry of elite politics, however. They are largely stories of generals, emperors, and presidents—precisely the kind of analysis that he earlier derided as "high-sounding dramas of princes and states" (Marx and Engels, 1947: 57). The popular politics of Marx's day receives much less attention. However, we can discern the outlines of a populist imaginary in the remarks he does make.

The most celebrated of these analyses is *The Eighteenth Brumaire of Louis Bonaparte*. Here Marx focuses on the brief period of French republican government between 1848 and 1851. For him this republic is built out of class struggle: factions of the *grande bourgeoisie* fighting for their own material interests, *petit bourgeois* republicans using the cloak of "democracy" to struggle against them, the *Lumpenproletariat* and rural peasants being instrumentalized as the demagogue Louis Bonaparte's power base. These conflicts are rendered in vivid detail to substantiate Marx's assertion that political interests are in essence class interests (Marx, 1852 [1996]: 102).

Among these careful characterizations of class politics, two absences stand out. Marx says fairly little about the proletariat, the class that he sees as the consistent victim of such elite struggles. He also refers to "the people" on occasion, but does not specify who or what they would consist of. For instance, Marx draws on these ideas when leveling criticisms against petty-bourgeois democrats in the republican parliament. With biting sarcasm, he mimes the pollyannaish claims of the democrats that they are the representatives of the people, therefore above class conflict, therefore their interests are the people's interests (62). These "bourgeois republicans" or "revolutionary bourgeoisie" are not representatives of the people, he says, but their enemy. In this sense, he firmly rejects instrumental forms of populism, ones that draw on the people as a basis of consent and political power without a more principled commitment to their opinions and interests.

Similarly, Marx describes the liquidation of the revolutionary proletariat as a condition of the consolidation of the bourgeois republic. On at least one occasion, he identifies the victims of the bourgeois republicans as "the people" (Marx, 1852 [1996]: 48). Because Marx had earlier been talking about the "revolutionary proletariat," the two groups are implicitly identified with one another in this passage. This is typical of his populist orientation: Marx's implicit imaginary often equates the proletariat with the people in at least a vague way, in distinction to the various other classes that represent reactionary interests.

The Civil War in France, written several decades later, continues this line of thought in light of the Paris Commune of 1871. The Commune began as a popular uprising that seized Paris and briefly formed itself into a radical, democratically elected socialist government. Marx views it as a second attempt to achieve the project that was launched in 1848. The political form of the Commune, a "social republic" that provides an alternative to monarchy, is inscribed within a class politics undertaken by the proletariat. By extension, the proletariat itself is a collectivity defined by class identity. Its political task is to end class rule—presumably by ending class as such (Marx, 1871 [1996]: 183).

While Marx uses the concept of the proletariat in a rigorous way, he occasionally substitutes more colloquial terms like "the working class" or "workers." He says of the Commune, for instance, that it "was the first revolution in which the working class was openly acknowledged as the only class capable of social initiative" (189). Similarly, he notes that "[t]he working class cannot simply lay hold of the ready-made state machinery, and wield it for its own purposes" (181). From the standpoint of political collectivity, these references function identically to those about the proletariat. They remain within the ambit of Marx's conception of class, and identify a normatively privileged revolutionary group on that basis.

On rare occasions Marx also refers to a rather different collectivity, "the people." In a passage lauding the popular character of legislation passed during the Commune, for instance, he characterizes it as "a government of the people by the people" (192). The reference is an ambivalent one. Marx praises the Commune's normative rectitude by noting that it is truly of the people. In the same breath, however, he lists the principal measures implemented by the Commune, which seem disappointingly shortsighted: abolishing night work for journeymen bakers, prohibiting workplace fines for the purpose of reducing wages, socializing abandoned workshops and factories with compensation to the former owners. For Marx, such measures indicate political myopia on the part of "the people" initiating them, and thus a certain dissatisfaction with populism itself.

When Marx does refer to the people, he does not characterize them as a universal, normatively privileged group that encompasses all of society—the notion that French revolutionaries struggled to articulate, for instance (Olson, 2016: 54–92)—but one that is limited and particular. In this sense, he hearkens back to a much earlier idea that was characteristic of the *ancien régime*: the people as a subjected, deprived remainder left over after other groups had distinguished themselves out as superior (Falconnet de la Bellonie, 1748: I: 184; Coyer, 1757; Voltaire, 1766 [1973]). This is likely an implicit acknowledgement on Marx's part of the impossibility of social unity under current conditions. It suggests that for him there can be no universal subject of politics within the current structures of capitalism. It is not surprising, then, that he tends to prefer "the proletariat" over "the people" as the normatively privileged political collectivity. It also goes some way towards explaining his ambivalence towards the people, at least insofar as one might conceptualize them as a unified, universalist collectivity.

In spite of his attention to the concrete details of actual politics, Marx tends to over-theorize "the proletariat," "workers," and other collective agents by substituting a theoretically specified class position for the concrete texture of actual politics. The concepts of class, material interests, and relation to the means of production flavor these accounts in subtle ways that render them artificial to an extent. They become theory-laden exercises in discovering that which one set out to find: a politics of class, articulated along specific, objective, economic criteria.

This is not simply a reductive conception of politics as class struggle. Rather, Marx shows an ambivalence towards the people that embraces their normative rectitude while assimilating them to a class. Actually existing mobilizations are implied to have a free-standing value in all of their complexity and authenticity, but they are also judged by the extent to which they follow the fault lines of material interests, construed according to a particular analysis of the structure of property in the capitalist economy. Class-in-itself is a heuristic that consistently shapes Marx's interpretations of actually existing populist politics, creating tensions within his analyses.

The extent to which Marx's political analysis begs questions of collectivity formation can be thrown into contrast by examining other accounts of the time. John Leighton, an Englishman trapped in the midst of the Paris Commune, gives a first-person report of the events unfolding around him. Without delving too deeply, it is interesting to note the textual and descriptive differences between his account and Marx's.

For instance, Leighton tries to estimate the political sympathies of the eighty members of the Commune's Municipal Council, the same one celebrated by Marx (Marx, 1871 [1996]: 184–5). In so doing, he makes clear the political heterogeneity of the core organizers:

> Firstly, ten or twelve men belonging to the International, who have both thought and studied and may be able to act, mixed with these several foreigners; secondly, a number of young men, ardent but inexperienced, some of whom are imbued with Jacobin principles; thirdly, and by far the largest portion, unsuccessful plotters in former revolutions, journalists, orators, and conspirators,—noisy, active and effervescent, having no particular tie amongst themselves except the absence of any common bond of unity with the two former divisions, and being confounded now with one, now with the other. (Leighton, 1871: 76–7)

Leighton does not see the Commune as the political expression of a revolutionary proletariat or any other class. Rather, he sees a complex mélange of political insurgents, some allied with the International Working Men's Association, some ardent and inexperienced Jacobins, and a large, chaotic collection of adventurers who do not seem to have any particular ties.

Leighton is also more sensitive to the concrete, material texture of the Commune's politics—not the elite maneuvering of Thiers and his generals, to which Marx devotes so much attention, but the actual politics of the Communards themselves. For instance, Leighton notes the sudden surge of political pamphlets, newspapers, and other printed materials in the heady atmosphere of the Commune. He lists the titles of thirty-nine journals of the sixty-one that came into existence with the Commune, many revealing a strongly populist orientation. Among these are *Le Cri du Peuple*, *L'Ami du Peuple*, *Le Tribun du Peuple*, and *La Souveraineté du Peuple*. Others have more explicitly socialist resonances: *La Sociale*, or *Le Drapeau Rouge*, named after the red socialist flag. Some reveal a Jacobin flavor from the first revolution: *Le Salut Public*, a reference to the committee used as the political platform for the Terror during the French Revolution, and *Le Bonnet Rouge*, named after the red cap that was a symbol of revolutionary republicanism (237).

Leighton's attention to the concrete details of the insurgency—its political heterogeneity, the material means of its political expression—throw Marx's more stylized analysis into contrast. Marx fails to capture many important facets of the rich texture of the actual politics of the time. This is a further manifestation of his ambivalence towards populism. His efforts to provide a rigorous grounding for socialism trump his express commitments to "the people." The people, in turn, is awkwardly defined as an expression of a theoretical conception of class.

Masses and Crowds

The tension between socialism and populism is articulated in other ways by other socialist visionaries. Marx frequently mentions Auguste Blanqui when he discusses the revolutionary politics of nineteenth-century France. In his account of the revolutions of 1848, for instance, Marx notes that:

> The well-known result of May [1848] was that Blanqui and associates, i.e. the real leaders of the proletarian party, the revolutionary communists, were removed from the public arena for the entire duration of the events we are considering. (1852 [1996]: 38)

Similarly, in his account of the Paris Commune, Marx refers to Blanqui as one of the chief representatives of the working class and obliquely mentions insurrections by his followers leading up to the Paris Commune (1871 [1996]: 175–6, 178).

Blanqui was a socialist insurgent who exercised a defining influence on many of the events that Marx theorized. He was a rather Socratic figure, possessing a single-minded, ascetic resolve in pursuing the goals that interested him, focusing on action rather than writing, and serving as a galvanizing presence for many young men eager to follow his example. Blanqui's activities frequently put him on the wrong side of the French government, to the extent that he spent half of his life in prison and came to be known as "the Imprisoned." As a result, his influence was largely felt in the movement that he inspired. The so-called Blanquists were a loose network of students and workers. Of the many strands of socialist thought and practice in their time, they were among the most focused on the actual politics of popular mobilization. Theirs was a practice of revolutionary populism taking the form of concrete, material politics, revolutionary community, and the continuation of a tradition begun during the French Revolution.

The leading Blanquist theoretician, and the closest of them to Blanqui, was Gustave Tridon (Hutton, 1981: 27–8). His book *Les Hébertistes* is one of the richest articulations of Blanquist thought. Writing as a member of the Paris Commune in 1871, Tridon reflects back on the various currents of revolutionary practice in the French Revolution. Examining that heritage, he criticizes both of the principal revolutionary factions, the Robespierrists and the Girondins, as insufficiently populist. It is the Hébertistes, the followers of the radical journalist Jacques Hébert, who were truest to the cause of the people. By moving them into focus, Tridon hopes to recuperate a revolutionary tradition that is not Robespierrist nor Girondin, but more genuinely populist (Tridon, 1871).

According to Tridon, both the Robespierrists and the Girondins place too much emphasis on elite politics and show insufficient trust in the people. In his eyes, the people are the great revolutionary subject. Their "mind burning with patriotic fever," they "push events forward and force the hand of fortune" (1871: 16). In this sense, he articulates a view more thoroughly populist than Marx's, as well as the French Revolutionaries whom he criticizes.

Tridon's hope is to revitalize a notion of revolutionary community that flourished briefly during the French Revolution. It consisted of the self-organization and direct rule of the most marginalized, which he describes as "the people, the plebeians, the populace" (1871: 17). These were the people who wore the red liberty cap, wooden peasant shoes, and the tricolor cockade, all symbols of the most radically republican sympathies at the time. In this earlier commune, ceremonies were established in which elected officials were held publicly to account for their actions. The Hébertistes, Marat, and likeminded revolutionaries defended these upwellings of popular democracy against the hypocrisy of Robespierre and the "learned oligarchy" of the Girondins. They made it their project to educate and empower the people, rather than to lead them in a way that would have been self-serving (1871: 18–21).

Following the ideas of Tridon's treatise, the Blanquists worked hard to create revolutionary community during their own time. They aimed to build bridges across class divides, rather than intensifying class conflict as their Marxist counterparts espoused. The principal expression of their efforts—seemingly trivial but quite effective—was a movement to provide burials for the poor and destitute. This Civil Burial movement focused on enhancing the dignity and status of ordinary people by according them the same public commemoration normally reserved for the rich and powerful. It created elaborate public displays attended by hundreds or thousands, the equivalent of an elaborate state funeral for people who were otherwise humble and unknown (Hutton, 1981: 53–6). By devising these ceremonies, the Blanquists displayed a keen awareness of the importance of group assembly, performativity, and ritual in creating a popular movement.

With these insights comes a notion of collectivity quite different from Marx's. Whereas Marx develops a structural analysis of capitalism based on the idea of class, then predicts actually existing mobilization and affect around those cleavages, the Blanquists take community directly as a goal to be achieved. They see revolutionary community as a project in itself, rather than as epiphenomenal to deeper economic processes.

Instead of emphasizing material interests as a basis of class analysis, the Blanquists enacted forms of politics that were literally material. Theirs was a politics of popular mobilization, grassroots organizing, armed rebellion, and barricades in the streets. In an insurrectionary pamphlet circulated in 1868, for instance, Auguste Blanqui tackles the question of how to take to the streets in the most concrete sense (Blanqui, 1868 [2006]). He draws on previous insurrections to detail the best ways to hinder the movement of cavalry by overturning carriages and tearing up cobblestones, and reflects concretely about the number of people who are needed for such a task. He considers the organization of barricades, noting that during the June uprising of 1830, 95 percent of the barricades saw no action (they "didn't light a single fuse"), and the rest were easily defeated (1868 [2006]: 258). He concludes that this was the fault of poor planning, disunity, and disorganization.

To build an effective popular movement where others have failed, Blanqui is deeply interested in the material means of popular unity. He says that the military has an "immense, irresistible" advantage in its organization, and he wants to give the people similar capabilities (1868 [2006]: 261). This is not simply a matter of publicity and discussion: Blanqui thinks of popular unity as built through action. He says that "[i]n a time of tyranny, writing is good, but when an enslaved pen remains powerless, fighting is better" (1868 [2006]: 263). To enable this, his attention is always focused on practical considerations of mass mobilization and popular uprising: the forms of popular unity and organization needed to get people into the streets in a politically effective manner. In this sense, the Blanquists' materialism is quite different from that of Marx. Where Marx focused on material interests, Blanqui is interested in the materiality of practice. This is materiality in the most tangible sense: a concern with the specific means of insurgency available for specific political actions.

The Blanquists had a complicated relationship with other strands of socialism. The tensions between socialism and populism are finely etched in these conflicts. The Blanquists were on-again, off-again members of the International Working Men's Association, the same "International" of which Marx was a founding member (Hutton, 1981: 29–30). Many of the Blanquists who were not killed or imprisoned at the end of the Paris Commune reassembled in London, where they were welcomed for a time by Marx. Several were elected to the International's General Council. By 1872, however, relations with Marx had soured and he engineered their removal from the Council.

The Blanquists published several pamphlets in indignant response, outlining their disagreements with Marx and the inner circle of the International. A polemic first volley was entitled *Internationale et Révolution*, and it attacked the International—and by extension, Marx—for their focus on economic analysis at the expense of politics, particularly the pursuit of working-class power (Arnaud et al., 1872). Marx and the International are alleged to be insufficiently political and insufficiently revolutionary; they are portrayed as guardians of the status quo rather than agents of revolution. A militant politics of armed struggle is needed to realize the insights about economic justice that the International has formulated. This goal is succinctly summarized in a delicate contrast between the strike, a means of economic action, and other, more forceful measures: "If the strike is a means of revolutionary action, the barricade is another such means and the most powerful of all" (1872: 15).

In essence, the Blanquists take the Marxist-Internationalists to task for their abstract internationalism and a corresponding lack of commitment to revolutionary community. As an alternative, they propose a return to the spirit of the revolutionary commune, the tradition of Hébert and Marat. They reject the elite conception of organization implied by the International in favor of a more broad-based one that connects revolutionary elements of the urban proletariat in cities across France. The challenge is to organize, arm, and strengthen this collectivity. Thus revolutionary politics will be communal, popular, and a politics of the street (Arnaud et al., 1872; Commune Révolutionnaire, 1874).

Friedrich Engels wrote a response to these manifestos. He faults the Blanquists for their vanguardism and says that Blanqui "is a socialist only in sentiment, in sympathy with the suffering of the people." Their problem is not with their sympathy for the plight of workers, nor with their revolutionary orientation, but with the lack of a systematic basis for either. They are socialists by instinct, not by theory, and their lack of a coherent theoretical analysis ultimately deprived their actions of meaning. The result, he claims, was the flawed program of the Paris Commune, in which so much was left unaddressed in the economic sphere (Engels, 1874).

The idea that the Blanquists were not really socialists is a polemic characterization on Engels's part—they were very much within the socialist camp, albeit not Marxists. This charge illustrates a broader point, however. The Blanquists were above all focused on a revolutionary form of populism. To that extent, they were seen by Engels and others as improperly socialist. The tensions between Marxists and Blanquists says much about the more general tensions between socialism and populism. In the first camp there is a seemingly rigorous analysis of material interests and class antagonism, accompanied by a corresponding ambivalence about the people. In the second camp is a robust revolutionary populism centered on concrete forms of collective action and material practice. It emphasizes material practice rather than material interests, and is thus seen as giving up too much of socialism in the course of articulating a genuinely populist politics.

FIN DE SIÈCLE: SOCIAL DEMOCRACY

The final decades of the nineteenth century displayed mass politics on a previously unseen scale. Crowds and masses were a recurrent preoccupation, and the turbulent street politics of the time provoked a streak of paranoid consternation among bourgeois strata. Writing in 1895, the pioneering social psychologist Gustave Le Bon summed up this sentiment elegantly: "Crowds are somewhat like the sphinx of ancient fable: it is necessary to arrive at a solution of the problems offered by their psychology or to resign ourselves to being devoured by them" (Le Bon, 1895 [1960]: 102).

Socialists like Auguste Blanqui were a vital part of this political transformation. Yet by the late nineteenth century they were joined by other powerful movements. Socialist internationalism ran up against the widespread nationalism of the era, forcing socialists to compete for the hearts and minds of the mobilized masses (Hanák, 1970: 58–66; Hobsbawm, 1992: 122–4). The result was a socialism much savvier about actually existing politics, and one that had squarely confronted questions of popular mobilization and collective unity.

Eduard Bernstein's thinking was shaped by these currents. Writing in the same decade as Le Bon, he marked out a powerful and unique socialist position as a series of departures from orthodox Marxism. He advocated an "evolutionary" rather than revolutionary approach, believing that political circumstances had changed in ways that rendered revolution obsolete as a political tactic. The true opportunity for pursuing socialist goals in the early twentieth century, he claimed, was through electoral politics. These views, derided by some as reactionary and bourgeois, sparked what came to be known as the Revisionist Debate in 1896–1898 (Tudor and Tudor, 1988). Bernstein's pioneering ideas about social democracy exercised an important political influence at the time that has only grown during subsequent decades. In this sense, he ranks as a thinker of profound importance whose impact on contemporary politics competes with that of Karl Marx.

For our purposes Bernstein is important not primarily for his embrace of revisionism, but for the broader synthesis of socialism and democracy that it describes. Indeed, a populist democratic politics is the primary presupposition of socialism advertised in the title of Bernstein's principal work, *The Presuppositions of Socialism and the Tasks of Social Democracy* (1899 [1993]). Writing in the immediate aftermath of the Revisionist Debate in 1899, Bernstein argues that democracy is a precondition of socialism, in the sense that the forms of freedom aimed at by socialists are only possible through political organization. In this sense, he sees the modern socialist movement as an ally of liberal democracy, rather than its class enemy. Liberalism has historically been allied with the bourgeoisie, he admits, but it has a broader role to play in the realization of a more radical egalitarianism. A suitably reconfigured liberalism can foster grassroots democracy, which in turn provides socialism with the unity and cohesion that allows it to form into a movement (1899 [1993]: 150–60).

Bernstein shows how grassroots democracy is threaded through socialism, both conceptually and in the vision of Marx and other writers. He does this through a series of critical reevaluations of both Marxism and Blanquism.

Writing at the end of a tumultuous century, Bernstein places Blanquism at the heart of Marxism. He writes that there was an "original inner connection" between Blanquism and Marxism, in the sense that Marx's writings of the late 1840s and early 1850s were completely, implicitly Blanquist (1899 [1993]: 38–9). Here he is referring specifically to Blanquist notions of revolution. The Paris Commune, he notes, was a point of reference for both the Blanquists and the Marx-Engels of *The Communist Manifesto*, but each could imagine the rule of the working class only as a dictatorial, centralized, revolutionary power "supported by the terrorist dictatorship of revolutionary clubs" (1899 [1993]: 152). In this, he rejects the polarity that Engels, for instance, saw between the two camps. Both of them were committed revolutionaries, Bernstein argues, and this revolutionism had its origin among the Blanquists.

For Bernstein, this observation is part of a broader rejection of revolution as the mode of socialism's enactment. He argues that social conditions have changed since the revolutions of 1848, the touchstone of revolutionary doctrine for both Marxists and Blanquists (1899 [1993]: 42–5). As a result, some of the Blanquists' concepts of politics as popular insurrection are dated. By extension, Marxists' implicit reliance on these ideas is also out of step with contemporary realities.

Another distortion in Marxism comes from its reliance on an implicit politics of conflict, particularly ideas of class conflict. Bernstein argues that Marx's idea of "class-in-itself" remains too far from actual political, social, and economic conditions. He writes, "[o]n the whole, nothing is more misleading than to infer a real similarity in conditions from a formal similarity of situation" (1899 [1993]: 106). Such a structural analysis focuses too singly on one facet of existence, a person's relation to the means of production, ignoring other aspects of social life. Strikingly for his time, Bernstein also notes that such an analysis ignores various forms of sentiment and attachment, "feelings of closeness," which can attenuate or enhance political affiliation between groups independently of class (1899 [1993]: 106). Because Marx ignores all of this, he subordinates the political to the economic and produces a distorted analysis of socialist politics (1899 [1993]: 41).

To bring socialist politics into line with contemporary social and political realities, Bernstein favors an evolutionary approach that would achieve socialism through piecemeal political reform. It would be based on a universal franchise, and what Bernstein calls the absence of class government, by which he means the absence of legal privileges of property, birth, or religion. The central idea is a universalized notion of citizenship in which the "social position of proletarian" is raised to that of citizen (1899 [1993]: 146). This gradualist strategy broadens the scope of political practices that can be considered properly socialist, particularly with reference to democratic politics. Bernstein argues that it reveals the idea of the "dictatorship of the proletariat," typically attributed to Auguste Blanqui, to be anachronistic. Instead, socialists should support a broad view of democratic politics that prominently features rich forms of grassroots democracy.

For Bernstein, the paradigm of this vision is the workers' cooperative movement. Cooperatives articulate an alternative to the politics of conflict by creating a "republican organization of the workshop." They thereby displace class domination with democracy, integrating the political with the economic. As such, he believes that the cooperative movement expresses forms of interaction that should lie at the heart of socialism. They would replace the ideal of centralized control with decentralized, local decision-making that harnesses the expertise of those who labor, enacting forms of popular participation that are at once economic and political. All of this reanimates and updates the ideals of the Paris Commune. It removes the focus on revolutionary insurgency that came from the Blanquist legacy and was adopted by Marx. In its place we have the Commune's profoundly popular impulse and its emphasis on self-organization and community. This, Bernstein argues, should be seen as the Commune's true legacy (1899 [1993]: 152–6).

Like the Blanquists, Bernstein's conception of politics is an importantly materialist one: the materiality of concrete, face-to-face, and local forms of interaction and organization. His primary focus is on the contribution that democracy can make to socialism. When socialism becomes a theory of piecemeal reform, it can use the governmental apparatus itself as a means of social change. Social policy can now become the answer to deprivation and inequality. By executing this shift of perspective, Bernstein extends attention to the concrete, specific materiality of politics into a new domain, the domain of institutions pursuing socialist goals of material equality.

The social-democratic fusion of socialism and populism played out in various ways in the early decades of the twentieth century. It remained a preoccupation for British Fabian socialists like Sidney and Beatrice Webb (Webb, 1923). This synthesis was developed in dramatic ways in Sweden as well. Populism was a vivid part of the social-democratic imaginary in Per Albin Hansson's idea of society as the "people's home" (*Folkhemmet*). This compelling image, formulated from the late 1920s to the early 1940s, formed a stern critique of capitalist hierarchy and alienation. Family members have an intrinsic value, Hansson argued. Similarly, in the people's home, members should be treated as equals rather than functioning as abstract suppliers of commodified labor. In this sense, the people's home is above all a notion of democratic community emphasizing solidarity, integration, full participation, and consensus (Tilton, 1990: 259). It is an imaginary rearticulation of populist community, though in a Swedish idiom rather different from that of the Paris Commune. Democracy and equality are central to this vision, so that the hierarchical mentality of class should give way to a society in which every person has her or his say, both politically and in the workplace. Through Hansson's leadership of the Social Democratic Party and two terms as prime minister, this imaginary became a basis of the paradigmatic Swedish social-democratic state (Tilton, 1990: 126–44). His use of "politics against markets" provides a well-developed realization of Bernstein's insight that socialist goals could be accomplished through state action as well as, and perhaps better than, through revolution (Esping-Andersen, 1985).

CONDITIONS OF POSSIBILITY

These episodes in the development of socialism reveal subtle tensions with populism. They are particularly seen in the ways socialists have imagined forms of collectivity like "the people" and attached different values to them. During the time separating Karl Marx and Eduard Bernstein, socialist notions of collectivity were considerably reworked. Marx articulates an abstract, structural assessment of material interests as the basis for a conception of class. In so doing, he frames a conception of collectivity based on a materialist history of politics, but in an abstract and ineffable sense. As a result, Marx's appeals to the people as a political subject are rather ambivalent.

In contrast, the Blanquists elaborate a vision in which collectivity is expressed in tangible, material form. It is a politics of popular mobilization and revolutionary community that takes the form of mutual aid, public ceremony, and collective action at the barricades and in the street.

Bernstein redraws these features in yet other ways. He also thinks of collectivity as a form of community, one involving cooperation and affective relations of fellow-feeling, as well as state policies promoting material equality. In both of these senses, he is closer to the Blanquists than to Marx. Their ideas of collectivity focus on revolutionary community, however, whereas Bernstein articulates these themes within a socialist vision of constitutional democracy. The result is a subtle change of tone, emphasis, and their imaginary effects. Bernstein's frame of reference becomes correspondingly more distant from Blanquist insights about direct popular action. He embraces populism, but it must compete with constitutional democracy for attention and pride of place. As Bernstein's attention becomes more heavily focused on party politics and social policy, he has less to say about the fine-grained texture of popular community and everyday politics that is so vivid among the Blanquists.

It is often said that socialism is in decline, particularly since the breakup of the Eastern Bloc, the conversion of China to capitalism, and the opening up of Cuba. This platitude ignores the vigorous growth and spread of social democracy across the globe, however. Many European parliamentary systems have parties that identify themselves as social democratic. More subtly, elements of social democracy have been incorporated into governments in all of the developed countries. Even those whose doctrinal commitments are primarily liberal or conservative maintain policy regimes that have recognizably social-democratic elements: they buffer the side effects of the capitalist economy by supporting the material health and equality of their populations. They do this in ways consistent with a wide variety of political goals and modalities, but with the (often explicit) purpose of attenuating social inequalities. Socialism might remain highly controversial, but its social-democratic form has become a ubiquitous structural characteristic of contemporary societies. It makes modern liberal democracy possible under capitalist economic conditions.

Although Bernstein's vision of social democracy was largely captive to constitutional democracy and electoral politics, it is possible to imagine a more deeply populist formulation of these ideals. Collectivity takes a powerful universalist form in contemporary social democracy. Aimed specifically at promoting social equality, it forms an important nexus between democratic politics and its material basis. A radical democratic politics is vulnerable to material inequalities, which can quickly become forms of marginalization and division. Social democracy is the one political vision that moves this concern to the center of its agenda. It uses politics in a comprehensive way to buffer the side effects of capitalism and provide freedom by decommodifying labor (Esping-Andersen, 1990). In so doing, it provides the material bases of political equality. This, in turn, gives citizens greater political and social freedom, including the ability to safeguard and promote their own political equality. As a principled, genuine form of populism, social democracy is the only one able to establish a virtuous circle that reflexively supports its own material basis (Olson, 2006; 2009). In short, it has the ability to provide its own conditions of possibility. Of all the populist imaginaries, it is best able to support a thoroughly populist politics.

Revolutionary doctrines like Blanquism put the people vividly at the center of their vision, but they do not effectively account for the material bases of democratic politics nor the problems that can be encountered there. Contemporary strands of social democracy have this capacity. It is important, however, not to conceive of such policies in an abstractly procedural way. To do so would be to forget the lesson of socialism's great populists. The Blanquists emphasized concrete forms of community; Bernstein, local and specific forms of workplace democracy; Hansson, the "people's home" as a metaphorical family. If taken seriously, these rich, communally oriented visions prevent populism from becoming an instrumental exercise in manufacturing consent. The challenge is to navigate between two opposing tendencies that we see at work in the history of socialism: avoiding a nostalgia about lost moments of populist unity, while also finding a genuinely populist way to articulate these ideals within complex electoral systems and capitalist economies.

As a history of the present, this short genealogy tells us some important things about contemporary populism. The people may haunt socialism as an elusive ideal and source of bad conscience, but socialism has the ability to reanimate democratic politics as a condition of its very possibility. As a fusion of socialism and populism, social democracy in particular has functional importance for supporting the material bases of democratic politics. It knits socialism and populism together not simply as conceptual positions, but as concrete forms of political action. In so doing, it holds out the possibility of a non-ambivalent reconciliation between the two, one that creates synergies rather than hauntings.[1]

Note

1 Special thanks to Ghislaine Taxy for piquing my interest in Auguste Blanqui. All translations are mine unless otherwise noted.

References

Agamben, G. 1998. *Homo Sacer: Sovereign Power and Bare Life*, trans. Daniel Heller-Roazen. Stanford: Stanford University Press.

Arnaud, A. et al. 1872. *Internationale et révolution: a propos du Congrès de la Haye par des réfugiés de la Commune, ex-membres du Conseil Général de l'Internationale*. London: De Graag and Cie.

Bernstein, E. 1899 [1993]. *Die Voraussetzungen des Sozialismus and die Aufgaben der Sozialdemokratie*, trans. H. Tudor as *The Preconditions of Socialism*. Cambridge: Cambridge University Press.

Blanqui, A. 1868 [2006]. "Instructions pour une prise d'armes," in *Maintenant, il faut des armes*, ed. Dominique Le Nuz. Paris: La Fabrique, 257–92.

Canovan, M. 1981. *Populism*. London: Junction.

Canovan, M. 1999. "Trust the people! Populism and the two faces of democracy," *Political Studies*, 47: 4–5.

Commune Révolutionnaire [Edouard Vaillant et al.]. 1874. "Aux communeux." 12 p. ([n.l.]: [n.p.]).

Coyer, G. F. 1757. 'Dissertation sur la nature du peuple," in *Bagatelles morales et dissertations par Mr. L'Abbé Coyer*, nouvelle edn. London: Knoch and Eslinger.

Engels, F. 1874. "Le programme des émigrés Blanquistes de la Commune," *Der Volksstaat*, 73 (26 June).

Esping-Andersen, G. 1985. *Politics Against Markets: The Social Democratic Road to Power*. Princeton: Princeton University Press.

Esping-Andersen, G. 1990. *The Three Worlds of Welfare Capitalism*. Princeton: Princeton University Press.

Falconnet de la Bellonie, C. 1748. *La psycantropie ou nouvelle théorie de l'homme*. Avignon: Louis Chambeau.

Filmer, R. 1991. *"Patriarcha" and Other Writings*. Cambridge: Cambridge University Press.

Hanák, P. 1970. "Die Volksmeinung währeng des letzten Kriegsjahres in Österreich-Ungarn," in R. Plaschka and K. Mack (eds), *Die Auflösung des Habsburgerreiches: Zusammenbruch und Neuorientierung im Donauraum*. Munich: Oldenbourg: 58–66.

Hobsbawm, E. 1992. *Nations and Nationalism since 1780: Programme, Myth, Reality*, 2nd edn. Cambridge: Cambridge University Press.

Hutton, P. 1981. *The Cult of the Revolutionary Tradition: The Blanquists in French Politics, 1864–1893*. Berkeley: University of California Press.

Kantorowicz, E. 1957. *The King's Two Bodies: A Study in Mediaeval Political Theology*. Princeton: Princeton University Press.

Laclau, E. 2005. *On Populist Reason*. London: Verso.

Le Bon, G. 1895 [1960]. *La psychologie des foules*, trans. as *The Crowd*. New York: Viking Press.

Leighton, J. 1871. *Paris under the Commune: Or, The Seventy-Three Days of the Second Siege*, 3rd edn. London: Bradbury and Evans.

Marx, K. 1847 [1920]. *The Poverty of Philosophy*, trans. H. Quelch. Chicago: Charles Kerr.

Marx, K. 1852 [1996]. "The eighteenth Brumaire of Louis Bonaparte," in *Later Political Writings*, trans. Terrell Carver. Cambridge: Cambridge University Press.

Marx, K. 1871 [1996]. "The civil war in France," in *Later Political Writings*, trans. Terrell Carver. Cambridge: Cambridge University Press.

Marx, K. and F. Engels. 1947. *The German Ideology*. New York: International.

McCormick, J. P. 2011. *Machiavellian Democracy*. Cambridge: Cambridge University Press.

Olson, K. 2006. *Reflexive Democracy: Political Equality and the Welfare State*. Cambridge: MIT Press.

Olson, K. 2009. "Reflexive democracy as popular sovereignty," in Boudewijn de Bruin and Christopher Zurn (eds), *New Waves in Political Philosophy*. London: Palgrave Macmillan.

Olson, K. 2016. *Imagined Sovereignties: The Power of the People and Other Myths of the Modern Age*. Cambridge: Cambridge University Press.

Tilton, T. 1990. *The Political Theory of Swedish Social Democracy: Through the Welfare State to Socialism*. New York: Oxford University Press.

Tridon, G. 1871. *Les Hébertistes*, 2nd edn. Bruxelles: Chez Tous les Libraires.

Tudor, H. and J. M. Tudor (eds). 1988. *Marxism and Social Democracy: The Revisionist Debate, 1896–1898*. Cambridge: Cambridge University Press.

Voltaire. 1766 [1973]. Letter to Damilaville, 1 April 1766. D13232, in T. Besterman (ed.), *The Complete Works of Voltaire*, Vol. 114: *Correspondence*. Banbury: Voltaire Foundation, 155–6.

Urbinati, N. 2014. *Democracy Disfigured: Opinion, Truth, and the People*. Cambridge: Harvard University Press.

Webb, S. 1923. "Constitutional problems of a cooperative society," Fabian Tract 202. London: The Fabian Society.

Index

Lightning Source UK Ltd.
Milton Keynes UK
UKHW030227150721
387195UK00003B/7

9 780198 846284